LAW AND ABORIGINAL PEOPLES IN CANADA

FIFTH EDITION

DAVID W. ELLIOTT

Associate Professor of Law
Carleton University

CANADIAN LEGAL STUDIES SERIES

Captus Press

Canadian Legal Studies Series
Law and Aboriginal Peoples in Canada, 5th edition

First Captus Press edition, 1992
Fifth edition, 2005

Captus Press Inc.
Units 14 & 15, 1600 Steeles Avenue West
Concord, Ontario, L4K 4M2, Canada
Telephone: (416) 736–5537
Fax: (416) 736–5793
Email: Info@captus.com
Internet: http://www.captus.com

Canadä *We acknowledge the financial support of the Government of Canada through the Book Publishing Industry Development Program (BPIDP) for our publishing activities.*

Library and Archives Canada Cataloguing in Publication

Elliott, David W. (David William), date
Law and aboriginal peoples in Canada / David W. Elliott — 5th ed.

(Canadian legal studies series)
Includes bibliographical references and index.
ISBN 1–55322–095–1

1. Native peoples — Legal status, laws, etc. — Canada. 2. Native peoples — Civil rights — Canada. 3. Constitutional amendments — Canada. I. Title. II. Series.

KE7709.5.L39 2005 342.7108'72 C2005–901916–6
KF8205.A2L39 2005

0 9 8 7 6 5 4 3 2 1
Printed and bound in Canada

Table of Contents

Preface xiii

Acknowledgements xiv

Organization and Guide to Symbols xiv

Main Text

1 Introduction 3

1. Scope of the Book 4
2. The People, the Change, and the Law 4
3. Mileposts 5

2 Who Is an Aboriginal Person? 13

1. Anthropological and Legal Descriptions. 14
2. Section 35 Aboriginal Peoples 14
3. Section 91(24) Indians 14
4. Categories of *Indian Act* Indians. 15
   (a) *Indian Act*. 15
   (b) Pre-April 17, 1982 Eligibility Procedures 15
   (c) Problems with Old System. 15
   (d) Movement for Change 16
   (e) 1985 Eligibility Reforms 17
   (f) Challenges Ahead 18
   (g) *Corbiere v. Canada (Minister of Indian and Northern Affairs)* . . . 19
5. Non-*Indian Act* Aboriginal Peoples 20
   (a) Non-Status Indians 20
   (b) Inuit 20
   (c) Métis 20

6. Treaty Indians 21
7. Claims Agreement Beneficiaries 21
8. Self-Definition Possibilities. 22
9. Aboriginal Status and Equality 22

3 Aboriginal Rights before *Calder* 30

1. Context 31
2. Background. 31
3. Aboriginal Concepts 31
4. Descriptions and Questions 32
5. Source of Aboriginal Rights 33
6. Alternative Approaches 33
7. Interrelationships 34
8. Evolution of Approaches 34
9. The Royal Proclamation of 1763. 34
10. *St. Catherine's Milling and Lumber Co. v. The Queen* 35
11. *Johnson and Graham's Lessee v. M'Intosh* 36
12. *Worcester v. Georgia* 37
13. *Connolly*. 38
14. Shadow of *St. Catherine's* 39

4 Aboriginal Rights from *Calder* to *Guerin* 43

1. *Calder* 44
   (a) Source of Aboriginal Title. 44
   (b) Proof. 45
   (c) Effect of European Sovereignty 45
   (d) Content 45
   (e) Extinguishment. 46
   (f) Enforcement 46
   (g) Compensation 46
2. Post-*Calder* Years 46
3. *Baker Lake* 47
4. *Guerin*. 47
5. Turning Point? 48

5 Indian Treaties. 51

1. Significance. 52
2. Definition. 52
3. Main Categories. 52
4. Size 52
5. Content 52
6. Participants. 53
7. Status 53

8. Interpretation And Enforcement . . . 53
9. Charlottetown Accord . . . 54
10. Treaty Problems . . . 54
11. *Simon* . . . 55
12. *Sioui* . . . 55
13. *Bear Island* . . . 56
14. *Badger* . . . 56
15. *Marshall* . . . 58
16. *Haida Nation* . . . 59
17. Clarification or Reconstruction? . . . 60

6 Legislative Jurisdiction . . . 65

1. Overview . . . 66
2. Level One: Statutes and Parliamentary Sovereignty . . . 66
3. Level Two: *Constitution Act, 1867* . . . 66
   (a) Validity . . . 66
   (b) Inoperativeness . . . 66
   (c) Inapplicability . . . 66
   (d) Invalidity . . . 67
4. Level Three: Section 88 of *Indian Act* . . . 67
5. Level Four: *Natural Resources Transfer Agreements* . . . 68
6. Level Five: Section 35(1) of *Constitution Act, 1982* . . . 68
7. *Cardinal* . . . 69
8. *Dick* . . . 69
9. *Delgamuukw* . . . 70
10. *Kitkatla* . . . 70
11. More Challenges . . . 71

7 *Constitution Act, 1982* and *Sparrow* . . . 75

1. Changes to *Constitution Act, 1982* . . . 76
2. Background . . . 76
3. Questions . . . 77
4. *Sparrow* . . . 77
   (a) Legal Situation before *Sparrow* . . . 77
   (b) Facts and Context . . . 78
   (c) Supreme Court's Decision . . . 78
   (d) Elements of Decision . . . 79
      (i) Proof and Content . . . 79
      (ii) Extinguishment . . . 80
      (iii) Fiduciary Duties and Crown Honour . . . 80
      (iv) Legal Status . . . 80
      (v) Entrenchment . . . 81
      (vi) Infringement . . . 81
      (vii) Justification . . . 81

8 Fiduciary Duties 86

1. Introduction 88
2. "Ordinary" Fiduciary Relationships 88
   (a) Character and Scope 88
   (b) Content 88
3. Source of Obligation 88
4. *Guerin* 89
   (a) Facts 89
   (b) Judgments 89
   (c) Features 89
   (d) Relationship to Land 90
5. *Sparrow* 90
   (a) Judgment 90
   (b) Features of *Sparrow* Duty 91
6. Content of Fiduciary Duty 91
   (a) *Guerin* Duty 91
   (b) Comparison with *Sparrow* Duty 92
7. General Trends 92
8. Modern Cases 93
   (a) *Grand Council of the Crees* 93
   (b) *Blueberry River* 93
   (c) *Badger*, *Gladstone*, and *Delgamuukw* 94
   (d) *Osoyoos* 95
   (e) *Wewaykum* 95
   (f) *Haida Nation* 97
9. Tentative Summary 98
   (a) Special Fiduciary Obligation 98
   (b) Specific Protection 98
   (c) Related But Distinct Forms 98
   (d) Scope of *Guerin* Duty 98
   (e) Scope of *Sparrow* Duty 98
   (f) Content 98
   (g) Reconciliation 98
   (h) Liberal Canons of Construction 98

9 Aboriginal Rights: I 108

1. Introduction 109
2. *Mabo* 109
3. *Van Der Peet* 110
   (a) Background 110
   (b) Basis of Aboriginal Rights: Land 111
   (c) Basis of Aboriginal Rights: Distinctive Societies 112
   (d) Section 35(1) 112
   (e) "Distinctive Practices" Test 112
   (f) A Missing Link? 113
   (g) McLachlin J.'s Criticisms 113
   (h) A Return to Land? 114

4. *Gladstone* . . . 116
5. *Pamajewon* . . . 117

10 Aboriginal Rights: II . . . 125

1. Introduction . . . 126
2. *Adams* . . . 126
3. *Delgamuukw* . . . 127
   (a) The Challenge . . . 127
   (b) The Litigation . . . 127
   (c) Changing Claims . . . 128
   (d) Aboriginal Evidence . . . 129
      (i) Collective Oral Histories . . . 129
      (ii) Personal and Family Histories . . . 129
      (iii) Chiefs' Territorial Affidavits . . . 129
      (iv) Beyond Hearsay Exceptions . . . 130
   (e) Aboriginal Title . . . 131
      (i) General Features . . . 131
      (ii) Exclusivity . . . 131
      (iii) Land Attachment . . . 132
      (iv) Identification . . . 132
      (v) Constitutional Status . . . 133
      (vi) Aboriginal Title and Other Aboriginal Rights . . . 133
   (f) Justification . . . 133
      (i) Justification Goals . . . 133
      (ii) Justification in *Delgamuukw* . . . 134
   (g) Self-Government . . . 134
   (h) Extinguishment . . . 135
      (i) Provincial Jurisdiction under *Constitution Act, 1867* . . . 135
      (ii) Provincial Jurisdiction under Section 88 of *Indian Act* . . . 136
      (iii) A Case for Deferral? . . . 136
4. *Mitchell* . . . 136
   (a) Recurring Questions . . . 136
   (b) Background . . . 136
   (c) Characterization . . . 137
   (d) Evidence . . . 138
   (e) Aboriginal Rights, Section 35(1), and Sovereign Incompatibility . . . 139
5. *Powley* . . . 140
6. *Haida Nation* . . . 143
   (a) Underlying Source and General Nature of s. 35(1) Duty to Consult . . . 143
   (b) Parties Subject to Duty . . . 144
   (c) Scope of Duty . . . 144
   (d) Content of Duty . . . 144
   (e) Relationship between Forms of Justification . . . 145

7. Basic Features 146
(a) General Aspects 146
(b) Identification 147
(c) Content 147
(d) Relationship to Crown 148
(e) Possession and Use 148
(f) Extinguishment and Restriction 148
(g) Justification 148
(h) Fiduciary Duty 149

11 Aboriginal Claims 162
1. General Questions 163
2. What Are Aboriginal Claims? 163
3. Alternative Approaches 163
(a) Courts 163
(b) Quasi-Judicial Tribunal 163
(c) Arbitration 163
(d) Representations before a Legislative Body 164
(e) Negotiations 164
4. Claims Process 164
(a) Procedure 164
(b) Development 164
5. Major Comprehensive Claims Agreements and Negotiations 166
6. Factors Influencing Settlement of Comprehensive Claims 167
(a) Issues 167
(b) Parties 168
(c) Non-Beneficiaries 168
(d) Development 168
(e) Other Forums 169
(f) Scope 169
(g) Other Factors 170
7. Some Key Land Claims Agreements 170
(a) 1971 Alaska Native Claims Settlement 170
(b) 1975 James Bay and Northern Quebec Agreement and 1978 Northeastern Quebec Agreement 171
(c) 1984 Western Arctic (Inuvialuit) Agreement 171
(d) 1992 Gwich'in Agreement 172
(e) 1993 Nunavut Agreement 172
(f) 1993 and Later Yukon Agreements 172
(g) 1993 Sahtu Dene and Metis Agreement 173
(h) Nisga'a Agreement 173
(i) 2003 Tlicho Agreement 176
(j) 2005 Labrador Agreement 177
(k) Sechelt Agreement-in-Principle 177
8. Some Specific Claims 178
9. "Other Claims" 178
(a) Oka 178

(i) People 178
(ii) Crisis 178
(iii) Background 179
(iv) Aftermath 180
(b) Ipperwash 180
10. Future Directions 180

12 Aboriginal Self-Government 190

1. Aboriginal Perspectives. 191
2. The Debate 191
3. Possible Alternatives 191
(a) Traditional Self-Government 191
(b) Legislated Self-Government 192
(i) *Indian Act* Self-Government 192
(c) Negotiated Self-Government. 193
(i) Guaranteed Participation 193
(ii) Public Government 193
(iii) Coordinated Ethnic Government 193
(A) James Bay and Northern Quebec Agreement . . . 194
(B) Sechelt Indian Band Self-Government Act 194
(C) Alberta Metis Settlements Legislation. 194
(D) Métis Act of Saskatchewan 194
(iv) Separate Ethnic Government 194
(A) Vuntut Gwitchin First Nation Self-Government Agreement 195
(B) Westbank Indian Self-Government Agreement. . . 196
(d) Judicial Self-Government. 196
4. A Common Law Right of Aboriginal Self-Government?. 197
5. Formal Constitutional Route 198
(a) Road to Charlottetown. 198
(b) Charlottetown Aboriginal Provisions. 199
(c) Rejection of Charlottetown 200
6. Federal Policy Route. 200
7. Royal Commission on Aboriginal Peoples 201
8. Assessment of Self-Government Initiatives 203

13 Concluding Note 212

Chapter Readings

1 Introduction 217

(a) Some Aboriginal Perspectives on Lands and Resources. 217
(b) Founding Peoples in Traditional Times. 219

2 Who Is an Aboriginal Person? 221

(a) General Status Provisions. 221
(b) *Canadian Bill of Rights and Charter* 222
(c) *Canada (A.G.) v. Lavell; Isaac et al. v. Bedard* 223
(d) 1985 *Indian Act* Status Provisions 228
(e) *Corbiere v. Canada (Minister of Indian and Northern Affairs)*. 231

3 Aboriginal Rights before *Calder* 236

(a) The Royal Proclamation of 1763 236
(b) *St. Catherine's Milling and Lumber Co. v. The Queen* 237
(c) *Johnson and Graham's Lessee v. M'Intosh* 242
(d) *Worcester v. Georgia* 250
(e) *Connolly v. Woolrich* and *Johnstone v. Connolly* 251

4 Aboriginal Rights from *Calder* to *Guerin* 255

(a) *Calder v. British Columbia (A.G.)* 255
(b) *Baker Lake v. Canada (Minister of Indian and Northern Affairs)* 263
(c) *Guerin v. The Queen* 265

5 Indian Treaties. 272

(a) Indian Treaty Map 272
(b) Report of the Commissioner for Treaty Number 11 272
(c) *Simon v. The Queen* 276
(d) *R. v. Sioui* 279
(e) *Ontario (A.G.) v. Bear Island Foundation*. 285
(f) *R. v. Badger* 286
(g) *R. v. Marshall* 291

6 Legislative Jurisdiction 299

(a) Some Provisions Relevant to Legislative Jurisdiction 299
(b) *Cardinal v. Alberta (A.G.)* 300
(c) *Dick v. The Queen* 304
(d) *Delgamuukw* 310
(e) *Kitkatla Band v. British Columbia (Minister of Small Business, Tourism and Culture)* 311

7 *Constitution Act, 1982* and *Sparrow*. 315

(a) Excerpts from *Constitution Act, 1982* 315
(b) 1983 Constitutional Accord. 316
(c) *R. v. Sparrow* 318

8 Fiduciary Duties 330

(a) *Guerin* 330
(b) *Sparrow* 330
(c) *Blueberry River Indian Band v. Canada (Department of Indian Affairs and Northern Development)* 331
(d) *Wewaykum Indian Band v. Canada* 333

9 Aboriginal Rights 338

(a) *Mabo v. State of Queensland (No. 2)* 338
(b) *R. v. Van der Peet* 341
(c) *R. v. Gladstone* 348
(d) *R. v. Pamajewon* 350

10 Aboriginal Rights and Title 353

(a) *R. v. Adams* 353
(b) *Delgamuukw v. British Columbia* 355
(c) *Mitchell v. Canada (Minister of National Revenue)* 362
(d) *R. v. Powley* 370
(e) *Haida Nation v. British Columbia (Minister of Forests)* 378

11 Aboriginal Claims 382

(a) Map of Comprehensive Land Claims in British Columbia 382
(b) Federal Policy for the Settlement of Native Claims. 382
(c) Land Provisions of Modern Treaties 391
(d) *Nisga'a Final Agreement in Brief* 398
(e) *Sechelt Agreement-in-Principle* 404
(f) Land Claims Agreement Dispute Resolution 408

12 Aboriginal Self-Government 410

(a) *Kaianerakowa* 410
(b) *Sechelt Indian Band Self-Government Act* 413
(c) *Vuntut Gwitchin First Nation Self-Government Agreement* 419
(d) Proposed Charlottetown Accord 429
(e) *Pamajewon* 433
(f) Highlights of *Report of the Royal Commission on Aboriginal Peoples* 434
(g) *People to People, Nation to Nation* 435

General Index 441

Table of Section References 443

Preface

This is mainly a descriptive book. It addresses some key aspects of Canadian law relating to Aboriginal peoples. The central concern is to say what the law is, not to dwell on broad sociological impacts or to theorize about possible alternatives. But law is a normative and social phenomenon. Simply by talking about it, we colour it with our own values and prejudices. I have tried to offset this tendency by including primary materials to help the reader form his or her own conclusions. As well, I feel I should provide some notice here of the perspective I bring to this book.

I share the view expressed in Alan Cairns' *Citizens Plus: Aboriginal Peoples and the Canadian State* (Vancouver: U.B.C. Press, 2000) and in John Barrows' *Recovering Canada, The Resurgence of Indigenous Law* (Toronto: University of Toronto Press, 2002) that difference and interconnectedness are *both* important to Aboriginal / non-Aboriginal relations. In my view, assimilation was clearly the wrong road. On the other hand, I think the modern stress on difference may lead Canadians to neglect common values. Paradoxically, one of these is the value of benefiting from cultures other than our own.

For balancing these goals, I think it would be unwise to rely too heavily on law and legal mechanisms. The law portrayed in this book is very significant to Aboriginal / non-Aboriginal relations. Law has a high profile, is enforceable, and has helped secure general recognition for Aboriginal rights. But law has also helped to perpetuate problems. Consider, for example, the longstanding sexual inequality of Aboriginal women under former s. 12(1)(b) of the federal *Indian Act*. Moreover, law often resolves one problem by introducing others. The legal approach attracts adversarial, judicially imposed, constitutionally hardened, "top-down" solutions to social challenges. It also tends to draw issues into the divisive mould of status, and away from the more inclusive context of needs and interests.

What kind of approach could play a bigger role in supplementing law-centred options? A detailed assessment of this question is beyond the scope of this book. I will merely venture here one possible avenue for exploration.

The 19th century Chief Shingwauk of the Garden River Band (also known now as the Garden River First Nation) had a vision of a "teaching wigwam". In this house, his children would learn both non-Aboriginal and Aboriginal ways, and would secure their own future. (See J.R. Miller, *Shingwauk's Vision: A History of Native Residential Schools* (Toronto: University of Toronto Press, 1996).) Tragically, the Chief's hopes were dashed on the rocks of residential school cultural imperialism and child abuse. But surely it was the execution, not the inspiration, of the vision thatd failed.

Why not try now to do real justice to the education vision? A modern approach would involve grassroots Aboriginal participation, strong support from the existing academic community, and adequate government funding. It would involve elders and Aboriginal professionals, Aboriginal as well as other knowledge, and parents as well as children. It would be complemented by effective measures to meet the housing, health, environmental, and other concrete needs so well documented in the 1996 *Report of the Royal Commission on Aboriginal Peoples*.

This approach would also be supplemented by greater emphasis in all Canadian schools on Aboriginal culture, languages, philosophy, and practical learning. The Chief's vision is not confined to courtrooms. It cannot work as a tool of either assimilation or isolation. Chief Shingwauk's vision includes us all.

Acknowledgements

I acknowledge with many thanks the assistance of the support staff at the Department of Law, staff at Captus Press (Randy Hoffman, Lily Chu, and Pauline Lai), and my family, including G.V. Elliott and W.K. Elliott in Surrey, B.C. They provided valuable help in preparing this volume for printing.

As well, I wish to thank the authors and publishers who have granted permission to reproduce their works herein.

David W. Elliott
Ottawa, 2005

Organization and Guide to Symbols

This book is divided into two sections:

- the **Main Text**, comprising thirteen chapters; and
- a **Chapter Readings** section, containing major decisions, statutes, and other supporting materials. The twelve units of the **Chapter Readings** correspond to the first twelve chapters of the **Main Text**. Individual materials in the **Main Text** and the **Chapter Readings** are linked throughout the book by key symbols.

Each chapter of the **Main Text** has a title page, which contains chapter highlights, a chapter synopsis, and a list of readings (marked by key symbols) in the relevant **Chapter Readings** unit. As well, within the **Main Text**, individual topics are linked (at the key symbols) to relevant readings, and *vice versa*.

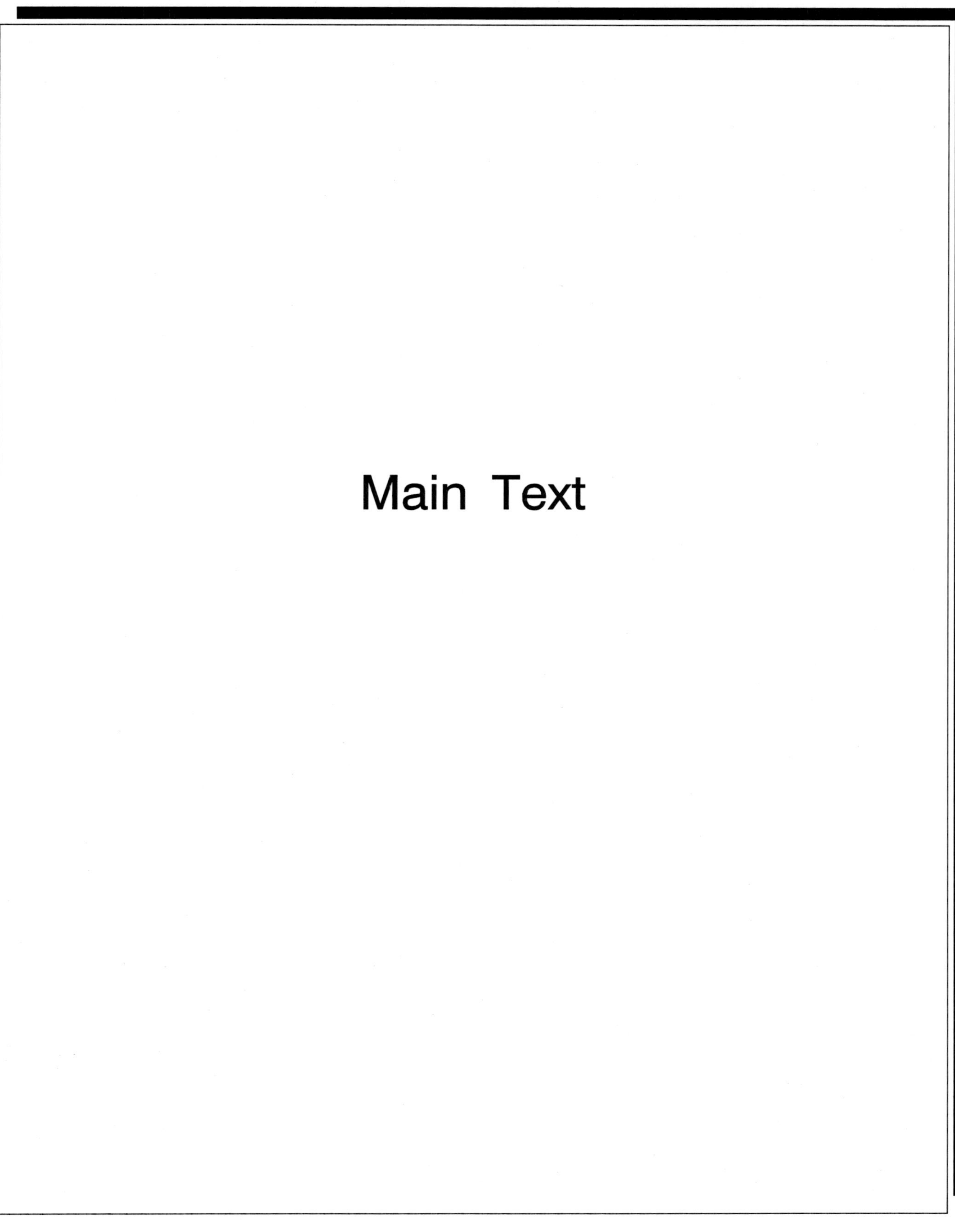

Main Text

Specific Links to Chapter Readings

Materials in the **Main Text** are linked to readings in the **Chapter Readings** section of the book in two ways. First, on most of the chapter title pages is a list of **Selected Readings**. Opposite the key symbol at the left margin is the part of the chapter (sometimes the entire chapter) of the **Main Text** that is addressed by the reading in question. After this you will see the name of the heading of the relevant reading, followed by the page number at which it starts. For example, on p. 13, a reading that addresses Parts 4(g) and 9 of Chapter 2 of the **Main Text** is the *Corbiere* case, and this case starts at p. 231 of the **Chapter Readings**.

Elsewhere in the **Main Text**, a key symbol refers to the location and page number of readings that are especially relevant to a particular topic. Look, for example, at p. 16. There you will see heading (d), **Movement for Change**, in Part 4 of Chapter 2 of the **Main Text**. The key symbol there refers you to Readings 2(b) and 2(c) of the **Chapter Readings**, which start at pp. 222 and 223, respectively.

1 Introduction

Chapter Highlights

- More than one million Aboriginal people in Canada are descendants of the first inhabitants of North America, who were here as long as 12,000 years ago.
- When non-Aboriginals arrived, they brought problems as well as benefits to the first peoples, and took over most of the first peoples' land.
- To see how the law affects Aboriginal peoples and their relationship with non-Aboriginals, it is necessary to start by looking at the past.
- Over the centuries, a number of developments have produced historic milestones that affect the law relating to Aboriginal peoples even today.
- Examining the role law has played in the past not only helps us understand it today, but also helps us to learn its potential — and its limits — as a tool for change in the future.

Synopsis

This book looks at some basic elements of the law relating to Canadian Aboriginal people. It deals with status, Aboriginal rights, treaties, legislative jurisdiction, the constitutional framework, fiduciary obligations, Aboriginal claims, and Aboriginal self-government. Underlying the law is a unique group of people with a rich past and a potentially limitless future. Their present, though, is clouded by injustice, marginalization, and poverty. Helping unlock their potential is a responsibility and an opportunity for all Canadians. How does law relate to this situation? How, and where, should it be used to address this challenge? It is useful to look first at the role of law in the past. **Chapter 1** considers some key historical mileposts with legal significance for Aboriginal peoples and the Aboriginal / non-Aboriginal relationship.

Selected Readings

🖹 links material in this chapter to the corresponding headings and page numbers of the relevant readings.

🖹 Entire Chapter Some Aboriginal Perspectives on Lands and Resources 217

🖹 Entire Chapter Founding Peoples in Traditional Times 219

1. SCOPE OF THE BOOK

The law relating to Canadian Aboriginal people is dramatic, complex, and extensive. This book is not a reference source for the entire subject. Its focus is not the social, economic, and political environment of Canadian Aboriginal people, but the law that relates to them. The book does not explore the many rich streams of indigenous customary law,[1] or the documents[2] and doctrines[3] of international law. Its focus is the law that is generally applied in Canadian courts. It looks at the constitutional and other basic elements of this law.

The book addresses the following questions:

1. Who is an Aboriginal person?
2. What are Aboriginal rights?
3. What are Indian treaties?
4. Who has legislative jurisdiction in regard to Aboriginal people?
5. How has the *Constitution Act, 1982* affected Aboriginal and treaty rights?
6. What is the scope of the special fiduciary obligation to Aboriginal peoples?
7. How has the government addressed Aboriginal rights claims?
8. What is Aboriginal self-government?

The book includes a **Chapter Readings** section that contains major decisions, statutes, and other material relevant to each of the chapters in the main text.

2. THE PEOPLE, THE CHANGE, AND THE LAW

Approximately one million Aboriginal people live in Canada. They are descendants of the first inhabitants of North America, people who were here as long as 12,000 years ago.[4] Since the 16th century, non-Aboriginal immigrants from Europe and elsewhere have taken over much of the continent's land and resources, irrevocably changing Aboriginal lives.[5]

The settlers brought with them the benefits of an industrial society. Today, Inuit families in remote corners of the Northwest Territories can use ski-doos and high-powered rifles to hunt caribou. They can watch television programs relayed over enormous distances by satellite.

But the settlers brought problems as well. Many of Canada's Aboriginal people grapple with extreme poverty, continuous unemployment, high infant mortality, and high rates of suicide, illness, and disease. Traditional land has been dug up, ploughed under, and paved over for mines, farms, roads, shopping centres, and golf courses. Cultures that used to thrive on hunting, fishing, and trapping are weakened as acid rain, dams, logging, and pollution undermine the resource base on the lands that remain. The technology that made the high-powered rifles for the Inuit is destroying their caribou herds. The television signals to remote fishing and trapping communities are beaming in soap operas, urban talk shows, and cigarette ads.[6]

The impact is especially acute for younger Aboriginal people. Cultural gaps compound generation gaps. Many young people are caught between a threatened traditional world and the bottom economic rung of the industrial world. For many, the choice may be poverty, unemployment, and alcoholism on a depressed reserve or poverty, unemployment, and alcoholism in the "skid row" section of an alien city. For them, there seems to be no place to turn.[7]

These are not simply Aboriginal issues. "Aboriginal" problems are often more general in scope.[8] So are many Aboriginal challenges. For example, all Canadians share — or should share — the responsibility for looking after the northern half of this continent. Aboriginal strengths have an important common dimension too. For example, traditional Aboriginal practices and philosophies tend to stress values neglected by the majority.[9] Values like consensus, conservation, sharing, and common good are well worth considering in a society preoccupied with competition, development, and individual gain.

We need to help Aboriginal people preserve their way of life, to let them plan their own ways of adapting.[10] We need to put an end to their special economic and social burdens so that they — and indeed all other disadvantaged Canadians — can enjoy more of the opportunities of the majority.

The typical reaction of lawyers and constitutional enthusiasts is to say, "How has law dealt with these challenges?" and, "What more should it be doing?" Certainly, we will be asking these questions in this book. Law has played a significant role here, and is being given an even increasingly major role. Canada has been moving steadily from legislative approaches to more judicial and constitutional approaches. Increasingly, the role of the politician is being supplemented by that of the judge.

At the same time, there is another trend developing: a transfer of responsibility from non-Aboriginal to Aboriginal managers. Will this trend overtake the movement toward greater reliance on law and courts? If it does, how far will the native management role extend? Will it be limited to uniquely Aboriginal concerns, or will it extend more broadly to the country as a whole?

Although law is a necessary tool of change, it is a double-edged sword. Many social challenges of Aboriginal peoples have been compounded by legal complexity and uncertainty. Courts can make relatively independent, enforceable decisions, but they are a cumbersome, authoritarian, and often inefficient forum for resolving complex social issues. Constitutional change, the ultimate legal mechanism, can rarely accommodate regional diversity, and invites further involvement by courts. In considering change, we should be aware of the limitations of law as well as its potential. We should not assume that better sanitation, more educational opportunities, adequate housing, and a sense of pride and purpose will come solely from constitutional amendments and courtroom verdicts. We should look beyond the law, and encourage active, continuous "grassroots" involvement by Aboriginal people, their non-Aboriginal neighbours, and accountable politicians.

3. MILEPOSTS

The law relating to Canadian Aboriginal peoples is bound up with the past.[11] As non-Aboriginal immigrants took over northern North America, they imposed their own laws to implement policies, defuse crises, formalize agreements, rationalize expansion, and shape future relations. Sometimes these new laws opened constructive forms of interaction; just as often they also generated new problems. Some of the most important laws have accompanied, followed, or even constituted key mileposts in Aboriginal / non-Aboriginal relations. Let us consider a few examples.

The first milepost lies well before recorded history. South of Old Crow, in what is now the Yukon Territory, archaeologists have found what may be remains of hunters' tools — chipped stone artifacts that may be over 12,000 years old.[12] Elsewhere in North America, there is strong evidence of human occupation that is nearly as old.[13] At a few sites, there are signs of even older occupation.[14] Some of these first people may have migrated from Asia over a Bering Sea land bridge during the later Ice Ages.[15] Some may have travelled by water as well.[16]

In any event, when Samuel de Champlain established a little settlement in Quebec in 1608, the Aboriginal peoples were already there, and had been there for many thousands of years. The continent was alive with myriad societies and cultures, each with its own institutions, traditions and beliefs, but all closely linked to the land and its resources.[17] These included the Mi'kmaq by the Atlantic Ocean, the Iroquoian peoples of the Eastern woodlands, Rocky Mountain and plains tribes who later formed the Blackfoot Confederacy, the Haida and many others along the northwest coast, subarctic peoples such as the Chipewyan, and the Inuit of the far north.[18] Much later, in the 1970s, this notion of prior traditional use and occupancy of land gained general protection at common law.[19]

The year 1608 provides a second milepost. Champlain's settlement grew into New France, the first relatively permanent non-Aboriginal colony in northern North America.[20] In New France, two driving forces were the fur trade and the church. The fur trade depended on the Aboriginal populations. Aboriginal allies trapped, provided transportation such as canoes, supplied native medicines and geographical knowledge, and formed the military alliances needed to protect supply routes.[21] Economic interdependence was accompanied by social interaction.[22] Intermarriage was common.[23] But interdependence and interaction were often resisted by the church. Missionary groups tried to set Indians apart from secular European influences so they could be converted and gradually "civilized".[24] Like so many other newcomers, they concentrated on trying to change Aboriginal peoples rather than trying to learn from them.

In the end, the missionaries' efforts left stronger legal imprints than those of the fur traders. Informal fur trade exchanges produced oral agreements rather than lasting written treaties. To isolate and then "civilize" their Indian charges, the religious orders acquired parcels of lands to be used for the benefit of the Indians.[25] Both the reserves and the segregation policy continued. They formed the foundations of the *Indian Act* of the 19th and 20th centuries.[26]

Another milepost was the creation, in the 15th and 16th centuries, of the Five (then Six) Nations Confederacy of the Iroquois. This organization of five and, later, six Aboriginal nations had a highly sophisticated system of traditional government and consensual decision-making.[27] It became a major political and military force on the continent.[28] Iroquois power tended to help the British, especially in the early years of their long struggle against France. The Iroquois helped ensure that the European law governing future Aboriginal / non-Aboriginal relations would be English.

When Britain won the Seven Years' War in 1760, her former Indian allies and enemies were upset and anxious.[29] Indians had long been angered by the sharp practices of English fur traders and land speculators. These abusive dealings escalated as the war drew to a close. A 1763 uprising by the Odawa chief Pontiac and his allies showed that Indian dissatisfaction could seriously threaten British control.[30] To provide for the government of the continent, and to address the concerns of the Indians, George III issued a royal proclamation on October 7, 1763. This wide-ranging document set aside a huge territory as a form of Indian reserve and provided other land and trading protections for Indians.[31]

Having gained most of North America after the middle of the 18th century, Britain then lost much of it in the American Revolution. After 1776, thousands of United Empire Loyalists migrated north from the rebellious colonies.[32] To make space for the newcomers, among them the Indian allies, the British government concluded Indian treaties in Upper Canada.[33] Unlike most of the peace accords of the 18th century, these were land cession treaties — Crown grants of money and other benefits in return for large areas of land. By the middle of the 19th century, land cession treaties had become more complex, and included reserves and hunting rights. In a final period, between 1871 and 1921, the Canadian government concluded the eleven "numbered" treaties in Ontario, the Prairies, and other parts of western Canada.[34]

On July 1, 1867, the *Constitution Act, 1867*[35] subjected Aboriginal and non-Aboriginal inhabitants of three Canadian colonies to a complex system of federal government. Section 91(24) of the Act gave Parliament exclusive legislative jurisdiction in relation to "Indians, and Lands reserved for the Indians". On the other hand, s. 92 also gave several powers capable of affecting Indians to provincial legislatures. Moreover, s. 109 gave the provinces the ownership of most Crown land. The stage was set for competing claims to power by federal and provincial governments, with Aboriginal people often caught in the middle.[36]

The *Constitution Act, 1867* may have also affected Aboriginal self-government. Courts have held that the Act's division of sovereign powers between the federal and provincial levels was intended to be exhaustive. Some courts say this arrangement precluded any continued power of sovereign Aboriginal government. Others argue that some rights of Aboriginal self-government continue.[37]

In the *St. Catherine's* case of 1888,[38] a federal-provincial conflict over natural resources led to a landmark judicial ruling on Indian title. The Privy Council held that the Indian people had a legal interest in the land by virtue of the Royal Proclamation of 1763. When the land was surrendered by treaty, the remaining ownership rights passed to the province. The case established the Royal Proclamation as the basis of Indian title in Canada for many decades afterward. It also increased the need for provincial involvement in government agreements involving Aboriginal lands.[39] Earlier in the century, an American legal decision had recognized Aboriginal rights based not only on the Proclamation, but also on the Indians' prior occupancy of land.[40] It would be a century and a half before this approach would be adopted in Canada.[41]

A year after Confederation, Parliament passed the first federal *Indian Act*.[42] This was a cradle-to-grave régime that governed — and in some ways, still governs — the lives of Aboriginal people identified as Indians. The Act defined Indians,[43] and affirmed their entitlement to live on the reserves set aside for them. It gave — and continues to give — certain tax exemptions for Indians residing on reserves. It imposed many restrictions on Indians. At different times these included alcohol prohibitions, claims restrictions, bans on traditional cultural and religious ceremonies such as the potlatch and the sun dance, and limits to the very rudimentary form of local government permitted under the Act.[44] The general idea was to set Indians aside from non-Aboriginal society so they could be exposed to European religion and customs and gradually "civilized". Despite later reforms,[45] and recent efforts at major change,[46] the *Indian Act* is still in place today.

Shortly after Confederation, the main focus in Aboriginal / non-Aboriginal relations shifted to a distinctive group of Aboriginal peoples, the Métis.[47] The Red River Métis were people of mixed Indian / non-Indian ancestry who forged a unique culture based on fur-trading, farming, and summer buffalo hunts. In the 1860s, plans were made to transfer the Red River colony to Canada, but the Métis and other inhabitants were not consulted. New settlers flowed into the Red River area, threatening Métis claims and lands. In 1869 and, again, in 1885, the fiery Métis leader Louis Riel led rebellions against Canadian authorities at Red River,

Manitoba, and Batoche, Saskatchewan, respectively. Louis Riel was hanged for treason, but for the Métis and many others he lives on as a hero.[48]

Native concerns did win some legal recognition. In 1870, when Rupert's Land and the Northwestern Territory were transferred to Canada, so was the formal responsibility for settling Indian claims in this vast area.[49] This had little effect on the far northern Aboriginal occupants, the Inuit, whose claims were not formally addressed for a hundred years.[50] In 1870, the *Manitoba Act* created Manitoba and provided for half-breed land grants.[51] Unfortunately, the grants were woefully mismanaged, and provided little benefit for the Métis.[52]

The *British North America Act* and the *Manitoba Act* were followed by other nation-building documents that also affect the constitutional situation of some Aboriginal peoples. For example, the order-in-council admitting British Columbia into Canada committed the federal government to a policy regarding Indians and their lands "as liberal as that hitherto pursued by the British Columbia Government."[53] The 1912 Ontario and Quebec *Boundaries Extension Acts* committed these provinces to dealing with Indian claims to the same extent that Canada had done so previously.[54] The 1930 *Natural Resources Transfer Agreements*[55] created a distinct hunting, fishing and trapping constitutional framework for Indians in the three Prairie provinces.[56]

In 1969, a federal White Paper proposed an end to separate Indian status, a conversion of reserve lands into Indian private property, and a phasing out of the federal Indian Affairs bureaucracy.[57] Native groups protested vehemently, regarding the proposal as a frontal attack on traditional rights and culture.[58] The White Paper was withdrawn. In the decades that followed, federal Aboriginal policy — and proposals from Aboriginal peoples — moved increasingly toward separate, constitutionally guaranteed Aboriginal status and rights.[59]

The year 1971 marked the beginning of the modern land claims agreement in North America. In that year the American federal government, the state of Alaska, and 80,000 Alaska natives concluded the continent's first modern land claims settlement, contained in the *Alaska Native Claims Settlement Act*.[60] This was followed by two very significant events in Canada. In the January 1973 *Calder* decision,[61] the Supreme Court rejected a Nisga'a claim to land in northwestern British Columbia. However, it came close to conceding that Aboriginal people might have a title to land on the basis of their own prior use and occupancy. Two years later, the federal and Quebec governments and nearly 16,000 James Bay Cree and northern Quebec Inuit signed the first Canadian land claims agreement. Since 1975 there have been nearly 20 land claims agreements, mainly in northern Canada.[62]

Another important modern milestone in Aboriginal / non-Aboriginal relations is April 17, 1982. The *Constitution Act, 1982*[63] was enacted on this date. The Act symbolized a tendency in late 20th century Canada to address social, economic, and political issues through legal and constitutional guarantees. It recognized and affirmed Aboriginal and treaty rights, protected rights of Aboriginal peoples from the *Charter*, and provided for a constitutional conference to determine what other rights of Aboriginal peoples should be included in the constitution. The Act led to further constitutional changes in 1984, including additional Aboriginal protections and a guarantee of more Aboriginal constitutional conferences. These conferences focused on the Aboriginal desire for constitutionally guaranteed Aboriginal self-government. This did not materialize. Some governments were concerned about entrenching self-government without first defining it. The conferences ended without agreement.[64]

Two later attempts at constitutional change also ended in failure. The Meech Lake Accord of 1987–1990, which ignored most Aboriginal demands, was killed in 1990.[65] The Charlottetown Accord of 1992 moved in the opposite direction. It promised entrenched Aboriginal self-government, an Aboriginal constitutional veto, and many other extensive constitutional guarantees. The Charlottetown Accord died when it was rejected by a majority of Canadians, including, apparently, many Aboriginal people.[66] Will Aboriginal self-government be entrenched as a result of some future constitutional agreement? Or will it be established "from the ground up" by changes to the *Indian Act*, negotiated agreements, and more informal Aboriginal initiatives? In this area, prediction is perilous.[67]

Section 15 of the *Constitution Act, 1982*, the equality guarantee, was postponed until April 17, 1985, to give governments time to reconcile their laws with it. One of the most discriminatory parts of the *Indian Act* deprived Indian women but not Indian men of their Indian status when they married non-Indian spouses. In 1985, with retroactive effect to April 17 of that year, Parliament enacted new Indian status provisions to redress some of the sexual discrimination issues under the former régime, and to give Indian bands greater power to administer their own membership provisions.

Although extraordinarily complex and far from perfect, the reform underscored a growing awareness of the special problems of Aboriginal women.[68]

The summer of 1990 yielded three mileposts. On May 31, 1990, the Supreme Court of Canada rendered its decision in *Sparrow*, holding that Aboriginal rights are entrenched subject to infringements that the courts consider to be constitutionally justified. By confirming that Aboriginal (and treaty) rights have entrenched status, subject to a judicial process of interest-balancing, the Supreme Court has given the judiciary a new leading role in shaping Aboriginal / non-Aboriginal relations.[69] A month later, Aboriginal M.L.A. Elijah Harper used parliamentary tactics to delay a provincial vote past a constitutional deadline and thereby killed the Meech Lake Accord.[70]

Also, in that long summer, members of the Kanesetake and Kahnawake reserves blockaded roads and a bridge to protest expansion of a golf course onto land at Oka that had been subject to Aboriginal claims since the 18th century. The protest escalated into some violent confrontations with police, armed forces, and others.[71] It was followed by a series of Aboriginal occupations and blockades in support of claims and grievances throughout most of the rest of the 1990s.[72]

In 1996 the *Royal Commission on Aboriginal Peoples*[73] called for dramatic new powers of Aboriginal self-government and for massive increases in public government funding for Aboriginal concerns. In its 1996 *Van der Peet* decision[74] and its 1997 *Delgamuukw* decision,[75] the Supreme Court clarified aspects of the proof, identification, and content of Aboriginal rights and Aboriginal title. The year 1998 brought the *Nisga'a Final Agreement*,[76] the first modern land claims agreement to be signed in British Columbia. April 1, 1999 marked the creation of Nunavut, a new territorial government controlled, effectively, by the Inuit of northern Canada.[77]

The first years of the new century brought mixed results. In 2003, the Supreme Court confirmed that the Métis can hold constitutionally protected Aboriginal rights, but it provided only a start at legally defining Métis.[78] More Yukon land claims agreements were signed,[79] but several remained unfinished, three decades after the Yukon negotiations had begun. There were claims agreements in the Northwest Territories[80] and northern Labrador,[81] but no final agreements from the more than 50 claim negotiations in the B.C. Treaty process. Although the federal government managed to establish a new specific treaty claims process,[82] it had to withdraw more controversial proposals for *Indian Act* reform.[83] Beyond the new legal mileposts, many Aboriginal people continued to live in the shadows of poverty, unemployment and illness.[84] Despite these hurdles, Aboriginal children were graduating from high school and university in significantly higher proportions.[85]

In retrospect, the turbulent summer of 1990 was symbolic of the choices that lie ahead. Which of its three markers — the constitutional and judicial initiative in *Sparrow*, the legislative action of Mr. Harper, or the confrontation at Oka — will lead to changes to the situation of Canadian Aboriginal peoples in the century to come? Are confrontation and legal change the only alternatives? The drawbacks of confrontation should be obvious to those who value tolerance and human life. On the other hand, we may need to go beyond purely legal expedients, to Aboriginal values, education, and practical support, and try to develop a more general appreciation of the rich potential of these varied and remarkable peoples in our midst. The law examined in this book, the law relating to Aboriginal peoples in Canada, is a complex and imperfect instrument. To study it is to see the need to look beyond it.

Notes

1. See, however, *Kaianerakowa*, described in **Reading 12(a)**. See also M. Gluckman, *Politics, Law and Ritual in Tribal Society* (Chicago: Aldine, 1965); Wa & D. Uukw, *The Spirit in the Land* (Gabriola, B.C.: Reflections Press, 1992); A. Mills, *Eagle Down is Our Law: Witsuit'en Law, Feasts and Land Claims* (Vancouver: U.B.C. Press, 1994); G. Friesen, A.C. Hamilton, and C.M. Sinclair, " 'Justice Systems' and Manitoba's Aboriginal People: An Historical Survey" in G. Friesen, *River Road: Essays on Manitoba and Prairie History* (Winnipeg: University of Manitoba Press, 1996), 49; James [sakéj] Youngblood Henderson, "First Nations' Legal Inheritances in Canada: The Mikmaq Model" (1996) 23 Man. L.J. 1 at 1–31; M.D. Walters, "According to the Old Customs of our Nation: Aboriginal Self-Government on the Credit River Mississauga Reserve, 1826–1847" (1998–1999) 30 Ottawa L. Rev. 1.
2. Some important international law documents of possible relevance to Canadian Aboriginal peoples: (i) Article 27 of the *International Covenant on Civil and Political Rights* says that members of ethnic, religious, or linguistic minorities within states "shall not be denied the right, in community with other members of their group, to enjoy their culture, to profess and practice their religion, or to use their own language": December 19, 1966, 999 U.N.T.S. 171, arts. 9–14 (entered into force March 23, 1976, accession by Canada May 19, 1976). In the 1981 *Lovelace* case, the United Nations Human Rights Committee held that former s. 12(1)(b) of the *Indian Act* violated Article 27's guarantee of the right to enjoy a minority culture in community with other members of the group: *Lovelace v. Canada*, Comm. No. R 6/24 (also known as Comm. No. 24/1977), GAOR 36th Sess., Supp. No. 40, U.N. Doc. A/36/40 (1981); (ii) Article 1(1) of the 1992 *United Nations Declaration on the Rights of Persons Belonging to National or Ethnic, Religious and Linguistic Minorities* says

that "[s]tates shall protect the existence and the national, cultural, religious, and linguistic identity of minorities within their respective territories and shall encourage conditions for the promotion of that identity": UNGA Res. 47/135 of December 18, 1992 (92nd plenary meeting of the G.A.); U.N. Doc. E/CN 4/Sub.2/1992/37 (U.N. Eide-Report 1992) at 36 (Annex); (iii) Articles 8 and 9 of the 1989 *International Labour Convention Concerning Indigenous and Tribal Peoples in Independent Countries* (I.L.O. Convention No. 169) guarantee respect for indigenous peoples' customs and existing laws, to the extent that these are consistent with national law and basic international human rights: Repr. in (1989) 28 I.L.M. 1382 (entered into force September 5, 1991, not yet acceded to by Canada); and (iv) Article 1(4) of the 1965 *International Convention on the Elimination of All Forms of Racial Discrimination* prohibits discrimination on the basis of ethnic and similar criteria: Annex to UNGA Res. 2106-A of December 21, 1965. Article 1(4) allows special measures for ensuring equality for certain races or ethnic groups, "providing, however, that such measures do not, as a consequence, lead to the maintenance of separate rights for different racial groups and that they shall not be continued until after the objectives for which they were taken have been achieved." Documents relating to the international law principle of self-determination are noted briefly in note 1 **Chapter 12**. For these and other international law documents, see S.J. Anaya, *Indigenous Peoples in International Law* (New York, Oxford University press, 1996).

3. For a brief discussion of the international law principle of self-determination and its possible application to Aboriginal peoples, see note 1 **Chapter 12**, below. This and other international law principles are discussed in S.J. Anaya, *supra* note 2.
4. See **Part 3**, below.
5. For general works on the economic, social, and related conditions of Aboriginal peoples in Canada, see J. Silman, ed., *Enough is Enough: Aboriginal Women Speak Out* (Toronto: The Women's Press, 1987); J. Sawchuk, "Native People, Social Conditions" in *The Canadian Encyclopedia*, Year 2000 ed. (Toronto: McClelland & Stewart, 1999) at 1594; H. McCue, "Native People, Education" in *The Canadian Encyclopedia, ibid.* at 1581; J.A. Price et al., "Native People, Economic Conditions" in *The Canadian Encyclopedia, ibid.* at 1580; T.K. Young, "Native People, Health" in *The Canadian Encyclopedia, ibid.* at 1584; G. York, *The Dispossessed: Life and Death in Native Canada* (Toronto: Lester, 1989); P. Comeau and A. Santin, *The First Canadians: A Profile of Canada's Native People Today* (Toronto: James Lorimer & Company, 1990); R. Hunter and R. Calihoo, *Occupied Canada: A Young White Man Discovers His Unsuspected Past* (Toronto: McClelland & Stewart, 1991); A.C. Hamilton and C.M. Sinclair, *Public Inquiry into the Administration of Justice and Aboriginal Peoples: Report of the Aboriginal Justice Inquiry of Manitoba*, vol. I (Winnipeg: Queen's Printer, 1991); L. Krotz, *Indian Country: Inside Another Canada* (Toronto: McClelland & Stewart, 1992); M. Boldt, *Surviving as Indians: The Challenge of Self-Government* (Toronto: University of Toronto Press, 1993); J.S. Frideres, *Native Peoples in Canada: Contemporary Conflicts*, 4th ed. (Scarborough, Ont.: Prentice Hall, 1993); D. Smith, *The Seventh Fire: The Struggle for Aboriginal Government* (Toronto: Key Porter Books, 1993): D.A. Long and O.P. Dickason, *Visions of the Heart: Canadian Aboriginal Issues* (Toronto: Harcourt Brace, 1996); and Royal Commission on Aboriginal Peoples, *Report of the Royal Commission on Aboriginal Peoples*, 5 vols. (Ottawa: Canada Communication Group, 1996) [hereinafter "*Report*"].
6. The problems go well beyond the effects of modern technology. For an earlier non-Aboriginal influence that generated ongoing problems, see J.R. Miller, *Shingwauk's Vision: A History of Native Residential Schools* (Toronto: University of Toronto Press, 1996); *Report*, vol. 1, chap. 10. For other problems, see *Report*, vol. 2, chap. 5, s. 1.2, 800–801: high levels of dependence on social assistance; *ibid.* at 802–803: poverty; *ibid.* at 802–803: high unemployment; *Report*, vol. 3, chap. 3, s. 1.1, 120–21: low life expectancy; *ibid.* at 137–42: high levels of infectious diseases; *ibid.* at 175–98 and chap. 4: poor living conditions and housing; and *Report*, vol. 3, chap. 3, s. 1.2, 108. See also 153–65 regarding "disturbingly high" rates of injury, violence, and self-destructive behaviour.
7. See Royal Commission on Aboriginal Peoples, *Choosing Life: A Special Report on Suicide Among Aboriginal People* (Ottawa: Canada Communication Group, 1995) at 30 (suicide) and *Report*, vol. 4, chap. 4, s. 3.3 at 164–65 (school-leaving rates) and *supra* note 5.
8. For example, the high level of Aboriginal incarceration in prisons may derive — at least in part — from the systemic bias against Aboriginal peoples in the Canadian criminal justice system: see *R. v. Gladue*, [1999] S.C.R. 688 at paras. 61–65, 68–69.
9. See, for example, J. Borrows, *Recovering Canada: The Resurgence of Indigenous Law* (Toronto: University of Toronto Press, 2002), chap. 2, regarding the potential contribution of traditional Aboriginal knowledge to environmental and planning law.
10. For one example, see D. Smith, *The Seventh Fire: The Struggle for Aboriginal Self-Government* (Toronto: Key Porter, 1993) at 206–207 (Aboriginal community and elder involvement in dispute resolution).
11. For general histories, see J.R. Miller, *Skyscrapers Hide the Heavens: A History of Indian-White Relations in Canada* (Toronto: University of Toronto Press, 2000); and O.P. Dickason, *Canada's First Nations: A History of Founding Peoples from Earliest Times*, 3d ed. (Don Mills, Ont.: Oxford University Press, 2002). Other general historical sources include P.A. Cumming and N.H. Mickenberg, *Native Rights in Canada*, 2d ed. (Toronto: Indian-Eskimo Association of Canada, 1972); B.G. Trigger and W.E. Washburn, eds., *The Cambridge History of the Native Peoples of the Americas: North America*, vol. 1 (New York: Cambridge University Press, 1996); A.J. Ray, *I Have Lived Here Since the World Began: An Illustrated History of Canada's Native Peoples* (Toronto: Lester Publishing, 1996).
12. J. Cinq-Mars, "La Place des Grottes du Poisson-Bleu dans la Préhistoire Béringienne" (1990) 1 *Revista Arqueologia Americana* 9: 26–27. See also R.E. Morlan and J. Cinq-Mars, "Ancient Beringians: Human Occupation in the Late Pleistocene of Alaska and the Yukon Territory" in D.M. Hopkins et al., eds., *Paleoecology of Beringia* (New York: Academic Press, 1982) at 381. Note, though, that dates indicated by the early evidence are subject to ongoing revision: S.J. Fiedel, *Prehistory of the Americas*, 2d ed. (New York: Cambridge University Press, 1992) at 58–59; Dickason, *ibid.* at 8; and *infra* note 14.
13. From southern Canada to Central America, scientists have found fluted spear points that appear to date to about 11,500 B.C., and are clearly made by humans: Fiedel, *ibid.* at 56–58. See also R. McGhee, "Prehistory", *The Canadian Encyclopedia*, Year 2000 ed. (Toronto: McClelland & Stewart, 1999) at 1885–88. Early Arctic occupation by Paleo-Eskimos and Dorset peoples dates to about 3000 B.C.: see R. McGhee, *Ancient People of the Arctic* (Vancouver: U.B.C. Press, 1996).

    Artifacts at Monte Verde, Chile, have been dated at about 12,500 B.P. See T.D. Dillehay and M.B. Collins, "Early Cultural Evidence from Monte Verde in Chile", *Nature*, 332: 150–52; T.D. Dillehay, *Monte Verdi, a Late Pleistocene Settlement in Chile* (Washington: Smithsonian Institution Press, 1989); and T.D. Dillehay, *The Settlement of the Americas: A New Prehistory* (New York: Basic Books, 2000). If migration to South America passed through North America, this suggests a date at least as old for North America.

14. Fiedel, *ibid.* at 53–56; Dickason, *supra* note 11 at 1–8.
15. D.M. Hopkins et al., eds., *Palaeontology of Beringia* (New York: Academic Press, 1982); B.M. Fagan, *The Great Journey: The Peopling of Ancient America* (New York: Thames and Hudson, 1987), chap. 5; Dickason, *supra* note 11 at 4.
16. Dickason, *supra* note 11 at 4–6; E.J. Dixon, *Quest for the Origins of the First Americans* (Albuquerque: University of New Mexico Press, 1993).
17. See **Readings 1(a) and 1(b)**.
18. See generally M.M.R. Freeman et al., "Native People" in *The Canadian Encyclopedia*, Year 2000 ed. (Toronto: McClelland & Stewart, 1999) at 1576–98; Dickason, *supra* note 11, chap. 4; *Report*, vol. 1, chap. 4.
19. See further, **Chapters 3**, **4**, **9** and **10**.
20. On relations between Aboriginal people and those of New France, see generally, R.G. Thwaites, ed., *The Jesuit Relations and Allied Documents* (Cleveland: The Burrows Bros. Co., 1986–1901); G. Lanctot, *A History of Canada* (Toronto: Clarke, Irwin & Co., 1964), col. II; W.J. Eccles, *France in America* (New York: Harper & Row, 1972); M. Trudel, *The Beginnings of New France, 1524–1663* (Toronto: McClelland and Stewart, 1973); C.J. Jaenen, *Friend and Foe: Aspects of French-Amerindian Cultural Contact in the Sixteenth and Seventeenth Centuries* (Toronto: McClelland & Stewart, 1976); C.J. Jaenen, *The Role of the Church in New France* (Toronto: McGraw-Hill Ryerson, 1976); J. Mathieu, entry on "New France", *The Canadian Encyclopedia*, Year 2000 ed. (Toronto: McClelland & Stewart, 1999) at 1622–23; J.R. Miller, *Skyscrapers Hide the Heavens*, *supra* note 11; P.A. Cumming and N.H. Mickenberg, *supra* note 11, chap. 11; C.J. Jaenen, *The Role of the Church in New France* (Ottawa: Canadian Historical Association, 1985); B.G. Trigger, *Natives and Newcomers: Canada's "Heroic Age" Reconsidered* (Kingston and Montreal: McGill-Queen's University Press, 1985), chaps. 4–6; Dickason, *supra* note 11, chap. 11.
21. The debt to the Indians went beyond the fur trade: local food, such as pumpkins and blueberries, tobacco, forced germination planting techniques, the use of toboggans for transporting wood in winter, and new terms such as *caribou*, were all adopted enthusiastically by the French: Trudel, *ibid.*, chap. 11.
22. As Trigger and others have pointed out, though, it was easier for French traders to adapt to Indian ways than Indians to European ways: B.G. Trigger, *supra* note 20 at 195.
23. Dickason, *supra* note 11 at 146–49.
24. See, for example, Cumming and Mickenberg, *supra* note 11 at 79–80, and Jaenen, *supra* note 20 at 11. Trigger, *supra* note 20, says that while the Recollects were concerned about the bad influence of the traders and interpreters who lived amongst the Indians (320), the Jesuits appreciated that the fur trade could be a source of influence with the Indians, and tried to control rather than limit it (331).
25. G.F.G. Stanley, "The First Indian 'Reserves' in Canada" (1950) 4 *Revue d'histoire de l'Amérique française* 178.
26. See further, **Chapter 2, Part 4**.
27. See, generally, L.H. Morgan, *League of Ho-dé-no-sau-nee or Iroquois* (New York: Sage and Brother, 1851); G.T. Hunt, *The Wars of the Iroquois: A Study in Intertribal Trade Relations* (Madison, Wisc.: University of Wisconsin Press, 1940); Elisabeth Tooker, "The League of the Iroquois: History, Politics, and Ritual" in B.T. Trigger, ed., *Handbook of North American Indians*, vol. 15 (Washington D.C.: Smithsonian Institution, 1978); B. Graymount, *The Iroquois in the American Revolution* (Syracuse: Syracuse University Press, 1972), chap. 1; F. Jennings, *The Ambiguous Iroquois Empire* (New York: Norton, 1984); E.J. Dickson-Gilmore, "Resurrecting the Peace: Traditionalist Approaches to Separate Justice in the Kahnawake Mohawk Nation" in R.A. Silverman and M.O. Nielsen, eds., *Aboriginal Peoples in Canadian Criminal Justice* (Toronto: Butterworths, 1992), chap. 20, in **Reading 12(a)**; Elisabeth Tooker, "The Five (Later Six) Nations Confederacy, 1550–1784" in E.S. Rogers and D.B. Smith, eds., *Aboriginal Ontario* (Toronto: Dundurn Press, 1994), chap. 5.
28. Appraisals of the geographical extent of Iroquois influence vary. Contrast Morgan, *ibid.*, and R. Wright, *Stolen Continents: The "New World" Through Indian Eyes Since 1492* (Toronto: Penguin, 1992) at 115, with Hunt, *ibid.*, and R.S. Allen, *His Majesty's Indian Allies: British Indian Policy in The Defence of Canada, 1774–1815* (Toronto: Dundurn Press, 1992) at 18. However, all agree that the Confederacy was a formidable and remarkably durable alliance.
29. For the period leading to the Royal Proclamation of 1763, see J.M. Sosin, *Whitehall and the Wilderness: The Middle West in British Colonial Policy, 1760–1775* (Lincoln: University of Nebraska Press, 1961); J. Stagg, *Anglo-Indian Relations in North America to 1763 and An Analysis of the Royal Proclamation of 7 October, 1763* (Ottawa: D.I.A.N.D., 1981).
30. Pontiac laid siege to the British fort at Detroit in the summer of 1763, the Odawa chief. Although Detroit did not fall, nine other forts did. See F. Parkman, *The Conspiracy of Pontiac* (New York: Collier Books, 1966, first pub. 1851); H. Peckham, *Pontiac and the Indian Uprising* (New York: Russell and Russell, 1947); Dickason, *supra* note 11 at 158–60.
31. On the Proclamation, see C.W. Avlord, "The Genesis of the Proclamation of 1763" (1908) 36 *Michigan Pioneer and Historical Society Collections* 20; P.A. Cumming and N.H. Mickenberg, *supra* note 11, chap. 4; B. Slattery, *The Land Rights of Indigenous Canadian Peoples as Affected by the Crown's Acquisition of their Territories, 1979, Parts I and II* (Saskatoon: Native Law Centre, University of Saskatchewan, 1979) [also a D.Phil. thesis, Oxford University, 1979]; J. Stagg, *Anglo-Indian Relations in North America to 1763 and An Analysis of the Royal Proclamation of 7 October, 1763* (Ottawa: D.I.A.N.D., 1981); G.S. Lester, *The Territorial Rights of the Inuit of the Canadian Northwest Territories: A Legal Argument*, 1981, chap. XIX. See further, **Chapter 3, Part 9**.
32. B. Graymount, *The Iroquois in the American Revolution* (Syracuse: Syracuse University Press, 1972); B.G. Wilson, "Loyalists", *The Canadian Encyclopedia*, Year 2000 ed. (Toronto: McClelland & Stewart, 1999) at 1374.
33. R.J. Surtees, "Land Cessions, 1763–1830" in E.S. Rogers and D.B. Smith, eds., *Aboriginal Ontario: Historical Perspectives on the First Nations* (Toronto: Dundurn Press, 1994), chap. 6; and **Chapter 5**.
34. See A. Morris, *The Treaties of Canada with the Indians of Manitoba and the North-West Territories* (Toronto: Belfords Clark, 1880); Cumming and Mickenberg, *supra* note 11, chap. 14; and **Chapter 5**.
35. (U.K.), 30 & 31 Vict., c. 3. (Originally called the *British North America Act, 1867*).
36. See further, **Chapter 6**.
37. See further, **Chapter 12**.
38. *St. Catherine's Milling and Lumber Co. v. The Queen* (1889), 14 App. Cas. 46 (J.C.P.C.), **Chapter 3, Part 10**.
39. See further, **Chapter 3, Part 10**.
40. *Johnson and Graham's Lessee v. M'Intosh* (1823), 8 Wheaton 543, 21 U.S. 240, 5 L. Ed. 681 (U.S.S.Ct.). See **Chapter 3, Part 11**.
41. **Chapter 4, Part 1**.
42. Now R.S.C. 1985, c. I-5. On post-Confederation Indian policy generally, see J. Leslie and R. Macguire for Treaties and Historical Research Branch, Department of Indian Affairs and Northern Development, *The Historical Development of the Indian Act*, 2d ed. (Ottawa: D.I.A.N.D., 1979); W. Daugherty and D. Madill for Treaties and Historical Research Branch, Department of Indian Affairs and Northern Development, 2d ed., *Indian Government under Indian*

Act Legislation, 1868–1951, 2d ed. (Ottawa: D.I.A.N.D., 1984); R.H. Bartlett, *The Indian Act of Canada*, 2d ed. (Saskatoon: University of Saskatchewan Native Law Centre, 1988); R.H. Bartlett, *Indian Reserves and Aboriginal Lands in Canada: A Study in Law and History* (Saskatoon: University of Saskatchewan Native Law Centre, 1990); *Report*, vol. 1, chap. 9 at 255–332.

43. In a manner that involved sexually discriminatory and other arbitrary criteria: see further, **Chapter 2, Part 4**.
44. See generally W. Moss and E. Gardner-O'Toole for Research Branch, Library of Parliament, *Aboriginal People: History of Discriminatory Laws*, rev. ed. (Ottawa: Supply and Services Canada, 1992) and *Report*, vol. 1, chap. 9, s. 9. Formal restrictions in the Act were accompanied by policy constraints, such as the Prairie travel pass requirements of the 1880s and early 1890s (*Report*, vol. 1, chap. 9, s. 9 at 296–97), and limits to the right to vote in federal and most provincial elections (*Report*, vol. 1, chap. 9, s. 9 at 299–300).
45. The alcohol prohibitions, travel limitations, bans on traditional cultural and religious ceremonies, and sexually discriminatory eligibility criteria have been repealed, and the local government restrictions have been eased.
46. That is, in Manitoba.
47. See generally, D. Redbird, *We are Métis: A Metis View of the Development of A Native Canadian People* (Willowdale, Ont.: Ontario Metis and Non-status Indian Assn., 1980); J.S.H. Brown, "Métis", *The Canadian Encyclopedia*, Year 2000 ed. (Vancouver: McClelland & Stewart, 1999) at 1447–79; D. Purich, *The Métis* (Toronto: Lorimer, 1988); M. Giraud (trans. G. Woodcock), *The Métis in the Canadian West* (Edmonton: University of Alberta Press, 1986); D.N. Sprague, *Canada and the Métis, 1869–1885* (Waterloo, Ont.: Wilfrid Laurier University Press, 1988); T.E. Flanagan, "The History of Métis Aboriginal Rights: Politics, Principle and Policy", [1990] 5 Can. J. L. & Soc. 71; Dickason, *supra* note 11, chaps. 20 and 21; *Report*, vol. 4, chap. 5.
48. See G.F.G. Stanley, *Louis Riel* (Toronto: Ryerson, 1963); M. Siggins, *Riel: A Life of Revolution* (Toronto: Harper Collins, 1994).
49. *Order of Her Majesty in Council admitting Rupert's Land and the Northwestern Territory into the Union*, June 23, 1870, clause 14 and sch. A, para. 8; See K. McNeil, *Native Claims in Rupert's Land and the North-Western Territory: Canada's Constitutional Obligations* (Saskatoon, University of Saskatchewan Native Law Centre, 1982).
50. J.R. Miller, *Skyscrapers Hide the Heavens*, *supra* note 11 at chap. 12; Dickason, *supra* note 11 at 55–56, 204–206, 357–63, 370–73, 379–80, and 405; and M.A. Freeman, "Inuit" in *The Canadian Encyclopedia*, Year 2000 ed. (Toronto: McClelland & Stewart, 1999) at 1183–84. See **Chapter 2, Part 5(c)**, and **Chapter 11, Parts 5 and 7**.
51. S.C. 1870, c. 3, s. 31, reprinted in R.S.C. 1985, App. II, no. 8.
52. G.F.G. Stanley, *The Birth of Western Canada* (Toronto: University of Toronto Press, 1961) at 244–45; D.N. Sprague, "Government Lawlessness in the Administration of the Manitoba Land Claims, 1870–1887" (1980) 10 Man. L.J. 415; P.L.A. Chartrand, "Aboriginal Rights: The Dispossession of the Métis" (1991) 29 Osgoode Hall L.J. 457, 470–72. For recent legislation relating to Alberta Métis, see **Chapter 12, Part 3(c)(iii)(C)**.
53. *Order of Her Majesty in Council Admitting British Columbia into the Union*, May 16, 1871, Schedule, clause 13.
54. *An Act to Extend the Boundaries of the Province of Quebec*, S.C., 1912, c. 45, s. 2(c); *An Act to Extend the Boundaries of the Province of Ontario*, S.C., 1912, c. 40, s. 2(a).
55. *Constitution Act, 1930* (U.K.), 21 Geo. V. c. 26, Schedules: *Manitoba, Memorandum of Agreement; Saskatchewan, Memorandum of Agreement; Alberta, Memorandum of Agreement.*
56. See further, **Chapter 6**.
57. Canada, *Statement of the Government of Canada on Indian Policy, 1969* (the "White Paper") (Ottawa: D.I.A.N.D., 1969).
58. See generally, S. Weaver, *Making Indian Policy: The Hidden Agenda 1968-79* (Toronto: University of Toronto, 1981).
59. Compare the White Paper with the proposals in the 1992 Charlottetown Accord: **Chapter 12, Part 5**; and compare Indian Chiefs of Alberta, *Citizens Plus A Presentation by the Indian Chiefs of Alberta to Right Honourable P.E. Trudeau*, June 1970 (Edmonton: Indian Association of Alberta, 1970) with the constitutional concerns conveyed in Canada, *Report of the Royal Commission on Aboriginal Peoples* (Ottawa: Canadian Communications Group Publishing, 1996): **Chapter 12, Part 5**. (The Commission operated independently of the federal government, and had significant Aboriginal representation.)
60. (U.S.). 85 Stat. 688. Public Law 92–203, 92nd Congress, H.R. 10367, December 18, 1971.
61. *Calder v. British Columbia (A.G.)*, [1973] S.C.R. 313: **Chapter 4, Part 1**.
62. See further, **Chapter 11**.
63. Schedule B to the *Canada Act 1982* (U.K.), 1982, c. 11.
64. See further, **Chapter 7, Parts 1–3**.
65. Largely as a result of actions by an Aboriginal legislator: see text, below.
66. S. Imai, *Aboriginal Law Handbook*, 2d ed. (Scarborough, Ont.: Carswell, 1999) at 17. It was supported generally by Inuit and Métis: D. Sanders, "Pre-Existing Rights: The Aboriginal Peoples of Canada" in G.-E. Beaudoin and E. Mendes, *The Canadian Charter of Rights and Freedoms*, 3d ed. (Scarborough, Ont.: Carswell, 1995), chap. 17 at 17–20. See further, **Chapter 11, Part 5**.
67. See further, **Chapter 12**.
68. See further, **Chapter 2, Part 4**.
69. See further, **Chapter 7, Part 4**.
70. **Chapter 11, Part 5**.
71. See further, **Chapter 11, Part 9**.
72. 1995 was especially turbulent. In May, Douglas Lake Indian band members blockaded a B.C. cattle ranch to protest charges of illegal gill-netting in privately-stocked lakes. In July, a salmon fishing dispute on the Miramichi River, N.B., involved illegal nets and a road blockade. In August, about thirty people occupied Gustafsen Lake ranch land in B.C., claiming it as a sacred Aboriginal sun dance site. After gun-fire exchanges with police and a 10-month trial, 15 protesters were convicted of offences such as mischief to property. In September, dissident Chippewa Indians occupied Ipperwash Provincial Park on Lake Huron, claiming that park development desecrated an Aboriginal burial ground. Earlier they had occupied a military base that had not been returned to the Chippewa as promised. During the park occupation, a confrontation with police resulted in the death of Aboriginal protester Mr. Dudley George. A provincial police officer was later convicted of criminal negligence in causing the death. See "Disputes Involving Aboriginal People During 1995" *Canadian Press Newstex*, December 11, 1995; "Policeman Guilty of Negligence", *ibid.*, April 28, 1997; S. Mertl, "Standoff Leader Cleared of Attempted Murder", *ibid.*, May 20, 1997.
73. *Report of the Royal Commission on Aboriginal Peoples*, 1996: **Chapter 12, Part 7**.
74. *R. v. Van der Peet*, [1996] 2 S.C.R. 507: **Chapter 9, Part 3**.
75. *Delgamuukw v. British Columbia*, [1997] 3 S.C.R. 1010: **Chapter 8, Part 3**.
76. Canada, British Columbia, Nisga'a Nation, *Nisga'a Final Agreement*, August 4, 1998: **Chapter 11, Part 7(h)**.
77. See **Chapter 11, Part 7(e)**. This was followed by the signing of the *Sechelt Agreement-in-Principle* on April 16, 1999, and the *Labrador Inuit Agreement-in-Principle* on May 10, 1999: **Chapter 11, Part 7(i)**.

78. *R. v. Powley*, [2003] 2 S.C.R. 207: see **Chapter 10, Part 5**.
79. See **Chapter 11, Part 7(f)**.
80. See **Chapter 11, Part 7(i)**.
81. See **Chapter 11, Part 7(j)**.
82. See **Chapter 11, Part 4(b)**.
83. See **Chapter 12, Part 3(b)(i)**.
84. Maple Leaf Web, an independent political affairs web-site at the University of Lethbridge, makes the following comment:

> Aboriginal infant mortality rates have seen improvements over the years, but the bigger picture remains bleak. Incidences of mental illness, alcoholism and foetal alcohol syndrome, suicide, family violence, injuries, diabetes, tuberculosis, HIV infection, obesity and hypertension are often several times higher than those in the non-aboriginal population. For instance, suicide rates among aboriginal people are around three times higher than the average, while Status Indians in BC can expect to live 7.5 years less than other British Columbians.... In addition, widespread poverty compounds these negative health indicators: *Native Health Care Issues*, <http://www.mapleleafweb.com/features/native/social-issues/health-care.html>, last modified, September 12, 2003.

See also Statistics Canada, *Aboriginal Peoples Survey 2001 Initial Findings: Well-being of the Non-reserve Aboriginal population* <http://www.statcan.ca/english/freepub/89-589-XIE/free.htm>.

85. Statistics Canada, *Education in Canada: Raising the Standard, data released 11 March 2003*, <http://12statcan.ca/english/census01/Products/Analytic/companion/educ/pdf/96FOO30XIE2001012.pdf>; Statistics Canada, *Aboriginal Peoples Survey 2001 Initial Findings: Well-being of the Non-reserve Aboriginal population,* ibid.; Department of Indian Affairs and Northern Development, *Aboriginal Peoples in the Workforce: The National Perspective, 24 September, 2003,* <http://www.ainc-inac.gc.ca/ai/awpi/fac_e.html>. Cf. H. Rubenstein and R. Clifton *The Challenge of Aboriginal Education,* (2003) Fraser Forum 24 for a more critical assessment of reserve-school outcomes. At the post-secondary level, June, 2003 marked a unique development: the opening of the first accredited and -operated university in Canada, the First Nations University of Canada. Formerly the Saskatchewan Federated Indian College, the FNUC has campuses in Regina, Prince Albert, and Saskatoon, and an enrolment of over 1200 students: <http://www.firstnationsuniversity.ca>. At the college level, see, for example, the Institute of Indigenous Government in British Columbia: <http://www.indigenous.bc.ca>.

2 Who Is an Aboriginal Person?

Chapter Highlights

- Many different traditional, social, and cultural groups of Canadian Aboriginal peoples belong to eleven major Aboriginal language families that include over 50 different languages.
- Canadian Aboriginal peoples include more than 45,000 Inuit, about 700,000 Indians subject to the federal *Indian Act*, and about 300,000 Métis people.
- The broadest legal category comprises "the Aboriginal peoples of Canada", whose existing Aboriginal and treaty rights are recognized and affirmed in the *Constitution Act, 1982*.
- Section 91(24) of the *Constitution Act, 1867* gives the federal Parliament exclusive legislative jurisdiction in relation to "Indians, and lands reserved for the Indians".
- Indians subject to the *Indian Act* are divided into a mass of statutory categories and subcategories with different legal entitlements.
- Other legal categories of Aboriginal person are created by treaties and modern land claims agreements.

Synopsis

Although all Aboriginal peoples have a common heritage in the first occupancy of North America, they belong to a rich variety of different cultures and societies. The Inuit tend to live in the Arctic and subarctic regions; Métis have distinct cultures that combine Aboriginal and non-Aboriginal worlds in unique cultural blends; and many *Indian Act* Indians live on reserves. The *Indian Act* itself is one of several formal documents that superimpose on Aboriginal peoples a mass of additional legal categories. These documents attach different legal consequences to different forms of Aboriginal status, affect everyday Aboriginal life, and add greatly to the complexity of this subject.

Selected Readings

🖹 links material in this chapter to the corresponding headings and page numbers of the relevant readings.

🖹 Entire Chapter	General Status Provisions	221
🖹 Parts 4(d), 9	*Canadian Bill of Rights* and *Charter*	222
	Canada (A.G.) v. Lavell; Isaac et al. v. Bedard	223
🖹 Part 4(e)	1985 *Indian Act* Status Provisions	228
🖹 Parts 4(g), 9	*Corbiere v. Canada (Minister of Indian and Northern Affairs)*	231
🖹 Part 5(c)	*R. v. Powley*	370

1. ANTHROPOLOGICAL AND LEGAL DESCRIPTIONS

Canadian Aboriginal people[†] are descendants of the first inhabitants of North America who live within the boundaries of Canada. In 2001, nearly one million people in Canada identified themselves as Aboriginal,[1] and over 1.3 million people in the country reported having at least some Aboriginal origins.[2] Aboriginal peoples are associated with a rich variety of traditional, social, and cultural groups.[3] For example, they belong to eleven major language families that comprise about 53 different languages. Of the total Aboriginal population there are over 45,000 Inuit[4] who live mainly in the Arctic and subarctic regions; over 700,000 Indians who are subject to the federal *Indian Act*;[5] and about 300,000 Métis[‡] of mixed Aboriginal and non-Aboriginal ancestry and non-status Indians with Indian ancestry who are ineligible to register under the *Indian Act*.[6] Most registered Indians belong to one of the 612 Indian bands[7] or First Nations[8] across the country. About 57% of registered Indians, or 31% of all people who identify themselves as Aboriginal, live on one of Canada's 2360 Indian reserves.[9] Over 49% of the total self-identifying Aboriginal population live in urban areas.[10]

The legal categories of Canadian Aboriginal peoples are complex, and relate only indirectly to their cultural situation. There are five main sets of legal distinctions:

(i) between "Aboriginal peoples" under s. 35 of the *Constitution Act, 1982*[11] and other Canadians;
(ii) between Indians under s. 91(24) of the *Constitution Act, 1867*[12] and other Canadians;
(iii) between Indians under the *Indian Act*[13] and Inuit, Métis and other non-*Indian Act* people;
(iv) between treaty and non-treaty Indians; and
(v) between claims agreement beneficiaries and other Aboriginal peoples.

2. SECTION 35 ABORIGINAL PEOPLES

Section 35(1) of the *Constitution Act, 1982*[14] recognizes and affirms the existing Aboriginal and treaty rights of the "Aboriginal peoples of Canada". Section 35(2) of the *Constitution Act, 1982* says that "[i]n this Act, 'Aboriginal peoples of Canada' includes the Indian, Inuit and Métis people of Canada." Two preliminary points are worth noting about this provision. First, because it uses the verb "includes", it is not necessarily exhaustive of the categories of peoples to be considered Aboriginal for the purposes of the *Constitution Act, 1982*. Second, the provision provides no further definition of who these Indian, Inuit, and Métis peoples are.

3. SECTION 91(24) INDIANS

Section 91(24) of the *Constitution Act, 1867*[15] (formerly called the *British North America Act, 1867*) gives the federal Parliament exclusive legislative jurisdiction in relation to "Indians, and lands reserved for the Indians". It has always been assumed that this provision includes Indians who are subject to the federal *Indian Act*, although neither s. 91(24) nor any other part of the *Constitution Act, 1867* supplies a definition of "Indians".

For a long time, it was unclear as to whether the term used in s. 91(24) extends to Inuit, previously known as Eskimos. In the 1939 *Reference Re Eskimos*,[16] the Supreme Court of Canada decided that "Indians" in s. 91(24) *does* include the Eskimos of northern Quebec, because Eskimos had traditionally been classified with Indians in official government records prior to 1867. The decision implies that s. 91(24) applies to *all* Canadian Inuit.

If this section is broad enough to include Inuit, it can be argued that it also includes Métis people and other non-*Indian Act* Indians.[17] If so, Parliament may have constitutional jurisdiction over

† Editorial commentary in this book uses the term Aboriginal rather than aboriginal. However, the lower case is retained if it is contained in passages quoted from other sources. The *Constitution Act, 1982* itself uses the lower case; the Supreme Court seems to be moving to the upper case. As well, editorial commentary in the book uses the phrase "Aboriginal people" to differentiate this general group from other people; it uses the phrase "Aboriginal peoples" to describe this general group with special reference to the diverse groups that comprise it.

‡ Editorial commentary in this book uses the spelling of Métis except when referring to formal names that use the spelling Metis. The former spelling is somewhat more common than the latter.

half again as many Aboriginal people as are now subject to the *Indian Act*. Sooner or later, the question will require judicial or constitutional resolution. The *Constitution Act, 1867* provides no clear indication of the outer scope of s. 91(24). Apart from suggesting the criterion of traditional government practice — *Re Eskimos* doesn't supply one either.

The position of s. 91(24) Indians is both complex and paradoxical. Many subjects that relate directly to Indian concerns — such as management of public property and natural resources — fall generally under provincial jurisdiction. Yet s. 91(24) is an exclusive federal power. On the other hand, Indians are not exempt from all provincial laws of general application.[18] When Parliament does act under s. 91(24), it exercises a discretionary power. It has no duty to legislate. Yet where Parliament or the Crown does act, Indians may be subject to special fiduciary presumptions or obligations imposed by the courts.[19]

4. CATEGORIES OF *INDIAN ACT* INDIANS

(a) *Indian Act*

Indian Act Indians fall under some or all of the provisions of the *Indian Act*, a federal statute first enacted in 1868[20] and patterned on pre-Confederation statutes.[21] There are many different categories of *Indian Act* Indians today, each with slightly different legal positions. To understand how this came about, it is useful to look back in time.

A key purpose of early legislation defining Indians was to prevent unauthorized persons from encroaching on Indian reserves. These reserves are parcels of land that were set aside for the use and benefit of Indians.[22] They were originally set aside to compensate Indians for the loss of larger areas of land, as places of refuge from baser European influences, and (rather paradoxically), as places where Indians could be gradually converted to European religions and customs.[23] This protective purpose was implemented and added to over the decades by provisions on alcohol restrictions, taxation immunity, financial management by a government overseer, gradual enfranchisement (ending of status), limited local government, and a host of other matters.[24] By the late 19th century, the *Indian Act* governed almost all aspects of the lives of those subject to it.

(b) Pre-April 17, 1982 Eligibility Procedures

The threshold of the *Indian Act* was its system for determining Indian status.[25] Before it was changed on April 17, 1985, this system had three important features. First, Indian status passed through the male line. A status Indian had to be either a male descendant of a group recognized as Indians in 1874,[26] or the wife or child of such a descendant. If an Indian man married a non-Indian woman, the woman gained Indian status. However, s. 12(1)(b) of the Act provided that if an Indian woman married a non-Indian man, she lost her Indian status.[27]

Second, Indian status, band membership, and residence on an Indian reserve resulted in different benefits.[28] Indian status gave (a) the right to uninsured health benefits and post-secondary educational benefits, and (b) for a reserve resident, tax immunity for real and personal property on the reserve. Band membership gave (a) an undivided share in reserve land and assets, (b) the right to live on a reserve if facilities were available, and (c) for a reserve resident, the right to participate in band council elections.

Third, Indian status and band membership were both determined by the provisions of the *Indian Act* and by the Department of Indian Affairs and Northern Development. Indian status almost automatically meant membership in one of the approximately 600 Indian bands. Thus, whoever had status benefits normally had band benefits too, so that the main distinction was between status-band Indians living off reserves and those living on reserves.

(c) Problems with Old System

Some kind of definition system was needed. Since the *Constitution Act, 1867* gave Parliament the power to legislate in regard to "Indians, and lands reserved for the Indians", it was necessary to determine who were "Indians". In particular, it was necessary to determine who were entitled to reside on Indian reserves. The old eligibility system accomplished this. Moreover, by passing Indian status through the male line, the system avoided splitting up nuclear families by keeping their status at the same time. Second, it limited the total number of status Indians, checking excessive demands on the many reserves with housing shortages.

However, the old system had a number of serious problems. First, although the system directly affected Aboriginal peoples, it was imposed unilaterally and gave Aboriginal peoples virtually no role in shaping it.

Second, the system conflicted with several aspects of traditional Indian custom. By concentrating on the European-type nuclear family, it ignored the importance of extended families in most traditional Indian societies. By carrying status through the male line, it upset Aboriginal societies with matrilineal traditions.[29]

Third, the system provided for a number of forms of arbitrary loss of status or enfranchisement. For example, at one time the only way an Indian could gain the right to vote was to give up Indian status and the band membership that went with it.[30] In some periods, Indians lost status on receiving a higher degree or professional or religious qualifications; conversely, they could lose it for being out of Canada for over five years without permission.[31] During the two world wars, Indians had to give up status for themselves and their families in order to serve in the armed forces.[32]

Fourth, the system based status at least partly on race. Aboriginal race-based distinctions had, and still have, significant constitutional supports.[33] On the other hand, they differentiate between people on the basis of a personal characteristic beyond their control.[34] In some cases, as with the *Indian Act*'s former alcohol restrictions, the distinctions resulted in personal disadvantage.[35] For reasons of fairness alone, they needed reform.

Finally, the system had one especially glaring drawback. It discriminated against women on the basis of their sex. Because status was the key to the legal right to live on a reserve, Indian women who married non-Indian spouses could find themselves deprived of the right to live among friends, extended families, and other relations. In contrast, a man marrying a non-Indian spouse suffered no such penalties.[36]

(d) Movement for Change

Readings 2(b) at p. 222 and 2(c) at p. 223

A catalyst for changing this situation was the 1960 *Canadian Bill of Rights*.[37] The *Bill* recognized a right of equality before the law that could only be excluded by express statutory language. This guarantee appeared to contradict the racial and sexual differentiation in the *Indian Act*. Legal confrontation seemed inevitable.

The first major *Bill of Rights* equality challenge was in *R. v. Drybones*.[38] Here a majority of the Supreme Court of Canada held that *Indian Act* prohibitions against being drunk in public denied Indians equality before the law. The judges said the provisions subjected Indians, on account of their race, to harsher treatment than others.[39] The *Indian Act* provisions imposed more severe penalties than those in a territorial liquor ordinance. It also applied over a wider area.

The legal challenge to the sexual differentiation was taken up by two Indian women who had lost their status as a result of marrying non-Indians. Mrs. Jeannette Lavell's name was deleted from the Indian Register after she married a non-Indian husband. She argued that s. 12(1)(b) violated her right to equality before the law. After losing the case at first instance, Mrs. Lavell succeeded in the Federal Court of Appeal. The Crown appealed to the Supreme Court of Canada, where her case was combined with that of Mrs. Yvonne Bedard.[40] Mrs. Bedard had left her reserve after marrying a non-Indian. After a separation from her husband, she returned. However, the band asked the District Superintendent to serve on Mrs. Bedard a notice to leave the reserve. Mrs. Bedard challenged s. 12(1)(b) in the Ontario Supreme Court, and succeeded.

Both women lost their case, however, in the Supreme Court of Canada. The position of the four dissenting judges in *Lavell* was quite simple: "If as in *Drybones*, discrimination by reason of race makes certain statutory provisions inoperative, the same result must follow as to statutory provisions which exhibit discrimination by reason of sex."[41]

However, four of the majority judges in *Lavell* redefined equality before the law in terms much weaker than in *Drybones*. In their view, it meant "equality in the administration and enforcement of the law by the law enforcement authorities and the ordinary Courts of the land."[42] They seemed to suggest that as long as a law was administered and enforced without discrimination to those to whom it applied, the fact that it treated them differently from others was irrelevant. Five majority judges added a second reason. They noted that s. 12(1)(b) defined Indian status. They said Indian status had to be defined before Parliament could exercise its s. 91(24) power in relation to "Indians, and lands reserved for the Indians". Although they recognized that Parliament could disable itself exercising from a specific constitutional power like this, they said it would have to do so in language stronger than that in the *Bill*.[43] They distinguished

Drybones on the ground that it was based not on the constitutional power in relation to Indians but on the criminal law power.[44]

Behind the dilution of equality and the complex argument about statutory intent may have lurked some policy considerations. Upholding the individual rights of Mrs. Lavell and Mrs. Bedard would have restricted the collective powers of band councils to manage reserve lands and to cope with severe housing shortages. Moreover, striking down the *Indian Act*'s eligibility provisions would have invalidated one of the main foundations of the Act. For judges in the 1960s, this would have been a bold step indeed.

Aboriginal women persisted.[45] In 1977, Mrs. Sandra Lovelace, a New Brunswick Aboriginal woman who lost status as a result of s. 12(1)(b), took her concerns to United Nations. The U.N. Human Rights Committee held that s. 12(1)(b) violated s. 27 of the *International Covenant on Civil and Political Rights*.[46] Section 27 guarantees members of ethnic minorities the right to enjoy their own culture "in community with other members of their group." Although it had no legal effect within Canada, the ruling put further moral pressure on the Canadian government to act.

On April 17, 1982, the *Canadian Charter of Rights and Freedoms* came into effect.[47] Section 15, the main equality provision, did not come into effect until three years later. Section 15 contained stronger, more specific equality guarantees than the *Bill*. Moreover, since s. 15 was part of the constitution itself, it was not subject to the "Parliamentary intent" argument that had blocked the application of the equality guarantee in *Lavell and Bedard*. Meanwhile, Aboriginal women kept up their calls for reform. Indian associations called for more Indian participation in controlling eligibility and band membership.

After several false starts, the reforms finally came in Bill C-31, which was proclaimed in force as of April 17, 1985.

(e) 1985 Eligibility Reforms

Reading 2(d) at p. 228

Bill C-31 changed an eligibility system that had been based on kinship and sex into one based mainly on blood. The Bill:

1. eliminated the main discriminatory provisions of the old *Indian Act* and reinstated those who had lost their status by discriminatory or arbitrary provisions;
2. maintained the different kinds of benefits flowing from Indian status, band membership, and reserve residence, except that children of a band member residing on a reserve are allowed to reside with the member on the reserve; and
3. allowed for the transfer of control of many of the criteria for band membership to the bands themselves, with the result that status and band membership criteria are no longer necessarily the same.

As a result of Bill C-31, the following people are eligible for Indian[48] status:[49]

1. those who had status before April 17, 1985;
2. members of a group declared by Cabinet to be a band;
3. those who lost status by sexually discriminatory provisions[50] or enfranchisement;[51]
4. children with both parents with status; and
5. children with one parent with status under one of the above categories.

People in categories one to four above have what might be called "primary" status. Their Indian status will be transmitted to their children, regardless of whom they marry. People in category five have what might be called "secondary" status. They can transmit Indian status to their children only if their spouse also has Indian status. If a person with secondary status marries a person without Indian status, the children of the marriage will not have Indian status, as they will not fall under any of these five categories.

Between 1985 and 2001, over 112,000 people gained *Indian Act* status by virtue of Bill C-31.[52] Of those who *re*-gained Indian status, three-quarters were women.[53]

Today, the following categories of people are automatically entitled to band membership:[54]

1. those who had band membership before April 17, 1985;
2. members of a group declared by Cabinet to be a band;
3. those who lost status by sexually discriminatory provisions and involuntary enfranchisement;[55] and
4. children with both parents with status and membership in the same band.

Bill C-31's band membership criteria vary according to whether an individual band opted to assume control of its membership by June 28,

1987. For bands that did *not* assume control by that date (about 65% of all bands), those who lost status through voluntary enfranchisement[56] and children with one parent with primary status and band membership, or with both parents with status and at least one of these with band membership, are also eligible for band membership. For the approximately 35% of all bands that *did* assume membership control by this date,[57] the band membership can be extended to almost anyone the band decides. However, existing rights cannot be altered by reason of a circumstance occurring before membership control was assumed.[58] Finally, a band can assume control of its membership at any time.

It is possible now, therefore, that a person may have status without band membership or band membership without status. Those with status but not band membership enjoy personal health and education benefits[59] and (if they reside on a reserve), tax immunity for their real and personal[60] property on a reserve. Those with band membership but not status enjoy a share of band assets (if they reside on a reserve), the right to tax immunity for their real property on the reserve, and, where the *Indian Act* elections process is in effect, the right to participate in *Indian Act* band council elections.[61]

Generally, then, the subcategory of *Indian Act* Indian with the most legal benefits is a status-band-reserve Indian. He or she is entitled to uninsured health benefits and post-secondary education assistance;[62] an undivided share in band reserve land and assets; reserve residence; the right to participate in band council elections; and tax immunity for real and personal property on the reserve. The subcategories with the fewest benefits are the band-only Indian, with an undivided share in band reserve land and assets; the reserve-only Indian, with reserve residence; and the status-only Indian, with uninsured health benefits and post-secondary education assistance. In between are other subcategories, such as status-reserve Indians, with uninsured health benefits and post-secondary education assistance and tax immunity for their real and personal property on the reserve.

(f) Challenges Ahead

The 1985 reforms ended the most direct forms of sexual discrimination in the old *Indian Act*. They restored the status and band membership of the most immediate victims of this discrimination. They also restored the status and, in some cases, the band membership of victims of some other forms of arbitrary enfranchisement. The reforms tried to compromise between the rights of these individuals and the desires of many band councils to have greater control of membership by splitting status and band membership, and giving bands the opportunity to exercise greater control over the latter.

This split does have a rationale. It gives band councils greater control over shared and group benefits, such as residence on reserve lands, and it retains government control over *per capita* benefits such as housing and education payments, which are dependent on the number of recipients.

On the other side of the ledger, the new scheme is extraordinarily complex.[63] As indicated, status and band membership are now split. There is a distinction between transferable and partly transferable status. Band membership may be automatic, conditional, or discretionary. There is now a mass of *Indian Act* subcategories, each with slightly different legal and practical consequences. Some differences are arbitrary. The right to band membership, for example, can depend on whether or not a band opted to assume membership control before June 28, 1987. Dependent children who have only one parent who has band membership and is residing on a reserve, can reside on the reserve with this parent, but the parent without band membership has no automatic right to reside there too.

There are other concerns.[64] For some bands, any continuing government control of either status or band membership is inconsistent with their own rights to control these questions, by virtue of treaties, self-government,[65] or sovereignty.[66] Some have attempted to by-pass key aspects of the *Indian Act* membership system, adding further to the complexity of the situation.[67]

From another perspective, although the more blatant sexual discrimination has been removed, the system still imposes some relative disadvantages at least partly on the basis of race.[68] The distinctions may be justified, but presumably the onus is on those who drew them.

Moreover, not all the consequences of sexual discrimination have been removed. Because of inadequate housing, many reserves lack facilities to accommodate the people who have been reinstated to status and band membership. Wealthy bands may be reluctant to share wealth with large numbers of newcomers. Children born to a reinstated Indian woman after she was reinstated can transmit their status only if they themselves marry spouses with Indian status. In contrast, children of a status Indian father who had married a non-status woman before April 17, 1985 can transmit status even if they marry non-Indian spouses.[69]

(g) *Corbiere v. Canada (Minister of Indian and Northern Affairs)*[70]

Reading 2(e) at p. 231

The situation of new off-reserve band members was aggravated by s. 77(1) of the *Indian Act* and similar restrictions in some customary band council selection procedures.[71] Section 77(1) limited the right to participate in *Indian Act* band council elections to band members who were "ordinarily resident on the reserve".[72] Section 77(2) imposed a similar restriction on the right to hold office in band councils. Lacking the capacity to influence band council decisions, off-reserve residents could not affect the very membership rules that could give them residency.

This dilemma reflected a structural tension in the *Indian Act* band / reserve structure. On one hand, band councils are responsible for many matters of predominantly local concern, such as health, traffic, and environmental regulations on the reserve itself.[73] These are matters in which reserve members have a special, sometimes exclusive, interest. On the other hand, some band council decisions can directly affect both off-reserve and on-reserve band members. As seen above, for example, decisions about reserve residency and housing can affect non-resident as well as resident band members. Moreover, band councils are authorized to spend band "capital" and "revenue" moneys,[74] and these moneys are to be spent for the benefit of the band as a whole.[75] By limiting voting and elected office to on-reserve members, s. 77 addressed the special local interests, but not the common interests.

Both the underlying structural problem and the special concerns of new off-reserve band members confronted the Batchewana Indian Band in Ontario. In 1985, 71.1% of this band membership lived on one of the band's three reserves.[76] However, largely because of the Bill C-38 amendments, by 1991 the off-reserve population had grown to comprise over 67% of all Batchewana Band members.[77] The band was subject to the *Indian Act* voting procedures. Thus, s. 77(1) required that band electors must be "ordinarily resident on the reserve". Housing funds were limited, and most non-residents had no immediate prospect of becoming reserve residents.

Mr. John Corbiere,[78] a former band council chief, sought a declaration that the residency requirement in s. 77(1) discriminated against off-reserve Batchewana Band members, contrary to s. 15(1) of the *Charter of Rights and Freedoms*, and that this discrimination was not justified under s. 1 of the *Charter*.

When the litigation reached the Supreme Court of Canada, the Court re-stated the issue to address the broader question of whether s. 77(1) constituted unjustified discrimination against all off-reserve band members.[79] The Court concluded that it did. However, the Court suspended the operation of its declaration of unconstitutionality for 18 months to enable the federal government to develop an electoral process to balance the rights of off-reserve and on-reserve band members.[80]

It had been suggested that s. 77(1) might violate an Aboriginal right to exclude off-reserve members from voting, and that Aboriginal rights were exempt from *Charter* requirements by virtue of s. 25 of the *Charter*. However, the Supreme Court said that no case had been made out for the application of s. 25 in this litigation,[81] and that no evidence had been presented on this issue in regard to other bands.[82] The important question of whether and how s. 25 and Aboriginal rights might affect the *Indian Act* was postponed to another day.

Applying the *Charter* equality criteria from the 1999 *Law* decision,[83] the five-judge main majority[84] said that (i) the s. 77(1) distinction imposed a relative disadvantage on off-reserve members; (ii) off-reserve band member status constituted a ground of discrimination that was analogous to those enumerated in s. 15 of the *Charter* because it was based on an immutable or virtually immutable personal characteristic; and (iii) the s. 77(1) distinction was discriminatory because it perpetuated the pre-existing disadvantage of off-reserve members, failed to take account of their important band and cultural interests, and thereby impugned their dignity in comparison with on-reserve members.[85]

Turning to s. 1 of the *Charter*, the main majority agreed that restricting voting rights was rationally related to the aim of limiting control of reserve affairs to those most closely affected. However, they concluded that a total bar on all off-reserve voting was not justified because it would be possible to achieve this aim with less intrusive measures.

The Court's suspension of its declaration of invalidity gave the federal government until November 20, 2000 to rectify the problem. On October 20, 2000, the federal government amended the *Indian Band Election Regulations* and the *Indian Referendum Regulations*[86] to give on-reserve band members the same voting rights in *Indian Act*[87] elections and referendums as on-reserve members. Further changes were contemplated in a proposed *First Nations Governance Act*, but it was withdrawn in 2003–2004: **Chapter 12(3)(b)(i)**.

5. NON-*INDIAN ACT* ABORIGINAL PEOPLES

(a) Non-Status Indians

The term "non-status Indian" usually describes people of Indian ancestry who are either unable to prove Indian status or no longer have it.[88] It includes people who once had status, or whose ancestors once had status, and subsequently lost it. Under the 1985 changes, almost every person who had status and lost it before 1985 was entitled to reinstatement. This also applied to many of their children and grandchildren. Also, there is no longer any legal provision for losing status under the *Indian Act*. One group who lost status before 1985 and did *not* regain status are women who became Indians solely as a result of marrying Indian men who then lost status through further marriages prior to 1985.[89] Also excluded are individuals who lack proof of ancestry or are too remotely related to people entitled to reinstatement.

(b) Inuit

The Inuit are a group of Aboriginal people with distinctive cultural and physical characteristics who have traditionally lived in the Arctic and subarctic regions of North America.[90] Although the Inuit have a common native language called Inuktitut, there are six different dialects in Canada spoken by eight main tribal groups.[91]

As seen, Inuit are specifically designated as one of the three "Aboriginal peoples of Canada" in s. 35(1) of the *Constitution Act, 1982*, and are considered to be "Indians" for the purposes of s. 91(24) of the *Constitution Act, 1867*. However, before 1975, no Canadian Inuit tribal group had a formal treaty with the Crown, and Inuit are excluded from the *Indian Act*. Similarly, while there are a number of federal programs for Inuit, there is no federal Inuit Act. On the other hand, Canadian Inuit are now beneficiaries in three main northern land claims agreements — the 1975 *James Bay and Northern Quebec Agreement*;[92] the 1984 *Western Arctic (Inuvialuit) Agreement*;[93] and the 1993 *Nunavut Agreement*;[94] and the 1993 *Northern Labrador Inuit Agreement*.[95]

(c) Métis

Reading 10(d) at p. 370

In a broad sense, the Métis[96] are descendants of mixed marriages between people of Indian or Inuit and European descent. These mixed marriages occurred at European settlements in New France, Acadia, Labrador, the Red River Valley, and elsewhere. They were especially common in the French and British fur trades that ranged from the coast to the Great Lakes region and interior of the continent.[97] In the late 18th century, many Métis people moved westward.[98] Métis in the Red River area of Manitoba played a crucial role in the beginnings of that province.[99] Today, Métis communities are especially distinct and organized in the Prairie provinces, while others live in the rural or urban areas dominated by non-Métis. In the 2001 census, almost 300,000 people identified themselves as Métis.[100]

Before modern land claims agreements, there were no formal Métis treaties similar to those signed with Indians.[101] There is no federal Métis Act. Before 1985, people who had been allotted half-breed lands or scrips were excluded from the *Indian Act*.[102] Only Alberta and Saskatchewan have enacted special legislation relating to Métis.[103] Once, in an adhesion to Treaty No. 3, a half-breed (Métis) community in western Ontario was dealt with separately and allotted two tracts of land adjacent to Rainy Lake.[104] The land was never granted. Section 31 of the *Manitoba Act* and early *Dominion Lands Acts* provided for granting land and transferrable land certificates called scrip to the half-breeds of Manitoba and the Northwest Territories.[105] The scheme was mismanaged and undermined by unscrupulous property dealers. Little land reached or remained with the Métis. Under most of the numbered treaties, Métis were generally given the option of either being treated as Indians and coming under the treaties, or taking scrip.[106]

Beyond the core idea of descent from mixed Aboriginal-European marriages, there is no single definition of Métis.[107] There are three main criteria possible:

1. links to an individual mixed marriage;
2. links to a Métis group such as a Métis organization; and
3. links to a distinct Métis community — either historic or contemporary, or both.

Moreover, there are at least three different means of establishing these links — self-identification (either explicit or implied), group or community acceptance (in the case of criteria 2 and 3 above), and third-party evidence, such as genealogical records. Clearly, the more specific the links required, and the more group and third-party evidence that is required, the narrower the definition of Métis.

The law has been as slow to define or describe Métis as governments have been in addressing their concern. The first national constitutional recognition since late 19th century references to "half-breeds" was in the *Constitution Act, 1982*. As seen in **Part 2** above, the Métis are one of three groups of Aboriginal peoples of Canada whose rights are recognized and affirmed in s. 35(1) of the *Constitution Act, 1982*. In 2003, the Supreme Court expressly affirmed that Métis people can hold Aboriginal rights under this section.[108] However, for the purpose of this section, the Court requires not only proof of mixed Aboriginal-European ancestry, but also evidence of a connection with a particular historic and ongoing Métis community.[109] Many people who self-identify as Métis and belong to Métis organizations could have trouble meeting these more demanding requirements.

There has been no Supreme Court ruling on whether Métis people are included in the term "Indians" in s. 91(24) of the *Constitution Act, 1867*. However, the facts that (i) the Court has already included Inuit in s. 91(24),[110] and (ii) Métis, like Indians and Inuit, have Aboriginal rights to be addressed,[111] suggests that Métis will eventually be included under this provision too. What criteria, if any, will be required for Métis status under s. 91(24), remains to be seen.

A related question is whether s. 91(24) applies to those who are non-status (i) as a result of having lost *Indian Act* status, or (ii) because they are band-only Indians or band-reserve Indians. The answer here may depend on whether applicants have Aboriginal ancestry. Generally, though, except for Inuit,[112] the scope of s. 91(24) has yet to be clearly defined.[113]

Until recently, another unanswered question was whether Métis are included as "Indians" for the purposes of the 1930 *Natural Resources Transfer Agreements*.[114] These Prairie constitutional documents have the general effect of exempting Indian food harvesting on certain lands from provincial wildlife legislation.[115] In 2003, the Supreme Court said that Métis were not intended to be included under these documents.[116] In the view of the Court, at the time Métis were not thought to need the special assistance and group treatment accorded to the Indians.[117] The Court cautioned that its findings about the *NRTA* did not necessarily apply to other constitutional documents.[118]

6. TREATY INDIANS

Treaty Indians[119] are those who (or whose ancestors) have entered into treaties with the Crown. Although virtually all treaty Indians are status Indians under the *Indian Act*, about one-half of the 608 bands of Indians have entered into treaties. Geographically, only about one-half to two-thirds of Canada is covered by the treaties. Many of the pre-Confederation treaties were little more than peace treaties or land sales agreements. The post-Confederation treaties normally granted to the Indian signatories reserves, hunting and fishing rights, and annual payments in money or goods.

7. CLAIMS AGREEMENT BENEFICIARIES

The modern form of treaty, dating from the 1975 *James Bay and Northern Quebec Agreement*, is the land claims agreement.[120] Typically, a land claims agreement covers a large number of topics, including guaranteed participation in administrative régimes and other forms of self-government. The largest land claims agreement in area, with the 18,000 members of the Tungavik Federation of Nunavut, covers 2.6 million square kilometres in the Northwest Territories — about one-quarter of the size of Canada. The smallest, depending on the criteria used, are the Northeastern Quebec Agreement with about 465 Naskapi Indians, and the smaller of the four Yukon agreements.

Ten land claims agreements have been concluded to date. Except for British Columbia and

Atlantic Canada, land claims agreements now cover most of the country that is not subject to treaties.

Claims agreement eligibility provisions vary from agreement to agreement. They generally establish a "charter" group defined in terms of ordinary residence in the agreement region, racial affiliation, or community recognition, and they extend membership to descendants of the Charter group. For example, under the *James Bay and Northern Quebec Agreement*, eligibility is open to people who on a specified date (i) were members of the eight Cree *Indian Act* bands, or (ii) had Cree, Indian, or Inuit ancestry and were ordinarily resident in the claims area or were recognized members of a Cree or Inuit community, and to (i) descendants of the above people, through either the male or female line, and (ii) lawful spouses of Inuit beneficiaries.[121]

Where claims agreements are accompanied by Aboriginal self-government agreements, Aboriginal people may qualify for both claims of beneficiary status and citizenship in the relevant Aboriginal government. Under the Yukon First Nation self-government agreements, citizenship criteria are determined for and by each First Nation government.[122]

8. SELF-DEFINITION POSSIBILITIES

Ideally, Aboriginal peoples should be able to define their status themselves. This general goal is consistent with Aboriginal aspirations for greater self-government.[123] It reflects the democratic notion that people should have maximum possible control over matters that concern them most directly. Those directly concerned are presumably the best-placed judges of who their fellow members are, and are most likely to be sensitive to their people's own cultural traditions.

However, this goal of self-definition may be tempered by some constraints. First, when government legislates in regard to one group only, or provides that group with benefits from public funds not provided to others, it also affects the interest of non-members and the interest of the public at large. For these reasons, where special legislation or publicly-funded benefits are tied to group membership, the relevant level of public government may be entitled to a role in helping determine the scope of that membership.

Second, the general goal of self-definition begs the question of the "self" who is intended to do the defining. Within any group, it is likely that more dominant interests will prevail over minority or weaker interests. Hence, it is reasonable to ask what arrangements are needed to help protect non-dominant Aboriginal interests. For example, should the *Canadian Charter of Rights and Freedoms* apply to Aboriginal eligibility criteria?[124]

Through the 1985 *Indian Act*, changes and eligibility provisions in recent land claims and self-government agreements have made it possible for Canada to move toward more self-definition. Subject to the possible constraints above, further reforms may be possible. For example, the more government allocates benefits on a group rather than *per capita* basis, the less it needs to try to control expenditures through detailed supervision of individual eligibility.

As for protecting non-dominant interests in internal Aboriginal affairs, perhaps Aboriginal groups should have greater freedom to fashion their own safeguards. Need these be statutory in nature? Where special public government benefits are not involved, must the *Charter* apply to internal Aboriginal matters? Are legal mechanisms necessarily superior to traditional Aboriginal methods for achieving internal consensus?

Finally, when further reforms are made, there should be some effort to reduce the number and complexity of the present forms of status. As a starting point, surely it would be possible to simplify the legal categories of status Indians and band Indians under the *Indian Act*.

9. ABORIGINAL STATUS AND EQUALITY

Readings 2(b) at p. 222, 2(c) at p. 223, and 2(e) at p. 231

As seen in this chapter, where the law distinguishes between Aboriginal peoples and other Canadians — or between specific groups of Aboriginal peoples — it opens the door to questions about equality. Status is a personal characteristic that is often immutable or difficult to change. Differential treatment based on immutable personal characteristics is likely to be regarded as discriminatory unless it can be seen to relate to the merits of a particular situation.

Thus, where the law attaches disadvantages directly to Aboriginal status, it raises the question of discrimination against Aboriginal peoples.[125] Conversely, where Aboriginal status is a condition for benefits, claimants may raise discrimination concerns where they feel that they have been unjustly denied the benefits. These claimants may comprise other Aboriginal peoples who have been denied the benefits, non-Aboriginals, or a combination of these two groups.

Where the claimants themselves are Aboriginal, their concern may be not the Aboriginal status itself. Instead, it may be some other personal characteristic — such as sex or place of residence — that was the basis for denying them a benefit linked to Aboriginal status.

On the other hand, where the law fails to accommodate relevant differences, it can be argued that the lack of differential treatment may itself be a form of discrimination.[126] Similarly, it is arguable that selective treatment is sometimes necessary to remove disadvantages experienced by certain social groups in comparison with others.[127] As well, some important constitutional provisions — such as s. 91(24) of the *Constitution Act, 1867* and ss. 25, 35, and 35.1 of the *Constitution Act, 1982* — do treat Aboriginal peoples differently.[128] Especially in regard to Aboriginal peoples, equality is a complex concept.

The main legal tools against legal discrimination are s. 1 of the *Canadian Bill of Rights* and s. 15 of the *Canadian Charter of Rights and Freedoms*.[129] Section 1 of the *Bill* guarantees protection against discrimination in regard to equality before the law in relation to federal and territorial laws.[130] Section 15 of the Charter contains a wider equality guarantee and discrimination protection and a proviso for affirmative action.[131] Moreover, while the *Canadian Bill of Rights* is a rebuttable interpretive tool that applies only to legislation under federal jurisdiction, the Charter can supersede all government action, and can be excluded only by an express use of the notwithstanding clause.

In its main Aboriginal equality decisions under the *Bill*, the Supreme Court moved between opposite poles of activism and restraint. In *Drybones*, for example, it was enough that Indians were subject to a disadvantage, on account of their race, that was not suffered by others.[132] However, the Court gave the *Bill*'s equality guarantee a much narrower interpretation in *Lavell*, limiting it to the administration and enforcement of laws and treating it as ineffective in the face of general distinctions contemplated in the Constitution.[133]

Under the *Charter*, the Court looks for s. 15(1) discrimination by means of a multiple-stepped analytical test. The Court asks if there is: (I) differential treatment; (II) differential treatment based on s. 15(1) enumerated or analogous grounds; and (III) substantive discrimination in the sense of an affront to human dignity, assessed by factors such as (i) pre-existing disadvantage in the claimant's group, (ii) correspondence between the ground of the distinction and the actual needs or circumstances of the relevant groups, (iii) the ameliorative purpose or effect of the provision in regard to a more disadvantaged general target group or to a disadvantaged specific target group, and (iv) the importance of the claimant's group's interest.[134]

The main Aboriginal *Charter* equality cases to date have involved Aboriginal groups who have been denied benefits conferred on other Aboriginal groups.[135] For example, *Corbiere*,[136] discussed earlier, concerned an *Indian Act* provision that denied off-reserve band members a right enjoyed by reserve resident band members — the right to vote in band council elections. The Court held that this provision violated s. 15(1), especially because the non-residence ground failed to correspond with the strong cultural and other interests of the off-reserve people in the assets and governance of the band.[137] Other claims involving this second situation have been less successful. In *Lovelace*,[138] the Court held that a government policy limiting casino proceeds to registered Indians did not discriminate against Métis and non-status Indians. Although non-band Indians had as much economic need as band Indians, the casino proceeds program was not intended to be a general benefits program, and exclusion of non-band Indians corresponded to their different general circumstances.[139] In the *Chippewas of Nawas* decision,[140] the Supreme Court dismissed an appeal from the Federal Court of Appeal in another claim that one Aboriginal group was denied a benefit enjoyed by the other. Because the Chippewas of Nawas live on the shores of Lake Huron, they were ineligible for the federal Aboriginal Fishing Strategy, which provides special fishing benefits for Aboriginal communities near tidal waters. The Court of Appeal stressed that the Strategy was a not a general purpose program, but was targeted at a group who were disadvantaged in relation to the general population (although not in relation to the claimants).[141] Because of this, the Strategy did not have to be appropriate to the specific needs and circumstances of the Nawash — it was enough that the Nawash were not a coastal community like the beneficiaries.[142] In other words, where there is a targeted ameliorative program, neither the disadvantaged nature of the claimants nor the lack of a precise fit between the exclusion and their needs and circumstances is likely to indicate discrimination.[143]

The third situation, where non-Aboriginals (or non-Aboriginals and some Aboriginals) allege discrimination on the basis of a benefit enjoyed by some Aboriginal groups, has not yet been considered by the Supreme Court of Canada. This situation occurred in *Kapp*,[144] where non-Aboriginal fishers and some Aboriginal fishers argued that the Pilot Fishery Program of the Aboriginal Fishing Strategy that gave special commercial fishing licences to three lower Fraser Valley bands was an unjustified violation of s. 15(1). The trial judge agreed, holding that because the eligible individuals in these bands were not financially disadvantaged, the program did not have an ameliorative purpose, and that it did not correspond with the needs and circumstances of the claimants. The British Columbia Supreme Court disagreed, saying that the relevant comparator group comprised all *bands* who were eligible to hold licences in the general area.[145] Because this broader group *could* be said to be disadvantaged generally,[146] the program did serve an ameliorative purpose, and by addressing their economic disadvantage, the program did correspond with actual needs and circumstances.

Regardless of the result of any further appeal in *Kapp*, there are several reasons why discrimination claims by non-Aboriginals will rarely succeed in regard to benefits enjoyed by Aboriginal groups. First, s. 15(1) analysis is undertaken in the context of the affirmative action provision in s. 15(2)[147] and, economically at least, Aboriginal peoples as a whole tend to be significantly disadvantaged.[148] If a program is intended to ameliorate the disadvantage of a specific group, it is unlikely to be deemed discriminatory on the basis of the other s. 15(1) contextual factors.[149] Moreover, in a situation such as *Kapp*, the more the comparator group approximates the general *Aboriginal* population (and not only a relatively advantaged group within it), the more likely it is that a *non*-Aboriginal discrimination claim will fail. Second, positive Aboriginal benefits may be justifiable as affirmative action under s. 15(2) of the Charter,[150] or as proportionate responses to pressing and substantial objectives under s. 1. Third, if a government provision implements a s. 35(1) Aboriginal or treaty right, that provision may be protected from Charter equality attack by virtue of s. 25 of the Charter.[151]

Beyond the constitutional framework, Canadian government faces two broader normative equality questions in its dealings with Aboriginal peoples. First, to what extent is government morally obliged to redress the past and continuing injustice suffered by Aboriginal peoples in Canada? Second, where should government redress this injustice and protect the distinctiveness of Aboriginal people by means of special legal measures? Both questions are fundamental, but each engages distinct equality issues.

Notes

1. Statistics Canada, *Aboriginal Peoples of Canada: A Demographic Profile* (Ottawa: Statistics Canada, release date, January 21, 2003), <http://www12.statcan.ca/english/census01/Products/Analytic/companion/abor/canada.cfm>). While the total Canadian population doubled between 1951 and 2001, the Canadian Aboriginal population grew by seven times during that period. In 2001, the Aboriginal population in Canada constituted 3.8% of the total Canadian population, as compared with Aboriginal population proportions of 1.5% in the United States, 2.2% in Australia, and 14% in New Zealand: *ibid.*
2. *Ibid.*
3. M.K. Foster, "Native People, Languages" in *The Canadian Encyclopedia*, Year 2000 ed. (Toronto: McClelland & Stewart, 1999) at 1453 and J.L. Steckley and B.D. Cummins, *Full Circle: Canada's First Nations* (Toronto: Prentice Hall, 2001), chap. 4.
4. *Ibid.*
5. Although the 2001 census identified about 558,000 registered Indians, enumeration was not permitted or completed on 30 Indian reserves and settlements: *ibid.* In that year, the federal government's Indian Register listed 690,101 registered Indians, a figure that has been growing by about 10,000 to 15,000 people per year. See Indian and Northern Affairs Canada, "Registered Indian Population by Type of Residence, December 1982–2001", in *Registered Indian Population by Sex and Residence 2002* (Ottawa: D.I.A.N.D., 2003).
6. In the 2001 census, 292,310 people reported themselves as *Métis*: *supra*, note 1. However, because of lack of a consensus on an exact definition of Métis, this figure is very approximate: see further **Part 5(c)**, below.
7. *Aboriginal Peoples of Canada: A Demographic Profile*, *supra* note 2. Generally speaking, a "band" is a body of Indians (i) for whose common use and benefit Crown lands have been set apart or moneys are held by the Crown, or (ii) a body declared by the federal Cabinet to be a band: *Indian Act*, R.S.C. 1985, c. I-8, s. 2(1). All but a very small number of bands have lands set apart for their use and benefit (reserves).
8. The is the term preferred by most bands. In the United States, the main Indian governmental organization is the tribe.
9. "Registered Indian Population by Type of Residence, December 1982-2001", *supra* note 5 (figure of 57%); *Aboriginal Peoples of Canada: A Demographic Profile*, *supra* note 1 (figure of 31%); and Corporate Information Management Indian Directorate, Indian and Northern Affairs Canada, 25 June 2004 (number of official reserves). Of the total number of reserves, 884 are occupied: *Report*, vol. 2, pt. 2, chap. 5, s. 1.2 at 807. Canadian reserves comprise a total of 3 million hectares. Section 2(1) of the current *Indian Act*, R.S.C. 1985, c. I-5, defines a reserve as "a tract of land, the legal title to which is vested in Her Majesty, that has been set apart by Her Majesty for the use and benefit of a band": para. (a). Except for some purposes the definition includes land of this kind after a less-than-absolute surrender: (definition of reserve, para. (b) and definition of "designated lands"). As well, Canadian land claims agreements have identified approximately 60 million hectares as being for the exclusive use of Aboriginal peoples. In the United States in

1995, there were 287 reservations, comprising a total of 22.68 million hectares: *Indians in Canada and the United States*, Communications Branch, Department of Indian Affairs and Northern Development, 1995.

10. *Ibid.*
11. Schedule B to the *Canada Act, 1982* (U.K.), 1982, c. 11.
12. (U.K.), 30 & 31 Vict., c. 3.
13. R.S.C. 1985, c. I-5. See **Reading 2(a)**.
14. Schedule B to the *Canada Act, 1982* (U.K.), 1982, c. 11. See **Reading 7(a)**.
15. See **Reading 2(a)**.
16. [1939] S.C.R. 104.
17. See C. Chartier, "Indian: Analysis of the Term" (1978) 43 Sask. L. Rev. 37; C. Bell, "Who are the Métis People in Section 35(2)?" (1991) 29 Alta. L. Rev. 351; B.W. Morse and J. Giokas, "Do the Métis Fall within Section 91(24) of the Constitution Act, 1867?" in Royal Commission on Aboriginal Peoples, *Aboriginal Self-Government: Legal and Constitutional Issues* (Ottawa: Supply and Services Canada, 1995), 140; D. McMahon and F. Martin, "The Métis and 91(24): Is Inclusion the Issue" in Royal Commission on Aboriginal Peoples, *Aboriginal Self-Government: Legal and Constitutional Issues* (Ottawa: Supply and Services Canada, 1995), 277.
18. See **Chapter 6, Part 3**.
19. See **Chapter 8**.
20. *An Act Providing for the Organization of the Department of the Secretary of State of Canada, and for the Management of Indian and Ordinance Lands*, 31 Vict. (1868), c. 4, s. 15.
21. See generally, Policy, Planning and Research Branch, Department of Indian and Northern Affairs, *The Historical Development of the Indian Act*, 1975; D.G. Smith, ed., *Canadian Indians and the Law: Selected Documents, 1663–1972* (McClelland & Stewart, 1975); O.P. Dickason, *Canada's First Nations: A History of Founding Peoples from Earliest Times*, 3d ed. (Don Mills, Ont.: Oxford University Press, 2002) at 238–39.
22. For the definition of reserve in the current *Indian Act*, R.S.C. 1985, c. I-5, see *supra* note 9.
23. See **Chapter 1, Part 3**. See also R.H. Bartlett, *Indian Reserves and Aboriginal Lands in Canada: A Study in Law and History* (Saskatoon: University of Saskatoon Native Law Centre, 1990), arguing that in Ontario, on the Prairies, and in northern Canada, reserves "were set apart as part of a policy of establishing homelands to the aboriginal peoples": 60. Bartlett says that in these areas there was an attempt to help preserve traditional ways of life while developing "more contemporary forms of economic development": *ibid.* At 131, Bartlett says more generally that "[r]eserves were established to provide for the survival and development of the aboriginal peoples, and in particular, to encourage the adoption of a settled and 'civilized' way of life." On the conflicting segregation-assimilation aims of post-Confederation Indian policy, see J. Leslie and R. Macguire for Treaties and Historical Research Branch, Department of Indian Affairs and Northern Development, *The Historical Development of the Indian Act*, 2d ed. (Ottawa: D.I.A.N.D., 1979); W. Daugherty and D. Madill for Treaties and Historical Research Branch, Department of Indian Affairs and Northern Development, 2d ed., *Indian Government under Indian Act Legislation, 1868–1951*, 2d ed. (Ottawa: D.I.A.N.D., 1984); and *Report*, vol. 1, chap. 9.
24. See W. Moss and E. Gardner-O'Toole for Research Branch, Library of Parliament, *Aboriginal People: History of Discriminatory Laws*, rev. ed. (Ottawa: Supply and Services Canada, 1992).
25. That is, eligibility to be registered as an Indian under the *Indian Act*.
26. Earlier Indian legislation also established an initial "Charter group" identified by blood and affiliation, and then provided for intermarriage with and descent from this group. The first clear specific legislative definition of "Indian" appears to be in *An Act for the better protection of the Lands and Property of the Indians in Lower Canada*, 13 and 14 Victoria (1850), c. 42. Section V of this Act defined Indians as:

    1st All persons of Indian blood, reputed to belong to the particular Body or Tribe of Indians interested in such lands, and their descendants.
    2nd All persons intermarried with any such Indians and residing amongst them, and the descendants of such persons.
    3rd All persons residing among such Indians, whose parents on either side were or are Indians of such Body or Tribe, or entitled to be considered as such, and
    4th All persons adopted in infancy by any such Indians, and residing in the Village or upon the lands of any such Tribe or Body of Indians, and their descendants.
27. This provision did not appear until 1876. In the first clear pre-Confederation legislation in 1850, intermarriage conferred status regardless of gender, and descendants could claim status through either the male or female line: *ibid.* In an 1851 amendment, though, the Act was changed to prevent non-Indian males from gaining status through marriage to Indians (14 & 15 Vic., c. 59, s. II.), and this amended eligibility scheme was repeated in the first federal Indian Act: *An Act Providing for the Organization of the Department of the Secretary of State of Canada, and for the Management of Indian and Ordinance Lands*, 31 Vict. (1868), c. 4, s. 15. Hence, the earliest legislative gender discrimination was against males. The 1869 *Enfranchisement Act* amended the 1868 legislation to provide for the first time that an Indian woman who married a non-Indian man lost her Indian status: *An Act for the Gradual Enfranchisement of Indians, the Better Management of Indian Affairs, and to Extend the Provisions of the Act 31 Victoria Cap. 42*, 32 & 33 Vic. (1869), c. 6, s. 6.
28. Earlier, Indian status had resulted in a number of disadvantages as well, from voting disabilities to mobility restrictions to alcohol restrictions, but by the 1980s most of these had been removed.
29. For general descriptions of Aboriginal traditions, see "Native People" in *The Canadian Encyclopedia*, Year 2000 ed. (Toronto: McClelland & Stewart, 1999) at 1576–97, and cross references therein.
30. See W. Moss and E. Gardner-O'Toole for Research Branch, Library of Parliament, *Aboriginal People: History of Discriminatory Laws*, rev. ed. (Ottawa: Supply and Services Canada, 1992). See also l'Heureux-Dubé J. in *Corbiere v. Canada (Minister of Indian and Northern Affairs)*, [1999] 2 S.C.R. 203 at para. 88, referring to L. Gilbert, *Entitlement to Indian Status and Membership Codes in Canada* (Scarborough, Ont.: Carswell, 1996) at 23–30.
31. *Ibid.*
32. *Ibid.*
33. See P.W. Hogg, *Constitutional Law of Canada*, Student Ed. 2004 (Scarborough, Ont.: Carswell, 2004), ss. 27.1(a), 27.9, and 52.9(b), discussing s. 91(24) of the *Constitution Act, 1867* and s. 25 of the *Constitution Act, 1982*.
34. Commenting on s. 15 of the *Constitution Act, 1982* and the Supreme Court's "immutable personal characteristic" requirement, P.W. Hogg said that "[w]hat does warrant a constitutional remedy is the claim that a person has been unfairly treated by reason of a condition over which the person has no control": *ibid.* at 1105. Although Hogg went on to note that s. 15 of the *Charter* affects Aboriginal peoples in only a limited way, the comment itself appeals to general considerations of fairness.
35. For example, the *Indian Act*'s former alcohol restrictions: see discussion of *R. v. Drybones*, [1970] S.C.R. 282 in

Part 2(4)(d), below. For the requirement of disadvantage in specific equality guarantees, see *Drybones*, *ibid.* at 297 and 298 and Hogg, *ibid.* at 961–66.

36. See generally *Report*, vol. 4, chap. 2, ss. 3.1 and 3.2.
37. S.C. 1960, c. 44, reprinted in R.S.C. 1985, App. III. See **Reading 2(b)**.
38. *R. v. Drybones*, [1970] S.C.R. 282. See further D.W. Elliott, "Canard: A Triad Returns" (1975) 25 U.T.L.J. 317.
39. *Ibid.* at 297 and 298.
40. *Canada (A.G.) v. Lavell; Isaac v. Bedard*, [1974] S.C.R. 1349, rev'g (1971), 22 D.L.R. (3d) 188 (F.C.A.: decision in Mrs. Lavell's case) and (1971), 25 D.L.R. (3d) 551 (O.H.C.: decision in Mrs. Bedard's case). See **Reading 2(c)**. See further D.W. Elliott, "Canard: A Triad Returns" (1975) 25 U.T.L.J. 317.
41. *Lavell*, *ibid.* at 1375.
42. *Ibid.* at 1373.
43. *Ibid.* at 1359–60.
44. *Ibid.* at 1370.
45. See J. Silman, ed., *Enough is Enough: Aboriginal Women Speak Out* (Toronto: The Women's Press, 1987).
46. See Human Rights Committee, United Nations, *Views under Article 5(4) of the Optional Protocol Concerning Communication No. R. 6/24*, December 29, 1977, July 30, 1981, reproduced in New Brunswick Human Rights Commission, *Selected Documents in the Matter of Lovelace v. Canada Pursuant to the International Covenant on Civil and Political Rights*, 1981, 156–64.
47. *Canadian Charter of Rights and Freedoms*, being Schedule B to the *Canada Act, 1982* (U.K.), 1982, c. 11. See **Reading 2(b)**.
48. As was before, "Indian" is defined as "a person who pursuant to this Act is registered as an Indian or is entitled to be registered as an Indian": (s. 2(1)).
49. *Indian Act*, R.S.C. 1985, c. I-5, ss. 4 to 7. The effect of the 1985 changes is described in detail in J. Woodward, *Native Law* (Toronto: Carswell, 1989), 5–51.
50. That is, women who lost status because of marriage to non-Indian men and any children enfranchised as a result (before 1974, the existing dependent minor children of women who "married out" were generally disenfranchised); illegitimate children of status women who were deregistered because the natural fathers were non-Indian; and children who lost status at age 21 because their mothers and paternal grandmothers had gained status by marriage (the "double-mother" rule).
51. That is, men who voluntarily gave up status, with the result that their wives and families lost it too; those who gave up status on earning university degrees or becoming members of professions or ministers; and those who lost status because they resided outside Canada for more than five years.
52. Department of Indian and Northern Affairs, "Figure 1.3, Percentage Change in Registered Indian and Bill V-31 Population, 1985 to 2001 (revised)" in *Basic Departmental Data, 2001* (Ottawa: D.I.A.N.D., 2001).
53. *Report*, vol. 4, chap. 2, s. 3.2 at 36–37.
54. *Indian Act*, R.S.C. 1985, c. I-5, s. 11(1).
55. *Supra* note 51.
56. *Supra* note 52.
57. By December 1995, this proportion had increased to just under 40%, a total of 240 bands: *Report*, vol. 4, chap. 2, s. 3.3 at 47.
58. *Indian Act*, R.S.C. 1985, c. I-5, s. 10, especially ss. 10(1) and 10(4).
59. For federal Indian and Inuit programs generally, see J. Woodward, *supra* note 49, chap. 19; and "D. Gottesman and J. Dempsey, Native People, Government Programs" in *The Canadian Encyclopedia*, Year 2000 ed. (Toronto: McClelland & Stewart, 1999) at 1584.
60. In regard to personal property, courts have construed the "on a reserve" requirement broadly. In *Williams v. Canada*, [1992] 1 S.C.R. 877, the Supreme Court listed several factors to be weighed in determining if income is closely enough connected to a reserve to fall within the exemption.
61. See, generally, *Indian Act*, R.S.C. 1985, c. I-5, s. 4.1.
62. The federal government also provides post-secondary educational assistance to Inuit students: *Indians in Canada and the United States, supra* note 9.
63. *Report*, vol. 4, chap. 2, s. 3.3 at 37–38 and 40.
64. For a useful general survey, see Megan Furi and Jill Wherrett for Library of Parliament, *Indian Status and Band Membership Issues* (Ottawa: Library of Parliament, 1996, rev'd. 2003).
65. See *Sawridge Band v. Canada*, *infra* note 123.
66. *Report*, *supra* note 63.
67. For example, in 1982 the council of the Mohawk community of Kahnawake, southwest of Montreal, asserted effective control of its membership outside the *Indian Act* procedure. It declared that band membership and related benefits would not be available to Kahnawake Mohawks who married or adopted non-Indians: see E.J. Dickson-Gilmore, *Iati-Onkweonwe*: Blood Quantum, Membership and the Politics of Exclusion in Kahnawake, (1999) 3 *Citizenship Studies* 27 at 36–37. In 1984, the council's Mohawk Citizenship Law defined Mohawk as "any person, male or female, whose name appears on the present band and reinstatement lists and whose blood quantum is 50% and more shall comprise the Kahnawake Mohawk Registry": *ibid.* at 37. The council then limited the right to vote to persons over 18 years who were then on the Band List and in the Mohawk Registry. As a result, about one-third of those who went to vote at the next council election were held to be disqualified: *ibid*.
68. For example, if a person with status under s. 6(2) of the Act (i.e, a person with only one parent with "primary" status under s. 6(1)) marries a person without Indian status or another person with status under s. 6(2), the children of the marriage will not have Indian status, since they will not have at least one parent with status under s. 6(1), as required in s. 6(2). If a person with primary status under s. 6(1) marries another person, the children will have Indian status: see s. 6(2).
69. See J. Holmes, *Bill C-31: Equality or Disparity? The Effects of the New Indian Act on Native Women* (Ottawa: Canadian Advisory Council on the Status of Women, 1986) at 22–24 and *Report*, vol. 4, chap. 2, s. 3.3 at 37–43.
70. *Corbiere v. Canada (Minister of Indian and Northern Affairs)*, [1999] 2 S.C.R. 203; aff'g. and varying [1997] 1 F.C. 689 (C.A.); aff'g. and varying (1993), 107 D.L.R. (4th) 582 (T.D.). *Corbiere and Lovelace* involved the application of the equality provisions of the *Charter* to different groups of Aboriginal peoples. The Supreme Court has not yet explored how far these provisions can apply to government measures for Aboriginal peoples that allegedly discriminate against non-Aboriginals (or groups that contain non-Aboriginals). See further, **Part 9**, below.

    For commentary, see P. Hughes, "Case Comment on *Corbiere v. Canada (Minister of Indian and Northern Affairs)*" (2001) 12 N.J.C.L. 69.
71. Under s. 74 of the *Indian Act*, the Minister of Indian and Northern Affairs has a discretion to declare that particular band councils are subject to the *Indian Act* system of elections. In practice, this enables a band to opt either for the *Indian Act* election system or for its own customary system of selecting band councillors. A small majority of bands are subject to customary systems of selection.
72. *Indian Act*, R.S.C. 1985, c. I-5, s. 77(1). (An eligible voter must also be at least 18 years of age.)
73. Section 81(1).
74. Sections 64(1) and 66(1).
75. Section 61(1).
76. See *Corbiere v. Canada (Minister of Indian and Northern Affairs)*, [1999] 2 S.C.R. 203 at para. 30. The reserves, the

Rankin, Goulais Bay, and Obadjiwan reserves, are all located near Sault St. Marie.

77. *Ibid.*
78. And three other Batchewana Band members.
79. Para. 50. The Court said the plaintiffs' statement of claim had not been limited solely to the Batchewana Band situation (para. 47), that many other bands were affected by the demographic trends affecting the Batchewana Band (para. 30), and that any principles developed in this case might apply to other bands (para. 50).
80. Paras. 24 and 118.
81. Paras. 20, 52, and 53. Although the Court did not say so expressly, it implied that the Batchewana Band had not established Aboriginal right to exclude off-reserve band member voting: see, for example, para. 22: "If another band could establish an Aboriginal right to restrict voting, as suggested by the Court of Appeal, that right would simply have precedence over the terms of the *Indian Act*; this is not a reason to restrict the declaration of invalidity to the Batchewana Band."
82. Para. 22.
83. *Law v. Canada (Minister of Employment and Immigration)*, [1999] 1 S.C.R. 497. In *Law*, the Court said [paras. 39 and 88] that s. 15 equality analysis involves three inquiries: (i) does the action impose differential treatment between the claimant and others? (ii) is the differential treatment based on one or more enumerated or analogous grounds of discrimination? and (iii) is the action substantively discriminatory? As with the other inquiries, the third inquiry is approached by asking if the action violates human dignity: paras. 54, 59, and 60–62. For this question, the Court said [at paras. 64–74, 88] that the following contextual factors are especially relevant: (i) preexisting disadvantage, (ii) correspondence between the ground on which the claim is made and the claimant's actual circumstances; (iii) absence of an ameliorative purpose or effect to the action for more disadvantaged people; and (iv) the severity and localized nature of the challenged activity.
84. McLachlin and Bastarache JJ. for themselves, Lamer C.J. and Cory and Major JJ. L'Heureux-Dubé J., for herself, Gonthier, Iacobucci and Binnie JJ., took a similar approach to the main majority. She differed mainly in regard to her approach to analogous grounds and discrimination under s. 15 of the *Charter*. For example, unlike the main majority, she felt that a characteristic may or may not constitute a ground analogous to those enumerated in s. 15, depending on the circumstances: paras. 6–11 (main majority); para. 61 (L'Heureux-Dubé J.).
85. The targeted rather than general ameliorative purpose of the benefits program and the correspondence between the ground of exclusion and the general circumstances of the claimant and beneficiary groups were critical in the Supreme Court's subsequent decision in *Lovelace v. Ontario*, [2000] 1 S.C.R. 950. Here Métis groups argued that the Ontario government's failure to extend proceeds from a reserve-based commercial casino to non-registered as well as *Indian Act* registered Indians and urban band members violated the equality guarantee in s. 15. The Court said the appropriate distinction here was between band and non-band Indians: para. 64. Non-band Indians did meet the requirements of the first two inquiries under the test in *Law* (*supra* note 83), and they could show preexisting disadvantage. However, the casino project had an ameliorative purpose, and the Court said that s. 15(1) must be read in light of the ameliorative goal of s. 15(2). Thus, when the Court considered if the distinction corresponded with actual circumstances, it focused on the circumstances of the program's target group as well as on those of the claimants. It said that band Indians, unlike non-band Indians, are subject to special reserve land use restrictions (para. 75) and have a tradition of involvement in gaming activities (para. 77). In this case, the band Indians had also been involved in the casino project on a partnership basis (para. 82). Similarly, when the Court looked at the ameliorative purpose of the project, it said that the key question was not whether the claimants were more or less disadvantaged than the target group, but whether the program was clearly directed at a specific disadvantaged group (paras. 85–87). In the Court's view, the project was clearly designed to ameliorate the situation of the band Indians (para. 87). Because of these factors, and because the claimants' had not shown that they had been denied any recognition as self-governing communities (para. 89), the Court concluded that there was no discrimination in effect.
86. SOR JUS 610-775, October 20, 2000.
87. SOR JUS 610-776, October 20, 2000.
88. "Non-status" used to be used in a broader sense to include Métis people and others of mixed Aboriginal and non-Aboriginal descent, but this use of the term is much less common now. The term "non-status" could also be used to describe those Indians who are band members without status. The problem with this use is that it groups those who are subject at least partly to the *Indian Act* together with those who are outside it. Because the term is imprecise, it is impossible to provide a clear estimate of the total number of non-status Indians. The large number of reinstatements in the decade following Bill C-31 will have significantly reduced the number of people who might be described as non-status.
89. See s. 7(1)(a) of *Indian Act*.
90. M.A. Freeman, "Inuit", *The Canadian Encyclopedia*, Year 2000 ed. (Toronto: McClelland & Stewart, 1999) at 1183; Dickason, *supra* note 21 at 68–75; R. McGhee, *Ancient People of the Arctic* (Vancouver: U.B.C. Press, 1996).
91. Freeman, *Ibid.*
92. **Chapter 11, Part 7(b)**. See also *James Bay and Northern Quebec Native Claims Settlement Act*, S.C. 1976–77; *Cree-Naskapi (of Quebec) Act*, S.C. 1984, c. 18.
93. **Chapter 11, Part 7(c)**. See also *Western Arctic (Inuvialuit) Claims Settlement Act*, S.C. 1984, c. 24, as am. S.C. 1988, c. 16, s. 1.
94. **Chapter 11, Part 7(e)**. Formal name: *Final Agreement between the Inuit of the Nunavut Settlement Area and Her Majesty in Right of Canada*. Federal ratifying legislation: *Nunavut Land Claims Agreement Act*, S.C. 1993, c. 29.
95. **Chapter 11, Part 7(j)**. Formal name: *Land Claims and Self-Government Agreement Between the Inuit of Labrador as Represented by the Labrador Inuit Association and the Queen in Right of Newfoundland and Labrador and the Queen in Right of Canada*.
96. See generally, D. Redbird, *We are Métis: A Metis View of the Development of A Native Canadian People* (Willowdale, Ontario: Ontario Metis and Non-status Indian Assn., 1980); D. Purich, *The Métis* (Toronto: Lorimer, 1988); M. Giraud (trans. G. Woodcock), *The Métis in the Canadian West* (Edmonton: University of Alberta Press, 1986); D.N. Sprague, *Canada and the Métis, 1869–1885* (Waterloo, Ont.: Wilfred Laurier University Press, 1988); T.E. Flanagan, "The History of Métis Aboriginal Rights: Politics, Principle and Policy", (1990) 5 *Can. J. of L. & Soc.* 71; Dickason, *supra* note 21, chaps. 20 and 21; J.S. Frideres, *Native Peoples in Canada: Contemporary Conflicts*, 4th ed. (Scarborough, Ont.: Prentice Hall, 1993) at 38–43; *Report*, vol. 4, chap. 5.
97. J.S.H. Brown, "Métis", *The Canadian Encyclopedia*, Year 2000 ed. (Toronto: McClelland & Stewart, 1999) at 1478–79.
98. *Ibid.* at 1477–79.
99. *Ibid.* and **Chapter 1, Part 3**.
100. The number of reported Métis in Canada was 292,310: Statistics Canada, "Largest Gains in Métis Population", in *Aboriginal Peoples of Canada: A Demographic Profile* (Ottawa: Statistics Canada, release date January 21,

2003), <http://www12.statcan.ca/english/census01/Products/Analytic/companion/abor/canada.cfm>.

101. Note, however, the adhesion to Treaty 3 mentioned below; see *infra* note 104; and note that several modern land claims agreements, such as the 1993 *Vuntut Gwitchin*, *Champagne and Aishihik*, *Teslin Tlingit*, and *Nacho Nyak Dun* agreements in the Yukon and the 1994 *Sahtu Dene and Metis Agreement*, include Métis beneficiaries: **Chapter 11, Parts 7(f) and (g)**.
102. R.S.C. 1970, c. 1-6, s. 12(1)(a).
103. Alberta enacted the *Metis Betterment Act* in 1938 to set aside land in the centre of the province for Métis settlements. See now the *Constitution of Alberta Amendment Act, 1990*, S.A, 1990, c.-22.2; *Metis Settlements Land Protection Act*, S.A., 1990, M-14.8; *Metis Settlements Accord Implementation Act*, S.A. 1990, M-14.5; *Metis Settlements Act*, S.A. 1990, M-14.3. See also **Chapter 12, Part 3(c)(iv)(B)**, last note.
104. Treaty No. 3 Between Her Majesty the Queen and the Saulteaux Tribe of the Ojibbeway Indians at the Northwest Angle on the Lake of the Woods with Adhesions, 1873 (Ottawa: Queen's Printer, 1966), Adhesion by Halfbreeds of Rainy River and Lake.
105. **Chapter 1, Part 3**.
106. See generally, P.A. Cumming and N.H. Mickenberg, eds., Native Rights in Canada, 2d ed. (Toronto: Indian-Eskimo Association of Canada, 1972), chap. 19; P.L.A. Chartrand, "Aboriginal Rights: The Dispossession of the Métis" (1991) 29 Osgoode Hall L.J. 457.
107. There are differences in the specific criteria used or emphasized by the national Métis organizations. For example, the Métis National Council defines Métis as "a person who self-identifies as Métis, is distinct from other Aboriginal peoples, is of Historic Métis Nation ancestry, and is accepted by the Métis Nation." The MNC describes the Historic Métis Nation as the Aboriginal people who resided in the Historic Métis National Homeland, that is, the traditional territory of the Métis or half-breeds in "west central North America": MNC General Assembly, Edmonton, September 27–28, 2002: <http://www.aboriginalcanada.gc.ca/abdt/interface/interface2.nsf/LaunchFrameSet?OpenAgent&RefDoc=1.html&URL=http://www.metisnation.ca/&altlang=http://www.metisnation.ca/&disp=e&end>. The Congress of Original Peoples stresses self-idenitification as a Métis, and rejects any geographical requirement: <http://www.aboriginalcanada. gc.ca/abdt/interface/interface2.nsf/LaunchFrameSet?OpenAgent&RefDoc=1.html&URL=http://www.abo-peoples.org/mainmenu.html&altlang=http://www.abo-peoples.org/mainmenu.html&disp=e&end> The Métis National Council's definition stresses European-Aboriginal ancestry, and, for membership in the MNC, requires proof of "Community acceptance as a Métis": <http://www.aboriginalcanada.gc.ca/abdt/interface/interface2.nsf/LaunchFrameSet?OpenAgent&RefDoc=1.html&URL=http://www.canadianmetis.com/&altlang=http://www.canadianmetis.com/&disp=e&end>
108. *R. v. Powley*, [2003] 2 S.C.R. 207: see **Chapter 10, Part 5**.
109. *Ibid.* at paras. 10, 18 *et seq.*
110. *Supra* note 16.
111. See *R. v. Powley*, *supra* note 108, and **Chapter 6, Part 3.**
112. **Part 3, above**.
113. See *Re Eskimos*, *supra* note 16.
114. See **Chapter 6, Part 5**.
115. *Ibid.*
116. *R. v. Blais*, [2003] 2 S.C.R. 236 at para 41: see **Chapter 6, Part 5.**
117. *Ibid.* at paras. 33 and 34.
118. *Ibid.* at para. 41.
119. The term "treaties" in this part refers primarily to the traditional Indian treaties that were concluded until the first part of the 20th century. The post-1970 modern land claims agreements — which are also technically a form of treaty — are referred to separately in **Part 7**, below. See further **Chapter 5**.
120. See further, **Chapter 11**.
121. *James Bay and Northern Quebec Agreement*, s. 3.2. Under the Yukon *Umbrella Final Agreement*, a beneficiary must (i) have at least 25% Indian ancestry, and (ii) be ordinarily resident in the Yukon between 1800 and 1940, or (iii) be a descendant of a person meeting these requirements or (iv) be recognized as having "a sufficient affiliation with a Yukon First Nation": *U.F.A.*, s. 3.2.0. Eligibility under the land claims agreements does not automatically end any status beneficiaries might have under the *Indian Act*.
122. For example, *Vuntut Gwitchin First Nation Self-Government Agreement*, Ottawa, Department of Indian Affairs and Northern Development, May 29, 1993, s. 10.1.1: see **Chapter 12, Part 3(c)(iv)(A)**. Self-government agreements are not to affect the rights of First Nations Citizens as Canadian citizens, or — except where otherwise provided in the agreements — their entitlement to all the "benefits, services, and protections" of other *Constitution Act, 1982* citizens: *ibid.* at s. 3.6.
123. *Quaere*, whether the right to control Aboriginal or Indian status is an inherent Aboriginal right pursuant to s. 35(1) of the *Constitution Act, 1982*? In *Sawridge Band v. Canada*, [1995] F.C.J. No. 1013 (F.C.T.D.), this claim was rejected by the trial court. (In June 1997, though, the Federal Court of Appeal held that the trial judge's decision gave rise to a reasonable apprehension of bias, and directed that the case be re-tried before another judge: "Judge Biased in Native-Status Ruling, Court Says" *The Globe and Mail* (June 6, 1997) A7). See also **Chapter 9** and **Chapter 12, Part 4**, on Aboriginal rights and Aboriginal self-government, respectively.
124. Does it apply at present? See ss. 25, 28, and 32 of the *Charter*.
125. Although examples of this are exceptional today, they were all too common in the past. After the early periods of Aboriginal-European contact, Aboriginal peoples in what is now Canada were generally regarded as British subjects, subject to specific legislative or policy restrictions: see, for example, *Sanderson v. Heap* (1909) 19 Man. R. 122 at 125 and *Sawridge Band v. Canada*, [1996] 1 F.C. 3 (C.A.) at para. 72. However, Inuit were denied the right to vote in federal elections until 1950, and registered Indians were not given this right until 1960. Registered Indians were subject to special alcohol restrictions until 1970. For other statutory or policy restrictions, see *J.R. Miller, Skyscrapers Hide the Heavens: A History of Indian-White Relations in Canada*, 3d ed. (Toronto: University of Toronto Press, 2000), chaps. 6 and 11; and Dickason, *supra* note 21, chaps. 19–22.
126. See, for example, *Andrews v. Law Society of British Columbia*, [1989]1 S.C.R. 143 at 164–69 reaffirmed in decisions such as *Eldridge v. British Columbia (A.G.) and Medical Services Commission*, [1997] 3 S.C.R. 624 at para. 61.
127. This is the general concept of affirmative action, given specific recognition in human rights and employment legislation, and in s. *15(2) of the Constitution Act, 1982*.
128. See P. Macklem, *Indigenous Difference and the Constitution of Canada* (Toronto: University of Toronto Press, 2001), arguing that because of the unique social and historical situation of Aboriginal peoples in Canada, they should have special constitutional rights, protections and powers to ensure that they have "equal citizenship" (e.g., pp. 5 and 288) with other Canadians.
129. See also s. 35(4) of the *Constitution Act, 1982*, guaranteeing equality to male and female persons in the enjoyment of s. 35(1) Aboriginal and treaty rights.
130. See especially **Parts 4(d)** and **Reading 2(b)**.
131. See especially **Parts 4(f)** and **4(g)** and **Reading 2(b)**.
132. *Supra* note 38 and accompanying text.

133. *Supra* note 40 and accompanying text.
134. These are essentially the contextual factors in *Law, supra* note 83, as modified by subsequent case law.
135. Cf. *Lavell* under the *Canadian Bill of RIghts*: it was alleged there that one group of registered Indians was denied benefits that were available to another group of registered Indians, as the result of a sexually discriminatory provision (former s. 12(1)(b) of the *Indian Act* regarding marriage by Indian women): *supra* note 133.
136. *Corbiere v. Canada (Minister of Indian and Northern Affairs)*, [1999] 2 S.C.R. 203.
137. *Ibid*., and **Part 4(g)**, above.
138. *Lovelace v. Ontario*, [2000] 1 S.C.R. 950.
139. Supra note 85. In the case of a specific targeted group such as the one here, the correspondence requirements are applied less rigorously than where the targeted groups are intended to be comprehensive.
140. *Chippewas of Nawash First Nation v. Canada (Minister of Fisheries and Oceans)*, [2003] S.C.C.A. No. 25 (September 18, 2003), dismissing without reasons or costs [2001] 1 C.N.L.R. 20 (F.C.A.), aff'g. [2000] F.C.J. 1833 (T.D.), rejecting a s. 15(1) claim and a claim for breach of fiduciary duty.
141. [2003] 3 F.C. 233 at paras. 46–48.
142. *Ibid*. at paras. 44, 45 and 49.
143. Although the Supreme Court approved this decision without reasons, the general presumption in favour of specifically targeted ameliorative programs seems consistent with the Court's reasoning in *Lovelace, supra* note 85.
144. *R. v. Kapp*, [2004] BCSC 958, rev'g. [2004] BCPC 151.
145. *R. v. Kapp*, [2004] BCSC 958 at para. 60.
146. "The learned trial judge found the members of the M.B.T. to be relatively financially advantaged. However, in my view it is the circumstances of the broader Aboriginal community that must be considered here, not just the M.B.T. While the M.B.T. may be relatively better off when compared with other Aboriginal communities, the comparator group is made up of the broader Aboriginal community whose members do not enjoy the relative advantages said by the respondents to arise from the fact that the M.B.T. members live in such close proximity to a major urban area": *ibid*. at para. 81.
147. And *vice versa*: see *Lovelace v. Ontario*, [2000] 1 S.C.R. 950 at paras. 42 and 61.
148. As noted in *Lovelace v. Canada*, [2000] 1 S.C.R. 950 paragraph 69: "Aboriginal peoples experience high rates of unemployment and poverty, and face serious disadvantages in the areas of education, health, and housing...." The Court also noted that "all aboriginal peoples have been affected "by the legacy of stereotyping and prejudice against Aboriginal peoples" (*Corbiere* ... at para. 66)": *ibid.*
149. As seen in *Lovelace* and *Chippewas of Nawash*.
150. After *Lovelace*, though, a s. 15(2) inquiry will likely be treated as an aspect of a larger analysis under s. 15(1): text at *supra* note 85.
151. See *R. v. Kapp*, [2004] BCSC 958 at paras. 29 and 30. Brenner J. held that s. 25 did not apply in this case because the right in question (an asserted Aboriginal commercial fishing right) had not been established as a s. 35(1) Aboriginal right (para. 31), and "something more than an "asserted right" or a negotiated agreement in the context of an asserted right is necessary": para. 35. Note, though, that, s. 35(1) rights are themselves subject to justified governmental infringement: on s. 35(1), see **Chapters 7, 9, and 10.**

3 Aboriginal Rights before *Calder*

Chapter Highlights

- The prior Aboriginal presence in North America is at the heart of the concept of Aboriginal rights.
- Aboriginal commentaries on Aboriginal rights tend to stress the need for a different perspective on justification of rights to land and resources; a communal, holistic, and spiritual view of land, natural resources and people; and an emphasis on the importance of land and self-government.
- Over the years, Canadian courts have developed three main approaches to describing the source of Aboriginal rights: the Royal Proclamation approach, the occupancy and use approach, and what might be called a "land and societies" approach.
- Until well into the 20th century, Canadian courts followed an 1888 decision of the Judicial Committee of the Privy Council and took the first approach; in contrast, American courts had long taken a wider view of the source of Aboriginal rights.

Synopsis

As an Aboriginal concept, Aboriginal rights are an expression of the Aboriginal connections to land, spirituality, sharing, and self-government. As a legal concept, the rights have had a narrower but evolving meaning. For a long time Canadian courts attributed Aboriginal rights to an 18th century prerogative instrument. Then they gave the rights a general common law status, on the basis of Aboriginal occupancy and use of land. Today the rights have constitutional status, and courts stress both the prior Aboriginal presence on land and the traditional organization of distinctive Aboriginal societies. This chapter looks at the early period in Canada, with an emphasis on the legal source and status of Aboriginal rights.

Selected Readings

🖹 links material in this chapter to the corresponding headings and page numbers of the relevant readings.

🖹	Part 2	Founding Peoples in Traditional Times	219
🖹	Part 3	Some Aboriginal Perspectives on Lands and Resources	217
🖹	Part 9	*The Royal Proclamation of 1763*	236
🖹	Part 10	*St. Catherine's Milling and Lumber Co. v. The Queen*	237
🖹	Part 11	*Johnson and Graham's Lessee v. M'Intosh*	242
🖹	Part 12	*Worcester v. Georgia*	250
🖹	Part 13	*Connolly v. Woolrich* and *Johnstone v. Connolly*	251

1. CONTEXT

Writing in 1988, one commentator called Aboriginal rights "the most undefined, uncertain, and fragile rights known to our law."[1] Although these rights are more defined today, they remain uncertain — still half hidden in a haze of complex legal interpretation. What *are* Aboriginal rights and Aboriginal title? How do they relate to Aboriginal self-government? Is judicial enforcement of Aboriginal rights the best hope for meeting the economic, social, and other challenges of Canadian Aboriginal people, and for unlocking their great cultural potential?[†]

2. BACKGROUND

Reading 1(b) at p. 219

People have lived in northern North America since very early times. They may have occupied the Old Crow area of what is now the Yukon Territory as long as 12,000 years ago.[2] Elsewhere, there is evidence that they have lived in what is now Canada since before the end of the last Ice Age.[3]

Without written records, we can only speculate about the hopes, fears, and plans of these earliest pre-Canadians. As the millennia move on, though, archaeological and anthropological evidence and oral traditions suggest an extraordinarily rich variety of traditional languages (over fifty are still spoken in Canada today), social structures, and patterns of life.[4] What is clear is that Aboriginal people lived here in North America long before the arrival of the Europeans, and continued to do so after newcomers came and claimed the land in the name of European governments. This prior Aboriginal presence is at the heart of the concept of Aboriginal rights.[5]

3. ABORIGINAL CONCEPTS

Reading 1(a) at p. 217

Our focus is on concepts of Aboriginal rights and title that are enforced in the courts of law. To help put these into perspective, we will first consider some concepts and concerns of Aboriginal writers. Although these writers do not speak with a single voice, a number of common themes recur.

The Aboriginal commentator LeRoy Little Bear suggested that courts have approached Aboriginal rights from the wrong direction. They have spent much time looking for the legal foundations of Aboriginal rights. Little Bear said the need for justification is on the other side:

> When the courts and the government say that the Indians' title is dependent on goodwill of the sovereign, and that the Indians' interest is a mere burden on the underlying title of the Crown, the question to ask is, "What did the Crown get its title from? And how?"[6]

Similarly, Anishinabek scholar John Borrows has said that:

> Aboriginal peoples have had their status redefined by Canada without persuasively sound juridical reasons. What could be more arbitrary than one nation substantially invalidating a politically distinct [people's] rights without providing an elementarily persuasive legal explanation? The Supreme Court has not effectively articulated how, and by what legal right, assertions of Crown sovereignty grant underlying title to the Crown or displace Aboriginal governance.[7]

For Aboriginal people, land has special importance. Summarizing Aboriginal testimony before it, the Royal Commission on Aboriginal Peoples said that:

> Aboriginal peoples have told us of their special relationship to the land and its resources. This relationship, they say, is both spiritual and material, not only one of livelihood, but of community and indeed of the continuity of their cultures.[8]

Speaking before the Commission, Elder Alex Stead of Winnipeg said:

> We are so close to the land. This is my body when you see this mother earth, because I live by it.[9]

Aboriginal commentators tend to stress the holistic, communal aspect of Aboriginal ownership of land. For example, Little Bear has said, "Indian ownership of property, like Indians' way of relating to the world, is holistic. Land is communally

† Parts of this chapter were based on the research for "Aboriginal Title", by D.W. Elliott, in B.W. Morse, ed., *Aboriginal Peoples and the Law: Indian, Métis and Inuit Rights in Canada* (Ottawa: Carleton University Press, 1985), and the book's proposed second edition, funded in part by the Law Foundation of Ontario.

owned; ownership rests not in any one individual, but rather belongs to the tribe as a whole, as an entity."[10] Georges Erasmus, former National Chief of the Assembly of First Nations and then Co-chair of the Royal Commission on Aboriginal Peoples, has said that Aboriginal title goes beyond land ownership:

> As First Nations, we believe that our aboriginal title includes ownership and jurisdiction over all lands and resources within our traditional areas....
>
> Land and jurisdiction over land go hand in hand. We have been pressing for fair land settlement to provide the basis for an economically viable life for our people, but we have also insisted on our right to aboriginal self-government over ... our traditional land, resources, and people.[11]

A position paper of the Union of British Columbia Indian Chiefs stressed the connection between land, native sovereignty, and inherent entitlement:

> The sovereignty of our Nations comes from the Great Spirit. It is not granted nor subject to the approval of any other Nation. As First Nations we have the sovereign right to jurisdictional rule within our traditional territories. Our lands are a sacred gift. The land is provided for the continued use, benefit and enjoyment of our people, and it is our ultimate obligation to the Great Spirit to care for and protect it.[12]

Speaking for the Innu of Ungava, Daniel Ashini expressed bitterness at the effects of the arrival of the Europeans:

> When the settlers first came to our land, we helped them. We taught them about the animals, and where they could find the great rivers of the Nitassinan. We showed them how to live and survive in this country, one of the coldest on earth. Canada was built by the fur trade in which the Innu were active participants. We traded animal furs for flour, cotton, rifles, alcohol, and other products. How could we have foreseen the tragic effects, for instance, that alcohol would have on our people? How could we have foreseen the industrial developments that would drive us off our land? When it began we didn't know how to fight against the giant companies that flooded and ravaged our land for hydroelectric power, mines, pulp and paper. This is how we were repaid for our generosity to the newcomers.[13]

These Aboriginal commentators stress the need for a different perspective on justification, a communal, holistic, and spiritual view of land, natural resources and people, and an emphasis on the importance of land and self-government. They convey a sense of bitterness at an historic process of dispossession, damage, and injustice.

As these passages suggest, there can be little moral support for an arbitrary and unilateral takeover of the land and governments of others, especially where land is central to culture. At the same time, this takeover involved an effective change in governmental control, and it imposed new common needs. Today, the first peoples and millions of others share a finite space, and few can easily leave. Public concerns such as conservation, safety, health, and the environment affect everyone, and demand general protection. All residents — Aboriginal and non-Aboriginal — have an interest in preserving resources such as lumber, game, and fish, and places such as forests, rivers, and parks. The means to meet these competing interests — room, resources, power, and money — are not unlimited. Dealing fairly with an arbitrary takeover, taking account of a change of sovereignty, and accommodating a shared present, are all parts of the modern challenge. These pressures and challenges converge whenever courts are called upon to decide how the law affects Aboriginal and non-Aboriginal relations. This is especially so in the important legal field of Aboriginal rights and Aboriginal title.

4. DESCRIPTIONS AND QUESTIONS

How do courts describe Aboriginal rights and Aboriginal title? There is no single comprehensive definition. Generally, though, courts describe Aboriginal rights as *rights of Aboriginal peoples which derive from their prior use and occupancy of land, in distinctive societies*.[14] Both the "land" and "societies" elements are considered relevant[15] although the emphasis varies with the nature of the right. For example, the Supreme Court sees Aboriginal title as "a sub-category of Aboriginal rights which deals solely with claims of rights to land."[16] Aboriginal title allows exclusive occupation and general use of land.[17] It requires proof of exclusive occupation prior to European sovereignty.[18] More specific Aboriginal rights are related to particular traditional activities. For an Aboriginal right other than Aboriginal title, courts require that a claimant show proof of "an element of a practice, custom or tradition integral to the distinctive culture of the Aboriginal group claiming the right."[19]

Until we consider Aboriginal rights (and the important Aboriginal right of Aboriginal title) in more depth, these descriptions provide only tentative guides. We will start by asking five basic questions about Aboriginal rights:[20]

1. What is the source of Aboriginal rights?
2. What is the status of Aboriginal rights?
3. What is the content of Aboriginal rights?
4. How, if at all, can Aboriginal rights be restricted?
5. To what extent are Aboriginal rights enforceable?

5. SOURCE OF ABORIGINAL RIGHTS

In determining the source of Aboriginal rights, courts have been looking for the origin of their status as legal rights. The Canadian legal system recognizes several different direct sources of law: (a) the constitution and legislation; (b) the royal prerogative; and (c) the common law itself.

The constitution is the most authoritative source of law. Aboriginal rights are mentioned in s. 35(1) of the *Constitution Act, 1982*.[21] However, this section does not create Aboriginal and treaty rights. It merely recognizes and affirms "existing" Aboriginal and treaty rights. Section 35(1) addresses the status of Aboriginal rights; for their source we must look elsewhere. But other constitutional enactments provide little help, and there has been little general recognition of Aboriginal title or rights in individual statutes.[22]

This leaves the royal prerogative and the common law. In modern government, the royal prerogative plays a minor and decreasing role, although it once had a more significant function. The common law is the most flexible and open-ended of these three sources. Not only is it used to interpret the first two sources, but it can also serve as an entry point for more indirect sources, such as custom, government practice, international law, and analogies to existing principles.

6. ALTERNATIVE APPROACHES

Over the years, Canadian courts have evolved three main approaches to describing the source of Aboriginal rights. One is based on the royal prerogative. The other two are based on the common law. For simplicity, we will call these three alternatives (i) the Royal Proclamation approach; (ii) the occupancy and use approach; and (iii) what might be called the "land and societies" approach.[23]

The Royal Proclamation approach assumes that Aboriginal rights must depend on some form of legislative or executive government recognition in order to have legal status. It holds that Aboriginal rights derive from government recognition in the Royal Proclamation of 1763, an early prerogative instrument that purported to reserve lands for Indians. For this approach, then, the context and the content of the Royal Proclamation is all-important.[24]

The occupancy and use approach holds that Aboriginal rights derive from common law recognition of traditional Aboriginal occupation and use of land before the assertion of European sovereignty. This approach dispenses with the need for legislative or executive recognition, so it is not tied to the Royal Proclamation. On the other hand, since it is linked to traditional activity that pre-dates the coming of the Europeans, it must grapple with a question that the Proclamation approach avoids: How and in what form did Aboriginal rights survive European sovereignty?

The land and societies approach involves common law recognition of Aboriginal peoples' prior occupation and use of land in North America in distinctive societies.[25] It has two distinct aspects: (i) occupation and use of land and (ii) membership in distinctive Aboriginal societies. Although both aspects are relevant to Aboriginal rights, the *identification* of Aboriginal rights may depend more on one than another, depending on the kind of right being claimed.

Under this approach, Aboriginal rights are seen as falling along a spectrum in regard to their proximity to land. They range from Aboriginal title, which involves exclusive occupation of land, to Aboriginal rights that are not tied to a particular territory. For rights other than Aboriginal title, the focus is on identifying those practices, traditions and customs that are integral to the distinctive traditional culture of the claimant Aboriginal group.[26] For Aboriginal title, the distinctive societies aspect is assumed, and the focus is on exclusive occupation of land.[27]

The approach has a close affinity with use and occupancy. At the same time, its distinctive practices test bears some resemblance to common law recognition of custom.[28] Finally, to the extent that it relates to pre-European practices, the land and societies approach requires some form of reconciliation between Aboriginal rights and European sovereignty.

7. INTERRELATIONSHIPS

The choice of approach to the source of Aboriginal rights can affect the content attributed to these rights. Although the content of the second approach can be broader than that of the first, both share a common general link in Aboriginal use of land. This link is also found in some and, possibly, all applications of the land and societies approach.

Under the Proclamation approach, the content of Aboriginal rights depends on the Royal Proclamation of 1763. Under the occupancy and use approach, the content depends on the nature of the traditional use of the land or related natural resources. For example, if traditional activity included certain forms of fishing, these constitute part of the Aboriginal rights. As noted in **Chapters 9** and **10**, the precise scope of the land and societies approach is yet to be established.[29] Since this approach appears to require the element of land as well as that of distinctive societies, the content of Aboriginal rights comprises the social use of land and related resources. If, however, this approach required no minimal link to land, Aboriginal rights might extend broadly to such areas as Aboriginal family laws and language customs, and to aspects of Aboriginal self-government that may be unrelated to land.[30]

Other basic questions may or may not be affected by the choice of approach. For example, both the Proclamation approach and the two solely common law-based approaches recognize Aboriginal rights that can be restricted in part or terminated ("extinguished") by legislation. The key questions here are presumably the same for all three approaches: (i) Can restriction or extinguishment be brought about by provincial as well as federal legislation? (ii) What indicates a legislative intent to restrict or extinguish? (iii) Can restriction or extinguishment be brought about by action of the Crown alone? and (iv) How have restriction and extinguishment been affected by the affirmation and recognition of Aboriginal rights in s. 35(1) of the *Constitution Act, 1982*?[31]

8. EVOLUTION OF APPROACHES

For the first century of Confederation, the first approach prevailed. The Royal Proclamation of 1763 was regarded as the sole source of Aboriginal rights.[32] Canadian courts abandoned the recognition-based approach in 1973, shifting the focus away from the Royal Proclamation. They adopted an occupancy and use approach similar to the one articulated in *Johnson v. M'Intosh*.[33] Aboriginal rights lost their dependence on the executive branch of government, but kept their close association with land.

Although the concept of native custom is an old one, the land and societies approach and its distinctive practices test are recent developments. As will be seen later, their contours have not yet been fully drawn.

9. THE ROYAL PROCLAMATION OF 1763[34]

Reading 3(a) at p. 236

On October 7, 1763, King George III of Britain issued a very important Royal Proclamation.[35] Britain had just gained mastery over much of the North American continent. The challenges now were to govern it and to establish peaceful relations with the Aboriginal peoples. The parts of the Proclamation that relate to this second challenge are reproduced in **Reading 3(a)**. According to the Supreme Court of Canada, a key objective of the Proclamation was:

> ...to provide a solution to the problems created by the greed which hitherto some of the English had all too often demonstrated in buying up Indian land at low prices. The situation was causing dangerous trouble among the Indians and the Royal Proclamation was meant to remedy this....[36]

The Proclamation set aside a huge tract of land in North America for Indians. It reserved the land to them "as their Hunting Grounds."[37] It prohibited grants or purchases of this land[38] or settlement on it[39] without a licence, and required that all non-Indians without a licence must leave.[40] It imposed similar restrictions on Indian reserve lands within British colonies or proprietary governments.[41] These lands could be purchased only by the Crown after a public meeting or by a proprietary government acting on instructions of the Crown.[42] In Indian territory outside the colonies, government and military officers were required to apprehend fugitives from justice.[43] A general provision required a licence for all trade with the Indians.[44] Nearly all these provisions are directed at protecting the Indians' possession or use of the lands reserved to them.[45]

Although the procedural parts of the Royal Proclamation have been repealed,[46] the non-procedural provisions that recognize Indian interests have not.[47] They probably still have legal force.[48]

Because of its legal character, the Proclamation was long regarded as a major source of Aboriginal rights. Indeed, by reserving lands for the Indians after describing them as "not having been ceded to or purchased by Us," the document suggests that the Indians *had* a pre-existing interest capable of being ceded or sold. On the other hand, the document does not refer expressly to any pre-existing interest. For the most part, it proceeds negatively, by imposing restrictions on non-Indians. Moreover, the scope of the "Hunting Grounds" provision is limited,[49] and the geographical scope of the Proclamation is extremely unclear.[50]

10. *ST. CATHERINE's MILLING AND LUMBER Co. v. THE QUEEN*[51]

Reading 3(b) at p. 237

It was the 1888 Privy Council decision in *St. Catherine's Milling and Lumber Co.* that established the Royal Proclamation approach to the source of Aboriginal rights. Speaking for the Judicial Committee, Lord Watson said that: "[The Indians'] possession, such as it was, can only be ascribed to the general provisions made by the royal proclamation in favour of all Indian tribes then living under the sovereignty and protection of the British Crown."[52] For decades afterward, Canadian courts assumed that Aboriginal rights are based solely on the Royal Proclamation of 1763. Not until the Supreme Court's *Calder* decision in 1973[53] did Canadian courts adopt the broader notion that Aboriginal rights are not dependent on government recognition in a document such as the Royal Proclamation, but can arise at common law by virtue of prior and continued occupancy and use of land.

But this does not relegate *St. Catherine's* to the archives. Much of what Lord Watson said about Indian title under the Royal Proclamation has been incorporated into the modern law of Aboriginal rights. The general framework in *St. Catherine's* has been applied to questions about content, restriction, and enforcement. This may be more than a matter of inertia. If the Proclamation can be regarded as a confirmation of Aboriginal rights, then it is reasonable to regard it as a reflection of these rights. Beyond this, *St. Catherine's* was the first major decision to relate Indian title and treaties to the Canadian federal system. Its pronouncements here have governed this area ever since.

Indeed, it was a federal-provincial dispute that led to the *St. Catherine's* case in the first place. Ontario challenged the federal government's right to grant a timber permit to the St. Catherine's Milling and Lumber Company. The grant was in 1883. In 1873, the Indians had surrendered their interest in the land by means of an Indian treaty. Who owned the land after the surrender? If the federal government did, the timber permit was valid. If the province did, the permit was invalid.

Who owned the land after the surrender depended on the application of the *Constitution Act, 1867*.[54] This, in turn, depended on the nature of the land before Confederation. If the land was public land before 1867, s. 109 of the *Constitution Act, 1867* would transfer it in that year to the province, subject to non-governmental interests. Thus, when the non-governmental Indian interest was surrendered, the province would gain the full unrestricted interest in the land. On the other hand, if the land was private land before 1867, s. 109 would not apply, and the land would go to the federal government after the treaty surrender.

The area in question was thought to be within the Indian Territory set aside by the Royal Proclamation of 1763. Thus, whether the land was public or private before Confederation was held to depend on the provisions of the Proclamation. If the Indian interest under the Proclamation was less than that of a fee simple,[55] the land would be regarded as public land before Confederation; if the Indian interest under the Proclamation was equivalent to a fee simple, the land would be regarded as private land before Confederation.

After identifying the Royal Proclamation as the basis of the Indian title, Lord Watson said that under that instrument, "the tenure of the Indians was a personal and usufructuary right, dependent on the good will of the Sovereign."[56] In other words, the Indian title was less than a full fee simple interest. For its part, the Crown had a beneficial as well as a nominal interest in the land. Thus, the land was "public" land. It could be said to belong to the province, subject to the non-provincial interest of the Indians. Hence s. 109 applied to it at the time of Confederation. When the Indians surrendered their interest by the 1873 treaty, the effect was like the expiry of a lease. The remaining interest went to the landlord, the province. Accordingly, the federal government's permit to the lumber company was invalid.

The federal government had argued that because s. 91(24) of the *Constitution Act, 1867* gave it legislative jurisdiction over Indians and lands reserved for the Indians, the Act created a presumption in favour of federal executive capacity in regard to these subjects too. They claimed that this included the ownership of all reserved lands after treaty surrenders. Lord Watson was willing to accept that s. 91(24) extended all lands reserved, "upon any terms or conditions."[57] He accepted that the section gave the federal government an implied executive capacity to conclude the treaty.[58] However, any federal ownership of the lands was negated by the express provisions to the contrary in s. 109.[59]

St. Catherine's had major implications for Aboriginal peoples and the federal system. While the federal government has (a) legislative jurisdiction in relation to Indians and lands reserved for the Indians, (b) administrative authority pursuant to this jurisdiction, and (c) the executive capacity to conclude treaties with Indians, provincial governments own the land subject to the Indian interest. Subject to contrary provisions in federal-provincial agreements,[60] they gain the benefit of any surrender to the Crown. Moreover, because provincial governments also own most public land *not* subject to Aboriginal interests, their participation is generally needed in agreements that transfer other land to Aboriginal peoples. Beyond this, as we will see later, provincial legislatures have jurisdiction in many areas that affect Aboriginal peoples.[61] Hence, despite the exclusive intent of s. 91(24), Aboriginal peoples must deal with two levels of public government.

11. *JOHNSON AND GRAHAM's LESSEE v. M'INTOSH*[62]

Reading 3(c) at p. 242

Although Canadian common law on Aboriginal rights did not free itself from the Proclamation until 1973, the U.S. Supreme Court had taken a broader use and occupancy approach as early as 1823. This was in Marshall C.J.'s decision in *Johnson v. M'Intosh*,[63] where he referred to "the title which occupancy gave to [the Indians]."[64] He called the Indian title a "right of possession".[65]

Thomas Johnson and others[66] had bought land from the Illinois and Piankeshaw Indians in 1773 and 1775. The area was originally part of the Indian Territory under the Royal Proclamation of 1763. The Indians then surrendered their lands to the U.S. government.[67] In 1818, M'Intosh bought from the U.S. government some of the same land that Johnson had bought in 1773 and 1775. When claimants under Johnson tried to have M'Intosh removed from the land, they failed. The U.S. Supreme Court held that the Indians' interest could only be alienated to the Crown (or to the U.S. government), not to Johnson.

This finding was not surprising. After all, Proclamation interests could be alienated only to or through the Crown or its agents. The Court, however, said the Indian interest was based not only on the Proclamation, but also on the fact of traditional Indian occupation of the land before the coming of the Europeans. The focus now was not on a government document of uncertain wording and scope. It was on an historical fact common to all Aboriginal peoples.

However, because it focused on an interest that pre-dated European sovereignty, this occupancy and use approach forced the Court to grapple with the relationship between the Indian interest and the effect of European territorial sovereignty. This, in turn, required a look at the basis on which this sovereignty had been acquired.

In examining the basis for European acquisition, Marshall C.J. said he would not assess the claim that the takeover might be justified by the introduction of Christianity and other aspects of European culture. Instead, he focused on whether the acquisition was consistent with existing state practice and law.

However, existing state practice and law presented a problem, because they were not well suited to what had happened in North America. By the early 18th century, there were two main common law doctrines about the acquisition of territorial sovereignty by European states. Under the conquest doctrine, the existing laws of inhabitants of a conquered colony continued until they were altered by the new sovereign.[68] Under the settlement doctrine, in uninhabited countries English law followed English settlers to the extent that local conditions permitted.[69] Neither of these two doctrines described the situation created by the arrival of European explorers, traders, and settlers in North America. Native and European populations were often too small and the land too large for military confrontations that could be described as "conquests". On the other hand, the land was by no means uninhabited, as the settlement doctrine assumed. The settlements themselves varied widely in nature and intensity. Even today, there is still controversy as to whether some parts of North America should be regarded as settled or conquered.[70]

Marshall C.J.'s response to these problems was to formulate a "discovery" doctrine that addressed the claims of European states, and an establishment concept to deal with how these claims were secured in practice. Discovery, he said, gave the first European state to discover lands in North America a right to claim sovereignty over these lands and to underlying ownership of them.[71] In relation to rival European powers, discovery gave this state the exclusive right to deal with their native inhabitants. It was entitled to try to establish its claims, either by purchasing Indian lands, or by establishing effective control.[72] Marshall C.J. said that in North America the newcomers had tended to take the latter course, a coercive course that amounted to conquest.[73]

Marshall C.J.'s discovery doctrine borrowed from the settlement notion that the discovering government claimed sovereignty and underlying ownership of all lands.[74] However, these lands were occupied, so the newcomers had to do more to make their claim effective. They did this, said Marshall C.J., by establishing effective control.[75] As with a traditional conquest, there was an expectation that prior property rights should survive the change of sovereignty, subject to actions to the contrary by the conqueror.[76] Thus, the Indian's pre-existing occupancy interest survived the change of sovereignty.[77]

However, the new government had interfered with the Indian interest in several ways. It had granted the land to third parties, even while it was occupied by the Indians.[78] It had permitted the Indians to be driven from their homes.[79] Moreover, it had limited the Indian interest so that it was alienable only to the Crown.[80] Although Marshall C.J. conceded that these measures were contrary to normal state practice and principles of natural justice, he felt that the Indians' warlike nature may have made them necessary.[81]

The discovery doctrine was restrictive in some respects, and ambiguous in others. Its moral foundations were weak; the very notion of "discovering" an inhabited land was highly presumptuous.[82] At some points, discovery seemed to relate only to relations between European states; at others, it seemed to extend to the European-Indian relationship. By combining aspects of both settlement and conquest, discovery and its establishment process were identical to neither.[83] On the other hand, *Johnson v. M'Intosh* did have potential to free Aboriginal rights from legislative or executive government recognition. It did suggest that the traditional acquisition doctrines must be modified to explain — if not justify — the situation in North America.[84] And it did give concrete significance to the fact that the Aboriginal people were here first.

12. *WORCESTER V. GEORGIA*[85]

🖹 Reading 3(d) at p. 250

Nine years after *Johnson v. M'Intosh*,[86] Marshall C.J. rendered a judgment with the capacity to extend Aboriginal rights beyond occupancy and use of land. The case involved the Cherokee territory, which stretched from south of the Great Smokey Mountains to the Ohio River. In the early part of the 19th century, the Cherokee Nation was a vigorous and creative society that combined hunting and farming. They had developed their own codified laws, constitution, written language, and newspaper.[87]

Like so many of their Aboriginal neighbours, though, the Cherokee were a nation under siege. Settlers wanted the rich land in the north. In the south, large tracts of land were needed for growing cotton.[88] Gold was discovered within Cherokee territory.[89] The federal government had a policy of encouraging the Cherokee to relocate further west.[90] In 1829, the state of Georgia enacted a statute purporting to extend its laws to the Cherokee territory, and stating that all laws made by the Cherokee Indians were null and void. A second Georgia law, passed in 1830, required that any white person residing in Cherokee territory must have the permission of the governor.

A Reverend Samuel Worcester was convicted under the 1830 Act and sentenced to four years of hard labour.[91] Reverend Worcester was a Vermont missionary who was preaching the gospel and translating the Bible at New Echota in the Cherokee territory. Although he was there with the permission of the Cherokees, he had no permission from the Georgia governor.

In *Worcester v. Georgia*,[92] Reverend Worcester argued before the U.S. Supreme Court that the state law was invalid. The Supreme Court agreed. Marshall C.J. said that the state laws had no effect in Cherokee territory. Why? Marshall C.J. said that the treaties with the Cherokees and federal statutes such as the *Trade and Intercourse Act* treated the Indians as distinct, self-governing political communities with territorial boundaries and the possession of the lands within these boundaries. He said that although the British king purchased Indian lands, alliances, and dependence, he "never intruded into the interior of their affairs, or interfered with their self-government, so far as that respected themselves only."[93] Marshall C.J. said that the constitution gave exclusive and unrestricted powers of war and peace, treaty-making, and commerce with the Indians to Congress. As well it gave treaties paramount power over state laws. Accordingly, the Georgia laws violated the constitution, laws, and treaties of the United States, and were invalid.[94]

Strictly speaking, the Georgia laws were not invalid because they violated a free-standing legal right of Cherokee self-government and community self-regulation. They were invalid because they violated treaties and statutes that Marshall C.J. felt maintained these rights. Marshall C.J.'s other arguments in favour of these broad rights were founded less on law, as in *Johnson v. M'Intosh*, and more on colonial policy alone.

Nevertheless, Marshall C.J.'s judgment opened the door to a potentially much wider view of the source of Aboriginal rights. On this view, arguably, what pre-dated and survived sovereignty as Aboriginal rights were not only rights to land but, possibly, all the internal laws, customs, and other practices of the pre-European Aboriginal community. This broader view gained currency in the United States, where courts affirmed the rights subject to the paramount power of Congress. It gained little support in Canada, where Aboriginal rights have long been linked to land. Somewhat paradoxically, perhaps, now that Parliament has *lost* its paramount power in relation to Indians, there has been some revival in Canada of a broader view that somewhat resembles the approach in *Worcester v. Georgia*.[95]

The American Supreme Court decision did little to help Reverend Worcester or the Cherokee. The Georgia Supreme Court refused to release Worcester and another missionary. They were forced to ask the governor for a pardon a year later.[96] Six years after the decision, almost the entire Cherokee population — about 16,000 people — were rounded up and moved to a new location more than 1,600 kilometres further west.[97] Over 4,000 Cherokee died on or immediately before the trip.[98] It became known as the Trail of Tears.

13. *CONNOLLY*[99]

Reading 3(e) at p. 251

One of the few early Canadian decisions to endorse the wider approach of *Worcester v. Georgia* was an 1867 Quebec Superior Court decision called *Connolly v. Woolrich*.[100] The question here was whether the common law could recognize an 1803 Cree customary marriage between a North-West Company trader and a Cree Indian lady in the Athabaska area. Quoting from *Worcester v. Georgia*, Monk J. held that at the time of the marriage "the Indian political and territorial rights, laws, and usages remained in full force"[101] in the area. He concluded that the native marriage customs could be recognized at common law, and that this marriage was valid. The outcome of Monk J.'s decision was affirmed by the Quebec Court of Appeal.[102]

Some have seen *Connolly v. Woolrich* as a basis for a broader approach to Aboriginal rights.[103] The Royal Commission on Aboriginal Peoples went further and saw Monk J.'s decision as supporting the concept of an inherent right of Aboriginal self-government.[104] It is helpful, though, to consider the decision in perspective. Monk J.'s judgment suggests that English sovereignty was not fully established in this area at the relevant time.[105] The Athabaska region was apparently outside Hudson Bay territory. Such European sovereignty as there was, was the minimal presence of the fur trade. Even within Hudson Bay territory at that time, the Hudson Bay Company had only power to enact laws that affected its own clerks and traders. Would Monk J.'s statement about the full force of existing political and territorial rights apply where English sovereignty was more fully established?

Monk J.'s decision should also be considered in the light of its appeal to the Quebec Court of Appeal in *Johnstone v. Connolly*.[106] Although they affirmed the decision below, the appeal judges all emphasized the limited English presence in the Athabaska area at the relevant time.[107] Moreover, the Court of Appeal judgments gave little support to the proposition that powers of self-government survive changes of sovereignty. Badgley J.A., with whom the other majority judges agreed, suggested that where there was a clear change of sovereignty, as in conquest, it was private rights and property that would survive: "The modern usage of nations would be violated *if private property should be confiscated and private rights annulled. Therefore the relations of the people to their ancient sovereign or government are dissolved*, but the relations to each other, and their customs and usages remain undisturbed."[108] If a clear change of sovereignty dissolves the prior relations to a former sovereign or government, it is difficult to see how self-government rights are supposed to continue.

In the early frontier situation at Athabaska, there had not yet been a clear change of sovereignty. All that existed was the "mere exclusive right of trading in furs with the inhabitants of the licensed country."[109] Clearly, this was not a situation that would last.

Arguably, though, Badgley J.A.'s decision in *Connolly* might support less sweeping propositions than the view that Aboriginal rights necessarily include self-government rights or are based generally on native customs. For, apart from Aboriginal rights, the common law can enforce native traditions such as marriage or adoption, simply as a form of customary law.[110] Although native custom would not be enough to create "existing Aboriginal rights" with entrenched status under the *Constitution Act, 1982*,[111] it would be enough to command common law support.

Beyond this, the Supreme Court has now said that Aboriginal rights are based on the fact of prior occupancy of the land and on the existence of practices integral to distinctive traditional cultures.[112] It has acknowledged, then, that Aboriginal rights do have a customary aspect, and that some of these customs are enforceable and constitutionally entrenched.

14. SHADOW OF *ST. CATHERINE's*

Subsequent Aboriginal rights case law in Canada has been heavily influenced by the 1888 *St. Catherine's* decision. What *St. Catherine's* decided about the relationship between Indian title and the Canadian federal system is still broadly applicable today. By appearing to attribute Aboriginal title solely to the Royal Proclamation of 1763, *St. Catherine's* set Canadian case law on a course that disregarded possible alternative sources and minimized the need to consider a further difficult and potentially embarrassing question: What is the source of *non*-Aboriginals' claims to northern North America? It took more than eighty years before the Supreme Court started to look at alternative routes. As indicated, some of the alternatives had already been considered in the United States long before *St. Catherine's*.

Notes

1. C. Bell and W.B. Henderson, "Aboriginal Rights" in *The Canadian Encyclopedia*, Year 2000 ed. (Toronto: McClelland & Stewart, 1999) at 4.
2. See **Chapter 1, Part 3**.
3. *Ibid.*
4. *Ibid.* See also entries on "Native People", *ibid.* at 1576–97; entry by M.K. Foster on "Native People, Languages", *ibid.* at 1585–87; and **Reading 1(b)**.
5. See *R. v. Van der Peet*, [1996] 2 S.C.R. 507 at para. 41.
6. "A Concept of Native Title" *CASNP Bulletin* (December 1976) 33.
7. John Borrows, *Recovering Canada: The Resurgence of Indigenous Law* (Toronto: University of Toronto Press, 2002) at 117.
8. Royal Commission on Aboriginal Peoples, *Report of the Royal Commission on Aboriginal Peoples*, vol. 2, chap. 4, s. 3.2 at 448 (hereinafter "*Report*"). See further, **Reading 1(a)**.
9. *Ibid.* at 435.
10. L. Little Bear, "The Aboriginal Peoples' Standard" in "Aboriginal Rights and the Canadian 'Grundnorm'", in J.R. Ponting, ed., *Arduous Journey: Canadian Indians and Decolonization* (Toronto: McClelland and Stewart, 1986) at 245–47.
11. Georges Erasmus, "Twenty Years of Disappointed Hopes", introduction to B. Richardson, ed., *Drumbeat* (Toronto: Summerhill Press, 1989) at 13.
12. Union of British Columbia Indian Chiefs, *Aboriginal Title and Rights Position Paper*, 1989, 1. See also *Report*, vol. 2, chap. 4, s. 3.2 at 448.
13. "David Confronts Goliath: The Innu of Ungava versus the NATO Alliance" in B. Richardson, ed., *Drumbeat*, 1989 at 52–53.
14. The two main sources for this general description are *R. v. Van der Peet*, [1996] 2 S.C.R. 507, especially paras. 32 and 41; and *Delgamuukw v. British Columbia*, [1997] 3 S.C.R. 1010, especially paras. 111–18, 124–32, 140–59.
15. Para. 74.
16. *Ibid.*
17. *Delgamuukw v. British Columbia*, [1997] 3 S.C.R. 1010 at para. 117.
18. *Delgamuukw v. British Columbia*, [1997] 3 S.C.R. 1010 at para. 143. In Aboriginal title cases, the Aboriginal claimants' connection to the land is assumed to be central to their distinctive culture or society: *Delgamuukw*, para. 151. For specific Aboriginal rights claims, the courts require evidence of the significance of the traditional practice to the culture or society in question: *R. v. Van der Peet*, *supra* note 14 at paras. 55–57.
19. *Ibid.* at para. 46. (The Court was speaking here in the context of s. 35(1) of the *Constitution Act, 1982*.)
20. These questions are highly interrelated. Because the question of the source of these rights is anterior to the other questions, the answers to it shape the answers to the others. For example, a finding about the source of Aboriginal rights can influence findings about their status, content and other features.
21. In s. 35(1).
22. Section 31 of the *Manitoba Act*, S.C. 1870, c. 3, did state that "it is expedient, towards the extinguishment of the Indian title to the lands of the Province," but it was restricted to compensation for claims of Métis people in the province of Manitoba. In fact, the Act resulted in little lasting monetary benefit for the Métis: see P.A. Cumming and N.H. Mickenberg, *Native Rights in Canada*, 2d ed. (Toronto: Indian-Eskimo Association of Canada, 1972) at 200–201 and P.L.A.H. Chartrand, "Aboriginal Rights: The Dispossession of the Métis" (1991) 29 Osgoode Hall L.J. 456. For a summary of some key legislative provisions arguably recognizing or otherwise supporting Aboriginal title or Aboriginal rights, see Cumming and Mickenberg, at 276–78. There is a major prerogative instrument relevant to Aboriginal rights, but since the prerogative power is dependent on common law interpretation, that instrument will be considered in the context of the common law: **Part 9**, below.
23. For other possible contrasting sources of Aboriginal title, see the distinction drawn between "recognized" and

"aboriginal" rights in G.S. Lester, *The Territorial Rights of the Inuit of the Canadian Northwest Territories: A Legal Argument* (D.Jur. Dissertation, York University, 1981) at 19–26; and between indigenous rights based on local customary law and "common law aboriginal title" in K. McNeil, *Common Law Aboriginal Title* (Oxford: Clarendon, 1989), chaps. 6 and 7.

24. Indian treaties are also possible sources of prerogative recognition, at least to the extent that they were not confirmed by legislation. As Hall J. said in *Calder v. British Columbia (A.G.)*, [1973] S.C.R. 313 at 394, "[s]urely the Canadian treaties, made with such solemnity on behalf of the Crown, were intended to extinguish the Indian title. What other purpose did they serve? If they were not intended to extinguish the Indian right, they were a gross fraud and that is not to be assumed." On the other hand, the treaties did not expressly acknowledge a pre-existing right, and Hall J.'s rhetorical question misses the possibility that the treaties were simply intended to extinguish any Indian title that *might* exist.
25. *R. v. Van der Peet*, [1996] 2 S.C.R. 507 at paras. 30, 31, and 35; **Part 4**, above.
26. *Van der Peet, ibid. at* para. 46; **Part 4**, above.
27. *Delgamuukw v. British Columbia*, [1997] 3 S.C.R. 1010 at paras. 143–51.
28. Although distinctive practices which amount to Aboriginal rights resemble customs, they are quite different from other forms of custom or Aboriginal custom. Generally speaking, an Aboriginal customary law is enforceable if it meets substantially the general common law criteria for enforceable customs. It should be long-standing, continuous, and clearly identifiable: see C.K. Allen, *Law in the Making*, 7th, ed., chap. II, including Excursus B. Canadian courts have tended to recognize Aboriginal customary law in the areas of native adoption and marriage: see, for example, the cases referred to in N. Zlotkin, "Judicial Recognition of Aboriginal Customary Law in Canada" [1984] 4 C.N.L.R. 1.

    In contrast, under the distinctive practices approach, an Aboriginal right is a custom or other pre-European Aboriginal practice or tradition that was important to the distinctive pre-European Aboriginal culture and survives the establishment of European sovereignty. It is based at least partly in prior Aboriginal occupation and use of land in North America. See **Chapter 9, Part 3**. Finally, while ordinary Aboriginal customary laws are subordinate to legislation, an Aboriginal right that meets the requirements of s. 35(1) of the *Constitution Act, 1982* prevails over unjustified governmental infringement. See further **Chapter 7**.
29. **Chapter 9, Parts 3** and **5**, and **Chapter 10, Parts 1** and **2**.
30. On self-government, see *R. v. Pamajewon* [*R. v. Jones*; *R. v. Gardner*], [1996] 2 S.C.R. 821, **Chapter 9, Part 5**, and **Chapter 12, Part 4**.
31. For this question, see **Chapters 7, 9** and **10**.
32. Courts tended to use the term "Indian title" in Proclamation cases.
33. The extent of this evolution should not be overstated. For example, although legislative, executive, or constitutional recognition is no longer required, where it is lacking courts generally require *common law* recognition of occupation and use of land. Moreover, since Royal Proclamation rights relate mainly to land and land use, what was said about them has been considered relevant to use and occupancy-based Aboriginal rights.
34. See generally J.M. Sosin, *Whitehall and the Wilderness: The Middle West in British Colonial Policy, 1760–1775* (Lincoln: Lincoln University of Nebraska Press, 1961); B. Slattery, *The Land Rights of Indigenous Canadian Peoples as Affected by the Crown's Acquisition of their Territories*, 1979, Parts I and II; J. Stagg, *Anglo-Indian Relations in North America to 1763 and An Analysis of the Royal Proclamation of 7 October, 1763*, 1981; G.S. Lester, *The Territorial Rights of the Inuit of the Canadian Northwest Territories: A Legal Argument*, 1981, chap. XIX; K. McNeil, *Common Law Aboriginal Title*, 1989; O.P. Dickason, *Canada's First Nations: A History of Founding Peoples from Earliest Times*, 3d ed. (Don Mills, Ont.: Oxford University Press, 2002) at 162–63; *Calder v. British Columbia (A.G.)*, [1973] S.C.R. 313 at 322–25 (Judson J.), 394–410 (Hall J.); *R. v. Sioui*, [1990] 1 S.C.R. 1025 at 1063–65.
35. *The Royal Proclamation of 1763*, R.S.C., 1985, Appendix II, No. 1.
36. *R. v. Sioui* (1990), 70 D.L.R. (4th) 427 at 457 (S.C.C.).
37. Paras. 1 and 2 of provisions relating to Indians (para. 1 commencing with the phrase "And whereas it is just and reasonable ...").
38. Paras. 1, 3 and 5.
39. Para. 3.
40. Para. 4.
41. Paras. 1, 3, 4, and 5.
42. Para. 5.
43. Para. 6.
44. Para. 7.
45. Cf. B. Slattery, *supra* note 34, chap. 11, Part IV, esp. 193; J. Stagg, *supra* note 34 at 20–24 (stressing land and trade); Dickason, *supra* note 34 at 163 (stressing land).
46. The *Quebec Act, 1774* (U.K.), c. 83 repealed the purely procedural aspects of the Proclamation. Note, though, that the *Quebec Act, 1774* (U.K.), c. 83 extended the boundaries of Quebec into much of the Royal Proclamation's Indian Territory. In what is now Canada, this reduced the Indian Territory to a much smaller region to the west of Lake Superior and south of Rupert's Land.
47. The repeal of the procedural provisions did not alter existing rights, titles, or possession: see *Ontario (A.G.) v. Bear Island Foundation* (1989), 58 D.L.R. (4th) 117 at 133 (O.C.A.).
48. The Crown has a prerogative capacity to manage its public lands, subject to statute: G.V. La Forest, *Natural Resources and Public Property under the Canadian Constitution* (Toronto: University of Toronto Press, 1969) at 20. The Crown could only impose new unilateral restrictions on private interests in conquered colonies (and even there only before a promise or grant of representative institutions: *Campbell v. Hall* (1774), 1 Cowp. Rep. 204 at 209; 98 E.R. 1045). However, it is arguable that the Proclamation generally affirmed existing Aboriginal title, rather than imposing on it significant new restrictions: see *Johnson v. M'Intosh* (1823), 8 Wheaton 543 at 595 (U.S.C.C.).
49. It does not apply to Rupert's Land: *Sigeareak E1-53 v. The Queen*, [1966] S.C.R. 645 at 650; or (except in regard to existing specific reserves) to Quebec: *R. v. Côté* (1993), 107 D.L.R. (4th) 28 at 39 (Q.C.A.).
50. See B. Slattery, *supra* note 34, Parts I and II; J. Stagg, *supra* note 34; G.S. Lester, *supra* note 34, chap. XIX; K. McNeil, *supra* note 34 at 274–75. McNeil argues that the Proclamation cannot apply to any part of Canada acquired by settlement, because "apart from statute the Crown has no legislative authority in settled colonies": 274. For British Columbia, see *Calder v. British Columbia (A.G.)* (1973), 34 D.L.R. (4th) 145 (S.C.C.); *R. v. Adolph*, [1986] B.C.J. No. 2125 (B.C. Co. Ct.); and *Delgamuukw v. British Columbia* (1991), 79 D.L.R. (4th) 185 at 306 (B.C.S.C.), aff'd on this point in (1993), 104 D.L.R. (4th) 470 at 521, 593–95 (B.C.C.A.).

    For British Columbia, see *Calder, ibid.* at 323 (Judson J.: Proclamation not applicable), 394–95 (Hall J.: Proclamation applicable); *R. v. Adolph*, [1986] B.C.J. No. 2125 (B.C. Co. Ct.); *Delgamuukw v. British Columbia* (1991), 79 D.L.R. (4th) 185 at 287-307 (B.C.S.C.) (McEachern C.J.B.B.: Proclamation not applicable) and (1993), 104 D.L.R. (4th) 470 at 521 (Macfarlane and

Taggart JJ.A.), 593 (Wallace J.A.), 751 (Hutcheon J.A., dissenting in part on other issues) (B.C.C.A.). All judges except Lambert J.A., dissenting, held that the Proclamation did not apply to British Columbia. Lambert J.A. discussed the issue but came to no conclusion on it: 732–36. For Quebec, see *R.* v. *Adams*, [1993] (Beauregard J.A.) at 130–31 (Rothman J.A., dissenting) (Q.C.A.); *R. v. Côté* (1993), 107 D.L.R. (4th) 28 at 43 (Q.C.A.).

51. *St. Catherine's Milling and Lumber Company v. The Queen* (1889), 14 App. Cas. 46 (J.C.P.C.: December 12, 1889), aff'g (1887) 13 S.C.R. 577, which aff'd (1887) 13 O.A.R. 148 (O.C.A.), which aff'd (1886) 10 OR 196 (Chancery Div.).
52. *St. Catherine's Milling and Lumber Company v. The Queen* (1889), 14 App. Cas. 46 at 54 (J.C.P.C.).
53. *Calder v. British Columbia (A.G.)*, [1973] S.C.R. 313: **Chapter 4, Part 1**.
54. (U.K.), 30 & 31 Vict., c. 3 (formerly *British North America Act, 1867*).
55. The greatest common law interest a private party can hold in land. For example, at common law, a fee simple interest lasts for an indefinite duration; cannot be unilaterally revoked by the Crown; is freely inheritable by all descendants; and is alienable without restriction to others.
56. *Supra* note 52.
57. *Ibid.* at 59.
58. *Ibid.* at 60.
59. *Ibid.* at 59.
60. Federal-provincial agreements have since provided generally that after surrender most — but not all — public interests accrue to the federal government: see G.V. La Forest, *supra* note 48.
61. **Chapter 6**.
62. (1823), 8 Wheaton 543, 21 U.S. 240, 5 L.Ed. 681 (U.S.S.Ct.).
63. *Johnson v. M'Intosh* was the second of five Aboriginal rights decisions by the Supreme Court of the United States under Chief Justice John Marshall. The other decisions were *Fletcher v. Peck* (1810), 6 Cranch 87, 2 Peters 308; *Cherokee Nation v. State of Georgia* (1831), 5 Peters 1, 8 L.Ed. 29; *Worcester v. Georgia* (1832), 6 Peters 515, 31 U.S. 530, 8 L.Ed. 483; and *Mitchel v. United States* (1835), 9 Peters 515 at 711, 9 L.Ed. 283.
64. (1823), 8 Wheaton 543 at 588.
65. *Ibid.* at 603.
66. Johnson was part of a land speculation syndicate called the Illinois-Wabash Company. On the eve of the American revolution, groups like this were buying up large tracts of land in the Indian Territory on the western side of the Appalachian mountains, contrary to the Royal Proclamation's prohibition on purchases directly from the Indians. See generally, R.A. Williams Jr., *The American Indian in Western Legal Thought: The Discourse of Conquest* (New York: Oxford University Press, 1990), chap. 7.
67. Treaty of Greenville, August 1775, which included the Kaskaskias (Illinois) and the Piankeshaw. See also Treaty of Ft. Wayne, Indiana, 7 June 1803; and Treaty with the Piankeshaws, 27 August 1804, proclaimed 6 February 1805, 7 Stat. 83, Article I. When it was purchased from the Indians, the land was within territory claimed by the colony of Virginia. Virginia had then ceded the territory to the United States government in 1776.
68. Blackstone's *Commentaries on the Laws of England*, 17th ed., 1830, Bk. 11, chap. 4 at 107–08; *Blankard v. Galdy* (1693), Halt K.B. 341, 90 E.R. 1089; *Campbell v. Hall* (1774), Cowp. 204 at 209–90, 98 E.B. 1045 at 1047–48; *Ruding v. Smith* (1821), 2 Con. 371, 161 E.R. 774 at 778; *Beaumont v. Bird* (1836), 1 Moo. P.C. 59; 12 E.R. 733. Although earlier decisions spoke generally of antecedent laws (except laws deemed morally unacceptable) remaining unchanged, this would presumably not include laws inconsistent with the change of sovereignty or relating to the new sovereign. In *Ruding*, for example, Lord Stowell of the Consistory Court said that "[e]ven with respect to the ancient inhabitants, no small portion of the ancient law [of the conquered country] is unavoidably superseded by the revolution of government that has taken place. The allegiance of the subjects, and all the law that relates to it — the administration of the law in the sovereign, and appellate jurisdictions — and all the laws connected with the exercise of the sovereign authority — must undergo alterations adapted to the change." In this sense, the rights that remained unchanged were private rights.
69. *Campbell v. Hall* (1774), Cowp. 204 at 209–90, 98 E.R. 1045 at 1047–48; Blackstone's *Commentaries on the Laws of England*, 17th ed., 1830, Bk. 11, chap. 4 at 106–107; *Freeman v. Fairlee* (1828), 1 Moo. Ind. App. 306 at 323–25, aff'd at 341; 18 E.R. 117 at 127–28, 137.
70. See, for example, D.W. Elliott, "Review of *The Territorial Rights of the Inuit of the Canadian Northwest Territories: A Legal Argument* (1982) 28 McGill L.J. 165 at 169–70 and compare K. McNeil, *Common Law Aboriginal Title*, 1989 with the views of the writers referred to in the McGill review.
71. *Supra* note 62 at 573, 585, 587, 592, and 595.
72. *Ibid.* at 578 and 587.
73. *Ibid.* at 590–92.
74. *Ibid.* at 595.
75. *Ibid.* at 570, 578, and 589.
76. *Ibid.* at 589.
77. *Ibid.* at 573.
78. *Ibid.* at 574.
79. *Ibid.* at 590–91.
80. *Ibid.* at 591. Marshall C.J. seemed to acknowledge that restrictions of this kind were made for "restraining the encroachments of the whites" (597), although he didn't link this protective purpose directly to this specific restriction.
81. *Ibid.* at 590–91. Marshall C.J. thought the hostility of the Indians provided "some excuse, if not justification" for what the newcomers had done: 580.
82. See *Mabo v. State of Queensland (No. 2)*, (1992), 107 A.L.R. 1 at 29–31 (**Chapter 9, Part 2**), rejecting this approach as an inadequate basis for refusing to recognize prior Aboriginal rights.
83. On balance, the resemblance to conquest was closer than that to settlement.
84. It also de-emphasized the differences between settlement and conquest. For Aboriginal people, rights of occupancy and use should not vary according to whether European acquisition more closely resembled the "settlement" or "conquest" label.
85. (1832), 6 Peters, 31 U.S. 515, 8 L.Ed. 483 (U.S.S.Ct.). See also Marshall C.J.'s decision in *Cherokee Nation v. State of Georgia* (1831), 5 Peters 1, 8 L.Ed. 25 (U.S.S.Ct.). In the earlier Cherokee case, Marshall C.J. had held that the Supreme Court could not hear a controversy between an Indian treaty and a state law because the treaties that had constitutional supremacy over state laws were treaties with foreign nations (20) whereas the Indians were treated in the treaties as "domestic dependent nations" (17).
86. (1823), 8 Wheaton 543, 21 U.S. 240, 5 L.Ed. 681 (U.S.S.Ct.).
87. See G.S. Woodward, *The Cherokees* (Norman: The University of Oklahoma Press, 1963), chap. X; R. Wright, *Stolen Continents: The "New World" Through Indian Eyes* (Toronto: Penguin Books, 1993), chap. 9.
88. L. Baker, *John Marshall: A Life in Law* (New York: Macmillan, 1974) at 733.
89. G.S. Woodward, *The Cherokees* (Norman: University of Oklahoma Press, 1963) at 159.
90. As early as 1802 President Jefferson had made a compact with the state of Georgia to attempt to remove all Indians from within the boundaries of Georgia, and to give the land to Georgia: W. G. McLoughlin, *Cherokees*

and Missionaries: 1789–1839 (New Haven, Conn.: Yale University Press, 1984) at 239. The Cherokees' situation worsened in 1828, with the election to the presidency of the hard-line proponent of removal, Andrew Jackson.

91. Ten other missionaries were arrested, but were released after agreeing either to sign an oath of allegiance to the state or to leave it. Only one colleague joined Worcester in challenging the Georgia law: W.G. McLoughlin, *Cherokees and Missionaries: 1789–1839* (New Haven, Conn.: Yale University Press, 1984) at 262.
92. (1832), 6 Peters, 31 U.S. 530, 8 L.Ed. 483 (U.S.S.Ct.).
93. *Ibid.* at 547.
94. *Ibid.* at 561.
95. See **Part 13**, below and **Chapter 9, Part 2**.
96. W.G. McLoughlin, *Cherokees and Missionaries: 1789–1839* (New Haven, Conn.: Yale University Press, 1984) at 298–99.
97. R. Wright, *Stolen Continents: The "New World" Through Indian Eyes* (Toronto: Penguin Books, 1993) at 221.
98. See G.S. Woodward, *The Cherokees* (Norman: The University of Oklahoma Press, 1963), chap. X; and R. Wright, *ibid.*
99. (1867), 11 L.C. Jur. 197, 17 R.J.R.Q. 75, 1 C.N.L.C. 70 (Q.S.C.); aff'd in *Johnstone et al. v. Connolly* (1869), 17 R.J.R.Q. 266; 1 R.L. (O.S.) 253 (Q.C.A.).
100. (1867), 11 L.C. Jur. 197, 17 R.J.R.Q. 75, 1 C.N.L.C. 70 (Q.S.C.); aff'd in *Johnstone et al. v. Connolly* (1869), 17 R.J.R.Q. 266; 1 R.L. (O.S.) 253 (Q.C.A.).
101. *Ibid.* at 82 (R.J.R.Q.).
102. *Johnstone et al. v. Connolly* (1869), 17 R.J.R.Q. 266; 1 R.L. (O.S.) 253. Except where otherwise indicated, page references are to the R.J.R.Q. In the Court of Appeal, Mackay J.A. concurred "substantially" with the judgment of Badgley J.A.: 345; Duval C.J. concurred in affirming the Superior Court's decision, for the reasons given by his colleagues: 1 R.L. (O.S.) 253 at 396; Caron J. was reported to have limited himself to a few brief comments, because he felt the case had been adequately discussed by his colleagues: 1 R.L. (O.S.) 253 at 396. Loranger J.A. dissented: 266.
103. See *Casimel et al. v. Insurance Corporation of British Columbia* (1993), 106 D.L.R. (4th) 720 at 727–28 (B.C.C.A.), where a three-judge panel held that native customary adoption could be the subject of Aboriginal rights.
104. As argued in the Royal Commission on Aboriginal Peoples, *Partners in Confederation: Aboriginal Peoples, Self-Government, and the Constitution* (Ottawa: Canada Communication Group, 1993) at 5–8; Royal Commission on Aboriginal Peoples, *Report of the Royal Commission on Aboriginal Peoples*, vol. 2, chap. 3, s. 2.3 at 186–90.
105. (1867), 11 L.C. Jur. 197 at 204. See also *ibid.* at 212.
106. *Johnstone et al. v. Connolly* (1869), 17 R.J.R.Q. 266; 1 R.L. (O.S.) 253 (Q.C.A.).
107. Badgley J., 331–33; Mackay J.A., 346–47; Loranger J.A., dissenting, on another point, 276. Caron J.A. and Duval C.J. agreed with the majority: 1 Review Légale 253 at 396.
108. Badgley J.A., 333–34 (emphasis added). (Cf. *Ruding v. Smith* (1821), 2 Con. 371 at 385, 161 E.R. 774 at 778). Loranger J., dissenting on another point, said that "civil" laws might survive, but stressed that "nulle loi étrangère *affectant l'order public* ou la moralité d'une nation, n'est, par elle, reconnue valable": 270 (emphasis added).
109. *Ibid.* at 334.
110. There is a sizable body of cases supporting the notion of native customary law. See, for example, *Re Noah Estate* (1961), 32 D.L.R. (2d) 185 (N.W.T.T.C.). For a comparison between Aboriginal rights and native customary law, see *supra* note 28.
111. Schedule B to the *Canada Act, 1982* (U.K.), 1982, c. 11: see **Chapter 7**.
112. *R. v. Van der Peet*, [1996] 2 S.C.R. 507 at para. 74: **Chapter 9, Part 3**.

4 Aboriginal Rights from *Calder* to *Guerin*

Chapter Highlights

- In the 1973 *Calder* decision the Supreme Court of Canada rejected the idea that Aboriginal title — and by implication, Aboriginal rights — depends solely on the Royal Proclamation of 1763.
- A majority of the Court said that Aboriginal title derives from traditional occupancy and use of land. However, the judges were badly split on a range of important new issues, including the question of what was required to show government extinguishment of Aboriginal title.
- In the 1984 *Guerin* decision, the Supreme Court confirmed that the common law recognizes Aboriginal title based on occupancy and use of land, but most of the other questions raised in *Calder* remained unanswered.

Synopsis

By uncoupling Aboriginal title from the Royal Proclamation of 1763, *Calder* opened a new legal threshold. Aboriginal title and rights were no longer at the mercy of the text and geographical limits of a government edict. Instead, they now rested on the much broader foundation of occupancy and use of land. This shift raised new questions. If Aboriginal rights pre-dated European sovereignty, how did the two interrelate? How were the rights to be proven? What was their content? How were they enforced? How did they fare against government regulation or extinguishment? Neither *Calder* nor the post-*Calder*-decade cases provided much guidance on these vital issues, and some of them remain with us today.

Selected Readings

🖹 links material in this chapter to the corresponding headings and page numbers of the relevant readings.

🖹 Part 1 *Calder v. British Columbia (A.G.)* 255

🖹 Part 3 *Baker Lake. v. Canada (Minister of Indian and Northern Affairs)*. 263

🖹 Part 4 *Guerin v. The Queen*. 265

1. *CALDER*[1]

Reading 4(a) at p. 255

For eighty-four years the Proclamation approach reigned supreme. The Royal Proclamation was seen as the sole source of Indian title, and the leading decision was that of Lord Watson in the *St. Catherine's Milling and Lumber Company* case.[2] Then, on January 31, 1973, came a revolution for Aboriginal rights in Canada. The *Calder* decision[3] shifted the source of Aboriginal rights from European government recognition to pre-European occupation and use of land. It freed them from the limitations of the Proclamation. But *Calder* was a typically Canadian revolution, tentative and equivocal, raising as many questions as it answered.

Calder began with a claim by the Nisga'a people of the Nass River area of British Columbia. They had lived in this area since long before it was called British Columbia. They had not surrendered the land by any treaty. In the late 1960s they went to court to claim that they had an Aboriginal title to the Nass River area, and that it had not been lawfully extinguished.[4]

The British Columbia courts said there was no Aboriginal title because the area was unknown to the British at the time of the Royal Proclamation of 1763. They added that any Aboriginal title that might have existed would have been extinguished by pre-Confederation proclamations and legislation of the colony of British Columbia. The British Columbia Court of Appeal stressed that there must be government recognition for Aboriginal title to exist.

In the Supreme Court of Canada, the Nisga'a lost again, on a technicality. British Columbia legislation required a fiat for legal actions that affected the Crown's own title to land. Pigeon J. held that an Aboriginal title claim did affect the Crown's title, and so a fiat was required.[5] Since none had been issued, the Nisga'a's claim could not proceed. Having addressed this procedural issue, Pigeon J. addressed no others. Speaking for three other judges, Judson J. agreed with Pigeon J.'s finding on the fiat requirement, giving it majority support.[6]

(a) Source of Aboriginal Title

Despite the focus on this technicality, *Calder* was a landmark. Why? Both Hall J. for three judges and Judson J. for three others supported the proposition that Aboriginal title may exist at common law, independently of the Royal Proclamation or other legislative or executive action.

Hall J. said that the Nisga'a derived their title from their possession of the land from time immemorial:

> ... [P]ossession is of itself proof of ownership. *Prima facie*, therefore, the Nishgas are the owners of the lands that have been in their possession from time immemorial.[7]

Hall J. drew heavily on *Johnson v. M'Intosh*, calling it the "*locus classicus* of the principles governing Aboriginal title."[8] In Hall J.'s view, "[t]he Aboriginal Indian title does not depend on treaty, executive order or legislative enactment."[9] In this view, the Royal Proclamation was no longer the sole source of Aboriginal title. Instead, it merely parallelled and supported a pre-existing legal occupancy right the Nisga'a had at common law.

Speaking for three other judges, Judson J. said that whatever Aboriginal title the Nisga'a might have had, had since been extinguished. But he went further, and speculated on the kind of rights the Nisga'a might have had if these had *not* been extinguished. Unlike Hall J., Judson J. felt that the Nisga'a could not claim rights based on the Royal Proclamation. In Judson J.'s view, the relevant part of the north Pacific coast was *terra incognita* in 1763, and could not have been included in the Proclamation. However, this did not necessarily end the question of Aboriginal title. In Judson J.'s view, when Lord Watson said in the *St. Catherine's* case that "[The Indians'] possession ... can only be ascribed to the Royal Proclamation," this merely meant that it was only necessary to look at the Proclamation because the land in question there was within the Proclamation's boundaries.[10] Judson J. continued:

> Although I think that it is clear that Indian title in British Columbia cannot owe its origin to the Proclamation of 1763, the fact is that when the settlers came, the Indians were there, organized in societies and occupying the land as their forefathers had done for centuries. This is what Indian title means.... What [the Nisga'a] are asserting in this action is that they had a right to continue to live on their lands as their forefathers had lived and that this right has never been lawfully extinguished.[11]

Thus, if Judson J. had not found that whatever title the Nisga'a were asserting had since been extinguished, he might well have agreed with Hall J. Quite likely he would have held that Aboriginal title exists independently of the Proclamation or other executive or legislative government recognition, by virtue of common law recognition of traditional occupation of land.[12]

If Aboriginal title is no longer tied exclusively to the Proclamation, it is no longer tied by the Proclamation's geographical limitations. As a result of *Calder*, unextinguished Aboriginal title and Aboriginal rights could exist at common law anywhere in Canada, wherever land had been occupied and used by Aboriginal peoples. This development helped spur the federal government to action. Within months, they agreed to negotiate the first major land claim based on Aboriginal title, and formulated a policy for negotiating Aboriginal title claims across Canada.

But *Calder* raised new questions, and left many old ones unresolved. There was agreement that Aboriginal title can derive from traditional use and occupancy of land, but there was little consensus beyond this.

(b) Proof

With the shift in emphasis from the Proclamation to pre-European occupancy, the Supreme Court raised two additional questions: (a) what should be required to prove Aboriginal title and rights? (b) how did Aboriginal title and rights survive the imposition of European sovereignty?[13]

Hall J. said proof of Indian title could be established by showing possession.[14] He found that the Nisga'a were at the time of their claim and "from time immemorial a distinctive cultural entity with concepts of ownership indigenous to their culture and capable of articulation under the common law."[15] That being established, the Nisga'a had shown a *prima facie* right of Aboriginal title.

Judson J.'s statement that "when the settlers came, the Indians were there, organized in societies, and occupying the land as their forefathers had done for centuries"[16] implies that he would have required proof of long traditional pre-European occupation of land by an organized society, and that he would have found the test to be satisfied in this case.

Neither judge was clear as to what specific elements must be proven, or whether individual forms of use of land must be proven separately or could be regarded as incidents of occupancy.

(c) Effect of European Sovereignty

In order to consider the effect of European sovereignty, the Court had either to explain, or to at least assume, the acquisition of European sovereignty. Hall J. took the first approach, but very briefly, while Judson J. took the second. As seen earlier,[17] the colonial common law rules of conquest and settlement did not clearly address the situation in North America, where conquest had not rarely taken the form of ordinary European military conflicts, and where settlement had taken place in lands that were already inhabited. Marshall C.J. had attempted to adapt the classic principles in *Johnson v. M'Intosh*, although with limited success.[18]

Historically, British Columbia seemed to resemble the situation of settlement, with the significant exception that the Aboriginal people were there when the settlers came. Hall J. appeared to consider settlement to be analogous to the establishment aspect of Marshall C.J.'s concept of discovery.[19] Hall J. said that the colonial common law principle that laws of conquered peoples continued until altered by the conqueror would apply "*a fortiori*" to the assertion of British sovereignty "by discovery or by declaration."[20] He interpreted *Johnson v. M'Intosh* as saying that Aboriginal title survives a change in sovereignty, "on discovery or on conquest."[21] Judson J. said nothing about the basis of European sovereignty and its effect on Aboriginal title.

Neither the brevity of Hall J. nor the silence of Judson J. was very satisfactory. Although Marshall C.J.'s analysis of the colonial American situation was ambiguous and somewhat archaic, it did attempt to grapple with the gap between the classic acquisition doctrines and state practice, and to relate both to the survival of Indian rights.[22] Hall J.'s suggestion that both doctrines have a similar effect was interesting, but needed elaboration. If Aboriginal rights survive the acquisition of European sovereignty, then courts need to clarify the acquisition as well as the rights.

(d) Content

Both Hall and Judson JJ. agreed that the content of Aboriginal title included occupation of land,[23] and the other forms of use referred to by Hall J. were all uses of land and resources on or in land and adjacent waters.[24] As well, both seemed to agree that the Indian interest did not preclude the Crown from having an underlying beneficial interest in the land.[25] Except for Judson J.'s reservations about the phrase "personal and usufructuary",[26] both judges seemed to assume that the description in *St. Catherine's* applies to

Indian title generally as well as the interest under the Proclamation.[27] Hall J., though, went on to describe the Indian interest as "a usufructuary right and a right to occupy the lands and to enjoy the fruits of the soil, the forest and of the rivers and streams."[28]

(e) Extinguishment

Hall and Judson JJ. agreed that extinguishment could be carried out consensually by treaty, and even unilaterally in some situations. Moreover, Judson J. did not seem to disagree with Hall J.'s contention that the onus is on government to prove extinguishment.[29] Hall J., though, said that government must show a "clear and plain intention" to extinguish unilaterally,[30] by "legislation specifically purporting to extinguish the Indian title."[31] For Judson J., extinguishment could be accomplished by government action inconsistent with the existence of an Aboriginal title.[32] Applying his specific legislation requirement, Hall J. found that pre-Confederation British Columbia colonial laws and proclamations had not extinguished the Nisga'a's Aboriginal title; applying his necessary inconsistency requirement, Judson J. found that they had.

Hall J.'s test suggests that only the legislature could extinguish unilaterally; for Judson J., this right extended to the Crown as well.[33]

(f) Enforcement

Hall J. seemed to agree with the Nisga'a's claim that they had a right of occupation "against the world except the Crown."[34] His approach to extinguishment suggests that the right could also be enforced against the Crown in the absence of a treaty surrender or legislative extinguishment. Judson J. repeated the statement in *St. Catherine's* that the Indian right was "dependent on the goodwill of the Sovereign."[35] He went on to find that colonial executive action had contributed to the extinguishment of the Nisga'a's title.

(g) Compensation

For Hall J., only express words could authorize an expropriation of Indian title without compensation;[36] Judson J. held that there could be no right to compensation in the absence of an express statutory requirement to this effect.[37]

On these crucial substantive issues, neither Hall J. nor Judson J. spoke for a majority of the Supreme Court of Canada. Small wonder, then, that there was little judicial consensus on Aboriginal title and Aboriginal rights in the post-*Calder* years. As we will see later, many of the issues that divided the Court in *Calder* still require resolution today.[38]

2. POST-*CALDER* YEARS

The highest Court supplied little more guidance in years after *Calder*. In two important decisions, it set some outer parameters for Aboriginal rights while saying almost nothing about Aboriginal title or Aboriginal rights themselves. *Derriksan*[39] involved a British Columbia Indian who defended himself against a charge of violating regulations under the federal *Fisheries Act* by claiming an Aboriginal right to fish. In a one-paragraph oral judgment, the Supreme Court said that assuming that there was an Aboriginal right to fish, arising from Indian occupation, any such right was subject to the federal regulations. The Court implied — but did not say — that, at the most, Aboriginal rights have common law status and are subject, like other common law rights, to otherwise competent legislation.

Kruger and Manuel[40] involved two British Columbia Indians who defended themselves against a charge of violating the provincial *Wildlife Act* by claiming, among other things, an Aboriginal right to hunt. The Court deemed it unnecessary to deal in detail with the Aboriginal rights claim. The Court concluded that the provincial statute was valid either by way of referential incorporation as a federal law,[41] or of its own force. Although the first alternative merely confirmed what had been said in *Derriksan*, the second alternative suggested that otherwise valid provincial laws could prevail over Aboriginal rights.[42]

In *Re Paulette*,[43] the Supreme Court found it possible to say even less about Aboriginal rights. Chief Paulette and other Indians of the Northwest Territories Mackenzie River area claimed that they had an Aboriginal title to Crown land and that this title interest could be protected by a *caveat* under the federal *Land Titles Act*. The trial judge looked at the proof and content of Aboriginal rights and their relationship to treaty rights, and agreed with both aspects of the claim.[44] However, the Supreme Court said simply that because the *Land Titles Act* only applied to interests on private land, not Crown land, it was unnecessary to consider the Aboriginal title claim.

Why did the Court seem to be avoiding the issue? In *Kruger*, Dickson J. said that "questions of

[Aboriginal title] should only be decided when title is directly in issue."[45] He said these questions "are woven with history, legend, politics and moral obligations" and should be considered on the basis of specific facts, rather than on a global basis.[46] Although this judicial caution was understandable, *Calder* had raised controversies of more than a factual nature. Clarification was needed.

3. *BAKER LAKE*[47]

Reading 4(b) at p. 263

A rare attempt during this period to pull together some common threads from *Calder* was the 1979 decision of Mahoney J. of the Federal Court Trial Division in *Baker Lake*.[48] In the late 1970s, the Inuit people of the Baker Lake area of the Northwest Territories sought a declaration that they had Aboriginal rights based on occupancy and use of the land, an injunction to prevent mining exploration activities from causing more interference with their caribou hunting, and related relief.

Mahoney J. considered whether decisions relevant to Aboriginal rights of Indians also apply to Inuit;[49] whether the Royal Proclamation applied to the Baker Lake area;[50] whether Aboriginal rights could exist apart from the Royal Proclamation, as suggested in *Calder*;[51] and what is required to prove or extinguish Aboriginal title. Mahoney J. formulated four criteria for proof of Aboriginal title that were widely used in subsequent years.[52] He required

1. that they [the plaintiffs, who are the Inuit] and their ancestors were members of an organized society;
2. that the organized society occupied the specific territory over which they assert the Aboriginal title;
3. that the occupation was to the exclusion of other organized societies;[53] and
4. that the occupation was an established fact at the time sovereignty was asserted by England.

Mahoney J. held that the Baker Lake Inuit met these criteria. However, he concluded that their Aboriginal title had been abridged by federal mining and lands legislation and permits. Mahoney J. anticipated the Supreme Court's later analysis in *Sparrow* by attempting to synthesize the tests of Judson and Hall JJ. in *Calder*. For Mahoney J., the relevant question was whether it was the necessary effect of statute to entirely abrogate Aboriginal title.[54]

Although *Baker Lake* supported the proposition that Aboriginal rights or title can arise at common law, by virtue of occupancy and use of land, not all decisions in the post-*Calder* era came to the same conclusion. In *Kanatewat*, for example, the Quebec Court of Appeal dismissed Aboriginal title as a vague, uncertain concept and doubted that an Aboriginal title existed in the area in question.[55] Beyond this issue, there was little clarity in the case law on the content, duration, and extinguishment of Aboriginal rights, and their relationship to other rights.

4. *GUERIN*[56]

Reading 4(c) at p. 265

In 1984, the Supreme Court rendered its decision in *Guerin*.[57] Although *Guerin* post-dated the *Constitution Act, 1982*, it was decided without express reference to that constitutional enactment, and may be usefully considered here for what it said about Aboriginal rights at common law.

Pursuant to s. 18(1) of the *Indian Act*,[58] the Musqueam Band in Vancouver surrendered reserve land for the purpose of a lease to a golf club, on terms negotiated for the band by Indian Affairs officials. Unfortunately, the Musqueam were not adequately consulted about the final terms, which proved to be much less favourable than promised to the band. The band sued the federal Crown for breach of a trust or fiduciary duty.

A trust can arise when one party assumes responsibility for the property of another, and exercises control over it. On the other hand, the courts have refused to enforce what are called "political trusts" in regard to subject matter that was originally created by the government itself.[59] The Federal Court of Appeal found that s. 18(1) of the *Indian Act* imposed at best a political trust, because its subject matter was not independent but created by statute.

The Supreme Court of Canada held that the Crown owed a duty to the Musqueam, and that this duty had been breached. The Court awarded the band $10 million in compensation. Seven of the eight judges found that there had been a breach of a fiduciary or trust obligation, while the eighth found that there had been a breach of the duties of an agent.

Dickson J. for four judges and Wilson J. for three judges responded to the political trust argument by saying that the Indians *did* have an interest independent of government. Dickson J., who addressed this issue more specifically, said the Indians' interest in the reserve land was the same as the aboriginal title interest from which the reserve interest was derived.[60] Aboriginal title, in turn, was independent of government because it did not depend on executive or legislative recognition. Dickson J. said that:

> In *Calder* ... this court recognized aboriginal title as a legal right derived from the Indians' historic occupation and possession of their tribal lands.[61]

This was not quite so, as in *Calder* Judson J., speaking for the three judges, had said that this was the best way to describe *what the Nisga'a were claiming* in that case.[62] Nonetheless, Wilson J. also seemed to assume that Aboriginal title had formal common law recognition, so that if full recognition had not occurred in *Calder*, it did occur retroactively in *Guerin*.

Dickson J. continued:

> In recognizing that the Proclamation is not the sole source of Indian title the *Calder* decision went beyond the judgment of the Privy Council in [the *St. Catherine's* case].... In this respect *Calder* is consistent with the position of Chief Justice Marshall in the leading American cases of [*Johnson v. M'Intosh* and *Worcester v. Georgia*]....
>
> In *Johnson v. M'Intosh* Marshall C.J., although he acknowledged the *Royal Proclamation* of 1763 as one basis for recognition of Indian title, was none the less of the opinion that the rights of the Indians in the lands they traditionally occupied prior to European colonization both predated and survived the claims to sovereignty made by the various European nations in the territories of the North American continent....
>
> ...
>
> The principle that a change in sovereignty over a particular territory does not in general affect the presumptive title of the inhabitants was approved by the Privy Council in *Amodu Tijani v. Secretary, Southern Nigeria*, [1921] 2 A.C. 399.[63]

Dickson J. said that although there could be no trust because the Indians' interest was not a true property interest, a fiduciary obligation arose at the time of the surrender. For Wilson J., the Crown did assume a full trust obligation at the time of the surrender. Before this, she said, the Crown owed a more general fiduciary obligation to the Musqueam.

What exactly *were* the sources of the fiduciary or trust obligation for Dickson and Wilson JJ.? If the Aboriginal title was a source, were other elements required?[64]

Guerin opened a new legal dimension in Aboriginal-government relations, one that is still largely uncharted.[65] Does the Crown owe fiduciary obligations to Aboriginal people in the absence of statutory provisions? Can the obligations attach to statutory commitments unconnected to Aboriginal title? Do they attach to health and social insurance benefits received by Aboriginal peoples? How do they relate to treaties and land claims agreements? And how does the *Guerin* obligation relate to the new constitutional fiduciary obligation in *Sparrow*?[66]

Guerin clarified the status of Aboriginal rights at common law, and linked this to the question of the Crown's fiduciary obligations to Aboriginal peoples, but the decision related neither of these issues to the *Constitution Act, 1982*, which had been proclaimed two years before. The link between the first two issues is interesting. Dickson J. said the reason the fiduciary obligation was legally enforceable was that the Indian title was independent of government recognition and arose from occupation and use of land.[67] There was less clarity about the nature and effect of the newly recognized Crown fiduciary obligation, a subject that will be considered in more detail in **Chapter 8**.

5. TURNING POINT?

By freeing Aboriginal title from the Royal Proclamation, *Calder* marked the beginning of the modern era in Aboriginal rights. But the judges agreed on only one main point: the idea that Aboriginal rights could derive from traditional use and occupancy of land. The post-*Calder* decade brought relatively little further clarification. This was a less-than-solid foundation on which to enshrine Aboriginal and treaty rights in the constitution.[68] As we will see later,[69] despite some major judicial efforts,[70] many old questions remain, and new ones are replacing those that have gone.[71]

Meanwhile, however, *Calder* did have a significant impact in another area. Shortly after the Supreme Court's decision in January 1973, the federal government reversed an earlier policy and decided that it would negotiate land claims agreements with Aboriginal title claimants.[72] Three decades later, nearly 20 land claims agreements had been signed throughout Canada. One of these was with the Nisga'a people of the Nass River area.[73]

Notes

1. *Calder v. British Columbia (A.G.)*, [1973] S.C.R. 313.
2. *St. Catherine's Milling and Lumber Company v. The Queen* (1888), 14 App. Cas. 46 (J.C.P.C.).
3. *Supra* note 1.
4. There was some question about the scope of this claim. At the Supreme Court level, Hall J. stressed that the claim did not challenge the Crown's paramount title, or the federal Crown's right to extinguish the Indian title: *ibid.* at 352. Pigeon J., on the other hand, thought the claim questioned the Crown's absolute title (426), so that a fiat was required: *infra* note 5. In regard to legislative power, the Nisga'a's claim might have affected provincial jurisdiction under s. 92(5) of the *Constitution Act, 1867* (by bringing the land under the exception to s. 109 of that Act: see **Chapter 3, Part 10**). However, this particular limitation would not have affected other legislative powers under s. 92 of the Act. See generally **Chapter 6**.
5. *Supra* note 1 at 426–27.
6. *Ibid.* at 345.
7. *Ibid.* at 375.
8. *Ibid.* at 380.
9. *Ibid.* at 390.
10. *Ibid.* at 322–23.
11. *Ibid.* at 328.
12. Had he done so, he would have been confronted with the ancillary question that faced Hall J.: what happened to this pre-existing right at the time of the assertion of British sovereignty?
13. This, in turn, suggested an additional question: what was the legal basis of European sovereignty itself?
14. *Ibid.* at 354.
15. *Ibid.* at 375.
16. *Ibid.* at 328.
17. **Chapter 3**, discussions of *Johnson v. M'Intosh* and *Worcester v. Georgia*.
18. *Ibid.*
19. *Ibid.* at 415–16. See also 383 and 388–89, contrasting discovery (and on 389, declaration) with conquest and **Chapter 3, Part 11**.
20. *Ibid.* at 389. Hall J. seemed to be treating discovery or declaration as analogous to settlement.
21. *Ibid.* at 383.
22. See *Johnson v. M'Intosh*, **Chapter 3, Part 11**.
23. *Ibid.* at 328 and 352.
24. *Ibid.*
25. *Ibid.* at 320 and 352.
26. *Ibid.* at 328, referring to the description in *St. Catherine's Milling and Lumber Company v. The Queen* (1889), 14 App. Cas. 46 at 54 (J.C.P.C.): **Chapter 3, Part 10**.
27. *Ibid.* at 320, 322–23 (Judson J.) and 380 (Hall J.).
28. *Ibid.* at 352.
29. *Ibid.* at 375 (Hall J.). Judson J. examined the evidence of extinguishment rather than requiring the Nisga'a to prove that there had been none.
30. *Ibid.* at 414.
31. *Ibid.* at 402.
32. *Ibid.* at 334–35. See also 337.
33. Judson J. attributed the extinguishment both to the ordinances of the Legislative Council of British Council and to the proclamations issued by Governor Douglas: *ibid.* at 333.
34. *Ibid.* at 352.
35. *Ibid.* at 328.
36. *Ibid.* at 352.
37. *Ibid.* at 344.
38. See **Chapters 7, 9** and **10**. In **Chapter 10**, see especially **Part 4**, questions in brackets. Compare the approach in *Calder* to that of the High Court of Australia in *Mabo v. State of Queensland (No. 2)* (1992), 107 A.L.R. 1; 175 C.L.R. 1: **Chapter 9, Part 2**; and with that of the British Columbia Court of Appeal in *Delgamuukw v. British Columbia* (1993), 104 D.L.R. (4th) 470.
39. *R. v. Derriksan* (1976), 71 D.L.R. (3d) 159n (S.C.C.).
40. *Kruger and Manuel v. The Queen*, [1978] 1 S.C.R. 104, December 1976.
41. By virtue of s. 88 of the *Indian Act* (now R.S.C. 1985, c. I-5), see **Chapter 6, Part 4**.
42. See **Chapter 6, Part 2**.
43. *Re Paulette et al. and Registrar of Land Titles (No. 2)*, [1977] 2 S.C.R. 628, aff'g (1976), 63 D.L.R. (3d) 1 (N.W.T.C.A.), which rev'd (1973), 42 D.L.R. (3d) 8 (N.W.T.S.C.).
44. *Re Paulette et al. and Registrar of Land Titles (No. 2)* (1974), 42 D.L.R. (3d) 8 (N.W.T.S.C.).
45. *Kruger and Manuel v. The Queen*, [1978] 1 S.C.R. 104.
46. *Ibid.*
47. *Baker Lake v. Canada (Minister of Indian and Northern Affairs)* (1970), 107 D.L.R. (3d) 513 (F.C.T.D.). See also D.W. Elliott, "*Baker Lake* and the Concept of Aboriginal Title" (1980) 18 Osgoode Hall L.J. 653.
48. *Ibid.*
49. Answer: Yes.
50. Answer: No.
51. Answer: Yes.
52. However, in a 1991 decision, the Supreme Court suggested, without explanation, that one or more of the criteria might be too strict: *Ontario (A.G.) v. Bear Island Foundation*, [1991] 2 S.C.R. 570 at 575.
53. Note, though, that where the right claimed is one of resource use rather than land occupancy, the courts do not require proof of exclusive traditional occupancy in the area in question: *R. v. Sparrow*, [1970] 1 S.C.R. 1075 at 1094–95. This may have been the criterion vaguely criticized in *Bear Island*, *ibid.*
54. *Ibid.* at 551. Mahoney J. applied the same test to the question as to whether a statute had abridged (i.e., restricted but not wholly extinguished) Aboriginal title.
55. *Société de Développment de la Baie James et al. v. Kanatewat et al.*, [1975] C.A. 166 at 176 (Q.C.A.).
56. *Guerin v. The Queen*, [1984] 2 S.C.R. 535, rev'g (1983) 143 D.L.R. (3d) 416 (F.C.A.), rev'g [1982] 2 F.C. 385 (F.C.T.D.) and (1982), 127 D.L.R. (3d) 170 (F.C.T.D.: supplementary reasons). See discussion of fiduciary implications of *Guerin* in **Chapter 8**.
57. *Guerin v. The Queen*, [1984] 2 S.C.R. 335.
58. R.S.C. 1952, c. 149, as am. (now R.S.C. 1985, c. I-5).
59. Such a trust might be enforced by political, but not legal, means. See *Alfred Kinloch v. Secretary of State for India in Council* (1882), 7 App. Cas. 619 and *Tito v. Waddell (No. 2)*, [1977] 3 All E.R. 129 (Ch.). For some post-*Guerin* references to this principle, see *Callie v. Canada*, [1991] 2 F.C. 379 at 391–94 (F.C.T.D.) and *Penikett v. Canada* (1987), 45 D.L.R. (4th) 108 at 124–26 (B.C.C.A.). A possible rationale for the political trust principle is that where the subject matter is Crown property or property derived from the Crown, the Crown's responsibility to manage it in the interests of the public at large should not be restricted by obligations to special beneficiaries.
60. *Ibid.* at 377.
61. *Supra* note 57 at 376.
62. **Part 1(a)**, above.
63. *Supra* note 57 at 377–78.
64. See **Chapter 8, Part 4**.
65. See **Chapter 8**.
66. See **Chapter 8, Part 7**.
67. Note that although Dickson C.J. quoted from Marshall C.J.'s discussion of the discovery doctrine in *Johnson v. M'Intosh*, (1823) 8 Wheaton 543 at 593–74 (U.S.S.Ct.)

(see **Chapter 3, Part 11**), Guerin did not provide new insight into the nature of European acquisition of sovereignty in Canada.

68. On the constitutionalization of Aboriginal rights and the *Sparrow* decision, see **Chapter 7**.
69. **Chapters 7, 9** and **10**.
70. E.g., *R. v. Van der Peet*, [1996] 2 S.C.R. 507, discussed in **Chapter 9, Part 3**. See also general propositions 1 to 23, in **Chapter 10, Part 4**.
71. See generally, **Chapter 10, Part 4**.
72. **Chapter 11, Part 4(b)**.
73. **Chapter 11, Part 7(h)**.

5 Indian Treaties

Chapter Highlights

- An Indian treaty is a solemn agreement between a group or nation of Aboriginal people and a representative of the Crown. It is intended to create obligations for both parties.
- Indian treaties are unique. They resemble both contracts and international treaties, but they are identical to neither.
- The four main categories of Indian treaties are early peace treaties, simple land cession treaties, the more complex Robinson and "numbered" treaties, and modern land claims agreements.
- Treaties can (but do not necessarily) extinguish Aboriginal rights, and can prevail over provincial laws and post-April 17, 1982, federal laws.
- The older treaties are especially subject to problems. These include the unequal bargaining position of the parties, cultural differences, inconsistencies in treaty benefits, and uncertain legal effects.
- More recently, courts have tried to redress some of these problems by a variety of interpretive presumptions.

Synopsis

Indian treaties are formal but paradoxical testaments to Aboriginal and non-Aboriginal attempts at understanding. Represented as solemn and just, they were erratically and unequally conceived, imperfectly understood, and inadequately performed. Although the treaties are unique to Aboriginal peoples, they were only concluded with some. Long neglected, treaties are now undergoing a revival. The old treaty process is being continued by modern land claims agreements. Existing treaty rights now have constitutional protection. The Supreme Court is trying to redress some of the old defects by construing treaty rights liberally. Nevertheless, serious problems remain, and more changes are needed.

Selected Readings

🖹 links material in this chapter to the corresponding headings and page numbers of the relevant readings.

🖹 Entire Chapter	Indian Treaty Map	272
🖹 Part 5	Report of the Commissioner for Treaty Number 11	272
🖹 Part 11	*Simon v. The Queen*	276
🖹 Part 12	*R. v. Sioui*	279
🖹 Part 13	*Ontario (A.G.) v. Bear Island Foundation*	285
🖹 Part 14	*R. v. Badger*	286
🖹 Part 15	*R. v. Marshall*	291
🖹 Part 16	*Haida Nation v. British Columbia (Minister of Forests)*	378

1. SIGNIFICANCE

> To those of us who are Treaty Indians, there are few things more important than the Treaties, the lands and the well being of our future generation.[1]

Indian treaties are formal but paradoxical testaments to Aboriginal and non-Aboriginal attempts at understanding.[2] Their roots stretch back into early history, but they are still highly relevant today. Represented as solemn, just, and lasting, they were erratically and unequally conceived, imperfectly understood, and inadequately performed. The treaties are unique to Aboriginal peoples, yet they were only concluded with some. Although many native parties considered them sacred, Indian treaties were made for the convenience of the newcomers, in aid of military, settlement, development, or transportation needs.

Today treaties are part of a new paradox. Neglected for hundreds of years, they have now undergone a revival.[3] Since the 1970s, the old treaty process has been continued by modern land claims agreements. Since 1982, existing treaty rights have been given constitutional protection under s. 35(1) of the *Constitution Act, 1982*. In recent decades, the Supreme Court has construed treaty rights very liberally. It stresses that treaty making and interpretation must be approached in light of the general principle of the honour of the Crown. The Court sees negotiated treaties as central to an historic reconciliation process between the Crown and Aboriginal peoples. The Court is moving treaties from the backstage to the spotlight.

2. DEFINITION

An Indian treaty is a solemn agreement between a group or nation of Aboriginal people and a representative of the Crown. It is intended to create obligations for both parties.[4] Typically, Aboriginal people agree to forego hostilities or claims related to land in return for Crown guarantees of protection, game rights, reserves, or other benefits. Although Indian treaties have been compared to international treaties[5] and contracts,[6] the Supreme Court says they are *sui generis*, not exactly like either.[7]

3. MAIN CATEGORIES

There are four main categories of Indian treaties. The first are the early peace treaties, mainly in the Maritimes in the 18th century.[8] The second include the simple land cession treaties, concluded in Upper Canada in the later 18th and earlier 19th centuries[9] and on Vancouver Island in the mid-19th century.[10] These were essentially land sales in return for cash grants.[11] The third are the Robinson treaties of 1850[12] and the numbered treaties of 1871 to 1921.[13] These were surrenders of large land areas in return for cash, annuities, reserves, and game rights and / or other benefits. The fourth comprise modern land claim agreements.[14] Typically, these include very large areas and complex governmental, social, and economic guarantees as well as modern equivalents of the benefits in the numbered treaties. Beyond this, an unknown number of less formal documents may now have Indian treaty status.[15]

4. SIZE

Since the early 18th century, hundreds of Indian treaties have been concluded in at least two-thirds of what is now Canada. Before the modern land claims era, the largest were the numbered treaties. These range from Treaty 1, that covers 17,000 square miles (44,030 square kilometres), to Treaty 11, that covers 372,000 square miles (963,476 square kilometres). Some modern land claims agreements are even larger. For example, the James Bay Agreement extends over 410,000 square miles (1.06 million square kilometres). The Nunavut Agreement covers an area three times the size of Alberta.[16]

5. CONTENT

Reading 5(b) at p. 272

In the Maritime peace treaties, the Indians generally agreed to refrain from hostilities and to acknowledge British sovereignty. Other commitments included undertakings not to disturb settlers or aid enemies of the Crown, and to submit disputes to British courts.[17] For its part, the Crown might guarantee the Indians the use of their existing lands and their existing hunting and fishing rights. Other Crown promises could include annual treaty presents, the same treatment "as any others of His Majesty's subjects" before British courts, the creation of trading posts, and the supply of food.[18]

After this early period, land became an increasingly important element of most treaties. For example, the Upper Canada and Vancouver Island land cession treaties were often land surrenders in return for cash grants or for smaller reserved areas for the Indians.[19] Reserves were an element of the Robinson treaties of 1850,[20] and reserves or similar lands have been a key element of all subsequent major treaties.

In the mid-19th century, treaty content became progressively more complex. All the numbered treaties contained education guarantees.[21] All numbered treaties provided for land for reserves; all except treaties 1 and 2 provided for hunting rights; all except treaties 1, 2, and 7 provided for fishing rights; and all except treaties 9 and 10 provided farming implements.[22] Treaty 6 contained a "medicine chest" provision that has been interpreted as providing free medicines but not exemptions from provincial medical taxes.[23] Modern land claims agreements may include land, resource rights, guaranteed participation in public bodies, tax exemptions, social and economic guarantees, and self-government provisions.

6. PARTICIPANTS

The Royal Proclamation of 1763 provided that lands reserved to Indians within settled colonies could be purchased "from the ... Indians" only for the Crown, in the Crown's name, "at some public Meeting or Assembly of the said Indians."[24] Typically, treaties have been signed by chiefs or other Aboriginal peoples' representatives on behalf of their tribes or nations. Just as Aboriginal rights are held collectively, by groups of Aboriginal peoples, it seems appropriate that Indian treaties should be concluded on behalf of Aboriginal groups, not individuals.[25]

As a result of its exclusive legislative power in s. 91(24) of the *Constitution Act, 1867* and the principle that executive power generally follows legislative power,[26] the federal government has full[27] and probably exclusive[28] constitutional executive power to negotiate Indian treaties.[29] However, the provinces own natural resources, subject to the Aboriginal interest, and are major beneficiaries of land cession treaties. Moreover, the provinces have the right to agree to the allotment of any reserve or other land from land surrendered in treaties.[30] Thus, it is desirable to have the provinces take part in land cession treaties (and land claims agreements) to help pay for them. Indeed, provinces must participate in some way if surrendered land is subsequently allocated as reserves.[31]

7. STATUS

Indian treaties:

1. can extinguish Aboriginal rights,[32] but some treaties preserve Aboriginal rights[33] and some do not affect Aboriginal rights;[34]
2. prevail over provincial laws that are subject to s. 88 of the *Indian Act*, where there is a conflict;[35]
3. could be restricted or extinguished by federal laws[36] enacted prior to April 17, 1982,[37] by virtue of the general principle of sovereignty of Parliament;[38] and
4. can be infringed by otherwise valid government action, but only if that infringement can be justified.[39]

As well, Indian treaties whose guarantees lack territorial boundaries may be held to prevail over regulations pursuant to a provincial statute if these guarantees are compatible with the purpose of the statute.[40] In the Prairie provinces, treaty rights have been modified, but not replaced, by the *Natural Resources Transfer Agreements*.[41]

8. INTERPRETATION AND ENFORCEMENT

In recent decades, the courts have stressed that treaties should be construed liberally,[42] especially where the bargaining position of the Aboriginal parties was weaker than that of the Crown.[43] This principle applies both to deciding whether a document is a treaty and to determining its content.[44] The principle has a number of corollaries. For example, treaties are to be interpreted with regard to the way their Indian signatories would have understood them,[45] and in the light of oral commitments that accompanied them.[46] However, the liberal construction principle may be applied less strictly to modern treaties[47] and to land claims agreements,[48] where bargaining positions are less unequal.

Although the relevant government could unilaterally restrict or extinguish treaty rights before April 17, 1982,[49] courts construe treaty right restrictions narrowly.[50] Government must show a "clear and plain intention" of any purported extinguishment and strict proof of the fact of extinguishment.[51] Any attempted restriction of an existing treaty right after

April 17, 1982, is subject to s. 35(1) of the *Constitution Act, 1982*. It is subject to an infringement/justification analysis patterned on that for Aboriginal rights in *Sparrow*.[52] Aboriginal and treaty rights can be infringed by the manner in which a law is administered, as well as by its content.[53] On the other hand, Aboriginal and treaty rights must be exercised with due concern for public safety, so that reasonable safety regulation does not constitute infringement.[54]

Although individual treaty promises should be specifically enforceable,[55] examples of successful judicial enforcement are uncommon.[56] However, the Crown may also be subject to a more general fiduciary duty to discharge treaty promises fairly,[57] and it may be that breach of such a duty will be enforceable.[58] Conversely, where treaty provisions are inadequate, Aboriginal people might prefer to try to have them set aside rather than enforced. It is unclear as to how far they could rely on contract analogies to do this.[59]

9. CHARLOTTETOWN ACCORD

A centrepiece of the failed Charlottetown Accord[60] of 1992 was negotiated self-government agreements that could become constitutionally enforceable treaties, pursuant to s. 35(1) of the *Constitution Act, 1982*.[61] These new self-government agreements were not supposed to derogate from existing s. 35(1) treaty rights.[62] As well, the Accord stated that all treaty rights should be interpreted liberally.[63] It committed the federal government and, where invited, the provincial governments, to negotiating clarifications and rectifications to existing treaties.[64] It also would have clarified that s. 91(24) of the *Constitution Act, 1867* includes Métis people.[65]

Some Aboriginal groups opposed the Accord on the ground that treaties in Canada should be on a nation-to-nation basis, and not as part of the Canadian constitution. Some objected to the involvement of provincial governments. Others were concerned about potential interference with government treaty responsibilities, and with the relatively open-ended mandate given to courts to define self-government after a five-year period.[66]

10. TREATY PROBLEMS

Treaty problems are legion. In the first place, Aboriginal peoples were generally in a weak bargaining position at the time the treaties were signed. Often it was clear that British settlement or development would come regardless of whether a treaty had been signed. There were not only differences in languages, but also in language traditions. Aboriginal signatories generally placed greater weight on oral commitments,[67] whereas non-Aboriginals relied on written documents. Treaty provisions were sometimes vague.[68] Assurances made orally were sometimes not repeated on paper.[69] These factors and cultural gaps between the parties increased the chances of differing views as to what had been agreed.[70]

Second, the Crown's commitments were generally modest in comparison with those of the Indians, and some were quite inappropriate to the situation of the Indians.[71] Even by contemporary standards, they tended to be meagre. Too often, they were not kept.[72]

Third, the multi-staged, piecemeal nature of the treaty-making process meant that some Aboriginal groups were left out or neglected. For example, no treaties were concluded by the government of New France, and many Aboriginal groups in Quebec are still without treaties. Few treaties were concluded in British Columbia, few land cession treaties in the Atlantic region, and — before the modern land claims agreement era — none with the Inuit of the Arctic. People who regarded themselves as Métis people were generally treated differently from Indians,[73] and were usually considered to be eligible for general treaty benefits. For example, Prairie Métis were entitled — at least in theory[74] — to individual issues of scrip rather than collective treaty rights.[75] Where scrip was promised, it was sometimes addressed outside the treaties,[76] sometimes in conjunction with them.[77] The sporadic nature of the process resulted in a patchwork of inconsistent approaches across the country. Even among the numbered treaties there were big disparities in benefits.[78] Between the traditional treaties and the modern land claims agreements, these disparities are still greater.

Fourth, there was — and, in several respects, still is — a lack of clarity regarding the legal nature of the Indian treaty. What are the minimum requirements for a valid treaty? Who are the parties? Are they only the signatories, or all those who have shared the treaty benefits?[79] Where *are* international or contractual analogies appropriate? Can a treaty limit or extinguish the Aboriginal rights of non-member Aboriginal groups?[80] Does it have other effects on third parties? Have third parties any rights, such as consultation rights, in the treaty-making process? To what extent does the law about the older treaties apply to modern land claims agreements?

Some of the leading treaty cases are considered in more detail below. In recent decades, especially, the highest Court has been making some significant changes.

11. *SIMON*[81]

🖹 Reading 5(c) at p. 276

How can Canadian society do justice to a promise made to Aboriginal people over two hundred years ago? The Supreme Court attempted to provide an answer to this question in the *Simon* case in Nova Scotia.

One afternoon in September 1980, Mr. James Simon was driving along the West Indian Road, a public highway beside the Shubenacadie Indian Reserve in Nova Scotia. He was stopped by the R.C.M.P. and charged with illegal possession of a rifle and shotgun cartridges during closed season, contrary to the provincial *Lands and Forests Act*.

Mr. Simon was a registered Indian and member of the Shubenacadie Indian Brook Band (No. 2) of the Mi'kmaq people. In 1752, the Governor of Nova Scotia and the Mi'kmaqs had entered into a "Treaty or Articles of Peace and Friendship Renewed" that stated that the Mi'kmaqs have "free liberty of hunting and Fishing as usual." Mr. Simon argued that the 1752 agreement was a treaty within the meaning of s. 88 of the *Indian Act*, which subordinated provincial laws to treaties.

The provincial court judge convicted Mr. Simon, saying that the 1752 agreement had been extinguished because of settlement and Crown grants and leases in the area. The Nova Scotia Supreme Court Appellate Division upheld the conviction. They had a long list of technical concerns. They said that the 1752 agreement was not a treaty because it was not made by competent parties; that it created no new right to hunt; that it had been extinguished in 1753 because of British-Indian hostilities; that Mr. Simon had not shown any connection by descent between himself and the original treaty signatories; and that the agreement was not a treaty within the meaning of s. 88 of the *Indian Act*.

The Supreme Court of Canada set aside the conviction. Speaking for the Court, Dickson J. said that "Indian treaties should be given a fair, large and liberal construction in favour of the Indians."[82] Using this as a benchmark, he rejected the conclusions of the courts below. He found that the Nova Scotia Governor, the Mi'kmaqs Chief, and three other Mi'kmaq signatories were competent to conclude a valid treaty. Dickson J. said this agreement provided a new protection for the right to hunt. He found the evidence too inconclusive to say the agreement had been terminated by hostilities. Since Mr. Simon was a member of the same body of Indians, and lived in the same area as the original signatories, it was unnecessary to go further and prove direct descent. Because the agreement was an exchange of solemn promises between the King's representative and the Indians, it was a treaty within the meaning of s. 88 of the *Indian Act*. As a result, the treaty prevailed over the restrictions in the provincial statute.

Regarding the argument that the agreement had been terminated by hostilities, on the model of international treaty law, Dickson J. said:

> An Indian treaty is unique; it is an agreement *sui generis* that is neither created nor terminated according to the rules of international law.[83]

Simon marked a new liberal approach to Indian treaties. Arguably, the decision introduced a presumption in favour of the existence and benefits of an Indian treaty, a presumption against its extinguishment, and a presumption against restrictive analogies drawn from other areas of law. On the other hand, precise tests for treaty existence, benefits, and extinguishment were left for another day. As well, it remained to be seen how far this liberal approach would apply to the modern and more sophisticated counterparts of the old treaties — modern land claims agreements.

12. *SIOUI*[84]

🖹 Reading 5(d) at p. 279

Sioui is notable both as a strong affirmation of the liberal approach to treaty interpretation started in *Simon*, and as a compromise approach to an unusual form of treaty.

Four Huron Band Indians from the Lorette Indian reserve in Quebec were charged with cutting down trees and camping and making fires in places not designated in Jacques-Cartier Park. These activities violated regulations under the provincial *Park Act*. The Indians argued that they were exercising ancestral customary and religious rights protected in a document signed in 1760 by British General James Murray. They maintained that this document constituted a treaty within the meaning of s. 88 of the *Indian Act*,[85] and was still valid. Hence, they argued, it could prevail over anything to the contrary in the provincial regulations. Although the Quebec Supreme Court upheld their convictions, both the Quebec Court of Appeal and the Supreme Court of Canada set them aside.

The Supreme Court was faced with three main questions: (a) Was the 1760 agreement a treaty? (b) If so, had the treaty rights been extinguished? and (c) Did the customary and religious guarantees in the treaty prevail over the regulations? The Court's answers to these questions were "yes", "no", and "yes", respectively.

For the first two questions, the Court built on the liberal approach in *Simon*.[86] They applied it to a document that initially looked like a unilateral government commitment. Their conclusion: It was a treaty. They required strict proof of any extinguishment. Their conclusion: The treaty had not been extinguished. This relaxed approach raised questions about the minimum requirements for treaty status and extinguishment. What other informal Aboriginal-government agreements might qualify as Indian treaties? What would qualify as extinguishment?

To answer the third main question, the Court had to deal with treaty guarantees that were relatively vague, and were not attached to a single geographical territory. The Court attempted a compromise approach to this kind of "non-territorial" treaty. They said the treaty's guarantees could prevail over provincial regulations, *provided* that the content of these guarantees was consistent with the general purpose of the enabling statute. Even by standards suitable to compromises, this was a complex solution.[87]

13. *BEAR ISLAND*[88]

🖹 Reading 5(e) at p. 285

In *Bear Island*, the Supreme Court settled one question about the parties to Indian treaties, but left several other important treaty questions unresolved, and cast doubt on a long-established test for Aboriginal rights.

In response to an Ontario government action seeking a declaration of clear title to land in northern Ontario, the Bear Island Foundation counterclaimed, on behalf of the Temagami Indians. They argued that the Temagami Indians had an Aboriginal title to the area, and that this title had not been extinguished by the Robinson-Huron Treaty of 1850 because the Temagami were not parties to the treaty. There were two basic questions underlying the litigation: (a) Did the Temagami originally have an Aboriginal right to the land? and (b) Had this right been extinguished by the Robinson-Huron Treaty of 1850?

The Supreme Court answered affirmatively to both questions.[89] They said that whatever the original status of the Temagami, their Aboriginal right had been extinguished by virtue of the Temagami's later adherence to the treaty. Rejecting the trial judge's finding that there was no Aboriginal peoples' right initially, the Supreme Court criticized the trial judge's application of the well-known criteria set down by Mahoney J. in *Baker Lake*, and then declared that the trial judge had been "misled".[90] They added enigmatically that "on the facts found by the trial judge the Indians exercised sufficient occupation of lands in question throughout the relevant period to establish an Aboriginal right."[91] They referred (without specific page references) to their decisions in *Simon* and *Sparrow*.[92] Did they mean that exclusive traditional occupation is not required to prove Aboriginal rights? Did they consider other aspects of Mahoney J.'s test incorrect?

On the scope of treaties, the Ontario Court of Appeal's decision suggested that an expressly worded treaty might be able to extinguish all Aboriginal title in a geographical area, whether or not all Aboriginal groups in the area were signatories.[93] The Supreme Court failed to address this question, saying merely that because the Temagami had accepted benefits from the treaty, they were subject to its burdens as well. The effects of treaties on third parties is a most important practical question; some guidance would have been useful. And on the extinguishment question, at what point does acceptance of treaty benefits affect Aboriginal title?

Toward the end of its decision, the Court said it was "conceded" that the breach of some of the treaty obligations amounted to a breach of the Crown's fiduciary obligations as well. Did the Court agree that there had been treaty breaches? Or that there had been fiduciary breaches? If the latter, do all treaty breaches amount to fiduciary breaches?

14. *BADGER*[94]

🖹 Reading 5(f) at p. 286

In *Badger*, the Supreme Court addressed the relationship between treaty rights and rights in privately-owned land; between treaty rights on the

Prairies and the *Natural Resources Transfer Agreements* of 1930;[95] between the *N.R.T.A.* and s. 35(1) of the *Constitution Act, 1982*;[96] and between treaty rights and s. 35(1).[97] In answering these questions, the Court reaffirmed, restated, and applied the liberal construction approach to treaties.

Mr. Badger and two other Treaty 8 status Indians claimed a right to hunt for food. Mr. Badger had hunted near a dilapidated but inhabited house. He was charged with shooting a moose outside the hunting season, contrary to licensing regulations under the Alberta *Wildlife Act*. Mr. Kiyawasew had hunted on a snow-covered farm field. Mr. Ominayak had hunted on uncleared muskeg, away from farms or dwellings. He and Mr. Kiyawasew were charged with hunting without a licence.

All three were convicted in the Alberta Provincial Court. They argued that: they had a treaty right to hunt for food on privately-owned land; their treaty hunting rights had not been extinguished or modified by the 1930 *Natural Resources Transfer Agreement*; and the Alberta *Wildlife Act* did not limit their treaty right to hunt for food in the treaty area. Mr. Badger and Mr. Kiyawasew lost their appeals in the higher courts. The Supreme Court of Canada allowed Mr. Ominayak's appeal, but directed that a new trial be held on the question of whether the *Wildlife Act*'s infringement of his right to hunt was justified.

Cory J. spoke for the five-judge main majority.[98] He started his analysis with the following observations:

> First, it must be remembered that a treaty represents an exchange of solemn promises between the Crown and the various Indian nations. It is an agreement whose nature is sacred.... Second, the honour of the Crown is always at stake in its dealing with Indian people.... It is always assumed that the Crown intends to fulfil its promises. No appearance of "sharp dealing" will be sanctioned.... Third, any ambiguities or doubtful expressions in the wording of the treaty or document must be resolved in favour of the Indians. A corollary to this principle is that any limitations which restrict the rights of Indians under treaties must be narrowly construed.... Fourth, the onus of proving that a treaty or aboriginal right has been extinguished lies upon the Crown. There must be "strict proof of the fact of extinguishment" and evidence of a clear and plain intention on the part of the government to extinguish treaty rights....[99]

Cory J. applied this approach to Treaty 8 and the *N.R.T.A.* He said the Treaty 8 right to hunt was subject to two limitations within the treaty itself: (i) the right did not apply to "such tracts as may be required or taken up from time to time for settlement, mining, lumbering, trading or other purposes,"[100] and (ii) the right was subject to government regulation for conservation purposes.[101] Then, he added that the *N.R.T.A.* imposed further modifications by restricting the hunting right to a right to hunt for food,[102] by extending its potential scope beyond the boundaries of the treaties to the entire area of the Prairie provinces,[103] and by limiting it within this area to "all unoccupied Crown lands and on any other lands to which the said Indians may have a right of access."[104]

Whether individual tracts were lands to which the Indians had a right of access depended on the wording of the individual treaty. In the case of Treaty 8, it depended on whether the lands were "required or taken up ... for settlement, mining, lumbering, trading or other purposes."[105] The historical context and oral history of Treaty 8 indicated that this provision would have been understood by the Indians at the time to exclude privately-owned land that was put to a visible use that was inconsistent with the right to hunt for food.[106] This was the test to be used.

Since the private land on which Mr. Badger and Mr. Kiyawasew had hunted was put to visible and inconsistent use, it fell outside the scope of the treaty and was not land to which the Indians had a right of access under the *N.R.T.A.* Hence the *N.R.T.A.*-modified treaty right did not apply to them. In the case of Mr. Ominayak, there was no such visible inconsistent use. Hence Mr. Ominayak had a right to hunt there for food. This right had been modified but not replaced by the *N.R.T.A.*[107] Thus, it was an "existing" treaty right to which s. 35 of the *Constitution Act, 1982* applied.

To determine if a *Sparrow*-type approach[108] should also be used for treaty rights, Cory J. started by noting some important differences between Aboriginal and treaty rights:

> Aboriginal rights flow from the customs and traditions of the native peoples.... [T]hey embody the right of native people to continue living as their forefathers lived. Treaty rights, on the other hand, are those contained in official agreements between the Crown and the native peoples. Treaties are analogous to contracts, albeit of a very solemn and special, public nature. They create enforceable obligations based on the mutual consent of the parties. It follows that the scope of treaty rights will be determined by their wording, which must be

> interpreted in accordance with the principles enunciated by this Court.[109]

However, Cory J. went on to say that treaty rights resemble Aboriginal rights in that both are unique, both can be abridged, and both engage the honour of the Crown. He added that the wording of s. 35(1) supports a common approach to both kinds of right. Hence, like infringements of Aboriginal rights, infringements of treaty rights must be justified.[110] In Cory J.'s view the safety component of the licensing regulations did not infringe the treaty rights, as Aboriginal and treaty rights must be assumed to be subject to reasonable safety regulation. The conservation component of the regulations infringed the treaty rights — not by their subject matter, but by the way they were administered.[111] Accordingly, Mr. Ominayak's case was referred back to trial to determine if there was justification for the infringement.

Badger stressed that, wherever possible, Indian treaties should be interpreted in favour of their Indian signatories.[112] It continued the emphasis in *Sioui* on the oral understandings accompanying the treaties. It established the "visible and inconsistent use" criterion for determining the scope of hunting for food on private land in the numbered treaties. It affirmed that pre-April 17, 1982, extinguishment of treaty rights requires "strict proof of the fact of extinguishment" as well as evidence of a clear and plain intention to extinguish. It held that treaty rights as modified by the *N.R.T.A.* qualify as "existing" rights subject to s. 35(1) of the *Constitution Act, 1982*. It applied the *Sparrow* infringement / justification test to treaty rights. It established that reasonable safety regulation is not an infringement of an Aboriginal or treaty right, but that in other respects both the content and the manner of administration of a law can infringe these rights. In a single decision, the Supreme Court did much to clarify Indian treaty law.

15. *MARSHALL*[113]

Reading 5(g) on p. 291

Mr. Donald John Marshall, Jr., a New Brunswick Mi'kmaq (Micmac) status Indian, caught and sold 463 pounds of eels, contrary to federal fisheries regulations. He had fished without a licence, with an illegal net, and during the closed season.[114]

Mr. Marshall claimed that several 1760–61 treaties entitled Mi'kmaqs to fish free of the regulations. The key treaty clause required the Indians not to "traffick, barter or exchange any commodities in any manner but with such persons or the managers of such Truck houses as shall be appointed or Established by His Majesty's Governor."[115]

To help determine the meaning of this clause, the Supreme Court of Canada considered extrinsic evidence outside the treaty text.[116] This evidence included a pre-treaty Aboriginal request for truckhouses "for the furnishing them with necessaries, in Exchange for their Peltry";[117] a pre-treaty government note that "there might be a Truckhouse established for the furnishing them with necessaries";[118] and historical evidence that the British sought peace with the Mi'kmaq, and supported trade as a means of helping the Mi'kmaq continue their traditional way of life.[119]

On the basis of this evidence, the seven-judge Court majority concluded that the trade restriction provision should be construed to contain a positive treaty right

(i) to trade;
(ii) to hunt, fish, and trap the goods needed to take part in this trade; and
(iii) to hunt, fish, and trap these goods to the extent that they yielded the Mi'kmaq a "moderate livelihood". Such a right was now constitutionally guaranteed and could be regulated only pursuant to s. 35(1) of the *Constitution Act, 1982*.

The two dissenting judges said the trade and truckhouse treaty rights were ended by both the Indian and government treaty parties shortly after the treaty was signed.[120] They said the core of the treaty was a requirement that the Mi'kmaq trade only with the British. Hence any implied trading right ended when the British truckhouses ended. In their view, the historical evidence indicated that the main aim of the treaties was to prevent the Mi'kmaq from maintaining alliances with the French. Thus, neither the treaty wording nor its context supported a freestanding trading right that survived the exclusive trade and truckhouse régime.[121]

The Supreme Court allowed no grace period for implementing the new requirements. Freed from closed season requirements, Atlantic Aboriginal fishermen began to exercise what they considered a constitutional right to catch lobster. There was speculation as to whether the ruling applied to non-status Indians. Pacific coast Aboriginal fishermen claimed similar commercial fishing rights under pre-Confederation treaties with the governor of Vancouver Island. Because of the closed season, non-Aboriginals were unable to fish.

There was an atmosphere of confrontation in the east coast lobster fishery. The West Nova Fishermen's Coalition applied to the Supreme Court to rehear *Marshall* on the issue of federal regulatory authority over the fisheries, claiming that the Court's decision had resulted in uncertainty in this regard. In an unusual forty-eight paragraph set of reasons, the Court dismissed the application.[122] The Court said *Marshall* had been misunderstood by both the Coalition and the Aboriginal parties. It said the treaty right in *Marshall*:

(i) is limited to the local communities in which the 1760–61 treaties were made;[123]
(ii) comprises only hunting, fishing, and gathering of things traditionally gathered,[124]
(iii) can evolve within limits, but, in the absence of a new agreement, "cannot be wholly transformed."[125]
(iv) can be regulated by government restrictions that do not deprive treaty-holders of the right to a moderate livelihood;[126]
(v) can be infringed where this is justified for conservation or other compelling and substantial public objectives;[127] and
(vi) even if a closed season or other restriction were not justified for one species, it might be justified for another.[128]

Through its rehearing motion judgment, the Court reined in *Marshall's* the potential scope. Even so, *Marshall* shows that general historical evidence can be used to interpret a treaty text trade restriction clause as a free-standing commercial harvesting right, protected constitutionally against general net, season, or other restrictions that govern non-treaty resource users. What other treaties can now yield such rights? Will the Court be able to formulate clear rules for assessing the application and weight of extrinsic evidence? Where will it draw the line between the evolution of a treaty right and its transformation? What weight should be given to oral and written evidence in more modern treaty situations, where extensive written evidence may be available?[129] How will the Court define a "moderate livelihood" in individual cases?[130] Will a test case be needed before every new attempt at government regulation?

Meanwhile, the federal government struggled to reach interim fishing agreements with the Mi'kmaq and other Atlantic Canada bands most directly affected by *Marshall*. By the end of July, 2002, it had reached agreements with 29 of 34 bands.[131] On August 1, 2002, it signed an agreement in principle with one of the most militant bands, the Burnt Church First Nation. The 1300 members of the band's reserve were to receive approximately $20 million of lobster, crab, and tuna licences, catch quotas, and training and other facilities in return for complying with federal regulations over a two year period.[132]

16. *HAIDA NATION*[133]

Reading 10(e) at p. 378

Haida Nation is considered in more detail in **Chapter 8, Part 8(f)** and in **Chapter 10, Part 6**. Here it can be noted that the decision made some important general comments about the principle of the honour of the Crown, treaties, and the general relationship between the Crown and Aboriginal peoples. The Court said that the principle behind both the special fiduciary duty of the Crown to Aboriginals and the justification requirements of s. 35(1) of the *Constitution Act, 1982* is the principle of the honour of the Crown. It continued:

> The honour of the Crown also infuses the processes of treaty making and treaty interpretation. In making and applying treaties, the Crown must act with honour and integrity, avoiding even the appearance of "sharp dealing" (*Badger*, at para. 41). Thus in *Marshall, supra,* at para. 4, the majority of this Court supported its interpretation of a treaty by stating that "nothing less would uphold the honour and integrity of the Crown in its dealings with the Mi'kmaq people to secure their peace and friendship...."
>
> Where treaties remain to be concluded, the honour of the Crown requires negotiations leading to a just settlement of Aboriginal claims: *R. v. Sparrow*, [1990] 1 S.C.R. 1075, at pp. 1105-6. Treaties serve to reconcile pre-existing Aboriginal sovereignty with assumed Crown sovereignty, and to define Aboriginal rights guaranteed by s. 35 of the *Constitution Act, 1982*. Section 35 represents a promise of rights recognition, and "[i]t is always assumed that the Crown intends to fulfil its promises" (*Badger, supra*, at para. 41). This promise is realized and sovereignty claims reconciled through the process of honourable negotiation. It is a corollary of s. 35 that the Crown act honourably in defining the rights it guarantees and in reconciling them with other rights and interests. This, in turn, implies a duty to consult and, if appropriate, accommodate.[134]

The Court sees government's underlying constitutional responsibility with regard to Aboriginal peoples to be one of reconciliation. It considers fair treaty making and fair treaty interpretation to be a key element of this responsibility.

17. CLARIFICATION OR RECONSTRUCTION?

After decades of neglect, the modern liberal approach to interpreting treaties has provided a positive change of direction. The Court says that treaties must be construed generously, with full regard to the perspective of the Aboriginal signatories. As indicated in *Haida Nation*, it considers fair negotiated treaties to be central to the Crown's responsibility of reconciliation with Aboriginal peoples. Less pronounced, but evident in decisions like *Badger* and the rehearing motion judgment in *Marshall*, are the Court's efforts to clarify specific aspects of treaty law. For example, the Court has confirmed that treaty rights are subject to the general constitutional infringement and justification principles that apply to Aboriginal rights, but are site-specific and species-specific in regard to their content.

As seen in this chapter, the clarification task is far from finished. Beyond this, courts may be able to reduce the *ad hoc* element in treaty interpretation by approaching it more systematically. Although treaty content is dependent on specific provisions and context, it may be possible to develop a general approach to determining the *degree* of protection that is appropriate in a particular case. For example, all treaties involve one or more contextual factors that are relevant to the Crown's treaty obligation. These can include the relative formality of the proceedings, the extent and nature of the government promise, the burden imposed on the Aboriginal parties, the importance of the Aboriginal interests, any relative bargaining inequality between the parties, the connection between the original parties and the claimants, any legitimate expectations, and relevant constitutional considerations. The stronger and more numerous these obligation factors, the higher the general level of protection that courts should give to the content of a particular treaty.

It should be kept in mind that judicial decisions impose third-party, constitutionally entrenched solutions on bilateral arrangements between the Crown and relevant Aboriginal peoples. Although judicial interpretation, clarification, and factor weighing can be useful where they are viable, some treaty obligations — especially in the earliest treaties — may be too unclear to yield much more than conjecture. Who can say with certainty, over two centuries after the fact, what was really meant by the "Truck houses" provision in *Marshall*? Such cases may require major reconstruction, and may be better suited to Aboriginal / government negotiation than to judicial surgery. In such cases, courts should normally suspend their decisions to provide the treaty parties time to fix the problem themselves.

Notes

1. Indian Chiefs of Alberta, *Citizens Plus*, 1970, 1.
2. See generally Canada, *Indian Treaties and Surrenders* (Toronto: Coles, 1971, reprint of Ottawa: Queen's Printer, 1891), 3 vols.; P.A. Cumming and N.H. Mickenberg, *Native Rights in Canada*, 2d ed. (Toronto: Indian-Eskimo Assn. of Canada, 1972), Part IV; G. Brown and R. Maguire, *Indian Treaties in Historical Perspective* (Ottawa: Dept. of Indian Affairs and Northern Development, 1979); A.J. Hall, "Indian Treaties" in *The Canadian Encyclopedia*, Year 2000 ed. (Toronto: McClelland & Stewart, 1999) at 1148–57; B.W. Morse, ed., *Aboriginal Peoples and the Law* (Ottawa: Carleton University Press, 1985), chaps. 4 and 5; O.P. Dickason, *Canada's First Nations: A History of Founding Peoples from Earliest Times*, 3d ed. (Don Mills, Ont.: Oxford University Press, 2002) at 153–55; J.S. Frideres, ed., *Native Peoples in Canada*, 4th ed. (Scarborough, Prentice-Hall, 1993), chap. 3; R.A. Reiter, *The Law of Canadian Indian Treaties* (Edmonton: Juris Analytica Publishing, 1995); Royal Commission on Aboriginal Peoples, *Report of the Royal Commission on Aboriginal Peoples*, vol. 1, chaps. 5 and 6 (hereinafter "*Report*").
3. The Charlottetown Accord, rejected in 1992, would have added another element to the revival. It provided for constitutionally enforceable self-government agreements and clarification of some existing treaties. See **Part 9**, below and **Chapter 12, Part 5**.
4. The Supreme Court has said that "what characterizes a treaty is the intention to create obligations, the presence of mutually binding obligations and a certain measure of solemnity": *Quebec (A.G.) v. Sioui*, [1990] 1 S.C.R. 1025 at 1044.
5. In *Simon v. The Queen*, [1985] 2 S.C.R. 387 at 404, the Supreme Court said that "it may be helpful in some instances to analogize the principles of international treaty law to Indian treaties," but then added that "these principles are not determinative." In *Quebec (A.G.) v. Sioui et al.*, [1990] 1 S.C.R. 1025 at 1056 (S.C.C.), addressing the early colonial situation, the Court said the European powers were forced to acknowledge that the Indians "had sufficient autonomy for the valid creation of solemn agreements which were called 'treaties', regardless of the strict meaning given to that word then and now by international law."
6. "Treaties are analogous to contracts, albeit of a very solemn and special, public nature": *R. v. Badger*, [1996] 1 S.C.R. 771 at para. 76.
7. *Simon v. The Queen*, [1985] 2 S.C.R. 387 at 404: *R. v. Badger*, [1996] 1 S.C.R. 771 at para. 78. Although they are similar to an international law treaty in terminology, in the independence of the Indian nations who concluded them in early times, and in their importance, Indian treaties do not follow the general rules of international law. For one thing, they are regarded by the government as agreements between the Crown and subjects of the

Crown. Moreover, unlike international treaties, they can create legal rights even before being implemented in specific legislation. Like contracts, Indian treaties are considered to be binding legal agreements, and may be subject to some of the same kind of protections that the law applies to contracts. On the other hand, Indian treaties involve groups rather than individuals, have a changing membership, and can prevail over some federal and provincial laws.

8. For example, the Treaty of 1752 with the Mi'kmaqs (eastern Nova Scotia) considered in the *Simon* case. Some other Maritime peace treaties: Treaty of 1725 with the Penobscots and others (Nova Scotia); Treaty of 1728 with the St. Johns and others (Nova Scotia and Acadia); Treaty of 1749 with the Chineto (Nova Scotia and Acadia); Treaty of 1749 with the St. Johns (Nova Scotia and Acadia); Treaty of 1760 with the Passamaquody and St. Johns (Nova Scotia); Treaty of 1760 with the Mi'kmaq of Richibucto (Nova Scotia); Treaty of 1761 with the Merimichy (Nova Scotia); Treaty of 1779 with the Merimichy and others (Cape Tormentine to the Bay of Chaleurs) Nova Scotia): R.A. Reiter, *supra* note 2, Part II, chap. V at 5–23. Like the other categories, this one is not exact. For example, one of the earliest peace treaties affecting what is now Canada was concluded in Albany in 1701 between the British and the Five Nations of the Iroquois Confederacy. Conversely, one Maritime peace treaty, in 1794, conveyed to the Indians a small portion of land "for their own use and for the future generations": Treaty Made with Mi'kmaqs on Miramichi, 1794, reproduced in P.A. Cumming and N.H. Mickenberg, eds., *Native Rights in Canada*, 2d ed. (Toronto: Indian-Eskimo Assn. of Canada, 1972) at 308–309.
9. For example, Treaty # 20 of 1818, considered in *Taylor and Williams* (1981), 34 O.R. 360 (O.C.A.). For a summary of these treaties, see R.A. Reiter, *supra* note 2, Part II, chap. V at 29–76.
10. For example, the 1851 Treaty with the Saalequun considered in *R. v. White and Bob* (1964), 50 D.L.R. (2d) 613 (B.C.C.A.), aff'd (1965), 52 D.L.R. (2d) 481n (S.C.C.). For a summary of the fourteen Vancouver Island treaties, see R.A. Reiter, Part II, chap. V at 1–21.
11. Sometimes the cash payment was extraordinarily low. For example, in Treaty No. 38 with the Six Nations in 1834, 22 chiefs were paid only six shillings each for surrendering a total of 50,000 acres of land. In other cases the compensation was in the form of annual payments, annuities, or goods, etc. In some cases smaller areas of land were reserved for the Indians from the parcels surrendered. See summaries in R.A. Reiter, *ibid.* at 1–76.
12. The Robinson-Superior Treaty and the Robinson-Huron Treaty. The latter was considered in *Ontario (A.G.) v. Bear Island Foundation*, [1991] 2 S.C.R. 570.
13. For example, Treaty Number 3, the 1871 "North West Angle Treaty" considered in *St. Catherine's Milling and Lumber Company v. The Queen* (1889), 14 App. Cas. 46 (J.C.P.C.). There were ten other numbered treaties, covering the Prairie provinces and parts of the territories, British Columbia, and Ontario. See A. Morris, *The Treaties of Canada with the Indians of Manitoba and the North-West Territories* (Toronto: Belfords Clark, 1880); Cumming and Mickenberg, *supra* note 2, chap. 14. Also associated with the numbered treaties were two small Ontario "catch-up" treaties, the Williams treaties of 1923.
14. These include the 1975 *James Bay Agreement*, the 1978 *Northeastern Quebec Agreement*, the 1984 *Inuvialuit Agreement*, and the 1993 *Nunavut Agreement*: see further **Chapter 11, Part 7**.
15. A good example is in *Quebec (A.G.) v. Sioui*, [1990] 1 S.C.R. 1025 (S.C.C.), **Part 13**, below, where the Court held that a safe conduct guarantee for the Lorette Hurons constituted a treaty. The guarantee was only one paragraph long and was not signed by the Hurons, but it had been preceded by formal negotiations, and it addressed fundamental issues, such as freedom of movement, customs, trade, and religion.
16. See further **Chapter 11, Part 7**.
17. *Supra* note 8.
18. The Crown made all these commitments in the Treaty of 1752 with the Mi'kmaqs (eastern Nova Scotia), reproduced in P.A. Cumming and N.H. Mickenberg, eds., *Native Rights in Canada*, 2d ed. (Toronto: Indian-Eskimo Assn. of Canada, 1972) at 307–308.
19. *Supra* note 11.
20. **Part 3**, above.
21. Department of Indian and Northern Affairs, *Treaty Agreements between the Indian People and the Sovereign in Right of Canada*, Treaties and Historical Research Centre (Chart), 1979.
22. *Ibid.*
23. *R. v. Johnston* (1966), 56 D.L.R. (2d) 749 (S.C.A.).
24. **Chapter 2**.
25. See *Pawis v. R.* (1979), 102 D.L.R. (3d) 602 at 612 (F.C.T.D.). *Contra*, *R. v. Blackfoot Band of Indians*, [1982] 4 W.W.R. 230 at 238 (F.C.T.D.).
26. See *Bonanza Creek Gold Mining Co. v. The King*, [1916] 1 A.C. 566 at 580 (J.C.P.C.).
27. *St. Catherine's Milling and Lumber Company v. The Queen* (1888), 14 App. Cas. 46 at 60 (J.C.P.C.). See also *R. v. Howard*, [1994] 2 S.C.R. 299 at para. 11.
28. The *St. Catherine's* decision, *ibid.*, implies this at 59. This restriction does not preclude provinces from being parties to Indian treaties between the federal government and Aboriginal people, or from negotiating separate agreements with Aboriginal people on matters under provincial jurisdiction.
29. Hence, an Indian treaty does not require ratification by statute or order-in-council to be valid, unless there is a prior legislative requirement to this effect: *R. v. Howard*, *supra* note 27 at para. 11 (S.C.C.).
30. *Ontario Mining v. Seybold*, [1903] A.C. 73, 82–83 (J.C.P.C.).
31. Unless the federal government were to expropriate the land: for the federal power to expropriate provincial land, see G.V. La Forest, *Natural Resources and Public Property under the Canadian Constitution* (Toronto: University of Toronto Press, 1969) at 150–55.
32. For example, *R. v. Howard*, *supra* note 27. See also *St. Catherines* and *Bear Island* cases.
33. For example, *Taylor and Williams*, *supra* note 9.
34. For example, *R. v. Denny* (1990), 55 C.C.C. (3d) 322 (N.S.C.A.D.).
35. For example, *R. v. White and Bob* (1966), 52 D.L.R. (2d) 481 (B.C.C.A.). Here two Vancouver Island Indians shot deer contrary to a British Columbia wildlife statute. The Court of Appeal said the 1854 treaty was a s. 88 *Indian Act* treaty and thus prevailed over the provincial law. Apart from s. 88, a provincial law enacted directly in relation to an Indian treaty would probably be invalid for invading s. 91(24) of the *Constitution Act, 1867*: see G.V. La Forest, *Natural Resources and Public Property under the Canadian Constitution* (Toronto: University of Toronto Press, 1969) at 178–79. Note that in the Prairie provinces, s. 88 of the *Indian Act* is superseded in part by the *Natural Resources Transfer Agreements*. See **Chapter 6, Parts 4 and 5**.
36. *R. v. Horseman*, [1990] 1 S.C.R. 901 at 936, regarding the *Constitution Act, 1930* that implemented the *Natural Resources Transfer Agreements*.
37. *R. v. Sikyea* (1964), 43 D.L.R. (2d) 150 (N.W.T.C.A.), aff'd (1965), 50 D.L.R. (2d) 80 (S.C.C.); *R. v. Horseman*, [1990] 1 S.C.R. 901 at 936; *R. v. Badger*, [1996] 1 S.C.R. 771 (April 3), 1996 at paras. 46 and 47.
38. **Chapter 6, Part 2** and *R. v. Sikyea*, *ibid.* Mr. Sikyea was a Northwest Territories Treaty 11 Indian charged with killing a migratory bird during closed season, contrary to

regulations under the federal *Migratory Birds Convention Act*, S.C. 1917, c. 18. In his defence, Mr. Sikyea relied on the hunting, fishing, and trapping guarantee in the 1921 treaty. Although his conviction at trial was set aside by the Northwest Territories Supreme Court, it was upheld by the Northwest Territories Court of Appeal and the Supreme Court of Canada. The higher courts ruled that where there was a clear contradiction between federal legislation and an Indian treaty, the legislation must prevail. Their unstated reason was the supremacy of legislation over executive actions such as Indian treaties.

Sikyea made no reference to s. 88 of the *Indian Act*, but the Supreme Court considered this provision in another clash between a treaty hunting right and a *Migratory Birds Convention Act* restriction. *R v. George* (1966), 55 D.L.R. (2d) 386 (S.C.C.). It was argued for Mr. George that s. 88 gave treaties precedence over all laws of general application, both provincial and federal. The Supreme Court of Canada rejected this argument. It said that "laws of general application" in s. 88 refers to provincial laws only. Thus, while treaty rights prevailed over provincial laws of general application, federal laws could prevail over treaty rights.

For laws enacted after April 17, 1982, the situation in *Sikyea* and *George* has changed: see text, *infra*.

39. *R. v. Badger*, [1996] 1 S.C.R. 771 (April 3), 1996 at paras. 73 and 75.
40. *Quebec (A.G.) v. Sioui*, [1990] 1 S.C.R. 1025. Note, however, that this result may be confined to fact situations similar to that in *Sioui*.
41. See *R. v. Badger*, [1996] 1 S.C.R. 771, **Part 15**, below, and (for the *N.R.T.A.*), **Chapter 6, Part 5**.
42. *R. v. Taylor* (1981), 34 O.R. (2d) 360 at 367 (O.C.A.); *Simon v. The Queen* (1985), 24 D.L.R. (4th) 390 at 409 (S.C.C.); *Saanichton Marina Ltd. v. Claxton* (1989), 36 B.C.L.R. (2d) 79 at 84; *Mitchell v. Peguis Indian Band*, [1990] 2 S.C.R. 85 at 142–43; *R. v. Côté* (1993), 107 D.L.R. (4th) 28 at 47 (Q.C.A.); *R. v. Little*, [1995] B.C.J. No. 2633 at para. 39 (B.C.C.A.); *R. v. Badger*, [1996] 1 S.C.R. 771 at para. 42.
43. *Supra* note 40 at 1036.
44. *Sioui*, *ibid.* at 1035–36.
45. *R. v. Badger*, [1996] 1 S.C.R. 771 at para. 52.
46. *Ibid.* at 55.
47. *R. v. Howard*, *supra* note 27 at para. 10 (S.C.C.).
48. *Eastmain Band et al. v. Federal Administrator*, [1993] 1 F.C. 501 at 515–16 (F.C.A.), leave to appeal refused in [1993] 3 S.C.R. vi.
49. **Part 7**, above.
50. *R. v. Badger*, [1996] 1 S.C.R. 771 at para. 41.
51. *Ibid.*
52. *Ibid.* at paras. 73 and 75.
53. *Ibid.* at para. 71.
54. *Ibid.* at para. 89.
55. In *R. v. Simon*, [1985] 1 S.C.R. 387 at 410, **Part 12**, below, the Supreme Court described a treaty as "an enforceable obligation." See also *R. v. Badger*, [1996] 1 S.C.R. 771 at para. 76.
56. See *Henry v. The King*, [1905] 2 Ex. C.R. 417 (Exch. Ct.); *Dreaver v. The King*, unreported, April 10, 1935; and *R. v. Johnston* (1966), 56 D.L.R. (3d) 749 (S.C.A.). For a more recent example of enforcement of treaty rights against third parties, see *Tsawout Indian Band v. Saanichton Marina*, [1989] B.C.J. No. 563 (B.C.C.A.). Here the British Columbia Court of Appeal upheld (i) a declaration that a marina development licence was invalid because it interfered with fishing rights guaranteed in an 1852 Indian treaty, and (ii) an injunction to stop construction on the project.
57. *Ontario (A.G.) v. Bear Island Foundation*, [1991] 2 S.C.R. 570. In *Badger, supra* note 50 at para. 9, Sopinka J. said for himself and Lamer C.J. that "treaties should be interpreted in a manner that maintains the integrity of the Crown, particularly the Crown's fiduciary obligation toward aboriginal peoples." Cory J. for the main majority referred several times (at paras. 41, 47, 78, and 97) to the fact that treaties involve the "honour of the Crown", although he used the phrase in support of a liberal construction or *Sparrow* approach (*R. v. Sparrow*, [1990] 1 S.C.R. 1075: **Chapter 7, Part 4**) to the treaty provisions rather than a specific enforceable fiduciary duty: see also **Part 15**, below and **Chapter 8, Part 7**.
58. *Ibid.*
59. See the contract analogies considered at first instance in *Re Paulette and Registrar of Titles (No. 2)* (1974), 39 D.L.R. (3d) 45 (N.W.T.S.C.). This decision was reversed on other grounds in (1976), 63 D.L.R. (3d) 1; and (1976), 72 D.L.R. (3d) 160 (S.C.C.). The Supreme Court noted the possible relevance of the concept of fundamental mistake in *Simon*, [1985] 2 S.C.R. 387, 404, but found it unnecessary to consider this further.
60. See further, **Chapter 12, Part 5**.
61. Draft Legal Text, proposed ss. 35.1 to 35.5 of *Constitution Act, 1982*. The parties to the agreement would have comprised the federal government, relevant groups of Aboriginal people, and the relevant provincial government(s).
62. *Ibid.*, proposed s. 35.2(7) of *Constitution Act, 1982*.
63. *Ibid.*, proposed s. 35.6(1).
64. *Ibid.*, proposed s. 35.6(2).
65. *Ibid.*, proposed s. 91A of *Constitution Act, 1867*.
66. See further, **Chapter 12, Part 5(c)**.
67. *R. v. Badger*, [1996] 1 S.C.R. 771 at para. 52.
68. For example, the "non-territorial" guarantee considered in *Quebec (A.G.) v. Sioui*, *supra* note 40 and **Part 13**, below.
69. *Ibid.*
70. See R. Fumoleau, *As Long as This Land Shall Last: A History of Treaty 8 and Treaty 11, 1870–1939* (Toronto: McClelland & Stewart, 1973); Treaty 7 Elders and Tribal Council with H. Carter et al., *The True Spirit and Original Intent of Treaty 7* (McGill-Queens: Montreal and Kingston, 1966); *Report*, vol. 1, chap. 6, s. 5 at 173–76.
71. For example, the agriculture provisions, especially inappropriate for nomadic peoples and in northern Canada.
72. For example, the failure to create reserves under Treaties 8 and 11. For a dramatic and disheartening illustration of this and of many of the other problems mentioned here, see R. Fumoleau, *As Long as This Land Shall Last* (Toronto: McClelland & Stewart, 1973). See further *Report*, vol. 1, chap. 6, s. 6 at 176–78.
73. "Government actors and the Métis themselves **[in early Manitoba]** viewed the Indians as a separate group with different historical entitlements": *R. v. Blais*, [2003] 2 S.C.R. 236 at para. 21.
74. See *infra*, notes 76 and 77.
75. The Supreme Court noted in Blais, *supra* note 73, at para. 34 that:

    > This perceived difference between the Crown's obligations to Indians and its relationship with the Métis was reflected in separate arrangements for the distribution of land. Different legal and political regimes governed the conclusion of Indian treaties and the allocation of Métis scrip. Indian treaties were concluded on a collective basis and entailed collective rights, whereas scrip entitled recipients to individual grants of land.

76. Section 31 of *Manitoba Act*, 1870 purported to extinguish "the Indian Title to the lands in the Province" and appropriated 1.4 million acres for distribution to the children of half-breed heads of families. However, it was an administrative disaster. Distribution of the benefits was delayed, so that many non-native settlers got the best lands first; land was distributed in individual lots rather than in the blocks favoured by the Métis. The Métis' negotiable certificates of entitlement to land ("scrip") ended up being

sold in large numbers to speculators. See **Chapter 1, Part 3**, note 51.

77. Treaty 8 contained a scrip option for Métis. This scrip was at first non-negotiable, but then became negotiable, and much was sold to speculators at a fraction of its value. In 1944, Indian Affairs officials removed 700 people from the Treaty 8 list because they had non-native fathers or grandfathers, causing massive dislocation. Most of the affected people were later returned to the Treaty. See P.A. Cumming and N.H. Mickenberg, *Native Rights in Canada*, 2d ed. (Toronto: Indian-Eskimo Association of Canada, 1972) at 202–204.
78. Compare, for example, the different per capita land allotments even among the numbered treaties: Department of Indian and Northern Affairs, *Treaty Agreements between the Indian People and the Sovereign in Right of Canada*, Treaties and Historical Research Centre (Chart), 1979.
79. See *Ontario (A.G.) v. Bear Island Foundation*, [1991] 2 S.C.R. 570 at 575, where the Court held that whatever the original signatory situation, the Temagami had subsequently adhered to the treaty by their actions.
80. An issue considered but not decided in *Ontario (A.G.) v. Bear Island Foundation* (1989), 58 D.L.R. (4th) 117 (O.C.A.), aff'd on different grounds in [1991] 2 S.C.R. 570 at 575.
81. *Simon v. The Queen*, [1985] 2 S.C.R. 387, rev'g 134 D.L.R. (3d) 76 (N.S.S.C.A.D.).
82. *Simon v. The Queen*, [1985] 2 S.C.R. 387 at 402.
83. *Ibid.* at 404.
84. *Quebec (A.G.) v. Sioui*, [1990] 1 S.C.R. 1025 (S.C.C.), aff'g [1987] R.J.Q. 1722 (Q.C.A.), which rev'd the decision of Desjardins J. (Q.S.C.), J.E. 85-947.
85. R.S.C. 1985, c. I-5 (formerly R.S.C. 1970, c. I-6).
86. *Simon v. The Queen*, [1985], 2 S.C.R. 387.
87. In *Sioui* the Court was able to use historical evidence outside the text to help determine the document's treaty status and the meaning of its commitments. Where historical evidence is absent, courts may be unable to do this. In the "bird's eye maple" case, for example, the New Brunswick Court of Appeal considered a reference to "Lawful Occasions" in an official's treaty-based promise. They held that in the absence of evidence of the historical context of the treaty, they could not infer a treaty right to harvest timber on Crown lands: *R. v. Peter Paul* (1998), 158 D.L.R. (4th) 231 (N.B.C.A.); varying (1997), 153 D.L.R. (4th) 131 (N.B.Q.B.); varying (1996), 145 D.L.R. (4th) 472 (N.B. Prov. Ct.). In *R. v. Peter Paul*, [1998] S.C.C.A. No. 298, November 5, 1998 (no reasons), the Supreme Court denied leave to appeal the New Brunswick Court of Appeal's decision.
88. *Ontario (A.G.) v. Bear Island Foundation*, [1991] 1 S.C.R. 570, aff'g (1989), 58 D.L.R. (4th) 117 (O.C.A.), which aff'd (1984), 15 D.L.R. (4th) 321 (O.H.C.).
89. *Ontario (A.G.) v. Bear Island Foundation*, [1991] 1 S.C.R. 570. The trial judge had said there was no Aboriginal right, and even if there were, it would have been extinguished either by virtue of the Temagami's participation in the treaty or by the treaty unilaterally: (1984), 15 D.L.R. (4th) 321 (O.H.C.). The Ontario Court of Appeal were even less willing to commit themselves. They started by assuming that the Aboriginal title existed. On this assumption, they said the right had been extinguished either (i) by virtue of the Temagami's participation in the treaty as signatories, (ii) by virtue of the Temagami's later adherence to the treaty; or (iii) by the treaty unilaterally: (1989), 58 D.L.R. (4th) 117.
90. *Ibid.* at 574–75.
91. *Ibid.*
92. *R. v. Sparrow*, [1990] 1 S.C.R. 1075.
93. *Ibid.*
94. *R. v. Badger*, [1996] 1 S.C.R. 771, (i) allowing the appeal of Ernest Clarence Ominayak and dismissing the appeals of Wayne Clarence Badger and Leroy Steven Kiyawasew: from [1993] 5 W.W.R. 7 (A.C.A.); aff'g a judgment of the Court of Queen's Bench aff'g the appellants' convictions for offences under the Alberta *Wildlife Act*; and (ii) directing a new trial for Ernest Clarence Ominayak.
95. See also **Chapter 6, Part 5**.
96. See also **Chapter 6, Part 6** and (for s. 35(1)), **Chapter 7**.
97. *Ibid.*
98. *R. v. Badger*, *supra* note 94, per Cory, La Forest, L'Heureux-Dubé, Gonthier, and Iacobucci JJ. Speaking for himself and Lamer C.J., Sopinka J. felt that the Treaty 8 rights had merged into the *N.R.T.A.*, which became the sole source of the rights (*ibid.* at paras. 2, 7, and 8). He said that the infringement / justification test applied in *R. v. Sparrow*, [1990] 1 S.C.R. 1075 to s. 35(1) of the *Constitution Act, 1982* (**Chapter 7, Part 4**) could be applied by analogy to the *N.R.T.A.* itself: paras. 13 and 14.
99. *Ibid.* at para. 41.
100. *Ibid.* at para. 51.
101. *Ibid.*
102. *Ibid.* at paras. 45–46. (This restriction also applied to the trapping and fishing rights referred to in the *N.R.T.A.*.)
103. *Ibid.*
104. *Ibid.* at para. 49.
105. *Ibid.* at para. 51.
106. *Ibid.* at para. 51.
107. This is where Sopinka J., for himself, and Lamer C.J., parted company from the main majority. Sopinka J. and Lamer J. felt that the *N.R.T.A.* had completely replaced the treaty rights, and suggested that a *Sparrow*-type test could be applied to determine if there had been unjustified infringement of the *N.R.T.A.*: *supra* note 94 at paras. 1–19.
108. See **Chapter 7, Part 4**.
109. *Ibid.* at para. 76.
110. *Ibid.* at para. 82. In Cory J.'s view, "it is equally if not more important to justify *prima facie* infringements of treaty rights."
111. For example, there was no category of licence suitable to Indian hunting for food (Cory J. dismissed a "subsistence" category as too restrictive), the Indians were given no preferential access to the limited supply of licences, and they were forced to pay in order to carry on a guaranteed treaty right: *ibid.* at para. 92.
112. Para. 41. Indeed, Cory J. said at para. 52 that treaties "must be interpreted in the sense that they would naturally have been understood by the Indians at the time of the signing...." Arguably, though, he was *not* suggesting that treaties must be interpreted *only* as the Indians would have understood them. Treaties were supposed to be bilateral arrangements, which involved both Indian and government perspectives. Instead, Cory J. was probably stressing that the Indian perspective at the time must be considered fully, and must not concealed or obscured by technical meanings or "rigid modern rules of construction": para. 52.
113. *R. v. Marshall*, [1999] 3 S.C.R. 456; rev'g. (1997), 159 N.S.R. (2d) 186, 468 A.P.R. 186, 146 D.L.R. (4th) 257, [1997] 3 C.N.L.R. 209, [1997] N.S.J. No. 131 (QL); which aff'd. [1996] N.S.J. No. 246 (QL. Provincial Court), convicting the accused of three offences under the federal *Fisheries Act*. See also [1999] 3 S.C.R. 533, motion for rehearing and stay of *R. v. Marshall*, September 17, 1999, reasons delivered by Lamer C.J. and L'Heureux-Dubé, Gonthier, McLachlin, Iacobucci and Binnie JJ.

    For commentary, see C. Bell and K. Buss, "The Promise of Marshall on the Prairies: A Framework for Analyzing Unfulfilled Treaty Promises" (2000) 63 Sask. L. Rev. 667; D. G. Bell, "Forum on *R. v. Marshall*: Was Amerindian Dispossession Lawful? The Response of 19th-Century Maritime Intellectuals" (2000) 23 Dal. L. J. 168; W.H. Hurlburt, "Case Comment on *R. v. Marshall*" (2000) 38 Alta. L. Rev. 563; T. Isaac, "The Courts, Government, and Public Policy: The Significance of *R. v. Marshall*"

(2000) 63 Sask. L. Rev. 701; R. Normey, "Angling for 'Common Intention': Treaty Interpretation in *R. v. Marshall*" (2000) 63 Sask. L. Rev. 646; L.I. Rotman, "'My Hovercraft Is Full of Eels': Smoking out the Message in *R. v. Marshall*" (2000) 63 Sask. L. Rev. 617; P. M. Saunders, "Getting Their Feet Wet: The Supreme Court and Practical Implementation of Treaty Rights in the *Marshall* Case" (2000) 23 Dal. L.J. 48; P.D. Palmater, "Forum on *R. v. Marshall*: An Empty Shell of a Treaty Promise: *R. v. Marshall* and the Rights of Non-Status Indians" (2000) 23 Dal. L.J. 102; J.P. McEvoy, "*Marshall v. Canada*: Lessons from Wisconsin" (2001) 12 N.J.C.L. 85; B. Edwards, "Case Comment on *R. v. Marshall*" (2001) 59 U.T. Fac. L. Rev. 107.

114. *R. v. Marshall*, [1999] 3 S.C.R. 456 at paras. 1 and 62.
115. *Ibid.* at para. 71.
116. Here (e.g., at paras. 11 and 81) the Court drew on the liberal approach to extrinsic evidence taken in *R. v. Taylor and Williams* (1981), 62 C.C.C. (2d) 227 at 236 (Ont. C.A.) (leave to appeal dismissed, [1981] 2 S.C.R. xi); *R. v. Sioui*, [1990] 1 S.C.R. 1025 at 1045; *R. v. Badger*, [1996] 1 S.C.R. 771 at para. 52; and (in the context of Aboriginal rights cases) *Delgamuukw v. British Columbia*, [1997] 3 S.C.R. 1010 at para. 87. At the same time (e.g., at paras. 13 and 81), the Court rejected the more restrictive approach to extrinsic evidence in *R. v. Horse*, [1988] 1 S.C.R. 187 at 210.
117. *Ibid.* at para. 97.
118. *Ibid.* at para. 58. See also para. 97.
119. *Ibid.* at paras. 25 and 102.
120. *Ibid.* at para. 101.
121. *Ibid.* (for example), paras. 102 and 112. At para. 112, McLachlin J., dissenting, added that "[t]o proceed from a right undefined in scope or modern counterpart to the question of justification would be to render treaty rights inchoate and the justification of limitations impossible."
122. *Rehearing Motion Judgement (R. v. Marshall)*, [1999] 3 S.C.R. 533, motion for rehearing and stay of *R. v. Marshall*, September 17, 1999.
123. *Ibid.* at paras. 18 and 38.
124. The Court said that things traditionally gathered would include wild fruit and berries, but not logging, or mining minerals or offshore natural gas deposits: *ibid.* at paras. 20 and 38.

    See also *R. v. Bernard*, 2003 NBBA 305 (C.A.). Here a majority of the New Brunswick Court of Appeal held that Mr. Joshua Bernard, a Mi'kmaq Indian from the Eel Ground reserve, had a treaty right to harvest and sell timber growing on Crown lands traditionally occupied by the Mirimachi Mi'kmaq. The Court held that the right was derived from the Mirimachi Treaty of 1761, had not been extinguished, and had been unjustifiably infringed by a provincial law that banned unauthorized possession of timber from Crown lands. The majority also held that the treaty right was not limited to the kinds of resources that were traditionally traded at the time of the treaty. The Supreme Court heard an appeal from this decision on January 17–18, 2005 and reserved its decision.
125. Para. 19 (referring to treaty rights in general).
126. (Thus it would not be infringed by government regulation that did permit a moderate livelihood): *ibid.* at paras. 36 and 37.
127. *Ibid.* at para. 3. (Government had elected not to try to justify a closed season on the eel fishery in this case.)
128. *Ibid.* at para. 21.
129. See, for example, *Benoit v. Canada*, 2003 FCA 236 (11 June, 2003), rev'g. 2002 FCT 243, leave to appeal to S.C.C. refused with costs and without reasons, [2004] S.C.C.A. No. 387, April 29, 2004. In Benoit, the Federal Court of Appeal suggested that the fact of oral Aboriginal evidence should not lead a judge to neglect written evidence. The Court of Appeal described the written evidence relating to Treaty 8 as "voluminous": para. 115. It concluded that the entire record, oral and written, did not support the trial judge's conclusion that Treaty 8 Indians had been promised an absolute immunity from taxation: paras. 117–19.
130. This was a contentious issue in *R. v. Bernard*, [2003] NBCA 55, notice of appeal to Supreme Court of Canada filed May 13, 2004, [2004] S.C.C.A. No. 467.
131. Canadian Press Newstext, "Burnt Church Natives Reach Agreement with Ottawa on Lobster Fishery", August 1, 2002, online: QL (CP02).
132. Minister of Indian and Northern Affairs, Backgrounder, *Key Elements of an Agreement-in-Principle for a Comprehensive Fisheries Agreement with Burnt Church*, August, 2002 <http://www.ainc-inac.gc.ca/index_e.html>; Canadian Press Newstext, *ibid.*
133. *Haida Nation v. British Columbia (Minister of Forests*, 2004 SCC 73, dismissing an appeal by the Crown and allowing an appeal by Weyerhaeuser Co. from [2002] 6 W.W.R. 243 (B.C.C.A.) with supplementary reasons in (2002), 10 W.W.R. 587 (B.C.C.A.) rev'g[2001] 2 C.N.L.R. 83 (B.C.S.C.).
134. *Ibid.* at paras. 19 and 20.

6 Legislative Jurisdiction

Chapter Highlights

- The relationship of Aboriginal interests to legislative jurisdiction is governed by five main sets of legal rules, each modifying those that precede them. They are as follows:
  - The principle of sovereignty of Parliament permits statutes to prevail over Aboriginal common law or prerogative interests, and above those interests in earlier or more general statutes.
  - The *Constitution Act, 1867* gives provincial legislatures powers that can affect Indians in some situations, subject to exclusive federal jurisdiction under s. 91(24) of the Act.
  - Section 88 of the *Indian Act* permits some provincial laws to affect Indians in circumstances in which these laws would normally be unconstitutional.
  - The *Natural Resources Transfer Agreements* empower the legislatures of the Prairie provinces to regulate Indian harvesting, subject to special protections for Indians.
  - Section 35(1) of the *Constitution Act, 1982* recognizes and affirms "the existing Aboriginal and treaty rights of the Aboriginal peoples of Canada."
- The job of making sense of these rules and their interrelationships has been given to the courts.

Synopsis

Since each of the sets of rules referred to above modifies those that precede them, the scope of one can affect the scope of the others. This, in turn, affects the degree to which an Aboriginal interest is affected by the legislative jurisdiction of the federal, provincial, or territorial legislatures. As a result, the legal effect of an Aboriginal interest can depend on a host of external factors, including geographical location, the presence of provincial enactments, and even the date of the legislation in question. How the courts have interpreted this complex constitutional framework is the subject of this chapter.

Selected Readings

🖹 links material in this chapter to the corresponding headings and page numbers of the relevant readings.

🖹 Entire Chapter	Some Provisions Relevant to Legislative Jurisdiction	299
🖹 Part 7	*Cardinal v. Alberta (A.G.)*	300
🖹 Part 8	*Dick v. The Queen*	304
🖹 Part 9	*Delgamuukw*	310
🖹 Part 10	*Kitkatla Band v. British Columbia (Minister of Small Business, Tourism, and Culture)*	311

1. OVERVIEW

The capacity of Canadian legislatures to affect Aboriginal peoples is governed by (a) the principle of Parliamentary sovereignty; (b) the *Constitution Act, 1867*; (c) s. 88 of *Indian Act*; (d) the *Natural Resources Transfer Agreements*; and (e) s. 35(1) of the *Constitution Act, 1982*. The rules that apply at each of these five main structural levels are subject to modifications or restrictions imposed at levels that follow them. All these rules are subject to interpretation and elaboration by the courts.

2. LEVEL ONE: STATUTES AND PARLIAMENTARY SOVEREIGNTY

At the most general level, in the absence of formal constitutional provisions to the contrary, the principle of sovereignty of Parliament has two main legal consequences. It permits statutes to prevail over the common law and over the royal prerogative power, and it permits newer or more specific legislation to prevail over that which is older or more general. Apart from statutes or constitutional provisions, the main legal basis for Aboriginal rights is the common law, while the main legal basis for Indian treaties is the royal prerogative power. Subject to formal constitutional provisions, then,[1] statutes can prevail over common law-based Aboriginal rights[2] and over common law-defined treaty rights.[3] However, a number of formal constitutional provisions affect this general situation.

3. LEVEL TWO: *CONSTITUTION ACT, 1867*

The *Constitution Act, 1867*[4] divides legislative jurisdiction between Parliament and the ten provincial legislatures. Section 91(24) of the *Constitution Act, 1867* gives Parliament exclusive legislative jurisdiction over "Indians, and lands reserved for the Indians".

As seen in **Chapter 2**, the term "Indians" presumably includes Indians under the federal *Indian Act*; includes the Inuit; and may include Métis.[5] The phrase "lands reserved for the Indians" includes both *Indian Act* reserves and lands reserved for the Indians in other provisions, such as the Royal Proclamation of 1763.[6] Because s. 91(24) contains two distinct heads of jurisdiction, federal power in relation to "Indians" is not limited to "lands reserved for the Indians", and power in relation to these lands is not limited to Indians.

As there is a general presumption that executive capacity follows legislative authority under the *Constitution Act, 1876*,[7] s. 91(24) gives rise to a corresponding federal capacity to negotiate Indian treaties.[8] However, for "lands reserved for the Indians", there is no such presumption regarding proprietary rights.[9] This is because s. 109 of the *Constitution Act, 1867* expressly confers full or residual ownership of pre-Confederation public lands on the provinces.[10]

As noted, the subject matters of s. 91(24) are under "exclusive" federal jurisdiction. Moreover, the opening words of s. 91 make it clear that the legislative authority of Parliament is supreme in its exclusive areas. On the other hand, the *Constitution Act, 1867* gives the provincial legislatures powers over a range of important subjects that are capable of affecting Indians or lands reserved for the Indians.[11] Also, s. 91(24) confers a power, rather than imposing a duty,[12] and that power has not been fully exercised.[13]

How do provincial laws fit into this jurisdictional scheme?

(a) Validity

Although s. 91(24) gives special authority to Parliament, the Supreme Court rejects the view that s. 91(24) creates sealed enclaves of federal power.[14] Instead, there is a "basic assumption" that Aboriginal peoples can be affected by provincial laws.[15] If there is no conflicting federal law, an otherwise valid provincial law can validly affect Indians or lands reserved for the Indians, as long as it is not "in relation to" either of these two branches of s. 91(24).[16] For example, a provincial labour law can regulate the labour relations of a band-owned Indian business on a reserve.[17]

(b) Inoperativeness

An otherwise valid provincial law that is inconsistent with a federal law is inoperative to the extent of the conflict.[18] Where there is no inconsistency, an otherwise valid provincial law is not inoperative, even where a federal law incorporates it by reference and provides for different penalties.[19]

(c) Inapplicability

An otherwise valid provincial law cannot impair the core aspects of the federal powers in s. 91(24) of the *Constitution Act, 1867*.[20] Thus an otherwise valid provincial law cannot impair the status or capacity of Indians as Indians (i.e., their "Indianness").[21] If a provincial law (i) is based only on the provincial jurisdiction provisions of the *Constitution Act, 1867*,[22] and (ii) has the *effect* but *not the purpose* of impairing s. 91(24) Indianness, that law will be inapplicable to Indians.[23] For example, a provincial game conservation and safety law that uniformally regulates all hunting, including Aboriginal hunting, might be held to have the effect but not the purpose of impairing Indianness.[24] If it is severable, the remainder of this law will be valid in regard to non-Indians.[25]

Indianness includes features that are central to who Indians are, such as Aboriginal rights.[26] A core attribute is "impaired" if it is ended[27] or significantly restricted.[28]

There appears to be a similar core of "Indian landness", reached where a provincial law impairs Indians' right of possession in reserve lands.[29]

(d) Invalidity

Provincial laws that single out Indians or lands reserved for the Indians for special treatment,[30] or have the purpose of impairing the status or capacity of Indians[31] or Indian reserved land,[32] are "in relation to" Indians and are wholly invalid.

4. LEVEL THREE: SECTION 88 OF *INDIAN ACT*

The formal distribution of legislative power in the Canadian federal system is entrenched in constitutional enactments such as the *Constitution Act, 1867*. It cannot be altered unilaterally by an ordinary statute of Parliament or a provincial legislature. However, one level of government can enact laws that incorporate laws of the other level as if they had been enacted by the first.

Parliament did this in 1951 when it enacted s. 88 (then numbered 87) of the *Indian Act*:[33]

> Subject to the terms of any treaty and any other Act of the Parliament of Canada, all laws of general application from time to time in force in any province are applicable to and in respect of Indians in the province, except to the extent that such laws are inconsistent with this Act or any order, rule, regulation or by-law made thereunder, and except to the extent that such laws make provision for any matter for which provision is made by or under this Act.

Section 88 applies only to *Indian Act* registered Indians and Indian band members,[34] not to other Indians or to Métis or Inuit.[35] If the subject matter were not *Indian Act* Indians, but lands reserved for the Indians, would s. 88 apply? The Supreme Court has not resolved this question unequivocally.[36]

The Supreme Court has said that the "laws of general application" to which s. 88 applies[37] are provincial, not federal laws.[38] These provincial laws are subordinate to: (i) inconsistent federal laws; (ii) inconsistent treaty provisions;[39] and (iii) provisions in or under[40] the *Indian Act* on the same subject matter.

A more difficult question is the nature of the provincial laws of general application to which s. 88 refers. Does s. 88 merely re-state the laws regarding federal paramountcy? Or does it "rescue" some provincial laws that would otherwise be invalid or inapplicable? If so, which provincial laws are rescued? In *Dick*, considered in **Part 8**, below, the Supreme Court took the latter approach. It held that s. 88 rescues provincial laws with uniform territorial application whose effect, *but not purpose*, is to impair Indianness.[41]

Summarizing the effect of *Dick* and other case law, the Supreme Court described the general character of s. 88 in *R. v. Côté*:[42]

> ...[section] 88 presently serves two distinct purposes. First, s. 88 serves an important jurisdictional purpose. Through the operation of the provision, provincial laws which would otherwise not apply to Indians under the federal and provincial division of powers are made applicable as incorporated federal law.... Second, s. 88 accords federal statutory protection to aboriginal treaty rights. The application of such generally applicable provincial laws through federal incorporation is expressly made "[s]ubject to the terms of any treaty." Section 88 accords a special statutory protection to aboriginal treaty rights from contrary provincial law through the operation of the doctrine of federal paramountcy.

Section 88 can be superseded by special constitutional provisions, such as the *Natural Resources Transfer Agreements*. However, s. 88 will still have effect where these provisions do not apply specifically. For example, a Prairie provincial resource protection law that does not involve game conservation may be invalid if it violates treaty rights contrary to s. 88.[43] Moreover, even if a provincial infringement of treaty rights were justified under

s. 35(1) of the *Constitution Act, 1982*, the law in question might still be held invalid under s. 88.[44]

The *Northwest Territories* Act,[45] the *Nunavut Act*,[46] and the *Yukon Act*[47] contain provisions that resemble s.88,[48] but refer to Inuit as well as Indians. Note that territorial legislative powers are subordinate to federal legislation and to provisions of land claims agreements in the territories.[49]

5. LEVEL FOUR: *NATURAL RESOURCES TRANSFER AGREEMENTS*

The three structural levels described above are further modified in the Prairie provinces. The *Natural Resources Transfer Agreements* (or *N.R.T.A.*) contained in the *Constitution Act, 1930*[50] give the legislatures of Alberta, Saskatchewan, and Manitoba special regulatory powers in relation to Indian game rights, provided that they do not interfere with specified kinds of Indian game subsistence harvesting.[51] The relevant provision of the *Manitoba Natural Resources Transfer Agreement* is s. 13:[52]

> In order to secure to the Indians of the Province the continuance of the supply of game and fish for their support and subsistence, Canada agrees that the laws respecting game in force in the Province from time to time shall apply to the Indians within the boundaries thereof, provided, however, that the said Indians shall have the right, which the Province hereby assures to them, of hunting, trapping and fishing game and fish for food at all seasons of the year on all unoccupied Crown lands and on any other lands to which the said Indians may have a right of access.

The Supreme Court has held that the "laws respecting game" in the *N.R.T.A.* are provincial, not federal laws.[53] In the *Cardinal* case, considered below, the Court addressed the relationship between the *N.R.T.A.* and the *Constitution Act, 1867*, and the meaning of "access" lands. In several other decisions, it has elaborated on the nature and extent of the harvesting rights permitted.[54] *Badger* established that the *N.R.T.A.* modified but did not replace hunting rights in the numbered treaties on the Prairies.[55]

The Court summarized the general intent and effect of the *N.R.T.A.* in *R. v. Blais*.[56] Referring to the Manitoba *N.R.T.A.*, it said:

> The broad purpose of the *NRTA* was to transfer control over land and natural resources to the three western provinces.
>
> ...
>
> The purpose of para. 13 of the *NRTA* is to ensure respect for the Crown's obligations to "Indians" with respect to hunting rights. It was enacted to protect the hunting rights of the beneficiaries of Indian treaties and the *Indian Act* in the context of the transfer of Crown land to the provinces. It took away the right to hunt commercially while protecting the right to hunt for food and expanding the territory upon which this could take place....[57]

The Court went on to hold that s. 13 had not been intended to include Métis.[58]

The *Northwest Territories* Act,[59] the *Nunavut Act*,[60] and the *Yukon Act*[61] contain provisions that resemble the *N.R.T.A.*,[62] but refer to Inuit as well as Indians. Unlike provincial laws, territorial statutes are subordinate to federal legislation, and to provisions of relevant land claims agreements.[63]

6. LEVEL FIVE: SECTION 35(1) OF *CONSTITUTION ACT, 1982*

All legislation under the above structures is subject to an additional restriction contained in s. 35(1) of the *Constitution Act, 1982*.[64] In *Sparrow*, the Supreme Court found that s. 35(1) guarantees "existing" Aboriginal rights[65] against unjustified governmental infringement.[66] Conversely, otherwise valid government action can in some cases constitute either a justified infringement of s. 35(1) rights or a permissible restriction on s. 35(1) rights.[67] In *Badger*, the Court held that the *Sparrow* test also applies to treaty rights, including treaty rights that were modified by the *Natural Resources Transfer Agreements*.[68] "Existing" rights are rights that were unextinguished as of April 17, 1982, the date on which most of the *Constitution Act, 1982*, including s. 5(1), was proclaimed in force.

How does s. 35(1) relate to other main levels of the constitutional framework? For example, can a provincial law extinguish, infringe, or otherwise affect s. 35(1) Aboriginal rights without being legislation "in relation to" s. 91(24) of the *Constitution Act, 1867*? Can s. 88 rescue provincial extinguishment or infringement that would be invalid because of s. 91(24) of the *Constitution Act, 1867*? How will public laws relate to Aboriginal laws that are protected by s. 35(1)?[69] How does s. 35(1) relate to s. 88? Does s. 88 require s. 35(1) justification, and if so, is it justifiable? If s. 88 can affect Aboriginal rights, can it also affect Aboriginal title? If a provincial law can justifiably infringe a s. 35(1) treaty right, can the law still be declared invalid because of conflict with the s. 88 treaty guarantee?[70] Some — but not all — of these questions were addressed in *Delgamuukw*, below.[71]

7. *CARDINAL*[72]

Reading 6(b) at p. 300

The foundations for much of the law on the *Natural Resources Transfer Agreements* and the relationship between s. 91(24) of the *Constitution Act, 1867* and provincial laws were laid in the 1974 Cardinal decision. Mr. Cardinal, an Alberta treaty Indian, had sold moose meat on a reserve to a non-Indian. Mr. Cardinal was charged with trafficking in big game, contrary to a provincial *Wildlife Act*. Mr. Cardinal was acquitted by the magistrate and the Alberta Supreme Court, but his acquittal was overturned by the Appellate Division of the Alberta Supreme Court and the Supreme Court of Canada. Mr. Cardinal argued that this was solely a federal matter under the *Constitution Act, 1867*, both before and after the *N.R.T.A.*

Did the *Natural Resources Transfer Agreements*[73] permit the Prairie provinces to legislate in regard to the game rights of Indians on reserves? More specifically, are Indian reserves "lands to which the Indians may have a right of access" under the *Natural Resources Transfer Agreements*? If the answer was yes, the *Agreements* permitted Prairie provinces to regulate hunting for commercial purposes on reserves. To answer these questions, the Supreme Court looked at the general constitutional situation under the *Constitution Act, 1867* before it had been modified for the Prairie provinces by the *Natural Resources Transfer Agreements*.

For the majority, the general situation under the *Constitution Act, 1867* was *not* one in which s. 91(24) built a jurisdictional wall around Indian reserves, shutting out all provincial legislation.[74] However, they felt there were *some* kinds of provincial laws on reserves that would have been *qua* Indians, were it not for the *Natural Resources Transfer Agreements*.[75] Compare this with the approach of the dissenting judges, who applied an "enclave theory" of interpretation to s. 91(24).[76] Although the enclave theory was rejected, it does not follow that provincial jurisdiction affecting Indians is unlimited. Trying to determine the precise limits of this jurisdiction — under the *Constitution Act, 1867*; s. 88 of the *Indian Act*; and the *Natural Resources Transfer Agreements* — has proved to be an extraordinarily difficult challenge.

8. *DICK*[77]

Reading 6(c) at p. 304

Mr. Arthur Dick and four companions shot a deer for food at Holdon Lake in British Columbia. Mr. Dick was a non-treaty Indian, a member of the Alkali Band, and a resident of the Alkali Lake Reserve. Holdon Lake is located outside the reserves but within the traditional hunting grounds of the Alkali Lake Band. Mr. Dick was charged with killing wildlife and possession of dead wildlife, contrary to the provincial *Wildlife Act*.[78] He was convicted by a provincial court judge, and his conviction was upheld by a majority of the British Columbia Court of Appeal, by a County Court judge, and by the Supreme Court of Canada.[79]

In *Cardinal*,[80] the Supreme Court had said that under the *Constitution Act, 1867*, while some provincial laws can affect Indians without being invalid, other provincial laws relate to Indians, *qua* Indians, and are considered to interfere with exclusive federal legislative jurisdiction under s. 91(24). In *Kruger and Manuel v. The Queen*,[81] the Court had said that at least one kind of provincial law that can apply to Indians is a law of general application. It described this as a law with uniform territorial application that does not impair Indian status or capacity. Since the provincial law in *Kruger* met these criteria, the Court felt it unnecessary to determine if the law were valid on its own, or if s. 88 of the *Indian Act* had referentially incorporated it as a federal law. Thus, *Kruger* left the role of s. 88 unresolved. It also failed to clarify if a law with the *effect* of impairing Indian status or capacity could qualify as a law of general application for the purposes of s. 88.[82] If it could not, it was difficult to see how s. 88 could referentially incorporate anything.

With this background, *Dick* promised to be a complex decision, and the Supreme Court lived up to the promise. The Court rejected the interpretation given to *Kruger* by Lambert J.A., dissenting, in the British Columbia Court of Appeal. The Supreme Court said that s. 88 rescues provincial laws of uniform territorial application that have the effect but not the purpose of impairing Indian status or capacity. In the situation at hand, the Court was prepared to assume that the *Wildlife Act* had the effect of impairing Indianness.[83] However, since it was not shown that the Act had the purpose of doing this (i.e., that it had the policy of singling out Indians for special treatment or otherwise impairing their status or capacity), it was a law of general application that was saved by s. 88.

Clearly, *Dick* increases the kinds of provincial laws that can apply to Indians. On the other hand, these rescued provincial laws exist only at federal, and, in some cases, Indian sufferance.

9. *DELGAMUUKW*[84]

Readings 6(d) at p. 310

In *Delgamuukw*[85] the Gitksan and Wet'suwet'en people argued in the Supreme Court of Canada that they had rights of Aboriginal title and Aboriginal self-government in regard to over 22,000 square miles (56,980 square kilometres) of west central British Columbia. One question before the Court was whether a province could extinguish Aboriginal rights before the enactment of the *Constitution Act, 1982*, either on its own authority or through the operation of s. 88 of the *Indian Act*.[86] Speaking for the majority, and probably for the entire Court,[87] Lamer C.J. answered "no" to both aspects of the question.

In the first situation, Lamer C.J. said that a provincial law that purported to extinguish Aboriginal rights would either be "in relation to" the lands reserved for the Indians in s. 91(24) of the *Constitution Act, 1867*,[88] or would interfere with the central core of "Indianness" at the heart of this section.[89] He said that this is because Aboriginal title and other Aboriginal rights tied to land are part of the "lands reserved for the Indians" jurisdiction in s. 91(24),[90] and because Aboriginal rights not tied to land are part of the "Indians" jurisdiction in s. 91(24).[91]

Lamer C.J. said this situation would not be changed if the laws in question were provincial laws of general application operating independently of s. 88 of the *Indian Act*. Such laws can only affect the subject matter of s. 91(24) if they (i) do not single out Indians for special treatment or (ii) are otherwise in relation to the subject matter of s. 91(24).[92] Since entrenchment requires a clear and plain intent to extinguish, any provincial law meeting this test would single out Indians for special treatment.[93] As well, such a law would interfere with the core of Indianness.[94]

Finally, Lamer C.J. rejected the argument that a provincial law of general application that purported to extinguish Aboriginal rights could be saved by s. 88 of the *Indian Act*. In his view, s. 88 "does not evince the requisite clear and plain intent to extinguish Aboriginal rights."[95] An alternative possible reason, not used by Lamer C.J. in this context, is that because s. 88 rescues only those provincial laws of general application that have the effect but not the purpose of interfering with Indianness, any provincial act with the "clear and plain intent" necessary to extinguish Aboriginal rights would be excluded because of its purpose of interfering with Indianness.

The clear and plain intent requirement applies only to extinguishment. Lamer J. said in *Delgamuukw* that both federal and provincial legislation can infringe Aboriginal rights and title, subject to the requirement of s. 35(1) justification.[96] On the other hand, Lamer J. also said that Aboriginal rights "are part of the core of Indianness at the heart of s. 91(24)."[97] This suggests that although Aboriginal rights will not be treated as an impermeable federal enclave,[98] division of powers requirements will be strictly applied to provincial infringements. Apart from the *Natural Resources Transfer Agreements*, s. 88 of the *Indian Act*, and the question of s. 35(1) justification, provincial infringement may be possible if is merely an incidental part of otherwise valid provincial legislation.[99] Second, and also subject to s. 35(1) justification, some provincial infringements may be capable of being rescued by s. 88 of the *Indian Act*.[100] Here, as seen, there must be no intent to single out Indians for special treatment or to impair their status or capacity. The more extensive the effect on Aboriginal rights, and the more vital the Aboriginal right to the community concerned, the higher these hurdles. Moreover, s. 88 only applies to Indians under the *Indian Act*.

10. *KITKATLA*[101]

Reading 6(e) at p. 311

Whether a provincial law singles out Indians for special treatment can be important to its validity. According to *Dick*,[102] such a law has the purpose of impairing the status or capacity of Indians. It is, therefore, either invalid or inapplicable to Indians. In *Kitkatla*, a provincial law allowed a Minister to override a general protection for heritage objects. Acting under this power, the Minister authorized the cutting of 40 of 120 culturally modified trees (CMTs) on Crown land. The Kitkatla Band argued, *inter alia*, that the provincial law singled out Indians. Because most heritage objects in the province were Aboriginal objects, the Band claimed that the law had a differential impact on Aboriginal peoples. The Supreme Court rejected this argument. It said that disproportionate effect by itself does not constitute "singling out".[103] The main thrust of this scheme was to **protect** heritage objects, so Aboriginal people were not subject to overall negative differential treatment.[104] Moreover, the law contained special protection for existing Aboriginal rights, and set a careful balance between competing resource and conservation needs.[105] Accordingly, there was no "singling out". Apart from this, the legislation fell under the provincial property and civil rights power in the *Constitution Act, 1867*.[106] Thus, it was valid.

11. MORE CHALLENGES

Although the case law on legislative jurisdiction and Aboriginal issues is extraordinarily complex, it would be wrong to blame this situation wholly on courts. In a federal system, the usual simple hierarchy between common law and statute law must be supplemented by a division of legislative powers. Provision must be made for conflicts and overlap between statutes of different jurisdictions. Canadian policy-makers added to the hierarchy in 1930. The *Natural Resources Transfer Agreements* gave Prairie provinces a special but qualified power to regulate aspects of Indian game harvesting, as part of a package that conferred on these provinces ownership of the natural resources within their jurisdiction. In 1951, policy-makers added another rung to the hierarchy. Section 88 gave provinces qualified federal power to enact certain kinds of laws affecting Indians.

With this many-layered constitutional and statutory framework, it is remarkable that courts have been able to achieve as much coherence as they have thus far. The arbitrary enclave theory has been rejected, but Aboriginal peoples are protected against undue provincial intrusion by the concept of "Indianness". Section 88 helps federal-provincial coordination and efficiency by rescuing some non-discriminatory provincial laws affecting Indians, but only to the extent that the federal government and Indian bands themselves permit. The *Natural Resources Transfer Agreements* have been interpreted in a manner that parallels s. 88 and shows sensitivity to the treaties.

In 1982, however, policy-makers added yet another level to the system of legislative jurisdiction through s. 35(1) of the *Constitution Act, 1982*.[107] This provision gives primacy to Aboriginal and treaty rights in situations determined, effectively, by courts.[108] As well, land claims agreements[109] and self-government agreements[110] are adding special regional levels of their own. For example, when the Yukon self-government agreements are all concluded, there will be fourteen First Nations governments in Yukon, each with legislative powers that can prevail over laws of the public territorial government and some laws of the federal government.[111] In British Columbia, Nisga'a laws can prevail over federal and provincial laws on matters such as Nisga'a citizenship,[112] culture and language,[113] lands,[114] child adoption (subject to some conditions),[115] and primary,[116] secondary,[117] and (subject to some conditions) post-secondary education, and Nisga'a laws are themselves elements of s. 35(1) treaty rights.[118] How courts will respond to these additional challenges remains to be seen.

Notes

1. That is, subject to modification or restriction by the provisions below.
2. Provincial legislation: see *Kruger and Manuel v. The Queen*, [1978] 1 S.C.R. 104; federal legislation: see *R. v. Derriksan* (1976), 71 D.L.R. (3d) 159 (S.C.C.). However, the capacity of provincial legislation to affect Aboriginal or treaty rights is limited by the *Constitution Act, 1867*, and the capacity of both federal and provincial legislation to affect Aboriginal or treaty rights is limited by the *Constitution Act, 1982*, as seen below.
3. For an example of a federal statute prevailing over a treaty right, see *Sikyea v. R.*, [1964] S.C.R. 642, predating the *Constitution Act, 1982*.
4. (U.K.), 30 & 31 Vict., c. 3.
5. **Chapter 2, Part 3**. Although in *R. v. Blais*, [2003] 2 S.C.R. 236 and *infra* at note 56, the Supreme Court said "Indians" excludes Métis for the purposes of the *Natural Resources Transfer Agreements*, the Court stressed (at para. 41) that this "in no way precludes a more liberal interpretation of other constitutional documents." Arguably, the contexts of the NRTA and of the *Constitution Act, 1867* are quite different.

   The questions of the precise reach of federal power under s. 91(24), the constitutionality of the *Indian Act*, and federal jurisdiction in regard to Métis and non-registered Aboriginal peoples were raised, but not addressed, in *Lovelace v. Ontario*, [2000] 1 S.C.C. 950 at para. 4. On the other hand, courts have evolved the notion of an inner core of "Indianness" and Aboriginality in s. 91(24). Within this federal core, provincial governments cannot legislate on their own: see **Part 3(c)**, below. If the core of s. 91(24) includes Aboriginality as well as Indianness, it would be difficult to argue that any group of Aboriginal persons is beyond the reach of this section.
6. *St. Catherine's Milling and Lumber Company v. The Queen* (1889), 14 App. Cas. 46 at 59 (J.C.P.C.), **Chapter 3, Part 10**.
7. See *Bonanza Creek Gold Mining Co. v. The King*, [1916] 1 A.C. 566 at 580 (J.C.P.C.).
8. *St. Catherine's Milling and Lumber Company v. The Queen* (1889), 14 App. Cas. 46 at 57–59 (J.C.P.C.), **Chapter 3, Part 10** and **Chapter 5, Part 6**.
9. *St. Catherine's*, *ibid.* at 59, and **Chapter 3, Part 10** and **Chapter 5, Part 10**.
10. *Ibid.* See also ss. 102 and 108 of the *Constitution Act, 1867*. Although Lord Watson does not use the language of presumption or rebuttal, it provides a bridge between

St. Catherine's and the doctrine in *Bonanza Creek, supra* note 7.

11. For example, s. 92(2) gives provincial legislatures power over direct taxation; s. 92(5), the management and sale of public lands and timber; s. 92(6), hospitals; s. 92(8), municipal institutions; s. 92(9), commercial licences; s. 92(11), the solemnization of marriage; and s. 92(14), the administration of justice. Three more provisions are worth noting: s. 92(13), "Property and Civil Rights in the Province", which has been construed widely to include such things as intraprovincial trade, labour relations, marketing, property rights, consumer protection, and probably traffic safety; s. 92(16), referring to "Generally all Matters of a merely local or private Nature in the Province"; and s. 93, conferring legislative jurisdiction in relation to education.
12. However, some exercises of this power may be subject to special fiduciary responsibilities in regard to Aboriginal peoples: see **Chapter 8**.
13. For example, there has been no "Inuit Act" corresponding to the federal *Indian Act* and, despite its wide range, the *Indian Act* does not address all aspects of Indian life.
14. See, for example, *Kitkatla Band v. British Columbia (Minister of Small Business*, [2002] 2 S.C.R. at para. 66; 1031; *R. v. Francis*, [1988] 1 S.C.R. 1025 at para. 4; *Dick v. The Queen*, [1985] 2 S.C.R. 309 at 326; *Four B Manufacturing Ltd. v. United Garment Workers of America*, [1980] 1 S.C.R. and the majority decision of Martland J. in *Cardinal v. Attorney General of Alberta*, [1974] S.C.R. 695.
15. *Kitkatla, ibid.*
16. *Cardinal v. Alberta (A.G.)*, [1974] S.C.R. 695, **Part 7**, below, rejecting the proposition that Indian reserves are exclusive federal enclaves within which no provincial law can be valid. However, a provincial law may validly affect the subject matter of s. 91(24) and still be inoperative or inapplicable in part: see **Parts 3(a) and 3(b)**, below.
17. *Four B Manufacturing Ltd. v. United Garment Workers of America*, [1980] 1 S.C.R. 1031. Similarly, a province-wide heritage conservation provision can affect Aboriginal culturally modified trees: *Kitkatla Band v. British Columbia (Minister of Small Business, Tourism and Culture), supra* note 14.
18. This is a result of the paramountcy principle expounded in *Citizen Insurance Co. v. Parsons* (1881–82), 7 A.C. 96 at 108 (J.C.P.C.); *Re Exported Natural Gas Tax*, [1982] 1 S.C.R. 1004 at 1031 (Laskin C.J., dissenting on another point); and *Multiple Access v. McCutcheon*, [1982] 2 S.C.R. 161 at 191. For consideration of the paramountcy principle in regard to s. 91(24) and provincial laws, see *Kruger v. The Queen*, [1978] 1 S.C.R. 104 at 114–15; *Simon* v, *The Queen*, [1985] 2 S.C.R. 387 at 411–14 *Derrickson v. Derrickson*, [1986] 1 S.C.R. 285 at 303; and *R. v. Côté*, [1996] 3 S.C.R. 139 at para. 86 (S.C.C.). For the inconsistency test, see *Multiple Access Ltd., ibid.*; *Derrickson, ibid.* at 303.
19. *R. v. Francis*, [1988] 1 S.C.R. 1025. Mr. Francis was convicted under the *New Brunswick Motor Vehicle Act* for a traffic offence that occurred on an Indian reserve. Section 6 of the *Indian Reserve Traffic Regulations* incorporated the New Brunswick statute by reference and provided for different penalties. Mr. Francis argued, *inter alia*, that the federal statute rendered the provincial statute inoperative by virtue of the paramountcy doctrine. The Supreme Court held that "federal and provincial laws that merely duplicate one another but do not conflict can exist side by side. A person may be charged with violating the provincial statute or the federal regulation": 1031.
20. This is a result of the general doctrine of interjurisdictional immunity: see *John Deere Plow Co. v. Wharton*, [1915] A.C. 330; *Manitoba (A.G.) v. Canada (A.G.)*, [1929] A.C. 260; *Commission du salaire minimum v. Bell Telephone Co. of Canada*, [1966] S.C.R. 767; *Registrar of Motor Vehicles v. Canadian American Transfer Ltd.*, [1972] S.C.R. 811; *Dick v. The Queen*, [1985] 2 S.C.R. 309; *Bell Canada v. Quebec (Commission de la santé et de la sécurité du travail)*, [1988] 1 S.C.R. 749; *Québec (Commission de transport de la Communauté urbaine) v. Canada (National Battlefields Commission)*, [1990] 2 S.C.R. 838; *Delgamuukw v. British Columbia*, [1997] 3 S.C.R. 1010 at paras. 177–81; *Ordon Estate v. Grail*, [1998] 3 S.C.R. 437 at paras. 81–82.
21. *R. v. Dick, ibid.*, and **Part 8**, below, using the "status and capacity" notion articulated in *Kruger and Manuel v. The Queen*, [1978] 1 S.C.R. 104 at 110.
22. Some laws of this kind may be referentially incorporated as federal legislation: see **Part 4**, below.
23. *Dick v. The Queen*, [1985] 2 S.C.R. 309 at 323–26.
24. *Delgamuukw v. B.C.*, [1997] 3 S.C.R. 1010 at para. 182.
25. **Part 8**, below.
26. *Delgamuukw v. B.C.*, [1997] 3 S.C.R. 1010 at para. 180.
27. E.g., where an Aboriginal right is extinguished: *Delgamuukw, ibid.* at para. 180.
28. See Delgamuukw, *ibid.* at para. 182, using a provincial law regulating hunting as an example of a law that "may very well" touch the core of Indianness.
29. This seems implicit in the following observation by Chouinard J. in *Derrickson v. Derrickson*, [1986] 1 S.C.R. 285 at 296: "The right of possession of lands on an Indian reserve is manifestly of the very essence of the exclusive legislative power under s. 91(24) of the *Constitution Act, 1867*. It follows that provincial legislation cannot apply, at least on its own strength, to the right of possession of Indian lands." See also *Re Stoney Plain Indian Reserve No. 135*, [1982] 1 W.W.R. 302 at 321–22 (A.C.A.) and *Stoney Creek Indian Band v. British Columbia*, [1998] B.C.J. No. 2468 (B.C.S.C) at para. 40.
30. *R. v. Sutherland*, [1980] 2 S.C.R. 451 at 455.
31. *R. v. Dick*, [1985] 2 S.C.R. 309, **Part 8**, below.
32. See *Derrickson*, *Stoney Plain* and *Stoney Creek* decisions, *supra* note 29.
33. R.S.C. 1985, c. I-5. For a detailed and critical examination of the genesis and operation of s. 88, see "'Still Crazy After All These Years: Section 88 of the Indian Act at Fifty", K. Wilkins, (2000) 38 Alta. L. Rev. (No. 2) 458. After probing the rather unrevealing historical evidence, Wilkins concludes that, at a minimum, s. 88 was probably intended to perpetuate the legal rights of Indians in provincial civil proceedings, and to insulate their treaty rights against provincial legislation: *ibid.* at para. 7.
34. *Ibid.* at s. 4.1.
35. *R. v. Alphonse*, [1993] 5 W.W.R. 401 at 420 (B.C.C.A.).
36. On one hand, because s. 88 refers to only the first of the two distinct branches of s. 91(24), it might be assumed that Parliament intended to leave the second branch unaffected: see Lysyk J. in *Stoney Creek Indian Band v. British Columbia*, [1999] 8 W.W.R. 709 (B.C.S.C.) at para. 36, rev'd. on other grounds in (1999), 179 D.L.R. (4th) 57 (B.C.C.A.), leave to appeal to S.C.C. dismissed in [1999] S.C.C.A. 539. On the other hand, both branches of s. 91(24) have a common subject matter in "Indians", so any legislation that involves "Lands reserved for the Indians" must also involve Indians.

    Although the Supreme Court found it unnecessary to resolve this question in *Derrickson v. Derrickson*, [1986] 1 S.C.R. 285, 298–96, Chouinard J. noted at 297 that "[i]t is far from settled however that s. 88 contemplates referential incorporation with respect to lands reserved for the Indians." On the other hand, in *Delgamuukw v. British Columbia*, [1997] S.C.R. 1010 at para. 182, Lamer J. suggested that s. 88 "extends the effect of provincial laws of general application which cannot apply to Indians *and Indian lands* because they touch on the Indianness at the core of s. 91(24)" (emphasis added). Lysyk J. concluded in *Stoney Creek Indian Band v. British Columbia*, [1998] B.C.J. No. 2468 (S.C.C.) at para. 36, that the weight of opinion favours the view that s. 88 does not rescue laws that affect the Indian lands core of s. 91(24).

37. These might be described as "section 88 laws of general application" as opposed to the "laws of general application" that, according to *Delgamuukw*, "apply [*ex*]*proprio vigore* [by their own force] to Indians and Indian lands": *Delgamuukw v. British Columbia*, [1997] 3 S.C.R. 1010 at para. 179.
38. *R. v. George*, [1966] S.C.R. 267.
39. *Simon v. The Queen*, [1985] S.C.R. 387. In *Quebec (A.G.) v. Sioui*, [1990] S.C.R. 102, the Court held that treaty guarantees without territorial precision could prevail over *regulations* made pursuant to a s. 88 law of general application, provided that the guarantees were consistent with the general purpose of these laws: See also **Chapter 5**.
40. E.g., band council by-laws.
41. *Dick v. The Queen*, [1985] 2 S.C.R. 309 at 323–26. It does not rescue laws that (a) are valid and not "in relation to" Indians or (b) are invalid because they single out Indians for special treatment or have the purpose of impairing Indianness. The former would not be "of general application", while the latter do not need rescuing.
42. *R. v. Côté*, [1996] 3 S.C.R. (S.C.C) para. 86.
43. *R. v. Sundown*, [1999] 1 S.C.R. 393, at para. 418.
44. See *R. v. Côté*, [1996] 3 S.C.R. 139, at paras. 84–88. In *Côté* itself, the relevant treaty right was held not to have been infringed. Note, though, that at para. 87, the Supreme Court referred to the possibility that s. 88 might be subject to an implicit justification requirement similar to that for s. 35(1) of the *Constitution Act, 1982*. See *Sundown*, *ibid.*, at para. 48, declining to address this issue, "important as it may be," because of a lack of significant argument on it. Arguably, because of its legislative character and its many conditions, s.88 does not confer the "broad, unstructured administrative discretion" prohibited in *R. v. Adams*, [1996] 3 S.C.R. 101, 131 at para. 50. Because of this, s. 35(1) justification would be required not for s. 88 itself, but for the provincial law that relies on it, as in *R. v. Alphonse*, [1993] 5 W.W.R. 401 (B.C.C.A.).
45. R.S.C. 1985, c. N-27.
46. S.C. 1998, c. 28.
47. S.C. 2002, c. 27.
48. *Ibid.*, ss. 22(1) (Inuit rather than Indians); 23(3) (Indians and Inuit); and 22(1) (Indians and Inuit, but only in regard to game conservation laws), respectively.
49. For the land claims agreements, see **Chapter 11, Part 6**.
50. (U.K.), 21 Geo. V. v. 26, Schedules: *Manitoba, Memorandum of Agreement; Saskatchewan, Memorandum of Agreement; Alberta, Memorandum of Agreement*. See G.V. La Forest, *Natural Resources and Public Property under the Canadian Constitution* (Toronto: University of Toronto Press, 1969) at 35–43.
51. Such as Indian hunting, trapping or fishing for food on unoccupied Crown land or "access" land, including reserves: *Cardinal v. Alberta (A.G.)*, [1974] S.C.R. 695. This leaves the Prairie provinces with special powers to regulate Indian commercial hunting (*Cardinal*), subject perhaps to s. 35(1) of the *Constitution Act, 1982*. Do these provisions apply to Métis as well as to Indians? See **Chapter 2, Part 5(c)**.
52. (U.K.), 21 Geo. V. v. 26, Schedules: *Manitoba, Memorandum of Agreement*. The Alberta and Saskatchewan Agreements each contain comparable provisions.
53. *Daniels v. White*, [1968] S.C.R. 517.
54. For example: *Daniels v. White*, [1968] 1 S.C.R. 517; *Frank v. The Queen*, [1978] 1 S.C.R. 95; *The Queen v. Mousseau*, [1980] 2 S.C.R. 89; *Elk v. The Queen*, [1980] 2 S.C.R. 166; *The Queen v. Sutherland*, [1980] 2 S.C.R. 451; *Moosehunter v. The Queen*, [1981] 1 S.C.R. 282; *R. v. Horse*, [1988] 1 S.C.R. 187; *R. v. Horseman*, [1990] 1 S.C.R. 901; *R. v. Badger*, [1996] 1 S.C.R. 771.
55. *R. v. Badger*, [1996] 1 S.C.R. 771, **Chapter 5, Part 15**. When a provincial law conflicts with treaty rights and is not given effect by the N.R.T.A., it may be inapplicable to Indians by virtue of s. 88 of the *Indian Act*: *R. v. Sundown*, [1999] 1 S.C.R. 393 at 417–18.
56. *R. v. Blais*, [2003] 2 S.C.R. 236, aff'g (2001), 198 D.L.R. (4th) 220 (M.C.A.), aff'g [1998] 10 W.W.R. 442, aff'g (1998), 130 Man. R. (2d) 114 (Prov. Ct.).
57. *Ibid.* at paras. 12 and 32.
58. *Ibid.*, para. 41.
59. R.S.C. 1985, c. N-27.
60. S.C. 1998, c. 28.
61. S.C. 2002, c. 27.
62. *Ibid.*, ss. 18(1), 19(1), and 19(3) respectively.
63. For the land claims agreements, see **Chapter 11, Part 6**.
64. Being Schedule B to the *Canada Act, 1982* (U.K.), 1982, c. 11.
65. Including land claims agreement rights: see s. 35(3).
66. *R. v. Sparrow*, [1987] 1 S.C.R. 1075: **Chapter 4**. This would appear to include otherwise valid provincial government action as well as federal government action: *Badger*, *supra* note 55. For a criticism of this position, see P.W. Hogg, *Constitutional Law of Canada*, 2004 Student ed. (Scarborough, Ont.: Carswell, 2004), heading 27.8 (i). See further **Chapter 10, Part 3(h)(i)**.
67. *R. v. Badger*, [1996] 1 S.C.R. 771, holding that reasonable safety regulation does not constitute infringement (para. 91), and that conservation regulation that is reasonable in the *Sparrow* sense may be a justifiable infringement if the manner of its application also complies with the *Sparrow* requirements (para. 89). Although *Badger* involved provincial regulations that were constitutionally supported by the *Natural Resource Transfer Agreements*, its broad language would appear to include all otherwise valid provincial government action as well as federal government action. (See *Badger*, para. 89, citing *R. v. Napoleon* (1985), 21 C.C.C. (3d) 515 (B.C.C.A.), a case involving provincial laws outside the scope of the *N.R.T.A.* (although subject to s. 88 of the *Indian Act*)).
68. *R. v. Badger*, [1996] 1 S.C.R. 771 at para. 77: **Chapter 5, Part 15**.
69. See **Parts 9 and 11**, below, and B. Slattery, "First Nations and the Constitution: A Question of Trust" (1992) Can. Bar. Rev. 260, especially 278–82.
70. In *R. v. Côte*, [1996] 3 S.C.R. 139 (S.C.C), the Court remarked that "[i]n the near future, Parliament will no doubt feel compelled to re-examine the existence and scope of **[s. 88 of the** *Indian Act*] in light of these uncertainties and in light of the parallel constitutionalization of treaty rights under s. 35(1)": para. 87. (In *Côté* itself, the issue did not arise, as the Court held that the regulation in question was not inconsistent with the treaty.)
71. **Part 9**. In regard to s.88, the Court appears to think that legislative change may be desirable.
72. *Cardinal v. Alberta (A.G.)*, [1974] S.C.R. 695, aff'g (1972), 22 D.L.R. (3d) 716 (A.S.C.A.D.), which rev'd the decision of the A.S.C., which upheld the decision of the Provincial Judge.
73. Incorporated into the *Constitution Act, 1930*.
74. *Cardinal v. Alberta (A.G.)*, [1974] S.C.R. 695 at 703.
75. For example, provincial game legislation in regarding to Indians on Indian reserves: *ibid.* at 704 at 706–707, and 708.
76. *Ibid.* at 716.
77. *Dick v. The Queen*, [1985] 2 S.C.R. 309, aff'g (1985), 23 D.L.R. (4th) 33 at 35 (B.C.C.A.), which aff'd the decisions of the County Court and Provincial Court judges.
78. There was evidence that the Alkali Band hunted for food and other subsistence purposes, and that this hunting was central to the Band's way of life. Despite this evidence, Mr. Dick and his colleagues chose not to rely on a claim to Aboriginal title or rights.
79. *Dick v. The Queen*, [1985] 2 S.C.R. 309.
80. *Cardinal v. Alberta (A.G.)*, [1974] S.C.R. 695.
81. [1978] 1 S.C.R. 104 (May 1977).

82. For the most part, the Court stressed that the key question (apart from whether there was uniform territorial application) was whether the law had the *purpose* of impairing Indian status or capacity. At one point, the Court said that mere differential impact is not enough to make a law other than one of general application. However, it then continued (*ibid.* at 110): "The line is crossed, however, when an enactment, though in relation to another matter, by its effect, impairs the status or capacity of a particular group."
83. Especially in light of the hunting evidence referred to in *supra* note 78.
84. *Delgamuukw v. British Columbia*, [1997] 3 S.C.R. 1010 (Supreme Court of Canada: December 11, 1997), varying (1993), 104 D.L.R. (4th) 470 (B.C.C.A.), which varied (1991), 79 D.L.R. (4th) 185 (B.C.S.C.). *Delgamuukw* is considered in detail in **Chapter 8, Part 8**, below. The discussion here highlights the application of the decision to the issue of legislative jurisdiction.
85. *Delgamuukw v. British Columbia*, [1997] 3 S.C.R. 1010.
86. R.S.C. c. I-5, as am.
87. Lamer C.J. spoke for six judges. In a brief separate judgment, McLachlin J. agreed with the Chief Justice's reasons: para. 209. On the issue of provincial extinguishment, La Forest J. said he agreed with the Chief Justice's "conclusion": para. 206. However, he did not indicate that he disagreed with the Chief Justice's *reasons* on this issue.
88. Paras. 174–76.
89. Paras. 174–75.
90. Paras. 173 and 175. Lamer C.J. said that the protection of s. 91(24) was not superseded by provincial ownership of public land pursuant to s. 109 of the *Constitution Act, 1982*. This was because s. 109 is subject to non-governmental interests (such as Aboriginal title): para. 175.
91. Paras. 177–78.
92. Para. 179. (In *R. v. Dick*, [1985] 2 S.C.R. 309 the Supreme Court regarded (a) singling out Indians for special treatment as roughly analogous to (b) having the purpose of impairing Indianness, and indicated that a law with either the purpose or the effect of impairing Indianness is a law in relation to the subject matter of s. 91(24)): see **Part 8**, above.) In *Kitkatla Band v. British Columbia (Minister of Small Business, Tourism and Culture)*, *infra* note 101 at para. 68, the Court said that disproportionate effect is different from "singling out", and is not fatal to jurisdiction in division of powers analysis.
93. Para. 180.
94. Para. 181.
95. Para. 183.
96. Para. 160.
97. Para. 181.
98. If they did, no provincial law could affect Aboriginal rights or title, even as an incidental aspect of provincial legislation whose main aspect fell within provincial jurisdiction.
99. Either the legislation itself might have this incidental effect, or a particular provision of the legislation may be regarded as incidental to the statutory scheme as a whole. In the latter case, the safeguards summarized in *Kitkatla Band v. British Columbia (Minister of Small Business, Tourism, and Culture)*, *infra* note 101 at para. 58 would apply.
100. To qualify for s. 88 protection, the provincial statute would have to be a law of general application, that is, intended neither to single out nor to impair the status and capacity of Indians, but to have the effect of impairing their status and capacity. The other terms of s. 88 (no inconsistent federal legislation and no laws in or under the *Indian Act* occupying the field) would have to be met as well.
101. *Kitkatla Band v. British Columbia (Minister of Small Business, Tourism and Culture)*, [2002] 2 S.C.R. 146, aff'g (2002) 183 D.L.R. (4th) 183 (B.C.C.A.), aff'g [1999] 7 W.W.R. 584 (S.C.) and [1999] 2 C.N.L.R. 176 (S.C.).
102. *Dick v. The Queen*, [1985] 2 S.C.R. 309, discussed in **Part 8**, above.
103. *Kitkatla Band*, *supra* note 101 at para. 68.
104. *Ibid.*, para. 70.
105. *Ibid.*, paras. 71 and 76.
106. *Ibid.*, para. 65.
107. **Chapter 7**.
108. *Ibid.*
109. **Chapter 11**.
110. **Chapter 12**.
111. **Chapter 12, Part 12(3)(iv)(A)**. Although the Yukon self-government agreements lack the constitutional status of s. 35(1) treaties (see, for example, Champagne and Aishihik First Nations Final Agreement, 29 May, 1993, s. 24.12.1), their implementation in federal statutes gives them superior constitutional status to territorial legislation.
112. *Nisga'a Final Agreement*, August 4, 1998, s. 40: see **Chapter 11, Part 7(h)**.
113. *Ibid.*, s. 43.
114. *Ibid.*, s. 45.
115. *Ibid.*, s. 99.
116. *Ibid.*, s. 101.
117. *Ibid.*, s. 105.
118. If a provincial law is inconsistent with a Nisga'a elementary education law, can the province still offer evidence that its law constitutes a justified infringement of an Aboriginal treaty right?

7 *Constitution Act, 1982* and *Sparrow*

Chapter Highlights

- The *Constitution Act, 1982* contained provisions that protect Aboriginal peoples' rights from the guarantees in the *Charter of Rights and Freedoms*; recognize and affirm existing Aboriginal and treaty rights (s. 35(1)); and require governments to hold an Aboriginal constitutional conference.
- The *Constitution Amendment Act, 1983* provided that rights in land claims agreements were existing treaty rights for the purposes of s. 35(1) above; guaranteed gender equality with regard to s. 35(1) rights; required governments to consult with Aboriginal peoples before amending certain constitutional provisions; and committed governments to at least two additional Aboriginal constitutional conferences.
- In its 1990 decision in *Sparrow*, the Supreme Court of Canada held that the existing Aboriginal and treaty rights of the Aboriginal peoples of Canada are guaranteed against unjustified government infringement.

Synopsis

In 1982, Canada's constitution-makers recognized and affirmed existing Aboriginal and treaty rights in the Constitution of Canada. However, they neglected to say what they meant by this recognition and affirmation. Were the rights merely constitutionally enshrined? Were they constitutionally guaranteed as well? If so, in what sense? Moreover, the constitution-makers provided no definition of the content of these rights. As we have seen, beyond asserting a general tie with traditional occupancy and use of land, the courts had provided little clarification on content either. Then, in *Sparrow*, the Supreme Court answered the question of status by declaring that unextinguished Aboriginal rights are protected against unjustified government infringement. The Court provided tests for the concepts of infringement and justification, and in doing so assumed broad new discretionary responsibilities. The question of content was left for another day.

Selected Readings

🗎 links material in this chapter to the corresponding headings and page numbers of the relevant readings.

🗎 Part 1	Excerpts from *Constitution Act, 1982*	315
🗎 Parts 1, 3	1983 Constitutional Accord	316
🗎 Part 4	*R. v. Sparrow*	318

1. CHANGES TO *CONSTITUTION ACT, 1982*[1]

Readings 7(a) at p. 315 and 7(b) at p. 316

The year 1982 was a watershed in Canadian constitutional history, and a turning point in the law relating to Canadian Aboriginal peoples. Rights with less than certain existence in the common law were suddenly enshrined in the written part of the Canadian constitution. Aboriginal-government relations and Aboriginal / non-Aboriginal relations were put into a more legal framework, and more under the control of lawyers and courts.

The main Aboriginal provisions came into effect in two main stages. The first stage was on April 17, 1982, when the *Constitution Act, 1982* was proclaimed. The Act contained three important sections: s. 25, which provides that *Charter* guarantees of rights and freedoms should not be construed as derogating from rights relating to Aboriginal peoples; s. 35, which recognizes and affirms the existing Aboriginal and treaty rights of the Aboriginal peoples of Canada (subsection 1), who include the Indian, Métis, and Inuit peoples of Canada (subsection 2); and s. 37 (now repealed), which provided for an Aboriginal constitutional conference within a year of April 17, 1982.

The second stage was on June 21, 1984, when the *Constitution Amendment Proclamation, 1983* was officially approved.[2] The Proclamation added four significant sections. Section 35(3) stated that, for greater certainty, "treaty rights" in s. 35(1) includes present and future land claims agreement rights; s. 35(4) guaranteed gender equality with respect to s. 35(1) rights; s. 35.1 committed governments to consult with Aboriginal peoples before amending constitutional provisions that directly affected them; and s. 37.1 (now repealed) committed governments to holding two additional Aboriginal conferences, the last to be held by April 17, 1987.

2. BACKGROUND

Federal government policy during the late 1970s and early 1980s aimed to dissuade French-speaking Canadians in Quebec from supporting separatism by offering them special guaranteed rights in a revised constitution. It sought to balance this with guaranteed rights for English-speaking minorities as well as guaranteed individual rights for Canadians generally. Against this background, Aboriginal Canadians sought constitutional protection of their own group rights.

In the spring of 1980, the federal government proposed a draft constitutional preamble that would include a provision to "enshrine the rights of our native peoples."[3] Instead of this, however, the proposed constitutional package, released in October 1980, contained only a negative non-derogation provision. It said *Charter* guarantees would not deny the existence of "any rights or freedoms that pertain to the native peoples of Canada."[4] There was a strong reaction from Aboriginal groups. When the constitutional package was considered by the Special Joint Committee of the Senate and the House of Commons on the Constitution of Canada, seventeen of the 104 groups who appeared before the Committee were groups representing Aboriginal people.[5] Nearly all Aboriginal groups sought — at the very least — a constitutional provision to entrench Aboriginal and treaty rights against federal and provincial legislation. Some sought recognition of sovereignty and Aboriginal governmental powers.[6]

On January 30, 1981, representatives of the three national Aboriginal organizations and political parties agreed to include a new provision as follows:

1. The Aboriginal and treaty rights of the Aboriginal peoples of Canada are hereby recognized and affirmed.
2. In this Act, "Aboriginal peoples of Canada" includes the Indian, Inuit and Métis peoples of Canada.

When the Parliamentary committee reported on February 23, it supported (a) the non-derogation clause, (b) a guaranteed constitutional conference for the "identification and definition" of the rights of Aboriginal peoples, and (c) the provision recognizing and affirming Aboriginal and treaty rights. On April 23, 1981, the House of Commons formally approved the revised package.[7] Meanwhile, the National Indian Brotherhood and the Native Council of Canada withdrew their support for the constitutional proposals, calling for an Aboriginal right to veto future constitutional amendments that affected them.

In the Constitutional Accord reached between the federal government and the nine provinces on November 5, 1981, the non-derogation and constitutional conference provisions were retained, but the recognition and affirmation provision was missing. Apparently some of the governments were concerned about the potential implications of this provision for government jurisdiction and expenditures, and for third party interests.[8] After a strong lobbying campaign by the aboriginal groups and the media and other supporters, the governments agreed on November 23 to reinstate the aboriginal and treaty rights recognition and affirmation, but prefaced by the word "existing".

The Assembly of First Nations and several other Aboriginal groups launched a court action in England against the package, claiming that it would interfere with treaty obligations still owed by the Imperial Crown. On January 23, 1982, the English Court of Appeal rejected this argument, saying that when Canada became independent, the Imperial Crown's treaty obligations had been transferred to Canada.[9]

The *Constitution Act, 1982* was proclaimed on April 17, 1982, except for the equality guarantee and the operation of a language guarantee in Quebec. The Aboriginal constitutional conference was held on March 15 and 16, 1983, and resulted in the *Constitution Amendment Proclamation, 1983*, as mentioned in **Part 1**, above.

This was to be the first and (so far) only general amendment to the *Constitution Act, 1982*. Three additional constitutional conferences were held as required, in 1984, 1985, and 1987. All focused on Aboriginal self-government. These were followed by the Meech Lake Accord of 1987–90, whose only Aboriginal provision would have been a non-derogation clause, and by the Charlottetown Accord, in which Aboriginal self-government was a major theme. As seen in **Chapter 12**, all these constitutional amendment initiatives ended in failure.

3. QUESTIONS

🖹 Reading 7(b) at p. 316

The constitutional amendments that did succeed raised several important constitutional questions. Most of these centred on the key provision: s. 35(1), which recognizes and affirms existing Aboriginal and treaty rights. Were the rights in this section enhanced, or entrenched? If the rights were entrenched, what rights were entrenched? What kind of action were they entrenched against? Did the same entrenchment rules apply to Aboriginal and treaty rights? What did the word "existing" mean? If it referred to rights that had not been extinguished at the time the *Constitution Act, 1982* was proclaimed, what was the test for extinguishment? If government action could still prevail over entrenched rights in some situations, what were these situations? Last but not least, what *kind* of Aboriginal and treaty rights were entrenched?

After eight inconclusive years, the Supreme Court supplied answers to some of these questions. What were the answers? What new questions were raised?

4. *SPARROW*[10]

🖹 Reading 7(c) at p. 318

(a) Legal Situation before *Sparrow*

Although traditional Aboriginal use and occupancy of land was a fact at the time of Confederation (and pre-dated it by perhaps 12,000 years),[11] for much of the 20th century Canadian courts did not recognize a general right based directly on this fact.[12] Non-legislative, non-treaty rights were thought to be limited to the qualified wording of an old prerogative instrument with shadowy boundaries, the Royal Proclamation of 1763.[13] As we saw in **Chapter 4**, it was not until *Calder* in 1973[14] that the Supreme Court moved toward recognizing a general occupancy-based right. Even then, only a minority accorded it full, unequivocal common law status.[15] Also, there was almost no consensus on other questions, such as proof, content, duration, liability to extinguishment, and compensability. On the eve of the *Constitution Act, 1982*, the highest Court had done little more to clarify this situation.[16] Lower court decisions were contradictory. One provincial appellate court declared that Aboriginal rights were simply too vague to recognize.[17] This was an unlikely foundation on which to base increased judicial responsibility.

Yet, increased judicial responsibility was an almost inevitable result of s. 35(1).[18] This provision required courts not only to clarify Aboriginal rights, but to say how they had been changed. Certainly, the mere fact of inclusion in the *Constitution Act, 1982* suggested something more than a continuation of the *status quo*. What was that something more? Were the rights to be entrenched, prevailing over inconsistent government action like *Charter* rights? But s. 35(1) was placed outside the *Charter*. It had no similar specific guarantee.[19] Another possibility was some form of enhancement short of entrenchment. This option would require further choices. Was unequivocal common law status intended? Real property status? Strong presumptions against restriction?

The entrenchment route posed even more complex dilemmas. As noted, if the rights were entrenched, courts would have to answer many difficult questions about the scope, manner, and effect of this entrenchment. Moreover, s. 35(1) lacked not only a specific guarantee, but also a justification provision like s. 1 of the *Charter*. That section permits legislative infringement that is specially justified in individual cases.[20] If the entrenchment route were taken, it might be necessary to impose at least some restrictions. For example, the reference to treaties in s. 35(1) and to treaties and land claims agreements in s. 35(3)[21] suggests that it could not have been intended to entrench Aboriginal rights against consensual alteration. Absolute entrenchment might be qualified by imposing limits of a chronological,[22] jurisdictional,[23] or other[24] nature, or by creating a justificatory test for individual cases, even though the *Constitution Act, 1982* itself provided none for s. 35(1) Aboriginal rights.

Finally, at the eleventh hour, the constitution-makers had entrenched not simply Aboriginal rights, but "existing" Aboriginal rights.[25] What exactly did this mean? Did it freeze all rights, subject to all government restrictions modifying them before April 17, 1982, and then entrench the rights against government restrictions after this date? Did it mean "unextinguished"? Did it refer to the legal status or scope of Aboriginal rights before April 17, 1982? Was some other meaning intended? The constitution-makers had hardly made things easy!

For eight years, there was no authoritative judicial response to these questions.[26] The Supreme Court's most important decision during this period was *R. v. Guerin*.[27] *Guerin* expressly recognized occupancy-based Aboriginal rights and articulated a special enforceable fiduciary duty,[28] but it said nothing about s. 35(1). Meanwhile, there was little agreement on the meaning of s. 35(1) in the lower courts.[29]

(b) Facts and Context

Without a doubt, *Sparrow*[30] was a landmark decision. It was the highest Court's first detailed look at s. 35(1). The decision provided some general guidelines for interpreting this complex provision, and articulated a new extinguishment / entrenchment / justification approach that would likely shape the Aboriginal people's legal landscape for decades to come. It was an ambitious attempt to deal fairly and generously with some of the strong claims and pressing needs of Aboriginal peoples.

On May 25, 1984, Mr. Sparrow, a Musqueam Indian, went fishing for salmon in the Fraser Valley delta area of British Columbia, a traditional Musqueam fishing place. He was using a 45-fathom drift net. However, in the spring of 1983, the Department of Fisheries had reduced the maximum net length in the Musqueam Band's Indian food fishing licence from 75 fathoms to 25 fathoms. Mr. Sparrow was charged under s. 61(1) of the *Fisheries Act*[31] with fishing with a drift net longer than permitted by licence.

Mr. Sparrow argued that he was fishing pursuant to an Aboriginal right guaranteed by s. 35(1) of the *Constitution Act, 1982*. At first, this was not successful: Mr. Sparrow was convicted by a provincial court judge, and the conviction was upheld by the British Columbia County Court. But the British Columbia Court of Appeal set aside the conviction and ordered a new trial. They held that Mr. Sparrow had provided adequate proof of an Aboriginal title to fish, and that the federal government had failed to show that the right had been extinguished. They said that since April 17, 1982, this right was entrenched against subsequent legislative extinguishment, and against all subsequent legislative regulation except that which could be justified according to certain criteria. However, the Court felt it had insufficient evidence in this case regarding (i) the alleged infringement of the Aboriginal right, and (ii) the facts that might justify the infringement. Hence the order for a new trial.

Until the British Columbia Court of Appeal's decision, most courts had said that s. 35(1) does not affect pre-April 17, 1982 legislation.[32] Since most decisions before *Sparrow* had not involved *post*-April 17, 1982, legislation, little had been said about it. In 1985, the Ontario Court of Appeal had suggested that Aboriginal rights are entrenched against all post-April 17, 1982 legislation,[33] but this comment was *obiter*. Thus, the concept of qualified entrenchment subject to a justification requirement was applied for the first time in the British Columbia Court of Appeal's decision in *Sparrow*.[34] This general approach was then adopted in several other jurisdictions.[35]

(c) Supreme Court's Decision

The Supreme Court's decision[36] followed closely in the footsteps of the British Columbia Court of Appeal. The main elements of the Supreme Court's reasoning are as follows:

1. "Existing" in s. 35(1) means (i) unextinguished as of April 17, 1982[37] (but does not mean subject to pre-April 17, 1982, regulatory regimes) and (ii) "affirmed in a contemporary form".[38]
2. The evidence of the Aboriginal right is scanty in parts, but is not seriously disputed and will be accepted.[39] It shows that the Musqueam band lived in the relevant area (although not to the exclusion of others) as an organized society,[40] long before the coming of the Europeans, and that salmon fishing was and is integral to their lives. It has been "an integral part of their distinctive culture".[41]
3. The test for extinguishment is not simply whether the government action is "necessarily inconsistent" with the continued existence of the Aboriginal right, but whether the Sovereign's intention to extinguish is "clear and plain".[42] In this case, it was not.
4. The Aboriginal right under discussion was to fish for food for (i) subsistence and (ii) ceremonial and social purposes. It will not be decided here if it extends to other purposes such as commercial purposes.[43]
5. Section 35(1) "affords Aboriginal peoples constitutional protection against provincial legislative power," a protection that would result in any event from the decision in *Guerin*.
6. Section 35(1) incorporates a fiduciary obligation toward Aboriginal peoples, and should be generously construed.
7. The Aboriginal right enshrined in s. 35(1) is not as susceptible to restriction as before April 17, 1982, since its new status in the constitution requires a different approach.[44] On the other hand, the right is not entrenched absolutely because the words "recognized and affirmed" are not absolute.[45] Moreover, the right is not entrenched subject to regulations in place on the eve of April 17, 1982, because that would constitutionalize "a crazy patchwork of regulations".[46]
8. Section 35(1) protects Aboriginal rights from infringement by government regulation, unless government is able to justify the infringement.
9. To show a *prima facie* infringement of s. 35(1) rights, those challenging the legislation must show that it (i) is an unreasonable limitation, (ii) has the effect of imposing undue hardship, or (iii) denies the right holders their preferred means of exercising the right.
10. To show justification, government must demonstrate (i) that it has a valid legislative objective; and (in a case such as this one) (ii) that it has given the Indian food fishing top priority after the legislative objective (i.e., conservation) has been met; and (iii) depending on the circumstances of the inquiry, that there has been minimum possible infringement with respect to the desired result, fair compensation for any expropriation, and consultation with the Aboriginal group concerned. The legislative objective must be "compelling and substantial", and could include (a) conserving and managing a natural resource, or (b) preventing harm to the Aboriginal people or the general populace. The "public interest" or mere "reasonableness" are not adequate criteria.
11. On the criteria required above, there was an Aboriginal right to fish for food, and this right was not extinguished. However, there was insufficient evidence in this case to permit a decision about infringement and justification. Accordingly, there should be a re-trial.

(d) Elements of Decision

A number of aspects of this decision merit a closer look.

(i) Proof and Content

On the question of proof of Aboriginal rights, the Court required little, and said little. It simply observed that the Musqueam had lived in the area as an organized society, and that the traditional fishing activity was integral to their distinctive culture.[47] It did not indicate which of these features, if any, were essential to the proof of Aboriginal rights, or if other necessary features were required and present. Although the comment above bore some resemblance to Mahoney J.'s test for proof in *Baker Lake*,[48] the Court did not mention this test. Because the existence of an Aboriginal right was not seriously disputed in *Sparrow*, elaboration was considered unnecessary.[49] In a later decision, though, the Court's short "integral to the distinctive culture" comment in *Sparrow* would become the nucleus of a major new test for proof and identification.[50]

In regard to the amount of proof needed, the Court took a very liberal approach. Although the evidence of traditional use was "scanty" in parts, the Court considered it sufficient that it was not seriously disputed.[51] Hence, once minimal proof is presented, the onus apparently shifts to government to produce serious evidence in rebuttal. This approach is necessary. Proof of Aboriginal right is often buried in the dust of centuries, beyond the reach of written records. At some point, though, the facts may be simply too distant for *any* clear measurement in an adjudicatory forum.

On the content of Aboriginal rights, *Sparrow* accepted the Musqueam's claim to an Aboriginal right to fish for food subsistence and ceremonial purposes.[52] It refrained from ruling on whether Aboriginal rights can extend to fishing for commercial purposes,[53] saying that this issue had not been argued in the courts below.[54] Apparently because the Musqueam's right to fish for food was not in question,[55] at least initially, the Court did not attempt to define or describe the general content and character of Aboriginal rights. The Court did say that British policy was "based on the [native population's] right to occupy their traditional lands," and that "there was from the outset never any doubt that sovereignty and legislative power, and indeed the underlying title, to [the natives' traditional lands] was vested in the Crown."[56] However, it did not go on to relate this observation to a general theory of Aboriginal rights. As with the issue of proof, a general description of Aboriginal rights was postponed until later.[57]

The Court stressed that Aboriginal rights were recognized and affirmed "in a contemporary form".[58] One result of this emphasis was the likelihood that modern *means* of fishing (and hunting), such as automated fishing equipment (and rifles for hunting) would be considered acceptable means of exercising the traditional right. This was consistent with the Court's liberal approach in modern treaty cases.[59]

(ii) Extinguishment

With respect to extinguishment,[60] the Court addressed a question that had gone unresolved since *Calder*. In *Calder*, Judson J. for three judges had held that government action amounting to complete dominion inconsistent with any conflicting interest, including Aboriginal title, was sufficient to extinguish it.[61] On the other hand, Hall J. for three other judges had concluded that the Sovereign's intention to extinguish must be clear and plain.[62]

In *Sparrow*, the Crown tried to build on Judson J.'s test. It argued that detailed government regulation of Indian fishing over the years was sufficiently inconsistent with the continuation of any Aboriginal fishing right to extinguish it.[63] The Court rejected this argument. The proper test, it said, is that of Hall J. in *Calder*.[64] Mere regulation, however detailed, is not enough to show a clear and plain intention to extinguish. By endorsing Hall J.'s test, the Court implied that necessary inconsistency is not enough, either, even in the stringent form proposed by Judson J.[65] On the other hand, the Court did not require that a clear and plain intention to extinguish be stated expressly. What role, if any, then, was envisaged for implied extinguishment?[66] The Court did not say,[67] and the question is not much clearer today.[68]

(iii) Fiduciary Duties and Crown Honour

In support of its view that s. 35(1) conditionally guarantees existing Aboriginal and treaty rights,[69] and in support of its justification requirement,[70] the Court referred in *Sparrow* to the *Guerin* decision on Crown fiduciary duties in regard to Aboriginal interests.[71] However, the Court used the fiduciary concept as an analogy or "guiding interpretative principle"[72] in *Sparrow*, not as the source of a directly enforceable equitable duty, as in *Guerin*. As will be seen in **Chapter 8**, the Court has since clarified that the constitutional justification duty in *Sparrow* and the fiduciary duty in *Guerin* are both distinct applications of the broader concept of the honour of the Crown.

(iv) Legal Status

On the question of the effect of s. 35(1), the Supreme Court suggested that the main choice was between (i) absolute entrenchment,[73] (ii) frozen rights,[74] and (iii) its compromise entrenchment / justification approach.[75] The Court rejected absolute entrenchment on the ground that "[r]ights that are recognized and affirmed are not absolute."[76] It rejected the view that s. 35(1) froze rights as of April 17, 1982, on the ground that "[that] would incorporate into the Constitution a crazy patchwork of regulations,"[77] dependent on the arbitrary fact of what happened to be in effect in a given area when the *Constitution Act, 1982* was proclaimed. Declining "these two extreme positions".[78] the Court adopted the third. It said s. 35(1) must be defined in light of the government's fiduciary responsibility with respect to Aboriginal peoples, and continued:

> [f]ederal power [under the *Constitution Act, 1867*] must be reconciled with federal duty [government's fiduciary responsibility], and the best way to achieve that reconciliation is to demand the justification of any government regulation that infringes upon or denies aboriginal rights.[79]

Thus, although Aboriginal rights were entrenched, they could be infringed under some circumstances. Apart from the specific content of the justification process, this approach parallelled the *Charter* breach / section justification approach the Court had already taken in regard to *Charter* rights.[80]

While the entrenchment-justification option was clearly preferable to the alternatives of absolute or frozen rights, and provides some symmetry with *Charter* jurisprudence, it was a complex approach. As we will see later, it raised a wide range of questions about the nature, scope, and effect of entrenchment, infringement, and justification.

Arguably, not all this complication was necessary. There was another possible option available to the Court in *Sparrow*. Although s. 52(1) of the *Constitution Act, 1982* entrenched the recognition and affirmation of existing Aboriginal rights in s. 35(1), it did not necessarily accord super-legislative status to the rights themselves. Unlike *Charter* rights, these rights were not expressly "guaranteed".[81] In this context, the Court might have looked at another possible option — enhanced status short of entrenchment.[82] It might have considered a strong constitutionally sanctioned *presumption* in favour of the existence of s. 35(1) rights and against its unilateral extinguishment or restriction. Such a presumption might have been used to clarify the confusion in the pre-1982 case law,[83] could have been as effective as entrenchment-justification, and would probably have been less convoluted. In any event, the enhancement option was not addressed.[84]

(v) Entrenchment

Having decided that Aboriginal rights are entrenched, the Court opened the door to more specific entrenchment questions. For example, are all Aboriginal rights[85] entrenched in the same way?[86] Are treaty rights entrenched in the same way as Aboriginal rights?[87] Are Aboriginal rights entrenched against all federal and provincial legislation or all federal and provincial government action of any kind?[88] Are the rights entrenched against all unjustified interference or all unjustified unilateral interference?[89] Apart from asserting that s. 35(1) protects Aboriginal rights against provincial legislation,[90] the Court did not answer these questions explicitly.

(vi) Infringement

The Court stressed that extinguishment is not the only possible form of government action capable of affecting Aboriginal rights.[91] It suggested that while extinguishment completely abrogates Aboriginal rights, it is possible to restrict Aboriginal rights short of ending them completely.[92] This was the kind of restriction the Court referred to as "regulation".[93]

The infringement an Aboriginal party is required to demonstrate is *prima facie* infringement.[94] Although this suggests minimal interference, *Sparrow* lists infringement criteria, such as "unreasonable limitation" and "undue hardship", that suggest that unreasonable or unjustified infringement must be shown. Moreover, if the latter were correct, it could be asked just how infringement differs from justification. The Court attempted to clarify this apparent "internal contradiction" in a later case.[95]

The infringement criteria themselves are open-ended. For example, what amounts to an "unreasonable" limitation of an Aboriginal right? What constitute "reasonable" food and ceremonial needs?[96] What constitutes a denial of a right-holder's "preferred" means of exercising that right?[97] When does a restriction "unnecessarily" infringe protected interests? What constitutes "undue time and money per fish caught," or "hardship ... in catching fish"?[98] Will what is reasonable at the time and place of one case be reasonable for another case two, twelve, or twenty-four months later, or in a neighbouring region? The Court did not comment.[99]

Must this weighing process begin afresh in every case, or will some categories of restriction not normally be regarded as infringements? As seen in **Chapters 9** and **10**, thus far the Court appears to have recognized two such *prima facie* categories.[100] While the category approach permits a more generalized approach, it risks undermining the *Sparrow* justification requirement — and with it the benefit of the *Sparrow* entrenchment protection.[101] Case-specific analysis seems to be a necessary consequence of *Sparrow*.

(vii) Justification

Before the enactment of the *Constitution Act, 1982*, the scope and existence of Aboriginal rights depended on whether or not they had been restricted (i.e., "regulated" or "abridged") or extinguished, and restriction and extinguishment depended on government intention. With the decision in *Sparrow* to accord Aboriginal rights entrenched status, it was necessary either to allow Aboriginal rights to prevail over government action in all situations, or to find some criterion other than government intention for determining when government action would be permitted to prevail. The Court chose the latter route. It said that government action will prevail over entrenched Aboriginal title to the extent that it is justified.[102] For post-section 35(1) government action, justification replaced government intention as a main test for validity.[103]

However, the shift was not complete. Justification replaced intention in regard to post-April 17, 1982 restriction or regulation, such as the licensing change challenged in *Sparrow* itself. However, it did not do so in regard to extinguishment by pre-April 17, 1982 government action, as seen above. Moreover, as seen, restriction that did not infringe escaped the justification requirements.

In at least one area, there was some question about the application of justification. What about post-April 17, 1982 extinguishment? Was it still possible, and thus subject to justification? Although a reference to "expropriation" in the *Sparrow* justification test suggested that it was, in a later decision the Court said that it was not.[104]

Justification in *Sparrow* was as subjective as infringement. The Court said valid legislative objectives must be "compelling and substantial", and it identified conservation and avoiding general harm as two eligible objectives.[105] It did not say how courts should determine what is "compelling and substantial". In *Gladstone*, discussed in **Chapter 9**, the Court has since said that judges should ask if an objective is directed at the general purposes of s. 35(1).[106] These criteria may be slightly less open-ended, although the purposes of s. 35(1) are formulated at a relatively general level.[107]

Which objectives other than conservation and preventing harm are compelling and substantial? *Gladstone* provided a list of possible examples.[108] Its concepts, such as "economic and regional fairness", rival those in *Sparrow* for subjectivity, and do not purport to be exhaustive.[109] For the criteria in *Sparrow*, are conservation and management objectives automatically valid?[110] What level of conservation is required?[111] Preservation of the resource to protect it from extinction? Preservation of the resource sufficient to maintain existing user levels? How will courts assess "harm to the general populace or to the Aboriginal peoples themselves"?

Other questions relate to the *Sparrow* criteria for assessing the manner in which a valid legislative objective has been implemented. How is it to be determined if there has been adequate consultation with the Aboriginal group in question? What conservation measures will require consultation? Which groups need to be consulted? How should the requirement of a priority allocation for Aboriginal users be assessed where land use interests rather than resource rights are involved?[112] What test should apply if the claimed right lacks in internal limits?[113] How is it determined if there has been minimum possible infringement to achieve the desired result? How are these questions to be monitored on an ongoing basis?[114]

How well equipped are courts to answer questions of this kind?[115] As will be seen in **Chapters 8 to 10**, the Court has worked hard since *Sparrow* to rise to the challenge, and has managed to fill in some of the larger gaps.[116] Nevertheless, the results have been mixed. In rejecting a "crazy patchwork of regulations" in 1990, was the Court substituting its own patchwork of judicial discretion?[117]

Notes

1. Schedule B to the *Canada Act, 1982* (U.K.), 1982, c. 11.
2. 1983, R.S.C. 1985, Appendix II, No. 46. See **Reading 7(b)**.
3. For this and subsequent constitutional developments, see E. McWhinney, *Canada and the Constitution: 1979–1982* (Toronto: University of Toronto Press, 1982); D. Milne, *The Canadian Constitution* (Toronto: James Lorimer, 1991); R. Sheppard and M. Valpy, *The National Deal: The Fight for a Canadian Constitution* (Toronto: Fleet Books, 1982); N. K. Zlotkin, *Unfinished Business: Aboriginal Peoples and the Constitutional Conference* (Kingston: Institute of Intergovernmental Relations, 1983); R. Romanow, J. Whyte, H. Leeson, *Canada ... Notwithstanding: The Making of the Constitution, 1976–1982* (Toronto: Carswell/Methuen, 1984); B. Schwartz, *First Principles, Second Thoughts: Aboriginal Peoples, Constitutional Reform and Canadian Statecraft* (Kingston: Institute of Intergovernmental Relations, 1985); D.W. Elliott, *The Legal Status of Aboriginal and Treaty Rights in Section 35(1) of the Constitution Act, 1982* (Ottawa: Canadian Bar Association, 1990) at 19–30.
4. Mr. Jean Chrétien, then Minister of Justice, later explained that the government did not propose a simple positive affirmation of rights because of concerns that this could result in other rights inadvertently being left out of the affirmation: Minutes of Proceedings and Evidence of the Special Joint Committee of the Senate and of the House of Commons on the Constitution of Canada, First Session of the Thirty-second Parliament, 1980–81, vol. 3 at 33.
5. D.W. Elliott, *The Legal Status of Aboriginal and Treaty Rights in Section 35(1) of the Constitution Act, 1982* (Ottawa: Canadian Bar Association, 1990) at 21.
6. *Ibid.*
7. The Senate approved it on April 24, 1981.
8. *Ibid.* at 24–25.
9. *The Queen v. Secretary of State for Foreign and Commonwealth Affairs*, [1982] 2 All E.R. 118 (C.A.: U.K.).
10. *R. v. Sparrow*, [1990] 1 S.C.R. 1075 (May 31, 1990) aff'g (1986), 36 D.L.R. (4th) 246 (B.C.C.A.) rev'g [1986] B.C.W.L.D. 599 (B.C. Co. Ct.) aff'g a conviction by Goulet Prov. Ct. J. The analysis of *Sparrow* here is adapted from D.W. Elliott, "In the Wake of *Sparrow*: A New Department of Fisheries?" (1991) 40 U.N.B.L.J. at 23–43. Used with permission.
11. **Chapter 1, Part 3**.
12. See **Chapters 3** and **4**.
13. **Chapter 3**. The Proclamation did focus on Indian rights to land: *ibid.*
14. *Calder v. British Columbia (A.G.)*, [1973] S.C.R. 313 at 344.
15. *Ibid.*

16. It did hold that claimed Aboriginal rights were subject to federal legislation (*R. v. Derriksan* (1977), 71 D.L.R. (3d) 159 (S.C.C.): a one-paragraph decision) and to some provincial legislation (*Kruger and Manuel v. The Queen*, [1978] 1 S.C.R. 104 (S.C.C.)).
17. *Kanatewat et al. v. The James Bay Development Corporation and Quebec (A.G.)*, [1975] C.A. 166 at 175 (Q.C.A.)
18. The literature on this section is voluminous. See, for example, K. Lysyk, "The Rights and Freedoms of the Aboriginal Peoples of Canada (ss. 25, 35 and 37)" in W. Tarnopolsky and G.A. Beaudoin, eds., *The Canadian Charter of Rights and Freedoms: Commentary* (Toronto: Carswell, 1982) at 467; K. McNeil, "The Constitutional Rights of the Aboriginal Peoples of Canada" (1982) 4 Sup. Ct. L. Rev. 255; D. Sanders, "The Rights of the Aboriginal Peoples of Canada" in S. Beck and I. Bernier, eds., *Canada and the New Constitution: The Unfinished Agenda*, vol. 1 (Montreal: Institute for Research on Public Policy, 1983); B. Slattery, "The Constitutional Guarantee of Aboriginal and Treaty Rights" (1983) 8 Queens L.J. 232; B. Schwartz, *First Principles, Second Thoughts: Aboriginal Peoples, Constitutional Reform and Canadian Statecraft*, *supra* note 3; K. McNeil, "The Constitutional Act, 1982, Sections 25 and 35" [1988] 1 C.N.L.R. 1; W.F. Pentney, "The Rights of the Aboriginal Peoples of Canada in the Constitution Act, 1982, Part II" (1988) 22 U.B.C. Law Rev. 207; and B. Slattery, "Understanding Aboriginal Rights" (1987) 66 Can. Bar Rev. 727.
19. The word "guaranteed" did appear in s. 35(4) of the *Constitution Act, 1982*, added in 1984. Arguably, though, the concern of this provision is to guarantee the equal enjoyment of s. 35(1) rights, not the rights themselves. If the latter effect had been intended it would have been a simple matter to add the word "guaranteed" to s. 35(1) itself.
20. "The *Canadian Charter of Rights and Freedoms* guarantees the rights and freedoms set out in it subject only to such reasonable limits prescribed by law as can be demonstrably justified in a free and democratic society": *Constitution Act, 1982*, being Schedule B to the *Canada Act, 1982* (U.K.), c. 11, s. 1.
21. Section 35(3), added in 1984, says that "For greater certainty, in subsection (1) 'treaty rights' includes rights that now exist by way of land claims agreements or may be so acquired."
22. For example, limiting entrenchment to post-April 17, 1982, government restrictions.
23. For example, limiting entrenchment to provincial government restrictions.
24. For example, limiting entrenchment to government restrictions not agreed to by the Aboriginal community concerned.
25. *Supra* note 1, s. 35(1).
26. **Chapter 4**.
27. *Guerin v. The Queen*, [1984] S.C.R. 335, **Chapter 4, Part 4** and **Chapter 8**.
28. See **Chapter 8, Parts 3 and 4**.
29. For example, while the Saskatchewan Queens Bench held that s. 35(1) treaty rights were not entrenched against pre-April 17, 1982 legislation: *R. v. Eninew* (1983), 1 D.L.R. (4th) 595 (S.Q.B.), upheld on somewhat different grounds in [1984] 2 C.N.L.R. 126 (S.C.A.), the Ontario Court of Appeal suggested in *R. v. Hare and Debassige* (1985), 20 C.C.C. (3d) 1 (O.C.A.) that s. 35(1) rights were entrenched against legislation enacted after, but not before, April 17, 1982; and a British Columbia decision. As we will see in **Part 4(b)**, below, the British Columbia took a very different approach in *Sparrow* itself.
30. *R. v. Sparrow*, [1990] S.C.R. 1075 (S.C.C.).
31. R.S.C. 1970, c. F-14.
32. For a typical early approach, see *R. v. Eninew* (1983), 1 D.L.R. (4th) 595 (Sask. Q.B.). See the other cases noted in D.W. Elliott, *The Legal Status of Aboriginal and Treaty Rights in Section 35(1)* (Ottawa: Canadian Bar Association, 1990), part 7.
33. *Supra* note 29 (in *Hare*).
34. About the time of the B.C. Court of Appeal's decision, an article appeared in the *Canadian Bar Review* articulating a similar approach. Professor Brian Slattery's article, "Understanding Aboriginal Rights" (1987) Can. Bar Rev. 727 at 782, was influential in subsequent decisions such as *R. v. Agawa* (1989), 65 O.R. (2d) 505 (O.C.A.) and *Sparrow* at the Supreme Court level.
35. For example, *R. v. N.T.C. Smokehouse Ltd.*, [1990] B.C.J. No. 434 (B.C. Co. Ct.) at 26; *R. v. Machatis*, [1990] A.J. No. 203 (A.Q.B.) at 11 and 16; and *R. v. Denny*, [1990] N.S.J. No. 56 (N.S.C.A.). Most dramatically, the Ontario Court of Appeal rejected its earlier approach in *R. v. Hare and Debassige* (1985), 20 C.C.C. (3d) 1 at 16, and supported a form of entrenchment / justification in *R. v. Agawa* (1989), 65 O.R. (2d) 505 (O.C.A.), reversing a decision of Vannini D.C.J. which had upheld six charges.
36. *R. v. Sparrow*, [1990] S.C.R. 1075 (S.C.C.), per Dickson C.J. and La Forest J. for the Court. The other members who participated in the decision were McIntyre, Lamer, Wilson, L'Heureux-Dubé, and Sopinka JJ.
37. *Ibid.* at 1091–93.
38. *Ibid.* at 1093.
39. *Ibid.* at 1095.
40. *Ibid.* at 1094.
41. *Ibid.* at 1099. See also 1094.
42. *Ibid.* at 1099.
43. *Ibid.* at 1101.
44. *Ibid.* at 1111.
45. *Ibid.* at 1109.
46. *Ibid.* at 1091.
47. *Ibid.* at 1094 and 1099.
48. *Baker Lake v. Canada (Minister of Indian and Northern Affairs)* (1980), 107 D.L.R. (3d) 513 at 545–45. (F.C.T.D.), **Chapter 4, Part 3**. Mahoney J.'s four requirements in *Baker Lake* had been cited and applied frequently in subsequent cases: see, for example, *Ontario (A.G.) v. Bear Island Foundation* (1984), 15 D.L.R. (4th) 321 at 335 (O.H.C.); *R. v. Cote*, [1989] 3 C.N.L.R. 141 at 156 (Que. Prov. Ct.); and *Jules v. Harper Ranch*, [1989] B.C.J. No. 861, Vancouver Reg. C890403, May 1989, at 52. Contrary to the *Baker Lake* test, the Court in *Sparrow* did not require exclusivity of use.
49. The Supreme Court quoted from the Court of Appeal's finding that there was no "serious dispute" in *Sparrow* about the existence of the Musqueam's Aboriginal right: 1095, referring to *R. v. Sparrow* (1987), 36 D.L.R. (4th) 246 at 254 (B.C.C.A.). See *R. v. Van der Peet*, [1996] 2 S.C.R. 507 at para. 2, making this point. On the other hand, the decision was ruling on the status of *all* s. 35(1) Aboriginal rights, many of which would be more contentious than the food fishing rights of the Musqueam.
50. *R. v. Van der Peet*, [1996] 2 S.C.R. 507, **Chapter 9, Part 3**.
51. *Ibid.* at 1095. See generally, the discussion of problems of evidence and proof in *Delgamuukw v. British Columbia* (1991), 79 D.L.R. (4th) 185 (B.C.S.C.) at 252–82 and 494–534.
52. It did not say what would qualify as ceremonial.
53. On one hand, recognizing an Aboriginal commercial fishing right would have been consistent with the Court's view that s. 35 requires Aboriginal rights to be construed generously, and "in a contemporary form" (1093). On the other hand, such a right could place holders of Aboriginal rights in a stronger position than the Aboriginal residents of the Prairie provinces, as these people are subject to the "for food" limitation of the *Natural Resources Transfer Agreements* (see **Chapter 6, Part 5**). It could also bring Aboriginal claimants into more obvious competition with non-Aboriginal commercial fishing interests.

54. The commercial fishing issue would re-surface again in the Court in 1996: see **Chapter 9, Parts 3 and 4**.
55. See *supra* note 49. This was the explanation given in *R. v. Van der Peet*, [1996] 2 S.C.R. 507 at para. 2.
56. *Ibid.* at 1103. These statements were relatively consistent with earlier legal doctrine on prior occupation. On sovereignty and underlying title, cf. *St. Catherine's Milling and Lumber Company v. The Queen* (1888), 14 App. Cas. 46 at 55 (J.C.P.C.); cited in *Calder v. British Columbia (A.G.)*, [1973] S.C.R. 313 at 322 (Judson J.) and 380 (Hall J.). Cf. *Quebec (A.G.) v. Sioui* (1990), 70 D.L.R. (4th) 427 at 450 (S.C.C.), in the context of early Aboriginal-European relations.
57. *R. v. Van der Peet*, [1996] 2 S.C.R. 507, **Chapter 9, Part 3**.
58. *Sparrow*, *supra* note 36 at 1093, quoting from B. Slattery, "Understanding Aboriginal Rights" (1987) 66 Can. Bar Rev. 727 at 782.
59. For example, *Simon v. The Queen* (1985), 24 D.L.R. (4th) 390 at 403 (S.C.C.) and *R. v. Badger*, [1996] 1 S.C.R. 771 at para. 41, and cf. the liberal approach to continuity in *R. v. Van der Peet*, [1996] 2 S.C.R. 507 at para. 65.
60. Extinguishment by government action after April 17, 1982 is no longer possible: *infra* note 104.
61. *Calder v. British Columbia (A.G.)*, [1973] S.C.R. 313 at 344. Judson J. quoted (at 335) from *U.S. v. Santa Fe Pacific R. Co.* (1941), 314 U.S. 339 at 347 (U.S.S.Ct.), which said Indian title can be extinguished "by the exercise of complete dominion adverse to the right of occupancy."
62. *Calder ibid.* at 404. Hall J. quoted (at 404) from *Lipan Apache Tribe v. U.S.* (1967), 180 Ct. Chill. 487 (U.S. Ct. Chill.), which said that "[i]n the absence of a 'clear and plain indication' in the public records that the sovereign 'intended to extinguish' all of the [claimants'] rights in their property, Indian title continues...." In *Lipan*, *supra*, the United States Supreme Court quoted in turn from *United States v. Santa Fe Pacific R.R.* 314 U.S. 339 at 353 (U.S.S.Ct.), the apparent origin of the "clear and plain" test.
63. *Sparrow*, *supra* note 36 at 1095–97.
64. *Ibid.* at 1099. The Court did not explain this choice. Was it influenced by the pro-Indian presumption in *Nowegijick v. The Queen*, [1983] 1 S.C.R. 29 at 36 (S.C.C.)? By the fact of s. 35(1)? By the common law presumption against expropriation of property?
65. That is, government action amounting to complete dominion inconsistent with any conflicting interest.
66. If it was rejecting necessary inconsistency, including Judson J.'s concept of complete dominion inconsistent with any conflicting interests, then the Court did not leave much room for implied extinguishment. Perhaps Judson J.'s test could reach the clear and plain intention threshold in a situation where the main or sole conflicting interests are Aboriginal rights. This might explain how the British Columbia Supreme Court could have found sufficient intention to extinguish in *Delgamuukw v. British Columbia* (1991), 79 D.L.R. (4th) 185 at 472–78 (B.C.S.C.), a case involving some of the same colonial enactments as *Calder*. Note, though, that the British Columbia Court of Appeal reversed this decision. It took the more restrictive view that under the clear and plain intention test, "there can only be extinguishment by necessary implication if the only possible interpretation of the statute is that Aboriginal rights were intended to be extinguished": (1993), 104 D.L.R. (4th) 470 at 524 (Macfarlane J.A. for himself and Taggart J.A., with Wallace J.A. agreeing in separate reasons). See further **Chapter 10, Part 3**.
67. Hall J. had provided little guidance in *Calder* itself. At 403–404 of *Calder*, he quoted from a decision indicating that in peacetime, extinguishment can only be affected with the consent of the Aboriginal peoples. At 401, he considered relevant the absence of "express words extinguishing aboriginal title" and of "legislation specifically purporting to extinguish the aboriginal title." At 413, he appeared to contemplate the possibility of extinguishment by implication, but said no such extinguishment had been authorized in *Calder*. The *Santa Fe* decision, the apparent origin of Hall J.'s "clear and plain" requirement, did contemplate implied extinguishment, but added that it "cannot be *lightly* implied": *supra* note 61 (emphasis added).
68. See **Chapter 10, Part 4**, proposition 17 and **Chapter 8, Part 6**. For an attempt at clarification below the Supreme Court level, see Macfarlane J.A.'s suggested test in *Delgamuukw v. British Columbia*, *supra* note 66 at 524.
69. *Sparrow*, *supra* note 36 at 1108–109.
70. *Ibid.* at 1115–17.
71. *Ibid.* esp. at 1108, referring to *Guerin v. The Queen*, [1984] 2 S.C.R. 335 (**Chapter 4, Part 4** and **Chapter 8, Parts 4** and **8**). The Court also referred in *Sparrow* to the concept of the honour of the Crown: *ibid.* at 1105 and 1108.
72. *Ibid.* at 1115.
73. Rejected in *Sparrow*, *supra* note 36 at 1109–10.
74. Rejected in *Sparrow*, *supra* note 36 at 1091, 1093, 1109.
75. Adopted in *Sparrow*, *supra* note 36 at 1109–10. Another option, not seriously considered, but referred to and dismissed in passing, was preservation of the *status quo*: 1106.
76. *Ibid.* at 1109.
77. *Ibid.* at 1091.
78. *Ibid.* at 1109–10.
79. *Ibid.* at 1109.
80. See especially *R. v. Oakes*, [1986] 1 S.C.R. 103 (S.C.R.), which was —and for the most part continues to be — the leading case on the interpretation to s. 1 of the *Charter*. In *Oakes*, the Court said s. 1 guarantees *Charter* rights and freedoms against limitations, except where a limit relates to an objective which is sufficiently important (it should be "pressing and substantial", for example), and is proportional to the objective in the sense that (i) there is a rational connection between the limit and the objective, (ii) the limit impairs the *Charter* right or freedom as little as possible to achieve the objective, and (iii) the effect of the limit is in proportion to the importance of the objective.
81. Compare the wording of ss. 1 and 35(1). Arguably, too, the word "guaranteed" in s. 35(4), which was added in 1984, refers to the equal enjoyment of the rights in s. 35(1), and not to the status of the rights themselves.
82. On this option, see D.W. Elliott, *The Legal Status of Aboriginal and Treaty Rights in Section 35(1)* (Ottawa: Canadian Bar Association, 1990), Part 5.
83. For example, the Court might have clarified if all Aboriginal rights have the same general status, and if status differences (other than those relating to extinguishment) prior to s. 35(1) are relevant to the status of the rights in this section. Are Proclamation-based rights different from occupancy-based rights? And are rights affected by European "conquest" different in status from rights affected by European "settlement"? (See generally **Chapters 3** and **4**.) Are Aboriginal rights different in areas settled by New France than those elsewhere? (On the latter question, see *R. v. Adams*, [1996] 3 S.C.R. 101, para. 33 and *R. v. Côté*, [1996] 3 S.C.R. 139 at paras. 46–53: **Chapter 10, Part 2**.)
84. Although it seriously considered only entrenchment options, the Court ended up enhancing some aspects of Aboriginal rights as *well* as adopting one form of entrenchment. As seen in **Part 4(d)(i)**, it took a very liberal approach to the existence and standard of proof required and, as seen in **Part 4(d)(ii)**, it tightened the requirements for proof of extinguishment. It attributed the latter development both to a general interpretation pre-

sumption in favour of Aboriginal rights (1110) and to its view of s. 35 as a kind of fiduciary promise to Aboriginal people (*ibid.*).

85. That is, whether they are Proclamation-based rights, occupancy-based rights, those from conquest areas, those from settlement areas, or those from areas formerly occupied by New France.
86. From later cases, the Court's answer would appear to be yes: see, for example, *R. v. Adams*, [1996] 3 S.C.R. 101 at para. 33 and *R. v. Côté*, [1996] 3 S.C.R. 139 at paras. 46–53, minimizing pre-section 35(1) differences in Aboriginal rights.
87. The answer is now, generally speaking, yes: *R. v. Badger*, [1996] 1 S.C.R. 771 at paras. 37, 77, 78, and 79; *R. v. Côté*, [1996] 3 S.C.R. 139 at para. 33, **Chapter 10, Part 4**.
88. Presumably the latter was included as well. In *Sparrow* itself, Mr. Sparrow's specific concern was that the net length restriction *in the Minister's licence* (itself an administrative action rather than legislation) was inconsistent with his Aboriginal rights. The Court seemed to treat both government legislation and administrative action generically as "regulation".
89. See text at *supra* note 21.
90. The Court said s. 35(1) "affords aboriginal peoples constitutional protection against provincial legislative power": 1105. The Court has since re-affirmed that s. 35(1) protections apply to provincial as well as federal laws: *R. v. Badger*, [1996] 1 S.C.R. 771 at para. 85; *R. v. Côté*, [1996] 3 S.C.R. 139 at para. 74.
91. *Sparrow*, 1097–98. (The Court's discussion did not extend to consensual arrangements affecting Aboriginal rights.)
92. *Ibid.*
93. The Court differentiated between (a) regulation in this sense and (b) "regulations" or "regulatory" as opposed to "statutes" and "statutory": e.g., *Sparrow*, *supra* note 36 at 1097 and 1111.
94. **Part 4(c)**, above.
95. In *R. v. Gladstone*, [1996] 2 S.C.R. 723 at paras. 43 and 52, the Court said that whereas at the infringement stage, the Court considers if the cumulative effect of the factors has been to limit the Aboriginal right, at the justification stage the relevant factors are considered separately: **Chapter 9, Part 4**. *Quaere*, if this proposition fully addresses the question of the relative importance of the infringement criteria?
96. Accurate statistics may be elusive, and the reasonableness requirement adds to the difficulty of the inquiry. In *R. v. Joseph*, [1990] B.C.J. No. 1749 (B.C.S.C.), a treaty case applying the *Sparrow* infringement and justification tests, it was conceded that the evidence regarding the adequacy of the Indians' catch for their needs was "vague and imprecise".
97. See *R. v. Joseph (No. 2)*, [1990] Y.J. No. 37 (Y. Terr. Ct.), where the Aboriginal people and, apparently, some of the enforcement officers thought the Indian food licence precluded fishing for grayling by means of rod and reel. Need the preferred means be a traditional means? Could it include personal preference? Where does "control" amount to "denial"?
98. *Sparrow*, *supra* note 36 at 1112.
99. In *Gladstone*, *supra* note 95 at para. 52, the Court cautioned that "[t]he [infringement] test as laid out in *Sparrow* is determined to a certain extent by the factual context in which it was articulated; the Court must take into account variations in the factual context of the appeal which affect the application of the test": para. 39.
100. Mere licensing requirements and safety regulation: see *R.* v. *Nikal*, [1996] 1 S.C.R. 1013 at paras. 91–96 and *R. v. Badger*, [1996] 1 S.C.R. 771 at para. 89, respectively, **Chapter 10, Part 4**.
101. A government restriction that is not an infringement is not subject to the *Sparrow* justification requirement.
102. *Sparrow*, *supra* note 36 at 1110.
103. For some of the key justification decisions since *Sparrow*, see **Chapter 10, Part 4**, proposition 21 below.
104. See now *R. v. Van der Peet*, [1996] 2 S.C.R. 507, para. 28: "Subsequent to s. 35(1) aboriginal rights cannot be extinguished and can only be regulated or infringed consistent with the justificatory test laid out by this Court in *Sparrow*...."
105. *Ibid.* at 1113.
106. *Gladstone*, *supra* note 95 at para. 72, **Chapter 9, Part 4**.
107. See *Gladstone*, *ibid.* at para. 72, where the Court said that compelling and substantial objectives "will be those directed at either the recognition of the prior occupation of North America by aboriginal peoples or ... at the reconciliation of aboriginal prior occupation with the assertion of the sovereignty of the Crown." See also **Chapter 10, Part 4**, proposition 21 below. Is it still relevant whether the objectives are "uncontroversial"?: *Sparrow*, 1113.
108. *Ibid.* at para. 75, and **Chapter 9, Part 4**.
109. *Ibid.*
110. Not necessarily, according to the Court in *R. v. Côté*, [1996] 3 S.C.R. 139 at para. 82.
111. See the reference to this controversy in *R. v. Nikal*, [1990] B.C.J. No. 2376 at 8–9.
112. See *Delgamuukw v. British Columbia*, [1991] B.C.J. No. 525 (B.C.S.C.) at 886–903, suggesting that multiple land use situations would require a more flexible process, more oriented to "reconciliation" than justification alone.
113. See *Gladstone*, *supra* note 95 at paras. 62–64, and **Chapter 9, Part 4**, modifying the *Sparrow* priority formula to take account of this situation.
114. For some of the key post-*Sparrow* decisions on these issues, see **Chapter 10, Part 4**, proposition 21 (justification). See also proposition 17 (extinguishment) and propositions 19 and 20 (infringement).
115. In the writer's view, Aboriginal issues are more than legal issues. Arguably, they require governmental expertise, political judgment, negotiated arrangements, and effective political involvement by Aboriginal peoples themselves more than they require open-ended judicial discretion. (For a more expansive view of the potential of courts in this area, see Royal Commission on Aboriginal Peoples, *Partners in Confederation: Aboriginal Peoples, Self-Government, and the Constitution* (Ottawa: R.C.A.P., 1993), and most of the sources cited in notes 66 and 100 therein.)
116. See also notes to **Part 4(d)** of this chapter indicating some of the major comments or clarifications since *Sparrow*.
117. On courts and constitutional discretion generally, see J.H. Ely, *Democracy and Distrust: A Theory of Judicial Review* (Cambridge, Mass.: Harvard University Press, 1980: an American analysis); P. Monahan, *Politics and the Constitution: The Charter, Federalism and the Supreme Court of Canada* (Toronto: Carswell, 1987); R. Knopff and F.L. Morton, *Charter Politics* (Scarborough: Nelson Canada, 1992); M. Mandel, *The Charter of Rights and the Legalization of Politics in Canada* (Toronto: Thompson, 1992); C.P. Manfredi, *Judicial Power and the Charter* (Toronto: McClelland & Stewart: 1993); W.A. Bogart, *Courts and Country: The Limits of Litigation and the Social and Political Life of Canada* (Toronto: Oxford University Press, 1994). For support for a broader judicial role, see D. Beatty, *Talking Heads and the Supremes: The Canadian Production of the Constitutional Review* (Toronto: Carswell, 1990). Although it is obviously too late to turn back from entrenchment, infringement, and justification, it is not too late to try to reduce uncertainty by seeking less subjective criteria wherever possible.

8 Fiduciary Duties

Chapter Highlights

- The Crown can owe a special fiduciary duty to Aboriginal peoples. This obligation is a particular application of the general concept of the honour of the Crown.
- Although the Crown's fiduciary duty to Aboriginal peoples bears some resemblance to ordinary fiduciary notions, it is unique.
- The Crown's fiduciary obligation to Aboriginal peoples does not exist at large, but in relation to specific Aboriginal interests.
- For the special Crown fiduciary duty to exist, there must be: a Crown undertaking to act for the benefit of Aboriginal peoples in regard to a specific, cognizable Aboriginal interest; Crown discretionary power to carry out the undertaking; and a corresponding vulnerability on the part of the Aboriginal peoples.
- The special Crown fiduciary duty is related to, but distinct from, the Crown's promissory duty to justify infringement rights that are recognized and affirmed in s. 35(1) of the *Constitution Act, 1982*. Both obligations are grounded in the general principle of the honour of the Crown. However, the former results from the Crown's assumption of discretionary control over specific Aboriginal interests, while the latter results from a Crown promise to protect constitutional rights and extends to rights that are either asserted or specific in nature.
- While the Crown's s. 35(1) promissory duty may have fiduciary features, it can apply outside fiduciary contexts to protect 35(1) rights that are neither defined nor resolved.
- The Crown's fiduciary duty requires a high standard of dealing in relation to Aboriginal peoples. The Crown is generally required to act in the best interests of the relevant Aboriginal group, although the precise content of the duty depends on the circumstances of the particular case and may be affected by the Crown's public and third party responsibilities. The s. 35(1) promissory duty requires a valid legislative objective, and conciliatory measures such as consultation and accommodation. Its content can also vary with the circumstances. Breach of the fiduciary duty can give rise to equitable relief; breach of the s. 35(1) duty renders a government infringement unconstitutional.

Synopsis

Under the general law, a fiduciary relationship is the equitable relationship that results when one party undertakes to act for the benefit of a second party, who depends on the discretionary power of the first to carry out the undertaking. The first party is subject to a fiduciary duty to the second. Although courts do not impose fiduciary obligations on the Crown, in some situations the Crown can owe a fiduciary duty to Aboriginal peoples, a duty that derives from the general principle of the honour of the Crown. It is important, then, to explore the (i) source, (ii) character, (iii) scope, and (iv) content of this obligation. All questions require a look at the foundation case of *Guerin*. It is also relevant to look at the 1990 *Sparrow* decision, which involves a related but distinct Crown duty. For the fourth question, the chapter considers how courts must balance government's public responsibilities with the high best interests standard required by the fiduciary duty.

Selected Readings

🖹 links material in this chapter to the corresponding headings and page numbers of the relevant readings.

🖹 Parts 4 and 6	*Guerin v. The Queen*	330
🖹 Parts 5 and 6	*R. v. Sparrow*	330
🖹 Part 8(b)	*Blueberry River Indian Band v. Canada (Department of Indian Affairs and Northern Development)*	331
🖹 Part 8(c)	*R. v. Badger*	286
	Delgamuukw v. British Columbia	355
🖹 Part 8(e)	*Wewaykum Indian Band v. Canada*	333
🖹 Part 8(f)	*Haida Nation v. British Columbia (Minister of Forests)*	378

1. INTRODUCTION

As we have seen, the Supreme Court said in *Guerin* that the Crown can owe a special fiduciary duty to the Aboriginal peoples of Canada.[1] In *Sparrow*, the Court said that the Crown is obliged to justify infringements of rights protected by s. 35(1) of the *Constitution Act, 1982*. This chapter focuses key questions about this obligation:[2] "What is the source of the obligation?" "What interests or concerns are protected by it?" It considers two other general questions: "What standard or content does the obligation require?"[3] and "Who is bound by it?"[4]

2. "ORDINARY" FIDUCIARY RELATIONSHIPS

Since the courts have said the Crown can owe a fiduciary duty to Aboriginal peoples, it is useful to look briefly at general fiduciary law. This will provide little more than background, though. The courts stress that the fiduciary relationship between Aboriginal peoples and the Crown is *sui generis*, or unique.

(a) Character and Scope

Defining the character and scope of the Crown's special fiduciary obligation is complicated by the lack of a clear definition of an "ordinary" fiduciary relationship. In 1985, Sir Anthony Mason described the fiduciary relationship as "a concept in search of a principle".[5] Although there has been progress,[6] the search is still far from complete.[7] In general terms, a fiduciary relationship might be described as the equitable relationship that results when one party undertakes to act for the benefit of a second party, who depends on the power of the first to carry out the undertaking.[8] In some circumstances, an obligation pursuant to a fiduciary relationship can impose an enforceable duty[9] on the fiduciary, or it may produce other tangible legal consequences.[10] The relationship can result from the status of the parties or from a specific fact situation.[11] A common form of status-based fiduciary relationship is a trust, which has special features of its own.[12]

As well, there is a general common law presumption against imposing legally enforceable trust obligations on the Crown.[13] Technically, it is incongruous to impose a trust obligation on government in regard to property that government itself originally created. Beyond this, though, the presumptions find support in two general policy concerns. First, an obligation that can demand exclusive regard for the interests of one group[14] could be difficult to reconcile with the Crown's responsibilities to the public as a whole.[15] Second, court-imposed duties could interfere with the Crown's political accountability for these responsibilities.[16]

(b) Content

Although there is considerable variation in statements about the content of an "ordinary" fiduciary duty, it might be described generally as a duty to act with loyalty and in the best interests of the beneficiary.[17] Loyalty to the beneficiary is often invoked,[18] and references to "utmost good faith"[19] and avoidance of conflict of interest are also common.[20] McLachlin J. has described "loyalty, good faith and avoidance of a conflict of duty and self-interest" as the "classic" fiduciary duties.[21] In *Lac Minerals*, La Forest J. said:

> The obligation imposed [where there is a specific category of fiduciary relationship] may vary in its specific substance depending on the relationship, though compendiously it can be described as the fiduciary duty of loyalty and will most often include the avoidance of a conflict of a duty and interest and a duty not to profit at the expense of the beneficiary.[22]

Generally speaking, then, it appears that the ordinary fiduciary standard can range from the "classic" duties of loyalty, utmost good faith, and conflict avoidance applicable to most situations to less onerous requirements, such as good faith and non-disclosure.[23] Normally, though, the beneficiary's interests should be considered first.

3. SOURCE OF OBLIGATION

Until recently, there was a lack of clarity about the general source of the Crown's fiduciary duty. Was it simply a special application of trust law, supported by the unique nature of interests such as

† Some of the earlier material in this chapter was adapted from D.W. Elliott, "Aboriginal Peoples in Canada and the United States and the Scope of the Special Fiduciary Relationship" (1996) 24 Man. L.J. 137. Reproduced with permission.

Aboriginal title, and by the Crown's special commitments to Aboriginal peoples?[24] Did it have an additional basis in s. 35(1) of the *Constitution Act, 1982*?[25] Did it go beyond the trust-type and s. 35(1) contexts above, and attach to virtually all aspects of the relationship between the Crown and Aboriginal peoples[26]? Was it a trust-type application of a general underlying principle of the honour of the Crown, a principle capable of other applications in other contexts?

In the 2004 *Haida Nation* decision, the Supreme Court took the latter approach. Building on its earlier decision in Wewaykum,[27] the Court said that the Crown's special fiduciary obligation to Aboriginal peoples is one application of the broader principle that underpins all aspects of the relationship between the Crown and Aboriginal peoples, the principle of the honour of the Crown.[28] Unlike the more general principle, the Crown's special fiduciary duty does not apply to all aspects of the relationship between the Crown-Aboriginal relationship. In particular, it is limited to specific, cognizable Aboriginal interests.[29]

4. *GUERIN*

🖹 Reading 8(a) at 330

The foundation case on the Crown's special fiduciary duty to Aboriginal peoples is the Supreme Court's 1984 decision in *Guerin*.[30] Here the Supreme Court held for the first time that the Crown can owe to Aboriginal peoples a fiduciary duty that is binding in law.[31] It remains the main authority on the scope and content of the duty.

(a) Facts

The facts in *Guerin* go back to the 1950s, when Indian Affairs officials arranged a surrender and lease of reserve land. Without consulting the band council, they negotiated lease terms that were far less favourable to the band than originally planned. The Supreme Court held that the Crown[32] owed the band a fiduciary duty to deal equitably with their land when surrendering it. The Court said the Crown had breached this duty, and must pay the band $10 million in compensation.[33]

(b) Judgments

Dickson and Wilson JJ. delivered the leading judgments.[34] Speaking for a plurality of the Court,[35] Dickson J. said there was a fiduciary relationship between the Crown and Indians. It was not an ordinary fiduciary relationship; it was *sui generis* in nature.[36] The relationship derived from the Indians' Aboriginal title and from the Crown's historic responsibility to protect Indian lands in transactions with third parties.[37] Because it derived from an interest that was independent of the Crown, the relationship could generate an obligation "in the nature of a private law duty,"[38] not just a political trust. The responsibility was confirmed by the specific *Indian Act* power to act on the Indians' behalf when surrendering their lands. The power gave rise to a concrete Crown fiduciary duty to the Indians.[39] This duty resembled a trust.[40] It obliged the Crown to act with "utmost loyalty"[41] in conducting the surrender. By securing a less desirable lease without proper consultation, the Crown had breached the duty.

For Wilson J., too, this was no ordinary relationship. Like Dickson J., Wilson J. said the fiduciary obligation was based on Aboriginal title and the Crown's historic responsibility for Indian lands, and was confirmed by the *Indian Act* surrender provisions.[42] She said the Crown had a fiduciary obligation "at large"[43] that crystallized into a full trust at the surrender.[44]

Estey J., the eighth judge, rejected the notion of trusts and related fiduciary duties. He said the relationship was one of agency.[45] Estey J. regarded the agency as existing "now and historically".[46] He saw it as reflecting a "community interest in protecting the rights of the native population in those lands to which they had a longstanding connection."[47] In the result, all eight judges linked the specific duty that arose on surrender to an earlier relationship between the Crown and the Indians in regard to Indian lands. Seven of the eight treated the surrender obligation as being at least "trust-like" in nature.[48]

(c) Features

There are several main features of the special duty established in *Guerin*. First, the duty is *sui generis*.[49] Hence, although it may resemble common law fiduciary and trust duties, it is not identical to them.[50] It has an historic foundation, it binds the Crown (which is not normally a fiduciary), and it protects an interest that is in itself unique. Second, the duty in *Guerin* is specifically enforceable.[51] It is not a mere "political trust",[52] nor is it simply a canon of interpretation.[53] It can be specifically enforced by equitable remedies, such as monetary compensation.[54] Third, the *Guerin* duty is a form of fiduciary duty.[55] In his plurality judgment, Dickson J. said the basic requirements for a fiduciary duty — a unilateral undertaking and discretionary power[56] — were present in historic documents such as the Royal Proclamation of 1763, and in the more specific surrender provisions of the *Indian Act*.[57] Fourth, this is a trust-like, private-law duty.[58] It applies to Aboriginal interests that are property-like in nature, although distinct from ordinary property.[59] It is based on, or derived from, Aboriginal interests in land.[60] Fifth, and related to the features above, this duty attaches to interests that are specific, cognizable and concrete, not mere assertions or claims.[61] Finally, the duty requires loyalty by way of prime consideration to the Aboriginal peoples' protected interests.

(d) Relationship to Land

Aboriginal or Indian land was central to the *Guerin* duty in two ways. First, the key instruments on which the duty was founded, the Royal Proclamation and the surrender provisions of the *Indian Act*, were concerned primarily with Indian land.[62] Second it is because the original Aboriginal title was not dependent on the Crown, but arose independently of the Crown, that the duty in *Guerin* was enforceable at law.[63] Were it not for this independent interest, the duty would have been a political trust, enforceable only in a moral sense.[64]

The Court did not limit the *Guerin* duty to *Indian Act* reserves or to Aboriginal title lands. The duty might extend to other land-based Aboriginal rights, or to specific quasi-proprietary benefits in Indian land treaties.[65] On the other hand, the duty would not appear to extend generally to broad public benefits, such as public health or other social services.[66]

5. *SPARROW*

🖹 Reading 8(b) at 330

Chapter 7 noted that the Supreme Court referred to the special fiduciary relationship in its 1990 *Sparrow* decision on s. 35(1) of the *Constitution Act, 1982*, but the chapter did not discuss the relationship between the constitutional obligation in *Sparrow* and the fiduciary duty in *Guerin*.[67] This relationship will be explored here.

(a) Judgment

As seen in **Chapter 7**, Mr. Sparrow, a Musqueam Indian, had challenged his conviction for violating a licence requirement under the federal *Fisheries Act*. He argued that he had an Aboriginal right to fish, protected under s. 35 of the *Constitution Act, 1982*. The Supreme Court agreed, and said the federal government must justify infringing this right. Because of lack of evidence of infringement and justification, the case was sent back to trial.[68]

To support the view that s. 35(1) provided a form of guarantee, and to support its justification requirement, the Court referred to the "unique" general relationship between the Crown and Aboriginal peoples;[69] the common law presumption in favour of treaties and statutes relating to Aboriginal peoples;[70] the finding in *Guerin* that the Crown owes a fiduciary obligation to Indians in regard to their lands; and the statement in *Taylor and Williams*[71] that the honour of the Crown is involved in the interpretation of Indian treaties.[72] The Court said that these cases supported "a general guiding principle for s. 35(1)"[73] — the principle that "the government has the responsibility to act in a fiduciary capacity with respect to Aboriginal peoples.

On the basis of this discussion, the Court said that the wording of s. 35(1)[74] should be treated as "a solemn promise that must be given meaningful content,"[75] and that this content was a requirement that the Crown justify any infringements of s. 35(1) rights. In particular, if the Crown could demonstrate a valid objective, it must also comply with a duty to consult with and accommodate the s. 35(1) interest in a variety of possible ways. These could include giving priority to s. 35(1) rights, prior consultation, and other forms of accommodation, such as compensation, in cases of expropriation.[76] In regard to this duty, the Court said that "the guiding interpretive principle" is the honour of the Crown,[77] and that the first consideration should be "[t]he special trust relationship and the responsibility of the government *vis-à-vis* aboriginals."[78]

The Court went on to formulate some specific examples of the justification criteria to be met. First, government must prove that it had a valid purpose for infringing a s. 35(1) right. Then it must show that it acted consistently with the honour of the Crown and the trust relationship between the Crown and Aboriginal peoples. However, failure to meet these criteria does not give rise to an equitable action, as in *Guerin*. Instead, it results in a declaration that the offending government regulation is unconstitutional and void.[79]

(b) Features of *Sparrow* Duty

Despite the references in *Sparrow* to fiduciary obligations and to the trust relationship, the s. 35(1) obligation is distinct from the fiduciary duty in *Guerin*. In general terms, the *Sparrow* obligation requires that government regulation must meet specific requirements in order to justify infringements of Aboriginal and treaty rights. The *Sparrow* obligation has four main features. First, like the duty in *Guerin*, this obligation is unique. It is not found outside the general relationship between the Crown and Aboriginal peoples. Second, this is a constitutional obligation in the most direct sense. Its immediate foundation is s. 35(1) of the *Constitution Act, 1982*. Because it is constitutionally entrenched, the *Sparrow* obligation can affect all government regulation, whether in individual administrative action, executive legislation, or statute. A key element of regulation is the notion of a rule,[80] an authoritative direction that is general in nature.[81] Hence the focus is on general government action. Third, the *Sparrow* obligation operates solely through an interpretive presumption, enforceable by a declaration of constitutional invalidity.[82] Courts look at government regulation that infringes s. 35(1) to determine if it meets judicial justification requirements. If it does not, the regulation is unconstitutional. There is no question here of a specific equitable action against the Crown, as there may be under *Guerin*.[83] Fourth, the subject matter of the *Sparrow* obligation is the existing Aboriginal and treaty rights that are constitutionally guaranteed under s. 35(1).[84] In other words, it is the *rights* that are the object of the Crown's duty, not all facets of its general relationship with Aboriginal peoples.[85]

How wide are these protected rights? As will be seen in **Chapters 9** and **10**, thus far the courts have tended to link Aboriginal rights to interests in land and natural resources. On the other hand, these interests can go well beyond Aboriginal title, and it is not clearly determined if *some* connection with land or resources will be required.[86] Even if such "non-land" interests as receipt of social services or general self-government powers were not automatically barred,[87] a link with traditional practices is required in the Aboriginal rights identification test formulated in *Van der Peet*.[88]

As well as Aboriginal rights, the *Sparrow* obligation extends to the existing treaty rights of the Aboriginal peoples of Canada. Section 35(3) defines treaty rights to include present and future land claims agreement rights.[89] Thus the *Sparrow* obligation can include both treaty rights that relate directly to land and those that do not.[90] Although most treaty provisions have some connection to land or related interests, some do not. An example of the latter is the "medicine chest" promise in Treaty No. 6,[91] which might well be interpreted more liberally today,[92] and should offer protection against unjustified infringement.[93] Unlike the obligations based on Aboriginal title or land, treaty obligations are limited to the terms of individual agreements. Depending on individual wording and on considerations such as relative bargaining positions, similar protection might be available for specific social services promises in land claims agreements.[94] As in the case of an Aboriginal right, though, a mere s. 35(1) treaty claim is insufficient to engage an enforceable Crown fiduciary obligation like that in *Guerin*. A specific, concrete interest is also needed, together with a specific Crown undertaking and evidence of Crown discretionary control.

What, then, is the connection between the *Guerin* duty and duty in *Sparrow*? Are they both distinct forms of fiduciary duty, despite the very specialized features of the latter? Or is there some other kind of link? In the *Haida Nation* decision, considered further in **Part (f)** below,[95] the Supreme Court shed some light on this question. Although the Court said that both duties share the underlying concept of the honour of the Crown, it appeared to suggest that only the *Guerin* duty is necessarily fiduciary in nature.[96] The Court treated the s. 35(1) duty as a distinct application of the Crown honour concept, triggered by a constitutional promise to protect Aboriginal and treaty rights.[97] Presumably, whether the s. 35(1) duty co-exists alongside a full *Guerin*-type fiduciary duty, has some fiduciary features, or is based on Crown honour alone, will depend on the individual context.[98]

6. CONTENT OF FIDUCIARY DUTY

Readings 4(c) at 265 and 7(c) at 318

(a) *Guerin* Duty

Guerin said that a fiduciary will be held to an exacting standard of conduct, and owes a duty of "utmost loyalty" to his principal.[99] Dickson J. saw the fiduciary duty as supporting the purpose of the surrender agreement, which was to prevent exploitation.[100] In the facts of this case, this required the

Crown to endeavour to keep its promises to the Indians, and to consult with the Indians before making any arrangement that would be less valuable for them.[101] Neither of these requirements had been followed, so the Court awarded the band $10 million in compensation. *Guerin* did not prescribe a set content for the fiduciary duty. It implied that the content will comprise whatever is equitable in the circumstances of the individual case.

(b) Comparison with *Sparrow* Duty

As in *Guerin*, the Supreme Court stressed in *Sparrow* that the Crown is held to a high standard.[102] However, unlike *Guerin*, *Sparrow* outlined a relatively detailed set of specific requirements for governments that seek to justify infringements of s. 35(1) rights. As these requirements are linked to the wording and context of the *Constitution Act, 1982*, they are discussed at greater length in **Chapters 7**,[103] **9**,[104] and **10**.[105]

Section 35(1) justification requires proof of a valid legislative objective, and proof of adequate government accommodation of the protected Aboriginal or treaty right. Accommodation measures might include: (i) giving the protected right priority after the valid objective, (ii) ensuring minimum possible infringement to achieve the objective, (iii) consulting where appropriate with the people concerned, and (iv) providing compensation in cases of expropriation.[106] *Sparrow* left the exact content of the Crown's duty to the circumstances of the individual case, but it supplied the framework and many of the criteria.

The *Sparrow* obligation exists alongside a collection of non-constitutional liberal canons of construction that can apply to Aboriginal peoples independently of s. 35(1). These canons are often not grounded in the notion of a Crown-Aboriginal fiduciary relationship.[107] Where they talk about a rationale for the canons, courts generally speak of the importance of remedying disadvantage.[108] In non-constitutional contexts, these liberal canons of interpretation can be rebutted or restricted by legislation. They may have no effect where the language of a statute is unambiguous,[109] or blocks a more liberal construction.[110] They can reach statutes and other documents or actions that are not connected to Aboriginal or treaty rights, although they may have less force when applied to statutes than to traditional treaties[111] or land claims agreements.[112] For example, although a statute aimed at Indian rights will be broadly construed, it will not necessarily be interpreted as the Aboriginal people would have understood it.[113]

7. GENERAL TRENDS

In the case law since *Guerin* and *Sparrow*, a few general trends are apparent. First, even before *Haida Nation*, most decisions tended[114] to treat *Guerin* and *Sparrow* as constituting two distinct forms of this obligation.[115] The *Sparrow* form relates solely to s. 35(1) Aboriginal interests, and the *Guerin* form relates typically to non-section 35(1) Aboriginal interests.

Second, most of the *Guerin*-type cases are concerned in some way with Aboriginal land, natural resource, or related interests;[116] When referring to the *Guerin*-type duty, the Supreme Court has tended to link it to land.[117] The duty is not limited to surrenders of reserve land,[118] the situation in *Guerin* itself. It includes interests derived from or related to Aboriginal land as well as to Aboriginal title itself.[119] Arguably, the *Guerin* duty can be applied to property-type interests in land cession or land recognition treaties and in land claims agreements.[120] Most major Canadian treaties involve cession or recognition of Aboriginal land, or deal with Aboriginal land interests.[121] This land component might have explained the view of some lower courts that governments have an ongoing fiduciary obligation to conduct treaty negotiations in good faith,[122] although since *Haida Nation* the treaty negotiation duty has been based more broadly on the concept of the honour of the Crown.[123] Another possibility is the extension of a *Guerin* duty to all Aboriginal treaties,[124] although this would involve a significant reinterpretation of the case law.[125]

Generally speaking, claims that clearly go beyond Aboriginal land or related interests have had only limited success to date.[126] Courts have agreed to consider fiduciary claims involving government funds for Indian housing[127] or litigation of native claims,[128] government supervision of band council elections,[129] and "protection".[130] However, they have done so in proceedings that require a minimal onus of proof and are preliminary and tentative in nature.[131]

Third, the content of the *Sparrow* promissory duty has become increasingly structured as the Supreme Court has added more detail regarding valid objectives and about forms and levels of accommodation.[132] Analogies to fiduciary law are less and less useful here, as the courts supply a justification and accommodation framework that was designed especially for the s. 35(1) context.

Fourth, under both the *Guerin* and *Sparrow* duties, the courts are attempting to fashion analytical devices for reconciling the special demands of the Crown's honour with competing public and third party needs.[133]

Fifth, there has been more attention to special problems, such as who is bound by the special duty,[134] when does the duty arise, and how long does it last.[135]

To explore these trends in more detail, it is helpful to look at some of the more important modern cases.

8. MODERN CASES

(a) *Grand Council of the Crees*

In the 1994 *Grand Council of the Crees* decision,[136] the Supreme Court held that when government exercises quasi-judicial functions in relation to parties to a hearing, it does not owe a special fiduciary duty to Aboriginal peoples. The exemption seems to apply only to *Guerin*-type duties, although its exact scope remains to be defined.

In this case, the James Bay Crees had claimed that by failing to disclose all information at a regulatory hearing, the National Energy Board had breached a specific fiduciary to provide full procedural fairness and act in their best interests. They seemed to be relying here on a *Guerin*-type duty. As well, they argued that by these actions, government had unjustifiably infringed their Aboriginal rights, contrary to the requirements in *Sparrow*.

The Supreme Court appeared to deal separately with the *Guerin* and *Sparrow*-based arguments. In regard to the first argument, it said:

> ...it must be remembered that not every aspect of the relationship between fiduciary and beneficiary takes the form of a fiduciary obligation ... The nature of the relationship between the parties defines the scope, and the limits, of the duties that will be imposed.[137]

The Court described the fiduciary relationship as one of utmost good faith,[138] and said that this is inconsistent with the quasi-judicial responsibilities of a regulatory body such as the National Energy Board.[139] Hence the Board should not be subject to a special fiduciary duty that could elevate the interests of one party over those of the other parties to a hearing.

Turning to the argument that there had been an unjustified infringement of the Crees' Aboriginal rights, the Court said:

> This Court, in *R. v. Sparrow*..., recognized the interrelationship between the recognition and affirmation of Aboriginal rights constitutionally enshrined in s. 35(1) of the *Constitution Act, 1982*, and the fiduciary relationship which has historically existed between the Crown and Aboriginal peoples. It is this relationship that indicates that the exercise of sovereign power may be limited or restrained when it amounts to an unjustifiable interference with Aboriginal rights.[140]

The Court rejected this branch of the Crees' argument too, but it did so on the ground of lack of evidence of a *prima facie* interference with Aboriginal rights. As a result, it is unclear if the quasi-judicial immunity applies to the *Sparrow* obligation as well as to the *Guerin* duty.[141] The extent of the quasi-judicial immunity is also unclear — does it apply to all functions of an agency such as the National Energy Board, or only to its quasi-judicial functions?

Grand Council of the Crees touched on one aspect of a larger issue: who is bound by the Crown's fiduciary obligation?[142] Thus far, the Supreme Court has only applied the special fiduciary duty in *Guerin* to the federal Crown. However, the s. 35(1) fiduciary justification obligation has been held to apply to the provincial Crown as well.[143] Apart from specific exemptions such as that in *Grand Council*, there seems no compelling reason that the *Guerin* duty should not apply at the provincial level as well.[144] As seen in **Chapter 6**, the fact that the *Constitution Act, 1867* gave exclusive legislation to Parliament in relation to "Indians, and lands reserved for the Indians" does not necessarily prevent the provinces from acting in regard to Aboriginal peoples.

(b) *Blueberry River*

Reading 8(c) at p. 331

The Supreme Court applied the *Guerin* duty positively in its 1995 decision in *Blueberry River*.[145] Following two surrenders involving the band's reserve land, the Department of Indian Affairs transferred both the surface interests and the mineral rights in the land to the Department of Veterans Affairs. The mineral rights transfer was not expressly authorized by the band, and contravened a long-standing departmental policy to lease rather than to sell reserve mineral rights. Although it became clear later that these rights had been included in the transfer and were valuable, the department failed to exercise its statutory power to revoke the transfer.

The Supreme Court found that the Crown had breached two fiduciary duties, both grounded in the surrender and post-surrender process. The first breach resulted from the mineral rights transfer; the second, from the failure to revoke it. Although the Court's two leading judgments differed as to the surrender that had generated the first fiduciary duty[146] and in their approaches to the duties themselves,[147] the subject matter of the fiduciary duties was clearly Indian land and resources connected to Indian land. *Guerin* was the only decision cited by Gonthier J. for the plurality; it was the main decision cited by McLachlin J. for the other three judges.

The Court made no mention of *Sparrow*. The main concern, as in *Guerin*, was with a set of specific government stewardship decisions affecting Indian land. There was no general regulatory provision, no argument claiming infringement of guaranteed Aboriginal or treaty rights, and no need to apply the constitutional canon of interpretation developed in regard to s. 35(1) of the *Constitution Act, 1982*.[148]

Blueberry River suggested that the content of the Crown's fiduciary duty varies according to the circumstances. For example, where there are specific competing public interests,[149] the level of the duty can be affected by the immediacy and significance of the interests, and by the extent of the conflict. In this case, where the question was whether to sell or lease the band's land for settlement by the veterans, the competing interest could not be allowed to affect the Crown's absolute duty to act in the best interests of the band. McLachlin J., with whom Gonthier J. concurred,[150] said that as the Crown faced competing interests of Indians and veterans, it may have been in a conflict of interest situation.[151] However, where the question concerned the adequacy of the price paid for the land, the veterans' competing interests became sufficiently compelling and immediate to be taken into account and balanced against that of the band. At this point a standard of reasonableness replaced the usual standard of the exclusive best interests of the fiduciaries. McLachlin J. required not that the band received the best possible price, but that the price was reasonable.[152]

(c) *Badger, Gladstone,* and *Delgamuukw*

🖹 Readings 5(f) at p. 286 (*Badger*) and 10(b) at p. 355 (*Delgamuukw*)

As the decisions on s. 35(1) of the *Constitution Act, 1982* are discussed in **Chapters 5**, **7**, **9**, and **10**, only a few of the most important *Sparrow* obligation cases will be considered here. As noted before, the *Sparrow* obligation is the basis for requiring governments to justify regulation that infringes Aboriginal and treaty rights. Although there have been some comments about the general nature of the obligation, increasingly the case law has focused on the detailed criteria for justification, especially its requirements for accommodating the guaranteed rights. *Badger*[153] in 1996 was the first major Supreme Court decision to apply the *Sparrow* test to treaty rights. For treaties, the Court saw the fiduciary concept as requiring fairness, reasonableness, and the keeping of promises. Referring to the honour of the Crown, the Court said that:

> Interpretations of treaties and statutory provisions which have an impact upon treaty or Aboriginal rights must be approached in a manner which maintains the integrity of the Crown. It is always assumed that the Crown intends to fulfil its promises. No appearance of "sharp dealing" will be sanctioned.[154]

It went on to say that:

> ...[I]t can properly be inferred that the concept of reasonableness forms an integral part of the **Sparrow** test. It follows that this concept should be taken into account in the consideration of the justification of an infringement.[155]

The Court added that the *Sparrow* justification criteria are generally applicable to cases involving treaty infringements.[156]

Sparrow had started to articulate these justification criteria, saying that government must show that it had a valid legislative objective and that it had attempted to accommodate the affected right in a variety of possible ways. In the 1996 *Gladstone* decision,[157] the Supreme Court worked on reconciling the demands of the special fiduciary obligation with the public and third party interests. *Gladstone* added economic and regional fairness and historical resource reliance by non-Aboriginal groups to *Sparrow*'s list of potentially valid legislative objectives.[158] *Gladstone* also refined the *Sparrow* concept of priority by requiring a less absolute form of priority for open-ended varieties of Aboriginal resource right.[159]

In its 1997 decision in *Delgamuukw*,[160] the Supreme Court applied the *Sparrow* justification test to Aboriginal title. Although it continued to refer to general fiduciary notions such as "the duty of honour and good faith of the Crown",[161] the Court focused on articulating the legislative objectives and accommodation measures that could satisfy the justification requirement, and on developing relationships between them. *Delgamuukw* said that:

> The manner in which the fiduciary duty operates with respect to the second stage of the justification test — both with respect to the standard of scrutiny and the particular form that the fiduciary duty will take — will be a function of the nature of Aboriginal title.[162]

In the Court's view, in cases of infringement of Aboriginal title, it is appropriate to look at a wide range of potentially valid legislative objectives,[163] and the most important accommodation measures will normally be consultation and compensation.[164] *Delgamuukw* suggests a contextual approach to accommodation, in which the level and nature of accommodation required varies with the circumstances, including the nature of the right infringed and the nature of the infringement.[165]

(d) *Osoyoos*

In *Osoyoos Indian Band v. Oliver (Town)*,[166] the Supreme Court applied the *Guerin* duty to a situation other than surrender. It applied the duty as an interpretation guide, and formulated an analytical approach for dealing with conflicting public and fiduciary duties.

The central question in *Osoyoos* was whether land that had been expropriated for a canal was still part of a reserve, and was therefore subject to Indian band taxation. The Supreme Court said that the Indian interest in reserve land and Aboriginal title are fundamentally similar, and that both are subject to a fiduciary duty owed by the Crown. The Court said that this duty applies to expropriation as well as surrender situations. In the case of an expropriation, the Indian interest is subject to public as well as special fiduciary duties. In such a case, government should decide first whether the public duty calls for a particular course of action. If so, government should then try to pursue that course of action with minimal disruption of the Indian interest.

One result of the fiduciary duty, it said, is that the expropriation document must show a clear and plain intention to remove land from a reserve. Here the document was unclear as to the extent of the interest taken. In order to minimize disruption of the Indian interest, the expropriation document should be construed as creating a lease rather than a full fee simple. As a result, the canal was still part of reserve land and was subject to Indian taxation.

Although the Court carried out its analysis mainly in the context of a *Guerin*-type duty, both the application of the duty and the emphasis on reconciliation of Aboriginal and public interests parallel the approach taken under s. 35(1) of the *Constitution Act, 1982*. In this regard, *Osoyoos* contrasts with cases in which government's competing interests were considered to be inconsistent with the performance of any fiduciary duty to individual parties. For example, in *Grand Council of the Crees*, considered above, the Court felt that the impartiality of a quasi-judicial body would be compromised by special obligations to any one party. In the *Fairford First Nation* case, one of several fiduciary claims was directed at Crown planning and financial support for public water control.[167] The Federal Court said that to impose a fiduciary duty here "would place the government in a conflict between its responsibility to act in the public interest and its fiduciary duty of loyalty to the Indian band to the exclusion of other interests."[168] Both *Osoyoos* and *Blueberry River* suggest that the Supreme Court is anxious to minimize these cases of "either-or" conflict, and to reconcile the competing interests wherever possible.[169]

(e) *Wewaykum*

Reading 8(d) at p. 333

The Supreme Court's 2002 *Wewaykum* decision[170] contained an extensive discussion of the Crown's special fiduciary obligation. In this case, each of two Indian bands claimed reserves occupied by the other. As well, each band sued the Crown for breach of the Crown's fiduciary duty in regard to the allocation of the land for the reserves.

The problem went back to 1907. Before this time, both parcels of land were originally listed in the name of the Wewaikai (Cape Mudge) Band. In 1907 the Crown transferred the first parcel to the Wewaykum (Campbell River) Band, but a clerical entry made it appear that the Wewaykum had been allocated *both* parcels.

At the time, neither party relied on the clerical entry. Nor did the bands object in 1938 when the Wewaikai and the Wewaykum obtained the first and second parcels, respectively, as reserves. The clerical error was finally corrected in 1943. In 1985, though, the Wewaykum launched a legal claim in regard to the second parcel. They argued that the Crown had breached its fiduciary duty in failing to uphold the clerical entry. Shortly after, the Wewaikai counterclaimed in regard to the first parcel. They argued that the Crown had breached its fiduciary duty in allowing the 1907 transfer in the first place.

These were not *Sparrow*-based claims that a regulation infringed existing Aboriginal rights.[171] The bands claimed compensation on the ground of the Crown's alleged failure to act in their best interests in allocating of *Indian Act* lands. They were alleging a *Guerin*-type stewardship context. On the other hand, there was no formal surrender, as in *Guerin*, and no expropriation, as in *Osoyoos*. The lands in question were not occupied by the bands who claimed them.[172] Regarding these lands, the claimants alleged a wide range of alleged fiduciary breaches, including failure to provide full disclosure and failure to protect against an improvident transaction.[173]

When the case reached the Supreme Court, it made several general statements about the scope and the content of the Crown's fiduciary obligations to Aboriginal peoples. Some of these are summarized below. Although *Wewaykum* involved a non-section 35(1) situation, the most general of the propositions could probably apply to s. 35(1) rights as well, as long as the latter are specific and cognizable:

1. The Crown's special fiduciary duty is not limited to s. 35(1) rights or to surrender situations.[174]
2. Not all aspects of the relationship between the Crown and Aboriginal peoples are subject to the Crown's fiduciary duty. "The fiduciary duty imposed on the Crown does not exist at large but in relation to specific Indian interests."[175]
3. For the special fiduciary duty to exist, (i) the Crown must have a discretionary control,[176] with a corresponding vulnerability for the Aboriginal peoples affected by it,[177] and (ii) the subject of the duty must be a cognizable Aboriginal interest.[178]
4. A cognizable Aboriginal interest should be (a) specific,[179] (b) significant to Aboriginal economies and culture,[180] and (c) capable of generating a private law kind of duty.[181]
5. Outside s. 35(1) situations, thus far the only kinds of Aboriginal interests that have met these requirements are Aboriginal interests in land.[182]
6. "The Crown can be no ordinary fiduciary; it wears many hats and represents many interests, some of which cannot help but be conflicting...."[183]
7. "The content of the Crown's fiduciary duty towards Aboriginal peoples varies with the nature and importance of the interest sought to be protected. It does not provide a general indemnity."[184]
8. Before an *Indian Act* reserve is created, the Crown may owe a fiduciary duty in relation to Aboriginal interests in *Indian Act* land, but if it exists, this duty is limited to loyalty, good faith, full disclosure where appropriate, and "ordinary prudence with a view to the best interest of the Aboriginal beneficiaries."[185]
9. "Once a reserve is created the content of the Crown's fiduciary duty expands to include the protection and preservation of the band's quasi-proprietary interest in the reserve from exploitation."[186]
10. Where there is a beneficial quasi-proprietary interest, equitable remedies such as dispossession or monetary compensation may be available.[187]
11. "Enforcement of equitable duties by equitable remedies is subject to the usual equitable defences, including laches and acquiescence."[188]

In the case at hand, the Court said that the Crown had not failed in its general good faith and prudence duties. Moreover, the stronger anti-exploitation duty did not arise because neither band had a beneficial interest in the land it claimed. In any event, in the past each band had effectively acquiesced in each other's presence on the land in question, and if there had been any fiduciary breach, it fell outside the statutory limitation period.

Wewaykum left many unanswered questions in its wake. For example, the Court needed to articulate the common and distinct features of the *Sparrow* and *Guerin* forms of obligation, to clarify if the *Sparrow* obligation was really fiduciary in nature, to indicate if any interests other than Aboriginal land will attract a non-section 35(1) fiduciary duty, and to indicate just how the content of the *Guerin* duty should relate public and third party interests.[189] Nevertheless, the decision summarized some of the general ingredients of the fiduciary notion; made a start at clarifying the kinds of interest that typically attract the *Guerin* duty; gave more precision to the potential content of this duty; and provided some guidance as to how it should be reconciled with the Crown's public responsibilities. For a fluid and amorphous area of the law, this was a welcome accomplishment.

(f) *Haida Nation*

Reading 10(e) at p. 378

The 2004 *Haida Nation* decision[190] is described in more detail in **Chapter 10**, but it contained an important clarification in regard to the special fiduciary duty of the Crown. In this case, it was argued that the Crown owed a fiduciary duty to the Haida, even though their Aboriginal rights and title had not been proven in the courts. It was also argued that the trust concept of "knowing receipt" applied in regard to these interests, and extended the Crown's fiduciary duty to a third party.

The Supreme Court repeated the proposition in *Wewaykum* that the Crown's fiduciary duty does not apply to all aspects of the Crown-Aboriginal relationship.[191] The Court said that the concept that does apply to all aspects of this relationship is the general principle of the honour of the Crown. The Court regarded the Crown fiduciary duty as just one particular application of the Crown honour principle, a principle that can apply in different ways depending on the context.[192] It repeated the *Wewaykum* position that the Crown fiduciary duty is limited to specific, cognizable Aboriginal interests, and does not extend to unproven or undefined s. 35(1) Aboriginal rights claims.[193]

However, this did not leave s. 35(1) claims unprotected; where the Crown knew or should have known of their existence, the Crown honour principle had a residual, non-fiduciary, application. The principle imposed on the Crown a duty to consult, and, if appropriate, to accommodate the Aboriginal claim by measures short of a requirement of full agreement with the claimants. As a result, this consultation-accommodation requirement is less rigorous than the full *Sparrow* justification obligation. The *Haida Nation* decision suggests that only proven or defined Aboriginal interests can attract the *Guerin* duty,[194] and that only proven or defined s. 35(1) rights can attract the full justification obligation in *Sparrow*.

In the light of *Haida Nation*, then, *Guerin* and *Sparrow* can be seen as related but distinct applications of the underlying Crown honour concept. The scope of the two duties can overlap. For example, the *Guerin* duty is concerned typically with Aboriginal interests in land, and part of the *Sparrow* obligation is based on Aboriginal rights, which derive in part from prior Aboriginal occupancy of land. As well, for the purposes of the *Guerin* duty, courts treat Indian reserve land interests as equivalent to Aboriginal title.[195] *Guerin*-type duties probably apply to at least some treaty rights[196] and might be extended to others. Moreover, it may be that all s. 35(1) Aboriginal rights have some relationship to land.[197] Conceivably, where s. 35(1) rights are sufficiently specific and defined, and where they are subject to special Crown commitments and discretionary controls, a litigant might have a choice between seeking justification or invalidation under *Sparrow* or specific remedy under *Guerin*.

Both under *Guerin* and *Sparrow*, the obligation requires a high standard of dealing on the part of the Crown. In some cases, it may be hard to distinguish between the content of the two obligations. For example, many of the requirements of the s. 35(1) justification tests considered in **Chapters 7**, **9**, and **10** may be relevant to *Guerin*-type duties.[198] Conversely, even in a non-regulatory context, government may have important public responsibilities to take into account, in some cases more than others.[199]

But despite the overlap and similarities, these obligations are not identical. *Sparrow* applies only to s. 35(1) Aboriginal and treaty rights, while *Guerin* focuses mainly on non-section 35(1) contexts. As noted in *Haida Nation*, the s. 35(1) duty can extend to claimed rights as well as those that have been defined or resolved; the *Guerin* duty is limited to specific, cognizable Aboriginal interests. *Guerin* focuses on land-related rights; *Sparrow* can affect non-land treaty commitments as well. Typically, *Guerin* reinforces government stewardship commitments in relation to particular Aboriginal interests; *Sparrow* mitigates the adverse effects of general public regulation on Aboriginal and treaty rights. *Guerin* provides an open-ended set of equitable remedies that can include monetary compensation; *Sparrow* holds government to a specific range of legislative objectives and forms of accommodation.

9. TENTATIVE SUMMARY

Canadian jurisprudence on Crown fiduciary obligations to Aboriginal peoples is young, elastic, and growing. No summary can be more than tentative. However, it may be helpful to summarize here some of the most basic features of the present law.

(a) Special Fiduciary Obligation

The Crown can owe a special fiduciary obligation between the Crown and Aboriginal peoples of Canada. This obligation is *sui generis*. Its source is the general principle of the honour of the Crown that applies to all the Crown's dealings with Aboriginal peoples.

(b) Specific Protection

The Crown's fiduciary obligation to Aboriginal peoples does not exist at large. Instead, it attaches to specific Aboriginal interests — either to proven or defined s. 35(1) rights or to cognizable interests such as Aboriginal land. The Crown's fiduciary obligation is one particular application of the general principle of the honour of the Crown.

(c) Related But Distinct Forms

The *Guerin* duty and the *Sparrow* duty are related but distinct applications of the underlying Crown honour concept. *Guerin* is a trust-like fiduciary obligation; *Sparrow* is a promissory obligation that may or may not be fiduciary in nature, depending on the context. *Sparrow* addresses s. 35(1) rights under the *Constitution Act*, 1982, whether or not these rights are legally defined or proven. Typically *Guerin* addresses cognizable Aboriginal interests other than s. 35(1) rights. However, where s. 35(1) rights are sufficiently specific, and where other fiduciary elements are present, a *Guerin*-type duty may apply to them as well. Where s. 35(1) rights are undefined or unproven, or where other fiduciary requirements are absent, the *Sparrow* duty can protect these rights under the general principle of the honour of the Crown.

(d) Scope of *Guerin* Duty

For the *Guerin* duty to exist, there must be a Crown undertaking to act for the benefit of Aboriginal peoples in regard to a cognizable Aboriginal interest; Crown discretionary power to carry out the undertaking; and a corresponding vulnerability on the part of the Aboriginal peoples. A cognizable Aboriginal interest is one that is (i) specific, (ii) significant to Aboriginal economies and culture, and (iii) capable of generating a private law kind of duty, and (iv) defined or proven.

(e) Scope of *Sparrow* Duty

For the *Sparrow* justification duty to exist, there must be at least *prima facie* evidence of infringement of proven or defined Aboriginal or treaty rights under s. 35(1) of the *Constitution Act, 1982*.

(f) Content

The Crown's fiduciary obligation requires a high standard of dealing in relation to Aboriginal peoples. The content of the *Guerin* duty includes requirements such as good faith and full disclosure, and prudence, and can include a duty to prevent exploitation of beneficial interests. The *Sparrow* duty takes the form of specific requirements for legislative objectives and for consultation and accommodation measures that can justify infringement of s. 35(1) Aboriginal and treaty rights. In each case, the precise level and nature of the content will depend on the circumstances of the particular case. For unproven or undefined s. 35(1) rights, the principle of the Crown's honour may impose a somewhat less rigorous obligation of a non-fiduciary nature.

(g) Reconciliation

Under both *Guerin* and *Sparrow*, courts try to reconcile the Crown's public and third party responsibilities with its obligation to Aboriginal peoples.

(h) Liberal Canons of Construction

The Crown's fiduciary obligation to Aboriginal peoples is supplemented and supported by a number of liberal canons of construction that apply uniquely to Aboriginal peoples. The canons reflect a general presumption that government documents and actions that relate especially to Aboriginal peoples should be construed in their favour. This, in turn, is an application of the general principle of the honour of the Crown.

Notes

1. *Guerin v. The Queen*, [1984] 2 S.C.R. 335: **Chapter 4, Part 4**, and **Reading 4(c)**.
2. For some Canadian commentaries on this relationship, see: L.C. Green, "Trusteeship and Canada's Indians" (1976) 3 Dal. L.J. 105; R.H. Bartlett, "You Can't Trust the Crown: the Federal Obligation of the Crown to the Indians: Guerin v. The Queen" (1984–85) 49 Sask. L. Rev. 367; B. Morse, "The Landmark Musqueam Case" (1985) 4 *Ont. Lawyers Weekly* 16; Editors "Crown's Fiduciary Obligation Towards Native Peoples" (1985) 1 Admin. L.J. 49; J. Hurley, "The Crown's Fiduciary Duty and Indian Title" (1985) 30 McGill L.J. 559; J.I. Reynolds and L.F. Harvey, "Re Guerin et al. (The Musqueam Case)" in *Indians and the Law II* (B.C.: Continuing Legal Education, 1985), chap. 1; D.P. Emond, "Case Comment: Guerin et al." (1985) 20 E.T.R. 61; D.M. Johnston, "A Theory of Crown Trust Towards Aboriginal Peoples" (1986) 18 Ottawa L. Rev. 308; W.R. McMurtry and A. Pratt, "Indians and the Fiduciary Concept, Self-government and the Constitution: Guerin in Perspective", [1986] 3 C.N.L.R. 19; D.W.M. Waters, "New Directions in the Employment of Equitable Doctrines: The Canadian Experience" in T.G. Youdan, ed., *Equity, Fiduciaries and Trusts* (Toronto: Carswell, 1989) at 411; R.H. Bartlett, "The Fiduciary Obligation of the Crown to the Indians" (1989) 53:2 Sask. L. Rev. 301; R.A. Reiter, "The Crown's Fiduciary Obligations to Indians", *The Fundamental Principles of Indian Law* (Edmonton: First Nations Resource Council, 1990), Part IV; B. Slattery, "First Nations and the Constitution: A Question of Trust" (1992) 71 Can. Bar Rev. 261; Pratt, A., "Aboriginal Self-Government and the Crown's Fiduciary Duty: Squaring the Circle or Completing the Circle?" (1993) 2 N.J.C.C. 163; M.J. Bryant, "Crown-Aboriginal Relationships in Canada: the Phantom of Fiduciary Law" (1993) 27 U.B.C. L. Rev. 19; M. Ellis, *Fiduciary Duties in Canada* (Toronto: Carswell, 1993), chap. 14, part 4; A. Lafontaine, "Fiduciary Obligations in the Context of Native Law — The Historical Context" in *UFO's — Unidentified Fiduciary Obligations: Conference Proceedings* (Winnipeg: Canadian Bar Association, May 28, 1994); P. Kennedy, "Case Law in Canada Since Guerin" in *UFO's* (above); P. Hutchins, "When do Fiduciary Obligations Arise?" in *UFO's* (above); E.J. Woodward and D. Jordan, "Who Benefits from Fiduciary Obligations?" in *UFO's* (above); G. Hannon, "Fiduciary Obligations — The Crown's Perspective" in *UFO's* (above); D.P. Owen, "Fiduciary Obligations and Aboriginal Peoples: Devolution in Action", [1994] 3 C.N.L.R. 1; R. Dupuis and K. McNeil for Royal Commission on Aboriginal Peoples, *Canada's Fiduciary Obligation to Aboriginal Peoples in the Context of Accession to Sovereignty by Quebec*, vol. 2 (Ottawa: Supply and Services, 1995) at 1; P.W. Hutchins et al., "When Do Fiduciary Obligations to Aboriginal People Arise?" (1995) 59 Sask. L. Rev. 97; L.I. Rotman, *Parallel Paths: Fiduciary Doctrine and the Crown-Native Title Relationship in Canada* (Toronto: University of Toronto Press, 1996); D.W. Elliott, "Much Ado About Dittos: Wewaykum and the Fiduciary Obligation of the Crown" (2003) 29 Queen's L.J. 1.
3. **Part 6**, below.
4. *Ibid.*
5. Sir Anthony Mason, "Themes and Prospects" in P.D. Finn, ed., *Essays in Equity* (Sydney: Law Book Co., 1985) 242 at 246, quoted by La Forest J. in *Lac Minerals Ltd. v. International Corona Resources Ltd.*, [1989] 2 S.C.R. 574 at 644.
6. Two earlier general descriptions of fiduciary relationships have found broad support from the Court in later decisions. In the first, in *Guerin*, *supra* note 1 at 384, Dickson J. quoted from E. Weinrib, "The Fiduciary Obligation" (1975) 25 U.T.L.J. 1 at 7, and added the comments quoted in **Part 4(b)**, below, at *infra* note 56. The other general description is that of Wilson J., dissenting, in *Frame v. Smith*, [1987] 2 S.C.R. 99 at 136:

   > Relationships in which a fiduciary obligation has been imposed seem to possess three general characteristics:
   >
   > (1) The fiduciary has scope for the exercise of some discretion or power.
   > (2) The fiduciary can unilaterally exercise that power or discretion so as to affect the beneficiary's legal or practical interests.
   > (3) The beneficiary is particularly vulnerable to or at the mercy of the fiduciary holding the discretion or power.

   [*Quaere*, whether the second requirement adds anything to the other two?]

   Reflecting on the case law since *Guerin* and *Frame*, La Forest J. has said that "...until recently the fiduciary duty could be described as a legal obligation in search of a principle.... [However, Supreme Court decisions over the past ten years or so have] led to the development of a 'fiduciary principle' which can be defined and applied with some measure of precision": La Forest J. for himself, L'Heureux-Dubé, Gonthier JJ. and possibly Iacobucci J. in *Hodgkinson v. Simms et al.*, [1994] S.C.R. 377 at 407. In *Blueberry River Indian Band v. Canada (Department of Indian Affairs and Northern Development)*, [1995] 4 S.C.R. 344 at 371–72, McLachlin J. attempted a synthesis of the general principles in *Frame*, *Norberg*, and *Hodgkinson*: *infra* note 7. However, the descriptions in *Guerin* and *Frame* are neither identical nor comprehensive and have been followed by considerable disagreement as to features that identify a fiduciary relationship, and *Hodgkinson* and *Blueberry* appear to fall short of consensus: *infra* note 7.
7. In *The Law of Fiduciaries* (Toronto: Carswell, 1981) at 51–92, J.C. Shepherd identified over seven competing theories that have been offered at various times to explain the fiduciary principle. Despite recognition accorded to the formulations by Dickson and Wilson JJ., and the optimistic comments in *Hodgkinson, ibid.*, the competition continues. In *Lac Minerals Ltd. v. International Corona Resources Ltd.*, [1989] 2 S.C.R. 574 at 599, the majority said vulnerability is indispensable to the existence of a fiduciary relationship, while La Forest J. (662) said it is not. In *Norberg v. Wynrib*, [1992] 2 S.C.R. 226 at 272–84, McLachlin J. stressed factors such as imbalance of power, potential for interference with interests, and an undertaking by the fiduciary. However, in *M.(K.) v. M.(H).*, [1992] 3 S.C.R. 6 at 63, La Forest J. said that sometimes a unilateral undertaking is unnecessary. In *Hodgkinson v. Simms et al.*, [1994] S.C.R. 377, La Forest J. (for three and possibly four members of a seven-judge court: see 480) said it is undesirable to overemphasize vulnerability (432), while Sopinka and McLachlin JJ., dissenting (for three judges) said vulnerability is indispensable (470). In *Hodgkinson*, La Forest J. described the formulation in *Frame* as a "rough and ready" although "useful" (408–409) guide for identifying one form of fiduciary relationship. He distinguished between recognized categories of fiduciary relationship "that have as their essence discretion, influence over interests, and an *inherent* vulnerability" (409, emphasis added by La Forest J.) and fact-based relationships involving characteristics such as "[d]iscretion, influence, vulnerability, and trust" (409), where "one party could have reasonably expected that the other party would act in the former's best interests ..." (409). Sopinka and McLachlin JJ. considered the question to be whether there is total assumption of power by the fiduciary, coupled with total reliance by the beneficiary. In *Blueberry River Indian Band v. Canada (Department of Indian Affairs and Northern Development)*, [1995] 4 S.C.R. 344 at 371–73, 405, McLachlin J. again stressed vulnera-

bility, and also referred to unilateral power and trust: 371 and 372. However, she spoke for three of seven judges. The other four did not expressly endorse her general comments, and seemed to emphasize expressed intent (i.e., the undertaking): *ibid.* at 358–59. See also P.D. Finn, "The Fiduciary Principle" in T.G. Youdan, ed., *Equity, Fiduciaries and Trusts* (Toronto: Carswell, 1989) 1 at 54, stressing action in another's interest and the expectations of the beneficiaries; *Canson Enterprises Ltd. v. Broughton & Co.*, [1991] 3 S.C.R. 534; and *McInerney v. MacDonald*, [1992] 2 S.C.R. 138.There appears to be somewhat less disagreement about the general standard or level of duty owed by a fiduciary: **Part 6**, below.

8. See, generally, *supra* notes 6 and 7.
9. See **Part 4**, below.
10. For example, a presumption of interpretation that can alter a court's construction of a document: see **Part 9(d),** below.
11. See R. Flannigan, "The Fiduciary Obligation" (1989) 9 *Oxford J. Legal Studies* 285 at 301; P.D. Finn, "The Fiduciary Principle" in T.G. Youdan, ed., *Equity, Fiduciaries and Trusts* (Toronto: Carswell, 1989) 1 at 31–33.
12. "A trust is an equitable relation binding on a person (who is called a trustee) to deal with property over which he has control (which is called the trust property), for the benefit of persons (who are called the beneficiaries or *cestuis que trust*), of whom he may himself be one, and anyone of whom may enforce the obligation": D.W.M. Waters, *Law of Trusts in Canada*, 2d ed. (Toronto: Carswell, 1984) at 5, referring to a definition in D.J. Hayton, ed., *Underhill's Law of Trusts and Trustees*, 13th ed. (London: Butterworths, 1979) at 1. For another important status-based form of fiduciary relationship, see G.H.L. Fridman, *The Law of Agency*, 6th ed. (London: Butterworths, 1983) at 9.
13. *Infra* note 64.
14. See the references to "utmost loyalty" and acting "exclusively for the benefit of the other", etc. in *infra* note 18.
15. See, for example, *Tito v. Waddell*, *ibid.* at 211, 217.
16. *Authorson v. Canada (Attorney General)* (2002), 58 O.R. (3d) 417 at para. 62.
17. For loyalty, see *infra* note 18. For best interests, see *Norberg v. Wynrib*, [1992] 2 S.C.R. 226 at 275; *Hodgkinson v. Simms*, [1994] 3 S.C.R. 377 at 409; *Blueberry*, *supra* note 132 at paras. 12 and 115.
18. Fiduciary duties have been said to call for "loyalty, good faith and avoidance of a conflict of duty and self-interest": *Canadian Aero Service Ltd. v. O'Malley*, [1974] S.C.R. 592 at 606 (S.C.C.), quoted by McLachlin J. in *Canson*, *supra* note 7 at 543 and *Norberg*, *supra* note 7 at 274 and 292; "loyalty": La Forest J. in *Lac*, *supra* note 7 at 646, quoted in *M.(K.)*, *supra* note 7 at 65; "utmost good faith and loyalty": La Forest in *McInerney*, *supra* note 7 at 149 (cf. M. Ellis, *supra* note 2 at 1–2). (Note the difference of emphasis by La Forest J. and Sopinka and McLachlin JJ. in *Hodgkinson*, *supra* note 6 at 59 and 161, respectively.) *Guerin*, *supra* note 1, involved a special fiduciary duty to Aboriginal peoples, but Dickson J. spoke in general terms there about the duty "of utmost loyalty" owed by "a fiduciary" (389). See also D.W.M. Waters, *Law of Trusts in Canada*, 2d ed. (Toronto: Carswell, 1984) at 710: "... [O]ne who undertakes a task on behalf of another must act exclusively for the benefit of the other, putting his own interests completely aside." Cf. *Grand Council of the Crees v. Canada (A.G.)* (1994), 112 D.L.R. (4th) 129 at 148 (S.C.C.), a case involving the special fiduciary duty, where the Court referred to a "relationship of utmost good faith": *Infra* note 137.
19. *Ibid.*
20. McLachlin J. in *Canson*, *supra* note 7 at 543 and *Norberg*, *supra* note 7 at 274 and 292, quoting from *Canadian Aero Service Ltd. v. O'Malley*, [1974] S.C.R. 592 at 606.
21. *Lac Minerals Ltd. v. International Corona Resources Ltd.*, [1989] 2 S.C.R. 574 at 646–47.
22. *Supra* note 21 at 646–47 (S.C.C.), and see *K.M. v. H.M.*, [1992] 3 S.C.R. 6 at 10. See also *Canson*, *supra* note 7, where La Forest J. appeared to distinguish between fiduciaries who hold property and those "who simply owe a duty of good faith and disclosure."
23. **Parts 4** and **5**, below.
24. See *Guerin v. The Queen*, [1984] 2 S.C.R. 335, **Part 4**, below.
25. This was the view taken in the previous edition of this book: see D.W. Elliott, *Law and Aboriginal Peoples in Canada*, 4th ed. (North York, Ont., Captus Press, 2000), chap. 8.
26. See *infra* note 85.
27. *Wewaykum Indian Band v. Canada*, 2002 SCC 79.
28. *Haida Nation v. Canada (Minister of Forests)*, 2004 SCC 73 at para. 18.
29. *Ibid.* and *Wewaykum, supra* note 27 at para. 81.
30. *Guerin v. The Queen*, [1984] 2 S.C.R. 335. In *Guerin*, seven of eight judges of the Supreme Court of Canada found the Crown in right of Canada in breach of a fiduciary or trust obligation owed to the Musqueam Indian Band in regard to a 1957 surrender of part of the band's reserve land pursuant to s. 18(1) of the *Indian Act*, R.S.C. 1952, c. 149, now R.S.C. 1985, c. I-5: **Chapter 4, Part 4**, and **Reading 4(b)**.
31. Although a number of pre-*Guerin* decisions referred to trust or trust-like Crown duties to Aboriginal peoples, none held expressly that there was a special legally enforceable obligation. In *St. Ann's Island Shooting and Fishing Club v. The King*, [1950] S.C.R. 211, the Supreme Court held that a federal official's failure to comply with a requirement in s. 51 of the *Indian Act* invalidated a lease of Indian lands and its renewal provision. Rand J. for three of the five judges referred to a political trust obligation to reinforce his conclusion that the language of the statute should be strictly construed in favour of the Indian band. He observed that "the language of the [*Indian Act*] embodies the accepted view that these aborigines are, in effect, wards of the State, whose care and welfare are a political trust of the highest obligation. For that reason, every such dealing with their privileges must bear the imprint of governmental approval ...": 219. For a discussion of *St. Ann's* and earlier Canadian cases, see L.I. Rotman, *Parallel Paths*, *supra* note 2, chap. 4.
32. The Court was referring here to the federal Crown, although it did not expressly preclude the possibility of fiduciary obligations attaching to the Crown in right of the provinces. On who is bound by fiduciary obligations, see further, **Part 9(a)**, below.
33. *Supra* note 30 at 364, 391, and 394–95.
34. There was no single set of majority reasons in *Guerin*. The plurality opinion was that of Dickson J., for four of the eight judges. Wilson J. spoke for three judges. Estey J. gave a separate opinion. Laskin C.J.C. did not take part in the judgment. See **Reading 4(c)**.
35. *Ibid.*
36. *Supra* note 30 at 385, 387.
37. *Ibid.* at 383. Dickson J.'s statement about the general requirements for a fiduciary relationship (at 384: *supra* note 30 and text opposite *infra* note 56) must be read together with his additional requirement (378–79 and 385) that where the prospective fiduciary is the Crown, the protected interest must be independent of government (here the interest in the reserve land derived from the independent Aboriginal title): text opposite *infra* note 38.

    In regard to the special situation of the Crown and the Indians, Dickson J. said (at 376) that:

    > The fiduciary relationship between the Crown and the Indians has its roots in the concept of Aboriginal, native or Indian title. The fact that Indian bands have a certain interest in

> lands does not, however, in itself give rise to a fiduciary relationship between Indians and the Crown. The conclusion that the Crown is a fiduciary depends upon the further proposition that the Indian interest in the land is inalienable except upon surrender to the Crown.

38. *Ibid.* at 385.
39. After describing the requirements for the special fiduciary relationship (*ibid.*), Dickson J. said (at 376) that "[t]he surrender requirement, and the responsibility it entails, are the source of a distinct fiduciary obligation owed by the Crown to the Indians." Later he said that "[w]hen, as here, an Indian band surrenders its interest to the Crown, a fiduciary obligation takes hold ..." (385). This suggests that although Aboriginal title and the Crown's historic undertaking were required for the general fiduciary relationship, a more specific provision, such as the *Indian Act* surrender power, is needed to give rise to an enforceable fiduciary duty.
40. At 387, Dickson J. said:

    > As would be the case with a trust, the Crown must hold surrendered land for the use and benefit of the surrendering band. The obligation is thus subject to principles very similar to those which govern the law of trusts....

    He said its remedy resembled compensation for breach of trust (*ibid.*), and that it also bore some resemblance to agency: 386–87.
41. *Ibid.* at 389. Cf. *infra* note 138 and the general duty of loyalty referred to at *infra* note 18.
42. *Ibid.* at 349.
43. *Guerin*, *supra*, 355. The content of this obligation was to hold the reserve land for the benefit of the Indian band before an *Indian Act* surrender.
44. *Ibid.*
45. Note that agency is itself a form of fiduciary relationship.
46. *Ibid.* at 394.
47. *Ibid.* at 392.
48. The differences between the approaches of Dickson and Wilson JJ. are less marked than they appear. Wilson J.'s "full-blown" (355) trust obligation was comparable in content to the "trust-like" (386) surrender fiduciary obligation of Dickson J. Dickson J. neither addressed nor precluded the possibility of specific fiduciary obligations arising before a surrender. Wilson J.'s general fiduciary obligation "at large" (355) would presumably require a specific transaction to impose specific duties in the Crown.
49. *Supra* note 36.
50. It is unclear as to how closely the special duty will be required to comply with the requirements of ordinary fiduciary duties referred to in **Part 2**, above. Moreover, general fiduciary law has been evolving rapidly over the past decade (*supra* notes 6 and 7), and it is not clear how this will affect the special duty in *Guerin*. *Guerin* has been referred to in several subsequent discussions of general fiduciary requirements: see the decisions in *supra* notes 6 and 7. On the other hand, in *Canson Enterprises Ltd. v. Broughton & Co.*, [1991] 3 S.C.R. 534 at 566, La Forest J. said *Guerin* involved "a fiduciary relation akin to a trust", with a fiduciary who holds property and who could be liable to pay compensation "on the same basis as for a breach of trust." He distinguished this from other situations where fiduciaries "simply owe a duty of good faith and disclosure."
51. *Guerin*, *supra* note 30 at 376.
52. *Ibid.* at 350–52, 378–79, 385; and *infra* note 64.
53. See **Part 6(b)**, below.
54. *Ibid.* at 363, 388–89, and *supra* text opposite note 33.
55. *Supra* notes 37 and 39.
56. *ibid.* at 384, Dickson J. said that "where by statute, agreement, or perhaps by unilateral undertaking, one party has an obligation to act for the benefit of another, and that obligation carries with it a discretionary power, the party thus empowered becomes a fiduciary": *ibid.* at 384. (However, he did not make the dependency of the principal on the fiduciary a prerequisite for every fiduciary obligation, at least some dependency would be the normal result of his requirement of discretionary power.)
57. *Ibid.* at 383 (unilateral Crown undertaking) and 383–84 (exclusive Crown discretionary power to dispose of Indian lands).
58. *Supra* notes 40 and 48, and see *Wewaykum Indian Band v. Canada*, 2002 SCC 79 at para. 74.
59. This was so even though Dickson J. considered that the Indians' "property" interest disappeared with the surrender: 386. However their interest, entitlement, or expectation might be labelled, it still related to proceeds from land (cf. Reynolds and Harvey, and Waters, *supra* note 2).
60. "It does not matter, in my opinion, that the present case is concerned with the interest of an Indian Band in a reserve rather than with unrecognized Aboriginal title in traditional tribal lands. The Indian interest is the same in both cases:" *Guerin, ibid.* at 379. However, there are clear differences between Aboriginal title and *Indian Act* interests for non-fiduciary purposes (e.g., the statutory occupancy rules that are unique to *Indian Act* reserve land). Hence Dickson J. must be taken to have meant "the same" — "for purposes of identifying a fiduciary duty": *Wewaykum Indian Band v. Canada*, 2002 SCC 79 at para. 77. In *Wewaykum*, the Court suggested that for the purposes of the *content* of a fiduciary duty, non-reserve Indian land might not stand as strong a footing as existing reserve land: *ibid.*
61. This feature, implicit in *Guerin*, was made explicit in *Haida Nation v. Canada (Minister of Forests)*, 2004 SCC 73 at para. 18.
62. In regard to the Proclamation, see **Chapter 3, Part 9**.
63. *Supra* note 30 at 352, 378–79 and 385 and *infra* note 64.
64. *Ibid.*, and *supra* note 52. The "political trust" doctrine is a judicial presumption against construing documents so as to impose legally enforceable fiduciary duties on the Crown in regard to property, funds, or other interests that were created by the legislative or executive branches of government. See, for example, *Kinloch v. Secretary of State for India in Council* (1882), 7 App. Cas. 619; *Hereford Ry. v. The Queen* (1894), 24 S.C.R. 1; *Tito v. Waddell (No. 2)*, [1977] 3 All E.R. 129 at 619 (Ch.); *Gardner et al. v. The Queen in Right of Ontario et al.* (1984), 7 D.L.R. (4th) 464 (O.H.C.); *Guerin v. The Queen*, [1984] 2 S.C.R. 335 at 371–72, 378–79, 350–52; *Penikett et al. v. The Queen* (1987), 45 D.L.R. (4th) 108 at 126 (B.C.C.A.); *Callie v. The Queen*, [1991] 2 F.C. 379 at 388–95 (F.C.T.D.); and Peter W. Hogg and Patrick J. Monahan, *Liability of the Crown*, 3rd ed. (Toronto: Carswell, 2000) at 259; *Authorson v. Canada (Attorney General)* (2002), 58 O.R. (3d) 417 at paras. 41–81.
65. For the possibility of an extension to other treaty interests, see *infra* note 125.
66. See also *infra* note 180.
67. **Chapter 7, Part 4(d)(iii)**. See **Reading 7(c)**.
68. See **Reading 7(c)**. See generally, D.W. Elliott, "In the Wake of *Sparrow*: A New Department of Fisheries?" (1991) 40 U.N.B.L.J. 23.
69. [1990] S.C.R. 1075 at 1108.
70. By the time of *Sparrow*, Canadian courts had developed a set of liberal canons of construction for interpreting documents that related especially to Aboriginal peoples. The most general of these presumed that "treaties and statutes relating to Indians should be liberally construed and doubtful expressions resolved in favour of the Indians": *Nowegijick v. The Queen*, [1983] 1 S.C.R. 29 at 36, cited in *Sparrow* (407). *Nowegijick* also endorsed a more specific canon for treaties. Quoting from the American

decision of *Jones v. Meehan* 175 U.S. 1 at 11 (U.S.S.Ct. 1889), the Court said treaties must be construed "in the sense in which they would naturally be understood by the Indians." Another more specific canon was expressed in *R. v. Horseman*, [1990] 1 S.C.R. 901 at 906–907, where Wilson J., dissenting, said "courts must be sensitive to the broader historical context in which [the] treaties were negotiated." Other examples of these canons of interpretation: *R. v. White and Bob* (1964), 50 D.L.R. (2d) 613 at 649, 651 (B.C.C.A.); *R. v. Sutherland* (1980), 113 D.L.R. (3d) 374 at 385 (S.C.C.); *Simon v. The Queen*, [1985] 2 S.C.R. 387 at 410; *R. v. Horse*, [1988] 1 S.C.R. 187 at 202–23 (S.C.C.); and *Horseman*, *ibid.* at 930 (Cory J.) (S.C.C.). See also *R. v. Sioui* (1990), 70 D.L.R. (4th) 427 at 435 (S.C.C.), released on the same day as *Sparrow*.

As the Court's citation of *Jones* suggests, the canons' content was very similar to that of their American counterparts. Unlike the American presumptions, though, the canons developed in Canada without relying on fiduciary concepts. (For a possible exception, see *R. v. Taylor and Williams* (1981), 34 O.R. (2d) 360 at 367 (O.C.A.), also cited in *Sparrow* (1107–108).) When the Supreme Court referred to *Jones*, *supra*, it drew no link to wardship or fiduciary responsibility. In *Jones* itself, the emphasis was more on imbalance of bargaining power than on wardship. Cf. *infra* note 94.

71. *R. v. Taylor and Williams* (1981), 34 O.R. (2d) 360 at 367 (O.C.A.).
72. As seen in *Haida Nation v. British Columbia (Minister of Forests)*, 2004 SCC 73 in **Part 8(f)**, below, it is the Crown honour notion, not the fiduciary notion, that now appears to be the more general guiding principle.
73. *Sparrow*, *supra* note 69 at 1108.
74. The Court said that although s. 35(1) contains no words expressly guaranteeing its rights, the words "recognition and affirmation" incorporate the general fiduciary relationship: *ibid.* at 1109.
75. *Sparrow*, *supra* note 69 at 1108.
76. *Ibid.* at 1107–19. See further, **Chapter 7, Parts 4(c) and 4(d)(vii)** and **Chapters 9** and **10**.
77. *Ibid.*
78. *Ibid.* at 1114.
79. By virtue of s. 52 of the *Constitution Act, 1982*. In *Sparrow* itself, the Court referred the case back to trial for evidence on the issues of infringement and justification.
80. See, for example, J.C. Strick, *The Economics of Government Regulation: Theory and Canadian Practice*, 2d ed. (Toronto: Thompson Educational Publishing, 1994) at 3.
81. See, for example, J. Jowell, "The Legal Control of Administrative Discretion" [1973] Pub. L. 178 at 178–85.
82. G. Hannon, *supra* note 2 at 12 and 20 (conclusions 2(a) and 2(b)), also see a difference between the *Sparrow* and *Guerin* approaches. *Contra*, Dupuis and McNeil, *supra* note 2 at 40. They suggest that *Sparrow* has merely extended to the legislative branch of government the enforceable compensable duty that *Guerin* imposed on the executive branch. M.J. Bryant, *supra* note 2 says that on one view the *Sparrow* approach may be seen to depart too much from "established principles of fiduciary law" (36), permitting courts either to freeze the content of the current obligation or to fashion it as they please. *Quaere*, whether the courts could or should have applied a full *Guerin*-type duty in the context of *Sparrow*?

    Compare the American approach discussed in D.W. Elliott, "Aboriginal Peoples in Canada and the United States and the Scope of the Special Fiduciary Relationship" (1996) 24 Man. L.J. 137 at 164–79.
83. **Part 4**, above.
84. Including constitutional enactments such as the *Natural Resources Transfer Agreements*, that themselves modify s. 35(1) Aboriginal and treaty rights: see *R. v. Badger*, [1996] 1 S.C.R 771 at para. 41.
85. At one point in *Sparrow*, the Court spoke about government's fiduciary responsibility "with respect to Aboriginal peoples" and said that "[t]he relationship between government and the Aboriginals is trust-like.": [1990] 1 S.C.R. 1075 at 1108. From this, it might be inferred that the fiduciary obligation is comprehensive, and attaches to *all* aspects of the relationship between Aboriginal peoples and government: see, for example, P. Hutchins, *supra* note 2 at 11–12 and D.P. Owen, *supra* note 2 at 15. However, these statements in *Sparrow* were made in the context of the rights protected by s. 35(1). Elsewhere, the Court called the fiduciary relationship "a general guiding principle *for s. 35(1)*": 1108 (emphasis added). It said "the words 'recognition and affirmation' [in s. 35(1) incorporate the fiduciary relationship": 1109. The context was clearly s. 35(1).
86. See especially **Chapter 10, Part 2**, where it is suggested that this would be a logical development.
87. For possible limits to interests of this kind, see *Wewaykum Indian Band v. Canada*, 2002 SCC 79, discussed below.
88. See *R. v. Van der Peet*, [1996] 2 S.C.R. 507, discussed in **Chapter 9, Parts 3 and 5** and **Chapter 12, Part 3(d)**. As well, it may be that the Court will require a cognizable Indian interest, and the Crown's undertaking of discretionary control in relation thereto in a way that invokes responsibility "in the nature of a private law duty."
89. These are incorporated into s. 35(1) through s. 35(3).
90. Can this result be reconciled with the political trust doctrine and the land-based fiduciary duty in *Guerin*? A short answer is that because the reference to "treaties" in the *Constitution Act, 1982* is unambiguous, there is no room here for an interpretative presumption such as the political trust doctrine. Moreover, a doctrine that evolved in regard to specific compensable equitable duties will not necessarily apply to presumptions of constitutional interpretation. Finally, as suggested later, even at the non-constitutional level, it might be possible to reconcile non-land treaty obligations with the political trust doctrine. This, however, would require significant reinterpretation of *Guerin*: see **Part 8**, below.
91. This says that "a medicine chest shall be kept at the house of each Indian Agent for the use and benefit of the Indians at the direction of such Agent," and promises assistance in the event of "any pestilence" or "a general famine": Treaty No. 6 Between Her Majesty the Queen and the Plains and Wood Cree Indians, at Fort Carlton, Fort Pitt and Battle River With Adhesions, August 23 and 28, 1876. See, generally, P.A. Barkwell, "The Medicine Chest Clause in Treaty No. 6", [1981] 4 C.N.L.R. 1.
92. In the past, the medicine chest provision has been held to guarantee Treaty No. 6 Indians free medicines, drugs, and medical supplies (see for example, *Dreaver v. The King*, [1935] 5 C.N.L.C. 92 at 115 (Exch. Ct.)), but not free hospital services (*R. v. Johnston* (1966), 56 W.W.R. 565 at 571 (S.C.A.)) or medical care (*R. v. Swimmer* (1971), 17 D.L.R. (3d) 476 at 481 (S.C.A.)).

    For the modern approach, see *R. v. Sioui*, [1990] 1 S.C.R. 1025 and *R. v. Wolfe* (1995), 129 D.L.R. (4th) 58 (S.C.A.). In *Wolfe*, the Saskatchewan Court of Appeal ordered that criminal prosecutions be stayed because they were based on Crown action that violated a non-land right in Treaty No. 6 (the right to have the Crown strictly enforce alcohol protection laws). The Court of Appeal said "*Sparrow* and *Bear Island* require that this law enforcement be undertaken in a manner which fulfils the Crown's fiduciary obligations": 64. In *Mitchell v. Peguis Indian Band et al.* (1990), 71 D.L.R. (4th) 193 at 230 (S.C.C.) La Forest J. contemplated payments in areas such as education, housing, and health and welfare as possible aspects of "treaty and ancillary obligations". A more liberal interpretation of Treaty No. 6 might or might not involve a guarantee of a particular level of services.

For example, the guarantee might be construed as affording services at least comparable to those enjoyed by other Canadians. If other Canadians were being subjected generally to cutbacks, these might be held to apply to Treaty No. 6 Indians too.

93. One non-land provision that is present in all the numbered treaties relates to education. Treaty 1, for example, promises that "Her Majesty agrees to maintain a school on each reserve ... whenever the Indians of the reserve should desire it.": Treaty No. 1 Between Her Majesty the Queen and The Chippewa and Cree Indians of Manitoba and Country Adjacent With Adhesions. August 3, 1871. A similar commitment is found in all the other numbered treaties. This commitment, too, would likely support more than a literal interpretation today. It could offer protection against unjustified infringement — for the treaties concerned, and subject to their individual wording and context.
94. For example, *James Bay and Northern Quebec Agreement, November 11, 1975*, ss. 14–17, 28–29. (See also the Agreement's main implementing legislation, the *James Bay and Northern Quebec Native Claims Settlement Act*, S.C. 1976–77, c. 32 and the *Loi Approuvant la Convention de la Baie James et du Nord Québécois*, S.Q. 1976, c. 46 (now L.C. c. 67)). For the other major land claims agreements, see **Chapter 11, Part 7**. Courts may be less willing to find fiduciary duties — or wide-ranging fiduciary duties — in modern land claims agreements than in the traditional treaties, on the ground that the element of bargaining disadvantage is now less significant: cf. *Eastmain, infra* note 112. Still, even a limited fiduciary tool might prove useful for Aboriginal peoples to help secure full implementation of land claims agreement commitments. There were many implementation problems relating to the health and social services provisions of the *James Bay and Northern Quebec Agreement*: W. Moss, "The Implementation of the James Bay and Northern Quebec Agreement" in B.W. Morse, ed., *Aboriginal Peoples and the Law* (Ottawa: Carleton University Press, 1985), chap. 11; and F. Cassidy and R.L. Bish, *Indian Government: Its Meaning in Practice* (Victoria: Oolican Books and The Institute for Research on Public Policy, 1989) at 149–52.
95. *Haida Nation v. British Columbia (Minister of Forests)*, 2004 SCC 73.
96. *Wewaykum Indian Band v. Canada*, 2002 SCC 79.
97. *Ibid.* at para. 20.
98. *Ibid.* at 389.
99. *Ibid.* at 389.
100. *Ibid.* at 383.
101. *Ibid.* at 389.
102. *Sparrow* at 1109.
103. Especially **Parts 4(c) and 4(d)(vii)**.
104. Especially **Part 4**.
105. Especially **Part 3(f)**.
106. **Chapter 7, Part 4(c)**.
107. E.g., *R. v. Badger*, [1996] 1 S.C.R. 771 at para. 41, where the principle of resolving ambiguities in favour of Aboriginal people was required independently of the fiduciary notion of the honour of the Crown; *Canada v. Poker*, [1995] 1 C.N.L.R. 85 (F.C.T.D.) at para. 38; *R. v. Alfred*, [1994] 3 C.N.L.R. 88 (B.C.S.C.); *R. v. Vincent* (1993), 12 O.R. (3d) 427 at 443 (O.C.A.); *R. v. Jones* (1993), 14 O.R. (3d) 421 at 434–35 (O.C.J. Prov. Div. referring, however, to *R. v. Taylor* (1981), 62 C.C.C. (2d) 227); *Mitchell v. Peguis Indian Band*, [1990] 2 S.C.R. 85 at 91, 98–99 (Dickson C.J.C.), 142–43 (La Forest J.); *R. v. Norn*, [1991] 3 C.N.L.R. 135 (Alta. Prov. Ct.) *R. v. Machatis*, [1991] 1 C.N.L.R. 154 at 159–60 (Alta. Q.B.); *R. v. Howard*, [1991] O.J. No. 548 (O.C.G.D.). In *Eastmain Band v. Canada (Federal Administrator)*, [1992] F.C.J. No. 1041 (F.C.A.), leave to appeal to S.C.C. dismissed, [1993] S.C.C.A. No. 23, the Court found the main basis for applying the liberal canon to treaties to be the historic bargaining disadvantage of the Aboriginal peoples (at 10). It then appeared to suggest that the canon could be reinforced by the special fiduciary relationship (at 18–19). *Contra*, an *obiter* comment in *Van der Peet*, suggesting that the special fiduciary relationship requires a generous interpretation not only of s. 35(1) but of treaties "and other statutory and constitutional enactments protecting the interests of Aboriginal peoples": *R. v. Van der Peet*, [1996] 2 S.C.R. 507 at para. 24.
108. "Underlying *Nowegijick* is an appreciation of societal responsibility and a concern with remedying disadvantage": Dickson C.J. in *Mitchell*, *ibid.* at 99. "From the perspective of the Indians, treaties were drawn up in a foreign language.. and incorporated references to legal concepts of a system of law with which Indians were unfamiliar": La Forest J. in *Mitchell*, *ibid.* at 142–43.
109. *R. v. Horse*, [1988] 1 S.C.R. 187 at 202 (S.C.C.); *R. v. Sundown*, [1988] 4 C.N.L.R. 116 (Sask. Q.B.); *Sagueen Indian Band v. The Queen*, [1989] 3 F.C. 186 at 203 (F.C.T.D.), aff'd. in [1990] 1 F.C. 403 (F.C.A.); *Sturgeon Lake Indian Band v. Canada (Minister of Indian Affairs and Northern Development*, (1995), 123 D.L.R. (4th) 93 (F.C.A.) (appeal to S.C.C. quashed for mootness in (1997) 149 D.I.R. (4th) 334 (S.C.C.)).
110. *Sagueen Indian Band et al. v. The Queen*, [1990] 1 F.C. 403 at 417 (F.C.A.).
111. *Mitchell v. Peguis Indian Band*, [1990] 2 S.C.R. 85 at 142–43 (S.C.C.). La Forest J. said that although statutes aimed at Indian rights should be construed broadly, the presumption that treaties should be interpreted as the Indians understood them should not apply to statutes. Treaties, he said, were the product of contractual negotiations in which one party, the Indians, were unfamiliar with the language and legal concepts employed, whereas with statutes the paramount objective is to determine the will of Parliament.
112. *Eastmain Band et al. v. Federal Administrator*, [1992] F.C.J. No. 1041 (F.C.A.) at 11, rejecting the full application of the canon to a land claims agreement. The Court said the Indian land claims agreement negotiators lacked the vulnerability of the Indians who negotiated the treaties. See also *R. v. Sioui*, [1990] 1 S.C.R. 1025 at 1036 (S.C.C.).
113. *Mitchell*, *supra* note 111, per La Forest J. Treaties, said La Forest J., were the product of contractual negotiations in which one party, the Indians, were unfamiliar with the language and legal concepts employed, whereas with statutes the paramount objective is to determine the will of Parliament. (La Forest J. spoke for three members of the Court. Four of the other five concurred with La Forest J.'s general analysis of the statute in question, although they did not comment on this proposition.) On the other hand, although a *treaty* will normally be construed as the Indians would have understood it, the Court has said that this presumption does not relieve it of the need to interpret the treaty to reflect the intention of both parties: *R. v. Sioui*, [1990] 1 S.C.R. 1025 at 1069. For the general principles applicable to the interpretation of treaties, see **Chapter 5, Part 8**.
114. The distinction between the two forms of the obligation is not always very clear. For example, in *Gitanyow First Nation v. Canada* (1999), 66 B.C.L.R. (3d) 165 (S.C.), the British Columbia Supreme Court imposed on governments a fiduciary duty to conduct treaty negotiations in good faith once they have been initiated, and cited both *Guerin* and *Sparrow* in support of the duty. *Wewaykum Indian Band v. Canada*, 2002 SCC 79, considered below, made several general statements about the Crown's fiduciary obligation, sometimes without making it explicit which features were common to s. 35(1) (*Sparrow*) and non-section 35(1) *Guerin*-type situations, and which were limited to the latter.

115. See cases listed in *infra* note 116. In *Dumont v. Canada (A.G.)* (1991), 91 D.L.R. (4th) 654, the Manitoba Court of Appeal said, "It is one thing for there to be a breach of a fiduciary duty, another for legislation to be unconstitutional."; and the approach in *Grand Council of the Crees v. Canada (A.G.)*, [1994] 1 S.C.R. 159, discussed below. In *Perry v. Ontario* (1997), 33 O.R. (3d) 705 (O.C.A.) the Ontario Court of Appeal suggested another possible distinction between the *Guerin* and *Sparrow* obligations. The claimant had argued that s. 35(1) imposes on the Crown a specific duty to negotiate Aboriginal rights claims, enforceable, if necessary, by a mandatory injunction. The Court refused to issue an injunction. One reason was its view that s. 35(1) "is a restraint against regulation improperly affecting Aboriginal rights, not an affirmative obligation to initiate negotiations with a view to such regulation": para. 73 (application for leave to appeal to S.C.C. dismissed, S.C.C. Bulletin, 1997, p. 22249).

The Court of Appeal attributed its reluctance to impose a positive obligation under s. 35(1) to the imprecise, evolving nature of Aboriginal rights: *ibid.* at para. 74. The Court might have added that s. 35(1) can affect statutes as well as Crown administrative action, and that courts are generally reluctant to impose positive obligations on Parliament. Beyond this, as noted earlier, regulation is characteristically a general government function, not a specific undertaking or engagement between government and an individual group.

116. For example, *Wewaykum Indian Band v. Canada*, 2002 SCC 79 (allocation of Indian land and establishment of reserves); *Ross River Dena Council Band v. Canada*, 2002 SCC 54 (establishment of reserves); *Osoyoos Indian Band v. Oliver* (Town), [2001] 3 S.C.R. 746 (expropriation of reserve land); *Opetchesaht Indian Band v. Canada*, [1997] 2 S.C.R. 119 (main issue the nature and extent of a hydro easement on reserve land); *Semiahmoo Indian Band v. Canada (District Manager)* (1997), 148 D.L.R. (4th) 523 (F.C.A.) (limitation statute barred remedy for breach of ongoing post-surrender fiduciary duty but not for pre-surrender fiduciary duty); *Chippewas of Kettle & Stony Point v. Canada (A.G.)* (1996), 31 O.R. (3d) 97 (O.C.A.), appeal to Supreme Court of Canada dismissed in [1998] 1 S.C.R. 756 (surrender of Indian lands not invalid, but fiduciary claim could proceed); *Blueberry River Indian Band v. Canada (Department of Indian Affairs and Northern Development)*, [1995] 4 S.C.R. 344 (Crown breached fiduciary duties in regard to transfer and failure to revoke a transfer of mineral rights in surrendered reserve land); *Holiday Park Developments Ltd. v. Canada*, [1994] F.C.J. No. 193 (F.C.T.D.) (Crown lease of reserve land: inappropriate form of proceedings for enforcing fiduciary duty); ; *Enoch Band of Stony Plain Indians v. The Queen*, [1994] 3 C.N.L.R. 41 (F.C.A.) (surrender of reserve land: interlocutory proceedings); *Hopton v. Pamajewon* (1993), 16 O.R. (3d) 390 (O.C.A.) (dedication of reserve land for a road, without consultation or surrender: fiduciary duty enforced by declaration) *Wewaikai Indian Band v. Canada*, [1992] F.C.J. No. 507 (F.C.T.D.) (entitlement to reserve land: interlocutory proceedings); *Lower Kootenay Indian Band v. Canada*, [1991] 2 C.N.L.R. 54 (F.C.T.D.) (lease of band land: a breach of fiduciary duty, but remedy barred by limitation statute); *Delgamuukw v. British Columbia* (1991), 79 D.L.R. (4th) 185 (B.C.S.C.) (Aboriginal title: declaration of fiduciary obligation on basis of both *Guerin* duty and *Sparrow* guarantee); *Montana Band v. Canada*, [1991] 2 F.C. 273 (F.C.T.D.) (surrender of reserve land: interlocutory proceedings); *Kruger et al. v. The Queen*, [1986] 1 F.C. 3 (F.C.A.) (Crown expropriation of reserve lands for airport; a fiduciary duty, but not breached).

117. "Fiduciary protection accorded to Crown dealings with Aboriginal interests in land (including reserve creation) has not to date been recognized by this Court in relation to Indian interests other than land outside the framework of s.35(1) of the *Constitution Act, 1982*: *Wewaykum Indian Band v. Canada*, 2002 SCC 79 at para. 81. See also list of Supreme Court of Canada decisions in previous endnote; *Canson Enterprises Ltd. v. Broughton & Co.*, [1991] 3 S.C.R. 534 at 578 (describing *Guerin* as "a situation in which one person has control of property which in the view of the court belongs to another"). Indian land and property related to Indian land are also stressed in *Mitchell v. Peguis Indian Band* (1990), 71 D.L.R. (4th) 193 at 226 ("From [since at least the signing of the Royal Proclamation of 1763], the Crown has always acknowledged that it is honour-bound to shield Indians from any efforts by non-natives to dispossess Indians of the property they hold *qua* Indians, i.e., their land base and the chattels on that land base"); and *Norberg v. Wynrib*, [1992] 2 S.C.R. 226 at 291 ("[*Guerin* said that] Aboriginal people [are] the beneficiaries of [a] fiduciary relationship with the Crown, which consequently has obligations with respect to dealings with land subject to aboriginal title").

118. See, for example, *Wewaykum, Ross River*, and *Osoyoos, ibid.*

119. *Supra* note 60.

120. In *Bear Island*, the Supreme Court observed that "[i]t is conceded that the Crown has failed to comply with some of its obligations under this agreement, *and thereby breached its fiduciary obligations to the Indians.*": *Ontario (A.G.) v. Bear Island Foundation*, [1991] 1 S.C.R. 570 at 576. Although the comment was *obiter*, it may have been more than a mere report on the position of the litigants. In *Ontario (A.G.) v. Bear Island Foundation*, [1995] O.J. 164, the Ontario Court (General Division) said this statement was "no more than an acknowledgment by the court of a submission made to it, that negotiations were ongoing between the parties (44–45)." Yet if the Supreme Court had had any reservations about the proposition that treaty violations could involve breaches of fiduciary obligations, it could have said so, whatever the agreement of the parties to the contrary. (The Court's main finding in *Bear Island* was that although the Temagami Indians had an Aboriginal right to the lands in question, this right had subsequently been extinguished by a treaty. The issue of treaty violations and another issue were not resolved here as they were the subject of negotiations between the parties.) For a provincial appellate court decision applying a *Sparrow*-type fiduciary interpretation to a non-land treaty right, see *R. v. Wolfe*, *supra* note 92.

121. See *Native Rights in Canada*, 2d ed. (Toronto: Indian-Eskimo Assn. of Canada, 1972), Part IV; G. Brown and R. Maguire, *Indian Treaties in Perspective (Ottawa: Dept. of Indian Affairs and Northern Development*, 1979); A.J. Hall, "Indian Treaties" in *The Canadian Encyclopedia*, Year 2000 ed. (Toronto: McClelland & Stewart, 1999) at 1148–56; B.W. Morse, ed., *Aboriginal Peoples and the Law* (Ottawa: Carleton University Press, 1985), chaps. 4 and 5; O.P. Dickason, *Canada's First Nations: A History of Founding Peoples from Earliest Times*, 3d ed. (Don Mills, Ont.: Oxford University Press, 2002) at 163–65; J.S. Frideres, ed., *Native Peoples in Canada*, 4th ed. (Scarborough, Ont.: Prentice-Hall, 1993), chap. 3; and **Chapter 5, Part 5**.

122. *Gitanyow First Nation v. Canada* (1999), 66 B.C.L.R. (3d) 165 (S.C.) at para. 65; *Nunavik Inuit v. Canada (Minister of Canadian Heritage)* (1998), 164 D.L.R. (4th) 463 (F.C.T.D.); *Chemainus First Nation v. British Columbia Assets and Lands Corporation*, [1999] 3 C.N.L.R. 8 (B.C.S.C.). Courts have not been very specific as to the particular form of this obligation (sometimes citing both *Guerin* and *Sparrow*, with little differentiation). However, in treaty negotiation, government's role is closer to stewardship and bilateral engagement than to general regulation, so that the *Guerin* model would seem more appropriate.

123. *Haida Nation v. British Columbia (Minister of Forests)*, 2004 SCC 73 at para. 20.
124. For example, the Federal Court has suggested that the presumption against Crown fiduciary obligations that involve public funds might not apply to treaty commitments: *Thomas and Peguis Indian Band v. Canada (Minister of Indian Affairs and Northern Development)*, [1991] 2 F.C. 433 at 449 (F.C.T.D.).
125. Some treaties lack any land-related component: see *Native Rights in Canada*, 2d ed. (Toronto: Indian-Eskimo Assn. of Canada, 1972), chap. 12; A.J. Hall, "Indian Treaties" in *The Canadian Encyclopedia*, Year 2000 ed. (Toronto: McClelland & Stewart, 1999) at 1149. These "non-land" treaties do not appear to be based on a specific, legally recognized interest that is wholly independent of government. Thus, they appear to lack the ingredient that was considered in *Guerin* to be essential to avoid the political trust doctrine. However, the political trust doctrine is itself only a presumption: *supra* note 64. Courts might decide that treaties signify the Crown's own *intention* to be equitably bound, despite presumptions to the contrary. Solemn and consensual, Indian treaties are as central to the historic Crown-Aboriginal relationship as the Crown's responsibility to protect Aboriginal land.

    Although it would involve a major reinterpretation of the rationale behind *Guerin*, a fiduciary presumption in favour of treaty promises would not necessarily impose fiduciary duties in all situations. For example, some treaty promises might be too abstract or general to generate specific, enforceable Aboriginal interests. Moreover, courts might be reluctant to infer fiduciary duties in situations involving modern land claims agreements. For example, some of these may have involved less inequality of bargaining power than most treaties: cf. *Eastmain*, *supra* note 112 at 11, rejecting the full application of the liberal canons of construction to a land claims agreement. Moreover, an agreement might provide explicitly for alternative dispute resolution procedures: e.g., *Vuntut Gwitchin First Nation Final Agreement* between the Government of Canada, the Vuntut Gwitchin First Nation and the Government of the Yukon, May 29, 1993, chap. 26: Dispute Resolution. In other cases, there may be little control or discretion delegated to the Crown.
126. "Fiduciary protection accorded to Crown dealings with Aboriginal interests in land (including reserve creation) has not to date been recognized by this Court in relation to Indian interests other than land outside the framework of s.35(1) of the *Constitution Act, 1982*": *Wewaykum Indian Band v. Canada*, 2002 SCC 79 at para. 81.
127. *Sandy Bay Band of Indians v. Minister of Indian Affairs and Northern Development* (sub. nom. *Desjarlais*), [1988] 2 C.N.L.R. 62 (F.C.T.D.).
128. *Derrickson v. The Queen in Right of Canada et al.*,[1991] F.C.J. No. 1150 (F.C.T.D.). *Contra, Lubicon Lake Indian Band v. Canada (Minister of Indian Affairs and Northern Development)*, [1987] 3 F.C. 174 (F.C.T.D.).
129. *Blackfoot Band of Indians No. 146 v. Canada (A.G.)*, [1986] F.C.J. No. 719 (F.C.T.D.).
130. *Montana Band of Indians v. Canada*, [1991] 2 F.C. 30 (F.C.A.).
131. *Desjarlais* (*supra* note 127) involved an application for an interlocutory injunction where all that was required was that the plaintiff show that the claim raised "a serious question". *Montana* (*supra* note 130), *Derrickson* (*supra* note 128), and *Blackfoot* (*supra* note 129) involved motions to strike out claims, where the defendants had to meet the high onus of showing that it was "plain and obvious" or "beyond doubt" that there was no reasonable cause of action.
132. See, for example, *R. v Gladstone*, [1996] 2 S.C.R. 723, and *Delgamuukw v. British Columbia*, [1997] 3 S.C.R. 1010, discussed in **Part 9(c)**, below.
133. See, for example, *Blueberry River Indian Band v. Canada (Department of Indian Affairs and Northern Development)*, [1995] 4 S.C.R. 344 and *Osoyoos Indian Band v. Oliver (Town)*, [2001] 3 S.C.R. 746, discussed in **Part 9(d)**, below.
134. See, for example, *Grand Council of the Crees v. Canada (A.G.)* (1994), 112 D.L.R. (4th) 129, discussed in **Part 9(a)**, below.
135. See, for example, *Wewaykum Indian Band v. Canada*, 2002 SCC 79, discussed in **Part 9(e)**, below.
136. *Grand Council of the Crees v. Canada (A.G.)* (1994), 112 D.L.R. (4th) 129.
137. *Ibid.* at 147. In this case, the Court went on to say that fiduciary obligations should not be imposed on quasi-judicial tribunals.
138. The Court spoke of "a relationship of utmost good faith between the Board and a party appearing before it": *ibid.* at 148. It suggested that even had there been a fiduciary duty here, the Board would have met its requirements because its procedure in relation to the claimants had been fair (148–49).

    The standard for most "ordinary" fiduciary duties normally requires loyalty: **Part 6**, above. Similarly, for the special fiduciary relationship, Dickson J. had said in *Guerin* "[a fiduciary's] duty is that of utmost loyalty to his principal": *supra* note 41. The Court gave no indication that it was now departing from *Guerin* and adopting a new, lower standard for fiduciary duties involving Aboriginal peoples. But the suggestion that the duty could be discharged merely by compliance with fair procedure does suggest a different level of obligation than in *Guerin*. Perhaps what is being suggested is that compliance with fair procedure is all that will be required where government must balance between Aboriginal and other concerns in an adjudicatory context, and that where the adjudicatory body is an independent quasi-judicial tribunal, like the Board, the presumption of procedural fiduciary duties may be rebutted altogether. This would not preclude fiduciary obligations by government in non-adjudicatory situations.
139. *Grand Council*, *supra* at .
140. *Ibid.* at 149.
141. Because of the constitutional status of the *Sparrow* function, it should not be precluded on the basis of the nature of the government functions involved. Of course, the presence of quasi-judicial functions might well influence the kind and level of accommodation needed to help satisfy the *Sparrow* justification test.
142. On this, see also W.A. McTavish, "Fiduciary Duties of the Crown in Right of Ontario" (1991) 25 L.S.U.C. 181; L.I. Rotman, "Provincial Fiduciary Obligations to First Nations: The Nexus Between Governmental Power and Responsibility" (1994) 32 Osgoode Hall L.J. 735; and Rotman, *Parallel Paths*, *supra* note 2, chap. 12. The main focus here is on the *Guerin*-type duty.
143. *R. v. Adams*, [1996] 3 S.C.R. 101 at para. 54; *R. v. Badger*, [1996] 1 S.C.R. 771 at para. 41.
144. For lower court decisions suggesting that a *Guerin*-type duty can apply to the provincial Crown, see *R. v. McPherson*, [1993] 1 W.W.R. 415 (Man. Prov. Ct.); *Gitanyow First Nation v. Canada*, *supra note* at para. 65 (referring to both *Sparrow* and *Guerin*).
145. *Blueberry River Indian Band v. Canada (Department of Indian Affairs and Northern Development)*, [1995] 4 S.C.R. 344, allowing an appeal and cross-appeal from (1993), 100 D.L.R. (4th) 504 (F.C.A.), which had dismissed an appeal and cross-appeal from [1988] 1 C.N.L.R. 73 (F.C.T.D.). Gonthier J. gave the reasons for four of the seven judges; McLachlin J. wrote for the other three. See **Reading 8(c)**.
146. The band first surrendered the mineral rights in reserve land to the Crown in trust "to lease" for their benefit. Five years later, the band surrendered the reserve to the

Crown in trust "to sale or lease". Gonthier J. for four judges found that the band had intended to include the mineral rights in the second surrender, so that the second surrender superseded the first. He concluded, though, that in light of the long-standing lease policy and the lack of express band authorization to sell the mineral rights, the Crown had breached its fiduciary duty to act in the band's best interests when it transferred these rights rather than leasing them for the band. McLachlin J. for the other three judges said the second surrender should not be interpreted so as to affect the mineral rights. Hence the first surrender's "lease" restriction on mineral rights still applied, and by violating it the Crown had breached its fiduciary duty to the Indians.

147. Both Gonthier and McLachlin JJ. agreed that the Crown had not violated its fiduciary duty in the surrender or transfer of the surface rights (354, 375–81). McLachlin J. noted that the Crown had provided the band with adequate information and had done nothing to prejudice the band's decision (372). McLachlin J. said the surface transfer price to the Department of Veteran's Affairs fell within the range of the appraisals, and was not unreasonable (380). Both judges agreed that the failure to revoke the mineral rights transfer was a continuing fiduciary breach that shielded the band from a key limitation statute (Gonthier J., at 354 [agreeing with McLachlin J.], 405–407). Both judges seemed to agree that beyond the duty to comply with the surrender terms there was a duty to act in the band's best interests (e.g., 362, 363, 365, 398, 405). For Gonthier J., the "sale or lease" discretion in the second surrender was modified by this "best interests" requirement. McLachlin J. said she would have considered this requirement in regard to the second surrender had she not found an enforceable violation of the "lease" term in the first (398).

Beyond this, the two judges seemed to differ significantly in their basic approaches to describing fiduciary duties: note 6, *supra*.

148. There was a *non*-constitutional liberal canon in *Blueberry*. Gonthier J. said that the *sui generis* nature of Aboriginal title requires courts to "go beyond the usual restrictions imposed by the common law" (358) and give effect to "the guiding principle that the decisions of Aboriginal peoples should be honoured and respected" (363). Rather ironically, this (for Gonthier J.) meant giving full effect to the surrender that gave the Crown technical authority to sell the mineral rights.

149. For an early discussion of the question of conflicting responsibilities, see the Federal Court of Appeal's decision in *Kruger v. R.* (1985), 17 D.L.R. (4th) 591 (F.C.A.). Dealings between the Department of Indian Affairs and the Department of Transport for leasing Indian lands had resulted in expropriation of the lands, and in the payment of compensation the band considered inadequate. The band claimed damages against the Crown for breach of its fiduciary duty. Two judges dismissed the claim on the ground that the Crown must be able to take into account competing national needs such as transport, and to arrive at compromises requiring concessions from each side: *ibid.* at 648: Urie J.A., Stone J.A., concurring at 657. Urie J. said there was evidence that the Indians' case had been represented strongly within government, and noted that the compensation paid was much closer to an independent evaluation than to the evaluation obtained by government: *ibid.* at 648. He went on to note that "the transport officials, too, owed a duty in the performance of their functions, not a direct duty to the Indians but a duty owed to the people of Canada as a whole, including the Indians, not to improvidently expend their moneys": *ibid.* A third judge said that the Crown's special fiduciary obligation was more rigorous, and could not be avoided by a plea of competing interests: *ibid.* at 607–608: Heald J.A.

Heald J.A. went on to find, however, that the band's claim was barred by statutory limitation requirements.

150. Gonthier J. concurred generally with McLachlin J.'s approach to the surrender of the surface rights: *ibid.* at para. 1.

151. *Ibid.* at para. 53, per McLachlin J. McLachlin J. said that if a conflict existed here, its effect was to require the Crown to raise a *prima facie* case that it had acted reasonably in regard to the sale price: *ibid.*, paras. 53–55.

152. McLachlin J. said that it was sufficient that the Crown show that the price obtained for the land fell within the range of the appraisals received. Once this was shown, the onus shifted to the band to show that the price was unreasonable: *Ibid.* at paras. 54 and 55. Gonthier J. concurred with this general approach at para. 1. Cf. the approach to compensation by Urie and Stone JJ. in *Kruger*, *supra* note 149 and the approach to conflicting duties in *Osoyoos Indian Band v. Oliver (Town)*, [2001] 3 S.C.R. 746, considered in **Part 9(d)**, below.

153. *R. v. Badger*, [1996] 1 S.C.R. 771.

154. *R. v. Badger*, [1996] 1 S.C.R. 771 at para. 41, per Cory J for the majority. The minority judges agreed (at para. 1) with Cory J.'s analysis of s. 35(1).

155. *Ibid.* at para. 73.

156. *Ibid.*

157. *R. v. Gladstone*, [1996] 2 S.C.R. 723, **Chapter 9, Part 4**. As will be seen in **Chapter 9**, the questions here were whether the Heiltsuk First Nation's commercial trade in herring spawn was an Aboriginal right protected by s. 35(1) of the *Constitution Act, 1982* and, if so, whether that right had been unjustifiably infringed. The majority held that although an Aboriginal right had been established and infringement had been shown, the case must be sent back to trial on the issue of justification.

Mention should also be made of *R. v. Adams*, [1996] 3 S.C.R. 101, decided a year before *Gladstone*. In *Adams*, the Supreme Court held that an unstructured discretionary power may constitute an infringement of s. 35(1) rights if it fails to provide the Crown with adequate direction for carrying out its fiduciary obligation to accommodate those rights para. 54.

158. *Ibid.* at para. 75.

159. *Ibid.* at para. 63.

160. *Delgamuukw v. British Columbia*, [1997] 3 S.C.R. 1010.

161. *Ibid.* at para. 169.

162. *Ibid.* at para. 166.

163. *Ibid.* at para. 165.

164. *Ibid.* at paras. 168 and 169.

165. See, for example, *ibid.* at paras. 166, 168, and 169.

166. *Osoyoos Indian Band v. Oliver (Town)*, [2001] 3 S.C.R. 746.

167. *Fairford First Nation v. Canada (A.G.)*, [1999] 2 F.C. 48 (F.C.T.D.). The case also involved several other fiduciary claims, all related to flooding from a provincial dam construction project that had involved federal planning and financial participation. Two of four other fiduciary claims related to a reserve land compensation agreement connected to the project. They were successful, and were held not to be barred by limitations acts. The first of these was based on the federal government's failure to act in a timely manner in ratifying the agreement (para. 228); the second was based on the federal government's failure to consult with the band regarding the compensation agreement during a relevant period of time (para. 285).

168. *Ibid.* at para. 67. The Courtsaid it would not impose this kind of conflict situation "[i]n the absence of legislative or constitutional provisions to the contrary": ibid. It should be noted, though, that the presence of a conflicting public interest was only one of a number of reasons the fiduciary duty claim was rejected in this case. The Court said that this fiduciary claim involved no relevant Crown undertaking (*ibid.* at para. 55), no course of conduct giving rise

to a reasonable expectation that a fiduciary duty would be assumed (paras. 59–60), no special Indian vulnerability (para. 64), and no direct connection to a surrender of Indian land (para. 63).

169. *Blueberry River* suggested that in cases of conflict, the fiduciary standard might be less demanding: **Part 8(b)**, above; *Osoyoos* suggests that in cases of conflict, the public responsibility might be met more minimally: presumably, reconciliation is required on both sides.
170. *Wewaykum Indian Band v. Canada*, 2002 SCC 79, aff'g [2000] 3 C.N.L.R. 303 (F.C.A.), which aff'd (1995), 99 F.T.R. 1 (F.C.T.D.). (*Wewaykum* was preceded by *Roberts v. Canada*, [1989] 1 S.C.R. 322 (C.A.); aff'g [1987] 1 F.C. 155 (T.D.), on a question of jurisdiction; and by (*Wewaykum Indian Band v. Wewayakai Indian Band*, [1991] 3 F.C. 420 (T.D.), on a question of procedure.) For a more extended discussion of this case, see *supra* note 1.
171. "There is no assertion of any entitlement in these lands under s. 35(1) of the *Constitution Act, 1982* ('existing aboriginal and treaty rights')": *ibid.* at para. 3. The Wewaikai and the Wewaykum had apparently settled in this area at about the same time as their non-Indian neighbours; the previous residents had been the Comox First Nation: para. 1.
172. The Wewaykum lived on Reserve 11 but claimed Reserve 12 as well; the Wewaikai lived on Reserve 12 but claimed Reserve 11 as well.
173. The Court remarked that "[t]he appellants seemed at times to invoke the 'fiduciary duty' as a source of plenary Crown liability covering all aspects of the Crown-Indian band relationship. This overshoots the mark": *Ibid.* at para. 81.
174. *Ibid.* at para. 79.
175. *Ibid.* at para. 81.
176. *Ibid.* at paras. 79, 80, 83, 85.
177. *Ibid.* at para. 80.
178. *Ibid.* at para. 85.
179. *Ibid.* at para. 80.
180. This requirement seems to be implied in Binnie J.'s observation that "[i]n this case we are dealing with land, which has generally played *a central role in Aboriginal economies and cultures*": *ibid.*, para. 80 (emphasis added).
181. *Ibid.* at para. 85. In this regard, Binnie J. said that "[a] quasi-proprietary interest (e.g., reserve land) could not be put on the same footing as a government benefits program. The latter will generally give rise to public law remedies only. The former raises considerations in the nature of a private law duty" (*Guerin*, at p. 385).
182. "In this case we are dealing with land, which has generally played a central role in aboriginal economies and cultures. Land was also the subject matter of *Ross River* ('the lands occupied by the Band'), *Blueberry River* and *Guerin* (disposition of existing reserves). Fiduciary protection accorded to Crown dealings with Aboriginal interests in land (including reserve creation) has not to date been recognized by this Court in relation to Indian interests other than land outside the framework of s. 35(1) of the *Constitution Act, 1982*": *ibid.* at para. 81. Earlier, Binnie J. noted with apparent approval that a Federal Court judge had rejected a fiduciary duty allegation on the ground that neither a *Guerin* reserve land situation nor s. 35(1) Aboriginal rights were involved: *ibid.* at para. 54, referring to *Nawash First Nation v. Canada (Minister of Indian and Northern Affairs)* (1999), 251 N.R. 220 (F.C.A.), at para. 6, per Rothstein J.A.
183. *Ibid.* at para. 96.
184. *Ibid.* at para. 86.
185. *Ibid.*
186. *ibid.*
187. *Ibid.*
188. *Ibid.*
189. Here it would be helpful to build on the approach started in *Blueberry River* (**Part 8(b)**, above) and *Osoyoos* (**Part 8(d)**, above).
190. *Haida Nation v. Canada (Minister of Forests)*, 2004 SCC 73.
191. *Ibid.* at para. 18.
192. *Ibid.* at paras. 18–20.
193. *Ibid.* at para. 18.
194. Note that the Supreme Court did not rule out the possibility of applying *Guerin*-type fiduciary duties to defined and proven s. 35(1) rights, in a suitable context.
195. *Supra* note 60.
196. Supra note 65, 120, and 125.
197. See **Chapter 9(3)(h)** and **Chapter 10(3)(e)(vi)**, below.
198. See, for example, *Fairford First Nation v. Canada (A.G.)*, [1999] 2 F.C. 48 (F.C.T.D.) at paras. 198–202 and *Halfway River First Nation v. British Columbia (Ministry of Forests)* (1999), 178 D.L.R. (4th) 666 (B.C.C.A.). In *Halfway*, the Court said the provincial Crown breached a fiduciary duty owed to the band in regard to its treaty rights, by failing to consult adequately before granting a forest cutting permit. The Crown was ordered to consult adequately. Although the majority had used the *Sparrow* analytical framework to arrive at the duty to consult, Huddart J.A. said that because the consultation was incomplete, he could not come to a final conclusion on the issue of justification under *Sparrow*.
199. **Parts 9(a),(b),(d), and (e),** below.

9 Aboriginal Rights: I

Chapter Highlights

- Aboriginal rights are *sui generis*, apply only to Aboriginal peoples, survived European sovereignty, and do not depend on formal legislative or executive government recognition.
- Aboriginal rights are based on "the prior occupation of North America by distinctive Aboriginal societies" (*Van der Peet*).
- Specific Aboriginal rights can be identified by a three-part test that looks, *inter alia*, at practices that were integral to the distinctive culture of the Aboriginal society in question.
- Aboriginal rights are communal, are alienable only to the Crown, and are guaranteed against unjustified government infringement occurring after April 17, 1982.

Synopsis

The Australian *Mabo* decision parallelled the modern Canadian position that Aboriginal rights predated and survived European sovereignty. In *Van der Peet*, the Supreme Court of Canada took a "land and societies" approach to describing the general basis of Aboriginal rights. It formulated a "distinctive practices" test for identifying specific Aboriginal rights. *Van der Peet* also distinguished between specific Aboriginal rights and Aboriginal title. Aboriginal title was said to be a form of Aboriginal right that relates solely to interests in land. However, the relationship between the two concepts, and between these concepts and the notion of land, was left uncharted. At the time of *Van der Peet*, the Court also re-stated the *Sparrow* justification test, and confronted the question of claims to constitutionally-guaranteed Aboriginal self-government.

Selected Readings

🖹 links material in this chapter to the corresponding headings and page numbers of the relevant readings.

🖹 Part 2	*Mabo v. State of Queensland (No. 2)*	338
🖹 Part 3	*R. v. Van der Peet*	341
🖹 Part 4	*R. v. Gladstone*	348
🖹 Part 5	*R. v. Pamajewon*	350

1. INTRODUCTION

Chapter 3 looked at Aboriginal rights before the Supreme Court's decision in *Calder*. **Chapter 4** explored the concept in the decades after *Calder*. **Chapter 7** examined *Sparrow*, where the Court outlined the status of Aboriginal rights in s. 35(1) of the *Constitution Act, 1982*. This chapter continues the inquiry by looking at Aboriginal rights after *Sparrow*, until the decision in *Van der Peet* in the summer of 1996. In *Van der Peet*, the Supreme Court formulated a general theory about the basis of Aboriginal rights and the purpose of s. 35(1), and developed a test for identifying Aboriginal rights in specific situations.

The chapter will look first at a pre-*Van der Peet* case — the Australian decision in *Mabo*. Then, after a detailed examination of *Van der Peet*, it will consider *Gladstone*, where the Court qualified its constitutional justification approach in *Sparrow*, and *Pamajewon*, the Court's first direct contact with the issue of Aboriginal self-government.

2. *MABO*[1]

Reading 9(a) at p. 338

Outside Canada, there was an extensive discussion of Aboriginal title and classical acquisition doctrines in the High Court of Australia's decision in *Mabo*. Although the decision has no weight as a precedent in Canada, it is helpful to see how another jurisdiction coped with similar — although not identical — problems.

Members of the Meriam people sought declarations that they had ownership or occupancy rights to the Murray Islands in the Torres Strait, Queensland, and that the State of Queensland could not extinguish their title. They had occupied these islands for generations before European contact. After the islands were formally annexed to Queensland on August 1, 1879, the Government of Queensland exercised effective administrative power over them.

Could the Meriam's rights be recognized at common law? Did the rights survive the change of sovereignty? Had they been extinguished since the change of sovereignty? If so, did extinguishment give rise to legal remedies?

The main majority judge, Brennan J., reviewed the classical acquisition doctrines. He said that three ways of acquiring sovereignty were by conquest, by cession, and by occupation of territory that was *terra nullius* (unknown land). The acquisition here was by settlement. Under the settlement doctrine, the Crown acquired not only sovereignty but title to the land, with an unlimited power to grant interests in it or to appropriate it. Land already inhabited by Aboriginal peoples was treated as if it were *terra nullius*, on the view that they were "uncivilized" or unchristian, or that their lands were uncultivated. As a result, their prior interests in land were ignored.

Brennan J. said the old justifications for refusing to recognize prior interests in the lands of Aboriginal inhabitants were outdated, inappropriate, and discriminatory.[2] Moreover, the survival of a native interest in land was not inconsistent with the acquisition of territory. With the acquisition, there was a change of sovereignty and the Crown obtained an underlying title to all the land. This enabled the Crown to dispose of the land or to appropriate the land for itself, under its prerogative power. However, until it had done either of these things, and subject to any legislative action, the pre-existing native title in land continued.[3]

Brennan J. then described the content of the interest that survives a change in sovereignty:

> (The term 'native title' conveniently describes the interests and rights of indigenous inhabitants in land, whether communal, group, or individual, possessed under the traditional laws acknowledged by, and the traditional customs observed by the indigenous inhabitants.)[4]

These traditional native rights had three main characteristics. First, they required a "traditional connection with the land".[5] Second, they were interests "in land".[6] Third, they were based on, and given their content, by "the traditional laws acknowledged by and the traditional customs observed by the indigenous inhabitants of a territory."[7]

Brennan J. held that although the Crown had a prerogative power to grant the land subject to the native title to others, or to appropriate the land for its own purposes, there must be a clear and plain intention to extinguish the native title. At the very least, the government's action must be inconsistent with the continued existence of the title.[8] With a few minor exceptions, the Meriam peoples' native title continued.[9]

Mabo supports extinguishment by Crown prerogative action alone, although the court was split on this issue. Its test for extinguishment, inconsistency, was less onerous than the clear and plain intention test in Canada, although a later Australian decision narrowed the gap.[10] Most significant, though, was *Mabo*'s clear rejection of the claim that Aboriginal rights disappear in the case of settlement. This is relevant to Canada, where most colonial acquisition resembled settlement. *Mabo* put considerable emphasis on native laws and customs for identifying specific Aboriginal rights. On the other hand, the rights contemplated in *Mabo* were clearly rights in land. *Mabo*, then, supported a general "customary land use" approach to the content of Aboriginal rights.

3. *VAN DER PEET*[11]

Reading 9(b) at p. 341

In *R. v. Van der Peet*, the Supreme Court moved closer to providing what was lacking in its 1990 decision in *Sparrow*[12] — a workable theory of the source, constitutional entrenchment, and content of Aboriginal rights. This was a landmark decision. It provided a general explanation of the basis of Aboriginal rights. It described the general purposes of s. 35(1) of the *Constitution Act, 1982*. It formulated a three-part test for identifying the content of Aboriginal rights in specific situations. Between the theory and the practical test, though, something was missing.

(a) Background

In September 1987, Dorothy Van der Peet, a Stó:lo Nation status Indian, sold ten sockeye salmon to a non-Indian for $50. The fish had been caught by other members of Mrs. Van der Peet's band, under a valid Indian food licence. The question here was not whether Stó:lo had a traditional right to fish salmon in the Fraser River for food or ceremonial purposes. It was whether the traditional right included the sale of fish. Federal regulatory provisions prohibited all kinds of sale or trade of fish.[13] When Mrs. Van der Peet was charged with violating these,[14] she claimed what the majority of the Supreme Court described as an Aboriginal right to sell, barter or trade salmon. She argued that this right prevailed over the regulations by virtue of s. 35(1) of the *Constitution Act, 1982*.

Mrs. Van der Peet's legal claim was part of a larger drama. As seen in earlier chapters, land and resources have special significance to Aboriginal peoples, both culturally and materially.[15] Trapped near the bottom of the economic ladder, many First Nations peoples are claiming Aboriginal rights to natural resources, for commercial as well as for food purposes.[16] On the other hand, natural resources like fish are declining amidst a storm of regulatory controversy and conflicting needs. In British Columbia, for example, the salmon fishing industry has been plagued by international quota disputes, habitat degradation, complaints of government mismanagement, federal-provincial bickering, high unemployment, and declining fish stocks.[17] Moreover, some commentators claim a still wider reach for judicially-guaranteed Aboriginal rights,[18] raising questions about the role of courts and the allocation of governmental authority. Although the analysis here focuses on the legal and conceptual implications of *Van der Peet*, these larger issues are not far below the surface.

Mrs. Van der Peet's conviction was upheld by most of the lower British Columbia courts[19] and by a majority of 7–2 in the Supreme Court of Canada.[20] Speaking for the majority of the Supreme Court, Lamer C.J. built on the version of the distinctive practices test favoured by the majority of the British Columbia Court of Appeal.[21] However, he attempted to put it into the context of a general theory of both Aboriginal rights and the purpose of s. 35(1) of the *Constitution Act, 1982*.

Lamer C.J. started with general interpretation issues. He said the fiduciary relationship between the Crown and Aboriginal peoples requires courts to give a liberal interpretation to provisions that protect these peoples, and to construe ambiguities in their favour. He noted that the meaning of s. 35(1) depends on the meaning of Aboriginal rights. Then he said that the basis of Aboriginal rights is the fact that when the Europeans came to North America, Aboriginal peoples were already occupying the land and participating in distinctive cultures.[22] He said the purpose of s. 35(1) is to reconcile this prior occupation of land by distinctive Aboriginal societies with the Crown's assertion of sovereignty.[23]

Lamer C.J. formulated a three-part "distinctive practices" test[24] for identifying specific Aboriginal rights. He said a court should first characterize precisely the Aboriginal claim, then determine if the activity in question was part of a pre-European contact practice that was integral to the distinctive culture in question, and then decide if there is sufficient continuity between the modern activity and the traditional practice. If the test identifies an Aboriginal right, the court can apply the extinguishment, infringement, and justification tests laid down in *Sparrow*[25] to determine if the right is protected by s. 35(1) of the *Constitution Act, 1982*. The aim, said Lamer C.J., is to determine if a practice was a "defining feature" of the Aboriginal culture in question.[26] He said courts should be sensitive both to the Aboriginal perspective and the need to approach this perspective "in terms which are cognizable to the non-Aboriginal legal system."[27]

For the characterization stage of the test, Lamer C.J. said a court should consider such factors as the action said to constitute an exercise of an Aboriginal right, the relevant government action, and the traditional practice said to give rise to the right.[28] He stressed that the characterization should be specific.[29] For the second stage of the test, Lamer J. said that "integral" means "central and significant",[30] and independent, not incidental significance.[31] The term "distinctive"[32] excludes features common to all societies,[33] but does not require uniqueness.[34] The focus should be on the particular Aboriginal community in question.[35] Both for evidentiary requirements and continuity, the courts should not apply standards that are too rigid or demanding.[36]

Applying the first part of the test, Lamer C.J. noted that Mrs. Van der Peet had only sold ten salmon, that there was no evidence of similar sales "on other occasions or on a regular basis,"[37] and that the regulations prohibited all sale or trade of fish caught under an Indian food fish licence.[38] Thus, he said, the relevant question was not whether Mrs. Van der Peet had an Aboriginal right to sell salmon commercially, but whether she could establish an Aboriginal right to exchange fish for money or other goods, i.e., other than in "the commercial marketplace".[39]

On the second part of the test, Lamer C.J. agreed with the trial judge that while the Stó:lo had traded traditionally in salmon, they did not do so on a large scale and in an organized way. The trade was only occasional, and was incidental to fishing for food and ceremonial purposes. Hence, the exchange of fish for money or other goods was not an integral part of the Stó:lo's distinctive traditional culture before contact with the Europeans. Finally, Lamer C.J. agreed that the Stó:lo's trade with Hudson's Bay Company officials was qualitatively different from the traditional practices, so that there was no continuity here. As a result, Mrs. Van der Peet could not claim an Aboriginal right today.

L'Heureux-Dubé and McLachlin JJ. dissented in separate judgments.[40] L'Heureux-Dubé agreed generally with the majority's approach to general interpretation principles[41] and to the basis of Aboriginal rights.[42] Although she also supported a distinctive practices test,[43] she would have applied it more broadly than the majority.[44] She found an Aboriginal right, but would have sent the case back to trial because of insufficient evidence on the issues of extinguishment, infringement, and justification. McLachlin J. would have focused the distinctive practices test on the question of a traditional right to derive sustenance from the land or natural resource in question.[45] She would have recognized a current right to secure a "moderate livelihood" from the land or resource, in a modern manner, subject to conservation and safety constraints.[46] She said Mrs. Van der Peet could claim such a right.[47] Since this right had not been extinguished but had been unjustifiably infringed, the conviction should be set aside.

(b) Basis of Aboriginal Rights: Land

Because it was unclear if fishing for non-food or non-ceremonial purposes could in fact be an Aboriginal right, the Court needed a test for identifying Aboriginal rights. Since it would be logical to relate such a test to the basic features of Aboriginal rights, the Court also needed a general theory of Aboriginal rights. As we saw in earlier chapters, the case law had moved from grounding Aboriginal rights in the Royal Proclamation of 1763 to basing them on prior occupancy and use of land.[48] On the other hand, the Supreme Court had not yet articulated a comprehensive general theory about the basis of Aboriginal rights.[49]

In his majority judgment in *Van der Peet*, Lamer C.J. suggested that the essence of Aboriginal rights is the Aboriginal peoples' prior occupation of land in distinctive societies. He said the basis of Aboriginal rights is the fact that:

> ...when Europeans arrived in North America, aboriginal peoples *were already here*, living in communities on the land, and participating in distinctive cultures, as they had done for centuries. It is this fact, and this fact above all others, which separates aboriginal peoples from all other minority groups in Canadian society and which mandates their special legal, and now constitutional, status.[50]

Aboriginal rights, said Lamer C.J. are "based in the prior occupation of North America by distinctive Aboriginal societies."[51]

Land, then, was clearly one of the two key components of the foundation of Aboriginal rights. Lamer C.J. included the prior Aboriginal relationship to land as a vital part of what sets off Aboriginal peoples from all other minorities and justifies the special legal status of Aboriginal rights.[52] At another point, Lamer C.J. referred to "the existence of distinctive Aboriginal communities occupying 'the land as their forefathers had done for centuries',"[53] and to a "pre-existing occupation and use of the land."[54] He said that the purpose of s. 35(1) is to reconcile this fact of prior occupation of land by distinctive Aboriginal societies with the Crown's assertion of sovereignty.[55] McLachlin J. put a similar emphasis on occupation of lands in her dissenting judgment.[56]

Some commentaries[57] and judgments[58] have favoured a much broader approach than this. They have claimed that Aboriginal rights extend far beyond land and land-related interests. They have tended to prefer law and custom as better reflections of traditional Aboriginal life. For support, they have relied on decisions such as *Connolly v. Woolrich*,[59] *Worcester v. Georgia*,[60] and *R. v. Sioui*.[61]

For their part, supporters of a more land-based approach to Aboriginal rights can stress that original occupation of North America,[62] with a close and distinctive relationship to the land,[63] is a claim no other group can make. Supporters of this approach might note that the wider comments in *Connolly*, *Worcester*, and *Sioui*[64] refer to situations in which European sovereignty was only imperfectly established,[65] and may be less applicable to later times.[66] They might argue that traditional laws and customs can be harder to prove than occupancy or use.[67] As well, they can claim that the concept of prior Aboriginal occupancy[68] has strong support both in historical government instruments[69] and in case law in the United States,[70] former British colonies,[71] Australia,[72] and Canada.[73]

(c) Basis of Aboriginal Rights: Distinctive Societies

The other main element of the majority's description of the basis of Aboriginal rights was prior participation *in distinctive Aboriginal societies*. Although the majority did not elaborate on the role of the "distinctive" requirement in this context,[74] the phrase as a whole may have been intended to reflect at least[75] two important features of the prior Aboriginal presence. First, the phrase clarifies that the prior occupancy and use on which Aboriginal rights are based was not fleeting and random but was well established and socially organized. Second, it underlines the fact that the prior occupancy was not individual, but communal in nature.

After speaking of prior occupancy by distinctive societies, Lamer C.J. said this is what distinguishes Aboriginal peoples from all other minority groups in Canada and justifies the special legal status of Aboriginal rights.[76] In other words, presumably, it is the prior occupancy of land by Aboriginal societies that is at the root of what is distinctive about Aboriginal rights. As will be seen, though, this interpretation appears to contrast with the meaning Lamer C.J. gave as "distinctive" later, in the context of identifying Aboriginal rights.[77]

This general tie between Aboriginal rights and land did not require that Aboriginal rights be synonymous with Aboriginal title. As Lamer C.J. said, "[a]boriginal title is the aspect of Aboriginal rights related specifically to Aboriginal claims to land."[78] Nevertheless, "[b]oth Aboriginal title and Aboriginal rights arise from the existence of distinctive Aboriginal communities occupying "the land as their forefathers had done for centuries."[79]

(d) Section 35(1)

Lamer C.J. said the purpose of s. 35(1) of the *Constitution Act, 1982* is to reconcile prior Aboriginal occupancy with Crown sovereignty.[80] On the purpose of s. 35(1),[81] the dissenting judgments in *Van der Peet* did not diverge fundamentally from that of Lamer C.J. Here, as in its general discussion of the basis of Aboriginal rights,[82] the Court's emphasis was on occupancy: i.e., on land.

(e) "Distinctive Practices" Test

Lamer C.J. stressed that the rights affirmed in s. 35(1) of the *Constitution Act, 1982* are not just rights, but *Aboriginal*.[83] He describes the purposes of the section as recognition of prior Aboriginal occupation of land by distinctive Aboriginal communities, and reconciliation of this fact with Crown sovereignty. He said that "[t]he content of Aboriginal rights must be directed at fulfilling both of these purposes."[84] Thus, he concluded, "the test for identifying the Aboriginal rights recognized and affirmed by s. 35(1) must be directed at identifying the crucial elements of those pre-existing distinctive societies."[85]

Lamer C.J. then articulated a three-part test for identifying specific Aboriginal rights:

1. *characterization of claim*: determine the precise nature and purpose of the modern activity claimed to be an Aboriginal right;[86]
2. *evaluation of traditional practice*: "determine whether the activity claimed to be an Aboriginal right is part of a practice, custom or tra-

dition which was, prior to contact with Europeans, an integral part of the distinctive aboriginal society of the aboriginal people in question";[87] and

3. *assessment of continuity between the traditional practice and the modern activity*: determine whether there is sufficient continuity between the traditional practice and the modern activity claimed as an Aboriginal right.[88]

To explore this test further, it is useful to look first at its relationship to the majority's description of the basis of Aboriginal rights.

(f) A Missing Link?

As suggested above, a coherent test for identifying Aboriginal rights today should relate to the basic nature of these rights. As Lamer C.J. said, although criteria should be applied in a modern context, courts must take account of the "Aboriginal" in "Aboriginal rights".[89] Because of the historical origin of Aboriginal rights, modern claims must have some basis in the traditional situation of Aboriginal peoples. But unless the law is to recognize *all* Aboriginal traditional practices as Aboriginal rights, courts must decide which aspect of the traditional situation should qualify as Aboriginal rights.

The need to highlight some, rather than all, possible aspects of traditional life is underlined by s. 35(1) of the *Constitution Act, 1982*. Since April 17, 1982, a finding that a right is an Aboriginal right is a finding that that right can prevail over all other legislation, federal or provincial. If, as Lamer C.J. said, s. 35(1) is intended not only to protect the fact of prior Aboriginal occupation but to reconcile it with Crown sovereignty, the scope of paramount Aboriginal rights cannot be co-extensive with the scope of traditional Aboriginal life. Non-designation as a s. 35(1) Aboriginal right does not, of course, limit other special rights to which Canadian Aboriginal peoples may be entitled.[90]

Lamer C.J. concluded that the test for identifying Aboriginal rights should look for the "crucial elements"[91] of traditional Aboriginal societies. As we have seen, the majority found that the crucial elements of these societies are traditional occupation of land and participation in distinct societies.[92] If the test for identifying Aboriginal rights is to reflect their basic nature, one would expect that this test would look for some link to land as well as — or as a part of — a distinctive society.[93]

Lamer C.J. said that in considering whether an Aboriginal rights claim can succeed, courts must look at the claimant's relationship to land as well as at the practices, traditions and customs[94] that are integral to the claimant's distinctive culture.[95] On the other hand, Lamer C.J. failed to make this relationship an explicit part of the distinctive practices test. At some points he seemed to suggest that this test is sufficient on its own to prove Aboriginal rights.[96] Moreover, although the Chief Justice's discussion of the basis of Aboriginal rights implied that land is part of the distinctiveness of Aboriginal cultures,[97] the discussion of the distinctive practices test did not. Lamer C.J.'s main concern here appears to have been less to distinguish Aboriginal cultures from those of other groups than to characterize and distinguish Aboriginal cultures on an individual basis.[98]

Starting with their general "land and societies" approach[99] to the basis of Aboriginal rights, then, the majority in *Van der Peet* seem to have ended up with a "societies" approach[100] to identifying Aboriginal rights in specific situations. What happened to the link to land? Had it no real importance in the first place? Was it implicit in the distinctive practices identification test? As will be seen later, these questions involve more than just theoretical consistency.

(g) McLachlin J.'s Criticisms

In her dissenting opinion in *Van der Peet*, McLachlin J. charged that the distinctive practices test on its own is "overinclusive, indeterminate, and ultimately categorical." For example, she said that the dictionary definition of "integral" means

> ...anything which can be said to be part of the aboriginal culture would qualify as an aboriginal right protected by the *Constitution Act, 1982*. This would confer constitutional protection on a multitude of activities, ranging from the trivial to the vital.[101]

The terms "integral" and "distinctive" did seem subjective, and capable of assessment by different and contradictory criteria. A conclusion based on quantity may conflict with one based on frequency, or one based on emphasis in traditional beliefs. The elasticity of these terms was illustrated by the very different ways they were applied in *Van der Peet* itself.[102]

The initial characterization process at the beginning was especially complex[103] and open-ended. At the Court of Appeal and Supreme Court levels, Mrs. Van der Peet's claim was characterized by seven different judges in five different ways.[104] Yet the characterization of an Aboriginal rights claim defines the assessment of the traditional activity. The wider the characterization, the more likely the claimant can prove a traditional practice, and *vice versa*.[105] In a very real way, characterization helps determine results.[106] McLachlin J. said the Chief Justice's emphasis on particularity "enabl[es] him to find no Aboriginal right where a different analysis might find one."[107] The Chief Justice might have made a similar observation about the opposite effect of the dissenting judgments.[108]

This uncertainty was exacerbated by conflicting views on the appropriate period in which to assess traditional practices. The majority focused on the pre-contact period. By doing this, they deprived themselves of most of the written records and firsthand oral experience normally required in courts. Lacking these tools, they had to come to a significant constitutional conclusion about a society far removed from them in culture and in time. L'Heureux-Dubé J.'s alternative suggestion that courts consider any twenty- to fifty-year time period would have traded this evidentiary uncertainty for chronological uncertainty.[109] As well, it could have minimized the element of prior occupancy at the heart of Aboriginal rights.[110]

The notion of continuity also posed indeterminateness problems, problems that are closely related to the issue of characterization. The broader the characterization, the more readily courts can find continuity. For example, the majority's right to "exchange fish for money or other goods"[111] is more vulnerable to continuity breaks than McLachlin's wider right to "[draw] a moderate livelihood from the fishery."[112] The decision also raised questions as to when continuity is broken by interrupted use or by extraneous influences. Although the majority said interruptions in an activity do not necessarily affect its status as an Aboriginal right, they did not indicate when an interruption becomes a final break. The majority said that European influence cannot break continuity unless it is the "sole" reason for a practice,[113] yet they considered it significant that the exchange of salmon between the Hudson's Bay Company and the Stó:lo occurred "primarily" because of European influences.[114]

McLachlin J.'s response to the problems of indeterminacy and categorical results[115] was to find a link between Aboriginal rights and land, on one hand, and "economic equivalency" on the other. Under her economic equivalency approach, a particular Aboriginal people have the right "to take from the resource the modern equivalent of what by Aboriginal law and custom it historically took."[116] Hence, if the claimants can show that they have traditionally derived "a moderate livelihood" from a natural resource, they may be able to establish an Aboriginal right to a moderate livelihood from that resource today, by modern means.[117] McLachlin J. claimed that this approach provides some of the internal limits that the majority's version of the distinctive practices test lacks.[118] As a result, it reduces indeterminateness, prevents categorical results, and avoids the need to add to the justification component of the *Sparrow* test for s. 35(1).

But economic equivalency and moderate livelihood have their own indeterminateness. To assess a modern economic equivalent to the value of an activity carried on as many as hundreds of years ago is a daunting goal. Moreover, what *is* a moderate livelihood? It has been suggested that "a moderate livelihood includes such basics as 'food, clothing and housing, supplemented by a few amenities', but not the accumulation of wealth...."[119] Does this mean an amount equivalent to the minimum wage, or more? Should the amount be the same for one group as for another? What happens if some members of a group are earning far more than a moderate livelihood, while others are barely surviving? Should the standard shift with the cost of living? With the inflation rate?[120]

Will the moderate livelihood test be applied to Aboriginal rights in future? On one hand, in *Gladstone*, a majority of the Supreme Court suggested that the place for assessing possible quantitative restrictions on the enjoyment of Aboriginal rights in relation to other rights is the justification branch of the infringement-justification test in *Sparrow*.[121] Despite McLachlin J.'s criticisms of this approach,[122] it does consider the relative priority to be accorded to Aboriginal rights in the forum in which they can be weighed explicitly against other interests, rather than in a relative vacuum.[123] On the other hand, in the more recent *Marshall* decision, the Supreme Court applied the moderate livelihood test to treaty rights.[124] It might well return to Aboriginal rights.

(h) A Return to Land?

There is no simple answer to the indeterminateness of the distinctive practices test. Courts cannot respect the special traditional origins of Aboriginal rights without producing an interest that is difficult to identify. On the other hand, they can do more than to say, as the majority said, that Aboriginal rights derive from practices important to the distinctive features of a particular traditional society. In this regard, McLachlin J.'s other main suggestion might provide some help: what might be needed is a meaningful relationship with land or its resources.

What kind of link to land is feasible? There are a number of possible approaches to linking Aboriginal rights and land:

(i) a *derivative* approach, requiring Aboriginal rights to be based on proof of Aboriginal title. This alternative was rejected explicitly in the Supreme Court's 1996 decision in *Adams*.[125]
(ii) a *nominal* approach, requiring only that activities giving rise to Aboriginal rights should "take place" on land. This approach would render any reference to land meaningless for identification purposes, as it would include virtually all forms of traditional activity. It would undermine the stress on prior occupancy in the majority's discussion of the basis of Aboriginal rights. It would be at odds with most existing case law. It would leave the distinctive practices test without form or content.
(iii) a *geographical* approach, requiring that activities giving rise to Aboriginal rights must occur only on specific areas of land. Although this approach describes some Aboriginal activities, it would be unduly restrictive as a general test for Aboriginal rights. It might exclude, for example, the sale by Mrs. Van der Peet, since that sale took place at her home, and not where the salmon were caught.
(iv) a *functional* approach, requiring that activities giving rise to Aboriginal rights must involve *some* form of use of land or its adjoining resources. Thus, the practices, traditions and customs that are integral to the distinctive culture of an Aboriginal society would be land or resource use activities. The degree of use would vary in individual situations, from full occupancy to non-site-specific use. This spectrum approach would avoid any necessary tie to Aboriginal title, would accommodate mobility of use, would permit a broad range of traditional activities to be classified as Aboriginal rights, would be consistent with the Royal Proclamation and the dominant case law, would reflect the discussion of the basis of Aboriginal rights in *Van der Peet* itself, and would bring clarity to the *Van der Peet* identification test.
(v) a *model* approach, stipulating that the closer an activity is linked to land or resource use, the lower the level of specific proof required to show that it is integral to a distinctive traditional society, and *vice versa*. This approach would leave the door open for recognition of forms of Aboriginal rights, such as language rights, that have no significant connection to land. On the other hand, it could add to courts' challenges in interpreting Aboriginal evidence.

The functional approach would not have resolved the controversy in *Van der Peet* itself. It requires that the practices, traditions and customs that are integral to the distinctive culture of an Aboriginal society must involve some use of land or its adjoining or related natural resources. Although the Stó:lo's traditional activity met this basic requirement, there was a controversy about the relative importance of the activity to the Stó:lo's traditional culture. Nevertheless, the functional approach could provide courts with a general core area within which traditionally significant activities would normally qualify for judicial protection.[126] Conversely, the functional approach would withhold s. 35(1) Aboriginal rights protection from activities outside this core area.[127] The functional approach could enable the Supreme Court to reconcile the *Van der Peet* identification test with the Court's own discussion of basic principles, and could give some general form to the rights the Court guaranteed in *Sparrow*. Arguably, the approach could provide clarity without being unduly restrictive. Moreover, it would not prevent courts from recognizing non-land customs outside s. 35(1), and from enforcing this custom in statutes, agreements, and special constitutional enactments.

Under the model approach, the practices, traditions and customs that are integral to the distinctive culture of an Aboriginal society are *characteristically* those that involve some use of land or its adjoining or related natural resources. Like the functional approach, this approach would not have resolved the specific controversy in *Van der Peet*. But by according primacy to land, it too could give a focal point to Aboriginal rights and their identification. Has the Court moved in the direction of the functional approach, or at least the model approach? On this question, see *Adams*,[128] *Delgamuukw*[129] and *Mitchell*[130] in **Chapter 10**.

4. *GLADSTONE*[131]

Reading 9(c) at p. 348

Gladstone was the second of a trilogy of commercial fishing cases decided at the same time as *Van der Peet*.[132] The case involved somewhat similar issues to *Van der Peet*, so we will focus mainly on *Gladstone*'s main contribution, which is an elaboration of the *Sparrow* doctrine of justification.

The Gladstones were both members of the Heiltsuk Band in British Columbia. They were charged with attempting to sell herring spawn on kelp without a licence, contrary to regulations under the federal *Fisheries Act*. In response, the Gladstones argued that the regulations violated their Aboriginal right to sell herring spawn on kelp commercially, contrary to s. 35(1) of the *Constitution Act, 1982*.

In the Supreme Court, the main majority judges found that the Heiltsuk had an unextinguished Aboriginal right to sell the spawn commercially and that the regulations infringed this right. However, they referred the case back to trial for more evidence on the issue of justification. L'Heureux-Dubé J. agreed in separate reasons. McLachlin J. also found that there was an unextinguished Aboriginal right, but she would have referred the case back to trial for more evidence on both infringement and justification. La Forest J., dissenting, held that there was no right to sell the spawn commercially in the sense claimed by the Gladstones, and that, in any event, any such right had been extinguished.[133]

Lamer C.J. for the main majority applied the three-part approach distinctive practices test developed in *Van der Peet*.[134] He distinguished between the right to exchange herring spawn on kelp for money or other goods, and a more extensive right to sell the spawn commercially. He said that "[t]his case, like N.T.C. Smokehouse, potentially creates problems at the characterization stage."[135] Although the Gladstones' actions were commercial, as in *Smokehouse*,[136] the regulations restricted all trade or sale. Hence, Lamer C.J. looked first to see if a less extensive non-commercial right could be established.[137] Applying the *Van der Peet* test, Lamer C.J. found that pre-contact trade in the spawn had been so extensive as to constitute an integral part of the distinctive culture of the Heiltsuk. Indeed, it was so extensive that Lamer C.J. felt it could be called "commercial" even though commercial transactions in the strict sense[138] did not arrive until the Europeans. Hence the pre-contact practice had sufficient continuity with the current activity.[139]

Lamer C.J. found that the right had not been extinguished, and was infringed within the terms of *Sparrow*.[140] Addressing the question of infringement, Lamer C.J. said it is the cumulative effect of the factors mentioned in *Sparrow* that matters, not the absence of any one factor.[141] On the issue of justification, Lamer C.J. said that while with food fishing the amount of exploitation is limited internally by the food needs of the users, commercial fishing has no such limits.[142] The *Sparrow* test required that all Aboriginal food and ceremonial fishery needs should be given priority after conservation.[143] If this test were applied to commercial Aboriginal fishing, it would replace the "internal" limits imposed by the needs of the rights holders with the potentially unlimited demands of the market. The result would be an unconfined and exclusive right over other potential users, including users who had had access in the past, and other Aboriginal users not subject to the special Aboriginal rights. To avoid this situation, government would be justified in imposing a less rigorous priority for Aboriginal commercial rights.[144]

Lamer C.J. said that "[t]he content of this priority — something less than exclusivity but which nonetheless gives priority to the Aboriginal right — must remain somewhat vague pending consideration of the government's actions in specific cases."[145] He said it would involve such factors as consultation, compensation where required, accommodations in the form of reduced licence fees, efforts to ensure that Aboriginal resource use participation reflected their proportion of the population, and the significance of the resource use to a particular band.[146]

Lamer C.J. then turned to a more general aspect of justification, the question of the kind of general goals government might invoke to help justify infringements of Aboriginal rights. He said this question should be considered in light of the *Van der Peet* principle that the purpose of s. 35(1) of the *Constitution Act, 1982* is to reconcile prior Aboriginal occupation with Crown sovereignty.[147] He said this purpose takes account of the fact that "distinctive Aboriginal communities exist within, and are a part of, a broader social, political, and economic community, over which the Crown is sovereign."[148] Accordingly, valid justification goals should not be limited to conservation and prevention of harm. Lamer C.J. continued:

> Although by no means making a definitive statement on this issue, I would suggest that with regards to the distribution of the fisheries resource after conservation goals have been met, objectives such as the pursuit of economic and regional fairness, and the recognition of the historical reliance upon, and participation in, the fishery by non-aboriginal groups, are the type of objectives which can (at least in the right circumstances) satisfy **[the compelling and substantial]** standard.[149]

L'Heureux-Dubé J. agreed with the main majority's discussion of Aboriginal peoples' commercial fishing priority and valid government objectives. Although McLachlin J. did not find it necessary to address the question of justification,[150] she made it clear in *Van der Peet* that she rejected both the notion of a less stringent priority and going beyond conservation or prevention of harm as valid government objectives.[151]

As noted in **Part 3(g)**, McLachlin J. felt that the *Gladstone* majority's expanded list of justification objectives and the new qualified priority concept were too indeterminate, and that they wrongly diluted s. 35(1) rights. It is true that valid legislative objectives can affect and even limit the accommodation measures required in the second part of the justification process. On the other hand, Lamer J. said that the additional legislative objectives *could* be valid, "[i]n the right circumstances", not that they *were* automatically valid. Moreover, the presence of a valid justification objective cannot justify infringement by itself; government must demonstrate acceptable accommodation as well. In this light, the wider objective list may be as much a broadening as a diluting agent, expanding the range of factors that government can consider when regulating s. 35(1) rights.

Perhaps the most critical element of justification is its second stage, where government must demonstrate that it has accommodated the s. 35(1) right. Here, *Gladstone*'s limited priority concept does not replace the absolute priority concept in *Sparrow*. Instead, the *Gladstone* concept offers an additional accommodation tool, for rights that lack the inherent limits found in *Sparrow*.

However, none of these considerations addresses McLachlin J.'s concern about the indeterminacy of the *Gladstone* approach. The *Gladstone* majority took one of the most complex aspects of s. 35(1) analysis and made it more complex. This concern, and possible responses, are considered further in **Chapter 10(3)(f)**.

5. *PAMAJEWON*[152]

Reading 9(d) at p. 350

In *Pamajewon*, the Supreme Court of Canada dismissed an Aboriginal self-government claim by applying the distinctive practices test, but without actually deciding if Aboriginal self-government can constitute an Aboriginal right under s. 35(1) of the *Constitution Act, 1982*.

The facts that resulted in this remarkable legal feat were relatively simple. Members of the Shawanaga First Nation and the Eagle Lake Band had been convicted of violating the *Criminal Code* because of high stakes gambling activities on their reserves. They argued that the gambling was protected by s. 35 of the *Constitution Act, 1982* either (i) as an Aboriginal right derived from Aboriginal title or (ii) as an Aboriginal right that was an incident of a broader inherent right to self-government.

On the self-government issue, the trial judge for the first claimant said that any possible right of Aboriginal self-government had been extinguished by either the Royal Proclamation of 1763, the Robinson Huron Treaty of 1859, or s. 91(24) of the *Constitution Act, 1867*. The other trial judge asserted that the relevant *Criminal Code* provision was constitutionally valid.

The Ontario Court of Appeal adopted the "distinctive practices" requirement stressed in *Delgamuukw*.[153] They said, "It is clear from cases such as *R. v. Sparrow*, that the common law recognizes Aboriginal rights which are integral to, or connected with, traditional Aboriginal practices, and land use."[154] They concluded that the claimed gambling right was neither a part of the claimants' historical cultures and traditions, *nor* an aspect of their use of their land.[155]

On the issue of self-government, Osborne J.A. said for the Court that:

> In my view, this claim is answered by *Sparrow* [where the Court said that ...] "there was from the outset never any doubt that sovereignty and legislative power, and indeed the underlying title, to such lands [were] vested in the Crown.[156]

Osborne J.A. went on to say that assuming that the claimants *had* an inherent right of self-government, there was no evidence here of any traditional practice of high stakes gambling, or traditional Aboriginal regulation of gambling. Next, they said that assuming that there *was* evidence of traditional activities of this kind, they had since been extinguished by federal criminal law enactments regulating gambling.

Like the Ontario Court of Appeal, the Supreme Court of Canada dismissed the argument that gambling could be seen as a generalized form of use of land.[157] As in *Van der Peet*, they said Aboriginal rights claims must be considered on a more specific basis.[158] Unlike the Court of Appeal, though, the Supreme Court declined to look for any more specific form of land use. Everything, they suggested, depended on whether the alleged rights were integral to the distinctive culture of the individual claimant group.[159] Like the Court of Appeal, the Supreme Court was willing to assume "without deciding"[160] that Aboriginal self-government can constitute an Aboriginal right within the meaning of s. 35(1) of the *Constitution Act, 1982*.

Applying the distinctive practices test, the Supreme Court concluded that the evidence did not establish that gambling, or that the regulation of gambling, was an integral part of the distinctive cultures of the claimant societies in this case. While there had been gambling, it had been informal, and on a small scale, and bore no resemblance to the commercial lotteries of the 20th century. Hence, the claimants in this case had not established an Aboriginal right.

The Court might have arrived at the same conclusion without needing to assess the prevalence and distinctiveness of traditional gambling, by requiring a link to a specific use of land or natural resources.[161] Gambling may have been an activity on the land, but it was not a direct use of the land of the same order as occupation, fishing, or the consumption of natural resources. Neither, for that matter, was the regulation of gambling.

By regarding land as a necessary foundation of Aboriginal rights, the Court could have given some minimal substantive content to the distinctive practices test.[162] It could have provided a concrete criterion for assessing broad claims involving self-government.[163] The Court did not take this position, or the more modest position that land is a *characteristic* foundation of Aboriginal rights.[164] Instead, it left to another day the task of clarifying Aboriginal rights and their relationship to Aboriginal self-government.[165]

Notes

1. *Mabo v. State of Queensland (No. 2)* (1992), 107 A.L.R. 1; 175 C.L.R. 1 (High Court of Australia).

   For commentary, see H.E. Maconachie, "*Mabo* v. *Queensland*" [No. 2] (1998) 56 Advocate 697.
2. For Brennan J.'s criticisms of the old approach, and his comments on its inapplicability to the present case, see *ibid.* at 21–29. As he noted, the land was not uninhabited. The traditional argument that lands with Aboriginal inhabitants could be considered *terra nullius* because the lands were uncultivated and the people were "uncivilized", not Christian, was inappropriate. (Assuming that the cultivation concept could or should be employed to help indicate greater densities of use, the land in this case was unquestionably cultivated, as the Meriam were traditional gardeners!)
3. *Ibid.* at 35–41.
4. *Ibid.* at 41.
5. *Ibid.* at 43
6. *Ibid.* at 41.
7. As examples of these interests, Brennan J. referred to "[t]he incidents of a particular native title relating to inheritance, the transmission or acquisition of rights and interest on death or marriage, the transfer of rights and interests in land and the grouping of persons to possess rights and interests in land ...": *ibid.* at 44. He said these "are matters to be determined by the laws of the indigenous inhabitants, provided those laws and customs are not so repugnant to natural justice, equity and good conscience that judicial sanctions under the new regime must be withheld ...": *ibid.*
8. *Ibid.* at 50.
9. Mason C.J. and McHugh J. agreed with Brennan J. Deane, Toowhee, and Gaudron JJ. said extinguishment required clear legislative action. They agreed that there was generally no extinguishment here. Dawson J., dissenting, agreed with the main majority that native title can be extinguished by the Crown acting alone. In his view the native title had been extinguished by the Crown's actions from the time of the change of sovereignty.
10. See *The Wik Peoples v. The State of Queensland and Ors*; *The Thayorre People v. The State of Queensland and Ors* (1996), A.H.C., No. 88 of 1996 and No. 88 of 1996 (High Court of Australia).
11. *R. v. Van der Peet*, [1996] 2 S.C.R. 507 (S.C.C.); aff'g [1993] 5 W.W.R. 459 (B.C.C.A.); rev'g [1991] 3 C.N.L.R. 161 (B.C.S.C.); rev'g [1991] 3 C.N.L.R. 155 (B.C. Prov. Ct.).

    For an introduction to the traditional cultural group involved in this case, see B. Thom, *Stó:lo Traditional Culture: A Short Ethnography of the Stó:lo People*, May 1996 <http://web20.mindlink.net/stolo/culture.htm>.

    For commentary on the case, see D. Lambert, "Case Comment: *Van Der Peet* and *Delgamuukw*: The Unresolved Issues" (1998) 32 U.B.C. L. Rev. 249; K. McNeil, "Case Comment on *R. v. Van der Peet* (1998) 36 Alta. L. Rev. 117; J. Rudin, "One Step Forward, Two Steps Back: The Political and Institutional Dynamics Behind the Supreme Court of Canada's Decisions in *R. v. Sparrow*, *R. v. Van Der Peet* and *Delgamuukw v. British Columbia*" (1998) 13 J.L. & Soc. Pol'y. 67; D. Stack, "Case Comment on *R. v. Van der Peet*" (1999) 62 Sask L. Rev. 471.
12. *R. v. Sparrow*, [1990] 1 S.C.R. 1075 at 1099: **Chapter 7, Part 4**, above. See also W.I.C. Binnie, "The Sparrow Doctrine: Beginning of the End or End of the Beginning" (1990) 15 Queen's L.J. 217; D.W. Elliott, "In the Wake of Sparrow: A New Department of Fisheries?" (1991) 40 U.N.B.L.J. 23.
13. Section 27(5) of the *British Columbia Fishery (General) Regulations*, SOR/84-248. Section 27(5) stipulated that "[n]o person shall sell, barter or offer to sell or barter any fish caught under the authority of an Indian food fish licence."
14. Ms. Van der Peet was charged under s. 61(1) of the *Fisheries Act*, R.S.C. 1970, c. F-14, with selling fish caught under the authority of an Indian food fish licence, contrary to s. 27(5) of the *British Columbia Fishery (General) Regulations*, SOR/84-248.
15. **Chapter 3, Part 3** and **Chapter 1, Part 3**. See testimony of Aboriginal witnesses, reported in Royal Commission

on Aboriginal Peoples, *Report of the Royal Commission on Aboriginal Peoples*, vol. 2 (Ottawa: Canada Communication Group, 1996), part 2, chap. 4, ss. 3.1 and 3.2. See also J. Cruikshank, *Through the Eyes of Strangers: A Preliminary Survey of Land Use History in the Yukon During the Late Nineteenth Century* (Whitehorse: Govt. of Yukon, 1974); P. Tennant, *Aboriginal Peoples and Politics: The Indian Land Question in British Columbia, 1849–1989* (Vancouver: U.B.C. Press, 1990); O.P. Dickason, *Canada's First Nations: A History of Founding Peoples from Earliest Times*, 3d ed. (Don Mills, Ont.: Oxford University Press, 2002), chaps. 1–4; and D. Newell, *Tangled Webs of History: Indians and the Law in Canada's West Coast Fisheries* (Toronto: University of Toronto Press, 1993), chap. 2.

16. A right to sell fish or to fish commercially was claimed not only in *Van der Peet* but in *R. v. N.T.C. Smokehouse Ltd.*, [1996] 2 S.C.R. 672 and *R. v. Gladstone*, [1996] 2 S.C.R. 723. See also S. Gilby, "The Aboriginal Right to a Commercial Fishery" (1995) 4 *Dal. J. Leg. Studies* at 231–52. Before 1992, Aboriginal people participated in the commercial fishery on the same general basis as non-Aboriginals. In 1992, the Department of Fisheries began the Aboriginal Fisheries Strategy, a program that allocated to signatory Indian bands in British Columbia a separate part of the salmon harvest for commercial purposes. For two contrasting assessments of the Aboriginal Fisheries Strategy, see M.H. Smith, *Our Home and Native Land?* (Victoria: Crown Western, 1995), chap. 9; and D. Newell, *ibid.* at 77–78. Unlike the AFS or other government policies, an Aboriginal right to fish commercially would be guaranteed constitutionally.
17. For a sample of the problems, see D.S. Boyer, "The Untamed Fraser: British Columbia Lifeline" *National Geographic* (July 1986) at 44–75; J.F. Roos, Pacific Salmon Commission, *Restoring Fraser River Salmon: A History of the International Pacific Salmon Fisheries Commission, 1937–1985* (Vancouver: P.S.F.C., 1991); G. Meggs, *Salmon and the Decline of the B.C. Fishery* (Vancouver: Douglas & McIntyre, 1992); D. Newell, *ibid.*; J. Allain and J.-D. Fréchette, Library of Parliament, *The Aboriginal Fisheries and the Sparrow Decision* (Ottawa: Supply and Services Canada, 1994); Report of the Fraser River Sockeye Public Review Board, *Fraser River Sockeye 1994: Problems and Discrepancies* (Ottawa: Public Works and Government Services Canada, 1995); T.L. Slaney, "Status of Anadromous Salmon and Trout in British Columbia and Yukon" 21:10 *Fisheries* at 20–35; Pacific Salmon Commission, *1995/96 Eleventh Annual Report* (Vancouver: P.S.C., 1996), chart at 53, showing catch declines in most of the southern regions of British Columbia.
18. For example, Royal Commission on Aboriginal Peoples, *Report of the Royal Commission on Aboriginal Peoples*, vol. 2 (Ottawa: Canada Communication Group, 1993), part 1 at 189. See also **Part 3(b)**, below and **Chapter 12, Part 4**.
19. Mrs. Van der Peet lost in the British Columbia Provincial Court ([1991] 3 C.N.L.R. 155, October 29, 1990); succeeded in the British Columbia Supreme Court ([1991] 3 C.N.L.R. 161, August 14, 1991); and then lost again in a majority decision of the British Columbia Court of Appeal ([1993] 5 W.W.R. 459, June 35, 1993).

    In the Court of Appeal the majority (Macfarlane J.A. for himself and Taggart J.A.; Wallace J.A. concurring separately) applied the "distinctive practices" test they had formulated in *Delgamuukw v. British Columbia*, [1993] 5 W.W.R. 97: see [1993] 5 W.W.R. 459 at 467–69, 482–83, applying [1993] 5 W.W.R. 97 at 124–25 (Wallace J.A. concurring at 183). They concluded that the Stó:lo's traditional trade in salmon was insufficient to be integral to their distinctive culture.

    Lambert and Hutcheon JJ.A. dissented. While the majority of the Court of Appeal related Aboriginal rights to occupancy and use of land (and by extension to resources such as water) (Macfarlane and Taggart JJ.A. at [1993] 5 W.W.R. 459 at 468 and Wallace J.A. at 487), Lambert J.A. said "[a]boriginal rights have their origin in the customs, traditions and practices [of the relevant aboriginal people]": 493. He said the customs, traditions and practices "which formed an integral part of the distinctive culture of the aboriginal people in question [at the relevant time]" gave rise to Aboriginal rights: 493. From here Lambert J.A. went on to articulate an Aboriginal right to a moderate livelihood from traditionally-used resources: 494–504. Applying this approach, Lambert J.A. said that because the traditional use of salmon was integral to Stó:lo culture, the Stó:lo should be entitled to catch enough in modern times to provide themselves with a "moderate livelihood": *ibid.* at 499–500. Hutcheon J.A. dissented on other grounds: *ibid.* at 513.
20. *R. v. Van der Peet*, [1996] 2 S.C.R. 507.
21. *Supra* note 11.
22. *Ibid.* at para. 30. This proposition is at the heart of the *Van der Peet* decision's general "land and societies" approach to the source of Aboriginal rights: see **Chapter 3, Part 6**. For the land component, see **Part 5(b)**, below; for the distinctive societies component, see **Part 3(c)**, below.
23. *Ibid.* at para. 31.
24. Or, as Lamer C.J. called it, the "integral to a distinctive culture" test: *R. v. Van der Peet*, [1996] 2 S.C.R. 507 at paras. 55, 56, 80. See also paras. 46, 48, 51–54, 55, 57–59, and 60–65.
25. *R. v. Sparrow*, [1990] 1 S.C.R. 1075.
26. *Van der Peet*, *supra* note 11 at para. 59.
27. *Ibid.* at para. 49.
28. Lamer C.J. in *R. v. Van der Peet*, [1996] S.C.R. 507 at para. 53.
29. *Ibid.*, heading above para. 51. Lamer C.J. said characterization should focus on the significance of actual practices to the distinctive culture of the claimant group, not on whether a general area of activity is significant for a broad ultimate goal such as livelihood: *ibid.* at para. 79.
30. *Ibid.* at para. 55. He said the practice must be such that without the practice the culture would be fundamentally altered: *ibid.* at para. 59.
31. *Ibid.* at para. 70. *Quaere*: assuming that the regulatory power claimed in *R. v. Pamajewon* [*R. v. Jones*; *R. v. Gardner*], [1996] 2 S.C.R. 821 could meet other aspects of the *Van der Peet* test, could it meet this one?
32. Lamer C.J. referred (*ibid.* at para. 45) to the Court's later statement in *Sparrow* that "for the Musqueam, the salmon fishery has always constituted *an integral part of their distinctive culture*": *R. v. Sparrow*, [1990] 1 S.C.R. 1075 at 1099. [Emphasis added by Lamer C.J.] As seen, the British Columbia Court of Appeal adapted this statement in their own different sets of reasons in *Van der Peet*: **Part 3(b)**, above. The term was also used in *Calder*, where Hall J. observed that the Nisga'a "are and were from time immemorial a distinctive cultural entity with concepts of ownership indigenous to their culture and capable of articulation under the common law": *Calder v. British Columbia (A.G.)*, [1973] S.C.R. 313 at 375. In *Calder* and *Sparrow*, the term appeared to be one means of describing Aboriginal rights; in *Van der Peet* it became a required element for identifying Aboriginal rights. Outside Aboriginal law the term "distinctive" is often associated with trademark law, where it refers to features that distinguish or identify: see, for example, *Canada (Registrar of Trade Marks) v. G.A. Hardie & Co.*, [1949] S.C.R. 483.
33. Such as "eating to survive": *Van der Peet*, *supra* note 11 at para. 56.
34. *Ibid.* at 71.
35. *Ibid.* at para. 69.
36. *Ibid.* at para. 68 (evidence) and paras. 64 and 65 (continuity).
37. *Ibid.* at para. 77.

38. *Ibid.* at para. 78.
39. *Ibid.* at para. 88.
40. *Ibid.*, commencing at paras. 95 and 224, respectively.
41. *Ibid.* at para. 141. However, L'Heureux-Dubé J. did not agree that consideration of the Aboriginal perspective should be balanced by a concern to incorporate this perspective into the common law: *ibid.* at para. 145.
42. L'Heureux-Dubé J. saw Aboriginal rights as "arising out of the historic occupation and use of native ancestral lands" (*ibid.* at para. 116) and as "part of a distinctive aboriginal culture" (*ibid.*). However, she suggested that these rights could include not only Aboriginal title and rights to hunt, fish or trap, and accompanying rights, but also "other matters, not related to land, that form part of a distinctive aboriginal culture": *ibid.* and para. 121. *Quaere*: how can a matter arise out of occupation and use of land, and not relate to land?
43. *Ibid.* at paras. 147–62.
44. L'Heureux-Dubé J. said courts must not limit their search to individual practices that are unique to Aboriginal cultures (*ibid.* at paras. 150–54, and see para. 180), and that courts should not limit themselves to pre-contact times when looking for distinctive traditional practices. She said a practice should be integral to the distinctive culture "*for a substantial continuous period of time*" (*ibid.* at para. 175, emphasis added by L'Heureux-Dubé J.) — either before or after European contact or sovereignty — and that a period of twenty to fifty years would qualify for these purposes (*ibid.* at 178).
45. McLachlin J. said the distinctive practices test was insufficient by itself to provide a satisfactory means of identifying Aboriginal rights: *ibid.* at para. 255. She said the test should be qualified by inquiring to see "what sort of practices have been identified as aboriginal rights in the past": para. 261. From this inquiry, McLachlin J. concluded that the right to live off the land and its resources had been recognized historically as a fundamental Aboriginal right: paras. 272 and 275. See further, **Part 3(g)**, below.
46. *Ibid.* at paras. 279 and 280, and **Part 3(g)**, below.
47. *Ibid.* at paras. 283–84.
48. **Chapter 3, Parts 5–8**; **Chapter 4**, and **Chapter 7**. As seen in **Chapter 4, Part 1**, *Calder v. British Columbia (A.G.)*, [1973] S.C.R. 313 was instrumental in suggesting that Indian title claims do not depend exclusively on the Royal Proclamation, but derive as well from common law recognition of Aboriginal occupancy and use of land prior to the arrival of the Europeans.
49. Although the two leading judgments in *Calder*, *ibid.*, strongly supported occupancy and use, they did not address the questions of content and basic features comprehensively; the post-*Calder* decisions (**Chapter 4**) did not add much more about the content of Aboriginal rights; and *Sparrow* (**Chapter 7**) was directed more to the status than content.
50. *Van der Peet*, *supra* note 11 at para. 30 [emphasis added by Lamer C.J.].
51. *Ibid.* at para. 35, suggesting that this view also has support in early American case law.
52. *Ibid.* at para. 30.
53. *Ibid.* at para. 33.
54. *Ibid.* at para. 37, saying that this feature and possession of the soil from time immemorial are as relevant to the identification of the interests that s. 35(1) was intended to protect, as it was in the early American case of *Worcester v. Georgia*, 31 U.S. (6 Pet.) 515.
55. *Ibid.* at para. 31.
56. McLachlin J. referred generally to "two fundamental principles" — "that the Crown took subject to *existing aboriginal interests in the lands they traditionally occupied and their adjacent waters* ... [and that the interests were to be removed only by treaty with compensation]": *ibid.* at para. 275 (emphasis added). She said an Aboriginal right is established "[i]n so far as an aboriginal people under internal law or custom had used the land and its waters in the past": para. 269. L'Heureux-Dubé J., dissenting, also saw land as important to the basis of Aboriginal rights, although she did not appear to regard it as vital to the content of Aboriginal rights: *supra* note 42.
57. For example, M. Walters, "British Imperial Constitutional Law and Aboriginal Rights: A Comment on *Delgamuukw v. British Columbia*" (1992) 17 Queen's L.J. 350, articulating a general theory about Aboriginal rights that extend beyond land and resources connected with land. (Although a compelling case can be made for "some sort of intermediary category between conquest and settlement," as suggested in note 85 of the article, there is still a question as to that category's general content. See also discussion paper of Royal Commission on Aboriginal Peoples, *Aboriginal Peoples, Self-Government, and the Constitution* (Ottawa: Canada Communication Group, 1993) and Royal Commission on Aboriginal Peoples, *Report of the Royal Commission on Aboriginal Peoples*, vol. 2 (Ottawa: Canada Communication Group, 1996), part 1 at 189.
58. In *Delgamuukw v. British Columbia*, [1993] 5 W.W.R. 97 at 290; *R. v. Van der Peet*, [1993] 5 W.W.R. 459 at 470; and their June 25, 1993, companion decisions in the British Columbia Court of Appeal, Lambert J.A., dissenting, supported an identification test for Aboriginal rights that was free of any necessary tie to land. Lambert J.A. also spoke for a three-judge Court of Appeal panel that held that native customary adoption can be the subject of Aboriginal rights: *Casimel et al. v. Insurance Corporation of British Columbia* (1993), 106 D.L.R. (4th) 720 at 727–28 (B.C.C.A.). See also *Manychief v. Poffenroth*, [1994] No. 907, 27 (A.Q.B.).
59. (1867) 17 R.J.R.Q. 75, 11 L.C. Jur. 197, 1 C.N.L.C. 70 (Q.S.C., cited in this note to R.J.R.Q.), **Chapter 3, Part 13**. In *Connolly*, Monk J. recognized the validity of an Indian customary marriage in the Athabaska Territory in 1803. He said that "the territorial rights, political organization, such as it was, or the laws and usages of the Indian tribes" continued in full force, even assuming that European law applied at trading posts in the region in question: 84. The Royal Commission Report used Monk J.'s decision to help support the proposition that Aboriginal rights are based generally on "unwritten sources such as long-standing custom and practice": *supra* note 57 at 189. The Report concluded that Aboriginal rights that continue past European sovereignty include "special linguistic, cultural, and religious rights", and other rights such as "rights of self-government": *ibid.*
60. (6 Peters) 515, 540, 547, 552, 557, 558 (1832), **Chapter 3, Part 12**.
61. *R. v. Sioui*, [1990] 1 S.C.R. 1025 at 1055: **Chapter 5, Part 13**. In *Worcester*, *ibid.*, and *Sioui*, the Supreme Court of the United States and the Supreme Court of Canada, respectively, commented about the British policy of treating Indians as nations, with internal autonomy.
62. For views on the antiquity of Aboriginal occupation, see **Chapter 1, Part 3**, notes 11 to 15.
63. For the special significance of land and related resources to Aboriginal peoples, see *supra* note 15.
64. *Supra* note 61.
65. Arguably, European presence, government and sovereignty in the Athabaska Territory in 1803 was minimal. Within Rupert's Land, the "governmental" powers of the Hudson's Bay Company applied only to its employees. The Athabaska area lay beyond even the territory of the Hudson's Bay Company. There was no true settlement in the Athabaska area — just a handful of forts and some early fur trade activity. Hence, Monk J.'s decision does not necessarily support the theory that all forms of pre-existing customs and laws, including self-government laws, survived the more complete changes of sovereignty that occurred later and elsewhere. Although the decision

was upheld by the majority of the Quebec Court of Appeal (in (1869), 17 R.J.R.Q. 266; 1 R.L. (O.S.) 253 (cited in this note to R.J.R.Q.)), their language was more restrained, and was inconsistent with any broad claim to common law self-government rights: 333–34. They too stressed the limited nature of the European presence in the region in 1803: Badgley: 332–33; Mackay: 346, 352; and Loranger J. (dissenting on another point): 276. (Duval J. concurred with his colleagues: *ibid.*)

Before quoting the comments in *Worcester*, Lamer C.J. noted that they referred to "British policy towards the Indians in the mid-eighteenth century": *Sioui*, *supra* note 61 at 1053. Lamer C.J.'s own comments were also made in the context of 18th century Indian-European relations. However, the Royal Commission discussion paper considered both comments to be "persuasive reasons for concluding that under the common law doctrine of Aboriginal rights, Aboriginal peoples have an inherent right to govern themselves within Canada": *supra* note 57 at 21. The Royal Commission report cited the same comments and came to a similar conclusion: *supra* note 57 at 192.

66. In most of North America, European sovereignty was imposed gradually, rather than overnight: see the comments by L'Heureux-Dubé J. in *R. v. Van der Peet*, [1996] 2 S.C.R. 507 at para. 167, about the difficulty of establishing an exact date for British sovereignty. In *Baker Lake v. Minister of I.A.N.D.*, [1980] 1 F.C. 518 at 562 (F.C.T.D.), Mahoney J. suggested that English sovereignty had been established in the Baker Lake area "probably no earlier than 1610 and certainly no later than May 2, 1670." Even in regard to the more standard "conquest" situation after the fall of New France, the Supreme Court has referred to the "transition" to British sovereignty: *R. v. Côté*, [1996] 3 S.C.R. 139 at paras. 4 and 42; *R. v. Adams*, [1996] 3 S.C.R. 1013 at paras. 4 and 32). Early situations might bear little resemblance to those later on.

67. On the potential difficulties of proof of Aboriginal custom, see K. McNeil, *Common Law Aboriginal Title* (Oxford: Oxford University Press, 1989) at 193.

68. Or use.

69. Rights associated with the occupation and use of land and adjoining resources were the main focus of protection in the Indian provisions of the Royal Proclamation of 1763: **Chapter 3, Part 9**. After an initial contact period, land rights became an increasingly central feature in Indian treaties: **Chapter 5, Part 5**.

70. See Lamer C.J. in *R. v. Van der Peet*, [1996] 2 S.C.R. 507, para. 36, referring to *Johnson v. M'Intosh*, 21 U.S. (8 Wheat.) 543 at 574 (1823). Marshall C.J. referred throughout to the Indian right "of possession": *ibid.* at 574, 580, 582, 583, 584, 588, 590, 591, 603; and of "occupancy": 574, 583, 588. This right was considered to have survived sovereignty at common law (with additional assistance from the Royal Proclamation of 1763), and to be capable of supporting a common law action in ejectment (592).

Although Marshall C.J.'s later decision in *Worcester v. Georgia* U.S. 515 (1832) affirmed a right of self-government as well as occupancy-based Aboriginal rights, the wider right appeared to be based heavily on its specific acknowledgment in early American peace treaties and federal legislation. In *Worcester* itself, the Supreme Court held that Georgia laws that interfered with the Cherokee were invalid on the ground that the state laws were "repugnant to the Constitution, laws, and treaties of the United States" (562). On *Worcester*, see also text referred to at notes 60 and 64.

See also *County of Oneida v. Oneida Indian Nation* 470 U.S. 226 (1985): "By the time of the Revolutionary War, several well-defined principles had been established governing the nature of a tribe's interest in its property and how those interests could be conveyed. It was accepted that Indian nations held 'aboriginal title' to lands they had inhabited from time immemorial" (at 233–34). "[This court has recognized at least implicitly that] Indians have a federal common-law right to sue to enforce their aboriginal land rights" (at 235).

71. Most later colonial decisions support the survival of antecedent Aboriginal rights associated with land, see *Wi Parata v. Bishop of Wellington* (1877), 3 N.Z. Jur. (N.S.) 72 at 77 (N.Z.S.C.): "native proprietary rights" (although there is also a reference to the "old laws of the country," the emphasis is on proprietary rights); *Cook et al. v. Sprigg*, [1899] A.C. 572 at 578 (J.C.P.C.): "private property"; *Nireaha Tamaki v. Baker*, [1900] A.C. 561 at 578 (J.C.P.C.): "possession and occupation of ... lands ... under a native title"; *Southern Nigeria (A.G.) v. Holt*, [1915] A.C. 599 at 609 (J.C.P.C.); *Amodu Tijani v. Secretary, Southern Nigeria*, [1921] 2 A.C. 399 at 407, 409–10 (J.C.P.C.); *Bakare Ajakaiye v. Lieutenant-Governor, Southern Provinces*, [1929] A.C. 679 at 682 (J.C.P.C.); *Adeyinka Oyekan v. Musendiku Adele*, [1957] 2 All E.R. 785 at 788 (J.C.P.C.): "rights equivalent to property".

72. *Mabo v. State of Queensland (No. 2)* (1992), 107 A.L.R. 1 at 41 (High Court of Australia): "[t]he preferable rule equates the indigenous inhabitants of a settled colony with the inhabitants of a conquered colony in respect of their rights and interests in land", see **Part 3**, above. (The remainder of the quotation refers to *Re Southern Rhodesia*, [1918] A.C. 211 at 233, 235 (J.C.P.C.), which spoke of rights in or equivalent to property as being the kind of private rights that could survive conquest.)

73. The "Indian title" referred to in *St. Catherine's Milling and Lumber Co. v. The Queen* (1888), 14 A.C. 46 at 55 (J.C.P.C.), **Chapter 3, Part 10**, was a land-based title ascribed to the Royal Proclamation of 1763. In *Calder v. British Columbia (A.G.)*, [1973] S.C.R. 313 at 375, **Chapter 4, Part 1**, Judson J. said that "when the settlers came, the Indians were there, organized in societies and occupying the land as their forefathers had done for centuries. This is what Indian title means...." Hall J. said that "[t]he issue here is whether any right or title the Indians possess *as occupants of the land from time immemorial* has been extinguished": *Ibid.* at 352 (emphasis added). In *R. v. Guerin*, [1984] 2 S.C.R. 335 at 376 (S.C.C.), **Chapter 4, Part 4**, Dickson J. summarized *Calder* as holding that Aboriginal title is "a legal right derived from the Indians' historic occupation and possession of their tribal lands." In *R. v. Sparrow*, [1990] 1 S.C.R. 1075 at 1094, the Court noted that "...the Musqueam have lived in the area as an organized society long before the coming of European settlers, and ... the taking of salmon was an integral part of their lives and remains so to this day." See also *Delgamuukw v. British Columbia* (1993), 104 D.L.R. (4th) 470 (B.C.C.A.) at paras. 496–97 and 573.

74. Elsewhere they said that the term excludes features common to all societies, but does not require uniqueness, and focuses on the particular Aboriginal community in question (*Van der Peet*, *supra* note 11 at paras. 56, 71, and 69, respectively, and **Part 3(b)**, above). However, they did not indicate if the term comprehends some elements *common to Aboriginal societies*.

75. For a more general common element, see the next paragraph.

76. See **Part 3(b)**, above, referring to *Van der Peet*, *supra* note 11 at para. 30.

77. **Part 3(f)**, below.

78. *Van der Peet*, *supra* note 11 at para. 33.

79. *Ibid.*

80. *Ibid.* at para. 31.

81. L'Heureux-Dubé J. said that "s. 35(1) constitutionalizes the common law doctrine of aboriginal rights which recognizes aboriginal interests arising out of the historic occupation and use of ancestral lands by natives" (para. 159), and stressed that the provision must be given a broad interpretation. McLachlin J. did not reject the

majority's description of s. 35(1), although she considered it incomplete. She said the section recognized a prior legal régime as well as prior occupation (para. 230). (Although McLachlin J. attributed this proposition to two passages she quoted from page 1105 of *Sparrow*, the connection is not clear. The second passage does support her other suggestion (at para. 230) that settlement of Aboriginal claims is part of the purpose of s. 35(1). However, the majority might argue that this goal is implied in their general notion of reconciliation and that its purposes are, in McLachlin J.'s words, "to preclude extinguishment and to provide a firm foundation for settlement of aboriginal claims" (para. 232)).

82. **Part 3(b)**, above. Note, however, L'Heureux-Dubé J.'s position on content: *supra* notes 42 and 44.
83. *Ibid.* at para. 17. [Emphasis added by Lamer C.J.].
84. *Ibid.* at para. 43.
85. *Ibid.* at para. 44.
86. *Ibid.* at paras. 51–54 and 76.
87. Lamer C.J. referring to this part of the *Van der Peet* test in *R. v. Adams*, [1996] 3 S.C.R. 101 at para. 37. See also *Van der Peet, ibid.* at paras. 55–59.
88. *Van der Peet, ibid.* at para. 63. In *Adams, ibid.* at paras. 37 and 47, this part is combined with the traditional practice evaluation in the second stage of the test.
89. *Ibid.* at para. 17.
90. In situations not meeting the requirements of s. 35(1) Aboriginal rights, there may still be a possibility of s. 35(1) treaty rights, including land claims agreement rights; legislative rights (i.e., under the *Indian Act*, R.S.C. 1985, c. I-5, as am.); native customary law rights (see, for example, N. Zlotkin, "Judicial Recognition of Aboriginal Customary Law in Canada", [1984] 4 C.N.L.R. 1); and international law rights. See **Chapter 12, Part 1**, note 1.
91. *Van der Peet, supra* note 11 at para. 44.
92. **Parts 3(b) and (c)**, above.
93. The test need not be narrow. The historical notion of land and the complexity of traditional Aboriginal life both militate against restricting this link to land to a literal sense. Constitutionally, "land" can include not only use of the surface, but mines (e.g., *British Columbia (A.G.) v. Canada (A.G.)* (1899), 14 A.C. 295 (J.C.P.C.)); minerals (*ibid.*); renewable resources such as timber (e.g., *St. Catherine's* decision, **Chapter 3, Part 10**); and adjoining waters and water resources, such as fish (e.g., *R. v. Robertson* (1882), 6 S.C.R. 52; *Re Provincial Fisheries* (1895), 26 S.C.R. 444 (S.C.C.)). Thus, traditional land use, not a narrow definition of land, can form the basis for the content of Aboriginal rights. Moreover, as many traditional Aboriginal societies were highly mobile, not all Aboriginal activities need be located on land that is subject to Aboriginal title: see *R. v. Adams*, [1996] 2 S.C.R. 101 at para. 27, **Chapter 10, Part 2**). As well, the Supreme Court said in *Adams* that Aboriginal rights need not involve a traditional connection to land that would be sufficient to establish a claim to Aboriginal title: *ibid.* at para. 26. Nor need the relationship to land prevent activities originally tied directly to land from evolving into modern forms. On the other hand, if traditional occupation and use is to have any significance at all, it should mean more than the nominal fact that traditional Aboriginal activities took place *on* land or adjacent water.
94. For convenience, in the remainder of this chapter the words "practice" and "practices" will refer to "practice, tradition, and custom" and "practices, traditions or customs", respectively.
95. *Ibid.* at para. 74.
96. For example, *ibid.* at paras. 63, 71.
97. *Ibid.* at para. 30 and **Part 3(i)**, above, second last para.
98. See, for example, his quotation (at para. 40) from *Mabo v. Queensland (No. 2)* (1992), 175 C.L.R. 1 at 58, and his statement that "[a]boriginal rights are not general and universal; their scope and content must be determined on a case by case basis.... The existence of the right will be specific to each aboriginal community": para. 69.
99. **Part 3(b)**, above.
100. That is, the distinctive practices test.
101. *Ibid.* at para. 256. McLachlin J. added that the majority's notions of distinctiveness and specificity were too imprecise to resolve this problem of overbreadth: *ibid.*
102. For example, the majority said the distinctive practices test requires the court to ask if a practice was sufficiently important to the defining features of a particular society. Yet L'Heureux-Dubé J. was able to apply the same test and conclude that the relevant question is whether a practice was sufficiently important "to the culture and social organization" of the Aboriginal society: para. 206, and see also paras. 157 and 162. Although McLachlin J. agreed with L'Heureux-Dubé J.'s interpretation of the test (*ibid.* at para. 255), she then dismissed the test itself as inadequate.
103. The characterization process was complicated by the majority's willingness to consider factors *other* than the appearance of the activity that is the subject of the claim: see para. 53.
104. For example, Macfarlane and Taggart JJ.A. characterized the claim as a right "to sell fish ... on a commercial basis": *R. v. Van der Peet*, [1993] 5 W.W.R. 459 at 469. Wallace J.A. described it as a right "to sell fish": *ibid.* at 477. Lambert J.A. characterized it, *inter alia*, as a right "to catch and ... sell sufficient salmon [to provide those fishing and their dependent families] with a moderate livelihood": *ibid.* at 499. In the Supreme Court, Lamer J. characterized the claim as a claimed right "to exchange fish for money or other goods": para. 77. L'Heureux-Dubé J. characterized it as a right "to sell, trade and barter fish for livelihood, support and sustenance purposes": *ibid.* at paras. 96, 191, 192, 199, 206, 221. McLachlin J. called the claim a right "to fish for sustenance": *ibid.* at paras. 227, 275, 294, 322, although her later descriptions of the content of the right were similar to that of Lambert J.A.

    There were also sharp differences as to what qualifies as "commercial". For the majority, a commercial transaction is a large-scale exchange for money or other goods: *ibid.* at para. 77; and see *R. v. N.T.C. Smokehouse Ltd.*, [1996] 2 S.C.R. 672 at paras. 17 and 18. L'Heureux-Dubé J. associated "purely" commercial transactions with the notions of profit: *ibid.* at paras. 189, 192, 194, 218. For L'Heureux-Dubé J., the purposes of Aboriginal activities "should be viewed on a spectrum, with aboriginal activities undertaken solely for food, at one extreme, those directed to obtaining purely commercial profit, at the other extreme, and activities relating to livelihood, support and sustenance, at the centre": para. 192: For McLachlin J., any sale is commercial: *ibid.* at paras. 236, 237.
105. For example, if the courts had decided to characterize all fishery uses other than food or ceremonial uses as "commercial" and requiring large-scale market transactions, then few traditional fishing practices would likely qualify as Aboriginal rights. Conversely, if courts characterized commercial and other uses as one aspect of a blanket right to benefit from fishing, courts would ensure that few practices would not qualify.
106. At the Supreme Court level, Lamer C.J. stressed the specific purpose of the claimed activity. By linking this purpose (in her words, the right to "sell, trade and barter": para. 96) to the wider objectives of "livelihood, support and sustenance" (*ibid.*), L'Heureux-Dubé J. would have broadened this approach. By focusing *only* on sustenance, McLachlin J. would have broadened it further.
107. *Ibid.* at para. 241. See also para. 239.
108. McLachlin J.'s own dissenting reasons illustrate the power of characterization. McLachlin J. considered Van der Peet's own claim to be a right to fish commercially: paras. 236, 237. McLachlin J., however, regarded this as

only the starting point to characterizing the traditional practice itself. "At its base," she said, "the right is not the right to trade, but the right to continue to use the resource in the traditional way to provide for the traditional needs, albeit in their modern form": para. 278; see also paras. 227, 272, 275, 318. For this case, McLachlin J. said the court should look to see if there was a corresponding traditional use of the fishery resource: paras. 276–78. If so, the claimant is entitled to the modern economic equivalent of the traditional use. Although McLachlin J.'s approach places quantitative limits on the modern enjoyment of Aboriginal rights, it would significantly expand the scope of traditional activities that could qualify as Aboriginal rights in the first place.

109. L'Heureux-Dubé J. provided no guidance as to *which* twenty- to fifty-year period to select.
110. As Lamer C.J. said (at para. 60), "[b]ecause it is the fact that distinctive aboriginal societies lived on the land prior to the arrival of Europeans that underlies the aboriginal rights protected by s. 35(1), it is to that pre-contact period that the courts must look in identifying aboriginal rights." McLachlin J. agreed with the majority that the relevant period is the traditional period, but suggested that courts should not become overly concerned to establish a precise moment of first European contact: paras. 247 and 248.
111. *Ibid.* at para. 77.
112. *Ibid.* at para. 279.
113. *Ibid.* at para. 73.
114. *Ibid.* at para. 89.
115. The majority had an answer to McLachlin J.'s criticisms about the categorical nature of the test: as seen in **Part 4**, below, they felt that concerns of this nature could be addressed elsewhere.
116. *Ibid.* at para. 279. The approach was first suggested in a Canadian context by Lambert J.A., dissenting in *Van der Peet*.
117. *Ibid.*
118. *Ibid.* at 279 and 302.
119. *R. v. Marshall*, [1999] 3 S.C.R. 456 at para. 59.
120. In the United States, where the moderate livelihood criterion has been criticized as uncertain, the best known use of the test has, at least, a fixed upper limit.
121. *Gladstone*, *infra* note 131, **Part 4**, below.
122. *Ibid.* at paras. 302–15. McLachlin J. argued, *inter alia*, that *Sparrow* and the Crown's fiduciary duty to Aboriginal peoples prohibits courts from justifying infringements of Aboriginal rights by reference to non-Aboriginal interests (paras. 303–307); that the *Gladstone* approach treats s. 35(1) rights as if they were subject to the s. 1 constraint in the *Charter* (para. 308); that the approach is indeterminate (para. 309); and that courts cannot constitutionally dilute the content of s. 35(1) rights (para. 315). On the other hand: (i) the court did not say in *Sparrow* that conservation and avoiding harm are the only possible justification factors, and even these factors contemplate interests of non-rights holders; (ii) the *Sparrow* application of the Crown's fiduciary duty to Aboriginal peoples is *sui generis*, and does not necessarily impose obligations identical to those of private fiduciaries: see D.W. Elliott, "Aboriginal Peoples in Canada and the United States and the Scope of the Special Fiduciary Relationship" (1966) Man. L.J. 137, part V and note 212 therein; (iii) although s. 35(1) rights lack the restraints in s. 1 of the *Charter*, they also lack its explicit guarantee; (iv) allocating priorities as between Aboriginal interests and other concerns will be an indeterminate exercise *wherever* it is carried out; and (v) courts cannot be said to act unconstitutionally by "modifying" s. 35(1) rights when it is they who have the responsibility of interpreting these rights in the first place.
123. See *Gladstone*, **Part 4**, below.
124. *R. v. Marshall*, [1999] 3 S.C.R. 456 at para. 59, **Chapter 6, Part 16**.
125. *R. v. Adams*, [1996] No. 87 at paras. 26 and 27 (S.C.C.).
126. Subject to the infringement and justification tests in *Sparrow*, **Chapter 7, Part 4** and *Gladstone*, **Part 4**, below.
127. For example, adoption, marriage, penal and gambling customs, and general regulatory régimes might not fall in this category unless a special tie to land could be shown.
128. *R. v. Adams*, [1996] 3 S.C.R. 101, **Chapter 10, Part 2.**
129. *Delgamuukw v. British Columbia*, [1997] 3 S.C.R. 1010, **Chapter 12, Part 3.**
130. *Mitchell v. Canada (Minister of National Revenue)*, [2001] 1 S.C.R. 911.
131. *R. v. Gladstone*, [1996] 2 S.C.R. 723 (August 21, 1996): Lamer C.J. and La Forest, L'Heureux-Dubé, Sopinka, Gonthier, Cory, McLachlin, Iacobucci, and Major JJ..
132. **Part 3**, above. The third case was *R. v. N.T.C. Smokehouse Ltd.*, [1996] 2 S.C.R. 672 (August 21, 1996): Lamer C.J. and La Forest, L'Heureux-Dubé, Sopinka, Gonthier, Cory, McLachlin, Iacobucci, and Major JJ. In *Smokehouse*, a company was charged with selling and purchasing fish caught without a commercial fishing licence, contrary to federal regulations. The company argued the regulations were invalid because they violated the constitutionally guaranteed right of the Sheshaht and Opetchesaht peoples to sell Chinook salmon commercially. The majority of the Court held that the traditional exchange of fish for money or other goods was infrequent and only incidental to its exchange for other purposes. They held that since there was no Aboriginal right to fish for money or other goods, there was also no Aboriginal right to fish commercially. In separate judgments, L'Heureux-Dubé J. and McLachlin J. dissented. All three judgments defined "commercially" differently.
133. La Forest J. was using the same clear and plain intention test as his colleagues: *ibid.* at para. 106. For La Forest J., the fact that the legislature had explicitly addressed the question of translating Aboriginal practices into statutory rights, and had explicitly addressed the latter's scope, showed a clear and plain intention to extinguish: paras. 111–12. Lamer C.J. for the main majority, and L'Heureux-Dubé and McLachlin JJ. held that the regulations merely regulated the fishery, and did not extinguish Aboriginal rights: paras. 34–37, 149 and 168, respectively. For L'Heureux-Dubé "the Government must address the aboriginal activities in question and explicitly extinguish them by making them no longer permissible": para. 148, referring to *Smokehouse*, para. 78. In *Van der Peet* McLachlin J. had said that a clear and plain intention to extinguish can be shown only where there is "acknowledgment of an aboriginal right, conflict of the right proposed with policy, and resolution of the two": para. 289. La Forest said in *Gladstone* that this "would, as a practical matter, render virtually meaningless the Crown's power to extinguish aboriginal rights": para. 116. Lamer C.J. for the majority said that "[w]hile to extinguish an aboriginal right the Crown does not, perhaps, have to use language which refers expressly to its extinguishment of aboriginal rights, it must demonstrate more than that, in the past, the exercise of an aboriginal right has been subject to a regulatory scheme": para. 34. *Quaere*, how much more?

    Clearly, the clear and plain intention test should be clearer! For one possible criterion for implicit extinguishment, see *Delgamuukw v. British Columbia* (1993), 104 D.L.R. (4th) 470 at 524 (B.C.C.A.). Note, though, that in *Gladstone* La Forest J. was arguing that the legislature had addressed the matter explicitly.
134. *Gladstone*, *supra* note 131 at para. 23 *et seq.* See *Van der Peet*, **Part 3**, above.
135. *Gladstone*, *supra* note 131 at para. 24.
136. *Supra* note 132.

137. *Gladstone*, *supra* note 131 at para. 24. Although logical, this approach requires courts to consider criteria other than an activity's own features when characterizing it, thus complicating an already uncertain process.
138. Note the range of possible meanings of "commercial" in this case, and in the judgments in *Van der Peet*, **Part 3**, above and *Smokehouse*, *supra* note 132.
139. *Contra*, La Forest J., dissenting, who found that the contexts of the modern activity and that of the traditional activities were entirely different: para. 95.
140. *R. v. Sparrow*, [1990] 1 S.C.R. 1075, **Chapter 7, Part 4**.
141. *Gladstone*, *supra* note 131 at para. 52.
142. *Ibid.* at paras. 58 and 59.
143. [And, presumably, after prevention of harm, if this goal were relevant]. *R. v. Sparrow*, [1990] 1 S.C.R. 1075 at 1116.
144. *Ibid.* at para. 66.
145. *Ibid.* at para. 63.
146. *Ibid.* at paras. 64, 68.
147. *Ibid.* at para. 72, referring to *Van der Peet*, para. 39.
148. *Ibid.* at para. 73.
149. *Ibid.* at para. 75.
150. This is because McLachlin J. thought the case should be referred back to trial for lack of sufficient evidence on the infringement and justification issues. She did say that these issues should be decided "according to the principles set out in *Van der Peet*": para. 174. However, in *Van der Peet*, McLachlin J. disagreed with the *Van der Peet* and *Gladstone* majorities on the issue of justification.
151. *Van der Peet*, paras. 302–15.
152. *R. v. Pamajewon* [*R. v. Jones*; *R. v. Gardner*], [1996] 2 S.C.R. 821, February 26, 1996 (decision) and August 21, 1996 (S.C.C. reasons: C.J.C., La Forest, Sopinka, Gonthier, Cory, McLachlin, Iacobucci and Major JJ, with L'Heureux-Dubé concurring in separate reasons); aff'g (1994) 21 O.R. (3d) 385 (O.C.A.: per Dubin C.J.O. and Osborne J.A. A third judge, Blair J.A., retired before the judgment was rendered and took no part in it); dismissing appeals from convictions by Carr Prov. Ct. J. and Flaherty Prov. Ct. J.
153. **Part 3**, above.
154. *R. v. Pamajewon* [*R. v. Jones*; *R. v. Gardner*] (1994), 21 O.R. (3d) 385 at 399 (O.C.A.). The use of the word "and" suggests that the Court felt that Aboriginal practices and land use should be treated conjunctively.
155. "[There] is no evidence to support a conclusion that gambling generally or high stakes gambling of the sort in issue here, were part of the First Nations' historic cultures and traditions, or an aspect of their use of their land": *ibid.* at 400. By treating these two requirements disjunctively here, the Court left it unclear as to whether they intended both to be necessary.
156. *Ibid.* at 400.
157. *R. v. Pamajewon* [*R. v. Jones*; *R. v. Gardner*], [1996] 2 S.C.R. 821. Lamer C.J. delivered the reasons for eight judges. L'Heureux-Dubé concurred in separate reasons, characterizing the activity slightly more broadly than her colleagues ("gambling"), applying her own version of the integral practices test, and going beyond this test to comment briefly on Aboriginal self-government.
158. *Ibid.* at para. 27 (*cf. R. v. Van der Peet*, [1996] 2 S.C.R. 507 at para. 69).
159. *Ibid.* at paras. 23 and 24.
160. *Ibid.*
161. I.e., by taking a "functional" approach to linking Aboriginal rights and land: see **Part 3(h)(iv)**, above.
162. For the apparent contradiction in *Van der Peet* between the emphasis on land as one of the foundations of Aboriginal rights, and the apparent neglect of land in the *Van der Peet* identification test, see **Part 3**, above.
163. Self-government activities that involve a direct use of land and do not conflict with Crown sovereignty (see **Chapter 10, Part 4** for this possible requirement) might well qualify as s. 35(1) Aboriginal rights under this approach. Examples might include Aboriginal self-regulation of occupancy of Aboriginal land or of consumption of natural resources.
164. I.e., a "model" approach to linking Aboriginal rights and land: see **Part 3(h)(v)**, above.
165. Only L'Heureux-Dubé J., in her separate concurring judgment, went beyond the case-specific incrementalism of the integral practices test. She said briefly that Aboriginal activities are subject to Parliamentary and some provincial legislative control as a result of the assertion of British sovereignty over Canadian territory: *ibid.* at para. 42. See further, **Chapter 12, Part 4**. As will be seen, there were some longer but inconclusive comments on Aboriginal self-government in *Mitchell v. Canada (Minister of National Revenue)*, [2002] 1 S.C.R. 911, discussed in **Chapter 10**.

10 Aboriginal Rights: II

Chapter Highlights

- Specific Aboriginal rights can exist independently of Aboriginal title.
- Aboriginal rights and title exist along a spectrum in regard to their degree of connection to land. Aboriginal title is a generalized form of Aboriginal right. It is an inalienable, communally held interest in land that arises from prior Aboriginal occupation of land and pre-existing Aboriginal law.
- Aboriginal title holders have the right to exclusive use of the land, but this use must not be irreconcilable with the nature of their traditional and ongoing attachment to it.
- Proof of Aboriginal title requires, *inter alia*, Aboriginal occupation prior to European sovereignty and exclusive Aboriginal occupation at sovereignty.
- Aboriginal title cannot be extinguished by provincial laws.
- To accommodate Aboriginal oral evidence, the rules of evidence should be relaxed, but not abandoned completely.
- Métis Aboriginal rights were established prior to effective European control, not prior to first contact or European sovereignty

Synopsis

The modern law of Aboriginal rights rests heavily on four landmark decisions — *Calder*, *Sparrow*, *Van der Peet*, and *Delgamuukw*. *Delgamuukw*, considered in this chapter, went a long way to clarify the content, status, and general nature of Aboriginal title. It also dealt in detail with s. 35(1) justification, with the relationship between Aboriginal rights and title and provincial laws, and with Aboriginal evidence. *Delgamuukw* built on the Court's earlier Aboriginal title decision in *Adams*, and *Delgamuukw*'s comments on issues such as Aboriginal evidence were revisited in the Court's later decision in *Mitchell*. More recently, *Powley* addressed the long-neglected question of Métis Aboriginal rights. Nevertheless, as seen in **Part 5**, below, many important Aboriginal rights and title questions remain to be answered.

Selected Readings

🗎 links material in this chapter to the corresponding headings and page numbers of the relevant readings.

🗎 Part 2	*R.* v. *Adams*	353
🗎 Part 3	*Delgamuukw v. British Columbia*	355
🗎 Part 4	*Mitchell v. Canada (Minister of National Revenue)*	362
🗎 Part 5	*R. v. Powley*	370
🗎 Part 6	*Haida Nation v. British Columbia (Minister of Forests)*	378

1. INTRODUCTION

Contemporary case law on Aboriginal rights and Aboriginal title rests heavily on four landmark modern decisions. In *Calder* in 1973, the Supreme Court established that Aboriginal title can be recognized at common law independently of government executive or legislative action.[1] The Court based the title on the prior occupancy and use of land by Aboriginal peoples. Then in *Sparrow*, in 1990, the Court said that Aboriginal rights are constitutionally entrenched by s. 35(1) of the *Constitution Act, 1982*, subject to the government's capacity to justify infringements in special cases.[2] The third landmark was the Court's 1996 decision in *Van der Peet*. Here the Supreme Court formulated a "land and societies" theory about the basis of Aboriginal rights and the purpose of s. 35(1), and developed a "distinctive practices" test for identifying Aboriginal rights in specific situations.[3]

While *Calder* was concerned with Aboriginal title, *Sparrow* and *Van der Peet* focused mainly on Aboriginal rights. *Van der Peet* did describe Aboriginal title as a subcategory of Aboriginal rights that deals solely with claims of rights to land, but the relationship between the rights and their subcategory remained unclear. Do Aboriginal rights depend on the existence of Aboriginal title? Is the test for identifying Aboriginal title identical to the test for specific Aboriginal rights? What is the status of Aboriginal title? How extensive is its content? What is the relationship of Aboriginal rights and title to land?

This chapter looks at *Adams*, which established that Aboriginal title does not depend on Aboriginal rights; at the landmark decision in *Delgamuukw*, which clarified the nature of Aboriginal title; at *Mitchell*, which explored specific issues such as characterization, evidence, and Aboriginal self-government; and at *Powley*, which applied the concept of Aboriginal rights to Métis peoples. **Chapter 10** concludes with a look at some of the basic features of common law Aboriginal rights — including Aboriginal title — today.

When studying these decisions, consider the relationship between Aboriginal rights and the Aboriginal claims that are the subject of **Chapter 11**. From one perspective, when the Supreme Court strengthens the legal and constitutional aspects of Aboriginal rights and makes them easier to prove, it encourages litigation as an alternative to land claims negotiations. From another perspective, by strengthening the legal and constitutional elements, the Court is facilitating the claims negotiation process. It is persuading governments to settle claims sooner and is helping to ensure a meaningful content for the agreements that are signed. Which perspective is right?

2. *ADAMS*[4]

Reading 10(a) at p. 353

Mr. George Adams was a Mohawk Indian who was a resident of the St. Regis (Akwesasne) Reserve in southern Quebec. He was charged with seine fishing without a permit, contrary to regulations under the federal *Fisheries Act*. He was fishing in Lake St. François, a part of the St. Lawrence River, at a site about 15 kilometres from the St. Regis Reserve. The site was once a marsh within the boundaries of a reserve, but the marshland was flooded in the mid-19th century and the adjacent reserve land had been ceded to the Crown. The Mohawk claimed traditional fishing rights throughout this region.[5]

The Crown argued that there was no Aboriginal title in this area in the first place because the colony of New France had not recognized it at the time of settlement. They claimed that any title that might have existed had been extinguished by the flooding or cession. Mr. Adams argued that he had an Aboriginal right to fish in the area; that it continued after the land was flooded and the adjacent land was ceded; and that this right was protected by s. 35(1) of the *Constitution Act, 1982*. Mr. Adams was unsuccessful before the Court of Session of the Peace[6] and the Quebec Superior Court,[7] and his conviction was upheld by a majority of the Quebec Court of Appeal.[8]

In separate reasons,[9] the majority of the Court of Appeal held that any fishing rights that may have existed in the area[10] ceased when the Mohawk's Aboriginal title ended in the 19th century. For Beauregard and Proulx JJ.A., Aboriginal fishing rights were an incident of Aboriginal title and could not exist independently of it.[11] Hence, the 19th century extinguishment of Aboriginal title in the adjacent reserve land ended any claim to fishing rights as well.[12] Rothman J.A., dissenting, held that Aboriginal fishing rights can and did exist independently from Aboriginal title, and that these rights were not lost with the flooding or cession in 1888.[13]

Speaking for the main majority of the Supreme Court, Lamer C.J. rejected the argument that Aboriginal rights not had been recognized by New France, "[f]or the reasons developed in *Côté*."[14] In *Côté*, the Court said it was not clear that the law of New France was unequivocally opposed to the existence of Aboriginal rights.[15] In that case the Court also said that the intent of s. 35(1) of the *Constitution Act, 1982* was to protect rights meeting the *Van der Peet* distinct practices test, regardless of formal governmental recognition or non-recognition.[16]

Lamer C.J. appeared to concede that the Mohawk's claim to occupancy of the area was not strong. He referred to evidence indicating that the area had been occupied between 1000 and 1500 A.D. by an Iroquois-speaking people of a lineage different from that of the Mohawks,[17] and said that the 19th century flooding and cession may have been enough to extinguish any title that may have existed.[18]

However, Lamer C.J. rejected the contention that Aboriginal rights cannot exist apart from Aboriginal title. He said that:

> [w]here an aboriginal group has shown that a particular activity, custom or tradition taking place on the land was integral to the distinctive culture of that group then, *even if they have not shown that their occupation and use of the land was sufficient to support a claim of title to the land*, they will have demonstrated that they have an aboriginal right to engage in that practice, custom or tradition.[19]

Lamer C.J. pointed out that although traditionally some Aboriginal peoples were nomadic, and so could not be expected to have established links to particular land, this:

> ...does not alter the fact that nomadic peoples survived through reliance on the land prior to contact with Europeans and, further, that many of the customs, practices and traditions of nomadic peoples that took place on the land were integral to their distinctive cultures.[20]

In other words, it was the reliance on the land, not reliance on a particular plot of land, that was central to the prior occupancy of Aboriginal peoples. This suggests, then, that although Aboriginal rights can exist independently of Aboriginal title, they are not necessarily wholly independent of land.[21]

3. *DELGAMUUKW*[22]

Reading 10(b) at p. 355

(a) The Challenge

"Let us face it, we are all here to stay."[23] Lamer C.J.'s last words in *Delgamuukw* referred to a pressing Canadian challenge. How do we ensure the peaceful, positive, and permanent coexistence of one million First Peoples and 31 million newcomers? The words also involved some questions about means. How should we address this challenge? Through negotiated settlements? Court decisions? Other ways? *Delgamuukw* — and these questions about means — are the subject of this part.[24]

The Supreme Court stressed in *Delgamuukw* that it favours negotiated settlements that are anchored in the law, especially in s. 35(1) of the *Constitution Act, 1982*.[25] The Court saw this provision as a "solid constitutional base on which subsequent negotiations can take place."[26] It suggested that courts have a supporting role here, developing the law and furthering the political negotiation process.[27] The Court tried to play this role in *Delgamuukw*, by clarifying and strengthening Aboriginal title.

Did the Supreme Court succeed? To explore this question, we will look first at the litigation in *Delgamuukw*, and then at the main questions addressed by the Supreme Court of Canada.[28]

(b) The Litigation

Delgamuukw started with a major loss for the claimants. In the British Columbia Supreme Court, representatives of about 7,000 Gitksan and Wet'suwet'en people claimed full ownership, self-government, and other Aboriginal rights, to over 22,000 square miles (56,980 square kilometres) of west central British Columbia. The trial judge, McEachern C.J., rejected the ownership and self-government claims. He declared that the claimants had Aboriginal rights of occupation and use, but that these had been extinguished by the Crown prior to British Columbia's entry into Confederation.[29] In coming to his conclusion, the trial judge assigned a limited role to Aboriginal oral evidence.[30] McEachern C.J. did say the Crown owed the Aboriginal people a fiduciary duty to let them use certain lands in the territory. But this was a pale concession. He limited the use to unoccupied Crown lands, and subjected it to laws of general application and adverse Crown needs.[31]

The Gitksan and Wet'suwet'en fared better in the British Columbia Court of Appeal.[32] A majority of the appeal court[33] did reject the claim to full ownership because of lack of evidence of exclusive occupation and clear boundaries. Moreover, the majority said that any Aboriginal self-government — in the sense of sovereign legislative powers —

had been ended by British sovereignty or by the exhaustive division of legislative powers in the *Constitution Act, 1867*.[34] However, the majority upheld the claimed Aboriginal rights of occupation and use of land and said that these rights had not been extinguished. Lambert and Hutcheon JJ.A., dissenting in part, agreed with the majority in regard to rights of occupation and use. However, they went on to accept the claim to ownership and to Aboriginal self-government (which Hutcheon J.A. regarded as a non-sovereign right of internal regulation).[35]

At the Supreme Court level, the Gitksan and Wet'suwet'en won a major victory. The highest Court took a liberal approach to admission and weight of oral Aboriginal evidence, gave strong, exclusive content to Aboriginal title, added to the requirements for its justifiable infringement, and denied provincial governments the capacity to extinguish Aboriginal rights.[36] The Supreme Court addressed five main sets of questions:

(i) Could the Gitksan and Wet'suwet'en's claims be changed informally in the course of the court proceedings?
(ii) What evidentiary value should be given to oral Aboriginal histories in Aboriginal rights cases? (And where should appellate courts interfere with trial judges' findings of fact?)
(iii) What is the general nature, content and status of Aboriginal title? (What is its content? How is it related to Aboriginal rights? What is the general nature of Aboriginal rights? What is required to prove Aboriginal title? How is it protected under s. 35(1) of the *Constitution Act, 1982*?[37] What justification principles apply to infringement of s. 35(1) Aboriginal title?)
(iv) What is required to argue a claim of guaranteed Aboriginal self-government rights?
(v) Could a province extinguish Aboriginal rights after its entry into Confederation, either on its own authority or through the operation of s. 88 of the *Indian Act*?[38]

(c) Changing Claims

Despite its technical appearance, this first issue in *Delgamuukw* was more than mere formality. It had a direct connection with the subject matter of this case. Although changing claims is not unique to Aboriginal litigation, it is likely to recur in this area of law. When the Gitksan and Wet'suwet'en appealed the British Columbia Court of Appeal's decision, they made two sets of changes to their claims. First, they changed their original claims of ownership and jurisdiction into claims of Aboriginal title and self-government, respectively.[39] Second, they replaced the original individual claims by 51 Gitksan and Wet'suwet'en chiefs and houses[40] with a collective claim by each of the Gitksan and Wet'suwet'en nations.[41] Neither change had been made by formal amendment to the pleadings. Should the changes be permitted informally?

The Supreme Court allowed the first set of changes, but not the second. For the first set, said Lamer C.J.,[42] the trial judge had already allowed a similar change, before the end of the trial. He had done this in an area where the law was uncertain, and the respondent governments had not contested the change by way of appeal. However, the second set of changes was another matter. Here no change had been allowed during the trial. Although the boundaries of the two nations' new claims coincided with those of the 51 chiefs' original claims, no evidence or argument had been addressed to the latter at trial. To allow this change could deprive the respondents of the opportunity to respond to the new claim. Thus the case must be sent back to trial. As a result, all the Court's reasons on substantive issues, from Aboriginal title to s. 35(1) of the *Constitution Act, 1982*, were technically *obiter dicta*.

There may have been little real alternative to this frustrating result. As Lamer C.J. suggested, if a claim is changed near the end of the trial, the other parties may be denied the opportunity to respond effectively to the new claim. The later the change, the greater the risk. The first changes came well before the trial's end. At this time the respondents could still adjust their own presentation of evidence and argument. The second set of changes followed the evidence and argument. They were too late.

A second possible distinction between the two sets of changes[43] is less convincing. Lamer C.J. said the first set could be justified in part because of the legal uncertainty about Aboriginal title and self-government. Yet the law about the second set of changes — the law about the parties and rules of evidence appropriate to Aboriginal title claims — was far from certain itself. Uncertainty clouded all aspects of this area of law.

Legal uncertainty not only helps justify changes of claim, but it makes them more likely. It requires appellate courts to choose between denials of hearings and costly and time-consuming referrals back to trial. One way to end this cycle is to provide a major clarification of the evidentiary and substantive law of Aboriginal title and Aboriginal rights. Did the Court provide this in *Delgamuukw*?

(d) Aboriginal Evidence[44]

The rules of evidence are as crucial to the outcome of litigation as is the substantive law. In *Delgamuukw*, the Court tried to build a bridge between the standard rules of evidence and Aboriginal evidence[45] in Aboriginal claims cases.[46] Arguably, though, this bridge was incomplete.

The 51 hereditary chiefs claimed traditional occupation and use of 133 contiguous but discrete territories, each separated by internal boundaries. To demonstrate this, and to show the significance of this land to their cultures, the claimants relied heavily on oral or partly oral evidence. This included collective oral histories (the adaawk of the Gitksan and the kungax of the Wet'suwet'en), personal and family histories, and chiefs' territorial affidavits of declarations by deceased persons.

(i) Collective Oral Histories

The adaawk and kungax were hearsay evidence, which is not generally admissible in courts.[47] The problem with hearsay is that it cannot be directly tested in court.[48] In court a witness must testify under oath, his or her credibility can be assessed at first hand, and all statements can be tested directly by cross-examination.[49] On the other hand, the hearsay rule has several exceptions and can be relaxed in appropriate situations. The Supreme Court has said that both the exceptions and the relaxation are subject to the two guiding principles of necessity and reliability.[50] Generally speaking, the hearsay rule is not applied where: (i) the evidence would not be available otherwise (a situation of "necessity") and (ii) there are alternative safeguards to ensure reliability.[51] One exception that meets these principles is "reputation" evidence.[52] This includes statements made by deceased persons about public or general rights.[53]

Stressing that there was no other way to prove the claimants' history,[54] McEachern C.J. admitted the adaawk and kungax as reputation evidence.[55] However, he concluded that they could be given little weight, and that he could use them only to confirm other evidence of the 133 individual territories.[56] This was mainly because the adaawk and kungax (i) lacked sufficient detail about the territories and their internal boundaries,[57] (ii) were part belief as well as fact,[58] and (iii) lacked sufficiently large and diverse verifying groups.[59] McEachern C.J. went on to conclude that the evidence was insufficient to prove these individual territories.[60]

How did the Supreme Court respond to these concerns? Lamer C.J. said that imprecision and small verifying groups are characteristic of all oral histories. Thus, the trial judge's refusal to give them independent weight would systematically undervalue all Aboriginal oral histories and would disregard the problem of finding alternative forms of proof. This, in turn, violated the instruction in *Van der Peet* to interpret Aboriginal peoples' evidence "in light of the difficulties inherent in adjudicating Aboriginal claims."[61]

(ii) Personal and Family Histories

McEachern C.J. also admitted the personal and family histories in regard to the internal boundaries,[62] but only as proof of land use within the past 100 years. He referred to anthropologists' concerns about oral recollection beyond this time. The Supreme Court addressed these concerns only indirectly. Lamer C.J. said that requiring definitive evidence of pre-contact Aboriginal activities on the territory in question was expecting too much. The evidence might still be useful to demonstrate pre-sovereignty occupation, if not to establish it conclusively.[63]

(iii) Chiefs' Territorial Affidavits

For the most part, McEachern C.J. refused to admit the claimant chiefs' territorial affidavits as independent evidence of the internal boundaries. He held that *in regard to these particular boundaries*, the affidavits did not fit the reputation exception to the rule against hearsay. In the first place, reputation requires general knowledge.[64] Outside the communities in which the affidavits were made, there was little evidence of knowledge of their content. Much of this content could not be regarded as general knowledge because it was disputed. Moreover, because they had been prepared in conjunction with the claims process, the affidavits lacked objectivity. There was an additional, "much more serious"[65] problem. In McEachern C.J.'s view, the evidence about the 133 territories and their internal boundaries contained too many inconsistencies to be credible.

The Supreme Court's first response to the affidavit concerns was to say that requiring general knowledge of Aboriginal oral histories ignores their local nature. As for controversy, Lamer C.J. said that Aboriginal rights claims "are almost always disputed and contested."[66] If the claims were uncontroversial, they wouldn't need to be decided by the courts. In Lamer C.J.'s view the claims process was slow because British Columbia had refused to recognize aboriginal title. Why should the claimants be penalized because of action (or *in*action!) beyond their control? Lamer C.J. noted that aboriginal communities must discuss their oral history to have it qualify as reputation. If this history were discounted because of its proximity to the claims process, aboriginal people could never use it to establish their claims in court. Perhaps because he regarded it as going to weight, not admissibility, Lamer C.J. did not deal directly with the trial judge's concerns about inconsistency.

(iv) Beyond Hearsay Exceptions

Thus the Supreme Court rejected most of the trial judge's concerns about the oral Aboriginal evidence. The Court said in *Delgamuukw* that Aboriginal oral histories are admissible as proof of Aboriginal rights claims, and should not be denied independent evidentiary weight on the grounds given by the trial judge.[67] The Court supported the use of personal and family histories. It said it would recognize affidavits of declarations by deceased persons, whether or not these were prepared as part of documentation for Aboriginal claims.[68] In the Court's view, this approach was necessary to take proper account of: (i) the Aboriginal perspective as well as Canadian legal and constitutional constraints, and (ii) the special evidentiary difficulties involved in proving rights that pre-date written records.

The Supreme Court's analysis was generous but incomplete. It made a strong case for admitting and considering oral Aboriginal evidence on grounds of necessity. This kind of evidence can provide both a perspective and material that may not otherwise be available. However, the Court said little about another key aspect of evidence — reliability. The Court did cite the vague caution in *Van der Peet* that the accommodation of Aboriginal evidence must not "strain 'the Canadian legal and constitutional structure'."[69] It conceded that Aboriginal oral evidence presents "challenges"[70] because it is subjective in parts, cannot always be tested in court, lacks detail, is disputed and controversial, and is generally too local to be broadly verified. Yet when the trial judge expressed concerns about how these features affect reliability, the Court responded with arguments about necessity.

The result was to neglect an important dimension of evidence and to leave trial judges without comprehensive guidelines. In *Delgamuukw*, it is unclear how the Court could find a "palpable and overriding error"[71] in the trial decision without having prescribed tangible evidentiary standards in the first place. After *Delgamuukw* relaxed the hearsay rule, there was a need for alternative safeguards to help replace those normally protected by the rule: physical presence, oath, and cross-examination.[72]

After *Delgamuukw*, then, trial judges needed a more systematic and balanced conceptual framework for considering oral Aboriginal evidence. This framework should require courts to admit non-prejudicial Aboriginal hearsay evidence where there is a threshold level of both necessity and reliability, and it should provide a recognized set of criteria for assessing its weight.

For determining necessity, the threshold should not be set high. All that need be asked is: "Could this evidence be the only way to prove the claim, or is it needed to provide the Aboriginal perspective?" For the reliability threshold, there should be some external[73] assurance of credibility.[74] This assurance might be provided by indicators such as outside corroboration, logical consistency, and contestability of the evidence, and the relative impartiality and expertise of the sources.[75]

Although the job of assessing the weight of evidence has a broader focus, it includes the same reliability indicators that are relevant to admissibility. For assessing the weight of evidence, the goal is to determine if it is sufficiently reliable and relevant to support the claim made. Before this can be done, it will be necessary to determine the strength of the external assurances of reliability. The assessment of the weight of the evidence will be tied closely to the level of the claim. The more specific, wide-ranging, or exclusive the claim, the higher the level of external assurances required, and *vice versa*.

Because most Aboriginal claims are rooted in pre-historical situations, the answer to the necessity question will normally be "yes". Moreover, because of the communal nature of Aboriginal claims, the telling and re-telling of most Aboriginal oral evidence,[76] and the role of trained elders as sources,[77] there will likely be some external assurance of reliability.[78] The real challenge comes with the weighing of the evidence. Generally speaking:

(i) the wider the supporting and verifying group,
(ii) the more consistent the oral evidence,
(iii) the greater its correlation with other forms of evidence, and

(iv) the deeper its exposure to criticism and debate,

the more likely it is to be reliable.[79] Similarly, the more impartial[80] and expert the sources, the greater their credibility. The overall weight of the evidence required will be inversely proportional to the level of the claim made. A claim to non-shared exclusive occupation of many highly specific territories will require stronger evidence than a claim to use or shared use rights to a less sharply defined area, and *vice versa*.[81]

Under this approach, there would be no advance assumption that oral Aboriginal evidence is automatically "more" or "less" reliable than conventional forms. This evidence is certainly different from other evidence, and may well require a distinctive approach, but its weight would depend on the circumstances of the individual claim.

But is assessing the evidence in support of an Aboriginal claim really a suitable job for courts at all? In the longer term, it might be better to commit this initial responsibility to an independent administrative tribunal. Such a body could be staffed by anthropologists, archaeologists, Aboriginal elders,[82] and similar specialists, as well as by lawyers. It would have some flexibility to go beyond the adversarial constraints of a judicial trial. A decision by this tribunal could be protected by a strong privative clause, ensuring that it need not and could not be reviewed by ordinary courts except for patent unreasonableness, gross procedural unfairness, or constitutional defects.

An Aboriginal claims fact-finding tribunal would operate within the general law of Aboriginal rights. If the tribunal decided that the evidence supported a particular claim, courts could determine the application of the legal rules of extinguishment, infringement, and justification, and could award appropriate legal remedies. Alternatively, and preferably, claimants and government might try to settle the claim by negotiation.

(e) Aboriginal Title

Before *Delgamuukw*, the law of Aboriginal title and Aboriginal rights resembled a framework dwelling in a half-built community. Courts had described Aboriginal title as a right based on traditional occupation. They had done little to identify its specific characteristics[83] or to explain its relationship to the broader community of Aboriginal rights.[84] Aboriginal rights had been developed substantially in recent years, but there were unfinished elements here, too. In *Delgamuukw*, the Supreme Court accomplished a substantial piece of conceptual construction, clarifying key aspects of Aboriginal title and rights.[85] As will be seen, though, several important questions remained to be answered.

The pre-*Delgamuukw* situation fuelled a wide-ranging dispute in the case itself. The parties supported very different notions of Aboriginal title and its relationship to the Aboriginal rights in s. 35(1) of the *Constitution Act, 1982*. The Gitksan and Wet'suwet'en argued that Aboriginal title amounts to an inalienable fee simple, constitutionalized by s. 35(1) of the *Constitution Act, 1982*. The respondents argued that s. 35(1) merely constitutionalizes the right to occupy and use land — perhaps exclusively — for the purpose of engaging in particular s. 35(1) Aboriginal rights. For them, Aboriginal title is wholly dependent on the identification of other specific Aboriginal rights.[86]

(i) General Features

Lamer C.J. rejected both positions. He said common law Aboriginal title is *sui generis*, neither a fee simple on one hand nor a non-proprietary interest on the other. Moreover, Aboriginal title is more than the sum of other specific Aboriginal rights. The Chief Justice described Aboriginal title as an inalienable, communally-held interest in land, which arises from both prior occupation and the pre-existing Aboriginal law that accompanied this occupation. Lamer C.J. said Aboriginal title allows exclusive use and occupation of land for a variety of purposes. However, there is an important qualification. The uses of the land must not be irreconcilable with the nature of the Aboriginal group's traditional and ongoing attachment to it.[87]

(ii) Exclusivity

Both the exclusivity of Aboriginal title and its land qualification are significant. With exclusivity, Aboriginal title holders have a potentially powerful means of protecting their lands from outside interference. To give effect to it, courts will have to allocate legal boundaries and priorities between constitutionally protected Aboriginal title and other exclusive property rights.

Exclusivity raises special questions about overlapping Aboriginal title claims. In his trial judgment in *Delgamuukw*, for example, McEachern C.J. noted that claims to the Gitksan-Wet'suwet'en claim area had been also made by the Tsimshian, Nisga'a, Kitwankool, Tahltan / Stikine, Tsetsaut, Kaska-Dene, and Carrier-Sekanni peoples.[88] He said that the latter's claim extended to over half the area claimed by the Wet'suwet'en.[89] How would these claims relate to Gitksan and Wet'suwet'en Aboriginal title?

At the Supreme Court level, Lamer C.J. and La Forest J. contemplated the possibility of "shared exclusivity" or "joint occupancy" between one or more nations of Aboriginal people.[90] On the other hand, Lamer C.J. urged other Aboriginal peoples with overlapping claims in the Gitksan-Wet'suwet'en area to intervene in any new litigation.[91] If they did not, would any Aboriginal title established by the Gitksan and Wet'suwet'en be immune to future shared-exclusivity claims? Would it preclude shared Aboriginal rights other than Aboriginal title?

Certainly the combination of exclusivity and overlapping Aboriginal claims lends weight to the need to articulate alternative criteria of reliability for oral Aboriginal evidence.[92] This may be as important for Aboriginal peoples themselves as for the Crown.

(iii) Land Attachment

According to Lamer C.J., the land attachment qualification to Aboriginal title is necessary to preserve the continuity of a community's title, to the present, and into the future.[93] The Chief Justice provided two examples of how the qualification would operate. If Aboriginal title was established with specific reference to hunting, Aboriginal title holders could not destroy the value of the land for hunting "(e.g., by strip mining it)".[94] Alternatively, if the title related especially to the land's ceremonial or cultural significance, the Aboriginal community could not destroy that value "(e.g., ... perhaps by turning it into a parking lot)".[95] If the community did want to use the land in a manner irreconcilable with their special attachment to it, they would have to surrender the land to the Crown, "in exchange for valuable consideration."[96]

Lamer C.J. stressed that this restriction does not limit Aboriginal title holders to their traditional practices. As long as the land's special value to the Aboriginal title is not destroyed, title holders are allowed "a full range of uses of the land".[97] On the other hand, when the land attachment qualification is added to the constitutional entrenchment and general inalienability of Aboriginal title, the result is a property right with higher legal status but narrower general content than the full fee simple.

What kind of uses short of strip mining and parking lots would destroy the land's special value? This will depend on: (i) the nature of that special value in individual cases, and (ii) on what is regarded as constituting destruction. The answer to these issues will require more litigation.[98]

(iv) Identification

If Aboriginal title has distinctive content, should this affect the way courts try to identify it? Lamer C.J. said it should. The test for identifying particular Aboriginal rights had been formulated in 1996, in *R. v. Van der Peet*.[99] It required that a particular practice, custom or tradition claimed to be an Aboriginal right must have been:

(i) exercised prior to European contact;
(ii) integral at that time "to the distinctive culture of the Aboriginal group claiming the right";[100] and
(iii) exercised with sufficient continuity between pre-contact and present times.

In *Delgamuukw* Lamer C.J. said that to prove Aboriginal title to land:

(i) the land must have been occupied[101] prior to sovereignty;
(ii) the occupation must have been exclusive at sovereignty; and
(iii) if present occupation is relied on as proof of pre-sovereignty occupation, there must be continuity between present and pre-sovereignty occupation.[102]

Lamer C.J. justified these modifications on pragmatic and theoretical grounds.[103] He said occupation of land is always central to Aboriginal culture. Hence Aboriginal title does not require explicit proof of the "integral to the distinctive culture" criterion in *Van der Peet*.[104] Next, since exclusivity is important to the content of Aboriginal title, proof of Aboriginal title requires evidence of exclusive occupation.[105] Finally, for identifying Aboriginal title, the time of sovereignty is preferable to contact because: (i) Aboriginal title is a burden on the title of the Crown, whose own title did not arise until it asserted sovereignty;[106] (ii) since occupation of land is itself of central significance to Aboriginal culture, it is irrelevant to ask if it might have resulted from European contact; and (iii) the date of sovereignty can be established more precisely than the date of contact.

Although these are all sound reasons, courts might be able to consolidate the new identification test with the *Van der Peet* test.[107] This should be possible, without losing the distinctive requirements for Aboriginal title. One version, which uses "tradition" to include a practice or custom, would be as follows:

> To prove aboriginal title or a particular aboriginal right, respectively, a claimant must demonstrate exclusive occupation at sovereignty, or a particular tradition integral to the claimant group's distinctive culture at contact, and must show continuity of the occupancy or tradition to the present.

An additional identification requirement may arise at a later stage. If the use of Aboriginal title land cannot be irreconcilable with an Aboriginal community's traditional special attachment to that land, title holders may have to identify the special purpose or purpose of their particular occupation. As well, it will be suggested later that in all identification analysis there may be room for a general connection to land.

(v) Constitutional Status

Does the distinctive content of Aboriginal title affect its status under s. 35(1) of the *Constitution Act, 1982*? Lamer C.J.'s answer was no. Although Aboriginal title may have special features, it has been constitutionalized by s. 35(1) as fully as other Aboriginal rights.[108] Moreover, this section did not create Aboriginal rights; it gave special status to Aboriginal rights existing as of April 17, 1982.[109] Hence the common law relationship between Aboriginal title and other Aboriginal rights applies to s. 35(1) rights. This makes sense. It would be peculiar if s. 35(1) constitutionalized all forms of common law Aboriginal right except one of the most central forms of all. Thus Aboriginal title — including the right to exclusive occupation — is protected constitutionally against all unjustified infringement by governments.

(vi) Aboriginal Title and Other Aboriginal Rights

Beyond the Court's imaginative exposition of Aboriginal title and Aboriginal rights, one basic question needs more attention. What substantive features, if any, has Aboriginal title in common with other Aboriginal rights? In other words, are Aboriginal rights open-ended concepts, unified simply by whatever was consider central to traditional Aboriginal cultures, or are they linked by a common substantive theme?[110] The first alternative allows flexibility and invites judicial discretion. The second may facilitate coherence and a more restrained role for courts.

Before *Delgamuukw*, the Supreme Court had not clearly chosen either alternative. In *Van der Peet* the Court had said that cultural importance and land are both relevant to Aboriginal rights.[111] On the other hand, the *Van der Peet* identification test seemed to use only the former.[112] In *Delgamuukw*, Lamer C.J. said that s. 35(1) Aboriginal rights "fall along a spectrum with respect to their degree of connection with the land."[113] At one end, he said, is Aboriginal title. This is the exclusive right to the land itself, derived from exclusive occupation at sovereignty. In the middle are traditions that still fall short of Aboriginal title, but are intimately linked to a particular piece of land. At the other end are traditions[114] that are integral to the claimant group's distinctive Aboriginal culture.[115] These may involve occupation and use of land that is not sufficient to support a claim of Aboriginal title.[116]

Did the Court finally say that all s. 35(1) rights, including those that are neither Aboriginal title nor site-specific,[117] involve some occupation and use of land? In *Delgamuukw*, the Court moved beyond the apparently open-ended *Van der Peet* test. It formulated a general framework for all particular Aboriginal rights and Aboriginal title: a varying link with land. Once, again, though, the Court stopped short of making the link explicit.[118] Next time, perhaps?

(f) Justification

(i) Justification Goals

Government can infringe s. 35(1) Aboriginal and treaty rights only if the infringement[119] is justified. Lamer C.J. said that justification should be considered in light of the two general goals of s. 35 — recognizing prior Aboriginal occupation, and reconciling this fact with the assertion of Crown sovereignty.[120] In support of these goals, justification can serve a number of related practical purposes. For governments, justification requirements can provide standards to follow in regulating Aboriginal rights. For Aboriginal groups, the requirements support legal remedies for unjust infringement, and can help protect s. 35(1) interests pending negotiated settlements. Moreover, by raising the cost of unilateral action, the requirements may encourage governments to seek negotiated solutions instead. *Delgamuukw*'s reformulation of justification was probably aimed at all of these ends.

(ii) Justification in Delgamuukw

Before focusing especially on justification for infringement of Aboriginal title, Lamer C.J. provided a restatement of pre-*Delgamuukw* justification law. He said that in order to justify an infringement of a s. 35(1) right, government must demonstrate evidence of a "compelling and substantial" legislative objective[121] and adequate consultation and accommodation in regard to the right. The latter requirements should be consistent with the Crown's special fiduciary obligations to Aboriginal peoples, in regard to their s. 35(1) interests.[122] Lamer C.J. said that valid legislative objectives can include:

(a) conservation of natural resources, such as fisheries;
(b) "the pursuit of economic and regional fairness";[123] and
(c) "the recognition of the historical reliance upon, and participation in, the fishery by non-Aboriginal groups."[124]

Consultation and accommodation measures can include:

(a) consulting with the affected Aboriginal group;
(b) giving priority to the protected Aboriginal right;
(c) ensuring minimum possible infringement to achieve the desired objective; and
(d) providing fair compensation for expropriation.[125]

Lamer C.J. then said that the kind of measure required and the degree of protection needed will depend on the individual context, including the nature of the Aboriginal right, the nature and severity of the infringement, and the extent to which other forms of consultation and accommodation are provided.[126] This factor-weighing approach built on the comment in *Gladstone* that the requirements of the fiduciary duty depend on the particular context.[127] In *Gladstone* the Court applied the varying standard approach to the justification measure of priority;[128] in *Delgamuukw* it extended this approach to the other possible measures.[129]

Turning to Aboriginal title in particular, Lamer C.J. said that infringements of this kind of Aboriginal interest can be justified with reference to a potentially wide range of legislative objectives, including the broader regional, economic, and non-Aboriginal reliance concerns referred to in the *Gladstone* decision.[130] Lamer C.J. then looked at consultation and accommodation. He said that an infringement of Aboriginal title *must* be preceded by consultation[131] and should normally be followed by compensation.[132] He provided concrete examples of both of these requirements,[133] and linked both their form and their extent to factors such as the nature of the right infringed and the extent of the infringement.

(g) Self-Government[134]

While title relates to occupation and use of land, the concept of government is potentially far broader. It extends to virtually all aspects of life. Governmental powers can range from minimal to vast. They can be binding, coercive, legislative, and paramount. They are likely to affect the entire population of a given territory. In their strongest form, they include the sovereign powers of an international state. Because of this indeterminate content, the notion of government is not susceptible to ready definition by courts. Because of its potential scope, government should probably not be subject to final definition by courts.[135] Arguably, basic questions about the shape of government should be made by accountable elected representatives.

It is not surprising, then, that the Supreme Court has been cautious in discussing self-government as a general judicial concept.[136] Lamer C.J. offered several specific reasons for this reticence. He said the trial judge's errors of fact made it impossible to determine whether a self-government right had been made out.[137] He said this was "not the right case" in which to formulate general principles on this issue.[138] The parties had emphasized self-government much less here than in the courts below. This was because the claim had been cast in a form inappropriate to s. 35(1). It had been made before the Supreme Court's judgment in *Pamajewon*.[139] "There," said Lamer C.J., "I held that rights to self-government, if they existed, cannot be framed in excessively general terms."[140] Finally, Lamer C.J. said the parties had failed to address the complex range of possible structures of self-government.[141]

As in *Pamajewon*, the Court has refused to say if Aboriginal self-government is an Aboriginal right enforceable at common law or protected by s. 35(1) of the *Constitution Act, 1982*.[142] As in *Pamajewon*, the Court has said that a right of self-government is not protected under s. 35(1) if it is advanced in broad terms. The Court has identified the possible range and variety of self-government, its relationship to other governments and people, and to those subject to it, as "difficult and central" concerns.[143]

The Court's caution on self-government contrasted with its emphasis on Aboriginal title. The trial judge's "errors of fact" and the nature of the pleadings were no obstacle to a major new statement about the character, content, and constitutional protection of Aboriginal title. Moreover, in describing the relationship between Aboriginal title and Aboriginal rights, the Court may have been suggesting that s. 35(1) Aboriginal rights are — to a greater or lesser degree — associated with land.[144] If so, this could rule out broad governmental powers and structures that are wholly unrelated to land.[145]

Nevertheless, there are some very real roles for Aboriginal self-government in the evolving picture of Aboriginal rights. First, traditional self-government is now an important part of proof of these rights. *Delgamuukw* makes it clear that Aboriginal title derives in part from pre-sovereignty systems of Aboriginal law.[146] Evidence of traditional governing laws and structures will be important in establishing Aboriginal title claims.[147] They are also a significant part of the *Van der Peet* identification test. Lamer C.J. has said that specific Aboriginal rights may be established at common law if they were recognized traditionally "by either *de facto* practice or by the Aboriginal system of governance."[148]

Second, individual traditional rights of governance might include community laws on the use of Aboriginal land and resources. If these satisfy the *Van der Peet* or *Delgamuukw* identification tests, there is no reason why they might not be recognized as aspects of Aboriginal rights or title. The power to enforce the laws, at least in regard to the Aboriginal right holders, would constitute a form of Aboriginal self-government.

Third, "government" incorporates a notion of choice and control. Recognition of Aboriginal land rights implies a degree of control over the land in question. Nowhere is this more apparent than with Aboriginal title. As Lamer C.J. has stressed in *Delgamuukw*, choice is an important aspect of Aboriginal title.[149] Effectively, then, Aboriginal title is very much a matter of self-government.

What about self-government that is unrelated to Aboriginal land and resources? Or broader concepts of self-government that may confer legislative powers? Or protection for these kinds of self-government under the *Constitution Act, 1982*? Although *Delgamuukw* didn't rule out these possibilities, it seemed to suggest that they should be pursued through negotiation, not litigation.

(h) Extinguishment

Section 35(1) of the *Constitution Act, 1982* protects Aboriginal rights only if they had not been extinguished by April 17, 1982.[150] The province of British Columbia argued that it had extinguished any remaining Aboriginal title in the province between 1871 and April 17, 1982. The Gitksan and Wet'suwet'en argued that the province had no jurisdiction to extinguish Aboriginal title, because it falls under exclusive federal jurisdiction by virtue of the *Constitution Act, 1867*.[151]

The Supreme Court addressed two questions: (i) Did British Columbia have jurisdiction to extinguish Aboriginal rights during this period? and (ii) Could a provincial law have the effect of extinguishing Aboriginal rights by virtue of s. 88 of the *Indian Act*?[152]

(i) Provincial Jurisdiction under Constitution Act, 1867

Lamer C.J.'s answer to both questions was "no". Section 91(24) of the *Constitution Act, 1867*[153] gives Parliament exclusive legislative jurisdiction in relation to "Indians, and Lands reserved for the Indians". Lamer C.J. said that since "Lands reserved for the Indians" includes all lands reserved, on any terms, it must include lands held pursuant to Aboriginal title.[154] Hence s. 91(24) gives Parliament exclusive legislative power in relation to Aboriginal title. Lamer C.J. said this power prevails over provincial ownership of Crown lands in s. 109 of the *Constitution Act, 1867*. Why? Section 109 is subject to interests such as Aboriginal title.[155] In Lamer C.J.'s view, it is logical that the level of government with primary constitutional responsibility for Aboriginal peoples' welfare should also have jurisdiction over Aboriginal title. The same logic also applied to jurisdiction over other Aboriginal rights tied to land, since some of these could be as fundamental to Aboriginal people as title itself.[156]

The Chief Justice found another protection for Aboriginal rights in the phrase "Indians" in s. 91(24). Lamer C.J. said that this provision protects a central core of "Indianness".[157] It encompasses Aboriginal rights, including those referred to in s. 35(1) of the *Constitution Act, 1982*. Indianness includes Aboriginal rights in relation to land, and also "practices, traditions, or customs which are not tied to land."[158] By analogy to the constitutional doctrine of interjurisdictional immunity,[159] provinces cannot legislate in relation to either kinds of Aboriginal rights.[160]

The province had argued that provincial laws of general application could extinguish Aboriginal rights. Lamer C.J. agreed that such laws can affect Aboriginal rights and other matters within s. 91(24). To do so, though, they must not single out these matters for special treatment. Then Lamer C.J. noted that at common law, extinguishment requires a "clear and plain intention" to extinguish.[161] Hence, the common law condition for extinguishment requires a provincial law to single out Indians for special treatment. This, in turn, would render the law *ultra vires* s. 91(24). Moreover, a provincial law that purported to extinguish Aboriginal rights would directly affect the quality of "Indianness" at the core of s. 91(24). As such, the law would be barred by the doctrine of interjurisdictional immunity,[162] and would not apply.[163]

(ii) Provincial Jurisdiction under Section 88 of Indian Act[164]

As seen in **Chapter 6**, provincial laws of general application that affect Indianness can sometimes be given effect by s. 88 of the *Indian Act.*[165] However, Lamer C.J. said s. 88 does not rescue provincial laws that purport to extinguish Aboriginal rights. In his view, s. 88 lacks a clear and plain intention required to extinguish Aboriginal rights.[166] As well, he thought the express reference to treaty rights in s. 88[167] shows a clear intention not to undermine Aboriginal rights.[168]

For the most part,[169] the Court's reasoning on the division of legislative powers is a logical extension of previous case law. As Lamer C.J. pointed out, the argument that s. 91(24) is limited to Indian reserves was rejected over a century ago.[170] Moreover, if Aboriginal rights are not part of the "Indianness" or "Indian land reservedness" cores of s. 91(24), it is difficult to imagine what would be part of it. Since Aboriginal rights cannot be extinguished without a clear and plain intention, it follows that no provincial law could extinguish Aboriginal rights without singling out matters in s. 91(24).

(iii) A Case for Deferral?

Although the Court's reasoning was logical, its potential consequences were sweeping. First, vast Aboriginal title areas of British Columbia and other non-treaty areas of Canada are now clearly subject to exclusive federal legislative jurisdiction in relation to "Indians, and Lands reserved for the Indians".[171] Second, the core of s. 91(24) — within which provinces cannot legislate independently — includes Aboriginal rights. To the extent that they affect Aboriginal rights, then, provincial game, environment, health, and similar laws must either have a dominant provincial aspect or lack any independent force. In the latter case, they cannot affect Aboriginal rights unless they are rescued by s. 88 of the *Indian Act.* If they purport to extinguish Aboriginal rights, s. 88 does not save them. Third, provincial laws enacted prior to April 17, 1982, cannot extinguish Aboriginal rights, without or with the help of s. 88.[172] Fourth, provincial governments may owe Canadian Aboriginal peoples immense sums in compensation for unconstitutional extinguishment between Confederation and April 17, 1982. While the Court said little about these implications in *Delgamuukw*, they would require some resolution later on.[173]

In light of potential consequences like these, courts may find it necessary to defer final rulings on injunctions or compensation until governments and claimants have had an opportunity to settle matters through negotiation. The alternative could well be economic paralysis, judicial backlogs, deterioration in Aboriginal and non-Aboriginal community relations, and yet more legal uncertainty.

4. *MITCHELL*[174]

🖹 Reading 10(c) at p. 362

(a) Recurring Questions

Some of the unfinished business in *Delgamuukw* returned in the Supreme Court's next major Aboriginal rights decision, *Mitchell*. This time the Court sounded a cautious note about evidence, made some new but inconclusive comments about sovereign incompatibility and self-government, and underlined the importance of the characterization of an Aboriginal claim.

(b) Background

The facts in *Mitchell* took place near the reserve that straddles two national and two provincial borders — the Akwesasne reserve. In the 1950s, Akwesasne Mohawks argued unsuccessfully that they had a right under the Jay Treaty of 1794 to take goods across the Canada-United States border, free of duty.[175] The Ontario Court of Appeal had dismissed a similar claim in a 1993 decision.[176]

In *Mitchell*, the Mohawks tried again, relying on an Aboriginal rights claim as well.

Akwesasne Mohawk Chief Michael Mitchell brought some American-bought household items into Canada. Canadian customs officers allowed him to proceed, but assessed him $142.88 in duty. When Chief Mitchell failed to pay, he was served a "Notice of Ascertained Forfeiture" for unpaid duty, taxes and penalties. In response, Chief Mitchell claimed an Aboriginal and treaty right to bring personal and community goods with him into Canada, free of customs or duties, for trade with other First Nations.

The Federal Court Trial Division[177] and the Federal Court of Appeal[178] dismissed Chief Mitchell's treaty rights argument, but both courts upheld his Aboriginal rights claim. The Crown appealed the Federal Court of Appeal's decision on Aboriginal rights, and the Supreme Court upheld the appeal.[179] The five-judge main majority[180] of the Supreme Court held that there was insufficient evidence that the Mohawk had traded north of the St. Lawrence River. They said that even if there were such trade, it would not have been integral to the distinctive traditional culture of the Mohawk. In a separate judgment, two other majority judges[181] agreed that even if there were occasional trade across the river, it was not a defining feature of traditional Mohawk society. They added that the claimed trading / mobility right could not constitute an Aboriginal right because it was incompatible with the Crown's authority to control movement across its international borders.

(c) Characterization

Before a court considers the validity of an Aboriginal rights claim, it decides if the claim itself has been properly characterized. This is a critical part of Aboriginal rights analysis. The nature and generality of the claim can have a determining effect on its ultimate success. In *Mitchell*, for example, the Supreme Court said that the claim was not simply a right to trade. Instead, the Court said the claim involved a right to bring goods *across the St. Lawrence River* for purposes of trade.[182] Then the Court rejected this claim because there was insufficient evidence of cross-river Mohawk trade in pre-contact times, and because there was no evidence that any such trade was integral to traditional Mohawk society. Geography was considered essential to the characterization of the claim, and geography was fatal to its success.

Because of the significance of characterization, it is important to explore the criteria that shape it. Chief Marshall claimed "the right to enter Canada from the United States with personal and community goods, without paying customs or duties, and the right to trade these goods with other First Nations."[183] McLachlin C.J. referred to the three characterization criteria set down in *Van der Peet*: the nature of the action in regard to which the claim is made, the nature of the governmental action said to conflict with the claimed right, and Aboriginal practice relied on to establish the right.[184] In effect, these criteria require consistency between the claimant's stated claim and its factual and evidentiary context.[185] McLachlin C.J. said the claimant's action was essentially one of trade, the government action was generally neutral in regard to characterization, and the Aboriginal practice relied on was, in essence, a trading right. In all three elements, cross-border or cross-river trade was an important factor. McLachlin C.J. concluded that the context supported a claimed "right to bring goods across the Canada-United States border for purposes of trade."[186]

However, other parts of McLachlin C.J.'s analysis suggest that the *Van der Peet* criteria are not the only possible elements of the characterization process. Not only must a claim be consistent with its factual and evidentiary context; it must not violate judicial principles for interpreting the scope of Aboriginal rights. For example, McLachlin C.J. said the claim should not be limited to trade with other First Nations, because courts do not restrict contemporary expressions of Aboriginal trading rights to specific trading partners.[187] She also rejected the attempt to exclude mobility rights from the claim, saying that "[a]n Aboriginal right, once established, generally encompasses other rights necessary to its meaningful exercise."[188]

As well, a suitable claim must be one that the courts consider appropriate for judicial resolution. In this regard, the claimed right should be quantifiable, enforceable, and reasonably — but not excessively — specific. McLachlin C.J. said the trial judge's limitation of the right to "small, non-commercial scale trade" could cause practical definitional problems.[189] She added that it would be impossible to enforce a restriction that limited trade to Aboriginal trading partners.[190]

McLachlin C.J. cautioned that "[a]n overly narrow characterization risks the dismissal of valid claims and an overly broad characterization risks distorting the right by neglecting the specific culture and history of the claimant's society"[191] She might have added that an overly broad characterization risks the acceptance of more claims than the courts feel they can manage, and that what is overly broad or narrow is a matter for the judgment of the court. Characterization is indeed a powerful — and highly discretionary — judicial tool for regulating the scope of Aboriginal rights claims.

(d) Evidence

Although *Delgamuukw* relaxed the barriers to considering oral Aboriginal evidence, it said little about the limits that remained, and how these should be applied. In *Mitchell*, McLachlin C.J. tried to provide more guidance on these limits.

On the admissibility of evidence, McLachlin C.J. said that evidence should be useful[192] in providing access to relevant facts, reliable, and non-prejudicial.[193] She said that oral Aboriginal histories can be useful in providing information that would not otherwise be available, and in offering the Aboriginal perspective.[194] She repeated the caution in *Delgamuukw* against "facilely rejecting oral histories simply because they do not convey 'historical' truth, contain elements that may be classified as mythology, lack precise detail, embody material tangential to the judicial process, or are confined to the community whose history is being recounted."[195]

On the weighing of evidence, McLachlin C.J. noted that although *Delgamuukw* had stressed that courts must give due weight to the Aboriginal perspective, it also said courts must not strain the Canadian legal and constitutional structure in order to do so.[196] McLachlin C.J. then tried to give this caution a more concrete content. She said that although Aboriginal evidence should not be undervalued, "neither should it be artificially strained to carry more weight than it can reasonably support."[197]

In *Mitchell*, McLachlin C.J. had no problem with the admissibility of the evidence. She said that Chief Mitchell's oral historical evidence was useful and reliable because he was an elder with a long training in the history of his community.[198] In her view, the problem was with the weighing of the evidence. The trial judge had relied on the following evidence to support his finding of pre-contact cross-border trade:

(i) an archaeological work saying that in pre-contact times the Iroquois had traded in copper originating from the north;
(ii) another book by the same archaeologist suggesting that there is evidence of pre-contact northerly trade by the Mohawks;
(iii) post-contact Mohawk treaties that emphasized trade; and
(iv) post-contact Mohawk participation in the Montreal-Albany fur trade.

McLachlin C.J. said that although Aboriginal evidence should not be undervalued, it must be at least "minimally cogent".[199] In this case, the discussion about copper trade did not prove that there was any direct trade in a northerly direction. The only evidence of this trade was "a single 'smoky chalcedony ceremonial (?) knife'."[200] She said that the trade emphasis in post-contact Mohawk treaties did not prove that there was cross-river trade in pre-contact times. Although she conceded that post-contact Mohawk participation in the Montreal-Albany fur trade could lead to an inference that there was a trade route in this area in pre-contact times, there was no other evidence to support this inference.[201] Since there was no minimally cogent evidence in favour of pre-contact cross-border trade, the claimed Aboriginal right was not established. McLachlin C.J. went on to say that even if the Court did defer to the trial judge's finding that there was evidence of pre-contact cross-border trade, there was no evidence that this trade was integral to the distinctive culture of the traditional Mohawk culture.[202]

McLachlin C.J. used the criterion of "usefulness" rather than "necessity",[203] and her analysis suggests that Aboriginal evidence will rarely be rejected on this ground.[204] However, her judgment provided little guidance as to when Aboriginal evidence should be held inadmissible on grounds of unreliability. It is helpful to know that oral histories should not be rejected simply because they do not convey "historical" truth, contain mythology, lack precise detail, contain tangential material, or are confined to the community in question.[205] But trial judges need to know whether and when any of these factors *are* relevant to the reliability of Aboriginal oral evidence. Similarly, the call for "minimally cogent evidence" provided no criteria for determining what *is* minimally cogent. As suggested in the discussion of *Delgamuukw*,[206] it might be helpful to apply a simple requirement of external corroboration to admissibility, and it should be possible to articulate factors relevant to the weighing of Aboriginal evidence.

(e) Aboriginal Rights, Section 35(1), and Sovereign Incompatibility

In the discussion of *Van der Peet* in **Chapter 9** and of *Delgamuukw* in this chapter, it was suggested that the identification test for Aboriginal rights did not fully reflect the common law description of the basis of these rights. The Court said Aboriginal rights were based on the use and occupancy of land by distinct societies. It then formulated an identification test that related only to the distinct societies element, except where Aboriginal title or specific areas of land were concerned. The idea of a wider relationship with land, which was said to be part of the basis of Aboriginal rights, was not pursued.

McLachlin C.J. continued this approach in *Mitchell*. For example, McLachlin C.J. said "an Aboriginal claimant must prove a modern practice, tradition or custom that has a reasonable degree of continuity with the practices, traditions or customs that existed prior to contact."[207] She referred to the comment in *Delgamuukw* that Aboriginal rights fall along a spectrum in regard to their degree of connection to land,[208] but focused only on connections to specific geographical land sites.[209] Binnie J., too, seemed to continue this approach in parts of his judgment.[210] However, he went on to say that:

> ...[a] finding of distinctiveness is a judgment that to fulfill the purpose of s. 35, a measure of constitutional space is required to accommodate particular activities (traditions, customs or practices) *rooted in the aboriginal peoples' prior occupation of the land*.[211] [Emphasis added.]

On its own, the *Van der Peet* test is empty at the core. As suggested earlier, it could be given coherence by a general link with land.

Nevertheless, it was another question about the *Van der Peet* identification test that was controversial in *Mitchell*. Although he did not stress the issue of Aboriginal self-government, Chief Mitchell asserted the right to bring trade goods across the international border, "as a citizen of the Mohawk nation".[212] The federal government argued that Aboriginal rights do not include rights incompatible with the authority of the Crown. It claimed that a key aspect of the sovereign authority of the British — and now Canadian — state is the control of movement over the state's international boundaries. McLachlin C.J. said she did not need to resolve this issue because of her finding that there was no minimally cogent evidence of a right to cross-border transit and trade.[213] However, she did observe that the sovereign incompatibility argument had not been argued in earlier s. 35(1) cases, and that the *Van der Peet* identification test makes no reference to it.[214]

McLachlin C.J.'s comments suggest three different possible approaches to this issue:

(i) that sovereign incompatibility was not a limitation on Aboriginal rights at common law;
(ii) that the common law limitation of sovereign incompatibility was removed by s. 35(1) of the *Constitution Act, 1982*; or
(iii) that the *Van der Peet* test is not comprehensive, and is subject to an implied restriction for sovereign incompatibility.

Clearly, McLachlin C.J.'s judgment did not support option (i). McLachlin C.J. felt that sovereign incompatibility was a restriction on Aboriginal rights at common law. Speaking of the common law, she said that "Aboriginal interests and customary laws were presumed to survive the assertion of sovereignty, and were absorbed into the common law as rights, *unless (1) they were incompatible with the Crown's assertion of sovereignty*, (2) they were surrendered voluntarily via the treaty process, or (3) the government extinguished them" [emphasis added].[215]

McLachlin C.J.'s judgment might appear to give some support to option (ii), the view that common law sovereign incompatibility was removed by s. 35(1) of the *Constitution Act, 1982*. Speaking about the effect of this section, she said that "it is important to note [that] the protection offered by s. 35(1) also extends beyond the Aboriginal rights recognized at common law."[216] She said that the Supreme Court had affirmed the *Van der Peet* test and the extinguishment, infringement and justification doctrines as the appropriate approach to Aboriginal rights claims, including those involving issues of Crown sovereignty.[217]

On the other hand, McLachlin C.J. made no final determination on this issue. Moreover, several considerations suggest that sovereign incompatibility may still be relevant to s. 35(1) Aboriginal rights. Some of these are noted in the separate majority judgment of Binnie J.

First, as Binnie J. said, "[t]he subject matter of [s. 35(1)] is 'existing' Aboriginal and treaty rights and they are said to be 'recognized and affirmed' not wholly cut loose from either their legal or historical origins."[218] Although the protection offered by s. 35(1) does extend beyond that of the common law, the Supreme Court has not used s. 35(1) to create new Aboriginal rights. Section 35(1) protects unextinguished common law rights against future unilateral extinguishment or unjustified infringement. It gives constitutional expression to the Crown's fiduciary obligation to Aboriginal peoples. It has also been applied to protect Aboriginal rights that were denied recognition by another European government in Canada.[219] However, these rights were not incompatible with British sovereignty. They were rights that would have survived if the first European sovereignty had been British sovereignty.

Second, the Supreme Court has construed the purpose of s. 35(1) as being the *reconciliation* of Aboriginal interests and Crown sovereignty, not the negation of one by the other. As Binnie J. noted in his separate judgment, the fact that sovereign incompatibility was sometimes widely construed in the past is not a reason to deny it any scope under s. 35(1). Binnie J. gave the deployment of a military force in Canada as an extreme example of the kind of action that would be subject to sovereign incompatibility. He cautioned, though, that the doctrine is a narrow one that need not be often invoked.[220] If so, this might help explain why the doctrine did not emerge in earlier s. 35(1) cases.

Third, as Binnie J. pointed out, Aboriginal peoples have access to the benefits of Canadian citizenship as well as membership in their own community. In Binnie J.'s view:

> Affirmation of the sovereign interest of Canadians as a whole, including aboriginal peoples, should not necessarily be seen as a loss of sufficient "constitutional space for aboriginal peoples to be aboriginal" (Donna Greschner, "Aboriginal Women, the Constitution and Criminal Justice", [1992] U.B.C. L. Rev. (Sp. ed.) 338 at 342).... In terms of sovereign incompatibility, it is a conclusion that the respondent's claim relates to national interests that all of us have in common rather than to distinctive interests that for some purposes differentiate an aboriginal community.[221]

If these considerations have weight, then option (iii) is a possibility in future, and the *Van der Peet* identification test may have to be revisited.

5. *POWLEY*[222]

🖹 Reading 10(d) at p. 370

In 2003, the Supreme Court tackled the long-neglected question of the Aboriginal rights of Métis people. In *Powley*, the Court affirmed and enforced the Aboriginal rights of two Métis persons under s. 35 of the *Constitution Act, 1982.* More generally, it provided a basis for a test for identifying Métis people and Métis Aboriginal rights under this section. In doing so, the Court approached Métis rights a little differently from the Aboriginal rights of Indian and Inuit peoples.

It was hardly surprising that the Supreme Court would uphold Métis Aboriginal rights. After all, Métis people are one of the three groups of Aboriginal peoples of Canada whose Aboriginal and treaty rights are recognized and affirmed by s. 35 of the *Constitution Act, 1982.* The provision implies that Métis can hold Aboriginal and treaty rights, and that any such rights should enjoy constitutional protection comparable to those of Indian and Inuit peoples.

However, two major challenges complicate judicial efforts to define and enforce Métis Aboriginal rights. First, it is not easy to define Métis people in legal terms. For the purpose of Aboriginal rights, a broad definition might include all people of mixed Indian (or Inuit) and European ancestry; narrower definitions would impose additional requirements, such as the existence of a distinct historic Métis community.[223]

Second, standard Aboriginal doctrine had failed to take account of the special historical situation of Métis people.[224] For example, the *Van der Peet* test for identifying Aboriginal rights required proof that a practice was integral to the distinctive culture of an Aboriginal community prior to European contact.[225] Without modification, this could exclude Métis, who resulted from the mixing of Aboriginals and Europeans.[226] Similarly, while Indian and Inuit Aboriginal rights were the rights of original inhabitants, Métis had one direct ancestral link to the original inhabitants and another to the new inhabitants. As a result, occupation by Métis communities pre-dated European control, not contact, and did not necessarily pre-date the assertion of European sovereignty.

On the definition question, the Supreme Court said that for the purposes of s. 35, Métis includes only those people of mixed Indian and European heritage who developed a separate group identity distinct from those of their Indian or Inuit ancestors.[227] Métis, it said, are identified by their association with a Métis community — historically and today. It said that "[a] Métis community can be defined as a group of Métis with a distinctive collective identity, living together in the same geographic area and sharing a common way of life."[228]

Section 35 Métis status requires an ancestral connection with a historical Métis community and membership in its modern counterpart. The Court declined to formulate a comprehensive list of criteria for determining Métis community association, but it said that three broad criteria are relevant: "self-identification, ancestral connection, and community acceptance".[229]

On the application of s. 35 to Métis Aboriginal rights, the Court agreed that these rights are subject to the same kind of protection as other Aboriginal rights, and are subject to the same general approach to extinguishment, characterization,[230] infringement[231] and justification.[232] The Court said that the purpose of s. 35 is to protect practices that are historically and currently important features of distinctive Aboriginal communities[233] — features such as the distinctive existence of the community or its relationship to the land.[234] However, these features and their context were somewhat different in the case of the Métis.

On the question of the basis and test for Métis Aboriginal rights, the Court said that the basis of Métis Aboriginal rights is somewhat different from that for Indian and Inuit Aboriginal rights. As a result, the general *Van der Peet* identification test would have to be modified slightly to accommodate Aboriginal Métis rights. In the Court's view, while the Aboriginal rights of Indian and Inuit peoples are grounded on pre-contact occupation, this cannot be the case for Métis people. In their case, courts should look for practices that were integral to a Métis community's distinctive existence and relation to the land prior to the date of effective control of European laws and customs.

In the case at hand, the Supreme Court agreed with the lower Ontario courts that Sault Ste. Marie Métis Steve Powley and his son Roddy should be acquitted of the charge of hunting moose without a licence and possessing game contrary to a provincial wildlife statute. The Supreme Court said that the right claimed by the Powleys should be characterized as a right to hunt for food in the Sault Ste. Marie area, not just a right to hunt moose there. It found that this was a right that had been integral to a distinctive pre-European control Métis community in the Sault Ste. Marie area, and that both the community and the right had continued to the present. The Powleys had shot the moose for food, and the Court found no reason to set aside the trial judge's finding that the Powleys had an ancestral connection and current membership ties to the Sault Ste. Marie Métis community. In the Supreme Court's view, the failure of provincial hunting regulations to make special provision for Métis subsistence hunting infringed the Métis Aboriginal right. Moreover, the government had not shown that this failure was justified for the purpose of conservation. Accordingly, the hunting regulations constituted an unjustified infringement of the *Powley*'s Métis Aboriginal right to hunt for food in the Sault Ste. Marie area.

Powley provided some long-needed clarification of the rights of a major group of Canadian Aboriginal people, but it left behind several pressing questions about Métis rights in particular, and Aboriginal rights in general.

For example, who exactly are Métis people for the purposes of s. 35 Aboriginal rights? The Court indicated that last-minute self-identification is unacceptable;[235] what will constitute long-standing self-identification? The Court called for objective evidence of involvement in and recognition by the relevant community"[236]; how rigorously should this requirement be applied? Are only local communities eligible for consideration, or can regional communities be considered as well?[237] The Court required "some proof that the claimant's ancestors belonged to the historic Métis community by birth, adoption, or other means";[238] what evidence and what "other means" are acceptable here? Which historical groupings of Métis people will be accepted as historical Métis communities, and which will not?[239] How much community continuity will be required from historical times to present? The Court seemed to recognize the tentative state of the existing law when it said, "The development of a more systematic method of identifying Métis rights-holders for the purpose of enforcing hunting regulations is an urgent priority."[240]

Powley provides another example[241] of the importance of how an Aboriginal claim is characterized. Because the Powleys' claim was characterized as a right to hunt for food, and not as a right to hunt moose for food, historical fluctuations in Métis moose hunting were deemed to be irrelevant, and the scope of the Aboriginal right was much broader in the end. What were the Court's main considerations in drawing the right this wide? Although the Powleys had claimed a right to hunt for food, and were able to show that traditional Métis subsistence hunting was not limited to moose, the regulatory regime in question was specifically concerned with moose hunting. How should a court decide which of the above factors should prevail? More discussion of the characterization criteria in *Van der Peet*[242] may have helped here.

The treatment of infringement needed more discussion too. *Sparrow* required that a claimant must show something more than a mere restriction in order to demonstrate an infringement of an Aboriginal right. To assess this, courts were to consider if there was an unreasonable limitation, undue hardship, or a denial of a preferred means of exercising a right.[243] In *Powley*, the mere fact that the relevant wildlife regulations did not specifically recognize the Aboriginal right, together with the general wildlife restrictions, was deemed enough to constitute infringement.[244] Are the *Sparrow* infringement qualifications — which, arguably, overlap with the question of justification — now obsolete? Is virtually any Aboriginal rights restriction an infringement? If not, what qualifications remain?

Other questions stem from the introduction of effective control as a test for the date of the historic Métis community. Aboriginal rights now have three relevant "prior" dates, depending on their context. Except for Aboriginal title, Aboriginal rights of Indian and Inuit people are assessed by reference to important practices carried on prior to first contact with the Europeans. Aboriginal title of Indian and Inuit people is assessed by reference to exclusive occupation prior to the assertion of European sovereignty. As a result of *Powley*, Aboriginal rights of Métis people are assessed by reference to important practices of their historic community prior to the establishment of effective control by the Europeans. How should the new expanded concept of Aboriginal rights be described? There are several possibilities, but one is that they are the rights that derive from the occupation and use of northern North America by distinctive Aboriginal communities prior to the coming or establishment of Europeans.

How will courts assess the time of the effective establishment of effective control through European laws and customs in a particular area? Although there was a general consensus on the relevant period in the *Powley* case,[245] effective control is a vague concept that could cause problems in more contentious historical situations.

Does *Powley* shed any light on the ongoing question of the role of the Aboriginal relationship to land as a means of identifying Aboriginal rights? The answer here is "not very much". As seen earlier, although the *Van der Peet* test was said to be grounded on prior occupation by distinctive societies, the test itself asked simply for practices, customs, and traditions that were integral to these distinctive societies, raising questions about the role of occupancy of land.[246] The Court said in *Powley* that:

> The pre-contact test in *Van der Peet* is based on the constitutional affirmation that aboriginal communities are entitled to continue those practices, customs and traditions that are integral to their distinctive existence or relationship to the land. By analogy, the test for Métis practices should focus on identifying those practices, customs and traditions that are integral to the Métis community's distinctive existence and relationship to the land.[247]

In the first sentence above, the Court may be requiring *either* integral practices *or* a relationship to land. But the concept of integral practices is broad enough to encompass those practices that relate to the relationship to land. Hence, the Court may be viewing these practices and the relationship to land conjunctively, as different aspects of an interrelated whole. If so, a relationship to land would be a necessary element of Aboriginal rights. Third, the Court may see a relationship to land as the characteristic indicator, but not necessarily the only indicator, of Aboriginal rights.[248] The ambiguity is not resolved in the second sentence above, where courts considering Métis Aboriginal rights claims are directed to look at both integral practices and the relationship to the land. Nor is it resolved when the Court says the Métis are included in s. 35 because of "their special status as peoples" that emerged between contact and European control,[249] not because of their "pre-contact occupation of Canadian territory",[250] and not merely because of their Métis Indian ancestry.[251] On the other hand, the Court notes that the distinctive Métis cultures emerged "in areas not yet open to colonization."[252] Moreover, it says that the purpose of s. 35 is:

> ...to recognize and affirm the rights of the Métis held by virtue of their direct relationship to this country's original inhabitants and by virtue of the continuity between their customs and traditions and those of their Métis predecessors.[253]

Generally, then, whether a relationship to land is an optional, characteristic, or necessary element of Métis and other Aboriginal rights remains to be seen.

Finally, *Powley* does not indicate if Métis people can hold rights to Aboriginal title. If they can, the relevant time for assessing Métis Aboriginal title may have to be moved to the date of effective control, for the same reasons that it was moved for non-title Aboriginal rights.

6. *HAIDA NATION*[254]

Reading 10(e) at p. 378

As seen in **Part 5**, *Delgamuukw* clarified several aspects of the s. 35(1) justification process, stressing the reconciliation and Crown honour notions behind the process, and developing a factor-weighing approach to the consultation and accommodation components of justification. However, these advances raised some important questions:

(a) What is the general nature and the underlying source of the s. 35(1) justification requirement? For example, is s. 35(1) justification a form of fiduciary duty? And how does this requirement fit into the general relationship between the Crown and Aboriginal peoples?
(b) Who is subject to the duty to consult and accommodate?
(c) Where does the duty to consult and accommodate arise? Is it limited to rights that have been defined in court or resolved in agreements?
(d) How much and what kind of consultation or accommodation is required?
(e) How do the various forms of consultation and accommodation relate to each other, and to the various legislative objectives that can justify infringement?

The Supreme Court answered many of these questions in *Haida Nation*,[255] a 2004 decision involving the Aboriginal rights and title claims made by the Haida of Haida Gwai, the Queen Charlotte Islands. In 1999, the Government of British Columbia had transferred a tree farm licence for logging rights on Haida Gwai's Graham Island and Moresby Island from Macmillan Bloedel Ltd. to Weyerhaeuser Co. Tree farm licences are the basis for determining annual allowable cuts and individual cutting licences. The Haida had occupied Haida Gwai since long before the coming of Europeans, had harvested old growth red cedar on the islands since before the assertion of British sovereignty in 1846, and had claimed title to Haida Gwai for over 100 years. The Haida argued that their s. 35(1) rights had been breached because the Crown and Weyerhaeuser had carried out the licence transfer replacements without consulting the Haida and accommodating their concerns.

The province argued that before Aboriginal claims are proven or settled, it could not know whom to consult, or how high a level of consultation or accommodation to provide. The Haida responded that without consultation and accommodation of their Aboriginal claims, there might be little left by the time the claims were formally resolved. Meanwhile, Weyerhaeuser disputed a British Columbia Court of Appeal finding that private companies can be subject to the Crown's fiduciary consultation and accommodation duties to Aboriginal peoples. A majority of that court had said that Weyerhaeuser was subject to the trust law doctrine of "knowing receipt".[256] The doctrine imposes a fiduciary duty on third parties who receive property that they must have known was held in trust for another.

The trial judge[257] held that there was a strong *prima facie* case for a Haida Aboriginal right to harvest the cedars and a reasonable *prima facie* case for Haida Aboriginal title. However, he said that the Crown should not be required to justify infringements of unproven rights, and concluded that the Crown had a moral, but not a legal, fiduciary duty to consult with and negotiate with the Haida. The majority of the British Columbia Court of Appeal held that both the Crown and Weyerhaeuser had a fiduciary duty to consult with and to accommodate the Haida.[258]

In a unanimous judgment given by McLachlin C.J.,[259] the Supreme Court held that a duty to consult can arise in regard to unproven or unsettled Aboriginal rights. The Court established parameters for both the scope and content of this duty and of a related duty to accommodate. On a broader plane, it restated the basis of the Crown's general constitutional relationship to Aboriginal peoples, linking them to a common underlying principle. Building on the earlier *Wewaykum* decision,[260] the Court differentiated between the fiduciary, treaty, and s. 35(1) consultation applications of this principle, and clarified that the duty to consult in regard to a claimed but unproven s. 35(1) Aboriginal right is *not* a form of fiduciary duty.[261]

(a) Underlying Source and General Nature of s. 35(1) Duty to Consult

In *Haida Nation*, the Supreme Court identified an underlying principle for both 35(1) of the *Constitution Act* and the general relationship between the Crown and Aboriginal peoples. It said that the concept that underlies both the constitutional provision and the general relationship is the principle of the honour of the Crown.[262] This principle requires the Crown to reconcile the prior presence of the Aboriginal peoples with the Crown's assertion of sovereignty, by determining, recognizing, and respecting the rights of the Aboriginal peoples.

The Court said the Crown honour principle applies to all phases of the treaty process. Where treaties are being concluded, the honour of the Crown requires fair dealing; where they have been concluded, the principle requires that the promises be kept; and where they have yet to be concluded, the principle requires negotiations that lead to fair agreements.[263] Beyond the treaty process, where the Crown has assumed discretionary control of a specific, cognizable Aboriginal interest, the honour of the Crown can take the shape of a trust-like fiduciary duty.[264]

The interest in the *Haida Nation* case was neither a treaty right nor any other form of established interest. Instead, it was a constitutional promissory interest — a claim to rights under s. 35(1) of the *Constitution Act, 1982,* a Crown commitment to recognize and affirm existing Aboriginal and treaty rights.[265] In the s. 35(1) context, the Crown honour principle requires consultation and, sometimes, accommodation before the rights can be infringed.[266] Moreover, said the Court, this requirement can arise before the rights themselves are legally proven or resolved. Otherwise, the rights would lack effective protection, and could be eroded or destroyed before they could be established.[267] In this case, the Haida were entitled to be consulted, and perhaps also positively accommodated, in regard to their claim.

(b) Parties Subject to Duty

It had been argued that the duty to consult and accommodate applied not only to the provincial Crown but to Weyerhaeuser, the private lumber company. The Court of Appeal had said that Weyerhaeuser was subject to the equitable "knowing receipt" doctrine that binds third parties who knowingly participate in a breach of trust or fiduciary duty.[268] However, the Supreme Court said that knowing receipt is a trust-type doctrine, and since the s. 35(1) duty to consult is not the same as the Crown's trust-type fiduciary duty to Aboriginal peoples, the s. 35(1) duty is not affected by the doctrine.[269] The Court went on to suggest that even the Crown's fiduciary duty to Aboriginal peoples is not an ordinary trust, and that the knowing receipt doctrine should not apply to it either. In the Court's view, there was no good reason — conceptual or practical — to subject third parties to the duty. Accordingly, it is a duty that applies only to the Crown. On the other hand, it is a duty that binds both the federal and provincial Crowns.[270]

(c) Scope of Duty

In the view of the Supreme Court, the duty to consult and, perhaps, accommodate arises wherever the Crown has "knowledge, real or constructive, of the potential existence of [an] Aboriginal right or title and [has] contemplated conduct that might adversely affect [it].[271] The Court said that the claimants should outline their claims clearly,[272] and that the claim should be "credible".[273] The Court acknowledged that it might be difficult to consult and accommodate before claims are resolved.[274] In its view, however, the law can differentiate between claims that are tenuous, those with *prima facie* strength, and those that are established.[275] Moreover, said the Court, a claim that is "dubious or peripheral" might require no more than notice.[276] On the other hand, if even claims of this nature can trigger consultation duties, the Court has set a low threshold for credibility. The breadth and subjectivity of these criteria may pose challenges for government efforts to formulate workable consultation and accommodation regulatory regimes.[277] Claimants are likely to dispute a government verdict that a particular claim is tenuous, *prima facie* strong, or established, or altogether lacking in credibility. More likely, these questions will be returned to the courts.[278]

(d) Content of Duty

The Supreme Court made it clear that *Haida Nation* was intended to establish only a "general framework" for the duty to consult and accommodate.[279] At the lowest, the duty requires only the presence of a structured consultation regime[280] and notice to an affected claimant of an impending decision or regulation.[281] At the top of the procedural spectrum, government could be required to provide for "formal participation in the decision-making process" and written reasons.[282]

As well, consultation has a substantive aspect, and must be meaningful.[283] The Court described preproof accommodation as "taking steps to avoid irreparable harm or to minimize the effects of infringement, pending final resolution of the underlying claim."[284] In a threshold case, there is a minimal requirement of good faith and reasonableness.[285] More specific accommodation requirements can range from offering disclosure,[286] providing feedback,[287] and being willing to discuss and change proposals,[288] to acting only with the claimants' consent.[289] However, the Court said that the latter requirement is limited to selected cases that involve established rights.[290]

The Court stressed that the level, the aspect, and the specific requirement of consultation depend on the circumstances of the individual case,[291] and on the guiding notions of the honour of the Crown and its obligation to reconcile Aboriginal and societal interests.[292] From the decision, some of the relevant factors appear to be the following:

(i) the strength of the Aboriginal claim;[293]
(ii) the significance of the claimed interest to the Aboriginal peoples;[294]
(iii) the risk and extent of the potential infringement of the claimed interest;[295]
(iv) the risk of irreparable harm to the claimed interest;[296]
(v) the extent to which government was aware, or should have been aware, of the above factors;[297] and
(vi) the capacity of a particular procedural and substantive measure to achieve a reasonable balance between the Aboriginal and societal interests.[298]

(e) Relationship between Forms of Justification

Haida Nation focused on consultation and accommodation, and said little about the other justification component, the requirement of a valid legislative objective. Under *Sparrow*, priority for Aboriginal rights is subject to compelling and substantial legislative objectives, such as conservation and public safety,[299] and *Gladstone* extended the list of valid legislative objectives.[300] How do these objectives relate to s. 35(1) consultation and accommodation? First, evidence of a valid legislative objective is, presumably, a prerequisite for a consideration of consultation and accommodation. Second, a valid federal objective such as conservation may prevail over an "exclusive" form of priority, such as the food fishing right in *Sparrow*.[301] However, the general factor-balancing approach in *Haida Nation* suggests that the relevant legislative objective has another role. The relative importance of the legislative objective is likely one of the key "societal" considerations[302] that a court will take into account in determining the appropriate level of consultation and accommodation. *Haida Nation* also suggests that all societal factors, not only those contained in the relevant legislative objective, will be relevant to this exercise.[303] Generally speaking, the more urgent the legislative objective and other relevant societal factors in a particular case, the lower the level of consultation or accommodation that may be needed.[304]

Another question that will require attention after *Haida Nation* is the relationship between the forms of consultation and accommodation themselves. For example, *Haida Nation* distinguished between established Aboriginal interests and Aboriginal interests that are unproven or unresolved. The former can attract fiduciary duties; the latter do not. In a case of infringement of s. 35(1) rights, the former can involve an Aboriginal veto in certain situations; the latter cannot. If fiduciary duties can apply to s. 35(1) rights, where will these apply instead of the usual s. 35(1) requirements of consultation and accommodation?[305] As between individual requirements, presumably the degree of accommodation in one form may influence the level that is appropriate in another form. For example, more compensation might be appropriate in cases where there has been less accommodation by way of priority resource use in the first place.

For the s. 35(1) consultation and accommodation process, the Supreme Court said that "regard may be had to the procedural safeguards of natural justice mandated by administrative law",[306] and the factor-balancing, varying level approach here has many similarities with the Court's modern approach to natural justice. In both situations the Court is taking a factor-based approach to determining both the appropriate level of protection and its most suitable form.[307] This is a flexible approach that enables courts to tailor individual solutions to the context of particular circumstances. It is also a fluid approach, one that puts a premium on judicial discretion.

On the other hand, there are limits to the natural justice analogy. First, the threshold for s. 35(1) consultation and accommodation is (a) an infringement of existing Aboriginal and treaty rights, (b) Crown knowledge or constructive knowledge that these rights have been claimed, and (c) proof of a valid legislative objective; natural justice requires little more than a public decision that seriously affects an individual's rights or other interests.[308]

Second, natural justice contains a single spectrum of possible procedural safeguards; s. 35(1) consultation and accommodation includes a spectrum of substantive safeguards as well. This raises questions as to the kind and weight of the contextual factors that will be likely to trigger higher level substantive protections. So far, the Court has said that positive ameliorative measures may be required where there is a strong *prima facie* interest and an apparently significant impact on it.[309] Conversely, Aboriginal consent will not be required in regard to unproven rights.[310]

Third, common law natural justice can be modified or excluded by ordinary statutes,[311] while the s. 35 duties prevail over all legislation, delegated or primary. Although this is a consequence of the constitutional and entrenched status of s. 35(1) rights, it does suggest that courts use special care and restraint in applying obligations that may be hard to change.

Fourth, while common law natural justice serves mainly as a means of protecting existing rights and enhancing citizen participation in administrative decisions, the Court regards the s. 35(1) duties as one of a reconciliation process that is intended to culminate with fair, negotiated, and respected treaties between the Crown and Aboriginal peoples. In other words, judicial protection is intended to facilitate executive and legislative reconciliation. This goal puts a special constraint on s. 35(1) protection. The levels of consultation and accommodation must be sufficiently rigorous to protect the rights before they are confirmed by agreement, but not so expansive that they are regarded as an alternative to negotiated settlements.

Haida Nation is a significant advance toward a more coherent framework for s. 35(1) justification and the broader relationship between the Crown and Aboriginal peoples. The Supreme Court has established Crown honour as the principle that grounds all aspects of the Crown-Aboriginal peoples relationship. Building on *Delgamuukw*, the Court has shown how justification is just one step along a reconciliation process that should culminate in fair, negotiated, and respected treaties with Aboriginal peoples. *Haida Nation* affirms that interim judicial protections are a necessary means to this end. The challenge now is to refine these protections,[312] and to ensure that the means do not overshadow the ends.

7. BASIC FEATURES

Today, a quarter-century after *Calder*,[313] many propositions about Aboriginal rights and title seem relatively well established. Many — but not all — of the gaps left by *Sparrow*[314] have been filled in. We now have a general theory about the basis of Aboriginal rights, a statement of the purpose of s. 35(1) and of the Crown's underlying legal responsibility in regard to Aboriginal interests, a picture of the general nature of Aboriginal title, tests for identifying Aboriginal rights and Aboriginal title, clarification of the impact of s. 35(1) on treaty rights, and a general framework for considering s. 35(1) infringement and justification. The *Sparrow* extinguishment-infringement-justification trilogy still causes problems, and many of the propositions below raise further questions. As in the fable, when one hat is removed, another appears in its place.[315] The summary below outlines some of the basic features and unresolved questions of Aboriginal rights today.

(a) General Aspects

Aboriginal rights:

1. *Are sui generis,*[316] and are not identical to ordinary common law concepts.[317] (Just how do they differ?)
2. *Apply only to Aboriginal peoples.*[318] (They apply to Métis peoples in a somewhat different way than to people of Indian ancestry.[319] Are there variations in the way they apply to Inuit?[320])
3. *Are recognized at common law.*[321] (Are they analogous to some common law concepts — custom,[322] adverse possession,[323] prescription?[324] How do they relate to the civil law concept of usufruct?[325])
4. *Survived the assertion of sovereignty and the acquisition of territory by Britain.*[326] (How does this fact relate to the colonial acquisition doctrines of conquest and settlement?[327] How exactly was European sovereignty established in northern North America? Do the differences between the colonial doctrines matter any more in Canada? How were Aboriginal rights affected by the assertion of sovereignty by France in New France?)[328]
5. *May have to be compatible with the sovereignty of the Crown.*[329] (Does this requirement apply to both common law Aboriginal rights and s. 35(1) Aboriginal rights, or only to common law Aboriginal rights?[330] What specific activities are incompatible?[331])
6. *Do not depend on formal legislative or executive government recognition.*[332] *Moreover,*

s. 35(1) Aboriginal rights are unaffected by any alleged non-recognition by the colonial French Crown.[333] (Has the Royal Proclamation any remaining relevance to Aboriginal rights in areas where it is applicable?[334] Where is it applicable?[335] Is there such a thing as a "conceded" Aboriginal interest, dependent on an historic grant?[336])

7. *Are based on "the prior occupation of North America by distinctive Aboriginal societies."*[337] (There are two key aspects of this general approach to Aboriginal rights: (i) the fact of prior Aboriginal occupancy[338] or use[339] of land[340], and (ii) traditional Aboriginal organization in distinctive cultures[341] or societies[342] with their own systems of Aboriginal law[343]. Are the two aspects connected? Are they equally important?[344])
8. *Include Aboriginal title, a species of Aboriginal right that relates solely to Aboriginal claims to land.*[345] (Is Aboriginal title the only special form of Aboriginal right?)
9. *Can be proven by oral Aboriginal evidence*[346] *that might not be permissible under ordinary rules of evidence.* (How far will courts permit variations from the ordinary evidentiary rules?[347] To what extent will they require alternative safeguards?)

(b) Identification

1. *To identify Aboriginal rights other than Aboriginal title:*
   (i) Characterize the modern activity that is the subject of an Aboriginal rights claim;
   (ii) Determine if prior to first European contact (in the case of Indian or Inuit peoples)[348] *or prior to the effective European control (in the case of Métis peoples),*[349] *the activity as characterized was an element of a practice, custom and or tradition that was integral to the distinctive culture of the claimants' traditional Aboriginal community;*
   (iii) Determine if there has been sufficient continuity between the traditional activity and the present activity that is the subject of the claim;[350] *and*
   (iv) (For Métis Aboriginal rights only), determine if the claimant's traditional community constitutes an historic Métis community, and if the claimants are members of the relevant contemporary Métis community.[351]

(Is any link to land implicit in these tests?[352] Are they subject to an implicit restriction in regard to sovereign incompatibility?[353] Do Aboriginal rights include Aboriginal self-government?[354] What factors govern characterization?[355] What is the meaning of "integral"?[356] What features are "distinctive"?[357] What establishes or breaks continuity?[358])

2. *To identify Aboriginal title:*
   (i) Determine if prior to European sovereignty the land that is the subject of the Aboriginal title claim was occupied exclusively by the Aboriginal community; and
   (ii) Determine if there has been sufficient continuity between the traditional occupation and the present occupation that is the subject of the claim.[359]

What constitutes "occupation"?[360] (Assuming that "shared exclusivity" is possible,[361] how will Aboriginal title rights be apportioned between joint occupants? If continuity depends on the absence of uses "inconsistent with continued use by future generations of aboriginals,"[362] what test of inconsistency will be employed?)

(c) Content

1. *The content of Aboriginal rights falls along a spectrum according to the degree of connection between the rights and land.*[363] (Must Aboriginal rights have some general association with land?[364] Or can they be entirely unrelated to land? What circumstances of the Aboriginal group are especially relevant?)
2. *The content of Aboriginal rights other than Aboriginal title varies according to the specific history, culture, and circumstances of the Aboriginal group in question.*[365] (For what *purposes* can traditional practices be recognized — food purposes, ceremonial purposes, commercial purposes, the purpose of trade for a moderate livelihood, etc.?)[366]
3. *Aboriginal title is the right to exclusive use and occupation of the land for purposes that are not irreconcilable with the nature of the group's attachment to that land.*[367] (The Supreme Court has said that activities that "destroy"[368] or "terminate"[369] the nature of the attachment are forbidden. Are lesser forms of interference with the attachment possible?)

(d) Relationship to Crown

Aboriginal rights:

1. *Co-exist with an underlying beneficial title held by the Crown.*[370] (Do the Crown's rights vary with the nature and extent of the Aboriginal rights?)
2. *Can be alienated only by surrender to the Crown.*[371] (What fiduciary obligations does this impose on the Crown?[372])

(e) Possession and Use

1. *Aboriginal rights are held communally rather than individually held.*[373] (Can they be shared by more than one Aboriginal group?[374])
2. *Can be exercised in a modern manner,*[375] *provided that there is general continuity with traditional practices.*[376] (What threshold is needed to establish continuity?)

(f) Extinguishment and Restriction

1. *Aboriginal rights can be unilaterally extinguished by otherwise valid pre-April 17, 1982 government action*[377] ***where government has demonstrated a clear and plain intention to extinguish.***[378] (What is the test for a clear and plain intention to extinguish? Must the intention to extinguish be explicit?[379] If not, what kind of implicit extinguishment qualifies?[380] Should the assertion of European sovereignty be regarded as a potential form of extinguishment? Does the clear and plain test apply to otherwise valid pre-April 17, 1982 government action that falls short of extinguishment?)
2. *Aboriginal title cannot be unilaterally extinguished by otherwise valid pre-April 17, 1982 provincial government action.*[381] (What compensation is due for past appropriations of Aboriginal title by provincial governments?)
3. *Aboriginal rights cannot be unilaterally extinguished by otherwise valid post-April 17, 1982 government action.*[382] (When is extinguishment unilateral, and when is it consensual? Are the Indian treaties all to be regarded as consensual arrangements? What is the difference between unilateral extinguishment, infringement, and restriction? As seen below, infringement and restriction are sometimes permitted.)
4. *Aboriginal rights cannot be infringed*[383] *by otherwise valid post-April 17, 1982 government action*[384] *unless that infringement can be justified.*[385] (What is the relative importance of the factors that suggest infringement?[386])
5. *Aboriginal rights can be restricted without infringement by otherwise valid post-April 17, 1982 government action,*[387] *such as reasonable safety legislation*[388] *and licensing requirements,*[389] *provided that the administration of the regulations does not constitute unjustified infringement.*[390] (Do any other kinds of government action escape the infringement / justification test in *Sparrow*?)

(g) Justification

1. *The requirement that Aboriginal rights cannot be infringed without adequate justification is based on the underlying principle of the honour of the Crown, which requires the Crown to reconcile its assertion of sovereignty with the pre-existence of Aboriginal societies, and on the Crown's promise of rights recognition in s. 35(1) of the Constitution Act, 1982.*[391] (Does this constitutional and promissory justification duty overlap with the special fiduciary duty discussed in **Chapter 8**?)
2. *Government may be able to justify infringing Aboriginal rights if it can demonstrate that it had a compelling and substantial objective for the infringement,*[392] *and that it offered reasonable consultation and — where applicable — accommodation to the Aboriginal groups affected by it.*[393] (How directly must Aboriginal groups be affected in order to be entitled to accommodation? See consultation and accommodation below.)
3. *Compelling and substantial objectives can include conservation, economic and regional fairness, and historical reliance on resources by non-Aboriginal groups,*[394] *but "public interest" is too broad a notion to qualify.*[395] (What other objectives can qualify?)
4. *Consultation and accommodation duties can arise in regard to claimed s. 35(1) rights that have not yet been proven or resolved by treaty, if the Crown was aware or should have been aware of the claims.*[396] (How strong should these claims be to attract minimal consultation or accommodation requirements?)
5. *Consultation and accommodation must be fair, reasonable,*[397] *in good faith, and carried out*

consistently with the underlying principle of the honour of the Crown.[398]

6. *Consultation can require mainly procedural protections such as notice, a structured consultation regime, formal participation in the decision-making process, and written reasons.*[399] (Could the notice requirement be met by mass notice in the media? Will formal participation rights extend to the legislative decision-making process?)
7. *Consultation also has a substantive aspect, and must be meaningful.*[400] (What is the difference between meaningful consultation and more general forms of accommodation?)
8. *As well as consultation, justification can require specific positive forms of accommodation, such as specific steps to avoid or ameliorate harm, acting only with Aboriginal agreement, affording priority to the Aboriginal interest, and providing compensation.*[401] (The Court has said that the requirement that government act only with agreement would not be imposed in regard to non-established rights;[402] in what kinds of situations would it apply to established rights?)
9. *Where accommodation requires that an Aboriginal right be given priority over other interests, this priority may be either absolute*[403] *(for Aboriginal rights with "internal limits")*[404] *or qualified*[405] *(for Aboriginal rights without "internal limits")*[406] *in nature.* (What forms of qualified priority are available?[407])
10. *The level of consultation or accommodation required will vary with the individual circumstances, including the strength and significance of the Aboriginal claim, the risk and extent of the potential infringement, and the relative importance of the relevant societal considerations.*[408] (What kinds of societal considerations will qualify here?)

(h) Fiduciary Duty

1. *Specific cognizable Aboriginal interests can be subject to a special Crown fiduciary duty.*[409] *This duty is distinct from the promissory consultation and accommodation duty in s. 35(1) of the Constitution Act, 1982*, although the two different forms of duty are based on the same underlying principle of Crown honour.[410] (Compare these propositions with the older view that infringements of 35(1) rights must be justified in a manner that is consistent with the Crown's fiduciary obligation.[411] In what circumstances will s. 35(1) rights be subject directly to the Crown's special fiduciary duty?)

Notes

1. **Chapter 3**.
2. **Chapter 7**.
3. **Chapter 9**.
4. *R. v. Adams*, [1996] 3 S.C.R. 101, rev'g [1993] 3 C.N.L.R. 98 (Q.C.A., Rothman J.A., dissenting), which aff'd [1985] 4 C.N.L.R. 39 (Q.S.C.), which aff'd [1985] 4 C.N.L.R. 123 (Q. Ct. Sess.).
5. The Mohawks controlled the St. Lawrence Valley between the end of the 15th and 16th centuries, and hunted and fished there for a period between the 17th and 18th centuries. Apparently there were no permanent Mohawk settlements in the St. Regis region until Mohawks settled at the St. Regis Jesuit mission in 1752. In 1784, Mohawks were granted land in the fishing site area, which was marshland at the time. By 1831 this land was regarded as part of a reserve. In the mid-19th century the marshland area was flooded for the construction of the Beauharnois Canal, and in 1888 the Mohawks ceded the higher adjoining land to the Crown.
6. Now the Court of Quebec.
7. The two lower courts held that the Mohawks had originally had an Aboriginal title to the area; that it was ended in the 19th century by the flooding (trial judge and Quebec Superior Court) and the cession (Quebec Superior Court); that the Mohawks had Aboriginal hunting and fishing rights that were independent of the Aboriginal title and continued after the title ended; but that the fishing rights were validly restricted by the regulations. (These two decisions pre-dated the Supreme Court's decision in *Sparrow*.)
8. *R. v. Adams*, [1993] 3 C.N.L.R. 98 (Q.C.A.).
9. By Beauregard and Proulx JJ.A. Proulx J.A. said Beauregard J.A.'s "very detailed and very convincing legal and historical study" made it unnecessary to elaborate further on the question of the existence and nature of the Mohawks' title to the lands in question (119). Proulx J.A. appeared to regard the cession (rather than the flood and the cession) as determinative in ending any fishing rights. Unlike Beauregard J.A., he felt that if fishing rights *had* continued, they would have prevailed over the regulation restrictions by virtue of the infringement-justification test in *Sparrow*.
10. The majority did not directly address the argument that New France had not recognized Aboriginal title. Beauregard J.A. said his conclusions were "[s]ubject to" this argument (*ibid.* at 109), and considered that there was insufficient proof of traditional possession of the fishing site area. However, Beauregard J.A. said the Mohawk had acquired a "conceded Indian title" to the area, since they had occupied it since the first part of the 18th century with the informal approval of local French authorities: *ibid.* at 110–11. Beauregard J.A. also felt that the Royal Proclamation of 1763 could be construed as protecting Indian interests that had been informally granted in this way before 1763.

    In *R. v. Côté* (1993), 107 D.L.R. (4th) 28 (Q.C.A.), in *obiter* comments, a differently constituted majority of the Quebec Court of Appeal questioned whether Aboriginal rights survived the colonization of New France. In their view, the French policy of arrogating all titles and rights to the French Crown may have been inconsistent with the continuation of any general Indian title: Baudouin J.A., with Tyndale J.A. concurring, *ibid.* at 43–44.
11. *Ibid.* at 115–18 (Beauregard J.A.) and at 120–24 (Proulx J.A.). Beauregard J.A. conceded that the right to fish could be separated from occupancy rights by means of a

specific treaty provision but said there was no such provision here (115).

12. The majority also rejected the argument that the fishing rights could be claimed as an incident of the title to the St. Regis Reserve 15 kilometres away. They said the original terms of settlement at St. Regis had included no special rights to fish in the Lake.
13. Rothman J.A. was not suggesting that Aboriginal rights are unconnected with use of land (or water), or that no traditional possession need be shown to support an Aboriginal right. His discussion was limited to Aboriginal hunting and fishing rights. He said that some pre-European possession should be shown as well as the traditional use in question. Rothman J.A.'s approach would require less stringent proof for an Aboriginal hunting, fishing, or other non-possessory land or resource use right than for an Aboriginal title. This would have benefited the Mohawks, who had a stronger case for fishing rights than for possessory rights. Rothman J.A. also saw his "independent" Aboriginal rights as surviving the extinguishment of the Aboriginal title. This need not necessarily follow. Presumably an Aboriginal title includes resource use rights such as fishing. Hence, barring evidence to the contrary, extinguishment of Aboriginal title should include extinguishment of Aboriginal fishing and other resource use rights.
14. *R. v. Adams*, [1996] 3 S.C.R. 101 at para. 33, referring to *R. v. Côté*, [1996] 3 S.C.R. 139, decided at the same time as *Adams*.
15. *Côté*, *ibid.* at paras. 46–49.
16. *Ibid.* at para. 52. See also *Adams*, *supra* note 14 at para. 33. *Quaere*, are there any common law limitations on Aboriginal rights, such as sovereign incompatibility, that constitute implied limits to the *Van der Peet* test, or does this test apply regardless of any implied common law limits? See discussion of *Mitchell* case in **Part 4**, below, under "Aboriginal Rights, Section 35(1), and Sovereign Incompatibility".
17. *Adams*, *supra* note 14 at para. 40.
18. *Ibid.* at 49.
19. *Ibid.* at para. 26. [Emphasis added by Lamer C.J.]
20. *Ibid.* at para. 27.
21. Further on, Lamer C.J. said that "[t]he recognition that aboriginal title is simply one manifestation of the doctrine of aboriginal rights should not create the impression that the fact that some aboriginal rights are linked to land use or occupation is unimportant": para. 30. This passage suggests at first that some Aboriginal rights may not be linked to land use or occupation in any sense. However, the "linkage" to which Lamer C.J. is referring here is simply the fact that some Aboriginal rights are "site-specific" in the sense that they are restricted to specific areas of land: para. 27. There is no suggestion that no connection whatever to land or land use is required. Like her separate concurring reasons in *Van der Peet* (para. 252), L'Heureux-Dubé J.'s separate concurring reasons in *Adams* (para. 64) and *Côté* (para. 98) suggest that Aboriginal rights can encompass practices "not related to land." However, compare this with para. 65 of her reasons in *Adams*, stressing the severability of Aboriginal rights *from Aboriginal title*.
22. *Delgamuukw v. British Columbia*, [1997] 3 S.C.R. 1010 (Supreme Court of Canada: December 11, 1997). The Supreme Court's decision is cited hereinafter as *Delgamuukw*. It varied (1993), 104 D.L.R. (4th) 470 (B.C.C.A.), which varied (1991), 79 D.L.R. (4th) 185 (B.C.S.C.).

    For commentary, see N. Bankes, "*Delgamuukw*, Division of Powers and Provincial Land and Resource Laws: Some Implications for Provincial Resource Rights" (1998) 32 U.B.C.L. Rev. 317; N. Bankes, "Case Comment on *Delgamuukw v. British Columbia*" (1998) 32 U.B.C. L. Rev. 317; R.H. Bartlett, "The Content of Aboriginal Title and Equality Before the Law" (1998) 61 Sask. L. Rev. 377; G. Borrows, "Sovereignty's Alchemy: An Analysis of *Delgamuukw* v. *British Columbia*" (1999) 37 Osgoode Hall L.J. 537; G. Christie, "*Delgamuukw* and the Protection of Aboriginal Land Interests" (2000–2001) 32 Ottawa L. Rev. 85; B. Donovan, "The Evolution and Present Status of Common Law Aboriginal Title in Canada: The Law's Crooked Path and the Hollow Promise of *Delgamuukw*" (2001) 35 U.B.C. L. Rev. 43; A. Emond, «l'Affaire *Delgamuukw* ou la réactualisation du droit américain au regard des conditions d'existence et d'extinction du titre aborigène au Canada» (1998) 39 Cahiers 849; W.F. Flanagan, "Piercing the Veil of Real Property Law: *Delgamuukw v. British Columbia*" (1998) 24 Queen's L.J. 279; P. Joffe, "Assessing the *Delgamuukw* Principles: National Implications and Potential Effects in Quebec" (2000) 45 McGill L.J. 154; D. Lambert, "Case Comment: *Van Der Peet* and *Delgamuukw*: The Unresolved Issues" (1998) 32 U.B.C. L. Rev. 249; B. Olthuis, "Defrosting *Delgamuukw* (or "How to Reject a Frozen Rights Interpretation of Aboriginal Title in Canada")" (2000–2001) 12 N.J.C.L. 385; A.D. Palmer, 'Evidence "Not in a Form Familiar to Common Law Courts"': Assessing Oral Histories in Land Claims Testimony After *Delgamuukw v. B.C.* (2000) 38 Alta. L. Rev. 1040; and J. Rudin, "One Step Forward, Two Steps Back: The Political and Institutional Dynamics Behind the Supreme Court of Canada's Decisions in *R.* v. *Sparrow, R. v. Van Der Peet* and *Delgamuukw v. British Columbia*" (1998) 13 J.L. & Soc. Pol'y. 67.
23. *Delgamuukw*, *ibid.* at para. 186.
24. The discussion in this part is a modified version of "Comment — *Delgamuukw*: Back to Court?" (1999) 26 Man. L.J. 1. Reproduced with permission.
25. Schedule B to the *Canada Act 1982* (U.K.), 1982, c. 11.
26. *R. v. Sparrow*, [1990] 1 S.C.R. 1075 at 1105, quoted in *Delgamuukw*, *supra* note 22 at para. 186.
27. This process needs all the help it can get. Progress in the comprehensive land claims negotiation process has been painfully slow. Since 1975, the year of the *James Bay and Northern Quebec Agreement*, nearly 20 modern land claims agreements have been signed and ratified. In British Columbia, over 50 land claims — including the claim of the Gitksan and Wet'suwet'en — have yet to be resolved. In that province, only the Nisga'a claim has been settled. The Nisga'a Treaty was signed in 1998... after 25 years of negotiation. For the current state of the negotiation process in British Columbia, see Government of British Columbia, *Present Status of B.C.T.C.* (British Columbia Treaty Consultation Process), online: <http//aaf.gov.bc.ca/aaf/treaty.status.htm>. See further, **Chapter 11**.
28. This discussion will not attempt to address all the significant issues that are raised by this complex decision, or even all aspects of the five highlighted here. In particular, it will not address the broader cultural, economic and social implications of *Delgamuukw*.
29. *Delgamuukw v. British Columbia* (1991), 79 D.L.R. (4th) 185, esp. parts 14 and 15 (B.C.S.C.).
30. *Ibid.*, especially at parts 7, 8, and 17.
31. *Ibid.* at 487–90.
32. *Delgamuukw v. British Columbia* (1993), 104 D.L.R. (4th) 470 (B.C.C.A.). The Gitksan and Wet'suwet'en appealed all of the British Columbia Supreme Court's decision except the fiduciary ruling.
33. Macfarlane J.A., Taggart JJ.A. concurring; and Wallace J.A. For a more detailed summary of these judgments, see D.W. Elliott, *Law and Aboriginal Peoples of Canada*, 3d ed. (North York, Ont.: Captus Press, 1997) at 72–73.
34. (U.K.), 30 & 31 Vict., c.3.
35. Lambert and Hutcheon JJ.A., dissenting, felt that a right to self-government was protected as an Aboriginal right by s. 35(1) of the *Constitution Act, 1982*. Lambert J.A. said Aboriginal self-government relates to internal Aborigi-

nal affairs, does not involve "ultimate legislative power" (728) and does not prevail over provincial law "in all circumstances": (*Delgamuukw v. British Columbia* (1993), 104 D.L.R. (4th) 470 at 727–28). He said Aboriginal self-government survived both sovereignty and the division of powers in the *Constitution Act, 1867*: *ibid.* at 727–30. Hutcheon J.A. suggested that Aboriginal self-government is subject to otherwise valid federal and provincial laws: *Ibid.* at 761–64.

36. As Sopinka J. had died earlier in the autumn, the decision was rendered by a six-judge court. The most extensive reasons were by Lamer C.J., who spoke for four judges. La Forest J. delivered concurring reasons for himself and L'Heureux-Dubé. La Forest J. agreed with Lamer C.J.'s conclusion and with many of the Chief Justice's reasons. La Forest J. disagreed with Lamer C.J. in four main respects. First, La Forest J. said the fact that the claimants sought a declaration of Aboriginal title but tried to prove complete control constituted an additional defect in the pleadings: para. 189. Second, La Forest thought Aboriginal title should not be defined more precisely than Dickson J. had described it in *Guerin v. The Queen*, [1984] 2 S.C.R. 335 at 381–82: para. 190. Third, La Forest J. disagreed with the use of statutes to help define Aboriginal title: para. 192. Fourth, La Forest J. felt Aboriginal title could be proven by reference to the principles derived from the criteria formulated in *R. v. Van der Peet*, [1996] 2 S.C.R. 507 for particular Aboriginal rights, rather through a separate test: paras. 193–99. McLachlin J. agreed with the Chief Justice, and said, "I add that I am in substantial agreement with the comments of Justice La Forest": para. 209. Apart from his reluctance to endorse the detailed exposition of the content of Aboriginal title, La Forest J.'s points of disagreement with Lamer C.J. were not fundamental. This commentary will focus on the reasons of the Chief Justice.
37. Schedule B to the *Canada Act 1982* (U.K.), 1982, c. 11.
38. R.S.C. c. I-5, as am.
39. The claimants made this change to their pleadings at the level of the Supreme Court of Canada. In the British Columbia Court of Appeal, Gitksan and Wet'suwet'en had attempted to change the original ownership and jurisdiction claims into a global claim of Aboriginal rights, said to include proprietary ownership, and self-government over land, resources, and people. The majority judges rejected this formulation, saying the claim should be limited to ownership, jurisdiction (which they understood to mean self-government), and other Aboriginal rights, not Aboriginal rights in a global sense. Without expressly limiting the claimants' "global" formulation, Lambert J.A. took a somewhat similar approach.
40. They claimed a total of 133 individual territories.
41. These two territories occupied the same area as the 133 individual territories. Thus, the external boundaries of the individual territories and those of the two collective territories were identical.
42. Lamer J. gave the main majority reasons for the Supreme Court: *supra* note 22.
43. Two other possible distinctions can be mentioned briefly here. *Failure to Appeal*: Lamer C.J. stressed that although the first set of changes could have been appealed, this had not been done. It could be inferred, therefore, that the respondents had not felt seriously prejudiced by it. Although Lamer C.J. did not say so specifically, the second set of changes were sought too late to have been appealed, so no such inference was possible. *Net Effect of Change*: The smaller the change, the more likely one would expect it to be permitted. Since two new territorial claims covered the same area as the 51 original claims, the claimants argued that the second set of changes made no net difference to the case, and should be allowed. Although Lamer C.J. conceded that this argument carried "considerable weight" (para. 76), he said it did not address the fact that the new collective claims had not been in issue at trial. Thus Lamer C.J. appears to have been willing to have assume that this set of changes could have made *some* difference to the form of the evidence and argument at trial.
44. The issue of Aboriginal oral evidence was related to the question as to where an appellate court should interfere with a trial judge's findings of fact. In *Delgamuukw*, the Supreme Court affirmed (at paras. 78 and 79) the general principle that an appellate court should normally defer to a trial judge's findings of fact, especially those based on the testimony and credibility of the witnesses, and on the law the trial judge applied to the facts. However, the Court said appellate intervention is justified "by the failure of a trial court to appreciate the evidentiary difficulties inherent in adjudicating aboriginal claims when, first, applying the rules of evidence and, second, interpreting the evidence before it": para. 80. Given the potential scope of this exception — and the way the Supreme Court applied it in *Delgamuukw* — is there much room for judicial deference in Aboriginal claims litigation? Given the rapidly evolving nature of the case law on Aboriginal rights — a fact acknowledged by the Court in *Delgamuukw* (at para. 79), the scope of this exception is likely to generate an abundance of appeals in this area.
45. On Aboriginal evidence, see M. Asch, "Errors in Delgamuukw: An Anthropological Perspective" in F. Cassidy, ed., *Aboriginal Title in British Columbia: Delgamuukw v. The Queen* (Lantzville: Oolican Books and the Institute for Research on Public Policy, 1992) at 221; M. Storrow and M. Bryant, "Litigating Aboriginal Rights Cases" in F. Cassidy, ed., *ibid.* at 178; G. Sherrott, "The Court's Treatment of the Evidence in *Delgamuukw v. B.C.*" (1992) 56 Sask. L. Rev. 441; J. Fortune, "Construing Delgamuukw: Legal Arguments, Historical Argumentation, and the Philosophy of History" (1993) 51 U.T. Fac. L. Rev. 80. M. Asch and C. Bell, "Definition and Interpretation of Fact in Canadian Aboriginal Title Litigation: An Analysis of Delgamuukw" (1994) 10 Queen's L.J. 503; and B.J. Gover and M.L. Macaulay, "'Snow Houses Leave No Ruins': Unique Evidence Issues in Aboriginal and Treaty Rights Cases" (1996) 60 Sask. L. Rev. 47; A.D. Palmer, 'Evidence "Not in a Form Familiar to Common Law Courts"': Assessing Oral Histories in Land Claims Testimony After *Delgamuukw v. B.C.* (2000) 38 Alta. L. Rev. 1040 J. Borrows, "Listening for a Change: The Courts and Oral Tradition" (2001) 39 Osgoode Hall L.J. I.
46. This development builds on an earlier series of decisions stressing the need to accommodate oral Aboriginal evidence in the context of Aboriginal treaty cases: see *R. v. Taylor* (1981), 62 C.C.C. (2d) 227 at 232; *Simon v. The Queen*, [1985] 2 S.C.R. 387 at 408; and *R. v. Sioui*, [1990] 1 S.C.R. 1025 at 1068, all referred to in *Delgamuukw*, *supra* note 22 at para. 87.
47. Hearsay evidence is an out-of-court statement or other communication made as proof of an assertion of fact contained in it: see J. Sopinka, S.N. Lederman, and Alan W. Bryant, *The Law of Evidence in Canada*, 2d ed. (Toronto: Butterworths, 1998) at 156. The common law "rule" against hearsay is that hearsay evidence is generally inadmissible. Cf. the description in *Subramanniam v. Public Prosecutor*, [1956] 1 W.L.R. 965 at 970, cited in *R. v. Smith* [1992] 2 S.C.R. 915 at 924; and M. N. Howard *et al.*, eds., *Phipson on Evidence*, 15th ed. (London: Sweet & Maxwell, 2000) at 557; Stanley Schiff, *Evidence in the Litigation Process*, 4th ed. (Scarborough, Ont.: Carswell, 1993), vol. 1 at 322.
48. *Ibid.*
49. As noted, for example, in *R. v. B.(K.G.)*, [1993] 1 S.C.R. 740.
50. See, for example, *R. v. Khan*, [1990] 2 S.C.R. 531; *R. v. Smith*, [1992] 2 S.C.R. 915, and *R. v. B.(K.G.)*, [1993] 1 S.C.R. 740, and *R. v. Rockey*, [1996] 3 S.C.R. 829 at

para. 17. The movement in the *Khan, Smith*, and *B.(K.G.)* trilogy from the "categorical" to the "principled" approach to hearsay rule exceptions is summarized in the first part of P. M. McCrea, "Judicial Law-Making: The Development of the Principled Exception to the Hearsay Rule — Implications for Preliminary Hearsay Recantations", (1998) 61(1) Sask. L. Rev. 199. Note that McEachern C.J.'s decision in *Delgamuukw* pre-dated *Smith* and *B.(K.G.)*.

51. *Ibid.*
52. See generally M. N. Howard *et al.*, eds., *Phipson on Evidence*, 15th ed. (London: Sweet & Maxwell, 2000) at 736.
53. These statements meet the necessity requirement because the dead cannot give further evidence. They meet the alternative safeguards requirement because public or general rights are subject to testing by the community as a whole.
54. *Delgamuukw v. British Columbia* (1991), 79 D.L.R. (4th) 185 at 258. Note that in *R. v. Smith*, [1992] 2 S.C.R. 915, the Supreme Court seemed to require a stricter test of necessity than this. In *Smith*, the Court said necessity referred to the situations where the evidence would be unavailable otherwise to prove the fact in issue. The Supreme Court said necessity did not mean "necessary to [a party's] case": 933.

    In a separate ruling on evidence, McEachern C.J. held that the telling and re-telling of oral history at public gatherings helped qualify the adaawk and kungax as general reputation: *Uukw v. British Columbia* (1987), 15 B.C.L.R. (2d) 326 (B.C.S.C.).
55. *Delgamuukw v. British Columbia* (1991), 79 D.L.R. (4th) 185 at 258. McEachern C.J. considered questions of evidence generally in Part 7 of his decision, and in the following separate rulings: *Uukw v. British Columbia* (1987), 15 B.C.L.R. (2d) 326 (B.C.S.C.) [oral histories]; *Delgamuukw v. British Columbia* (1988), 32 B.C.L.R. (2d) 152 (B.C.S.C.) [opinion evidence]; *Delgamuukw v. British Columbia* (1988), 32 B.C.L.R. (2d) 156 (B.C.S.C.) [legal professional privilege]; *Delgamuukw v. British Columbia* (1989), 38 B.C.L.R. (2d) 165 (B.C.S.C.) [historical documents and opinions]; *Delgamuukw v. British Columbia* (1989), 38 B.C.L.R. (2d) 176 (B.C.S.C.) [learned treatises].
56. *Delgamuukw v. British Columbia* (1991), 79 D.L.R. (4th) 185 at 281. McEachern C.J. said, "I do not find [the adaawk and kungax] helpful as evidence of use of specific territories at particular times in the past: *ibid.* at 260.
57. *Ibid.* at 259–60.
58. *Ibid.* at 243–48 (a concern of McEachern C.J. with much of the oral evidence).
59. *Ibid.* at 259. (McEachern C.J. also expressed concern at the claimants' attempts to support the adaawk and kungax by reference to anthropological accounts — which he found unreliable — and to historical accounts — which he said provided little to support pre-contact events: *ibid.* at 260).
60. *Ibid.* at 505, 515. However, McEachern C.J. said the evidence — mainly the archaeological, linguistic, and (in part) historical and Aboriginal genealogical evidence — did establish an Aboriginal presence in the area "for a long, long time before sovereignty" (*ibid. at 282*). Moreover, he concluded that inferences from this evidence and the Aboriginal territorial affidavits established Aboriginal rights in two territories comprising much of the area of the 133 territories originally claimed: *ibid.* at 522–23.
61. *Delgamuukw*, *supra* note 22 at para. 98, referring to *R. v. Van der Peet*, [1996] 2 S.C.R. 507, heading to para. 68.
62. Also under the reputation evidence exception to the hearsay rule: see *Delgamuukw v. British Columbia* (1991), 79 D.L.R. (4th) 185 at 255.
63. *Delgamuukw*, *supra* note 22 at para. 101.
64. M. N. Howard *et al.*, eds., *Phipson on Evidence*, 15th ed. (London: Sweet & Maxwell, 2000) at 736.
65. *Ibid.* at 507.
66. *Delgamuukw*, *supra* note 22 at para. 106.
67. *Delgamuukw*, *supra* note 22 at para. 98. Although the trial judge said that his concerns about the evidentiary reliability of the adaawk and kungax affected their evidentiary weight rather than their admissibility, the Supreme Court stressed the general implications of these concerns, and appeared to treat this question as essentially one of admissibility: *ibid.* The confusion is partly because some of the same factors that are relevant to establishing a threshold of admissibility (such as the size of the verifying group) may also be relevant to the issue of evidentiary weight; partly because of the Supreme Court's tendency to respond to the trial judge's reliability concerns with arguments about necessity; and partly because of the Supreme Court's failure to note that the trial judge's concerns were mainly about the evidentiary reliability of the adaawk and kungax *in relation to the 133 specific territories claimed* (see, for example, *Delgamuukw v. British Columbia* (1991), 79 D.L.R. (4th) at 259–60).
68. *Delgamuukw*, *supra* note 22 at paras. 99–107.
69. *Delgamuukw*, *supra* note 22 at para. 82, quoting from *R. v. Van der Peet*, [1996] 2 S.C.R. 507 at para. 49.
70. *Delgamuukw*, *supra* note 22 at para. 87.
71. *Delgamuukw*, *supra* note 22 at para. 78
72. The Supreme Court has said in other cases that to receive a hearsay statement, it is necessary to show circumstances "which substantially negate" the possibility that the evidence was not reliable (*R. v. Smith*, [1992] 2 S.C.R. 915 at 933); or "some other fact or circumstance that compensates for, or stands in the stead of the oath, presence, and cross-examination" (*R. v. B.(K.G.)*, [1993] 1 S.C.R. 740 at 791) that would normally be available in open court. In *R. v. B.(K.G.)* at 788–96, the Supreme Court provided illustrations of the kind of "substitute *indicia* of trustworthiness [that] might permit reception of prior inconsistent statements, bearing in mind that the question of reliability is a matter for the trial judge, to be decided on the particular circumstances of the case." Similar guidance is needed for Aboriginal oral evidence.
73. External to the party submitting the evidence.
74. Cf. the Supreme Court's *Smith* and *B.(K.G.)* decisions, *supra* note 72.
75. This is an illustrative, rather than exhaustive, list, drawn from the general considerations that appear to animate some of the main existing hearsay exceptions, such as the reputation exception: see for example, M.N. Howard *et al.*, eds., *Phipson on Evidence*, 15th ed. (London: Sweet & Maxwell, 2000) at 736.
76. J. Fortune, "Construing Delgamuukw: Legal Arguments, Historical Argumentation, and the Philosophy of History" (1993) 51 U.T. Fac. L. Rev. 80 at 93; *Uukw v. British Columbia* (1987), 15 B.C.L.R. (2d) 326 (B.C.S.C.).
77. See M. Jackson et al., "The Address of the Gitksan and Wet'suwet'en Hereditary Chiefs to Chief Justice McEachern of the Supreme Court of British Columbia" [1988] 1 C.N.L.R. 17 at 35–36, stressing the specialized training and study necessary before elders become experts in maintaining an Aboriginal peoples' oral traditions.
78. For these and other positive assurances of reliability typical in Aboriginal oral traditions, see also C. McLeod, "The Oral Histories of Canada's Northern People, Anglo-Canadian Evidence Law, and Canada's Fiduciary Duty to First Nations: Breaking Down the Barriers of the Past" (1992) 30 Alta. L. Rev. (No. 4) 1276; and B.J. Gover and M.L. Macaulay, "'Snow Houses Leave No Ruins': Unique Evidence Issues in Aboriginal and Treaty Rights Cases" (1996), 60 Sask. L. Rev. 47.

    Not all commentators agree on the significance of all the factors: see, for example, the cautions raised in M. Pylypchuk, "The Value of Aboriginal Records as Legal Evidence in Canada: An Examination of Sources" (1991) 32 Archivaria 51 at 54–55 M.J. Kaplan, "Proof and Extinguishment of Aboriginal Title to Indian Lands" 41 A.L.R. Fed. 425 at 436; Dr. Bruce Trigger, in "Time and Traditions: Essays in Archaeological Interpretation": P. Drucker, Cultures of the North Pacific Coast (San Francisco: Chandler, 1965) at 246.

At the reliability threshold, however, the question is simply whether there is *some* external assurance of reliability in the case at hand. The challenge of tallying up the force of the assurances and counterarguments in the case comes later, when the weight of the evidence is assessed.

79. These are not the only possible *indicia* of the reliability of the evidence itself. But they seem consistent with the spirit of past exceptions to the hearsay rule, and can be applied to the context of oral Aboriginal evidence. Together with the *indicia* of the reliability of the sources (suggested below), they could help provide trial judges with a starting point.
80. Clearly, absolute impartiality is unattainable. The fact that evidence was produced in the midst of a claim may not carry as much weight as evidence generated in other circumstances, but it may gain more credibility from other factors. For example, evidence from elders is likely to carry more weight than evidence generated by members of a claims litigation or negotiating committee.
81. The trial judge's own approach pointed in this direction. McEachern C.J. indicated that his conclusion that the claimants had established traditional use in a portion of the general area in question was based more on avoiding the risk of "unfairness" than on an inference from the evidence (*Delgamuukw v. British Columbia* (1991), 79 D.L.R. (4th) 185 at 522). However, his most serious evidentiary concerns were with the evidence offered in support of the 133 highly detailed territorial claims.
82. Other than elders from the Aboriginal community making a claim in a particular case.
83. The Supreme Court had described Aboriginal title as a right to "occupy and possess certain lands": *Guerin v. The Queen*, [1984] 2 S.C.R. 335 at 382. It had done little to define the nature and extent of this occupation and possession. Was it exclusive? Was it proprietary? Had it any limits other than a bar on alienation?
84. The Court had characterized Aboriginal title as "a subcategory of aboriginal rights which deals solely with claims of rights to land": *R. v. Van der Peet*, [1996] 2 S.C.R. 507 at para. 74; see also para. 34. Although the Court had indicated that Aboriginal rights are not necessarily derivative of Aboriginal title, it had not said if Aboriginal title must be derivative of particular Aboriginal rights. Indeed, in *Van der Peet* the Court had formulated an Aboriginal rights identification test that focused on particular Aboriginal rights. Was Aboriginal title simply the sum of the individual Aboriginal rights that could be proven in a given location? How would the claimants show that occupation of an area was "integral" to their culture? To prove Aboriginal title, must claimants establish exclusive use? If so, where did this fit into the *Van der Peet* test? See further, D.W. Elliott, *ibid.* at 73–91.
85. Lamer C.J. acknowledges academic works at several points in this part of his reasons. The following appear to have been especially influential in contributing to the Court's views on Aboriginal title: K. McNeil, *Common Law Aboriginal Title* (Oxford: Clarendon Press, 1989); K. McNeil, "The Meaning of Aboriginal Title" in M. Asch, ed., *Aboriginal and Treaty Rights in Canada: Essays on Law, Equality and Respect for Difference* (Vancouver: U.B.C. Press, 1997) at 135; B. Slattery, "The Constitutional Guarantee of Aboriginal and Treaty Rights" (1982–83) 8 Queen's L.J. 232; B. Slattery, *Ancestral Lands, Alien Laws: Judicial Perspectives on Aboriginal Title* (Saskatoon: University of Saskatchewan Native Law Centre, 1983); and B. Slattery, "Understanding Aboriginal Rights" (1987) 64 Can. Bar Rev. 727.
86. The respondents' position was almost the converse of the unsuccessful argument in *R. v. Adams*, [1996] 3 S.C.R. 101 that Aboriginal rights are dependent on Aboriginal title.
87. *Delgamuukw*, *supra* note 22 at para. 128: For Lamer C.J., this restriction applies both to the use and the disposition of the land. On use, he said: "For example, if occupation is established with reference to the use of the land as a hunting ground, then the group that successfully claims Aboriginal title to that land may not use it in such a fashion as to destroy its value for such a use (e.g., by strip mining it). Similarly, if a group claims a special bond with the land because of its ceremonial or cultural significance, it may not use the land in such a way as to destroy that relationship (e.g., by developing it in such a way that the bond is destroyed, perhaps by turning it into a parking lot.)": *ibid.* On disposition, he said: "It is for this reason also that lands held by virtue of aboriginal title may not be alienated. Alienation would bring to an end the entitlement of the aboriginal people to occupy the land and would terminate their relationship with it": para. 129. This, however, did not preclude "the possibility of surrender to the Crown in exchange for valuable consideration": para. 131.
88. *Delgamuukw v. British Columbia* (1991), 79 D.L.R. (4th) 185 at 522, 505.
89. *Ibid.* at 519.
90. *Delgamuukw*, *supra* note 22 at paras. 158 and 196, respectively.
91. *Ibid.* at 185.
92. Discussed in section (d) above.
93. *Delgamuukw*, *supra* note 22 at paras. 126 and 127.
94. *Delgamuukw*, *supra* note 22 at para. 128.
95. *Ibid.* at para. 129.
96. *Ibid.* at para. 131. Note, however, that here Lamer C.J. seemed to contemplate a conversion of Aboriginal title to non-Aboriginal title, not an absolute surrender.
97. *Ibid.* at para. 132.
98. On the uncertainty likely here, see W.F. Flanagan, "Piercing the Veil of Real Property: *Delgamuukw v. British Columbia*" (1998) 24 Queen's L.J. 279 at paras. 47–54.
99. See *R. v. Van der Peet*, [1996] S.C.R. 507, esp. paras. 44–74 and D.W. Elliott, "Fifty Dollars of Fish: A Comment on Van der Peet" (1997) 35 Alta. L. Rev. 759 at 761–62.
100. *R. v. Van der Peet*, [1996] 2 S.C.R. 507 at para. 51.
101. Lamer C.J. said that proof of occupancy could be shown either by physical evidence of occupation (as the respondents argued) or by evidence of recognition of occupation in Aboriginal laws (as the claimants argued): para. 147.
102. See generally *Delgamuukw*, *supra* note 22 at para. 143.
103. For a thorough analysis supporting similar modifications, see K. McNeil, "Aboriginal Title and Aboriginal Rights: What's The Connection?" (1997) 36 Alta. L. Rev. 117.
104. *Delgamuukw*, *supra* note 22 at para. 151.
105. Lamer C.J. stressed that this need not preclude shared exclusive occupation: para. 158.
106. *Ibid.*
107. In his separate majority judgment, La Forest J. took one possible approach to consolidation. He identified Aboriginal title by reference to four factors he regarded as key to the *Van der Peet* test: precision, specificity, continuity, and centrality: *Delgamuukw*, *supra* note 22 at para. 193. But these are very general criteria, and La Forest found it necessary to qualify them. Despite them, for example, La Forest J. conceded that: (i) title boundaries need not be drawn in great detail, (ii) for title, sovereignty is more relevant than contact, (iii) occupation is evidence of centrality, and (iv) occupation must be exclusive (although this need not preclude shared exclusive occupation) (at paras. 193–99).
108. *Delgamuukw*, *supra* note 22 at para. 133. The Court had already indicated in *Van der Peet* that Aboriginal title is a component of both common law and s. 35(1) Aboriginal rights: *R. v. Van der Peet*, [1996] 2 S.C.R. 507 at

para. 33. There was no reason why the special content of Aboriginal title should affect its status.

109. *Delgamuukw*, *supra* note 22 at para. 133. Lamer C.J. also said that common law Aboriginal rights are not exhaustive of the content of s. 35(1), and referred to *R. v. Côté*, [1996] 3 S.C.R. 139 at para. 136. This probably means that Aboriginal rights that are defeated by a common law or similar technicality (not extinguishment) are still protected by s. 35(1) if they meet the requirements of the *Van der Peet* or *Delgamuukw* identification tests.

110. These questions were complicated by the fact that common law Aboriginal rights were constitutionalized in 1982 by s. 35(1) of the *Constitution Act, 1982*. The Court had suggested in *Van der Peet* that Aboriginal title is a component of both common law and s. 35(1) Aboriginal rights: *R. v. Van der Peet*, [1996] 2 S.C.R. 507 at para. 33. However, in *R. v. Côté*, [1996] 3 S.C.R. 139 at para. 52, the Court indicated that Aboriginal rights that might not be recognized at common law could still be recognized for the purposes of s. 35(1) if they satisfied the requirements of the *Van der Peet* test. Were the answers to these questions the same for common law and s. 35(1) Aboriginal rights?

111. It said Aboriginal rights are based on "the prior occupation of North America by distinctive aboriginal societies": *R. v. Van der Peet*, [1996] 2 S.C.R. 507 at para. 35.

112. As noted above, the *Van der Peet* test required that an alleged right be "an element of a practice, custom or tradition integral to the distinctive culture of the aboriginal group claiming the right": *R. v. Van der Peet*, [1996] 2 S.C.R. 507 at para. 46. On its own, then, it seemed open-ended. *R. v. Adams*, [1996] 3 S.C.R. 101 and *R. v. Côté*, [1996] 3 S.C.R. 139 were also ambiguous in this respect. When the Court spoke of the content of Aboriginal rights in these decisions, it did so solely by reference to their relationship to land: *Adams*, para. 30 and *Côté*, para. 39. Yet the wording in both cases left open the possibility that the Court also contemplated Aboriginal rights wholly unrelated to land.

113. *Delgamuukw*, *supra* note 22 at para. 138.

114. And practices and customs.

115. *Delgamuukw*, *supra* note 22 at para. 138.

116. (Or, one might add, of a site-specific Aboriginal right). Lamer C.J.'s full "spectrum" discussion is as follows: "The picture which emerges from *Adams* is that the aboriginal rights which are recognized and affirmed by s. 35(1) fall along a spectrum with respect to their degree of connection with the land. At the one end, there are those aboriginal rights which are practices, customs and traditions that are integral to the distinctive aboriginal culture of the group claiming the right. However, the 'occupation and use of the land' where the activity is taking place is not 'sufficient to support a claim of title to the land' ([*Adams*] at para. 26). Nevertheless, those activities receive constitutional protection. In the middle, there are activities which, out of necessity, take place on land and indeed, might be intimately related to a particular piece of land. Although an aboriginal group may not be able to demonstrate title to the land, it may nevertheless have a site-specific right to engage in a particular activity": *Delgamuukw*, *supra* note 22 at para. 138.

117. The passage quoted above (from para. 138 of *Delgamuukw*) appears to suggest that all Aboriginal rights have some connection with land, even though at one end of the spectrum that connection may be too indirect to support a claim of Aboriginal title or even a claim to a site-specific activity.

118. The suggestion that there is such a link seems at first to clash with Lamer C.J.'s discussion of s. 91(24) of the *Constitution Act, 1867*. Here he says that "[aboriginal rights] also encompass practices, customs and traditions which are not tied to land ...": *ibid.* at para. 178. But the "tie" to which Lamer C.J. refers here is the special tie of rights that are site-specific (para. 176) or "relate" or are "in relation to" (para. 176) land in the strict sense of the division of federal / provincial legislative jurisdiction. Rights that lack this special tie might still have a more general substantive link with land.

See **Chapter 9, Part 3(h)** for a discussion of different possible approaches to linking Aboriginal rights and land.

119. For the general test for infringement, see *R. v. Sparrow*, [1990] 1 S.C.R. 1075 at 1111–12. For important post-*Sparrow* discussions of infringement, see *R. v. Badger*, [1996] 1 S.C.R. 771 at paras. 75–98; *R. v. Nikal*, [1996] 1 S.C.R. 1013 at paras. 86–108; *R. v. Gladstone*, [1996] 2 S.C.R. 723 at paras. 39–53; and *R. v. Adams*, [1996] 3 S.C.R. 101 at paras. 52–55. Although Lamer C.J. focused on justification in *Delgamuukw*, infringement and justification are two sides of the same coin, so that it might have been useful to consider the two concepts together. As well, it would have been helpful to examine the ruling in *Badger* (at para. 89) that there is a boundary between (i) restriction short of infringement (whether justified or not) at least for reasonable provision for safety, and (ii) infringement (whether justified or not).

120. *Delgamuukw*, *supra* note 22 at para. 161.

121. *Delgamuukw*, *supra* note 22 at para. 161. The phrase is from *R. v. Sparrow*, [1990] 1 S.C.R. 1075 at 1075, 1113. Lamer J. repeated his statement in government in *R. v. Gladstone*, [1996] 2 S.C.R. 723 at para. 72 that compelling and substantial objectives are those that are directed at either of the two main goals of s. 35(1) in regard to Aboriginal rights.

122. *Delgamuukw*, *supra* note 22 at para. 165.

123. *Ibid.* at para. 161, referring to *Gladstone*, para. 75.

124. *Ibid.*

125. *Ibid.* at para. 162, quoting from *R. v. Sparrow*, [1990] 1 S.C.R. 1075 at 1119.

126. This general proposition is extrapolated from Lamer C.J.'s comments about consultation and compensation: *Delgamuukw*, *supra* note 22 at paras. 166–69.

127. *R. v. Gladstone*, [1996] 2 S.C.R. 723 at para. 56.

128. *Ibid.* In regard to priority, the Court distinguished in *Gladstone* between "self-limiting" rights, such as Aboriginal food rights, and rights such as commercial rights, whose only limits were supply and demand. While the former could be given full priority over other interests, permitting exclusive use in some situations, the latter should be given a less stringent non-exclusive form of priority: para. 62. Factors relevant to this latter form of priority are: (i) evidence of participatory measures, such as reduced licence fees; (ii) priority in government regulatory objectives; (iii) resource use by rights holders relative to their percentage of the population; (iv) accommodation of different kinds of Aboriginal rights to a particular resource; (v) the relative importance of the resource to Aboriginal rights holders; and (vi) government's criteria for allocating licences between different users (*Gladstone*, para. 64).

129. *Delgamuukw*, *supra* note 22 at paras. 163, 166.

130. *Delgamuukw*, *supra* note 22 at para. 161, referring to *Gladstone*, para. 75. In referring to the situations mentioned in *Gladstone*, the Court continued its pragmatic approach to justification objectives — proceeding more by way of specific examples of legitimate objectives than under any general theoretical rubric.

131. In the Court's view, this requirement resulted from the element of choice in the content of Aboriginal title: para. 168.

132. The Court felt that this requirement resulted from the important economic aspect of Aboriginal title: para. 169.

133. The Court's approach to justification under s. 35(1) is more pragmatic than its approach to s. 1 of the *Charter*. Instead of purporting to apply a general framework for assessing proportionality, under the general rubric of the test in *R. v. Oakes*, [1986] 1 S.C.R. 103 at 138–39, the Court approaches s. 35(1) justification more by way of

specific examples of legitimate objectives and of required or possible consultation or accommodation.
134. See also **Chapter 12, Part 4**.
135. If courts recognize Aboriginal self-government as a distinct Aboriginal right under s. 35(1) of the *Constitution Act, 1982*, the definition they give it will be constitutionally entrenched.
136. In *Delgamuukw*, for example, it said far less about self-government than the lower court judges: see **Part 3(b)**, above.
137. *Delgamuukw*, *supra* note 22 at para. 170.
138. *Ibid.*
139. *R. v. Pamajewon*, [1996] 2 S.C.R. 821.
140. *Delgamuukw*, *supra* note 22 at para. 170.
141. Lamer C.J. pointed out that there are many different possible models, "each differing with respect to their conception of territory, citizenship, jurisdiction, internal government organization, etc.": *Delgamuukw*, *supra* note 22 at para. 170.
142. This seems to leave untouched the ruling of the majority of the Court of Appeal in *Delgamuukw* that no Aboriginal self-government with legislative powers superior to Parliament or the provincial legislatures survived the assertion of sovereignty: *Delgamuukw v. British Columbia* (1991), 104 D.L.R. (4th) 470 at 518–19, 591–93, and **Part 3(b)**, above. In *R. v. Ignace* (1998), 156 D.L.R. (4th) 713 (B.C.C.A.) rendered after the Supreme Court's decision in *Delgamuukw*, the British Columbia Court of Appeal reaffirmed this position, and said that nothing in the Supreme Court's decision casts doubt on it: paras. 10–11, They noted that the Court said in *Pamajewon* and *Delgamuukw* that self-government rights, if they exist, cannot be framed in excessively general terms: para. 11.
143. *Delgamuukw*, *supra* note 22 at para. 171.
144. See **Part (e)**, above.
145. Of course, if they were agreed to by governments and Aboriginal groups concerned, powers and structures of this kind could be constitutionally protected as s. 35(1) treaty rights. Cf. *Nisga'a Final Agreement*, August 4, 1998, chaps. 11 and 12.
146. See *Delgamuukw*, *supra* note 22 at para. 147.
147. *Ibid.*
148. *Delgamuukw*, *supra* note 22 at para. 159.
149. "[T]he right to choose to what uses land can be put [subject to the restriction against destroying the value of the land to the community]": *Delgamuukw*, *supra* note 22 at para. 129.
150. (The date of the enactment of s. 35(1)). See *R. v. Sparrow*, [1990] 1 S.C.R. 1075 at 1091–93.
151. (U.K.), 30 & 31 Vict., c. 3.
152. R.S.C. 1985, c. I-5, as am.
153. (U.K.), 30 & 31 Vict., c. 3.
154. *Delgamuukw*, *supra* note 22 at para. 174.
155. Section 109: All Lands, Mines, Minerals and Royalties belonging to the several Provinces of Canada ... at the Union ... shall belong to the several Provinces ... *subject to any Trusts existing in respect thereof, and to any Interest other than that of the Province in the same* (emphasis added).
156. *Delgamuukw*, *supra* note 22 at para. 176.
157. *Delgamuukw*, *supra* note 22 at para. 181, referring *inter alia*, to *Dick v. The Queen*, [1985] 2 S.C.R. 309 at 326 and 315.
158. *Delgamuukw*, *supra* note 22 at para. 178.
159. On interjurisdictional immunity, see P.W. Hogg, *Constitutional Law of Canada*, 2004 student ed. (Scarborough, Ont.: Carswell, 2004) in heading 15(8) (generally) and heading 27.2(c) (in regard to s. 91(24) of the *Constitution Act, 1867*).
160. *Delgamuukw*, *supra* note 22 at para. 178.
161. *Delgamuukw*, *supra* note 22 at para. 180. The requirement is from *R. v. Sparrow*, [1990] 1 S.C.R. 1075 at 1099.
162. *Supra* note 158.
163. *Delgamuukw*, *supra* note 22 at para. 181.
164. See also N. Bankes, "*Delgamuukw*, Division of Powers and Provincial Land and Resource Laws: Some Implications for Provincial Resource Rights" (1998) 32 U.B.C.L. Rev. 317; Kent McNeil, "Aboriginal Title and Section 88 of the *Indian Act*" (2000) 34 U.B.C. L. Rev. 159; and **Chapter 6, Parts 4** and **9**.
165. See *Dick v. The Queen*, [1985] 2 S.C.R. 309. Section 88 provides that: "Subject to the terms of any treaty and any other Act of Parliament, all laws of general application from time to time in force in any province are applicable to and in respect of Indians in the province, except to the extent that those laws are inconsistent with this Act or any order, rule, regulation, or by-law made thereunder, and except to the extent that those laws make provision for any matter for which provision is made by or under this Act." Note that some provincial laws may affect Aboriginal interests without affecting Indianness as well: *Kitkatla Band v. British Columbia (Minister of Small Business, Tourism and Culture)*, [2002] 2 S.C.R. 146 at paras. 75–78.
166. *Delgamuukw*, *supra* note 22 at para. 183.
167. *Supra* note 154.
168. *Delgamuukw*, *supra* note 22 at para. 183. In this context, "undermine" appears to refer to the word "extinguish" in the sentence above.
169. It is rather surprising, though, that Lamer C.J. rejected the province's referential incorporation argument by saying simply that s. 88 does not show the clear and plain intent required to extinguish Aboriginal rights. Since s. 88 is only a general enabling provision, arguably the relevant intention is not just that of s. 88, but also that of the provincial legislation seeking support from s. 88. Thus, because:
    (i) extinguishment of Aboriginal rights requires a clear and plain legislative intent to extinguish;
    (ii) provincial legislation with the intent of affecting the core area of s. 91(24) cannot be referentially incorporated by s. 88 (see *Dick v. The Queen*, [1985] 2 S.C.R. 309, where the Supreme Court held that the kind of provincial law that is "rescued" by s. 88 is a law of uniform territorial application whose effect *but not purpose or intent* is to impair Indianness); and
    (iii) Aboriginal rights are part of the core area of s. 91(24) of the *Constitution Act, 1867*, it follows that s. 88 cannot referentially incorporate provincial laws purporting to extinguish Aboriginal rights.
170. See *Delgamuukw*, *supra* note 22 at para. 174, referring to *St. Catherine's Milling and Lumber Co. v. The Queen* (1888), 14 A.C. 46 at 59 (J.C.P.C.). Note that the clear and plain intention requirement applies only to extinguishment. It would not prevent s. 88 from rescuing certain provincial laws of general application that infringe but do not extinguish Aboriginal rights. Of course, a provincial law rescued by s. 88 might still fail the justification test in *Sparrow*: see *R. v. Alphonse*, [1993] 5 W.W.R. 401 (B.C.C.A.).

    Whether there are other impediments to provincial extinguishment of Aboriginal rights or title is considered in **Chapter 6, Part 9**.
171. *Constitution Act, 1867* (U.K.). 30 & 31 Vict., c. 3, s. 91(24).
172. And now neither federal nor provincial laws enacted after April 17, 1982 can unilaterally extinguish Aboriginal rights. Cf. the "plenary but good faith" power of Congress to acquire American Indian lands: *Lone Wolf v. Hitchcock*, 187 U.S. 553 at 565 (1903), as modified by decisions such as *U.S. v. Sioux Nation of Indians*, 448 U.S. 371 (1980).

173. *Skeetchestn Indian Band v. British Columbia*, [2000] B.C.J. No. 177 (B.C. Prov. Ct.) concerned an Aboriginal title claim to 1,000 acres of land near Kamloops, B.C., known as the 6 Mile Ranch. The question was simply if Aboriginal title could be registered under the B.C. *Land Title Act*. The judge said no. However, the main action, yet to be resolved, involved the broader issue of the rival claims of Aboriginal title and provincially conferred fee simple title. The judge said that:

> [para45] The Supreme Court of Canada decision in *Delgamuukw* does not address the issue of registration of aboriginal title. Nor does it cast any light on the impact that aboriginal rights have on privately owned lands as opposed to Crown lands.... *Delgamuukw* does not say that this is so with respect to fee simple title. It suggests no mechanism for reconciling fee simple and aboriginal rights.
>
> [para46] This case pits aboriginal title against fee simple title. Most of the fee simple lands in this province are derived from Crown grants issued in an era when government knew less about their obligations to aboriginals than now. Many of these lands have been developed at substantial cost to their owners. Can this be ignored? Can aboriginal rights extend to fee simple lands? Is it possible to reconcile aboriginal title and fee simple title at this late stage? Should the fee simple title be declared null and void as requested by the Band or is the Band's claim reduced to a claim in damages if aboriginal rights were in fact wrongfully and irrevocably infringed by fee simple grants? These are only some of the questions that arise in this litigation.

174. *Mitchell v. Canada (Minister of National Revenue)*, [2001] 1 S.C.R. 911; rev'g. [1999] 1 F.C. 375 (F.C.A.); aff'g. in part [1997] 4 C.N.L.R. 103 (F.C.T.D.).
175. See *Francis v. The Queen*, [1956] S.C.R. 618, holding that the Jay Treaty is not an "Indian treaty" for the purposes of s.88 of the *Indian Act*.
176. *R. v. Vincent* (1993), 12 O.R. (3d) 427, leave to appeal to S.C.C. refused [1993] 3 S.C.R. ix.
177. [1997] 4 C.N.L.R. 103 (F.C.T.D.).
178. [1999] 1 F.C. 375 (F.C.A.).
179. *Mitchell*, *supra* note 174.
180. McLachlin C.J. for herself and Gonthier, Iacobucci, Arbour, and LeBel JJ.
181. Binnie J. for himself and Major JJ.
182. *Ibid.* at para. 57.
183. *Ibid.* at para. 16.
184. *Ibid.* at para. 15, referring to the following statement by Lamer C.J. in *R. v. Van der Peet*, [1996] S.C.R. 507 at para. 53: "To characterize an applicant's claim correctly, a court should consider such factors as the nature of the action which the applicant is claiming was done pursuant to an aboriginal right, the nature of the governmental regulation, statute or action being impugned, and the tradition, custom or practice being relied upon to establish the right."
185. In this regard, the factual context comprises the claimant's action in exercising the alleged Aboriginal right and government action in allegedly infringing it. The evidentiary context comprises the subject matter (not necessarily the veracity) of the claimant's evidence.
186. *Mitchell*, *supra* note 174 at para. 16.
187. *Ibid.* at para. 20. Ironically, this did not stop the majority from requiring that the Mohawk prove the existence of pre-contact trade with relatively specific trading partners, First Nations living to the north of the St. Lawrence River. In some cases, then, claimants may have to prove traditional practices that are more specific than their contemporary counterparts.
188. *Ibid.* at para. 22.
189. *Ibid.* at para. 21.
190. *Ibid.* at para. 20.
191. *Ibid.* at para. 15.
192. *Ibid.* at para. 30. Note how the notion of usefulness goes beyond that of necessity used in *Delgamuukw*.
193. *Ibid.* Even where evidence is otherwise admissible, courts have a discretion to exclude it if its probative value is outweighed by its prejudicial, misleading, or similarly negative effects: see *R.* v. *Jabarianha*, [2001] 3 S.C.R. 430 at para. 17.
194. *Ibid.* at para. 32.
195. *Ibid.* at para. 34.
196. *Ibid.* at para. 38.
197. *Ibid.* at para. 39.
198. *Ibid.* at para. 35.
199. *Ibid.* at para. 42.
200. *Mitchell* at para. 47.
201. *Ibid.* at para. 50.
202. *Ibid.* at para. 59.
203. *Ibid.* at para. 30.
204. *Ibid.* at para. 32, where McLachlin C.J. says that "[a]boriginal oral histories can offer evidence of ancestral practices and their significance that would not otherwise be available" and that "oral histories may provide the aboriginal perspective on the right claimed." It is hard to envisage a situation in which a claimant's oral Aboriginal history would *not* help supply the Aboriginal perspective.
205. *Ibid.* at para. 34.
206. See **Part 3(d)(iv)**, above.
207. *Ibid.* at para. 12. Although McLachlin C.J. said this requirement was "[s]tripped to its essentials", the "essentials" did not seem to include any connection to land. For a similar approach, see Binnie J. at para. 96.
208. *Ibid.* at para. 56.
209. McLachlin C.J. said although most general trade rights are more "free-ranging" than hunting and fishing rights, and "lack an inherent connection to a specific tract of land", the trade right in this case was just one aspect of a claimed right to cross an international boundary for trade: *ibid.* at paras. 56 and 57. Hence, the claimants must show that their traditional practices had a geographical connection to the specific land in question.

    A broader approach would require either a connection to a specific area of land or a general connection that required simply that the traditional activity involved the use of land or its resources. Traditional trade in natural resources, over a specified territory, would meet both of these requirements.
210. At para. 96, Binnie J. paraphrased the standard *Van der Peet* identification, without any reference to land. At para. 72, he seemed to distinguish between Aboriginal rights that relate to economic and cultural activity and those that are "land-based" interests.
211. *Ibid.* at para. 164. Does this imply that the traditional activities that receive s. 35(1) protection must be, or characteristically are, "rooted in the aboriginal peoples' prior occupation of the land"?
212. *Ibid.* at para. 69, where Binnie J. quoted from this observation by Létourneau J.A. in the Federal Court of Appeal. See also paras. 136, 137, and 161.
213. *Ibid.* at para. 64.
214. *Ibid.* at para. 63.
215. *Ibid.* at para. 10. See also para. 62.
216. *Ibid.* at para. 11.
217. *Ibid.* at para. 63.
218. *Ibid.* at para. 150.
219. See *R. v. Côté*, [1996] 3 S.C.R. 139 at paras. 50–54; and *R. v. Adams*, [1996] 3 S.C.R. 101 at para. 33.
220. Binnie J. went on to conclude that the international mobility / trading right claimed by Chief Mitchell was incom-

patible with the right of a sovereign state to control movement across its borders, and could not, therefore, constitute an Aboriginal right.

221. *Ibid.* at para. 164.
222. *R. v. Powley*, [2003] 2 S.C.R. 207 [*Powley*], aff'g. and dismissing cross-appeal from (2001), 53 O.R. (3d) 35, 196 D.L.R. (4th) 221 (C.A.), aff'g. (2000), 47 O.R. (3d) 30 (O.C.J.), aff'g. [1999] 1 C.N.L.R. 153, 58 C.R.R. (2d) 149 (O.C.P.D.).

   Powley can be compared with *R. v. Blais*, [2003] 2 S.C.R. 207, decided on the same day, where the Supreme Court held that the term "Indians" in para. 13 of the 1930 Manitoba *Natural Resources Transfer Agreement* does not include Métis people.
223. See *Powley*, para. 10, where the Supreme Court rejects the broader option.
224. Summarized briefly at paras. 10 and 11.
225. *R. v. Van der Peet*, [1996] 2 S.C.R. 507 at para. 44, and **Chapter 9, Part 3**.
226. See *Van der Peet*, *ibid.* at para. 67, where the Supreme Court recognized that changes might be needed to accommodate the special situation of the Métis.
227. *Powley*, para. 10.
228. Para. 12.
229. Para. 30.
230. Para. 19.
231. Para. 47.
232. Para. 48.
233. Para. 18.
234. Para. 37.
235. Para. 31.
236. Para. 33.
237. The Court did not address this question. Counsel had not made submissions on it, and the Court did not consider it necessary to decide the question in this case: para. 12.
238. Para. 32.
239. Decisions immediately after *Powley* suggested that the requirement of an association with an historic Métis community could prove to be a major hurdle to s. 35 Métis rights: see *R. v. Hopper*, [2004] N.B.J. No. 107 (Prov. Ct.); *R. v. Daigle*, [2004] NBQB 79. *R. c. Chiasson*, [2004] NBBR 80 (Q.B.).
240. Para. 49. It added that Métis community identification problems "must not be exaggerated as a basis for defeating their rights under the Constitution of Canada": *ibid.*
241. See also *R. v. Van der Peet*, [1996] 2 S.C.R. 507 at para. 53 and *Mitchell v. Canada (Minister of National Revenue*, [2001] 1 S.C.R. 911 at para. 16.
242. *R. v. Van der Peet*, *ibid.*
243. *R. v. Sparrow*, [1990] 1 S.C.R. 1075 at pp. 1111–12.
244. *Powley*, para. 47.
245. In the Sault Ste. Marie region, there was a tangible change of policy in the middle of the 19th century. At that time, the British government abandoned its traditional policy of discouraging white settlement in the area, and sent William B. Robinson to negotiate Indian treaties to help pave the way for resource development and the establishment of a development of a town at Sault Ste. Marie: para. 39.
246. **Chapter 9, Part 3**.
247. *Powley*, para. 31.
248. Cf. The options canvassed in **Chapter 9, Part 3(h)**.
249. Para. 17.
250. *Ibid.*
251. Para. 36: "While the fact of prior occupation grounds aboriginal rights claims for the Inuit and the Indians, the recognition of Métis rights in s. 35 is not reducible to the Métis' Indian ancestry."
252. Para. 17.
253. Para. 29.
254. *Haida Nation v. British Columbia (Minister of Forests*, 2004 SCC 73, dismissing an appeal by the Crown and allowing an appeal by Weyerhaeuser Co. from [2002] 6 W.W.R. 243 (B.C.C.A.) with supplementary reasons in (2002), 10 W.W.R. 587 (B.C.C.A.) rev'g. [2001] 2 C.N.L.R. 83 (B.C.S.C.). See also *Taku River Tlingit First Nation v. British Columbia (Project Assessment Director)*, 2004 SCC 74, released on November 18, 2004, the same day as *Haida Nation.* In *Taku River*, the Supreme Court held that the s. 35(1) duty to consult with and accommodate had been met, but that in this case the consultation / accommodation process was not yet complete.
255. *Ibid.*
256. *Haida Nation v. British Columbia (Minister of Forests* (2002), 10 W.W.R. 587 (B.C.C.A.) at para. 65.
257. Kelleher J. in *Haida Nation v. British Columbia (Minister of Forests*), [2001] 2 C.N.L.R. 83 (B.C.S.C.).
258. *Haida Nation v. British Columbia (Minister of Forests* (2002), 10 W.W.R. 587 (B.C.C.A.), Lambert J.A. for himself and Finch C.J. There were two sets of reasons by the British Columbia Court of Appeal in this case. In the first set, in [2002] 6 W.W.R. 243 (B.C.C.A.), issued on February 27, 2002, Lambert J.A., for himself, Finch C.J. and Low J.A., issued a declaration that both the provincial Crown and Weyerhaeuser had a fiduciary duty under s. 35(1) to consult the Haida and to accommodate their interests. The second set of reasons was in (2002), 10 W.W.R. 587 (issued by the Court of Appeal on August 19, 2002 in response to an argument by Weyerhaeuser that the Court of Appeal (a) could not have declared a private company to be subject to a fiduciary duty because the proceedings had been brought under a statute in which relief was limited to bodies that exercise statutory (not contractual) powers, and (b) should not have declared Weyerhaeuser to be subject to the duty. The majority of the Court of Appeal held that a more restricted version of their original application should be issued, in regard to both the province and Weyerhaeuser. In their view, this was only an interim declaration, and the governing statute permitted interim relief against bodies that exercise non-statutory powers. Low J.A. dissented on the ground that the statute permitted no relief against non-statutory bodies, and that, in any event, the question as to whether Weyerhaeuser was bound had not been raised in the pleadings.
259. McLachlin C.J. for a seven-judge court in *Haida Nation v. British Columbia (Minister of Forests*, 2004 SCC 73.
260. *Ibid.* at para. 18, referring to *Wewaykum Indian Band v. Canada,* [2002] 4 S.C.R. 245 at para. 79.
261. *Haida Nation*, *supra* note 256 at para. 18.
262. *Ibid.* at para. 16. The Court referred to the use of this concept in *R. v. Badger*, [1996] 1 S.C.R. 771 at para. 41 and *R. v. Marshall*, [1999] 3 S.C.R. 456. See also *R. v. Sparrow*, [1990] 1 S.C.R. 1075 at 1114–19; *R. v. Gladstone*, [1996] 2 S.C.R. 723 at para. 56; *Delgamuukw*, *supra* note 22 at para. 163; and **Chapter 8**.
263. *Haida Nation*, *ibid.* at paras. 18 and 19.
264. *Ibid.* at para. 18.
265. *Ibid.* at para. 20: "Section 35 represents a promise of rights recognition...."
266. *Ibid.* at para. 15.
267. *Ibid.* at para. 33.
268. *Haida Nation v. British Columbia (Minister of Forests* (2002), 10 W.W.R. 587 (B.C.C.A.) at para. 65.
269. *Haida Nation*, *supra* note 256 at para. 54.
270. The Court rejected the province's argument that s. 109 of the *Constitution Act, 1867* gave it the exclusive right to the land, pointing out that the s. 109 interest is subject to "any interest other than that of the Province in the same": *Ibid.* at para. 59.
271. *Ibid.* at para. 64.
272. *Ibid.* at para. 36.
273. *Ibid.* at para. 37.
274. *Ibid.*
275. *Ibid.* at para. 36.
276. *Ibid.* at para. 37.

277. For an example of a government consultation and accommodation regime, see *Provincial Policy for Consultation with First Nations*, October 2002.
278. One possible government approach would be to institute mass advance notice of proposed regulatory measures, on the pattern of the former *Federal Regulatory Plan* and the present Quebec *Regulations Act,* S.Q. 1986, c. 22. A well-publicized prepublication scheme might address the notice requirement for regulations, but could fall short of other consultation and accommodation requirements.
279. *Haida Nation*, *supra* note 256 at para. 11.
280. *Ibid.* at para. 51.
281. *Ibid.* at para. 37.
282. *Ibid.* at para. 44.
283. *Ibid.,* paras. 40 and 46. This substantive element was foreshadowed in *Delgamuukw*, where Lamer C.J. had said that s. 35(1) consultation always has a good faith element, and will normally be "significantly deeper than mere consultation": *Delgamuukw*, para. 168.
284. *Haida Nation*, *ibid.* at para. 47.
285. *Ibid.* at para. 42. Cf. *Nikal*, where Cory J. suggested that "the concept of reasonableness forms an integral part of the *Sparrow* test for justification": *R. v. Nikal*, [1996] 1 S.C.R. 1013 at para. 110.
286. *Haida Nation*, *ibid.* at para. 43.
287. *Ibid.* at para. 46.
288. *Ibid.* at paras. 43 and 46, respectively.
289. *Ibid.* at para. 48.
290. *Ibid.*
291. *Ibid.* at para. 40.
292. *Ibid.* at para. 46.
293. *Ibid.* at paras. 40 and 44.
294. *Ibid.* at para. 44.
295. *Ibid.* at paras. 40 and 44.
296. *Ibid.* at para. 44.
297. *Ibid.* at para. 64.
298. *Ibid.* at para. 46.
299. *R. v. Sparrow*, [1990] 1 S.C.R. 1075 at 1116.
300. *R. v. Gladstone*, [1996] 2 S.C.R. 723 at para. 75.
301. *Sparrow*, *supra* note 161.
302. See *Haida Nation*, *supra* note 256 at para. 46.
303. The Court said that the scope and the content of the consultation duty "will vary with the circumstances" *(Ibid.* at para. 40). When it referred (at para. 46) to "societal interests", it did not suggest that only some would be relevant. For a similar non-restrictive approach, see *Delgamuukw*, *supra* note 22 at paras. 166–69.
304. For example, an emergency conservation measure to counter a sudden wildlife threat would presumably require less elaborate consultation than routine measures. (*Quaere* whether certain kinds of high priority legislative objective — such as conservation — will normally need less consultation or accommodation than others?) Since consultation and accommodation levels are determined in the light of the individual circumstances, societal considerations — such as safety, public access, etc. — may be relevant to these levels even where they are not central to the legislative objective of the government action.
305. As well, because of the equitable basis of fiduciary duties, they would presumably be limited to situations where the constitutional s. 35(1) promissory duty failed to provide adequate relief.
306. *Haida Nation*, *supra* note 256 at para. 41.
307. For natural justice, see David W. Elliott, "Suresh and the Common Borders of Administrative Law: Time for the Tailor?" (2002) Sask. Law Rev. 469, 480–81. The rules of natural justice require that a party adversely affected by proposed government action should be given a prior opportunity to respond on its own behalf. The right may require one or more of a variety of procedural protections, depending on the circumstances. On the other hand, common law natural justice is presumed not to apply to "legislative" functions, while s. 35(1) infringements are often legislative in nature. As seen in that article, factor-balancing is applied to other areas of administrative and constitutional law as well.
308. Cf. *Baker v. Minister of Citizenship and Immigration*, [1999] 2 S.C.R. 817 at para. 20.
309. *Haida Nation*, *supra* note 256 at para. 47.
310. *Ibid.* at para. 48. It remains to be seen what combination of contextual factors will give rise to an Aboriginal veto.
311. See, for example, *Ocean Port Hotel v. British Columbia (General Manager, Liquor and Licensing Branch)*, [2001] 2 S.C.R. 781 at para. 22.
312. For example, the list of relevant contextual factors might be expanded to include the following:
    - (i) the strength of the Aboriginal claim (its content and extent, and the degree to which it has been proven or addressed by agreement);
    - (ii) the significance of the claimed interest to the Aboriginal peoples;
    - (iii) the risk and extent of the potential infringement of the claimed interest;
    - (iv) the risk of irreparable harm to the claimed interest;
    - (v) the extent to which government was aware or should have been aware, of the above factors;
    - (vi) the relative weight of the legislative objectives and other societal considerations;
    - (vii) the relevance of the infringement to these objectives and considerations; and
    - (vi) the capacity of a particular procedural and substantive measure to achieve a reasonable balance between the Aboriginal and societal interests.
313. *Calder v. British Columbia (A.G.)*, [1973] S.C.R. 313, **Chapter 4, Part 1**.
314. *R. v. Sparrow*, [1990] 1 S.C.R. 1075, **Chapter 7, Part 4**.
315. T. Suess Geisel, *The 500 Hats of Bartholomew Cubbins*, 1939.
316. *Guerin v. The Queen*, [1984] 2 S.C.R. 335 at 382: **Chapter 4, Part 4**; *Canadian Pacific Ltd. v. Paul*, [1988] 2 S.C.R. 654 at 678 (S.C.C.); *R. v. Sparrow*, [1990] 1 S.C.R. 1075 at 1108, 1112: **Chapter 7, Part 3**; *R. v. Badger*, [1996] 1 S.C.R. 771 at para. 78 (S.C.C.): **Chapter 5, Part 15**; *R. v. Van der Peet*, [1996] 2 S.C.R. 507: **Chapter 9, Part 3**; and *Delgamuukw v. British Columbia*, [1997] 3 S.C.R. 1010 at paras. 82 and 112: **Part 3**, above. Aboriginal rights are like treaty rights in this respect: *Simon* v. *The Queen*, [1985] 2 S.C.R. 387; *Badger*, *ibid.*
317. For comments on this question, see *R. v. Adams,* [1996] 3 S.C.R. 101 at para. 33: **Part 2**, above; and *Delgamuukw*, *ibid.*
318. *R. v. Nikal*, [1996] 1 S.C.R. 1013 at para. 95 (S.C.C.).
319. For example, in *R. v. Powley*, [2003] 2 S.C.R. 207 at para. 17, **Part 3**, above, the Supreme Court said that the relevant period for considering if Métis traditions were integral to their distinctive historical culture is after European contact and prior to the establishment of European control (not prior to European contact, as for other Aboriginal rights.) See also *Van der Peet*, *supra* note 225 at para. 67, **Chapter 9, Part 3**.
320. See *Baker Lake v. Canada (Minister of Indian and Northern Affairs)*, [1979] 1 F.C. 487 at 555–56 (F.C.T.D.).
321. *Calder et al.* v. *British Columbia (A.G.)*, [1973] S.C.R. 313: **Chapter 4, Part 1**; *Guerin v. The Queen*, [1984] 2 S.C.R. 335 at 378 (S.C.C.); *Delgamuukw v. British Columbia* (1993), 104 D.L.R. (4th) 470 at 493 (B.C.C.A.); *R. v. Pamajewon*; *R. v. Gardner* (1994), 21 O.R. (3d) 385 at 397 (O.C.A.); and *R. v. Van der Peet*, *supra* note 225 at para. 28.
322. See *R. v. Badger*, *supra* note 262 at para. 76.

323. See *Delgamuukw v. British Columbia* (1993), 104 D.L.R. (4th) 470 at 650–51 (B.C.C.A.: Lambert J.A., dissenting (not prescriptive)).
324. See *Calder v. British Columbia (A.G.)*, [1973] S.C.R. 313 at 351 (Hall J.: not prescriptive).
325. "[T]he tenure of the Indians was a personal and usufructuary right": *St. Catherine's Milling and Lumber Co. v. The Queen* (1888), 14 App. Cas. 46 at 54 (J.C.P.C.), **Chapter 3, Part 10**.
326. *Guerin v. The Queen*, [1984] 2 S.C.R. 335 at 378–89: **Chapter 4, Part 4**.
327. See *Amodu Tijani v. Southern Nigeria (Secretary)*, [1921] 2 A.C. 399 at 403 (J.C.P.C.: situation in part of colonial Africa); *Calder et al.* v. *British Columbia (A.G.)*, [1973] S.C.R. 313; *Guerin v. The Queen*, [1984] 2 S.C.R. 335 at 378–89 (S.C.C.); *Mabo v. State of Queensland (No. 2)* (1992) 107 A.L.R. 1 at 21–42 (H.C. Aust.), **Chapter 9, Part 2**); *Delgamuukw v. British Columbia* (1993), 104 D.L.R. (4th) 470 at 495, 565–71 (Wallace J.A.) and 640–43 (Lambert J.A., dissenting) (B.C.C.A.); and *Mitchell v. Canada (Minister of National Revenue*, [2001] 1 S.C.R. 911 at paras. 10 and 62 (main majority judgment) and 67 (separate majority judgment).
328. *R. v. Adams*, [1996] 3 S.C.R. 101 at para. 33, **Part 2**, above; and *R. v. Côté*, [1996] 3 S.C.R. 139 at paras. 46–53.
329. *Mitchell v. Canada (Minister of National Revenue*, [2001] 1 S.C.R. 911 at paras. 10 and 62 (main majority judgment, implying that the principle may apply to common law Aboriginal rights) and paras. 144 *et seq.* (separate majority judgment, asserting that the principle applies to both common law and s. 35(1) Aboriginal rights).
330. See *Mitchell*, *ibid.* where two majority judges held that sovereign incompatibility can apply to both common law and s. 35(1) Aboriginal rights (paras. 144 *et seq.*), while the main majority found it unnecessary to address the doctrine's applicability to s. 35(1) Aboriginal rights (para. 64).
331. In *Mitchell*, *ibid.*, the two separate majority judges said that a claimed right of trade and mobility across Canada's international boundary, on the basis of Aboriginal citizenship, was incompatible with Canadian sovereignty: para. 163. They said an extreme example of sovereign incompatibility would be the deployment of a private independent military force in Canada: para. 153.
332. *Guerin*, *supra* note 326 at 376. Nor are they necessarily precluded by a possible lack of formal government recognition: see *R. v. Côté*, *supra* note 328 at paras. 51–53 and *R. v. Adams*, *supra* note 328 at para. 33, **Part 2**, above.
333. *R. v. Adams*, *ibid.* at para. 33, and *R. v. Côté*, *ibid.* at paras. 46–53.
334. See *Calder v. British Columbia (A.G.)*, [1973] S.C.R. 313 at 322–23 (Judson J.: not a source of Aboriginal rights), 394–95 (Hall J.: supports the prior occupation source), in **Chapter 3, Part 9**, and *Delgamuukw*, *supra* note 22 at para. 114: not a source, but recognized Aboriginal title.
335. See **Chapter 3, Part 9**.
336. See *R. v. Adams*, [1993] 3 C.N.L.R. 98 at 131 (Q.C.A.).
337. *R. v. Van der Peet*, *supra* note 225 at para. 35, **Chapter 9, Part 3**; see also paras. 56 and 74. Similarly, at para. 30, Lamer C.J. said that Aboriginal rights are based on the fact that "when Europeans arrived in North America, aboriginal peoples were already here, living in communities on the land, and participating in distinctive cultures, as they had done for centuries." He went on to say that "[i]t is this fact, and this fact above all others, which separates aboriginal peoples from all other minority groups in Canadian society and which mandates their special legal, and now constitutional, status": *ibid.*, and see **Chapter 9, Part 3(b)**. See also *Delgamuukw*, *supra* note 22 at para. 114, referring to Aboriginal title.
338. (Or "occupation"): *ibid.* at paras. 30, 32, 41, 43, 49, 50.
339. For the reference to "use" as well as occupation, see *ibid.* at para. 76.
340. *Ibid.* at paras. 30, 31, 42, 43, 44, 60.
341. *Ibid.* at para. 30.
342. *Ibid.* at para. 31.
343. *Delgamuukw*, *supra* note 22 at para. 114.
344. See *ibid.* at para. 74.
345. *R. v. Van der Peet*, *supra* note 225 at paras. 33 and 74, **Chapter 9, Part 3**. See also *R. v. Côté*, [1996] 3 S.C.R. 139 at para. 125, **Part 2**, above and *Delgamuukw*, *supra* note 22 at para. 137, **Part 3**, above.
346. For example, oral histories and affidavits of declarations by deceased persons: *Delgamuukw*, *supra* note 22 at paras. 98–107.
347. At paras. 29–39 of *Mitchell*, *supra* note 174, McLachlin C.J. provided a more cautious restatement of the oral Aboriginal evidence discussion in *Delgamuukw*. At para. 39 of *Mitchell*, she stressed that "[t]here is a boundary that must not be crossed between a sensitive application and a complete abandonment of the rules of evidence." At para. 51. she said that "[s]parse, doubtful and equivocal evidence cannot serve as the foundation for a successful claim."
348. *R. v. Van der Peet*, note 225 at paras. 44 and 60, **Chapter 9, Part 3**.
349. *R. v. Powley*, [2003] 2 S.C.R. 207 at paras. 18 and 37, **Part 5**, above.
350. *R. v. Van der Peet*, *supra* note 225 at paras. 17, 36, and 67, **Chapter 9, Part 3**.
351. *Powley supra* note 349 at para. 24. Community membership is assessed by means of self-identification, evidence of an ancestral connection to the historic community, and acceptance by the contemporary community: *ibid.* at paras. 31–33.
352. *Delgamuukw*, *supra* note 22 at para. 138, saying that s. 35(1) Aboriginal rights "fall along a spectrum with respect to their degree of connection with the land." See also *R. v. Van der Peet*, *supra* note 225: **Chapter 9, Part 3**, and *R. v. Adams*, *supra* note 328 at para. 33, **Part 2**, above.
353. See *Mitchell*, *supra* note 174 at paras. 10, 61–64, and 111–73.
354. See *Delgamuukw v. British Columbia* (1993), 104 D.L.R. (4th) 470 at 520 (Macfarlane and Taggart JJ.A.), 591 (Wallace J.A.), 728 (Lambert J.A., dissenting), 761–64 (Hutcheon J.A.) (B.C.C.A.) and *Delgamuukw*, *supra* note 22 at paras. 170–71, **Part 3**; *R. v. Van der Peet*, *supra* note 225, **Chapter 9, Part 3**; and *R. v. Pamajewon* [*R. v. Jones*; *R. v. Gardner*], [1996] 2 S.C.R. 821, **Chapter 9, Part 5**, and **Chapter 12, Part 4**.
355. See the factors listed in *Van der Peet*, *supra* note 225 at para. 53, **Chapter 9, Part 3**, and considered in *Mitchell*, *supra* note 174, **Chapter 10, Part 4** (see also discussion of characterization in **Part 3(c)**, above). How broadly should these factors be construed? Which should prevail? Are the *Van der Peet* factors the only considerations affecting characterization?
356. *Van der Peet*, *supra* note 225 at para. 55: "central"; *R. v. N.T.C. Smokehouse Ltd.*, [1996] 2 S.C.R. 672 at para. 14: "a central, significant or defining feature of the distinctive cultures": *Mitchell*, *supra* note 174 at paras. 54 and 65: a "defining feature" of the traditional culture. In *Smokehouse,* the main criterion of significance was relative frequency — here the majority said the traditional exchange of fish was too infrequent to meet the test. L'Heureux-Dubé J., dissenting, disagreed. In *Van der Peet*, the majority said an integral practice must also be "independently significant": para. 70, **Chapter 9, Part 3**. See paras. 86–91, for an attempt to draw boundaries between "integral" and "incidental". Is the purpose of a practice relevant to whether it is integral? In *R. v. Gladstone*, [1996] 2 S.C.R. 723, La Forest J. disagreed with the majority, stressing that the purpose of the modern activity was dif-

ferent from that of the traditional activity, and was therefore not integral: paras. 95–96, **Chapter 9, Part 4**.

357. *Van der Peet*: "defining features" of a culture: *supra* note 225 at paras. 56 and 59. How are these identified? The majority in *Van der Peet* said distinctiveness excludes features common to all cultures (e.g., "eating to survive": para. 56) but does not require uniqueness (para. 71). Where should the line between the two be drawn? The majority in *Van der Peet* said the practices, customs and traditions must have existed prior to contact with the Europeans: para. 60, **Chapter 9, Part 4.** (L'Heureux-Dubé and McLachlin JJ., in separate dissenting reasons, considered this requirement too restrictive and proposed different alternatives: see paras. 178 and 246, respectively.)
358. *Ibid.* at paras. 64, 65, and 73. In *Van der Peet*, the majority considered it relevant that the salmon trade between the Stó:lo and the Hudson's Bay Company was significant to the Stó:lo "*primarily* as a result of European influences": para. 89 (emphasis added), **Chapter 9, Part 3**. See also *Delgamuukw*, *supra* note 22 at paras. 152–54.
359. *R. v. Van der Peet*, *supra* note 225 at paras. 17, 36, and 67: **Chapter 9, Part 3**.
360. Does occupation require continuous physical presence? Does it require the capacity to control activities in the area in question? Any presence in the area that is integral to the distinctive traditional culture? See Hon. Justice D.L. Lambert, "*Van der Peet* and *Delgamuukw*: Ten Unresolved Issues" (1998) 32 U.B.C. L. Rev. 249 at paras. 26–30.
361. *Delgamuukw*, *supra* note 22 at para. 158.
362. *Ibid.* at paras. 152–54.
363. *Delgamuukw*, *supra* note 22 at para. 138.
364. Beyond, for example, the requirement that they be "site-specific"? See *Delgamuukw*, *supra* note 22 at para. 138.
365. *R. v. Kruger*, [1978] 1 S.C.R. 104 at 109; *Delgamuukw v. British Columbia* (1993), 104 D.L.R. (4th) 470 at 493, 496 (B.C.C.A.); *R. v. Van der Peet*, *supra* note 225 at paras. 69, 71; *R. v. Gladstone*, *supra* note 127 at para. 65.
366. See *R. v. Van der Peet*, *supra* note 225; *R. v. Gladstone*, *supra* note 127: *R. v. Smokehouse*, [1996] 2 S.C.R. 672.
367. *Delgamuukw*, *supra* note 22 at paras. 117 and 127–32.
368. *Ibid.* at para. 129.
369. *Ibid.* at 130.
370. *Amodu Tijani v. Southern Nigeria (Secretary)*, [1921] 2 A.C. 399 at 403 (J.C.P.C.); *Calder v. British Columbia (A.G.)*, [1973] S.C.R. 313 at 351 (Hall J., referring to Indian title); *Sparrow*, *supra* note 22 at 1103 (S.C.C.).
371. *St. Catherine's Milling and Lumber Co. v. The Queen* (1888), 14 App. Cas. 46 at 54 (P.C.); *Smith v. The Queen*, [1983] 1 S.C.R. 554 at 568–69; *Delgamuukw v. British Columbia* (1993), 104 D.L.R. (4th) 470 at 495 (B.C.C.A.) and *Delgamuukw*, *supra* note 22 (S.C.C.) at paras. 129 and 131.
372. See **Chapter 8**.
373. *Sparrow*, *supra* note 26 at 1108 and 1112 (S.C.C.); *Pasco v. C.N.R. Co.* (1989), 56 D.L.R. (4th) 404 at 410 (B.C.C.A.); *Twinn v. Canada*, [1987] 2 F.C. 450 at 462 (F.C.T.D.): *Delgamuukw v. British Columbia* (1993), 104 D.L.R. (4th) 470 at 495 (B.C.C.A.) and *Delgamuukw* (S.C.C.) *supra* note 22 at para. 115.
374. See *Ontario (A.G.) v. Bear Island Foundation*, [1991] 2 S.C.R. 570 at 575. For Aboriginal title, the answer is "yes": *Delgamuukw*, *supra* note 22 at para. 158. Is this true of other Aboriginal rights as well?
375. *R. v. Sparrow*, *supra* note 26 at 1093.
376. *R. v. Van der Peet*, *supra* note 225 at paras. 54, 63–65, **Chapter 9, Part 3**.
377. *R. v. Badger*, *supra* note 262 at para. 77. Aboriginal rights are similar to treaty rights in regard to extinguishment.
378. *Sparrow*, *supra* note 26 at 1099; *R. v. Gladstone*, *supra* note 127 at para. 31.
379. Perhaps not, said the Court in *R. v. Gladstone*, *supra* note 127 at para. 34, **Chapter 9, Part 4**.
380. "... [The Crown] must demonstrate more than that, in the past, the exercise of an aboriginal right has been subject to a regulatory scheme": Gladstone, *ibid.* at para. 34. How much more? See the test suggested by Macfarlane J.A. in *Delgamuukw v. British Columbia* (1993), 104 D.L.R. (4th) 470 at 524 (B.C.C.A.).
381. *Delgamuukw*, *supra* note 22 at para. 175.
382. *R. v. Van der Peet*, [1996] 2 S.C.R. 507 at para. 28, **Chapter 9, Part 3**. Aboriginal rights are probably similar to treaty rights in this respect.
383. For the general test for infringement, see *R. v. Sparrow*, *supra* note 26 at 1075, 1111–12, **Chapter 7, Part 3**. For important post-*Sparrow* discussions of infringement, see *R. v. Badger*, *supra* note 262 at paras. 75–98; *R. v. Nikal*, [1996] 1 S.C.R. 1013 at para. 86–108; *R. v. Gladstone*, *supra* note 127 at paras. 39–53; and *R. v. Adams*, *supra* note 328 at paras. 52–55.
384. *Sparrow*, *ibid.* at 1111–12, **Chapter 7, Part 3**; *R. v. Gladstone*, *supra* note 127 at para. 39, **Chapter 9, Part 4**. This principle applies to either federal (see *Sparrow* and *Gladstone*) or otherwise valid provincial (*R. v. Badger*, *supra* note 262 at para. 91; *R. v. Côté*, *supra* note 328 at para. 74; and *Delgamuukw*, *supra* note 22 at para. 160) government action. It is said to apply to treaty rights as well as Aboriginal rights: *R. v. Badger*, *supra* note 262 at paras. 37, 77, 78, and 79; *R. v. Côté*, *supra* note 328 at para. 33.
385. *Sparrow*, *ibid.* at 1075, 1111–19 (S.C.C.) (Aboriginal rights); *R. v. Badger*, *supra* note 262 at para. 77 (treaty rights).
386. In *R. v. Gladstone*, *supra* note 127, the Court said it was the "cumulative effect" of the factors that matters: para. 52, but did not indicate if some factors are more important than others. See *R. v. Powley*, [2003] S.C.R. 207 at para. 47, according little importance to the factors, and emphasizing the fact of the restriction.
387. This includes either federal (*Sparrow*, *ibid.*) or otherwise valid provincial (see *R. v. Badger*, *supra* note 262 at para. 89 and **Chapter 6, Part 6**) government action. Aboriginal rights are similar to treaty rights in this respect: *Badger*.
388. *R. v. Badger*, *supra* note 262 at para. 89.
389. *R. v. Nikal*, [1996] 1 S.C.R. 1013 at paras. 91–96 (S.C.C.).
390. *Badger*, *supra* note 262 at paras. 89–99.
391. *Haida Nation v. British Columbia (Minister of Forests)*, 2004 SCC 73 at paras. 17–20 and para. 20, **Part 6**, above.
392. *Sparrow*, *supra* note 26 at 1113 (S.C.C.), **Chapter 7, Part 3**.
393. Under the general approach pioneered in *Sparrow,* courts were to ask if the Aboriginal interest was given priority over other interests; "whether there has been as little infringement as possible in order to effect the desired result; whether, in a situation of expropriation, fair compensation is available; and, whether the aboriginal group in question has been consulted with respect to the conservation measures being implemented": *R. v. Sparrow*, *supra* note 26 at 1113, 1116, and 1119, **Chapter 7, Part 3**. The Supreme Court has elaborated on this approach in later decisions, most notably *Delgamuukw v. British Columbia*, *supra* note 22, **Part 3**, above; and *Haida Nation*, *supra* note 391, **Part 6**, above. The individual consultation and accommodation components are described below.
394. "The paramount regulatory objective is the conservation of the resource.... The Minister's authority extends to other compelling and substantial public objectives that may include economic and regional fairness, and recognition of the historical reliance upon, and participation in, the fishery by non-aboriginal groups": *R. Marshall*, [1999] 3 S.C.R. 533 at paras. 40 and 41, respectively, **Chapter 5, Part 16**. See also *R. v. Sparrow, supra* note 26 at 1075, 1113; *R. v. Gladstone*, *supra* note 127 at paras. 54–75; *Delgamuukw v. British Columbia*, *supra* note 22 at

160–61. (Note that the requirement of a valid legislative objective and the other justification requirements apply to both Aboriginal and treaty rights: *R. v. Badger*, *supra* note 262 at paras. 75–98; *R. v. Côté*, *supra* note 328 at para. 33.)

395. *R. v. Sparrow, ibid.*, **Chapter 7, Part 3**.
396. *Haida Nation*, *supra* note 391 at para. 27, **Part 6**, above.
397. For this part of the justification test, the general concept of reasonableness is important: see *R.* v. *Badger*, *supra* note 262 at para. 73; *R. v. Nikal*, [1996] 1 S.C.R. 1013 at paras. 91–96, 109–10.
398. *Haida Nation*, *supra* note 391 at para. 27, **Part 6**, above. Cf. *Sparrow*, *supra* note 26 at 1113–19, **Chapter 7, Part 3**, emphasizing consistency with the Crown's fiduciary duty to Aboriginal peoples. *Haida Nation* clarified that the s. 35(1) consultation and accommodation duty is not itself fiduciary, but shares the underlying Crown honour concept with the Crown's special fiduciary duty to Aboriginal peoples: paras. 16–20 and 54.
399. *Haida Nation*, *ibid.* at paras. 43–44.
400. *Ibid.* at paras. 40–42.
401. *Ibid.* at paras. 46–49; and *Sparrow*, *supra* note 26 at 1113. See also *Delgamuukw*, *supra* note 22 at paras. 165–69, saying, *inter alia*, that justification for infringement of Aboriginal title always requires consultation in good faith, ordinarily requires fair compensation, and may require other measures such as reduced licensing fees for using lands.
402. *Haida Nation*, *ibid.* at para. 48.
403. I.e., ensuring that the Aboriginal use is exercised fully before other uses are permitted.
404. See *R. v. Gladstone*, *supra* note 127 at para. 58, **Chapter 9, Part 4**, distinguishing between rights such as subsistence food rights that are internal in the sense that they have finite and ascertainable limits, and commercial rights that have no such limits.
405. I.e., ensuring that the Aboriginal use is exercised fully before other uses are permitted.
406. See *Gladstone*, *ibid.* at para. 64 and (in the context of Aboriginal title *Delgamuukw* (S.C.C.)) *supra* note 22 at para. 167.
407. See *R. v. Gladstone*, *supra* note 127 at para. 64; and (in the context of Aboriginal title) *Delgamuukw*, *supra* note 22 at para. 167. So far, the Court has approached this question by offering examples of qualified priority: *ibid.* In *Gladstone*, *ibid.*, the Court referred to this as "something less than exclusivity ... which nevertheless gives priority to the aboriginal right": para. 63. The Court conceded that the content of this priority "must remain somewhat vague pending consideration of the government's actions in specific cases": *ibid.*
408. *Haida Nation*, *ibid.* at paras. 40–45.
409. *Guerin v. The Queen*, [1984] 2 S.C.R. 335 at 384. Aboriginal rights are probably similar to treaty rights in this respect: see *Ontario (A.G.) v. Bear Island Foundation*, [1991] 2 S.C.R. 570 at 575 (*obiter*: treaty). See further *Haida Nation*, *ibid.* at paras. 18 and 54, **Part 6**, above. See further, **Chapter 8**.
410. *Haida Nation*, *ibid.* at para. 18
411. *Sparrow*, *supra* note 26 at 1114–19, **Chapter 7, Part 3**; and *Delgamuukw*, *supra* note 22 at para. 162, **Chapter 10, Part 3**. See further, **Chapter 8**.

11 Aboriginal Claims

Chapter Highlights

- The federal government recognizes two main categories of Aboriginal claims — comprehensive claims based on continuing Aboriginal rights and title to land and resources, and specific claims relating to obligations that arise from treaties, statutes, or the administration of Indian assets. As well, other claims may be accepted on a discretionary basis.
- The federal government and Aboriginal claimants generally follow a negotiation approach to resolving Aboriginal claims.
- Nearly twenty comprehensive land claims agreements have been concluded in Canada to date. These are highly complex documents, both in their negotiation processes and their content, and can vary significantly in both respects.
- The number of settlements is small in comparison with the overall number of cases. Some claims, such as those at Oka, do not fit the comprehensive / specific categories.

Synopsis

Negotiation is not the only possible approach to dealing with Aboriginal claims. Other possible alternatives include resolution by courts, adjudication before a quasi-judicial tribunal, arbitration, and representations before a legislative body. The negotiation approach has a number of distinct advantages, however. It permits consideration of a wide range of issues, participation by the Aboriginal groups most closely involved, ratification by elected officials, and constitutional entrenchment of guarantees. Negotiation is the most common approach in Canada today, although its practical application has been marked by problems and controversy. For all claims, for example, the pace of settlement has been disappointingly slow. In this regard, it may be useful to consider factors that appear to have affected the speed of the negotiation process in individual cases. The completed land claims agreements are massive arrangements that can extend to hundreds of pages. Because of their significance for beneficiaries and non-beneficiaries alike, and their permanent constitutional status, they are worth examining in some detail.

Selected Readings

🖹 links material in this chapter to the corresponding headings and page numbers of the relevant readings.

🖹 Parts 3(e), 4, 5, 6	Federal Policy for the Settlement of Native Claims	382
🖹 Part 5	Map of Comprehensive Land Claims in British Columbia	382
🖹 Part 7	Land Provisions of Modern Treaties	391
	Land Claims Agreement Dispute Resolution	408
🖹 Part 7(f)	*Vuntut Gwitchin First Nation Self-Government Agreement*	419
🖹 Part 7(h)	*Nisga'a Final Agreement in Brief*	398
🖹 Part 7(k)	*Sechelt Agreement-in-Principle*	404

1. GENERAL QUESTIONS

This chapter addresses five main questions: (a) What are Aboriginal claims? (b) What are some of the main alternative approaches for dealing with Aboriginal title or comprehensive claims? (c) Why have some comprehensive claims been settled, and others not? (d) What are some of the main land claims agreements to date? (e) What is the future of the Aboriginal comprehensive claims process? The chapter also looks briefly at specific claims involving unfulfilled government commitments, and at one of the oldest unresolved claims — the claim of the Mohawk people at Oka.

2. WHAT ARE ABORIGINAL CLAIMS?

Aboriginal claims are claims made by Aboriginal people. The federal government recognizes two main categories of Aboriginal claims — comprehensive and specific claims.[1] Comprehensive claims are claims based on continuing Aboriginal rights and title to land and resources.[2] Specific claims relate to the fulfilment of lawful obligations arising from Aboriginal treaties, statutes, or the administration of Indian assets.[3] As well, the federal government may accept certain other kinds of claim on a discretionary basis, on the ground that they meet the spirit, if not the letter, of the specific and comprehensive claims policies.[4]

Both comprehensive and specific claims can have important constitutional aspects. They may involve Aboriginal constitutional concerns, and can be addressed in treaties and land claims agreements that receive protection under s. 35(1) of the *Constitution Act, 1982*. This chapter focuses on claims based primarily on Aboriginal title and pursued in the federal government's comprehensive claims forum.[5] Claims and agreements addressed primarily in the constitutional arena, such as those leading to the Charlottetown accord, are considered in **Chapter 11**.

3. ALTERNATIVE APPROACHES

(a) Courts

Generally, the courts have been a slow, expensive, and uncertain means of dealing with Aboriginal title claims. The *Tlingit-Haida* litigation in Alaska[6] took more than thirty-three years to resolve; the Calder case, four years to decide; *Sparrow* took six; and *Delgamuukw* took more than ten.[7] and there may yet be a decision from the Supreme Court of Canada. The judicial forum is a winner-loser forum, with limited facilities for designing multiparty compromises. It is expensive, and almost always requires legal representation. It is riddled with technical obstacles, such as standing requirements, evidentiary restrictions, and time limitations. Canadian judges are not directly accountable to the government, to the general public, or to Aboriginal groups. A judicial solution is imposed on the parties from above.

(b) Quasi-Judicial Tribunal

One alternative to the court process is a quasi-judicial tribunal with expertise in the area of claims. One such tribunal was the Indian Claims Commission that operated in the United States from 1946 to 1978. However, the experience with the Commission was a disappointment. Its procedures rapidly became as adjudicatory, formal and limited as those of ordinary courts. It ended with a huge backlog of unfinished business.[8] One observer estimated that through litigation expenses, the Commission cost the United States $1.2 billion in order to dispense $1 billion in compensation.[9] A quasi-judicial tribunal can have some independence of government, depending on its structure. On the other hand, governments may be reluctant to voluntarily entrust decisions involving large public expenditures to a body beyond their control.[10] Like courts, a quasi-judicial tribunal imposes solutions from above, rather than permitting the parties themselves to build them.

(c) Arbitration

An individual arbitrator may permit greater flexibility than a court or court-like tribunal, while retaining some of their impartiality. As with judicial bodies, though, governments may be reluctant to lose control of a wide variety of issues involving large expenditures and broad public interests. For example, although the federal government often appoints land claims negotiators from outside the public service, the process is not arbitration, as the negotiators follow federal instructions, and their decisions can be overruled. A variation on the arbitrator model would be an independent body or inquiry that would recommend agreements to the federal government rather than making binding decisions on its own.

(d) Representations before a Legislative Body

The *Alaska Native Claims Settlement Act*[11] was the result of successive draft settlement bills to Congressional committees by the federal American government and the Alaska Federation of Natives. A comparable Canadian approach would involve consideration of Aboriginal and government proposals by a Parliamentary committee. This approach presupposes concrete settlement proposals and a high level of consensus on key issues. In the Canadian context, it also assumes that a legislative committee's recommendations will be accepted by the government in power.

(e) Negotiations

Reading 11(b) at p. 382

In the negotiation approach, representatives of an Aboriginal claimant group and government(s) enter into bargaining discussions aimed at securing agreements acceptable to both. Negotiations are more flexible than judicial or quasi-judicial approaches. They involve claimants and governments directly. They result in consensual rather than imposed solutions.[12] These features help explain why the negotiation approach is the federal government's preferred approach to Aboriginal claims today.

Recently, the Supreme Court has said that in some circumstances government may have a general constitutional obligation to pursue treaty negotiations. In *Haida Nation*, it said that:

> Where treaties remain to be concluded, the honour of the Crown requires negotiations leading to a just settlement of Aboriginal claims: *R. v. Sparrow*, [1990] 1 S.C.R. 1075, at pp. 1105-6. Treaties serve to reconcile pre-existing Aboriginal sovereignty with assumed Crown sovereignty, and to define Aboriginal rights guaranteed by s. 35 of the *Constitution Act, 1982*. Section 35 represents a promise of rights recognition, and "[i]t is always assumed that the Crown intends to fulfil its promises" (*Badger, supra*, at para. 41). This promise is realized and sovereignty claims reconciled through the process of honourable negotiation.[13]

Presumably this duty requires good faith negotiations similar to those envisaged by the Court in the 1998 *Quebec Secession Reference*.[14]

4. CLAIMS PROCESS

Reading 11(b) at p. 382

(a) Procedure

Although the federal government's claims negotiation process has since undergone several changes, the general procedure[15] is as follows. First, an Aboriginal claimant group must establish the validity of its claim. For a comprehensive claim, claimants must provide evidence of traditional and continuing use and occupancy of land, not dealt with by treaty or eliminated by other lawful means.[16] For a specific claim, they must normally show a breach of one of a number of recognized kinds of lawful obligation under treaty or other government action.[17]

If a claim is accepted, the claimants and the government attempt to negotiate rights and benefits to address the claimed Aboriginal title or compensation for the unfulfilled obligation. Comprehensive claims are normally preceded by preliminary framework agreements to set the parameters of the discussions. If negotiations are successful, they will lead first to agreements-in-principle and then to final agreements that are signed, ratified, and then implemented. Except where it provides to the contrary, a completed final agreement is constitutionally entrenched as an existing treaty right by s. 35(1) of the *Constitution Act, 1982*.

(b) Development

Although individual situations varied, there was very limited room for negotiation in most of the old treaties. The Indians were at a bargaining disadvantage, and the government tended to follow a standard form.[18] After the last of the numbered treaties and two follow-up treaties in southern Ontario in 1923,[19] even this limited negotiation approach fell into relative disuse. Between 1927[20] and 1951,[21] federal legislation prohibited raising money or hiring counsel for Aboriginal claims without express government consent.[22]

In 1969, the federal government's "White Paper"[23] on Indian policy dismissed Aboriginal claims based on Aboriginal title as being too "general and undefined" to be regarded as specific claims capable of specific remedies. However, the paper did say government should recognize Indian claims based on "lawful obligations". It recommended the creation of an Indian Claims Commission to address this kind of claims. Although the

Claims Commission approach lasted only a short while,[24] the government continued to recognize specific claims based on lawful obligations.

Then, in January 1973, the Supreme Court indicated in *Calder* that Aboriginal title might be cognizable at common law.[25] In August of that year, the federal government announced a new policy. After reaffirming its commitment to address specific claims based on lawful obligations, the government said it would negotiate comprehensive claims based on unextinguished Aboriginal title. The following year, it established an Office of Native Claims to deal with both kinds of claims through negotiations.

The federal government elaborated its comprehensive claims policy more formally in 1981.[26] That policy statement stressed the importance of the finality of land claims settlement.[27] It called for rights and benefits in exchange for the extinguishment of Aboriginal title claims.[28] Its emphasis was on lands, wildlife rights, and monetary compensation. It also contemplated subsurface rights, corporate structures, taxation immunities, and programs.[29] It opposed non-finite financial grants and discouraged "new indeterminate programs geared solely to Natives."[30]

By 1985, though, only three comprehensive claims had been resolved. Negotiations in the Yukon were stalled after Yukon Indians had rejected the most recent proposed package. Aboriginal groups were criticizing the claims process. A federal task force recommended:

(i) permitting alternatives to extinguishment;
(ii) continuing *Indian Act* status where Aboriginal claimants desired this;
(iii) negotiating subsurface resource rights where desired;
(iv) permitting the negotiation of self-government provisions in the agreements; and
(v) taking a more graduated approach to the negotiation process, including the greater use of early "framework" agreements.[31]

Most of these recommendations were accepted.[32]

However, the federal government did continue to include extinguishment provisions in most proposed agreements. The 1995 Hamilton Report[33] condemned this practice, as did the Royal Commission on Aboriginal Peoples in a 1995 interim report[34] and in its final report in 1996.[35] Another Aboriginal concern was the lack of independence of the federal government.[36] Its position as negotiator and arbiter gave it the appearance of a judge in its own cause. In its 1993 Red Book on policy, the Liberal Party of Canada said it would develop a more independent claims process. In 1996 the Royal Commission on Aboriginal Peoples charged that the federal government had an unduly restrictive approach to land and treaty claims,[37] and recommended the creation of an independent treaty tribunal to oversee land claims and self-government treaty negotiations and to rule on specific claims.[38]

Federal policy involved a regional innovation in British Columbia, where most of the province is subject to Aboriginal claims. In 1993, the federal government, the provincial government, and the First Nations of the province established a tripartite independent British Columbia Treaty Commission to facilitate and co-ordinate the negotiation process in the province.[39]

Meanwhile, the federal government outlined a formal specific claims policy in 1982.[40] It said that by "lawful obligation" it meant "[n]on-fulfilment of a treaty or agreement between Indians and the Crown"; "[a] breach of an obligation arising out of the *Indian Act* or other statutes pertaining to Indians and regulations thereunder"; "[a] breach of an obligation arising out of government administration of Indian funds or other assets"; and "[a]n illegal disposition of Indian land."[41] It added that it was also willing to go "beyond lawful obligation" to address lack of uncompensated federal acquisition of or harm to reserve land, or clear cases of fraud by federal officials acquiring or disposing of this land. Critics have argued that this process leaves out many kinds of claim, such as wildlife rights and self-government,[42] or treaty claims based on grounds such as duress or mistake, and leaves the federal government as a judge in its own cause.[43]

In 1991, the federal government created an independent Indian Specific Claims Commission with authority to report on the validity of a specific claim rejected by government and on compensation criteria in cases of disagreement between government and claimants.[44] These powers were only advisory, though, and there has been little positive government response to Commission reports.[45] On June 27, 1996, the five specific claims commissioners submitted a joint letter calling for an end to the Commission.[46] They said their work had been seriously undermined by lack of government response, and recommended that the Commission be replaced by a decision-making body.[47]

Legislation to restructure the specific claims process was finally enacted in December, 2003.[48] A new Canadian Centre for the Independent Resolution of First Nations Specific Claims is to be created to deal with claims to compensation arising from the result of government treaty, legislative, or administrative obligations. A Commission would help First Nations with research and dispute resolution efforts, while a Tribunal could decide on unresolved questions of validity and compensation. In the first instance, the Commission is to assist a First Nation to negotiate its claim with the Minister of Indian Affairs and Northern Development.[49] If the Minister refuses to enter negotiations, the Commission must try to facilitate resolution, by means of "any appropriate dispute resolution process."[50] If this is unsuccessful, the Commission can refer the issue to the Tribunal.[51] A similar process applies to unresolved issues of compensation.[52] The Tribunal is to operate at arms' length from the Commission, with adjudicators who hold office during good behaviour for terms of three to five years, with a possibility of renewal.[53] The Tribunal's procedure is to be quasi-judicial,[54] and its decisions are to be final, apart from the possibility of judicial review.[55] Until this new process is started,[56] the old Indian Claims Commission continues to function.

Although the new process does not address comprehensive and self-government claims, it is arguable that their more open-ended policy content requires a more direct governmental role. For specific claims, where the issues are narrower, and tend to focus on accountability and compensation, greater independence and finality seem both feasible and desirable. In this context, can government ensure adequate independence by hiring adjudicators for renewable terms of only three to five years?

5. MAJOR COMPREHENSIVE CLAIMS AGREEMENTS AND NEGOTIATIONS

🖹 Readings 11(a) and 11(b) at p. 382

The first modern land claims settlement in North America was the 1971 *Alaska Native Claims Settlement Act*,[57] affecting 80,000 Alaska natives. In Canada, the main agreements concluded to date are as follows:

1. The *James Bay and Northern Quebec Agreement*,[58] signed in 1975 with 6,500[59] James Bay Cree and 4,200 northern Quebec Inuit.
2. The *Northeastern Quebec Agreement*,[60] signed in 1978 with 465 Quebec Naskapi of the Naskapi Band of Schefferville.
3. The *Western Arctic (Inuvialuit) Agreement*,[61] signed in 1984 with 2,500 Inuvialuit in the western Arctic.
4. The *Gwich'in Agreement*,[62] signed in 1992 with 2,200 Gwich'in in the northwestern Northwest Territories.
5. The *Nunavut Agreement*,[63] signed in 1993 with 17,500 Inuit of the northeastern Northwest Territories.
6. The *Vuntut Gwitchin*, *Champagne and Aishihik*, *Teslin Tlingit*, and *Na-cho Ny'a'k Dun* agreements,[64] signed in 1993 with a total of about 2,500 Yukon Indians in four Yukon Indian First Nations. These were followed by the *Little Salmon-Carmacks* and *Selkirk* agreements in 1997 (over 500 beneficiaries each), the *Trondëk Hwëch'in Agreement* of 1998 (over 700 beneficiaries), *the Ta'an Kwäch'än Council Agreement of 2002* (over 400 beneficiaries), the *Kluane Agreement* of 2003 (over 100 beneficiaries), and the *Kwanlin Dün Agreement* of 2004 (over 900 beneficiaries).
7. The *Sahtu Dene and Metis Agreement*,[65] signed in 1994 with 2,400 Dene and Metis in the western Northwest Territories.
8. The *Nisga'a Final Agreement*[66] signed in 1998 with 5,800 Nisga'a of northwestern British Columbia.
9. The *Tlicho Agreement,*[67] signed in 2003 with 3,000 Dogrib people of southwestern N.W.T.
10. The *Labrador Inuit Agreement,*[68] signed in 2005 with 5,000 Inuit and native settlers of northern Labrador.

As well, over fifty other comprehensive claims are being negotiated in British Columbia within the framework of a special B.C. Treaty Commission process established in 1993. As seen in **Part 7(k)** below, an Agreement-in-Principle was initialled in 1999 with the 900 Sechelt people north of Vancouver, but in May 2000 the negotiations stalled. By early 2005, agreements in principle had been signed with the Maa-nulth First Nations on Vancouver Island, the Lheidli T'enneh band of the Prince George region, the Sliammon Indian Band of the Powell River area and the Tsawwassen First Nation south of Vancouver.[69] Elsewhere, there are discussions with the Deh Cho of southwestern N.W.T., the Conseil des Atikamekw et des Montagnais north of the St. Lawrence River in Quebec, the Innu Nation of Labrador, and the northern Quebec Inuit in regard to the offshore area adjacent to northern Quebec and Labrador.

6. FACTORS INFLUENCING SETTLEMENT OF COMPREHENSIVE CLAIMS

Reading 11(b) at p. 382

Apart from the recent *Tlicho* and *Labrador Inuit* agreements, the completed land claims agreements referred to above have all been signed and ratified in legislation.[70] Negotiations on the *James Bay and Northern Quebec Agreement* took two years to complete. The *Inuvialuit Agreement* was negotiated in seven years. In contrast, the Yukon claim took over twenty years to produce final agreements, and this has happened in only ten of fourteen areas of the original claim. Other claims are in varying states of progress, impasse, or delay.

Why have land claims negotiations produced agreements in some cases, but not in others? Why has the process been so slow, especially in some cases? Although every land claims situation is unique, it may be possible to isolate a few relevant factors. In considering these, it is important to keep in mind that a land claims agreement that is readily reached is not necessarily a successful agreement over the longer term.

(a) Issues

One factor is the distance between the parties on the issues. In the negotiations leading to the 1971 *Alaska Native Claims Settlement Act*,[71] lack of wide differences on the issues between the Alaska natives and government representatives helped ensure agreement after a relatively short discussion period. Conversely, in the early years of the Dene / Metis claim, progress was hampered by the wide gap between the concept of a separate native state in the 1976 Dene Declaration and the federal government's unequivocal rejection of this concept. The November 1990 Dene / Metis Agreement-in-Principle fell apart in July 1991 partly because of the reluctance of three of the five regions to give up Aboriginal and treaty rights in exchange for the benefits of the land claims agreement. Similarly, differences on the issue of extinguishment helped prevent agreement on the 1984 Yukon Agreement-in-Principle.

The 1985 Coolican *Task Force to Review Comprehensive Claims Policy* blamed much of the lack of progress in claims negotiations on the federal government. As seen,[72] two of the Task Force's concerns were

(i) "the insistence of the federal government on finality and on the blanket extinguishment of all Aboriginal rights"[73]; and
(ii) government's "refusal to include political rights, decision-making power on land and resources management boards, [and revenue-sharing and offshore rights] in the negotiations."[74]

The federal government's 1986 *Comprehensive Land Claims Policy*[75] followed Coolican's suggestions and adopted a more flexible, more expansive approach.[76]

Despite the policy shift, differences over extinguishment continued to present obstacles. For example, the final agreement concluded by the Inuit of the Eastern Arctic[77] was opposed by some southern Aboriginal representatives because of the precedent it was thought to set for other parts of the country. Moreover, the negotiation process continued at a glacial pace. To try to speed it up, the Prime Minister announced in September 1990 that the federal government would no longer limit itself to negotiating six claims at one time.[78] The years 1992 and 1993 finally brought some apparent results. Seven land claims agreements were concluded, although six of these were with fragments of groups whose negotiations had failed on a more global basis.

A key issue today is Aboriginal self-government.[79] Although the Coolican report advocated including "political" rights in land claims negotiations, it was not clear as to just how negotiators should balance Aboriginal desires for Aboriginal self-government with traditional notions of public government.

Clearly, Aboriginal needs may vary greatly in different regions, and in agreements so far a wide variety of possible approaches is emerging. In the south, for example, municipal / regional-type Aboriginal self-government on the Sechelt and Nisga'a patterns provide two possible models[80]; in the James Bay region[81] and much of the north,[82] agreements include guaranteed Aboriginal participation in public government bodies with power to advise or to make reviewable decisions. Agreements in the Yukon involve both guaranteed participation[83] *and* special municipal / territorial powers[84] with varying degrees of paramountcy over laws of general application.

Philosophically, each of these approaches requires a balancing of basic goals. They must try to reconcile traditional public government concepts based on residency and majority rule with ethnic government provisions based on race and special minority rights. They must address difficult practical questions, such as "Which laws prevail where?" and "What impact will proposed schemes have on affected beneficiaries and their neighbours?" Even "public" government proposals may require extensive political change. For example, the *Nunavut Agreement* was accompanied by a political accord to establish a new territory in which Inuit beneficiaries will form a majority. This political change required extensive consultation to secure agreement on the division of the Northwest Territories.[85]

(b) Parties

The degree of unity or disunity among claimant groups and between government parties can be a relevant factor. In the Dene / Metis claim, progress was slowed by lack of agreement between the Dene and the Metis, and between the two northern regions on one hand and those of the south on the other. For their part, the Dene / Metis people have had concerns about the location of the proposed territory of Nunavut, a key element of the Eastern Arctic claim. In the *James Bay and Northern Quebec Agreement*, though, the Northern Quebec Inuit and James Bay Cree maintained a consistent united front. In the Yukon, consensus was sometimes stronger between Indian and Métis than between individual bands.

Until recently, land claims talks in British Columbia were stalled by disagreements between the federal and provincial governments, especially regarding the latter's role in the process. In Quebec, things got off to a slow start until Mr. Justice Malouf's judgment in *Kanatewat*[86] helped persuade Quebec to enter the negotiations. In the Yukon, claims negotiations had to be considered in the context of territorial aspirations for constitutional development. In contrast, intergovernmental tensions were largely absent in Alaska, where statehood had already been achieved and where control of natural resources remained with the federal government.

A succession of different parties can also slow negotiations. Over a period of three decades, the Yukon claim had countless changes of federal negotiators. Especially in the earlier years, this generally required starting all over again.

(c) Non-Beneficiaries

Resolution of claims can be complicated by the impact of claims on third party non-beneficiaries. The greater the proximity of the non-beneficiaries, the greater the complications. Land claims settlements diminish non-beneficiary access to land and use of natural resources. Unless they are carefully planned and perceived as fair, special benefits can result in disruption and resentment among ineligible neighbours.

Proximity to reluctant or concerned non-beneficiaries was a significant factor in the Yukon claim. Concerns about the potential impact of a settlement slowed negotiation in the early years, and must still be taken into account. In resource-dependent British Columbia, claims negotiations arouse special opposition among non-beneficiary forestry and fisheries interests. A good example of a group pressing non-beneficiary concerns (unsuccessfully) in court is the *Fishermen's Alliance* case.[87]

Overlap between two or more Aboriginal claims is also a potentially important factor. It was one of the relatively few factors that slowed the Inuvialuit (C.O.P.E.) negotiations. It complicates progress in Northern Quebec and Labrador, where there are claims by the Naskapi-Montagnais Innu Association, and the Conseil des Atikamekw et des Montagnais, and an agreement with the Labrador Inuit Association. It is a major challenge there and in British Columbia, where many of the dozens of claims overlap.

(d) Development

Major economic development can play a big role in accelerating negotiations. The *Alaska Native Claims Settlement Act* was prompted by the discovery of massive reserves of oil in the Prudhoe Bay area of northern Alaska and proposals to construct an oil pipeline from northern to southern Alaska. The James Bay Hydro development gave the Quebec government incentive to negotiate the *James Bay and Northern Quebec Agreement* and to complete the *Northeastern Quebec Agreement*. The discovery of natural gas in the Beaufort sea sped up the Inuvialuit claim negotiations. In 1977, a Canadian-American agreement to build a natural gas pipeline quickened the pace of Yukon land claims negotiations; when it became clear that the pipeline would not be built, the pace slowed accordingly. It is ironic and unfortunate that land claims negotiations about the natural resources of a region are often hastened by a phenomenon that has the potential to destroy them.

(e) Other Forums

The judicial forum can have both an accelerating or slowing effect on the pace of land claim negotiations. In Alaska, the great length of the *Tlingit* litigation[88] illustrated the snail-like pace of the court route, and encouraged all parties to seek an expeditious negotiated settlement out-of-court. In British Columbia, although the Supreme Court of Canada's mixed but partly positive response to the Nisga'a's claim[89] encouraged the federal government to adopt a positive approach to negotiating Aboriginal claims, the decision did little to speed the negotiation of the Nisga'a's own claim. The *Kanatewat* litigation[90] both slowed and facilitated the James Bay negotiations: it slowed them by diverting time and money but speeded them by encouraging Quebec to enter the negotiations. The *Sparrow*[91] decision accorded entrenched status to Aboriginal rights, but it may have had an ambivalent effect on claims. On one hand, the stronger Aboriginal rights seem, the greater Aboriginal peoples' leverage in land claims negotiations; on the other hand, stronger Aboriginal rights may make their holders less willing to exchange or define them in land claims agreements.

Similarly, the constitutional forum created pursuant to s. 37 (now spent) and s. 37.1 (now repealed) of the *Constitution Act, 1982* had a mixed effect on land claims negotiations. Sections 37 and 37.1 formalized national conferences aimed at securing formal constitutional amendments on self-government and other Aboriginal matters.[92] The conferences were followed by negotiations on the Meech Lake and Charlottetown Accords.[93] Although these constitutional forums may have helped land claims negotiations by focusing interest on Aboriginal issues, they attracted time and resources from the claims forum. In places such as the Yukon, land claims negotiations were delayed because of uncertainty as to how the two forums should interrelate.

It is possible that eventually land claims negotiations could become an adjunct of self-government negotiations, rather than *vice versa*. As well, recent case law on Aboriginal rights may encourage a shift away from the old land claims emphasis on certainty toward a more fluid concept of ongoing equity. These developments could help reduce discrepancies between different Aboriginal claimant groups. On the other hand, they may make it difficult to maintain that settlements are final and conclusive when key elements — such as Aboriginal rights, treaty rights, and self-government — are subject to ongoing constitutional redefinition.

(f) Scope

Agreement may be easier to secure by postponing some issues to a later stage in negotiations, or even until after the settlement as a whole. The parties involved took the latter approach in Alaska, concluding a brief 27-section statute that left many issues to be worked out later. One benefit was a relatively short pre-settlement negotiation period.[94]

In Canada, the requirement of an agreement-in-principle before a final agreement gives the parties involved an opportunity to postpone disagreement on specific issues to later stages. For example, the Dene / Metis Agreement-in-Principle left many topics — such as the objectives of the agreement, the amending process, overlapping claims with adjoining Aboriginal groups, and the precise composition of the arbitration board to resolve disputes respecting the agreement — to further negotiations.

After a recommendation in the 1985 Coolican report, another initial stage, the "framework agreement", was added to the negotiation process to encourage early consensus and certainty on preliminary matters such as representation, agenda, and procedure.

Another means of narrowing scope initially or postponing issues is regionalization. By the summer of 1990, it was clear that the Dene / Metis Agreement-in-Principle would not be fully supported by all five regions involved. Although the two northern groups generally supported it, the three in the south had major concerns. Rather than trying to salvage the entire agreement, the federal government suspended the existing negotiations and started talks with the two northern groups. Subsequent negotiations led to a final agreement between the federal government and the Gwich'in of the Mackenzie Delta in 1992, and between the federal government and the Sahtu Dene and Metis in 1993. Regionalization is also a feature of the current Yukon negotiations. A key Aboriginal concern with the unsuccessful 1984 Agreement-in-Principle was that it paid inadequate individual attention to the fourteen Yukon Aboriginal communities. Moreover, some of these communities seemed more disposed to accept a land claims settlement than others. Later, an Umbrella Final Agreement and a Model Self-Government Agreement were created to provide a general structure for negotiating Yukon First Nation agreements with the individual communities.[95]

The ultimate postponement mechanism is an "add-on" clause providing for the negotiation of additional benefits *after* the conclusion of the final agreement. For example, the *Inuvialuit Agreement* contains clauses stating that the agreement does not deprive Inuvialuit of "any future constitutional rights for Aboriginal people that may be applicable to them",[96] and that they shall be entitled to be treated no less favourably than any other native people with respect to institutions of public government.[97] The Yukon *Umbrella Final Agreement* and *Draft Model Self-Government Agreement* contain add-on clauses for the Yukon settlement as a whole,[98] and there is a special provision to ensure that each Yukon First Nation is entitled to renegotiate self-government provisions that are "no less favourable" than any special self-government provisions secured by any other Yukon First Nations.[99]

Postponement of topics through the expedients above may encourage early consensus, maintain momentum, and help avoid a general stalemate over specific issues, but it has potential disadvantages. For example, the generalities and ambiguities of the Alaska settlement have had to be litigated in the courts. Failure to address the general objectives of the Dene / Metis claim in the Dene / Metis may have simply postponed the breakdown over basic issues two summers later. Regionalization may make earlier agreements possible with specific groups, but raises difficult challenges for consistency and coordination between regions. The new regional Yukon settlement is far more complex than the earlier Yukon proposals, with great potential for jurisdictional conflicts between federal, territorial, and fourteen new First Nations governments. "Add-on" clauses undermine certainty. In an extreme case, they could convert a "final" agreement into one more stage in a perpetual negotiation process.

(g) Other Factors

Some of the other factors that may affect the speed of negotiations include: (i) the format of the negotiations, (ii) the personalities of the negotiators, (iii) geographical distances between the negotiating parties (certainly a hindrance in the past in the case of the Yukon claim); and (iv) support or opposition from outside groups (e.g., non-beneficiary interest groups, other governments, and regional or national Aboriginal associations).

The land claims approach is a very complex and relatively slow approach to resolution of Aboriginal land claims issues. Because of the operation of some of the factors referred to above, in Canada, Aboriginal representatives and other parties had concluded only two fully completed land claims agreements in the decade since negotiations began in 1973.[100] On the positive side, there has been considerable progress in the last decade. After the Inuvialuit Agreement in 1984, seven more land claims agreements were signed and ratified in legislation in the early 1990s,[101] followed by one in 1998[102] and two more in 2003 and 2005[103].

As seen, both the Yukon and Dene / Metis negotiations have resulted in smaller regional agreements with some of the groups in the original claim areas.[104] The final agreement between the federal government and 17,500 Inuit has produced the largest land claim area in the world — a two-million square-kilometre region in the northern and northeastern Northwest Territories — and a timetable for the creation of a new northern territory.[105] In 1993, following recommendations of a joint task force,[106] the B.C. Treaty Commission was created. As noted in **Part 4**, this is an independent body entrusted with facilitating claims negotiations in this province.[107] In August 1998, an agreement was finally[108] signed with the Nisga'a, outside the auspices of the Treaty Commission.[109] As well, both the federal and British Columbia treaty processes have produced numerous preliminary agreements.[110]

7. SOME KEY LAND CLAIMS AGREEMENTS

Readings 11(c) at p. 391 and 11(f) at p. 408

(a) 1971 Alaska Native Claims Settlement

The *Alaska Native Claims Settlement*[111] was the first large North American land claims agreement. The emphasis was on cash and land in return for the extinguishment of the native peoples' claims to Aboriginal rights.

The 80,000 Alaska natives (with one-quarter or more Alaska native blood, or recognized as an Alaska native by a native village) were granted \$962.5 million[112] and 62,500 square miles (161,847 square kilometres) of surface and subsurface rights in fee simple.[113] The lands were immune from tax for twenty years. They are held and administered by 225 village corporations and 13 village corporations. Individual Alaska natives were issued shares in these corporations, shares that were to be inalienable for twenty years.

There were no special game rights beyond those exercisable on native lands, although in 1978, the state of Alaska passed a law recognizing subsistence activities for native and non-native Alaskans on public lands in the state. A general land use planning body was established.

(b) 1975 James Bay and Northern Quebec Agreement and 1978 Northeastern Quebec Agreement

The focus in the *James Bay and Northern Quebec Agreement*[114] and the *Northeastern Quebec Agreement*[115] was on game rights, land use planning, some social and economic programs, and cash and land. These benefits were provided in exchange for the extinguishment of the Aboriginal peoples' claims to Aboriginal rights. This was the first modern Canadian land claims agreement, a result of the massive James Bay hydro-electric project in James Bay Cree and northern Quebec Inuit traditional territory. It was really a "two-in-one" agreement, with one part for the James Bay Cree and the other for the northern Quebec Inuit.

The 6,500[116] Cree[117] received 2,095 square miles (5,426 square kilometres) of "reserve"-type lands, alienable only to the Crown.[118] The 4,200 Inuit[119] received 3,251 square miles (8,420 square kilometres) of similar lands.[120]

About half the Cree lands are very similar to *Indian Act* reserves, subject to band council jurisdiction, and governed locally by band councils. Other native governments exist in the form of municipal corporations and regional councils.

Beneficiaries have exclusive game rights over the lands described above and over an additional 59,000 square miles (152,809 square kilometres). Throughout the remainder of the 410,000 square mile (1,061,900 square kilometre) agreement region, beneficiaries have exclusive game rights to certain species and are exempt from closed seasons.

Beneficiaries have the right to representation on environmental screening and land use advisory bodies, on fish and game advisory bodies, and on an economic development committee. Special health, education, justice, and economic programs were established. Monetary compensation of $225 million ($21,000 per beneficiary in 1975 dollars) was paid, and the James Bay power project was re-rerouted slightly.

Like most of the land claims agreements that follow it, the *James Bay Agreement* is a very long document.[121] Although part of the length is required to address the special needs of two different claimant groups, much of the agreement addresses technical questions and matters of detail.[122] As a result of the *Constitution Act, 1982*, as amended in 1984,[123] both the detail and more basic elements are all constitutionally entrenched.

The *James Bay and Northern Quebec Agreement* was followed in 1978 by the *Northeastern Quebec Agreement*,[124] which contained similar provisions for 465 Naskapi Indians in the Schefferville area of northeastern Quebec.

For beneficiaries of the *James Bay and Northern Quebec Agreement*, there have been numerous concerns,[125] including disagreements with government over the latter's obligations in regard to economic and social programs. A special concern for the Cree was the Quebec government's plan to proceed with a Phase II of the power project in the heart of the agreement region. After a massive Cree lobbying and publicity campaign, New York state decided not to purchase a large quantity of power from Quebec, and the Quebec government decided in 1992 to postpone Phase II.

Like other land claims agreements, the *James Bay and Northern Quebec Agreement* provides for amendment by consent of the parties.[126] Thus, because of the constitutional status of the *Agreement*, any attempt by a secessionist Quebec government to alter its basic provisions without the consent of either the James Bay Crees, the northern Quebec Inuit, or the federal government, would be unconstitutional.[127]

(c) 1984 Western Arctic (Inuvialuit) Agreement

The main emphasis in this agreement[128] was on land and game rights. In exchange for the extinguishment of their Aboriginal rights claims, the 2,500 Inuvialuit of the northwestern N.W.T.[129] received 90,643 square kilometres of inalienable, untaxable "fee simple" land in the N.W.T.[130] Of this land, 12,949 square kilometres included subsurface rights.

The Inuvialuit have exclusive game rights on their own lands, and exclusive or preferential game rights to certain species throughout the agreement region. These include exclusive and preferential game rights in a newly created National Wilderness Park in the northern Yukon Territory. As in *James*

Bay, the agreement provides for guaranteed Inuvialuit representation in the region on land-use planning bodies, environmental screening bodies, and wildlife and fisheries advisory bodies.

The administration of the agreement is done by the Inuvialuit corporations concerned with land, investment, and development; local government at the community level is administered though local Inuvialuit corporations. Financial compensation was $62.5 million in 1984 dollars,[131] plus $17.5 million (1984) for economic and social development funds.

As with the other land claims agreements, the provisions of the *Inuvialuit Agreement* are constitutionally entrenched. In the event of a dispute, interpretation of the provisions of the agreement is carried out by an arbitration board whose members must include Inuvialuit appointees.

(d) 1992 Gwich'in Agreement

The *Gwich'in Agreement*[132] was the first settlement in the area of the unsuccessful Dene / Metis claim. The N.W.T. portion of the Gwich'in region was subject to Treaty 11, and the Gwich'in ceded certain Treaty 11 rights[133] in addition to their claimed Aboriginal rights. The agreement stresses land quantum (although proportionately less than the *Inuvialuit* and *Nunavut* agreements) and subsurface rights, and contains the first resource royalty sharing provision in a Canadian land claims agreement.

In exchange for the cession of treaty rights and extinguishment of Aboriginal rights claims, 2,300 Gwich'in[134] received 17,818 square kilometres.[135] Like the Inuvialuit, the Gwich'in have exclusive game rights on their own lands, and exclusive or preferential game rights to certain species throughout the agreement region. These include exclusive and preferential game rights in any national parks to be created in the agreement region. As in *James Bay* and *Inuvialuit* agreements, the agreement provides for guaranteed Gwich'in representation in the region on land use planning bodies, environmental screening bodies, and wildlife harvesting advisory bodies.

The administration of the agreement is by the Gwich'in Tribal Council and by organizations designated by it, including settlement corporations established to manage settlement funds. Financial compensation included cash payments totalling $75 million, to be paid over fifteen years,[136] and a percentage of government resource royalties in the Mackenzie Valley area. Dispute resolution is to be settled by an arbitration panel with guaranteed Gwich'in representation on it.

(e) 1993 Nunavut Agreement

In terms of land area, the *Nunavut Agreement*[137] is the largest land claims agreement in the world. It has a large allotment of land per beneficiary, and involved the largest number of beneficiaries at the time it was signed.[138] Unlike any other land claims agreement, *Nunavut* is accompanied by an agreement to create a new Canadian territory in the area of the land claims agreement.

The agreement involved 17,500 Inuit[139] living roughly northeast of the tree line in the Northwest Territories. In exchange for surrendering their claims to Aboriginal rights, the Inuit were allotted 351,000 square kilometres of land,[140] including 37,000 square kilometres with subsurface rights.

Inuit have exclusive or preferential game rights to certain species in the settlement area; involvement in the establishment and management of new parks; guaranteed representation on bodies affecting matters such as land use and planning, water management, environmental screening, and wildlife harvesting; resource revenue sharing; and financial compensation of $1.17 billion over fourteen years. As well, there are preferential requirements for government hiring and contracts. As in the *Inuvialuit Agreement*, disputes are to be resolved through arbitration structures.

As part of the agreement, the federal government committed itself to a process to create the new territory of Nunavut on April 1, 1999. In this huge territory, lying generally northeast of the tree line in the present Northwest Territories, Inuit constitute a large majority of the population. The boundary for the new territory was approved by a majority of N.W.T. residents in a referendum on May 4, 1992. On October 30 of that year, the federal and territorial governments and the Tungavut Federation of Nunavut (the Inuit negotiating organization) signed a political accord on the powers of a Nunavut Territorial Government. Federal legislation to create the new territory received royal assent in 1993.[141]

(f) 1993 and Later Yukon Agreements

Reading 12(c) at p. 419

Like the *Gwich'in* and *Sahtu Dene and Metis* agreements, the ten Yukon First Nation final agreements[142] with about 5,000 Yukon Indians[143] are examples of smaller land claims agreements[144] within an area originally subject to a single claim.[145] Like the *Sahtu Dene and Metis Agreement*, the Yukon agreements also involve a significant proportion of Métis beneficiaries.

However, the Yukon First Nation final agreements have several unique features. First, they are all based on a single framework agreement, called an "*Umbrella Final Agreement*"[146], or *U.F.A.* This document is intended to govern the negotiation of individual land claims "final agreements" for the fourteen Yukon First Nations, representing over 6,500 Yukon Indians. It contains detailed provisions[147] that are to be incorporated, with regional variations, into each of the fourteen individual agreements. Second, although the first four First Nations final agreements required government ratification by legislation, subsequent federal ratification requires only an order in council. Third, these agreements do not entirely extinguish Aboriginal rights on settlement lands. These rights are extinguished only to the extent that they are inconsistent with settlement provisions. Fourth, although the Yukon First Nations final agreements provide for guaranteed participation in public government bodies, they are accompanied by Yukon First Nations self-government agreements.[148] These permit each First Nation to exercise separate governmental powers that can prevail over those of the existing territorial government. Although both the First Nations final agreements and the First Nations self-government agreements will have legal status, only the former are deemed to be "land claims agreements" for the purposes of s. 35(1) of the *Constitution Act, 1982*.[149]

The *Umbrella Final Agreement* contemplates the transfer of 41,440 square kilometres of land to the fourteen First Nations.[150] About 25,900 square kilometres of this land will include subsurface rights.[151] The *U.F.A.* also provides for $248 million[152] in financial compensation,[153] guaranteed harvesting and natural resources rights, resource revenue sharing, park management rights, and tax assistance.

Two of the first individual agreements to be reached were with the First Nation representing the Aboriginal people of the northern community of Old Crow.[154] These and the three other sets of First Nations agreements were formally signed in May 1993.[155]

The Yukon final agreements are complex and long.[156] All provisions in the final agreements are constitutionally entrenched. Many address matters that are highly technical or subject to change. For example, one section of the 414-page *Vuntut Gwitchin First Nation Final Agreement* stipulates that in some situations the Vuntut Gwitchin shall be allocated the lesser of either "the first 40 moose" in the Total Allowable Harvest[157] set by the government or the number of moose required to satisfy the Vuntut Gwitchin's "Subsistence needs".[158] The allowable harvest concept was pioneered in the Yukon claim. It provides a sophisticated means of reconciling conservation and other needs with priority harvesting rights for Aboriginal people. But is it necessary to entrench a 40-moose requirement as part of the Constitution of Canada?[159]

(g) 1993 Sahtu Dene and Metis Agreement

The *Sahtu Dene and Metis Agreement*[160] with 2,400 Sahtu Dene and Metis people in the Mackenzie Valley and Great Bear Lake region of the N.W.T. is broadly similar to its predecessor in the former Dene / Metis claim area, the *Gwich'in Agreement*. However, the *Sahtu Dene and Metis Agreement* involves a significant proportion of Metis beneficiaries,[161] a higher *per capita* allotment of land,[162] and a lower proportion of land with subsurface rights.[163] The Sahtu Dene and Metis settlement area occupies 280,000 square kilometres, an area fourth in size after that of the *Nunavut*, *James Bay*, and *Inuvialuit* agreements.

(h) Nisga'a Agreement[164]

🖹 Reading 11(d) at p. 398

On August 4, 1998, representatives of approximately 5,800 Nisga'a people from the Lower Nass valley of British Columbia, the federal government, and the government of British Columbia signed the *Nisga'a Final Agreement*.[165] After a long ratification process,[166] this landmark modern treaty came into effect on May 11, 2000.

The *Nisga'a Agreement* is significant in three respects. In the first place, this is the first land claims agreement in any province since the *James Bay* and *Northeastern Quebec* agreements of the 1970s. Second, however, the *Nisga'a Agreement* is also remarkable for the long time it took to achieve. It followed two decades of negotiations[167] and over a century of earlier efforts by the Nisga'a to protect and reclaim their culture and their land.[168] Third, the *Nisga'a Agreement* is notable for its status and content. This is the first modern treaty to contain constitutionally entrenched Aboriginal legislative powers that can prevail over federal and provincial laws.

The agreement focuses on the lower Nass Valley, the heart of Nisga'a's traditional homeland. About 2,200 Nisga'a lived in this valley at the time of the agreement, mainly in the villages of New Aiyansh (Gitlakdamiks), Canyon City (Gitwinksihlkw), Greenville (Lax Galtsap), and Kincolith (Gingolx). Kincolith, the westernmost village, has been accessible only by air or water, although a road link was planned under the agreement. About 100 non-natives lived in the area, mainly at the village of Nass Camp east of New Aiyansh.

Traditionally, the Nisga'a fished salmon and oolichan, hunted game such as mountain goats and bears, gathered clams, berries and herbs, and cut the giant red cedar for houses, totem poles, and canoes.[169] At the time of the agreement, these traditional pursuits were supplemented by logging. However, the unemployment rate ranged between 50% and 70%.[170] Housing shortages, alcoholism, and suicides were serious problems.[171] On the other hand, the Nisga'a were the first band to run their own school board, in 1976.[172] Nisga'a language and culture are compulsory until grade 7, and optional in high school. Student drop-out rates declined from about 80% in the 1960s and 1970s to about 20% in the late 1990s.[173] A Nisga'a college was established in 1994. At the time of the signing, the Nisga'a Tribal Council operated in conjunction with an advisory health board and operated its own hospital and development corporation.[174]

The *Nisga'a Final Agreement* applies to Nisga'a people who meet the agreement's eligibility requirements, including Nisga'a ancestry and a maternal Tribal connection.[175] It allocates to these people 1,992 square kilometres of land in the lower Nass valley,[176] a small fraction of the 25,000 square kilometres claimed by the Nisga'a as their full traditional territory.[177] The Nisga'a are to have both surface and subsurface mineral rights;[178] forest resources[179] (and forest management rights after a five-year transition period); a portion of the Canadian Nass River salmon catch and other fish and wildlife rights;[180] environmental control rights;[181] $190 million in general compensation;[182] and an additional $24.5 million for fishing conservation and commercial fishing purposes.[183] An agreement separate from the *Nisga'a Final Agreement* provides for commercial salmon fishing rights.[184]

The main agreement provides for constitutionally entrenched institutions of self-government, including a Nisga'a Lisims Central Government and governments for the four main Nisga'a villages.[185] As well, there are three "urban locals" for the approximately 60% of Nisga'a people who live outside the lower Nass area — mainly in Prince Rupert, Terrace, and Vancouver.[186] Elections to Nisga'a government must be held at least every five years.[187] Subject to residency, age, and other requirements in the Nisga'a constitution or Nisga'a law, all Nisga'a citizens can vote in Nisga'a elections and hold office in Nisga'a government.[188]

The Nisga'a central (Lisims) Government is empowered to enact laws that prevail over federal and provincial laws of general application to the extent of any conflict. This paramount[189] power includes such subjects as Nisga'a government, Nisga'a citizenship, Nisga'a language and culture (with prohibitory powers on Nisga'a lands only), Nisga'a lands, Nisga'a assets, and devolution of cultural assets.[190] On Nisga'a lands it has paramount powers over delivery of health services,[191] Aboriginal faith healers,[192] child and family services consistent with provincial standards,[193] Nisga'a adoption of Nisga'a children,[194] and pre-school to grade 12 education.[195] At the local level, the laws of the four Nisga'a village governments have paramountcy over federal and provincial laws in areas such as administration of village government[196] and regulation and zoning of village lands.[197]

Nisga'a governmental powers extend to other subjects on a limited basis. To the extent of a conflict, federal and provincial laws of general application prevail over Nisga'a laws in regard to public order, peace, and safety,[198] buildings and public works,[199] traffic and transportation,[200] solemnization of marriage,[201] social services,[202] health services (other than delivery),[203] gambling and gaming,[204] and intoxicants.[205]

The Nisga'a Lisims Government is empowered to create a Nisga'a Police Service, with a full range of police responsibilities.[206] It can create community correction services.[207] There is to be a Nisga'a Court with civil and some criminal jurisdiction.[208] It will resemble the Provincial Court of British Columbia,[209] but its members will be appointed by the Nisga'a Lisims Government,[210] it can review decisions of Nisga'a public institutions,[211] and it can apply traditional Nisga'a methods and values in adjudicating and sentencing.[212]

Nisga'a law does not extend to employment standards,[213] industrial relations,[214] and occupational health and safety.[215] Although Nisga'a government authority does not encompass the general field of criminal law,[216] it includes the limited jurisdiction over "public order, peace, or safety"[217] noted above and power to impose fines, restitution, imprisonment, or other penalties for violation of Nisga'a laws.[218] The Nisga'a Police Service can enforce criminal as well as civil law,[219] and the Nisga'a Court's jurisdiction will include prosecutions under Nisga'a laws.[220]

On one hand, then, Nisga'a government power is not unlimited. It includes the usual responsibilities of ordinary municipalities, and it is subject in some areas to federal and provincial federal laws. On the other hand, Nisga'a government power exceeds that of ordinary municipalities in at least four respects. First, the Nisga'a Lisims Government can legislate beyond local boundaries, on all Nisga'a lands. Second, the Nisga'a Lisims Government has general responsibilities in areas such as health, education, corrections, justice, and social services. Third, in some areas both Nisga'a Lisims Government laws and Nisga'a village government laws can prevail over federal and provincial legislation. Fourth, Nisga'a government power is entrenched in the Constitution of Canada. In contrast, all laws of ordinary municipal governments are subject to the jurisdiction of provincial legislatures.

The agreement subjects Nisga'a government and its institutions to the *Canadian Charter of Rights and Freedoms*, "bearing in mind the free and democratic nature of Nisga'a Government as set out in this Agreement."[221] The intended effect of this qualification is not self-evident.[222]

The *Indian Act* no longer applies to the Nisga'a Nation and its people, except for the purpose of determining whether a person is an "Indian".[223] The *Indian Act* tax exemptions for individual Nisga'a people will be phased out over a period of eight to twelve years.[224]

Although the *Nisga'a Final Agreement* contemplates Nisga'a government taxation of the property of non-Nisga'a living on Nisga'a lands,[225] non-Nisga'a residents have no right to vote or run for office in Nisga'a elections. The agreement does require that the Nisga'a government "consult" with non-Nisga'a residents on matters that affect them "significantly and directly".[226]

The agreement attempts to provide certainty without extinguishing Aboriginal rights and title. It says the Treaty is a "full and final" settlement of Nisga'a Aboriginal rights, which sets out exhaustively the Nisga'a s. 35 rights.[227] It specifies that the Nisga'a agree to release any Aboriginal rights that are not in the Treaty or are different from the Nisga'a s. 35 rights in the Treaty.[228]

The total cost of the agreement is expected to be about $490 million.[229] Apart from increases for inflation,[230] the cash component is $190 million, about $32,000 per beneficiary. Over half the total estimated cost and almost 80% of the cash component will be paid for by the federal government.[231]

The *Nisga'a Final Agreement* has been opposed by fishing groups,[232] non-Nisga'a who live within lands allocated to the Nisga'a,[233] the British Columbia Liberal party,[234] the provincial Reform party, the federal Conservative Alliance (formerly Reform) party, Aboriginal groups such as the neighbouring Gitanyow, and others. Critics other than the Aboriginal groups[235] argued that the agreement:

(i) is arbitrarily preferential and potentially divisive, creating constitutionally-guaranteed governments based on race and other arbitrary inequalities that could split the province along ethnic and linguistic lines;
(ii) privileges specific interests over the general public interest, by giving some Nisga'a laws paramountcy over federal and provincial laws of general application;
(iii) is undemocratic, denying non-native residents the right to vote;
(iv) is unconstitutional, because it (a) conflicts with the principle that the *Constitution Act, 1867* divided primary legislative jurisdiction exhaustively between Parliament and the provincial legislatures, (b) by-passes the constitutional requirement of royal assent for valid legislation, and (c) deprives citizens of the right to vote, contrary to s. 3 of the *Charter*.[236]
(v) violated British Columbia's *Constitutional Amendment Approval Act*,[237] because it made effective changes to the Constitution of Canada without the public referendum required under this Act.
(vi) is slanted toward collective rather than individual interests within the Aboriginal community; and
(vii) is too expensive.

Several neighbouring Aboriginal peoples were concerned about overlapping claims. The Nisga'a treaty area includes territories claimed by the Gitanyow, Gitksan, and Tahltan peoples.[238] Gitanyow representatives argued that the Crown breached its fiduciary obligations to them by concluding the Nisga'a Treaty before resolving the Gitanyow's territorial claims in the Nisga'a Treaty area.[239] In preliminary litigation, a legal challenge by the Gitanyow received qualified judicial support.[240] Within the Nisga'a community, the dissident Nisga'a House of Sga'nism challenged the authority of the Nisga'a Tribal Council to conclude the agreement. In early litigation, this challenge was unsuccessful.[241]

Supporters of the agreement,[242] including the Nisga'a, the federal and provincial governments, and others, argued that the agreement:

(i) is based more on Aboriginal property and cultural rights than on race;
(ii) contains legislative powers that are vital to the Nisga'a, but not that disruptive to others;
(iii) must restrict voting by non-native residents in order to protect Aboriginal self-government from the growing size of non-Aboriginal populations;
(iv) will end the legal and economic uncertainty of Aboriginal rights and title litigation;
(v) is not unconstitutional, as it (a) was not extinguished by the division of powers or other provisions in the *Constitution Act, 1867*, (b) did not by-pass the requirement of assent, and (c) is not affected by the voting guarantee in s. 3 of the *Charter*;[243]
(vi) did not require a British Columbia referendum or a Part V constitutional amendment, because s. 35(1) of the *Constitution Act, 1982* permits a land claims treaty to automatically substitute one form of existing constitutional rights (i.e., Aboriginal rights) for another (i.e., treaty rights);[244] and
(vii) is needed as a matter of justice to the Nisga'a.

In the *Campbell* case,[245] discussed in **Chapter 12, Part 4**, a British Columbia Supreme Court judge rejected most of the constitutional challenges to the Treaty, and further litigation was discontinued when the politician who had led the court challenge became premier. Beyond the issues canvassed in *Campbell*, a number of more general questions may be relevant to a general assessment of this important treaty. First, do concerns about the financial cost of agreement take full account of what the Nisga'a have lost in the past? Second, does criticism of the collectivist aspects of the agreement undervalue the communal nature of traditional Aboriginal rights and culture? Third, does effective self-government require constitutionally entrenched paramountcy over some decisions of generally elected legislatures?[246] Fourth, does effective local control require the potential partial disenfranchisement of non-beneficiary residents?[247] Fifth, if a land claims agreement incorporates sufficient public interest and third party safeguards, and is adequately explained, is a public referendum an unwelcome threat or a source of potential long-term public support?

From April 2, 2002 to May 15, 2002, the provincial government conducted a mail-in referendum on the B.C. treaty process. Voters were to agree or disagree with eight statements that reflected provincial government treaty policy. The support rate in the responses ranged between 84.5% and 94.5%.[248] Of those who responded, 87% agreed that "[a]boriginal self-government should have the characteristics of local government, with the powers delegated from Canada and B.C."[249] Another 91% of those who responded agreed that "[e]xisting tax exemptions for Aboriginal people should be phased out."[250] But these results masked weaknesses. For example, most of the questions seemed to be worded to elicit positive responses. One statement said that "[p]arks and protected areas should be maintained for the use and benefit of all British Columbians."[251] Not surprisingly, 95% of those who replied agreed. Churches, opposition critics, and Aboriginal groups attacked the referendum as counterproductive, misleading, and interfering. They refused to vote. Overall, fewer than 36% of eligible voters participated in the referendum,[252] little more than for municipal elections.

(i) 2003 Tlicho Agreement

The Tlicho[253] people were the third group in the former Dene / Metis claim region to negotiate a land claims agreement. Like the Gwich'in and the Sahtu Dene, about 3,000 Tlicho people live in the Treaty 11 area of the Northwest Territories, and have relinquished the right to claim most Treaty 11 rights.[254] In their 1993 land claims agreement,[255] the Tlicho retain the right to annual Treaty 11 treaty payments, and to "payment of the salaries of teachers to instruct the children of the Indians."[256]

The *Tlicho Agreement* provides for 39,000 square kilometres of fee simple-type land,[257] including both surface and subsurface rights. The land will be allocated in a single block, surrounding the four main Tlicho communities.[258] Non-Tlicho Citizens are allowed access to these lands for non-commercial purposes, subject to Tlicho laws.[259] The agreement also provides for wildlife and related resource rights,[260] for mineral royalties[261], and for financial compensation of $152 million over fourteen years.[262]

This was the first N.W.T. land claims agreement to include distinct self-government provisions alongside the land, resource, and financial components. The agreement establishes a central Tlicho Government with regional powers and four Tlicho Community Governments with local powers. Federal legislation of general application will prevail over Tlicho laws,[263] and Tlicho laws will prevail over other federal legislation.[264] Normally, Tlicho law will supersede territorial law.[265] Non-Tlicho Citizens can vote in Tlicho community government elections if they resided in the relevant community in the six months before the election and in the Tlicho traditional region of the N.W.T. in the two years before the election.[266] On the other hand, only Tlicho Citizens can serve as community government chiefs,[267] and no more than half of the seats on community government councils can be held by non-Tlicho citizens.[268] The Tlicho have agreed not to exercise land rights beyond those provided in the agreement. However, they may still claim additional non-land rights, in relation to matters such as self-government.[269] If any such rights are added to the Agreement, they are subject to federal laws relating to important national interests.[270] If the government should decline to negotiate additional rights, the Tlicho reserve the right to establish them in the courts.[271]

(j) 2005 Labrador Agreement

The Labrador Inuit Land Claims Agreement[272] involves over 5,000 northern Labrador Inuit who live mainly in the communities of Nain, Hopedale, Makkovik, Postville, and Rigolet. The Agreement sets aside 15,799 square kilometres as Labrador Inuit Lands, subject to fee simple-type ownership, and creates a Torngat Mountains National Park Reserve, in which the Inuit have special rights. There are resource revenue sharing arrangements both on Inuit lands and in the broader Settlement Area, including a special resource sharing arrangement in the Voisey's Bay nickel region. Labrador Inuit are to receive $140 million in monetary compensation over a fifteen year period.[273]

Although the *Labrador Agreement* resembles the general pattern of the *Nisga'a* and *Tlicho* agreements, it contains some distinctive provisions. Like the others, the *Labrador Agreement* provides for separate self-government institutions, both at the regional level (the Nunatsiavut Government) and at the local level (Inuit Community Governments). As in the other agreements, Aboriginal laws tend to prevail over conflicting laws of general application in regard to internal, social, and cultural matters, while laws of general application tend to prevail for basic standards of health, safety, and security.[274] However, the *Labrador Agreement* also gives a general paramountcy to federal legislation relating to peace, order and good government, criminal law or procedure, general human rights, or health and safety.[275] This is somewhat similar to a provision in the *Tlicho Agreement*, but the Tlicho provision applies only to Agreement rights negotiated in future.[276] Like the *Tlicho Agreement*, the *Labrador Agreement* expressly permits non-beneficiary existing residents to vote and run for election in Inuit Community Government elections.[277] However, the *Labrador Agreement* makes a limited quota of voting rights and seats available for non-beneficiary new residents as well.[278] Also of note is the *Labrador Agreement*'s two-part approach to certainty. The Labrador Inuit cede all their Aboriginal rights in and to subsurface resources in Labrador Inuit Aboriginal lands,[279] whereas other Labrador Inuit Aboriginal rights are to continue as modified in the land claims agreement.[280]

(k) Sechelt Agreement-in-Principle

🖹 Reading 11(e) at p. 404

Two agreements in principle were concluded in the spring of 1999. On April 16, 1999, the Sechelt Land Claims Agreement-in-Principle was concluded between the federal and British Columbia governments and 900 members of the Sechelt Indian Band north of Vancouver. Less than a month later, on the Atlantic coast, the May 10 Labrador Inuit Land Claims Agreement-in-Principle was signed by the federal and Newfoundland and Labrador governments and almost 5,000 Labrador Inuit. As seen, the Labrador Agreement-in-Principle is now a treaty. For the Sechelt, this has not yet happened.

Perhaps because the Sechelt are in a semi-urban location, with a large non-beneficiary population and many competing pressures for space, the Sechelt AIP allocated them only 933 hectares of new land.[281] On the other hand, the AIP included a significant cash component of $42.0 million,[282] and other benefits, such as gravel and timber. Under the AIP, the Sechelt would have retained their unique form of delegated self-government.[283] Like the Nisga'a, they would have agreed to give up their tax exempt status.[284]

In late May 2000, though, the Sechelt said that they would be withdrawing from the negotiations and taking their land claims to the courts.[285] The Sechelt were unsatisfied with the land quantum, the end of the tax exemption, and provisions barring future claims.[286] The Sechelt Chief was reported to have said that the governments had failed to adjust their bargaining position to take account of the Supreme Court's decision in *Delgamuukw*.[287]

8. SOME SPECIFIC CLAIMS

As with comprehensive claims the number of specific claims settlements is small in comparison with overall number of cases.[288] A relatively typical case involved the Mississauga First Nation near Blind River, Ontario.[289] In 1982, the Mississauga First Nation claimed that the northern boundary of their reserve had been surveyed incorrectly in the 1850s.[290] After a federally appointed fact finder concurred generally with this claim, the federal government accepted its validity. Together with the Ontario government, it entered into negotiations with the Mississauga. In 1982, the parties reached a tentative agreement, which was made available for public comment. The proposed settlement was strongly opposed by local non-Aboriginal residents, many of whom had lumber or tourist interests or cottages in the affected area. They disputed the fact finder's assessment of the boundary issue and argued strongly for a monetary, rather than a land, settlement. After several compromises, a final agreement was concluded in 1995.

9. "OTHER CLAIMS"

The federal government's tidy comprehensive / specific dichotomy is not always adequate to address the complex reality of claims.[291] For example, the Yukon claim and those in the southwestern Northwest Territories are in areas partly or wholly covered by treaties. Until the Supreme Court held that they were subject to the treaty, the Temagami First Nation had asserted an Aboriginal title claim in the midst of the area of the Robinson Huron Treaty. The Lubicon Lake Cree of Alberta have argued that Treaty 8 is inapplicable to them because their ancestors were not included in it.[292] The Golden Lake Algonquin at Algonquin Park take a similar position in regard to the treaties of Upper Canada and Ontario.[293]

(a) Oka

Another claim that defies simple categories, and has remained unresolved for nearly two centuries, is the claim of "the people of the Pines", the Mohawk people of Oka in Quebec.[294]

(i) People

The more than 1,600 Kanesatake Mohawk Indians are one of seven Mohawk communities in Canada. They have close ties with the much larger neighbouring Mohawk community of Kahnawake. About one-half of the Kanesatake Mohawk people live either within the boundaries of the town of Oka, Quebec, or on lands west of the town. Although both of these kinds of lands have been purchased or set aside for the Kanesatake Mohawks, they are not a formal *Indian Act* reserve. The close juxtaposition of Mohawk and non-Mohawk people in and around Oka, living on different categories of land, presents challenges for cooperative local government.

The challenge is compounded by a diversity of political traditions among Kanesatake Mohawks themselves.[295] Some support an *Indian Act* system of elected band councils. Others support a system of band councils under the *Indian Act*, but chosen by customary procedures. A third group, the "People of the Longhouse", also follow customary procedures but reject any federal authority, including the *Indian Act*, in Mohawk matters. Yet another group, who tend to identify with Longhouse views, belong to a Mohawk self-policing / defensive organization, the Mohawk Warrior Society. Like other Mohawk, Kanesatake Mohawks — especially the Longhouse people and the warriors — tend to support a strong concept of Mohawk sovereignty.

Many non-Indian Oka residents live on lands purchased from a Roman Catholic missionary order, the Sulpicians. They have a municipal government structure that is subject, in turn, to the jurisdiction of the province of Quebec.

(ii) Crisis

In March 1989, the mayor of Oka announced plans to extend a privately leased golf course on municipally owned land.[296] The town planned to buy adjoining land from a private developer so that the golf course could be extended from nine holes to eighteen. However, the land was claimed by the Kanesatake Mohawk Indians, who regarded it as part of "the Pines", a sacred ancestral area. They protested vehemently. The proposal was suspended during sporadic negotiations between the Mohawks, the town, and the federal and provincial governments.

In March 1990, when negotiations hit a low point, the town announced that it was going ahead with the proposal. On March 10, 1990, after another unsuccessful public protest, the Kanesatake Mohawks erected barriers across roads leading into the Pines. There were more unproductive negotiations. On April 26 and June 29, the town obtained injunctions requiring the roadblocks to be dismantled. The injunctions were disregarded. On July 10, Oka Mayor Jean Ouellette asked the Quebec Provincial Police to enforce the injunctions. On July 11, over one hundred officers attacked the barricades. There was an exchange of gunfire. One officer, Corporal Marcel Lemay, was killed. The police withdrew.

On the same day, in support of the Kanesatake Mohawks, the Kahnawake Mohawks blockaded the Mercier Bridge south of Montreal, causing huge traffic jams. The confrontations turned into a 78-day standoff (20 days less in the case of the Kahnawake) that involved Mohawk warriors, the Quebec provincial police, and, after August 13, the Canadian army. Supported by their powerful allies at Kahnawake, the Kanesatake Mohawks demanded full ownership of the disputed land, movement toward recognition of full Mohawk sovereignty, and other guarantees, such as commitments that external police forces would not enter Mohawk lands. The standoff at the Mercier Bridge ended on August 29; at Oka, the crisis finally ended when the Mohawks came out from behind their barricades on September 26, 1990.

(iii) Background

The roots of the problems at Oka are centuries deep. Before the Europeans came, the area near what is now Oka was apparently used by the St. Lawrence Iroquoians, a group of people other than the Mohawks.[297] The Mohawks controlled the St. Lawrence Valley for much of the first half of the 17th century. They hunted, fished, and trapped (but apparently did not settle) there during most of that century.[298] In 1717, the Governor of New France granted the area around what is now Oka, known as the Lake of Two Mountains, to the Roman Catholic Sulpician order, for the use and benefit of the Indians under their care.[299] In 1721, Mohawks then residing at a Sulpician mission in the Montreal area, and some Nipissing and Algonquin people, moved to the new mission. The Indians claimed afterwards that the Sulpicians had promised them land of their own in the Lake of the Two Mountains area; the Sulpicians maintained that it was they who owned and controlled the land.

By 1743 there were about 700 Indians at the new site.[300] They continued to claim that the land was theirs. Ongoing disputes festered over the parcels of land allotted to individual Indians and the amount of wood they could cut. Later in the century, the Indians claimed that the British had agreed to recognize their ownership of the land in return for their support during the Seven Years' War and the American Revolution. In 1841, a colonial ordinance confirmed the Sulpicians' ownership of the land,[301] but the conflict continued. The Mohawks sent petitions to the Governor of Canada and to Parliament pressing their case, to no avail. In 1852, eleven Mohawks and four Algonquians were excommunicated.[302]

Ignored, then rebuffed and penalized, the Indians continued to assert their claims. In 1868 and 1869, a Mohawk chief tried to distribute the land to his people, to force the Sulpicians to leave: he was arrested.[303] By the end of 1869, most of the Mohawks had left the Catholic church, and most of the Algonquins had left the settlement for new lands in Maniwaki. The Catholic church was destroyed in a fire, and several Indians were charged with arson.[304] The Sulpicians starting selling off large areas of land to non-Indians. There were more violent protests and petitions and appeals from the Mohawks. A Mohawk chief travelled to England to press their claims. A Mohawk called Angus Corinth sued the Sulpicians over land ownership. In 1912, the Judicial Committee ruled in favour of the Sulpicians, but said that they might be subject to some trust obligations owed to the Indians.[305]

In 1945, the federal government purchased all the Sulpicians' unsold lands except those being used for religious purposes.[306] The purchase excluded a significant area, including the area that later became known as "the Pines". In 1947, the remaining common lands were expropriated by the province of Quebec and then transferred to the adjoining municipality of Oka. The municipality cleared part of this area (including part of the Pines) in 1959. It leased the cleared land to a private non-profit corporation, the *Club de Golf Oka Inc.*, for the operation of a nine-hole golf course. Despite another Mohawk protest, this time before a

Parliamentary committee in 1961, the project went ahead. The Mohawks submitted a comprehensive claim to the area in 1975, but this was rejected on the grounds that

(i) the Mohawks had not shown that they had possessed the land from time immemorial;
(ii) any Aboriginal title that might have originally existed had since been extinguished; and
(iii) Mohawk settlement came after, rather than before, a European presence in the area.[307]

The Indians also made a specific claim, but it was rejected in 1986 because the Oka band had not shown any outstanding obligation on the part of the federal Crown. The ground was laid for the events of 1990.

(iv) Aftermath

After the conflict, some Mohawk warriors were convicted and given short prison sentences. The golf course extension was halted. The federal government intensified its policy of purchasing lands for the use of the Mohawks. On the other hand, Mohawk demands for full sovereignty were rejected. There was public disapproval of the methods of the warriors and disgust at those who threw stones at Mohawk women, children and older people who had tried to cross the Mercier Bridge in the midst of the standoff. There was a great increase in public awareness of the plight of the Mohawks at Kanesatake, and of the sovereignty claims being made by the Mohawk in general.

On June 14, 2001, after a decade of discussion, the federal government proclaimed in force the *Kanesatake Interim Land Base Governance Act*.[308] The Act recognized existing federal land purchases for the Kanesatake Mohawk.[309] It gave the Mohawk Council of Kanesatake jurisdiction to make laws in relation to wildlife and fish, construction, zoning, and related activities on Kanesatake lands.[310] These laws complied with general standards prescribed in a schedule to the Act, unless the Council first negotiated a land use harmonization agreement with the Municipality of Oka.[311] Although Kanesatake lands would be "Lands reserved for the Indians" under s. 91(24) of the *Constitution Act, 1867*, they would not be a reserve under *Indian Act*.[312] Meanwhile, though, the Mohawk's larger land claim in the region remained largely unresolved. The three-centuries-old battle continued.

(b) Ipperwash[313]

Another complex claim outside the standard categories is that of the Chippewas of Kettle and Stony Point in southwestern Ontario. In negotiations and treaties between 1818 and 1827, the Chippewa Nation gave up rights to a large area of land by the shore of Lake Huron, and kept five tracts that became the reserve of the Chippewas of Kettle and Stony Point band. In 1927, the band surrendered 377 acres of the reserve, which were then sold to private owners. They then sold 108 acres of the land to the Government of Ontario, who designated it as Ipperwash Provincial Park. In 1942, with the onset of the Second World War, the Department of National Defence appropriated over 2,000 acres of the reserve for use as a training facility (Camp Ipperwash). In 1944, the federal government expanded Camp Ipperwash to include all the land surrendered in 1927, except for the park.

For decades after the war had ended, the Chippewas tried unsuccessfully to get the military use lands back. The federal government gave the Chippewas some compensation and hunting and fishing rights on the land, but it agreed to return the land only when it was no longer needed for military purposes.

By the spring of 1993, the land had still not been returned. Some of it was contaminated, and the government said it needed more time to clean it up. A group of Chippewas moved in to occupy it. After court actions and confrontations with the occupying Chippewas, the federal government withdrew military personnel from the Camp in the spring of 1995.

In the fall of 1995, a group of Chippewas occupied Ipperwash Park, which contained the site of an ancient Aboriginal burial ground. There was a confrontation on September 6, 1995. Armed Ontario Provincial Police moved in to remove the occupiers. Band member Mr. Dudley George was shot and killed. An O.P.P. officer was found guilty of negligence causing death. On January, 1996, the federal government appointed a negotiator to expedite the return of Camp Ipperwash. In an Agreement-in-Principle on June 18, 1996, the federal government agreed to pay to clean up the Camp and to support research on issues involving the park.

10. FUTURE DIRECTIONS

The claims process directly involves the parties — the Aboriginal groups directly affected and the governments — in fashioning agreements that reconcile

Aboriginal and public interests. It allows arrangements that are impossible in ordinary courts, or before quasi-judicial claims commissions, and is likely to be more sensitive to "grassroots" regional concerns than national constitutional conferences. Unlike task force reports, commissions of inquiry, and *Indian Act* reforms, land claims settlements can result in binding agreements with constitutional force by virtue of s. 35(3).

Yet there is no reason for complacency. As seen, the process has been painfully slow, both for comprehensive and specific claims. In recent years, the federal government has taken numerous measures to increase the rate of settlements. For comprehensive claims, for example, it has split up large claim areas and has negotiated them as segments. It has also made recent land claims agreements more generous, more governmental, more separate,[314] and more open-ended.[315]

However, while separate structures may respond to pluralist needs, they can also generate duplication and conflict, as well as discourage cooperative approaches to common social interests. Open-endedness must also be handled with care. If Aboriginal rights are to be retained rather than extinguished, it is in the interest of all parties to ensure that agreements cannot be re-cast by litigation. As well, a systematic and predictable process for periodic review of all agreements would be preferable to *ad hoc* catch-up provisions.

To help speed the process as a whole, it is necessary to ensure that comprehensive, specific, and other Aboriginal claims negotiations have high government policy priority and adequate funding.

It would be a mistake, though, to aim for speed at the cost of third-party consultation and public involvement. Support from the public, especially from non-beneficiaries in the immediate area of claims agreements, is vital to their success. Could a non-beneficiary representative be included at negotiations? Shouldn't all land claims agreements be subject to a requirement of individual legislative ratification?[316] Could parliamentary committees consider proposed agreements before they are approved in legislation?

Although a threshold of certainty is important, other matters require greater flexibility. At present, the administrative *minutiae* of agreements can be constitutionally frozen as of the settlement date, with little chance of change without formal amendments or cumbersome mediation / arbitration proceedings.[317] Consideration could be given to a two-level approach in which general agreement principles are entrenched, but implementation plans[318] and technical details are not.

Potentially, the negotiation process seems to be the best available means of addressing claims based on Aboriginal title, treaty problems, and disputes such as that at Oka. The challenge is to translate the potential into practice — into achieving agreements, and making them work once the ink is dry.

Notes

1. See further, Department of Indian Affairs and Northern Development, *Federal Policy for the Settlement of Native Claims*, March 1993 (updated on ongoing basis).
2. These are formally defined as claims "based on the concept of continuing Aboriginal rights and title which have not been dealt with by treaty or other legal means": *ibid.*; Currently, a comprehensive claim must include evidence of "some continuing use and occupancy of the land": *ibid.* at 5. Compare with *R. v. Adams*, [1996] 3 S.C.R. 101 at para. 26, where the Supreme Court said that Aboriginal rights are "not limited to those circumstances where an aboriginal group's relationship with the land is of a kind sufficient to establish title to the land."
3. The federal government defines these as claims "arising from alleged non-fulfilment of Indian treaties and other lawful obligations, or the improper administration of lands and other assets under the *Indian Act* or formal agreements": *ibid.* at i.
4. *Ibid.* at 29.
5. For a general work that includes treaty-based land claims, see K. Coates, ed., *Aboriginal Land Claims in Canada*, 1992.
6. *Tlingit and Haida Indians of Alaska v. United States*, 389 F.2d. 778 (Ct. C. 1968).
7. In *Delgamuukw*, the trial before the British Columbia Supreme Court lasted 374 days, involved 61 trial witnesses, 15 additional witnesses on commission, 53 territorial affidavits, and 30 out-of-court deponents, and about 90,000 pages of evidence, argument, and exhibits. The combined trial and appeal decisions occupy 753 pages of the Dominion Law Reports: 455 for the British Columbia Supreme Court decision (excluding maps), and 298 for the Court of Appeal decision (excluding maps).
8. B.W. Morse, "The Resolution of Land Claims" in B.W. Morse, ed., *Aboriginal Peoples and the Law: Indian, Métis and Inuit Rights in Canada*, rev. 1st ed. (Ottawa: Carleton University Press, 1991) at 617, 668–69.
9. R. Barsh, "Indian Land Claims Policy in the United States" (1982) 58 North Dakota Law Rev. 7, quoted in Morse, *ibid.* at 667.
10. However, in 2003 the Canadian federal government enacted legislation creating a quasi-judicial tribunal to deal with unresolved specific claims: see end of **Part 4(b)**, below.
11. Public Law 92–203, 92nd Congress, H.R. 10367, December 18, 1971.
12. For other comments on the advantages of negotiations, see Royal Commission on Aboriginal Peoples, *Report of the Royal Commission on Aboriginal Peoples*, vol. 2, chap. 4, s. 6.2 at 562 (hereinafter "*Report*").
13. *Haida Nation v. British Columbia (Minister of Forests)*, 2004 SCC 73 at para. 20.
14. *See Reference re Secession of Quebec*, [1998] 2 S.C.R. 217 esp. at paras. 88–104. By analogy with the *Quebec Secession Reference*, negotiations should be principled and should take account of the legitimate interests of the other parties. Note, however, that while secession negotiations would be required only in the event of a clear

expression of a desire to secede, made by the clear majority in a province, Aboriginal claims negotiations are required now.

15. For the special procedure in British Columbia, see <http://www.bctreaty.net/files/hdbk-treaty.html>.
16. *Supra* note 1 at 5–6. They must also show proof of an organized society, occupation of the territory claimed since the assertion of sovereignty by European nations, and more or less exclusive occupation of the territory: *ibid.* at 5. These requirements may need modification in light of the Supreme Court's decisions in *R. v. Van der Peet*, [1996] 2 S.C.R. 507 and *R. v. Adams*, [1996] 3 S.C.R. 101.
17. For these, see **Part 8**, below.
18. See O.P. Dickason, *Canada's First Nations: A History of Founding Peoples from Earliest Times*, 3d ed. (Don Mills, Ont.: Oxford University Press, 2002) at 257–63 and accompanying notes. See also **Chapter 5**.
19. Treaty Made October 31, 1923 Between His Majesty the King and the Chippewa Indians (Ottawa: Queen's Printer, 1957); Treaty Made November 15, 1923 Between His Majesty the King and the Mississauga Indians (Ottawa: Queen's Printer, 1957).
20. S.C. 1927, c. 32, s. 6.
21. S.C. 1951, c. 149.
22. Consent was rarely given: see W.R. Morrison, *A Survey of the History and Claims of the Native Peoples of Northern Canada* (Ottawa: Indian & Northern Affairs, 1983).
23. *Statement of the Government of Canada on Indian Policy* (Ottawa: Queen's Printer, 1969).
24. From 1969 to 1977. The effectiveness of the office of the Indian Commissioner was hindered by its association with the White Paper. Most Aboriginal people were vehemently opposed to the main thrust of the White Paper, which was to put an end to special Indian status.
25. **Chapter 4**.
26. Minister of Indian Affairs and Northern Development, *In All Fairness: A Native Claims Policy — Comprehensive Claims* (Ottawa: D.I.A.N.D., 1981). See discussion in *Report*, vol. 2, chap. 5, s. 5.2 at 533–44. The specific claims policy is discussed below.
27. *Ibid.* at 19.
28. *Ibid.*
29. *Ibid.* at 23–25.
30. *Ibid.* at 24–25.
31. M. Coolican, Chair, Task Force to Review Comprehensive Claims Policy, *Living Treaties, Lasting Agreements* (Ottawa: D.I.A.N.D., December 1985).
32. Department of Indian Affairs and Northern development, *Comprehensive Land Claims Policy*, 1986. See **Reading 11(b)** and *Federal Policy for the Settlement of Native Claims*, *supra* note 1. The graduated approach followed since 1986 is generally as follows: When resources permit, a government negotiator is appointed. Parties aim at concluding a statement of intent, then a framework agreement to govern the overall approach, then an agreement-in-principle and, finally, a final agreement that can be ratified and implemented in legislation. All agreements must have the approval of the parties before the next step can be taken.
33. A.C. Hamilton, *Canada and Aboriginal Peoples: A New Partnership* (Ottawa: D.I.A.N.D., 1995).
34. *Treaty Making in the Spirit of Co-existence: An Alternative to Extinguishment* (Ottawa: Canada Communication Group, 1995).
35. Royal Commission on Aboriginal Peoples, *Report of the Royal Commission on Aboriginal Peoples*, vol. 2, chap. 4, s. 5.2 at 542–44. On one hand, extinguishment is anathema to most Aboriginal groups, representing a termination of sacred rights. On the other hand, extinguishment serves the practical concern of legal certainty. The challenge is to eliminate the negative aspects of extinguishment while maintaining certainty. If Aboriginal rights continue past implementation of a land claims agreement, courts could define new aspects of Aboriginal rights that were not anticipated by the parties. This could disrupt existing public and third party interests, and upset the balance negotiated in the agreement. The Hamilton Report (A.C. Hamilton, *Canada and Aboriginal Peoples: A New Partnership* (Ottawa: D.I.A.N.D., 1995, 114) and the Royal Commission on Aboriginal Peoples (*Report*, *ibid.*) suggested defining the context of unextinguished Aboriginal rights in as much detail as possible, using quit claim assurances, and incorporating dispute resolution processes. At the same time Hamilton and the Royal Commission also urged that the language incorporating all these safeguards must be "clear, plain and understandable to everyone" (*Report*, vol. 2, chap. 2, s. 5.2 at 543), an exacting requirement. See further G. Otis and A. Émond, "L'Identité auchtotone dans les traités contemporains de l'extinction à l'affirmation du titre ancestral" (1996) 41 McGill L.J. 543.
36. See, for example, Association of Iroquois and Allied Indians, Grand Council Treaty No. 3 and the Union of Ontario Indians, *A New Proposal for Claims Resolution in Ontario*, 1981.
37. *Report*, vol. 2, chap. 4, ss. 5.4 and 5.5.
38. *Report*, vol. 5, Appendix A, Recommendation 2.4.29; *Report*, vol. 2, chap. 4, s. 6.4. The *Report* did not propose that the tribunal have an active decision-making role in regard to the substantive aspects of land claims and self-government negotiations. Although the government might be technically in a conflict of interest position in these negotiations if it were a private party, its obligations go beyond those of private parties. For example, the government has a responsibility to take into account all interests — those of Aboriginal claimants, those of Aboriginal and non-Aboriginal non-claimants — in order to accommodate general public needs such as conservation, control of pollution, transportation access, and national security. If it transferred effective decision-making power on issues of this kind to an independent tribunal, government would arguably be abdicating control over its public responsibilities. On the other hand, government must address Aboriginal claims fairly, expeditiously, and consistently with the Crown's special fiduciary obligations: an independent facilitator might be able to assist with this.
39. See *supra* note 15 and *Report*, vol. 2, chap. 4, s. 5.2.
40. Department of Indian Affairs and Northern Development, *Outstanding Business: A Native Claims Policy — Specific Claims* (Ottawa: D.I.A.N.D.), 1982. See discussion in *Report*, vol. 2, chap. 5, s. 5.2 at 544–48.
41. *Outstanding Business*, *ibid.* at 20.
42. Indian Commission of Ontario, *Discussion Paper Regarding First Nation Land Claims* (Toronto: Indian Commission of Ontario, 1990) at 22.
43. W.B. Henderson and D.T. Ground, "Survey of Aboriginal Land Claims" (1994) 26 *Ottawa L.C.* 187 at 216. See *ibid.* at 216–17 for a more extensive list of criticisms of the process.
44. Orders-in-Council P.C. 1991-1329 and 1992-1730. The Commission may also provide information or mediation services on request. See further, Indian Claims Commission, "ICC Creation and History", in <http://www.indianclaims.ca/english/about/history.html>.
45. "The Indian Specific Claims Commission has completed 18 inquiries into claims made by Indian bands. But the reports on how the federal government can reach settlements have not been acted on": J. Aubry, "Land [*sic*] Claims Commissioners Resigning to Protest Inaction" *Ottawa Citizen* (July 13, 1996) A1. "The commission has investigated and reported on 18 claims. Recommendations in six of them have been accepted by Ottawa": R. Platiel, "Advisory Group Moves to Spur Settlement of Native Claims" *The Globe and Mail* (July 16, 1996) A4.

See also Henderson and Ground, *supra* note 43 at 223–24.
46. J. Aubry, *ibid.* at A1, A2 and R. Platiel, A4.
47. *Ibid.* Cf. *Report*, vol. 5, Appendix A, Recommendation 2.4.33.
48. *Specific Claims Resolution Act*, S.C. 2003, c. 23.
49. *Ibid.* at ss. 28–30.
50. *Ibid.* at s. 31.
51. *Ibid.* at s. 32.
52. *Ibid.* at ss. 33–35.
53. *Ibid.* at s. 41(5). A majority of adjudicators must be members of the bar: s. 41(2).
54. *Ibid.* at ss. 62–70.
55. *Ibid.* at s.71.
56. Six months after the enactment of the new legislation, it had not been proclaimed in effect.
57. American legislation: the *Alaska Native Claims Settlement Act*, 1971, 85 Stat. 688, enacted December 18, 1971. Although the Alaska natives lobbied strongly for the content they wanted in settlement legislation, and presented a draft bill to Congress, the 1971 Act was not preceded by a signed native-government agreement.
58. Federal implementing legislation: *James Bay and Northern Quebec Native Claims Settlement Act*, S.C. 1976–77, c. 32; *Cree-Naskapi (of Quebec) Act*, S.C. 1984, c. 18.
59. Unless otherwise indicated, population figures refer to the approximate number of beneficiaries at the time of the signing of land claims agreements. In the case of early agreements, current beneficiary numbers will be significantly higher.
60. Federal implementing legislation: *Northeastern Quebec Agreement* Regulations, SOR/78-502, February 23, 1978.
61. Federal implementing legislation: *Western Arctic (Inuvialuit) Claims Settlement Act*, S.C. 1984, c. 24, as am. S.C. 1988, c. 16, s. 1.
62. Formal name: *Comprehensive Land Claim Agreement between Her Majesty in Right of Canada and the Gwich'in as represented by the Gwich'in Tribal Council*. Federal implementing legislation: *Gwich'in Land Claim Settlement Act*, S.C. 1992, c. 53.
63. Formal name: *Final Agreement between the Inuit of the Nunavut Settlement Area and Her Majesty in Right of Canada*. Federal implementing legislation: *Nunavut Land Claims Agreement Act*, S.C. 1993, c. 29.
64. Federal implementing legislation: *Yukon First Nations Land Claims Settlements Act*, S.C. 1994, c. 34; *Yukon First Nations Self-Government Act*, S.C. 1994, c. 35; *Yukon Surface Rights Act*, S.C. 1994, c. 43; all in force on February 14, 1995.
65. Federal implementing legislation: *Sahtu Dene and Metis Land Claim Settlement Act*, S.C. 1994, c. 27.
66. Federal implementing legislation: *Nisga'a Final Agreement Act*, S.C. 2000, c. 7.
67. Formal name: *Land Claims and Self-Government Agreement Among the Tlicho and the Government of the Northwest Territories and the Government of Canada*. Signed: 25 August 2003. Federal implementing legislation: *Tlicho Land Claims and Self Government Act*, S.C. 2005, c. 1.
68. Formal name: *Land Claims and Self-Government Agreement Between the Inuit of Labrador as Represented by the Labrador Inuit Association and the Queen in Right of Newfoundland and Labrador and the Queen in Right of Canada.* Signed: 22 January 2005.
69. British Columbia Treaty Commission, online: <http://www.bctreaty.net/files_2/updates.html>.
70. *Supra* notes 49–59.
71. 85 Stat. 688.
72. **Part 3(e)**, above.
73. *Supra* note 31 at 13.
74. *Ibid.* (Were these matters of federal intransigence, as the Coolican Task Force suggested? Did any of them involve legitimate policy differences?)
75. *Supra* note 32.
76. See Department of Indian Affairs and Northern Development, *Federal Policy for the Settlement of Native Claims*, March 1993 at 8–11, in **Reading 11(b)**.
77. *Inuvialuit Agreement*, *infra* note 128.
78. See *Federal Policy for the Settlement of Native Claims*, *supra* note 76 at 11.
79. See further **Chapter 12**.
80. Note, however, that the 1986 *Sechelt Indian Band Self-Government Act* was negotiated and enacted separately from the Sechelt band's comprehensive land claim.
81. For example, in *James Bay* and in *Northeastern Quebec* agreements: *infra* note 113.
82. For example, the *Inuvialuit, Gwich'in* and *Nunavut* agreements, 46, **Parts 7(c), (d), and (e)**, below.
83. See, for example, the Yukon *Comprehensive Land Claim Umbrella Final Agreement*, *infra* note 146 at s. 2.12.0 on "Boards" and s. 24.4.0 on "Participation".
84. See, for example, the Yukon *Comprehensive Land Claim Umbrella Final Agreement*, *infra* note 146, chap. 24 on "Yukon Indian Self-Government" (other than s. 24.4.0) and the *Draft Yukon Model Self-Government Agreement*, November 19, 1991.
85. Dickason, *supra* note 18 at 406–408.
86. *Kanatewat et al. v. The James Bay Development Corporation and Quebec (A.G.)*, [1974] R.P. 38 (Q.C.S.); rev'd a year later in [1975] C.A. 166 (Q.C.A.).
87. *Pacific Fishermen's Defence Alliance et al. v. The Queen et al.*, [1987] 2 C.N.L.R. 115 (F.C.T.D.).
88. *Tlingit and Haida Indians of Alaska v. United States*, 177 F. Supp. 452 (Ct. Cl. 1959) and 389 F.2d. 778 (Ct. Cl. 1968). A statute enacted in 1935 authorized the Tlingit and Haida to pursue their claim in court, but three decades passed before the last of the two decisions in their favour: see K. Lysyk, "Approaches to Settlement of Indian Title Claims: The Alaskan Model" (1973) 8 U.B.C. L. Rev. 321.
89. In *Calder v. British Columbia (A.G.)*, [1973] S.C.R. 313, three of the four-judge majority who dismissed the Nisga'a's application acknowledged that apart from the question of extinguishment, the Nisga'a may have originally had an Aboriginal title to the land: **Chapter 4, Part 1**.
90. **Chapter 4, Part 3**.
91. [1990] 1 S.C.R. 1075, **Chapter 7, Part 4**.
92. **Chapter 12, Part 5**.
93. *Ibid.*
94. For a strongly critical view of the *content* of the *Alaska Agreement*, see T.R. Berger, *Village Journey: The Report of the Alaska Native Review Commission*, 1985.
95. **Part 7(f)**, below.
96. *Inuvialuit Final Agreement*, *infra* note 128.
97. *Ibid.* at s. 4(3).
98. The "future constitutional rights" provision is in s. 2.2.4 of the *Umbrella Final Agreement*, *infra* note 146. Section 6.5 of the November 19, 1991 *Draft Model Self-Government Agreement* permits a review in five years' time to determine, *inter alia*, if "other self-government agreements in Canada have more effectively incorporated self-government provisions respecting any matters considered in this Agreement," and, if so, to determine the process required to incorporate more effective provisions.
99. The right to re-negotiation arises (i) where a First Nation has secured self-government provisions that are more favourable than those contained in the November 19, 1991 *Draft Model Self-Government Agreement*, and (ii) where it would be practical to include no-less-favourable provisions for the other First Nations requesting them: see s. 6.3 of this Agreement.
100. The 1975 *James Bay Agreement* and the 1978 *Northeastern Quebec Agreement*, **Part 7(b)**, below.
101. The *Gwich'in* (1992) and *Nunavut* (1993) agreements; the *Vuntut Gwitchin*, *Na'cho n'y'ak Dun*, *Teslin Tlingit* and *Champagne and Aishihik* agreements (1993); and the

Sahtu Dene and Metis Agreement (1993): **Parts 7(d), (e), (f)**, and **(g)**, below.
102. The *Nisga'a Agreement*: **Part 7(h)**, below.
103. The 2003 *Tlicho Agreement* and the 2005 *Labrador Inuit Agreement*: **Parts 7(i)** and **(j)**, below.
104. **Part 6(f)**, above.
105. **Part 7(e)**, below.
106. *B.C. Claims Task Force Report*, July 3, 1991. The recommendations were accepted by the federal government on November 13, 1991.
107. **Part 4(b)**, above.
108. The Nisga'a negotiations pre-dated the Treaty Commission. Comprehensive claims discussions with the Nisga'a began in 1974. However, the British Columbia government did not agree to participate until late in 1990.
109. See **Part 7(h)**, below.
110. See Department of Indian Affairs and Northern Development, online: Agreements <http://www.ainc-inac.gc.ca/pr/agr/index_e.html#FinalAgreements2>; and British Columbia Treaty Process, online: Negotiation Update <http://www.bctreaty.net/files_2/updates.html>.
111. American federal implementing legislation: the *Alaska Native Claims Settlement Act, 1971*, 85 Stat. 688, enacted December 18, 1971.
112. About $12,000 per beneficiary in 1971 dollars.
113. About .8 square miles (2 square kilometres) per beneficiary, in comparison with .2 square miles (.5 square kilometres) per beneficiary in most of the Canadian numbered treaties.
114. Signed on November 11, 1975. Federal implementing legislation: *James Bay and Northern Quebec Native Claims Settlement Act*, S.C. 1976–77; *Cree-Naskapi (of Quebec) Act*, S.C. 1984, c. 18.
115. Signed on January 31, 1978. Federal implementing legislation: *Northeastern Quebec Agreement* Regulations, SOR/78-502, February 23, 1978.
116. Today the combined Cree and Inuit population affected by the agreement totals almost 19,000 people.
117. Beneficiaries must have Cree ancestry and residence in the area, recognition as a member of a Cree community in the area, or membership in one of the Indian bands in the area.
118. About .3 square miles (.8 square kilometres) per beneficiary.
119. Eligible beneficiaries must have Inuit ancestry and either a Quebec birthplace, ordinary residence in the area, or recognition as a member of an Inuit community in the area.
120. (About .8 square miles (2 square kilometres) per beneficiary). On lands, see further, **Reading 11(c)**, s. 1.
121. It is 455 pages long.
122. For example, one provision stipulates that at Kativik Regional Government meetings, "[t]he secretary must attend every sitting of the executive committee and of the council and draw up minutes of all the acts and proceedings thereof in registers kept for those purposes and called: 'Minute Book of the Executive Committee' and 'Minute Book of the Council,' respectively": *James Bay and Northern Quebec Agreement*, s. 13, sched. 2 (the Kativik Act, Part II), s. 71, para. 1. Although this provision is included in a schedule, the same schedule also contains such basic matters as the jurisdiction of the Regional Government.
123. See *Constitution Act, 1982*, ss. 35(1) and 35(3): **Chapter 7, Part 2**.
124. Federal implementing legislation: *Northeastern Quebec Agreement* Regulations, SOR/78-502, February 23, 1978.
125. See, for example, Grand Council of the Crees, *Sovereign Injustice: Forcible Inclusion of the James Bay Crees and Cree Territory into a Sovereign Quebec* (Nemaska, Québec: Grand Council of the Crees, 1995) at 249–75.
126. Section 2.15. Most of the key provisions of the *Agreement* can be amended *only* by consent of the relevant parties: see, for example, s. 5.6 regarding *Land Regime*.
127. *Supra* note 123 at 277–81, and authorities noted there.
128. Signed on June 5, 1984. Federal implementing legislation: *Western Arctic (Inuvialuit) Claims Settlement Act*, S.C. 1984, c. 24, as am. S.C. 1988, c. 16, s. 1.
129. (Eligible beneficiaries must have Canadian citizenship and (a) Inuvialuit ancestry and birthplace in the region, or acceptance as a member of an Inuvialuit corporation or (b) residence in the region for specified periods of time).
130. (About 36.4 square kilometres per beneficiary: the highest *per capita* land allotment in land claims agreements thus far). On the land provisions of this Agreement, see further **Reading 11(c)**, s. 2.
131. About $64,800 per beneficiary in 1984 dollars. By the time the payments were completed, the financial compensation was worth $152 million in 1997 dollars.
132. Formal name: *Comprehensive Land Claim Agreement between Her Majesty in Right of Canada and the Gwich'in as represented by the Gwich'in Tribal Council*. Signed on April 22, 1992. Federal implementing legislation: *Gwich'in Land Claim Settlement Act*, S.C. 1992, c. 53.
133. For example, the right to reserves under the treaty (none had ever been set aside in the region), to annual payments, and to hunting, fishing, and trapping equipment.
134. Eligible beneficiaries must have Canadian citizenship and (a) Inuvialuit ancestry and birthplace in the region, or acceptance as a member of an Inuvialuit corporation or (b) residence in the region for specified periods of time.
135. (About 16,264 square kilometres in the northwestern N.W.T. — of which 4,299 square kilometres includes subsurface rights — and 1,554 square kilometres in the Yukon, of inalienable, untaxable fee simple land, or 7.7 square kilometres per beneficiary).
136. About $34,000 per beneficiary in 1990 dollars.
137. Signed on May 25, 1993. Formal name: *Final Agreement between the Inuit of the Nunavut Settlement Area and Her Majesty in Right of Canada*. Federal implementing legislation: *Nunavut Land Claims Agreement Act*, S.C. 1993, c. 29 (received royal assent on June 10, 1993; brought into force by order in council on July 9, 1993). For the land provisions of this Agreement, see **Reading 10(c)**, s. 3.
138. The James Bay and Northern Quebec Agreement currently has the largest number of beneficiaries (19,000). It included 10,700 Cree and Inuit when it was signed in 1975.
139. An eligible beneficiary must be an Inuk by "Inuit customs and usages", must self-identify as an Inuk, and must be associated with the Nunavut settlement area.
140. (At about 20 square kilometres per beneficiary, this is also a relatively high amount in *per capita* terms.) For the land provisions of this Agreement, see further **Reading 11(c)**, s. 3.
141. *Nunavut Land Claims Agreement Act*, S.C. 1993, c. 29 (received royal assent on June 10, 1993; brought into force by order in council on July 9, 1993). See also Nunavut Implementation Commission, *Footprints in the Snow: A Comprehensive Report of the Nunavut Implementation Commission Concerning the Establishment of the Nunavut Government*, March 31, 1995; Nunavut Implementation Commission, *Footprints 2: A Second Comprehensive Report of the Nunavut Implementation Commission Concerning the Establishment of the Nunavut Government*, October 21, 1996.
142. The *Vuntut Gwitchin Agreement First Nations Final Agreement* (and the *Vuntut Gwitchin Agreement First Nations Self-Government Agreement*), involving over 500 beneficiaries centred in the Old Crow area; the *Champagne and Aishihik First Nations Final Agreement* (and the *Champagne and Aishihik First Nations Self-Government Agreement*, involving over 900 beneficiaries centred in the

Haines Junction, Champagne and Aishihik areas; *Teslin Tlingit Council Final Agreement* (and the *Teslin Tlingit Council Self-Government Agreement*): involving over 600 beneficiaries centred in the Teslin area; the *First Nation of Na-cho Ny'a'k Dun Final Agreement* (and the *First Nation of Na-cho Ny'a'k Dun Self-Government Agreement*): involving over 400 beneficiaries centred in the Mayo area; the *Little Salmon-Carmacks First Nations Final Agreement* (and the *Little Salmon-Carmacks First Nations Self-Government Agreement*), involving over 500 beneficiaries centred in the Little Salmon-Carmacks area; the *Selkirk First Nations Final Agreement* (and the *Selkirk First Nations Self-Government Agreement*), involving over 500 beneficiaries centred in the Pelly Crossing area; the *Tronděck Hwěch'in Final Agreement* (and the *Tronděck Hwěch'in Self-Government Agreement*), involving over 700 beneficiaries in the Dawson City area; the Kwäch'än Council *First Nation Final Agreement* (and the *Ta'an Kwäch'än Council First Nation Self-Government Agreement*), involving over 400 beneficiaries centred in the Lake Laberge / north Whitehorse area; the Kluane *First Nation Final Agreement* (and the *Kluane First Nation Self-Government Agreement*), involving over 100 beneficiaries centred in the Burwash Landing / Kluane area; and the *Kwanlin Dün First Nation Agreement* (and the *Kwanlin Dün First Nation Self-Government Agreement*), involving over 900 beneficiaries centred in the McIntyre area of Whitehorse). The first four sets of agreements were signed on May 29, 1993. They were implemented federally in the *Yukon First Nations Land Claims Settlements Act*, S.C. 1994, c. 34; *Yukon First Nations Self-Government Act*, S.C. 1994, c. 35; *Yukon Surface Rights Act*, S.C. 1994, c. 43; all proclaimed in force on February 14, 1995. The *Little Salmon-Carmacks* and *Selkirk* agreements were concluded in 1997; the *Tronděck Hwěch'in* agreements, in 1998; the *Ta'an Kwäch'än Council* agreements, in 2002; the *Kluane* agreements, in 2003; and the *Kwanlin Dün* agreements, in 2004. Note that population figures are estimates for the time of signing; because of population growth, current beneficiary numbers will now be significantly larger in the case of the earlier agreements.

143. The current number of beneficiaries is significantly higher than this: see comment at end of note 142, *ibid*. An eligible beneficiary must normally be either a Canadian citizen with at least 25% Yukon ancestry and ordinary Yukon residence during a specified period, or a Canadian citizen who is a descendant of such as person. An eligible beneficiary may not be enrolled under more than one Yukon Indian First Nation Agreement.

144. Between them, the four Yukon First Nations were to receive, *inter alia*, almost $180 million in financial benefits and over 16,000 square miles (41,437 square kilometres) of land.

145. The total area of the Yukon claim involves the entire territory below the North Slope in the Arctic. The claim involves fourteen Yukon Indian First Nations representing a total of over 7,000 Indians.

146. *Umbrella Final Agreement between the Government of Canada, the Council for Yukon Indians, and the Government of Yukon*. Signed on May 29, 1993 the federal government, the Government of Yukon, and the Council for Yukon Indians. (See also the *Umbrella Final Agreement Implementation Plan*.) Registered and non-status Indians or Métis have a history of cooperation in Yukon. The Council for Yukon Indians was formed in 1973 to negotiate the claim of all fourteen Yukon bands. It was a successor to the Yukon Native Brotherhood, established in 1970 to represent Status Indians. In 1975, the Yukon Association for Non-Status Indians, created three years earlier, joined with the Council for Yukon Indians. The C.Y.I. was renamed the Council of Yukon First Nations in August 1995.

147. On such matters as dispute resolution, and implementation, eligibility, and enrolment, land (reserves, settlement land, tenure, access, expropriation, surface rights regulation, quantum, boundaries, and land use planning), heritage sites, natural resources (water, fish and wildlife, forest resources, non-renewable resources), and financial matters (compensation, taxation, economic development, resource royalty sharing, and training).

148. These are to be patterned on a November 29, 1991, *Model Self-Government Agreement*: see **Chapter 12, Part 3(b)(iv)(A)**.

149. (The First Nations transboundary agreements will also qualify as land claims agreements within the meaning of s. 35 of the *Constitution Act, 1982*.) See generally s. 1 (definition of "Settlement Agreement"), s. 2.2.1, and s. 24.12.1, of the *Umbrella Final Agreement*. The *Umbrella Final Agreement* expressly leaves open the possibility that the self-government agreements may receive protection in future constitutional amendments (s. 24.12.2). This kind of protection was contemplated in the unsuccessful *Charlottetown Accord* of 1992.

150. (Although this constitutes an average of about 6.4 square kilometres per beneficiary, the proportions are to vary among individual First Nations agreements.) For the land provisions of these Agreements, see further, **Reading 11(c)**, s. 4.

151. (About 63% on average; although, again, proportions will vary among individual First Nations.)

152. (In 1990 dollars.)

153. (About $38,000 per beneficiary in 1990 dollars.)

154. (i) The *Vuntut Gwitchin (originally spelled "Gwich'in") First Nation Final Agreement*, which incorporates two transboundary agreements, the *Gwich'in Transboundary Agreement* and the *Old Crow / Inuvialuit Reciprocal Harvesting Agreement*; and (ii) the *Vuntut Gwitchin First Nation Self-Government Agreement*.

155. All were formally signed on May 29, 1993. In some cases, earlier versions had been signed a year before. Federal legislation ratifying the settlement and self-government agreements was introduced in the House of Commons on May 31, 1994 and was given Royal Assent on July 7, 1994. Federal legislation on settlement surface rights received Royal Assent on December 15, 1994. The federal ratifying legislation came into force on February 14, 1995.

156. The *Teslin Tlingit Council Final Agreement*, for example, is 409 pages in length. (The non-entrenched *Umbrella Final Agreement* is 292 pages long; the non-entrenched *Umbrella Agreement Implementation Plan*: 212 pages; and the non-entrenched *Teslin Tlingit Council Self-Government Agreement*, 43 pages.)

157. This is defined as "the total number of animals of a Freshwater Fish or Wildlife species which, in the manner established by this chapter, are deemed not to be required for Conservation": s. 16.2.0.

158. Section 16.9.1.3.

159. The Yukon agreements are accompanied by a non-entrenched implementation agreement, the *Umbrella Agreement Implementation Plan*. This channels technical operational matters away from the entrenched final agreements. Perhaps the concept of non-entrenched side-agreements could be used more widely. They could filter out more technical issues or matters that might need adjustment from time to time. They might spare parties the need to resort to formal amendment or to time-consuming dispute resolution procedures.

160. Signed on September 6, 1993. Federal implementing legislation: *Sahtu Dene and Metis Land Claim Settlement Act*, S.C. 1994, c. 27.

161. (About one-sixth of all beneficiaries.)

162. (About 41,437 square kilometres for 2,400 beneficiaries, or about 17 square kilometres per beneficiary.) For the land provisions of this Agreement, see further, **Reading 11(c)**, s. 5.

163. (About 4% of all land, compared to about 14% for the Gwich'in.)
164. For some general discussions of the agreement, see "*The Nisga'a Treaty*" (1998–99) 120 *B.C. Studies* 1 at 1–110 (special volume); T.R. Berger, *The Importance of the Nisga'a Treaty to Canadians*, Corry Lecture at Queen's University, February 10, 1999, online: <http://www.nisgaa.org>; D. Sanders, "We Intend to Live Here Forever: A Primer on the Nisga'a Treaty" (1999) 33 U.B.C. L. Rev. 103; G. Gibson, "Comments on the Draft Nisga'a Treaty" (1999) 120 *BC Studies* at 55; G. Gibson, *A Principled Analysis of the Nisga'a Treaty* in *Public Policy Sources #27* (Vancouver: The Fraser Institute, spring, 1999).
165. *Nisga'a Final Agreement*, between The Nisga'a Nation, Her Majesty the Queen in Right of Canada, and Her Majesty the Queen in Right of British Columbia, August 4, 1998.
166. To become effective, the Agreement required ratification by a majority of all eligible Nisga'a voters, and by provincial and federal legislation. The Agreement was ratified by 61% of eligible Nisga'a voters, or 73% of those who cast ballots, on November 8 and 9, 1998: see *House of Sga'nism, Nisilada v. Canada*, [2000] B.C.J. No. 831 (B.C.S.C.) at para. 25. The provincial ratifying legislation, the *Nisga'a Final Agreement Act*, S.B.C. 1999, c. 2, received royal assent on April 26, 1997, after the provincial government invoked closure when only 12 of the 25 chapters had been discussed on a clause-by-clause basis. The federal ratifying legislation, the *Nisga'a Final Agreement Act*, S.C. 2000, c. 7, received royal assent on April 13, 2000.
167. Formal negotiation of the Nisga'a claim began in 1976, but was hampered by the refusal of the Government of British Columbia to participate. Subject to the Indian interest, virtually all the land in question was owned by the province. Moreover, provincial jurisdiction and administration would be directly affected by any settlement. Thus provincial involvement was crucial. British Columbia agreed to participate in the negotiations in 1990, and an Agreement-in-Principle was initialled in February 1996. The *Nisga'a Final Agreement* was signed on August 4, 1998. See further, Department of Indian and Northern Affairs, *Nisga'a Final Treaty Agreement Backgrounder: History of Negotiations With the Nisga'a Tribal Council* (Ottawa: D.I.A.N.D.), July 23, 1998, catalogue no. S-B009-005-EE-A1.
168. Early Nisga'a contact with Europeans dates back to the late 18th century. From then until well into the 19th century, the Nisga'a were ravaged by epidemics of smallpox and measles: "The Nisga'a: A Journey Through Time" *Vancouver Sun* (July 16, 1998) A11. A Hudson's Bay post called Fort Simpson operated on the Nass River from 1831–34: D. Raunet, *Without Surrender Without Consent*, rev'd. ed. (Vancouver, B.C.: Douglas & McIntyre, 1984) 37–42. Anglican church missions were established in 1867 (at Kincolith) and 1878 (at Aiyansh): *ibid.*, chaps. 4 and 5. In the 1880s the government instituted a reserve system in the area: *ibid.* at 80–85. Pursuant to it, the Nisga'a were allocated a tiny fraction of the lands they traditionally claimed.

    In 1884, a federal law banned the potlatch, a vital traditional ceremony for the Nisga'a and other west coast Aboriginal peoples: *ibid.*, chap. 8, and R.R. Gadacz, "Potlatch" in *The Canadian Encyclopedia*, Year 2000 ed. (Toronto: McClelland & Stewart, 1999) at 1878–79. The potlatch marked special occasions, confirmed official positions, honoured those who had died, and was accompanied by a distribution of wealth to others. Ironically, this monument to community life and sharing was strenuously opposed by Christian churches, who saw it as a symbol of waste and decadence. The ban was in place until 1951.

    In 1890 the Nisga'a formed a Land Committee to pursue their claims to their traditional lands. They petitioned to Victoria, to Ottawa, and to the Judicial Committee of the Privy Council in London, but to no avail: Raunet, chap. 9. In 1927, the federal government prohibited all persons from raising funds for native land claims without special federal permission. The ban lasted until 1951.

    In 1967, under the leadership of Frank Calder, a Nisga'a chief and elected MLA, the Nisga'a sought a court declaration that they had Aboriginal title to the Nass Valley. As seen in **Chapter 4**, the Nisga'a themselves lost the *Calder* case on a legal technicality. However, the Supreme Court's decision in this case did strengthen the concept of Aboriginal rights. It also convinced the federal government to begin a formal process for negotiating Aboriginal title claims.
169. Raunet, *ibid.* chap. 2.
170. "The World of the Nisga'a" *Vancouver Sun* (August 1, 1998) A12–A13.
171. *Ibid.*
172. "Nisga'a Proud of their School System" *Vancouver Sun* (July 31, 1998) A17.
173. *Ibid.*
174. "The Nisga'a: A Journey Through Time". *Vancouver Sun* (July 16, 1998) A11.
175. For the key eligibility provision, see *Nisga'a Final Agreement (NFA)*, chap. 20, subpara. 1(a): "An individual is eligible to be enrolled under this Agreement if that individual is (a) of Nisga'a ancestry and their mother was born into one of the Nisga'a tribes." The agreement also requires, in effect, that the Nisga'a constitution provide that every Canadian citizen who is enrolled under the agreement is entitled to be a Nisga'a citizen: *NFA*, chap. 11, subpara. 9(p.) and chap. 1 (definition of Nisga'a participant).
176. *NFA*, chap. 3, para. 2. (Assuming that there are approximately 5,800 eligible Nisga'a, this constitutes about .33 square kilometres per beneficiary, or about .83 square kilometres per beneficiary presently residing in the Treaty area.)
177. "The World of the Nisga'a" *Vancouver Sun* (August 1, 1998) A12–A13.
178. *NFA*, chap. 3, para. 19.
179. *NFA*, chap. 5.
180. *NFA*, chap. 8.
181. *NFA*, chap. 10.
182. "How Costs are Shared and Land Allocated" *Vancouver Sun* (July 30, 1998) A13.
183. Canada is to make a net contribution of $10 million to a fisheries conservation trust, and to provide the Nisga'a with $11.5 million to enable them to increase their participation in the coastal commercial fishery: *NFA*, chap. 8, schedules F and G, respectively. For a summary of other contributions in areas such as forestry and training, see "How Costs are Shared and Land Allocated" *Vancouver Sun* (July 30, 1998) A13.
184. *NFA*, chap. 8, paras. 21–27. For a comment on the general role of separate "side agreements" in the Nisga'a Treaty and other settlements, see T. Dickson, "Self-Government by Side Agreement?" (2004) 49 McGill L.J. 419.
185. *NFA*, chap. 11.
186. *NFA*, chap. 11, para. 13.
187. *NFA*, chap. 11, subpara. 9(k)(i).
188. *NFA*, chap. 11, subpara. 9(k)(ii).
189. In relation to general public governments; the power is subject to the Nisga'a constitution.
190. *NFA*, chap. 11, paras. 33 (a general provision) and 116 (devolution of cultural property). In these areas, in the event of a conflict, a Nisga'a law prevails over a federal or provincial law.
191. *NFA*, chap. 11, para. 84.
192. *NFA*, chap. 11, para. 88.

193. *NFA*, chap. 11, para. 89.
194. *NFA*, chap. 11, para. 99.
195. *NFA*, chap. 11, para. 101. Although para. 100 authorizes the Nisga'a to enact pre-school to grade 12 education laws subject to certain curriculum, examination, and other standards, para. 101 stipulates that Nisga'a laws will prevail over federal or provincial laws to the extent of any inconsistency or conflict.
196. *NFA*, chap. 11, paras. 35 and 36.
197. *NFA*, chap. 11, paras. 47 to 49.
198. *NFA*, chap. 11, para. 62.
199. *NFA*, chap. 11, para. 71.
200. *NFA*, chap. 11, para. 74.
201. *NFA*, chap. 11, para. 76.
202. *NFA*, chap. 11, para. 78.
203. *NFA*, chap. 11, para. 82.
204. *NFA*, chap. 11, para. 108.
205. *NFA*, chap. 11, para. 111.
206. *NFA*, chap. 12, paras. 1 to 22.
207. *NFA*, chap. 12, paras. 23 to 29.
208. *NFA*, chap. 12.
209. See, for example, *NFA*, chap. 11, paras. and subparas. 38(b), 41(b), 42, and 47.
210. *NFA*, chap. 12, 37.
211. *NFA*, chap. 12, subpara. 38(a). Judicial review decisions are subject to appeal to the Supreme Court of British Columbia for errors of law or jurisdiction: chap. 12, para. 46.
212. *NFA*, chap. 12, subpara. 41(d). However, the Nisga'a Court may not impose "a sanction or penalty different in nature from those generally imposed by provincial or superior courts in Canada, without the person's consent": chap. 12, para. 44.
213. *NFA*, chap. 11, para. 67.
214. *Ibid.*
215. *Ibid.*.
216. *NFA*, chap. 11, para. 61.
217. *NFA*, chap. 11, paras. 59 to 62.
218. *NFA*, chap. 11, para. 129.
219. *NFA*, chap. 12, subpart. 1(b).
220. *NFA*, chap. 12, subpara. 38(b).
221. *NFA*, chap. 2, para. 9.
222. Section 1 of the *Charter* refers to "reasonable limits prescribed by law as can be demonstrably justified in a free and democratic society." Does para. 9 mean that Nisga'a laws that violate *Charter* provisions are subject not to the usual s. 1 *Charter* test, but to a requirement that they relate reasonably to the purpose of the *Nisga'a Final Agreement*?
223. *NFA*, chap. 18, para. 18.
224. *NFA*, chap. 16, paras. 5 and 6.
225. This would depend on negotiations between the Nisga'a and Canada and / or British Columbia: *NFA*, chap. 16, subpara. 3 (b).
226. *NFA*, chap. 11, para. 21. See also paras. 19, 20, 22, and 23.
227. *NFA*, chap. 2, para. 22.
228. *NFA*, chap. 2, paras. 26 and 27.
229. "How Costs are Shared and Land Allocated" *Vancouver Sun* (July 30, 1998) A13. A later Sun article put the figure at $487 million: P. O'Neil, "Bells Ring in B.C.'s Historic Nisga'a Deal" *Vancouver Sun* (April 14, 2000) A3. If natural resources costs are included, this figure would be higher: see, D. Sanders, "We Intend to Live Here Forever: A Primer on the Nisga'a Treaty" (1999) 33 U.B.C. L. Rev. 103.
230. See, for example, the indexation factors in Schedule A to chap. 14.
231. "How Costs are Shared and Land Allocated" *Vancouver Sun* (July 30, 1998) A13.
232. The B.C. Fisheries Survival Coalition.
233. Represented by the B.C. Citizens First coalition.
234. The Liberal Party of B.C. and the Reform Party of B.C.
235. See, for example, Office of the Official Opposition, Liberal Caucus of British Columbia, *The Nisga'a Template: Facts the Government isn't Sharing* (Victoria, B.C., 1998); G. Gibson, "Comments on the Draft Nisga'a Treaty" (1999) 120 *BC Studies* 55; and G. Gibson, *A Principled Analysis of the Nisga'a Treaty* in *Public Policy Sources #27* (Vancouver: The Fraser Institute, spring, 1999). Note that not all of these critics have stressed all of these arguments, and that some critics stress other concerns.
236. See *Campbell v. British Columbia (A.G.)* 2000), 189 D.L.R. (4th) 333 (B.C.S.C.), discussed in **Chapter 12, Part 4.**
237. R.S.B.C. 1996, Chap. 67, requiring a public referendum in British Columbia on proposed constitutional changes. Non-compliance with this Act is a key concern of the British Columbia Liberal Party: see Office of the Official Opposition, Liberal Caucus of British Columbia, "The Nisga'a Template: Facts the Government Isn't Sharing" (Victoria: B.C. Liberal Caucus, 1998) at 4, point # 6. The Liberal Party is challenging the legality of the Treaty process in Court, arguing, *inter alia*, that it contravenes this Act.
238. N. Sterritt, "The Nisga'a Treaty: Competing Claims Ignored!" (1999) 120 *BC Studies* 73.
239. See, for example, C. McInnes, "Nisga'a's Neighbours Vow to Defend Overlapping Claims" *Vancouver Sun* (August 1998); online: <nisgaa_treaty19.html>; and following note.
240. The British Columbia Supreme Court has said that although the Crown does not have a legal obligation to negotiate Aboriginal claims, once it enters negotiations it has a legal obligation to negotiate in good faith: *Gitanyow First Nation v. Canada*, [1999] 3 C.N.L.R. 89 (B.C.S.C.)..
241. *House of Sga'nism, Nisilada v. Canada,* [2000] B.C.J. No. 831 (B.C. Prov. Ct.); (application for interlocutory injunction refused); aff'd in [2000] B.C.J. No. 821 (B.C.C.A.); and Canadian Press, "Dissident Nisga'a Will Continue Battling Treaty" *Vancouver Sun* (April 30, 2000) B8.
242. See, generally, S. Baade, "Aboriginal Self-Government in British Columbia: The Nisga'a Agreement-in-Principle" (1997) 3 Appeal 42; J. Gosnell, Sr., "Hereditary Chief and President of the Nisga'a Tribal Council" *Vancouver Sun* (August 5, 1998) A10; Glen Clark, former premier of B.C., "The Aim is Justice, Reconciliation, and Certainty, the Premier Says", *ibid.* at A5; T.R. Berger, "Nisga'a Won't Knuckle Under", *ibid.* at A19; D. Sanders, "We Intend to Live Here Forever: A Primer on the Nisga'a Treaty" (1999) 33 U.B.C. L. Rev. 103. Not all the supporters make or stress all the arguments cited here. Some are concerned with other issues. For example, H. Foster, in "Honouring the Queen's Flag: A Legal and Historical Perspective on the Nisga'a Treaty" (1999) 120 *BC Studies* 11, argues that the agreement does address the overlap question.
243. See *Campbell v. British Columbia (A.G.)*, *supra* note 236, discussed in **Chapter 12, Part 4.**
244. See, for example, former premier Glen Clark, "The Aim is Justice, Reconciliation, and Certainty, the Premier Says", *ibid.*: "[The framers of the Constitution] created a ready-made slot within Section 35, into which the Nisga'a Treaty fits, without changing the Constitution itself"; and H. Foster, *ibid.* at 30–33. Cf. Ted McWhinney, M.P., "Constitutional Rights Could be Endangered by Treaties" *Vancouver Sun* (August 28, 1998) A19. In McWhinney's view, the "ready-made slot" interpretation was probably not intended when s. 35(3) was drafted. However, since that interpretation could permit future treaties to derogate automatically from the existing division of legislative powers and from *Charter* rights, McWhinney urged that the issue be resolved by the Supreme Court of Canada.
245. *Campbell v. British Columbia (A.G.)*, *supra* note 236.
246. One alternative approach would retain Aboriginal paramountcy in the specific areas required, subject to a general federal power to legislate in relation to the peace, order, and good government of Canada, criminal law or

criminal procedure, and the human rights, health and safety of all Canadians: this is the approach taken in the Inuit Land Claims Agreement, s. 2.22.2: see **Chapter 11, Part 7(j)**. A second alternative would permit Aboriginal paramountcy to be overridden where the federal or provincial overriding legislation is otherwise valid constitutionally and is publicly and expressly renewed at least every five years. This approach would be patterned on s. 33 of the *Constitution Act, 1982*. A third alternative, more dependent on judicial discretion than the first two, would permit a general public legislation to prevail in areas of *prima facie* Aboriginal paramountcy, where the general legislation was accompanied by a legitimate justification for the override. The model here is the reviewable judicial independence override contemplated in *Re Remuneration of Provincial Court Judges*, [1997] 3 S.C.R. 3 at paras. 180–84. All three alternatives could combine a high level of effective Aboriginal finality with residual general public interest safeguards.

247. For a possible alternative, see ss. 17.40.7 and 17.40.11 of the *Labrador Inuit Land Claims Agreement*: **Part 7(j)**, below. These sections give non-beneficiary residents the right to vote for and to hold office in Inuit Community Government Councils, subject to the requirement that at least 75% of Inuit Community Government Council seats be reserved for (a) beneficiaries, (b) non-beneficiaries who were ordinarily resident in Inuit communities at the time of the signing of the Agreement-in-Principle, and (c) descendants of the non-beneficiaries in category (b).
248. Centre for Research and Information on Canada (CRIC), *Referendum on Aboriginal Treaties in British Columbia*, http://www.cric.ca/en_html/guide/referendum/referendum_bc.html; *The Globe and Mail*, "Only 36% of Eligible Voters Cast Ballots" and "Referendum Results", July 4, 2002, A8.
249. *Ibid.*
250. *Ibid.*
251. *Ibid.*
252. *Ibid.*
253. Formerly called Dogrib.
254. Section 2.6.1.
255. *Land Claims and Self-Government Agreement Among the Tlicho and the Government of the Northwest Territories and the Government of Canada*. Signed: 25 August 2003.
256. Section 2.6.1.
257. Section 18.1. The land is to be exempt from expropriation, except in special circumstances: s. 20.1.1.
258. Map referred to in the appendix to Chapter 18 of Tlicho Agreement. The communities are Behcho Ko (Rae-Edzo), Wha Ti (Lac la Martre), Gameti (Rae Lakes), and Wekweti (Snare Lake).
259. Section 19.2.
260. E.g., the right to harvest all species of wildlife at all times of the year (s. 10.1.1(a) and the right to harvest furbearers on Tlicho lands at all times of the year (s. 10.1.1(b)); and guaranteed representation on a Renewable Resources Board (ss. 12.2.2. to 12.3.5) Land and Water Board (ss. 22.3.3 to 22.3.6).
261. The Tlicho are to have just over 10% of the first $2 million in government mineral royalties in each calendar year and just over 2% of additional government mineral royalties in that calendar year (s. 25.1.1).
262. Appendix to Chapter 24 of Tlicho Agreement: Capital Transfer Payments Schedule (24.1.1).
263. Section 7.7.2.
264. *Ibid.*
265. Section 7.7.3.
266. Section 8.2.3.
267. Section 8.2.4.
268. Section 8.2.7.
269. Section 2.10.2.
270. Section 2.10.10.
271. Sections 2.10.3 to 2.10.5.
272. *Land Claims and Self-Government Agreement Between the Inuit of Labrador as Represented by the Labrador Inuit Association and the Queen in Right of Newfoundland and Labrador and the Queen in Right of Canada*. Signed: 22 January 2005.
273. Schedule 19A of Section 19. The payments are to be in 1997 dollars, indexed to 2003 value.
274. *Labrador Inuit Agreement*, chap. 7.
275. *Labrador Inuit Agreement*, part. 2.22.2:

> Notwithstanding any other provision of the Agreement, if there is a Conflict between an Inuit Law or a Bylaw of an Inuit Community Government and:
> (a) a federal Law in relation to the peace, order and good government of Canada; or
> (b) a federal Law that relates specifically to the criminal law or criminal procedure, the recognition and protection of human rights of all Canadians, or the protection of health and safety of all Canadians,
>
> the federal Law prevails to the extent of the Conflict.

See also part 2.22.1, providing that where an Inuit law does not have paramountcy, and conflicts with a federal or provincial law of general application, the latter prevails to the extent of the paramountcy.

276. *Supra* note 270. The *Nisga'a Agreement* does not have a comparable provision.
277. The Agreement reserves 75% of Inuit Community Council seats for beneficiaries and for non-beneficiaries who were ordinarily resident in Inuit communities before May 10, 1999: part 17.40.7.
278. Non-beneficiary new residents can hold up to 25% of the seats in Community Councils, with corresponding voting rights, depending on the ratio of their voting population to that of the total number of eligible Community voters: part 17.40.11.
279. Parts 2.11.2 and 2.11.3.
280. Parts 2.11.4 and 2.11.5. See also the quit claim in part 2.11.6.
281. Section 2.2.1.
282. Sections 1.1 and 16.3.1. This amount was later raised to $50 million: J. Steffenhagen and P. Willcocks, "Treaty Process on Life Support, Chief Says: The Decision to Pursue Native Rights Claims Through the Courts Puts the B.C. Treaty Process into Crisis" *The Vancouver Sun* (June 1, 2000) A7. In addition, and outside the terms of the AIP, the federal government provided a one-time grant of $1.5 million for economic development initiatives and planning.
283. Sections 15.1.0 to 15.3.0. Section 15.5.3 provides that "[t]he Parties agree that the provisions relating to Sechelt governance will not be constitutionally protected treaty rights, unless specifically provided for in the Final Agreement."
284. Section 17.3.0.
285. J. Steffenhagen and P. Willcocks, *supra* note 282.
286. *Ibid.*
287. *Ibid. Delgamuukw v. British Columbia*, [1997] S.C.R. 1010 is discussed in **Chapter 10, Part 3**.
288. "It is estimated that there are 600 specific claims on behalf of Indian First Nations alone, a number that is undoubtedly low. Some 300 of these are (or have been) in the specific claims process, and about 75 have been settled: W.B. Henderson and D.T. Ground, "Survey of Aboriginal Land Claims" (1994) 26 *Ottawa L.R.* 187 at 199. "The Department of Indian Affairs is dealing with about 225 specific claims, but Indian leaders estimate there are more than 2,000 across the country": J. Aubry, "Land [*sic*] Claims Commissioners Resigning to Protest Inaction" *Ottawa Citizen* (July 13, 1996) A2. See generally, the annual reports of the Indian Claims Commission: main website at <www.indianclaims.ca>.

289. See S. Griess, *Examination of the Northern Boundary Dispute of the Mississauga Indian Reserve*, Honours. Essay, Department of Law, Carleton University, 1994 [unpublished].
290. They had made two earlier, unsuccessful, attempts at challenging the northern boundary, in 1892 and 1976.
291. As seen, the government has attempted to address this problem by recognizing a category of "other claims" on a discretionary basis: *supra* note 4. See discussion in *Report*, vol. 2, chap. 4, s. 5.2 at 548–49.
292. The Ontario Temagami First Nation made a similar argument, but this was rejected on the ground that they had adhered to the Robinson-Huron Treaty by enjoying its benefits: *Ontario (A.G.) v. Bear Island Foundation*, [1991] 1 S.C.R. 570 at 575.
293. J.L. Steckley and B.D. Cummins, *Full Circle: Canada's First Nations* (Toronto: Prentice Hall, 2001), chap. 14.
294. The account below attempts to synthesize the materials in R.C. Daniel, "The Oka Indians vs. the Seminary of St. Sulpice", in *A History of Native Claims Processes in Canada, 1867–1979* (Ottawa: Department of Indian Affairs and Northern Development, Research Branch, 1983); L. Villeneuve and D. Francis, "The Oka Indians" in *The Historical Background of Indian Reserves and Settlements in the Province of Quebec* (Ottawa: Department of Indian Affairs and Northern Development, Research Branch, 1984); Dept. of Indian and Northern Affairs and Northern Development, *Overview of the Oka Issue* (Ottawa: D.I.A.N.D., 1990); House of Commons Standing Committee on Aboriginal Affairs, *Fifth Report of the Standing Committee on Aboriginal Affairs* (Ottawa: Queen's Printer, 1991); M. Tugwell, *The Legacy of Oka* (Toronto: The Mackenzie Institute, 1991); G. York and L. Pindera, *People of the Pines: The Warriors and the Legacy of Oka* (Toronto: Little, Brown & Co., 1991); Dickason, *supra* note 18 at 326–31; J.S. Frideres, *Native Peoples in Canada: Contemporary Conflicts* (Scarborough, Ont.: Prentice-Hall, 1993), chap. 10 at 367–406; J.R. Miller, "Great White Father Knows Best: Oka and the Land Claims Process" (reprint), in K.S. Coates and R. Fisher, eds., *Out of the Background: Readings on Canadian Native History* (Toronto: Copp Clark, 1996) at 367.
295. See generally Frideres, *ibid.* at 387–90.
296. For a short account of these events and the crisis that followed, see Frideres, *ibid.* at 397–404.
297. See J.B. Jamieson, "Trade and Warfare: The Disappearance of the St. Lawrence Iroquois" (1990) 39 *Man in the Northeast* 79; B. Trigger and J. Prendergast, "Saint Lawrence Indians" in W.C. Sturtevant, ed., *Handbook of North American Indians*, vol. 15 (Washington: Smithsonian Institute, 1978) at 357–61; *R. v. Adams*, [1993] 3 C.N.L.R. 98 at 109–35, 119 (Q.C.A.); D.R. Snow, *The Iroquois* (Oxford: Blackwell, 1994).
298. See *R. v. Adams*, [1996] 3 S.C.R. 101 at paras. 16, 22, 41, 44, 45.
299. *People of the Pines*, *supra* note 294 at 86.
300. Miller, *supra* note 294.
301. 4 Vict., c. 42 (1841).
302. *People of the Pines*, *supra* note 294 at 90.
303. *Ibid.* at 91–92.
304. After a series of hung juries, the Indians were finally acquitted: A.R. Hassard, "When the Oka Seminary Went Up in Flames" in *Famous Canadian Trials* (Toronto: Carswell, 1924) at 106–23.
305. *Corinthe et al. v. Seminary of St. Sulpice of Montreal*, [1912] 5 D.L.R. 263 at 267 (J.C.P.C.).
306. *Native Peoples in Canada*, *supra* note 294 at 384.
307. Frideres, *supra* note 294 at 381.
308. S.C. 2001, c.8. The Act implemented land use agreements signed between the Kanesatake Mohawks and the federal government on June 22, 2000 and December 21, 2000.
309. Section 4.
310. Section 7. See also s. 6.
311. Section 13.
312. Section 4.
313. See generally, P. Edwards, *One Dead Indian: The Premier, The Police, and The Ipperwash Crisis* (Toronto: Stoddart Publishing, 2003 and J.L. Steckley and B.D. Cummins, Full Circle: Canada's First Nations (Toronto: Prentice Hall, 2001), chap. 20.
314. While self-government was once seen mainly as guaranteed participation in the governmental mainstream, it can now mean separate governmental structures with parallel or superior jurisdiction to that of existing public governments.
315. While earlier agreements required a general extinguishment of Aboriginal rights claims, some of the more recent agreements cede certain Aboriginal rights while preserving others. More recent agreements also contain "catch-up" provisions to ensure that they can be re-negotiated to match later, more generous, settlements.
316. In the Yukon, now that the first four agreements have been ratified, future First Nation Final Agreements — agreements with constitutional effect — can be implemented merely by order in council: see *Umbrella Final Agreement*, s. 2.2.12.
317. For examples, see *supra* note 122 and text referred to in *supra* note 159. The formal dispute resolution amendment processes are not only extraordinarily complex, but vary considerably from one agreement to the other: see further **Reading 11(f)** at p. 408.
318. For example, the non-entrenched implementation plans referred to in *supra* note 159.

12 Aboriginal Self-Government

Chapter Highlights

- Aboriginal spokespeople tend to call for a form of self-government that is inherent, entrenched, enforceable, and, to some extent, sovereign.
- As a legal concept, self-government has a wide range of possible meanings, from outright international status to voluntary internal self-regulation. Most approaches proposed in Canada today fall between these two extremes.
- Alternatives include traditional, legislated, negotiated, and "judicial" self-government, as well as self-government by formal constitutional amendment or policy recognition.
- The Supreme Court has not recognized a general right of Aboriginal self-government, although the federal government recognizes such right as a matter of government policy.
- The Royal Commission on Aboriginal Peoples combined recommendations for separate legal structures of self-government, such as an eventual separate Aboriginal Parliament, with practical recommendations for increasing Aboriginal self-sufficiency and self-control in matters such as health, housing, and education.

Synopsis

Self-government promises greater participation by those affected by government decisions, more responsive government decisions, and less dependence. At the same time, the interests of one group within Canada must be balanced against the needs of the wider community. The more governmental the interests, the more they will affect third parties. As for Aboriginal claims in general, the negotiation approach has some advantages for addressing Aboriginal self-government claims. These include flexibility, participation by those directly concerned, approval by elected officials, and possible legislative or constitutional protection. Self-government will have to vary with individual situations. However, the most effective arrangements may be those that address concrete problems without generating unnecessary legal barriers.

Selected Readings

🖹 links material in this chapter to the corresponding headings and page numbers of the relevant readings.

🖹 Part 3(a)	*Kaianerakowa*	410
🖹 Part 3(c)(iii)(B)	*Sechelt Indian Band Self-Government Act*	413
🖹 Part 3(c)(iv)(A)	*Vuntut Gwitchin First Nation Self-Government Agreement*	419
🖹 Part 4	*R. v. Pamajewon*	433
🖹 Part 5(b)	Proposed Charlottetown Accord	429
🖹 Part 7	Highlights of *Report of the Royal Commission on Aboriginal Peoples*	434
	People to People, Nation to Nation	435

1. ABORIGINAL PERSPECTIVES

It would be futile to seek a single catch-all concept of Aboriginal self-government,[1] even among Aboriginal peoples. The history and present situations of Aboriginal peoples across the country are just as diverse as those of their non-Aboriginal counterparts. Varying local and regional needs will require different answers.

On the other hand, Aboriginal spokespeople have been relatively consistent in demanding recognition of a form of self-government that is inherent, entrenched, enforceable, and, to some extent, sovereign. We originally had self-government, they say; we should continue to have it. An Assembly of First Nations position paper expressed this concern with simplicity and eloquence:

> Our Creator, Mother Earth, put First Nations on this land to care for and live in harmony with all her creation. We cared for our earth, our brothers and sisters in the animal world, and each other. These responsibilities give us our inherent, continuing right to self-government. This right flows from our original occupation of this land from time immemorial.[2]

2. THE DEBATE

There is considerable consensus about the desirability of self-government for Aboriginal peoples. Like all people, Aboriginal peoples should be able to have the greatest possible control over governing their own lives. Greater self-government means less dependence on others. It increases the chances that community decisions will reflect the interests of their members. Originally, Aboriginal peoples did govern their own affairs. Their influence over their own affairs was restricted by colonists and other newcomers. The challenge now is how to translate the goal of Aboriginal self-government into reality.

Part of this reality is the presence in Canada today of many who cannot claim Aboriginal ancestry, and who cannot now easily leave. Another part is Canada's status as international state, with its own claims to sovereignty, territorial integrity, and responsibility for all those within its borders.

On one hand, this means that if Aboriginal self-government is to be effective, it should be enforceable against non-Aboriginals as well as Aboriginals. On the other hand, this also means that if Aboriginal self-government is to be fair, it should take into account the interests of non-Aboriginals and the larger community as well as those of Aboriginal peoples themselves.

How much self-control can individual groups exercise within a larger polity without threatening its viability or effective operation? How much pluralism is workable in government? Even in the vast spaces of Canada, no person or group lives in a vacuum. Special rights for some can result in restrictions for others. The more public or governmental these rights, the more likely that third parties will be affected.

There are other questions about the status and context of Aboriginal self-government. Should it be protected constitutionally? If constitutional protection is not always forthcoming or desirable, what are the other possibilities? Should it be subject to the *Canadian Charter of Rights and Freedoms*? Beyond these questions are the practical challenges of organizing on-the-ground resources, training, and facilities that will be needed to make Aboriginal self-government work effectively. These challenges are at least as important as the theoretical ones.

3. POSSIBLE ALTERNATIVES

At one extreme, full Aboriginal self-government might be equated with international status. In this sense it could help justify the secession of Aboriginal states from Canada. At another extreme, Aboriginal self-government might mean internal self-regulation, enforced by voluntary moral constraints rather than by law in the courts. Most approaches proposed or considered in Canada today fall between these two extremes.[3] But within them are so many possibilities that Aboriginal self-government can mean vastly different things, depending on the speaker and the context. The categories below are not the only possible ones,[4] nor are they necessarily mutually exclusive.

(a) Traditional Self-Government

Reading 12(a) at p. 410

Traditional systems of Aboriginal self-government are not generally enforceable in the courts of Canada, but may have strong support within Aboriginal communities.[5] For example, the Mohawk people of Ontario, Quebec and northeastern United States have a traditional system of self-government that operates alongside the *Indian Act* and other legislative structures. The traditional constitution of the Iroquois Confederacy is called *Kaianerakowa*, the Great Law of Peace. The Great Law is based on an elaborate clan and federal system that has specific requirements on such matters as emigration, foreign nations, war, referenda, festivals, and funerals.[6]

Increasingly, Aboriginal peoples are asserting greater effective control of government programs by applying their own traditional methods to areas formerly administered by federal or provincial administrators. For example, in many communities, native healing circles and lodges are being used to address social problems formerly handled by social workers.[7] Native-run health clinics, such as Anishnawabe Health in Toronto, make use of traditional healers.[8] At Pangnirtung, Baffin Island, a local mental health committee consults with Inuit elders on all decisions.[9] Some communities use native justice circles, in which local judges consult with neighbours and affected community members before sentencing Aboriginal offenders.[10] Most schools formerly under federal control are now run by bands, which emphasize native staff and traditional teachings.[11] Native-run child welfare agencies are developing.[12]

(b) Legislated Self-Government

Aboriginal self-government that is created and protected by ordinary legislation will be described here as legislated self-government. It is unilaterally created and can be unilaterally changed by majority vote in Parliament. It is produced at least in part by elected politicians. The best example of this unilateral approach is the federal *Indian Act*.

(i) Indian Act Self-Government

Although the federal *Indian Act*[13] was imposed from outside, and has been regarded as a highly restrictive, "colonial" piece of legislation, it does contain some structures of self-government.[14] For example, band members can select their own band council governments. A chief and two to twelve councillors are chosen either by native custom or by elections from among adult band members.[15]

The band council has municipal-type legislative and administrative responsibilities over the reserve and powers over band membership and funds. Since 1988, band councils can tax reserve property,[16] and can negotiate block funding over multiple-year periods. Band council jurisdiction extends to areas such as traffic, curfews, water supply, and fish and game.[17] Its subject matter is narrower than that on which Cabinet can legislate. Band council by-laws:

1. must not be inconsistent with the *Indian Act* or regulation made under it by Cabinet or the Minister;[18] and
2. are subject to disallowance by the Minister.[19]

The Cabinet and the Minister have exercised their paramount legislative power and disallowance power much less in recent years.

Some of the problems with *Indian Act* self-government are:

1. its relatively restricted scope, limited essentially to status reserve residents;
2. its complexity;
3. the centralist structure of the *Indian Act*; and
4. the small size (often less than 500 people), isolation, and limited resource base of most bands and reserves.

Some bands, though, such as the Squamish, Six Nations and The Pas bands, have exercised their *Indian Act* powers extensively.[20] Under — and sometimes despite — the *Indian Act* framework, many bands have been extending their responsibilities in areas such as education, health care, and social services.[21] Two other important areas are economic development[22] and native policing.[23] Some bands control their own policing, either by contract with the R.C.M.P. and / or provincial forces,[24] or through their own police forces.[25] Two of the best known of the latter are the Six Nations police and the Peacekeepers force at Kahnawake.[26]

In 2002, the federal government introduced in Parliament a proposed *First Nations Governance Act*[27] (*FNGA*). The *FNGA* was the centrepiece of a package of *Indian Act* and related reform initiatives by the federal government in 2002. Other legislative initiatives included a more independent specific claims resolution process,[28] increased control over band lands,[29] and provisions for storage and management of First Nations statistics.[30]

Although the FNGA changes were to apply on a transitional basis, pending the negotiation of self-government agreements, they would significantly alter the governance provisions of the *Indian Act*.[31] The FNGA would have:

1. permitted bands to write their own leadership selection, administration, and fiscal and accountability codes;[32]
2. required bands to write code guidelines on leadership selection (for selection codes); council membership, rule-making, and access to information (for administration codes) and

on budgets, loans, salaries, and debts (for fiscal codes);[33]

3. imposed federal government default codes where band codes are not made within a two-year deadline;[34]
4. conferred on bands expanded local and regional law-making powers,[35] ended the requirement of Ministerial approval for former band by-laws, and curtailed the Governor in Council's power to enact regulations in areas of band jurisdiction.[36]
5. given bands legal capacity, including power to contract, hold property, and borrow money;[37]
6. ended the Ministerial approval requirement for band fiscal decisions, but required independent audits[38] and provided for Ministerial remedial orders in the event of serious band financial problems;[39]
7. required compliance with Canadian human rights legislation, subject to consideration of aboriginal community needs and aspirations, "to the extent consistent with principles of gender equality";[40] and
8. required leadership codes to "respect the rights of all members of the band" but would have permitted them to balance members' interests, "including the different interests of members residing on and off the reserve."[41]

Aboriginal reaction was largely critical.[42] Some groups rejected changes to the *Indian Act* in favour of a more "nation-to-nation" approach that would directly implement inherent Aboriginal self-government. Others objected to accountability mechanisms, such as the provision for default federal controls where codes were not made in time. Most complained of inadequate consultation. The proposed legislation was dropped when Mr. Paul Martin became Prime Minister in the winter of 2003–04. The *Indian Act* self-government controversy continued.

(c) Negotiated Self-Government

In Canada today, self-government structures cannot be created without involving substantial Aboriginal participation. In the case of treaties or land claims agreements, Aboriginal groups can participate directly in negotiation. In the case of self-government, through an ordinary statute such as the *Sechelt Indian Band Self-Government Act*,[43] the final legislation was preceded by extensive negotiation. The product of most negotiated self-government is an agreement that may or may not be constitutionally protected as an existing treaty under s. 35(1) of the *Constitution Act, 1982*.

(i) Guaranteed Participation

One self-government approach found in land claims agreements is guaranteed participation in public structures of government. Guaranteed participation is an important element in all land claims agreements, and the key governmental element in the earlier agreements.[44] Typically, Aboriginal people are guaranteed a certain portion of seats — perhaps a third or a half — on an administrative advisory or decision-making body. The James Bay Cree and Northern Quebec Inuit have guaranteed representation in areas such as education, game, environmental and development control, and justice.[45]

A variation on guaranteed advisory power is guaranteed representation in legislative bodies. In New Zealand and the state of Maine, Aboriginal peoples have guaranteed participation in legislatures. The 1992 Charlottetown Accord proposed guaranteed Aboriginal representation in an elected Senate and in the House of Commons.[46] A 1996 proposal suggested that when the Northwest Territories were split in 1999, Aboriginal people should be guaranteed eight special seats in a 22-seat legislature for the new western territory. Thus far, this proposal has not been implemented.

(ii) Public Government

Aboriginal people are, of course, free to participate in the ordinary structures of public government throughout the country, and several have made significant contributions in recent times.[47] Where Aboriginal people constitute a potential majority of the electorate, their opportunity for influence is enhanced. This is the case for the Inuit in the northeastern Arctic region of Canada. The Inuit's land claims agreement was followed by the creation of the territory of Nunavut in the former northeastern N.W.T. Elections and residence in this new territory are open to all, but the demographic situation will give the Inuit a large majority for the foreseeable future. Under the *James Bay and Northern Quebec Agreement*, the Northern Quebec Inuit have a form of public government at the local level.

(iii) Coordinated Ethnic Government

The coordinated ethnic government approach provides for a governmental structure that is ethnic at the local level, but coordinated with provincial or territorial structures at the regional and provincial or territorial level. Examples of this approach can be found in the 1975 *James Bay Agreement* and the 1986 *Sechelt Indian Band Self-Government Act*.[48]

(A) JAMES BAY AND NORTHERN QUEBEC AGREEMENT

Under the *James Bay Agreement*, the James Bay Cree have governments that are ethnic at the local level, exercising the powers of band councils, but without the ministerial or cabinet controls in the *Indian Act*. These local governments are coordinated with provincial structures at the regional level, where there is a Cree Regional Authority. The Inuit have public, not coordinated ethnic, local government structures, which they dominate demographically, and a coordinated regional government, the Kativik Regional Government. Both the Cree and the Inuit have guaranteed participation in advisory bodies, as noted above.

(B) SECHELT INDIAN BAND SELF-GOVERNMENT ACT[49]

Reading 12(b) at p. 413

Under the *Sechelt Indian Band Self-Government Act*, the Aboriginal governing body has federal powers as a band council in regard to more than 900 status Sechelt Indians.[50] In its capacity as a district council, it also has provincial powers over the more than 500 non-Indians who live in the area.[51] When it acts as a district council, the governing body is advised by an advisory group that includes non-Indians. The band-district council can enter into agreements with the province for exercising municipal-type powers.[52] The band's municipal and regional powers go beyond those exercised by band councils.[53]

The band council can determine its own membership through a membership code.[54] Although the band owns its former *Indian Act* reserve land in fee simple,[55] the land is deemed to be s. 91(24) land under the *Constitution Act, 1867*.[56] Section 87 of the *Indian Act*[57] applies to those Sechelt who are Indians under the *Indian Act*.[58] Generally, the *Indian Act* applies to the Sechelt where the *Sechelt Act* does not.[59] The *Sechelt Act* is without prejudice to the Sechelt's comprehensive land claim.

The Sechelt approach has been criticized because it lacks constitutional protection.[60] On the other hand, this protection may be possible at a later date, either together with or separately from a Sechelt land claim agreement. In the meantime, the Sechelt have been able to secure substantial practical and formal control over their own affairs.

(C) ALBERTA METIS SETTLEMENTS LEGISLATION[61]

Alberta first enacted a *Metis Population Betterment Act* in 1938 to set aside land in the centre of the province for Métis settlements.[62] Following concerns over the administration of the lands, the Alberta government has enacted a set of statutes to protect the land, to clarify its management, and to outline a form of expanded local and regional government for the Métis. Under the legislation, eight Métis settlement corporations exercise powers similar to those of municipalities, while a General Council administers policies affecting land development, finance, membership, and hunting, fishing and trapping. Although most General Council policies can be overruled by the relevant Alberta government minister, there is provision for special protection for General Council policies that relate to hunting, fishing, and trapping.[63]

(D) MÉTIS ACT OF SASKATCHEWAN[64]

In contrast, Métis self-government in Saskatchewan is still mainly at the planning and discussion level. In 1995, the Métis Nation of Saskatchewan Secretariat Incorporated was established to administer the interests of the Métis Nation of Saskatchewan. In 2002, *The Métis Act* of Saskatchewan replaced this corporation with the Métis Nation-Saskatchewan Secretariat Inc.[65] The Act also provided for a bilateral process between the Saskatchewan government and the Métis Nation-Saskatchewan for discussions and a possible memorandum of agreement on such issues as "capacity building", land, harvesting, and governance.[66]

(iv) Separate Ethnic Government

Under separate ethnic government, there are distinct and separate Aboriginal governmental structures at the local, regional, and — in some areas — provincial or territorial level. Although there are links with provincial or territorial governments, within designated areas Aboriginal governments can operate as parallel systems and can exercise provincial-type or territorial-type powers that prevail over those of the province or territory in which they are located. The earliest examples of separate ethnic government can be found in the self-government agreements that accompany the First Nations Final agreements in the Yukon.[67] One of these, the 1993 *Vuntut Gwitchin First Nation Self-Government Agreement*, will be explored in more detail here.

(A) VUNTUT GWITCHIN FIRST NATION SELF-GOVERNMENT AGREEMENT[68]

Reading 12(c) at p. 419

As seen in **Chapter 11**, the *Vuntut Gwitchin First Nation Self-Government Agreement*[69] is part of a more general package. Following the blueprint in the *Umbrella Final Agreement*,[70] there are also self-government provisions in the *Vuntut Gwitchin*[71] *First Nation Final Agreement*.[72] This Agreement provides for guaranteed Yukon Indian participation in settlement structures and other structures of public government in many of the areas affecting the Vuntut Gwitchin's land claims agreement. The provisions of the *First Nation Final Agreement* tend to emphasize guaranteed Yukon Indian involvement in common governmental structures, especially in regard to land and natural resources.[73]

In contrast, the *Vuntut Gwitchin First Nation Self-Government Agreement*[74] emphasizes *separate* self-government. Under it, the Vuntut Gwitchin First Nation government has power to establish its own constitution[75] to address such matters as its own governmental structure[76] and the membership criteria for Vuntut Gwitchin First Nation Citizens.[77] In keeping with its dual role as settlement manager as well as governing body, the First Nation has exclusive legislative power over the administration of settlement benefits[78] as well as more general legislative powers in relation to most of the subject areas that are conferred on the territorial legislature by s. 17 of the *Yukon Act*.[79]

Section 13.3 of *Vuntut Gwitchin First Nation Self-Government Agreement* gives the First Nation jurisdiction to enact laws affecting both Vuntut Gwitchin Citizens and other people on Vuntut Gwitchin settlement land, in relation to 23 categories of the subject matter.[80] Section 13.2 gives the First Nation legislative powers that apply to Vuntut Gwitchin Citizens in Yukon, both on and off Vuntut Gwitchin settlement land, in relation to 15 categories of subject matter.[81] Separate sections confer emergency legislative powers[82] and legislative powers in relation to the administration of justice[83] and taxation.[84] The First Nation can enact property taxes on residents on settlement land and may be able to enact other forms of direct taxes, such as income and sales taxes on citizens on settlement land.[85]

Even where the First Nation has not enacted any laws, in an area within its legislative jurisdiction it can compel the territorial government to negotiate the transfer of the administration of programs or services.[86] To ensure that the First Nation has sufficient money to administer programs and services, the agreement requires the federal government to negotiate with it a self-government financial transfer agreement. This agreement is to provide the First Nation

> with resources to enable the Vuntut Gwitchin First Nation to provide public services at levels reasonably comparable to those generally prevailing in Yukon, at reasonably comparable levels of taxation.[87]

Vuntut Gwitchin laws would have legislative paramountcy over public territorial or municipal laws in Yukon.[88] Vuntut Gwitchin paramountcy is considerably broader than the normal "necessary inconsistency" test[89] that applies to relations between federal and provincial laws.[90] Vuntut Gwitchin legislation would need simply to occupy the field occupied by the public territorial law in order to prevail.[91] Beyond this, the *Vuntut Gwitchin First Nation Self-Government Agreement* contemplates paramountcy of Vuntut Gwitchin laws over federal laws in an unspecified number of areas.[92]

Some Vuntut Gwitchin laws apply and can override public territorial laws *beyond* Settlement Land.[93] Conceivably, Vuntut Gwitchin legislation *on* Settlement Land could affect government or interests off Settlement Land.[94] The Vuntut Gwitchin government can delegate any of its powers to any legal entity in Canada, including organizations and institutions outside Yukon.[95]

All the powers above can be exercised by the other Yukon First Nations that have concluded final agreements. When all final agreements are concluded, they will be available to all fourteen Yukon First Nations.

First Nations jurisdiction is discretionary. There is no general restriction on *when* a First Nations government or its delegate can legislate in an area previously occupied by the Government of Yukon. Subject only to a requirement of notice or consultation,[96] this can be done in most subject areas[97] at will. Hence, potential First Nations jurisdiction can serve as a lever to help compel the public territorial government to conclude agreements on their terms.

It will be interesting to see how cooperative self-government (in the guaranteed Aboriginal participation provisions of the Final Agreements) and separate self-government (in the self-government agreements) will interrelate in the Yukon. Arguably, the success of the first approach depends on the vitality of the public government in which participation is guaranteed. Is it possible to implement the second approach while ensuring that public government remains worth participating in?

The self-government arrangements raise other important questions.[98] Two features, however, stand out: their complexity and their strong emphasis on separate Aboriginal jurisdiction. After all the self-government agreements are concluded, the Yukon will have (a) a public territorial government subject to guaranteed representation requirements,[99] (b) a federal government with powers in certain areas, and (c) fourteen governments with provincial-type legislative powers. Where there is an overlap, the self-government agreements provide that the powers of the fourteen Aboriginal governments will prevail over those of the territorial government. They may also prevail over some of the powers of the federal government. The fourteen Aboriginal governments will be able to assume, relinquish, or delegate their legislative powers. They will be entitled to exercise administrative responsibility with or without Aboriginal rights legislation. These different forms of government will be subject to agreements on taxation room, financial revenue transfers, etc.

The governmental arrangements will affect approximately 30,000 Yukoners, about one-quarter of whom are Aboriginal people and will be settlement beneficiaries. Most Aboriginal and non-Aboriginal Yukoners live in a small number of adjacent or intermixed communities.[100] Will the self-government arrangements accommodate vital needs, or will they flood this population in a sea of jurisdictions so complex that public government or any government will be unworkable? Are the arrangements a necessary recognition of diversity, or will they reinforce and encourage divisions between Aboriginal and non-Aboriginal Yukoners?

The Yukon self-government arrangements are part of a scheme that is meant to address long-standing claims and injustices. They are intended to be in place permanently. The settlement scheme will constitute the greatest single change to the Yukon Territory since its creation in the 19th century. Should it be a model for Aboriginal self-government elsewhere too?

(B) WESTBANK INDIAN SELF-GOVERNMENT AGREEMENT

In 2003, the federal government and the B.C. Westbank First Nation signed the Westbank First Nation Self-Government Agreement.[101] The Agreement enables the Westbank First Nation to take over administration of most subjects that were previously subject to federal control under the *Indian Act*. It gives the Westbank First Nation legislative jurisdiction over Westbank lands, Westbank members on these lands and, in some cases, other persons on these lands. Specific First Nation powers include subjects such as land and resource management, landlord and tenant relations, health services, culture and language, education, public works, and community services.[102] In the event of conflicts, the Agreement specifies where Westbank First Nation, federal, or provincial laws will prevail.[103] There is a supremacy clause for federal legislation regarding peace, order, and good government,[104] and Westbank First Nation laws are not to affect federal legislation on subjects as criminal law, the health and safety of all Canadians, and broadcasting and telecommunications.[105] Westbank lands continue to be treated as reserves,[106] and its members continue to be subject to tax immunity on these lands, pursuant to the *Indian Act*.[107] The Agreement is not a s. 35(1) treaty, and is without prejudice to future self-government agreements[108] or to changes that may result from future lands claims agreements.[109]

About 350 Westbank members and about 8,000 non-members live on the Westbank reserve lands, which are located near Kelowna, B.C. The Agreement continues the Westbank First Nation's powers to tax property on Westbank lands, including that of non-member residents.[110] Under the Agreement, non-member reserve residents are to have "input" on matters that "directly and significantly" affect them.[111] Opponents to the Agreement expressed the concern that it requires non-residents to pay property taxes to the First Nation Government, but denies them the right to vote in its elections.[112] Supporters pointed out that this situation existed prior to the Agreement.

(d) Judicial Self-Government

Aboriginal self-government that is defined and enforced primarily by courts might be described in a short form as "judicial" self-government. Judicial self-government could result from the development of an inherent right of self-government at common law. Alternatively, it could result from a constitutional or legislative provision that proclaims an inherent right of Aboriginal self-government but leaves the nature and specific characteristics of self-government mainly to definition by the courts. The second of these approaches, together with constitutionally legislated self-government, was contemplated in the ill-fated 1992 Charlottetown Accord, considered in **Part 5**, below. The common law situation has been referred to earlier and will be re-visited briefly here.

4. A COMMON LAW RIGHT OF ABORIGINAL SELF-GOVERNMENT?

Reading 12(e) at p. 433

It has been suggested that Aboriginal self-government has already been implicitly recognized by the courts as a form of Aboriginal right.[113] Is this so? *Is* Aboriginal self-government now regarded by the courts as a form of common law Aboriginal right?

This question was addressed earlier.[114] As seen, earlier commonwealth opinion and earlier Canadian case law tends to support the view that Aboriginal rights are derived from and related to land or natural resources.[115] Below the Supreme Court, most — but not all[116] — decisions have rejected the notion of an inherent right of Aboriginal self-government or sovereignty.[117] Most courts that have addressed the question have said that if any Aboriginal self-government rights did survive British sovereignty, they were ended by the *Constitution Act, 1867*[118] or legislation enacted pursuant to it.[119] Both the Judicial Committee[120] and the Supreme Court[121] have said that the division of primary[122] legislative jurisdiction between federal and provincial governments in 1867 was intended to be exhaustive.[123]

The Supreme Court itself has not decided if Aboriginal self-government is or is not a common law Aboriginal right. However, it did say in *Sparrow* that "there was from the outset never any doubt that sovereignty and legislative power, and indeed the underlying title, to [Indian traditional lands is] vested in the Crown...."[124] While this statement is not unequivocal,[125] it seems inconsistent with the survival of paramount Aboriginal laws.

In *Pamajewon*,[126] discussed in **Chapter 9**, the Supreme Court did deal with an Aboriginal self-government claim. However, it did so without deciding generally if Aboriginal self-government can constitute an Aboriginal right. Members of the Shawanaga First Nation and the Eagle Lake Band had argued that gambling on their reserves was an Aboriginal right that was itself an incident of a broader inherent right to Aboriginal self-government. The majority of the Court said that "[a]ssuming without deciding that s. 35(1) includes self-government claims, the applicable legal standard is nonetheless that laid out in *Van der Peet* [the distinctive practices test]."[127] They held that the evidence did not establish that gambling, high stakes gambling, or the regulation of gambling were traditional practices integral to the distinctive cultures of the two Aboriginal claimant groups. Accordingly, no Aboriginal right was established.

Only L'Heureux-Dubé J. went further, in a separate concurring judgment. She quoted her earlier statement in *Van der Peet* that the jurisdiction of Parliament and, to an extent, of the provincial legislatures over the activities of Aboriginal people "is the result of the British assertion of sovereignty over Canadian territory."[128]

The Court's statement in *Sparrow* and L'Heureux-Dubé J.'s comments in *Pamajewon* and *Van der Peet*[129] suggest that at least some forms of common law Aboriginal self-government would be inconsistent with Canadian sovereignty. Certainly the Court's current case-by-case approach to Aboriginal rights is not conducive to broad self-government claims.[130] Since the distinctive practices test requires evidence of traditional practices that are independently distinctive, the Court's present approach does not encourage self-government claims that depend on showing regulation over other traditional practices.[131]

Despite the caution in the highest court, there are many unanswered questions, and more self-government litigation seems likely. A recent example was *Campbell*.[132] Here, Williamson J. of the British Columbia Supreme Court upheld some provisions of the Nisga'a treaty on the basis of a pre-treaty self-government right at common law. Provincial Liberal party members had challenged the constitutionality of treaty provisions[133] that conferred primary legislative powers,[134] including some that conferred primary and paramount[135] legislative powers, on Nisga'a government.[136] They argued, *inter alia*,[137] that these provisions violated the constitutional principle of the exhaustion of legislative powers[138] and the prohibition against abdication of legislative power.[139]

Williamson J. replied that the division of public legislative jurisdiction in ss. 91 and 92 and in similar provisions of the *Constitution Act, 1867* was "internal" to the federal and provincial legislatures.[140] Although he conceded that ss. 91 and 92 diminished the status of Aboriginal primary legislative power, he said they were not intended to affect the continued existence of this power.[141] In Williamson J.'s view, this power was part of an unwritten constitutional principle of Aboriginal self-government, protected by the Act's Preamble.[142] Williamson J. thought the existence of this power was supported by the fact of judicial enforcement of Aboriginal custom.[143] In his view, this power was also supported by the fact that Canadian courts have enforced Aboriginal custom.[144]

Williamson J. said the Nisga'a themselves had originally exercised identifiable governmental powers.[145] After the change in sovereignty, these powers were diminished. Until 1982, they were subject to extinguishment.[146] Subject to this, however, they continued to exist as primary legislative powers. Thus, the Nisga'a treaty's self-government provisions did not create new constitutional rights. Instead, they merely defined existing Aboriginal rights, and were not invalid.[147]

Campbell raises basic legal questions about public as well as Aboriginal powers. For example, what were the minimum features of British and Canadian sovereignty? Did they include exclusive, as well as supreme, law-making authority? If so, was this public authority consistent with the continued existence of primary or paramount Aboriginal legislative power? Were the legislative powers in the *Constitution Act, 1867* merely an internal arrangement, irrelevant to the continuation of Aboriginal legislative authority? If the establishment of sovereignty brought Parliamentary supremacy by the time of Confederation, did the *Constitution Act, 1982* bring Aboriginal legislative supremacy in some areas in 1982?

The legal questions about common law Aboriginal self-government are equally important. Assuming the existence of such a right, can it include (i) primary legislative power, (ii) paramount legislative power, (iii) the power to develop enforceable consensual customary law, (iv) the power to formulate laws for the management of Aboriginal title and rights, or (v) some combination of the above? If Aboriginal self-government does not include alternative (i) or alternative (ii), are treaties provisions that confer these powers merely defining existing Aboriginal rights? Are such treaty provisions invalid without further constitutional amendment? Is Aboriginal self-government an unwritten principle of the Canadian Constitution? If so, does it include primary or paramount legislative power? Just how do unwritten constitutional principles affect the powers conferred in the text of the *Constitution Act, 1867*? Is court enforcement of Aboriginal custom evidence of an Aboriginal self-government right to legislate? If the decision in *Campbell* is appealed, some of these questions may be re-visited.[148]

Apart from the legal issues addressed above,[149] *should* courts recognize a common law right of Aboriginal self-government? This highly normative[150] question is difficult to answer in the abstract, partly because of the many different possible forms of common law Aboriginal self-government. Nevertheless, a few general questions may be relevant. First, how adequate are the alternatives to common law Aboriginal self-government? Second, to what extent does a particular approach to self-government require formulation and application by lawyers and judges rather than by negotiators and politicians? Third, how effectively does a particular approach balance the need for pluralism with the common concerns of Canadians as a whole? The answers to these questions are bound to vary, not only with the particular form of self-government contemplated, but with the perspectives of those who ask them.

5. FORMAL CONSTITUTIONAL ROUTE

(a) Road to Charlottetown

Many Aboriginal groups were unhappy with the *Constitution Act, 1982* in April 1982. They wanted an entrenched right of Aboriginal self-government. The 1983 Aboriginal constitutional conference resulted in constitutional protection for land claims agreements, an Aboriginal gender equality guarantee, a right to consultation before governments amend Aboriginal provisions, and a number of other guarantees, but no entrenched right of self-government.[151]

In October 1983, the House of Commons "Penner Committee" on Indian self-government recommended that Indian First Nations be given (a) constitutionally-entrenched, provincial-type powers; (b) an expanded land base; (c) an Indian-federal tribunal to arbitrate inter-governmental disputes; (d) sole control over participation in Indian government; and (e) guaranteed, unconditional federal government funding.[152] The federal government replied positively, but stressed the potential for non-constitutional self-government arrangements as well.[153]

Three additional Aboriginal constitutional conferences followed the conference of 1983. All three focused on the issue of entrenched Aboriginal self-government. None produced amendments. At the 1984 conference, a federal proposal for negotiated delegated self-government was rejected by the four national Aboriginal associations.[154] At the 1985 conference, the federal government proposed a "contingent rights" approach. It would entrench a general concept of self-government, with specific content to depend on negotiations. This was opposed by the Assembly of First Nations and by three provinces. At the 1987 conference, the federal government proposed a similar approach, but with a more specific entrenched right of self-government. This, too, was unsuccessful. Most Aboriginal groups wanted immediate entrenchment of a constitutional right of Aboriginal self-government, with details to be negotiated later. In contrast, most governments wanted to negotiate agreements on the nature of Aboriginal self-government first, before entrenching it in the constitution.[155]

At the end of April 1987, little more than a month after the last Aboriginal conference, the first ministers secured unanimous agreement at Meech Lake on major constitutional amendments to secure Quebec's support for the *Constitution Act, 1982*.[156] Quebec would get special constitutional guarantees, while the self-government guarantees were being denied to the Aboriginal peoples. The early version of the Meech Lake Accord made no mention of Aboriginal peoples. The later Langevin version provided only a non-derogation provision to protect rights of Aboriginal peoples from the new distinct society clause.

Aboriginal people were strongly opposed to the Accord.[157] Mr. Elijah Harper, a Manitoba Aboriginal M.L.A., played a crucial role in toppling it. The Accord required unanimous support from Parliament and the provincial legislative assemblies by midnight of Saturday, June 23, 1990. On Friday before the deadline, Mr. Harper withheld the unanimous consent needed to permit the Manitoba legislature to continue its debate and move to a vote. Debate on the Accord ended in Manitoba, ending any chance of unanimous support by the following evening.[158]

When the next wave of constitutional change swept the country, the reformers tried to ensure that this time Aboriginal concerns would be addressed.[159] In its September 1991 paper, *Shaping Canada Together: Proposals*,[160] the federal government proposed a new constitutional "Canada clause". This would acknowledge "that the Aboriginal peoples were historically self-governing," and would recognize "their rights within Canada."[161] The government proposed "an amendment to the Constitution to entrench a general justiciable right to Aboriginal self-government within the Canadian federation and subject to the [*Charter*], with the nature of the right to self-government described so as to facilitate [its interpretation] by the courts."[162] To allow the parties to agree on the content of this right, its enforceability would be delayed for up to ten years.[163] This general approach was followed with modifications in the February 28, 1992, Beaudoin-Dobbie Committee Report[164] and the June 11, 1992, Status Report of the Multilateral Meetings on the Constitution.

(b) Charlottetown Aboriginal Provisions

🖹 Reading 12(d) at p. 429

The Charlottetown Accord[165] was signed on August 28, 1992. Its 51-page legal version was released on October 9, less than two weeks before the October 22 referendum. The centre-piece of the Accord's many Aboriginal provisions was an entrenched inherent right of self-government. This was to be implemented by negotiation, if possible, but after a delay of five years it could be defined by the courts.[166]

Other key provisions included recognition of Aboriginal people and their governments in the Accord's "Canada clause";[167] guaranteed representation in the new elected Senate;[168] dispensation for Aboriginal governments from the *Charter's* right to vote and qualify as a member of a legislative assembly;[169] inclusion of Aboriginal governments in the *Charter's* application and "override" provisions;[170] a right to initiate processes to clarify, implement, of rectify treaties;[171] an Aboriginal gender-equality guarantee;[172] a guarantee of at least four more Aboriginal constitutional conferences to be held by the year 2002;[173] the right to prior consultation at a constitutional conference[174] and a veto[175] in regard to proposed constitutional amendments directly referring to Aboriginal peoples or their governments; a clarification that s. 91(24) of the *Constitution Act, 1867* includes all the Aboriginal people of Canada;[176] constitutional protection for Alberta Métis lands and their governing body;[177] and a provision for the negotiation of constitutional accords between the federal, Ontario, and western provincial governments and Métis people.[178] As well, there were numerous non-derogation provisions to ensure that Aboriginal peoples, their governments, and their rights would not be prejudiced by other provisions in the Accord.[179] Other provisions, such as changes to the rules for the creation of new provinces, would have affected Aboriginal peoples indirectly.[180]

From one perspective, the Charlottetown Aboriginal provisions would have constituted sweeping gains for Canadian Aboriginal peoples. One commentator called them "a historic (though imperfect) achievement."[181] Another was more critical, asking:

> If Aboriginal peoples are progressively differentiated from other Canadians by a spate of reinforcing constitutional amendments, what sense of shared Canadian citizenship will develop within the Aboriginal and the larger Canadian community?[182]

(c) Rejection of Charlottetown

Canadians rejected the Charlottetown Accord[183] for different, and sometimes conflicting, reasons. Some non-Quebeckers felt there had been too many concessions to Quebec; some Quebeckers felt there had been too few. Many felt they had been given inadequate time to comprehend the meaning of the complex 51-page Draft Legal Text. Some Aboriginal peoples felt that decades of planning, lobbying, and negotiating had been suddenly and catastrophically overturned.[184] For others, the end of the Accord removed a serious threat to the treaties.[185] Some were concerned about the impact of the Aboriginal self-government provisions on the individual rights of Aboriginal women.[186] Others were relieved to see the end of a document that failed to deal with them as equal sovereign nations.[187] Still others shared the general concern that, once again, a Canadian government had failed to consult adequately with the people.[188]

6. FEDERAL POLICY ROUTE

In 1995, acting on an election promise,[189] two federal government ministers issued a policy statement saying that:

> [t]he government of Canada recognizes the inherent right of self-government as an existing Aboriginal right under section 35 of the *Constitution Act, 1982*. It recognizes, as well, that the inherent right may find expression in treaties, and in the context of the Crown's relationship with treaty First Nations.[190]

The wording of this "recognition" is misleading. It may suggest that federal recognition of an inherent rights of self-government under s. 35 has legal constitutive effect. In fact, only the courts can determine the meaning of self-government for the purposes of s. 35. What the statement really does is treat self-government *as if it were* an inherent right under s. 35, and express a willingness to negotiate its content. This approach falls short of a commitment to constitutionally entrench a general inherent right of self-government. On the other hand, it does come to terms with the fact that, so far, the general entrenchment approach has not succeeded. It invites Aboriginal groups and other parties to address the practical shape of self-government without wasting time and effort on litigation.

The federal policy statement proposed the negotiation of self-government agreements with individual Aboriginal groups. It listed a wide range of potential subjects for negotiation, including governing structures, education, health, social services, administration and enforcement of Aboriginal laws, Aboriginal courts, policing, land and natural resources management, and housing.[191] In areas such as these, the federal government envisaged the exercise of Aboriginal "jurisdiction". In other specified areas,[192] the government envisaged "some measure of Aboriginal jurisdiction or authority," but with primary law-making power remaining with the federal or provincial governments.[193] Finally, the government listed a number of other subjects, such as defence, external relations, banking, law and order, and broadcasting, in which it would not give up its law-making authority.[194] It said that "where the other parties agree," it would be prepared to have the resulting agreements constitutionally entrenched as treaty rights within the meaning of s. 35(1) of the *Constitution Act, 1982*.[195]

The federal policy contained a number of parameters. It said Aboriginal self-government "does not include a right of sovereignty in the international law sense, and will not result in sovereign independent Aboriginal nation states."[196] Aboriginal self-government was to operate "within the framework of the Canadian constitution."[197] The policy said Aboriginal governments must be subject to the *Charter*[198] and accountable to their members and clients.[199] It said that the government's fiduciary duty should diminish as Aboriginal self-government powers increase.[200]

More specific federal initiatives followed. In December 1994, the Indian Affairs Minister announced a pilot program to transfer Indian Affairs programs in the province of Manitoba to Manitoba First Nations, and in 1998 the federal government signed a framework agreement for discussing fiscal relations, elections, and government structures with the Anishinabek Nation, representing over 30 Ontario First Nations. The 1998 *Mi'kmaq Education Act* transferred substantial pre-University education authority to nine Mi'kmaq bands.[201] The 1999 *First Nations Land Management Agreement Act* gave 14 First Nations wide powers to manage land on reserves, including power to hold reserve property and to divide matrimonial real property after divorces.[202]

7. ROYAL COMMISSION ON ABORIGINAL PEOPLES

Readings 12(f) at p. 434 and 12(g) at p. 435

Meanwhile, on May 31, 1991, the federal government announced the creation of a Royal Commission on Aboriginal Peoples. The mandate was vast — the Commission was to examine all aspects of the situation of Aboriginal peoples in Canada.[203] The Commission held 178 days of formal hearings.[204] Between 1991 and 1966, the Commission issued numerous background papers and preliminary reports on topics such as Aboriginal self-government,[205] Arctic relocation,[206] suicide,[207] fiduciary obligations and Quebec secession,[208] extinguishment,[209] and justice.[210] *The Right of Aboriginal Self-Government and the Constitution: A Commentary*[211] proposed a constitutional amendment to recognize an inherent right of Aboriginal self-government in terms similar to that included in the ill-fated Charlottetown Accord. In *Partners in Confederation: Aboriginal Peoples, Self-Government, and the Constitution*,[212] referred to earlier,[213] the Royal Commission argued that Canadian common law already recognizes an inherent right of Aboriginal self-government, a right it said is already entrenched in the constitution.

In 1996, the Commission released the *Report of the Royal Commission on Aboriginal Peoples* in five volumes and six parts — two volumes on history, governance, land, and treaties; one more volume on social problems, women's issues, elders, Métis, and off-reserve Indians; and two final volumes of recommendations, together with a summary.[214] The 3,537 pages of the *Report* detailed the massive social, cultural, and economic challenges facing Canadian Aboriginal peoples. It attributed many of them to non-Aboriginal newcomers and their governments. The *Report* called for hundreds of far-reaching changes to the relationship between Aboriginal and non-Aboriginal peoples in Canada, including:

1. a Proclamation to acknowledge past mistakes made in relation to Aboriginal peoples and to commit governments to a new "bilateral nation-to-nation" relationship with Aboriginal peoples;[215]
2. creation of an Aboriginal Parliament, first to advise[216] and then (as a third Parliamentary chamber) to supplement[217] the existing House of Commons and Senate;
3. governmental[218] and constitutional[219] recognition that an inherent right of sovereign[220] Aboriginal self-government is guaranteed in the *Constitution Act, 1982*;
4. an Aboriginal constitutional veto in regard to matters directly affecting constitutional rights of Aboriginal peoples;[221]
5. dual Aboriginal / Canadian citizenship for Aboriginal peoples, to be reflected in dual Aboriginal / Canadian passports for Aboriginal peoples;[222]
6. treaty negotiations on a "nation-to-nation" basis[223] under the auspices of permanent independent treaty tribunals;[224] and
7. additional $1.5 billion and $2 billion of annual government spending for Aboriginal peoples, for 15 and 20 years,[225] respectively, on such subjects as long-term economic development agreements,[226] small business assistance,[227] venture capital corporations,[228] a ten-year initiative for Aboriginal development and training,[229] expansion of healing centres and lodges,[230] "training of 10,000 Aboriginal professionals" in health and social services,[231] housing funds,[232] improvement of water and sewage systems,[233] Aboriginal language instruction where desired and warranted by numbers,[234] Aboriginal advisory committees to school boards,[235] Aboriginal teacher education programs,[236] a Métis and Aboriginal scholarship fund,[237] an Aboriginal languages foundation,[238] programs for Aboriginal women,[239] youth,[240] Métis,[241] Northerners,[242],[243] settlement of Aboriginal claims[244] and implementing self-government.[245]

It is beyond the scope of this book to assess these recommendations in detail.[246] Only a few tentative observations will be offered here. First, for the economic and social problems identified — from poor housing to infectious diseases to high suicide rates, very large sums of well-spent money do seem essential.[247] Second, the land claims process should, indeed, be expedited, and old treaty grievances addressed. Third, for greater self-reliance, greater Aboriginal control of Aboriginal affairs is vital. To its credit, the *Report* urged major action on all of these issues.

On the other hand, could the *Report* have achieved these objectives with less reliance on legalistic foundations and on formal and separate implementing mechanisms? The Commission asserted that s. 35(1) of the *Constitution Act, 1982* contains an inherent right of self-government.[248] It called upon governments to acknowledge this legal situation.[249] It formulated many of its recommendations as if they depended on it. Yet interpretation of the existing law is in the hands of courts, not royal commissions or governments. Thus far the courts have not recognized the existence of a general inherent right of self-government in s. 35(1).[250] It is conceivable that they might not recognize such a right in future. If they do, their recognition might not be on the terms suggested by the Commission.

The *Report* suggested that in this case, "the way to resolve this uncertainty [would be] with a constitutional amendment."[251] Thus, the Commission's approach calls for formal constitutional amendment if its own case law interpretation is incorrect. Elsewhere, the Commission indicated that it would prefer formal constitutional amendment, if possible, in any event. It said that although most of its proposals do not require constitutional amendment, this approach would be "clearer and surer" for areas such as self-government, the treaty implementation process, an Aboriginal constitutional veto, Métis protections,[252] and jurisdictional changes to s. 91(24) of the *Constitution Act, 1867*.[253] It suggested further constitutional changes to include an Aboriginal member of the Supreme Court,[254] and to create an Aboriginal house of Parliament.[255]

Need the *Report* have relied so heavily on judicial interpretation, or on formal constitutional amendment as an alternative or supplement to it? Could reliance on these legal forums shift effective control of self-government and related issues from elected politicians and Aboriginal peoples to lawyers and judges? Alternatively, could the more practical aspects of Aboriginal self-control, self-reliance, and self-government be implemented *as a simple matter of fundamental government policy*,[256] rather than being imposed as a matter of law? Would they be any less important as a result? Or any less effective?

It is possible that the *Report*'s many practical recommendations could be overshadowed by some of its more formal general proposals. On one hand, the Report grapples with improving water quality on reserves, fighting infectious diseases, and encouraging young people to stay in school; on the other hand, it proposes an Aboriginal Parliament, dual Aboriginal peoples / Canadian citizenship, and an Aboriginal constitutional veto. Is a separate Aboriginal Parliament the most direct route to fixing poor plumbing on reserves? Would dual Aboriginal / Canadian citizenship do much to fight tuberculosis? Would a separate Aboriginal constitutional veto encourage young people to stay in school? In light of finite government resources, would reform efforts be better spent fighting practical concerns directly?

Although the *Report*'s emphasis on Aboriginal nations highlights the distinctiveness of Aboriginal societies, it could also generate fragmentation.[257] Since not all Aboriginal peoples meet the *Report's* criteria for Aboriginal nationhood,[258] existing Aboriginal distinctions could be replaced with a new class system. And what of the common ground between Aboriginal peoples and other Canadians? Many basic needs — such as environmental control, transportation safety, and fire protection — require joint action, not separate efforts. Others, such as health, may be of general, as well as special, concern. Even some special goals, such as Aboriginal economic development, require bridges, not legal boundaries. While the Commission did not advocate sovereignty-association, as some seek for Quebec,[259] many of the Commission's recommendations de-emphasize common ties in favour of separate national status.[260] Are assimilation or the *status quo* the only possible alternatives to the latter?[261]

There is much to be said for a pragmatic approach to self-government and other key Aboriginal issues, an approach that puts concrete assistance above constitutional drafts and negotiated arrangements above litigation in courts. The many practical recommendations in this *Report*[262] should not be neglected. Moreover, although the negotiation process has potential problems, it seems preferable to most of the alternatives.[263] Here, the *Report*'s general stress[264] on the importance of negotiated land claims and self-government agreements seems very appropriate.

Although the Commission's work was unprecedented in scope, it was, arguably, incomplete. Political scientist Alan Cairns says the Commission overlooked the fact that Aboriginal peoples are also Canadian citizens, whose lives are intermeshed with those of other citizens.[265] In particular, Cairns says the Commission's emphasis on separate land-based Aboriginal governments neglected the large urban Aboriginal population, who comprise roughly 45% of all Aboriginal people in Canada.[266] Cairns argues that because of their very small size, even the land-based Aboriginal governments would be dependent on other governments for many services.[267] More generally, Cairns suggests that there was a contradiction between the Commission's heavy emphasis on constitutional separateness and the interdependence implicit in its many local-level recommendations in areas such as health, education, and housing.[268] Cairns asks if Aboriginal disengagement from common citizenship would encourage an attitude of sharing and fellow-feeling from the majority society.[269] These are significant concerns, although it may be noted that Cairns does not indicate how he would balance the common citizenship and the "plus" in his own preferred concept of "citizens plus."[270]

The federal government responded to the *Report* in 1997 in *Gathering Strength — Canada's Aboriginal Action Plan*.[271] The *Plan* formally apologized for the historical injustices suffered by the Aboriginal peoples, especially through the residential school system. Although the *Plan* agreed with the *Report*'s emphasis on partnership and change, the federal government said its vision of partnership includes common goals as well as diversity.[272]

Attempting to counter some of the negative message of the *Report*, the *Plan* stressed what the federal government regarded as accomplishments in regard to claims settlements and self-government, and in economic, social, health, cultural, and educational areas. The government said it was determined to work with Aboriginal peoples to intensify efforts in these areas.

The *Plan* rejected past assimilation, and said the government was open to discussion regarding the *Report*'s suggestions for restructuring federal institutions. On the other hand, there was no mention of constitutional vetos, Aboriginal passports, or an Aboriginal Parliament. Despite the *Plan*'s practical orientation, it was not accompanied by a significant increase in federal government Aboriginal funding.

8. ASSESSMENT OF SELF-GOVERNMENT INITIATIVES

All people should be able to control their own affairs as effectively as possible. Canadian Aboriginal peoples have made a strong case for special forms of self-government that reflect their unique cultures and historical and constitutional situation. At the same time, Aboriginal self-government involves responsibilities as well as powers. It can affect non-Aboriginal as well as Aboriginal citizens, and must co-exist with the general norms of public government and equal treatment for all Canadians. To succeed in the long term, it should be able to encourage general support by all those it affects.

With these considerations in mind, it may be possible to develop some preliminary criteria for assessing Aboriginal self-government initiatives. The list is by no means exhaustive, but suggests a few tentative questions that might be asked:

1. Does the initiative accommodate the needs and objectives of the Aboriginal people concerned?
2. Does it recognize the diversity of conditions of Aboriginal peoples across the country while maintaining a general parity of benefits among Aboriginal groups?
3. Is it subject to debate and ratification by elected representatives of the public at the provincial or territorial level and the federal level?
4. Is it clear, comprehensible, and defined, or does it place wide definition powers in the hands of unelected judges or administrators?
5. Does it provide adequate safeguards for individual Aboriginal people and minority Aboriginal groups subject to them, and adequate means of ongoing general Aboriginal control?
6. Does it provide adequate safeguards for non-Aboriginal people affected by it?
7. Does it specify that the Aboriginal government or government power is part of the Canadian state?
8. Does it minimize unnecessary conflict and duplication of powers and responsibilities?
9. Does it involve practical measures, such as education, including job and management training, and adequate economic support?

Notes

1. Some Aboriginal groups and other commentators see self-government as an aspect of a broader international law right of indigenous peoples to self-determination: Grand Council of the Crees, *Sovereign Injustice: Forcible Inclusion of the James Bay Crees and Cree Territory into a Sovereign Quebec* (Nemaska, Québec: Grand Council of the Crees, 1995), chaps. 1 and 2, and authorities noted there, comparing Aboriginal and Québec nationalist concepts of self-determination. See also M.J. Bryant, "Aboriginal Self-Determination: The Status of Canadian Aboriginal Peoples at International Law" (1992) 56 Sask. L. Rev. 267; B. Berg, "Introduction to Aboriginal Self-Government In International Law: An Overview" (1992) 56 Sask. L. Rev. 375; and S.J. Anaya, *Indigenous Peoples in International Law* (New York: Oxford University Press, 1996), esp. chaps. 2 and 3 and 109–12.

   Although the notion of self-determination is not well-defined, it might be described generally as the right of a people to freely determine their political status. This right may help legitimate independence or secession in the case of domination of overseas colonies or oppression of a minority by a metropolitan state. Otherwise, self-determination is generally subject to the right of existing states to territorial integrity. See art. 1, para. 2 and art. 2, para. 4 of the *United Nations Charter*; arts. 2 and 6 of the *Declaration on the Granting of Independence to Colonial Countries and Peoples*; art. 1, para. 1 of the *International Covenant on Civil and Political Rights* (self-determination and minority rights, respectively); art. 1, para. 1 of the *International Covenant on Economic, Social and Cultural Rights* (self-determination); and arts. 1, 2, and 7 of the *Declaration on Principles of International Law Concerning Friendly Relations and Co-operation among States in Accordance with the Charter of the United Nations*.

In regard to indigenous peoples, a United Nations Commission on Human Rights subcommittee working group has been attempting to achieve consensus, *inter alia*, on a form of internal self-determination that would support a "right to autonomy or self-government in matters relating to [indigenous peoples'] internal and local affairs": *Draft United Nations Declaration on the Rights of Indigenous Peoples*, August 23, 1993 (reproduced in [1994] 1 C.N.L.R. 48), art. 31 (see also arts. 3, 4, and 21). It is this internal form of self-determination — self-government without separate national status — that is most commonly asserted in regard to Aboriginal peoples. *Quaere*: does this form of self-determination include a right to maintain *existing* national status? For example, do Aboriginal peoples in the region of the *James Bay and Northern Quebec Agreement* retain a self-determination right to remain within Canada in the event of an attempted secession by Quebec? See *Sovereign Injustice*, *supra*, and authorities noted there, arguing that they do.

Finally, note that the legal effect of international law norms within Canada depends on their status in the international community and on whether they are incorporated into and consistent with Canadian domestic law: see L.C. Green, *International Law: A Canadian Perspective*, 2d ed. (Toronto: Carswell, 1988) at 76–90.

2. Assembly of First Nations First Circle on the Constitution, *First Nations and the Constitution: Discussion Paper*, November 21, 1991 at 8, quoted in Royal Commission on Aboriginal Peoples, *The Right of Aboriginal Self-Government and the Constitution: A Commentary*, 1992, 6. See also Assembly of First Nations Conference, *A Declaration of The First Nations*, December 1980, reprinted in Shin Imai, Katharine Logan, and Gary Stein, *Aboriginal Law Handbook*, 2d ed. (Scarborough, Ont.: Carswell, 1999) at 122.
3. "'Inherent' does not connote a desire to separate from the Canadian state": R. Kuptana, President of the Inuit Tapirisat of Canada, quoted in Royal Commission on Aboriginal Peoples, *The Right of Aboriginal Self-Government and the Constitution: A Commentary* (Ottawa, 1995) at 7; "We are not seeking sovereignty from Canada, we are not seeking separation, we are seeking recognition within the Canadian confederation": Yvon Dumont, Métis National Council, *ibid.* at 8; "The inherent right of Aboriginal self-government does not include a right of sovereignty in the international law sense ...": Minister of Indian Affairs and Northern Development and Federal Interlocutor for Métis and Non-Status Indians, *Aboriginal Self-government: The Government of Canada's Approach to Implementation of the Inherent Right and the Negotiation of Aboriginal Self-Government* (Ottawa: D.I.A.N.D., 1995) at 4.
4. See Royal Commission on Aboriginal Peoples, *Report of the Royal Commission on Aboriginal Peoples* (hereinafter "*Report*"), vol. 2, chap. 3, s. 3.1 at 245–78, distinguishing between Aboriginal "nation government" (245–65); Aboriginal "public government" (264–72); and Aboriginal "community of interest governments" (272–78).
5. See generally, F. Cassidy and R.L. Bish, *Indian Government: Its Meaning in Practice* (Lantzville, B.C.: Oolichan, 1989), chap. 4.
6. E.J. Dickson-Gilmore, "Resurrecting the Peace: Traditionalist Approaches to Separate Justice in the Kahnawake Mohawk Nation", R.A. Silverman and M.O. Nielson, eds., *Aboriginal Peoples and Canadian Criminal Justice* (Toronto: Butterworths, 1992) at 259, 264–66; R.S. Allen, *His Majesty's Indian Allies: British Indian Policy in The Defence of Canada, 1774–1815* (Toronto: Dundurn Press, 1992) at 13–14; and **Reading 12(a)**.
7. L.A. Schiendeen, "The Aboriginal Healing Lodge: A First Step" (1992) 50 Sask. L. Rev. 427; D. Smith, *The Seventh Fire: The Struggle for Aboriginal Government* (Toronto: Key Porter, 1993) at 47–51; D.A. Long and T. Fox, "Circles of Healing: Illness, Healing, and Health among Aboriginal People in Canada" in D.A. Long and O.P. Dickason, *Visions of the Heart: Canadian Aboriginal Issues* (Toronto: Harcourt Brace, 1996), chap. 9; R. Ross, *Returning to the Teachings: Exploring Aboriginal Justice* (Toronto: Penguin, 1996); Royal Commission on Aboriginal Peoples, *Report of the Royal Commission on Aboriginal Peoples*, vol. 3, chap. 3, s. 3.2.
8. D. Smith, *ibid.* at 166–77.
9. Royal Commission on Aboriginal Peoples, *Report of the Royal Commission on Aboriginal Peoples*, vol. 2, chap. 3, s. 1.3 at 127.
10. D. Smith, *The Seventh Fire: The Struggle for Aboriginal Government* (Toronto: Key Porter, 1993) at 16–18. See also the community justice pilot projects discussed in Royal Commission on Aboriginal Peoples, *Aboriginal Peoples and the Justice System: Report of the National Round Table on Aboriginal Justice Issues* (Ottawa: Canadian Communication Services, 1993) at 383–404.
11. D. Smith, *ibid.* at 19–21.
12. D. Smith, *ibid.* at 19–21.
13. R.S.C. 1985, c. I-8.
14. See, generally, *Indian Act*, R.S.C. 1985, c. I-8, especially ss. 74–86; R.H. Bartlett, *The Indian Act of Canada*, 2d ed. (Saskatoon: University of Saskatchewan Native Law Centre, 1988), chap. IV.A; J. Woodward, *Native Law* (Toronto: Carswell, 1989), chap. 7.
15. *Ibid.* at ss. 74, 77.
16. *Ibid.* at s. 83(1).
17. *Ibid.* at s. 81.
18. *Ibid.*
19. *Ibid.* at s. 82(2).
20. F. Cassidy and R.L. Bish, *supra* note 5 at 43–46.
21. See **Part (b)**, above and F. Cassidy and R.L. Bish, *ibid.* See also L. Krotz, *Indian Country: Inside Another Canada* (Toronto: McClelland and Stewart, 1992).
22. See, for example, P.D. Elias, *Development of Aboriginal People's Communities* (North York: Captus Press, 1991); Royal Commission on Aboriginal Peoples, *Sharing the Harvest: The Road to Self-Reliance: Report of the National Round Table on Aboriginal Economic Development and Resources* (Ottawa: Canadian Communication Services, 1993) at 32–34, 249–68.
23. *Ibid.*
24. J.L. Steckley and B.D. Cummins, *Full Circle: Canada's First Nations* (Toronto: Prentice Hall, 2001), chap. 22, using as a case study the Ashinibeck Police Force.
25. See, for example, Shin Imai, Katharine Logan, and Gary Stein, *Aboriginal Law Handbook*, 2d ed. (Scarborough, Ont.: Carswell, 1999) at 371–72.
26. P. Moon, "Mohawk Community Finds Inner Peace" *The Globe and Mail* (May 10, 1994) A1 and A4; "Native Self-policing Growing Force" *The [Toronto] Globe and Mail* (May 11, 1994) A4. On the relationship between the *Indian Act*-based Peacekeepers approach and more traditionalist approaches at Kahnawake, see E.J. Dickson-Gilmore, "Resurrecting the Peace: Traditionalist Approaches to Separate Justice in the Kahnawake

Mohawk Nation", R.A. Silverman and M.O. Nielsen, eds., *Aboriginal Peoples and Canadian Criminal Justice* (Toronto: Butterworths, 1992) at 259.

27. *An Act respecting leadership selection, administration and accountability of Indian bands, and to make related amendments to other Acts*. Introduced originally on June 14, 2002 as Bill C-61, and reinstated on October 9, 2002 at Committee stage, before second reading, as Bill c-7.
28. Bill C-6, reinstated on October 9, 2002 after second reading, and enacted as the *Specific Claims Resolution Act*, S.C. 2003, c. 23. See **Chapter 12, Part 4(b)**.
29. Through an extension of the existing *First Nations Land Management Act*, S.C. 1999, c. 24. When it was first enacted in 1999, this act gave 14 First Nations greater legal powers of land management, and enabled them to appoint their own justices of the peace to deal with offences on these lands.
30. In the draft *First Nations Fiscal and Statistical Management Act*, made public in 2002. In 2004–2005, this proposal and those referred to *supra* notes 27–29 were consolidated into Bill C-20, now the *First Nations Fiscal and Statistical Management Act*, S.C. 2005, c. 9 (royal assent, 23 March 2005).
31. The FNGA proposals would not have affected existing self-governance provisions in the *Cree-Naskapi (of Quebec) Act*, S.C. 1984, c. 18; the *Sechelt Indian Band Self-Government Act*, S.C. 1986, c. 27; the *Nisga'a Final Agreement Act*, S.C. 2002, c. 7; and the *Yukon First Nations Self-Government Act*, S.C. 1994, c. 35.
32. Section 4.
33. Sections 5, 6, and 7, respectively.
34. Ss. 32 and 36. As well, although bands that use customary leadership procedures could adopt custom leadership codes, this could be done for only two years: s. 5(3). After this time, they were to adopt electoral leadership codes under s. 5, or they would be subject to default electoral regulations made by the Governor in Council pursuant to ss. 32 and 36.
35. For example, the new powers would have extended to natural resources and to culture and language: ss. 17(1)(a) and (b), respectively.
36. Section 33.
37. Section 15.
38. Sections 8 and 9.
39. Section 10.
40. Section 41.
41. Section 5(5).
42. The Assembly of First Nations, representing most status Indians, was strongly opposed to the package. The Congress of Aboriginal Peoples supported it, and the National Aboriginal Women's Association gave qualified support to its human rights provisions.
43. S.C. 1986, c. 27.
44. In Nunavut, the key governmental element is the creation of a new territory in which Inuit constitute a majority (**Chapter 11, Part 7(e)**); in the Yukon, it is separate self-government agreements (**Chapter 11, Part 7(f)** and **Chapter 12, Part 3(b)(iv)(A)**).
45. *Ibid.*
46. **Part 5**, below.
47. For example, Mr. Elijah Harper, the Manitoba M.L.A. who played an influential role in ending the Meech Lake Accord; Ms. Nellie Cournoyea, former government leader, Northwest Territories; Ms. Ethel Blondin-Andrews, M.P.; and Mr. Paul Okalik, government leader, Nunavut.
48. **Part 3(b)(iv)(B)**, below.
49. S.C. 1986, c. 27. See also the companion British Columbia statute, the *Sechelt Indian Government District Enabling Act*, S.B.C. 1987, c. 16, proclaimed in force on July 23, 1987.
50. See further, J.P. Taylor and G. Paget, "Federal / Provincial responsibility and the Sechelt", D.C. Hawkes, *Aboriginal Peoples and Government Responsibility*, 1989, chap. 8.
51. Powers conferred both under the federal *Sechelt* act and under the British Columbia *Sechelt Indian Government District Enabling Act*, S.B.C. 1987, c. 16, proclaimed in force on July 23, 1987.
52. For example, it levies taxes on behalf of the province in return for full municipal taxes and obtains the rest of its funding through a block funding arrangement with the federal government.
53. The powers include taxation, zoning, roads, education, welfare, game, businesses, estates, and, generally, "matters related to the good government of the Band, its members or Sechelt lands": *Sechelt Indian Band Self-Government Act*, S.C. 1986, c. 27, s. 14. See also s. 15, enabling the band council to exercise powers conferred on it by the legislature of British Columbia.
54. Section 10(2). This right is subject to *Indian Act* membership rights in existence immediately prior to the establishment of the code.
55. The band itself has decided that the land cannot be alienated except by a 75% referendum vote.
56. Section 31.
57. The section that confers a tax immunity on Indians who are on, or have an interest, in reserve lands.
58. Section 35(1).
59. *Ibid.*
60. *Supra* note 50 at 297.
61. *Metis Settlements Land Protection Act*, S.A. 1990, c. M-14.8; *Metis Settlements Act*, S.A. 1990, c. M-14.3; *Metis Settlements Accord Implementation Act*, S.A. 1990, c. M-14.5; and *Constitution of Alberta Amendment Act*, 1990, c. 22.2.
62. S.A. 1938, c. 6 (later called *Metis Betterment Act*).
63. See generally, C.E. Bell, *Alberta's Metis Settlements Legislation: An Overview of Ownership and Management of Settlement Lands* (Regina: Canadian Plains Research Centre, University of Regina, 1994).
64. *The Métis Act*, S.S. M-14.01, effective January 28, 2002.
65. *Ibid.*, ss. 5 and 17.
66. *Ibid.*, s. 3.
67. See **Chapter 11, Part (7)(f)**.
68. *Vuntut Gwitchin First Nation Self-Government Agreement*, Ottawa, Department of Indian Affairs and Northern Development, May 29, 1993.
69. See **Reading 12(c)**. For further discussions of the Yukon self-government agreements, see M.S. Whittington, "Aboriginal Self-Government in Canada" in M.S. Whittington and G. Williams, eds., *Canadian Politics in the 1990s* (Toronto: Nelson Canada, 1995) at 3, 11–18; P.W. Hogg and M.E. Turpel, "Implementing Aboriginal Self-Government: Constitutional and Jurisdiction Issues" in Royal Commission on Aboriginal Peoples, *Aboriginal Self-Government: Legal and Constitutional Issues* (Ottawa: Canada Communications Group, 1995) 375 at 389–440.
70. (Updated subsequently to May 29, 1993.) On its own, the *Umbrella Final Agreement* is a non-legal "framework" agreement. However, it is to be incorporated in the legally binding Yukon First Nation final agreements that are to be concluded with each of the fourteen First Nations. As well as the *Umbrella Final Agreement*, each final agreement is to add provisions specific to the individual First Nation that signs it.
71. Originally spelled "Gwich'in".
72. (Updated version: May 29, 1993). The *Vuntut Gwitchin First Nation Self-Government Agreement* incorporates two transboundary agreements, the *Gwich'in Transboundary Agreement* and the *Old Crow / Inuvialuit Reciprocal Harvesting Agreement*: ss. 25.5.0 and 25.6.0 of the *Vuntut Gwitchin First Nation Self-Government Agreement*, respectively.
73. These governmental structures include the Yukon Land Use Planning Council, Regional Land Use Planning Commissions, the Yukon Development Assessment Board, the Yukon Heritage Resources Board, the Yukon Geo-

graphical Place Names Board, the Yukon Water Board, the Fish and Wildlife Management Board, Renewable Resources Councils, the Dispute Resolution Board, the Surface Rights Board, and the Kluane National Park Management Board.

74. This is based on the *Draft Model Self-Government Agreement* of November 19, 1991, a blueprint agreement that serves, for most self-government matters, a function similar to that served for the settlement as a whole by the *Umbrella Final Agreement*, *supra* note 70.
75. *Ibid.* at s. 10.1.
76. *Ibid.* at s. 10.1.2.
77. *Ibid.* at s. 10.1.1.
78. And exclusive legislative power over internal government matters: *ibid.* at s. 13.1.
79. R.S.C. 1985, c. Y-2. The main forms of more general First Nation legislative powers are described below.
80. These include "gathering, hunting, trapping or fishing and the protection of fish, wildlife and habitat" (s. 13.3.4), "control or prohibition of the operation and use of vehicles" (s. 13.3.13), and "establishment, maintenance, provision, operation or regulation of local services and facilities" (s. 13.3.13). A closing category relates to "matters coming within the good government of Citizens on Settlement Land" (s. 13.3.23).
81. These relate to subject matter such as "adoption by and of Citizens" (s. 13.2.6.), "inheritance, wills, intestacy and administration of estates of Citizens including rights and interests in Settlement Land" (s. 13.2.9), and "solemnization of marriage of Citizens" (s. 13.2.12).
82. *Ibid.* at s. 13.4.0.
83. *Ibid.* at s. 13.6.0.
84. *Ibid.* at s. 14.0.
85. *Ibid.* at s. 14.1.
86. *Ibid.* at s. 17.0.
87. *Ibid.* at s. 16.1. Cf. the equalization provision in s. 36(2) of the *Constitution Act, 1982*.
88. The key paramountcy provisions in the *Vuntut Gwitchin First Nation Self-Government Agreement* are ss. 13.5.2 and 13.5.3.
89. Section 13.5.4 of the *Vuntut Gwitchin First Nation Self-Government Agreement.*
90. The express contradiction test was affirmed by the Supreme Court in *Bank of Montreal v. Hall*, [1990] 1 S.C.R. 121 (applying the test established in *Multiple Access Ltd. v. McCutcheon*, [1982] 2 S.C.R. 161).
91. Section 13.5.3 of the *Vuntut Gwitchin First Nation Self-Government Agreement.*
92. Section 13.5.2 of the *Vuntut Gwitchin First Nation Self-Government Agreement* requires negotiations to identify the areas in which Vuntut Gwich'in First Nation laws will prevail over federal laws.
93. See, generally, s. 13.3 of the *Vuntut Gwitchin First Nation Self-Government Agreement.*
94. For example, liquor control, licensing and regulating of businesses, environmental, and health standards laws.
95. Section 12.0 of the *Vuntut Gwitchin First Nation Self-Government Agreement.*
96. Section 13.5.5 of the *Vuntut Gwitchin First Nation Self-Government Agreement* requires that "[w]here the Yukon reasonably foresees that a Yukon Law of General Application which it intends to enact may have an impact on a law enacted by the Vuntut Gwitchin First Nation, the Yukon shall Consult with the Vuntut Gwitchin First Nation before introducing the Legislation in the Legislative Assembly." The First Nation is subject to a reciprocal obligation: s. 13.5.5. This consultation requirement gives the Government of Yukon an advance opportunity to declare its own legislation inoperative in regard to First Nations Citizens or Settlement Land (s. 13.5.6) or to attempt to negotiate an accommodation agreeable to the First Nation (s. 13.5.7.1). A First Nation with notice of impending Yukon legislation has no corresponding need to declare its own legislation inoperative, since its legislation would prevail over the Yukon legislation: s. 13.5.3.
97. As noted above, special agreements are contemplated in the areas of administration of justice and taxation: *supra* notes 83 and 84. However, for administration of justice, First Nations can enact enforcement measures without prior agreement: s. 13.6.4.1.
98. For example: (1) What kind of political control will beneficiaries have over First Nation governments? (2) Will First Nation governments be subject to the *Charter*? (Although the self-government agreements do not themselves refer to the *Charter*, the *Yukon First Nations Self-Government Act*, S.C. 1994. c. 35, which implements them, is a federal law subject to the *Charter*. Whittington, *supra* note 69 at 13, and Hogg and Turpel, *supra* note 69 at 417 contend that this is sufficient to subject the self-government agreements to the *Charter* as well.) (3) What kind of financial control, access to information, etc., will be allowed for individual Yukon Indian people? (4) How much of the agreement is known now, and how much will depend on future agreements? Are these future agreements subject to approval in advance, or can they be examined after they have been concluded?
99. Under the Yukon Final Agreements.
100. An exception is the northern community of Old Crow, whose population is almost all Aboriginal.
101. Westbank First Nation Self-Government Agreement between Her Majesty the Queen in Right of Canada and Westbank First Nation, October 3, 2003. Federal implementing legislation: *Westbank First Nation Self-Government Act*, S.C. 2004, c. 17 (royal assent 6 May, 2004).
102. See especially Parts VI to XXIII.
103. See generally Part V, and specific sections conferring legislative jurisdiction.
104. Section 31: "In the event of a conflict between a Westbank Law and a federal law that relates to the peace, order and good government of Canada, the federal law shall prevail to the extent of the conflict."
105. *Ibid.* s. 39.
106. *Ibid.* s. 5.
107. Section 276 (f).
108. *Ibid.* s. 23.
109. *Ibid.*, s. 4.
110. Section 275.
111. *Ibid.* s. 54(a): "Non-Members living on Westbank Lands or having an interest in Westbank Lands shall be provided in Westbank Law with mechanisms through which they may have input into proposed Westbank Law and proposed amendments to Westbank Law that directly and significantly affect such non-Members."
112. Peter O'Neill, B.C. Indian Bill Splits Conservatives", *The Vancouver Sun* (22 April, 2004), A5.
113. Royal Commission on Aboriginal Peoples, *Partners in Confederation: Aboriginal Peoples, Self-Government, and the Constitution* (Ottawa: Canada Communication Group, 1993); Royal Commission on Aboriginal Peoples, *Report of the Royal Commission on Aboriginal Peoples*, vol. 2, chap. 3, s. 2.3 at 184–213.
114. **Chapter 3, Parts 7, 12**, and **13**; **Chapter 9, Part 5**; and **Chapter 10, Part 3(g)**.
115. *Ibid.*, especially **Chapter 8, Part 5(b)**.
116. Some exceptions: *Eastmain Band v. Gilpin*, [1987] 3 C.N.L.R. 54 at 67 (Q.C.S.); *Delgamuukw v. British Columbia* (1992), 104 D.L.R. (4th) 470 at 726–31 (Lambert J.A., dissenting), and 761–64 (Hutcheon J.A., dissenting); *Casimel et al. v. Insurance Corporation of British Columbia* (1993), 106 D.L.R. (4th) 720 at 726–28 (B.C.C.A.: a three-judge panel affirming "aboriginal rights of social self-regulation"); and *Campbell v. British Columbia (A.G.)*, (2000), 189 D.L.R. (4th) 333 (B.C.S.C.).
117. See, for example, *Ontario (A.G.) v. Bear Island Foundation* (1984), 15 D.L.R. (4th) 321 at 341 and 407 (O.H.C.), aff'd. without comment on this issue in (1989), 58 D.L.R. (4th)

117 (O.C.A.) and [1991] 2 S.C.R. 570; [1991] *Director of Support and Enforcement v. Nowegijick*, [1989] 2 C.N.L.R. 27 at 33 (Prov. Ct., Family Div.); *Delgamuukw v. British Columbia* (1991), 79 D.L.R. (4th) 185 (B.C.S.C.); *Delgamuukw v. British Columbia* (1992), 104 D.L.R. (4th) 470 at 518–20 and 590–93 (B.C.C.A.); *R. v. S.V.*, [1994] O.J. No. 2454 (O.C.J. — Prov. Div.) at paras. 12–13.

118. E.g., *Delgamuukw v. British Columbia* (1993), 104 D.L.R. (4th) 470 at 519 (Macfarlane and Taggart J.A.), 592 (Wallace J.A.) (B.C.C.A.). Lambert J.A., dissenting, felt that self-government rights survived (687–89); Hutcheon J.A. felt that a right of self-regulation that was subordinate to provincial laws of general application survived (763–64). See also *Campbell v. British Columbia (A.G.)*, *supra* note 116, discussed below.

119. *R. v. Pamajewon*, *infra* note 126 at 410, and **Chapter 9, Part 5**. The Royal Commission on Aboriginal Peoples discounted these views, arguing that there is a lack of evidence of clear and plain legislative intention to end Aboriginal self-government rights: *Report*, vol. 2, chap. 3, s. 2.3 at 207. Arguably, the Commission's position rests on at least four unproven assumptions: (i) that Aboriginal rights include Aboriginal self-government rights; (ii) that self-government rights survived the establishment of British and Canadian sovereignty; (iii) that the Supreme Court's extinguishment test for Aboriginal rights applies to claimed governmental rights in the same way as it applies to Aboriginal rights generally; and (iv) that, conceding all the previous assumptions, courts will be unable to find clear and plain evidence of any intention to exclude non-public governmental power.

120. See, for example, *Canada (A.G.) v. Ontario (A.G.)*, [1937] A.C. 326 at 353–54.

121. See, for example, *Jones v. New Brunswick (A.G.)*, [1975] 2 S.C.R. 182 at 195. See also *Ontario (A.G.) v. Bear Island Foundation* (1984), 15 D.L.R. (4th) 321 at 405 (O.H.C.), aff'd without reference to this point by the O.C.A. and S.C.C. Arguably, the 1982 constitutional changes have not changed this position. Although they may have restricted the sovereignty of the federal and provincial legislatures, they did not purport to transfer any restricted powers to other orders of government.

122. Non-delegated.

123. See, for example, *Ontario (A.G.) v. Canada (A.G.)*, [1912] A.C. 571 at 581, 583–84; *Bank of Toronto v. Lambe* (1887), 12 App. Cas. 575 at 587; *Union Colliery Co. v. Bryden*, [1899] A.C. 580 at 584–85; *Canada (A.G.) v. Ontario (A.G.)* [1937] A.C. 326 at 353–54; *Nova Scotia (A.G.) v. Canada (A.G.)*, [1951] S.C.R. 31; *Murphy v. C.P.R.*, [1958] S.C.R. 636 at 636, 643; *Jones v. New Brunswick (A.G.)*, [1975] S.C.R. 182 at 195; and *Reference Re Same-Sex Marriage*, 2004 SCC 79 at para. 34. In the view of the Royal Commission on Aboriginal Peoples, federal and provincial jurisdiction is exclusive of provincial and federal jurisdiction, respectively, and not of Aboriginal jurisdiction: *Report*, vol. 2, chap. 3, s. 2.3 at 209–12. The Commission said the term "exclusive" in ss. 91 and 92 of the *Constitution Act, 1867* "does not address the question of inherent Aboriginal jurisdiction and does not affect it": *Report*, *ibid.* at 210. However, the word "exclusive" is not qualified, as the Commission suggests, but — within the bounds of the *Constitution Act, 1867* — absolute. Moreover, as the *Report* indicated in its discussion of *Connolly v. Woolrich* (1867), 11 L.C. Jur. 197 (Q.S.C.) (*Report*, *ibid.* at 186–88), the concept of Indian title was not unknown at the time of Confederation. See also *Campbell v. British Columbia (A.G.)*,(2000), 189 D.L.R. (4th) 333 (B.C.S.C.), discussed below, taking a similar approach to that of the Royal Commission.

124. *R. v. Sparrow* (1990), 70 D.L.R. (4th) 385 at 404 (S.C.C.).

125. Although the matter is not free from doubt, the use of the terms "sovereignty", "legislative power", and "underlying title" here suggest matters not just of policy, but law. Conversely, although the Court said in *Sioui* that the British avoided interfering in the internal affairs of the Indians (*Quebec (A.G.) v. Sioui* (1990), 70 D.L.R. (4th) 427 at 450 (S.C.C.)), it seemed to be referring more to policy than law.

126. *R. v. Pamajewon*; *R. v. Gardner*, [1996] 2 S.C.R. 821: **Chapter 8, Part 7**, and **Readings 8(d) and 11(e)**.

127. *Ibid.* at para. 24.

128. *Ibid.* at para. 42, quoting from *R. v. Van der Peet*, [1996] 2 S.C.R. 507 at para. 117.

129. *Supra* notes 126 and 128, respectively.

130. In *Pamajewon*, *supra* note 126, the Court rejected the contention that Aboriginal self-government was an aspect of a broad notion of use of Aboriginal reserve land (para. 27).

131. The integral practices test formulated in *Van der Peet*, *supra* note 128, requires specific traditional practices that are independently integral to distinctive cultures, not practices that are incidental to the former: **Chapter 8, Part 5(a)**. Would regulation or control of another practice, or of practices generally, possess the requisite specificity and independence?

132. *Campbell v. British Columbia (A.G.)* (2000, 189 D.L.R. (4th) 333 (B.C.S.C.).

133. Strictly speaking, they challenged only the legislation implementing the treaty.

134. I.e., independent or non-delegated.

135. I.e., capable of prevailing over federal or provincial statutes in the event of a conflict.

136. They also argued that the provisions denying non-residents on Nisga'a lands the right to vote in Nisga'a elections violated s. 3 of the *Charter*.

137. They also argued that the provisions by-passed the constitutional requirement of royal assent to legislation.

138. *Supra* note 123.

139. The principle that, subject to the *Constitution Act, 1867*, the legislative powers of Canadian legislatures are exclusive as well as supreme, and can be delegated to subordinate agencies, but not abdicated to other bodies: see, for example, *Hodge v. The Queen* (1883), 9 A.C. 117 at 132–33; *Nova Scotia (A.G.) v. Canada (A.G.)*, [1951] S.C.R. 31.

140. *Ibid.* at paras. 75–81.

141. *Ibid.* and 179. Williamson J. said the unqualified wording of s. 91(24) of the *Constitution Act, 1867* did not affect this: para. 82.

142. *Ibid.* at para. 81. Williamson J. suggested that because the exclusivity of the distribution of public legislative powers is internal to Parliament and the provincial legislatures, the result is a "gap" in the text of the Constitution. This is filled by the unwritten constitutional Preamble principle of Aboriginal self-government, under the "gap" theory expounded in the *Provincial Court Judges Reference*, [1997] 3 S.C.R. 3 and the *Reference Re Secession of Quebec*, [1998] 2 S.C.R. 217. See *Campbell*, *ibid.* at paras. 65–70.

143. Williamson J. said Aboriginal custom had been enforced by Canadian courts after Confederation, and therefore must be "law": *ibid.* at para. 86. In his view, the argument that custom was non-legislative because it was consensual was irrelevant. In his view, legitimacy is more important to law than coerciveness (para. 106), and distinguishing between legislation and Aboriginal customs involves a failure to consider this issue from an Aboriginal perspective: para. 107.

144. *Ibid.* at paras. 83–86. For Williamson J., the argument that Aboriginal custom is not sufficiently coercive to resemble legislative power was not convincing: paras. 106 and 107.

On the question of Aboriginal custom and its relationship to Aboriginal rights, see **Chapter 3, Part 13**.

145. *Ibid.* at para. 20. Williamson J. said it was unnecessary to use the strict *Van der Peet* test for proving Aboriginal rights, as required for Aboriginal self-government in

Pamajewon, because "it is treaty rights and not aboriginal rights which are the subject of this proceeding": para. 9. But by Williamson J.'s own reasoning, the validity of the treaty self-government rights was dependent on the prior existence of comparable common law self-government rights.

146. *Ibid.* at para. 179.
147. Williamson J. also said the requirement of royal assent does not apply to legislative powers as limited as those of the Nisga'a (*ibid.* at paras. 144–150), and that the denial of voting rights to non-Nisga'a residents did not violate s. 3 of the *Charter* since it applied only to Parliament and the provincial legislatures, and that in any case, s. 3 was subject to the Aboriginal exception in s. 25 of the *Charter*: paras. 151–66.
148. Many other questions may arise on appeal. For example, if legislative power under the Aboriginal right of self-government is subject to federal and provincial laws, do entrenched treaty provisions merely define existing Aboriginal rights where they give Aboriginal legislation paramountcy over conflicting federal and provincial statutes? Is judicial enforcement of Aboriginal custom a recognition of primary legislative jurisdiction, when judicial enforcement of other forms of custom is not? How far can evidence of executive policy be used in support of the scope of Aboriginal self-government?
149. In the present part, and in **Chapter 3, Parts 7, 12, and 13**; **Chapter 9, Part 5**, and **Chapter 10, Part 3(g)**.
150. The normative nature of the question is recognized in P. Macklem, "Normative Dimensions of the Right of Aboriginal Self-Government" in Royal Commission on Aboriginal Peoples, *Aboriginal Self-Government: Legal and Constitutional issues* (Ottawa: Canada Communications Group, 1995) at 1. Many of the relevant normative considerations are questions of balance. For example, one might include the notion of balancing group equality with individual equality, empowerment with responsibility, heterogeneity with efficiency, minority rights with majoritarian accountability, and cultural difference with national cohesion.
151. **Chapter 7, Parts 1 and 2**.
152. House of Commons Special Committee on Indian Self-Government, *Indian Self-Government in Canada*, Report of the special Committee, October 20, 1983.
153. J.C. Munro, Minister of Indian Affairs and Northern Development, *Response of the Government of Canada to the Report of the Special Committee on Indian Self-Government*, March 5, 1984.
154. The Assembly of First Nations, representing status Indians under the *Indian Act*, the Native Council of Canada (now the Congress of Aboriginal Peoples), representing non-status and off-reserve Indians, the Inuit Tapirisat of Canada, representing Inuit people, and the Métis National Council, representing Métis people.
155. See generally, D. Sanders, "An Uncertain Path: The Aboriginal Constitutional Conferences" in J.M. Weiler and R.M. Elliot, eds., *Litigating the Values of a Nation: the Canadian Charter of Rights and Freedoms* (Toronto: Carswell, 1986) at 63.
156. On the Meech Lake Accord, see P.W. Hogg, *Meech Lake Accord Annotated* (Toronto: Carswell, 1988); K.E. Swinton and C.J. Rogerson, *Competing Constitutional Visions: The Meech Lake Accord* (Toronto: Carswell, 1988); M. Behiels, ed., *The Meech Lake Primer: Conflicting Views of the 1987 Constitutional Accord* (Ottawa: University of Ottawa Press, 1989); D. Milne, *The Canadian Constitution* (Toronto: Lorimer, 1991), chaps. 6 and 7; P.J. Monahan, *Meech Lake: The Inside Story* (Toronto: University of Toronto Press, 1991).
157. See, for example, the trenchant criticisms summarized in T. Hall, "What are We? Chopped Liver? Aboriginal Affairs in the Constitutional Politics of Canada in the 1980s" in Behiels, *ibid.* at 423–56.
158. Monahan, *ibid.*, chap. 8; D.W. Elliott, ed., *Introduction to Public Law Sourcebook*, 5th ed. (North York, Ont.: Captus Press, 2000), chap. 11.
159. See generally P.H. Russell, *Constitutional Odyssey: Can Canadians Become a Sovereign People?* (Toronto: University of Toronto Press, 1993), chap. 11; *Report*, vol. 1, chap. 7, s. 1 at 202–17; and the commentaries in *infra* note 165.
160. September 25, 1991.
161. *Ibid.* at 52–53.
162. *Ibid.* at 52.
163. The federal proposal also contained provisions promising Aboriginal participation in the constitutional deliberations then going on and an entrenched constitutional process to address Aboriginal matters not dealt with in this process, and to monitor negotiation of self-government agreements; and guaranteed Aboriginal representation in a reformed Senate.
164. Special Joint Committee of the Senate and the House of Commons, *Report of the Special Joint Committee on a Renewed Canada*, February 28, 1992.
165. See generally, K. McRoberts and P.J. Monahan, eds., *The Charlottetown Accord, the Referendum, and the Future of Canada* (Toronto: University of Toronto Press, 1993); R.M. Campbell, "The Rise and Fall of the Charlottetown Accord" in *The Real Worlds of Canadian Politics*, 3d ed. (Peterborough: Broadview Press, 1994), chap. 3; A.C. Cairns, "The Charlottetown Accord: Multinational Canada v. Federalism" in C. Cook, ed., *Constitutional Predicament: Canada After the Referendum of 1992* (Montreal & Kingston: McGill-Queen's University Press, 1994) at 25.
166. Draft Final Agreement, proposed ss. 35.1 to 35.5 of *Constitution Act, 1982*.
167. *Ibid.*, proposed s. 2 of *Constitution Act, 1867*.
168. *Ibid.*, proposed s. 21(1)(c) of *Constitution Act, 1867*.
169. *Ibid.*, proposed amendment to s. 3 of *Constitution Act, 1982*.
170. *Ibid.*, proposed s. 33.1 of *Constitution Act, 1982*.
171. *Ibid.*, proposed s. 35.6 of *Constitution Act, 1982*.
172. *Ibid.*, proposed s. 35.7 of *Constitution Act, 1982*.
173. *Ibid.*, proposed s. 35.9 of *Constitution Act, 1982*.
174. *Ibid.*, proposed s. 35.8 of *Constitution Act, 1982*.
175. *Ibid.*, proposed s. 45.1 of *Constitution Act, 1982*.
176. *Ibid.*, proposed s. 91A of *Constitution Act, 1867*.
177. *Ibid.*, proposed s. 24 of *Alberta Act*.
178. Charlottetown Accord: Consensus Report on the Constitution (the political agreement), August 28, 1982, s. 56.
179. Draft Final Agreement, proposed ss. 2(2), 2(4) and 127 of *Constitution Act, 1867*, and s. 35.6(6) of *Constitution Act, 1982*.
180. Proposed s. 2 of *Constitution Act, 1871*.
181. R. Jhappan, "Aboriginal Self-Government" *Canadian Forum*, October 1992 at 15–16.
182. A.C. Cairns, "The Charlottetown Accord: Multinational Canada v. Federalism" in C. Cook, ed., *Constitutional Predicament: Canada after the Referendum of 1992* (Montreal & Kingston: McGill-Queen's University Press, 1994) at 47.
183. On October 22, 1992.
184. For example, the national leadership of the four main Aboriginal associations — the Assembly of First Nations, the Native Council of Canada (now the Congress of Aboriginal Peoples), the Inuit Tapirisat of Canada, and the Métis National Council — all of which supported the Accord. Although the main national leadership of the Assembly of First Nations played an especially forceful role in the negotiations leading to the Accord, referendum polling stations indicated that 60% of those voting on Indian reserves opposed the Accord: P.H. Russell, *Constitutional Odyssey: Can Canadians Become a Sovereign People?* 2d ed. (Toronto: University of Toronto Press, 1993) at 194, referring to an article in *The [Toronto] Globe and Mail*, dated October 28, 1992.
185. This was especially true of some Prairie Indian groups.

186. For example, the Native Women's Association of Canada. The Association was concerned not only that Aboriginal self-government might prejudice equality rights of Aboriginal women, but that Aboriginal women were insufficiently represented in the constitutional process. The Association's equality challenge to the negotiating process was rejected in *Native Women's Association v. Canada*, [1994] 3 S.C.R. 627.
187. A concern, for example, of numerous Mohawk people in Ontario and Quebec.
188. For a summary of these and other Aboriginal concerns, see J. Tully, "Diversity's Gambit Declined" in C. Cook, ed., *Constitutional Predicament: Canada after the Referendum of 1992* (Montreal & Kingston: McGill-Queen's University Press, 1994) at 191–94, and accompanying notes.
189. See Liberal Party of Canada, *Creating Opportunity: The Liberal Plan for Canada* (the "Red Book") (Ottawa: Liberal Party of Canada, 1993) at 98.
190. Minister of Indian Affairs and Northern Development and Federal Interlocutor for Métis and Non-Status Indians, *Aboriginal Self-Government: The Government of Canada's Approach to Implementation of the Inherent Right and the Negotiation of Aboriginal Self-Government* (Ottawa: D.I.A.N.D., 1995) at 3. Cf. Government of Ontario and First Nations of Ontario, *Statement of Political Relationship*, August 6, 1991, reprinted in Shin Imai, Katharine Logan, and Gary Stein, *Aboriginal Law Handbook*, 2d ed. (Scarborough, Ont.: Carswell, 1999) at 123.
191. *Ibid.* at 5–6.
192. Such as divorce, some administration of justice issues, environmental protection and emergency preparedness.
193. *Ibid.* at 6.
194. *Ibid.* at 6–8.
195. *Ibid.* at 8. The government said (at 10) that it was also prepared to consider constitutional protection of self-government arrangements in the *Sechelt Indian Band Self-Government Act* in British Columbia, the *Cree-Naskapi (of Quebec) Act*, and the *Yukon First Nations Self-Government Act*.
196. *Ibid.* at 4.
197. *Ibid.* at 3.
198. *Ibid.* at 4.
199. *Ibid.* at 12–13.
200. *Ibid.* at 12.
201. S.C. 1998, c. 24.
202. S.C. 1999, c. 24. The legislation, which was criticized by some Aboriginal groups as piecemeal, permits other First Nations to acquire the new land management powers.

    As well as these group developments, there have been numerous self-government agreements with individual bands. An example is the 2003 Westbank First Nation Self-Government Agreement: **Part 3(C)(iv)(B)**, above.
203. Royal Commission on Aboriginal Peoples, "The Commission's Terms of Reference (P.C. 1991–1596)" in *Report of the Royal Commission on Aboriginal Peoples* (hereinafter "*Report*") (Ottawa: Canada Communications Group Publishing, 1996), vol. 1, Appendix A at 699–702.
204. *Highlights*, x. The presentations at the hearings were summarized in M. Cassidy Ginger Group Consultants for Royal Commission on Aboriginal Peoples, *Overview of the First Round — Public Hearings* (Ottawa: Royal Commission on Aboriginal Peoples, 1992).
205. *The Right of Aboriginal Self-Government and the Constitution: A Commentary* (Ottawa: R.C.A.P., 1992); *Partners in Confederation: Aboriginal Peoples, Self-Government, and the Constitution* (Ottawa: R.C.A.P., 1993).
206. *The High Arctic Relocation: A Report on the 1953–55 Relocation and Summary of Supporting Information*, 3 vols. (Ottawa: R.C.A.P., 1994).
207. Royal Commission on Aboriginal Peoples, *Choosing Life: A Special Report on Suicide Among Aboriginal People* (Ottawa: Canada Communication Group, 1995).
208. *Canada's Fiduciary Obligation to Aboriginal Peoples in the Context of Accession to Sovereignty by Quebec*, 2 vols. (Ottawa: Canada Communication Group, 1995).
209. *Treaty Making in the Spirit of Co-existence: An Alternative to Extinguishment* (Ottawa: Canada Communication Group, 1995).
210. *Report of the National Round on Criminal Justice* (Ottawa: Supply and Services, 1993); *Bridging the Cultural Divide: A Report on Aboriginal Peoples and Criminal Justice in Canada* (Ottawa: Supply & Services, 1996). For other works on this important topic, see Nova Scotia, Royal Commission on the Donald Marshall, Jr. Prosecution, *Royal Commission on the Donald Marshall, Jr. Prosecution: Digest of Findings and Recommendations* (Halifax: Royal Commission on the Donald Marshall Jr. Prosecution, 1989); Law Reform Commission of Canada, *Aboriginal Peoples and Criminal Justice: Equality, Respect, and the Search for Justice* (Ottawa: L.R.C. Canada, 1991); Manitoba, Manitoba Aboriginal Justice Inquiry (Hamilton Inquiry), *Report of the Aboriginal Justice Inquiry of Manitoba: The Justice System and Aboriginal People*, vol. 1 (Winnipeg, 1992); R.A. Silverman and M.O. Nielsen, eds., *Aboriginal Peoples and Canadian Criminal Justice* (Toronto: Butterworths, 1992).
211. *Supra* note 205.
212. *Ibid.*
213. *Supra* note 143.
214. *People to People, Nation to Nation: Highlights from the Report of the Royal Commission on Aboriginal Peoples* (Ottawa: Canada Communication Group, 1996) (hereinafter "*Highlights*"). See **Reading 12(g)**.
215. *Report*, vol. 5, Appendix A, 150, Recommendation 2.2.7; *Report*, vol. 2, chap. 2, s. 6.1 at 65–66, and chap. 3, s. 4 at 312–14.
216. *Report*, vol. 5, Appendix A, 173, Recommendation 2.3.51; *Report*, vol. 2, chap. 2, s. 4.4 at 375–82.
217. "A third chamber of Parliament would be a logical extension of three orders of government.... If a third chamber is to be established, it should have real power. By this, we mean the power to initiate legislation and to require a majority vote to initiate legislation and to require a majority vote on matters crucial to the lives of Aboriginal Peoples.... We recognize that, to accomplish this objective, the constitution would have to be amended. To move immediately in this area, we suggest a staged approach, which would not require a constitutional amendment initially": Royal Commission on Aboriginal Peoples, *Report*, vol. 2, chap. 3, s. 4.4 at 377–78.
218. *Report*, vol. 5, Appendix A, 158, Recommendations 2.3.4 to 2.3.16; *Report*, vol. 2, chap. 3, s. 2.3 at 184–244, especially at 223–25.
219. *Report*, vol. 5, Appendix A, 255, Recommendation 5.5.3 (Constitutional recognition is to be part of the agenda of "any future constitutional conference convened by the government of Canada": see also Recommendation 5.5.1); *Report*, vol. 2, chap. 3, s. 2 and vol. 5, chap. 5, s. 2.1 at 126–27.
220. *Report*, vol. 5, Appendix A, 162, Recommendation 2.3.12.
221. *Report*, vol. 5, Appendix A, 255, Recommendation 5.5.2 (A constitutional veto for Aboriginal Peoples is to be "one matter for consideration at any future [constitutional] conference"); *Report*, vol. 5, chap. 5, s. 2.3 at 130.
222. *Report*, vol. 5, Appendix A, 161, Recommendations 2.3.8 (dual citizenship) and 2.3.9 (dual passports); *Report*, vol. 2, chap. 3, s. 2.1 at 237–40.
223. *Report*, vol. 5, Appendix A, Recommendation 2.2.8(h).
224. *Report*, vol. 5, Appendix A at 148–54, Recommendations 2.2.2 to 2.2.1; *Report*, vol. 2, chap. 2 and vol. 5, chap. 1, s. 2.2.
225. In 1992–93, the federal government spent $6 billion and the provincial governments spent $5.6 billion, a total of $11.6 billion per year, for Aboriginal peoples: *Highlights*, 138.

226. *Report*, vol. 5, Appendix A, Recommendation 2.5.1.
227. *Ibid.*, Recommendation 2.5.23.
228. *Ibid.*, Recommendation 2.5.32.
229. *Ibid.*, Recommendation 2.5.36.
230. *Ibid.*, Recommendation 3.3.5.
231. *Ibid.*, Recommendation 3.3.14.
232. *Ibid.*, Recommendations 3.4.1 to 3.4.15.
233. *Ibid.*, Recommendation 3.4.4.
234. *Ibid.*, Recommendation 3.5.6(a).
235. *Ibid.*, Recommendation 3.5.7.
236. *Ibid.*, Recommendation 3.5.14.
237. *Ibid.*, Recommendation 3.5.22.
238. *Ibid.*, Recommendation 3.6.10.
239. *Ibid.*, Recommendations 4.2.1 to 4.2.3.
240. *Ibid.*, Recommendations 4.4.1 to 4.4.10.
241. *Ibid.*, Recommendations 4.5.1 to 4.5.10.
242. *Ibid.*, Recommendations 4.6.1 to 4.6.22.
243. *Ibid.*, Recommendations 4.7.1 to 4.7.26.
244. *Ibid.*, Recommendation 2.4.4.
245. *Ibid.*, Recommendations 2.3.17 to 2.3.26.
246. For an overview, see A.C. Cairns, *Citizens Plus: Aboriginal Peoples and the Canadian State* (Vancouver: U.B.C. Press, 2000), chap. 4.
247. The qualification "well-spent" is important. As well, amounts ideally required would have to be tempered by the capacity of governments to pay and the needs of others at the bottom of the economic scale. Subject to these qualifications, the case for a major financial commitment is compelling.
248. *Report*, vol. 2, chap. 3, s. 2.3 at 202–13.
249. *Report*, vol. 5, Appendix A at 158, Recommendations 2.3.4 to 2.3.16, especially Recommendation 2.3.4(a); *Report*, vol. 2, chap. 3, s. 2.3 at 184–244, especially at 223–25.
250. See **Part 4**, above. The Commission's argument that an inherent Aboriginal right of self-government is entrenched by virtue of s. 35(1) of the *Constitution Act, 1982* is based on its argument that there is an existing inherent right of Aboriginal self-government at common law: *Report*, vol. 2, chap. 2, s. 2.3 at 202 and 204. On this question, see **Part 4**, above.
251. *Report*, vol. 5, chap. 5, s. 2.1 at 126.
252. The *Report* said protection of the *Metis Settlements Act* would require a constitutional amendment in any event: vol. 5, chap. 5, s. 2.2 at 127.
253. *Ibid.* at 134. "Taken together," the Commission said, "the changes we propose to protect Aboriginal interests would constitute a comprehensive amendment to the constitution": *Report*, vol. 5, chap. 5, s. 2.4 at 133.
254. *Ibid.* at 129.
255. *Report*, vol. 2, chap. 3, s. 4.4 at 377–78.
256. But not the hybrid government "policy statement of the law" approach recommended by the Commission in *Report*, vol. 5, Appendix A at 158, Recommendation 2.3.4(a) *et seq.*
257. Cf. A.C. Cairns' question about the parallel relationships proposed in the Charlottetown Accord: "At what point do good fences cease to make good neighbours and instead make strangers of fellow citizens?": A.C. Cairns, "The Charlottetown Accord: Multinational Canada v. Federalism" in C. Cook, ed., *Constitutional Predicament: Canada after the Referendum of 1992* (Montreal & Kingston: McGill-Queen's University Press, 1994) at 51.
258. The *Report* said that "[a]n Aboriginal or treaty nation is an indigenous society, possessing its own political organization, economy, culture, language and territory": vol. 2, chap. 2, s. 7.7 at 88, and that "an Aboriginal nation is a sizeable body of Aboriginal people with a shared sense of national identity that constitutes the predominant population in a certain territory or collection of territories": vol. 2, chap. 3, s. 2.2 at 178. The Commission identified as examples of Aboriginal nations, "the Huron, the Mohawk, Nisga'a, the Haida, and the Métis of Red River, among others" (*Report*, *ibid.*) and the Mi'kmaq, the Innu, the Anishnabe, the Blood ... the Inuvialuit, the western Métis Nation "and other peoples whose bonds have stayed intact, despite government interference" (*Highlights*, 25). It said that "[o]rdinarily, an Aboriginal nation should comprise at least several thousand people": *Report*, vol. 2, chap. 3, s. 2.2 at 179.

    Most of the 320,000 self-identified Aboriginal people who live in cities — approximately 45% of the total self-identified Aboriginal population (*Highlights*, 117) — will lack territorial bases of their own. Some urban Aboriginal people may be affiliated with groups with sufficiently large territorial bases, but would live outside the special territorial jurisdiction negotiated for those groups. Some Aboriginal people will lack any affiliation with groups with large territorial bases. See *Report*, vol. 2, chap. 3, s. 2.3 at 179–80 for the Commission's attempt to cope with these complications.
259. The Commission said that "[t]o say that Aboriginal peoples are nations is not to say that they are nation-states seeking independence from Canada": *Highlights*, xi, and unlike the sovereignty-association sought by the Parti-Québécois, the Commission did not recommend international sovereignty.
260. For example, concepts such as dual citizenship and passports, separate Parliamentary bodies, and a "nation-to-nation" relationship all stress separate status, with relatively little emphasis on common ties. The *Report* also argued that Canadian Aboriginal peoples have an international law right of self-determination: *Report*, vol. 2, chap. 3, s. 2.2, and see *supra* note 1.
261. See also *Citizens Plus: Aboriginal Peoples and the Canadian State* (Vancouver: U.B.C. Press, 2000), chaps. 4 and 5.
262. See, for example, the subjects referred to above in regard to the *Report*'s proposal that governments spend an additional $1.5 to $2 billion per year on Aboriginal peoples.
263. **Chapter 11, Part 3.**
264. That is, apart from the "nation-to-nation" negotiating structure proposed in *Report*, vol. 5, Appendix A, Recommendation 2.2.8(h).
265. A.C. Cairns, *Citizens Plus: Aboriginal Peoples and the Canadian State* (Vancouver, U.B.C. Press, 2000).
266. *Ibid.* at 122–26, 154. The Commission did make some non-land Aboriginal government proposals for Métis people, who are mainly (65%) urban. These included national and provincial Métis governments with voluntary membership off Métis lands: Canada, *Report of the Royal Commission on Aboriginal Peoples* (Ottawa: Canadian Communications Group Publishing, 1996), vol. 2(1), *Restructuring the Relationship* at 153–62. Cairns criticizes the Commission for failing to consider the workability of these proposals: Cairns, *ibid.* at 138.
267. Cairns, *ibid.* at 138–42.
268. *Ibid.* at 158–59.
269. *Ibid.* at 159–60.
270. Cairns says this concept puts more emphasis on common citizenship, "although the 'plus' concept has expansive possibilities": *ibid.* at 183.
271. Ottawa: Minister of Indian Affairs and Northern Development, 1997.
272. The differences (and some of the similarities) between the *Report's* vision and that of the federal government can be seen in the following passage from the *Plan*:

    > The Royal Commission on Aboriginal Peoples concluded that fundamental change is needed in the relationship between Aboriginal and non-Aboriginal people in Canada. The Royal Commission's vision included rebuilding Aboriginal nationhood; supporting effective and accountable Aboriginal governments; establishing government-to-government relationships between Canada and Aboriginal nations; and taking

practical steps to improve the living conditions of Aboriginal people. It called for a partnership based on the four principles of mutual respect and recognition, responsibility and sharing.

The Government of Canada agrees with the Commission's conclusion that Aboriginal and non-Aboriginal people must work together, using a non-adversarial approach, to shape a new vision of their relationship and to make that vision a reality. In that spirit, Canada is undertaking to build a renewed partnership with Aboriginal people and governments.

Canada's vision of partnership means celebrating our diversity while sharing common goals. It means developing effective working relationships with Aboriginal organizations and communities. Above all, it means all levels of government, the private sector, and individuals working together with Aboriginal people on practical solutions to address their needs. Our common aim should be to help strengthen Aboriginal communities and economies, and to overcome the obstacles that have slowed progress in the past.

13 Concluding Note

Chapter Highlights

- Four decades ago, the main agreements with Aboriginal peoples were the traditional treaties — archaic, uncertain, meagre, and incomplete. Today, many former non-treaty areas are subject to constitutionally entrenched, comprehensive land claims agreements.
- Three decades ago, few Canadian courts supported Aboriginal rights outside the Royal Proclamation. Today, Aboriginal rights are not only recognized at common law but are also entrenched in the Constitution.
- Two decades ago, Indian women were campaigning to remove sexual discrimination in the paternalistic *Indian Act*. Today, most of the sexual discrimination is gone, the paternalism has been reduced, and recent changes could bring major amendments and end the Department of Indian Affairs.
- Less than two decades ago, the common law focused on land and land use. Today, Aboriginal representatives, many government officials, and the Royal Commission on Aboriginal Peoples call for more guaranteed Aboriginal self-government.

Synopsis

After centuries of neglect, the situation of Canadian Aboriginal peoples is moving to centre stage. Aboriginal / non-Aboriginal relations are being touched by winds of change. Reformers are turning more to special legal safeguards and government structures. Informal accommodations, administrative arrangements, and policy statements are being replaced by legal mechanisms — by common law presumptions, equitable obligations, statutory provisions, and constitutional guarantees. Problems that used to be viewed as economic or social — or simply ignored — are now candidates for separate government solutions. These are, in many ways, positive developments. They have raised the profile of Aboriginal issues. They provide stronger and more permanent forms of protection. They encourage diversity and self-control. But these developments also carry risks. In seeking legal solutions, let us remember that rules and courts are imperfect and offer only partial answers to complex social challenges. Let us not overlook more consensual and accountable avenues of change. And, in emphasizing separate structures, let us not neglect common problems and common opportunities. Ultimately, we must all travel — or sink — together.

Canadian law relating to Aboriginal peoples has been changing at an astounding rate. Four decades ago, the main agreements with Aboriginal peoples were the traditional treaties — archaic, uncertain, meagre, and incomplete. Today, many former non-treaty areas are subject to constitutionally entrenched, comprehensive land claims agreements.

Little more than three decades ago, few Canadian courts supported Aboriginal rights outside the Royal Proclamation. Today, Aboriginal rights are not only recognized at common law but are entrenched in the Constitution.

Two decades ago, Indian women were campaigning to remove sexual discrimination in the paternalistic *Indian Act*. Today, most of the sexual discrimination is gone, paternalism has been reduced, and recent changes could bring major amendments and end the Department of Indian Affairs.

Less than two decades ago, the common law focused on land and land use. Since then, many Aboriginal representatives, many government officials, and the Royal Commission on Aboriginal Peoples have called for more guaranteed Aboriginal self-government.

In many ways, this greater recognition is a positive development. After losing military power and their pivotal role in the fur trade, Aboriginal peoples languished near the bottom of the list of social priorities. When they were approached, it was on non-Aboriginal terms. Non-Aboriginal rights policies and structures were imposed unilaterally, often with disastrous consequences.

Small wonder, then, that many people seek leverage and protection in legal rights and constitutional guarantees. It is not surprising that they should want to replace imposed structures with Aboriginal powers. It is understandable that people should desire maximum possible control over their own destinies

However, this trend also carries some risks. The increasing legalization and constitutionalization of Aboriginal / non-Aboriginal rights relations can bring more litigation and conflict. Open-ended constitutional proposals and complex land claims agreements are breeding grounds for lawyers. The extension of Aboriginal rights to governmental jurisdiction could transfer more power from Aboriginal and elected public representatives to judges. Unless its scope is carefully defined, the notion of special Aboriginal fiduciary obligations could reduce Aboriginal law to a state of ongoing uncertainty.

The drive for more legal rights could become an end in itself. It could overshadow more mundane and more concrete concerns. The old politics of paternalism could be replaced with a new politics of difference. In celebrating what divides us we could risk overlooking what we have in common.

What do we have in common? We share a land of great potential wealth and opportunity. All cultures can bring special strengths to the challenge of using and preserving it as effectively as possible. Technology can help in using the land efficiently; Aboriginal values can help in using it carefully.

We also face common problems. Keeping our health, supporting roofs over our heads, protecting our environment, reducing social conflicts, and educating our children concern us all. In areas like these, we need both to bring all Canadians closer to reasonable standards and to benefit from Aboriginal wisdom in the process. Stopping mercury poisoning, preventing teen suicides, and encouraging university graduates will require more than constitutional guarantees and sovereignty declarations. In claims agreements, for example, we need to focus on land, training, funding, and shared arrangements as much as on new jurisdictions or paramountcy clauses. For self-government, change should not stop at separate structures. There should be more emphasis on cooperation, more room for Aboriginal involvement in the mainstream, and more Aboriginal leadership in Canadian public government.

For these challenges, we should be leaning *less* on courts and the law. The common law needs clarity more than it needs *ad hoc* intervention or political change by unelected reformers. Nor should we try to make every Aboriginal issue a constitutional issue. As this book demonstrates, in the relationship between Aboriginal and non-Aboriginal peoples, the law is, at best, an incomplete and imperfect tool.

Nor is it always an appropriate tool. As well as the challenges above, Aboriginal and non-Aboriginal Canadians have something else in common. We have an identity that transcends our status as individuals; as people with First Nations, Inuit, Métis, or other ancestry; as followers of different religions; as speakers of different languages; as residents of the various provinces or territories; or even as Canadians. We are all citizens of the world. Although boundaries, protection, and legal guarantees have a place, we must also work for greater cooperation, greater communication, and greater equity in the distribution of the riches of the planet.

The cover page of a 1982 Parliamentary committee report on Indian self-government depicted a Two Row Wampum.[1] In this symbol Indian people and non-Indians travel in vessels side by side, but separately from each other. If it extends to include rows for the Métis and Inuit peoples as well, this vivid image highlights the distinctiveness of Aboriginal peoples. In other respects, though, all Canadians and all humanity travel on a single, increasingly fragile and interdependent, blue craft in the heavens. Ultimately we must all travel — or sink — together.

Note

1. Canada, House of Commons, *Indian Self-Government: Report of the Special Committee on Indian Self-Government* (the "Penner Committee"), First Session of the Thirty-second Parliament, 1980–81–82–83, October 20, 1983, front cover; description on back cover.

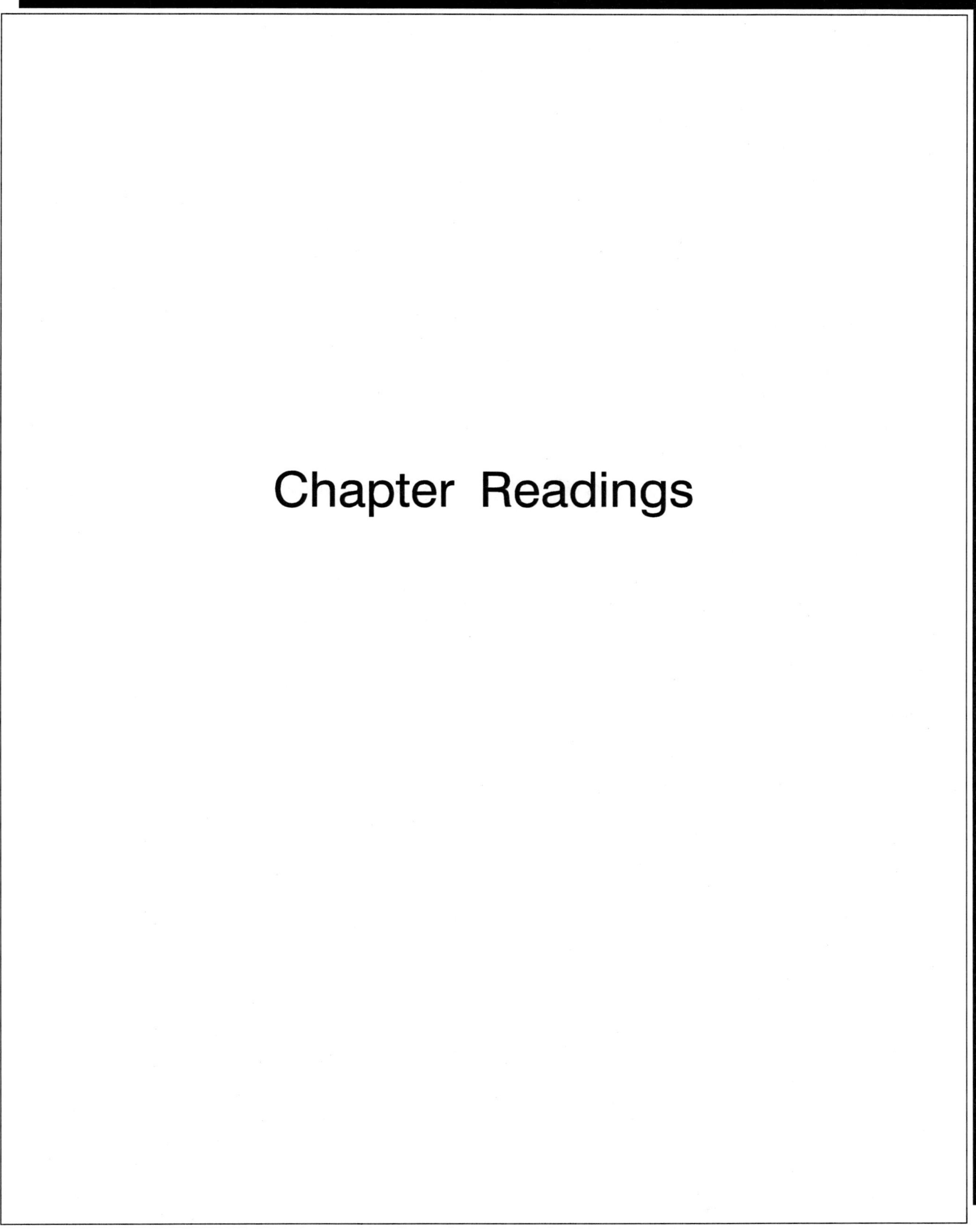

Chapter Readings

Purpose

The **Chapter Readings** that follow provide an introductory resource base for the topics addressed in the **Main Text** above, and offer a possible gateway to more advanced work in this field. Together with the endnotes that follow the chapters in the **Main Text**, the materials here should help the reader to approach the subject critically, to move beyond it, and to develop his or her own understanding of some of its main contours and challenges.

General Structure and Links to Main Text

The **Chapter Readings** are organized into twelve units. Each unit contains material that relates to the corresponding chapter in the text. Thus, the material in unit one (the **Introduction** unit of the **Chapter Readings** on p. 217) relates to **Chapter 1** (the **Introduction** chapter of the text beginning on p. 3). This general correspondence does not preclude other links between the **Chapter Readings** and the **Main Text**. In a broader sense, for example, the **Introduction** unit of the **Chapter Readings** is very relevant to the **Main Text** as a whole.

Each individual unit of the **Chapter Readings** is divided into parts. Typically, each part comprises extracts from a major decision, statute, or other basic primary or secondary work. Thus, a reference to "**Readings 2(b)**" in the **Main Text** is to the reading in Part (b) of unit 2 of the **Chapter Readings** (in this example, the excerpt on the *Canadian Bill of Rights*). Where the focus is on a specific aspect of a decision, the **Chapter Reading** part refers the reader to relevant extract, and to the portions that address the specific aspect.

Specific Links to Main Text

The 🗎 symbol in the **Chapter Readings** section links individual parts of this section with individual parts of the corresponding chapters of the **Main Text**, or with other parts of the **main text**. Thus, the key symbol shown opposite **Part 2(b)** of the **Chapter Readings** indicates that the reading in that part (the *Canadian Bill of Rights*) is especially relevant to **Chapter 2, Part 4(d)** of the text.

1 Introduction

(a) Some Aboriginal Perspectives on Lands and Resources†

See **Chapter 1** and **Chapter 3, Part 3**.

The themes of Nógha's songs and prophecies — nurturing communities, making a living, caring for the land — recurred throughout the Commission's public hearings. We have no hesitation in saying that these themes unite all Canadians. In a country that still derives much of its culture and wealth from the land and its natural resources, this should not be surprising. Over the course of our travels and meetings, the individuals and organizations that spoke to us about such issues, whether Aboriginal or non-Aboriginal, showed a common concern for social and economic well-being, for finding ways to provide for their children and future generations.

But while there are definite similarities, we also learned that there are profound differences between Aboriginal people and other Canadians over fundamental issues associated with lands and resources. As Chief Tony Mercredi of Fort Chipewyan in Alberta reminded us, much of the problem stems from the power imbalance in the current relationship:

> Envision, if you will, a circle. The Creator occupies the centre of the circle and society ... revolves around the Creator.
>
> This system is not based on hierarchy. Rather, it is based on harmony. Harmony between the elements, between and within ourselves and within our relationship with the Creator. In this circle there are only equals.
>
> Now, envision a triangle. This triangle represents the fundamental elements of the Euro-Canadian society. Authority emanates from the top and filters down to the bottom. Those at the bottom are accountable to those at the top, that is control. Control in this society is not self-imposed, but rather exercised by those at the top upon those beneath them.
>
> In this system the place of the First Nations peoples is at the bottom. This is alien to the fundamental elements of our society, where we are accountable only to the Creator, our own consciences and to the maintenance of harmony.
>
> By having the institutions and regulations of the Euro-Canadian society imposed upon us, our sense of balance is lost.
>
> Chief Tony Mercredi
> Athabasca Chipewyan First Nation Community
> Fort Chipewyan, Alberta,
> 18 June 1992

The songs of the prophet Nógha convey this idea of harmony in the relationship between the earth and all those who inhabit the lands and waters. This fundamental tenet of Aboriginal spirituality was repeated to us many times during the hearings by individuals like Elder Alex Skead in Winnipeg:

> We are so close to the land. This is my body when you see this mother earth, because I live by it. Without that water, we dry up, we die. Without food from the animals, we die, because we got to live on that. That's why I call that spirit, and that's why we communicate with spirits. We thank them every day that we are alive....
>
> Elder Alex Skead
> Winnipeg, Manitoba
> 22 April 1992

. . . .

† Royal Commission on Aboriginal Peoples, "Lands and Resources: Background," *Report of the Royal Commission on Aboriginal Peoples: Restructuring the Relationship*, vol. 2 (Ottawa: Canada Communication Group, 1996), chap. 4, s. 3.1: "Lessons from the Hearings" at 434–38. Notes omitted. Reproduced with the permission of the Minister of Public Works and Government Services, 2004 and courtesy of the Privy Council Office.

At the core of Aboriginal peoples' world view is a belief that lands and resources are living things that both deserve and require respect and protection. Grand Chief Harold Turner of the Swampy Cree Tribal Council stressed that his people were "placed on Mother Earth to take care of the land and to live in harmony with nature":

> The Creator gave us life, inherent rights and laws which governed our relationship with nations and all peoples in the spirit of coexistence. This continues to this day.
>
> We as original caretakers, not owners of this great country now called Canada, never gave up our rights to govern ourselves and thus are sovereign nations. We, as sovereign nations and caretakers of Mother Earth, have a special relationship with the land.
>
> Our responsibilities to Mother Earth are the foundation of our spirituality, culture and traditions.... Our ancestors did not sign a real estate deal, as you cannot give away something you do not own.
>
> Grand Chief Harold Turner
> Swampy Cree Tribal Council
> The Pas, Manitoba,
> 20 May 1992

Aboriginal peoples believe, therefore, that lands and resources are their common property, not commodities to be bought and sold. Chief George Desjarlais of the West Moberly community in British Columbia told us that the principle of sharing formed the basis of arrangements made between his people and the Crown:

> We are treaty people. Our nations entered into a treaty relationship with your Crown, with your sovereign. We agreed to share our lands and territories with the Crown. We did not sell or give up our rights to our land and territories. We agreed to share our custodial responsibility for the land with the Crown. We did not abdicate it to the Crown. We agreed to maintain peace and friendship among ourselves and with the Crown.
>
> Chief George Desjarlais
> West Moberly First Nation
> Fort St. John, British Columbia,
> 20 November 1992

Aboriginal people also understand the treaties as instruments through which land-based livelihood and future self-sufficiency for themselves and the newcomers were secured. The late John McDonald, then Vice-Chief of the Prince Albert Tribal Council, stated emphatically that Aboriginal peoples never gave up their rights to take part in the governance and management of lands and resources:

> If the wealth of our homelands was equitably shared with us and if there is no forced interference in our way of life, we could fully regain and exercise our traditional capacity to govern, develop and care for ourselves from our natural resources. This is what was intended by the Creator, this is what our elders believe to be the true significance of our treaties. First Nations agreed to share the wealth of their homelands with the Crown, the Crown agreed to protect the First Nations and their homelands from forced interference into their way of life, i.e., culture, economy, social relations, and provide development and material assistance.
>
> Vice-Chief John McDonald
> Prince Albert Tribal Council
> La Ronge, Saskatchewan,
> 28 May 1992

Many of the Aboriginal people who appeared before us expressed bitterness at the way they had been treated by society. Elder Moses Smith of the Nuu-chah-nulth Nation on Vancouver Island particularly objected to the assumption that Aboriginal people had not been making proper use of their lands and resources before the settlers arrived:

> We got absolutely the short end of the stick. And to quote what was said, what was said of us, we, as Nuu-chah-nulth people, "These people, they don't need the land. They make their livelihood from the sea."... So there we have just mere little rock piles on the west coast of Vancouver Island, the territory of the Nuu-chah-nulth Nation. Rock piles! Rock piles!
>
> Moses Smith
> Nuu-chah-nulth Nation
> Port Alberni, British Columbia,
> 20 May 1992

(b) Founding Peoples in Traditional Times†

See **Chapter 1** and **Chapter 3, Part 2**.

One point is becoming increasingly clear: New World prehistory was as filled with significant developments as that of the Old World in the fascinating story of man's cultural evolution. Whatever the degree of overseas influence, the civilizations that evolved in the New World were distinctively their own; American Olmec and Chinese Shang each had their dragons, but they are not easily confused, any more than the split animal motif of the Northwest Coast could be with that of the Chou or Ch'in dynasties. What is more, varied as New World cultures were, they fit into a hemisphere-wide pattern; like Europeans on the other side of the Atlantic, they shared a basic civilization. Their "formidable originality" has led Joseph Needham, director of the East Asian History of Science Library, Cambridge, and Lu Gwei-Djen, associate director, to place them on a par with the Old World civilizations of the Han, the Gupta, and the Hellenistic Age.[39]

. . . .

At the time of the first known European contact with North America, that of the Norse in about A.D. 1000, by far the majority of Canada's original peoples were hunters and gatherers, as could be expected from the country's northern location.[1] This way of life, based on regulated patterns that had evolved over thousands of years, grew out of an intimate knowledge of resources and the best way of exploiting them. Anthropologist Robin Ridington has made the point that their technology consisted of knowledge rather than tools.[2] It was by means of this knowledge of their ecosystems, and their ingenuity in using them to their own advantage, that Amerindians had been able to survive as well as they did with a comparatively simple technology.

Because of Canada's extended coast line (the longest in the world), many of them were sea-oriented; however, the great variety in the country's geographical regions (Arctic, Subarctic, Northeast, Great Plains, Plateau, and Northwest Coast) ensured many variations on fundamentally similar ways of life. For the most part, the population was thinly scattered, as this mode of subsistence is land-intensive; the most widely accepted estimate is about 500,000, although recent demographic studies have pushed the possible figure to well over 2 million.[3] The principal population concentrations were on the Northwest Coast, where abundant and easily available resources had allowed for a sedentary life, and in what is today's southern Ontario, where various branches of Iroquoians practised farming. The Iroquoian groups may have totalled about 60,000 if not more, and the Northwest Coast could have counted as many as 200,000 souls, making it "one of the most densely populated nonagricultural regions in the world."[4] Most of these people had been in their locations for thousands of years; as Wright has pointed out, only in the Arctic and the interior of British Columbia had there been comparatively recent migrations (A.D. 1000 and A.D. 700 respectively).[5]

These people spoke about fifty languages that have been classified into twelve families, of which six were exclusive to present-day British Columbia. By far the most widespread geographically were those within the Algonkian group, spread from the Rocky Mountains to the Atlantic and along the coast from the Arctic to Cape Fear; Cree and Inuktitut had the widest geographical ranges. This accords with Rogers's hypothesis, that by the proto-historic period areas that were once glaciated (most of Canada and a portion of the northern United States) had fewer languages than areas that had been unglaciated. While Canada was completely covered with ice during the last glaciation, except for parts of the Yukon and some adjacent regions, the strip along the Pacific coast was freed very early. According to Rogers' calculations, once-glaciated areas average eighteen languages per million square miles, and unglaciated regions 52.4 languages per million square miles (2,590,000 square kilometres).[6] Following the rule of thumb of linguistics that greater diversity of language indicates longer occupation, then the settlement of Canada can be judged to be compa-

† From *Canada's First Nations: A History of Founding Peoples from Earliest Times*, 1st ed., by Olive Patricia Dickason (Toronto: McClelland & Stewart, 1992) at 62–66, 432–33.

ratively recent — for the most part, dating to no more than about 15,000 years ago. In any event, the Athapaskan languages spoken in the unglaciated Northwest are more diversified than the Algonkian spoken in the once-glaciated taiga that stretches from the Rockies to the Atlantic coast. Intrusive Iroquoian-Siouan languages have been aptly described as islands in an Algonkian sea. In Canada, as in the two Americas generally, the greater language diversity of the Pacific coast indicates settlement prior to the rest of the country, although this has not so far been backed up archeologically.[7] At the present, one can only speculate about the villages and campsites that have been drowned by rising sea levels following the retreat of the glaciers.

All of these peoples, whether mobile or sedentary, lived within cultural frameworks that met social and individual needs by emphasizing the group as well as the self. This was true even among those peoples, particularly in the Far North, whose groupings were fluid, depending on the season and availability of food. The social organization of Amerindians, like their languages, displayed a wider variety than was the case in Europe. However, with the exception of some aspects of the chiefdoms of the Northwest Coast, the only area in Canada where that type of social organization developed,[8] Amerindians shared the general characteristics of pre-stated societies in that they were egalitarian to the extent that their sexual division of labour and responsibility allowed,[9] and they were regulated by consensus....

Notes

39. Needham and Lu, *Trans-Pacific Echoes*, p. 64.

. . . .

1. Canada's ecology, subsistence bases, and population distribution for 1500 are mapped in R. Cole Harris, ed., *Historical Atlas of Canada*, 1 (Toronto: University of Toronto Press, 1987), plates 17, 17A, and 18. Seasonal Algonkian and Iroquoian cycles are schematized in plate 34.
2. Robin Ridington, "Technology, world view, and adaptive strategy in a northern hunting society," *Canadian Review of Sociology and Anthropology*, 19, 4 (1982), pp. 469–81.
3. Russell Thornton, *American Indian Holocaust and Survival. A Population History Since 1492* (Norman: University of Oklahoma Press, 1987), p. 32. Ethnologist June Helm, University of Iowa, divides the Subarctic into the shield with associated Hudson Bay lowlands and Mackenzie borderlands, the cordillera, the Alaska plateau, and the region south of the Alaska range. The first division, that of the Subarctic shield and borderlands, covers approximately three-quarters of the land mass of the Arctic. June Helm, ed., *Handbook of North American Indians, 6: Subarctic* (Washington, D.C.: Smithsonian Institution, 1981), p. 1.
4. Robert T. Boyd, "Demographic History, 1774–1874," in Wayne Suttles, ed., *Handbook of North American Indians, 7: Northwest Coast* (Washington, D.C.: Smithsonian Institution, 1990), p. 135. Richard Inglis, curator of ethnology, Royal British Columbia Museum, estimates the pre-contact population for the west coast from California to Alaska at 500,000. (*Vancouver Sun*, 21 November 1987.)
5. Harris, ed., *Historical Atlas of Canada*, plate 9.
6. Ruth Gruhn, "Linguistic Evidence in Support of the Coastal Route of Earliest Entry into the New World," *Man*, new series, 23, 2 (1988), pp. 77–79.
7. See Harris, ed., *Historical Atlas of Canada*, plate 66, on linguistic evidence indicating extremely ancient habitation of the Northwest Coast. The discovery of a longhouse dated to 9,000 years ago near Mission, B.C., appears to be an archeological break-through. See *Alberta Report*, 18, 34 (1991), pp. 50–51.
8. There is some evidence that chiefdoms had appeared among some of the Iroquois. See William C. Noble, "Tsouharissen's Chiefdom: An Early Historic 17th Century Neutral Iroquoian Ranked Society," *Canadian Journal of Archaeology*, 9, 2 (1985), pp. 131–46.
9. An offshoot of the sexual division of labour and responsibility was that it prevented celibacy. See Reuben Gold Thwaites, ed., *Jesuit Relations and Allied Documents*, 73 vols. (Cleveland: Burrows Bros., 1896–1901), XVI, p. 163. Another consequence was the clear definition of roles, a major factor in the harmony that prevailed in the encampments. (*Ibid.*, VI, pp. 233–34.)

2 Who Is an Aboriginal Person?

(a) General Status Provisions

See **Chapter 2**.

CONSTITUTION ACT, 1867†

VI. Distribution of Legislative Powers

Powers of the Parliament

91. It shall be lawful for the Queen, by and with the Advice and Consent of the Senate and House of Commons, to make Laws for the Peace, Order, and good Government of Canada, in relation to all Matters not coming within the Classes of Subjects by this Act assigned exclusively to the Legislatures of the Provinces; and for greater Certainty, but not so as to restrict the Generality of the foregoing Terms of this Section, it is hereby declared that (notwithstanding anything in this Act) the exclusive Legislative Authority of the Parliament of Canada extends to all Matters coming within the Classes of Subjects next herein-after enumerated; that is to say, —

. . . .

(24) Indians, and Lands reserved for the Indians.

CONSTITUTION ACT, 1982‡

The *Constitution Act, 1982* is reproduced in part in **Reading 7(a)** because of its importance to Aboriginal and treaty rights. Note that s. 35(2) of this Act refers to the holders of these rights as the "Aboriginal peoples of Canada". It says that "Aboriginal peoples of Canada includes the Indian, Inuit and Métis peoples of Canada." However, it provides no further definition of these terms.

*INDIAN ACT**

S. 2, definition of Indian:

Interpretation

2.(1) In this Act
"Indian" means a person who pursuant to this Act is registered as an Indian or is entitled to be registered as an Indian

---

† *Constitution Act, 1867* (U.K.) 30431 Vict., c. 3; R.S.C. 1985, App. II, No. 5, s. 91(24).

‡ *Constitution Act, 1982*, being Schedule B of the *Canada Act, 1982*, (U.K.) 1982, c. 11; R.S.C. 1985, App. II, No. 44, as am. by the *Constitutional Amendment Proclamation, 1983*, (SI/84-102) at ss. 25, 35, 35.1, and 37.1.

* *Indian Act*, R.S.C. 1985, c. I-5, as am., s. 2(1).

(b) *Canadian Bill of Rights and Charter*

See **Chapter 2, Parts 4(d) and 9.**

THE CANADIAN BILL OF RIGHTS†

The Parliament of Canada, affirming that the Canadian Nation is founded upon principles that acknowledge the supremacy of God, the dignity and worth of the human person and the position of the family in a society of free men and free institutions;

Affirming also that men and institutions remain free only when freedom is founded upon respect for moral and spiritual values and the rule of law;

And being desirous of enshrining these principles and the human rights and fundamental freedoms derived from them in a *Bill of Rights* which shall reflect the respect of Parliament for its constitutional authority and which shall ensure the protection of these rights and freedoms in Canada:

THEREFORE Her Majesty, by and with the advice and consent of the Senate and House of Commons of Canada, enacts as follows:

Part I
Bill of Rights

1. It is hereby recognized and declared that in Canada there have existed and shall continue to exist without discrimination by reason of race, national origin, colour, religion or sex, the following human rights and fundamental freedoms, namely,

- (a) the right of the individual to life, liberty, security of the person and enjoyment of property, and the right not to be deprived thereof except by due process of law;
- (b) the right of the individual to equality before the law and the protection of the law;
- (c) freedom of religion;
- (d) freedom of speech;
- (e) freedom of assembly and association; and
- (f) freedom of the press.

2. Every law of Canada shall, unless it is expressly declared by an Act of the Parliament of Canada that it shall operate notwithstanding the *Canadian Bill of Rights*, be so construed and applied as not to abrogate, abridge or infringe or to authorize the abrogation, abridgment or infringement of any of the rights or freedoms herein recognized and declared, and in particular, no law of Canada shall be construed or applied so as to

- (a) authorize or effect the arbitrary detention, imprisonment or exile of any person;
- (b) impose or authorize the imposition of cruel and unusual treatment or punishment;
- (c) deprive a person who has been arrested or detained
  - (i) of the right to be informed promptly of the reason for his arrest or detention,
  - (ii) of the right to retain and instruct counsel without delay, or
  - (iii) of the remedy by way of *habeas corpus* for the determination of the validity of his detention and for his release if the detention is not lawful;
- (d) authorize a court, tribunal, commission, board or other authority to compel a person to give evidence if he is denied counsel, protection against self incrimination or other constitutional safeguards;
- (e) deprive a person of the right to a fair hearing in accordance with the principles of fundamental justice for the determination of his rights and obligations;
- (f) deprive a person charged with a criminal offence of the right to be presumed innocent until proved guilty according to law in a fair and public hearing by an independent and impartial tribunal, or of the right to reasonable bail without just cause; or
- (g) deprive a person of the right to the assistance of an interpreter in any proceedings in which he is involved or in which he is a party or a witness, before a court, commission, board or other tribunal, if he does not understand or speak the language in which such proceedings are conducted.

---

† *The Canadian Bill of Rights*, S.C. 1960, c. 44, reprinted in R.S.C. 1985, App. III.

3. The Minister of Justice shall, in accordance with such regulations as may be prescribed by the Governor in Council, examine every proposed regulation submitted in draft form to the Clerk of the Privy Council pursuant to the *Regulations Act* and every Bill introduced in or presented to the House of Commons, in order to ascertain whether any of the provisions thereof are inconsistent with the purposes and provisions of this Part and he shall report any such inconsistency to the House of Commons at the first convenient opportunity.

4. The provisions of this Part shall be known as the *Canadian Bill of Rights*.

Part II

5.(1) Nothing in Part I shall be construed to abrogate or abridge any human right or fundamental freedom not enumerated therein that may have existed in Canada at the commencement of this Act.

(2) The expression "law of Canada" in Part I means an Act of the Parliament of Canada enacted before or after the coming into force of this Act, any order, rule or regulation thereunder, and any law in force in Canada or in any part of Canada at the commencement of this Act that is subject to be repealed, abolished or altered by the Parliament of Canada.

(3) The provisions of Part I shall be construed as extending only to matters coming within the legislative authority of the Parliament of Canada.

CANADIAN *CHARTER OF RIGHTS AND FREEDOMS*†

[See also s. 25 (as am.), and subsection 4 of s. 35 (as am.) in **Reading 7(a)**.]

Equality Rights

15.(1) Every individual is equal before and under the law and has the right to equal protection and equal benefit of the law without discrimination and, in particular, without discrimination based on race, national or ethnic origin, colour, religion, sex, age or mental or physical disability.

(2) Subsection (1) does not preclude any law, program or activity that has as its object the amelioration of conditions of disadvantaged individuals or groups including those that are disadvantaged because of race, national or ethnic origin, colour, religion, sex, age or mental of physical disability.

. . . .

26. The guarantee in this *Charter* of certain rights and freedoms shall not be construed as denying the existence of any other rights or freedoms that exist in Canada.

. . . .

28. Notwithstanding anything in this *Charter*, the rights and freedoms referred to in it are guaranteed equally to male and female persons.

(c) *Canada (A.G.) v. Lavell; Isaac et al. v. Bedard*‡

See **Chapter 2, Parts 4(d) and 9**.

NOTE

Because of former s. 12(1)(b) of the *Indian Act*, Mrs. Jeannette Lavell and Mrs. Yvonne Bedard lost their Indian status after they married non-Indian men. They argued that s. 12(1)(b) discriminated against them on the basis of sex, and should be declared inoperative because of conflict with the equality guarantees in the *Canadian Bill of Rights*.

---

† *Canadian Charter of Rights and Freedoms*, being Schedule B to the *Canada Act 1982* (U.K.), 1982, c. 11.

‡ [1974] S.C.R. 1349 at 1359–62, 1365–67, 1370–73, 1375, 1390 (S.C.C.), rev'g (1971), 22 D.L.R. (3d) 188 (F.C.A.: decision in Mrs. Lavell's case) and (1971), 25 D.L.R. (3d) 551 (O.H.C.: decision in Mrs. Bedard's case).

EXTRACT

Martland and Judson JJ., concurred with Ritchie J.

[RITCHIE J. for himself, Fauteux C.J., and Martland and Judson JJ.:]

I have had the advantage of reading the reasons for judgment prepared for delivery by my brother Laskin.

These appeals, which were heard together, are from two judgments holding that the provisions of s. 12(1)(b) of the *Indian Act*, R.S.C. 1970, c. I-6, are rendered inoperative by s. 1(b) of the *Canadian Bill of Rights*, R.S.C. 1970, App. III, as denying equality before the law to the two respondents.

Both respondents were registered Indians and "Band" members within the meaning of s. 11(b) of the *Indian Act* when they elected to marry non-Indians and thereby relinquished their status as Indians in conformity with the said s. 12(1)(b) which reads as follows:

> **12.**(1) The following persons are not entitled to be registered, namely,
>
> (b) a woman who married a person who is not an Indian, unless that woman is subsequently the wife or widow of a person described in section 11.

It is contended on behalf of both respondents that s. 12(1)(b) of the Act should be held to be inoperative as discriminating between Indian men and women and as being in conflict with the provisions of the *Canadian Bill of Rights* and particularly s. 1 thereof which provides:

> **1.** It is hereby recognized and declared that in Canada there have existed and shall continue to exist without discrimination by reason of race, national origin, colour, religion or sex, the following human rights and fundamental freedoms, namely,
>
> (b) the right of the individual to equality before the law and the protection of the law;

. . . .

In my opinion the exclusive legislative authority vested in Parliament under s. 91(24) could not have been effectively exercised without enacting laws establishing the qualifications required to entitle persons to status as Indians and to the use and benefit of Crown "lands reserved for Indians". The legislation enacted to this end was, in my view, necessary for the implementation of authority so vested in Parliament under the Constitution.

To suggest that the provisions of the *Bill of Rights* have the effect of making the whole *Indian Act* inoperative as discriminatory is to assert that the Bill has rendered Parliament powerless to exercise the authority entrusted to it under the Constitution of enacting legislation which treats Indians living on reserves differently from other Canadians in relation to their property and civil rights. The proposition that such a wide effect is to be given to the *Bill of Rights* was expressly reserved by the majority of this Court in the case of *R.* v. *Drybones* (1969), 9 D.L.R. (3d) 473 at pp. 485–86, [1970] 3 C.C.C. 355, [1970] S.C.R. 282, to which reference will hereafter be made, and I do not think that it can be sustained.

What is at issue here is whether the *Bill of Rights* is to be construed as rendering inoperative one of the conditions imposed by Parliament for the use and occupation of Crown lands reserved for Indians. These conditions were imposed as a necessary part of the structure created by Parliament for the internal administration of the life of Indians on reserves and their entitlement to the use and benefit of Crown lands situated thereon, they were thus imposed in discharge of Parliament's constitutional function under s. 91(24) and in my view can only be changed by plain statutory language expressly enacted for the purpose. It does not appear to me that Parliament can be taken to have made or intended to make such a change by the use of broad general language directed at the statutory proclamation of the fundamental rights and freedoms enjoyed by all Canadians, and I am therefore of opinion that the *Bill of Rights* had no such effect.

. . . .

The contention that the *Bill of Rights* is to be construed as overriding all of the special legislation imposed by Parliament under the *Indian Act* is, in my view, fully answered by Pigeon J., in his dissenting opinion in the *Drybones* case where he said, at pp. 489–90:

> If one of the effects of the *Canadian Bill of Rights* is to render inoperative all legal provisions whereby Indians as such are not dealt with in the same way as the general public, the conclusion is inescapable that Parliament, by the enactment of the Bill, has not only fundamentally altered the status of the Indians in that indirect fashion but has also made any future use of federal legislative authority over them subject to the requirement of expressly declaring

> every time "that the law shall operate notwithstanding the *Canadian Bill of Rights*". I find it very difficult to believe that Parliament so intended when enacting the Bill. If a virtual suppression of federal legislation over Indians as such was meant, one would have expected this important change to be made explicitly, not surreptitiously, so to speak.

That it is membership in the band which entitles an Indian to the use and benefit of lands on the reserve is made plain by the provisions of ss. 2 and 18 of the *Indian Act*. Section 2(1)(a) reads as follows:

> **2.**(1) In this Act
>
> "band" means a body of Indians
>
> (a) for whose use and benefit in common, lands, the legal title to which is vested in Her Majesty, have been set apart before, on or after the 4th day of September 1951.

Section 18 reads as follows:

> **18.**(1) Subject to this Act, reserves are held by Her Majesty for the use and benefit of the respective bands for which they were set apart; and subject to this Act and to the terms of any treaty or surrender, the Governor-in-Council may determine whether any purpose for which lands in a reserve are used or are to be used is for the use and benefit of the band.

. . . .

In my view the meaning to be given to the language employed in the *Bill of Rights* is the meaning which it bore in Canada at the time when the Bill was enacted, and it follows that the phrase "equality before the law" is to be construed in light of the law existing in Canada at that time.

In considering the meaning to be attached to "equality before the law" as those words occur in s. 1(b) of the Bill, I think it important to point out that in my opinion this phrase is not effective to invoke the egalitarian concept exemplified by the 14th Amendment of the U.S. Constitution as interpreted by the Courts of that country: see *R.* v. *Smythe* (1971), 19 D.L.R. (3d) 480, 3 C.C.C. (2d) 366, [1971] S.C.R. 680, *per* Fauteux C.J.C., at pp. 482 and 484–85. I think rather that, having regard to the language employed in the second paragraph of the preamble to the *Bill of Rights*, the phrase "equality before the law" as used in s. 1 is to be read in its context as a part of "the rule of law" to which overriding authority is accorded by the terms of that paragraph.

In this connection I refer to *Stephen's Commentaries on the Laws of England*, 21st ed., vol. III (1950), where it is said at p. 337:

> Now the great constitutional lawyer Dicey, writing in 1885 was so deeply impressed by the absence of arbitrary ... governments present and past, that he coined the phrase "the rule of law" to express the regime under which Englishmen lived; and he tried to give precision to it in the following words which have exercised a profound influence on all subsequent thought and conduct.
>
>> That the "rule of law," which forms a fundamental principle of the constitution has three meanings, or may be regarded from three different points of view.

The second meaning proposed by Dicey is the one with which we are here concerned and it was stated in the following terms:

> It means again equality before the law or the equal subjection of all classes to the ordinary law of the land administered by the ordinary courts; the "rule of law" in this sense excludes the idea of any exemption of officials or others from the duty of obedience to the law which governs other citizens or from the jurisdiction of the ordinary courts.

"Equality before the law" in this sense is frequently invoked to demonstrate that same law applies to the highest official of Government as to any other ordinary citizen, and in this regard Professor F.R. Scott, in delivering the Plaunt Memorial Lectures on *Civil Liberties and Canadian Federalism* (1959), speaking of the case of *Roncarelli* v. *Duplessis* (1959), 16 D.L.R. (2d) 689, [1959] S.C.R. 121, had occasion to say:

> ... it is always a triumph for the law to show that it is applied equally to all without fear or favour. This is what we mean when we say that all are equal before the law.

The relevance of these quotations to the present circumstances is that "equality before the law" as recognized by Dicey as a segment of the rule of law, carries the meaning of equal subjection of all classes to the ordinary law of the land as administered by the ordinary Courts, and in my opinion the phrase "equality before the law" as employed in s. 1(b) of the *Bill of Rights* is to be treated as meaning equality in the administration or application of the law by the law enforcement authorities and the ordinary Courts of the land. This construction is, in my view, supported by the provision of paras. (a) and (g) of s. 2 of the Bill which clearly indicate to me that it was equality in the administration and enforcement of the law with which Parliament was concerned when it guaranteed the continued existence of "equality before the law".

Turning to the *Indian Act* itself, it should first be observed that by far the greater part of that Act is concerned with the internal regulation of the lives of Indians on reserves and that the exceptional provisions dealing with the conduct of Indians off reserves and their contracts with other Canadian citizens fall into an entirely different category.

It was, of course necessary for Parliament, in the exercise of s. 91(24) authority, to first define what Indian meant, and in this regard s. 2(1) of the Act provides that:

> "Indian" means a person who pursuant to this Act is registered as an Indian or is entitled to be registered as an Indian;

It is therefore clear that registration is a necessary prerequisite to Indian Status....

. . . .

A careful reading of the Act discloses that s. 95 (formerly s. 94, R.S.C. 1952, c. 149) is the only provision therein made which creates an offence for any behaviour of an Indian off a reserve and it will be plain that there is a wide difference between legislation such as s. 12(1)(b) governing the civil rights of designated persons living on Indian reserves to the use and benefit of Crown lands, and criminal legislation such as s. 95 which creates an offence punishable at law for Indians to act in a certain fashion when off a reserve. The former legislation is enacted as a part of the plan devised by Parliament, under s. 91(24) for the regulation of the internal domestic life of Indians on reserves. The latter is criminal legislation exclusively concerned with behaviour of Indians off a reserve.

Section 95 (formerly s. 94) reads, in part, as follows:

> **95.** An Indian who
> (b) is intoxicated ...
>
> off a reserve, is guilty of an offence and is liable on summary conviction to a fine of not less than ten dollars and not more than fifty dollars or to imprisonment for a term not exceeding three months or to both fine and imprisonment.

These were the provisions that were at issue in the case of *R.* v. *Drybones* (1969), 9 D.L.R. (3d) 473, [1970] 3 C.C.C. 355, [1970] S.C.R. 282, where this Court held that they could not be construed and applied without exposing Indians as a racial group to a penalty in respect of conduct as to which the Parliament of Canada had imposed no sanctions on other Canadians who were subject to Canadian laws regulating their conduct, which were of general application in the Northwest Territories where the offence was allegedly committed and in which there are no Indian reserves.

In that case the decision of the majority of this Court was that the provision of s. 94(b), as it then was, could not be enforced without bringing about inequality between one group of citizens and another and that this inequality was occasioned by reason of the race of the accused. It was there said, at pp. 484–85:

> ... I am ... of opinion that an individual is denied equality before the law if it is made an offence punishable at law, on account of his race, for him to do something which his fellow Canadians are free to do without having committed any offence or having been made subject to any penalty.
>
> It is only necessary for the purpose of deciding this case for me to say that in my opinion s. 94(b) of the *Indian Act* is a law of Canada which creates such an offence and that it can only be construed in such manner that its application would operate so as to abrogate, abridge or infringe one of the rights declared and recognized by the *Bill of Rights*. For the reasons which I have indicated I am therefore of opinion that s. 94(b) is inoperative.
>
> For the purpose of determining the issue raised by this appeal it is unnecessary to express any opinion respecting the operation of any other section of the *Indian Act*.

And it was later said, at pp. 485–86:

> The present case discloses laws of Canada which abrogate, abridge and infringe the right of an individual Indian to equality before the law and in my opinion if those laws are to be applied in accordance with the express language used by Parliament in s. 2 of the *Bill of Rights*, then s. 94(b) of the *Indian Act* must be declared to be inoperative.
>
> It appears to me to be desirable to make it plain that these reasons for judgment are limited to a situation in which, under the laws of Canada, it is made an offence punishable at law on account of race, for a person to do something which all Canadians who are not members of that race may do with impunity; in my opinion the same considerations do not by any means apply to all the provisions of the *Indian Act*.

Having regard to the express reservations contained in these passages, I have difficulty in understanding how that case can be construed as having decided that any sections of the *Indian Act*, except s. 94(b) are rendered inoperative by the *Bill of Rights*.

The *Drybones* case can, in my opinion, have no application to the present appeals as it was in no way concerned with the internal regulation of the lives of Indians on reserves or their right to the use and benefit of Crown lands thereon, but rather deals exclusively with the effect of the *Bill of Rights* on a section of the *Indian Act* creating a crime with attendant penalties for the conduct by Indians off a reserve in an area where non-Indians, who were also governed by federal law, were not subject to any such restriction.

The fundamental distinction between the present case and that of *Drybones*, however, appears to me to be that the impugned section in the latter case could not be enforced without denying equality of treatment in the administration and enforcement of the law before the ordinary Courts of the land to a racial group, whereas no such inequality of treatment between Indian men and women flows as a necessary result of the application of s. 12(1)(b) of the *Indian Act*.

To summarize the above, I am of the opinion:

1. that the *Bill of Rights* is not effective to render inoperative legislation, such as s. 12(1)(b) of the *Indian Act*, passed by the Parliament of Canada in discharge of its constitutional function under s. 91(24) of the *British North America Act, 1867*, to specify how and by whom Crown lands reserved for Indians are to be used;
2. that the *Bill of Rights* does not require federal legislation to be declared inoperative unless it offends against one of the rights specifically guaranteed by s. 1, but where legislation is found to be discriminatory, this affords an added reason for rendering it ineffective;
3. that equality before the law under the *Bill of Rights* means equality of treatment in the enforcement and application of the laws of Canada before the law enforcement authorities and the ordinary Courts of the land, and no such inequality is necessarily entailed in the construction and application of s. 12(1)(b).

I would allow the appeal of the *Attorney-General of Canada* v. *Lavell*, reverse the judgment of the Federal Court of Appeal and restore the decision of Judge B.W. Grossberg. In accordance with the terms of the order of the Federal Court of Appeal granting leave to appeal to this Court, the appellant will pay to the respondent her solicitor-and-client costs of the appeal and the application for leave. There should be no further order as to costs.

On the appeal of *Isaac et al.* v. *Bedard*, a question was raised in this Court as to the jurisdiction of the trial Court. In view of the conclusion reached on the merits, no decision is now necessary on that question. The appeal to this Court should be allowed, the judgment at trial should be reversed and the action dismissed. Under the circumstances, there should be no order as to costs in that case in any Court.

Hall and Spence JJ., concurred with Laskin J.

[Abbott J., dissenting, wrote brief separate reasons concurring with Laskin J.]

. . . .

[LASKIN J., dissenting, for himself and Hall and Spence JJ.:]

... In my opinion, unless we are to depart from what was said in *Drybones*, both appeals now before us must be dismissed. I have no disposition to reject what was decided in *Drybones*; and on the central issue of prohibited discrimination as catalogued in s. 1 of the *Canadian Bill of Rights*, it is, in my opinion, impossible to distinguish *Drybones* from the two cases in appeal. If, as in *Drybones*, discrimination by reason of race makes certain statutory provisions inoperative, the same result must follow as to statutory provisions which exhibit discrimination by reason of sex.

. . . .

[PIGEON J.:]

I agree in the result with Ritchie J. I certainly cannot disagree with the view I did express in *R.* v. *Drybones* (1969), 9 D.L.R. (3d) 473 at pp. 489–90, [1970] 3 C.C.C. 355, [1970] S.C.R. 282, that the enactment of the *Canadian Bill of Rights* was not intended to effect a virtual suppression of federal legislation over Indians. My difficulty is Laskin J.'s strongly reasoned opinion that, unless we are to depart from what was said by the majority in *Drybones*, these appeals should be dismissed because, if discrimination by reason of race makes certain statutory provisions inoperative, the same result must follow as to statutory provisions which exhibit discrimination by reason of sex. In that end, it appears to me that, in the circumstances, I need not reach a firm conclusion on that point. Assuming the situation is such as Laskin J., says, it cannot be improper for me to adhere to what was my dissenting view, when a majority of those who did not agree with it in respect of a particular section of the *Indian Act*, R.S.C. 1970, c. I–6, now adopt it for the main body of this important statute.

(d) 1985 *Indian Act* Status Provisions†

See **Chapter 2, Part 4**(**e**).

Indian Register

5.(1) There shall be maintained in the Department an Indian Register in which shall be recorded the name of every person who is entitled to be registered as an Indian under this Act.

(2) The names in the Indian Register immediately prior to April 17, 1985 shall constitute the Indian Register on April 17, 1985.

(3) The Registrar may at any time add to or delete from the Indian Register the name of any person who, in accordance with this Act, is entitled or not entitled, as the case may be, to have his name included in the Indian Register.

(4) The Indian Register shall indicate the date on which each name was added thereto or deleted therefrom.

(5) The name of a person who is entitled to be registered is not required to be recorded in the Indian Register unless an application for registration is made to the Registrar.

6.(1) Subject to section 7, a person is entitled to be registered if

(a) that person was registered or entitled to be registered immediately prior to April 17, 1985;
(b) that person is a member of a body of persons that has been declared by the Governor in Council on or after April 17, 1985 to be a band for the purposes of this Act;
(c) the name of that person was omitted or deleted from the Indian Register, or from a band list prior to September 4, 1951, under subparagraph 12(1)(a)(iv), paragraph 12(1)(b) or subsection 12(2) or under subparagraph 12(1)(a)(iii) pursuant to an order made under subsection 109(2), as each provision read immediately prior to April 17, 1985 or under any former provision of this Act relating to the same subject-matter as any of those provisions.
(d) the name of that person was omitted or deleted from the Indian Register, or from the Indian Register, or from a band list prior to September 4, 1951, under subparagraph 12(1)(a)(iii) pursuant to an order made under subsection 109(1), as each provision read immediately prior to April 17, 1985 or under any former provision of this Act relating to the same subject-matter as any of those provisions;
(e) the name of that person was omitted or deleted from the Indian Register, or from a band list prior to September 4, 1951.
  (i) under section 13, as it read immediately prior to September 4, 1951, or under any former provision of this Act relating to the same subject-matter as that section or
  (ii) under section 111, as it read immediately prior to July 1, 1920, or under any former provision of this Act relating to the same subject-matter as that section; or
(f) that person is a person both of whose parents are or, if no longer living, were at the time of death entitled to be registered under this section.

(2) Subject to section 7, a person is entitled to be registered if that person is a person one of whose parents is or, if no longer living, was at the time of death entitled to be registered under subsection (1).

(3) For the purposes of paragraph (1)(f) and subsection (2).

(a) a person who was no longer living immediately prior to April 17, 1985 but who was at the time of death entitled to be registered shall be deemed to be entitled to be registered under paragraph (1)(a); and

† *Indian Act*, ss. 5–13.3, R.S.C. 1985, c. I-5, as am.

(b) a person described in paragraph (1)(c), (d) or (e) who was no longer living on April 17, 1985 shall be deemed to be entitled to be registered under that paragraph.

7.(1) The following persons are not entitled to be registered:

(a) a person who was registered under paragraph 11(1)(f), as it read immediately prior to April 17, 1985, or under any former provision of this Act relating to the same subject-matter as that paragraph, and whose name was subsequently omitted or deleted from the Indian Register under this Act; or
(b) a person who is the child of a person who was registered or entitled to be registered under paragraph 11(1)(f), as it read immediately prior to April 17, 1985, or under any former provision of this Act relating to the same subject-matter as that paragraph, and is also the child of a person who is not entitled to be registered.

(2) Paragraph (1)(a) does not apply in respect of a female person who was, at any time prior to being registered under paragraph 11(1)(f), entitled to be registered under any other provision of this Act.

(3) Paragraph (1)(b) does not apply in respect of the child of a female person who was, at any time prior to being registered under paragraph 11(1)(f), entitled to be registered under any other provision of this Act.

Band Lists

8. There shall be maintained in accordance with this Act for each band a Band List in which shall be entered the name of every person who is a member of that band.

9.(1) Until such time as a band assumes control of its Band List, the Band List of that band shall be maintained in the Department by the Registrar.

(2) The names in a Band List of a band immediately prior to April 17, 1985 shall constitute the Band List of that band on April 17, 1985.

(3) The Registrar may at any time add to or delete from a Band List maintained in the Department the name of any person who, in accordance with this Act, is entitled or not entitled, as the case may be, to have his name included in that List.

(4) A Band List maintained in the Department shall indicate the date on which each name was added thereto or deleted there from.

(5) The name of a person who is entitled to have his name entered in a Band List maintained in the Department is not required to be entered therein unless an application for entry therein is made to the Registrar.

10.(1) A band may assume control of its own membership if it establishes membership rules for itself in writing in accordance with this section and if, after the band has given appropriate notice of its intention to assume control of its own membership, a majority of the electors of the band gives its consent to the band's control of its own membership.

(2) A band may, pursuant to the consent of a majority of the electors of the band,

(a) after it has given appropriate notice of its intention to do so, establish membership rules for itself; and
(b) provide for a mechanism for reviewing decisions on membership.

(3) Where the council of a band makes a by-law under paragraph 81 (p. 4) bringing this subsection into effect in respect of the band, the consents required under subsections (1) and (2) shall be given by a majority of the members of the band who are of the full age of eighteen years.

(4) Membership rules established by a band under this section may not deprive any person who had the right to have his name entered in the Band List for that band, immediately prior to the time the rules were established, of the right to have his name so entered by reason only of a situation that existed or an action that was taken before the rules came into force.

(5) For greater certainty, subsection (4) applies in respect of a person who was entitled to have his name entered in the Band List under paragraph 11(1)(c) immediately before the band assumed control of the Band List if that person does not subsequently cease to be entitled to have his name entered in the Band List.

(6) Where the conditions set out in subsection (1) have been met with respect to a band, the council of the band shall forthwith give notice to the Minister in writing that the band is assuming control of its own membership and shall provide the Minister with a copy of the membership rules for the band.

(7) On receipt of a notice from the council of a band under subsection (6), the Minister shall, if the

conditions set out in subsection (1) have been complied with forthwith

- (a) give notice to the band that it has control of its own membership; and
- (b) direct the Registrar to provide the band with a copy of the Band List maintained in the Department.

(8) Where a band assumes control of its membership under this section, the membership rules established by the band shall have effect from the day on which notice is given to the Minister under subsection (6), and any additions to or deletions from the Band List of the band by the Registrar on or after that day are of no effect unless they are in accordance with the membership rules established by the band.

(9) A band shall maintain its own Band List from the date on which a copy of the Band List is received by the band under paragraph (7)(b), and, subject to section 13.2 the Department shall have no further responsibility with respect to that Band List from that date.

(10) A band may at any time add to or delete from a Band List maintained by it the name of any person who, in accordance with the membership rules of the band, is entitled or not entitled, as the case may be, to have his name included in that list.

(11) A Band List maintained by a band shall indicate the date on which each name was added thereto or deleted therefrom.

11.(1) Commencing on April 17, 1985, a person is entitled to have his name entered in a Band List maintained in the Department for a band if

- (a) the name of that person was entered in the Band List for that band, or that person was entitled to have his name entered in the Band List for that band, immediately prior to April 17, 1985;
- (b) that person is entitled to be registered under paragraph 6(1)(b) as a member of that band;
- (c) that person is entitled to be registered under paragraph 6(1)(c) and ceased to be a member of that band by reason of the circumstances set out in that paragraph; or
- (d) that person was born on or after April 17, 1985 and is entitled to be registered under paragraph 6(1)(f) and both parents of that person are entitled to have their names entered in the Band List or, if no longer living, were at the time of death entitled to have their names entered in the Band List.

(2) Commencing on the day that is two years after the day that an Act entitled *An Act to amend the Indian Act*, introduced in the House of Commons on February 28, 1985, is assented to, or on such earlier day as may be agreed to under section 13.1, where a band does not have control of its Band List under this Act, a person is entitled to have his name entered in a Band List maintained in the Department for the band

- (a) if that person is entitled to be registered under paragraph 6(1)(d) or (e) and ceased to be a member of that band by reason of the circumstances set out in that paragraph; or
- (b) if that person is entitled to be registered under paragraph 6(1)(f) or subsection 6(2) and a parent referred to in that provision is entitled to have his name entered in the Band List or, if no longer living, was at the time of death entitled to have his name entered in the Band List.

(3) For the purposes of paragraph (1)(d) and subsection (2), a person whose name was omitted or deleted from the Indian Register or a band list in the circumstances set out in paragraph 6(1)(c), (d) or (e) who was no longer living on the first day on which he would otherwise be entitled to have his name entered in the Band List of the band of which he ceased to be a member shall be deemed to be entitled to have his name so entered.

(4) Where a band amalgamates with another band or is divided so as to constitute new bands, any person who would otherwise have been entitled to have his name entered in the Band List of that band under this section is entitled to have his name entered in the Band List of the amalgamated band or the new band to which he has the closest family ties, as the case may be.

12. Commencing on the day that is two years after the day that an Act entitled *An Act to amend the Indian Act*, introduced in the House of Commons on February 28, 1985, is assented to, or on such earlier day as may be agreed to under section 13.1, any person who

- (a) is entitled to be registered under section 6, but is not entitled to have his name entered in the Band List maintained in the Department under section 11, or
- (b) is a member of another band,

is entitled to have his name entered in the Band List maintained in the Department for a band if the council of the admitting band consents.

13. Notwithstanding sections 11 and 12, no person is entitled to have his name entered at the same time in more than one Band List maintained in the Department.

13.1.(1) A band may, at any time prior to the day that is two years after the day that the day that an Act entitled *An Act to amend the Indian Act*, introduced in the House of Commons on February 28, 1985, is assented to, decide to leave the control of its Band List with the Department if a majority of the electors of the band gives its consent to that decision.

(2) Where a band decides to leave the control of its Band List with the Department under subsection (1), the council of the band shall forthwith give notice to the Minister in writing to that effect.

(3) Notwithstanding a decision under subsection (1), a band may, at any time after that decision is taken, assume control of its Band List under section 10.

13.2.(1) A band may, at any time after assuming control of its Band List under section 10, decide to return control of the Band List to the department if a majority of the electors of the band gives its consent to that decision.

(2) Where a band decides to return control of its Band List to the Department under subsection (1), the council of the band shall forthwith give notice to the Minister in writing to that effect and shall provide the Minister with a copy of the Band List and a copy of all the membership rules that were established by the band under subsection 10(2) while the band maintained its own Band List.

(3) Where a notice is given under subsection (2) in respect of a Band List, the maintenance of that Band List shall be the responsibility of the Department from the date on which the notice is received and from that time the Band List shall be maintained in accordance with the membership rules set out in section 11.

13.3. A person is entitled to have his name entered in a Band List maintained in the Department pursuant to section 13.2 if that person was entitled to have his name entered, and his name was entered, in the Band List immediately before a copy of it was provided to the Minister under subsection 13.2(2), whether or not that person is also entitled to have his name entered in the Band List under section 11.

(e) *Corbiere v. Canada (Minister of Indian and Northern Affairs)*†

See **Chapter 2, Parts 4(g) and 9.**

NOTE

Although band councils can make decisions affecting off-reserve band members, s. 77(1) of the *Indian Act* limited the right to vote in band council elections to band members "ordinarily resident on the reserve". Mr. John Corbiere and three other members of the Batchewana Band in Ontario argued that this provision violated off-reserve band members' right to equality before the law in comparison with reserve residents, contrary to s. 15 of the *Charter*. They went on to argue that this breach was not justified under s. 1 of the *Charter*.

The Supreme Court agreed. However, the Court suspended its declaration of unconstitutionality for 18 months to give the federal government time to make the necessary legislative changes. The government announced its intent to make the amendments needed to give off-reserve members equal voting rights, and invited Aboriginal input on these and any further changes that might be consistent with the *Charter*.

The band had argued that it had an Aboriginal right to exclude off-reserve members from voting. How did the Court respond to this? In regard to the *Charter*, this was the first Supreme Court decision to recognize off-reserve band member status

† [1999] 2 S.C.R. 203; aff'g. and varying [1997] 1 F.C. 689 (C.A.); aff'g. and varying (1993), 107 D.L.R. (4th) 582 (T.D.).

as an "analogous ground" for the purposes of s. 15. What other *Indian Act* categories of people might qualify for analogous ground status? How does the Court's decision in *Corbiere* affect the many bands who select band council members by custom, rather than under the *Indian Act*? Should off-reserve members have precisely the same band voting rights as reserve residents? If not, what viable alternatives are likely to be acceptable under the *Charter*? On October 20, 2000, the government amended the *Indian Band Election Regulations* and the *Indian Referendum Regulations* to give on-reserve band members the same voting rights in *Indian Act* elections and referendums as on-reserve members. It proposed more wide-ranging electoral changes to the *Indian Act*, but withdrew them in 2003–04: see **Chapter 12(3)(b)(i)**.

EXTRACT

[L'Heureux-Dubé J. gave separate reasons for herself, Gonthier, Iacobucci and Binnie JJ., summarized at the end of this extract. The extract here is from the main majority judgment.

McLACHLIN and BASTARACHE JJ., for themselves, Lamer C.J. and Cory and Major JJ.:]

. . . .

[para3] The narrow issue raised in this appeal is whether the exclusion of off-reserve members of an Indian band from the right to vote in band elections pursuant to s. 77(1) of the *Indian Act*, R.S.C., 1985, c. I-5, is inconsistent with s. 15(1) of the *Canadian Charter of Rights and Freedoms*. There is no need for us to describe the steps applicable to a s. 15(1) analysis. They have been affirmed with great precision by Iacobucci J. in *Law* v. *Canada (Minister of Employment and Immigration)*, S.C.C., No. 25374, judgment rendered March 25, 1999.

[para4] The first step is to determine whether the impugned law makes a distinction that denies equal benefit or imposes an unequal burden. The Act's exclusion of off-reserve band members from voting privileges on band governance satisfies this requirement.

[para5] The next step is to determine whether the distinction is discriminatory. The first inquiry is whether the distinction is made on the basis of an enumerated ground or a ground analogous to it. The answer to this question will be found in considering the general purpose of s. 15(1), i.e. to prevent the violation of human dignity through the imposition of disadvantage based on stereotyping and social prejudice, and to promote a society where all persons are considered worthy of respect and consideration.

[para6] We agree with L'Heureux-Dubé J. that Aboriginality-residence (off-reserve band member status) constitutes a ground of discrimination analogous to the enumerated grounds. [Editorial note: see the brief summary of the reasons of L'Heureux-Dubé, Gonthier, Iacobucci and Binnie JJ. at the end of this extract.] However, we wish to comment on two matters: (1) the suggestion by some that the same ground may or may not be analogous depending on the circumstances; and (2) the criteria that identify an analogous ground.

. . . .

[para10] If it is the intention of L'Heureux-Dubé J.'s reasons to affirm contextual dependency of the enumerated and analogous grounds, we must respectfully disagree. If "Aboriginality-residence" is to be an analogous ground (and we agree with L'Heureux-Dubé J. that it should), then it must always stand as a constant marker of potential legislative discrimination, whether the challenge is to a governmental tax credit, a voting right, or a pension scheme. This established, the analysis moves to the third stage: whether the distinction amounts, in purpose or effect, to discrimination on the facts of the case.

. . . .

[para13] What then are the criteria by which we identify a ground of distinction as analogous? The obvious answer is that we look for grounds of distinction that are analogous or like the grounds enumerated in s. 15 — race, national or ethnic origin, colour, religion, sex, age, or mental or physical disability. It seems to us that what these grounds have in common is the fact that they often serve as the basis for stereotypical decisions made not on the basis of merit but on the basis of a personal characteristic that is immutable or changeable only at unacceptable cost to personal identity. This suggests that the thrust of identification of analogous grounds at the second stage of the Law analysis is to reveal grounds based on characteristics that we cannot change or that the government has no legitimate interest in expecting us to change to receive equal treatment under the law. To put it another way, s. 15 targets the denial of equal treatment on grounds that are actually immutable, like race, or

constructively immutable, like religion. Other factors identified in the cases as associated with the enumerated and analogous grounds, like the fact that the decision adversely impacts on a discrete and insular minority or a group that has been historically discriminated against, may be seen to flow from the central concept of immutable or constructively immutable personal characteristics, which too often have served as illegitimate and demeaning proxies for merit-based decision making.

[para14] L'Heureux-Dubé J. ultimately concludes that "Aboriginality-residence" as it pertains to whether an Aboriginal band member lives on or off the reserve is an analogous ground. We agree. L'Heureux-Dubé J.'s discussion makes clear that the distinction goes to a personal characteristic essential to a band member's personal identity, which is no less constructively immutable than religion or citizenship. Off-reserve Aboriginal band members can change their status to on-reserve band members only at great cost, if at all.

[para15] Two brief comments on this new analogous ground are warranted. First, reserve status should not be confused with residence. The ordinary "residence" decisions faced by the average Canadians should not be confused with the profound decisions Aboriginal band members make to live on or off their reserves, assuming choice is possible. The reality of their situation is unique and complex. Thus no new water is charted, in the sense of finding residence, in the generalized abstract, to be an analogous ground. Second, we note that the analogous ground of off-reserve status or Aboriginality-residence is limited to a subset of the Canadian population, while s. 15 is directed to everyone. In our view, this is no impediment to its inclusion as an analogous ground under s. 15. Its demographic limitation is no different, for example, from pregnancy, which is a distinct, but fundamentally interrelated form of discrimination from gender. "Embedded" analogous grounds may be necessary to permit meaningful consideration of intra-group discrimination.

[para16] Having concluded that the distinction made by the impugned law is made on an analogous ground, we come to the final step of the s. 15(1) analysis: whether the distinction at issue in this case in fact constitutes discrimination. In plain words, does the distinction undermine the presumption upon which the guarantee of equality is based — that each individual is deemed to be of equal worth regardless of the group to which he or she belongs?

[para17] Applying the applicable Law factors to this case — pre-existing disadvantage, correspondence and importance of the affected interest — we conclude that the answer to this question is yes. The impugned distinction perpetuates the historic disadvantage experienced by off-reserve band members by denying them the right to vote and participate in their band's governance. Off-reserve band members have important interests in band governance which the distinction denies. They are co-owners of the band's assets. The reserve, whether they live on or off it, is their and their children's land. The band council represents them as band members to the community at large, in negotiations with the government, and within Aboriginal organizations. Although there are some matters of purely local interest, which do not as directly affect the interests of off-reserve band members, the complete denial to off-reserve members of the right to vote and participate in band governance treats them as less worthy and entitled, not on the merits of their situation, but simply because they live off-reserve. The importance of the interest affected is underlined by the findings of the Royal Commission on Aboriginal Peoples, Report of the Royal Commission on Aboriginal Peoples (1996), vol. 1, Looking Forward, Looking Back, at pp. 137-91. The Royal Commission writes in vol. 4, Perspectives and Realities, at p. 521:

> Throughout the Commission's hearings, Aboriginal people stressed the fundamental importance of retaining and enhancing their cultural identity while living in urban areas. Aboriginal identity lies at the heart of Aboriginal peoples' existence; maintaining that identity is an essential and self-validating pursuit for Aboriginal people in cities.

And at p. 525:

> Cultural identity for urban Aboriginal people is also tied to a land base or ancestral territory. For many, the two concepts are inseparable.... Identification with an ancestral place is important to urban people because of the associated ritual, ceremony and traditions, as well as the people who remain there, the sense of belonging, the bond to an ancestral community, and the accessibility of family, community and elders.

[para18] Taking all this into account, it is clear that the s. 77(1) disenfranchisement is discriminatory. It denies off-reserve band members the right to participate fully in band governance on the arbitrary basis of a personal characteristic. It reaches the cultural identity of off-reserve Aboriginals in a stereotypical way. It presumes that Aboriginals living off-reserve are not interested in maintaining meaningful participation in the band or in preserving their cultural identity, and are therefore less deserving members of

the band. The effect is clear, as is the message: off-reserve band members are not as deserving as those band members who live on reserves. This engages the dignity aspect of the s. 15 analysis and results in the denial of substantive equality.

[para19] The conclusion that discrimination exists at the third stage of the Law test does not depend on the composition of the off-reserve band members group, its relative homogeneity or the particular historical discrimination it may have suffered. It is the present situation of the group relative to that of the comparator group, on-reserve band members, that is relevant. All parties have accepted that the off-reserve group comprises persons who have chosen to live off-reserve freely, persons who have been forced to leave the reserve reluctantly because of economic and social considerations, persons who have at some point been expelled then restored to band membership through Bill C-31 (*An Act to amend the Indian Act*, S.C. 1985, c. 27), and descendants of these people. It is accepted that off-reserve band members are the object of discrimination and constitute an underprivileged group. It is also accepted that many off-reserve band members were expelled from the reserves because of policies and legal provisions which were changed by Bill C-31 and can be said to have suffered double discrimination. But Aboriginals living on reserves are subject to the same discrimination. Some were affected by Bill C-31. Some left the reserve and returned. The relevant social facts in this case are those that relate to off-reserve band members as opposed to on-reserve band members. Even if all band members living off-reserve had voluntarily chosen this way of life and were not subject to discrimination in the broader Canadian society, they would still have the same cause of action. They would still suffer a detriment by being denied full participation in the affairs of the bands to which they would continue to belong while the band councils are able to affect their interests, in particular by making decisions with respect to the surrender of lands, the allocation of land to band members, the raising of funds and making of expenditures for the benefit of all band members. The effect of the legislation is to force band members to choose between living on the reserve and exercising their political rights, or living off-reserve and renouncing the exercise of their political rights. The political rights in question are related to the race of the individuals affected, and to their cultural identity. As mentioned earlier, the differential treatment resulting from the legislation is discriminatory because it implies that off-reserve band members are lesser members of their bands or persons who have chosen to be assimilated by the mainstream society.

[para20] We have been asked to consider the possible application of s. 25 of the *Charter*. This section provides that rights accorded in the *Charter* must not be construed as abrogating or derogating from the rights of Aboriginals. We agree with L'Heureux-Dubé J. that given the limited argument on this issue, it would be inappropriate to articulate general principles pertaining to s. 25 in this case. Suffice it to say that a case for its application has not been made out here.

[para21] Having found that s. 77(1) is discriminatory, we must address the s. 1 argument of the appellants. The applicable test was recently described by Iacobucci J. in *Egan* v. *Canada*, [1995] 2 S.C.R. 513, at para. 182. We are satisfied that the restriction on voting is rationally connected to the aim of the legislation, which is to give a voice in the affairs of the reserve only to the persons most directly affected by the decisions of the band council. It is admitted that although all band members are subject to some decisions of the band council, most decisions would only impact on members living on the reserve. The restriction of s. 15 rights is however not justified under the second branch of the s. 1 test; it has not been demonstrated that s. 77(1) of the *Indian Act* impairs the s. 15 rights minimally. Even if it is accepted that some distinction may be justified in order to protect legitimate interests of band members living on the reserve, it has not been demonstrated that a complete denial of the right of band members living off-reserve to participate in the affairs of the band through the democratic process of elections is necessary. Some parties and interveners have mentioned the possibility of a two-tiered council, of reserved seats for off-reserve members of the band, of double-majority votes on some issues. The appellants argue that there are important difficulties and costs involved in maintaining an electoral list of off-reserve band members and in setting up a system of governance balancing the rights of on-reserve and off-reserve band members. But they present no evidence of efforts deployed or schemes considered and costed, and no argument or authority in support of the conclusion that costs and administrative convenience could justify a complete denial of the constitutional right. Under these circumstances, we must conclude that the violation has not been shown to be demonstrably justified.

[para22] With regard to remedy, the Court of Appeal was of the view that it would be preferable

to grant the Batchewana Band a permanent constitutional exemption rather than to declare s. 77(1) of the *Indian Act* to be unconstitutional and without effect generally. With respect, we must disagree.... We do not think this is a case where a possible expansion of the constitutional exemption remedy should be considered. There is no evidence of special circumstances upon which this possibility might be raised. The evidence before the Court is that there are off-reserve members of most if not all Indian bands in Canada that are affected by s. 77(1) of the *Indian Act*, and no evidence of other rights that may be relevant in examining the effect of s. 77(1) with regard to any band other than the Batchewana Band. If another band could establish an Aboriginal right to restrict voting, as suggested by the Court of Appeal, that right would simply have precedence over the terms of the *Indian Act*; this is not a reason to restrict the declaration of invalidity to the Batchewana Band.

[para23] Where there is inconsistency between the *Charter* and a legislative provision, s. 52 of the *Constitution Act*, 1982 provides that the provision shall be rendered void to the extent of the inconsistency. We would declare the words "and is ordinarily resident on the reserve" in s. 77(1) of the *Indian Act* to be inconsistent with s. 15(1) but suspend the implementation of this declaration for 18 months. We would not grant a constitutional exemption to the Batchewana Band during the period of suspension, as would normally be done according to the rule in *Schachter* [v. *Canada*, [1992] 2 S.C.R. 679]. The reason for this is that in the particular circumstances of this case, it would appear to be preferable to develop an electoral process that will balance the rights of off-reserve and on-reserve band members. We have not overlooked the possibility that legislative inaction may create new problems. Such claims will fall to be dealt with on their merits should they arise.

[para24] We would therefore dismiss the appeal and modify the remedy by striking out the words "and is ordinarily resident on the reserve" in s. 77(1) of the *Indian Act* and suspending the implementation of the declaration of invalidity for 18 months, with costs to the respondents. We would answer the restated constitutional questions as follows:

1. Do the words "and is ordinarily resident on the reserve" contained in s. 77(1) of the *Indian Act*, R.S.C., 1985, c. I-5, contravene s. 15(1) of the *Canadian Charter of Rights and Freedoms*, either generally or with respect only to members of the Batchewana Indian Band?

   Yes, in their general application.

2. If the answer to question 1 is in the affirmative, is s. 77(1) of the *Indian Act* demonstrably justified as a reasonable limit pursuant to s. 1 of the *Canadian Charter of Rights and Freedoms*?

   No.

[L'Heureux-Dubé, for herself, Gonthier, Iacobucci and Binnie JJ., arrived at a similar result. However, she held that whether a ground is analogous or not depends on the context of the alleged discrimination; and that the factors for determining if a ground is analogous include (i) its importance to a person's identity, personhood, or belonging, and (ii) the political powerlessness, disadvantage, or vulnerability of the group affected, as well as (iii) the immutability of the ground in question.]

3 Aboriginal Rights before *Calder*

(a) The Royal Proclamation of 1763†

See **Chapter 3, Part 9**.

And whereas it is just and reasonable, and essential to our Interest, and the security of our Colonies, that the several Nations or Tribes of Indians with whom We are connected, and who live under our protection, should not be molested or disturbed in the Possession of such Parts of Our Dominions and Territories as, not having been ceded to or purchased by Us, are reserved to them or any of them, as their Hunting Grounds — We do therefore, with the Advice of our Privy Council, declare it to be our Royal Will and Pleasure, that no Governor or Commander-in-chief in any of our Colonies of Quebec, East Florida, or West Florida, do presume, upon any Pretence whatever, to grant Warrants of Survey, or pass any Patents for Lands beyond the Bounds of their respective Governments, as described in their Commissions; as also that no Governor or Commander-in-Chief in any of our other Colonies or Plantations in America do presume for the present, and until our further Pleasure be Known, to grant warrants of Survey, or pass Patents for any Lands beyond the Heads or Sources of any of the Rivers which fall into the Atlantic Ocean from the West and North West, or upon any Lands whatever, which, not having been ceded to or purchased by Us as aforesaid, are reserved to the said Indians, or any of them.

And We do further declare it to be Our Royal Will and Pleasure, for the present as aforesaid, to reserve under our Sovereignty, Protection, and Dominion, for the use of the said Indians, all the Lands and Territories not included within the Limits of Our Said New Governments, or within the Limits of the Territory granted to the Hudson's Bay Company, as also all the Lands and Territories lying to the Westward of the Sources of the Rivers which fall into the Sea from the West and North West as aforesaid:

And We do hereby strictly forbid, on Pain of our Displeasure, all our loving subjects from making any Purchase or Settlements whatever, or taking Possession of any of the Lands above reserved, without our especial leave and Licence for the Purpose first obtained.

And, We do further strictly enjoin and require all Persons whatever who have either wilfully or inadvertently seating themselves upon any Lands within the Countries above described, or upon any other Lands which, not having been ceded to or purchased by Us, are still reserved to the said Indians as aforesaid, forthwith to remove themselves from such Settlements.

And Whereas Great Frauds and Abuses have been committed in purchasing Lands of the Indians, to the Great Prejudice of our Interests, and to the Great Dissatisfaction of the said Indians; In Order, therefore, to prevent such Irregularities for the future, and to the End that the Indians may be convinced of our Justice and determined Resolution to remove all reasonable Cause of Discontent, We do, with the Advice of our Privy Council, strictly enjoin and require, that no private Person do presume to make any Purchase from the said Indians of any Lands reserved to the said Indians, within

† R.S.C. 1985, Appendix II, No. 1. George III, United Kingdom. October 7, 1763. The extract reproduced here deals specifically with Indian people.

those parts of our Colonies where, We have thought proper to allow Settlement; but that, if at any Time any of the said Indians should be inclined to dispose of the said Lands, the same shall be Purchased only for Us, in our Name, at some public Meeting or Assembly of the said Indians, to be held for the Purpose of the Governor or Commander-in-Chief of our Colony respectively within which they shall lie; and in case they shall lie within the limits of any Proprietary Government, they shall be purchased only for the Use and in the name of such Proprietaries, conformable to such Directions and Instructions as We or they shall think proper to give for the Purpose; And We do, by the Advice of our Privy Council, declare and enjoin, that the Trade with the said Indians shall be free and open to all our Subjects whatever, provided that every Person who may incline to Trade with the said Indians do take out a Licence for carrying on such Trade from the Governor or Commander-in-Chief of any of our Colonies respectively where such Person shall reside, and also give Security to observe such Regulations as We shall at any Time think fit, by ourselves or by our Commissaries to be appointed for this Purpose, to direct and appoint for the Benefit of the said Trade:

And We do hereby authorize, enjoin, and require the Governors and Commanders-in-Chief of all our Colonies respectively, as well those under Our immediate Government as those under the Government and Direction of Proprietaries, to grant such Licences without Fee or Regard, taking especial care to insert therein a Condition, that such Licence shall be void, and the Security forfeited in the case the Person to whom the same is granted shall refuse or neglect to observe such Regulations as We shall think proper to prescribe as aforesaid.

And We do further expressly enjoin and require all Officers whatever, as well Military as those Employed in the Management and Direction of Indian Affairs, within the Territories reserved as aforesaid for the Use of the said Indians, to seize and apprehend all Persons whatever, who standing charged with Treason, Misprisons of Treason, Murders, or other Felonies or Misdemeanors, shall fly from Justice and take Refuge in the said Territory, and to send them under a proper Guard to the Colony where the Crime was committed of which they stand accused, in order to take their Trial for the same.

Given at our Court at St. James'
the 7th Day of October, 1763,
in the Third Year of our Reign.
God Save the King

(b) *St. Catherine's Milling and Lumber Co. v. The Queen*†

See **Chapter 3, Part 10**.

NOTE

Ontario challenged the federal government's right to grant a timber permit to a lumber company. Ontario claimed that after the Indian interest in the land had been surrendered by treaty, the full beneficial interest in the land went to the province. The federal government said the interest went to them. Resolution of this dispute required an examination of the nature of Indian title before Confederation.

EXTRACT

[LORD WATSON for the Judicial Committee of the Privy Council:]

On the 3rd of October, 1873, a formal treaty or contract was concluded between commissioners appointed by the Government of the Dominion of Canada, on behalf of Her Majesty the Queen, of the one part, and a number of chiefs and headmen duly chosen to represent the Salteaux tribe of Ojibbeway

† (1889), 14 App. Cas. 46 at 46, 51–60 (J.C.P.C.), aff'g (1887) 13 S.C.R. 577 (S.C.C.), which aff'd (1887) 13 O.A.R. 148 (O.C.A.), which aff'd (1886) 10 OR 196 (Chancery Div.).

Indians, of the other part, by which the latter, for certain considerations, released and surrendered to the Government of the Dominion, for Her Majesty and her successors, the whole right and title of the Indian inhabitants whom they represented, to a tract of country upwards of 50,000 square miles in extent. By an article of the treaty it is stipulated that, subject to such regulations as may be made by the Dominion Government, the Indians are to have right to pursue their avocations of hunting and fishing throughout the surrendered territory, with the exception of those portions of it which may, from time to time, be required or taken up for settlement, mining, lumbering, or other purposes.

Of the territory thus ceded to the Crown, an area of not less than 32,000 square miles is situated within the boundaries of the Province of Ontario; and, with respect to that area, a controversy has arisen between the Dominion and Ontario, each of them maintaining that the legal effect of extinguishing the Indian title has been to transmit to itself the entire beneficial interest of the lands, as now vested in the Crown, freed from incumbrance of any kind, save the qualified privilege of hunting and fishing mentioned in the treaty.

Acting on the assumption that the beneficial interest in these lands had passed to the Dominion Government, their Crown Timber Agent, on the 1st of May, 1883, issued to the appellants, the St. Catherine's Milling and Lumber Company, a permit to out and carry away one million feet of lumber from a specified portion of the disputed area. The appellants having availed themselves of that licence, a writ was filed against them in the Chancery Division of the High Court of Ontario, at the instance of the Queen on the information of the Attorney-General of the Province, praying —

1. a declaration that the appellants have no rights in respect of the timber cut by them upon the lands specified in their permit;
2. an injunction restraining them from trespassing on the premises and from cutting any timber thereon;
3. an injunction against the removal of timber already cut; and
4. decree for the damage occasioned by their wrongful acts.

The Chancellor of Ontario, on the 10th of June, 1885, decided with costs against the appellants, in terms of the first three of these conclusions, and referred the amount of damage to the Master in Ordinary. The judgment of the learned Chancellor was unanimously affirmed on the 20th of April, 1886, by the Court of Appeal for Ontario, and an appeal taken from their decision to the Supreme Court of Canada was dismissed on the 20th of June, 1887, by a majority of four of the six judges constituting the court.

Although the present case relates exclusively to the right of the Government of Canada to dispose of the timber in question to the appellant company, yet its decision necessarily involves the determination of the larger question between that government and the province of Ontario with respect to the legal consequences of the treaty of 1873. In these circumstances, Her Majesty, by the same order which gave the appellants leave to bring the judgment of the Court below under the review of this Board, was pleased to direct that the Government of the Dominion of Canada should be at liberty to intervene in this appeal, or to argue the same upon a special case raising the legal question in dispute. The Dominion Government elected to take the first of these courses, and their Lordships have had the advantage of hearing from their counsel an able and exhaustive argument in support of their claim to that part of the ceded territory which lies within the provincial boundaries of Ontario.

The capture of Quebec in 1759, and the capitulation of Montreal in 1760, were followed in 1763 by the cession to Great Britain of Canada and all its dependencies, with the sovereignty, property, and possession, and all other rights which had at any previous time been held or acquired by the Crown of France. A royal proclamation was issued on the 7th of October, 1763, shortly after the date of the Treaty of Paris, by which His Majesty King George erected four distinct and separate Governments, styled respectively, Quebec, East Florida, West Florida, and Grenada, specific boundaries being assigned to each of them. Upon the narrative that it was just and reasonable that the several nations and tribes of Indians who lived under British protection should not be molested or disturbed in the "possession of such parts of Our dominions and territories as, not having been ceded to or purchased by us, are reserved to them or any of them as their hunting grounds," it is declared that no governor or commander-in-chief in any of the new colonies of Quebec, East Florida, or West Florida, do presume on any pretence to grant warrants of survey or pass any patents for lands beyond the bounds of their respective governments, or "until Our further pleasure be known," upon any lands whatever which, not having been ceded or purchased as aforesaid, are reserved to the said Indians or any of them. It was further declared "to be Our Royal will, for the present, as aforesaid, to reserve under Our sovereignty, protection, and dominion, for the use of the said Indians, all the land and territories not included within the limits of Our said three new Governments, or within the limits of the territory granted to the Hudson's Bay Company." The proclamation also enacts that no private person shall make any purchase from the Indians of lands reserved to them within those colonies where settlement was permitted, and that all purchases must be on behalf of the Crown, in a public assembly of the Indians, by the governor or commander-in-chief of the colony in which the lands lie.

The territory in dispute has been in Indian occupation from the date of the proclamation until 1873. During that interval of time Indian affairs have been administered successively by the Crown, by the Provincial Governments, and (since the passing of the *British North America Act, 1867*), by the Government of the Dominion. The policy of these administrations has been all along the same in this respect, that the Indian inhabitants have been precluded from entering into any transaction with a subject for the sale or transfer of their interest in the land, and have only been permitted to surrender their rights to the Crown by a formal contract, duly ratified in a meeting of their chiefs or head men convened for the purpose. Whilst there have been changes in the administrative authority, there has been no change since the year 1763 in the character of the interest which its Indian inhabitants had in the lands surrendered by the treaty. Their possession, such as it was, can only be ascribed to the general provisions made by the royal proclamation in favour of all Indian tribes then living under the sovereignty and protection of the British Crown. It was suggested in the course of the argument for the Dominion, that inasmuch as the proclamation recites that the territories thereby reserved for Indians had never "been ceded to or purchased by" the Crown, the entire property of the land remained with them. That inference is, however, at variance with the terms of the instrument, which show that the tenure of the Indians was a personal and usufructuary right, dependent upon the good will of the Sovereign. The lands reserved are expressly stated to be "parts of Our dominions and territories;" and it is declared to be the will and pleasure of the sovereign that, "for the present," they shall be reserved for the use of the Indians, as their hunting grounds, under his protection and dominion. There was a great deal of learned discussion at the Bar with respect to the precise quality of the Indian right, but their Lordships do not consider it necessary to express any opinion upon the point. It appears to them to be sufficient for the purposes of this case that there has been all along vested in the Crown a substantial and paramount estate, underlying the Indian title, which became a plenum dominium whenever that title was surrendered or otherwise extinguished.

By an Imperial statute passed in the year 1840 (3 & 4 Vict. c. 35), the provinces of Ontario and Quebec, then known as Upper and Lower Canada, were united under the name of the Province of Canada, and it was, *inter alia*, enacted that, in consideration of certain annual payments which Her Majesty had agreed to accept by way of civil list, the produce of all territorial and other revenues at the disposal of the Crown arising in either of the united Provinces should be paid into the consolidated fund of the new Province. There was no transfer to the Province of any legal estate in the Crown lands, which continued to be vested in the Sovereign; but all moneys realized by sales or in any other manner became the property of the Province. In other words, all beneficial interest in such lands within the provincial boundaries belonging to the Queen, and either producing or capable of producing revenue, passed to the Province, the title still remaining in the Crown. That continued to be the right of the Province until the passing of the *British North America Act, 1867*. Had the Indian inhabitants of the area in question released their interest in it to the Crown at any time between 1840 and the date of that Act, it does not seem to admit of doubt, and it was not disputed by the learned counsel for the Dominion, that all revenues derived from its being taken up for settlement, mining, lumbering, and other purposes would have been the property of the Province of Canada. The case maintained for the appellants is that the Act of 1867 transferred to the Dominion all interest in Indian lands which previously belonged to the Province.

The Act of 1867, which created the Federal Government, repealed the Act of 1840, and restored the Upper and Lower Canadas to the condition of separate Provinces, under the titles of Ontario and Quebec, due provision being made (s. 142) for the division between them of the property and assets of the United Province, with the exception of certain items specified in the fourth schedule, which are still held by them jointly. The Act also contains careful provisions for the distribution of legislative powers and of revenues and assets between the respective Provinces included in the Union, on the one hand, and the Dominion, on the other. The conflicting claims to the ceded territory maintained by the

Dominion and the Province of Ontario are wholly dependent upon these statutory provisions. In construing these enactments, it must always be kept in view that, wherever public land with its incidents is described as "the property of" or as "belonging to" the Dominion or a Province, these expressions merely import that the right to its beneficial use, or to its proceeds, has been appropriated to the Dominion or the Province, as the case may be, and is subject to the control of its legislature, the land itself being vested in the Crown.

S. 108 enacts that the public works and undertakings enumerated in Schedule 3 shall be the property of Canada. As specified in the schedule, these consist of public undertakings which might be fairly considered to exist for the benefit of all the Provinces federally united, of lands and buildings necessary for carrying on the customs or postal service of the Dominion, or required for the purpose of national defence, and of "lands set apart for general public purposes". It is obvious that the enumeration cannot be reasonably held to include Crown lands which are reserved for Indian use. The only other clause in the Act by which a share of what previously constituted provincial revenues and assets is directly assigned to the Dominion is s. 102. It enacts that all "duties and revenues" over which the respective legislatures of the United Provinces had and have power of appropriation, "except such portions thereof as are by this Act reserved to the respective legislatures of the Provinces, or are raised by them in accordance with the special powers conferred upon them by this Act," shall form one consolidated fund, to be appropriated for the public service of Canada. The extent to which duties and revenues arising within the limits of Ontario, and over which the legislature of the old Province of Canada possessed the power of appropriation before the passing of the Act, have been transferred to the Dominion by this clause, can only be ascertained by reference to the two exceptions which it makes in favour of the new provincial legislatures.

The second of these exceptions has really no bearing on the present case, because it comprises nothing beyond the revenues which provincial legislatures are empowered to raise by means of direct taxation for Provincial purposes, in terms of s. 92(2). The first of them, which appears to comprehend the whole sources of revenue reserved to the provinces by s. 109, is of material consequence. S. 109 provides that "all lands, mines, minerals, and royalties belonging to the several Provinces of Canada, Nova Scotia, and New Brunswick, at the union, and all sums then due or payable for such lands, mines, minerals, or royalties, shall belong to the several Provinces of Ontario, Quebec, Nova Scotia, and New Brunswick, in which the same are situate or arise, subject to any trusts existing in respect thereof, and to any interest other than that of the Province in the same". In connection with this clause it may be observed that, by s. 117, it is declared that the Provinces shall retain their respective public property not otherwise disposed of in the act, subject to the right of Canada to assume any lands or public property required for fortifications or for the defence of the country. A different form of expression is used to define the subject-matter of the first exception, and the property which is directly appropriated to the Provinces; but it hardly admits of doubt that the interests in land, mines, minerals, and royalties, which by s. 109 are declared to belong to the Provinces, include, if they are not identical with, the "duties and revenues" first excepted in s. 102.

The enactments of s. 109 are, in the opinion of their Lordships, sufficient to give to each Province, subject to the administration and control of its own Legislature, the entire beneficial interest of the Crown in all lands within its boundaries, which at the time of the union were vested in the Crown, with the exception of such lands as the Dominion acquired right to under s. 108, or might assume for the purposes specified in s. 117. Its legal effect is to exclude from the "duties and revenues" appropriated to the Dominion, all the ordinary territorial revenues of the Crown arising within the Provinces. That construction of the statute was accepted by this Board in deciding *Attorney-General of Ontario v. Mercer*, where the controversy related to land granted in fee simple to a subject before 1867, which became escheat to the Crown in the year 1871. The Lord Chancellor (Earl Selborne) in delivering judgment in that case, said: "It was not disputed, in the argument for the Dominion at the bar, that all territorial revenues arising within each Province from 'lands' (in which term must be comprehended all estates in land), which at the time of the union belonged to the Crown, were reserved to the respective Provinces by s. 109; and it was admitted that no distinction could, in that respect, be made between lands then ungranted, and lands which had previously reverted to the Crown by escheat. But it was insisted that a line was drawn at the date of the union, and that the words were not sufficient to reserve any lands afterwards escheated which at the time of the union were in private hands, and did not then belong to the Crown. Their Lordships indicated an opinion to the effect that the escheat would not, in the special circumstances of that case, have passed to the Province as "lands"; but they held that it fell within the class of rights reserved to the Provinces as "royalties" by s. 109.

Had its Indian inhabitants been the owners in fee simple of the territory which they surrendered by the treaty of 1873, *Attorney-General of Ontario v. Mercer* might have been an authority for holding that the Province of Ontario could derive no benefit from the cession, in respect that the land was not vested in the Crown at the time of the union. But that was not the character of the Indian interest. The Crown has all along had a present proprietary estate in the land, upon which the Indian title was a mere burden. The ceded territory was at the time of the union, land vested in the Crown, subject to "an interest other than that of the Province in the same", within the meaning of s. 109; and must now belong to Ontario in terms of that clause, unless its rights have been taken away by some provision of the Act of 1867 other than those already noticed.

In the course of the argument the claim of the Dominion to the ceded territory was rested upon the provisions of s. 91(24), which in express terms confer upon the Parliament of Canada power to make laws for "Indians, and lands reserved for the Indians". It was urged that the exclusive power of legislation and administration carried with it, by necessary implication, any patrimonial interest which the Crown might have had in the reserved lands. In reply to that reasoning, counsel for Ontario referred us to a series of provincial statutes prior in date to the Act of 1867, for the purpose of shewing that the expression "Indian reserves" was used in legislative language to designate certain lands in which the Indians had, after the royal proclamation of 1763, acquired a special interest by treaty or otherwise, and did not apply to land occupied by them in virtue of the proclamation. The argument might have deserved consideration if the expression had been adopted by the British Parliament in 1867, but it does not occur in s. 91(24), and the words actually used are, according to their natural meaning, sufficient to include all lands reserved, upon any terms or conditions, for Indian occupation. It appears to be the plain policy of the Act that, in order to ensure uniformity of administration, all such lands, and Indian affairs generally, shall be under the legislative control of one central authority.

Their Lordships are, however, unable to assent to the argument for the Dominion founded on s. 92(24). There can be no *a priori* probability that the British Legislature, in a branch of the statute which professes to deal only with the distribution of legislative power, intended to deprive the Provinces of rights which are expressly given them in that branch of it which relates to the distribution of revenues and assets. The fact that the power of legislating for Indians, and for lands which are reserved to their use, has been entrusted to the Parliament of the Dominion is not in the least degree inconsistent with the right of the Provinces to a beneficial interest in these lands, available to them as a source of revenue whenever the estate of the Crown is disencumbered of the Indian title.

By the treaty of 1873 the Indian inhabitants ceded and released the territory in dispute, in order that it might be opened up for settlement, immigration, and such other purpose as to Her Majesty might seem fit, "to the Government of the Dominion of Canada", for the Queen and Her successors for ever. It was argued that a cession in these terms was in effect a conveyance to the Dominion Government of the whole rights of the Indians, with consent of the Crown. That is not the natural import of the language of the treaty, which purports to be from beginning to end a transaction between the Indians and the Crown; and the surrender is in substance made to the Crown. Even if its language had been more favourable to the argument of the Dominion upon this point, it is abundantly clear that the commissioners who represented Her Majesty, whilst they had full authority to accept a surrender to the Crown, had neither authority nor power to take away from Ontario the interest which had been assigned to that province by the Imperial Statute of 1867.

These considerations appear to their Lordships to be sufficient for the disposal of this appeal. The treaty leaves the Indians no right whatever to the timber growing upon the lands which they gave up, which is now fully vested in the Crown, all revenues derivable from the sale of such portions of it as are situate within the boundaries of Ontario being the property of that Province. The fact, that it still possesses exclusive power to regulate the Indians' privilege of hunting and fishing, cannot confer upon the Dominion power to dispose, by issuing permits or otherwise, of that beneficial interest in the timber which has not passed Ontario. Seeing that the benefit of the surrender accrues to her, Ontario must, of course, relieve the Crown, and the Dominion, of all obligations involving the payment of money which were undertaken by Her Majesty, and which are said to have been in part fulfilled by the Dominion Government. There may be other questions behind, with respect to the right to determine to what extent, and at what periods, the disputed territory, over which the Indians still exercise their avocations of hunting and fishing, is to be taken up for settlement or other purposes, but none of these questions are raised for decision in the present suit.

Their Lordships will therefore humbly advise Her Majesty that the judgment of the Supreme Court of Canada ought to be affirmed, and the appeal dismissed. It appears to them that there ought to be no costs of the appeal.

(c) *Johnson and Graham's Lessee v. M'Intosh*†

See **Chapter 3, Part 11.**

NOTE

In 1775 the Piankeshaw Indians sold land along the Ohio and Wabash rivers to Johnson. Later they surrendered to the United States government a large tract that included this land. When M'Intosh bought some of the same land from the American government in 1818, claimants under Johnson argued that the land was theirs. Was the 1775 sale valid? What was the nature of the Indian interest in the land?

EXTRACT

This was an action for ejectment for lands in the state and district of Illinois, claimed by the plaintiff under a purchase and conveyance from the Piankeshaw Indians, and by the defendant, under a grant by the United States. It came up on a case stated, upon which there was a judgment below for the defendant. The case stated set out the following facts:

. . . .

[Here the report describes the facts of the case. In 1609, James I of England issued letters patent to create the colony of Virginia. The area granted was vast. It included the land later in dispute in this case, an area along the Ohio and Wabash rivers, inhabited by the Piankeshaw Indians. On October 18, 1775, the Piankeshaw Indians sold this land to a group of settlers that included Thomas Johnson. On May 6, 1776, the colony of Virginia declared its independence of Great Britain, and on December 20, 1783, Virginia authorized the transfer of land within its boundaries to the United States. On July 20, 1818, the United States government sold to William M'Intosh the same land (now within the boundaries of the state of Illinois) which the Piankeshaw Indians had purported to sell to Thomas Johnson. William M'Intosh entered it and claimed ownership by virtue of his grant from the United States government. But Thomas Johnson's heirs (and the lessee of one of his heirs) *also* claimed the land, and they brought an action of ejectment to have M'Intosh removed from it. They based their claim on the Piankeshaw Indians' 1775 sale to Thomas Johnson.]

Judgment being given for the defendant on the case stated, the plaintiffs brought this writ of error.

. . . .

[MARSHALL C.J. for the Court:]

The plaintiffs in this cause claim the land, in their declaration mentioned, under two grants, purporting to be made, the first in 1773, and the last in 1775, by the chiefs of certain Indian tribes, constituting the Illinois and the Piankeshaw nations; and the question is, whether this title can be recognized in the courts of the United States?

The facts as stated in the case agreed, show the authority of the chiefs who executed this conveyance, so far as it could be given by their own people; and likewise show that the particular tribes for whom these chiefs acted were in rightful possession of the land they sold. The inquiry, therefore, is, in a great measure, confined to the power of the Indians to

† (1823), 8 Wheaton 543 at 543, 562, 571–74, 576–97, 604–05; 21 U.S. 240, 5 L.Ed. 681 (U.S.S.Ct.).

give, and of private individuals to receive, a title which can be sustained in the courts of this country.

As the right of society to prescribe those rules by which property may be acquired and preserved is not, and cannot be drawn into question; as the title to lands, especially, is and must be admitted to depend entirely on the law of the nation in which they lie; it will be necessary, in pursuing this inquiry, to examine, not singly those principles of abstract justice, which the Creator of all things has impressed on the mind of his creature man, and which are admitted to regulate, in a great degree, the rights of civilized nations, whose perfect independence is acknowledged; but those principles also which our own government has adopted in the particular case, and given us as the rule for our decision.

On the discovery of this immense continent, the great nations of Europe were eager to appropriate to themselves so much of it as they could respectively acquire. Its vast extent offered an ample field to the ambition and enterprise of all; and the character and religion of its inhabitants afforded an apology for considering them as a people over whom the superior genius of Europe might claim an ascendency. The potentates of the old world found no difficulty in convincing themselves that they made ample compensation to the inhabitants of the new, by bestowing on them civilization and Christianity, in exchange for unlimited independence. But, as they were all in pursuit of nearly the same object, it was necessary, in order to avoid conflicting settlements, and consequent war with each other, to establish a principle which all should acknowledge as the law by which the right of acquisition, which they all asserted, should be regulated as between themselves. This principle was that discovery gave title to the government by whose subjects, or by whose authority, it was made, against all other European governments, which title might be consummated by possession.

The exclusion of all other Europeans, necessarily gave to the nation making the discovery the sole right of acquiring the soil from the natives, and establishing settlements upon it. It was a right with which no Europeans could interfere. It was a right which all asserted for themselves, and to the assertion of which, by others, all assented.

Those relations which were to exist between the discoverer and the natives, were to be regulated by themselves. The rights thus acquired being exclusive, no other power could interpose between them.

In the establishment of these relations, the rights of the original inhabitants were, in no instance, entirely disregarded; but were necessarily, to a considerable extent, impaired. They were admitted to be the rightful occupants of the soil, with a legal as well as just claim to retain possession of it, and to use it according to their own discretion; but their rights to complete sovereignty, as independent nations, were necessarily diminished, and their power to dispose of the soil as their own will, to whomsoever they pleased, was denied by the original fundamental principle that discovery gave exclusive title to those who made it.

While the different nations of Europe respected the right of the natives, as occupants, they asserted the ultimate dominion to be in themselves; and claimed and exercised as a consequence of this ultimate dominion, a power to grant the soil, while yet in possession of the natives. These grants have been understood by all to convey a title to the grantees, subject only to the Indian right of occupancy.

The history of America, from its discovery to the present day, proves, we think, the universal recognition of these principles.

. . . .

In this first effort made by the English government to acquire territory on this continent, we perceive a complete recognition of the principle which has been mentioned. The right of discovery given by this commission is confined to countries "then unknown to all Christian people;" and of these countries Cabot was empowered to take possession in the name of the King of England, thus asserting a right to take possession, notwithstanding the occupancy of the natives, who were heathens, and at the same time admitting the prior title of any Christian people who may have made a previous discovery.

The same principle continued to be recognized. The charter granted to Sir Humphrey Gilbert, in 1578, authorized him to discover and take possession of such remote, heathen and barbarous lands as were not actually possessed by any Christian prince or people. This charter was afterwards renewed to Sir Walter Raleigh, in nearly the same terms.

By the charter of 1606, under which the first permanent English settlement on this continent was made, James I granted to Sir Thomas Gates and others, those territories in America lying on the sea-coast, between the thirty-fourth and forty-fifth degrees of north latitude, and which either belonged to that monarch, or were not then possessed by any other Christian prince or people. The grantees were divided into two companies at their own request. The first, or southern colony, was directed to settle between the thirty-fourth and forty-first degrees of north latitude; and the second, or northern colony, between the thirty-eighth and forty-fifth degrees.

. . . .

[Marshall C.J. examined several other historic Crown charters and grants which conveyed territory to their recipients in unqualified terms.]

Thus has our whole country been granted by the crown while in the occupation of the Indians. These grants purport to convey the soil as well as the right of dominion to the grantees. In those governments which were denominated royal, where the right to the soil was not vested in individuals, but remained in the crown, or was vested in the colonial government, the king claimed and exercised the right of granting lands, and of dismembering the government at his will. The grants made out of the two original colonies, after the resumption of their charters by the crown, are examples of this. The governments of New England, New York, New Jersey, Pennsylvania, Maryland, and a part of Carolina, were thus created. In all of them, the soil, at the time the grants were made, was occupied by the Indians. Yet almost every title within those governments is dependent on these grants. In some instances, the soil was conveyed by the crown unaccompanied by the powers of government, as in the case of the northern neck of Virginia. It has never been objected to this, or to any other similar grant, that the title as well as possession was in the Indians when it was made, and that it passed nothing on that account.

These various patents cannot be considered as nullities; nor can they be limited to a mere grant of the powers of government. A charter intended to convey political power only, would never contain words expressly granting the land, the soil and the waters. Some of them purport to convey the soil alone; and in those cases in which the powers of government, as well as the soil, are conveyed to individuals, the crown has always acknowledged itself to be bound by the grant. Though the power to dismember regal governments was asserted and exercised, the power to dismember proprietary governments was not claimed; and, in some instances, even after the powers of government were revested in the crown, the title of the proprietors to the soil was respected.

. . . .

Further proofs of the extent to which this principle has been recognized, will be found in the history of the wars, negotiations and treaties which the different nations, claiming territory in America, have carried on and *held* with each other.

The contests between the cabinets of Versailles and Madrid, respecting the territory on the northern coast of the Gulf of Mexico, were fierce and bloody, and continued until the establishment of a Bourbon on the throne of Spain produced such amicable dispositions in the two crowns as to suspend or terminate them.

Between France and Great Britain, whose discoveries as well as settlements were nearly contemporaneous, contests for the country, actually covered by the Indians, began as soon as their settlements approached each other, and were continued until finally settled in the year 1763, by the treaty of Paris.

Each nation had granted and partially settled the country, denominated by the French, Acadie, and by the English, Nova Scotia. By the twelfth article of the treaty of Utrecht, made in 1703, His Most Christian Majesty ceded to the Queen of Great Britain, "all Nova Scotia or Acadie, with its ancient boundaries." A great part of the ceded territory was in the possession of the Indians, and the extent of the cession could not be adjusted by the commissioners to whom it was to be referred.

The treaty of Aix la Chapelle, which was made on the principle of the *status ante bellum*, did not remove this subject of controversy. Commissioners for its adjustment were appointed, whose very able and elaborate, though unsuccessful arguments, in favour of the title of their respective sovereigns, show how entirely each relied on the title given by discovery to lands remaining in the possession of Indians.

After the termination of this fruitless discussion, the subject was transferred to Europe, and taken up by the cabinets of Versailles and London. This controversy embraced not only the boundaries of New England, Nova Scotia, and that part of Canada which adjoined those colonies but embraced our whole western country also. France contended not only that the St. Lawrence was to be considered as the center of Canada, but that the Ohio was within that colony. She founded this claim on discovery, and on having used that river for the transportation of troops, in a war with some southern Indians.

This river was comprehended in the chartered limits of Virginia; but, though the right of England to a reasonable extent of country, in virtue of her discovery of the sea-coast, and of the settlements she made on it, was not to be questioned; her claim of all the lands to the Pacific Ocean, because she had discovered the country washed by the Atlantic, might, without derogating from the principle recognized by all, be deemed extravagant. It interfered, too, with claims of France, founded on the same principle. She therefore sought to strengthen her original title to the lands in controversy, by insisting that it had been acknowledged by France in the Fifteenth article of the treaty of Utrecht. The dispute respecting the construction of that article has no tendency to impair the principle that discovery gave a title to lands still remaining in the possession of the Indians. Whichever title prevailed, it was still a title to land occupied by the Indians, whose right of occupancy neither controverted, and neither had then extinguished.

These conflicting claims produced a long and bloody war, which was terminated by the conquest of the whole country east of the Mississippi. In the treaty of 1763, France ceded and guarantied to Great Britain, all Nova Scotia, or Acadie, and Canada, with their dependencies; and it was agreed that the boundaries between the territories of the two nations, in America, should be irrevocably fixed by a line drawn from the source of the Mississippi, through the middle of that river and lakes Maurepas and Ponchartrain, to the sea. This treaty expressly cedes, and has always been understood to cede, the whole country, on the English side of the dividing line, between the two nations, although a great and valuable part of it was occupied by the Indians. Great Britain, on her part, surrendered to France all her pretensions to the country west of the Mississippi. It has never been supposed that she surrendered nothing, although she was not in actual possession of a foot of land. She surrendered all right to acquire the country; and any after attempt to purchase it from Indians would have been considered and treated as a invasion of the territories of France.

By the twentieth article of the same treaty, Spain ceded Florida, with its dependencies, and all the country she claimed east or south-east of the Mississippi, to Great Britain. Great part of this territory also was in possession of the Indians.

By a secret treaty, which was executed about the same time, France ceded Louisiana to Spain; and Spain has since retroceded the same country to France. At the time both of its cession and retrocession, it was occupied chiefly by the Indians.

Thus, all the nations of Europe, who have acquired territory on this continent, have asserted in themselves and have recognized in others, the exclusive right of the discoverer to appropriate the land occupied by the Indians. Have the American states rejected or adopted this principle?

By the treaty which concluded the war of our revolution, Great Britain relinquished all claim, not only to the government, but to the "propriety and territorial rights of the United States," whose boundaries were fixed in the second article. By this treaty, the powers of government, and the right to soil, which had previously been in Great Britain, passed definitively to these states. We had before taken possession of them, by declaring independence; but neither the declaration of independence, nor the treaty confirming it, could give us more than that which we before possessed, or to which Great Britain was before entitled. It has never been doubted, that either the United States, or the several states, had a clear title to all the lands within the boundary lines described in the treaty, subject only to the Indian right of occupancy, and that the exclusive power to extinguish that right was vested in that government which might constitutionally exercise it.

Virginia, particularly, within those chartered limits the land in controversy lay, passed an act in the year 1779, declaring her "exclusive right of preemption from the Indians, of all the lands within the limits of her own charted territory, and that no person or persons whatsoever, have, or ever had, a right to purchase any land within the same, from any Indian nation, except only persons duly authorized to make such purchase, formerly for the use and benefit of the colony, and lately for the commonwealth." The act then proceeds to annul all deeds made by Indians to individuals, for the private use of the purchasers.

Without ascribing to this act the power of annulling vested rights, or admitting it to countervail the testimony furnished by the marginal note opposite to the title of law, forbidding purchases from the Indians, in the revisals of the Virginia statutes, stating that law to be repealed, it may safely be considered as an unequivocal affirmance, on the part of Virginia, of the broad principle which had always been maintained that the exclusive right to purchase from the Indian resided in the government.

In pursuance of the same idea, Virginia proceeded, at the same session, to open her land office, for the sale of that country which now constitutes Kentucky — a country, every acre of which was then claimed and possessed by Indians, who maintained their title with as much persevering courage as was ever manifest by any people.

The states, having within their chartered limits different portions of territory covered by Indians, ceded that territory, generally to the United States, on conditions expressed in their deeds of cession, which demonstrate the opinion that they ceded the soil as well as jurisdiction, and that in doing so they granted a productive fund to the government of the Union. The lands in controversy lay within the chartered limits of Virginia, and were ceded with the whole country north-west of the river Ohio. This grant contained reservations and stipulations which could only be made by the owners of the soil; and concluded with a stipulation that "all the lands in the ceded territory, not reserved, should be considered as a common fund, for the use and benefit of such of the United States as have become, or shall become, members of the confederation" &c., according to their usual respective proportions in the general charge and expenditure, and shall be faithfully and *bona fide* disposed of for that purpose, and for no other use or purpose whatsoever.

The ceded territory was occupied by numerous and warlike tribes of Indians; but the exclusive right of the United States to extinguish their title, and to grant the soil, has never, we believe, been doubted.

After these states became independent, a controversy subsisted between them and Spain respecting boundary. By the treaty of 1795, this controversy was adjusted, and Spain ceded to the United States the territory in question. This territory, though claimed by both nations, was chiefly in the actual occupation of Indians.

The magnificent purchase of Louisiana was the purchase from France of a country almost entirely occupied by numerous tribes of Indians, who are in fact independent. Yet any attempt of others to intrude into that country would be considered as an aggression which would justify war.

Our late acquisitions from Spain are of the same character; and the negotiations which preceded those acquisitions recognize and elucidate the principle which has been received as the foundation of all European title in America.

The United States, then, have unequivocally acceded to that great and broad rule by which its civilized inhabitants now hold this country. They hold, and assert in themselves, the title by which it was acquired. They maintain, as all other have maintained, that discovery gave an exclusive right to extinguish the Indian title of occupancy, either by purchase or by conquest; and gave also a right to such a degree of sovereignty as the circumstances of the people would allow them to exercise.

The power now possessed by the government of the United States to grant lands, resided, while we were colonies, in the crown, or its grantees. The validity of the titles given by either has never been questioned in our courts. It has been exercised uniformly over territory in possession of the Indians. The existence of this power must negative the existence of any right which may conflict with, and control it. An absolute title to lands cannot exist, at the same time, in different persons, or in different governments. An absolute, must be an exclusive title, or at least a title which excludes all others not compatible with it. All our institutions recognize the absolute title of the crown, subject only to the Indian right of occupancy, and recognized the absolute title of the crown to extinguish that right. This is incompatible with an absolute and complete title in the Indians.

We will not enter into the controversy, whether agriculturists, merchants, and manufacturers, have a right, on abstract principles, to expel hunters from the territory they possess, or to contract their limits. Conquest gives a title which the courts of the conqueror cannot deny, whatever the private and speculative opinions of individuals may be, respecting the original justice of the claim which has been successfully asserted. The British government, which was then our government, and whose rights have passed to the United States, asserted a title to all the lands occupied by Indians within the chartered limits of the British colonies. It asserted also a limited sovereignty over them, and the exclusive right of extinguishing the title which occupancy gave to them. These claims have been maintained and established as far west as the river Mississippi, by the sword. The title to a vast portion of the lands we now hold, originates in them. It is not for the courts of this country to question the validity of this title, or to sustain one which is incompatible with it.

Although we do not mean to engage in the defense of those principles which Europeans have applied to Indian title, they may, we think, find some excuse, if not justification, in the character and habits of the people whose rights have been wrested from them.

The title by conquest is acquired and maintained by force. The conqueror prescribes its limits. Humanity, however, acting on public opinion, has established, as a general rule, that the conquered shall not be wantonly oppressed, and that their condition shall remain as eligible as is compatible with the objects of the conquest. Most usually they are incorporated with the victorious nation and become subjects or citizens of the government with which they are connected. The new and old members of the society mingle with each other; the distinction between them is gradually lost, and they make one people. Where this incorporation is practicable, humanity demands, and a wise policy requires, that the rights of the conquered to property should remain unimpaired; that the new subjects should be governed as equitably as the old, and that confidence in their security should gradually banish the painful sense of being separated from the ancient connections, and united by force to strangers.

When the conquest is complete, and the conquered inhabitants can be blended with the conquerors, or safely governed as a distinct people, public opinion, which not even the conqueror can disregard, imposes these restraints upon him; and he cannot neglect them without injury to his fame, and hazard to his power.

But the tribes of Indians inhabiting this country were fierce savages, whose occupation was war, and whose subsistence was drawn chiefly from the forest. To leave them in possession of their country was to leave the country a wilderness; to govern them as a distinct people was impossible, because they were as brave and high spirited as they were fierce, and were ready to repel by arms every attempt on their independence.

What was the inevitable consequence of this state of things? The Europeans were under the necessity either of abandoning the country, and relinquishing their pompous claims to it, or of enforcing those claims by the sword, and by the adoption of principles adapted to the condition of a people with whom it was impossible to mix, and who could not be governed as a distinct society, or of remaining in their neighborhood and exposing themselves and their families to the perpetual hazard of being massacred.

Frequent and bloody wars, in which the whites were not always the aggressors, unavoidably ensued. European policy, numbers and skill, prevailed. As the white population advanced, that of the Indians necessarily receded. The country in the immediate neighborhood of the agriculturalists became unfit for them. The game fled into thicker and more unbroken forests, and the Indians followed. The soil, to which the crown originally claimed title, being no longer occupied by its ancient inhabitants, was parcelled out accordingly to the will of the sovereign power, and taken possession of by persons who claimed immediately from the crown, or mediately, through its grantees or deputies.

That law which regulates, and ought to regulate in general, the relations between the conqueror and conquered, was incapable of application to a people under such circumstances. The resort to some new and different rule, better adapted to the actual state of things, was unavoidable. Every rule which can be suggested will be found to be attended with great difficulty.

However extravagant the pretension of converting the discovery of an inhabited country into conquest may appear, if the principle has been asserted in the first instance, and afterwards sustained; if a country has been acquired and held under it; if the property of the great mass of the community originates in it, it becomes the law of the land, and cannot be questioned. So, too, with respect to the concomitant principle, that the Indian inhabitants are to be considered merely as occupants, to be protected, indeed, while in peace, in the possession of their lands, but to be deemed incapable of transferring the absolute title to others. However this restriction may be opposed to natural right, and to the usages of civilized nations, yet, if it be indispensable to that system under which the country has been settled, and be adapted to the actual condition of the two people, it may, perhaps be supported by reason, and certainly cannot be rejected by courts of justice.

This question is not entirely new in this court. The case of *Fletcher v. Peck* grew out of a sale made by the state of Georgia of a large tract of country within the limits of that state, the grant of which was afterwards resumed. The action was brought by a sub-purchaser, on the contract of sale, and one of the covenants in the deed was, that the state of Georgia was, at the time of sale, seized in fee of the premises. The real question presented by the issue was, whether the seisin in fee was in the state of Georgia, or in the United States. After stating that this controversy between the several states and the United States had been compromised, the court thought it necessary to notice the Indian title, which, although entitled to the respect of all courts until it should be legitimately extinguished, was declared not to be such as to be absolutely repugnant to a seisin in fee on the part of the state.

This opinion conforms precisely to the principle which has been supposed to be recognized by all European governments, from the first settlement of America. The absolute ultimate title has been considered as acquired by discovery, subject only to the Indian title of occupancy, which title the discoverers possessed the exclusive right of acquiring. Such a right is no more incompatible with a seisin in fee than a lease for years, and might as effectually bar an ejectment.

Another view has been taken of this question, which deserves to be considered. The title of the crown, whatever it might be, could be acquired only by a conveyance from the crown. If an individual might extinguish the Indian title for his own benefit, or, in other words, might purchase it, still he could acquire only that title. Admitting their power to change their laws or usages, so far as to allow an individual to separate a portion of their lands from the common stock, and hold it in severalty, still it is a part of their territory, and is held under them, by a title dependent on their laws. The grant derives its efficacy from their will; and, if they choose to resume it, and make a different disposition of the land, the courts of the United States cannot interpose for the protection of the title. The person who purchases lands from the Indians, within their territory, incorporates himself with them, so far as respects the property purchased; holds their title under their protection, and subject to their laws. If they annul the grant, we know of no tribunal which can revise and set aside the proceeding. We know of no principle which can distinguish this case from a grant made to a native Indian, authorizing him to hold a particular tract of land in severalty.

As such a grant could not separate the Indian from his nation, nor give a title which our courts could distinguish from the title of his tribe, as it might still be conquered from, or ceded by his tribe, we can perceive no legal principle which will authorize a court to say that different consequences are attached to this purchase, because it was made by a stranger. By the treaties concluded between the United States and the Indian nations, whose title the plaintiffs claim, the country comprehending the lands in controversy has been ceded to the United States, without any reservation of their title. These nations had been at war with the United States, and had an unquestionable right to annul any grant they had made to American citizens. Their cession of the country, without a reservation of this land, affords a fair presumption that they considered it as of no validity. They ceded to the United States this very property, after having used it in common with other lands, as their own, from the date of their deeds to the time of cession; and the attempt now made is to set up their title against that of the United States.

The proclamation issued by the King of Great Britain, in 1763, has been considered, and we think with reason, as constituting an additional objection to the title of the plaintiffs.

By that proclamation, the crown reserved under its own dominion and protection, for the use of the Indians, "all the land and territories lying to the westward of the sources of the rivers which fall into the sea from the west and north-west," and strictly forbade all British subjects from making any purchases or settlements whatever, or taking possession of the reserved lands.

It has been contended that, in this proclamation, the King transcended his constitutional powers; and the case of *Campbell v. Hall* (reported by Cowper) is relied on to support this position.

It is supposed to be a principle of universal law that, if an uninhabited country be discovered by a number of individuals, who acknowledge no connection with, and owe no allegiance to, any government whatever, the country becomes the property of the discoverers, so far at least as they can use it. They acquire a title in common. The title of the whole land is in the whole society. It is to be divided and parcelled out according to the will of the society, expressed by the whole body, or by that organ which is authorized by the whole to express it.

If the discovery be made, and possession of the country be taken, under the authority of an existing government, which is acknowledged by the emigrants, it is supposed to be equally well settled that the discovery is made for the whole nation, that the country becomes a part of the nation, and that the vacant soil is to be disposed of by that organ of the government which has constitutional power to dispose of the national domains, by that organ in which all vacant territory is vested by law.

According to the theory of the British constitution, all vacant lands are vested in the crown, as representing the nation; and the exclusive power to grant them is admitted to reside in the crown, as a branch of the royal prerogative. It has been already shown that this principle was as fully recognized in America as in the island of Great Britain. All the lands we hold were originally granted by the crown; and the establishment of a regal government has never been considered as impairing its right to grant lands within the chartered limits of such colony. In addition to the proof of this principle, furnished by the immense grants, already mentioned, of lands lying within the chartered limits of Virginia, the continuing right of the crown to grant lands lying within that colony was always admitted. A title might be obtained, either by making an entry with the surveyor of a county, in pursuance of law, or by an order of the governor-in-council, who was the deputy of the King, or by an immediate grant from the crown. In Virginia, therefore, as well as elsewhere in the British dominions, the complete title of the crown to vacant lands was acknowledged.

So far as respected the authority of the crown, no distinction was taken between vacant lands and lands occupied by the Indians. The title, subject only to the right of occupancy by the Indians, was admitted to be in the King, as was his right to grant that title. The lands, then, to which this proclamation referred, were lands which the King has a right to grant, or to reserve for the Indians.

According to the theory of the British constitution, the royal prerogative is very extensive so far as respects the political relations between Great Britain and foreign nations. The peculiar situation of the Indians, necessarily considered in some respects, as a dependent, and in some respects as a distinct people, occupying a country claimed by Great Britain, and yet too powerful and brave not to be dreaded as formidable enemies, required that means should be adopted for the preservation of peace, and that their friendship should be secured by quieting their alarms for their property. This was to be effected by restraining the encroachments of the whites; and the power to do this was never, we believe, denied by the colonies to the crown.

In the case of *Campbell* against *Hall*, that part of the proclamation was determined to be illegal which imposed a tax on a conquered province, after a government had been bestowed upon it. The correctness of this decision cannot be questioned, but its application to the case at bar cannot be admitted. Since the expulsion of the Stuart family, the power of imposing taxes, by proclamation, has never been claimed as a branch of the regal prerogative; but the powers of granting, or refusing to grant, vacant lands, and of restraining encroachments on the Indians, have always been asserted and admitted.

The authority of this proclamation, so far as it respected this continent, has never been denied, and the titles it gave to lands have always been sustained in our courts.

. . . .

It has never been contended that the Indian title amounted to nothing. Their right of possession has never been questioned. The claim of government extends to the complete ultimate title, charged with this right of possession, and to the exclusive power of acquiring that right. The object of the crown was to settle the sea-coast of America; and when a portion of it was settled, without violating the rights of others, by persons professing their loyalty, and soliciting the royal sanction of an act, the consequences of which were ascertained to be beneficial, it would have been as unwise as ungracious to expel them from their habitations because they had obtained the Indian title otherwise than through the agency of government. The very grant of a charter is an assertion of the title of the crown, and its words convey the same idea. The country granted is said to be "our island called Rhode Island;" and the charter contains an actual grant of the soil, as well as of the powers of government.

The letter was written a few months before the charter was issued, apparently at the request of the agents of the intended colony, for the sole purpose of preventing the trespasses of neighbors, who were disposed to claim some authority over them. The King, being willing himself to ratify and confirm their title, was, of course, inclined to quiet them in their possession.

This charter, and this letter, certainly sanction a previous unauthorized purchase from Indians, under the circumstances attending that particular purchase, but are far from supporting the general proposition that a title acquired from the Indians would be valid against a title acquired from the crown, or without the confirmation of the crown.

The acts of the several colonial assemblies, prohibiting purchases from the Indians, have also been relied on, as proving that, independent of such prohibitions, Indian deeds would be valid. But we think this fact, at most, equivocal. While the existence of such purchases would justify their prohibition, even by colonies which considered Indian deeds as previously invalid, the fact that such acts have been generally passed, is strong evidence of the general opinion that such purchases are opposed by the soundest principles of wisdom and national policy.

After bestowing on this subject a degree of attention which was more required by the magnitude of the interest in litigation, and the able and elaborate arguments of the bar, than by its intrinsic difficulty, the court is decidedly of opinion that the plaintiffs do not exhibit a title which can be sustained in courts of the United States, and that there is no error in the judgment which was rendered against them in the District Court of Illinois.

Judgment affirmed with costs.

(d) *Worcester v. Georgia*†

See **Chapter 3, Part 12.**

NOTE

Missionary Reverend Worcester was convicted of living in Cherokee territory, Georgia, without a state licence. Worcester argued that the licence requirement violated Indian treaties, federal American laws, and the Constitution of the United States.

EXTRACT

[MARSHALL C.J. for the majority of the Court:]

. . . .

The first step, then, in the inquiry, which the constitution and laws impose on this court, is an examination of the rightfulness of this claim.

America, separated from Europe by a wide ocean, was inhabited by a distinct people, divided into separate nations, independent of each other and of the rest of the world, having institutions of their own, and governing themselves by their own laws. It is difficult to comprehend the proposition, that the inhabitants of either quarter of the globe could have rightful original claims of dominion over the inhabitants of the other, or over the lands they occupied; or that the discovery of either by the other should give the discoverer rights in the country discovered, which annulled the pre-existing rights of its ancient possessors.

. . . .

[The principle established by the European maritime powers] ... was, 'that discovery gave title to the government by whose subjects or by whose authority it was made, against all other European governments, which title might be consummated by possession.' (8 Wheat. 573.)

This principle, acknowledged by all Europeans, because it was the interest of all to acknowledge it, gave to the nation making the discovery, as its inevitable consequence, the sole right of acquiring the soil and of making settlements on it. It was an exclusive principle which shut out the right of competition among those who had agreed to it; not one which could annul the previous rights of those who had not agreed to it. It regulated the right given by discovery among the European discoverers; but could not affect the rights of those already in possession, either as aboriginal occupants, or as occupants by virtue of a discovery made before the memory of man. It gave the exclusive right to purchase, but did not found that right on a denial of the right of the possessor to sell.

. . . .

Certain it is, that our history furnishes no example, from the first settlement of our country, of any attempt on the part of the crown to interfere with the internal affairs of the Indians, farther than to keep out the agents of foreign powers, who, as traders or otherwise, might seduce them into foreign alliances. The king purchased their lands when they were willing to sell, at a price they were willing to take; but never coerced a surrender of them. He also purchased their alliance and dependence by subsidies; but never intruded into the interior of their affairs, or interfered with their self-government, so far as respected themselves only.

. . . .

From the commencement of our government, congress has passed acts to regulate trade and intercourse with the Indians; which treat them as nations, respect their rights, and manifest a firm purpose to afford that protection which treaties stipulate. All these acts, and especially that of 1802, which is still in force, manifestly consider the several Indian nations as distinct political communities, having territorial boundaries, within which their authority is exclusive, and having a right to all the lands within those boundaries, which is not only acknowledged, but guaranteed by the United States.

---

† (1832), 6 Peters, 31 U.S. 515, 8 L.Ed. 483 at 542–45, 547, 556–61 (U.S.S.Ct.). See also Marshall C.J.'s decision in *Cherokee Nation v. State of Georgia* (1831), 5 Peters 1, 8 L.Ed. 25 (U.S.S.Ct.).

. . . .

[The Constitution] ... gave the United States in congress assembled the sole and exclusive right of 'regulating the trade and managing all the affairs with the Indians, not members of any of the states: provided, that the legislative power of any state within its own limits be not infringed or violated.'

. . . .

[The Constitution] confers on congress the powers of war and peace; of making treaties, and of regulating commerce with foreign nations, and among the several states, and with the Indian tribes. These powers comprehend all that is required for the regulation of our intercourse with the Indians. They are not limited by any restrictions on their free actions. The shackles imposed on this power, in the confederation, are discarded.

The Indian nations had always been considered as distinct, independent political communities, retaining their original natural rights, as the undisputed possessors of the soil, from time immemorial, with the single exception of that imposed by irresistible power, which excluded them from intercourse with any other European potentate than the first discoverer of the coast of the particular region claimed: and this was a restriction which those European potentates imposed on themselves, as well as on the Indians.

. . . .

The very fact of repeated treaties with them recognizes it; and the settled doctrine of the law of nations is, that a weaker power does not surrender its independence — its right to self government, by associating with a stronger, and taking its protection.... The Cherokee nation, then, is a distinct community occupying its own territory, with boundaries accurately described, in which the laws of Georgia can have no force, and which the citizens of Georgia have no right to enter, but with the assent of the Cherokees themselves, or in conformity with treaties and with the Acts of Congress. The whole intercourse between the United States and this nation is, by our own Constitution and laws, vested in the government of the United States.

[Marshall C.J. held that the state law was invalid not only because it dealt with a matter entrusted exclusively to Congress, but also because it conflicted with federal treaties with the Cherokees and federal legislation affecting them. M'Lean J. delivered a similar separate opinion, and Baldwin J. dissented.]

(e) *Connolly v. Woolrich*† and *Johnstone v. Connolly*‡

See **Chapter 3, Part 13**.

NOTE

After joining the North-West Company as a clerk, William Connolly married a Cree Indian lady in the Athabaska region in 1803 in accordance with the Cree custom of the era. Connolly later re-married his second cousin in Lower Canada. After Connolly's death, the eldest son of Connolly's native marriage claimed a share of the estate. The claim depended, in part, on whether the native marriage could be recognized at common law.

EXTRACT

[MONK J. for the Quebec Superior Court:]

. . . .

... [T]he Athabaska region was, by a general clause, excepted, from the grant of King Charles [to the Hudson Bay Company in 1670]; for although neither the laws of France, nor those of her contiguous colonies, may have obtained at those distant

† (1867), 11 L.C. Jur. 197, 17 R.J.R.Q. 75, 1 C.N.L.C. 70 (Q.S.C.); aff'd in *Johnstone et al. v. Connolly* (1869), 17 R.J.R.Q. 266; 1 R.L. (O.S.) 253 (Q.C.A.).

‡ (1869), 17 R.J.R.Q. 266; 1 R.L. (O.S.) 253 (Q.C.A.); aff'g (1867), 11 L.C. Jur. 197, 17 R.J.R.Q. 75, 1 C.N.L.C. 70 (Q.S.C.).

posts in 1670, the date of the Hudson Bay Charter, yet I think it is beyond all doubt that the Athabaska, and other regions bordering on it, belonged to the Crown of France at that time, to the same extent and by the same means, as the countries around Hudson Bay belonged to the Crown of England, that is to say, by discovery, by hunting, and trading explorations — with this difference, that in the case of the French traders there was a kind of occupation, whereas the English never occupied or settled any part of the Hudson Bay coast till 1669. I will assume, however, for the purposes of argument, that, in both these cases the principle of public law applied, viz., that in the case of a colony (though they were not plantations or colonies in the proper or legal sense of the terms) acquired by discovery and occupancy, which is a plantation in the strict and original meaning of the word, the law of the parent states then in being was immediately and *ipso facto* in force in these new settlements — that is to say, at Athabaska and on the Hudson Bay; and that the discoverers and first inhabitants of these places carried with them their own inalienable birthright, the laws of their country. Yet they took with them only so much of these laws as was applicable to the condition of an infant colony.

. . . .

... [E]ven admitting, for the sake of argument, the existence prior to the Charter of Charles, of the common law of France, and that of England, at these two trading posts or establishments respectively, yet will it be contended that the territorial rights, political organization such as it was, or the laws and usages of the Indian tribes, were abrogated — that they ceased to exist when those two European nations began to trade with the aboriginal inhabitants? In my opinion, it is beyond controversy that they did not — that so far from being abolished, they were left in full force, and were not even modified in the slightest degree in regard to the civil rights of the natives. As bearing upon this point, I cannot do better than to cite [the decision of the United States Supreme Court in *Worcester v. Georgia*]:

> America, separated from Europe by a wide ocean, was inhabited by a distinct people, divided into separate nations, independent of each other and of the rest of the world, having institutions of their own, and governing themselves by their own laws. It is difficult to comprehend the proposition, that the inhabitants of either quarter of the globe could have rightful original claims of dominion over the inhabitants of the other, or over the lands they occupied; *or that the discovery of either by the other should give the discoverer rights in the country discovered, which annulled the pre-existing rights of its ancient possessors.* [Emphasis added by Monk J.]

. . . .

I have no hesitation in saying that ... the Indian political and territorial rights, laws, and usages remained in full force — both at Athabaska and in the Hudson Bay region, previous to the Charter of 1670, and even after that date, as will appear hereafter....

. . . .

... [The words of the Hudson Bay Charter] were intended to concede a vast extent of country, round the whole coast of Hudson's Bay and the rivers flowing into it....

. . . .

Assuming this to be true, yet the Athabaska would not be included within the western boundaries of the Company's territory. [Monk J. noted that the Athabaska River flows into the Arctic Ocean and not first into Hudson Bay.]

. . . .

... [A]dmitting, for the purpose of conceding to the defendant all that can be granted, that in 1803, the Athabaska district was included within the western limits of the Hudson Bay territories, still that portion of the Common Law of England which would prevail there, had a very restricted application — [under the terms of the Charter] it could be administered and enforced only among, and in favor of, and against those "*who belonged to the Company or were living under them.*" [Emphasis added by Monk J.] It did not apply to the Indians, nor were the native laws or customs abolished or modified, and this is unquestionably true with regard to their civil rights.... The Charter did introduce the English law, but did not, at the same time, make it applicable generally or indiscriminately — it did not abrogate the Indian laws and usages. The Crown has not done so.

. . . .

... When Connolly went to Athabaska, in 1803, he found the Indian usages as they had existed for ages, unchanged by European power or Christian legislation. He did not take English law with him, for his settlement there was not preceded by discoveries made either by himself or English adventurers, nor was it an uninhabited or unoccupied country.

. . . .

[BADGLEY J.A. (Quebec Court of Appeal):]

It was only in 1820, that the Hudson Bay Company obtained from the British Government, *a Royal Decree*, to trade over the Rebaska [Athabaska] country, not as forming part of their charter grant, but only under a trading licence for 20 years, to trade therein, which was renewed in 1836, for a similar period. The acceptance of these licences is a strong confirmation of the fact, that as it really was, that the charter did not cover the Rebaska country. It is plain then, the Rebaska was nor in the charter grant, in 1803, not at any subsequent period.... [Even for the area it did cover, although the charter gave the power to make regulations conforming wherever possible to the laws of England], "[t]hey were to be solely for the administration of the company's affairs, and the government of their own *employés*, and were to be administered within the company's own territorial establishments...."

. . . .

... It is plain, therefore, that neither the common nor the statutory enactments of England and Great Britain, had any footing in Rebaska, in 1803, or before or since that time. It is also true to say that the law of England could not legally be introduced or enforced as the law of even conquered countries, by the mere power of the prerogative, much less could it be so into countries which were neither ceded nor conquered. It is true that conquest gives a title which the courts of the conqueror cannot deny, whatever may be the speculative opinion of individuals, respecting the original justice of the claim which has been successfully asserted. But, although this title is acquired and maintained by force, humanity, resting on public opinion, has prescribed rules and limits, by which it may be governed, and, hence it is very unusual, even in case of conquest, to do more than displace the former Sovereign, and assume dominion over the conquered country, as in the instance of this country, and its cession by France. The modern usage of nations would be violated if private property should be confiscated and private rights annulled. Therefore the relations of the people to their ancient sovereign or government are dissolved, but the relations to each other, and their customs and usages remain undisturbed. If this is the actual result of conquest, and its limits are restricted in this manner, it is manifest, that the mere exclusive right of trading in furs with the inhabitants does not interfere with the local or national customs of those people. The legislative power alone can change the local law, and substitute, by its mere power, some other, but, even the legislature, would not exercise that power over countries where the local nations have been left in territorial possession, as the Crees of Rebaska. There is nothing to show that the Indian title of the Crees, in the Rebaska territory, has ever been interfered with, or set aside.... It is unquestionable that the law of England, common or statutory, was never introduced or established, even by implication, beyond the area of the company's territorial grant; it certainly did not control the Indians of the Cree nation, outside of that area, nor apply to white men, in those outside districts who were not in the service of the H.B. Company.

. . . .

[MACKAY J.A. (Quebec Court of Appeal):]

Concurring, as I do substantially in the judgment of my brother Badgley, I might have remained silent, [but I will express my own views at length because of the novelty of this case and its importance to the parties.]

. . . .

... Rat River [where Connolly was stationed in Athabaska] was not in Rupert's Land. It was without the limits of the H.B. Coy. Territory proper....

. . . .

... [In any event, even within H.B. Coy Territory proper, the charter was] peculiar and operating a different thing from the founding of a colony. It invited no settlement.... It was a grant to fur traders of sole rights to trade and making them laws of the whole territory on fee simple, with the rights to make laws ... for the good government of the company and its servants....

. . . .

... [I]t is proved that Rat River was not comprehended in that charter [to the Hudson Bay Company]. [The witness] talks of that charter having regulated the country. What country? Surely, it could not regulate a country other than that of the charter.

. . . .

[Duval J.A. is reported to have "[c]oncurred in the judgment of the Court for the reasons given by his colleagues": 1 Revue Légale (O.S.) 253, 396. Caron J.A. is reported to have said that he agreed with the majority of the court, and to have limited himself to a few brief comments so as not simply to repeat his colleagues' reasons: *ibid.*]

. . . .

[LORANGER J.A. (Quebec Court of Appeal), dissenting (trans.):]

. . . .

... [The] evidence shows that Rat River, located in the District of Athabaska, was outside Hudson's Bay territory, and that the introduction of English law into the latter territory, supposing that it was introduced, would not have affected actions outside these limits.

. . . .

But assuming, for the purposes of the argument, that Athabaska was within the limits of Hudson Bay territory in 1803, is it certain that the laws of England would be in force? This is a secondary point which in my view is academic. However, to do justice to the parties who have raised it, I would like to examine it.... [I]n a discovery, conquest, or cession of a new country, the civil laws of the people discovered, conquered, or ceded, do not follow the laws of the [new] sovereign in the sense that the new sovereign's civil laws are not automatically binding on the new subjects.

. . . .

I conclude that the claim of the appellant that English laws were in force in Athabaska in 1803, and that these regulated the marriage of Connolly is unfounded. Were the Indians' customs in force?

. . . .

... [N]o foreign law affecting the public order or morality of a nation is recognised as valid on its own....

[Loranger J.A. went on to hold that because the Cree customs recognized polygamy, they could not constitute a "marriage" that could be recognized in the courts of Quebec.]

4 Aboriginal Rights from *Calder* to *Guerin*

(a) *Calder v. British Columbia (A.G.)*†

See **Chapter 4, Part 1.**

NOTE

The Nisga'a (formerly called Nishga) Indians of northwestern British Columbia sought a declaration that they had and continued to have Aboriginal title to an area around the Nass River. The provincial government argued, *inter alia*, that any Aboriginal title had been extinguished by colonial laws and proclamations, and that the Nisga'a had failed to obtain a fiat (a formal permission) that was needed to authorize the declaration proceedings.

EXTRACT

[JUDSON J. for himself, MARTLAND and RITCHIE JJ.:]

. . . .

No treaty or contract with the Crown or the Hudson's Bay Company has ever been entered into with respect to the area by anyone on behalf of the Nishga Nation. Within the area there are a number of reserves but they comprise only a small part of the total land. The Nishga Nation did not agree to or accept the creation of these reserves. The Nishgas claim that their title arises out of aboriginal occupation; that recognition of such a title is a concept well embedded in English law; that it is not dependent on treaty, executive order or legislative enactment. In the alternative they say that if executive or legislative recognition ever was needed, it is to be found in the *Royal Proclamation* of 1763, in Imperial statutes acknowledging that what is now British Columbia was "Indian Territory", and in Royal instructions to the Governor of British Columbia. Finally, they say that their title has never been extinguished.

. . . .

Any Canadian inquiry into the nature of the Indian title must begin with *R.* v. *St. Catherine's Milling & Lumber Co.* v. *The Queen* (1885), 10 O.R. 196; aff'd (1886), 13 O.A.R. 148; aff'd (1887), 13 S.C.R. 577; aff'd (1888), 14 App. Cas. 46. This case went through the Ontario Courts, the Supreme Court of Canada and ended in the Privy Council. The Crown in right of the Province sought to restrain the milling company from cutting timber on certain lands in the District of Algoma. The company pleaded that it held a licence from the Dominion Government which authorized the cutting. In 1873, by a treaty known as the North-West Angle Treaty No. 3, the Dominion had extinguished the Indian title.

The decision throughout was that the extinction of the Indian title ensured to the benefit of the Province and that it was not possible for the Dominion to preserve that title so as to oust the vested right of the Province to the land as part of the public domain of Ontario. It was held that the Crown had at all times a present proprietary estate, which title, after Confederation, was in the Province, by virtue of s. 109 of the *B.N.A. Act*. The Indian title was a mere burden upon that title which, following the cession of the lands under the treaty, was extinguished.

† [1973] S.C.R. 313 at 317–23, 325–36, 338–339, 342–47, 351–54, 368, 375–76, 383, 387–90, 394–95, 400–401, 404–405, 413–14, 426–27.

The reasons for judgment delivered in the Canadian Courts in the *St. Catherine's* case were strongly influenced by two early judgments delivered in the Supreme Court of the United States by Chief Justice Marshall — *Johnson and Graham's Lessee* v. *M'Intosh* (1823), 8 Wheaton 543, 21 U.S. 240, and *Worcester* v. *State of Georgia* (1832), 6 Peters 515, 31 U.S. 530. In *Johnson* v. *M'Intosh* the actual decision was that a title to lands, under grants to private individuals, made by Indian tribes or nations north-west of the river Ohio, in 1773 and 1775, could not be recognized in the Courts of the United States. In *Worcester* v. *Georgia*, the plaintiff, who was a missionary, was charged with residing among the Cherokees without a licence from the State of Georgia. His defence was that his residence was in conformity with treaties between the United States and the Cherokee nation and that the law under which he was charged was repugnant to the constitution, treaties and laws of the United States. The Supreme Court made a declaration to this effect. Both cases raised the question of aboriginal title to land. The following passage from [*Worcester* v. *Georgia*], 8 Wheaton at pp. 587–88 gives a clear summary of the views of the Chief Justice:

. . . .

[Judson J. quoted from the passage that contained Marshall C.J.'s statement that "[a]ll our institutions recognize the absolute title of the crown, subject only to the Indian right of occupancy; and recognize the absolute title of the crown to extinguish that right."]

The description of the nature of Indian title in the Canadian Courts in the *St. Catherine's* case is repeated in the reasons delivered in the Privy Council. I quote from 14 App. Cas. at pp. 54–55:

[Judson J. quoted the paragraph commencing with the words "The territory in dispute".]

. . . .

There can be no doubt that the Privy Council found that the Proclamation of 1763 was the origin of the Indian title — "Their possession, such as it was, can only be ascribed to the ... royal proclamation in favour of all Indian tribes then living under the sovereignty and protection of the British Crown."

I do not take these reasons to mean that the Proclamation was the exclusive source of Indian title. The territory under consideration in the *St. Catherine's* appeal was clearly within the geographical limits set out in the Proclamation. It is part of the appellants' case that the Proclamation does apply to the Nishga territory and that they are entitled to its protection. They also say that if it does not apply to the Nishga territory, their Indian title is still entitled to recognition by the Courts. These are two distinct questions.

I say at once that I am in complete agreement with judgments of the British Columbia Courts in this case that the Proclamation has no bearing upon the problem of Indian title in British Columbia. I base my opinion upon the very terms of the Proclamation and its definition of its geographical limits and upon the history of the discovery, settlement and establishment of what is now British Columbia.

. . . .

It is clear, as the British Columbia Courts have held, and whose reasons I adopt, that the Nishga bands represented by the appellants were not any of the several nations or tribes of Indians who lived under British protection and were outside the scope of the Proclamation.

The British Columbia Courts have dealt with the history of the discovery and settlement of their Province. This history demonstrates that the Nass Valley, and, indeed, the whole of the Province could not possibly be within the terms of the Proclamation.

. . . .

The area in question in this action never did come under British sovereignty until the Treaty of Oregon in 1846. This treaty extended the boundary along the 49th parallel from the point of termination, as previously laid down, to the channel separating the Continent from Vancouver Island, and thus through the Gulf Islands to Fuca's Straits. The Oregon Treaty was, in effect, a treaty of cession whereby American claims were ceded to Great Britain. There was no mention of Indian rights in any of these Conventions or the treaty.

. . . .

Although I think that it is clear that Indian title in British Columbia cannot owe its origin to the Proclamation of 1763, the fact is that when the settlers came, the Indians were there, organized in societies and occupying the land as their forefathers had done for centuries. This is what Indian title means and it does not help one in the solution of this problem to call it a "personal or usufructuary right".

What they are asserting in this action is that they had a right to continue to live on their lands as their forefathers had lived and that this right has never been lawfully extinguished. There can be no question that this right was "dependent on the goodwill of the Sovereign".

It was the opinion of the British Columbia Courts that this right, if it ever existed, had been lawfully extinguished, that with two societies in competition for land — the white settlers demanding orderly settlement and the Indians demanding to be let alone — the proper authorities deliberately chose to set apart reserves for Indians in various parts of the territory and open up the rest for settlements. They held that this had been done when British Columbia entered Confederation in 1871 and that the Terms of Union recognized this fact.

. . . .

The reasons for judgment next deal with a series of Proclamations by James Douglas as Governor of the Colony of British Columbia. The first is dated December 2, 1858, and it is stated to be a Proclamation having the force of law to enable the Governor of British Columbia to have Crown lands sold within the said Colony. It authorized the Governor to grant any land belonging to the Crown in the Colony.

The second Proclamation is dated February 14, 1859. It declared that all lands in British Columbia and all mines and minerals thereunder belonged to the Crown in fee. It provided for the sale of these lands after surveys had been made and the lands were ready for sale, and that due notice should be given of such sales.

The third Proclamation is dated January 4, 1860. It provided for British subjects and aliens who take the oath of allegiance acquiring unoccupied and unreserved and unsurveyed Crown land, and for the subsequent recognition of the claim after the completion of the survey.

The fourth Proclamation is dated January 20, 1860. It provided for the sale of certain lands by private contract and authorized the Commissioner of Land and all Magistrates and Gold Commissioners to make these sales at certain prices.

The fifth Proclamation of January 19, 1861, dealt with further details of land sales.

The sixth Proclamation, dated January 19, 1861, reduced the price of land.

The seventh Proclamation, dated May 28, 1861, dealt with conditions of pre-emption and limited the right to 160 acres per person.

The eighth Proclamation, dated August 27, 1861, was a consolidation of the laws affecting the settlement of unsurveyed Crown lands in British Columbia.

The ninth Proclamation, dated May 27, 1863, dealt with the establishment of mining districts.

Then follow four Ordinances enacted by the Governor by and with the consent of the Legislative Council of British Columbia. The first is dated April 11, 1865. It repeats what the Proclamation had previously said, namely, that all lands in British Columbia and all mines and minerals therein, not otherwise lawfully appropriated, belong to the Crown in fee. It goes on to provide for the public sale of lands and the price; that unless otherwise specially announced at the time of the sale, the conveyance of the lands shall include all trees and all mines and minerals within and under the same (except mines of gold and silver). It also deals with rights of pre-emption; of unoccupied, unsurveyed and unreserved Crown lands "not being the site of an existent or proposed town, or auriferous land or an Indian reserve or settlement under certain conditions".

The next Ordinance, dated March 31, 1866, restricts those who may acquire lands by pre-emption under the Ordinance of April 11, 1865. British subjects or aliens who take the oath of allegiance have this right but it does not extend without special permission of the Governor to companies or "to any of the Aborigines of this Colony or the Territories neighbouring thereto".

The third Ordinance is dated March 10, 1869. It deals with the payment of purchase money for preemption claims.

The last Ordinance is dated June 1, 1870, and is one to amend and consolidate the laws affecting Crown lands in British Columbia.

The result of these Proclamations and Ordinances was stated by Gould J., at the trial in the following terms [8 D.L.R. (3d) at pp. 81–82]. I accept his statement, as did the Court of Appeal:

> The various pieces of legislation referred to above are connected, and in many instances contain references *inter se*, especially XIII. They extend back well prior to November 19, 1866, the date by which, as a certainty, the delineated lands were all within the boundaries of the Colony of British Columbia, and thus embraced in the land legislation of the Colony, where the words were appropriate. All thirteen reveal a unity of intention to exercise, and the legislative exercising, of absolute sovereignty over all the lands of British Columbia, a sovereignty inconsistent with any conflicting interest, including one as to "aboriginal title, otherwise known as the Indian title", to quote the statement of claim.

> The legislation prior to November 19, 1866, is included to show the intention of the successor and connected legislation after that date, which latter legislation certainly included the delineated lands.

. . . .

[This brings] to mind what was said on the subject of extinguishment of Indian title in *United States* v. *Santa Fe Pacific R. Co.* (1941), 314 U.S. 339 at p. 347:

> Nor is it true, as respondent urges, that a tribal claim to any particular lands must be based upon a treaty, statute, or other formal government action. As stated in the *Cramer* case, "The fact that such right of occupancy finds no recognition in any statute or other formal governmental action is not conclusive." [261 U.S. at 229.]
>
> Extinguishment of Indian title based on aboriginal possession is of course a different matter. The power of Congress in that regard is supreme. The manner, method and time of such extinguishment raise political, not justiciable issues. *Buttz* v. *Northern Pacific Railroad, supra*, [119 U.S. 55], p. 66. As stated by Chief Justice Marshall in *Johnson* v. *M'Intosh, supra*, [8 Wheaton 543], p. 586, "the exclusive right of the United States to extinguish" Indian title has never been doubted. And whether it be done by treaty, by the sword, by purchase, by the exercise of complete dominion adverse to the right of occupancy, or otherwise, its justness is not open in inquiry in the courts. [*Beecher* v. *Wetherby*, 95 U.S. 517, 525.]

To the same effect are the reasons delivered in the Privy Council in *Re Southern Rodesia*, [1919] A.C. 211.

. . . .

In the Department of Indian Affairs and Northern Development there exists a Nass River Agency that administers the area in question. The reserves generally correspond with the fishing places that the Indians had traditionally used. The Government of the original Crown colony and, since 1871, the Government of British Columbia have made alienations in the Nass Valley that are inconsistent with the existence of an aboriginal title. These have already been referred to and show alienations in fee simple and by way of petroleum and natural gas leases, mineral claims and tree farm licences.

Further, the establishment of the railway belt under the Terms of Union is inconsistent with the recognition and continued existence of Indian title....

. . . .

There was no reservation of Indian rights in respect of the railway belt to be conveyed to the Dominion Government.

. . . .

The appellants submit that [Treaty 8 in north-eastern British Columbia] constituted a recognition of their rights by the Dominion in 1899. Whether this involved a recognition of similar rights over the rest of the Province of British Columbia is another matter. The territorial limitations of the treaty and the fact that the Indians of north-eastern British Columbia were included with those in the Northwest Territories may have some significance. But the answer of the Province is still the same — that original Indian title had been extinguished in the Colony of British Columbia prior to Confederation and that there were no Indian claims to transfer to the Dominion beyond those mentioned in term 13 of the Terms of Union.

In the United States an issue closely comparable with the one now before us was dealt with in three fairly recent cases in the Supreme Court. These cases are: *United States* v. *Alcea Band of Tillamooks et al.* (1946), 329 U.S. 40; *United States* v. *Alcea Band of Tillamooks et al.* (1951), 341 U.S. 48; *Tee-Hit-Ton Indians* v. *United States* (1955), 348 U.S. 272.

. . . .

... In the first *Tillamooks* case, the majority had clearly said that there was no difference between compensation for the taking of reserves (*Shoshone* and *Klamath*) and for claims under original Indian Title, and that both claims came under the Fifth Amendment. The Second Tillamooks case receded from this position and held that the claim had to be dealt with under the legislation of 1935 and not under the Fifth Amendment.

The next case is *Tee-Hit-Ton Indians* v. *United States* (1955), 348 U.S. 272. The United States had taken certain timber from Alaskan lands which the Indians said belonged to them. They asked for compensation. In this case compensation claimed did not arise from any statutory direction to pay. The petition was founded on the Fifth Amendment and the aboriginal claim against the lands upon which the timber stood. The suit was one which could be brought as a matter of procedure under a jurisdictional Act of 1946 permitting suits for Indian claims accruing after that date. The Court held that the recovery in the *Tillamooks* cases [329 U.S. 40 and

341 U.S. 48] was based upon a statutory direction to pay for the aboriginal title in the special jurisdictional Act for the purpose of equalizing the Tillamooks with the neighbouring tribes and not that there had been a compensable taking under the Fifth Amendment.

Again, I say this was, in effect, an adoption of the opinion of Mr. Justice Black in the *Tillamooks* case that the basis of recovery was statutory.

The relevant portion of the Fifth Amendment provides as follows: "... nor shall private property be taken for public use, without just compensation." The finding of the Court in the second *Tillamooks* case was therefore that aboriginal title did not constitute private property compensable under the Amendment.

This position is spelled out in the *Tee-Hit-Ton* case. In the opinion of the Court, at p. 279, in discussing the nature of aboriginal Indian title, it is said:

> This is not a property right but amounts to a right of occupancy which the sovereign grants and protects against intrusion by third parties but which right of occupancy may be terminated and such lands fully disposed of by the sovereign itself without any legally enforceable obligation to compensate the Indians.

In my opinion, in the present case, the sovereign authority elected to exercise complete dominion over the lands in question, adverse to any right of occupancy which the Nishga Tribe might have had, when, by legislation, it opened up such lands for settlement, subject to the reserves of land set aside for Indian occupation.

We were not referred to any cases subsequent to *Tee-Hit-Ton* on the problem of compensation for claims arising out of original Indian title. The last word on the subject from the Supreme Court of the United States is, therefore, that there is no right to compensation for such claims in the absence of a statutory direction to pay. An *Indian Claims Commission Act* was, in fact, passed by Congress in 1946. I note the concluding paragraph in the reasons for judgment in *Tee-Hit-Ton* [348 U.S. at pp. 290–91]. In my opinion, it has equal application to the appeal now before us:

> In the light of the history of Indian relations in this Nation, no other course would meet the problem of the growth of the United States except to make congressional contributions for Indian lands rather than to subject the Government to an obligation to pay the value when taken with interest to the date of payment. Our conclusion does not uphold harshness as against tenderness toward the Indians, but it leaves with Congress, where it belongs, the policy of Indian gratuities for the termination of Indian occupancy of Government-owned land rather than making compensation for its value a rigid constitutional principle.

For the foregoing reasons I have reached the conclusion that this action fails and that the appeal should be dismissed.

There is the further point raised by the respondent that the Court did not have jurisdiction to make the declaratory order requested because the granting of a fiat under the *Crown Procedure Act*, R.S.B.C. 1960, c. 89, was a necessary prerequisite to bringing the action and it had not been obtained. While it is not necessary, in view of my conclusion as to the disposition of this appeal, to determine this point, I am in agreement with the reasons of my brother Pigeon dealing with it.

I would dismiss the appeal and would make no order as to costs.

[HALL J., dissenting, for himself, Ritchie, and Laskin JJ.:]

This appeal raises issues of vital importance to the Indians of northern British Columbia and, in particular, to those of the Nishga tribe. The Nishga tribe has persevered for almost a century in asserting an interest in the lands which their ancestors occupied since time immemorial. The Nishgas were never conquered nor did they at any time enter into a treaty or deed of surrender as many other Indian tribes did throughout Canada and in southern British Columbia. The Crown has never granted the lands in issue in this action other than a few small parcels later referred to prior to the commencement of the action.

. . . .

When asked to state the nature of the right being asserted and for which a declaration was being sought, counsel for the appellants described it as "an interest which is a burden on the title of the Crown; an interest which is usufructuary in nature; a tribal interest inalienable except to the Crown and extinguishable only by legislative enactment of the Parliament of Canada". The exact nature and extent of the Indian right or title does not need to be precisely stated in this litigation. The issue here is whether any right or title the Indians possess as occupants of the land from time immemorial has been extinguished. They ask for a declaration that there has been no extinguishment. The precise nature and value of that right or title would, of course, be most relevant in any litigation that might follow extinguishment in the future because in such an event, according to common law, the expropriation of private rights by the Government under the prerogative necessitates the payment of compensation: *Newcastle Breweries Ltd.* v. *The King*, [1920] 1 K.B. 854. Only express words to that effect in an enactment would authorize a taking without compensation. This proposition has been extended to Canada in *City of Montreal* v. *Montreal Harbour Com'rs*, [1926] 1 D.L.R. 840, 47 Que. K.B. 163, [1926] A.C. 299. The principle is so much part of the common law that it even exists in time of war as was made clear in *Attorney-General* v. *DeKeyser's Royal Hotel Ltd.*, [1920] A.C. 508, and *Burmah Oil Co. (Burmah Trading) Ltd.* v. *Lord Advocate*, [1965] A.C. 75. This is not a claim to title in fee but is in the nature of an equitable title or interest [see *Cherokee Nation* v. *State of Georgia* (1831), 5 Peters 1, 30 U.S. 1], a usufructuary right and a right to occupy the lands and to enjoy the fruits of the soil, the forest and of the rivers and streams which does not in any way deny the Crown's paramount title as it is recognized by the law of nations. Nor does the Nishga claim challenge the federal Crown's right to extinguish that title. Their position is that they possess a right of occupation against the world except the Crown and that the Crown has not to date lawfully extinguished that right. The essence of the action is that such rights as the Nishgas possessed in 1858 continue to this date. Accordingly, the declaratory judgment asked for implies that the *status quo* continues and this means that if the right is to be extinguished it must be done by specific legislation in accordance with the law.

The right to possession claimed is not prescriptive in origin because a prescriptive right presupposes a prior right in some other person or authority. Since it is admitted that the Nishgas have been in possession since time immemorial, that fact negatives that anyone ever had or claimed prior possession.

. . . .

Unlike the method used to make out title in other contexts, proof of the Indian title or interest is to be made out as a matter of fact. In *Amodu Tijani* v. *Secretary, Southern Nigeria*, [1921] 2 A.C. 399, Lord Haldane said at pp. 402–04:

> Their Lordships make the preliminary observation that in interpreting the native title to land, not only in Southern Nigeria, but other parts of the British Empire, much caution is essential. There is a tendency, operating at times unconsciously, to render that title conceptually in terms which are appropriate only to systems which have grown up under English law. But this tendency has to be held in check closely. As a rule, in the various systems of native jurisprudence throughout the Empire, there is no such full division between property and possession as English lawyers are familiar with. A very usual form of native title is that of a usufructuary right, which is a mere qualification of or burden on the radical or final title of the Sovereign where that exists. In such cases the title of the Sovereign is a pure legal estate, to which beneficial rights may or may not be attached. But this estate is qualified by a right of beneficial user which may not assume definite forms analogous to estates.... [Emphasis added.]

. . . .

Possession is of itself at common law proof of ownership: Cheshire, *Modern Law of Real Property*, 10th ed., p. 659, and Megarry and Wade, *Law of Real Property*, 3rd ed., p. 999. Unchallenged possession is admitted here.

. . . .

What emerges from the foregoing evidence is the following: the Nishgas in fact are and were from time immemorial a distinctive cultural entity with concepts of ownership indigenous to their culture and capable of articulation under the common law having, in the words of Dr. Duff, "developed their cultures to higher peaks in many respects than in any other part of the continent north of Mexico"....

. . . .

While the Nishga claim has not heretofore been litigated, there is a wealth of jurisprudence affirming common law recognition of aboriginal rights to possession and enjoyment of lands of aborigines precisely analogous to the Nishga situation here.

. . . .

The dominant and recurring proposition stated by Chief Justice Marshall in *Johnson* v. *M'Intosh* is that on discovery or on conquest the aborigines of newly-found lands were conceded to be the rightful occupants of the soil with a legal as well as a just claim to retain possession of it and to use it according to their own discretion, but their rights to complete sovereignty as independent nations were necessarily diminished and their power to dispose of the soil on their own will to whomsoever they pleased was denied by the original fundamental principle that discovery or conquest gave exclusive title to those who made it.

Chief Justice Marshall had occasion in 1832 once more to adjudicate upon the question of aboriginal rights in *Worcester* v. *State of Georgia* (1832), 6 Peters 515, 31 U.S. 530, 8 L.Ed. 483.

. . . .

Chief Justice Marshall in his judgment in *Johnson* v. *M'Intosh* referred to the English case of *Campbell* v. *Hall* (1774), 1 Cowp. 204, 98 E.R. 1045. This case was an important and decisive one which has been regarded as authoritative throughout the Commonwealth and the United States. It involved the rights and status of residents of the Island of Grenada which had recently been taken by British arms in open war with France. The judgment was given by Lord Mansfield. In his reasons he said at pp. 208–09:

> A great deal has been said, and many authorities cited relative to propositions, in which both sides seem to be perfectly agreed; and which, indeed are too clear to be controverted. The stating of some of those propositions which we think quite clear, will lead us to see with greater perspicuity, what is the question upon the first point, and upon what hinge it turns. I will state the propositions at large, and the first is this:
>
> A country conquered by the British arms becomes a dominion of the King in the right of his Crown; and, therefore, necessarily subject to the Legislature, and Parliament of Great Britain.
>
> The 2d is, that the conquered inhabitants once received under the King's protection, become subjects, and are to be universally considered in that light, not as enemies or aliens.
>
> . . . .
>
> The 5th, that the laws of a conquered country continue in force, until they are altered by the conqueror: the absurd exception as to pagans, mentioned in *Calvin's* case [(1608), 7 Co. Rep. 1a, Moore (K.B.) 790 *sub nom. Case del Union, del Realm, D'Escose, ove Angleterre*, 72 E.R. 908], shews the universality and antiquity of the maxim. For that distinction could not exist before the Christian era; and in all probability arose from the mad enthusiasm of the Croisades. In the present case the capitulation expressly provides and agrees, that they shall continue to be governed by their own laws, until His Majesty's further pleasure be known.
>
> The 6th, and last proposition is, that if the King (and when I say the King, I always mean the King without the concurrence of Parliament,) has a power to alter the old and to introduce new laws in a conquered country, this legislation being subordinate, that is, subordinate to his own authority in Parliament, he cannot make any new change contrary to fundamental principles: he cannot exempt an inhabitant from that particular dominion; as for instance, from the laws of trade, or from the power of Parliament, or give him privileges exclusive of his other subjects; and so in many other instances which might be put.

A fortiori the same principles, particularly Nos. 5 and 6, must apply to lands which become subject to British sovereignty by discovery or by declaration.

. . . .

Surely the Canadian treaties, made with much solemnity on behalf of the Crown, were intended to extinguish the Indian title. What other purpose did they serve? If they were not intended to extinguish the Indian right, they were a gross fraud and that is not to be assumed....

. . . .

If there was no Indian title extant in British Columbia in 1899, why was [Treaty 8] negotiated and ratified?

Parallelling and supporting the claim of the Nishgas that they have a certain right or title to the lands in question is the guarantee of Indian rights contained in the Proclamation of 1763. This Proclamation was an Executive Order having the force and effect of an Act of Parliament and was described by Gwynn J., in *St. Catherine's Milling* case at p. 652 as the "Indian Bill of Rights": see also *Campbell* v. *Hall*. Its force as a statute is analogous to the status of Magna Carta which has always been considered to be the law throughout the Empire. It was a law which followed the flag as England assumed jurisdiction over newly-discovered or acquired lands or territories. It follows, therefore, that the *Colonial Laws Validity Act*, 1865 (U.K.), c. 63, applied to make the Proclamation the law of British Columbia. That it was regarded as being the law of England is clear from the fact that when it was deemed advisable to amend it the amendment was affected by an Act of Parliament, namely the *Quebec Act* of 1774 [1774 (U.K.) (14 Geo. III), c. 83].

. . . .

The aboriginal Indian title does not depend on treaty, executive order or legislative enactment. Sutherland J., delivering the opinion of the Supreme Court of the United States in *Cramer et al.* v. *United States* (1923), 67 L.Ed. 622, 261 U.S., 219, dealt with the subject as follows [p. 626]:

> The fact that such right of occupancy finds no recognition in any statute or other formal governmental action is not conclusive....

. . . .

... [I]t cannot be challenged that while the west coast lands were mostly unexplored as of 1763 they were certainly known to exist and that fact is borne out by the wording of the paragraph in the Proclamation previously quoted.

This important question remains: were the rights either at common law or under the Proclamation extinguished? Tysoe J.A., said in this regard at p. 95 [13 D.L.R. (3d)] of his reasons: "It is true, as the appellants have submitted, that nowhere can one find express words extinguishing Indian title...". [Emphasis added.]

The parties here agree that if extinguishment was accomplished, it must have occurred between 1858 and when British Columbia joined Confederation in 1871. The respondent relies on what was done by Governor Douglas and by his successor, Frederick Seymour, who became Governor in 1864.

Once aboriginal title is established, it is presumed to continue until the contrary is proven....

. . . .

It would, accordingly, appear to be beyond question that the onus of proving that the Sovereign intended to extinguish the Indian title lies on the respondent and that intention must be "clear and plain". There is no such proof in the case at bar; no legislation to that effect.

The Court of Appeal also erred in holding that there "is no Indian Title capable of judicial interpretation ... unless it has previously been recognized either by the Legislature or the Executive Branch of Government" [see p. 70]. Relying on *Cook et al.* v. *Sprigg*, [1899] A.C. 572, and other cases, the Court of Appeal erroneously applied what is called the Act of State Doctrine....

. . . .

The Act of State doctrine has no application in the present appeal for the following reasons: (a) It has never been invoked in claims dependent on aboriginal title. An examination of its rationale indicates that it would be quite inappropriate for the Courts to extend the doctrine to such cases; (b) It is based on the premise that an Act of State is an exercise of the Sovereign power which a municipal Court has no power to review: see *Salaman* v. *Secretary of State-in-Council of India*, [1906] 1 K.B. 613 at pp. 639–40; *Cook* v. *Sprigg*, *supra*, at p. 578.

. . . .

If in any of the Proclamations or actions of Douglas, Seymour or of the Council of the Colony of British Columbia there are elements which the respondent says extinguish by implication the Indian title, then it is obvious from the Commission of the Governor and from the Instructions under which the Governor was required to observe and neither the Commission nor the Instructions contain any power or authorization to extinguish the Indian title, then it follows logically that if any attempt was made to extinguish the title it was beyond the power of Governor or of the Council to do so and, therefore, *ultra vires*.

. . . .

Having reviewed the evidence and cases in considerable detail and having decided that if the Nishgas ever had any right or title that it had been extinguished, Tysoe J.A., was inexorably driven to the conclusion which he stated as follows [p. 94]:

> As a result of these pieces of legislation the Indians of the Colony of British Columbia became in law trespassers on and liable to actions of ejectment from lands in the Colony other than those set aside as reserves for the use of Indians. [Emphasis added.]

Any reasoning that would lead to such a conclusion must necessarily be fallacious. The idea is self-destructive. If trespassers, the Indians are liable to prosecution as such, a proposition which reason itself repudiates.

. . . .

[PIGEON J.:]

. . . .

For all those reasons, I have to hold that the preliminary objection that the declaration prayed for, being a claim of title against the Crown in the right of the Province of British Columbia, the Court has no jurisdiction to make it in the absence of a fiat of the Lieutenant-Governor of that Province. I am deeply conscious of the hardship involved in holding that the access to the Court for the determination of the plaintiffs' claim is barred by sovereign immunity from suit without a fiat. However, I would point out that in the United States, claims in respect of the taking of lands outside of reserves and not covered by any treaty were not held justiciable until legislative provisions had removed the obstacle created by the doctrine of immunity. In Canada, immunity from suit has been removed by legislation at the federal level and in most Provinces. However, this has not yet been done in British Columbia.

I would therefore dismiss the appeal and make no order as to costs.

Appeal dismissed.

(b) *Baker Lake v. Canada (Minister of Indian and Northern Affairs)*†

See **Chapter 4, Part 3**.

NOTE

The Inuit people of the Baker Lake area of the Northwest Territories sought a declaration that they had Aboriginal title to the area. They also asked for an injunction to prevent mining exploration companies from interfering with their claimed Aboriginal right to hunt caribou. Could the Inuit prove an Aboriginal title? The exploration was carried out pursuant to federal legislation. Could (pre-April 17, 1982) legislation authorize interference with Aboriginal rights?

EXTRACT

[MAHONEY J.:]

. . . .

While the *Royal Proclamation* of 1763, various statutes and almost all the decided cases refer to Indians and do not mention Inuit or Eskimos, the term "Indians", in Canadian constitutional law, includes the Inuit: *Re Eskimos*, [1939] 2 D.L.R. 417, [1939] S.C.R. 104 *sub nom. Reference as to whether "Indians" in 91(24) of the* B.N.A. Act, 1867, *includes Eskimo inhabitants of Quebec*. In the absence of their exclusion from that term, either expressly or by compelling inference, decisions relevant to the aboriginal rights of Indians in Canada apply to the Inuit. In light of the *Sigeareak* decision, *supra*, the *Royal Proclamation* must be dismissed as a source of aboriginal title in Rupert's Land. However, the Proclamation is not the only source of aboriginal title in Canada.

. . . .

In the result, [Judson J.] held [in *Calder*] that "Indian title" to have been extinguished. The dissenting judgment, which held the aboriginal title, with certain exceptions, not to have been extinguished, was delivered by Hall J., with Spence and Laskin JJ., concurring. Pigeon J., disposed of the matter exclusively on the procedural ground that the plaintiffs had not obtained the required *fiat* to sue the Crown in right of British Columbia, a conclusion concurred in by Judson, Martland and Ritchie JJ. While it appears that the judgment of Pigeon J., embodies the *ratio decidendi* of the Supreme Court, the clear agreement of the other six judges on the point is solid authority for the general proposition that the law of Canada recognizes the existence of an aboriginal title independent of the *Royal Proclamation* or any other prerogative Act or legislation. It arises at common law....

. . . .

... The *Calder* decision renders untenable, in so far as Canada is concerned, the defendants' arguments that no aboriginal title exists in a settled, as distinguished from a conquered or ceded, colony and that there is no aboriginal title unless it has

† (1979), 107 D.L.R. (3d) 513 (F.C.T.D.) at 513, 540–42, 550–51, 557–58.

been recognized by statute or prerogative act of the Crown or by treaty having statutory effect.

PROOF OF ABORIGINAL TITLE

The elements which the plaintiffs must prove to establish an aboriginal title cognizable at common law are:

1. That they and their ancestors were members of an organized society.
2. That the organized society occupied the specific territory over which they assert the aboriginal title.
3. That the occupation was to the exclusion of other organized societies.
4. That the occupation was an established fact at the time sovereignty was asserted by England.

. . . .

The plaintiffs argue that any such extinguishment must be effected expressly. They find support for that proposition in the judgment of Mr. Justice Hall in the *Calder* case, *supra*. The defendants argue that extinguishment may be the necessary result of legislation even though the intention is not expressed. They find support for their position in the judgment of Mr. Justice Judson in the *Calder* case.

At p. 208 D.L.R., p. 402 S.C.R., Mr. Justice Hall, referring to the "Indian title" in issue, said:

> It being a legal right, it could not thereafter be extinguished except by surrender to the Crown or by competent legislative authority, *and then only by specific legislation*. [Emphasis mine.]

After citing a number of authorities, he concluded his discussion of the particular point, at p. 210 D.L.R., p. 404 S.C.R., as follows:

> It would, accordingly, appear to be beyond question that the onus of proving that the Sovereign intended to extinguish the Indian title lies on the respondent and that *the intention must be "clear and plain"*. [Emphasis mine.]

If I understand the plaintiffs well, they argue that, to extinguish aboriginal title, legislation must state expressly that such extinguishment is its object.

I have perused the authorities cited by Mr. Justice Hall and one upon which he appears to have relied for the qualification embraced in the phrases I have emphasized is the following passage from the opinion of Davis J., for the United States Court of Claims in *Lipan Apache Tribe* v. *United States* (1967), 180 Ct.Cl. 487 at p. 492:

> The correct inquiry is, not whether the Republic of Texas accorded or granted the Indians any rights, but whether that sovereign extinguished their pre-existing occupancy rights. Extinguishment can take several forms; it can be effected "by treaty, by the sword, by purchase, by the exercise of complete dominion adverse to the right of occupancy, or otherwise...". *United States* v. *Santa Fe Pac. R.R.*, supra, 314 U.S. at 347. While the selection of a means is a governmental prerogative, the actual act (or acts) of extinguishment must be plain and unambiguous. *In the absence of a "clear and plain indication" in the public records that the sovereign "intended to extinguish all of the [claimants'] rights" in their property, Indian title continues.* Id. at 353. [Emphasis added by Hall J.]

It is apparent that the phrase "clear and plain intention" has its origin in the *Santa Fe* decision, *supra*. The issue, which gave rise to the phrase, was whether a band's acceptance of a reservation in 1881 had effected an extinguishment, by voluntary cession, of the aboriginal title to lands which were subject to the Act of Congress of July 27, 1866, which had granted those lands to the railway. The Act provided, in part, that:

> **2.** The United States shall extinguish, as rapidly as may be consistent with public policy and the welfare of the Indians, and only by their voluntary cession, the Indian title to all lands falling under the operation of this act and required in the donation to the road named in the act.

That is clearly the expression of avowed solicitude Mr. Justice Douglas had in mind when he said, at pp. 353–54:

> We search the public records in vain for any clear and plain indication that Congress in creating the Colorado River reservation was doing more than making an offer to the Indians, including the Walapais, which it was hoped would be accepted as a compromise of a troublesome question. We find no indication that Congress by creating that reservation intended to extinguish all of the rights which the Walapais had in their ancestral home. That Congress could have effected such an extinguishment is not doubted. But an extinguishment cannot be lightly implied in view of the avowed solicitude of the Federal Government for the welfare of its Indian wards.

No Canadian legislation requiring that legislative extinguishment of aboriginal title be effected in a particular way, has been brought to my attention. There are numerous Canadian authorities which have held that the aboriginal right to hunt, even when confirmed by treaty, is subject to regulation by competent legislation. The decision in *Sikyea* v. *The Queen* (1964), 50 D.L.R. (2d) 80, [1964] S.C.R. 642, [1965] 2 C.C.C. 129, delivered by Mr. Justice Hall for the Court, is an example. The right freely to hunt as one's ancestors did, over particular land, had been an important incident of most, if not all, aboriginal titles yet asserted in Canada. It is the right proved here. It is, nonetheless, a right that has been abridged by legislation of general application making no express mention of any intention to deal with aboriginal title in any way.

I cannot accept the plaintiffs' argument that Parliament's intention to extinguish an aboriginal title must be set forth explicitly in the pertinent legislation. I do not agree that Mr. Justice Hall went that far. Once a statute has been validly enacted, it must be given effect. If its necessary effect is to abridge or entirely abrogate a common law right, then that is the effect that the Courts must give it. That is as true of an aboriginal title as of any other common law right. Section 1(a) of the *Canadian Bill of Rights* does not make the aboriginal title in issue here an exception to the general rule.

. . . .

No real doubt as to the validity of the mining laws has been raised in my mind. I do not, therefore, intend to recite them, except to the extent necessary to deal with the questions of whether, by virtue of the aboriginal title, the Inuit have "rights previously acquired" within the meaning of s. 29(11) of the *Canada Mining Regulations* and are "holders of surface rights" within the meaning of s. 8 of the *Territorial Lands Act*.

With the exception of a number of parcels in the hamlet itself, I am entirely satisfied that the entire territory in issue remains "territorial lands" within the meaning of the *Territorial Lands Act* and "public lands" within the meaning of the *Public Lands Grants Act*. They are subject to the *Canada Mining Regulations*. To the extent that their aboriginal rights are diminished by those laws, the Inuit may or may not be entitled to compensation. That is not sought in this action. There can, however, be no doubt as to the effect of competent legislation and that, to the extent it does diminish the rights comprised in an aboriginal title, it prevails. That point was succinctly made by Laskin C.J.C., for the Court, in *R.* v. *Derrikson* (1976), 71 D.L.R. (3d) 159n at p. 160, 31 C.C.C. (2d) 575n, [1976] 6 W.W.R. 480n:

> On the assumption that Mr. Sanders is correct in his submission (which is one which the Crown does not accept) that there is an aboriginal right to fish in the particular area arising out of Indian occupation and that this right has subsequent reinforcement (and we express no opinion of the correctness of this submission), we are all of the view that the *Fisheries Act*, R.S.C. 1970, c. F–14, and the Regulations thereunder which, so far as relevant here, were validly enacted, have the effect of subjecting the alleged right to controls imposed by the Act and Regulations.

It was reiterated in *Kruger and Manuel* v. *The Queen*, *supra*.

[Mahoney J. went on to hold that the Aboriginal rights of the Baker Lake Inuit had been validly abridged by mining permits granted under the Canada Mining Regulations.]

(c) *Guerin v. The Queen*†

See **Chapter 4, Part 4** and **Chapter 8, Parts 4 and 6.**

NOTE

The Musqueam Band in Vancouver surrendered reserve land so it could be leased to a golf club. The lease was negotiated for the Band by the federal Department of Indian Affairs and Northern Development. Its terms proved to be much less favourable than those originally shown to the Band. Had the Band any legal remedy?

---

† [1984] 2 S.C.R. 335 at 348–49, 365, 375–85, 389, 391–93 (S.C.C.); rev'g (1983), 143 D.L.R. (3d) 416 (F.C.A.), rev'g [1982] 2 F.C. 385 (F.C.T.D.) and (1982), 127 D.L.R. (3d) 170 (F.C.T.D.: supplementary reasons).

There was a sequel to the situation in Guerin in the summer of 2003, when the Musqueam Band purchased for itself the remaining terms of the golf club lease.

EXTRACT

[DICKSON J. for himself, Beetz, Chouinard, and Lamer JJ.:]

The question is whether the appellants, the chief and councillors of the Musqueam Indian Band, suing on their own behalf and on behalf of all other members of the band, are entitled to recover damages from the federal Crown in respect of the leasing to a golf club of land on the Musqueam Indian Reserve. Collier J., of the Trial Division of the Federal Court, declared that the Crown was in breach of trust [[1982] 2 F.C. 385, 10 E.T.R. 61, and 127 D.L.R. (3d) 170, [1982] 2 F.C. 445 (supplementary reasons)]. He assessed damages at $10,000,000. The Federal Court of Appeal allowed a Crown appeal, set aside the judgment of the Trail Division and dismissed the action [143 D.L.R. (3d) 416, [1983] 2 F.C. 656, [1983] 2 W.W.R. 686, 13 E.T.R. 245, 45 N.R. 181].

GENERAL

Before adverting to the facts, reference should be made to several of the relevant sections of the *Indian Act*, R.S.C. 1952, c. 149, as amended. Section 18(1) provides in part that reserves shall be held by Her Majesty for the use of the respective Indian bands for which they were set apart. Generally, lands in a reserve shall not be sold, alienated, leased or otherwise disposed of until they have been surrendered to Her Majesty by the band for whose use and benefit in common the reserve was set apart [s. 37]. A surrender may be absolute or qualified, conditional or unconditional [s. 38(2)]. To be valid, a surrender must be made to Her Majesty, assented to by a majority of the electors of the band, and accepted by the Governor-in-Council [s. 39(1)].

The gist of the present action is a claim that the federal Crown was in breach of its trust obligations in respect of the leasing of approximately 162 acres of reserve land to the Shaughnessy Heights Golf Club of Vancouver. The band alleged that a number of the terms and conditions of the lease were different from those disclosed to them before the surrender vote and that some of the lease terms were not disclosed to them at all. The band also claimed failure on the part of the federal Crown to exercise the requisite degree of care and management as a trustee.

. . . .

[Dickson J. went on to relate the facts in detail and to discuss the lower court decisions. He continued:]

FIDUCIARY RELATIONSHIP

The issue of the Crown's liability was dealt with in the courts below on the basis of the existence or non-existence of a trust. In dealing with different consequences of a "true" trust, as opposed to a "political" trust, Le Dain J. noted that the Crown could be liable only if it were subject to an "equitable obligation enforceable in a court of law". I have some doubt as to the cogency of the terminology of "higher" and "lower" trusts, but I do agree that the existence of an equitable obligation is the *sine qua non* for liability. Such an obligation is not, however, limited to relationships which can be strictly defined as "trusts". As will presently appear, it is my view that the Crown's obligations *vis-à-vis* the Indians cannot be defined as a trust. That does not, however, mean that the Crown owes no enforceable duty to the Indians in the way in which it deals with Indian land.

In my view, the nature of Indian title and the framework of the statutory scheme established for disposing of Indian land places upon the Crown an equitable obligation, enforceable by the courts, to deal with the land for the benefit of the Indians. This obligation does not amount to a trust in the private law sense. It is rather a fiduciary duty. If, however, the Crown breaches this fiduciary duty it will be liable to the Indians in the same way and to the same extent as if such a trust were in effect.

The fiduciary relationship between the Crown and the Indians has its roots in the concept of aboriginal, native or Indian title. The fact that Indian bands have a certain interest in lands does not, however, in itself give rise to fiduciary relationship between the Indians and the Crown. The conclusion that the Crown is a fiduciary depends upon the further proposition that the Indian interest in the land is inalienable except upon surrender to the Crown.

An Indian band is prohibited from directly transferring its interest to a third party. Any sale or lease of land can only be carried out after a surrender has taken place, with the Crown then acting on the band's behalf. the Crown first took this responsibility upon itself in the *Royal Proclamation* of 1763 [R.S.C. 1970, App. II, No. 1]. It is still recognized in the surrender provisions of the *Indian Act*. The surrender requirement, and the responsibility it entails, are the source of a distinct fiduciary obligation owed by the Crown to the Indians. In order to explore the character of this obligation, however, it is first necessary to consider the basis of aboriginal title and the nature of the interest in land which it represents.

The Existence of Indian Title

In *Calder et al.* v. *A.-G. B.C.* (1973), 34 D.L.R. (3d) 145, [1973] S.C.R. 313, [1973] 4 W.W.R. 1, this court recognized aboriginal title as a legal right derived from the Indians' historic occupation and possession of their tribal lands. With Judson and Hall JJ. writing the principal judgments, the court split three-three on the major issue of whether the Nishga Indians' aboriginal title to their ancient tribal territory had been extinguished by general land enactments in British Columbia. The court also split on the issue of whether the *Royal Proclamation* of 1763 was applicable to Indian lands in that province. Judson and Hall JJ. were in agreement, however, that aboriginal title existed in Canada (at least where it has not been extinguished by appropriate legislative action) independently of the *Royal Proclamation* of 1763. Judson J. stated expressly that the Proclamation was not the "exclusive" source of Indian title [at pp. 152–53, 156 D.L.R., pp. 322–23, 328 S.C.R.]. Hall J. said [at p. 200 D.L.R., p. 390 S.C.R.] that "aboriginal Indian title does not depend on treaty, executive order or legislative enactment".

The *Royal Proclamation* of 1763 reserved [at p. 127]

> ... under our Sovereignty, Protection, and Dominion, for the use of the said Indians, all the Lands and Territories not included within the Limits of Our said Three new Governments or within the limits of the Territory granted to the Hudson's Bay Company, as also all the Lands and Territories lying to the Westward of the Sources of the Rivers which fall into the Sea from the West and North West as aforesaid.

In recognizing that the Proclamation is not the sole source of Indian title the *Calder* decision went beyond the judgment of the Privy Council in *St. Catherine's Milling & Lumber Co.* v. *The Queen* (1888), 14 App. Cas. 46. In that case Lord Watson acknowledged the existence of aboriginal title but said it had its origin in the *Royal Proclamation*. In this respect *Calder* is consistent with the position of Chief Justice Marshall in the leading American cases of *Johnson and Graham's Lessee* v. *M'Intosh* (1823), 8 Wheaton 543, 21 U.S. 240, and *Worcester* v. *State of Georgia* (1832), 6 Peters 515, 31 U.S. 530, cited by Judson and Hall JJ. in their respective judgments.

In *Johnson* v. *M'Intosh* Marshall C.J., although he acknowledged the *Royal Proclamation* of 1763 as one basis for recognition of Indian title, was none the less of opinion that the rights of Indians in the lands they traditionally occupied prior to European colonization both predated and survived the claims to sovereignty made by various European nations in the territories of the North American continent. The principle of discovery which justified these claims gave the ultimate title in the land in a particular area to the nation which had discovered and claimed it. In that respect at least the Indians' rights in the land were obviously diminished; but their rights of occupancy and possession remained unaffected, Marshall C.J., explained this principle as follows, at pp. 573–74:

> The exclusion of all other Europeans, necessarily gave to the nation making the discovery the sole right of acquiring the soil from the natives, and establishing settlements upon it.... It was a right which all asserted for themselves, and to the assertion of which, by others, all assented.
>
> Those relations which were to exist between the discoverer and the natives, were to be regulated by themselves. The rights thus acquired being exclusive, no other power could interpose between them.
>
> In the establishment of these relations, the rights of the original inhabitants were, in no instance, entirely disregarded; but were necessarily, to a considerable extent, impaired. <u>They were admitted to be the rightful occupants of the soil, with a legal as well as just claim to retain possession of it</u>, and to use it according to their own discretion; but their rights to complete sovereignty, as independent nations, were necessarily diminished, and their power to dispose of the soil at their own will, to whomsoever they pleased, was denied by the original fundamental principle, that discovery gave exclusive title to those who made it. [Emphasis added.]

The principle that a change in sovereignty over a particular territory does not in general affect the presumptive title of the inhabitants was approved by the Privy Council in *Amodu Tijani* v. *Secretary, Southern Nigeria*, [1921] 2 A.C. 399. That principle supports the assumption implicit in *Calder* that Indian title is an independent legal right which, although recognized by the *Royal Proclamation* of 1763, none the less predates it. For this reason

Kinloch v. *Secretary of State for India*, *supra*; *Tito* v. *Waddell*, *supra*, and the other "political trust" decisions are inapplicable to the present case. The "political trust" cases concerned essentially the distribution of public funds or other property held by the government. In each case the party claiming to be beneficiary under a trust depended entirely on statute, ordinance or treaty as the basis for its claim to an interest in the funds in question. The situation of Indians is entirely different. Their interest in their lands is a pre-existing legal right not created by *Royal Proclamation*, by s. 18(1) of the *Indian Act*, or by any other executive order or legislative provision.

It does not matter, in my opinion, that the present case is concerned with the interest of an Indian band in a reserve rather than with unrecognized aboriginal title in traditional tribal lands. The Indian interest in the land is the same in both cases: see *A.-G. Que.* v. *A.-G. Can.* (1920), 56 D.L.R. 373 at pp. 378–79, [1921] 1 A.C. 401 at pp. 410–11 (the *Star Chrome* case). It is worth noting, however, that the reserve in question here was created out of the ancient tribal territory of the Musqueam band by the unilateral action of the Colony of British Columbia, prior to Confederation.

The Nature of Indian Title

In the *St. Catherine's Milling* case, *supra*, the Privy Council held that the Indians had a "personal and usufructuary right" [p. 54] in the lands which they had traditionally occupied. Lord Watson said that "there has been all along vested in the Crown a substantial and paramount estate, underlying the Indian title, which became a *plenum dominium* whenever the title was surrendered or otherwise extinguished" [at p. 55]. He reiterated this idea, stating that the Crown "has all along had a present proprietary estate in the land, upon which the Indian title was a mere burden" [at p. 58]. This view of aboriginal title was affirmed by the Privy council in the *Star Chrome* case. In *Amodu Tijani, supra*, Viscount Haldane, adverting to the *St. Catherine's Milling* and *Star Chrome* decisions, explained the concept of a usufructuary right as "a mere qualification of or burden on the radical or final title of the Sovereign" [p. 403]. He described the title of the Sovereign as a pure legal estate, but one which could be qualified by a right of "beneficial user" that did not necessarily take the form of an estate in land. Indian title in Canada was said to be one illustration "of the necessity for getting rid of the assumption that the ownership of land naturally breaks itself up into estates, conceived as creatures of inherent legal principle" [p. 403]. Chief Justice Marshall took a similar view in *Johnson* v. *M'Intosh*, *supra*, saying, "All our institutions recognize the absolute title of the Crown, subject only to the Indian right of occupancy" [p. 588].

It should be noted that the Privy Council's emphasis on the personal nature of aboriginal title stemmed in part from constitutional arrangements peculiar to Canada. The Indian territory at issue in *St. Catherine's Milling* was land which in 1867 had been vested in the Crown subject to the interest of the Indians. The Indians' interest was "an interest other than that of the Province", within the meaning of a s. 109 of the *Constitution Act*, 1867. Section 109 provides:

> **109.** All Lands, Mines, Minerals, and Royalties belonging to the several Provinces of Canada, Nova Scotia, and New Brunswick at the Union, and all Sums then due or payable for such Lands, Mines, Minerals, or Royalties, shall belong to the several Provinces of Ontario, Quebec, Nova Scotia, and New Brunswick in which the same are situate or arise subject to any Trusts existing in respect thereof, and to any interest other than that of the Province in the same.

When the land in question in *St. Catherine's Milling* was subsequently disencumbered of the native title upon its surrender to the federal government by the Indian occupants in 1873, the entire beneficial interest in the land was held to have passed, because of the personal and usufructuary nature of the Indians' right, to the Province of Ontario under s. 109 rather than to Canada. The same constitutional issue arose recently in this court in *Smith et al.* v. *The Queen* (1983), 147 D.L.R. (3d) 237, [1983] 1 S.C.R. 554, 47 N.R. 132 *sub nom. Government of Canada* v. *Smith*, in which the court held that the Indian right in a reserve, being personal, could not be transferred to a grantee, whether an individual or the Crown. Upon surrender the right disappeared "in the process of release".

No such constitutional problem arises in the present case, since in 1938 the title to all Indian reserves in British Columbia was transferred by the provincial government to the Crown in right of Canada.

It is true that in contexts other than the constitutional the characterization of Indian title as "a personal and usufructuary right" has sometimes been questioned. In *Calder, supra*, for example, Judson J. intimated at p. 156 D.L.R., p. 328 S.C.R., that this characterization was not helpful in determining the nature of Indian title. In *A.-G. Can.* v. *Giroux*

(1916), 30 D.L.R. 123, 53 S.C.R. 172, Duff J., speaking for himself and Anglin J., distinguished *St. Catherine's Milling* on the ground that the statutory provisions in accordance with which the reserve in question in *Giroux* had been created conferred beneficial ownership on the Indian band which occupied the reserve. In *Cardinal* v. *A.-G. Alta.* (1973), 40 D.L.R. (3d) 553, [1974] S.C.R. 695, 13, C.C.C. (2d) 1, Laskin J., dissenting on another point, accepted the possibility that Indians may have a beneficial interest in a reserve. The Alberta Court of Appeal in *Western Industrial Contractors Ltd.* v. *Sarcee Developments Ltd.* (1979), 98 D.L.R. (3d) 424, [1979] 3 W.W.R. 631 *sub nom. Western Int'l Contractors Ltd.* v. *Sarcee Developments Ltd.*, 15 A.R. 309, accepted the proposition that an Indian band does indeed have a beneficial interest in its reserve. In the present case this was the view as well of Le Dain J. in the Federal Court of Appeal. See also the judgment of Kellock J. in *Miller* v. *The King*, [1950] 1 D.L.R. 513, [1950] S.C.R. 168, in which he seems implicitly to adopt a similar position. None of these judgments mentioned in the *Star Chrome* case, however, in which the Indian interest in land specifically set aside as a reserve was held to be the same as the "personal and usufructuary right" which was discussed in *St. Catherine's Milling*.

It appears to me that there is no real conflict between the cases which characterize Indian title as a beneficial interest of some sort, and those which characterize it a personal, usufructuary right. Any apparent inconsistency derives from the fact that in describing what constitutes a unique interest in land the courts have almost inevitably found themselves applying a somewhat inappropriate terminology drawn from general property law. There is a core of truth in the way that each of the two lines of authority has described native title, but an appearance of conflict has none the less arisen because in neither case is the categorization quite accurate.

Indians have a legal right to occupy and possess certain lands, the ultimate title to which is in the Crown. While their interest does not, strictly speaking, amount to beneficial ownership, neither is its nature completely exhausted by the concept of a personal right. It is true that the *sui generis* interest which the Indians have in the land is personal in the sense that it cannot be transferred to a grantee, but it is also true, as will presently appear, that the interest gives rise upon surrender to a distinctive fiduciary obligation on the part of the Crown to deal with the land for the benefit of the surrendering Indians. These two aspects of Indian title go together, since the Crown's original purpose in declaring the Indians' interest to be inalienable otherwise than to the Crown, was to facilitate the Crown's ability to represent the Indians in dealings with third parties. The nature of the Indians' interest is therefore best characterized by its general inalienability coupled with the fact that the Crown is under an obligation to deal with the land on the Indians' behalf when the interest is surrendered. Any description of Indian title which goes beyond these two features is both unnecessary and potentially misleading.

The Crown's Fiduciary Obligation

The concept of fiduciary obligation originated long ago in the notion of breach of confidence, one of the original heads of jurisdiction in chancery. In the present appeal its relevance is based on the requirement of a "surrender" before Indian land can be alienated.

The *Royal Proclamation* of 1763 provided that no private person could purchase from the Indians any lands that the Proclamation had reserved to them, and provided further that all purchases had to be by and in the name of the Crown, in a public assembly of the Indians held by the governor or commander-in-chief of the colony in which the lands in question lay. As Lord Watson pointed out in *St. Catherine's Milling, supra*, at p. 54, this policy with respect to the sale or transfer of the Indians' interest in land has been continuously maintained by the British Crown, by the governments of the colonies when they became responsible for the administration of Indian affairs, and, after 1867, by the federal government of Canada. Successive federal statutes, predecessors to the present *Indian Act*, have all provided for the general inalienability of Indian reserve land except upon surrender to the Crown, the relevant provisions in the present Act being ss. 37–41.

The purpose of this surrender requirement is clearly to interpose the Crown between the Indians and prospective purchasers or lessees of their land, so as to prevent the Indians from being exploited. This is made clear in the *Royal Proclamation* itself, which prefaces the provision making the Crown an intermediary with a declaration that "great Frauds and Abuses have been committed in purchasing Lands of the Indians, to the great Prejudice of our Interest and to the great Dissatisfaction of the said Indians...". Through the confirmation in the *Indian Act* of the historic responsibility which the Crown has undertaken, to act on behalf of the Indians so as to protect their interests in transactions with third parties, Parliament has conferred upon the Crown a discretion to decide for itself where the Indians' best interests really lie. This is the effect of s. 18(1) of the Act.

This discretion on the part of the Crown, far from ousting, as the Crown contends, the jurisdiction of the courts to regulate the relationship between the Crown and Indians, has the effect of transforming the Crown's obligation into a fiduciary one. Professor Ernest Weinrib maintains in his article "The Fiduciary Obligation", 25 *U.T.L.J.* 1 (1975), at p. 7, that "the hallmark of a fiduciary relation is that the relative legal positions are such that one party is at the mercy of the other's discretion". Earlier, at p. 4, he puts the point in the following way:

> [Where there is a fiduciary obligation] there is a relation in which the principal's interests can be affected by, and are therefore dependent on, the manner in which the fiduciary uses the discretion which has been delegated to him. The fiduciary obligation is the law's blunt tool for the control of this discretion.

I make no comment upon whether this description is broad enough to embrace all fiduciary obligations. I do agree, however, that where by statute, agreement, or perhaps by unilateral undertaking, one party has an obligation to act for the benefit of another, and that obligation carries with it a discretionary power, the party thus empowered becomes a fiduciary. Equity will then supervise the relationship by holding him to the fiduciary's strict standard of conduct.

It is sometimes said that the nature of fiduciary relationships is both established and exhausted by the standard categories of agent, trustee, partner, director, and the like. I do not agree. It is the nature of the relationship, not the specific category of actor involved that gives rise to the fiduciary duty. The categories of fiduciary, like those of negligence, should not be considered closed: see, *e.g.*, *Laskin* v. *Bache & Co. Inc.* (1971), 23 D.L.R. (3d) 385 at p. 392, [1972] 1 O.R. 465 (C.A.); *Goldex Mines Ltd.* v. *Revill et al.* (1974), 54 D.L.R. (3d) 672 at p. 680, 7 O.R. 216 (C.A.) at p. 224.

It should be noted that fiduciary duties generally arise only with regard to obligations originating in a private law context. Public law duties, the performance of which requires the exercise of discretion, do not typically give rise to a fiduciary relationship. As the "political trust" cases indicate, the Crown is not normally viewed as a fiduciary in the exercise of its legislative or administrative function. The mere fact, however, that it is the Crown which is obligated to act on the Indians' behalf does not of itself remove the Crown's obligation from the scope of the fiduciary principle. As was pointed out earlier, the Indians' interest in land is an independent legal interest. It is not a creation of either the legislative or the executive branches of government. The Crown's obligation to the Indians with respect to that interest is therefore not a public law duty. While it is not a private law duty in the strict sense either, it is none the less in the nature of a private law duty. Therefore, in this *sui generis* relationship, it is not improper to regard the Crown as a fiduciary.

Section 18(1) of the *Indian Act* confers upon the Crown a broad discretion in dealing with surrendered land. In the present case, the document of surrender, set out in part earlier in these reasons, by which the Musqueam band surrendered the land at issue, confirms this discretion in the clause conveying the land to the Crown "in trust to lease ... upon such terms as the Government of Canada may deem most conducive to our Welfare and that of our people". When, as here, an Indian band surrenders its interest to the Crown, a fiduciary obligation takes hold to regulate the manner in which the Crown exercises its discretion in dealing with the land on the Indians' behalf.

. . . .

[Dickson J. elaborated on the nature of the fiduciary obligation of the Crown to the Indians, saying it was not a trust. As to whether there had been a breach of this obligation, Dickson J. concluded that:]

In obtaining without consultation a much less valuable lease than that promised, the Crown breached the fiduciary obligation it owed the band. It must make good the loss suffered in consequence.

. . . .

[Dickson J. then dealt with limitation of action, laches, and the measure of damages. Wilson J., with whom Ritchie and MacIntyre JJ. agreed, said, *inter alia*, that:]

While I am in agreement that s. 18 does not *per se* create a fiduciary obligation in the Crown with respect to Indian reserves, I believe that it recognizes the existence of such an obligation. The obligation has its roots in the aboriginal title of Canada's Indians as discussed in *Calder et al.* v. *A.-G. B.C.* (1973), 34 D.L.R. (3d) 145, [1973] S.C.R. 313, [1973] 4 W.W.R. 1. In that case the court did not find it necessary to define the precise nature of Indian title because the issue was whether or not it had been extinguished. However, in *St. Catherine's Milling & Lumber Co.* v. *The Queen* (1888), 14 App. Cas. 46 Lord Watson, speaking for the Privy Council, had stated at p. 54 that "the tenure of the Indians [is] a personal and usufructuary right". That description of the Indians' interest in reserve lands was approved by this court most recently in *Smith et al.* v. *The Queen* (1983), 147 D.L.R. (3d) 237, [1983] 1 S.C.R. 554, 47 N.R. 132 *sub nom. Government of Canada* v. *Smith*. It should be noted that no constitutional issue such as arose in the *St. Catherine's* and *Smith* cases arises in this case since title to Indian reserve land in British Columbia was transferred to the Crown in right of Canada in 1938: see British Columbia Orders-in-Council 208 and 1036 passed pursuant to art. 13 of the Terms of Union of 1870 [see R.S.C. 1970, App. II, No. 10].

. . . .

[In a separate judgment, Estey J. said *inter alia*, that after a "surrender" of Indian lands to effect an alternate use of the land for the benefit of the Indians, the relationship between the Crown and the Indians resembles that of an agency.]

5 Indian Treaties

(a) Indian Treaty Map†

See **Chapter 5.**

Map 1 (on p. 273) shows areas covered by the major land treaties and the first land claims agreements.

The shaded area marked "1763" indicates land exempted from most of the Indian provisions of the *Royal Proclamation* of 1763.

(b) Report of the Commissioner for Treaty Number 11‡

See **Chapter 5, Part 5.**

D.C. Scott, Esq.
Deputy Superintendent General
Department of Indian Affairs
Ottawa

Sir: — I have the honour to submit herewith the report on treaty made by me on authority granted by Order-in-Council, dated March 14, last, as Commissioner to negotiate a treaty with the Indians occupying the territory north of the 60th parallel and along the Mackenzie river and the Arctic ocean.

I left Edmonton on June 8, 1921, accompanied by Inspector W.B. Bruce, Constable Wood and Constable Campbell, of the Royal Canadian Mounted Police. Constable Campbell acted as my clerk for the summer.

Arriving at Fort McMurray on June 11, we left there on the 14th in a houseboat, the property of the Hudson's Bay Company, which company had made all arrangements for the transportation of the treaty party during the summer in the North.

We arrived at Fort Fitzgerald on June 18, crossed the portage to Fort Smith, and boarded the SS. *Mackenzie River* on June 20 for Fort Providence, at which place the first adhesion to Treaty 11 was to be taken. July 5 was the date set for the meeting of the Indians and myself to take place at Fort Providence, and, in order to arrive in good time, I thought it better for me and my party to proceed there by the SS. *Mackenzie River*, and let the houseboat take us up again at this point. The transportation of the houseboat across the portage at Fort Smith took several days.

On our arrival at Fort Providence, on June 20, I found the Indians were not at the post, as we were there before the date set for the meeting, so word was sent of my arrival, and the majority of the Prov-

† Map — "Indian Treaties" from *The Canadian Encyclopedia*, 2d ed., vol. II (Edmonton: Hurtig, 1988) at 1057. *The Canadian Encyclopedia* used by permission of McClelland & Stewart Ltd., The Canadian Publishers.

‡ Ottawa, October 12, 1921 (Ottawa: Queen's Printer, 1926).

INDIAN TREATIES

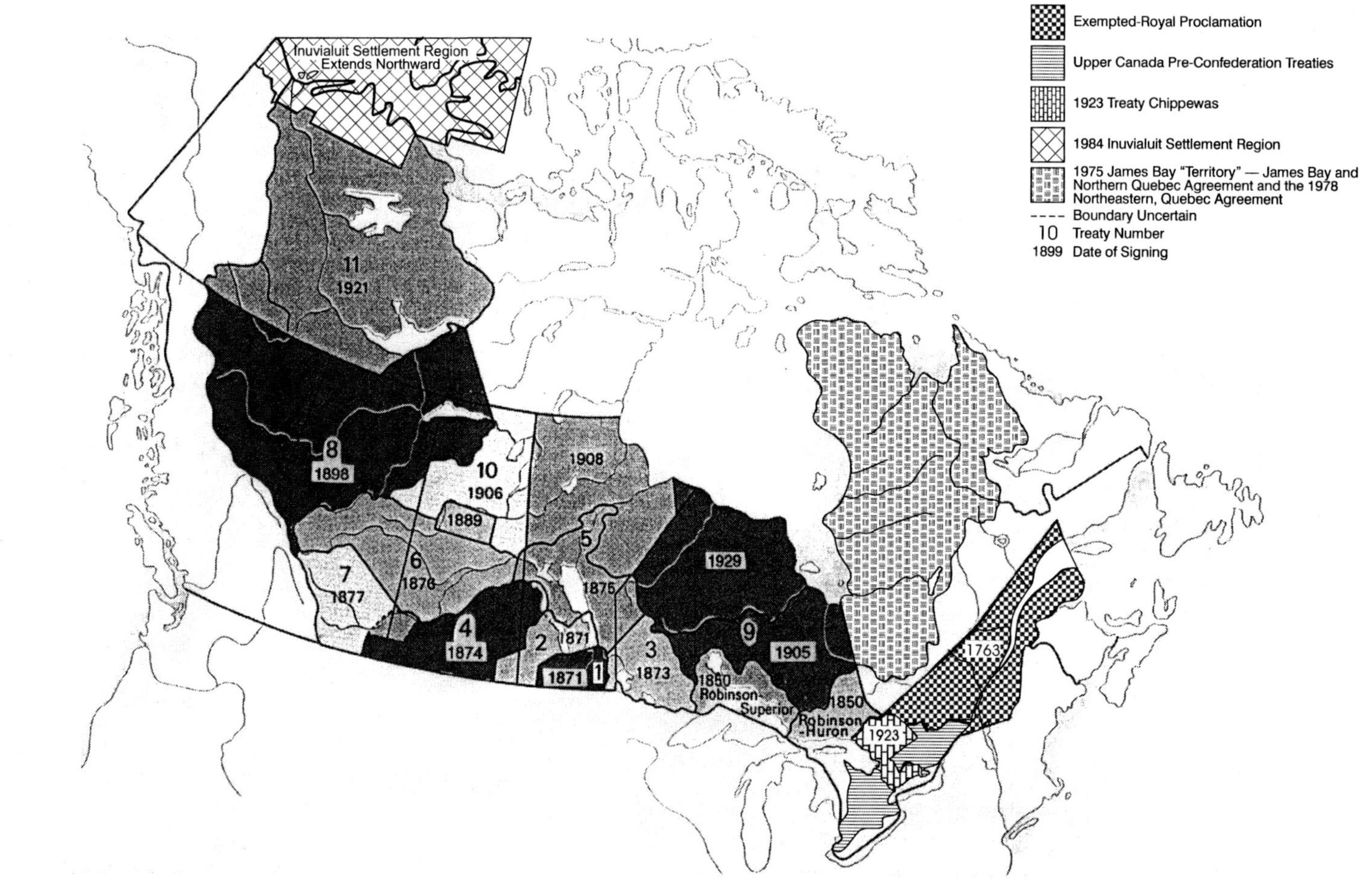

NOTE: This map includes the main traditional Indian treaties (from 1850 to 1923), and the three earliest land claims agreements (of 1975, 1978, and 1984).

idence Indians living at Willow Lake arrived on June 25, those at Trout Lake not till July 2. I had several meetings with them, and explained the terms of treaty. They were very apt in asking questions, and here, as in all the other posts where the treaty was signed, the questions asked and the difficulties encountered were much the same. The Indians seemed afraid, for one thing, that their liberty to hunt, trap and fish would be taken away or curtailed, but were assured by me that this would not be the case, and the Government will expect them to support themselves in their own way, and, in fact, that more twine for nets and more ammunition were given under the terms of this treaty than under any of the preceding ones; this went a long way to calm their fears. I also pointed out that any game laws made were to their advantage, and, whether they took treaty or not, they were subject to the laws of the Dominion. They also seemed afraid that they would be liable for military service if the treaty was signed, that they would be confined on the reserves, but, when told that they were exempt from military service, and that the reserves mentioned in the treaty would be of their own choosing, for their own use, and not for the white people, and that they would be free to come and go as they pleased, they were satisfied.

H.A. Conroy
Commr. Treaty No. 11

. . . .

TREATY NUMBER ELEVEN, 1921, WITH SUBSEQUENT ADHESIONS

Articles of a Treaty made and concluded on the several dates mentioned therein in the year of Our Lord One thousand Nine hundred and Twenty-One, between His Most Gracious Majesty George V, King of Great Britain and Ireland and the British Dominions beyond the Seas, by His Commissioner, Henry Anthony Conroy, Esquire of the City of Ottawa, of the One Part, and Slave, Dogrib, Loucheux, Hare and other Indians, inhabitants of the territory within the limits hereinafter defined and described, by their Chiefs and Headmen, hereunto subscribed, of the other part: —

WHEREAS, the Indians inhabiting the territory hereinafter defined have been convened to meet a commissioner representing His Majesty's Government of the Dominion of Canada at certain places in the said territory in this present year of 1921, to deliberate upon certain matters of interest to His Most Gracious Majesty, of the one part, and the said Indians of the other.

AND WHEREAS, the said Indians have been notified and informed by His Majesty's said commissioner that it is His desire to open for settlement, immigration, trade, travel, mining, lumbering and such other purposes as to His Majesty may seem meet, a tract of country bounded and described as hereinafter set forth, and to obtain the consent thereto of His Indian subjects inhabiting the said tract, and to make a treaty, so that there may be peace and goodwill between them and His Majesty's other subjects, and that His Indian people may know and be assured of what allowances they are to expect and receive from His Majesty's bounty and benevolence.

AND WHEREAS, the Indians of the said tract, duly convened in council at the respective points named hereunder, and being requested by His Majesty's Commissioner, to name certain Chiefs and Headmen, who should be authorized on their behalf to conduct such negotiations and sign any treaty to be founded thereon, and to become responsible to His Majesty for the faithful performance by their respective bands of such obligations as shall be assumed by them, the said Indians have therefore acknowledged for that purpose the several chiefs and Headmen who have subscribed thereto.

AND WHEREAS, the said Commissioner has proceeded to negotiate a treaty with the Slave, Dogrib, Loucheux, Hare and other Indians inhabiting the district hereinafter defined and described, which has been agreed upon and concluded by the respective bands at the dates mentioned hereunder, the said Indians do hereby cede, release, surrender and yield up to the Government of the Dominion of Canada, for His Majesty the King and His Successors forever, all their rights, titles, and privileges whatsoever to the lands included within the following limits, that is to say:

> Commencing at the northwesterly corner of the territory ceded under the provisions of Treaty Number Eight; thence northeasterly along the height-of-land to the point where it intersects the boundary between the Yukon Territory and the Northwest Territories; thence northwesterly along the said boundary to the shore of the Arctic ocean; thence easterly along the said shore to the mouth of Coppermine river; thence southerly and southeasterly along the left bank of the said river to Lake Gras by way of Point

lake; thence along the southern shore of Lake Gras to a point situated northwest of the most western extremity of Aylmer lake; thence along the southern shore of Aylmer lake and following the right bank of the Lockhart river to Artillery lake; thence along the western shore of Artillery lake and following the right bank of the Lockhart river to the site of Old Fort Reliance where the said river enters Great Slave lake, this being the northeastern corner of the territory ceded under the provisions of Treaty Number Eight; thence westerly along the northern boundary of the said territory so ceded to the point of commencement; comprising an area of approximately three hundred and seventy-two thousand square miles.

AND ALSO, the said Indian rights, titles and privileges whatsoever to all other lands wherever situated in the Yukon Territory, the Northwest Territories or in any other portion of the Dominion of Canada.

To have and to hold the same to His Majesty the King and His Successors forever.

AND His Majesty the King hereby agrees with the said Indians that they shall have the right to pursue their usual vocations of hunting, trapping and fishing throughout the tract surrendered as heretofore described, subject to such regulations as may from time to time be made by the Government of the Country acting under the authority of His Majesty, and saving and excepting such tracts as may be required or taken up from time to time for settlement, mining, lumbering, trading or other purposes.

AND His Majesty the King hereby agrees and undertakes to lay aside reserves for each band, the same not to exceed in all one square mile for each family of five, or in that proportion for larger or smaller families;

PROVIDED, however, that His Majesty reserves the right to deal with any settlers within the boundaries of any lands reserved for any band as He may see fit; and also that the aforesaid reserves of land, or any interest therein, may be sold or otherwise disposed of by His Majesty's Government for the use and benefit of the said Indians entitled thereto, with their consent first had and obtained; but in no wise shall the said Indians, or any of them, be entitled to sell or otherwise alienate any of the lands allotted to them as reserves.

It is further agreed between his Majesty and His Indian subjects that such portions of the reserves and lands above indicated as may at any time be required for public works, buildings, railways, or roads of whatsoever nature may be appropriated for that purpose by His Majesty's Government of the Dominion of Canada, due compensation being made to the Indians for the value of any improvements thereon, and an equivalent in land, money or other consideration for the area of the reserve so appropriated.

And in order to show the satisfaction of His Majesty with the behaviour and good conduct of His Indian subjects, and in extinguishment of all their past claims herein above mentioned, He hereby, through his Commissioner, agrees to give each Chief a present of thirty-two dollars in cash, to each Headman, twenty-two dollars, and to every other Indian of whatever age of the families represented, at the time and place of payment, twelve dollars.

HIS MAJESTY, also agrees that during the coming year, and annually thereafter, He will cause to be paid to the said Indians in cash, at suitable places and dates, of which the said Indians shall be duly notified, to each Chief twenty-five dollars, to each Headman fifteen dollars, and to every other Indian of whatever age five dollars, to be paid only to heads of families for the members thereof, it being provided for the purposes of this Treaty that each band having at least thirty members may have a Chief, and that in addition to a Chief, each band may have Councillors or Headmen in the proportion of two to each two hundred members of the band.

FURTHER, His Majesty agrees that each Chief shall receive once and for all a silver medal, a suitable flag and a copy of this Treaty for the use of his band; and during the coming year, and every third year thereafter, each Chief and Headman shall receive a suitable suit of clothing.

FURTHER, His Majesty agrees to pay the salaries of teachers to instruct the children of said Indians in such manner as His Majesty's Government may deem advisable.

FURTHER, His Majesty agrees to supply once and for all to each Chief of a band that selects a reserve, ten axes, five hand-saws, five augers, one grindstone, and the necessary files and whetstones for the use of the band.

FURTHER, His Majesty agrees that, each band shall receive once and for all equipment for hunting, fishing and trapping to the value of fifty dollars for each family of such band, and that there shall be distributed annually among the Indians equipment, such as twine for nets, ammunition and trapping to the value of three dollars per head for each Indian who continues to follow the vocation of hunting, fishing and trapping.

FURTHER, His Majesty agrees that, in the event of any of the Indians aforesaid being desirous of following agricultural pursuits, such Indians shall receive such assistance as is deemed necessary for that purpose.

AND the undersigned Slave, Dogrib, Loucheux, Hare and other Chiefs and Headmen, on their own behalf and on behalf of all the Indians whom they represent, do hereby solemnly promise and engage to strictly observe this Treaty, and also to conduct and behave themselves as good loyal subjects of His Majesty the King.

THEY promise and engage that they will, in all respects, obey and abide by the law; that they will maintain peace between themselves and others of His Majesty's subjects, whether Indians, half-breeds or whites, now inhabiting and hereafter to inhabit any part of the said ceded territory; that they will not molest the person or property of any inhabitant of such ceded tract, or of any other district or country, or interfere with or trouble any person passing or travelling through the said tract or any part thereof, and that they will assist the officers of His Majesty in bringing to justice and punishment any Indian offending against the stipulations of this Treaty, or infringing the law in force in the country so ceded.

IN WITNESS WHEREOF, His Majesty's said Commissioner and the said Chiefs and Headmen have hereunto set their hands at the places and times set forth in the year herein first above written.

SIGNED AT PROVIDENCE on the twenty-seventh day of June, 1921, by His Majesty's Commissioner and the Chiefs and Headmen in the presence of the undersigned witnesses, after having been first interpreted and explained.

(c) *Simon v. The Queen*†

See **Chapter 5, Part 12.**

NOTE

Mr. Simon, a Mi'kmaq Indian, was charged with possession of a rifle and ammunition contrary to a provincial wildlife act. He relied on a 1752 agreement between the Nova Scotia governor and the Mi'kmaqs, which promised the Mi'kmaq "free liberty of Hunting & Fishing as usual". The provincial government raised several concerns about the status and effect of the 1752 agreement. Was it an Indian treaty? What did it guarantee? Could it protect Mr. Simon?

EXTRACT

[DICKSON C.J. for the Court:]

This case raises the important question of the interplay between the treaty rights of native peoples and provincial legislation. The right to hunt, which remains important to the livelihood and way of life of the Micmac people, has come into conflict with game preservation legislation in effect in the Province of Nova Scotia. The main question before this Court is whether, pursuant to a Treaty of 1752 between the British Crown and the Micmac, and to s. 88 of the *Indian Act*, R.S.C. 1970, c. I–6, the appellant, James Matthew Simon, enjoys hunting rights which preclude his prosecution for offences under the *Lands and Forests Act*, R.S.N.S. 1967, c. 163.

. . . .

The Treaty of 1752, the relevant part of which states at article 4 that the Micmacs have "free liberty of Hunting & Fishing as usual," provides:

. . . .

> 4. It is agreed that the said Tribe of Indians shall not be hindered from, but have free liberty of Hunting & Fishing as usual: and that if they shall think a Truckhouse needful at the River Chibenaccadie or any other place of their resort, they shall have the same built and proper Merchandize lodged therein, to be Exchanged for what the Indians shall have to dispose of,

† [1985] 2 S.C.R. 387 at 390, 392–93, 401–402, 404–408, 410, 413–14 (S.C.C.), rev'g 134 D.L.R. (3d) 76 (N.S.S.C.A.D.).

> and that in the mean time the said Indians shall have free liberty to bring for Sale to Halifax or any other Settlement within this Province, Skins, feathers, fowl, fish or any other thing they shall have to sell, where they shall have liberty to dispose thereof to the best Advantage. [Emphasis added.]

. . . .

The Treaty was entered into for the benefit of both the British Crown and the Micmac people, to maintain peace and order as well as to recognize and confirm the existing hunting and fishing rights of the Micmac. In my opinion, both the Governor and the Micmac entered into the Treaty with the intention of creating mutually binding obligations which would be solemnly respected. It also provided a mechanism for dispute resolution. The Micmac Chief and the three other Micmac signatories, as delegates of the Micmac people, would have possessed full capacity to enter into a binding treaty on behalf of the Micmac. Governor Hopson was the delegate and legal representative of His Majesty The King. It is fair to assume that the Micmac would have believed that Governor Hopson, acting on behalf of His Majesty The King, had the necessary authority to enter into a valid treaty with them. I would hold that the Treaty of 1752 was validly created by competent parties.

. . . .

The majority of the Nova Scotia Court of Appeal seemed to imply that the Treaty contained merely a general acknowledgement of pre-existing non-treaty aboriginal rights and not an independent source of protection of hunting rights upon which the appellant could rely. In my opinion, the Treaty, by providing that the Micmac should not be hindered from but should have free liberty of hunting and fishing as usual, constitutes a positive source of protection against infringements on hunting rights.

. . . .

Such an interpretation accords with the generally accepted view that Indian treaties should be given a fair, large and liberal construction in favour of the Indians. This principle of interpretation was most recently affirmed by this Court in *Nowegijick* v. *The Queen*, [1983] 1 S.C.R. 29. I had occasion to say the following at p. 36:

> It is legal lore that, to be valid, exemptions to tax laws should be clearly expressed. It seems to me, however, that treaties and statutes relating to Indians should be liberally construed and doubtful expressions resolved in favour of the Indians.... In *Jones* v. *Meehan*, 175 U.S. 1 (1899), it was held that Indian treaties "must ... be construed, not according to the technical meaning of [their] words ... but in the sense in which they would naturally be understood by the Indians."

. . . .

[Dickson C.J.C. added that the words "as usual" should not be construed so as to limit the Mi'kmaq to 1752 hunting methods or to hunting for non-commercial purposes.]

In considering the impact of subsequent hostilities on the peace Treaty of 1752, the parties looked to international law on treaty termination. While it may be helpful in some instances to analogize the principles of international treaty law to Indian treaties, the principles are not determinative. An Indian treaty is unique; it is an agreement *sui generis* which is neither created nor terminated according to the rules of international law.

. . . .

... Once it has been established that a valid treaty has been entered into, the party arguing for its termination bears the burden of proving the circumstances and events justifying termination. The inconclusive and conflicting evidence presented by the parties makes it impossible for this Court to say with any certainty what happened on the eastern coast of Nova Scotia 233 years ago. As a result, the Court is unable to resolve this historical question. The Crown has failed to prove that the Treaty of 1752 was terminated by subsequent hostilities.

I would note that there is nothing in the British conduct subsequent to the conclusion of the Treaty of 1752 and the alleged hostilities to indicate that the Crown considered the terms of the Treaty at an end.

. . . .

... The respondent submits that absolute title in the land covered by the Treaty lies with the Crown and, therefore, the Crown has the right to extinguish any Indian rights in such lands. The respondent further submits, based on *Isaac*, that the Crown, through occupancy by the white man under Crown grant or lease, has, in effect, extinguished native rights in Nova Scotia in territory situated outside of reserve lands. As the appellant was stopped on a highway outside the Shubenacadie Reserve, the respondent argues that the Treaty of 1752 affords no defence to the appellant regardless of whether the treaty is itself valid.

In my opinion, it is not necessary to come to a final decision on the respondent's argument. Given the serious and far-reaching consequences of a finding that a treaty right has been extinguished, it seems appropriate to demand strict proof of the fact of extinguishment in each case where the issue arises. As Douglas J. said in *United States* v. *Santa Fe Pacific R. Co.*, *supra*, at p. 354, "extinguishment cannot be lightly implied."

. . . .

The respondent tries to meet the apparent right of the appellant to transport a gun and ammunition by asserting that the treaty hunting rights have been extinguished. In order to succeed on this argument it is absolutely essential, it seems to me, that the respondent lead evidence as to where the appellant hunted or intended to hunt and what use has been and is currently made of those lands. It is impossible for this Court to consider the doctrine of extinguishment "in the air"; the respondent must anchor that argument in the bedrock of specific lands. That has not happened in this case. In the absence of evidence as to where the hunting occurred or was intended to occur, and the use of the lands in question, it would be impossible to determine whether the appellant's treaty hunting rights have been extinguished.

. . . .

The respondent argues that the appellant has not shown that he is a direct descendant of a member of the original Micmac Indian Band covered by the Treaty of 1752.

. . . .

With respect, I do not agree with the Appellate Division on this point. In my view, the appellant has established a sufficient connection with the Indian band, signatories to the Treaty of 1752. As noted earlier, this Treaty was signed by Major Jean Baptiste Cope, Chief of the Shubenacadie Micmac tribe, and three other members and delegates of the tribe. The Micmac signatories were described as inhabiting the eastern coast of Nova Scotia. The appellant admitted at trial that he was a registered Indian under the *Indian Act*, and was an "adult member of the Shubenacadie-Indian Brook Band of Micmac Indians and was a member of the Shubenacadie Band Number 02".

The appellant is, therefore, a Shubenacadie-Micmac Indian, living in the same area as the original Micmac Indian tribe, party to the Treaty of 1752.

This evidence alone, in my view, is sufficient to prove the appellant's connection to the tribe originally covered by the Treaty. True, this evidence is not conclusive proof that the appellant is a direct descendant of the Micmac Indians covered by the Treaty of 1752. It must, however, be sufficient, for otherwise no Micmac Indian would be able to establish descendancy. The Micmacs did not keep written records. Micmac traditions are largely oral in nature. To impose an impossible burden of proof would, in effect, render nugatory any right to hunt that a present-day Shubenacadie Micmac Indian would otherwise be entitled to invoke based on this Treaty.

. . . .

Section 88 of the *Indian Act* stipulates that, "Subject to the terms of any treaty ... all laws of general application from time to time in force in any province are applicable to and in respect of Indians in the province...."

. . . .

In my view, Parliament intended to include within the operation of s. 88 all agreements concluded by the Crown with the Indians that would otherwise be enforceable treaties, whether land was ceded or not.

. . . .

... The Treaty was an exchange of solemn promises between the Micmacs and the King's representative entered into to achieve and guarantee peace. It is an enforceable obligation between the Indians and the white man and, as such, falls within the meaning of the word "treaty" in s. 88 of the *Indian Act*.

. . . .

In my opinion, s. 150 of the *Lands and Forests Act* of Nova Scotia restricts the appellant's right to hunt under the Treaty. The section clearly places seasonal limitations and licensing requirements, for the purposes of wildlife conservation, on the right to possess a rifle and ammunition for the purposes of hunting. The restrictions imposed in this case conflict, therefore, with the appellant's right to possess a firearm and ammunition in order to exercise his free liberty to hunt over the lands covered by the Treaty. As noted, it is clear that under s. 88 of the *Indian Act* provincial legislation cannot restrict native treaty rights. If conflict arises, the terms of the treaty prevail. Therefore, by virtue of s. 88 of the *Indian Act*, the clear terms of article 4 of the Treaty must prevail over s. 150(1) of the provincial *Lands and Forests Act*.

(d) *R. v. Sioui*†

See **Chapter 5, Part 13**.

NOTE

Four Huron Band Indians were charged with cutting trees and making fires in a provincial park, contrary to regulations under the provincial park act. In their defence, they relied on a 1760 document in which Governor James Murray had assured the Hurons of "the free Exercise of their Religion, their Customs, and Liberty of trading with the English." The document was not signed by the Hurons. It referred to no particular territory. Was it a treaty? What was its effect?

EXTRACT

[LAMER J. for the Court:]

Facts and Relevant Legislation

The four respondents were convicted by the Court of Sessions of the Peace of cutting down trees, camping and making fires in places not designated in Jacques-Cartier Park contrary to ss. 9 and 37 of the *Regulation respecting the Parc de la Jacques-Cartier* [Order-in-Council 3108–81, November 11, 1981 (1981), 113 *O.G.* II, 3518], adopted pursuant to the *Parks Act*, R.S.Q. 1977, c. P–9. The regulations state that:

> **9.** In the Park, users may not:
>
> 1. Destroy, mutilate, remove or introduce any kind of plant or part thereof.
>
> . . . .
>
> However, the collection of edible vegetable products is authorized solely for the purpose of consumption as food on the site, except in the preservation zones where it is forbidden at all times;
>
> . . . .
>
> **37.** Camping and fires are permitted only in the places designated and arranged for those purposes.

The *Parks Act*, under which the foregoing regulations were adopted, provides the following penalties for an offence:

> **11.** Every person who infringes this act or the regulations is guilty of an offence and liable on summary proceedings, in addition to the costs, to a fine of not less than $50 nor more than $1,000 in the case of an individual and to a fine of not less than $200 nor more than $5,000 in the case of a corporation.

The respondents appealed unsuccessfully to the Superior Court against this judgment by way of trial *de novo*. However, the Court of Appeal allowed their appeal and acquitted the respondents, Jacques J.A. dissenting.

The respondents are Indians within the meaning of the *Indian Act*, R.S.C. 1985, c. I–5 (formerly R.S.C. 1970, c. I–6), and are members of the Huron Band on the Lorette Indian Reserve. They admit that they committed the acts with which they were charged in Jacques-Cartier Park, which is located outside the boundaries of the Lorette Reserve. However, they alleged that they were practising certain ancestral customs and religious rites which are the

† [1990] 1 S.C.R. 1025 at 1030–31, 1035–36, 1043–45, 1052–53, 1055–56, 1060–61, 1066–74 (S.C.C.); aff'g [1987] R.J.Q. 1722 (Q.C.A.), which rev'd the decision of Desjardins J. (Q.S.C.: J.E. 85–947).

subject of a treaty between the Hurons and the British, a treaty which brings s. 88 of the *Indian Act* into play and exempts them from compliance with the regulations. Section 88 of the *Indian Act* states that:

> **88.** Subject to the terms of any treaty and any other Act of Parliament, all laws of general application from time to time in force in any province are applicable to and in respect of Indians in the province, except to the extent that those laws are inconsistent with this Act or any order, rule, regulation or by-law made thereunder, and except to the extent that those laws make provision for any matter for which provision is made by or under this Act.

The document the respondents rely on in support of their contentions is dated September 5, 1760, and signed by Brigadier General James Murray. It reads as follows:

> THESE are to certify that the CHIEF of the HURON Tribe of Indians, having come to me in the name of His Nation, to submit to His BRITANNICK MAJESTY, and make Peace, has been received under my Protection, with his whole Tribe; and henceforth no English Officer or party is to molest, or interrupt them in returning to their Settlement at LORETTE; and they are received upon the same terms with the Canadians, being allowed the free Exercise of their Religion, their Customs, and Liberty of trading with the English: — recommending it to the Officers commanding the Posts, to treat them kindly.
>
> Given under my hand at Longueil, this 5th day of September, 1760.
>
> By the Genl's Command, JA. MURRAY
JOHN COSNAN,
Adjut. Genl.

The Hurons had been in the Quebec area since about 1650, after having had to leave their ancestral lands located in territory which is now in Ontario. In 1760, they were settled at Lorette on land given to them by the Jesuits 18 years earlier and made regular use of the territory of Jacques-Cartier Park at that time.

. . . .

As the Chief Justice said in *Simon*, *supra*, treaties and statutes relating to Indians should be liberally construed and uncertainties resolved in favour of the Indians [at p. 257 C.C.C., p. 409 D.L.R.]. In our quest for the legal nature of the document of September 5, 1760, therefore we should adopt a broad and generous interpretation of what constitutes a treaty.

In my opinion, this liberal and generous attitude, heedful of historical fact, should also guide us in examining the preliminary question of the capacity to sign a treaty, as illustrated by *Simon* and *White and Bob*.

Finally, once a valid treaty is found to exist, that treaty must in turn be given a just, broad and liberal construction....

. . . .

Legal Nature of the Document of September 5, 1760

Constituent Elements of a Treaty

In *Simon* this court noted that a treaty with the Indians is unique, that it is an agreement *sui generis* which is neither created nor terminated according to the rules of international law. In that case the accused had relied on an agreement concluded in 1752 between Governor Hopson and the Micmac Chief Cope, and the Crown disputed that this was a treaty. The following are two extracts illustrating the reasons relied on by the Chief Justice in concluding that a treaty had been concluded between the Micmacs and the British Crown [at pp. 250–51 and 257 C.C.C., pp. 401 and 409 D.L.R.]:

> In my opinion, both the Governor and the Micmac entered into the treaty with the intention of creating mutually binding obligations which would be solemnly respected. It also provided a mechanism for dispute resolution.
>
> . . . .
>
> The treaty was an exchange of solemn promises between the Micmacs and the King's representative entered into to achieve and guarantee peace. It is an enforceable obligation between the Indians and the white man and, as such, falls within the meaning of the word "treaty" in s. 88 of the *Indian Act*.

From these extracts it is clear that what characterizes a treaty is the intention to create obligations, the presence of mutually binding obligations and a certain measure of solemnity....

. . . .

The decision of the Ontario Court of Appeal in *R.* v. *Taylor and Williams* (1981), 62 C.C.C. (2d) 227, 34 O.R. (2d) 360, also provides valuable assistance by listing a series of factors which are relevant to analysis of the historical background. In that case the court had to interpret a treaty, and not determine the legal nature of a document, but the factors mentioned may be just as useful in determining the existence of a treaty as in interpreting it. In particular, they assist in determining the intent of the parties to enter into a treaty. Among these factors are:

1. continuous exercise of a right in the past and at present;
2. the reasons why the Crown made a commitment;
3. the situation prevailing at the time the document was signed;
4. evidence of relations of mutual respect and esteem between the negotiators; and
5. the subsequent conduct of the parties.

. . . .

I consider that, instead, we can conclude from the historical documents that both Great Britain and France felt that the Indian nations had sufficient independence and played a large enough role in North America for it to be good policy to maintain relations with them very close to those maintained between sovereign nations.

The mother countries did everything in their power to secure the alliance of each Indian nation and to encourage nations allied with the enemy to change sides. When these efforts met with success, they were incorporated in treaties of alliance or neutrality. This clearly indicates that the Indian nations were regarded in their relations with the European nations which occupied North America as independent nations. The papers of Sir William Johnson [*The Papers of Sir William Johnson*, 14 volumes], who was in charge of Indian affairs in British North America, demonstrate the recognition by Great Britain that nation-to-nation relations had to be conducted with the North American Indians....

. . . .

This "generous" policy which the British chose to adopt also found expression in other areas. The British Crown recognized that the Indians had certain ownership rights over their land, it sought to establish trade with them which would rise above the level of exploitation and give them a fair return. It also allowed them autonomy in their internal affairs, intervening in this area as little as possible.

Whatever the similarities between a document recording the laying down of arms by French soldiers or Canadians and the document at issue, the analogy does not go so far as to preclude the conclusion that the document was none the less a treaty.

Such a document could not be regarded as a treaty so far as the French and the Canadians were concerned because under international law they had no authority to sign such a document: they were governed by a European nation which alone was able to represent them in dealings with other European nations for the signature of treaties affecting them. The colonial powers recognized that the Indians had the capacity to sign treaties directly with the European nations occupying North American territory. The *sui generis* situation in which the Indians were placed had forced the European mother countries to acknowledge that they had sufficient autonomy for the valid creation of solemn agreements which were called "treaties", regardless of the strict meaning given to that word then and now by international law. The question of the competence of the Hurons and of the French or the Canadians is essential to the question of whether a treaty exists. The question of capacity has to be examined from a fundamentally different viewpoint and in accordance with different principles for each of these groups. Thus, I reject the argument that the legal nature of the document at issue must necessarily be interpreted in the same way as the capitulations of the French and the Canadians. The historical context which I have briefly reviewed even supports the proposition that both the British and the Hurons could have intended to enter into a treaty on September 5, 1760. I rely, in particular, on Great Britain's stated wish to form alliances with as many Indians as possible and on the demoralizing effect for the French, the Canadians and their allies which would result from the loss of this longstanding Indian ally whose allegiance to the French cause had until then been very seldom shaken.

. . . .

I am therefore of the view that the document of September 5, 1760, is a treaty within the meaning of s. 88 of the *Indian Act*. At this point, the appellant raises two arguments against its application to the present case. First, he argues that the treaty has been extinguished. In the event that it has not been, he argues that the treaty is not such as to render ss. 9 and 37 of the *Regulation respecting the Parc de la Jacques-Cartier* inoperative. Let us first consider whether on May 29, 1982, the date on which the respondents engaged in the activities which are the subject of the charges, the treaty still had any legal effects.

. . . .

Legal Effects of Treaty of September 5, 1760, on May 29, 1982

Neither the documents nor the legislative and administrative history to which the appellant referred the court contain any express statement that the treaty of September 5, 1760, has been extinguished. Even assuming that a treaty can be extinguished implicitly, a point on which I express no opinion here, the appellant was not able in my view to meet the criterion stated in *Simon* regarding the quality of evidence that would be required in any case to support a conclusion that the treaty had been extinguished. That case clearly established that the onus is on the party arguing that the treaty has terminated to show the circumstances and events indicating it has been extinguished. This burden can only be discharged by strict proof, as the Chief Justice said at p. 253 C.C.C., p. 405 D.L.R.:

> Given the serious and far-reaching consequences of a finding that a treaty right has been extinguished, it seems appropriate to demand strict proof of the fact of extinguishment in each case where the issue arises.

The appellant did not submit any persuasive evidence of extinguishment of the treaty....

. . . .

The question that arises at this point is as to whether the treaty is capable of rendering ss. 9 and 37 of the regulations inoperative. To answer this it will now be necessary to consider the territorial scope of the rights guaranteed by the treaty, since the appellant recognizes that the activities with which the respondents are charged are customary or religious in nature.

Territorial Scope of Rights Guaranteed by Treaty of September 5, 1760

Although the document of September 5th is a treaty within the meaning of s. 88 of the *Indian Act*, that does not necessarily mean that the respondents are exempt from the application of the *Regulation respecting the Parc de la Jacques-Cartier*. It is still necessary that the treaty protect activities of the kind with which the respondents are charged cover the territory of Jacques-Cartier Park. The appellant argues that the territorial scope of the treaty does not extend to the territory of the park. The respondents, on the other hand, argue that the treaty confers personal rights on them and that they are in no way seeking to assert rights of a territorial nature.

Although this case does not involve a territorial claim as such, in that the Hurons are not claiming control over territory, I am of the view that exercise of the right they are claiming has an essential territorial aspect. The respondents argue that they have a right to carry on their customs and religious rites in a specific territory, namely, that of the park. The substantive content of the right cannot be considered apart from its territorial content. Just as it would distort the nature of a right of way to consider it while ignoring its territorial aspect, one cannot logically disregard the territorial aspect of the substantive rights guaranteed by the treaty of September 5, 1760. The respondents must therefore show that the treaty guaranteed their right to carry on their customs and religious rites in the territory of Jacques-Cartier Park.

The treaty gives the Hurons the freedom to carry on their customs and their religion. No mention is made in the treaty itself of the territory over which these rights may be exercised. There is also no indication that the territory of what is now Jacques Cartier Park was contemplated. However, for a freedom to have real value and meaning, it must be possible to exercise it somewhere. That does not mean, despite the importance of the rights concerned, that the Indians can exercise it anywhere. Our analysis will be confined to setting the limits of the promise made in the treaty, since the respondents have at no time based their argument on the existence of aboriginal rights protecting the activities with which they are charged.

The respondents suggest that the treaty gives them the right to carry on their customs and religion in the territory of the park because it is part of the territory frequented by the Hurons in 1760, namely, the area between the Saguenay and the St-Maurice. In their submission, customs as they existed at the time of the treaty and as they might reasonably be expected to develop subsequently are what the British Crown undertook to preserve and foster.

The appellant argued in the Court of Appeal that the free exercise of the customs mentioned in the document of September 5, 1760, has to be limited to the Lorette territory, a territory of 40 arpents by 40 arpents. In this court, he argues that even if the treaty covers the activities with which the respondents are charged, these rights must be exercised in accordance with the legislation designed to protect users of the park and to preserve it. He further argues that, except as regards the cutting of trees, the legislation only affects the way in which the right can be exercised, not the substance of the right. This should be a sufficient basis for requiring the Hurons to observe the legislation. In his intervention, the Attorney-General of Canada argues that the respondents' claim is essentially a territorial one and that in order to establish their rights, the respondents must show a connection between the rights claimed and their exercise in a given territory. He is of the view that the document in the present case does not connect the freedom of exercise of religion, customs and trade with the English to any territory.

In my view, the treaty essentially has to be interpreted by determining the intention of the parties on the territorial question at the time it was concluded. It is not sufficient to note that the treaty is silent on this point. We must also undertake the task of interpreting the treaty on the territorial question with the same generous approach toward the Indians that applied in considering earlier questions. Now as then, we must do our utmost to act in the spirit of *Simon*.

The historical context, which has been used to demonstrate the existence of the treaty, may equally assist us in interpreting the extent of the rights contained in it. As MacKinnon J.A. said in *Taylor and Williams, supra*, at 232:

> Cases on Indian or aboriginal rights can never be determined in a vacuum. It is of importance to consider the history and oral traditions of the tribes concerned, and the surrounding circumstances at the time of the treaty, relied on by both parties, in determining the treaty's effect.

Before I again turn to history, the problems raised by the territorial question should be briefly stated. There are two rights in opposition here: the provincial Crown's right of ownership over the territory of the park and the Hurons' right to exercise their religion and ancestral customs on this land. The ownership right suggests that ordinarily the Crown can do whatever it likes with its land. On the other hand, a very special importance seems to attach to territories traditionally frequented by the Hurons so that their traditional religious rites and ancestral customs will have their full meaning. Further, the Hurons are trying to protect the possibility of carrying on these rites and customs near Lorette on territory which they feel is suited to such purposes.

. . . .

... The interpretation which I think is called for when we give the historical context its full meaning is that Murray and the Hurons contemplated that the rights guaranteed by the treaty could be exercised over the entire territory frequented by the Hurons at the time, so long as the carrying on of the customs and rites is not incompatible with the particular use made by the Crown of this territory.

. . . .

... [I]n view of the absence of any express mention of the territorial scope of the treaty, it has to be assumed that the parties to the treaty of September 5th intended to reconcile the Hurons' need to protect the exercise of their customs and the desire of the British conquerors to expand. Protecting the exercise of the customs in all parts of the territory frequented when it is not incompatible with its occupancy is in my opinion the most reasonable way of reconciling the competing interests. This, in my view, is the definition of the common intent of the parties which best reflects the actual intent of the Hurons and of Murray on September 5, 1760. Defining the common intent of the parties on the question of territory in this way makes it possible to give full effect to the spirit of conciliation, while respecting the practical requirements of the British. This gave the English the necessary flexibility to be able to respond in due course to the increasing need to use Canada's resources, in the event that Canada remained under British suzerainty. The Hurons, for their part, were protecting their customs wherever their exercise would not be prejudicial to the use to which the territory concerned would be put. The Hurons could not reasonably expect that the use would forever remain what it was in 1760. Before the treaty was signed, they had carried on their customs in accordance with restrictions already imposed by an occupancy incompatible with such exercise. The Hurons were only asking to be permitted to continue to carry on their customs on the lands frequented to the extent that those customs did not interfere with enjoyment of the lands by their occupier. I readily accept that the Hurons were probably not aware of the legal consequences, and in particular of the right to occupy to the exclusion of others, which the main European legal systems attached to the concept of private ownership. None the less I cannot believe that the Hurons ever believed that the treaty gave them the right to cut down trees in the garden of a house as part of their right to carry on their customs.

Jacques-Cartier Park falls into the category of land occupied by the Crown, since the province has set it aside for a specific use. What is important is not so much that the province has legislated with respect to this territory but that it is using it, is in fact occupying the space. As occupancy has been established, the question is whether the type of occupancy to which the park is subject is incompatible with the exercise of the activities with which the respondents were charged, as these undoubtedly constitute religious customs or rites. Since, in view of the situation in 1760, we must assume some limitation on the exercise of rights protected by the treaty, it is up to the Crown to prove that its occupancy of the territory cannot be accommodated to a reasonable exercise of the Hurons' rights.

The Crown presented evidence on such compatibility but that evidence did not persuade me that exercise of the rites and customs at issue here is incompatible with the occupancy.

Jacques-Cartier Park is a park that falls within the class of conservation parks. The *Parks Act*, R.S.Q. 1977, c. P–9, describes them in the following way:

> **1.** ...
> (c) "conservation park" means a park primarily intended to ensure the permanent protection of territory representative of the natural regions of Québec, or of natural sites presenting exceptional features, while rendering them accessible to the public for the purposes of education and cross-country recreation;

Cross-country recreation is given the following definition, again in s. 1 of the Act:

> (e) "cross-country recreation" means a type of recreation characterized by the use of little frequented territory and the use of relatively simple equipment;

Under the *Regulation respecting the Parc de la Jacques-Cartier*, the park is divided into environmental zones, which are portions of the park for moderate use set aside for the discovery and exploration of the environment, and preservation zones, for limited use and set aside for the conservation, observation and enjoyment of the environment.

For the exercise of rites and customs to be incompatible with the occupancy of the park by the Crown, it must not only be contrary to the purpose underlying that occupancy, it must prevent the realization of that purpose. First, we are dealing with Crown lands, lands which are held for the benefit of the community. Exclusive use is not an essential aspect of public ownership. Secondly, I do not think that the activities described seriously compromise the Crown's objectives in occupying the park. Neither the representative nature of the natural region where the park is located nor the exceptional nature of this natural site are threatened by the collecting of a few plants, the setting up of a tent using a few branches picked up in the area or the making of a fire according to the rules dictated by caution to avoid fires. These activities also present no obstacle to cross-country recreation. I therefore conclude that it has not been established that occupancy of the territory of Jacques-Cartier Park is incompatible with the exercise of Huron rites and customs with which the respondents are charged.

Conclusion

For all these reasons, I would dismiss the appeal with costs.

I would dispose of the constitutional questions stated by the Chief Justice as follows:

1. Does the following document, signed by General Murray on 5 September 1760, constitute a treaty within the meaning of s. 88 of the *Indian Act* [R.S.C. 1970, c. I–6]?

   > "THESE are to certify that the Chief of the Huron tribe of Indians, having come to me in the name of His Nation, to submit to His BRITANNICK MAJESTY, and make Peace, has been received under my protection, with his whole Tribe; and henceforth no English Officer or party is to molest, or interrupt them in returning to their Settlement at LORETTE; and they are received upon the same terms with the Canadians, being allowed the free Exercise of their Religion, their Customs, and Liberty of trading with the English: — recommending it to the Officers commanding the Posts, to treat them kindly.
   >
   > Given under my hand at Longueil, this 5th day of September, 1760.
   >
   > By the Genl's Command, JA. Murray
   > John Cosnan,
   > Adjut. Genl."

   Answer: Yes.

2. If the answer to question 1 is in the affirmative, was the "treaty" still operative on 29 May 1982, at the time when the alleged offences were committed?

   Answer: Yes.

3. If the answer to questions 1 and 2 are in the affirmative, are the terms of the document of such a nature as to make ss. 9 and 37 of the *Regulation respecting the Parc de la Jacques-Cartier* [Order-in-Council 3108–81, *Gazette*

officielle du Québec, Part II, November 25, 1981, pp. 3518 *et seq.*] made under the *Parks Act* [R.S.Q., c. P–9] unenforceable in respect of the respondents?

Answer: Yes.

Appeal dismissed.

(e) *Ontario (A.G.) v. Bear Island Foundation*†

See **Chapter 5, Part 14**.

NOTE

Representatives of the Temagami Band claimed Aboriginal rights in an area covered by an 1850 Indian treaty. They argued that the treaty did not apply to them because their ancestors had not signed it. Were they bound by the treaty?

EXTRACT

[BY THE COURT:]

The respondent Attorney-General for Ontario brought action against the appellant, the Bear Island Foundation, after the latter had registered cautions against tracts of unceded land north of Lake Nipissing, Ontario, on behalf of the Temagami Band of Indians. By this action, the respondent sought a declaration that the Crown in right of Ontario has clear title to the land in question and that the appellants have no interest therein, and further sought certain injunctive relief. The foundation counterclaimed and sought a declaration of quiet title on the ground that the Temagami have a better right to possession of all the lands by virtue of their aboriginal rights in the land. Ontario claimed that the Temagami had no aboriginal right in relation to the land, or that any right they might have had has been extinguished, either by treaty or unilateral act of the sovereign.

Steele J. [15 D.L.R. (4th) 321, 49 O.R. (2d) 353] found that the appellants had no aboriginal right to the land, and that even if such a right had existed, it had been extinguished by the Robinson-Huron Treaty of 1850, to which the Temagami band was originally a party or to which it had subsequently adhered. These findings were essentially factual, and were drawn from the mass of historical documentary evidence adduced over the course of 130 days of trial. Steele J. also dismissed the counterclaim.

Reference may be made here to the reasons why Steele J. refused to find that the Indians had established an aboriginal right. The gist of these reasons may be found in the following passage from his reasons for judgment, at p. 341:

> ... I will deal with the entitlement of the defendants; to aboriginal rights in the Land Claim Area. I find that the defendants have failed to prove that their ancestors were an organized band level of society in 1763; that, as an organized society, they had exclusive occupation of the Land Claim Area in 1763; or that, as an organized society, they continued to exclusively occupy and make aboriginal use of the Land Claim Area from 1763 or the time of coming of settlement to the date the action was commenced.

An appeal to the Ontario Court of Appeal [58 D.L.R. (4th) 117, [1989] 2 C.N.L.R. 73, 68 O.R. (2d) 394] was dismissed. On the assumption that an aboriginal right existed, the court held that that right had been extinguished either by the Robinson-Huron Treaty or by the subsequent adherence to that treaty by the Indians, or because the treaty constituted a unilateral extinguishment by the sovereign.

This case, it must be underlined, raises for the most part essentially factual issues on which the courts below were in agreement. On such issues, the rule is that an appellate court should not reverse the trial judge in the absence of palpable and overriding error which affected his or her assessment of the facts.... The rule is all the stronger in the face of

† [1991] 2 S.C.R. 570 at 573–76 (S.C.C.), aff'g (1989), 58 D.L.R. (4th) 117 (O.C.A.), which aff'd (1984), 15 D.L.R. (4th) 321 (O.H.C.).

concurrent findings of both courts below. We have undertaken a detailed examination of the facts on this basis. We do not take issue with the numerous specific findings of fact in the courts below, and it is, therefore, not necessary to recapitulate them here.

It does not necessarily follow, however, that we agree with all the legal findings based on those facts. In particular, we find that on the facts found by the trial judge the Indians exercised sufficient occupation of the lands in question throughout the relevant period to establish an aboriginal right: see in this context, *R.* v. *Simon* (1985), 24 D.L.R. (4th) 390, 23 C.C.C. (3d) 238, [1985] 2 S.C.R. 387, and *R.* v. *Sparrow* (1990), 70 D.L.R. (4th) 385, 56 C.C.C. (3d) 263, [1990] 1 S.C.R. 1075. In our view, the trial judge was misled by the considerations which appear in the passage from his reasons quoted earlier.

It is unnecessary, however, to examine the specific nature of the aboriginal right because, in our view, whatever may have been the situation upon the signing of the Robinson-Huron Treaty, that right was in any event surrendered by arrangements subsequent to that treaty by which the Indians adhered to the treaty in exchange for treaty annuities and a reserve. It is conceded that the Crown has failed to comply with some of its obligations under this agreement, and thereby breached its fiduciary obligations to the Indians. These matters currently form the subject of negotiations between the parties. It does not alter the fact, however, that the aboriginal right has been extinguished.

For these reasons, the appeal is dismissed.

Appeal dismissed.

(f) *R. v. Badger*†

See **Chapter 5, Part 14** and **Chapter 8, Part 8(c)**

NOTE

Mr. Badger and two other Treaty 8 Indians were convicted of hunting contrary to the Alberta *Wildlife Act*. All had hunted for food on privately-owned land within the area of Treaty 8. Mr. Badger had hunted near a run-down but occupied house, Mr. Kiyawasew had hunted in a farm field, while Mr. Ominayak had hunted on uncleared land away from farms or dwellings. The Supreme Court had to determine if hunting under these circumstances was protected by Treaty 8, how the *Natural Resources Transfer Agreements* affected the treaty right, and how this situation was affected by s. 35(1) of the *Constitution Act, 1982*.

EXTRACT

[CORY J. for himself, La Forest, L'Heureux-Dubé, Gonthier, and Iacobucci JJ.:]

[para20] Three questions must be answered on this appeal. First, do Indians who have status under Treaty No. 8 have the right to hunt for food on privately owned land which lies within the territory surrendered under that Treaty? Secondly, have the hunting rights set out in Treaty No. 8 been extinguished or modified as a result of the provisions of para. 12 of the 1930 *Natural Resources Transfer Agreement*, 1930 (*Constitution Act, 1930*, Schedule 2)? Thirdly, to what extent, if any, do s. 26(1) and s. 27(1) of the *Wildlife Act*, S.A. 1984, c. W–9.1, apply to the appellants?

. . . .

[para31] The relevant part of Treaty No. 8, made 21 June 1899, provides:

> And Her Majesty the Queen hereby agrees with the said Indians that they shall have right to pursue their usual vocations of hunting, trapping and fishing throughout the tract surrendered as heretofore described, subject to such regulations as may from time to time be made by the Government of the country, acting under the authority of Her Majesty, and saving and excepting such tracts as may be required or taken up from

† [1996] 1 S.C.R. 771; April 3, 1996.

time to time for settlement, mining, lumbering, trading or other purposes.

. . . .

[Cory J. referred to s. 1 of the *Constitution Act, 1930*, giving constitutional effect to the *Natural Resources Transfer Agreements*; to paragraph 12 of the *Natural Resources Transfer Agreement*; and to s. 35(1) of the *Constitution Act, 1982*.]

[para35] Sections 26(1) and 27(1) of the *Wildlife Act* provide:

> **26.**(1) A person shall not hunt wildlife unless he holds a licence authorizing him, or is authorized by or under a licence, to hunt wildlife of that kind.
>
> **27.**(1) A person shall not hunt wildlife outside an open season or if there is no open season for that wildlife.

. . . .

[para40] Treaty No. 8 ... guaranteed that the Indians "shall have the right to pursue their usual vocations of hunting, trapping and fishing". The Treaty, however, imposed two limitations on the right to hunt. First, there was a geographic limitation. The right to hunt could be exercised "throughout the tract surrendered ... saving and excepting such tracts as may be required or taken up from time to time for settlement, mining, lumbering, trading or other purposes". Second, the right could be limited by government regulations passed for conservation purposes.

. . . .

[Here Cory J. summarized the general principles that should govern judicial interpretation of treaties: see text referred to in **Chapter 5, Part 15** at note 96.]

[para43] The issue at this stage is whether the *NRTA* extinguished and replaced the Treaty No. 8 right to hunt for food. It is my conclusion that it did not.

. . . .

[para47] ... The decisions of this Court [such as *R. v. Horseman*, [1990] 1 S.C.R. 901] confirm that para. 12 of the *NRTA* did, to the extent that its intent is clear, modify and alter the right to hunt for food provided in Treaty No. 8.... However ... [t]reaty rights can only be amended where it is clear that effect was intended.... [The Treaty No. 8 right to hunt has only been altered or modified by the *NRTA* to the extent that the *NRTA* evinces a clear intention to effect such a modification....

. . . .

[para50] ... [T]hree preliminary points should be made. First, the "right of access" in the *NRTA* does not refer to a general right of access but, rather, it is limited to a right of access for the purposes of hunting....

[para51] Second, because the various treaties affected by the *NRTA* contain different wording, the extent of the treaty right to hunt on privately owned land may well differ from one treaty to another.... Under Treaty No. 8, the right to hunt for food could be exercised "throughout the tract surrendered" to the Crown "saving and excepting such tracts as may be required or taken up from time to time for settlement, mining, lumbering, trading or other purposes." Accordingly, if the privately owned land is not "required or taken up" in the manner described in Treaty No. 8, it will be land to which the Indians had a right of access to hunt for food.

[para52] Third, the applicable interpretive principles must be borne in mind. Treaties and statutes relating to Indians should be liberally construed ... [and] a court must take into account the context in which the treaties were negotiated, concluded and committed to writing. The treaties, as written documents, recorded an agreement that had already been reached orally and they did not always record the full extent of the oral agreement.... [T]he the words in the treaty must not be interpreted in their strict technical sense nor subjected to rigid modern rules of construction. Rather, they must be interpreted in the sense that they would naturally have been understood by the Indians at the time of the signing....

[para53] The evidence led at trial indicated that in 1899 the Treaty No. 8 Indians would have understood that land had been "required or taken up" when it was being put to a use which was incompatible with the exercise of the right to hunt....

. . . .

[para58] ... [T]he oral promises made by the Crown's representatives and the Indians' own oral history indicate that it was understood that land would be taken up and occupied in a way which precluded hunting when it was put to a visible use that was incompatible with hunting....

. . . .

[para66] In summary, then, the geographical limitation on the right to hunt for food is derived from the terms of the particular treaty if they have not been modified or altered by the provisions of paragraph 12 of the *NRTA*. In this case, the geographical limitation on the right to hunt for food provided by Treaty No. 8 has not been modified by para. 12 of the *NRTA*. Where lands are privately owned, it must be determined on a case-by-case basis whether they are "other lands" to which Indians had a "right of access" under the Treaty. If the lands are occupied, that is, put to visible use which is incompatible with hunting, Indians will not have a right of access. Conversely, if privately owned land is unoccupied and not put to visible use, Indians, pursuant to Treaty No. 8, will have a right of access in order to hunt for food. The facts presented in each of these appeals must now be considered.

. . . .

[Cory J. concluded that the lands on which Mr. Badger and Mr. Kiyawasew were hunting were put to visible use. Hence they did not have existing treaty rights to hunt that could be protected under the *Constitution Act, 1982*. In Mr. Ominayak's case, though, the land in question was not being put to any visible use inconsistent with any Indian right to hunt for food. Accordingly, it fell under the category of "other lands" where the treaty right to hunt for food is not restricted by the *N.R.T.A.*

Since the relevant provisions of the *N.R.T.A.* did not restrict the treaty right in this case, the next question was whether there were any other government restrictions, and whether these constituted infringements under s. 35(1) of the *Constitution Act, 1982*. Cory J. started by noting Treaty 8's proviso that the right to hunt was "subject to such regulations as may from time to time be made by the Government of the country."]

[para70] ... In light of the existence of [the conservation laws in existence prior to signing the Treaty], the Indians would have understood that, by the terms of the Treaty, the government would be permitted to pass regulations with respect to conservation. This concept was explicitly incorporated into the *NRTA* in a modified form providing for Provincial regulatory authority in the field of conservation.... It follows that by the terms of both the Treaty and the *NRTA*, provincial game laws would be applicable to Indians so long as they were aimed at conserving the supply of game. However, the provincial government's regulatory authority under the Treaty and the *NRTA* did not extend beyond the realm of conservation. It is the constitutional provisions of s. 12 of the *NRTA* authorizing provincial regulations which make it unnecessary to consider s. 88 of the *Indian Act* and the general application of provincial regulations to Indians.

[para71] The licensing provisions contained in the *Wildlife Act* are in part, but not wholly, directed towards questions of conservation. At first blush, then, they may seem to form part of the permissible government regulation which can establish the boundaries of the existing right to hunt for food. However, the partial concern with conservation does not automatically lead to the conclusion that s. 26(1) is permissible regulation. It must still be determined whether the manner in which the licensing scheme is administered conflicts with the hunting right provided under Treaty No. 8 as modified by the *NRTA*.

. . . .

[para73] ... [I]t seems logical and appropriate to apply the recently formulated *Sparrow* test in these circumstances. I would add that it can properly be inferred that the concept of reasonableness forms an integral part of the *Sparrow* test. It follows that this concept should be taken into account in the consideration of the justification of an infringement. As a general rule the criteria set out in *Sparrow, supra*, should be applied. However, the reasons in *Sparrow, supra*, make it clear that the suggested criteria are neither exclusive nor exhaustive. It follows that additional criteria may be helpful and applicable in the particular situation presented.

. . . .

[para75] In *Sparrow, supra*, certain criteria were set out pertaining to justification at pp. 1111 and following. While that case dealt with the infringement of aboriginal rights, I am of the view that these criteria should, in most cases, apply equally to the infringement of treaty rights.

[para76] There is no doubt that aboriginal and treaty rights differ in both origin and structure. Aboriginal rights flow from the customs and traditions of the native peoples. To paraphrase the words of Judson J. in *Calder, supra*, at p. 328, they embody the right of native people to continue living as their forefathers lived. Treaty rights, on the other hand, are those contained in official agreements between the Crown and the native peoples. Treaties are analogous to contracts, albeit of a very solemn and special, public nature. They create enforceable obligations based on

the mutual consent of the parties. It follows that the scope of treaty rights will be determined by their wording, which must be interpreted in accordance with the principles enunciated by this Court.

[para77] This said, there are also significant aspects of similarity between aboriginal and treaty rights. Although treaty rights are the result of mutual agreement, they, like aboriginal rights, may be unilaterally abridged.... It follows that limitations on treaty rights, like breaches of aboriginal rights, should be justified.

. . . .

[para79] The wording of s. 35(1) of the *Constitution Act, 1982* supports a common approach to infringements of aboriginal and treaty rights. It provides that "[t]he existing aboriginal and treaty rights of the aboriginal peoples of Canada are hereby recognized and affirmed". In *Sparrow, supra*, Dickson C.J. and La Forest J. appeared to acknowledge the need for justification in the treaty context....

. . . .

[para80] This standard of scrutiny requires that the Crown demonstrate that the legislation in question advances important general public objectives in such a manner that it ought to prevail....

. . . .

[para82] In summary, it is clear that a statute or regulation which constitutes a *prima facie* infringement of aboriginal rights must be justified. In my view, it is equally if not more important to justify *prima facie* infringements of treaty rights....

. . . .

[para85] ... [A]ny *prima facie* infringement of the rights guaranteed under Treaty 8 or the *NRTA* must be justified. How should the infringement of a treaty right be justified? Obviously, the challenged limitation must be considered within the context of the treaty itself. Yet, the recognized principles to be considered and applied in justification should generally be those set out in *Sparrow, supra*. There may well be other factors that should influence the result. The *Sparrow* decision itself recognized that it was not setting a complete catalogue of factors. Nevertheless, these factors may serve as a rough guide when considering the infringement of treaty rights.

[para86] The licensing provisions of the *Wildlife Act* address two objectives: public safety and conservation. These objectives, in and of themselves, are not unconstitutional. However, it is evident from the wording of the Act and its regulations that the manner in which the licensing scheme is set up results in a *prima facie* infringement of the Treaty No. 8 right to hunt as modified by the *NRTA*. The statutory scheme establishes a two-step licensing process. The public safety component is the first one that is engaged.

[para87] Under s. 15(1)(c) of the *Wildlife Act*, the Lieutenant Governor in Council may pass regulations which "specify training and testing qualifications required for the obtaining and holding of a licence or permit"....

. . . .

[Reg. 50/87, s. 2(2) passed pursuant to this section required all hunters to take gun safety courses and pass hunting competency tests and accordingly protected all hunters, including Indians.]

[para88] Standing on its own, the requirement that all hunters take gun safety courses and pass hunting competency tests makes eminently good sense. This protects the safety of everyone who hunts, including Indians. It has been held on a number of occasions that aboriginal or treaty rights must be exercised with due concern for public safety....

. . . .

[para90] Accordingly, it can be seen that reasonable regulations aimed at ensuring safety do not infringe aboriginal or treaty rights to hunt for food. Similarly these regulations do not infringe the hunting rights guaranteed by Treaty 8 as modified by the *NRTA*.

[para90] While the general safety component of the licensing provisions may not constitute a *prima facie* infringement, the conservation component appears to present just such an infringement. Provincial regulations for conservation purposes are authorized pursuant to the provisions of the *NRTA*. However, the routine imposition upon Indians of the specific limitations that appear on the face of the hunting licence may not be permissible if they erode an important aspect of the Indian hunting rights. This Court has held on numerous occasions that there can be no limitation on the method, timing and extent of Indian hunting under a Treaty. I would add that a Treaty as amended by the *NRTA* should be considered in the same manner....

. . . .

[para91] ... in this case, s. 12 of the *NRTA* specifically provides that the provincial government may make regulations for conservation purposes, which affect the Treaty rights to hunt. Accordingly, Provincial regulations pertaining to conservation will be valid so long as they are not clearly unreasonable in their application to aboriginal people.

. . . .

[Cory J. said that although the provincial regulatory scheme had the valid purpose of conservation, the *application* of the scheme infringed the treaty right. This was because the scheme: (i) could deny to an Indian who had passed the safety requirements a licence to hunt for food; (ii) provided no category of "hunting for food" licences, and included a subsistence hunting licence that was too minimal and restricted to allow the right to hunt for food in the sense contemplated in Treaty No. 8; and (iii) gave Indians no preferential access to the limited number of licences, and no exemption from the licence fee.]

[para94] The present licensing system denies to holders of treaty rights as modified by the *NRTA* the very means of exercising those rights. Limitations of this nature are in direct conflict with the treaty right. Therefore, it must be concluded that s. 26(1) of the *Wildlife Act* conflicts with the hunting right set out in Treaty No. 8 as modified by the *NRTA*.

[para95] Accordingly, it is my conclusion that the appellant, Mr. Ominayak, has established the existence of a *prima facie* breach of his treaty right. It now falls to the government to justify that infringement.

[para96] In my view justification of provincial regulations enacted pursuant to the *NRTA* should meet the same test for justification of treaty rights that was set out in *Sparrow, supra*....

. . . .

[para98] In the present case, the government has not led any evidence with respect to justification. In the absence of such evidence, it is not open to this Court to supply its own justification. Section 26(1) of the *Wildlife Act* constitutes a *prima facie* infringement of the appellant Mr. Ominayak's treaty right to hunt. Yet, the issue of conservation is of such importance that a new trial must be ordered so that the question of justification may be addressed.

. . . .

[para100] The hunting rights confirmed by Treaty No. 8 were modified by para. 12 of the *NRTA* to the extent indicated in these reasons. Paragraph 12 of the *NRTA* provided for a continuing right to hunt for food on unoccupied land.

[para101] Mr. Badger and Mr. Kiyawasew were hunting on occupied land to which they had no right of access under Treaty No. 8 or the *NRTA*. Accordingly, ss. 26(1) and 27(1) of the *Wildlife Act* do not infringe their constitutional right to hunt for food.

[para102] However, Mr. Ominayak was exercising his constitutional right on land which was unoccupied for the purposes of this case. Section 26(1) of the *Wildlife Act* constitutes a *prima facie* infringement of his Treaty right to hunt for food. As a result of their conclusions, the issue of justification was not considered by the courts below. Therefore, in his case, a new trial must be ordered so that the issue of justification may be addressed.

[para103] The appeals of Mr. Badger and Mr. Kiyawasew are dismissed.

[para104] The appeal of Mr. Ominayak is allowed and a new trial directed so that the issue of the justification of the infringement created by s. 26(1) of the *Wildlife Act* and any regulations passed pursuant to that section may be addressed.

[Sopinka J., for himself and Lamer C.J. agreed with Cory J.'s disposition of the appeal and with his analysis of the relationship between Treaty No. 8, the *Natural Resources Transfer Agreement* (*NRTA*), and s. 35 of the *Constitution Act, 1982*. However, Sopinka J. felt that the effect of the *Natural Resources Transfer Agreement* was not to modify the treaty rights it affected, but to replace them. Hence, for Sopinka J., the question as to the impact of the legislation on the claimed hunting rights should be examined pursuant to the *Natural Resources Transfer Agreement*, and not pursuant to s. 35(1) of the *Constitution Act, 1982*. However, Sopinka J. considered that a test analogous to the s. 35(1) infringement-justification test developed in *Sparrow* was also appropriate to the *Natural Resources Transfer Agreement*.]

(g) *R. v. Marshall*†

See **Chapter 5, Part 15.**

NOTE

Mr. Donald John Marshall, Jr., a Nova Scotia Mi'kmaq, caught and sold 463 pounds of eels. He did so without a licence, with an illegal net, and during closed season. When he was charged with violating federal fisheries regulations, Mr. Marshall claimed that several treaties from 1760–61 gave Mi'kmaqs a treaty right to fish and trade in fish. The key clause in the treaty text prevented Mi'kmaqs from trading, except with "such persons or the managers of such Truck houses as shall be appointed or Established by His Majesty's Governor." Both the majority and the dissenting judges in the Supreme Court looked at evidence outside the text of the treaty to help determine the meaning of this clause. Why were their conclusions so different?

Worried about their jobs in the east coast lobster fishery, the West Nova Fishermen's Coalition applied to the Supreme Court to rehear aspects of this decision. The *Marshall* rehearing motion judgment is appended at the end of the extracts from the *Marshall* decision. To what extent does this judgment limit the scope of the majority decision in *Marshall*?

EXTRACT

[BINNIE J. for himself, Lamer C.J., and L'Heureux-Dubé, Cory, Iacobucci, and Binnie JJ.:]

[para2] ...The appellant says that [the Mi'kmaq people] are entitled to continue to [harvest and trade fish, including eels] now by virtue of a treaty right agreed to by the British Crown in 1760. As noted by my colleague, Justice McLachlin, the appellant is guilty as charged unless his activities were protected by an existing aboriginal or treaty right. No reliance was placed on any aboriginal right; the appellant chooses to rest his case entirely on the Mi'kmaq treaties of 1760–61.

[para3] The trial judge ([1996] N.S.J. No. 246 (QL) (Prov. Ct.)) accepted as applicable the terms of a *Treaty of Peace and Friendship* signed on March 10, 1760 at Halifax. The parties disagree about the existence of alleged oral terms, as well as the implications of the "trade clause" written into that document.... The treaties were entered into in a period where the British were attempting to expand and secure their control over their northern possessions. The subtext of the Mi'kmaq treaties was reconciliation and mutual advantage.

[para4] I would allow this appeal because nothing less would uphold the honour and integrity of the Crown in its dealings with the Mi'kmaq people to secure their peace and friendship, as best the content of those treaty promises can now be ascertained. In reaching this conclusion, I recognize that if the present dispute had arisen out of a modern commercial transaction between two parties of relatively equal bargaining power, or if, as held by the courts below, the short document prepared at Halifax under the direction of Governor Charles Lawrence on March 10, 1760 was to be taken as being the "entire agreement" between the parties, it would have to be concluded that the Mi'kmaq had inadequately protected their interests. However, the courts have not applied strict rules of interpretation to treaty relationships.... The appellant says the treaty allows him to fish for trade. In my view, the 1760 treaty does affirm the right of the Mi'kmaq people to continue to provide for their own sustenance by taking the products of their hunting, fishing and other gathering activities, and trading for what in 1760 was termed "necessaries". This right was always subject to regulation. The Crown does not suggest that the regulations in question accommodate the treaty right. The Crown's case is that no such treaty right exists. Further, no argument was made that the treaty right was extinguished prior to 1982, and no justification was offered by the Crown for the several prohibitions at issue in this case. Accordingly, in my view, the appellant is entitled to an acquittal.

† [1999] 3 S.C.R. 456, September 17, 1999 reasons for judgment of Lamer C.J. and L'Heureux-Dubé, Cory, Iacobucci, and Binnie JJ. (majority) and Gonthier and McLachlin JJ. (dissenting); followed by [1999] 3 S.C.R. 533, November 17, 1999, reasons for judgment on motion for rehearing and stay, of Lamer C.J. and L'Heureux-Dubé, Gonthier, McLachlin, Iacobucci and Binnie JJ.

[para5] The starting point for the analysis of the alleged treaty right must be an examination of the specific words used in any written memorandum of its terms.... Embree Prov. Ct. J. was satisfied that the written terms applicable to this dispute were contained in a *Treaty of Peace and Friendship* entered into by Governor Charles Lawrence on March 10, 1760...:

...

> ...And I do further engage that we will not traffick, barter or Exchange any Commodities in any manner but with such persons or the managers of such Truck houses as shall be appointed or Established by His Majesty's Governor at Lunenbourg or Elsewhere in Nova Scotia or Accadia. [emphasis added by Binnie J.].

[para6] The underlined portion of the document, the so-called "trade clause", is framed in negative terms as a restraint on the ability of the Mi'kmaq to trade with non-government individuals. A "truckhouse" was a type of trading post. The evidence showed that the promised government truckhouses disappeared from Nova Scotia within a few years and by 1780 a replacement regime of government licensed traders had also fallen into disuse while the British Crown was attending to the American Revolution. The trial judge ... rejected the Crown's argument that the trade clause amounted to nothing more than a negative covenant. He found, at para. 116, that it reflected a grant to the Mi'kmaq of the positive right to "bring the products of their hunting, fishing and gathering to a truckhouse to trade". The Court of Appeal ... held that the trade clause does not grant the Mi'kmaq any rights. Instead, the trade clause represented a "mechanism imposed upon them to help ensure that the peace was a lasting one, by obviating their need to trade with enemies of the British".... When the truckhouses disappeared, said the court, so did any vestiges of the restriction or entitlement, and that was the end of it.

[para7] The appellant's position is that the truckhouse provision not only incorporated the alleged right to trade, but also the right to pursue traditional hunting, fishing and gathering activities in support of that trade. It seems clear that the words of the March 10, 1760 document, standing in isolation, do not support the appellant's argument....

. . . .

[Binnie J. proceeded to justify looking beyond the text of the treaty]:

[para10] Firstly, Even in a modern commercial context, extrinsic evidence is available to show that a written document does not include all of the terms of an agreement....

[para11] Secondly, even in the context of a treaty document that purports to contain all of the terms, this Court has made clear in recent cases that extrinsic evidence of the historical and cultural context of a treaty may be received even absent any ambiguity on the face of the treaty....

[para12] Thirdly, where a treaty was concluded verbally and afterwards written up by representatives of the Crown, it would be unconscionable for the Crown to ignore the oral terms while relying on the written terms....

[para13] The narrow approach applied by the Court of Appeal to the use of extrinsic evidence apparently derives from the comments of Estey J. in *R.* v. *Horse*, [1988] 1 S.C.R. 187, where, at p. 201, he expressed some reservations about the use of extrinsic materials, such as the transcript of negotiations surrounding the signing of Treaty No. 6, except in the case of ambiguity....

[para14] Subsequent cases have distanced themselves from a "strict" rule of treaty interpretation, as more recently discussed by Cory J., in *R.* v. *Badger*, [1996] 1 S.C.R. 771, at para. 52....

. . . .

...The special rules are dictated by the special difficulties of ascertaining what in fact was agreed to. The Indian parties did not, for all practical purposes, have the opportunity to create their own written record of the negotiations. Certain assumptions are therefore made about the Crown's approach to treaty making (honourable) which the Court acts upon in its approach to treaty interpretation (flexible) as to the existence of a treaty (*R.* v. *Sioui*, [1990] 1 S.C.R.1025, at p. 1049), the completeness of any written record (the use, e.g., of context and implied terms to make honourable sense of the treaty arrangement: *Simon* v. *The Queen*, [1985] 2 S.C.R. 387, and *R.* v. *Sundown*, [1999] 1 S.C.R. 393), and the interpretation of treaty terms once found to exist (*Badger*). The bottom line is the Court's obligation is to "choose from among the various possible interpretations of the common intention [at the time the treaty was made] the one which best reconciles" the Mi'kmaq interests and those of the British Crown (emphasis added) (*Sioui*, per Lamer J., at p. 1069). In *R.* v. *Taylor and Williams* (1981), 62 C.C.C. (2d)

227 (leave to appeal refused, [1981] 2 S.C.R. xi), the Crown conceded that points of oral agreement recorded in contemporaneous minutes were included in the treaty (p. 230) and the court concluded that their effect was to "preserve the historic right of these Indians to hunt and fish on Crown lands" (p. 236). The historical record in the present case is admittedly less clear-cut, and there is no parallel concession by the Crown.

. . . .

[para20] While the trial judge drew positive implications from the negative trade clause (reversed on this point by the Court of Appeal), such limited relief is inadequate where the British-drafted treaty document does not accord with the British-drafted minutes of the negotiating sessions and more favourable terms are evident from the other documents and evidence the trial judge regarded as reliable. Such an overly deferential attitude to the March 10, 1760 document was inconsistent with a proper recognition of the difficulties of proof confronted by aboriginal people....

. . . .

[para25] ...[T]he British saw the Mi'kmaq trade issue in terms of peace (as the Crown expert Dr. Stephen Patterson testified, "people who trade together do not fight, that was the theory"). Peace was bound up with the ability of the Mi'kmaq people to sustain themselves economically. Starvation breeds discontent. The British certainly did not want the Mi'kmaq to become an unnecessary drain on the public purse of the colony of Nova Scotia or of the Imperial purse in London, as the trial judge found. To avoid such a result, it became necessary to protect the traditional Mi'kmaq economy, including hunting, gathering and fishing....

. . . .

[para30] ...The subject of trading with the British government as distinguished from British settlers, however, did not arise until after the Indians had first requested truckhouses. The limitation to government trade came as a response to the request for truckhouses, not the other way around....

. . . .

[para35] In my view, all of this evidence, reflected in the trial judgment, demonstrates the inadequacy and incompleteness of the written memorial of the treaty terms by selectively isolating the restrictive trade covenant. Indeed, the truckhouse system offered such advantageous terms that it hardly seems likely that Mi'kmaq traders had to be compelled to buy at lower prices and sell at higher prices. At a later date, they objected when truckhouses were abandoned. The trade clause would not have advanced British objectives (peaceful relations with a self-sufficient Mi'kmaq people) or Mi'kmaq objectives (access to the European "necessaries" on which they had come to rely) unless the Mi'kmaq were assured at the same time of continuing access, implicitly or explicitly, to a harvest wildlife to trade....

. . . .

[para37] ...[It has been argued that the] law sees a finality of interpretation of historical events where finality, according to the professional historian, is not possible. The reality, of course, is that the courts are handed disputes that require for their resolution the finding of certain historical facts. The litigating parties cannot await the possibility of a stable academic consensus. The judicial process must do as best it can. In this particular case, however, there was an unusual level of agreement amongst all of the professional historians who testified about the common intention of the participants regarding the treaty obligations entered into by the Crown with the Mi'kmaq....

. . . .

[para40] In my view, the Nova Scotia judgments erred in concluding that the only enforceable treaty obligations were those set out in the written document of March 10, 1760, whether construed flexibly (as did the trial judge) or narrowly (as did the Nova Scotia Court of Appeal)....

. . . .

[para52] I do not think an interpretation of events that turns a positive Mi'kmaq trade demand into a negative Mi'kmaq covenant is consistent with the honour and integrity of the Crown....

. . . .

[para54] ...[T]here is no suggestion in the negotiating records that the truckhouse system was a sort of transitional arrangement expected to be temporary, it only became temporary because the King unexpectedly disallowed the enabling legislation passed by the Nova Scotia House of Assembly; and the notion that

the truckhouse was merely a response to a trade restriction overlooks the fact the truckhouse system offered very considerable financial benefits to the Mi'kmaq which they would have wanted to exploit, restriction or no restriction. The promise of access to "necessaries" through trade in wildlife was the key point, and where a right has been granted, there must be more than a mere disappearance of the mechanism created to facilitate the exercise of the right to warrant the conclusion that the right itself is spent or extinguished.

. . . .

[para56] My view is that the surviving substance of the treaty is not the literal promise of a truckhouse, but a treaty right to continue to obtain necessaries through hunting and fishing by trading the products of those traditional activities subject to restrictions that can be justified under the *Badger* test.

. . . .

[para58] ...What is contemplated [here] is not a right to trade generally for economic gain, but rather a right to trade for necessaries. The treaty right is a regulated right and can be contained by regulation within its proper limits.

[para59] The concept of "necessaries" is today equivalent to the concept of what Lambert J.A., in *R.* v. *Van der Peet* (1993), 80 B.C.L.R. (2d) 75 (C.A.), at p. 126, described as a "moderate livelihood". Bare subsistence has thankfully receded over the last couple of centuries as an appropriate standard of life for aboriginals and non-aboriginals alike. A moderate livelihood includes such basics as "food, clothing and housing, supplemented by a few amenities", but not the accumulation of wealth....

. . . .

[Binnie J. concluded that the three fisheries regulations unjustifiedly infringed Mr. Marshall's constitutionally guaranteed treaty right to catch and trade fish for a moderate livelihood.]

. . . .

[McLACHLIN J., dissenting, for herself and Gonthier J.:]

. . . .

[After considering the extrinsic evidence, McLachlin J. concluded that shortly after the signing of the treaties of 1760-61, both government and Aboriginal parties put an end to the provision regarding exclusive trading and truckhouses. She said that in any event, this treaty clause did not support an independent right to fish.]:

. . . .

[para87] ...The clause is short, the words simple. The Mi'kmaq covenant that they will "not traffick, barter or Exchange any Commodities in any manner <u>but with [British agents]</u>" (emphasis added). The core of this clause is the obligation on the Mi'kmaq to trade only with the British. Ancillary to this is the implied promise that the British will establish truckhouses where the Mi'kmaq can trade. These words do not, on their face, confer a general right to trade.

. . . .

[para102] The historical context, as the trial judge points out, supports the view that the British wanted the Mi'kmaq to maintain their traditional way of life and that trade was important to the Mi'kmaq. From this, Binnie J. suggests that the purpose of the treaty trading regime was to promote the self-sufficiency of the Mi'kmaq, and finds a treaty right to hunt, to fish, and to trade for sustenance. Yet, with respect, the historical record does not support this inference. The dominant purpose of the treaties was to prevent the Mi'kmaq from maintaining alliances with the French. To this end, the British insisted on a treaty term that the Mi'kmaq trade exclusively with British agents, at British trading outlets — the truckhouses. Implicit in this is the expectation that the Mi'kmaq would continue to trade. But it does not support the inference that the treaty clause conveyed a general right to trade and to sustenance. The treaty reference to the right to bring goods to truckhouses was required by and incidental to the obligation of the Mi'kmaq to trade with the British, and cannot be stretched to embrace a general treaty right to trade surviving the exclusive trade and truckhouse regime. To do so is to transform a specific right agreed to by both parties into an unintended right of broad and undefined scope.

. . . .

[para112] To proceed from a right undefined in scope or modern counterpart to the question of justification would be to render treaty rights inchoate and the justification of limitations impossible. How

can one meaningfully discuss accommodation or justification of a right unless one has some idea of the core of that right and its modern scope? How is the government, in the absence of such definition, to know how far it may justifiably trench on the right in the collective interest of Canadians? How are courts to judge whether the government that attempts to do so has drawn the line at the right point? Referring to the "right" in the generalized abstraction risks both circumventing the parties' common intention at the time the treaty was signed, and functioning illegitimately to create, in effect, an unintended right of broad and undefined scope.

. . . .

[The West Nova Fishermen's Coalition applied to the Supreme Court for: a rehearing of this decision on the question of the federal regulatory authority over the fisheries; a further trial on whether the regulation of a Mi'kmaq treaty right could be justified on conservation or other grounds; and a stay of the judgment pending the rehearing and further trial. Extracts from *R. v. Marshall*, [1999] 3 S.C.R. 533, dismissing the rehearing motion, are reproduced here.]

[THE COURT:]

[para2] Those opposing the motion object in different ways that the Coalition's motion rests on a series of misconceptions about what the September 17, 1999 majority judgment decided and what it did not decide. These objections are well founded. The Court did not hold that the Mi'kmaq treaty right cannot be regulated or that the Mi'kmaq are guaranteed an open season in the fisheries. Justification for conservation or other purposes is a separate and distinct issue at the trial of one of these prosecutions. It is up to the Crown to decide whether or not it wishes to support the applicability of government regulations when prosecuting an accused who claims to be exercising an aboriginal or treaty right.

[para3] The Attorney General of Canada, in opposing the Coalition's motion, acknowledges that the Crown did not lead any evidence at trial or make any argument on the appeal that the licensing and closed season regulations which restricted the exercise of the treaty right were justified in relation to the eel fishery. Accordingly, the issue whether these restrictions could have been justified in this case formed no part of the Court's majority judgment of September 17, 1999, and the constitutional question posed in this prosecution was answered on that basis.

. . . .

[para11] ...[T]his was a prosecution of a private citizen. It required the Court to determine whether certain precise charges relating to the appellant's participation in the eel fishery could be sustained. The majority judgment of September 17, 1999 was limited to the issues necessary to dispose of the appellant's guilt or innocence.

. . . .

[para14] As stated in para. 56 of the September 17, 1999 majority judgment, the treaty right was "to continue to obtain necessaries through hunting and fishing by trading the products of those traditional activities subject to restrictions that can be justified under the *Badger* test" (emphasis added). The *Badger* test (*R.* v. *Badger*, [1996] 1 S.C.R. 771) will be discussed below. The Crown, as stated, did not offer any evidence or argument justifying the licensing and closed season restrictions (referred to in the statute and regulations as a "close time") on the appellant's exercise of the collective treaty right, such as (for example) a need to conserve and protect the eel population. The eel population may not in fact require protection from commercial exploitation....

[para15] ...The issues of concern to the Coalition largely relate to the lobster fishery, not the eel fishery, and, if necessary, can be raised and decided in future cases that involve the specifics of the lobster fishery. It is up to the Crown to initiate enforcement action in the lobster and other fisheries if and when it chooses to do so....

[para16] The Coalition argues that a rehearing and a further trial are necessary because of "uncertainty" about the authority of the government to manage the fisheries. The Attorney General of Canada, acting on behalf of the federal government which regulates the fisheries, opposes the Coalition's position.

[para17] In the event of another prosecution under the regulations, the Crown will (as it did in this case) have the onus of establishing the factual elements of the offence. The onus will then switch to the accused to demonstrate that he or she is a member of an aboriginal community in Canada with which one of the local treaties described in the September 17, 1999 majority judgment was made, and was engaged in the exercise of the community's col-

lective right to hunt or fish in that community's traditional hunting and fishing grounds. The Court's majority judgment noted in para. 5 that no treaty was made by the British with the Mi'kmaq population as a whole:

> ...the British signed a series of agreements with individual Mi'kmaq communities in 1760 and 1761 intending to have them consolidated into a comprehensive Mi'kmaq treaty <u>that was never in fact brought into existence</u>. The trial judge, Embree Prov. Ct. J., found that by the end of 1761 all of the Mi'kmaq villages in Nova Scotia had entered into separate but similar treaties. [Emphasis added.]

The British Governor in Halifax thus proceeded on the basis that local chiefs had no authority to promise peace and friendship on behalf of other local chiefs in other communities, or to secure treaty benefits on their behalf. The treaties were local and the reciprocal benefits were local. In the absence of a fresh agreement with the Crown, the exercise of the treaty rights will be limited to the area traditionally used by the local community with which the "separate but similar" treaty was made. Moreover, the treaty rights do not belong to the individual, but are exercised by authority of the local community to which the accused belongs, and their exercise is limited to the purpose of obtaining from the identified resources the wherewithal to trade for "necessaries".

[para19] At the end of the day, it is always open to the Minister (as it was here) to seek to justify the limitation on the treaty right because of the need to conserve the resource in question or for other compelling and substantial public objectives, as discussed below. Equally, it will be open to an accused in future cases to try to show that the treaty right was intended in 1760 by both sides to include access to resources other than fish, wildlife and traditionally gathered things such as fruits and berries. The word "gathering" in the September 17, 1999 majority judgment was used in connection with the types of the resources traditionally "gathered" in an aboriginal economy and which were thus reasonably in the contemplation of the parties to the 1760-61 treaties. While treaty rights are capable of evolution within limits, as discussed below, their subject matter (absent a new agreement) cannot be wholly transformed. Certain unjustified assumptions are made in this regard by the Native Council of Nova Scotia on this motion about "the effect of the economic treaty right on forestry, minerals and natural gas deposits offshore". The Union of New Brunswick Indians also suggested on this motion a need to "negotiate an integrated approach dealing with all resources coming within the purview of fishing, hunting and gathering which includes harvesting from the sea, the forests and the land". This extended interpretation of "gathering" is not dealt with in the September 17, 1999 majority judgment, and negotiations with respect to such resources as logging, minerals or offshore natural gas deposits would go beyond the subject matter of this appeal.

[para20] The September 17, 1999 majority judgment did not rule that the appellant had established a treaty right "to gather" anything and everything physically capable of being gathered. The issues were much narrower and the ruling was much narrower. No evidence was drawn to our attention, nor was any argument made in the course of this appeal, that trade in logging or minerals, or the exploitation of off-shore natural gas deposits, was in the contemplation of either or both parties to the 1760 treaty; nor was the argument made that exploitation of such resources could be considered a logical evolution of treaty rights to fish and wildlife or to the type of things traditionally "gathered" by the Mi'kmaq in a 1760 aboriginal lifestyle....

[para21] The fact the Crown elected not to try to justify a closed season on the eel fishery at issue in this case cannot be generalised, as the Coalition's question implies, to a conclusion that closed seasons can never be imposed as part of the government's regulation of the Mi'kmaq limited commercial "right to fish". A "closed season" is clearly a potentially available management tool, but its application to treaty rights will have to be justified for conservation or other purposes. In the absence of such justification, an accused who establishes a treaty right is ordinarily allowed to exercise it. As suggested in the expert evidence filed on this motion by the Union of New Brunswick Indians, the establishment of a closed season may raise very different conservation and other issues in the eel fishery than it does in relation to other species such as salmon, crab, cod or lobster, or for that matter, to moose and other wildlife. The complexities and techniques of fish and wildlife management vary from species to species and restrictions will likely have to be justified on a species-by-species basis.

[para22] ...As this and other courts have pointed out on many occasions, the process of accommodation of the treaty right may best be resolved by consultation and negotiation of a modern agreement for participation in specified resources by the Mi'kmaq rather than by litigation....

[para23] The various governmental, aboriginal and other interests are not, of course, obliged to reach an agreement. In the absence of a mutually satisfactory solution, the courts will resolve the points of conflict as they arise case by case. The decision in this particular prosecution is authority only for the matters adjudicated upon. The acquittal ought not to be set aside to allow the Coalition to address new issues that were neither raised by the parties nor determined by the Court in the September 17, 1999 majority judgment.

[para24] The Government's power to regulate the treaty right is repeatedly affirmed in the September 17, 1999 majority judgment....

. . . .

[para26] As for the specific matter of licences, the conclusion of the majority judgment was not that licensing schemes as such are invalid, but that the imposition of a licensing restriction on the appellant's exercise of the treaty right had not been justified for conservation or other public purposes....

. . . .

[para30] No useful purpose would be served for those like the Coalition who are interested in justifying a closed season in the lobster fishery if a rehearing or a new trial were ordered in this case, which related only to the closed season in the eel fishery....

. . . .

[para33] ...Section 43 of the Act sets out the basis of a very broad regulatory authority over the fisheries which may extend to the native fishery where justification is shown.... [On the other hand,] [s]pecific criteria must be established for the exercise by the Minister of his or her discretion to grant or refuse licences in a manner that recognizes and accommodates the existence of an aboriginal or treaty right.

. . . .

[para35] Despite the limitations on the Court's ability in a prosecution to address broader issues not at issue between the Crown and the defence, the majority judgment of September 17, 1999 nevertheless referred to the Court's principal pronouncements on the various grounds on which the exercise of treaty rights may be regulated. These include the following grounds:

[para36] (a) The treaty right itself is a limited right. The September 17, 1999 majority judgment referred to the "narrow ambit and extent of the treaty right" (para. 57). In its written argument, the Coalition says that the only regulatory method specified in that judgment was a limit on the quantities of fish required to satisfy the Mi'kmaq need for necessaries. This is not so. What the majority judgment said is that the Mi'kmaq treaty right does not extend beyond the quantities required to satisfy the need for necessaries. The Court stated at para. 61 of the September 17, 1999 majority judgment: Catch limits that could reasonably be expected to produce a moderate livelihood for individual Mi'kmaq families at present-day standards can be established by regulation and enforced without violating the treaty right. In that case, the regulations would accommodate the treaty right. Such regulations would not constitute an infringement that would have to be justified under the *Badger* standard. [Underlining added by McLachlin J., replacing emphasis by italics in September 17, 1999 judgment.]

[para37] In other words, regulations that do no more than reasonably define the Mi'kmaq treaty right in terms that can be administered by the regulator and understood by the Mi'kmaq community that holds the treaty rights do not impair the exercise of the treaty right and therefore do not have to meet the *Badger* standard of justification.

[para38] Other limitations apparent in the September 17, 1999 majority judgment include the local nature of the treaties, the communal nature of a treaty right, and the fact it was only hunting and fishing resources to which access was affirmed, together with traditionally gathered things like wild fruit and berries.... [T]he Mi'kmaq treaty right to hunt and trade in game is not now, any more than it was in 1760, a commercial hunt that must be satisfied before non-natives have access to the same resources for recreational or commercial purposes. The emphasis in 1999, as it was in 1760, is on assuring the Mi'kmaq equitable access to identified resources for the purpose of earning a moderate living....

[para39] Only those regulatory limits that take the Mi'kmaq catch below the quantities reasonably expected to produce a moderate livelihood or other limitations that are not inherent in the limited nature of the treaty right itself have to be justified according to the *Badger* test.

[para40] (b) The paramount regulatory objective is the conservation of the resource....

[para41] (c) The Minister's authority extends to other compelling and substantial public objectives which may include economic and regional fairness, and recognition of the historical reliance upon, and participation in, the fishery by non-aboriginal groups....

[para42] In the case of any treaty right which may be exercised on a commercial scale, the natives constitute only one group of participants, and regard for the interest of the non-natives, as stated in *Gladstone, supra*, may be shown in the right circumstances to be entirely legitimate....

[para43] (d) Aboriginal people are entitled to be consulted about limitations on the exercise of treaty and aboriginal rights....

[para44] (e) The Minister has available for regulatory purposes the full range of resource management tools and techniques, provided their use to limit the exercise of a treaty right can be justified. If the Crown establishes that the limitations on the treaty right are imposed for a pressing and substantial public purpose, after appropriate consultation with the aboriginal community, and go no further than is required, the same techniques of resource conservation and management as are used to control the non-native fishery may be held to be justified. Equally, however, the concerns and proposals of the native communities must be taken into account, and this might lead to different techniques of conservation and management in respect of the exercise of the treaty right.

[para45] ...[The Coalition argued, in effect, that] if a treaty right would be disruptive, its existence should be denied or the treaty right should be declared inoperative. This is not a legal principle. It is a political argument. What is more, it is a political argument that was expressly rejected by the political leadership when it decided to include s. 35 in the *Constitution Act, 1982*....

[para46] At no stage of this appeal, either before or after September 17, 1999, has any government requested a stay or suspension of judgment. The Coalition asks for the stay based on its theory that the ruling created broad gaps in the regulatory scheme, but for the reasons already explained, its contention appears to be based on a misconception of what was decided on September 17, 1999. The appellant should not have his acquittal kept in jeopardy while issues which are much broader than the specifics of his prosecution are litigated. The request for a stay of the acquittal directed on September 17, 1999, is therefore denied.

. . . .

[para47] In the event the respondent Attorney General of Canada or the intervener Attorney General for New Brunswick should determine that it is in the public interest to apply for a stay of the effect of the Court's recognition and affirmation of the Mi'kmaq treaty right in its September 17, 1999 majority judgment, while leaving in place the acquittal of the appellant, the Court will entertain argument on whether it has the jurisdiction to grant such a stay, and if so, whether it ought to do so in this case.

Disposition

[para48] The Coalition's motion is dismissed with costs.

6 Legislative Jurisdiction

(a) Some Provisions Relevant to Legislative Jurisdiction

See **Chapter 6**. See also **Chapter 2, Parts 2 and 3**, and **Chapter 7, Parts 1 to 3**.

INDIAN ACT†

General Provincial Laws Applicable to Indians

88. Subject to the terms of any treaty and any other Act of the Parliament of Canada, all laws of general application from time to time in force in any province are applicable to and in respect of Indians in the province, except to the extent that such laws are inconsistent with this Act or any order, rule, regulation or by-law made thereunder, and except to the extent that such laws make provision for any matter for which provision is made by or under this Act. [R.S., c. 149, s. 87.]

MANITOBA NATURAL RESOURCES TRANSFER AGREEMENT‡

13. In order to secure to the Indians of the Province the continuance of the supply of game and fish for their support and subsistence, Canada agrees that the laws respecting game in force in the Province from time to time shall apply to the Indians within the boundaries thereof, provided, however, that the said Indians shall have the right, which the Province hereby assures to them, of hunting, trapping and fishing game and fish for food at all seasons of the year on all unoccupied Crown lands and on any other lands to which the said Indians may have a right of access.

MEECH LAKE ACCORD*

9) Sections 40 and 42 of the *Constitution Act, 1982* are replaced and the following substituted therefor:

. . . .

41. An Amendment to the Constitution of Canada in relation to the following matters may be made by proclamation issued by the Governor General under the Great Seal of Canada only where authorized by resolutions of the Senate and House of Commons and of the legislative assembly of each province:

. . . .

(i) notwithstanding any other law or practice, the establishment of new provinces

. . . .

16) Nothing in section 2 of the *Constitution Act, 1867* (the distinct society provision) affects section 25 or 27 of the *Canadian Charter of Rights and Freedoms*, section 35 of the *Constitution*

---

† R.S.C. 1985, c. I-5, s. 88.

‡ Implemented in *Manitoba Natural Resources Act*, S.C. 1930, c. 29; confirmed in *Constitution Act, 1930*, R.S.C. 1985, App. II, No. 26. [Note: the Alberta and Saskatchewan Agreements contain comparable provisions.]

* Proposed *Constitution Amendment, 1987*. [This was the legislative part of the proposed Meech Lake Accord. It was agreed to on June 3, 1987 but failed to secure unanimous legislative authorization by June 3, 1990.]

Act, 1982 or class 24 of section 91 of the *Constitution Act, 1867.*

REPORT OF THE SPECIAL COMMITTEE TO STUDY THE PROPOSED COMPARISON RESOLUTION TO THE MEECH LAKE ACCORD†

... New Brunswick has proposed a return to the pre-1982 situation thereby ensuring that the two territories could aspire to provincehood under the same conditions as the other provinces created since 1867.

9) Your Committee agrees with the position of New Brunswick and the territories on the creation of new provinces and recommends that this be dealt with in a Comparison Resolution.

. . . .

Representatives of aboriginal groups testified that instead of being one of the items on the agenda of annual First Ministers Constitutional Conferences, a separate process be devoted specifically to aboriginal matters. They recommended that these conferences would be held every three years.

10) Your Committee agrees with the suggestion of the leadership of the aboriginal groups and recommends that a Comparison Resolution should provide for a separate process of constitutional conferences every three years. The first such conference should be convened no later than one year after such Resolution comes into force.

(b) *Cardinal v. Alberta (A.G.)*‡

See **Chapter 6, Part 7.**

NOTE

Mr. Cardinal sold moose on an Indian reserve to a non-Indian, contrary to Alberta conservation legislation. The *Natural Resources Transfer Agreements* permit Prairie provinces to regulate commercial hunting in (among other places) "lands to which the Indians have a right of access." To determine if this phrase included reserves, the Court looked at the general constitutional scheme that was modified by the *N.R.T.A.*: the division of powers in the *Constitution Act, 1867*.

EXTRACT

Fauteux C.J., and Abbott J., concurred with Martland J.

[MARTLAND J. for himself:]

On December 8, 1970, the appellant, a treaty Indian, at his home on an Indian reserve, in the Province of Alberta, sold a piece of moose meat to a non-Indian. He was charged with a breach of s. 37 of the *Wildlife Act*, R.S.A. 1970, c. 391, which provides:

> **37.** No person shall traffic in any big game or any game bird except as is expressly permitted by this Act or by the regulations.

The trial judge found that the appellant had trafficked in big game within the meaning of this section. The appellant was acquitted on the ground that the *Wildlife Act* is *ultra vires* of the Alberta Legislature in its application to the appellant as an Indian on an Indian reserve. A case was stated on this legal issue, which was considered by a Judge of the Supreme Court of Alberta, who held that the decision was correct. An appeal was taken to the Appellate Division of the Supreme Court of Alberta, which allowed the appeal and overruled the judg-

† (The Charest Report), Canada, House of Commons, Ottawa, May 1990, at p. 7.

‡ [1974] S.C.R. 695 at 697–704, 706–10, 716–17, 721 (S.C.C.), aff'g (1972), 22 D.L.R. (3d) 716 (A.S.C.A.D.), which rev'd the decision of the A.S.C., which upheld the decision of the Provincial Court judge.

ment of the Court below [5 C.C.C. (2d) 193, 22 D.L.R. (3d) 716 *sub nom. R.* v. *Cardinal*, 17 C.R.N.S. 110 *sub nom. A.-G. Alta.* v. *Cardinal*]. The present appeal is brought, with leave, to this Court.

Section 91(24) of the *British North America Act, 1867*, gives to the Parliament of Canada exclusive authority to legislate in respect of:

> **91.**(24) *Indians*, and Lands reserved for the *Indians*.

An agreement was made between the Government of Canada and the Government of Alberta, dated December 14, 1929, hereinafter referred to as "the Agreement", for the transfer by the former to the latter of the interest of the Crown in all Crown lands, mines and minerals within the Province of Alberta, and the provisions of the *Alberta Act, 1905* (Can.), c. 3, were modified as in the Agreement set out.

Paragraphs 10 to 12 inclusive appear in the Agreement under the heading "Indian Reserves", and it is paras. 10 and 12 which are of importance in considering this appeal. They provide as follows [schedule to *Alberta Natural Resources Act, 1930* (Alta.), c. 21, and 1930 (Can.), c. 3].

> **10.** All lands included in Indian reserves within the province, including those selected and surveyed but not yet confirmed, as well as those confirmed, shall continue to be vested in the Crown and administered by the Government of Canada for the purposes of Canada, and the Province will from time to time, upon the request of the Superintendent General of Indian Affairs, set aside, out of the unoccupied Crown land hereby transferred to its administration, such further areas as the said Superintendent General may, in agreement with the appropriate Minister of the Province, select as necessary to enable Canada to fulfil its obligations under the treaties with the Indians of the Province, and such areas shall thereafter be administered by Canada in the same way in all respects as if they had never passed to the Province under the provisions hereof.

> **12.** In order to secure to the Indians of the Province the continuance of the supply of game and fish for their support and subsistence, Canada agrees that the laws respecting game in force in the Province from time to time shall apply to the Indians within the boundaries thereof, provided however, that the said Indians shall have the right, which the Province hereby assures to them, of hunting, trapping and fishing game and fish for food at all seasons of the year on all unoccupied Crown lands and on any other lands to which the said Indians may have a right of access.

This Agreement was approved by the Parliament of Canada and the Legislature of the Province of Alberta and, thereafter, it and also agreements between the Government of Canada and the Provinces of Manitoba, Saskatchewan and British Columbia were confirmed by the *British North America Act, 1930* (U.K.), c. 26. Section 1 of that Act provided:

> **1.** The agreements set out in the Schedule to this Act are hereby confirmed and shall have the force of law notwithstanding anything in the *British North America Act, 1867*, or any Act amending the same, or any Act of the Parliament of Canada, or in any Order-in-Council or terms or conditions of union made or approved under any such Act as aforesaid.

Paragraphs 10 and 12 of the Agreement were, therefore, given the force of law, notwithstanding anything in the *British North America Act, 1867*. The question in issue on this appeal is as to whether s. 12 was effective so as to make the provisions of the *Wildlife Act* applicable to the appellant, a treaty Indian, in respect of an act which occurred on an Indian reserve in the Province of Alberta.

The submission of the appellant is that the Parliament of Canada has exclusive legislative authority to legislate to control the administration of Indian reserves and that provincial laws cannot apply on such a reserve unless referentially introduced through federal legislation. It is contended that the phrase "on all unoccupied Crown lands and on any other lands to which the said Indians may have a right of access" does not include Indian reserve lands and that the only laws to which Indians are subject, while on a reserve, are the laws of Canada. Paragraph 12, it is said, can only have application to Indians in Alberta outside the Indian reserves.

. . . .

As indicated earlier, the appellant starts from the proposition that, prior to the making of the Agreement, Indian reserves were enclaves which were withdrawn from the application of provincial legislation, save by way of reference by virtue of federal legislation. On this premise it is contended that para. 12 should not be construed so as to make provincial game legislation applicable within Indian reserves.

I am not prepared to accept this initial premise. Section 91(24) of the *British North America Act, 1867*, gave exclusive legislative authority to the Canadian Parliament in respect of Indians and over lands reserved for the Indians. Section 92 gave to each Province, in such Province, exclusive legislative power over the subjects therein defined. It is well established, as illustrated in *Union Colliery Co. of B.C.* v. *Bryden*, [1899] A.C. 580, that a Province cannot legislate in relation to a subject-matter exclusively assigned to the federal Parliament by s. 91. But it is also well established that provincial legislation enacted under a heading of s. 92 does not necessarily become invalid because it affects something which is subject to federal legislation. A vivid illustration of this is to be found in the Privy Council decision a few years after the *Union Colliery* case in *Cunningham et al.* v. *Tomey Homma*, [1903] A.C. 151, which sustained provincial legislation, pursuant to s. 92(1), which prohibited Japanese, whether naturalized or not, from voting in provincial elections in British Columbia.

A provincial Legislature could not enact legislation in relation to Indians, or in relation to Indian reserves, but this is far from saying that the effect of s. 91(24) of the *British North Act, 1867*, was to create enclaves within a Province within the boundaries of which provincial legislation could have no application. In my opinion, the test as to the application of provincial legislation within a reserve is the same as with respect to its application within the Province and that is that it must be within the authority of s. 92 and must not be in relation to a subject-matter assigned exclusively to the Canadian Parliament under s. 91. Two of those subjects are Indians and Indian reserves, but if provincial legislation within the limits of s. 92 is not construed as being legislation in relation to those classes of subjects (or any other subject under s. 91) it is applicable anywhere in the Province, including Indian reserves, even though Indians or Indian reserves might be affected by it. My point is that s. 91(24) enumerates classes of subjects over which the federal Parliament has the exclusive power to legislate, but it does not purport to define areas within a Province within which the power of a Province to enact legislation, otherwise within its powers, is to be excluded.

There have been a number of cases in provincial Courts in which para. 12 of the Agreement, or its equivalent in the Manitoba and Saskatchewan Agreements, was not applicable, which have considered the question of the application of provincial laws to Indians, and their application within Indian reserves....

. . . .

In none of these cases is it decided that a provincial game law, of general application, would not affect an Indian outside a reserve. Legislation of this kind does not relate to Indians, *qua* Indians, and the passage above quoted would, in my opinion, be applicable to such legislation. The *Jim* case and the *Rodgers* case held that such legislation did not apply to an Indian on an Indian reserve. The *Morley* case is inconsistent with the idea that no provincial legislation can apply within an Indian reserve, save by reference in a federal statute.

I now turn to a consideration of the effect of para. 12 of the Agreement.

It has been noted that this paragraph along with paras. 10 and 11, appears under the heading "Indian Reserves". It begins with the words:

> In order to secure to the Indians of the Province the continuance of the supply of game and fish for their support and subsistence, Canada agrees that the laws respecting game in force in the Province from time to time shall apply to the Indians within the boundaries thereof....

The opening words of the paragraph define its purpose. It is to secure to the Indians of the Province a continuing supply of game and fish for their support and subsistence. It is to achieve that purpose that Indians within the boundaries of the Province are to conform to provincial game laws, subject, always, to their right to hunt and fish for food. This being the purpose of the paragraph, it could not have been intended that the controls which would apply to Indians in relation to hunting and fishing for purposes other than for their own food, should apply only to Indians not on reserves.

Furthermore, if the paragraph were to be so restricted in its scope, it would accomplish nothing towards its purpose. Cases decided before the Agreement, such as *R.* v. *Martin*, *supra*, had held that general legislation by a Province, not relating to Indians, *qua* Indians, would apply to them. On their facts, these cases dealt with Indians outside reserves. The point is that the provisions of para. 12 were not required to make provincial game laws apply to Indians off the reserve.

In my opinion, the meaning of para. 12 is that Canada, clothed as it was with legislative jurisdiction over "Indians, and Lands reserved for the Indians", in order to achieve the purpose of the section, agreed to the imposition of provincial controls over hunting and fishing, which, previously, the Province might not have had power to impose. By its express wording, it provides that the game laws of the Province shall apply "to Indians within the boundaries thereof". To me this must contemplate their application to all Indians within the Province, without restriction as to where, within the Province, they might be.

This view is supported by an examination of the state of the law, in Alberta, at the time the Agreement was made. At that time, s. 69 of the *Indian Act*, R.S.C. 1927, c. 98, provided as follows:

> **69.** The Superintendent General may, from to time, by public notice, declare that, on and after a day therein named, the laws respecting game in force in the province of Manitoba, Saskatchewan or Alberta, or the Territories, or respecting such game as is specified in such notice, shall apply to Indians within the said province or Territories, as the case may be, or to Indians in such parts thereof as to him seems expedient.

The Superintendent General was thus empowered to declare that Alberta laws respecting game should apply to "Indians within the said province" or "in such parts thereof as to him seems expedient". Being a provision of the *Indian Act*, the section must have contemplated the possible exercise of the power with respect to Indians on reserves when it spoke of "Indians within the said province".

When para. 12 was drafted, it stated its general purpose and then went on to provide that the game laws of the Province should apply "to Indians within the boundaries thereof". This is practically the same as the words "Indians within the said province" in s. 69, and, in my opinion, it was intended to have the same meaning and application.

Section 69 ceased to have any effect in Alberta, Saskatchewan and Manitoba after the enactment of the *British North America Act, 1930*, which gave the agreements therein mentioned the force of law, notwithstanding anything in the *British North America Act, 1867*, or any amendments to it, or any Act of the Parliament of Canada. Section 69 disappeared from the *Indian Act* enacted in 1951 (Can.), c. 29, which then introduced s. 87 [now s. 88] to which reference will be made later, and which provided:

> **87.** Subject to the terms of any treaty and any other Act of the Parliament of Canada, all laws of general application from time to time in force in any province are applicable to and in respect of Indians in the province, except to the extent that such laws are inconsistent with this Act or any order, rule, regulation or by-law made thereunder, and except to the extent that such laws make provision for any matter for which provision is made by or under this Act.

The appellant places emphasis on the words in the proviso to para. 12 of the Agreement "on any other lands to which the said Indians may have a right of access". The contention is that para. 10 provided for continuance of the vesting of title in Indian reserves in the federal Crown, as well as for the creation of additional reserves, and that, in these lands, the Indians who reside thereon have an interest considerably greater than a mere "right of access". The use of that phrase, it is submitted, is inconsistent with any reference to reserve lands, and therefore, as the proviso, by the terms used, does not apply to Indian reserves, the section as a whole, must be taken not to have application to them.

I am unable to agree that the broad terms used in the first portion of para. 12 can be limited, inferentially, in this way. In my view, having made all Indians within the boundaries of the Province, in their own interest, subject to provincial game laws, the proviso, by which the Province assured the defined rights of hunting and fishing for food, was drawn in broad terms. The proviso assures the right to hunt and fish for food on Indian reserves, because there can be no doubt that, whatever additional rights Indian residents on a reserve may have, they certainly have the right of access to it. This view was expressed by the Saskatchewan Court of Appeal in the *Smith* case to which reference has already been made.

For these reasons, I am of the opinion that para. 12 of the Agreement made the provisions of the *Wildlife Act* applicable to all Indians, including those on reserves, and governed their activities throughout the Province, including reserves. By virtue of s. 1 of the *British North America Act, 1930*, it has the force of law, notwithstanding anything contained in the *British North America Act, 1867*, any amendment thereto, or any federal statute.

Having reached this conclusion, it is not necessary, in the circumstances of this case, to determine the meaning and effect of s. 88 [formerly s. 87] of the *Indian Act*, R.S.C. 1970, c. I–6.

I would dismiss the appeal.

Judson and Ritchie JJ. concurred with Martland J.
Hall and Spence JJ. concured with Laskin J.
Pigeon J. concured with Martland J.

. . . .

[LASKIN J., dissenting:]

. . . .

Where land in a Province is, as in the present case, an admitted Indian reserve, its administration and the law applicable thereto, so far at least as Indians thereon are concerned, depend on federal legislation. Indian reserves are enclaves which, so long as they exist as reserves, are withdrawn from provincial regulatory power. If provincial legislation is applicable at all, it is only by referential incorporation through adoption by the Parliament of Canada. This is seen in the *Indian Act*, with which I will deal later in these reasons.

The significance of the allocation of exclusive legislative power to Parliament in relation to Indian reserves merits emphasis in terms of the kind of enclave that a reserve is. It is a social economic community unit, with its own political structure as well according to the prescriptions of the *Indian Act*. The underlying title (that is, upon surrender) may well be in the Province, but during its existence as such a reserve, in my opinion, is no more subject to provincial legislation than is federal Crown property; and it is no more subject to provincial regulatory authority than is any other enterprise falling within exclusive federal competence.

. . . .

History, which is highly relevant here, denies the equation of Indian reserves with lands to which Indians may have a right of access. Legal logic also denies the equation in a situation where they are separately dealt with as they are here and in the same document. To treat Indian reserves as coming within the description of "lands to which Indians have a right of access", as did the Alberta Appellate Division, is to describe them in terms of their lowest rather than of their highest legal signification. Indians have at least a right of occupancy of reserves, and this is a larger interest than a mere right of access which, as this Court held in *Prince and Myron* v. *The Queen*, [1964] 3 C.C.C. 2, [1964] S.C.R. 81, 41 C.R. 403, may exist in privately-owned lands. I see no justification for enlarging the category of what I may call, for short, access lands beyond lands which strictly fall within that description and have no higher legal quality....

(c) *Dick v. The Queen*†

See **Chapter 6, Part 8**.

[BEETZ J. for the Court:]

The Facts

The facts are not in dispute. They are summarized by Lambert J.A., dissenting in the British Columbia Court of Appeal whose reasons for judgment are reported: *R.* v. *Dick*, *ante* p. 35, 3 C.C.C. (3d) 481, 41 B.C.L.R. 173. At p. 37 *ante*, Lambert J.A. related the facts:

> Arthur Dick is a member of the Alkali Lake Band of the Shuswap people. He lives on the Alkali Lake Reserve in the Chilcotin District of the County of Cariboo. He is a non-treaty Indian.
>
> The Alkali Lake Band is comprised of about 10 families, or approximately 350 people, all told. They subsist in large measure by foraging. They catch fish for food and they kill deer and moose for food and other uses.
>
> The Shuswap word for May is "Pellcwewlemten". It means "time to go fishing". In response to this imperative Arthur Dick and two other band members, with two members of the Canoe Creek Band, set off on May 4, 1980, for Gustafsen Creek, where they intended to catch fish. On the way they passed Holdon Lake. There Arthur Dick killed a deer with a rifle. His purpose was to provide food for the members of the foraging party and for other band members. The carcass, cut up in pieces, was taken on to Gustafsen Creek where a provincial conservation

† [1985] 2 S.C.R. 309 at 312–30 (S.C.C.), aff'g. (1985), 23 D.L.R. (4th) 33 at 35 (B.C.C.A.), which aff'd. the decisions of the County Court and Provincial Court judges.

> officer and four R.C.M.P. constables found the five Indians in possession of dip nets, a number of rainbow trout, and the deer meat.

One precision should perhaps be added. The killing of the deer occurred in the traditional hunting grounds of the Alkali Lake Band but outside a reserve. I now return to the recital of the facts by Lambert J.A. [at pp. 37–38 *ante*]:

> The *Wildlife Act*, R.S.B.C., [1979] c. 433, said it was a closed season for hunting for deer. So Arthur Dick was charged under the Act with two counts; first, with killing wildlife, to wit: one deer, at a time not within the open season, contrary to s. 3(1); and secondly, with possession of wildlife that was dead, to wit: parts of one deer, during a closed season, contrary to s. 8. It was also a closed season for fishing in Gustafsen Creek. All five Indians were charged with respect to the fishing, and those charges are the subject-matter of a separate appeal by the Crown, raising quite different issues from those raised in this appeal.
>
> The trial took place before His Honour Judge Gilmour, a judge of the provincial court. The evidence was extensive. The accused was convicted on the first count and sentenced to a fine of $50. No conviction was entered on the second count. The accused appealed. His appeal was heard by His Honour Judge Andrews, sitting as a judge of the County Court of the County of Cariboo. The appeal was dismissed. Both Judge Gilmour and Judge Andrews reserved judgment and each of them prepared full and carefully considered written reasons.
>
> An application has now been made to this court, under s. 114 of the *Offence Act*, R.S.B.C. 1979, c. 305, for leave to appeal on a ground or grounds involving a question or questions of law alone.

Leave to appeal was granted by the Court of Appeal but the appeal was dismissed, Lambert J.A. dissenting.

Appellant further appealed to this Court by leave of this Court.

The Issues

Appellant and respondent appear to agree in substance as to the issues raised by this appeal, save one. But they express them differently and I find it preferable to rephrase them as follows:

1. Is the practice of year-round foraging for food so central to the Indian way of life of the Alkali Lake Shuswap that it cannot be restricted by ss. 3(1) and 8(1) of the *Wildlife Act*, R.S.B.C. 1979, c. 433, without impairment of their status and capacity as Indians, and invasion of the federal field under s. 91(24) of the *Constitution Act, 1867*?
2. If the answer to the first question is in the affirmative and, consequently, the *Wildlife Act* cannot apply *ex proprio vigore* to the appellant, then is this Act a law of general application referentially incorporated into federal law by s. 88 of the *Indian Act*, R.S.C. 1970, c. I–6, which provides:

> **88.** Subject to the terms of any other Act of the Parliament of Canada, all laws of general application from time to time in force in any province are applicable to and in respect of Indians in the province, except to the extent that such laws are inconsistent with this Act or any order, rule, regulation or by-law made thereunder, and except to the extent that such laws make provision for any matter for which provision is made by or under this Act.

. . . .

In addition, a constitutional question was stated by the Chief Justice:

> Are ss. 3(1)(c) and 8(1) of the *Wildlife Act*, R.S.B.C. 1979, c. 433, constitutionally inapplicable in the circumstances of this case on the ground that the restriction imposed by such sections affects the appellant *qua* Indian and therefore may only be enacted by the Parliament of Canada pursuant to s. 91(24) of the *Constitution Act, 1867*?

. . . .

One issue that does not arise is that of aboriginal title or rights. In its factum, the appellant expressly states that he has "not sought to prove or rely on the Aboriginal Title or Rights in the case at bar". As in the *Kruger and Manuel* case, the issue will accordingly not be dealt with any more than the related or included question whether the Indians' right to hunt is a personal right or, as has been suggested by some learned authors, is a right in the nature of a *profit à prendre* or some other interest in land covered by the expression "Lands reserved for the Indians", rather than the word "Indians" in s. 91(24) of the *Constitution Act, 1867*: see Lysyk, Kenneth, "The Unique Constitutional position of the Canadian Indian" (1967), 45 *Can. Bar Rev.* 513 at 518–19; Jordan, Anthony, "Government, Two — Indians, One" (1978), 16 *Osgoode Hall L.J.* 709 at 719. No submission was made on this last point and in this Court, as well apparently as in the courts below, the case has been argued as if the Indians' right to hunt were a personal one.

The First Issue

Appellant's main submission which was apparently presented in the Court of Appeal as an alternative argument, is that the *Wildlife Act* strikes at the core of Indianness, that the question stated in the first issue should accordingly be answered in the affirmative and that the *Wildlife Act*, while valid legislation, should be read down so as not to apply to appellant in the circumstances of the case at bar.

. . . .

In the Court of Appeal, Seaton J.A. concluded as follows at p. 37 *ante*:

> The decisions under attack were primarily decisions of fact. To the extent that there were questions of law alone, I am not persuaded that error has been shown. I would grant leave, but dismiss the appeal.

MacDonald J.A. refrained from expressing any views on the merits of the three issues raised in the Court of Appeal. At p. 48 *ante*, he concluded: "My opinion is that none of the three issues involves a question of law alone. I would therefore dismiss the appeal."

The reasons of Lambert J.A., dissenting, are quite elaborate. For the greater part, they expound the similarities and differences between the case at bar and *Kruger and Manuel* and his understanding of the tests adopted in the latter case to determine whether a law is one of general application, a matter to which I will return in dealing with the second issue. But he used the same tests to answer the question stated in the first issue, namely, whether the application of the *Wildlife Act* to appellant would regulate him *qua* Indian. Here is what he wrote at p. 45 *ante*:

> ... it seems to me that the same tests as are applied to determine whether the application of a provincial law to a particular group of Indians in a particular activity is the application of a law of general application, should also be applied to determine whether the application of a provincial law to a particular group of Indians in a particular activity is legislation in relation to Indians in their Indianness.
>
> So, subject to the question of referential incorporation, which I will come to next, it is my opinion that the evidence and argument which I have set out in Part III of these reasons require the conclusion that the *Wildlife Act* should be "read down" in order to preserve its constitutionality. That "reading down" would prevent it from applying to Arthur Dick in his activity in this case.

It is well worth quoting substantial parts of the evidence and argument set out in Part III of the reasons of Lambert J.A., which, as I just said, were also relied upon by him to resolve the first issue. He wrote, at pp. 39–40, and pp. 42–44 *ante*:

> In *Kruger and Manuel* v. *The Queen*, *supra*, the two accused were members of the Penticton Indian Band. They shot four deer for food on unoccupied Crown land on the traditional hunting grounds of the Penticton Indian Band. It was the closed season under the *Wildlife Act* and Kruger and Manuel did not have a sustenance permit which would have allowed them to shoot a deer during the closed season. They were convicted. Their appeal to Judge Washington took the form of a trial *de novo*. It was allowed. The Crown appealed to this Court. That appeal was also allowed and the convictions were restored; 24 C.C.C. (2d) 120, 60 D.L.R. (3d) 144, [1975] 5 W.W.R. 167. Kruger and Manuel appealed to the Supreme Court of Canada. Their appeal was dismissed. Mr. Justice Dickson's reasons were the reasons of the full court of nine.
>
> . . . .
>
> The evidence in this appeal goes much further than the agreed facts in *Kruger and Manuel* v. *The Queen*. Here there is evidence which indicates that the line demarking laws of general application from other enactments has been crossed. In *Kruger and Manuel* v. *The Queen* the only relevant evidence was the statement in the agreed facts that the accused had hunted deer during the closed season on land that was the traditional hunting grounds of the Penticton Indian Band. There was no evidence that the statutory restrictions on the right to hunt impaired the status and capacities of Kruger and Manuel as Indians. There was no evidence that it would be impracticable to hunt sufficient meat during the open season. There was no evidence as to the amount of meat obtained through hunting, the amount of meat needed to feed an Indian family for a year, or the amount of meat allowed to Indians under the prevailing hunting quotas. Finally, there was no evidence to indicate that hunting was central to the way of life of the Penticton Indian Band. There was, in the words of Mr. Justice Dickson, an "absence of clear evidence" that the provisions in the *Wildlife Act* crossed the line demarking laws of general application from other enactments.

> The situation is entirely different in the present appeal where, in my opinion, the evidence indicates that the line has been crossed.
>
> Nine members of the Alkali Lake Band and three members of the Canoe Creek Band gave evidence. They described their lives and the significance of the rituals of food gathering. They told of their dependence on moose and deer for food and for traditional and valued items of daily clothing and ceremonial clothing. Their evidence was placed in its cultural framework by Dr. Michael Asch, an anthropologist.
>
> In 1980, the year in which Arthur Dick shot the deer at Holdon Lake, there were 45 active hunters in the Alkali Lake Band. They took 117 deer and 48 moose in the year. That provided a yield of 65 to 70 pounds of meat for every man, woman and child in the Band. The meat was shared out among band members in accordance with the institutional practices of the Shuswap people.
>
> . . . .
>
> In my opinion, it is impossible to read the evidence without realizing that killing fish and animals for food and other uses gives shape and meaning to the lives of the members of the Alkali Lake Band. It is at the centre of what they do and what they are.
>
> In my opinion, this case is distinguishable from *Kruger and Manuel* v. *The Queen* (1977), 34 C.C.C. (2d) 377, 75 D.L.R. (3d) 434, [1978] 1 S.C.R. 104, because here the appellant has led evidence which, in my opinion, establishes that the *Wildlife Act* in its application to hunting for food impairs the status and capacities of the Alkali Lake Band members and crosses the line demarking laws of general application from other enactments.

And, before concluding at p. 48 *ante*, Lambert J.A. wrote:

> Indeed, I would add that if the facts in this case do not place the killing of the deer within the central core of Indianness, if there is one, or within the boundary that outlines the status and capacities of the Alkali Lake Band, then it is difficult to imagine other facts that would do so.

In *Cardinal* v. *A.-G. Alta.* (1973), 13 C.C.C. (2d) 1 at p. 9, 40 D.L.R. (3d) 553 at p. 562, [1974] S.C.R. 695 at p. 706, it had already been held, apart from any evidence, that provincial game laws do not relate to Indians *qua* Indians. In the case at bar, there was considerable evidence capable of supporting the conclusions of Lambert J.A. to the effect that the *Wildlife Act* did impair the Indianness of the Alkali Lake Band, as well as the opposite conclusions of the courts below.

I am prepared to assume, without deciding, that Lambert J.A. was right on this point and that appellant's submission on the first issue is well taken.

I must confess at being strengthened in this assumption by what Lambert J.A. said at p. 46 *ante*:

> The question of whether provincial legislation affects Indians as Indians, or Indians in their Indianness, to put it another way, is at the root of both arguments that I have considered in this appeal. I think it is worth adding that I have derived some sense of the nature of Indianness from the fact that the Indians in Alberta, Saskatchewan and Manitoba have the right to hunt and fish for food at all seasons of the year [see the Natural Resources Agreements and the *Constitution Act, 1930*, R.S.C. 1970, Appendix No. 25], and the treaty Indians in British Columbia also have that right: see *R.* v. *White and Bob* (1965), 52 D.L.R. (2d) 481n, [1965] S.C.R. vi. I think that those rights are characteristic of Indianness, at least for those Indians, and if for those Indians, why not for the Alkali Lake Band of the Shuswap people?

On the basis of this assumption and subject to the question of referential incorporation which will be dealt with in the next chapter, it follows that the *Wildlife Act* could not apply to the appellant *ex proprio vigore*, and, in order to preserve its constitutionality, it would be necessary to read it down to prevent its applying to appellant in the circumstances of this case.

The Second Issue

In holding that the tests adopted by this Court in *Kruger and Manuel* to determine whether a law is one of general application are the same tests which should be applied to determine whether the application of the *Wildlife Act* to appellant would regulate him in his Indianness, Lambert J.A. fell into error, in my respectful opinion. And this error resulted from a misapprehension of what was decided in *Kruger and Manuel* as to the nature of a law of general application.

The tests which Lambert J.A. applied in reviewing the evidence in his above-quoted reasons are perfectly suitable to determine whether the application of the *Wildlife Act* to the appellant would have the effect of regulating him *qua* Indian, with the consequential necessity of a reading down if it did; but, apart from legislative intent and colourability, they have nothing to do with the question whether the *Wildlife Act* is a law of general application. On the contrary, it is precisely because the *Wildlife Act* is a law of general application that it would have to be read down were it not for s. 88 of the *Indian Act*. If the special impact of the *Wildlife Act* on Indians had been the very result contemplated by the Legislature and pursued by it as a matter of policy, the Act could not be read down because it would be in relation to Indians and clearly *ultra vires*.

The *Wildlife Act* does not differ in this respect from a great many provincial labour laws which are couched in general terms and which, taken literally, would apply to federal works and undertakings. So to apply them, however, would make them regulate such works and undertakings under some essentially federal aspects. They are accordingly read down as not to apply to federal works and undertakings: *Reference re Minimum Wage Act of Saskatchewan* (1948), 91 C.C.C. 366, [1948] 3 D.L.R. 801, [1948] S.C.R. 248 *sub nom. Reference as to applicability of Minimum Wage Act of Saskatchewan to an employee of a Revenue Post Office*; *Com'n du salaire minimum* v. *Bell Telephone Co. of Canada (1966)*, 59 D.L.R. (2d) 145, [1966] S.C.R. 767, 66 C.L.L.C. para. 14, 154; *Letter Carriers' Union of Canada* v. *Canadian Union of Postal Workers et al.* (1973), 40 D.L.R. (3d) 105, [1975] 1 S.C.R. 178, [1974] 1 W.W.R. 452. But it has never been suggested, so far as I know, that, by the same token, those provincial labour laws cease to be laws of general application.

In his reasons for judgment, Lambert J.A. relied on two passages of *Kruger and Manuel* which he quoted and commented. The first passage is to be found at p. 381 C.C.C., p. 438 D.L.R., p. 110 S.C.R.:

> If the law does extend uniformly throughout the jurisdiction the intention and effects of the enactment need to be considered. The law must not be "in relation to" one class of citizens in object and purpose. But the fact that a law may have graver consequences to one person than to another does not, on that account alone, make the law other than one of general application. There are few laws which have a uniform impact. The line is crossed, however, when an enactment, though in relation to another matter, by its effect, impairs the status or capacity of a particular group.

The second passage of *Kruger and Manuel* quoted by Lambert J.A. is at pp. 382–83 C.C.C., pp. 439–40 D.L.R., p. 112 S.C.R.:

> Game conservation laws have as their policy the maintenance of wildlife resources. It might be argued that without some conservation measures the ability of Indians or others to hunt for food would become a moot issue in consequence of the destruction of the resource. The presumption is for the validity of a legislative enactment and in this case the presumption has to mean that in the absence of evidence to the contrary the measures taken by the British Columbia Legislature were taken to maintain an effective resource in the Province for its citizens and not to oppose the interests of conservationists and Indians in such a way as to favour the claims of the former. If, of course, it can be shown in future litigation that the Province has acted in such a way as to oppose conservation and Indian claims to the detriment of the latter — to "preserve moose before Indians" in the words of Gordon J.A., in *R. ex rel. Clinton* v. *Strongquill* (1935), 105 C.C.C. 262, [1953] 2 D.L.R. 264, 8 W.W.R. (N.S.) 247 —|it might very well be concluded that the effect of the legislation is to cross the line demarking laws of general application from other enactments. It would have to be shown that the policy of such an Act was to impair the status and capacities of Indians. Were that so, s. 88 would not operate to make the Act applicable to Indians. But that has not been done here and in the absence of clear evidence the Court cannot so presume.

Lambert J.A. then emphasized the importance of the effect of the legislation as opposed to its purpose. At p. 42 *ante*, of his reasons he wrote:

> ... evidence about the motives of individual members of the Legislature or even about the more abstract "intention of the legislature" or "legislative purpose of the enactment" is not relevant. What is relevant is evidence about the effect of the legislation. In fact, evidence about its "application".

With all due deference, it seems to me that the correct view is the reverse one and that what Dickson J., as he then was, referred to in *Kruger and Manuel* when he mentioned laws which had crossed the line of general application were laws which, either overtly or colourably, single out Indians for special treatment and impair their status as Indians. Effect and intent are both relevant. Effect can evidence intent. But in order to determine whether a law is not one of general application, the intent, purpose or policy of the legislation can certainly not be ignored: they form an essential ingredient of a law which discriminates between various classes of persons, as opposed to a law of general application. This, in my view, is what Dickson J. meant when in the above-quoted passage, he wrote: "It would have to be shown that the policy of such an Act was to impair the status and capacities of Indians".

. . . .

Reference should also be made to a later "company case", *Multiple Access Ltd.* v. *McCutcheon et al.* (1982), 138 D.L.R. (3d) 1, [1982] 2 S.C.R. 161, 18 B.L.R. 138, where it was held, *inter alia*, that ss. 113 and 114 of the *Securities Act*, R.S.O. 1970, c. 426, applied to federally incorporated companies. Dickson J. as he then was, delivered the reasons of the majority — but there was no division on this point — at p. 18 D.L.R. p. 183 S.C.R., Dickson J. wrote:

> It is well established that the provinces have the power, as a matter of property and civil rights, to regulate the trade in corporate securities in the province, provided the statute does not single out federal companies for special treatment or discriminate against them in any way. There must be no impairment of status or of the essential power to raise capital for corporate purposes. But federal incorporation does not render a company immune from securities regulation of general application in a province.

It has already been held in *Kruger and Manuel* that on its face, and in form, the *Wildlife Act* is a law of general application. In the previous chapter, I have assumed that its application to appellant would have the effect of regulating the latter *qua* Indian. However, it has not been demonstrated, in my view, that this particular impact has been intended by the provincial legislator. While it is assumed that the *Wildlife Act* impairs the status or capacity of appellant, it has not been established that the legislative policy of the *Wildlife Act* singles out Indians for special treatment or discriminates against them in any way.

I accordingly conclude that the *Wildlife Act* is a law of general application within the meaning of s. 88 of the *Indian Act*.

It remains to decide whether the *Wildlife Act* is a law of general application within the meaning of s. 88 of the *Indian Act*.

In *Kruger and Manuel*, Dickson J. wrote at p. 384 C.C.C., p. 442 D.L.R., p. 115 S.C.R.:

> There is in the legal literature a judicial controversy respecting whether s. 88 referentially incorporates provincial laws of general application or whether such laws apply to Indians *ex proprio vigore*. The issue was considered by this Court in *Natural Parents* v. *Superintendent of Child Welfare et al.* (1975), 60 D.L.R. (3d) 148, [1976] 2 S.C.R. 751, [1976] 1 W.W.R. 699.

This controversy has so far remained unresolved in this Court.

I believe that a distinction should be drawn between two categories of provincial laws. There are, on the one hand, provincial laws which can be applied to Indians without touching their Indianness, like traffic legislation; there are on the other hand, provincial laws which cannot apply to Indians without regulating them *qua* Indians.

Laws of the first category, in my opinion, continue to apply to Indians *ex proprio vigore* as they always did before the enactment of s. 88 in 1951, then numbered s. 87 — 1951 (Can.), c. 29 — and quite apart from s. 88 — *vide R.* v. *Hill* (1907), 15 O.L.R. 406, where an Indian was convicted of unlawful practice of medicine contrary to a provincial medical act, and *R.* v. *Martin* (1917), 29 C.C.C. 189, 39 D.L.R. 635, 41 O.L.R. 79, where an Indian was convicted of unlawful possession of intoxicating liquor, contrary to a provincial temperance act.

I have come to the view that it is to the laws of the second category that s. 88 refers. I agree with what Laskin C.J.C. wrote in *Natural Parents* v. *Superintendent of Child Welfare et al.* (1975), 60 D.L.R. (3d) 148 at p. 156, [1976] 2 S.C.R. 751 at p. 763, [1976] 1 W.W.R. 699:

> When s. 88 refers to "all laws of general application from time to time in force in any province" it cannot be assumed to have legislated a nullity but, rather, to have in mind provincial legislation which, *per se*, would not apply to Indians under the *Indian Act* unless given force by federal reference.
>
> I am fully aware of the contention that it is enough to give force to the several opening provisions of s. 88, which, respectively, make the "provincial" reference subject to the terms of any treaty and any other federal Act and subject also to inconsistency with the *Indian Act* and orders, rules, regulations or by-laws thereunder. That contention would have it that s. 88 is otherwise declaratory. On this view, however, it is wholly declaratory save perhaps in its reference to "the terms of any treaty", a strange reason, in my view, to explain all the other provisions of s. 88. I think too that the concluding words of s. 88, "except to the extent that such laws make provision for any matter for which provision is made by or under this Act" indicate clearly that Parliament is indeed effecting incorporation by reference.

I also adopt the suggestion expressed by Professor Lysyk, as he then was, *op. cit.*, p. 552:

> Provincial laws of general application will extend to Indians whether on or off reserves. It has been suggested that the constitution permits this result without the assistance of section 87 of the

> *Indian Act*, and that the only significant result of that section is, by expressly embracing *all* laws of general application (subject to the exceptions stated in the section), to contemplate extension of particular laws which otherwise might have been held to be so intimately bound up with the essential capacities and rights inherent in Indian status as to have otherwise required a conclusion that the provincial legislation amounted to an inadmissible encroachment upon section 91(24) of the *British North America Act*.

The word "all" in s. 88 is telling but, as was noticed by the late Chief Justice, the concluding words of s. 88 are practically decisive: it would not be open to Parliament, in my view, to make the *Indian Act* paramount over provincial laws simply because the *Indian Act* occupied the field. Operational conflict would be required to this end. But Parliament could validly provide for any type of paramountcy of the *Indian Act* over other provisions which it alone could enact, referentially or otherwise. It is true that the paramountcy doctrine may not have been as precise in 1951 as it has become at a later date, but it is desirable to adopt a construction of s. 88 which accords with established constitutional principles.

In a supplementary factum, appellant argues that a prospective incorporation into the *Indian Act* of future provincial laws which would regulate the appellant *qua* Indian, involves interdelegation of powers of a type held unconstitutional in *A.-G. N.S. et al.* v. *A.-G. Can. et al.*, [1950] 4 D.L.R. 369, [1951] S.C.R. 31. In my opinion, *A.-G. Ont.* v. *Scott* (1955), 114 C.C.C. 224, 1 D.L.R. (2d) 433, [1956] S.C.R. 137, and *Coughlin* v. *Ontario Highway Transport Board et al.* (1968), 68 D.L.R. (2d) 384, [1968] S.C.R. 569, provide a complete answer to this objection.

I accordingly conclude that, in view of s. 88 of the *Indian Act*, the *Wildlife Act* applies to appellant even if, as I have assumed, it has the effect of regulating him *qua* Indian.

. . . .

I would answer the constitutional question as follows:

> Sections 3(1) and 8(1) of the *Wildlife Act*, being laws of general application in the Province of British Columbia, are applicable to the appellant either by referential incorporation under s. 88 of the *Indian Act*, or of their own force.

Conclusions

I would dismiss the appeal and make no order as to costs.

Appeal dismissed.

(d) *Delgamuukw*†

See **Chapter 6, Part 9**.

Delgamuukw is reproduced in part in **Reading 10(b)** at p. 355 as it is the leading modern decision on the nature of Aboriginal title. However, in the last part of the decision, the Court made some important comments on the relationship of Aboriginal title to federal and provincial legislative jurisdiction: see especially paragraphs 175, 178 and 183 in the *Delgamuukw* extract. What is the result of these comments?

† [1997] 3 S.C.R. 1010 (December 11, 1997); varying (1993), 104 D.L.R. (4th) 470 (B.C.C.A.); which varied (1991), 79 D.L.R. (4th) 185 (B.C.S.C.).

(e) *Kitkatla Band v. British Columbia (Minister of Small Business, Tourism and Culture)*†

See **Chapter 6, Part 10**.

NOTE

A provincial statute banned the removal of heritage objects (CMTs) from sites showing evidence of human habitation before 1846. As an exception, though, it conferred a Ministerial discretion to grant site alteration permits in areas outside Indian reserves or areas in which Aboriginal title had been established. Exercising this discretion, the Minster granted a permit to a timber company to remove 40 of 120 CMTs in an area subject to Aboriginal title.

The Kitkatla Band claimed Aboriginal title to the area, and said they owned all the CMTs. Among other things, they sought a declaration that the statutory provisions were unconstitutional because they were laws in relation to s. 91(24) the *Constitution Act, 1867* and were not saved by s. 88 of the *Indian Act*. Why didn't the Supreme Court agree that a declaration should issue? Would the Court's decision have been different if there were proof here (a) that existing Aboriginal rights were affected, or (b) that important Kitkatla cultural interests were adversely affected?

EXTRACT

[LEBEL J. for himself, McLACHLIN C.J. and GONTHIER, IACOBUCCI, MAJOR, BINNIE, and ARBOUR JJ.]:

. . . .

[para50] The appellants, in support of their claim, assert that the preservation of the CMTs as living trees is required in order to safeguard evidence of their cultural heritage including the work, activities and endeavours of their forebears. Indeed, they argue that the CMTs constitute the only physical record of their heritage. Unfortunately, the evidence supporting these claims is sparse. Aside from an affidavit sworn by the appellant Chief Hill, there is very little evidence as to the extent to which these trees in the Kumealon had been related to or incorporated into the culture of the Band. In this respect, according to other evidence, the firm of archeologists hired by Interfor identified these CMTs and brought their existence to the attention of the appellants. The constitutional questions must be reviewed in the context of this factual record, with its particular weaknesses. I will now turn to the constitutional issues.

. . . .

[para52] ... In this case, the issues raised by the parties concern the use and protection of property in the province. The Act imposes limitations on property rights in the province by reason of their cultural importance. At first blush, this would seem to be a provincial matter falling within the scope of s. 92(13) of the *Constitution Act, 1867*. This view will have to be tested through a proper pith and substance analysis, in order to establish the relationship between the impugned provisions and the federal power on Indian affairs.

. . . .

[para58] ... In my view, Dickson C.J.'s test [in *General Motors of Canada Ltd. v. City National Leasing*, [1989] 1 S.C.R. 641 at 666–69] could be restated in the following form:

1. Do the impugned provisions intrude into a federal head of power, and to what extent?
2. If the impugned provisions intrude into a federal head of power, are they nevertheless part of a valid provincial legislative scheme?
3. If the impugned provisions are part of a valid provincial legislative scheme, are they sufficiently integrated with the scheme?

† *Kitkatla Band v. British Columbia (Minister of Small Business, Tourism and Culture)*, [2002] 2 S.C.R. 146 at paras. 50, 57–58, 60–71, and 74–78, aff'g (2002) 183 D.L.R. (4th) 183 (B.C.C.A.), aff'g [1999] 7 W.W.R. 584 (S.C.) and [1999]2 C.N.L.R. 176 (S.C.).

. . . .

[para60] Paragraphs (c) and (d) of s. 13(2) have as their purpose the protection of certain aboriginal heritage objects from damage, alteration, or removal. In other words, the purpose of these paragraphs is heritage conservation, specifically the heritage of the aboriginal peoples of British Columbia. The protection extends to all aboriginal rock paintings or aboriginal rock carvings that have historical or archaeological value, as well as to heritage objects, including artifacts, features, materials or other physical evidence of human habitation or use before 1846, which in effect consists almost entirely of aboriginal cultural artifacts.

[para61] Paragraph (a) of s. 12(2), on the other hand, provides the minister responsible for the operation of the Act as a whole with the discretion to grant a permit authorizing one of the actions prohibited under s. 13(2)(c) and (d). In other words, this paragraph provides a tempering of the absolute protection otherwise provided by s. 13(2)(c) and (d).

[para62] The purpose of such a provision seems obvious when one considers the nature of heritage conservation legislation generally and its specific application in the context of British Columbia. No heritage conservation scheme can provide absolute protection to all objects or sites that possess some historical, archaeological, or cultural value to a society. To grant such an absolute protection would be to freeze a society at a particular moment in time. It would make impossible the need to remove, for example, buildings or artifacts of heritage value which, nevertheless, create a public health hazard or otherwise endanger lives. In other cases, the value of preserving an object may be greatly outweighed by the benefit that could accrue from allowing it to be removed or destroyed in order to accomplish a goal deemed by society to be of greater value. It cannot be denied that ss. 12(2)(a) and 13(2)(c) could sometimes affect aboriginal interests. As will be seen below, these provisions form part of a carefully balanced scheme. As recommended by the Court in *Delgamuukw*, *supra*, it is highly sensitive to native cultural interests. At the same time, it appears to strike an appropriate balance between native and non-native interests....

[para63] Consequently, any heritage conservation scheme inevitably includes provisions to make exceptions to the general protection the legislation is intended to provide. Such a permissive provision strikes a balance among competing social goals.

H. Effect of the Provisions

[para64] Having looked at the purpose of these provisions, I turn now to consider their effects. Sections 12(2)(a) and 13(2)(c) and (d) grant the Minister a discretion to allow the alteration or removal of aboriginal heritage objects. We have no evidence before us with respect to the total number of aboriginal heritage objects which may be covered by this legislation. Nor do we have any evidence as to how often the Minister has exercised the discretion to permit the removal or destruction of aboriginal heritage objects of whatever type. We know only that, in the present case, the permit granted to the respondent Interfor allowed it to cut 40 out of about 120 standing CMTs within seven identified cutblocks. Thus, the practical effect, in this case anyway, is to permit the destruction of what are alleged to be Kitkatla heritage objects (although there is no specific proof here that the 40 CMTs in question were indeed the products of Kitkatla ancestors) while protecting 80 CMTs from alteration and removal. In addition, all CMTs allowed to be logged must be catalogued and an archival record of them must be retained. In other words, the effect here is the striking of a balance between the need and desire to preserve aboriginal heritage with the need and desire to promote the exploitation of British Columbia's natural resources.

I. Effect on Federal Powers

[para65] Given this analysis of the purpose and effect of the legislation in order to characterize the impugned provisions, the Court must then determine whether the pith and substance of ss. 12(2)(a) and 13(2)(c) and (d) fall within a provincial head of power or if, rather, they fall within a federal head of power. If the Court characterizes these provisions as a heritage conservation measure that is designed to strike a balance between the need to preserve the past while also allowing the exploitation of natural resources today, then they would fall squarely within the provincial head of power in s. 92(13) of the *Constitution Act, 1867* with respect to property and civil rights in the province.

[para66] On the other hand, one cannot escape the fact that the impugned provisions directly affect the existence of aboriginal heritage objects, raising the issue of whether the provisions are in fact with respect to Indians and lands reserved to Indians, a federal head of power under s. 91(24) of the *Constitution Act, 1867*. In considering this question, the

Court must assess a number of factors. First, the Court must remember the basic assumption that provincial laws can apply to aboriginal peoples; First Nations are not enclaves of federal power in a sea of provincial jurisdiction: see *Cardinal* v. *Attorney General of Alberta*, [1974] S.C.R. 695. The mere mention of the word "aboriginal" in a statutory provision does not render it *ultra vires* the province.

[para67] Second, it is clear that legislation which singles out aboriginal people for special treatment is *ultra vires* the province: see *Four B Manufacturing Ltd.* v. *United Garment Workers of America*, [1980] 1 S.C.R. 1031. For example, a law which purported to affect the Indian status of adopted children was held to be *ultra vires* the province: see *Natural Parents* v. *Superintendent of Child Welfare*, [1976] 2 S.C.R. 751. Similarly, laws which purported to define the extent of Indian access to land for the purpose of hunting were *ultra vires* the provinces because they singled out Indians: see *Sutherland*, *supra*; *Moosehunter* v. *The Queen*, [1981] 1 S.C.R. 282. Further, provincial laws must not impair the status or capacity of Indians: see *Kruger* v. *The Queen*, [1978] 1 S.C.R. 104, at p. 110; *Dick*, *supra*, at pp. 323–24.

[para68] Nevertheless, "singling out" should not be confused with disproportionate effect. Dickson J. (as he then was) said in *Kruger*, *supra*, at p. 110, that "the fact that a law may have graver consequence to one person than to another does not, on that account alone, make the law other than one of general application".

[para69] In the present case, the impugned provisions cannot be said to single out aboriginal peoples, at least from one point of view. The provisions prohibit everyone, not just aboriginal peoples, from the named acts, and require everyone, not just aboriginal peoples, to seek permission of the Minister to commit the prohibited acts. In that respect, the impugned provisions treat everyone the same. The impugned provisions' disproportionate effects can be attributed to the fact that aboriginal peoples have produced by far the largest number of heritage objects in British Columbia. These peoples have been resident in British Columbia for thousands of years; other British Columbians arrived in the last two hundred years.

[para70] A more serious objection is raised with respect to the issue of whether permitting the destruction of aboriginal heritage objects impairs the status or capacity of Indians. The appellants' submission seeks to situate these cultural interests, along with aboriginal rights, at the "core of Indianness", *Delgamuukw*, *supra*, at para. 181. However, as pointed out above, little evidence has been offered by the appellants with respect to the relationship between the CMTs and Kitkatla culture in this area. The appellants argue that aboriginal heritage objects constitute a major portion of their identity and culture in a way that non-aboriginal heritage objects do not go to the centre of non-aboriginal identity. Consequently, they argue, aboriginal people are singled out for more severe treatment. I would reject this argument. Because British Columbia's history is dominated by aboriginal culture, fewer non-aboriginal objects and sites receive protection than aboriginal objects and sites. The Act provides a shield, in the guise of the permit process, against the destruction or alteration of heritage property. When one considers the relative protection afforded aboriginal and non-aboriginal heritage objects, the treatment received by both groups is the same, and indeed is more favourable, in one sense to aboriginal peoples.

[para71] In any case, it should be remembered that the Act cannot apply to any aboriginal heritage object or site which is the subject of an established aboriginal right or title, by operation of s. 35(1) of the *Constitution Act, 1982* and by operation of s. 8 of the *Heritage Conservation Act* (and, by implication, s. 12(7) of that Act which states that a permit does not grant a right to alter or remove an object without the consent of the party which has title to the object or site on which the object is situated). The Act is tailored, whether by design or by operation of constitutional law, to not affect the established rights of aboriginal peoples, a protection that is not extended to any other group. On the whole, then, I am of the opinion that ss. 12(2)(a) and 13(2)(c) and (d) of the Act are valid provincial law and that they do not single out aboriginal peoples or impair their status or condition as Indians.

. . . .

[para74] The doctrine of paramountcy does not appear applicable in this case, as no valid federal legislation occupies the same field. There are provisions in the *Indian Act* with respect to aboriginal heritage conservation, but they are confined to objects on reserve lands. As I noted above, the *Heritage Conservation Act* does not apply to aboriginal heritage objects or sites which are the subject of an established aboriginal right or title by virtue both of s. 35(1) of the *Constitution Act, 1982* and s. 8 of the Act itself, which is declaratory of that fact. In any case, the CMTs in question in this case are not located on an Indian reserve but on Crown land.

[para75] I thus find that there is no intrusion on a federal head of power. It has not been established that these provisions affect the essential and distinctive core values of Indianness which would engage the federal power over native affairs and First Nations in Canada. They are part of a valid provincial legislative scheme. The legislature has made them a closely integrated part of this scheme. The provisions now protect native interests in situations where, before, land owners and business undertakings might have disregarded them, absent evidence of a constitutional right.

[para76] The Act purports to give the provincial government a means of protecting heritage objects while retaining the ability to make exceptions where economic development or other values outweigh the heritage value of the objects. In the British Columbia context, this generally means that the provincial government must balance the need to exploit the province's natural resources, particularly its rich abundance of lumber, in order to maintain a viable economy that can sustain the province's population, with the need to preserve all types of cultural and historical heritage objects and sites within the province. Given the overwhelming prevalence of aboriginal heritage objects in the province and, in this particular case, the ubiquitous nature of CMTs, legislation which sought to permit the striking of this balance but which did not attempt to extend this to aboriginal heritage objects and sites would inevitably fall very far short of its goal, if in fact it would not in most respects gut the purposes of the Act.

[para77] Given this conclusion, it will not be useful to discuss the doctrine of interjurisdictional immunity. It would apply only if the provincial legislation went to the core of the federal power. (See *Ordon Estate* v. *Grail*, [1998] 3 S.C.R. 437, at para. 81; *Delgamuukw*, *supra*, at paras. 177–78, per Lamer C.J.) In these circumstances, no discussion of the principle governing the application of s. 88 of the *Indian Act* would be warranted.

VII. CONCLUSION AND DISPOSITION

[para78] Heritage properties and sites may certainly, in some cases, turn out to be a key part of the collective identity of people. In some future case, it might very well happen that some component of the cultural heritage of a First Nation would go to the core of its identity in such a way that it would affect the federal power over native affairs and the applicability of provincial legislation. This appeal does not raise such issues, based on the weak evidentiary record and the relevant principles governing the division of powers in Canada. In the circumstances of this case, the overall effect of the provision is to improve the protection of native cultural heritage and, indeed, to safeguard the presence and the memory of the cultural objects involved in this litigation, without jeopardizing the core values defining the identity of the appellants as Indians. For these reasons, I would dismiss the appeal, without costs. The constitutional questions should be answered as follows:

- Is s. 12(2)(a) in respect of the subject matter of s. 13(2)(c) and (d) of the *Heritage Conservation Act* in pith and substance law in relation to Indians or Lands reserved for the Indians, or alternatively, is the law in relation to property, and, therefore, within the exclusive legislative competence of the Province under s. 92(13) of the *Constitution Act, 1867*?

  Answer: Section 12(2)(a) in respect of the subject matter in s. 13(2)(c) and (d) of the *Heritage Conservation Act* is in pith and substance law within the legislative competence of the Province under s. 92(13) of the *Constitution Act, 1867*.

- If the impugned provisions of the *Heritage Conservation Act* are within provincial jurisdiction under s. 92(13) of the *Constitution Act, 1867* do they apply to the subject matter of s. 13(2)(c) and (d) of the *Heritage Conservation Act*?

  Answer: Yes.

- If the impugned provisions do not apply to the appellants *ex proprio vigore*, do they nonetheless apply by virtue of s. 88 of the *Indian Act*?

  Answer: No need to answer.

7 *Constitution Act, 1982* and *Sparrow*

(a) Excerpts from *Constitution Act, 1982*†

See **Chapter 7, Part 1**.

NOTE: Clauses or sections resulting from the 1983 amendments are in **bold print**.

General

25. The guarantee in this Charter of certain rights and freedoms shall not be construed so as to abrogate or derogate from any aboriginal, treaty or other rights or freedoms that pertain to the aboriginal peoples of Canada including

(a) any rights or freedoms that have been recognized by the *Royal Proclamation* of October 7, 1763; and

(b) any rights or freedoms that **now exist by way of land claims agreements or may be so acquired**.

. . . .

PART II: RIGHTS OF THE ABORIGINAL PEOPLES OF CANADA

35.(1) The existing aboriginal and treaty rights of the aboriginal peoples of Canada are hereby recognized and affirmed.

(2) In this Act, "aboriginal peoples of Canada" includes the Indian, Inuit and Métis peoples of Canada.

(3) For greater certainty, in subsection (1) "treaty rights" includes rights that **now exist by way of land claims agreements or may be so acquired**.

(4) Notwithstanding any other provision of this Act, the aboriginal and treaty rights referred to in subsection (1) **are guaranteed equally to male and female persons**.

35.1. The government of Canada and the provincial governments are committed to the principle that, before any amendment is made to Class 24 of section 91 of the *Constitution Act, 1867*, to section 25 of this Act or to this Part,

(a) a constitutional conference that includes in its agenda an item relating to the proposed amendment, composed of the Prime Minister of Canada and the first ministers of the provinces, will be convened by the Prime Minister of Canada, and

(b) the Prime Minister of Canada will invite representatives of the aboriginal peoples of Canada to participate in the discussions on that item.

. . . .

PART IV.I: CONSTITUTIONAL CONFERENCES

37.1.(1) In addition to the conference convened in March 1983, at **least two constitutional** conferences composed of the Prime Minister of Canada and the first ministers of the provinces shall be convened by the Prime Minister of Canada, the first within three years after April 17, 1982 and the second within five years after that date.

---

† *Constitution Act, 1982*, being Schedule B of the *Canada Act, 1982*, (U.K.) 1982, c. 11; R.S.C. 1985, App. II, No. 44, as am. by the *Constitutional Amendment Proclamation, 1983*, (SI/84-102) at ss. 25, 35, 35.1, and 37.1.

(2) Each conference convened under sub-section (1) shall have included in its agenda **constitutional matters** that directly affect the aboriginal peoples of Canada, and the Prime Minister of Canada shall invite representatives of those peoples to participate in the discussions on **those matters**.

(3) The Prime Minister of Canada shall invite elected representatives of the governments of the Yukon Territory and the Northwest Territories to participate in the discussions on any item on the agenda of a conference convened under subsection (1) that, in the opinion of the Prime Minister, directly affects the Yukon Territory and the Northwest Territories.

(4) Nothing in this section shall be construed so as to derogate from subsection 35(1).

(b) 1983 Constitutional Accord†

See **Chapter 7, Parts 1 and 3.**

Whereas pursuant to section 37 of the *Constitution Act, 1982*, a constitutional conference composed of the Prime Minister of Canada and the first ministers of the provinces was held on March 15 and 16, 1983, to which representatives of the aboriginal peoples of Canada and elected representatives of the governments of the Yukon Territory and the Northwest Territories were invited;

And whereas it was agreed at that conference that certain amendments to the *Constitution Act, 1982* would be sought in accordance with section 38 of that Act;

And whereas that conference had included in its agenda the following matters that directly affect the aboriginal peoples of Canada:

AGENDA

1. Charter of Rights of the Aboriginal Peoples (expanded Part II) including:
   - Preamble
   - Removal of "Existing", and expansion of section 35 to include recognition of modern treaties, treaties signed outside Canada and before Confederation, and specific mention of "Aboriginal Title" including the rights of aboriginal peoples of Canada to a land and water base (including land base for the Métis)
   - Statement of the particular rights of aboriginal peoples
   - Statement of principles
   - Equality
   - Enforcement
   - Interpretation
2. Amending formula revisions, including:
   - Amendments on aboriginal matters not to be subject to provincial opting out [Section 42]
   - Consent clause
3. Self-government.
4. Repeal of Section 42(1)(e) and (f).
5. Amendments to Part III, including:

   Equalization
Cost-sharing
Service delivery } Resourcing of aboriginal governments
6. Ongoing process, including further first ministers conferences and the entrenchment of necessary mechanisms to implement rights.

And whereas that conference was unable to complete its full consideration of all the agenda items;

And whereas it was agreed at that conference that future conferences be held at which those agenda items and other constitutional matters that directly affect the aboriginal peoples of Canada will be discussed;

NOW THEREFORE the Government of Canada and the provincial governments hereby agree as follows:

1. A constitutional conference composed of the Prime Minister of Canada and the first minis-

† *1983 Constitutional Accord on Aboriginal Rights*, agreed to on March 15 and 16, 1983, and including the amendments later enacted in the *Constitution Amendment Proclamation* (SI/84-102).

ters of the provinces will be convened by the Prime Minister of Canada within one year after the completion of the constitutional conference held on March 15 and 16, 1983.

2. The conference convened under subsection (1) shall have included in its agenda those items that were not fully considered at the conference held on March 15 and 16, 1983, and the Prime Minister of Canada shall invite representatives of the aboriginal peoples of Canada to participate in the discussions on those items.
3. The Prime Minister of Canada shall invite elected representatives of the governments of the Yukon Territory and the Northwest Territories to participate in the discussions on any item on the agenda of the conference convened under subsection (1) that, in the opinion of the Prime Minister, directly affects the Yukon Territory and the Northwest Territories.
4. The Prime Minister of Canada will lay or cause to be laid before the Senate and House of Commons, and the first ministers of the provinces will lay or cause to be laid before their legislative assemblies, prior to December 31, 1983, a resolution in the form set out in the Schedule to authorize a proclamation to be issued by the Governor General under the Great Seal of Canada to amend the *Constitution Act, 1982*.
5. In preparation for the constitutional conferences contemplated by this Accord, meetings composed of ministers of the governments of Canada and the provinces, together with representatives of the aboriginal peoples of Canada and elected representatives of the governments of the Yukon Territory and the Northwest Territories, shall be convened at least annually by the government of Canada.
6. Nothing in this Accord is intended to preclude, or substitute for, any bilateral or other discussions or agreements between governments and the various aboriginal peoples and, in particular, having regard to the authority of Parliament under Class 24 of section 91 of the *Constitution Act, 1867*, and to the special relationship that has existed and continues to exist between the Parliament and government of Canada and the peoples referred to in that Class, this Accord is made without prejudice to any bilateral process that has been or may be established between the government of Canada and those peoples.
7. Nothing in this Accord shall be construed so as to affect the interpretation of the Constitution of Canada.

. . . .

SCHEDULE

Motion for a resolution to authorize His Excellency the Governor General to issue a proclamation respecting amendments to the Constitution of Canada.

Whereas the *Constitution Act, 1982* provides that an amendment to the Constitution of Canada may be made by proclamation issued by the Governor General under the Great Seal of Canada where so authorized by resolutions of the Senate and House of Commons and resolutions of the legislative assemblies as provided for in section 38 thereof;

And Whereas the Constitution of Canada, reflecting the country and Canadian society, continues to develop and strengthen the rights and freedoms that it guarantees;

And Whereas, after a gradual transition of Canada from colonial status to the status of an independent and sovereign state, Canadians have, as of April 17, 1982, full authority to amend their Constitution in Canada;

And Whereas historically and equitably it is fitting that the early exercise of that full authority should relate to the rights and freedoms of the first inhabitants of Canada, the aboriginal peoples;

Now Therefore the [Senate] [House of Commons] [legislative assembly] resolves that His Excellency the Governor General be authorized to issue a proclamation under the Great Seal of Canada amending the Constitution of Canada as follows:

Proclamation Amending the Constitution of Canada

1. Paragraph 25(b) of the *Constitution Act, 1982* is repealed and the following substituted therefor:

   "(b) any rights or freedoms that **now exist by way of land claims agreements or may be so acquired**".

2. Section 35 of the *Constitution Act, 1982*, is amended by adding thereto the following subsections:

   "(3) For greater certainty, in subsection (1) "treaty rights" includes rights that **now exist by way of land claims agreements or may be so acquired.**

   (4) Notwithstanding any other provision of this Act, the aboriginal and treaty rights referred to in subsection (1) **are guaranteed equally to male and female persons.**"

3. The said Act is further amended by adding thereto, immediately after section 35 thereof, the following section:

   "**35.1.** The government of Canada and the provincial governments are committed to the principle that, before any amendment is made to Class 24 of section 91 of the *Constitution Act, 1867*, to section 25 of this Act or to this Part,

   (a) a constitutional conference that includes in its agenda an item relating to the proposed amendment, composed of the Prime Minister of Canada and the first ministers of the provinces, will be convened by the Prime Minister of Canada, and

   (b) the Prime Minister of Canada will invite representatives of the aboriginal peoples of Canada to participate in the discussions on that item."

4. The said Act is further amended by adding thereto, immediately after section 37 thereof the following Part.

   "Part IV.1 — Constitutional Conferences

   37.1.(1) In addition to the conference convened in March 1983, at **least two constitutional** conferences composed of the Prime Minister of Canada and the first ministers of the provinces shall be convened by the Prime Minister of Canada, the first within three years after April 17, 1982 and the second within five years after that date.

   (2) Each conference convened under subsection (1) shall have included in its agenda **constitutional matters** that directly affect the aboriginal peoples of Canada, and the Prime Minister of Canada shall invite representatives of those peoples to participate in the discussions on **those matters**.

   (3) The Prime Minister of Canada shall invite elected representatives of the governments of the Yukon Territory and the Northwest Territories to participate in the discussions on any item on the agenda of a conference convened under subsection (1) that, in the opinion of the Prime Minister, directly affects the Yukon Territory and the Northwest Territories.

   (4) **Nothing in this section shall be construed so as to derogate from subsection 35(1).**"

5. The said Act is further amended by adding thereto, immediately after section 54 thereof, the following section:

   "**54.1.** Part IV.1 and this section are repealed on April 18, 1987".

6. The said Act is further amended by adding thereto the following section:

   "**61.** A reference to the *Constitution Acts, 1867 to 1982* shall be deemed to include a reference to the *Constitution Amendment Proclamation, 1983*".

7. This Proclamation may be cited as the ***Constitution Amendment Proclamation, 1983***.

Signed at Ottawa this 16th day of March, 1983 by the Government of Canada and the provincial governments.

(c) *R. v. Sparrow*†

See **Chapter 7, Part 4** and **Chapter 8, Parts 5 and 6.**

NOTE

Mr. Sparrow was charged with fishing with a drift net longer than permitted under a federal fishing licence. Mr. Sparrow argued that the net length restriction was inconsistent with s. 35(1) of the *Constitution Act, 1982*. For the first time, the Supreme Court was called upon to decide the effect of s. 35(1) on government regulation.

EXTRACT

[DICKSON C.J. and LA FOREST J. for the Court:]

† [1990] 1 S.C.R. 1075 at 1082–83, 1088–95, 1097–99, 1101–103, 1105–106, 1108–21, referring an issue back to trial, and aff'g (1986), 36 D.L.R.(4th) 246 (B.C.C.A.), which rev'd [1986] B.C.W.L.D. 599 (B.C. Co. Ct.: Vancouver, which aff'd the conviction by Goulet P.C.J.).

This appeal requires this court to explore for the first time the scope of s. 35(1) of the *Constitution Act, 1982*, and to indicate its strength as a promise to the aboriginal peoples of Canada. Section 35(1) is found in Part II of that Act, entitled "Rights of the Aboriginal Peoples of Canada", and provides as follows:

> **35.**(1) The existing aboriginal and treaty rights of the aboriginal peoples of Canada are hereby recognized and affirmed.

The context of this appeal is the alleged violation of the terms of the Musqueam food fishing licence which are dictated by the *Fisheries Act*, R.S.C. 1970, c. F–14, and the regulations under that Act. The issue is whether Parliament's power to regulate fishing is now limited by s. 35(1) of the *Constitution Act, 1982*, and, more specifically, whether the net length restriction in the licence is inconsistent with that provision.

Facts

The appellant, a member of the Musqueam Indian Band, was charged under s. 61(1) of the *Fisheries Act* of the offence of fishing with a drift-net longer than that permitted by the terms of the band's Indian food fishing licence. The fishing which gave rise to the charge took place on May 25, 1984, in Canoe Passage which is part of the area subject to the band's licence. The licence, which had been issued for a one-year period beginning March 31, 1984, set out a number of restrictions including one that drift-nets were to be limited to 25 fathoms in length. The appellant was caught with a net which was 45 fathoms in length. He has throughout admitted the facts alleged to constitute the offence, but has defended the charge on the basis that he was exercising an existing aboriginal right to fish and that the net length restriction contained in the band's licence is inconsistent with s. 35(1) of the *Constitution Act, 1982*, and therefore invalid.

. . . .

Acting under its regulation-making powers, the Governor-in-Council enacted the *British Columbia Fishery (General) Regulations*, SOR/84-248. Under these regulations (s. 4), everyone is, *inter alia*, prohibited from fishing without a licence, and then only in areas and at the times and in the manner authorized by the Act or regulations. That provision also prohibits buying, selling, trading or bartering fish other than those lawfully caught under the authority of a commercial fishing licence. Section 4 reads:

> **4.**(1) Unless otherwise provided in the Act or in any Regulations made thereunder in respect of the fisheries to which these Regulations apply or in the *Wildlife Act* (British Columbia), no person shall fish except under the authority of a licence or permit issued thereunder.
>
> (2) No person shall fish for any species of fish in the Province or in Canadian fisheries waters of the Pacific Ocean except in areas and at times authorized by the Act or any Regulations made thereunder in respect of the fisheries to which these Regulations apply.
>
> (3) No person who is the owner of a vessel shall operate that vessel or permit it to be operated in contravention of these Regulations.
>
> (4) No person shall, without lawful excuse, have in his possession any fish caught or obtained contrary to the Act or any Regulations made thereunder in respect of the fisheries to which these Regulations apply.
>
> (5) No person shall buy, sell, trade or barter or attempt to buy, sell, trade or barter fish or any portions thereof other than fish lawfully caught under the authority of a commercial fishing licence issued by the Minister or the Minister of Environment for British Columbia.

The regulations make provision for issuing licences to Indians or a band "for the sole purpose of obtaining food for that Indian and his family and for the band", and no one other than an Indian is permitted to be in possession of fish caught pursuant to such a licence. Subsections 27(1) and (4) of the Regulations read:

> **27.**(1) In this section "Indian food licence" means a licence issued by the Minister to an Indian or a band for the sole purpose of obtaining food for that Indian and his family or for the band.
>
> . . . .
>
> (4) No person other than an Indian shall have in his possession fish caught under the authority of an Indian food fish licence.

As in the case of other licences issued under the Act, such licences may, by s. 12 of the regulations, be subjected to restrictions regarding the species and quantity of fish that may be taken, the places and times when they may be taken, the manner in which they are to be marked and, most important here, the type of gear and equipment that may be used. Section 12 reads as follows:

> **12.**(1) Subject to these Regulations and any regulations made under the Act in respect of the fisheries to which these Regulations apply and for the proper management and control of such fisheries, there may be specified in a licence issued under these Regulations
>
> (a) the species of fish and quantity thereof that is permitted to be taken;
> (b) the period during which and the waters in which fishing is permitted to be carried out;
> (c) the type and quantity of fishing gear and equipment that is permitted to be used and the manner in which it is to be used;
> (d) the manner in which fish caught and retained for educational or scientific purposes is to be held or displayed;
> (e) the manner in which fish caught and retained is to be marked and transported; and
> (f) the manner in which scientific or catch data is to be reported.
>
> (2) No person fishing under the authority of a licence referred to in subsection (1) shall contravene or fail to comply with the terms of the licence.

Pursuant to these powers, the Musqueam Indian Band, on March 31, 1984, was issued an Indian food fishing licence as it had since 1978 "to fish for salmon for food for themselves and their family" in areas which included the place where the offence charged occurred, the waters of Ladner Reach and Canoe Passage therein described. The licence contained time restrictions as well as the type of gear to be used, notably "one Drift net twenty-five (25) fathoms in length".

The appellant was found fishing in the waters described using a drift-net in excess of 25 fathoms. He did not contest this, arguing instead that he had committed no offence because he was acting in the exercise of an existing aboriginal right which was recognized and affirmed by s. 35(1) of the *Constitution Act, 1982*.

Analysis

We will address first the meaning of "existing" aboriginal rights and the content and scope of the Musqueam right to fish. We will then turn to the meaning of "recognized and affirmed", and the impact of s. 35(1) on the regulatory power of Parliament.

"Existing"

The word "existing" makes it clear that the rights to which s. 35(1) applies are those that were in existence when the *Constitution Act, 1982*, came into effect. This means that extinguished rights are not revived by the *Constitution Act, 1982*. A number of courts have taken the position that "existing" means being in actuality in 1982: *R.* v. *Eninew* (1983), 7 C.C.C. (3d) 443 at p. 446 1 D.L.R. (4th) 595, 28 Sask. R. 168 (Sask. Q.B.), affirmed 12 C.C.C. (3d) 365, 10 D.L.R. (4th) 137, 32 Sask. R. 237 (Sask. C.A.); see also *Ontario (Attorney-General)* v. *Bear Island Foundation* (1984), 15 D.L.R. (4th) 321, 49 O.R. (2d) 353 (H.C.J.); *R.* v. *Hare and Debassige* (1985), 20 C.C.C. (3d) 1, [1985] 3 C.N.L.R. 139 (Ont. C.A.); *Steinhauer* v. *The Queen* (1985), 63 A.R. 381, 15 C.R.R. 175 (Alta. Q.B.); *Martin* v. *The Queen* (1985), 65 N.B.R. (2d) 21, 17 C.R.R. 375 (N.B.Q.B.); *R.* v. *Agawa* (1988), 43 C.C.C. (3d) 266, 53 D.L.R. (4th) 101, 28 O.A.C. 201.

Further, an existing aboriginal right cannot be read so as to incorporate the specific manner in which it was regulated before 1982. The notion of freezing existing rights would incorporate into the Constitution a crazy patchwork of regulations. Blair J.A. in *Agawa, supra*, had this to say about the matter, at p. 283:

> Some academic commentators have raised a further problem which cannot be ignored. The *Ontario Fishery Regulations* contain detailed rules which vary for different regions in the province. Among other things, the regulations specify seasons and methods of fishing, species of fish which can be caught and catch limits. Similar detailed provisions apply under the comparable fisheries regulations in force in other provinces. These detailed provisions might be constitutionalized if it were decided that the existing treaty rights referred to in s. 35(1) were those remaining after regulation at the time of the proclamation of the *Constitution Act, 1982*.

As noted by Blair J.A., academic commentary lends support to the conclusion that "existing" means "unextinguished" rather than exercisable at a certain time in history. Professor Slattery, "Understanding Aboriginal Rights" (1987), 66 *Can. Bar Rev.* 727 at pp. 781–82, has observed the following about reading regulations into the rights:

> This approach reads into the Constitution the myriad of regulations affecting the exercise of aboriginal rights, regulations that differed considerably from place to place across the country. It does not permit differentiation between regulations of long-term significance and those enacted to deal with temporary conditions, or between reasonable and unreasonable restrictions. Moreover, it might require that a constitutional amendment be enacted to implement

> regulations more stringent than those in existence on 17 April 1982. This solution seems unsatisfactory.

See also Professor McNeil, "The Constitutional Rights of the Aboriginal Peoples of Canada" (1982), 4 *Sup. Ct. L. Rev.* 255, at p. 258 (*q.v.*); Pentney, "The Rights of the Aboriginal Peoples of Canada in the *Constitution Act, 1982*, Part II, Section 35: The Substantive Guarantee" (1987), 22 *U.B.C. Law Rev.* 207.

The arbitrariness of such an approach can be seen if one considers the recent history of the federal regulation in the context of the present case and the fishing industry. If the *Constitution Act, 1982*, had been enacted a few years earlier, any right held by the Musqueam Band, on this approach, would have been constitutionally subjected to the restrictive regime of personal licences that had existed since 1917. Under that regime, the Musqueam catch had, by 1969, become minor or non-existent. In 1978, a system of band licences was introduced on an experimental basis which permitted the Musqueam to fish with a 75-fathom net for a greater number of days than other people. Under this regime, from 1977 to 1984, the number of band members who fished for food increased from 19 persons using 15 boats, to 64 persons using 38 boats, while 10 other members of the band fished under commercial licences. Before this regime, the band's food fish requirement had basically been provided by band members who were licensed for commercial fishing. Since the regime introduced in 1978 was in force in 1982, then, under this approach, the scope and content of an aboriginal right to fish would be determined by the details of the band's 1978 licence.

The unsuitability of the approach can also be seen from another perspective. Ninety-one other tribes of Indians, comprising over 20,000 people (compared with 540 Musqueam on the reserve and 100 others off the reserve) obtain their food fish from the Fraser River. Some or all of these bands may have an aboriginal right to fish there. A constitutional patchwork quilt would be created if the constitutional right of these bands were to be determined by the specific regime available to each of those bands in 1982.

Far from being defined according to the regulatory scheme in place in 1982, the phrase "existing aboriginal rights" must be interpreted flexibly so as to permit their evolution over time. To use Professor Slattery's expression, in "Understanding Aboriginal Rights", *ibid.* at p. 782, the word "existing" suggests that those rights are "affirmed in a contemporary form rather than in their primeval simplicity and vigour". Clearly, then, an approach to the constitutional guarantee embodied in s. 35(1) which would incorporate "frozen rights" must be rejected.

The Aboriginal Right

We turn now to the aboriginal right at stake in this appeal. The Musqueam Indian Reserve is located on the north shore of the Fraser River close to the mouth of that river and within the limits of the City of Vancouver. There has been a Musqueam village there for hundreds of years. This appeal does not directly concern the reserve or the adjacent waters, but arises out of the band's right to fish in another area of the Fraser River estuary known as Canoe Passage in the South Arm of the river, some 16 kilometres (about 10 miles) from the reserve. The reserve and those waters are separated by the Vancouver International Airport and the Municipality of Richmond.

The evidence reveals that the Musqueam have lived in the area as an organized society long before the coming of European settlers, and that the taking of salmon was an integral part of their lives and remains so to this day....

. . . .

In this court, however, the respondent contested the Court of Appeal's finding, contending that the evidence was insufficient to discharge the appellant's burden of proof upon the issue. It is true that for the period from 1867 to 1961, the evidence is scanty. But the evidence was not disputed or contradicted in the courts below and there is evidence of sufficient continuity of the right to support the Court of Appeal's finding, and we would not disturb it.

What the Crown really insisted on, both in this court and the courts below, was that the Musqueam Band's aboriginal right to fish had been extinguished by regulations under the *Fisheries Act*.

. . . .

It is this progressive restriction and detailed regulation of the fisheries which, respondent's counsel maintained, have had the effect of extinguishing any aboriginal right to fish. The extinguishment need not be express, he argued, but may take place where the sovereign authority is exercised in a manner "necessarily inconsistent" with the continued enjoyment of aboriginal rights. For this proposition, he particularl relied on *St. Catherine's Milling & Lumber Co.* v. *T Queen* (1888), 14 App. Cas. 46 (P.C.); *Calder* v *G. B.C.* (1973), 34 D.L.R. (3d) 145, [1973]

313, [1973] 4 W.W.R. 1; *Hamlet of Baker Lake* v. *Minister of Indian Affairs and Northern Development* (1979), 107 D.L.R. (3d) 513, [1980] 1 F.C. 518, [1980] 5 W.W.R. 193 (T.D.), and *Ontario (Attorney-General)* v. *Bear Island Foundation*, *supra*. The consent to its extinguishment before the *Constitution Act, 1982*, was not required; the intent of the sovereign could be effected not only by statute but by valid regulations. Here, in his view, the regulations had entirely displaced any aboriginal right. There is, he submitted, a fundamental inconsistency between the communal right to fish embodied in the aboriginal right, and fishing under a special licence or permit issued to individual Indians (as was the case until 1977) in the discretion of the Minister and subject to terms and conditions which, if breached, may result in cancellation of the licence. The *Fisheries Act* and its regulations were, he argued, intended to constitute a complete code inconsistent with the continued existence of an aboriginal right.

At bottom, the respondent's argument confuses regulation with extinguishment. That the right is controlled in great detail by the regulations does not mean that the right is thereby extinguished. The distinction to be drawn was carefully explained, in the context of federalism, in the first fisheries case, *A.-G. Can.* v. *A.-G. Ont.*, [1898] A.C. 700. There, the Privy Council had to deal with the interrelationship between, on the one hand, provincial property, which by s. 109 of the *Constitution Act, 1867*, is vested in the provinces (and so falls to be regulated *qua* property exclusively by the provinces) and, on the other hand, the federal power to legislate respecting the fisheries thereon under s. 91(12) of that Act. The Privy Council said the following in relation to the federal regulation [at pp. 712–13]:

> ... the power to legislate in relation to fisheries does necessarily to a certain extent enable the Legislature so empowered to affect proprietary rights. An enactment, for example, prescribing the times of the year during which fishing is to be allowed, or the instruments which may be employed for the purpose (which it was admitted the Dominion Legislature was empowered to pass) might very seriously touch the exercise of proprietary rights, and the extent, character, and scope of such legislation is left entirely to the Dominion Legislature. The suggestion that the power might be abused so as to amount to a practical confiscation of property does not warrant the imposition by the Courts of any limit upon the absolute power of legislation conferred. The supreme legislative power in relation to any subject-matter is always capable of abuse, but it is not to be assumed that it will be improperly used; if it is, the only remedy is an appeal to those by whom the Legislature is elected.

In the context of aboriginal rights, it could be argued that, before 1982, an aboriginal right was automatically extinguished to the extent that it was inconsistent with a statute. As Mahoney J. stated in *Baker Lake, supra*, at p. 551:

> Once a statute has been validly enacted, it must be given effect. If its necessary effect is to abridge or entirely abrogate a common law right, then that is the effect that the courts must give it. That is as true of an aboriginal title as of any other common law right.

[See also *Ontario (Attorney-General)* v. *Bear Island Foundation*, *supra*, at pp. 407–08.] That in Judson J.'s view was what had occurred in *Calder*, *supra*, where, as he saw it, a series of statutes evinced a unity of intention to exercise a sovereignty inconsistent with any conflicting interest, including aboriginal title. But Hall J. in that case stated [at p. 210] that "the onus of proving that the Sovereign intended to extinguish the Indian title lies on the respondent and <u>that intention must be 'clear and plain'</u>". [Emphasis added.] The test of extinguishment to be adopted, in our opinion, is that the Sovereign's intention must be clear and plain if it is to extinguish an aboriginal right.

There is nothing in the *Fisheries Act* or its detailed regulations that demonstrates a clear and plain intention to extinguish the Indian aboriginal right to fish. The fact that express provision permitting the Indians to fish for food may have applied to all Indians and that for an extended period permits were discretionary and issued on an individual rather than a communal basis in no way shows a clear intention to extinguish. These permits were simply a manner of controlling the fisheries, not defining underlying rights.

We would conclude then that the Crown has failed to discharge its burden of proving extinguishment. In our opinion, the Court of Appeal made no mistake in holding that the Indians have an existing aboriginal right to fish in the area where Mr. Sparrow was fishing at the time of the charge. This approach is consistent with ensuring that an aboriginal right should not be defined by incorporating the ways in which it has been regulated in the past.

. . . .

The scope of the existing Musqueam right to fish must now be delineated. The anthropological evidence relied on to establish the existence of the right suggests that, for the Musqueam, the salmon fishery has always constituted an integral part of their distinctive culture. Its significant role involved not only consumption for subsistence, but also consumption of salmon on ceremonial and social occasions. The Musqueam have always fished for reasons connected to their culture and physical survival. As we stated earlier, the right to do so may be exercised in a contemporary manner.

. . . .

In the courts below, the case at bar was not presented on the footing of an aboriginal right to fish for commercial or livelihood purposes. Rather, the focus was and continues to be on the validity of a net length restriction affecting the appellant's food fishing licence. We therefore adopt the Court of Appeal's characterization of the right for the purpose of this appeal, and confine our reasons to the meaning of the constitutional recognition and affirmation of the existing aboriginal right to fish for food and social and ceremonial purposes.

"Recognized and Affirmed"

We now turn to the impact of s. 35(1) of the *Constitution Act, 1982*, on the regulatory power of Parliament and on the outcome of this appeal specifically.

Counsel for the appellant argued that the effect of s. 35(1) is to deny Parliament's power to restrictively regulate aboriginal fishing rights under s. 91(24) ("Indians and Lands Reserved for the Indians"), and s. 91(12) ("Sea Coast and Inland Fisheries"). The essence of this submission, supported by the intervener, the National Indian Brotherhood Assembly of First Nations, is that the right to regulate is part of the right to use the resource in the band's discretion. Section 35(1) is not subject to s. 1 of the *Canadian Charter of Rights and Freedoms*, nor to legislative override under s. 33. The appellant submitted that, if the regulatory power continued, the limits on its extent are set by the word "inconsistent" in s. 52(1) of the *Constitution Act, 1982*, and the protective and remedial purposes of s. 35(1). This means that aboriginal title entails a right to fish by any non-dangerous method chosen by the aboriginals engaged in fishing. Any continuing governmental power of regulation would have to be exceptional and strictly limited to regulation that is clearly not inconsistent with the protective and remedial purposes of s. 35(1). Thus, counsel for the appellant speculated, "in certain circumstances, necessary and reasonable conservation measures *might* qualify" [Emphasis added.] — where for example such measures were necessary to prevent serious impairment of the aboriginal rights of present and future generations, where conservation could only be achieved by restricting the right and not by restricting fishing by other users, and where the aboriginal group concerned was unwilling to implement necessary conservation measures. The onus of proving a justification for restrictive regulations would lie with the government by analogy with s. 1 of the *Charter*.

In response to these submissions and in finding the appropriate interpretive framework for s. 35(1), we start by looking at the background of s. 35(1).

It is worth recalling that while British policy towards the native population was based on respect for their right to occupy their traditional lands, a proposition to which the *Royal Proclamation* of 1763 bears witness, there was from the outset never any doubt that sovereignty and legislative power, and indeed the underlying title, to such lands vested in the Crown: see *Johnson* v. *M'Intosh*, 8 Wheaton 543 (1823) (U.S.S.C.); see also the *Royal Proclamation* itself [R.S.C., 1985, App. II, No. 1, pp. 406]; *Calder, supra, per* Judson J. at p. 156, Hall J. at pp. 195, 208. And there can be no doubt that over the years the rights of the Indians were often honoured in the breach [for one instance in a recent case in this court, see *Canadian Pacific Ltd.* v. *Paul* (1988), 53 D.L.R. (4th) 487, [1988] 2 S.C.R. 654, 91 N.B.R. (2d) 43.]. As MacDonald J. stated in *Pasco* v. *C.N.R.* (1985), 69 B.C.L.R. 76 at p. 79, (1986), 1 C.N.L.R. 35 (S.C.): "We cannot recount with much pride the treatment accorded to the native people of this country."

For many years, the rights of the Indians to their aboriginal lands — certainly as legal rights — were virtually ignored....

. . . .

It is obvious from its terms that the approach taken towards aboriginal claims in the 1973 statement constituted an expression of a policy, rather than a legal position: see also Canada, Department of Indian Affairs and Northern Development, *In All Fairness: A Native Claims Policy — Comprehensive Claims* (1981), pp. 11–12; Slattery, "Understanding Aboriginal Right" (1987), 66 *Can. Bar Rev.* 726 at p. 730. As recently as *Guerin* v. *The Queen* (1984), 13 D.L.R. (4th) 321, [1984] 2 S.C.R. 335, [1984] 6 W.W.R. 481, the federal government argued in this court that any federal obligation was of a political character.

It is clear, then, that s. 35(1) of the *Constitution Act, 1982*, represents the culmination of a long and difficult struggle in both the political forum and the courts for the constitutional recognition of aboriginal rights. The strong representations of native associations and other groups concerned with the welfare of Canada's aboriginal peoples made the adoption of s. 35(1) possible and it is important to note that the provision applies to the Indians, the Inuit and the Métis. Section 35(1), at the least, provides a solid constitutional base upon which subsequent negotiations can take place. It also affords aboriginal peoples constitutional protection against provincial legislative power. We are, of course, aware that this would, in any event, flow from the *Guerin* case, *supra*, but for a proper understanding of the situation, it is essential to remember that the *Guerin* case was decided after the commencement of the *Constitution Act, 1982*. In addition to its effect on aboriginal rights, s. 35(1) clarified other issues regarding the enforcement of treaty rights: see Sanders, "Pre-existing Rights: The Aboriginal Peoples of Canada", Beaudoin and Ratushny, (eds.), *The Canadian Charter of Rights and Freedoms*, 2nd Ed., especially at p. 730.

In our opinion, the significance of s. 35(1) extends beyond these fundamental effects. Professor Lyon in "An Essay on Constitutional Interpretation" (1988), 26 *Osgoode Hall L.J.* 95, says the following about s. 35(1), at p. 100:

> ... the context of 1982 is surely enough to tell us that this is not just a codification of the case law on aboriginal rights that had accumulated by 1982. Section 35 calls for a just settlement for aboriginal peoples. It renounces the old rules of the game under which the Crown established courts of law and denied those courts the authority to question sovereign claims made by the Crown.

The approach to be taken with respect to interpreting the meaning of s. 35(1) is derived from general principles of constitutional interpretation, principles relating to aboriginal rights, and the purposes behind the constitutional provision itself. Here, we will sketch the framework for an interpretation of "recognized and affirmed" that, in our opinion, gives appropriate weight to the constitutional nature of these words.

In *Reference re Language Rights under the Manitoba Act, 1870* (1985), 19 D.L.R. (4th) 1, [1985] 1 S.C.R. 721, [1985] 4 W.W.R. 385, this court said the following about the perspective to be adopted when interpreting a constitution, at p. 19.:

> The constitution of a country is a statement of the will of the people to be governed in accordance with certain principles held as fundamental and certain prescriptions restrictive of the powers of the legislature and government. It is, as s. 52 of the *Constitution Act, 1982* declares, the "supreme law" of the nation, unalterable by the normal legislative process, and unsuffering of laws inconsistent with it. The duty of the judiciary is to interpret and apply the laws of Canada and each of the provinces, and it is thus our duty to ensure that the constitutional law prevails.

The nature of s. 35(1) itself suggests that it be construed in a purposive way. When the purposes of the affirmation of aboriginal rights are considered, it is clear that a generous, liberal interpretation of the words in the constitutional provision is demanded....

. . . .

In *Guerin, supra*, the Musqueam Band surrendered reserve lands to the Crown for lease to a golf club. The terms obtained by the Crown were much less favourable than those approved by the band at the surrender meeting. This court found that the Crown owed a fiduciary obligation to the Indians with respect to the lands. The *sui generis* nature of Indian title, and the historic powers and responsibility assumed by the Crown constituted the source of such a fiduciary obligation. In our opinion, *Guerin*, together with *R.* v. *Taylor and Williams* (1981), 62 C.C.C. (2d) 227, 34 O.R. (2d) 360 (C.A.), ground a general guiding principle for s. 35(1). That is, the government has the responsibility to act in a fiduciary capacity with respect to aboriginal peoples. The relationship between the government and aboriginals is trust-like, rather than adversarial, and contemporary recognition and affirmation of aboriginal rights must be defined in light of this historic relationship.

We agree with both the British Columbia Court of Appeal below and the Ontario Court of Appeal that the principles outlined above, derived from *Nowegijick, Taylor and Williams* and *Guerin*, should guide the interpretation of s. 35(1). As commentators have noted, s. 35(1) is a solemn commitment that must be given meaningful content: Lyon, *ibid.*; *Pentney, ibid.*; Schwartz, "Unstarted Business: Two Approaches to Defining s. 35 — 'What's in the Box?' and 'What Kind of Box?'", ch. XXIV, in *First Principles, Second Thoughts* (Montreal: Institute for Research on Public Policy, 1986); Slattery, *ibid.*; and Slattery, "The Hidden Constitution: Aboriginal Rights in Canada" (1984), 32 *Am. J. of Comp. Law* 361.

In response to the appellant's submission that s. 35(1) rights are more securely protected than the rights guaranteed by the *Charter*, it is true that s. 35(1) is not subject to s. 1 of the *Charter*. In our opinion, this does not mean that any law or regulation affecting aboriginal rights will automatically be of no force or effect by the operation of s. 52 of the *Constitution Act, 1982*. Legislation that affects the exercise of aboriginal rights will none the less be valid, if it meets the test for justifying an interference with a right recognized and affirmed under s. 35(1).

There is no explicit language in the provision that authorizes this court or any court to assess the legitimacy of any government legislation that restricts aboriginal rights. Yet, we find that the words "recognition and affirmation" incorporate the fiduciary relationship referred to earlier and so import some restraint on the exercise of sovereign power. Rights that are recognized and affirmed are not absolute. Federal legislative powers continue, including, of course, the right to legislate with respect to Indians pursuant to s. 91(24) of the *Constitution Act, 1867*. These powers must, however, now be read together with s. 35(1). In other words, federal power must be reconciled with federal duty and the best way to achieve that reconciliation is to demand the justification of any government regulation that infringes upon or denies aboriginal rights. Such scrutiny is in keeping with the liberal interpretive principle enunciated in *Nowegijick, supra*, and the concept of holding the Crown to a high standard of honourable dealing with respect to the aboriginal peoples of Canada as suggested by *Guerin* v. *The Queen*, *supra*.

We refer to Professor Slattery's "Understanding Aboriginal Rights", *ibid.*, with respect to the task of envisioning a s. 35(1) justificatory process. Professor Slattery, at p. 782, points out that a justificatory process is required as a compromise between a "patchwork" characterization of aboriginal rights whereby past regulations would be read into a definition of the rights, and a characterization that would guarantee aboriginal rights in their original form unrestricted by subsequent regulation. We agree with him that these two extreme positions must be rejected in favour of a justificatory scheme.

Section 35(1) suggests that while regulation affecting aboriginal rights is not precluded, such regulation must be enacted according to a valid objective. Our history has shown, unfortunately all too well, that Canada's aboriginal peoples are justified in worrying about government objectives that may be superficially neutral but which constitute *de facto* threats to the existence of aboriginal rights and interests. By giving aboriginal rights constitutional status and priority, Parliament and the provinces have sanctioned challenges to social and economic policy objectives embodied in legislation to the extent that aboriginal rights are affected. Implicit in this constitutional scheme is the obligation of the legislature to satisfy the test of justification. The way in which a legislative objective is to be attained must uphold the honour of the Crown and must be in keeping with the unique contemporary relationship, grounded in history and policy, between the Crown and Canada's aboriginal peoples. The extent of legislative or regulatory impact on an existing aboriginal right may be scrutinized so as to ensure recognition and affirmation.

The constitutional recognition afforded by the provision, therefore, gives a measure of control over government conduct and a strong check on legislative power. While it does not promise immunity from government regulation in a society that, in the twentieth century, is increasingly more complex, interdependent and sophisticated, and where exhaustible resources need protection and management, it does hold the Crown to a substantive promise. The government is required to bear the burden of justifying any legislation that has some negative effect on any aboriginal right protected under s. 35(1)....

. . . .

Section 35(1) and the Regulation of the Fisheries

Taking the above framework as guidance, we propose to set out the test for *prima facie* interference with an existing aboriginal right and for the justification of such an interference. With respect to the question of the regulation of the fisheries, the existence of s. 35(1) of the *Constitution Act, 1982*, renders the authority of *R.* v. *Derriksan*, *supra*, inapplicable. In that case, Laskin C.J.C., for this court, found that there was nothing to prevent the *Fisheries Act* and the regulations from subjecting the alleged aboriginal right to fish in a particular area to the controls thereby imposed. As the court of Appeal in the case at bar noted, the *Derriksan* line of cases established that, before April 17, 1982, the aboriginal right to fish was subject to regulation by legislation and subject to extinguishment. The new <u>constitutional</u> status of that right enshrined in s. 35(1) suggests that a different approach must be taken in deciding whether regulation of the fisheries might be out of keeping with constitutional protection.

The first question to be asked is whether the legislation in question has the effect of interfering with an existing aboriginal right. If it does have such an effect, it represents a *prima facie* infringement of s. 35(1). Parliament is not expected to act in a manner contrary to the rights and interests of aboriginals, and, indeed, may be barred from doing so by the second stage of s. 35(1) analysis. The inquiry with respect to interference begins with a reference to the characteristics or incidents of the right at stake. Our earlier observations regarding the scope of the aboriginal right to fish are relevant here. Fishing rights are not traditional property rights. They are rights held by a collective and are in keeping with the culture and existence of that group. Courts must be careful, then, to avoid the application of traditional common law concepts of property as they develop their understanding of what the reasons for judgment in *Guerin, supra*, at p. 339, referred to as the "*sui generis*" nature of aboriginal rights: see also Little Bear, "A Concept of Native Title", [1982] 5 *Can. Legal Aid Bul.* 99.

While it is impossible to give an easy definition of fishing rights, it is possible, and, indeed, crucial, to be sensitive to the aboriginal perspective itself on the meaning of the rights at stake. For example, it would be artificial to try to create a hard distinction between the right to fish and the particular manner in which that right is exercised.

To determine whether the fishing rights have been interfered with such as to constitute a *prima facie* infringement of s. 35(1), certain questions must be asked. First, is the limitation unreasonable? Secondly, does the regulation impose undue hardship? Thirdly, does the regulation deny to the holders of the right their preferred means of exercising that right? The onus of proving a *prima facie* infringement lies on the individual or group challenging the legislation. In relation to the facts of this appeal, the regulation would be found to be a *prima facie* interference if it were found to be an adverse restriction on the Musqueam exercise of their right to fish for food. We wish to note here that the issue does not merely require looking at whether the fish catch has been reduced below that needed for the reasonable food and ceremonial needs of the Musqueam Indians. Rather the test involves asking whether either the purpose or the effect of the restriction on net length unnecessarily infringes the interests protected by the fishing right. If, for example, the Musqueam were forced to spend undue time and money per fish caught or if the net length reduction resulted in a hardship to the Musqueam in catching fish, then the first branch of the s. 35(1) analysis would be met.

If a *prima facie* interference is found, the analysis moves to the issue of justification. This is the test that addresses the question of what constitutes legitimate regulation of a constitutional aboriginal right. The justification analysis would proceed as follows. First, is there a valid legislative objective? Here the court would inquire into whether the objective of Parliament in authorizing the department to enact regulations regarding fisheries is valid. The objective of the department in setting out the particular regulations would also be scrutinized. An objective aimed at preserving s. 35(1) rights by conserving and managing a natural resource, for example, would be valid. Also valid would be objectives purporting to prevent the exercise of s. 35(1) rights that would cause harm to the general populace or to aboriginal peoples themselves, or other objectives found to be compelling and substantial.

The Court of Appeal below held, at p. 96, that regulations could be valid if reasonably justified as "necessary for the proper management and conservation of the resource *or in the public interest*". [Emphasis added.] We find the "public interest" justification to be so vague as to provide no meaningful guidance and so broad as to be unworkable as a test for the justification of a limitation on constitutional rights.

The justification of conservation and resource management, on the other hand, is surely uncontroversial. In *Kruger and Manuel* v. *The Queen* (1977), 34 C.C.C. (2d) 377, 75 D.L.R. (3d) 434, [1978] 1 S.C.R. 104, the applicability of the *Wildlife Act*, S.B.C. 1966, c. 55, to the appellant members of the Penticton Indian Band was considered by this court. In discussing that Act, the following was said about the objective of conservation [at p. 382]:

> Game conservation laws have as their policy the maintenance of wildlife resources. It might be argued that without some conservation measures the ability of Indians or others to hunt for food would become a moot issue in consequence of the destruction of the resource. The presumption is for the validity of a legislative enactment and in this case the presumption has to mean that in the absence of evidence to the contrary the measures taken by the British Columbia Legislature were taken to maintain an effective resource in the Province for its citizens and not to oppose the interests of conservationists and Indians in such a way as to favour the claims of the former.

While the "presumption" of validity is now outdated in view of the constitutional status of the aboriginal rights at stake, it is clear that the value of conservation purposes for government legislation and action has long been recognized. Further, the conservation and management of our resources is consistent with aboriginal beliefs and practices, and, indeed, with the enhancement of aboriginal rights.

If a valid legislative objective is found, the analysis proceeds to the second part of the justification issue. Here, we refer back to the guiding interpretive principle derived from *Taylor and Williams* and *Guerin, supra*. That is, the honour of the Crown is at stake in dealings with aboriginal peoples. The special trust relationship and the responsibility of the government *vis-à-vis* aboriginals must be the first consideration in determining whether the legislation or action in question can be justified.

The problem that arises in assessing the legislation in light of its objective and the responsibility of the Crown is that the pursuit of conservation in a heavily used modern fishery inevitably blurs with the efficient allocation and management of this scarce and valued resource. The nature of the constitutional protection afforded by s. 35(1) in this context demands that there be a link between the question of justification and the allocation of priorities in the fishery. The constitutional recognition and affirmation of aboriginal rights may give rise to conflict with the interests of others given the limited nature of the resource. There is a clear need for guidelines that will resolve the allocational problems that arise regarding the fisheries. We refer to the reasons of Dickson J. in *Jack* v. *The Queen*, *supra*, for such guidelines.

In *Jack*, the appellants' defence to a charge of fishing for salmon in certain rivers during a prohibited period was based on the alleged constitutional incapacity of Parliament to legislate such as to deny the Indians their right to fish for food. They argued that art. 13 of the British Columbia Terms of Union imposed a constitutional limitation on the federal power to regulate. While we recognize that the finding that such a limitation had been imposed was not adopted by the majority of this Court, we point out that this case concerns a different constitutional promise that asks this Court to give a meaningful interpretation to recognition and affirmation. That task requires equally meaningful guidelines responsive to the constitutional priority accorded aboriginal rights. We therefore repeat the following passage from *Jack*, at p. 261:

> Conservation is a valid legislative concern. The appellants concede as much. Their concern is in the allocation of the resource after reasonable and necessary conservation measures have been recognized and given effect to. They do not claim the right to pursue the last living salmon until it is caught. Their position, as I understand it, is one which would give effect to an order of priorities of this nature: (i) conservation; (ii) Indian fishing; (iii) non-Indian commercial fishing; or (iv) non-Indian sports fishing; the burden of conservation measures should not fall primarily upon the Indian fishery.
>
> I agree with the general tenor of this argument.... With respect to whatever salmon are to be caught, the priority ought to be given to the Indian fishermen, subject to the practical difficulties occasioned by international waters and the movement of the fish themselves. But any limitation upon Indian fishing that is established for a valid conservation purpose overrides the protection afforded the Indian fishery by art. 13, just as such conservation measures override other taking of fish.

The constitutional nature of the Musqueam food fishing rights means that any allocation of priorities after valid conservation measures have been implemented must give top priority to Indian food fishing. If the objective pertained to conservation, the conservation plan would be scrutinized to assess priorities. While the detailed allocation of maritime resources is a task that must be left to those having expertise in the area, the Indians' food requirements must be met first when that allocation is established. The significance of giving the aboriginal right to fish for food top priority can be described as follows. If, in a given year, conservation needs required a reduction in the number of fish to be caught such that the number equalled the number required for food by the Indians, then all the fish available after conservation would go to the Indians according to the constitutional nature of their fishing right. If, more realistically, there were still fish after the Indian food requirements were met, then the brunt of conservation measures would be borne by the practices of sport fishing and commercial fishing.

The decision of the Nova Scotia Court of Appeal in *R.* v. *Denny*, judgment rendered March 5, 1990 (unreported) [since reported 55 C.C.C. (3d) 322, 94 N.S.R. (2d) 253, [1990] 2 C.N.L.R. 115], addresses the constitutionality of the Nova Scotia Micmac Indians' right to fish in the waters of Indian Brook and the Afton River, and does so in a way that accords with our understanding of the constitutional nature of aboriginal rights and the link between allocation and justification required for government regulation of the exercise of the rights. Clarke C.J.N.S., for a unanimous court, found that the *Nova Scotia Fishery Regulations* enacted pursuant to the federal *Fisheries Act* were in part inconsistent with the constitutional rights of the appellant Micmac Indians. Section 35(1) of the *Constitution Act, 1982*, provided the appellants with the right to a top priority allocation of any surplus of the fisheries resource which might exist after the needs of conservation had been taken into account. With respect to the issue of the Indians' priority to a food fishery, Clarke C.J.N.S. noted that the official policy of the federal government recognizes that priority. He added the following, at pp. 22–23 [p. 339 C.C.C.]:

> I have no hesitation in concluding that factual as well as legislative and policy recognition must be given to the existence of an Indian food fishery in the waters of Indian Brook, adjacent to the Eskasoni Reserve, and the waters of the Afton River after the needs of conservation have been taken into account....
>
> . . . .
>
> To afford user groups such as sports fishermen (anglers) a priority to fish over the legitimate food needs of the appellants and their families is simply not appropriate action on the part of the federal government. It is inconsistent with the fact that the appellants have for many years, and continue to possess an aboriginal right to fish for food. The appellants have, to employ the words of their counsel, a "right to share in the available resource". This constitutional entitlement is second only to conservation measures that may be undertaken by federal legislation.

Further, Clarke C.J.N.S. found that s. 35(1) provided the constitutional recognition of the aboriginal priority with respect to the fishery, and that the regulations, in failing to guarantee that priority, were in violation of the constitutional provision. He said the following, at p. 25 [pp. 340–41 C.C.C.]:

> Though it is crucial to appreciate that the rights afforded to the appellants by s. 35(1) are not absolute, the impugned regulatory scheme fails to recognize that this section provides the appellants with a priority of allocation and access to any surplus of the fisheries resource once the needs of conservation have been taken into account. Section 35(1), as applied to these appeals, provides the appellants with an entitlement to fish in the waters in issue to satisfy their food needs, where a surplus exists. To the extent that the regulatory scheme fails to recognize this, it is inconsistent with the Constitution. Section 52 mandates a finding that such regulations are of no force and effect.
>
> . . . .

In *Eninew*, Hall J.A. found, at p. 368, that "the treaty rights can be limited by such regulations as are reasonable". As we have pointed out, management and conservation of resources is indeed an important and valid legislative objective. Yet, the fact that the objective is of a "reasonable" nature cannot suffice as constitutional recognition and affirmation of aboriginal rights. Rather, the regulations enforced pursuant to a conservation or management objective may be scrutinized according to the justificatory standard outlined above.

We acknowledge the fact that the justificatory standard to be met may place a heavy burden on the Crown. However, government policy with respect to the British Columbia fishery, regardless of s. 35(1), already dictates that, in allocating the right to take fish, Indian food fishing is to be given priority over the interests of other user groups. The constitutional entitlement embodied in s. 35(1) requires the Crown to ensure that its regulations are in keeping with that allocation of priority. The objective of this requirement is not to undermine Parliament's ability and responsibility with respect to creating and administering over-all conservation and management plans regarding the salmon fishery. The objective is rather to guarantee that those plans treat aboriginal peoples in a way ensuring that their rights are taken seriously.

Within the analysis of justification, there are further questions to be addressed, depending on the circumstances of the inquiry. These include the questions of whether there has been as little infringement as possible in order to effect the desired result; whether, in a situation of expropriation, fair compensation is available, and whether the aboriginal group in question has been consulted with respect to the conservation measures being implemented. The aboriginal peoples, with their history of conservation-consciousness and interdependence with natural resources, would surely be expected, at the least, to be informed regarding the determination of an appropriate scheme for the regulation of the fisheries.

We would not wish to set out an exhaustive list of the factors to be considered in the assessment of justification. Suffice it to say that recognition and affirmation requires sensitivity to and respect for the rights of aboriginal peoples on behalf of the government, courts and indeed all Canadians.

Application to this Case — Is the Net Length Restriction Valid?

The Court of Appeal below found that there was not sufficient evidence in this case to proceed with an analysis of s. 35(1) with respect to the right to fish for food. In reviewing the competing expert evidence, and recognizing that fish stock management is an uncertain science, it decided that the issues at stake in this appeal were not well adapted to being resolved at the appellate court level.

Before the trial, defence counsel advised the Crown of the intended aboriginal rights defence and that the defence would take the position that the Crown was required to prove, as part of its case, that the net length restriction was justifiable as a necessary and reasonable conservation measure. The trial judge found s. 35(1) to be inapplicable to the appellant's defence, based on his finding that no aboriginal right had been established. He therefore found it inappropriate to make findings of fact with respect to either an infringement of the aboriginal right to fish or the justification of such an infringement. He did, however, find that the evidence called by the appellant

> ... casts some doubt as to whether the restriction was necessary as a conservation measure. More particularly, it suggests that there were more appropriate measures that could have been taken if necessary; measures that would not impose such a hardship on the Indians fishing for food. That case was not fully met by the Crown.

According to the Court of Appeal, the findings of fact were insufficient to lead to an acquittal. There was no more evidence before this court. We also would order a retrial which would allow findings of fact according to the tests set out in these reasons.

The appellant would bear the burden of showing that the net length restriction constituted a *prima facie* infringement of the collective aboriginal right to fish for food. If an infringement were found, the onus would shift to the Crown which would have to demonstrate that the regulation is justifiable. To that end, the Crown would have to show that there is no underlying unconstitutional objective such as shifting more of the resource to a user group that ranks below the Musqueam. Further, it would have to show that the regulation sought to be imposed is required to accomplish the needed limitation. In trying to show that the restriction is necessary in the circumstances of the Fraser River fishery, the Crown could use facts pertaining to fishing by other Fraser River Indians.

In conclusion, we would dismiss the appeal and the cross-appeal and affirm the Court of Appeal's setting aside of the conviction. We would, accordingly, affirm the order for a new trial on the questions of infringement and whether any infringement is none the less consistent with s. 35(1), in accordance with the interpretation set out here.

For the reasons given above, the constitutional question must be answered as follows:

Question:

> Is the net length restriction contained in the Musqueam Indian Band Indian Food Fishing Licence dated March 30, 1984, issued pursuant to the *British Columbia Fishery (General) Regulations* and the *Fisheries Act*, R.S.C. 1970, c. F–14, inconsistent with s. 35(1) of the *Constitution Act, 1982*?

Answer:

> This question will have to be sent back to trial to be answered according to the analysis set out in these reasons.

Appeal and cross-appeal dismissed.

8 Fiduciary Duties

(a) *Guerin*†

See **Chapter 8, Parts 4(c) and 6.**

Guerin is a leading decision on the Crown's fiduciary obligations to Aboriginal peoples. *Guerin* is reproduced in part in **Reading 4(c)** at p. 265, as it is also a key decision on the nature of Aboriginal title. For portions of *Guerin* that relate especially to fiduciary relations, see the material under the subheading "Fiduciary Relationship" in the *Guerin* extract and the last paragraph of the extract. In *Guerin*, note the link between the finding that Aboriginal title is independent of government, and the conclusion that the Crown's special fiduciary duty to Aboriginal peoples is not just an unenforceable "political trust".

(b) *Sparrow*‡

See **Chapter 7, Part 4.**

Sparrow applied the notion of Crown-Aboriginal fiduciary obligations to the special context of s. 35(1) of the *Constitution Act, 1982*. *Sparrow* is reproduced in part in **Reading 7(c)** at p. 318, as it is the key decision on the effect of that constitutional provision on the status of Aboriginal and treaty rights. For portions of *Sparrow* that relate especially to fiduciary relations, see the material under the subheadings "Recognized and Affirmed" and "Section 35(1) and the Regulation of the Fisheries" in the *Sparrow* extract. As a result of *Sparrow*, government can infringe s. 35(1) rights only if it complies with a number of fiduciary-type requirements prescribed by the Court.

---

† [1984] 2 S.C.R. 335 at 348–49, 365, 375–85, 389, 391–93 (S.C.C.); rev'g (1983), 143 D.L.R. (3d) 416 (F.C.A.), rev'g [1982] 2 F.C. 385 (F.C.T.D.) and (1982), 127 D.L.R. (3d) 170 (F.C.T.D.: supplementary reasons).

‡ [1990] 1 S.C.R. 1075 at 1082–83, 1088–95, 1097–99, 1101–103, 1105–106, 1108–21, referring an issue back to trial, and aff'g (1986), 36 D.L.R.(4th) 246 (B.C.C.A.), which rev'd [1986] B.C.W.L.D. 599 (B.C. Co. Ct.: Vancouver, which aff'd the conviction by Goulet P.C.J.).

(c) *Blueberry River Indian Band v. Canada (Department of Indian Affairs and Northern Development)*†

See **Chapter 8, Part 8(b).**

NOTE

An Indian Band surrendered reserve land to the Crown "to lease" and then surrendered it "to sale or lease". Apparently by oversight, the Department of Indian Affairs transferred the mineral rights, as well as surface rights, to the surrendered land to another department. This was against a longstanding departmental policy of reserving the mineral rights in surrendered reserve lands. Although it became clear a year later that the mineral rights had been transferred, and were extremely valuable, D.I.A.N.D. did nothing to correct its error. Those claiming on behalf of the Band argued, *inter alia*, that D.I.A.N.D. had breached its fiduciary duties to them in making the second surrender, in transferring the mineral rights, and in then failing to correct the transfer.

EXTRACT

[GONTHIER J. for himself and La Forest, L'Heureux-Dubé, and Sopinka JJ.:]

. . . .

[para7] ... In my view, when determining the legal effect of dealings between aboriginal peoples and the Crown relating to reserve lands, the *sui generis* nature of aboriginal title requires courts to go beyond the usual restrictions imposed by the common law, in order to give effect to the true purpose of the dealings.

. . . .

[Gonthier J. found that in the second of the two surrenders, the Indian band had intended to surrender both their surface lands and subsurface rights for sale as well as for lease. He concluded that the second of the two surrenders varied the terms of the first, which had referred only to leasing of mineral rights.]

[para14] ... I would be reluctant to give effect to this surrender variation if I thought that the Band's understanding of its terms had been inadequate, or if the conduct of the Crown had somehow tainted the dealings in a manner which made it unsafe to rely on the Band's understanding and intention. However, neither of these situations arises here [since the evidence shows that the Band intended to include both the surface and mineral rights in the 1945 surrender]....

. . . .

[para16] The terms of the 1945 surrender transferred I.R. 172 to the Crown "in trust to sell or lease the same to such person or persons, and upon such terms as the Government of the Dominion of Canada may deem most conducive to our welfare and that of our people". By taking on the obligations of a trustee in relation to I.R. 172, the DIA was under a fiduciary duty to deal with the land in the best interests of the members of the Beaver Band. This duty extended to both the surface rights and the mineral rights.

[para17] In my view, it is critical to the outcome of this case that the 1945 agreement was a surrender in trust, to sell or lease.... Because of the scope of the discretion granted to the DIA, it would have been open to the DIA to sell the surface rights in I.R. 172 to the Director, *Veterans' Land Act* (DVLA), while continuing to lease the mineral rights for the benefit of the Band, as per the 1940 surrender agreement.

[para18] Why this option was not chosen is a mystery. As my colleague McLachlin J. observes, the DIA had a long-standing policy, pre-dating the 1945 surrender, to reserve out mineral rights for the benefit of the aboriginal peoples when surrendered Indian lands were sold off. This policy was adopted precisely because reserving mineral rights was thought to be "conducive to the welfare" of aboriginal peoples in all cases. The existence and rationale

† [1995] 4 S.C.R. 344, allowing an appeal and cross-appeal from (1993), 100 D.L.R. (4th) 504 (F.C.A.), which had dismissed an appeal and cross-appeal from [1988] 1 C.N.L.R. 73 (F.C.T.D.).

of this policy ... justifies the conclusion that the DIA was under a fiduciary duty to reserve, for the benefit of the Beaver Band, the mineral rights in I.R. 172 when it sold the surface rights to the DVLA in March 1948. In other words, the DIA should have continued to lease the mineral rights for the benefit of the Band as it had been doing since 1940. Its failure to do so can only be explained as "inadvertence".

[para19] The DIA's failure to continue the leasing arrangement could be excused if the Department had received a clear mandate from the Band to sell the mineral rights ... [but it did not.].... Given these circumstances, the DIA was under a fiduciary duty to continue the leasing arrangement which had been established in the 1940 surrender. It was a violation of the fiduciary duty to sell the mineral rights to the DVLA in 1948.

. . . .

[para21] In her reasons, McLachlin J. amply demonstrates that between July 15, 1949 and August 9, 1949, the DIA became aware of two facts: (1) the mineral rights in I.R. 172 were potentially of considerable value; and (2) the mineral rights had been sold to the DVLA in 1948. It should also be recalled that the DIA had a long-standing policy of reserving mineral rights for the benefit of aboriginal peoples when selling Indian lands. Given these circumstances, it is rather astonishing that no action was taken by the DIA to determine how the mineral rights could have been sold to the DVLA. Little effort would have been required to detect the error which had occurred.

[para22] As a fiduciary, the DIA was required to act with reasonable diligence. In my view, a reasonable person in the DIA's position would have realized by August 9, 1949 that an error had occurred, and would have exercised the s. 64 power to correct the error, reacquire the mineral rights, and effect a leasing arrangement for the benefit of the Band. That this was not done was a clear breach of the DIA's fiduciary duty to deal with I.R. 172 according to the best interests of the Band.

[para23] Thus, I conclude that the appellants may recover any losses stemming from transfers by the DVLA after August 9, 1949 as such losses fall within the 30-year limitation period imposed by the *British Columbia Limitation Act*, and are not barred by any other provision of that Act as explained in the reasons of McLachlin J.

[para24] For the reasons given above, I would allow the appeal in the manner stated by McLachlin J. and remit the action to the Federal Court, Trial Division, for assessment of damages accordingly. I would also allow the cross-appeal for the reasons given by her. In the circumstances, I would award costs to the appellants throughout, and would make no order as to costs on the cross-appeal.

[McLachlin J., for herself, Cory and Major JJ. held that the first surrender precluded the sale or transfer of the mineral rights pursuant to the second surrender. However, assuming that the second surrender could permit the transfer of mineral rights, McLachlin J. felt that D.I.A.N.D. breached this duty in failing to reserve the potentially valuable mineral rights, and then failing to correct the error when it was discovered.

McLachlin J. (with whom Gonthier J. agreed) held that there was no fiduciary breach in regard to the price received for the land:]

. . . .

[para55] This evidence does not appear to support the trial judge's conclusion that the Crown was in breach of its fiduciary obligation to sell the land at a fair value. In finding a breach despite this evidence, the trial judge misconstrued the effect of the onus on the Crown. The Crown adduced evidence showing that the sale price lay within a range established by the appraisals. This raised a prima facie case that the sale price was reasonable. The onus then shifted to the Bands to show it was unreasonable. The Bands did not adduce such evidence. On this state of the record, a presumption of breach of the Crown's fiduciary duty to exact a fair price cannot be based on a failure to discharge the onus upon it. I note that the trial judge made no finding as to the true value of the property, nor any finding that it was significantly greater than $70,000, deferring this to the stage of assessment of damages.

[para56] I conclude that the trial judge erred in concluding that the Crown breached its fiduciary duty to the Band by selling the land for $70,000.

(d) *Wewaykum Indian Band v. Canada*†

See **Chapter 8, Part 8(e).**

NOTE

Each of two Indian bands claimed reserves that were occupied by the other. As well as suing each other, each band sued the Crown for breach of its fiduciary duty in regard to the original allocation of the lands. The Crown had transferred one of the two parcels of land from one band to another. However, an erroneous clerical entry made it appear that both parcels were transferred. One band claimed that the Crown had breached its fiduciary duty by failing to uphold the clerical entry (although neither band had relied on it in the past). The other band claimed that the Crown had breached its fiduciary duty by allowing the transfer to take place in the first place (although the band had not settled on that land, and it was not an existing reserve at the time). To complicate matters further, this situation did not involve a formal surrender, as in *Guerin*, or an expropriation of existing reserve land, as in *Osoyoos Indian Band v. Oliver (Town)*, [2001] 3 S.C.R. 746.

The lower courts dismissed the claims, as did the Supreme Court. The Supreme Court took the opportunity to make a number of general comments about the scope and content of the Crown's fiduciary obligation to Aboriginal peoples. How does the law in *Wewaykum* differ from that stated in *Guerin* and *Sparrow*? Has the Supreme Court applied sensible limitations, or unduly narrow constraints, to this area of law?

EXTRACT

[BINNIE J. for the Court:]

[para1] Two Indian bands on the east coast of Vancouver Island lay claim to each other's reserve land. The reserves, which have been in the possession of the incumbent band since about the end of the 19th century, are located two miles from each other. The inhabitants of both reserves are members of the Laich-kwil-tach First Nation which, in the mid-1800s, managed to displace the Comox First Nation from this area of British Columbia.

[para2] Each band claims that but for various breaches of fiduciary duty on the part of the federal Crown, its people would be in possession of <u>both</u> reserves. Members of the other band, on this view, should be in possession of neither.

[para3] There is no assertion of any entitlement in these lands under s. 35(1) of the *Constitution Act, 1982* ("existing aboriginal and treaty rights").

[para4] Although the bands seek formal declarations of trespass and possession and injunctive relief against each other, each acknowledges the hardship that such a result would cause the other, and each band therefore says it would be satisfied with financial compensation from the federal Crown. The Cape Mudge appellants say their compensation should be in the range of $12.2 to $14.8 million for Reserve No. 11 and the Campbell River appellants say their claim is about $4 million for Reserve No. 12. In short, if the appellant bands' claims are allowed, each band will stay where it is but will receive substantial funds by way of "equitable compensation" plus costs on a solicitor-client scale.

. . . .

[para 31] The trial judge found that the Cape Mudge Band had not in fact resided in the area now designated Reserve No. 11. Its members had used the rich fishing grounds in the vicinity in common with other Laich-kwil-tach peoples, but had landed their catch elsewhere along the shoreline.

[para 32] When a particular reserve was provisionally allocated at the band level, the practice was for a departmental official to write out a band's name in full for the first entry, and for every successive reference (in an unfortunate economy of effort) the official would simply put quotation or "ditto" marks. Thus by 1902, the Schedule (unlike the 1892 Schedule) showed an allocation to the Cape Mudge Band

† *Wewaykum Indian Band v. Canada*, [2002] 4 S.C.R. 245 at paras. 1–4, 31–32, 43, 79, 80–83, 85–86, 94–97, 100–102, 111–12, 121–24, 134–35, and 138, aff'g. [2000] 3 C.N.L.R. 303 (F.C.A.), which aff'd. (1995), 99 F.T.R. 1 (F.C.T.D.).

("Wewayakay") of both Reserve No. 11 and Reserve No. 12 as follows:

Reserve No	Reserve Name	Tribe or Band
1	Salmon River	Laichkwiltach, Kahkahmatsis band
... *[listing of reserves 2 to 6 omitted]*		
7	Village Bay	We-way-akay band
8	Open Bay	" "
9	Drew Harbour	" "
10	Cape Mudge	" "
11	Campbell River	" "
12	Quinsam	" "

(Source: Joint Record, vol. 8, p. 1325)

. . . .

[para41] The effect of the 1907 Resolution [a resolution allotting Reserve No. 11 to the We way akum (Weyaykum) Indian Band] was ineptly recorded by Indian Affairs in Ottawa in a handwritten addition to the 1902 Schedule as follows:

Reserve No	Reserve Name	Tribe or Band
1	Salmon River	Laichkwiltach, Kahkamatsis band
... *[listing of reserves 2 to 6 omitted]*		
7	Village Bay	We-way-akay band
8	Open Bay	" "
9	Drew Harbour	" "
10	Cape Mudge	" "
11	Campbell River	We-way-akum band
12	Quinsam	" "

(Source: Joint Record, vol. 8, p. 1453)

[para42] As is apparent, through a further unfortunate economy of effort, the handwritten note of "We-way-akum band" opposite Reserve No. 11 was not accompanied by any amendment to the Schedule to clarify the status of Reserve No. 12, whose ditto marks remained unchanged. The trial judge characterized this as the "ditto mark error". He found, amply supported by the evidence, that the handwritten correction was intended to refer only to Reserve No. 11, and that there was no intention (or basis) to make any change to Reserve No. 12, which was not part of the 1907 Resolution. The "difference of opinion", on the evidence, was confined at that time to Reserve No. 11. On a correct interpretation, therefore, the ditto marks opposite Reserve No. 12 continued to refer to the "Wewayakay" (Cape Mudge) Band, despite the confusion introduced by the subsequent handwritten notation against Reserve No. 11.

[para43] In light of the trial judge's findings that the "ditto mark error" was the result of a simple slip, and that there was no demonstrated reason for the 1907 Resolution to have precipitated the re-allocation not only of Reserve No. 11 but of Reserve No. 12 as well, which contradicted the intention of the parties, it is difficult not to see the Campbell River Band's position as an overly technical attempt to rely on what it conceives to be "the letter of the law"....

. . . .

[para79] ... All members of the Court accepted in *Ross River* that potential relief by way of fiduciary remedies is not limited to the s. 35 rights (*Sparrow*) or existing reserves (*Guerin*). The fiduciary duty, where it exists, is called into existence to facilitate supervision of the high degree of discretionary control gradually assumed by the Crown over the lives of aboriginal peoples....

. . . .

[para80] This *sui generis* relationship had its positive aspects in protecting the interests of aboriginal peoples historically (recall, e.g., the reference in *Royal Proclamation, 1763*, R.S.C. 1985, App. II, No. 1, to the "great Frauds and Abuses [that] have been committed in purchasing Lands of the Indians"), but the degree of economic, social and proprietary control and discretion asserted by the Crown also left aboriginal populations vulnerable to the risks of government misconduct or ineptitude. The importance of such discretionary control as a basic ingredient in a fiduciary relationship was underscored in Professor E. Weinrib's statement, quoted in *Guerin*, *supra*, at p. 384, that: "...the hallmark of a fiduciary relation is that the relative legal positions are such that one party is at the mercy of the other's discretion." ...

[para81] But there are limits. The appellants seemed at times to invoke the "fiduciary duty" as a source of plenary Crown liability covering all aspects of the Crown-Indian band relationship. This overshoots the mark. The fiduciary duty imposed on the Crown does not exist at large but in relation to specific Indian interests. In this case we are dealing with land, which has generally played a central role in aboriginal economies and cultures. Land was also the subject matter of *Ross River* ("the lands occupied by the Band"), *Blueberry River* and *Guerin* (disposition of existing reserves). Fiduciary protection accorded to Crown dealings with aboriginal interests in land (including reserve creation) has not to date been recognized by this Court in relation to Indian interests

other than land outside the framework of s. 35(1) of the *Constitution Act, 1982*.

[para82] Since *Guerin*, Canadian courts have experienced a flood of "fiduciary duty" claims by Indian bands across a whole spectrum of possible complaints....

. . . .

[para83] I offer no comment about the correctness of the disposition of these particular cases on the facts, none of which are before us for decision, but I think it desirable for the Court to affirm the principle, already mentioned, that not all obligations existing between the parties to a fiduciary relationship are themselves fiduciary in nature (*Lac Minerals, supra*, at p. 597), and that this principle applies to the relationship between the Crown and aboriginal peoples. It is necessary, then, to focus on the particular obligation or interest that is the subject matter of the particular dispute and whether or not the Crown had assumed discretionary control in relation thereto sufficient to ground a fiduciary obligation.

. . . .

[para85] I do not suggest that the existence of a public law duty necessarily excludes the creation of a fiduciary relationship. The latter, however, depends on identification of a cognizable Indian interest, and the Crown's undertaking of discretionary control in relation thereto in a way that invokes responsibility "in the nature of a private law duty", as discussed below.

N. Application of Fiduciary Principles to Indian Lands

[para86] For the reasons which follow, it is my view that the appellant bands' submissions in these appeals with respect to the existence and breach of a fiduciary duty cannot succeed:

1. The content of the Crown's fiduciary duty towards aboriginal peoples varies with the nature and importance of the interest sought to be protected. It does not provide a general indemnity.
2. Prior to reserve creation, the Crown exercises a public law function under the *Indian Act* — which is subject to supervision by the courts exercising public law remedies. At that stage a fiduciary relationship may also arise but, in that respect, the Crown's duty is limited to the basic obligations of loyalty, good faith in the discharge of its mandate, providing full disclosure appropriate to the subject matter, and acting with ordinary prudence with a view to the best interest of the aboriginal beneficiaries.
3. Once a reserve is created the content of the Crown's fiduciary duty expands to include the protection and preservation of the band's quasi-proprietary interest in the reserve from exploitation.
4. In this case, as the appellant bands have rightly been held to lack any beneficial interest in the other band's reserve, equitable remedies are not available either to dispossess an incumbent band that is entitled to the beneficial interest, or to require the Crown to pay "equitable"compensation for its refusal to bring about such a dispossession.
5. Enforcement of equitable duties by equitable remedies is subject to the usual equitable defences, including laches and acquiescence.

. . . .

[para94] Insofar as the appellant bands contend for a broad application of a fiduciary duty at the stage of reserve creation in non-s. 35(1) lands (as distinguished from their other arguments concerning existing reserves and reserve disposition), it is necessary to determine what the imposition of a fiduciary duty adds at that stage to the remedies already available at public law. The answer, I think, is twofold. In a substantive sense the imposition of a fiduciary duty attaches to the Crown's intervention the additional obligations of loyalty, good faith, full disclosure appropriate to the matter at hand and acting in what it reasonably and with diligence regards as the best interest of the beneficiary. In *Blueberry River* McLachlin J. (as she then was), at para. 104, said that "[t]he duty on the Crown as fiduciary was 'that of a man of ordinary prudence in managing his own affairs'".... Secondly, and perhaps more importantly, the imposition of a fiduciary duty opens access to an array of equitable remedies, about which more will be said below.

[para95] In this case the intervention of the Crown was positive, in that the federal government sought to create reserves for the appellant bands out of provincial Crown lands to which these particular bands had no aboriginal or treaty right. As explained, the people of the Laich-kwil-tach First Nation arrived in the Campbell River area at about the same time as the early Europeans (1840–1853). Government intervention from 1871 onwards was

designed to protect members of the appellant bands from displacement by the other newcomers.

[para96] When exercising ordinary government powers in matters involving disputes between Indians and non-Indians, the Crown was (and is) obliged to have regard to the interest of all affected parties, not just the Indian interest. The Crown can be no ordinary fiduciary; it wears many hats and represents many interests, some of which cannot help but be conflicting: *Samson Indian Nation and Band v. Canada*, [1995] 2 F.C. 762 (C.A.). As the Campbell River Band acknowledged in its factum, "[t]he Crown's position as fiduciary is necessarily unique" (para. 96). In resolving the dispute between Campbell River Band members and the non-Indian settlers named Nunns, for example, the Crown was not solely concerned with the band interest, nor should it have been. The Indians were "vulnerable" to the adverse exercise of the government's discretion, but so too were the settlers, and each looked to the Crown for a fair resolution of their dispute. At that stage, prior to reserve creation, the Court cannot ignore the reality of the conflicting demands confronting the government, asserted both by the competing bands themselves and by non-Indians. As Dickson J. said in *Guerin*, *supra*, at p. 385:

> It should be noted that fiduciary duties generally arise only with regard to obligations originating in a private law context. Public law duties, the performance of which requires the exercise of discretion, do not typically give rise to a fiduciary relationship. [Emphasis added.]

[para97] Here, as in *Ross River*, the nature and importance of the appellant bands' interest in these lands prior to 1938, and the Crown's intervention as the exclusive intermediary to deal with others (including the province) on their behalf, imposed on the Crown a fiduciary duty to act with respect to the interest of the aboriginal peoples with loyalty, good faith, full disclosure appropriate to the subject matter and with "ordinary" diligence in what it reasonably regarded as the best interest of the beneficiaries. As the dispute evolved into conflicting demands between the appellant bands themselves, the Crown continued to exercise public law duties in its attempt to ascertain "the place they wish to have" (as stated at para. 24), and, as a fiduciary, it was the Crown's duty to be even-handed towards and among the various beneficiaries. An assessment of the Crown's discharge of its fiduciary obligations at the reserve-creation stage must have regard to the context of the times. The trial judge concluded that each of these obligations was fulfilled, and we have been given no persuasive reason to hold otherwise....

. . . .

[para100] ... [Once a reserve is created] ... ordinary diligence must be used by the Crown to avoid invasion or destruction of the band's quasi-property interest by an exploitative bargain with third parties or, indeed, exploitation by the Crown itself. (Of course, there will also be cases dealing with the ordinary accountability by the Crown, as fiduciary, for its administrative control over the reserve and band assets.)

[para101] The Cape Mudge appellants contend that the Crown breached its fiduciary duty with respect to its two reserves (while attacking the trial judge's rejection of this factual premise) by permitting (or even encouraging) the *1907 Resolution*. They have been deprived of their legal interest in Reserve No. 11, they say, by an "exploitative bargain". They gave away 350 acres for nothing.

[para102] While the reserves were not constituted, as a matter of law, until 1938, I would be prepared to assume that, for purposes of this argument, the fiduciary duty was in effect in 1907. The Cape Mudge Band argument is nevertheless unconvincing. I do not accept what, with respect, is its shaky factual premise, i.e., that the band "gave away" Reserve No. 11 as opposed to entering a quit claim in favour of a sister band with a superior interest. More importantly, this argument rests on a misconception of the Crown's fiduciary duty. The Cape Mudge forbears, whose conduct is now complained of, were autonomous actors, apparently fully informed, who intended in good faith to resolve a "difference of opinion" with a sister band. They were not dealing with non-Indian third parties (*Guerin*, at p. 382). It is patronizing to suggest, on the basis of the evidentiary record, that they did not know what they were doing, or to reject their evaluation of a fair outcome. Taken in context, and looking at the substance rather than the form of what was intended, the 1907 Resolution was not in the least exploitative.

. . . .

[para111] It seems to me both branches of the doctrine of laches and acquiescence apply here, namely: (i) where "the party has, by his conduct done that which might fairly be regarded as equivalent to a waiver", and (ii) such conduct "results in circumstances that make the prosecution of the action

unreasonable" *(M. (K.) v. M. (H.), supra*, at pp. 76 and 78). Conduct equivalent to a waiver is found in the declaration, representations and failure to assert "rights" in circumstances that required assertion, as previously set out.

Unreasonable prosecution arises because, relying on the status quo, each band improved the reserve to which it understood its sister band made no further claim. All of this was done with sufficient knowledge "of the underlying facts relevant to a possible legal claim" *(M. (K.) v. M. (H.), supra*, at p. 79).

[para112] I conclude therefore that the claims of the appellant bands were rightly rejected on their merits by the trial judge....

. . . .

[para121] The Cape Mudge Band argues that the limitation periods otherwise applicable in this case should not be allowed to operate as "instruments of injustice" (factum, at para. 104). However, the policies behind a statute of limitations (or "statute of repose") are well known.... Witnesses are no longer available, historical documents are lost and difficult to contextualize, and expectations of fair practices change. Evolving standards of conduct and new standards of liability eventually make it unfair to judge actions of the past by the standards of today. As the Law Reform Commission of British Columbia wrote in support of an "ultimate" 30-year limitation period in 1990:

> If there are limitation periods, conduct which attracts legal consequences is more likely to be judged in light of the standards existing at the time of the conduct than if there are no restrictions on the plaintiff's ability to litigate. This rationale for the limitation of actions is of increasing importance, given the rate at which attitudes and norms currently change. New areas of liability arise continually in response to evolving sensitivities. (*Report on the Ultimate Limitation Period: Limitation Act, Section 8*, at p. 17)

[para122] The need for repose is evident in this case. Each band had settled and legitimate expectations with respect to the reserve it now inhabits. Each band still recognizes the need for repose of its sister band (thus seeking compensation from the Crown rather than dispossession of its sister band). Each band claims repose for itself, thus pleading the limitation period in its own defence against the other band.

[para123] This is not to say that historical grievances should be ignored, or that injustice necessarily loses its sting with the passage of the years. Here, however, the bands had independent legal advice at least by the 1930s, and were aware at that time of the material facts, if not all the details, on which the present claims are based. While the feeling may not have been unanimous, each band membership elected not to disturb its neighbours. The conduct of each band between 1907 and 1936 suggests that not only was the other band's open and notorious occupation of its reserve acknowledged, but such occupation was considered, as between the bands, to be fair and equitable.

. . . .

[para134] The appellants contend that every day they are kept out of possession of the other band's reserve is a fresh breach, and a fresh cause of action. As a result, their respective claims are not yet statute barred (and could never be). For instance, the Campbell River Band claims in its factum, at par. 111, that

> [t]he fact that Campbell River has been legally entitled to Quinsam since 1938, at the latest, gives it a presently enforceable right. Two additional consequences flow from this: (1) the Crown's fiduciary duty to safeguard Campbell River's right to its reserve against alienation has also subsisted since the legislation was passed; and (2) Cape Mudge has committed a continuous trespass since it first took possession of Quinsam. Both of these wrongs were committed anew each day and caused fresh damages each day.

The Cape Mudge Band's factum, at para. 98, makes analogous arguments.

[para135] Acceptance of such a position would, of course, defeat the legislative purpose of limitation periods. For a fiduciary, in particular, there would be no repose. In my view such a conclusion is not compatible with the intent of the legislation....

. . . .

[para138] I would therefore dismiss the appeals with costs.

9 Aboriginal Rights

(a) *Mabo v. State of Queensland (No. 2)*†

See **Chapter 9, Part 2**.

NOTE

The Meriam Aboriginal people of northern Australia sought declarations that they had Aboriginal title to the Murray Islands and that this title could not be extinguished by the State of Queensland. Did their Aboriginal title survive the change of sovereignty that occurred when the control of the area passed to Europeans? If so, how, and in what form?

EXTRACT

[MASON C.J. and McHUGH J.:]

We agree with the reasons for judgment of Brennan J. and with the declaration which he proposes.

In the result, six members of the Court (Dawson J. dissenting) are in agreement that the common law of this country recognizes a form of native title which, in the cases where it has not been extinguished, reflects the entitlement of the indigenous inhabitants, in accordance with their laws or customs, to their traditional lands and that, subject to the effect of some particular Crown leases, the land entitlement of the Murray Islanders in accordance with their laws or customs is preserved, as native title, under the law of Queensland. The main difference between those members of the Court who constitute the majority is that, subject to the operation of the *Racial Discrimination Act, 1975* (Cth), neither of us nor Brennan J. agrees with the conclusion to be drawn from the judgments of Deane, Toohey and Gaudron JJ. that, at least in the absence of clear and unambiguous statutory provision to the contrary, extinguishment of native title by the inconsistent grant is wrongful and gives rise to a claim for compensatory damages. We note that the judgment of Dawson J. supports the conclusion of Brennan J. and ourselves on that aspect of the case since his Honour considers that native title, where it exists, is a form of permissive occupancy at the will of the Crown.

We are authorized to say that the other members of the Court agree with what is said in the preceding paragraph about the outcome of the case.

The formal order to be made by the Court accords with the declaration proposed by Brennan J. but is cast in a form which will not give rise to any possible implication affecting the status of land which is not the subject of the declaration in par. 2 of the formal order.

[BRENNAN J. (Mason C.J., with McHugh J., concurring):]

. . . .

Whatever the justification advanced in earlier days for refusing to recognize the rights and interests in land of the indigenous inhabitants of settled colonies, an unjust and discriminatory doctrine of that kind can no longer be accepted.... A common law doctrine founded on unjust discrimination in the enjoyment of civil and political rights demands reconsideration. It is contrary both to international standards and to the fundamental values of our common law to entrench a discriminatory rule which, because of the supposed position on the scale of

† (1992), 107 A.L.R. 1; 175 C.L.R. 1 (High Court of Australia) at 7, 29, 34, 41, 50–52, 55–56.

social organization of the indigenous inhabitants of a settled colony, denies them a right to occupy their traditional lands.

. . . .

... [I]t is not a corollary of the Crown's acquisition of a radical title to land in an occupied territory that the Crown acquired absolute beneficial ownership of that land to the exclusion of the indigenous inhabitants. If the land were desert and uninhabited, truly a *terra nullius*, the Crown would take an absolute beneficial title (an allodial title) to the land: ... there would be no other proprietor. But if the land were occupied by the indigenous inhabitants and their rights and interests in the land are recognized by the common law, the radical title which is acquired with the acquisition of sovereignty cannot itself be taken to confer an absolute beneficial title to the occupied land. Nor is it necessary to the structure of our legal system to refuse recognition to the rights and interests in land of the indigenous inhabitants. The doctrine of tenure applies to every Crown grant of an interest in land, but not to rights and interests which do not owe their existence to a Crown grant.

. . . .

The preferable rule [to the recognition doctrine] ... is that a mere change in sovereignty does not extinguish native title to land. (The term "native title" conveniently describes the interests and rights of indigenous inhabitants in land, whether communal, group or individual, possessed under the traditional laws acknowledged by and the traditional customs observed by the indigenous inhabitants.) The preferable rule equates the indigenous inhabitants of a settled colony with the inhabitants of a conquered colony in respect of their rights and interests in land and recognizes in the indigenous inhabitants of a settled colony the rights and interests recognized by the Privy Council in *In re Southern Rhodesia* as surviving to the benefit of the residents of a conquered colony.

If native title survives the Crown's acquisition of sovereignty as, in my view, it does, it is unnecessary to examine the alternative arguments advanced to support the rights and interests of the Meriam people to their traditional land.... [I]n my opinion, the common law of Australia rejects the notion that, when the Crown acquired sovereignty over territory which is now part of Australia it thereby acquired the absolute beneficial ownership of the land therein, and accepts that the antecedent rights and interests in land possessed by the indigenous inhabitants of the territory survived the change in sovereignty. Those antecedent rights and interests thus constitute a burden on the radical title of the Crown.

. . . .

After this lengthy examination of the problem, it is desirable to state in summary form what I hold to be the common law of Australia with reference to land titles:

1. The Crown's acquisition of sovereignty over the several parts of Australia cannot be challenged in an Australian municipal court.
2. On acquisition of sovereignty over a particular part of Australia, the Crown acquired a radical title to the land in that part.
3. Native title to land survived the Crown's acquisition of sovereignty and radical title. The rights and privileges conferred by native title were unaffected by the Crown's acquisition of radical title but the acquisition of sovereignty exposed native title to extinguishment by a valid exercise of sovereign power inconsistent with the continued right to enjoy native title.
4. Where the Crown has validly alienated land by granting an interest that is wholly or partially inconsistent with a continuing right to enjoy native title, native title is extinguished to the extent of the inconsistency. Thus native title has been extinguished by grants of estates of freehold or of leases but not necessarily by the grant of lesser interests (e.g., authorities to prospect for minerals).
5. Where the Crown has validly and effectively appropriated land to itself and the appropriation is wholly or partially inconsistent with a continuing right to enjoy native title, native title is extinguished to the extent of the inconsistency. Thus native title has been extinguished to parcels of the waste lands of the Crown that have been validly appropriated for use (whether by dedication, setting aside, reservation or other valid means) and used for roads, railways, post offices and other permanent public works which preclude the continuing concurrent enjoyment of native title. Native title continues where the waste lands of the Crown have not been so appropriated or used or where the appropriation and use is consistent with the continuing concurrent enjoyment of native title over the land (e.g., land set aside as a national park).

6. Native title to particular land (whether classified by the common law as proprietary, usufructuary or otherwise), its incidents and the persons entitled thereto are ascertained according to the laws and customs of the indigenous people who, by those laws and customs, have a connection with the land. It is immaterial that the laws and customs have undergone some change since the Crown acquired sovereignty provided the general nature of the connection between the indigenous people and the land remains. Membership of the indigenous people depends on biological descent from the indigenous people and on mutual recognition of a particular person's membership by that person and by the elders or other persons enjoying traditional authority among those people.
7. Native title to an area of land which a clan or group is entitled to enjoy under the laws and customs of an indigenous people is extinguished if the clan or group, by ceasing to acknowledge those laws, and (so far as practicable) observe those customs, loses its connection with the land or on the death of the last of the members of the group or clan.
8. Native title over any parcel of land can be surrendered to the Crown voluntarily by all those clans or groups who, by the traditional laws and customs of the indigenous people, have a relevant connection with the land but the rights and privileges conferred by native title are otherwise inalienable to persons who are not members of the indigenous people to whom alienation is permitted by the traditional laws and customs.
9. If native title to any parcel of the waste lands of the Crown is extinguished, the Crown becomes the absolute beneficial owner.

These propositions leave for resolution by the general law the question of the validity of any purported exercise by the Crown of the power to alienate or to appropriate to itself waste lands of the Crown. In Queensland, these powers are and at all material times have been exercisable by the Executive Government subject, in the case of the power of alienation, to the statutes of the State in force from time to time. The power of alienation and the power of appropriation vested in the Crown in right of a State are also subject to the valid laws of the Commonwealth, including the *Racial Discrimination Act*. Where a power has purportedly been exercised as a prerogative power, the validity of the exercise depends on the scope of the prerogative and the authority of the purported repository in the particular case.

. . . .

As the Crown holds the radical title to the Murray Islands and as native title is not a title created by grant nor is it a common law tenure, it may be confusing to describe the title of the Meriam people as conferring "ownership", a term which connotes an estate in fee simple or at least an estate of freehold. Nevertheless, it is right to say that their native title is effective as against the State of Queensland and as against the whole world unless the State, in valid exercise of its legislative or executive power, extinguishes the title. It is also right to say that the Murray Islands are not Crown land because the land has been either "reserved for or dedicated to public purposes" or is "subject to ... lease". However, that does not deny that the Governor in Council may, by appropriate exercise of his statutory powers, extinguish native title. The native title has already been extinguished over land which has been leased pursuant to powers conferred by the *Land Act* in force at the time of the granting or renewal of the lease.

Accordingly, title to the land leased to the Trustees of the Australian Board of Missions has been extinguished and title to Dauar and Waier may have been extinguished. It may be that areas on Mer have been validly appropriated for use for administrative purposes the use of which is inconsistent with the continued enjoyment of the rights and interests of Meriam people in those areas pursuant to Meriam law or custom and, in that event, native title has been extinguished over those areas. None of these areas can be included in the declaration.

I would therefore make a declaration in the following terms:

Declare —

1. that the land in the Murray Islands is not Crown land within the meaning of that term in s. 5 of the *Land Act, 1962–1988* (Q.);
2. that the Meriam people are entitled as against the whole world to possession, occupation, use and enjoyment of the island of Mer except for that parcel of land leased to the Trustees of the Australian Board of Missions and those parcels of land (if any) which have been validly appropriated for use for administrative purposes the use of which is inconsistent with the continued enjoyment of the rights and privileges of Meriam people under native title;

3. that the title of the Meriam people is subject to the power of the Parliament of Queensland and the power of the Governor in Council of Queensland to extinguish that title by valid exercise of their respective powers, provided any exercise of those powers is not inconsistent with the laws of the Commonwealth.

(b) *R. v. Van der Peet*†

See **Chapter 9, Part 3.**

NOTE

Ms. Dorothy Van der Peet, a Stó:lo Indian, sold ten salmon contrary to federal fishing regulations. She argued that she had a constitutionally protected Aboriginal right to sell the fish. Speaking for the seven-judge majority of the Court, Lamer C.J. said the question required a look at the general nature and content of Aboriginal rights in the context of the *Constitution Act, 1982*. Note the sharply contrasting approach to these issues by one of the two dissenting judges, McLachlin J.

Van der Peet was decided on the same day as two other trade or commercial fishing cases from British Columbia. In *R. v. N.T.C. Smokehouse Ltd.*, [1996] 2 S.C.R. 672, a majority of the Supreme Court found that an Aboriginal group's traditional exchange of fish was insufficient to satisfy the distinctive practices test, and concluded that there was no Aboriginal right. In *R. v. Gladstone*, [1996] 2 S.C.R. 723, a majority of the Supreme Court held that a traditional Aboriginal trade in herring spawn met the requirements of the distinctive practices test, but then sent the case back to trial for further evidence on the issue of justification under s. 35(1) of the *Constitution Act, 1982*.

EXTRACT

[LAMER C.J. for himself, La Forest, Sopinka, Gonthier, Cory, Iacobucci, and Major JJ.:]

. . . .

[para15] I now turn to the question which, as I have already suggested, lies at the heart of this appeal: how should the aboriginal rights recognized and affirmed by s. 35(1) of the *Constitution Act, 1982* be defined?

. . . .

[para24] ... Because of [the fiduciary relationship between the Crown and the aboriginal peoples], and its implication of the honour of the Crown, treaties, s. 35(1), and other statutory and constitutional provisions protecting the interests of aboriginal peoples, must be given a generous and liberal interpretation.... This general principle must inform the Court's analysis of the purposes underlying s. 35(1), and of that provision's definition and scope.

. . . .

[para28] In identifying the basis for the recognition and affirmation of aboriginal rights it must be remembered that s. 35(1) did not create the legal doctrine of aboriginal rights; aboriginal rights existed and were recognized under the common law.... At common law aboriginal rights did not, of course, have constitutional status, with the result that Parliament could, at any time, extinguish or regulate those rights....; it is this which distinguishes the aboriginal rights recognized and affirmed in s. 35(1) from the aboriginal rights protected by the common law. Subsequent to s. 35(1) aboriginal rights cannot be extinguished and can only be regulated or infringed consistent with the justificatory test laid out by this Court in *Sparrow*, *supra*.

† [1996] 2 S.C.R. 507 (L'Heureux-Dubé and McLachlin JJ. dissenting, August 21, 1996); rev'g [1993] 5 W.W.R. 459 (B.C.C.A.); rev'g [1991] 3 C.N.L.R. 161 (B.C.S.C.); rev'g [1991] 3 C.N.L.R. 155 (Prov. Ct.).

. . . .

[para30] In my view, the doctrine of aboriginal rights exists, and is recognized and affirmed by s. 35(1), because of one simple fact: when Europeans arrived in North America, aboriginal peoples were already here, living in communities on the land, and participating in distinctive cultures, as they had done for centuries. It is this fact, and this fact above all others, which separates aboriginal peoples from all other minority groups in Canadian society and which mandates their special legal, and now constitutional, status.

[para31] More specifically, what s. 35(1) does is provide the constitutional framework through which the fact that aboriginals lived on the land in distinctive societies, with their own practices, traditions and cultures, is acknowledged and reconciled with the sovereignty of the Crown. The substantive rights which fall within the provision must be defined in light of this purpose; the aboriginal rights recognized and affirmed by s. 35(1) must be directed towards the reconciliation of the pre-existence of aboriginal societies with the sovereignty of the Crown.

[para32] That the purpose of s. 35(1) lies in its recognition of the prior occupation of North America by aboriginal peoples is suggested by the French version of the text....

. . . .

[para34] The position of Judson and Hall JJ. [in *Calder*] on the basis for aboriginal title is applicable to the aboriginal rights recognized and affirmed by s. 35(1). Aboriginal title is the aspect of aboriginal rights related specifically to aboriginal claims to land; it is the way in which the common law recognizes aboriginal land rights. As such, the explanation of the basis of aboriginal title in *Calder*, *supra*, can be applied equally to the aboriginal rights recognized and affirmed by s. 35(1). Both aboriginal title and aboriginal rights arise from the existence of distinctive aboriginal communities occupying "the land as their forefathers had done for centuries".

. . . .

[para37] ... Marshall C.J.'s essential insight [in *Worcester* v. *Georgia*] that the claims of the Cherokee must be analyzed in light of their pre-existing occupation and use of the land — their "undisputed" possession of the soil "from time immemorial" — is as relevant for the identification of the interests s. 35(1) was intended to protect as it was for the adjudication of Worcester's claim.

. . . .

[para40] ... To base aboriginal title in traditional laws and customs, as was done in *Mabo*, is ... to base that title in the pre-existing societies of aboriginal peoples. This is the same basis as that asserted here for aboriginal rights.

[para41] Academic commentators have also been consistent in identifying the basis and foundation of the s. 35(1) claims of aboriginal peoples in aboriginal occupation of North America prior to the arrival of Europeans. As Professor David Elliott, at p. 25, puts it in his compilation *Law and Aboriginal Peoples of Canada* (2nd Ed.), the "prior aboriginal presence is at the heart of the concept of aboriginal rights". Professor Macklem has, while also considering other possible justifications for the recognition of aboriginal rights, described prior occupancy as the "familiar" justification for aboriginal rights, arising from the "straightforward conception of fairness which suggests that, all other things being equal, a prior occupant of land possesses a stronger claim to that land than subsequent arrivals": Patrick Macklem, "Normative Dimensions of an Aboriginal Right of Self-Government" (1995), 21 *Queen's L.J.* 173, at p. 180. Finally, I would note the position of Professor Pentney who has described aboriginal rights as collective rights deriving "their existence from the common law's recognition of [the] prior social organization" of aboriginal peoples....

. . . .

[para43] The Canadian, American and Australian jurisprudence thus supports the basic proposition put forward at the beginning of this section: the aboriginal rights recognized and affirmed by s. 35(1) are best understood as, first, the means by which the Constitution recognizes the fact that prior to the arrival of Europeans in North America the land was already occupied by distinctive aboriginal societies, and as, second, the means by which that prior occupation is reconciled with the assertion of Crown sovereignty over Canadian territory. The content of aboriginal rights must be directed at fulfilling both of these purposes....

. . . .

[para44] In order to fulfil the purpose underlying s. 35(1) — i.e., the protection and reconciliation of the interests which arise from the fact that prior to the arrival of Europeans in North America aboriginal peoples lived on the land in distinctive societies, with their own practices, customs and traditions — the test for identifying the aboriginal rights recognized and affirmed by s. 35(1) must be directed at identifying the crucial elements of those pre-existing distinctive societies. It must, in other words, aim at identifying the practices, traditions and customs central to the aboriginal societies that existed in North America prior to contact with the Europeans.

[para45] In *Sparrow*, *supra* ... at p. 1099 Dickson C.J. and La Forest J. identified the Musqueam right to fish for food in the fact that

> The anthropological evidence relied on to establish the existence of the right suggests that, for the Musqueam, the salmon fishery has always constituted an integral part of their distinctive culture. Its significant role involved not only consumption for subsistence purposes, but also consumption of salmon on ceremonial and social occasions. The Musqueam have always fished for reasons connected to their cultural and physical survival. [Emphasis added.]

. . . .

[para46] In light of the suggestion of *Sparrow*, *supra*, and the purposes underlying s. 35(1), the following test should be used to identify whether an applicant has established an aboriginal right protected by s. 35(1): in order to be an aboriginal right an activity must be an element of a practice, custom or tradition integral to the distinctive culture of the aboriginal group claiming the right.

. . . .

[para49] In assessing a claim for the existence of an aboriginal right, a court must take into account the perspective of the aboriginal people claiming the right.

. . . .

[para51] Related to this is the fact that in assessing a claim to an aboriginal right a court must first identify the nature of the right being claimed; in order to determine whether a claim meets the test of being integral to the distinctive culture of the aboriginal group claiming the right, the court must first correctly determine what it is that is being claimed....

. . . .

[para53] To characterize an applicant's claim correctly, a court should consider such factors as the nature of the action which the applicant is claiming was done pursuant to an aboriginal right, the nature of the governmental regulation, statute or action being impugned, and the tradition, custom or practice being relied upon to establish the right.

. . . .

[para55] To satisfy the integral to a distinctive culture test the aboriginal claimant must do more than demonstrate that a practice, tradition or custom was an aspect of, or took place in, the aboriginal society of which he or she is a part. The claimant must demonstrate that the practice, tradition or custom was a central and significant part of the society's distinctive culture. He or she must demonstrate, in other words, that the practice, tradition or custom was one of the things which made the culture of the society distinctive — that it was one of the things that truly made the society what it was.

[para56] ... To recognize and affirm the prior occupation of Canada by distinctive aboriginal societies it is to what makes those societies distinctive that the court must look in identifying aboriginal rights. The court cannot look at those aspects of the aboriginal society that are true of every human society (e.g., eating to survive), nor can it look at those aspects of the aboriginal society that are only incidental or occasional to that society; the court must look instead to the defining and central attributes of the aboriginal society in question. It is only by focusing on the aspects of the aboriginal society that make that society distinctive that the definition of aboriginal rights will accomplish the purpose underlying s. 35(1).

. . . .

[para58] ... The significance of the tradition, practice or custom does not serve to identify the nature of a claim of acting pursuant to an aboriginal right; however, it is a key aspect of the court's inquiry into whether a tradition, practice or custom has been shown to be an integral part of the distinctive culture of an aboriginal community. The significance of the practice, tradition or custom will inform a court

as to whether or not that practice, tradition or custom can be said to be truly integral to the distinctive culture in question.

[para59] A practical way of thinking about this problem is to ask whether, without this practice, tradition or custom, the culture in question would be fundamentally altered or other than what it is. One must ask, to put the question affirmatively, whether or not a practice, tradition or custom is a defining feature of the culture in question.

. . . .

[para60] The time period that a court should consider in identifying whether the right claimed meets the standard of being integral to the aboriginal community claiming the right is the period prior to contact between aboriginal and European societies....

. . . .

[para63] ... It is precisely those present practices, customs and traditions which can be identified as having continuity with the practices, customs and traditions that existed prior to contact that will be the basis for the identification and definition of aboriginal rights under s. 35(1). Where an aboriginal community can demonstrate that a particular practice, custom or tradition is integral to its distinctive culture today, and that this practice, custom or tradition has continuity with the practices, customs and traditions of pre-contact times, that community will have demonstrated that the practice, custom or tradition is an aboriginal right for the purposes of s. 35(1).

. . . .

[para64] The evolution of practices, customs and traditions into modern forms will not, provided that continuity with pre-contact practices, customs and traditions is demonstrated, prevent their protection as aboriginal rights.... It may be that for a period of time an aboriginal group, for some reason, ceased to engage in a practice, tradition or custom which existed prior to contact, but then resumed the practice, tradition or custom at a later date. Such an interruption will not preclude the establishment of an aboriginal right.

. . . .

[para67] ... [T]he manner in which the aboriginal rights of other aboriginal peoples are defined is not necessarily determinative of the manner in which the aboriginal rights of the Métis are defined.

. . . .

[para69] Courts considering a claim to the existence of an aboriginal right must focus specifically on the traditions, customs and practices of the particular aboriginal group claiming the right.

. . . .

[para70] In identifying those practices, customs and traditions that constitute the aboriginal rights recognized and affirmed by s. 35(1), a court must ensure that the practice, custom or tradition relied upon in a particular case is independently significant to the aboriginal community claiming the right. The practice, custom or tradition cannot exist simply as an incident to another practice, custom or tradition but must rather be itself of integral significance to the aboriginal society....

[para71] The standard which a practice, custom or tradition must meet in order to be recognized as an aboriginal right is not that it be distinct to the aboriginal culture in question; the aboriginal claimants must simply demonstrate that the practice, custom or tradition is distinctive. A tradition or custom that is distinct is one that is unique — "different in kind or quality, unlike".... A culture with a distinct tradition must claim that in having such a tradition it is different from other cultures; a claim of distinctness is, by its very nature, a claim relative to other cultures or traditions. By contrast, a culture that claims that a practice, custom or tradition is distinctive — "distinguishing, characteristic" — makes a claim that is not relative; the claim is rather one about the culture's own practices, customs or traditions considered apart from the practices, customs or traditions of any other culture. It is a claim that this tradition or custom makes the culture what it is, not that the practice, custom or tradition is different from the practices, customs or traditions of another culture....

. . . .

[para74] ... [A]boriginal rights and aboriginal title are related concepts; aboriginal title is a sub-category of aboriginal rights which deals solely with claims of rights to land. The relationship between aboriginal title and aboriginal rights must not, however, confuse the analysis of what constitutes an aboriginal right.

Aboriginal rights arise from the prior occupation of land, but they also arise from the prior social organization and distinctive cultures of aboriginal peoples on that land. In considering whether a claim to an aboriginal right has been made out, courts must look at both the relationship of an aboriginal claimant to the land and at the practices, customs and traditions arising from the claimant's distinctive culture and society. Courts must not focus so entirely on the relationship of aboriginal peoples with the land that they lose sight of the other factors relevant to the identification and definition of aboriginal rights.

. . . .

[para85] ... The findings of fact made by Scarlett Prov. Ct. J. suggest that the exchange of salmon for money or other goods, while certainly taking place in Sto:lo society prior to contact, was not a significant, integral or defining feature of that society.

[para86] First, Scarlett Prov. Ct. J. found that, prior to contact, exchanges of fish were only "incidental" to fishing for food purposes....

[para87] For similar reasons, the evidence linking the exchange of salmon to the maintenance of kinship and family relations does not support the appellant's claim to the existence of an aboriginal right. Exchange of salmon as part of the interaction of kin and family is not of an independent significance sufficient to ground a claim for an aboriginal right to the exchange of fish for money or other goods.

[para88] Second, Scarlett Prov. Ct. J. found that there was no "regularized trading system" amongst the Sto:lo prior to contact.... [T]his indicates that the exchange of salmon was not widespread in Sto:lo society. Given that the exchange of salmon was not widespread it cannot be said that, prior to contact, Sto:lo culture was defined by trade in salmon....

[para89] Third, the trade engaged in between the Sto:lo and the Hudson's Bay Company ... does not have the necessary continuity with Sto:lo culture pre-contact to support a claim to an aboriginal right to trade salmon. Further, [this trade] can be seen as central or significant to the Sto:lo primarily as a result of European influences; activities which become central or significant because of the influence of European culture cannot be said to be aboriginal rights.

[para90] Finally, Scarlett Prov. Ct. J. found that the Sto:lo were at a band level of social organization rather than at a tribal level. As noted by the various experts, one of the central distinctions between a band society and a tribal society relates to specialization and division of labour. In a tribal society there tends to be specialization of labour — for example, specialization in the gathering and trade of fish — whereas in a band society division of labour tends to occur only on the basis of gender or age. The absence of specialization in the exploitation of the fishery is suggestive, in the same way that the absence of regularized trade or a market is suggestive, that the exchange of fish was not a central part of Sto:lo culture....

[para91] For these reasons, then, I would conclude that the appellant has failed to demonstrate that the exchange of fish for money or other goods was an integral part of the distinctive Sto:lo society which existed prior to contact. The exchange of fish took place, but was not a central, significant or defining feature of Sto:lo society. The appellant has thus failed to demonstrate that the exchange of salmon for money or other goods by the Sto:lo is an aboriginal right recognized and affirmed under s. 35(1) of the *Constitution Act, 1982*.

[para92] Since the appellant has failed to demonstrate that the exchange of fish was an aboriginal right of the Sto:lo, it is unnecessary to consider the tests for extinguishment, infringement and justification laid out by this Court in *Sparrow*, *supra*.

. . . .

[McLACHLIN J., dissenting:]

. . . .

[para227] My conclusions on this appeal may be summarized as follows. The issue of what constitutes an aboriginal right must, in my view, be answered by looking at what the law has historically accepted as fundamental aboriginal rights. These encompass the right to be sustained from the land or waters upon which an aboriginal people have traditionally relied for sustenance. Trade in the resource to the extent necessary to maintain traditional levels of sustenance is a permitted exercise of this right. The right endures until extinguished by treaty or otherwise. The right is limited to the extent of the aboriginal people's historic reliance on the resource, as well as the power of the Crown to limit or prohibit exploitation of the resource incompatible with its responsible use. Applying these principles, I conclude that the Sto:lo possess an aboriginal right to fish

commercially for purposes of basic sustenance, that this right has not been extinguished, that the regulation prohibiting the sale of any fish constitutes a *prima facie* infringement of it, and that this infringement is not justified. Accordingly, I conclude that the appellant's conviction must be set aside.

. . . .

[para246] ... I agree with the Chief Justice that history is important. A recently adopted practice would generally not qualify as being aboriginal. Those things which have in the past been recognized as aboriginal rights have been related to the traditional practices of aboriginal peoples....

[para247] I cannot agree with the Chief Justice, however, that it is essential that a practice be traceable to pre-contact times for it to qualify as a constitutional right. Aboriginal rights find their source not in a magic moment of European contact, but in the traditional laws and customs of the aboriginal people in question.

. . . .

[para255] I agree with the Chief Justice, at para. 46, that to qualify as an aboriginal right "an activity must be an element of practice, custom or tradition integral to the distinctive culture of the aboriginal group claiming the right". I also agree with L'Heureux-Dubé J. that an aboriginal right must be "integral" to a "distinctive aboriginal group's culture and social organization". To say this is simply to affirm the foundation of aboriginal rights in the laws and customs of the people. It describes an essential quality of an aboriginal right. But, with respect, a workable legal test for determining the extent to which, if any, commercial fishing may constitute an aboriginal right, requires more....

[para256] My first concern is that the proposed test is too broad to serve as a legal distinguisher between constitutional and non-constitutional rights. While the Chief Justice in the latter part of his reasons seems to equate "integral" with "not incidental", the fact remains that "integral" is a wide concept, capable of embracing virtually everything that an aboriginal people customarily did.... The Chief Justice attempts to narrow the concept of "integral" by emphasizing that the proposed right must be part of what makes the group "distinctive", the "specific" people which they are, stopping short, however, of asserting that the practice must be unique to the group and adhere to none other. But the addition of concepts of distinctness and specificity do not, with respect, remedy the overbreadth of the test. Minor practices, falling far short of the importance which we normally attach to constitutional rights, may qualify as distinct or specific to a group. Even the addition of the notion that the characteristic must be central or important rather than merely "incidental", fails to remedy the problem; it merely poses another problem, that of determining what is central and what is incidental to a people's culture and social organization.

[para257] The problem of overbreadth thus brings me to my second concern, the problem of indeterminacy. To the extent that one attempts to narrow the test proposed by the Chief Justice by the addition of concepts of distinctiveness, specificity and centrality, one encounters the problem that different people may entertain different ideas of what is distinctive, specific or central. To use such concepts as the markers of legal rights is to permit the determination of rights to be coloured by the subjective views of the decision-maker rather than objective norms, and to invite uncertainty and dispute as to whether a particular practice constitutes a legal right.

[para258] Finally, the proposed test is, in my respectful opinion, too categorical. Whether something is integral or not is an all or nothing test....

. . . .

[para261] In my view, the better approach to defining aboriginal rights is an empirical approach. Rather than attempting to describe *a priori* what an aboriginal right is, we should look to history to see what sort of practices have been identified as aboriginal rights in the past. From this we may draw inferences as to the sort of things which may qualify as aboriginal rights under s. 35(1). Confronted by a particular claim, we should ask, "Is this like the sort of thing which the law has recognized in the past?"

. . . .

[para264] For centuries, it has been established that upon asserting sovereignty the British Crown accepted the existing property and customary rights of the territory's inhabitants. Illustrations abound....

. . . .

[para268] This much is clear: the Crown, upon discovering and occupying a "new" territory, recognized

the law and custom of the aboriginal societies it found and the rights in the lands they traditionally occupied that these supported.

. . . .

[para272] [The Royal Proclamation of 1763 and the treaties] ... bear testimony to the acceptance by the colonizers of the principle that the aboriginal peoples who occupied what is now Canada were regarded as possessing the aboriginal right to live off their lands and the resources found in their forests and streams to the extent they had traditionally done so. The fundamental understanding — the Grundnorm of settlement in Canada — was that the aboriginal people could only be deprived of the sustenance they traditionally drew from the land and adjacent waters by solemn treaty with the Crown, on terms that would ensure to them and to their successors a replacement for the livelihood that their lands, forests and streams had since ancestral times provided them. (In making this comment, I do not foreclose the possibility that other arguments might be made with respect to areas in Canada settled by France.) ...

[para273] ... [The lack of treaties in much of British Columbia does not negate] the fundamental proposition acknowledged generally throughout Canada's history of settlement that the aboriginal occupants of particular territories have the right to use and be sustained by those territories.

. . . .

[para275] It thus emerges that the common law and those who regulated the British settlement of this country predicated dealings with aboriginals on two fundamental principles. The first was the general principle that the Crown took subject to existing aboriginal interests in the lands they traditionally occupied and their adjacent waters, even though those interests might not be of a type recognized by British law. The second, which may be viewed as an application of the first, is that the interests which aboriginal peoples had in using the land and adjacent waters for their sustenance were to be removed only by solemn treaty with due compensation to the people and its descendants. This right to use the land and adjacent waters as the people had traditionally done for its sustenance may be seen as a fundamental aboriginal right. It is supported by the common law and by the history of this country. It may safely be said to be enshrined in s. 35(1) of the *Constitution Act, 1982*.

. . . .

[para277] If an aboriginal people can establish that it traditionally fished in a certain area, it continues to have a similar right to do so, barring extinguishment or treaty. The same justice that compelled those who drafted treaties with the aboriginals in the nineteenth century to make provision for the continuing sustenance of the people from the land, compels those dealing with aboriginals with whom treaties were never made, like the Sto:lo, to make similar provision.

[para278] The aboriginal right to fish may be defined as the right to continue to obtain from the river or the sea in question that which the particular aboriginal people have traditionally obtained from the portion of the river or sea. If the aboriginal people show that they traditionally sustained themselves from the river or sea, then they have a prima facie right to continue to do so, absent a treaty exchanging that right for other consideration. At its base, the right is not the right to trade, but the right to continue to use the resource in the traditional way to provide for the traditional needs, albeit in their modern form. However, if the people demonstrates that trade is the only way of using the resource to provide the modern equivalent of what they traditionally took, it follows that the people should be permitted to trade in the resource to the extent necessary to provide the replacement goods and amenities. In this context, trade is but the mode or practice by which the more fundamental right of drawing sustenance from the resource is exercised.

. . . .

[para282] ... [T]he evidence conclusively establishes that over many centuries, the Sto:lo have used the fishery not only for food and ceremonial purposes, but also to satisfy a variety of other needs. Unless that right has been extinguished, and subject always to conservation requirements, they are entitled to continue to use the river for these purposes. To the extent that trade is required to achieve this end, it falls within that right.

[para283] I agree with L'Heureux-Dubé J. that the scale of fishing evidenced by the case at bar falls well within the limit of the traditional fishery and the moderate livelihood it provided to the Sto:lo.

[para284] For these reasons I conclude that Mrs. Van der Peet's sale of the fish can be defended as

an exercise of her aboriginal right, unless that right has been extinguished.

[McLachlin J. went on to find that the right had not been extinguished, that it had been infringed by government regulation, and that the government had failed to justify the infringement.

L'Heureux-Dubé J. also dissented in separate reasons. She supported a broader version of the distinctive practices test than that of the majority. L'Heureux-Dubé J. also felt that relevant traditional practices need not be limited to the pre-contact period.]

(c) *R. v. Gladstone*†

See **Chapter 9, Part 4**. See also **Chapter 8, Part 8(c)**.

NOTE

Two Heiltsuk Band members were charged with attempting to sell herring spawn on kelp without a licence, contrary to regulations under the *Fisheries Act*. They argued that the regulations violated their s. 35(1) Aboriginal right to sell herring spawn on kelp commercially. The majority of the Court found an unextinguished infringed Aboriginal right to fish commercially, but referred the matter back to trial on the question of s. 35(1) justification. The extracts here relate to the justification issue.

EXTRACT

[LAMER C.J. for himself and Sopinka, Gonthier, Cory, Iacobucci and Major JJ.:]

. . . .

[para57] ... [T]he aboriginal right in this case is, unlike the right at issue in *Sparrow*, without internal limitation.

[para58] ... In a situation where the aboriginal right is internally limited, so that it is clear when that right has been satisfied and other users can be allowed to participate in the fishery, the notion of priority, as articulated in *Sparrow*, makes sense. In that situation it is understandable that in an exceptional year, when conservation concerns are severe, it will be possible for aboriginal rights holders to be alone allowed to participate in the fishery, while in more ordinary years other users will be allowed to participate in the fishery after the aboriginal rights to fish for food, social and ceremonial purposes have been met.

[para59] Where the aboriginal right has no internal limitation, however ... the notion of priority, as articulated in *Sparrow*, would mean that where an aboriginal right is recognized and affirmed that right would become an exclusive one. Because the right to sell herring spawn on kelp to the commercial market can never be said to be satisfied while the resource is still available and the market is not sated, to give priority to that right in the manner suggested in *Sparrow* would be to give the right-holder exclusivity over any person not having an aboriginal right to participate in the herring spawn on kelp fishery.

. . . .

[para62] Where the aboriginal right is one that has no internal limitation then the doctrine of priority ... requires that the government demonstrate that, in allocating the resource, it has taken account of the existence of aboriginal rights and allocated the resource in a manner respectful of the fact that those rights have priority over the exploitation of the fishery by other users.

. . . .

† [1996] 2 S.C.R. 723 (August 21, 1996): Lamer C.J. and La Forest, L'Heureux-Dubé, Sopinka, Gonthier, Cory, McLachlin, Iacobucci and Major JJ.

[para63] The content of this priority — something less than exclusivity but which nonetheless gives priority to the aboriginal right — must remain somewhat vague pending consideration of the government's actions in specific cases....

[para64] Questions relevant to the determination of whether the government has granted priority to aboriginal rights holders are those enumerated in *Sparrow* relating to consultation and compensation, as well as questions such as whether the government has accommodated the exercise of the aboriginal right to participate in the fishery (through reduced licence fees, for example), whether the government's objectives in enacting a particular regulatory scheme reflect the need to take into account the priority of aboriginal right holders, the extent of the participation in the fishery of aboriginal rights holders relative to their percentage of the population, how the government has accommodated different aboriginal rights in a particular fishery (food versus commercial rights, for example), how important the fishery is to the economic and material well-being of the band in question, and the criteria taken into account by the government in, for example, allocating commercial licences amongst different users....

. . . .

[para67] ... [I]t was not contemplated by *Sparrow* that the recognition and affirmation of aboriginal rights should result in the common law right of public access in the fishery ceasing to exist with respect to all those fisheries in respect of which [exists] an aboriginal right to sell fish commercially. As a common law, not constitutional, right, the right of public access to the fishery must clearly be second in priority to aboriginal rights; however, the recognition of aboriginal rights should not be interpreted as extinguishing the right of public access to the fishery.

[para68] That this should not be the case becomes particularly clear when it is remembered that, as was noted above, the existence of aboriginal rights varies amongst different aboriginal peoples, with the result that the notion of priority applies not only between aboriginals and other Canadians, but also between those aboriginal peoples who have an aboriginal right to use the fishery and those who do not....

. . . .

[para72] In *Van der Peet* the purposes underlying s. 35(1)'s recognition and affirmation of aboriginal rights were identified, at para. 39, as

> first, the means by which the constitution recognizes the fact that prior to the arrival of Europeans in North America the land was already occupied by distinctive aboriginal societies, and as, second, the means by which that prior occupation is reconciled with the assertion of Crown sovereignty over Canadian territory.

. . . .

[para73] Aboriginal rights are recognized and affirmed by s. 35(1) in order to reconcile the existence of distinctive aboriginal societies prior to the arrival of Europeans in North America with the assertion of Crown sovereignty over that territory; they are the means by which the critical and integral aspects of those societies are maintained. Because, however, distinctive aboriginal societies exist within, and are a part of, a broader social, political and economic community, over which the Crown is sovereign, there are circumstances in which, in order to pursue objectives of compelling and substantial importance to that community as a whole (taking into account the fact that aboriginal societies are a part of that community), some limitation of those rights will be justifiable. Aboriginal rights are a necessary part of the reconciliation of aboriginal societies with the broader political community of which they are part; limits placed on those rights are, where the objectives furthered by those limits are of sufficient importance to the broader community as a whole, equally a necessary part of that reconciliation.

. . . .

[para75] ... [W]ith [regard] to the distribution of the fisheries resource after conservation goals have been met, objectives such as the pursuit of economic and regional fairness, and the recognition of the historical reliance upon, and participation in, the fishery by non-aboriginal groups, are the type of objectives which can (at least in the right circumstances) satisfy this standard. In the right circumstances, such objectives are in the interest of all Canadians and, more importantly, the reconciliation of aboriginal societies with the rest of Canadian society may well depend on their successful attainment.

[L'Heureux-Dubé and McLachlin JJ. gave separate reasons. La Forest J. dissented on the grounds (i) that the interest claimed did not resemble the traditional trading interest because the contexts were different, and (ii) that if there had been any Aboriginal right, it had been extinguished.]

(d) *R. v. Pamajewon*†

See **Chapter 9, Part 5**. See also **Chapter 12, Part 4**.

NOTE

Members of the Shawanaga First Nation and the Eagle Lake Band were convicted of violating the *Criminal Code* because of high stakes gambling activities on their reserves. They argued that the gambling was protected by s. 35 of the *Constitution Act, 1982*, either as an Aboriginal right derived from Aboriginal title or as an Aboriginal right that was an incident of a broader inherent right to self-government.

EXTRACT

[LAMER C.J. for himself, La Forest, Sopinka, Gonthier, Cory, Mclachlin, Iacobucci and Major JJ.:]

. . . .

[para20] Leave to appeal to this Court was granted on June 1, 1995, [1995] 2 S.C.R. viii. On July 6, 1995 the following constitutional question was stated:

> Are s. 201, s. 206 or s. 207 of the *Criminal Code*, separately or in combination, of no force or effect with respect to the appellants, by virtue of s. 52 of the *Constitution Act, 1982* in the circumstances of these proceedings, by reason of the aboriginal or treaty rights within the meaning of s. 35 of the *Constitution Act, 1982* invoked by the appellants?

Analysis

[para23] The resolution of the appellants' claim in this case rests on the application of the test, laid out by this Court in *R.* v. *Van der Peet*, S.C.C., No. 23803, released August 21, 1996, for determining the aboriginal rights recognized and affirmed by s. 35(1) of the *Constitution Act, 1982*. The appellants in this case are claiming that the gambling activities in which they took part, and their respective bands' regulation of those gambling activities, fell within the scope of the aboriginal rights recognized and affirmed by s. 35(1). *Van der Peet, supra* lays out the test for determining the practices, traditions and customs which fall within s. 35(1) and, as such, provides the legal standard against which the appellants' claim must be measured.

[para24] The appellants' claim involves the assertion that s. 35(1) encompasses the right of self-government, and that this right includes the right to regulate gambling activities on the reservation. Assuming without deciding that s. 35(1) includes self-government claims, the applicable legal standard is nonetheless that laid out in *Van der Peet, supra*. Assuming s. 35(1) encompasses claims to aboriginal self-government, such claims must be considered in light of the purposes underlying that provision and must, therefore, be considered against the test derived from consideration of those purposes. This is the test laid out in *Van der Peet, supra*. In so far as they can be made under s. 35(1), claims to self-government are no different from other claims to the enjoyment of aboriginal rights and must, as such, be measured against the same standard.

[para25] In *Van der Peet, supra* the test for identifying aboriginal rights was said to be as follows, at para. 46:

> in order to be an aboriginal right an activity must be an element of a tradition, custom or practice integral to the distinctive culture of the aboriginal group claiming the right.

In applying this test the Court must first identify the exact nature of the activity claimed to be a right and must then go on to determine whether, on the evidence presented to the trial judge, and on the facts as found by the trial judge, that activity could be said to be (*Van der Peet*, at para. 59) "a defining feature of the culture in question" prior to contact with Europeans.

† [*R.* v. *Jones*; *R.* v. *Gardner*], [1996] 2 S.C.R. 821, February 26, 1996 (decision) and August 21, 1996 (S.C.C. reasons: Lamer C.J.C., La Forest, Sopinka, Gonthier, Cory, McLachlin, Iacobucci and Major JJ, with L'Heureux-Dubé concurring in separate reasons); aff'g (1994), 21 O.R. (3d) 385 (O.C.A.: Dubin C.J.O. and Osborne J.A. A third judge, Blair J.A., retired before the judgment was rendered and took no part in it); dismissing appeals from convictions by Carr Prov. Ct. J. and Flaherty Prov. Ct. J.

[para26] I now turn to the first part of the *Van der Peet* test, the characterization of the appellants' claim. In *Van der Peet, supra* the Court held at para. 53 that

> To characterize an applicant's claim correctly, a court should consider such factors as the nature of the action which the applicant is claiming was done pursuant to an aboriginal right, the nature of the governmental regulation, statute or action being impugned, and the tradition, custom or practice being relied upon to establish the right.

... the most accurate characterization of the appellants' claim is that they are asserting that s. 35(1) recognizes and affirms the rights of the Shawanaga and Eagle Lake First Nations to participate in, and to regulate, gambling activities on their respective reserve lands.

[para27] The appellants themselves would have this Court characterize their claim as to "a broad right to manage the use of their reserve lands". To so characterize the appellants' claim would be to cast the Court's inquiry at a level of excessive generality. Aboriginal rights, including any asserted right to self-government, must be looked at in light of the specific circumstances of each case and, in particular, in light of the specific history and culture of the aboriginal group claiming the right. The factors laid out in *Van der Peet*, and applied, *supra*, allow the Court to consider the appellants' claim at the appropriate level of specificity; the characterization put forward by the appellants would not allow the Court to do so.

[para28] I now turn to the second branch of the *Van der Peet* test, the consideration of whether the participation in, and regulation of, gambling on the reserve lands was an integral part of the distinctive cultures of the Shawanaga or Eagle Lake First Nations. The evidence presented at both the *Pamajewon* and *Gardner* trials does not demonstrate that gambling, or that the regulation of gambling, was an integral part of the distinctive cultures of the Shawanaga or Eagle Lake First Nations. In fact, the only evidence presented at either trial dealing with the question of the importance of gambling was that of James Morrison.... While Mr. Morrison's evidence does demonstrate that the Ojibwa gambled, it does not demonstrate that gambling was of central significance to the Ojibwa people. Moreover, his evidence in no way addresses the extent to which this gambling was the subject of regulation by the Ojibwa community. His account is of informal gambling activities taking place on a small-scale; he does not describe large-scale activities, subject to community regulation, of the sort at issue in this appeal.

[para29] ... upon review of the evidence I find myself in agreement with the conclusion arrived at by Osborne J.A. when he said first, at p. 400, that there "is no evidence to support a conclusion that gambling generally or high stakes gambling of the sort in issue here, were part of the First Nations' historic cultures and traditions, or an aspect of their use of their land" and, second, at p. 400, that "there is no evidence that gambling on the reserve lands generally was ever the subject matter of aboriginal regulation". I also agree with the observation made by Flaherty Prov. Ct. J. in the *Gardner* trial when he said that

> ... commercial lotteries such as bingo are a twentieth century [phenomenon] and nothing of the kind existed amongst aboriginal peoples and was never part of the means by which these societies were traditionally sustained or socialized

[para30] Given this evidentiary record, it is clear that the appellants have failed to demonstrate that the gambling activities in which they were engaged, and their respective Bands' regulation of those activities, took place pursuant to an aboriginal right recognized and affirmed by s. 35(1) of the *Constitution Act, 1982*.

Conclusion

[para31] These are my reasons for dismissing the appeal and for affirming the decision of the Court of Appeal upholding the trial judge's conviction of the various appellants for violating ss. 201 and 206 of the *Code*. There will be no order as to costs.

[para32] For the reasons given above, the constitutional question [para20] must be answered as follows:

. . . .

Answer: No.

[L'HEUREUX-DUBÉ J., concurring:]

[In her separate concurring reasons, L'Heureux-Dubé J. said the claimed right should be characterized as an Aboriginal right to gamble. She found that in the circumstances of this case, the claimed right did not meet the requirements of her formulation of the distinctive practices test. She continued:]

. . . .

[para41] The appellants have also asserted that s. 35(1) encompasses a broad right of self-government, and that this right includes the authority to regulate gambling activities on the reservation. Given the conclusion I have reached regarding gambling as a practice in these particular bands, it is unnecessary for me to even consider the question of self-government.

[para42] However, to the extent that it is necessary to deal with this issue, I merely refer to my reasons in *Van Der Peet*, *supra*, at para. 117, where I stated:

> ... The common feature of [lands on which aboriginal rights can exist] is that the Canadian Parliament and, to a certain extent, provincial legislatures have a general legislative authority over the activities of aboriginal people, which is the result of the British assertion of sovereignty over Canadian territory.

[para43] In addition, I am also in general agreement with the reasons of Osborne J.A. in the Court of Appeal (1995), 21 O.R. (3d) 385, at p. 400, where he states with respect to this case:

> If the Shawanaga First Nation and Eagle Lake Band had some rights of self-government which existed in 1982 (I am prepared to assume that they did), the right of governance asserted must be viewed like other claimed aboriginal rights; it must be given an historic context. Here, there is no evidence that gambling on the reserve lands generally was ever the subject matter of aboriginal regulation. Moreover, there is no evidence of an historic involvement in anything resembling the high stakes gambling in issue in these cases.

[para44] Accordingly, I would dispose of this appeal and answer the constitutional question in the manner proposed by the Chief Justice.

10 Aboriginal Rights and Title

(a) *R. v. Adams*†

See **Chapter 10, Part 2.**

NOTE

Mr. Adams was charged with fishing without a permit, contrary to federal regulations, in an area formerly within the boundaries of New France. Although the area had been flooded, and adjacent Indian land had been ceded, Mr. Adams argued that he still had an Aboriginal right to fish in the in the region, and that this right was protected by s. 35(1) of the *Constitution Act, 1982*. The key question was whether Aboriginal rights can continue independently of Aboriginal title. A majority of the Quebec Court of Appeal said the two are inseparable — if title ends, so do all Aboriginal rights. Another question was whether the alleged non-recognition of Aboriginal rights by the government of New France affected Mr. Adams' claim to an Aboriginal right protected by s. 35(1).

EXTRACT

[LAMER C.J. for himself, La Forest, Sopinka, Gonthier, Cory, Mclachlin, Iacobucci, and Major JJ.:]

. . . .

Aboriginal Title and Aboriginal Rights

[para25] As was noted at the outset, the fundamental question to be answered in this case is as to whether a claim to an aboriginal right to fish must rest in a claim to aboriginal title to the area in which the fishing took place. In other words, this Court must determine whether aboriginal rights are inherently based in aboriginal title to the land, or whether claims to title to the land are simply one manifestation of a broader based conception of aboriginal rights. The reasons of this Court in *Van der Peet* demonstrate that it is the latter characterization of the relationship between aboriginal rights and aboriginal title that is correct.

[para26] In *Van der Peet*, at para. 43, aboriginal rights were said to be best understood as,

> ...first, the means by which the Constitution recognizes the fact that prior to the arrival of Europeans in North America the land was already occupied by distinctive aboriginal societies, and as, second, the means by which that prior occupation is reconciled with the assertion of Crown sovereignty over Canadian territory.

From this basis the Court went on to hold, at para. 46, that aboriginal rights are identified through the following test:

> ...in order to be an aboriginal right an activity must be an element of a practice, custom or tradition integral to the distinctive culture of the aboriginal group claiming the right.

What this test, along with the conceptual basis which underlies it, indicates, is that while claims to aboriginal title fall within the conceptual framework of aboriginal rights, aboriginal rights do not exist solely where a claim to aboriginal title has been made out. Where an aboriginal group has shown that a particular activity, custom or tradition taking place on the

† [1996] 3 S.C.R. 101 (October 3, 1996), rev.g [1993] 3 C.N.L.R. 98 (Q.C.A., Rothman J.A., dissenting), which aff'd [1985] 4 C.N.L.R. 39 (Q.S.C.), which aff'd [1985] 4 C.N.L.R. 123 (Q.Ct. Sess.).

land was integral to the distinctive culture of that group then, even if they have not shown that their occupation and use of the land was sufficient to support a claim of title to the land, they will have demonstrated that they have an aboriginal right to engage in that practice, custom or tradition. The *Van der Peet* test protects activities which were integral to the distinctive culture of the aboriginal group claiming the right; it does not require that that group satisfy the further hurdle of demonstrating that their connection with the piece of land on which the activity was taking place was of a central significance to their distinctive culture sufficient to make out a claim to aboriginal title to the land. *Van der Peet* establishes that s. 35 recognizes and affirms the rights of those peoples who occupied North America prior to the arrival of the Europeans; that recognition and affirmation is not limited to those circumstances where an aboriginal group's relationship with the land is of a kind sufficient to establish title to the land.

[para27] To understand why aboriginal rights cannot be inexorably linked to aboriginal title it is only necessary to recall that some aboriginal peoples were nomadic, varying the location of their settlements with the season and changing circumstances. That this was the case does not alter the fact that nomadic peoples survived through reliance on the land prior to contact with Europeans and, further, that many of the customs, practices and traditions of nomadic peoples that took place on the land were integral to their distinctive cultures. The aboriginal rights recognized and affirmed by s. 35(1) should not be understood or defined in a manner which excludes some of those the provision was intended to protect.

[para28] Moreover, some aboriginal peoples varied the location of their settlements both before and after contact. The Mohawks are one such people; the facts accepted by the trial judge in this case demonstrate that the Mohawks did not settle exclusively in one location either before or after contact with Europeans. That this is the case may (although I take no position on this point) preclude the establishment of aboriginal title to the lands on which they settled; however, it in no way subtracts from the fact that, wherever they were settled before or after contact, prior to contact the Mohawks engaged in practices, traditions or customs on the land which were integral to their distinctive culture.

[para29] Finally, I would note that the Court in *Van der Peet* did address itself to this question, holding at para. 74 that:

> Aboriginal rights arise from the prior occupation of land, but they also arise from the prior social organization and distinctive cultures of aboriginal peoples on that land. In considering whether a claim to an aboriginal right has been made out, courts must look at both the relationship of an aboriginal claimant to the land <u>and</u> at the practices, customs and traditions arising from the claimant's distinctive culture and society. Courts must not focus so entirely on the relationship of aboriginal peoples with the land that they lose sight of the other factors relevant to the identification and definition of aboriginal rights. [Emphasis in original.]

This analysis supports the position adopted here.

[para30] The recognition that aboriginal title is simply one manifestation of the doctrine of aboriginal rights should not, however, create the impression that the fact that some aboriginal rights are linked to land use or occupation is unimportant. Even where an aboriginal right exists on a tract of land to which the aboriginal people in question do not have title, that right may well be site specific, with the result that it can be exercised only upon that specific tract of land. For example, if an aboriginal people demonstrates that hunting on a specific tract of land was an integral part of their distinctive culture then, even if the right exists apart from title to that tract of land, the aboriginal right to hunt is nonetheless defined as, and limited to, the right to hunt on the specific tract of land. A site-specific hunting or fishing right does not, simply because it is independent of aboriginal title to the land on which it took place, become an abstract fishing or hunting right exercisable anywhere; it continues to be a right to hunt or fish on the tract of land in question.

Aboriginal Rights and The Colony of New France

[para31] ...The aboriginal right to fish claimed in this instance relates to a tract of territory, specifically Lake St. Francis, which falls within the boundaries of New France prior to 1763. The respondent argues that this claimed right should be rejected as the French colonial regime never legally recognized the existence of aboriginal title or any incident aboriginal right to fish prior to the commencement of British sovereignty.

. . . .

[para32] ... [T]he respondent submits that regardless of the actual fishing practices of the Mohawks both

prior to and during the French regime, the French Crown never formally recognized any legal right of the Mohawks to fish in Lake St. Francis, and thus no such right was received into the common law with the transition to British sovereignty in 1763.

[para33] For the reasons developed in [*R. v. Côté*, [1996] S.C.J. No. 93 (S.C.C.), at paras. 51–53], this argument must be rejected. The respondent's characterization of the status of aboriginal rights under French colonial law is open to question, although, as in *Côté*, I need not decide the point here. What is important is that, as explained in *Van der Peet*, [1996] S.C.J. No. 77, the purpose of the entrenchment of s. 35(1) was to extend constitutional protection to the practices, customs and traditions central to the distinctive culture of aboriginal societies prior to contact with Europeans. If the exercise of such practices, customs and traditions effectively continued following contact in the absence of specific extinguishment, such practices, customs and traditions are entitled to constitutional recognition subject to the infringement and justification test outlined in *Sparrow*, [1990] 1 S.C.R. 1075 and more recently, in *Gladstone*, [1996] S.C.J. No. 79. The fact that a particular practice, custom or tradition continued following the arrival of Europeans, but in the absence of the formal gloss of legal recognition from the European colonizers, should not undermine the protection accorded to aboriginal peoples. Section 35(1) would fail to achieve its noble purpose of preserving the integral and defining features of distinctive aboriginal societies if it only protected those defining features which were fortunate enough to have received the legal approval of British and French colonizers.

The Van der Peet Test

[para34] I now turn to the claim made by the appellant in this case. The appellant argues that the Mohawks have an aboriginal right to fish in Lake St. Francis. In order to succeed in this argument the appellant must demonstrate that, pursuant to the test laid out by this Court in *Van der Peet*, fishing in Lake St. Francis was "an element of a tradition, custom, practice or law integral to the distinctive culture" of the Mohawks. For the reasons given below, I am of the view that the appellant has satisfied this test. Given that this is so, it will be unnecessary to address the appellant's argument that the Mohawks have aboriginal title to the lands in the fishing area that gives rise to an incidental right to fish there. The appellant himself rests his claim primarily on the existence of a free-standing aboriginal right to fish in Lake St. Francis; since I accept this argument it is unnecessary to consider any subsidiary arguments the appellant makes.

[Lamer C.J. found that the fishing rights claimed by Mr. Adams met the requirements of the *Van der Peet* test, that the rights had not been extinguished, and that they had been unjustifiably infringed by the fishery regulations. On the question of infringement, Lamer C.J. said the Minister's unstructured discretion to grant or withhold permits caused undue hardship and denied Mr. Adams his preferred means of exercising his rights. Lamer C.J. said the Act failed the *Sparrow* justification test because (i) the Act's purpose of enhancing sports fishing was not a compelling and substantial objective, and (ii) the Act failed to give first priority after conservation to Indian food fishing. Accordingly, Mr. Adams' conviction was set aside. L'Heureux-Dubé J. concurred in separate reasons.]

(b) *Delgamuukw v. British Columbia*†

See **Chapter 6, Part 9** and **Chapter 10, Part 3**. See also **Chapter 8, Part 8(c)**.

NOTE

The Gitksan and Wet'suwet'en peoples claimed Aboriginal title and self-government rights in regard to a large area of west central British Columbia. In response to their claims, the Supreme Court addressed five main sets of questions:

† [1997] 3 S.C.R. 1010 (December 11, 1997); varying (1993), 104 D.L.R. (4th) 470 (B.C.C.A.); which varied (1991), 79 D.L.R. (4th) 185 (B.C.S.C.).

1. Could the claims be changed informally in the course of the court proceedings?
2. What evidentiary weight should be given to oral Aboriginal histories?
3. What is the general nature, content and status of Aboriginal title? How is it related to Aboriginal rights? What is needed to prove it? How is it protected under s. 35(1) of the *Constitution Act, 1982*? What justification principles apply to its infringement?
4. What is required to argue a claim of guaranteed Aboriginal self-government rights?
5. Can a province extinguish Aboriginal rights after its entry into Confederation, either on its own authority or through the operation of s. 88 of the *Indian Act*?

Extracts from Lamer C.J.'s main majority opinion are reproduced here. McLachlin J. said [at para. 209] that she was "in substantial agreement" with the separate majority reasons of La Forest J. (for himself and L'Heureux-Dubé.)

EXTRACT

[LAMER C.J. for himself, Cory, Mclachlin and Major JJ.:]

[1. Changing Claims]

. . . .

[para73] In their pleadings, the appellants, 51 Chiefs representing most of the houses of the Gitksan and Wet'suwet'en nations, originally advanced 51 individual claims on their own behalf and on behalf of their houses for "ownership" and "jurisdiction" over 133 distinct territories which together comprise 58,000 square kilometres of northwestern British Columbia. On appeal, that original claim was altered in two different ways. First, the claims for ownership and jurisdiction have been replaced with claims for aboriginal title and self-government, respectively. Second, the individual claims by each house have been amalgamated into two communal claims, one advanced on behalf of each nation. However, there were no formal amendments to the pleadings to this effect, and the respondents accordingly argue that claims which are central to this appeal are not properly before the Court. Furthermore, the respondents argue that they have suffered prejudice as a result because they might have conducted the defence quite differently had they known the case to meet.

[para74] I reject the respondents' submission with respect to the substitution of aboriginal title and self-government for the original claims of ownership and jurisdiction. Although it is true that the pleadings were not formally amended, the trial judge, at p. 158, did allow a *de facto* amendment to permit "a claim for aboriginal rights other than ownership and jurisdiction". Had the respondents been concerned about the prejudice arising from this ruling, they could have appealed accordingly. However, they did not, and, as a result, the decision of the trial judge on this point must stand.

[para75] Moreover, in my opinion, that ruling was correct because it was made against the background of considerable legal uncertainty surrounding the nature and content of aboriginal rights, under both the common law and s. 35(1)....

. . . .

[para76] However, no such amendment was made with respect to the amalgamation of the individual claims brought by the 51 Gitksan and Wet'suwet'en Houses into two collective claims, one by each nation, for aboriginal title and self-government. Given the absence of an amendment to the pleadings, I must reluctantly conclude that the respondents suffered some prejudice. The appellants argue that the respondents did not experience prejudice since the collective and individual claims are related to the extent that the territory claimed by each nation is merely the sum of the individual claims of each house; the external boundaries of the collective claims therefore represent the outer boundaries of the outer territories. Although that argument carries considerable weight, it does not address the basic point that the collective claims were simply not in issue at trial. To frame the case in a different manner on appeal would retroactively deny the respondents the opportunity to know the appellants' case.

[para77] This defect in the pleadings prevents the Court from considering the merits of this appeal. However, given the importance of this case and the fact that much of the evidence of individual territorial holdings is extremely relevant to the collective claims now advanced by each of the appellants, the correct remedy for the defect in pleadings is a new trial.... Moreover, as I will now explain, there are other reasons why a new trial should be ordered.

. . . .

[2. Oral Aboriginal Histories]

[para80] ... As I said in *R.* v. *Van der Peet*, [1996] 2 S.C.R. 507, at para. 68:

> In determining whether an aboriginal claimant has produced evidence sufficient to demonstrate that her activity is an aspect of a practice, custom or tradition integral to a distinctive aboriginal culture, *a court should approach the rules of evidence, and interpret the evidence that exists*, with a consciousness of the special nature of aboriginal claims, and of the evidentiary difficulties in proving a right which originates in times where there were no written records of the practices, customs and traditions engaged in. *The courts must not undervalue the evidence presented by aboriginal claimants simply because that evidence does not conform precisely with the evidentiary standards that would be applied in, for example, a private law torts case.* [Emphasis added.]

. . . .

[para82] ... [A]lthough the doctrine of aboriginal rights is a common law doctrine, aboriginal rights are truly *sui generis*, and demand a unique approach to the treatment of evidence which accords due weight to the perspective of aboriginal peoples. However, that accommodation must be done in a manner which does not strain "the Canadian legal and constitutional structure" (at para. 49).

. . . .

[para107] The trial judge's treatment of the various kinds of oral histories did not satisfy the principles I laid down in *Van der Peet*. These errors are particularly worrisome because oral histories were of critical importance to the appellants' case. They used those histories in an attempt to establish their occupation and use of the disputed territory, an essential requirement for aboriginal title. The trial judge, after refusing to admit, or giving no independent weight to these oral histories, reached the conclusion that the appellants had not demonstrated the requisite degree of occupation for "ownership". Had the trial judge assessed the oral histories correctly, his conclusions on these issues of fact might have been very different.

[para108] In the circumstances, the factual findings cannot stand. However, given the enormous complexity of the factual issues at hand, it would be impossible for the Court to do justice to the parties by sifting through the record itself and making new factual findings. A new trial is warranted, at which the evidence may be considered in light of the principles laid down in *Van der Peet* and elaborated upon here. In applying these principles, the new trial judge might well share some or all of the findings of fact of McEachern C.J.

. . . .

[3a. Content of Aboriginal Title]

[para117] ... [T]he content of aboriginal title can be summarized by two propositions: first, that aboriginal title encompasses the right to exclusive use and occupation of the land held pursuant to that title for a variety of purposes, which need not be aspects of those aboriginal practices, customs and traditions which are integral to distinctive aboriginal cultures; and second, that those protected uses must not be irreconcilable with the nature of the group's attachment to that land....

. . . .

[para125] The content of aboriginal title contains an inherent limit that lands held pursuant to title cannot be used in a manner that is irreconcilable with the nature of the claimants' attachment to those lands. This limit on the content of aboriginal title is a manifestation of the principle that underlies the various dimensions of that special interest in land — it is a *sui generis* interest that is distinct from "normal" proprietary interests, most notably fee simple.

. . . .

[para127] ... [T]he relationship of an aboriginal community with its land] should not be prevented from continuing into the future. As a result, uses of the lands that would threaten that future relationship are, by their very nature, excluded from the content of aboriginal title.

[para128] Accordingly, in my view, lands subject to aboriginal title cannot be put to such uses as may be irreconcilable with the nature of the occupation of that land and the relationship that the particular group has had with the land which together have given rise to aboriginal title in the first place....

[para129] It is for this reason also that lands held by virtue of aboriginal title may not be alienated. Alienation would bring to an end the entitlement of the

aboriginal people to occupy the land and would terminate their relationship with it....

. . . .

[para131] ... [W]hat I have just said regarding the importance of the continuity of the relationship between an aboriginal community and its land, and the non-economic or inherent value of that land, should not be taken to detract from the possibility of surrender to the Crown in exchange for valuable consideration. On the contrary, the idea of surrender reinforces the conclusion that aboriginal title is limited in the way I have described. If aboriginal peoples wish to use their lands in a way that aboriginal title does not permit, then they must surrender those lands and convert them into non-title lands to do so.

[3b. Relationship between Aboriginal Title and Aboriginal Rights]

. . . .

[para138] ... [T]he aboriginal rights which are recognized and affirmed by s. 35(1) fall along a spectrum with respect to their degree of connection with the land. At the one end, there are those aboriginal rights which are practices, customs and traditions that are integral to the distinctive aboriginal culture of the group claiming the right. However, the "occupation and use of the land" where the activity is taking place is not "sufficient to support a claim of title to the land" (at para. 26). Nevertheless, those activities receive constitutional protection. In the middle, there are activities which, out of necessity, take place on land and indeed, might be intimately related to a particular piece of land. Although an aboriginal group may not be able to demonstrate title to the land, it may nevertheless have a site-specific right to engage in a particular activity.

. . . .

... [A]boriginal title confers more than the right to engage in site-specific activities which are aspects of the practices, customs and traditions of distinctive aboriginal cultures. Site-specific rights can be made out even if title cannot. What aboriginal title confers is the right to the land itself.

[para139] Because aboriginal rights can vary with respect to their degree of connection with the land, some aboriginal groups may be unable to make out a claim to title, but will nevertheless possess aboriginal rights that are recognized and affirmed by s. 35(1), including site-specific rights to engage in particular activities....

[3c. Proof of Aboriginal Title]

[para140] In addition to differing in the degree of connection with the land, aboriginal title differs from other aboriginal rights in another way. To date, the Court has defined aboriginal rights in terms of activities. As I said in *Van der Peet* (at para. 46):

> in order to be an aboriginal right an *activity* must be an element of a practice, custom or tradition integral to the distinctive culture of the aboriginal group claiming the right. [Emphasis added.]

Aboriginal title, however, is a right to the land itself. Subject to the limits I have laid down above, that land may be used for a variety of activities, none of which need be individually protected as aboriginal rights under s. 35(1). Those activities are parasitic on the underlying title.

[para141] This difference between aboriginal rights to engage in particular activities and aboriginal title requires that the test I laid down in *Van der Peet* be adapted accordingly....

. . . .

Since the purpose of s. 35(1) is to reconcile the prior presence of aboriginal peoples in North America with the assertion of Crown sovereignty, it is clear from this statement that s. 35(1) must recognize and affirm both aspects of that prior presence — first, the occupation of land, and second, the prior social organization and distinctive cultures of aboriginal peoples on that land. To date the jurisprudence under s. 35(1) has given more emphasis to the second aspect. To a great extent, this has been a function of the types of cases which have come before this Court under s. 35(1) — prosecutions for regulatory offences that, by their very nature, proscribe discrete types of activity.

[para142] The adaptation of the test laid down in *Van der Peet* to suit claims to title must be understood as the recognition of the first aspect of that prior presence. However, as will now become apparent, the tests for the identification of aboriginal rights to engage in particular activities and for the identification of aboriginal title share broad similari-

ties. The major distinctions are first, under the test for aboriginal title, the requirement that the land be integral to the distinctive culture of the claimants is subsumed by the requirement of occupancy, and second, whereas the time for the identification of aboriginal rights is the time of first contact, the time for the identification of aboriginal title is the time at which the Crown asserted sovereignty over the land.

[para143] In order to make out a claim for aboriginal title, the aboriginal group asserting title must satisfy the following criteria: (i) the land must have been occupied prior to sovereignty, (ii) if present occupation is relied on as proof of occupation pre-sovereignty, there must be a continuity between present and pre-sovereignty occupation, and (iii) at sovereignty, that occupation must have been exclusive.

[3d. Aboriginal Title and Section 35(1) of Constitution Act, 1982]

[Note: At para. 133, Lamer J. said that Aboriginal title was included in the common law rights that were constitutionalized by s. 35(1) of the *Constitution Act, 1982*. As such, Aboriginal title was protected against infringements by federal or provincial governments, unless these infringements could be justified. Later, Lamer C.J. considered how the existing test for justification applied to Aboriginal title]:

[para161] The test of justification [of section 35(1) aboriginal or treaty] rights has two parts, which I shall consider in turn. First, the infringement of the aboriginal right must be in furtherance of a legislative objective that is compelling and substantial....

. . . .

The conservation of fisheries [is one compelling and substantial objective].... But legitimate government objectives also include "the pursuit of economic and regional fairness" and "the recognition of the historical reliance upon, and participation in, the fishery by non-aboriginal groups" (para. 75). By contrast, measures enacted for relatively unimportant reasons, such as sports fishing without a significant economic component (*R.* v. *Adams*, [1996] 3 S.C.R. 101) would fail this aspect of the test of justification.

[para162] The second part of the test of justification requires an assessment of whether the infringement is consistent with the special fiduciary relationship between the Crown and aboriginal peoples. What has become clear is that the requirements of the fiduciary duty are a function of the "legal and factual context" of each appeal (*R.* v. *Gladstone*, [1996] 2 S.C.R. 723, at para. 56).

. . . .

[para165] The general principles governing justification laid down in *R.* v. *Sparrow*, [1990] 1 S.C.R. 1075, and embellished by *Gladstone*, operate with respect to infringements of aboriginal title. In the wake of *Gladstone*, the range of legislative objectives that can justify the infringement of aboriginal title is fairly broad.... In my opinion, the development of agriculture, forestry, mining, and hydroelectric power, the general economic development of the interior of British Columbia, protection of the environment or endangered species, the building of infrastructure and the settlement of foreign populations to support those aims, are the kinds of objectives that are consistent with this purpose and, in principle, can justify the infringement of aboriginal title. Whether a particular measure or government act can be explained by reference to one of those objectives, however, is ultimately a question of fact that will have to be examined on a case-by-case basis.

[para166] The manner in which the fiduciary duty operates with respect to the second stage of the justification test — both with respect to the standard of scrutiny and the particular form that the fiduciary duty will take — will be a function of the nature of aboriginal title. Three aspects of aboriginal title are relevant here. First, aboriginal title encompasses the right to exclusive use and occupation of land; second, aboriginal title encompasses the right to choose to what uses land can be put, subject to the ultimate limit that those uses cannot destroy the ability of the land to sustain future generations of aboriginal peoples; and third, that lands held pursuant to aboriginal title have an inescapable economic component.

[para167] The exclusive nature of aboriginal title is relevant to the degree of scrutiny of the infringing measure or action. For example, if the Crown's fiduciary duty requires that aboriginal title be given priority, then it is the altered approach to priority that I laid down in *Gladstone* which should apply. What is required is that the government demonstrate (*Gladstone*, at para. 62) "both that the process by which it allocated the resource and the actual allocation of the resource which results from that process reflect the prior interest" of the holders of aboriginal title in the land. By analogy with *Gladstone*, this might entail, for example, that governments accom-

modate the participation of aboriginal peoples in the development of the resources of British Columbia, that the conferral of fee simples for agriculture, and of leases and licences for forestry and mining reflect the prior occupation of aboriginal title lands, that economic barriers to aboriginal uses of their lands (e.g., licensing fees) be somewhat reduced. This list is illustrative and not exhaustive....

[para168] Moreover, the other aspects of aboriginal title suggest that the fiduciary duty may be articulated in a manner different than the idea of priority.... First, ... [since aboriginal title involves a discretion as to how land is used, the fiduciary relationship may be satisfied by consulting aboriginal peoples about the uses to which their land is put.] There is always a duty of consultation. Whether the aboriginal group has been consulted is relevant to determining whether the infringement of aboriginal title is justified, in the same way that the Crown's failure to consult an aboriginal group with respect to the terms by which reserve land is leased may breach its fiduciary duty at common law: *Guerin*. The nature and scope of the duty of consultation will vary with the circumstances. In occasional cases, when the breach is less serious or relatively minor, it will be no more than a duty to discuss important decisions that will be taken with respect to lands held pursuant to aboriginal title. Of course, even in these rare cases when the minimum acceptable standard is consultation, this consultation must be in good faith, and with the intention of substantially addressing the concerns of the aboriginal peoples whose lands are at issue. In most cases, it will be significantly deeper than mere consultation. Some cases may even require the full consent of an aboriginal nation, particularly when provinces enact hunting and fishing regulations in relation to aboriginal lands.

[para169] Second, aboriginal title, unlike the aboriginal right to fish for food, has an inescapably economic aspect, particularly when one takes into account the modern uses to which lands held pursuant to aboriginal title can be put.... In keeping with the duty of honour and good faith on the Crown, fair compensation will ordinarily be required when aboriginal title is infringed. The amount of compensation payable will vary with the nature of the particular aboriginal title affected and with the nature and severity of the infringement and the extent to which aboriginal interests were accommodated. Since the issue of damages was severed from the principal action, we received no submissions on the appropriate legal principles that would be relevant to determining the appropriate level of compensation of infringements of aboriginal title. In the circumstances, it is best that we leave those difficult questions to another day.

[4. Self-Government]

[para170] In the courts below, considerable attention was given to the question of whether s. 35(1) can protect a right to self-government, and if so, what the contours of that right are. The errors of fact made by the trial judge, and the resultant need for a new trial, make it impossible for this Court to determine whether the claim to self-government has been made out. Moreover, this is not the right case for the Court to lay down the legal principles to guide future litigation. The parties seem to have acknowledged this point, perhaps implicitly, by giving the arguments on self-government much less weight on appeal. One source of the decreased emphasis on the right to self-government on appeal is this Court's judgment in *R.* v. *Pamajewon*, [1996] 2 S.C.R. 821. There, I held that rights to self-government, if they existed, cannot be framed in excessively general terms. The appellants did not have the benefit of my judgment at trial. Unsurprisingly, as counsel for the Wet'suwet'en specifically concedes, the appellants advanced the right to self-government in very broad terms, and therefore in a manner not cognizable under s. 35(1).

[para171] The broad nature of the claim at trial also led to a failure by the parties to address many of the difficult conceptual issues which surround the recognition of aboriginal self-government. The degree of complexity involved can be gleaned from the *Report of the Royal Commission on Aboriginal Peoples*, which devotes 277 pages to the issue. That report describes different models of self-government, each differing with respect to their conception of territory, citizenship, jurisdiction, internal government organization, etc.. We received little in the way of submissions that would help us to grapple with these difficult and central issues. Without assistance from the parties, it would be imprudent for the Court to step into the breach. In these circumstances, the issue of self-government will fall to be determined at trial.

. . . .

[5. Capacity of Province to Extinguish Aboriginal Title]

[para175] ... [A]lthough on surrender of aboriginal title the province would take absolute title, jurisdic-

tion to accept surrenders lies with the federal government. The same can be said of extinguishment — although on extinguishment of aboriginal title, the province would take complete title to the land, the jurisdiction to extinguish lies with the federal government.

. . . .

[para178] ... Laws which purport to extinguish [the rights that are recognized and affirmed by s. 35(1)] ... touch the core of Indianness which lies at the heart of s. 91(24), and are beyond the legislative competence of the provinces to enact. The core of Indianness encompasses the whole range of aboriginal rights that are protected by s. 35(1). Those rights include rights in relation to land; that part of the core derives from s. 91(24)'s reference to "Lands reserved for the Indians". But those rights also encompass practices, customs and traditions which are not tied to land as well; that part of the core can be traced to federal jurisdiction over "Indians". Provincial governments are prevented from legislating in relation to both types of aboriginal rights.

. . . .

[para183] ... I see nothing in the language of [section 88 of the *Indian Act*] which even suggests the intention to extinguish aboriginal rights. Indeed, the explicit reference to treaty rights in s. 88 suggests that the provision was clearly not intended to undermine aboriginal rights.

. . . .

[6. Disposition and Concluding Remarks]

[para184] For the reasons I have given above, I would allow the appeal in part, and dismiss the cross-appeal. Reluctantly, I would also order a new trial.

[para185] I conclude with two observations. The first is that many aboriginal nations with territorial claims that overlap with those of the appellants did not intervene in this appeal, and do not appear to have done so at trial. This is unfortunate, because determinations of aboriginal title for the Gitksan and Wet'suwet'en will undoubtedly affect their claims as well. This is particularly so because aboriginal title encompasses an exclusive right to the use and occupation of land, i.e., to the exclusion of both non-aboriginals and members of other aboriginal nations. It may, therefore, be advisable if those aboriginal nations intervened in any new litigation.

[para186] Finally, this litigation has been both long and expensive, not only in economic but in human terms as well. By ordering a new trial, I do not necessarily encourage the parties to proceed to litigation and to settle their dispute through the courts.

[In separate reasons (with which McLachlin J. expressed substantial agreement), La Forest J. (for himself and L'Heureux-Dubé J.) agreed with the Chief Justice's conclusion. However, La Forest J. said, "I disagree with various aspects of his reasons and in particular, with the methodology he uses to prove that Aboriginal peoples have a general right of occupation of certain lands" (often referred to as "aboriginal title": para. 187). La Forest J. felt that courts should refrain from trying to define Aboriginal title in detail. For him, it is sufficient to say that Aboriginal title (i) is based on traditional use and occupation of the land, (ii) is inalienable except to the Crown, and (iii) attracts a fiduciary obligation which is owed by the Crown: para. 190. La Forest J. said the *Van der Peet* test for proof of Aboriginal title requires "precision, specificity, continuity, and centrality": para. 193. For him, proof of occupancy should not subsume the requirements of precision, specificity, and centrality. Instead, occupancy should be taken as proof of the latter. La Forest J. agreed generally with the Chief Justice on the issues of justification of infringement of Aboriginal title, self-government, provincial extinguishment either independently or under s. 88 of the *Indian Act*, and the desirability of addressing cases of this kind through negotiation.]

SOME QUESTIONS ON *DELGAMUUKW*

1. Why did the Supreme Court accept the first set of changes of claims, but reject the second? What principles underlie — or should underlie — a court's approach to informal changes of this kind? Did the rejection of the second set of changes render the rest of this 65-page decision *obiter dicta*? Does this matter?
2. Why do standard evidentiary rules generally prohibit oral and hearsay (out-of-court) evidence? What are the (i) risks and (ii) benefits

of using oral Aboriginal histories in courts as independent proof of specific issues of fact? Can Aboriginal or treaty claims be raised effectively in courts *without* recourse to oral Aboriginal histories? What are the likely implications of the Supreme Court's evidentiary approach for future Aboriginal litigation? For the comprehensive claims process?

3. Where does Aboriginal title lie on the judicial spectrum that positions Aboriginal rights in regard to their connection to land? Are there any Aboriginal rights with no connection *whatever* to land? What rights does Aboriginal title give its owners? In what sense does it confer exclusive rights? What are the implications of Aboriginal title for non-aboriginals on the land in question, or for Aboriginal people without title to it? What are the special limits to the uses to which Aboriginal title can be put?
4. How do the requirements for identifying Aboriginal title differ from those for other Aboriginal rights, in regard to: (i) what must be shown, and (ii) the relevant date for showing it? How does Lamer C.J.'s approach to identifying Aboriginal title differ from that of La Forest J.? Which do you prefer?
5. Is the content of common law Aboriginal title the same as the content of Aboriginal title guaranteed by s. 35(1) of the *Constitution Act, 1982*? Is s. 35(1) Aboriginal title guaranteed in the same way as other Aboriginal rights? What are the main (i) forms and (ii) levels of scrutiny, of justification of infringement of s. 35(1) Aboriginal rights? How do the requirements for justifying infringement of Aboriginal title differ from the justification requirements in *Sparrow*? Where priority is required, what kind of priority must be accorded to Aboriginal title? Are consultation and compensation always required when Aboriginal title is infringed? What factors will govern the fairness and adequacy of consultation and compensation?
6. Why did the Supreme Court decline to say much about the Aboriginal self-government issue? Do *Delgamuukw* and *Pamajewon* provide any indication of the Court's likely future approach to self-government claims? Has the discussion of Aboriginal rights in *Delgamuukw* any relevance to the judicial concept of Aboriginal self-government?
7. Most Crown land south of the 60th parallel is owned — subject to Aboriginal claims — by provincial governments. Virtually all privately-owned land in this part of Canada results from fee simple grants issued by provincial governments. How are Crown and private land in the provinces affected by the Court's finding that after 1871 provinces cannot extinguish Aboriginal rights either on their own, or with reference to s. 88 of the *Indian Act*? Why is the Supreme Court's ruling especially significant in British Columbia?
8. Will *Delgamuukw* boost or weaken the land claims negotiation process? Consider its possible effects on the Sechelt and other negotiations discussed in **Chapter 11, Part 7**.

(c) *Mitchell v. Canada (Minister of National Revenue)*†

See **Chapter 10, Part 4**.

NOTE

Akwesasne Mohawk Chief Michael Mitchell claimed an Aboriginal and treaty right to bring personal and community goods into Canada, free of with customs or duties, to trade with other First Nations. The lower courts dismissed the treaty claim but upheld the Aboriginal rights claim. The Crown's appeal on the Aboriginal rights issue was upheld in the Supreme Court of Canada.

† *Mitchell v. Canada (Minister of National Revenue)*, [2001] 1 S.C.R. 911 at paras. 1–3, 9–10, 12, 15, 19–20, 25, 30–31, 33–42, 51, 53–55, 57, 60–65, 76, 126–28, 135, 141, 144–46, 149–51, 153–55, 160, 164–65, and 171–74, rev'g [1999] 1 F.C. 375, 167 D.L.R. (4th) 702, 233 N.R. 129 (F.C.A.), aff'g in part [1997] 4 C.N.L.R. 103, 134 F.T.R. 1 (F.C.T.D.).

The main majority judgment of McLachlin C.J. illustrates the importance of characterization and evidentiary rules for a case like this. As well, the two judgments are also relevant to the questions of the nature of Aboriginal rights, sovereignty and self-government. On these last two issues, which are addressed in **Chapter 12, Part 4**, see especially paras. 9–10, 61–64, and 76–172.

EXTRACT

[McLACHLIN C.J. for herself, Gonthier, Iacobucci, Arbour and Lebel JJ.:]

[para1] This case raises the issue of whether the Mohawk Canadians of Akwesasne have the right to bring goods into Canada from the United States for collective use and trade with other First Nations without paying customs duties. Grand Chief Michael Mitchell claims that his people have an aboriginal right that ousts Canadian customs law. The government replies that no such right exists, first because the evidence does not support it and second because such a right would be fundamentally contrary to Canadian sovereignty. At the heart of the case lies the question of the evidence that must be adduced to establish an aboriginal right.

[para2] Chief Mitchell is a Mohawk of Akwesasne, a Mohawk community located just west of Montreal, and a descendant of the Mohawk nation, one of the polities comprising the Iroquois Confederacy prior to the arrival of Europeans. On March 22, 1988, Chief Mitchell crossed the international border from the United States into Canada, arriving at the Cornwall customs office. He brought with him some blankets, bibles, motor oil, food, clothing, and a washing machine, all of which had been purchased in the United States. He declared the goods to the Canadian customs agents but asserted that he had aboriginal and treaty rights which exempted him from paying duty on the goods. After some discussion, the customs agents notified Chief Mitchell that he would be charged $142.88 in duty, and they permitted him to continue into Canada. Chief Mitchell, along with other Mohawks of Akwesasne, presented everything but the motor oil to the Mohawk community of Tyendinaga. The gifts were intended to symbolize the renewal of the historic trading relationship between the two communities. The oil was taken to a store in Akwesasne territory for resale to members of that community. In September of 1989, Chief Mitchell was served with a Notice of Ascertained Forfeiture claiming $361.64 for unpaid duty, taxes and penalties.

[para3] I conclude that the aboriginal right claimed has not been established. The sparse and tenuous evidence advanced in this case to prove the existence of pre-contact Mohawk trading north of the Canada-United States boundary simply cannot support the claimed right. Even if deference is paid to the trial judge on this finding, any such trade was clearly incidental, and not integral, to the Mohawk culture. As a result, Chief Mitchell must pay duty on the goods he imported to Canada.

. . . .

[para9] ...English law, which ultimately came to govern aboriginal rights, accepted that the aboriginal peoples possessed pre-existing laws and interests, and recognized their continuance in the absence of extinguishment, by cession, conquest, or legislation.... At the same time, however, the Crown asserted that sovereignty over the land, and ownership of its underlying title, vested in the Crown: *Sparrow*, *supra*. With this assertion arose an obligation to treat aboriginal peoples fairly and honourably, and to protect them from exploitation, a duty characterized as "fiduciary" in *Guerin* v. *The Queen*, [1984] 2 S.C.R. 335.

[para10] Accordingly, European settlement did not terminate the interests of aboriginal peoples arising from their historical occupation and use of the land. To the contrary, aboriginal interests and customary laws were presumed to survive the assertion of sovereignty, and were absorbed into the common law as rights, unless (1) they were incompatible with the Crown's assertion of sovereignty, (2) they were surrendered voluntarily via the treaty process, or (3) the government extinguished them.... Barring one of these exceptions, the practices, customs and traditions that defined the various aboriginal societies as distinctive cultures continued as part of the law of Canada: see *Calder* v. *Attorney-General of British Columbia*, [1973] S.C.R. 313....

. . . .

[para. 12] ... [To establish an aboriginal right], an aboriginal claimant must prove a modern practice, tradition or custom that has a reasonable degree of continuity with the practices, traditions or customs that existed prior to contact.... [The practice, custom or tradition] must be a "defining feature" of the aboriginal society, such that the culture would be "fundamentally altered" without it....

. . . .

[para15] In *Van der Peet, supra*, at para. 53, the majority of this Court provided three factors that should guide a court's characterization of a claimed aboriginal right: (1) the nature of the action which the applicant is claiming was done pursuant to an aboriginal right; (2) the nature of the governmental legislation or action alleged to infringe the right, i.e. the conflict between the claim and the limitation; and (3) the ancestral traditions and practices relied upon to establish the right. The right claimed must be characterized in context and not distorted to fit the desired result. It must be neither artificially broadened nor narrowed. An overly narrow characterization risks the dismissal of valid claims and an overly broad characterization risks distorting the right by neglecting the specific culture and history of the claimant's society: see *R.* v. *Pamajewon*, [1996] 2 S.C.R. 821.

. . . .

[para19] I conclude that the *Van der Peet* factors of the impugned action, the governmental action or legislation with which it conflicts, and the ancestral practice relied on, all suggest the claim here is properly characterized as the right to bring goods across the Canada-United States boundary at the St. Lawrence River for purposes of trade.

[para20] It may be tempting for a claimant or a court to tailor the right claimed to the contours of the specific act at issue.... However, narrowing the claim cannot narrow the aboriginal practice relied upon, which is what defines the right.... [McLachlan J. rejected attempts to limit the claim to trade with other First Nations in Canada or to "small, non-commercial scale trade", and said that mobility rights could not be excluded from it. She said that whether or not the claimed right was subject to duty or taxes should be considered at the infringement stage of analysis.]

. . . .

[para25] Properly characterized, then, the right claimed in this case is the right to bring goods across the St. Lawrence River for the purposes of trade.

. . . .

[para30] The flexible adaptation of traditional rules of evidence to the challenge of doing justice in aboriginal claims is but an application of the time-honoured principle that the rules of evidence are not "cast in stone, nor are they enacted in a vacuum".... Underlying the diverse rules on the admissibility of evidence are three simple ideas. First, the evidence must be useful in the sense of tending to prove a fact relevant to the issues in the case. Second, the evidence must be reasonably reliable; unreliable evidence may hinder the search for the truth more than help it. Third, even useful and reasonably reliable evidence may be excluded in the discretion of the trial judge if its probative value is overshadowed by its potential for prejudice.

[para31] In *Delgamuukw*, mindful of these principles, the majority of this Court held that the rules of evidence must be adapted to accommodate oral histories, but did not mandate the blanket admissibility of such evidence or the weight it should be accorded by the trier of fact; rather, it emphasized that admissibility must be determined on a case-by-case basis (para. 87). Oral histories are admissible as evidence where they are both useful and reasonably reliable, subject always to the exclusionary discretion of the trial judge.

. . . .

[para33] The second factor that must be considered in determining the admissibility of evidence in aboriginal cases is reliability: does the witness represent a reasonably reliable source of the particular people's history? The trial judge need not go so far as to find a special guarantee of reliability. However, inquiries as to the witness's ability to know and testify to orally transmitted aboriginal traditions and history may be appropriate both on the question of admissibility and the weight to be assigned the evidence if admitted.

[para34] ... Oral histories reflect the distinctive perspectives and cultures of the communities from which they originate and should not be discounted simply because they do not conform to the expectations of the non-aboriginal perspective. Thus, *Delgamuukw* cautions against facilely rejecting oral histories simply because they do not convey "historical" truth, contain elements that may be classified as mythology, lack precise detail, embody material tangential to the judicial process, or are confined to the community whose history is being recounted.

[para35] In this case, the parties presented evidence from historians and archaeologists. The aboriginal perspective was supplied by oral histories of elders such as Grand Chief Mitchell. Grand Chief Mitchell's testimony, confirmed by archaeological and historical evidence, was especially useful because he was

trained from an early age in the history of his community. The trial judge found his evidence credible and relied on it. He did not err in doing so and we may do the same.

. . . .

[para36] The second facet of the *Van der Peet* approach to evidence, and the more contentious issue in the present case, relates to the interpretation and weighing of evidence in support of aboriginal claims once it has cleared the threshold for admission.... This Court has not attempted to set out "precise rules" or "absolute principles" governing the interpretation or weighing of evidence in aboriginal claims.... [T]his process is generally the domain of the trial judge, who is best situated to assess the evidence as it is presented, and is consequently accorded significant latitude in this regard. Moreover, weighing evidence is an exercise inherently specific to the case at hand.

[para37] Nonetheless, the present case requires us to clarify the general principles laid down in *Van der Peet* and *Delgamuukw* regarding the assessment of evidence in aboriginal right claims. The requirement that courts interpret and weigh the evidence with a consciousness of the special nature of aboriginal claims is critical to the meaningful protection of s. 35(1) rights. As Lamer C.J. observed in *Delgamuukw*, the admission of oral histories represents a hollow recognition of the aboriginal perspective where this evidence is then systematically and consistently undervalued or deprived of all independent weight (para. 98). Thus, it is imperative that the laws of evidence operate to ensure that the aboriginal perspective is "given due weight by the courts" (para. 84).

[para38] Again, however, it must be emphasized that a consciousness of the special nature of aboriginal claims does not negate the operation of general evidentiary principles. While evidence adduced in support of aboriginal claims must not be undervalued, neither should it be interpreted or weighed in a manner that fundamentally contravenes the principles of evidence law, which, as they relate to the valuing of evidence, are often synonymous with the "general principles of common sense" (Sopinka and Lederman, *supra*, at p. 524).... As Lamer C.J. emphasized in *Delgamuukw*, *supra*, at para. 82:

> [A]boriginal rights are truly *sui generis*, and demand a unique approach to the treatment of evidence which accords due weight to the perspective of aboriginal peoples. However, that accommodation must be done in a manner which does not strain "the Canadian legal and constitutional structure" [*Van der Peet* at para. 49].... [Emphasis added.]

[para39] There is a boundary that must not be crossed between a sensitive application and a complete abandonment of the rules of evidence. As Binnie J. observed in the context of treaty rights, "[g]enerous rules of interpretation should not be confused with a vague sense of after-the-fact largesse" (*R.* v. *Marshall*, [1999] 3 S.C.R. 456, at para. 14). In particular, the *Van der Peet* approach does not operate to amplify the cogency of evidence adduced in support of an aboriginal claim. Evidence advanced in support of aboriginal claims, like the evidence offered in any case, can run the gamut of cogency from the highly compelling to the highly dubious. Claims must still be established on the basis of persuasive evidence demonstrating their validity on the balance of probabilities. Placing "due weight" on the aboriginal perspective, or ensuring its supporting evidence an "equal footing" with more familiar forms of evidence, means precisely what these phrases suggest: equal and due treatment. While the evidence presented by aboriginal claimants should not be undervalued "simply because that evidence does not conform precisely with the evidentiary standards that would be applied in, for example, a private law torts case" (*Van der Peet*, *supra*, at para. 68), neither should it be artificially strained to carry more weight than it can reasonably support. If this is an obvious proposition, it must nonetheless be stated.

[para40] With these principles in mind, I turn now to the consideration of whether the evidence offered in the present case in fact supports an aboriginal right to bring goods across the St. Lawrence River for the purposes of trade.

. . . .

[An archaeological study said that the Iroquois obtained copper originating in the Great Lakes area, but did not say that they obtained it directly through trade with their northern neighbours. Although an expert witness referred to a possible northerly trade, the only evidence for this was a single chalcedony knife. The Chief's own oral testimony did not discuss Mohawk trading activity north of the St. Lawrence. In the view of McLachlin J., the other pre-contact and post-contact evidence was no better].

. . . .

[para42] ... In this case ... the "little direct evidence" relied upon by the trial judge is, at best, tenuous and scant, and is perhaps better characterized as an absence of even minimally cogent evidence....

. . . .

[para51] ... Sparse, doubtful and equivocal evidence cannot serve as the foundation for a successful claim. With respect, this is exactly what has occurred in the present case. The contradiction between McKeown J.'s statement that little direct evidence supports a cross-river trading right and his conclusion that such a right exists suggests the application of a very relaxed standard of proof (or, perhaps more accurately, an unreasonably generous weighing of tenuous evidence). The *Van der Peet* approach, while mandating the equal and due treatment of evidence supporting aboriginal claims, does not bolster or enhance the cogency of this evidence. The relevant evidence in this case — a single knife, treaties that make no reference to pre-existing trade, and the mere fact of Mohawk involvement in the fur trade — can only support the conclusion reached by the trial judge if strained beyond the weight they can reasonably hold.... I conclude that the claimant has not established an ancestral practice of transporting goods across the St. Lawrence River for the purposes of trade.

. . . .

[para53] In view of the paucity of evidence of Mohawk trade north of the St. Lawrence River, I need not consider the argument that, even if it were established, any Mohawk trading right should be characterized as inherently subject to border controls, tolls and duties imposed by other peoples, as recognized by ancestral aboriginal custom.

[para54] Even if deference were granted to the trial judge's finding of pre-contact trade relations between the Mohawks and First Nations north of the St. Lawrence River, the evidence does not establish this northerly trade as a defining feature of the Mohawk culture....

. . . .

[para55] The importance of trade — in and of itself — to Mohawk culture is not determinative of the issue. It is necessary on the facts of this case to demonstrate the integrality of this practice to the Mohawk in the specific geographical region in which it is alleged to have been exercised (i.e., north of the St. Lawrence River), rather than in the abstract. This Court has frequently considered the geographical reach of a claimed right in assessing its centrality to the aboriginal culture claiming it....

. . . .

[para57] In the present case, however, the right to trade is only one aspect, and perhaps a peripheral one, of the broader claim advanced by Chief Mitchell: the right to convey goods across an international boundary for the purposes of trade....

. . . .

[para60] The claimed right in the present case implicates an international boundary and, consequently, imports a geographical element into the inquiry. Instead of asking whether the right to trade — in the abstract — is integral to the Mohawk people, this Court must ask whether the right to trade across the St. Lawrence River is integral to the Mohawks. The evidence establishes that it is not. Even if the trial judge's generous interpretation of the evidence were accepted, it discloses negligible transportation and trade of goods by the Mohawks north of the St. Lawrence River prior to contact. If the Mohawks did transport trade goods across the St. Lawrence River for trade, such occasions were few and far between.... Participation in northerly trade was therefore not a practice integral to the distinctive culture of the Mohawk people. It follows that no aboriginal right to bring goods across the border for the purposes of trade has been established.

. . . .

[para61] The conclusion that the right claimed is not established on the evidence suffices to dispose of this appeal. I add a note, however, on the government's contention that s. 35(1) of the *Constitution Act, 1982* extends constitutional protection only to those aboriginal practices, customs and traditions that are compatible with the historical and modern exercise of Crown sovereignty. Pursuant to this argument, any Mohawk practice of cross-border trade, even if established on the evidence, would be barred from recognition under s. 35(1) as incompatible with the Crown's sovereign interest in regulating its borders.

[para62] This argument finds its source in the doctrine of continuity, which governed the absorption of aboriginal laws and customs into the new legal regime upon the assertion of Crown sovereignty over

the region. As discussed above, this incorporation of local laws and customs into the common law was subject to an exception for those interests that were inconsistent with the sovereignty of the new regime: see Slattery, *supra*, at p. 738; see also *Delgamuukw* v. *British Columbia*, [1993] 5 W.W.R. 97 (B.C.C.A.), at paras. 1021–24, per Lambert J.A.; Mabo, *supra*, at p. 61, per Brennan J.; *Inasa* v. *Oshodi*, [1934] A.C. 99 (P.C.); and *R.* v. *Jacobs*, [1999] 3 C.N.L.R. 239 (B.C.S.C.).

[para63] This Court has not expressly invoked the doctrine of "sovereign incompatibility" in defining the rights protected under s. 35(1). In the *Van der Peet* trilogy, this Court identified the aboriginal rights protected under s. 35(1) as those practices, customs and traditions integral to the distinctive cultures of aboriginal societies: *Van der Peet*, *supra*, at para. 46. Subsequent cases affirmed this approach to identifying aboriginal rights falling within the aegis of s. 35(1) (*Pamajewon*, *supra*, at paras. 23–25; Adams, *supra*, at para. 33; Côté, *supra*, at para. 54; see also: Woodward, *supra*, at p. 75) and have affirmed the doctrines of extinguishment, infringement and justification as the appropriate framework for resolving conflicts between aboriginal rights and competing claims, including claims based on Crown sovereignty.

[para64] The Crown now contends that "sovereign incompatibility" is an implicit element of the *Van der Peet* test for identifying protected aboriginal rights, or at least a necessary addition. In view of my conclusion that Chief Mitchell has not established that the Mohawks traditionally transported goods for trade across the present Canada-U.S. border, and hence has not proven his claim to an aboriginal right, I need not consider the merits of this submission. Rather, I would prefer to refrain from comment on the extent, if any, to which colonial laws of sovereign succession are relevant to the definition of aboriginal rights under s. 35(1) until such time as it is necessary for the Court to resolve this issue.

VI. CONCLUSION

[para65] I would allow the appeal. Chief Mitchell must pay the duty claimed by the government. I note that the government has undertaken to pay Chief Mitchell's costs.

. . . .

[BINNIE J. for himself and Major J.:]

[para66] I have read the reasons of the Chief Justice and I concur in the result and with her conclusion that even if Mohawks did occasionally trade goods across the St. Lawrence River with First Nations to the north, this practice was not on the evidence a "defining feature of the Mohawk culture" (para. 54) or "vital to the Mohawk's collective identity" (para. 60) in pre-contact times. There are, however, some additional considerations that have led me to conclude that the appeal must be allowed.

. . . .

[para76] The importance of the Crown's argument is that even if the respondent's claim could be said to be distinctive and integral to Mohawk culture, it would still not give rise to an aboriginal right. The Crown says it fails the basic requirement of compatibility with the sovereignty of the legal regimes that came afterwards. The question also arises, as noted, whether acceptance of it would advance or undermine the s. 35(1) objective of reconciliation.

. . . .

[para126] It is true that in *R.* v. *Pamajewon*, [1996] 2 S.C.R. 821, the Court warned, at para. 27, against casting the Court's aboriginal rights inquiry "at a level of excessive generality". Yet when the claim, as here, can only properly be construed as an international trading and mobility right, it has to be addressed at that level.

[para127] In the constitutional framework envisaged by the respondent, the claimed aboriginal right is simply a manifestation of the more fundamental relationship between the aboriginal and non-aboriginal people. In the Mohawk tradition this relationship is memorialized by the "two-row" wampum....

. . . .

[para128] ... [I]n the "two-row" wampum there are two parallel paths. In one path travels the aboriginal canoe. In the other path travels the European ship. The two vessels co-exist but they never touch. Each is the sovereign of its own destiny.

. . . .

[In Binnie J.'s view, the modern expression of the two-row wampum is the concept of "shared sovereignty" endorsed in the final *Report of the Royal Commission on Aboriginal Peoples*].

[para135] ... [T]he Royal Commission itself sees aboriginal peoples as full participants with non-aboriginal peoples in a shared Canadian sovereignty. Aboriginal peoples do not stand in opposition to, nor are they subjugated by, Canadian sovereignty. They are part of it.

. . . .

[para141] I return to the comment of McLachlin J., dissenting in the result, in *Van der Peet*, *supra*, at para. 227 that "[t]he issue of what constitutes an aboriginal right must, in my view, be answered by looking at what the law has historically accepted as fundamental aboriginal rights". There was a presumption under British colonial law that the Crown intended to respect the pre-existing customs of the inhabitants that were not deemed to be unconscionable (e.g., Blackstone in *Commentaries on the Laws of England* (4th ed. 1770), Book I, at p. 107, gave the example, now discredited, of "infidel" laws) or incompatible with the new sovereignty: *Campbell* v. *Hall* (1774), 1 Cowp. 204, 98 E.R. 1045 (K.B.), at pp. 1047–48; *Delgamuukw* v. *British Columbia*, [1993] 5 W.W.R. 97 (B.C.C.A.), at paras. 1021–24....

. . . .

[para144] Reference has already been made to the fact that one of several sources of the concept of aboriginal rights, now significantly modified by the more generous principles of constitutional interpretation, is traditional British colonial law. Many of the cases decided by the Judicial Committee of the Privy Council were concerned with rights of property created under a former regime. In *Amodu Tijani* v. *Southern Nigeria (Secretary)*, [1921] 2 A.C. 399, at p. 407, it was confirmed that "A mere change in sovereignty is not to be presumed as meant to disturb rights of private owners" (emphasis added). More recently, Lord Denning, speaking for the Privy Council in *Oyekan* v. *Adele*, [1957] 2 All E.R. 785, at p. 788, said: "In inquiring ... what rights are recognized, there is one guiding principle. It is this: The courts will assume that the British Crown intends that the rights of property of the inhabitants are to be fully respected" (emphasis added). As with the modern law of aboriginal rights, the law of sovereign succession was intended to reconcile the interests of the local inhabitants across the empire to a change in sovereignty.

[para145] The concept of a presumption was endorsed by Hall J. in *Calder*, *supra*, at p. 402:

> The appellants rely on the presumption that the British Crown intended to respect native rights; therefore, when the Nishga people came under British sovereignty ... they were entitled to assert, as a legal right, their Indian title. [Emphasis added.]

[para146] It was subsequently affirmed that aboriginal rights could exist independently of "aboriginal title" (*Van der Peet*, *supra*, at para. 74; *Adams*, *supra*, at para. 26). Further, [in] *Guerin* v. *The Queen*, [1984] 2 S.C.R. 335, Dickson J. emphasized the "legal" character of the resulting aboriginal right: "[i]n *Calder* ... this Court recognized aboriginal title as a legal right derived from the Indians' historic occupation and possession of their tribal lands" (p. 376 (emphasis added)), and then went on to state the proposition that the Indians were "the rightful occupants of the soil, with a legal as well as just claim to retain possession of it, and to use it according to their own discretion" (p. 378 (emphasis added; emphasis in original deleted)).

. . . .

[para149] Care must be taken not to carry forward doctrines of British colonial law into the interpretation of s. 35(1) without careful reflection....

[para150] Yet the language of s. 35(1) cannot be construed as a wholesale repudiation of the common law. The subject matter of the constitutional provision is "existing" aboriginal and treaty rights and they are said to be "recognized and affirmed" not wholly cut loose from either their legal or historical origins. One of the defining characteristics of sovereign succession and therefore a limitation on the scope of aboriginal rights, as already discussed, was the notion of incompatibility with the new sovereignty....

[para151] Prior to *Calder*, *supra*, "sovereign incompatibility" was given excessive scope. The assertion of sovereign authority was confused with doctrines of feudal title to deny aboriginal peoples any interest at all in their traditional lands or even in activities related to the use of those lands. To acknowledge that the doctrine of sovereign incompatibility was sometimes given excessive scope in the past is not to deny that it has any scope at all, but it is a doctrine that must be applied with caution.

. . . .

[para153] However, important as they may have been to the Mohawk identity as a people, it could not be said, in my view, that pre-contact warrior activities

gave rise under successor regimes to a legal right under s. 35(1) to engage in [, for example,] military adventures on Canadian territory. Canadian sovereign authority has, as one of its inherent characteristics, a monopoly on the lawful use of military force within its territory.... Section 35(1) should not be interpreted to throw on the Crown the burden of demonstrating subsequent extinguishment by "clear and plain" measures (*Gladstone*, *supra*, at para. 31) of a "right" to organize a private army, or a requirement to justify such a limitation after 1982 under the *Sparrow* standard. This example, remote as it is from the particular claim advanced in this case, usefully illustrates the principled limitation flowing from sovereign incompatibility in the s. 35(1) analysis.

[para154] In my opinion, sovereign incompatibility continues to be an element in the s. 35(1) analysis, albeit a limitation that will be sparingly applied. For the most part, the protection of practices, traditions and customs that are distinctive to aboriginal cultures in Canada does not raise legitimate sovereignty issues at the definitional stage.

[para155] I proceed to the next step keeping in mind that the respondent's claim must respond not only to the historical requirements that have traditionally preoccupied aboriginal law but also to the reconciliation objective that lies at the heart of the purposive interpretation of s. 35(1).

. . . .

[para160] Control over the mobility of persons and goods into one country is, and always has been, a fundamental attribute of sovereignty....

. . . .

[para163] ... In my view ... the international trading/mobility right claimed by the respondent as a citizen of the Haudenosaunee (Iroquois) Confederacy is incompatible with the historical attributes of Canadian sovereignty.

[para164] The question that then arises is whether this conclusion is at odds with the purpose of s. 35(1), i.e. the reconciliation of the interests of aboriginal peoples with Crown sovereignty? In addressing this question it must be remembered that aboriginal people are themselves part of Canadian sovereignty as discussed above.... Affirmation of the sovereign interest of Canadians as a whole, including aboriginal peoples, should not necessarily be seen as a loss of sufficient "constitutional space for aboriginal peoples to be aboriginal" (Donna Greschner, "Aboriginal Women, the Constitution and Criminal Justice", [1992] U.B.C. L. Rev. (Sp. ed.) 338, at p. 342).... In my view, reconciliation of these interests in this particular case favours an affirmation of our collective sovereignty.

11. IMPLICATIONS FOR INTERNAL ABORIGINAL SELF-GOVERNMENT

[para165] In reaching that conclusion, however, I do not wish to be taken as either foreclosing or endorsing any position on the compatibility or incompatibility of internal self-governing institutions of First Nations with Crown sovereignty, either past or present.... [T]he sovereign incompatibility principle has not prevented the United States (albeit with its very different constitutional framework) from continuing to recognize forms of internal aboriginal self-government which it considers to be expressions of residual aboriginal sovereignty....

. . . .

[para171] ... [The question here] is not about post-1982 extinguishment. It is about the prior question of whether the claimed international trading and mobility right could, as a matter of law, have arisen in the first place.

[para172] It was, of course, an expression of sovereignty in 1982 to recognize existing aboriginal rights under s. 35(1) of the *Constitution Act, 1982*. However, if the claimed aboriginal right did not survive the transition to non-Mohawk sovereignty, there was nothing in existence in 1982 to which s. 35(1) protection of existing aboriginal rights could attach. It would have been, of course, quite within the sovereign's power to confer specific border privileges by treaty, but the respondent's claim to a treaty right was dismissed.

[para173] In my respectful view the claimed aboriginal right never came into existence and it is unnecessary to consider the Crown's argument that whatever aboriginal rights in this respect may have existed were extinguished by border controls enforced by Canada prior to April 17, 1982.

CONCLUSION

[para174] I would allow the appeal.

(d) *R. v. Powley*†

See **Chapter 2, Part 5(c)** and **Chapter 10, Part 5**.

NOTE

Mr. Steve Powley and his son Roddy were Métis who lived in the Sault Ste. Marie area. They were charged with violating a provincial game act by hunting a moose without a licence. In their defence, they argued that they had an Aboriginal right to hunt for food without a licence, and that this right was protected by s. 35(1) of the *Constitution Act, 1982*.

Like the Ontario courts, the Supreme Court of Canada agreed. It said there was evidence here that an historic Métis community had hunted in the Sault Ste. Marie area, and that hunting was an integral part of Métis culture before the assertion of effective European control. The Court went on to conclude that the infringement of this right had not been justified.

Note how the Supreme Court requires not only mixed Aboriginal and European heritage, but also proof of an association with a particular historic and modern Métis community, before a person may be eligible to claim rights under s. 35(1) of the *Constitution Act, 1982.* Will many Canadian Métis people be able to meet both requirements?

EXTRACT

[THE COURT:]

I. INTRODUCTION

1 This case raises the issue of whether members of the Métis community in and around Sault Ste. Marie enjoy a constitutionally protected right to hunt for food under s. 35 of the *Constitution Act, 1982*. We conclude that they do.

2 On the morning of October 22, 1993, Steve Powley and his son, Roddy, set out hunting. They headed north from their residence in Sault Ste. Marie, and at about 9 a.m., they shot and killed a bull moose near Old Goulais Bay Road.

3 Moose hunting in Ontario is subject to strict regulation. The Ministry of Natural Resources ("MNR") issues Outdoor Cards and validation stickers authorizing the bearer to harvest calf moose during open season. People wishing to harvest adult moose must enter a lottery to obtain a validation tag authorizing them to hunt either a bull or a cow in a particular area, as specified on the tag. The number of tags issued for a given season depends on the calculations of MNR biologists, who estimate the current adult moose population and the replacement rate for animals removed from the population. The validation tag requirement and seasonal restrictions are not enforced against Status Indians, and the MNR does not record Status Indians' annual harvest. (See *MNR Interim Enforcement Policy on Aboriginal Right to Hunt and Fish for Food* (1991).)

4 After shooting the bull moose near Old Goulais Bay Road, Steve and Roddy Powley transported it to their residence in Sault Ste. Marie. Neither of them had a valid Outdoor Card, a valid hunting licence to hunt moose, or a validation tag issued by the MNR. In lieu of these documents, Steve Powley affixed a handwritten tag to the ear of the moose. The tag indicated the date, time, and location of the kill, as required by the hunting regulations. It stated that the animal was to provide meat for the winter. Steve Powley signed the tag, and wrote his Ontario Métis and Aboriginal Association membership number on it.

5 Later that day, two conservation officers arrived at the Powleys' residence. The Powleys told the officers they had shot the moose. One week later, the Powleys were charged with unlawfully hunting moose and knowingly possessing game hunted in contravention of the *Game and Fish Act*, R.S.O. 1990, c. G-1. They both entered pleas of not guilty.

† *R . v. Powley*, [2003] 2 S.C.R. 207 at paras. 1–41 and 44–55, aff'g. (and dismissing cross-appeal from) (2001), 53 O.R. (3d) 35, 196 D.L.R. (4th) 221 (C.A.), aff'g. (2000), 47 O.R. (3d) 30 (O.C.J.), aff'g. [1999] 1 C.N.L.R. 153, 58 C.R.R. (2d) 149 (O.C.P.D.).

6 The facts are not in dispute. The Powleys freely admit that they shot, killed, and took possession of a bull moose without a hunting licence. However, they argue that, as Métis, they have an aboriginal right to hunt for food in the Sault Ste. Marie area that cannot be infringed by the Ontario government without proper justification. Because the Ontario government denies the existence of any special Métis right to hunt for food, the Powleys argue that subjecting them to the moose hunting provisions of the *Game and Fish Act* violates their rights under s. 35(1) of the *Constitution Act, 1982*, and cannot be justified.

7 The trial court, Superior Court, and Court of Appeal agreed with the Powleys. They found that the members of the Métis community in and around Sault Ste. Marie have an aboriginal right to hunt for food that is infringed without justification by the Ontario hunting regulations. Steve and Roddy Powley were therefore acquitted of unlawfully hunting and possessing the bull moose. Ontario appeals from these acquittals.

8 The question before us is whether ss. 46 and 47(1) of the *Game and Fish Act*, which prohibit hunting moose without a licence, unconstitutionally infringe the respondents' aboriginal right to hunt for food, as recognized in s. 35(1) of the *Constitution Act, 1982*.

II. ANALYSIS

9 Section 35 of the *Constitution Act, 1982* provides:

> **35.**(1) The existing aboriginal and treaty rights of the aboriginal peoples of Canada are hereby recognized and affirmed.
>
> (2) In this Act, "aboriginal peoples of Canada" includes the Indian, Inuit and Métis peoples of Canada.

10 The term "Métis" in s. 35 does not encompass all individuals with mixed Indian and European heritage; rather, it refers to distinctive peoples who, in addition to their mixed ancestry, developed their own customs, way of life, and recognizable group identity separate from their Indian or Inuit and European forebears. Métis communities evolved and flourished prior to the entrenchment of European control, when the influence of European settlers and political institutions became pre-eminent. The Royal Commission on Aboriginal Peoples describes this evolution as follows:

> Intermarriage between First Nations and Inuit women and European fur traders and fishermen produced children, but the birth of new Aboriginal cultures took longer. At first, the children of mixed unions were brought up in the traditions of their mothers or (less often) their fathers. Gradually, however, distinct Métis cultures emerged, combining European and First Nations or Inuit heritages in unique ways. Economics played a major role in this process. The special qualities and skills of the Métis population made them indispensable members of Aboriginal/non-Aboriginal economic partnerships, and that association contributed to the shaping of their cultures.... As interpreters, diplomats, guides, couriers, freighters, traders and suppliers, the early Métis people contributed massively to European penetration of North America.
>
> The French referred to the fur trade Métis as coureurs de bois (forest runners) and bois brulés (burnt-wood people) in recognition of their wilderness occupations and their dark complexions. The Labrador Métis (whose culture had early roots) were originally called "livyers" or "settlers", those who remained in the fishing settlements year-round rather than returning periodically to Europe or Newfoundland. The Cree people expressed the Métis character in the term Otepayemsuak, meaning the "independent ones". (*Report of the Royal Commission on Aboriginal Peoples: Perspectives and Realities*, vol. 4, at pp. 199–200 ("RCAP Report"))

The Métis developed separate and distinct identities, not reducible to the mere fact of their mixed ancestry: "What distinguishes Métis people from everyone else is that they associate themselves with a culture that is distinctly Métis" (RCAP Report, vol. 4, at p. 202).

11 The Métis of Canada share the common experience of having forged a new culture and a distinctive group identity from their Indian or Inuit and European roots. This enables us to speak in general terms of "the Métis". However, particularly given the vast territory of what is now Canada, we should not be surprised to find that different groups of Métis exhibit their own distinctive traits and traditions. This diversity among groups of Métis may enable us to speak of Métis "peoples", a possibility left open by the language of s. 35(2), which speaks of the "Indian, Inuit and Métis peoples of Canada".

12 We would not purport to enumerate the various Métis peoples that may exist. Because the Métis are explicitly included in s. 35, it is only necessary for our purposes to verify that the claimants belong to an identifiable Métis community with a sufficient degree of continuity and stability to support a site-specific aboriginal right. A Métis community can be defined as a group of Métis with a distinctive collective identity, living together in the same geographic

area and sharing a common way of life. The respondents here claim membership in the Métis community centred in and around Sault Ste. Marie. It is not necessary for us to decide, and we did not receive submissions on, whether this community is also a Métis "people", or whether it forms part of a larger Métis people that extends over a wider area such as the Upper Great Lakes.

13 Our evaluation of the respondents' claim takes place against this historical and cultural backdrop. The overarching interpretive principle for our legal analysis is a purposive reading of s. 35. The inclusion of the Métis in s. 35 is based on a commitment to recognizing the Métis and enhancing their survival as distinctive communities. The purpose and the promise of s. 35 is to protect practices that were historically important features of these distinctive communities and that persist in the present day as integral elements of their Métis culture.

14 For the reasons elaborated below, we uphold the basic elements of the *Van der Peet* test (*R.* v. *Van der Peet*, [1996] 2 S.C.R. 507) and apply these to the respondents' claim. However, we modify certain elements of the pre-contact test to reflect the distinctive history and post-contact ethnogenesis of the Métis, and the resulting differences between Indian claims and Métis claims.

A. The *Van der Peet* Test

15 The core question in *Van der Peet* was: "How should the aboriginal rights recognized and affirmed by s. 35(1) of the *Constitution Act, 1982* be defined?" (para. 15, per Lamer C.J.). Lamer C.J. wrote for the majority, at para. 31:

> [W]hat s. 35(1) does is provide the constitutional framework through which the fact that aboriginals lived on the land in distinctive societies, with their own practices, traditions and cultures, is acknowledged and reconciled with the sovereignty of the Crown. The substantive rights which fall within the provision must be defined in light of this purpose; the aboriginal rights recognized and affirmed by s. 35(1) must be directed towards the reconciliation of the pre-existence of aboriginal societies with the sovereignty of the Crown.

16 The emphasis on prior occupation as the primary justification for the special protection accorded aboriginal rights led the majority in *Van der Peet* to endorse a pre-contact test for identifying which customs, practices or traditions were integral to a particular aboriginal culture, and therefore entitled to constitutional protection. However, the majority recognized that the pre-contact test might prove inadequate to capture the range of Métis customs, practices or traditions that are entitled to protection, since Métis cultures by definition post-date European contact. For this reason, Lamer C.J. explicitly reserved the question of how to define Métis aboriginal rights for another day. He wrote at para. 67:

> [T]he history of the Métis, and the reasons underlying their inclusion in the protection given by s. 35, are quite distinct from those of other aboriginal peoples in Canada. As such, the manner in which the aboriginal rights of other aboriginal peoples are defined is not necessarily determinative of the manner in which the aboriginal rights of the Métis are defined. At the time when this Court is presented with a Métis claim under s. 35 it will then, with the benefit of the arguments of counsel, a factual context and a specific Métis claim, be able to explore the question of the purposes underlying s. 35's protection of the aboriginal rights of Métis people, and answer the question of the kinds of claims which fall within s. 35(1)'s scope when the claimants are Métis. The fact that, for other aboriginal peoples, the protection granted by s. 35 goes to the practices, customs and traditions of aboriginal peoples prior to contact, is not necessarily relevant to the answer which will be given to that question.

17 As indicated above, the inclusion of the Métis in s. 35 is not traceable to their pre-contact occupation of Canadian territory. The purpose of s. 35 as it relates to the Métis is therefore different from that which relates to the Indians or the Inuit. The constitutionally significant feature of the Métis is their special status as peoples that emerged between first contact and the effective imposition of European control. The inclusion of the Métis in s. 35 represents Canada's commitment to recognize and value the distinctive Métis cultures, which grew up in areas not yet open to colonization, and which the framers of the *Constitution Act, 1982* recognized can only survive if the Métis are protected along with other aboriginal communities.

18 With this in mind, we proceed to the issue of the correct test to determine the entitlements of the Métis under s. 35 of the Constitution Act, 1982. The appropriate test must then be applied to the findings of fact of the trial judge. We accept *Van der Peet* as the template for this discussion. However, we modify the pre-contact focus of the *Van der Peet* test when the claimants are Métis to account for the important

differences between Indian and Métis claims. Section 35 requires that we recognize and protect those customs and traditions that were historically important features of Métis communities prior to the time of effective European control, and that persist in the present day. This modification is required to account for the unique post-contact emergence of Métis communities, and the post-contact foundation of their aboriginal rights.

(1) Characterization of the Right

19 The first step is to characterize the right being claimed: *Van der Peet*, *supra*, at para. 76. Aboriginal hunting rights, including Métis rights, are contextual and site-specific. The respondents shot a bull moose near Old Goulais Bay Road, in the environs of Sault Ste. Marie, within the traditional hunting grounds of that Métis community. They made a point of documenting that the moose was intended to provide meat for the winter. The trial judge determined that they were hunting for food, and there is no reason to overturn this finding. The right being claimed can therefore be characterized as the right to hunt for food in the environs of Sault Ste. Marie.

20 We agree with the trial judge that the periodic scarcity of moose does not in itself undermine the respondents' claim. The relevant right is not to hunt moose but to hunt for food in the designated territory.

(2) Identification of the Historic Rights-Bearing Community

21 The trial judge found that a distinctive Métis community emerged in the Upper Great Lakes region in the mid-17th century, and peaked around 1850. We find no reviewable error in the trial judge's findings on this matter, which were confirmed by the Court of Appeal. The record indicates the following: In the mid-17th century, the Jesuits established a mission at Sainte-Marie-du-Sault, in an area characterized by heavy competition among fur traders. In 1750, the French established a fixed trading post on the south bank of the Saint Mary's River. The Sault Ste. Marie post attracted settlement by Métis — the children of unions between European traders and Indian women, and their descendants (A. J. Ray, "An Economic History of the Robinson Treaties Area Before 1860" (1998) ("Ray Report"), at p. 17). According to Dr. Ray, by the early 19th century, "[t]he settlement at Sault Ste. Marie was one of the oldest and most important [Métis settlements] in the upper lakes area" (Ray Report, at p. 47)....

. . . .

22 ... Dr. Ray elaborated: "By the time of Vidal's visit to the Sault Ste. Marie area, the people of mixed ancestry living there had developed a distinctive sense of identity and Indians and Whites recognized them as being a separate people" (Ray Report, at p. 56).

23 In addition to demographic evidence, proof of shared customs, traditions, and a collective identity is required to demonstrate the existence of a Métis community that can support a claim to site-specific aboriginal rights. We recognize that different groups of Métis have often lacked political structures and have experienced shifts in their members' self-identification. However, the existence of an identifiable Métis community must be demonstrated with some degree of continuity and stability in order to support a site-specific aboriginal rights claim. Here, we find no basis for overturning the trial judge's finding of a historic Métis community at Sault Ste. Marie. This finding is supported by the record and must be upheld.

(3) Identification of the Contemporary Rights-Bearing Community

24 Aboriginal rights are communal rights: They must be grounded in the existence of a historic and present community, and they may only be exercised by virtue of an individual's ancestrally based membership in the present community. The trial judge found that a Métis community has persisted in and around Sault Ste. Marie despite its decrease in visibility after the signing of the Robinson-Huron Treaty in 1850. While we take note of the trial judge's determination that the Sault Ste. Marie Métis community was to a large extent an "invisible entity" ([1999] 1 C.N.L.R. 153, at para. 80) from the mid-19th century to the 1970s, we do not take this to mean that the community ceased to exist or disappeared entirely.

25 Dr. Lytwyn describes the continued existence of a Métis community in and around Sault Ste. Marie despite the displacement of many of the community's members in the aftermath of the 1850 treaties....

26 The advent of European control over this area thus interfered with, but did not eliminate, the Sault Ste. Marie Métis community and its traditional practices, as evidenced by census data from the 1860s through the 1890s. Dr. Lytwyn concluded from this

census data that "[a]lthough the Métis lost much of their traditional land base at Sault Ste. Marie, they continued to live in the region and gain their livelihood from the resources of the land and waters" (Lytwyn Report, at p. 32). He also noted a tendency for underreporting and lack of information about the Métis during this period because of their "removal to the peripheries of the town", and "their own disinclination to be identified as Métis" in the wake of the Riel rebellions and the turning of Ontario public opinion against Métis rights through government actions and the media (Lytwyn Report, at p. 33).

27 We conclude that the evidence supports the trial judge's finding that the community's lack of visibility was explained and does not negate the existence of the contemporary community. There was never a lapse; the Métis community went underground, so to speak, but it continued. Moreover, as indicated below, the "continuity" requirement puts the focus on the continuing practices of members of the community, rather than more generally on the community itself, as indicated below.

28 The trial judge's finding of a contemporary Métis community in and around Sault Ste. Marie is supported by the evidence and must be upheld.

(4) Verification of the Claimant's Membership in the Relevant Contemporary Community

29 While determining membership in the Métis community might not be as simple as verifying membership in, for example, an Indian band, this does not detract from the status of Métis people as full-fledged rights-bearers. As Métis communities continue to organize themselves more formally and to assert their constitutional rights, it is imperative that membership requirements become more standardized so that legitimate rights-holders can be identified. In the meantime, courts faced with Métis claims will have to ascertain Métis identity on a case-by-case basis. The inquiry must take into account both the value of community self-definition, and the need for the process of identification to be objectively verifiable. In addition, the criteria for Métis identity under s. 35 must reflect the purpose of this constitutional guarantee: to recognize and affirm the rights of the Métis held by virtue of their direct relationship to this country's original inhabitants and by virtue of the continuity between their customs and traditions and those of their Métis predecessors. This is not an insurmountable task.

30 We emphasize that we have not been asked, and we do not purport, to set down a comprehensive definition of who is Métis for the purpose of asserting a claim under s. 35. We therefore limit ourselves to indicating the important components of a future definition, while affirming that the creation of appropriate membership tests before disputes arise is an urgent priority. As a general matter, we would endorse the guidelines proposed by Vaillancourt Prov. J. and O'Neill J. in the courts below. In particular, we would look to three broad factors as indicia of Métis identity for the purpose of claiming Métis rights under s. 35: self-identification, ancestral connection, and community acceptance.

31 First, the claimant must self-identify as a member of a Métis community. This self-identification should not be of recent vintage: While an individual's self-identification need not be static or monolithic, claims that are made belatedly in order to benefit from a s. 35 right will not satisfy the self-identification requirement.

32 Second, the claimant must present evidence of an ancestral connection to a historic Métis community. This objective requirement ensures that beneficiaries of s. 35 rights have a real link to the historic community whose practices ground the right being claimed. We would not require a minimum "blood quantum", but we would require some proof that the claimant's ancestors belonged to the historic Métis community by birth, adoption, or other means. Like the trial judge, we would abstain from further defining this requirement in the absence of more extensive argument by the parties in a case where this issue is determinative. In this case, the Powleys' Métis ancestry is not disputed.

33 Third, the claimant must demonstrate that he or she is accepted by the modern community whose continuity with the historic community provides the legal foundation for the right being claimed. Membership in a Métis political organization may be relevant to the question of community acceptance, but it is not sufficient in the absence of a contextual understanding of the membership requirements of the organization and its role in the Métis community. The core of community acceptance is past and ongoing participation in a shared culture, in the customs and traditions that constitute a Métis community's identity and distinguish it from other groups. This is what the community membership criterion is all about. Other indicia of community acceptance might include evidence of participation in community activities and testimony from other members about

the claimant's connection to the community and its culture. The range of acceptable forms of evidence does not attenuate the need for an objective demonstration of a solid bond of past and present mutual identification and recognition of common belonging between the claimant and other members of the rights-bearing community.

34 It is important to remember that, no matter how a contemporary community defines membership, only those members with a demonstrable ancestral connection to the historic community can claim a s. 35 right. Verifying membership is crucial, since individuals are only entitled to exercise Métis aboriginal rights by virtue of their ancestral connection to and current membership in a Métis community.

35 In this case, there is no reason to overturn the trial judge's finding that the Powleys are members of the Métis community that arose and still exists in and around Sault Ste. Marie. We agree with the Court of Appeal that, in the circumstances of this case, the fact that the Powleys' ancestors lived on an Indian reserve for a period of time does not negate the Powleys' Métis identity. As the Court of Appeal indicated, "E.B. Borron, commissioned in 1891 by the province to report on annuity payments to the Métis, was of the view that Métis who had taken treaty benefits remained Métis and he recommended that they be removed from the treaty annuity lists" ((2001), 53 O.R. (3d) 35, at para. 139, per Sharpe J.A.). We emphasize that the individual decision by a Métis person's ancestors to take treaty benefits does not necessarily extinguish that person's claim to Métis rights. It will depend, in part, on whether there was a collective adhesion by the Métis community to the treaty. Based on the record, it was open to the trial judge to conclude that the rights of the Powleys' ancestors did not merge into those of the Indian band.

(5) Identification of the Relevant Time Frame

36 As indicated above, the pre-contact aspect of the *Van der Peet* test requires adjustment in order to take account of the post-contact ethnogenesis of the Métis and the purpose of s. 35 in protecting the historically important customs and traditions of these distinctive peoples. While the fact of prior occupation grounds aboriginal rights claims for the Inuit and the Indians, the recognition of Métis rights in s. 35 is not reducible to the Métis' Indian ancestry. The unique status of the Métis as an Aboriginal people with post-contact origins requires an adaptation of the pre-contact approach to meet the distinctive historical circumstances surrounding the evolution of Métis communities.

37 The pre-contact test in *Van der Peet* is based on the constitutional affirmation that aboriginal communities are entitled to continue those practices, customs and traditions that are integral to their distinctive existence or relationship to the land. By analogy, the test for Métis practices should focus on identifying those practices, customs and traditions that are integral to the Métis community's distinctive existence and relationship to the land. This unique history can most appropriately be accommodated by a post-contact but pre-control test that identifies the time when Europeans effectively established political and legal control in a particular area. The focus should be on the period after a particular Métis community arose and before it came under the effective control of European laws and customs. This pre-control test enables us to identify those practices, customs and traditions that predate the imposition of European laws and customs on the Métis.

38 We reject the appellant's argument that Métis rights must find their origin in the pre-contact practices of the Métis' aboriginal ancestors. This theory in effect would deny to Métis their full status as distinctive rights-bearing peoples whose own integral practices are entitled to constitutional protection under s. 35(1). The right claimed here was a practice of both the Ojibway and the Métis. However, as long as the practice grounding the right is distinctive and integral to the pre-control Métis community, it will satisfy this prong of the test. This result flows from the constitutional imperative that we recognize and affirm the aboriginal rights of the Métis, who appeared after the time of first contact.

39 The pre-control test requires us to review the trial judge's findings on the imposition of European control in the Sault Ste. Marie area. Although Europeans were clearly present in the Upper Great Lakes area from the early days of exploration, they actually discouraged settlement of this region. J. Peterson explains:

> With the exception of Detroit, Kaskaskia and Cahokia, the French colonial administration established no farming communities in the Great Lakes region. After 1763, only partly in response to the regionwide resistance movement known as Pontiac's Rebellion, the British likewise discouraged settlement west of Lake Ontario. Desire to keep the peace and to monopolize the profits of the Great Lakes Indian trade were the over-

> riding considerations favouring this policy. To have simultaneously encouraged an influx of white farmers would have upset both the diplomatic alliance with the native inhabitants inherited from the French and the ratio between humans and animals on the ground, straining the fur-bearing capacities of the region. (J. Peterson, "Many roads to Red River: Métis genesis in the Great Lakes region, 1680–1815", in *The New Peoples: Being and Becoming Métis in North America* (1985), 37, at p. 40)
>
> This policy changed in the mid-19th century, as British economic needs and plans evolved. The British sent William B. Robinson to negotiate treaties with the Indian tribes in the regions of Lake Huron and Lake Superior. One of his objectives as Treaty Commissioner was to obtain land in order to allow mining, timber and other development, including the development of a town at Sault Ste. Marie (Lytwyn Report, *supra*, at p. 29).

40 The historical record indicates that the Sault Ste. Marie Métis community thrived largely unaffected by European laws and customs until colonial policy shifted from one of discouraging settlement to one of negotiating treaties and encouraging settlement in the mid-19th century. The trial judge found, and the parties agreed in their pleadings before the lower courts, that "effective control [of the Upper Great Lakes area] passed from the Aboriginal peoples of the area (Ojibway and Metis) to European control" in the period between 1815 and 1850 (para. 90). The record fully supports the finding that the period just prior to 1850 is the appropriate date for finding effective control in this geographic area, which the Crown agreed was the critical date in its pleadings below.

(6) Determination of Whether the Practice is Integral to the Claimants' Distinctive Culture

41 The practice of subsistence hunting and fishing was a constant in the Métis community, even though the availability of particular species might have waxed and waned. The evidence indicates that subsistence hunting was an important aspect of Métis life and a defining feature of their special relationship to the land (Peterson, *supra*, at p. 41; Lytwyn Report, supra, at p. 6). A major part of subsistence was the practice at issue here, hunting for food.

. . . .

44 This evidence supports the trial judge's finding that hunting for food was integral to the Métis way of life at Sault Ste. Marie in the period just prior to 1850.

(7) Establishment of Continuity Between the Historic Practice and the Contemporary Right Asserted

45 Although s. 35 protects "existing" rights, it is more than a mere codification of the common law. Section 35 reflects a new promise: a constitutional commitment to protecting practices that were historically important features of particular aboriginal communities. A certain margin of flexibility might be required to ensure that aboriginal practices can evolve and develop over time, but it is not necessary to define or to rely on that margin in this case. Hunting for food was an important feature of the Sault Ste. Marie Métis community, and the practice has been continuous to the present. Steve and Roddy Powley claim a Métis aboriginal right to hunt for food. The right claimed by the Powleys falls squarely within the bounds of the historical practice grounding the right.

(8) Determination of Whether or Not the Right Was Extinguished

46 The doctrine of extinguishment applies equally to Métis and to First Nations claims. There is no evidence of extinguishment here, as determined by the trial judge. The Crown's argument for extinguishment is based largely on the Robinson-Huron Treaty of 1850, from which the Métis as a group were explicitly excluded.

(9) If There Is a Right, Determination of Whether There Is an Infringement

47 Ontario currently does not recognize any Métis right to hunt for food, or any "special access rights to natural resources" for the Métis whatsoever (appellant's record, at p. 1029). This lack of recognition, and the consequent application of the challenged provisions to the Powleys, infringe their aboriginal right to hunt for food as a continuation of the protected historical practices of the Sault Ste. Marie Métis community.

(10) Determination of Whether the Infringement Is Justified

48 The main justification advanced by the appellant is that of conservation. Although conservation is clearly a very important concern, we agree with the trial judge that the record here does not support this

justification. If the moose population in this part of Ontario were under threat, and there was no evidence that it is, the Métis would still be entitled to a priority allocation to satisfy their subsistence needs in accordance with the criteria set out in *R. v. Sparrow*, [1990] 1 S.C.R. 1075. While preventative measures might be required for conservation purposes in the future, we have not been presented with evidence to support such measures here. The Ontario authorities can make out a case for regulation of the aboriginal right to hunt moose for food if and when the need arises. On the available evidence and given the current licensing system, Ontario's blanket denial of any Métis right to hunt for food cannot be justified.

49 The appellant advances a subsidiary argument for justification based on the alleged difficulty of identifying who is Métis. As discussed, the Métis identity of a particular claimant should be determined on proof of self-identification, ancestral connection, and community acceptance. The development of a more systematic method of identifying Métis rights-holders for the purpose of enforcing hunting regulations is an urgent priority. That said, the difficulty of identifying members of the Métis community must not be exaggerated as a basis for defeating their rights under the Constitution of Canada.

50 While our finding of a Métis right to hunt for food is not species-specific, the evidence on justification related primarily to the Ontario moose population. The justification of other hunting regulations will require adducing evidence relating to the particular species affected. In the immediate future, the hunting rights of the Métis should track those of the Ojibway in terms of restrictions for conservation purposes and priority allocations where threatened species may be involved. In the longer term, a combination of negotiation and judicial settlement will more clearly define the contours of the Métis right to hunt, a right that we recognize as part of the special aboriginal relationship to the land.

B. The Request for a Stay

51 With respect to the cross-appeal, we affirm that the Court of Appeal had jurisdiction to issue a stay of its decision in these circumstances. This power should continue to be used only in exceptional situations in which a court of general jurisdiction deems that giving immediate effect to an order will undermine the very purpose of that order or otherwise threaten the rule of law: Reference re Manitoba Language Rights, [1985] 1 S.C.R. 721. We note that the Powleys' acquittal would have remained valid notwithstanding the stay. It was, however, within the Court of Appeal's discretion to suspend the application of its ruling to other members of the Métis community in order to foster cooperative solutions and ensure that the resource in question was not depleted in the interim, thereby negating the value of the right.

52 The initial stay expired on February 23, 2002, and more than a year has passed since that time. The Court of Appeal's decision has been the law of Ontario in the interim, and chaos does not appear to have ensued. We see no compelling reason to issue an additional stay. We also note that it is particularly important to have a clear justification for a stay where the effect of that stay would be to suspend the recognition of a right that provides a defence to a criminal charge, as it would here.

III. CONCLUSION

53 Members of the Métis community in and around Sault Ste. Marie have an aboriginal right to hunt for food under s. 35(1). This is determined by their fulfillment of the requirements set out in *Van der Peet*, modified to fit the distinctive purpose of s. 35 in protecting the Métis.

54 The appeal is dismissed with costs to the respondents. The cross-appeal is dismissed.

55 The constitutional question is answered as follows:

> Are ss. 46 and 47(1) of the *Game and Fish Act*, R.S.O. 1990, c. G.1, as they read on October 22, 1993, of no force or effect with respect to the respondents, being Métis, in the circumstances of this case, by reason of their aboriginal rights under s. 35 of the *Constitution Act, 1982*?

Answer: Yes.

(e) *Haida Nation v. British Columbia (Minister of Forests)*†

See **Chapter 5, Part 16, Chapter 8, Part 8(f)**, and **Chapter 10, Part 6.**

NOTE

The Haida people claimed Aboriginal rights and title to Haida Gwai (the Queen Charlotte Islands). They argued that the provincial government had a legal duty to consult with them before transferring a tree farm licence on Haida Gwai from one logging company to another. The British Columbia Supreme Court said there could be no legal duty to consult, because the title claim had not been proven in court. The British Columbia Court of Appeal disagreed, and held both the provincial Crown and the transferee logging company to a fiduciary duty to consult. The Supreme Court of Canada upheld the consultation requirement in regard to the province. The Court said that a duty to consult can arise wherever the Crown knows or should have known of a credible claim to Aboriginal rights. It added that this duty is sometimes accompanied by an obligation to minimize the harm in question. On the other hand, the Court said that the duty to consult is not a fiduciary duty, and does not bind parties other than the Crown.

What was the Supreme Court's response to the argument that there should be no duty to consult where legal rights had not yet been established? Will governments face practical problems in trying to ascertain the potential Aboriginal claimants in a given area? If unproven or unresolved Aboriginal rights don't attract a fiduciary duty, what is the basis for the consultation duty? What factors did the court consider relevant to the question of the extent of the duty to consult, and to whether and how much accommodation is appropriate? How do these factors resemble or contrast with the factors relevant to the administrative law concept of the rules of natural justice? What was the Court's response to the argument that the consultation duty should bind the logging company as well?

Taku River Tlingit First Nation v. British Columbia (Project Assessment Director), 2004 SCC 74 also involved s. 35(1) consultation issues, and was released on the same day as *Haida Nation*. The Supreme Court said that although the Crown was under a s. 35(1) duty to consult with and accommodate the *Taku River Tlingit* in regard to a proposed mining road in far northern British Columbia, that duty had been met. The Court stressed that "[w]here consultation is meaningful, there is no ultimate duty to reach agreement" (para. 2), but added that here neither the process nor the consultation was complete.

EXTRACT

[McLACHLIN C.J. for the Court:]

11 This case is the first of its kind to reach this Court. Our task is the modest one of establishing a general framework for the duty to consult and accommodate, where indicated, before Aboriginal title or rights claims have been decided. As this framework is applied, courts, in the age-old tradition of the common law, will be called on to fill in the details of the duty to consult and accommodate.

. . . .

16 The government's duty to consult with Aboriginal peoples and accommodate their interests is grounded in the honour of the Crown. The honour of the Crown is always at stake in its dealings with Aboriginal peoples: see for example *R. v. Badger*, [1996] 1 S.C.R. 771, at para. 41; *R. v. Marshall*, [1999] 3 S.C.R. 456. It is not a mere incantation, but rather a core precept that finds its application in concrete practices.

. . . .

18 The honour of the Crown gives rise to different duties in different circumstances. Where the Crown has assumed discretionary control over specific Aboriginal interests, the honour of the Crown gives rise to a fiduciary duty: *Wewaykum Indian*

† *Haida Nation v. British Columbia (Minister of Forests)* 2004 SCC 73, dismissing an appeal by the Crown and allowing an appeal by Weyerhaeuser Co. from [2002] 6 W.W.R. 243 (B.C.C.A.) with supplementary reasons in (2002), 10 W.W.R. 587 (B.C.C.A.) rev'g [2001] 2 C.N.L.R. 83 (B.C.S.C.).

Band v. Canada, [2002] 4 S.C.R. 245, 2002 SCC 79, at para. 79. The content of the fiduciary duty may vary to take into account the Crown's other, broader obligations. However, the duty's fulfilment requires that the Crown act with reference to the Aboriginal group's best interest in exercising discretionary control over the specific Aboriginal interest at stake. As explained in *Wewaykum*, at para. 81, the term "fiduciary" does not connote a universal trust relationship encompassing all aspects of the relationship between the Crown and Aboriginal peoples:

> ... "fiduciary duty" as a source of plenary Crown liability covering all aspects of the Crown-Indian band relationship ... overshoots the mark. The fiduciary duty imposed on the Crown does not exist at large but in relation to specific Indian interests.

Here, Aboriginal rights and title have been asserted but have not been defined or proven. The Aboriginal interest in question is insufficiently specific for the honour of the Crown to mandate that the Crown act in the Aboriginal group's best interest, as a fiduciary, in exercising discretionary control over the subject of the right or title.

19 The honour of the Crown also infuses the processes of treaty making and treaty interpretation. In making and applying treaties, the Crown must act with honour and integrity, avoiding even the appearance of "sharp dealing" (*Badger*, at para. 41). Thus in *Marshall*, *supra*, at para. 4, the majority of this Court supported its interpretation of a treaty by stating that "nothing less would uphold the honour and integrity of the Crown in its dealings with the Mi'kmaq people to secure their peace and friendship ...".

20 Where treaties remain to be concluded, the honour of the Crown requires negotiations leading to a just settlement of Aboriginal claims: *R. v. Sparrow*, [1990] 1 S.C.R. 1075, at pp. 1105–6. Treaties serve to reconcile pre-existing Aboriginal sovereignty with assumed Crown sovereignty, and to define Aboriginal rights guaranteed by s. 35 of the *Constitution Act, 1982*. Section 35 represents a promise of rights recognition, and "[i]t is always assumed that the Crown intends to fulfil its promises" (*Badger, supra*, at para. 41). This promise is realized and sovereignty claims reconciled through the process of honourable negotiation. It is a corollary of s. 35 that the Crown act honourably in defining the rights it guarantees and in reconciling them with other rights and interests. This, in turn, implies a duty to consult and, if appropriate, accommodate.

. . . .

32 The jurisprudence of this Court supports the view that the duty to consult and accommodate is part of a process of fair dealing and reconciliation that begins with the assertion of sovereignty and continues beyond formal claims resolution. Reconciliation is not a final legal remedy in the usual sense. Rather, it is a process flowing from rights guaranteed by s. 35(1) of the *Constitution Act, 1982*. This process of reconciliation flows from the Crown's duty of honourable dealing toward Aboriginal peoples, which arises in turn from the Crown's assertion of sovereignty over an Aboriginal people and de facto control of land and resources that were formerly in the control of that people. As stated in *Mitchell v. M.N.R.*, [2001] 1 S.C.R. 911, 2001 SCC 33, at para. 9, "[w]ith this assertion [sovereignty] arose an obligation to treat aboriginal peoples fairly and honourably, and to protect them from exploitation ..." (emphasis added).

33 To limit reconciliation to the post-proof sphere risks treating reconciliation as a distant legalistic goal, devoid of the "meaningful content" mandated by the "solemn commitment" made by the Crown in recognizing and affirming Aboriginal rights and title: *Sparrow*, *supra*, at p. 1108. It also risks unfortunate consequences. When the distant goal of proof is finally reached, the Aboriginal peoples may find their land and resources changed and denuded. This is not reconciliation. Nor is it honourable.

. . . .

36 This leaves the practical argument. It is said that before claims are resolved, the Crown cannot know that the rights exist, and hence can have no duty to consult or accommodate. This difficulty should not be denied or minimized. As I stated (dissenting) in *Marshall, supra*, at para. 112, one cannot "meaningfully discuss accommodation or justification of a right unless one has some idea of the core of that right and its modern scope". However, it will frequently be possible to reach an idea of the asserted rights and of their strength sufficient to trigger an obligation to consult and accommodate, short of final judicial determination or settlement. To facilitate this determination, claimants should outline their claims with clarity, focussing on the scope and nature of the Aboriginal rights they assert and on the alleged infringements. This is what happened here, where the chambers judge made a preliminary evidence-based assessment of the strength of the Haida claims

to the lands and resources of Haida Gwaii, particularly Block 6.

37 There is a distinction between knowledge sufficient to trigger a duty to consult and, if appropriate, accommodate, and the content or scope of the duty in a particular case. Knowledge of a credible but unproven claim suffices to trigger a duty to consult and accommodate. The content of the duty, however, varies with the circumstances, as discussed more fully below. A dubious or peripheral claim may attract a mere duty of notice, while a stronger claim may attract more stringent duties. The law is capable of differentiating between tenuous claims, claims possessing a strong *prima facie* case, and established claims. Parties can assess these matters, and if they cannot agree, tribunals and courts can assist. Difficulties associated with the absence of proof and definition of claims are addressed by assigning appropriate content to the duty, not by denying the existence of a duty.

. . . .

39 The content of the duty to consult and accommodate varies with the circumstances. Precisely what duties arise in different situations will be defined as the case law in this emerging area develops. In general terms, however, it may be asserted that the scope of the duty is proportionate to a preliminary assessment of the strength of the case supporting the existence of the right or title, and to the seriousness of the potentially adverse effect upon the right or title claimed.

. . . .

43 Against this background, I turn to the kind of duties that may arise in different situations. In this respect, the concept of a spectrum may be helpful, not to suggest watertight legal compartments but rather to indicate what the honour of the Crown may require in particular circumstances. At one end of the spectrum lie cases where the claim to title is weak, the Aboriginal right limited, or the potential for infringement minor. In such cases, the only duty on the Crown may be to give notice, disclose information, and discuss any issues raised in response to the notice. "'[C]onsultation' in its least technical definition is talking together for mutual understanding": T. Isaac and A. Knox, "The Crown's Duty to Consult Aboriginal People" (2003), 41 Alta. L. Rev. 49, at p. 61.

44 At the other end of the spectrum lie cases where a strong *prima facie* case for the claim is established, the right and potential infringement is of high significance to the Aboriginal peoples, and the risk of non-compensable damage is high. In such cases deep consultation, aimed at finding a satisfactory interim solution, may be required. While precise requirements will vary with the circumstances, the consultation required at this stage may entail the opportunity to make submissions for consideration, formal participation in the decision-making process, and provision of written reasons to show that Aboriginal concerns were considered and to reveal the impact they had on the decision. This list is neither exhaustive, nor mandatory for every case. The government may wish to adopt dispute resolution procedures like mediation or administrative regimes with impartial decision-makers in complex or difficult cases.

45 Between these two extremes of the spectrum just described, will lie other situations.....

. . . .

47 When the consultation process suggests amendment of Crown policy, we arrive at the stage of accommodation. Thus the effect of good faith consultation may be to reveal a duty to accommodate. Where a strong *prima facie* case exists for the claim, and the consequences of the government's proposed decision may adversely affect it in a significant way, addressing the Aboriginal concerns may require taking steps to avoid irreparable harm or to minimize the effects of infringement, pending final resolution of the underlying claim. Accommodation is achieved through consultation, as this Court recognized in *R. v. Marshall*, [1999] 3 S.C.R. 533, at para. 22: "... the process of accommodation of the treaty right may best be resolved by consultation and negotiation".

48 This process does not give Aboriginal groups a veto over what can be done with land pending final proof of the claim. The Aboriginal "consent" spoken of in *Delgamuukw* is appropriate only in cases of established rights, and then by no means in every case. Rather, what is required is a process of balancing interests, of give and take.

. . . .

54 [In regard to the alleged fiduciary duty imposed on Weyerhaeuser] it is alleged that third parties might have a duty to consult and accommodate on the basis of the trust law doctrine of "knowing

receipt". However, as discussed above, while the Crown's fiduciary obligations and its duty to consult and accommodate share roots in the principle that the Crown's honour is engaged in its relationship with Aboriginal peoples, the duty to consult is distinct from the fiduciary duty that is owed in relation to particular cognizable Aboriginal interests. As noted earlier, the Court cautioned in Wewaykum against assuming that a general trust or fiduciary obligation governs all aspects of relations between the Crown and Aboriginal peoples. Furthermore, this Court in *Guerin v. The Queen*, [1984] 2 S.C.R. 335, made it clear that the "trust-like" relationship between the Crown and Aboriginal peoples is not a true "trust", noting that "[t]he law of trusts is a highly developed, specialized branch of the law" (p. 386). There is no reason to graft the doctrine of knowing receipt onto the special relationship between the Crown and Aboriginal peoples. It is also questionable whether businesses acting on licence from the Crown can be analogized to persons who knowingly turn trust funds to their own ends.

[The Chief Justice said that the Crown can require third parties to act consistently with consultation requirements, and that third parties can be held liable for negligence or dishonesty. She said that s. 109 of the *Constitution Act, 1867* did not shield the province from a consultation duty, because this provision was subject to Aboriginal interests. In this case, she said, the Haida had a *prima facie* case for Aboriginal title and a strong *prima facie* case for harvesting Aboriginal red cedar. These claims had long been known to the province, and could be seriously affected by logging. As a result, the provincial Crown had a duty to consult the Haida, not just before issuing individual cutting permits, but before granting or transferring a tree farm licence. This was because the tree farm licence incorporated the planning decisions that governed annual and long-term timber harvests. Since it had failed to consult the Haida about the licence transfer, the provincial Crown had breached its duty. Whether accommodation was also required would depend on the consultation results. However, the Chief Justice thought that the strength of the Haidas' claims and the seriousness of the potential impact on their interests "may well require significant accommodation" (para. 77) before the claims were finally resolved.]

11 Aboriginal Claims

(a) Map of Comprehensive Land Claims in British Columbia†

See **Chapter 11, Part 5**. See also **Chapter 11, Part 7(h)**.

The map that appears on p. 383 is adapted from the original coloured version prepared by the Department of Indian Affairs and Northern Development. The boundaries of individual claims areas are indicated by numbers. They are current to the dates indicated.

(b) Federal Policy for the Settlement of Native Claims‡

See **Chapter 11, Parts 3(e), 4, 5 and 6**.

COMPREHENSIVE CLAIMS

Objectives of Comprehensive Claims Settlements

The primary purpose of comprehensive claims settlements is to conclude agreements with Aboriginal groups that will resolve the debates and legal ambiguities associated with the common law concept of Aboriginal rights and title. Uncertainty with respect to the legal status of lands and resources, which has been created by a lack of political agreement with Aboriginal groups, is a barrier to economic development for all Canadians and has hindered the full participation of Aboriginal peoples in land and resource management. The comprehensive claims process is intended to lead to agreement on the special rights Aboriginal peoples will have in the future with respect to lands and resources. It is not an attempt to define what rights they may have had in the past.

Negotiated comprehensive claims settlements provide for the exchange of undefined Aboriginal rights over an area of traditional use and continuing occupancy, for a clearly defined package of rights and benefits codified in a constitutionally protected settlement agreement. The objective is to negotiate modern treaties that provide a clear, certain and long-lasting definition of rights to land and resources.

---

† Map: Treaty Negotiations in British Columbia. Reproduced with permission of the Ministry of Aboriginal Affairs, Province of British Columbia. The map represents the situation at its time of publication in 1998. Since then, the Nisga'a claim has been settled by the 1998 **Nisga'a Final Agreement** (ratified in 2000): see **Chapter 11, Part 7(h)**.

‡ *Federal Policy for the Settlement of Native Claims* (Ottawa: Indian and Northern Affairs Canada, 1993) at 5–11, 19–24, 29–30. Published under the authority of the Honourable Pauline Browes, Minister of Indian Affairs and Northern Development, Ottawa, 1993. Reproduced with the permission of the Minister of Public Works and Government Services, 2004. Note: Aspects of the Policy such as details of acceptance criteria are updated on an ongoing basis to reflect developments in case law.

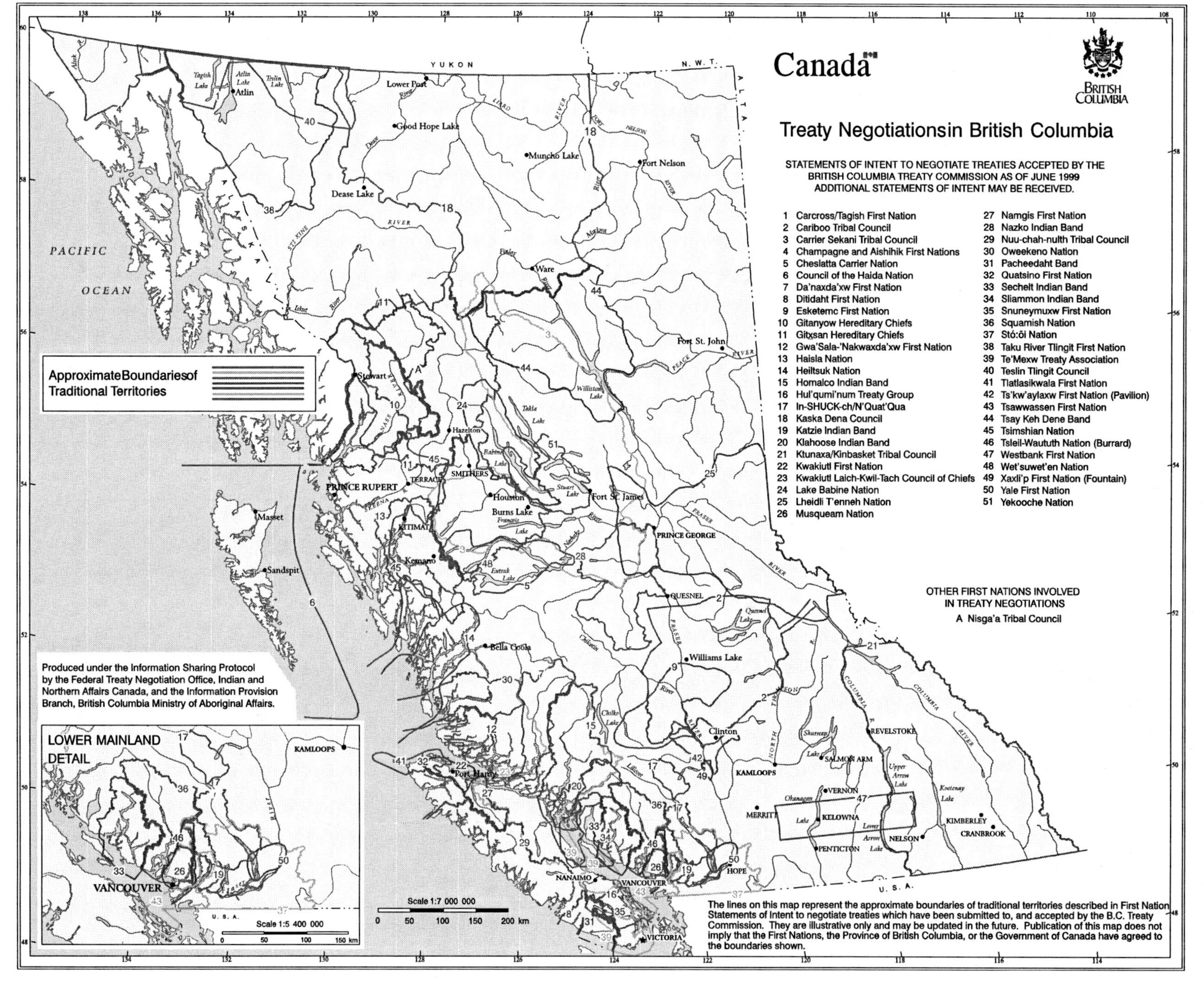
Canada
British Columbia
Treaty Negotiationsin British Columbia
STATEMENTS OF INTENT TO NEGOTIATE TREATIES ACCEPTED BY THE BRITISH COLUMBIA TREATY COMMISSION AS OF JUNE 1999
ADDITIONAL STATEMENTS OF INTENT MAY BE RECEIVED.
1 Carcross/Tagish First Nation
2 Cariboo Tribal Council
3 Carrier Sekani Tribal Council
4 Champagne and Aishihik First Nations
5 Cheslatta Carrier Nation
6 Council of the Haida Nation
7 Da'naxda'xw First Nation
8 Ditidaht First Nation
9 Esketemc First Nation
10 Gitanyow Hereditary Chiefs
11 Gitxsan Hereditary Chiefs
12 Gwa'Sala-'Nakwaxda'xw First Nation
13 Haisla Nation
14 Heiltsuk Nation
15 Homalco Indian Band
16 Hul'qumi'num Treaty Group
17 In-SHUCK-ch/N'Quat'Qua
18 Kaska Dena Council
19 Katzie Indian Band
20 Klahoose Indian Band
21 Ktunaxa/Kinbasket Tribal Council
22 Kwakiutl First Nation
23 Kwakiutl Laich-Kwil-Tach Council of Chiefs
24 Lake Babine Nation
25 Lheidli T'enneh Nation
26 Musqueam Nation
27 Namgis First Nation
28 Nazko Indian Band
29 Nuu-chah-nulth Tribal Council
30 Oweekeno Nation
31 Pacheedaht Band
32 Quatsino First Nation
33 Sechelt Indian Band
34 Sliammon Indian Band
35 Snuneymuxw First Nation
36 Squamish Nation
37 Stó:lō Nation
38 Taku River Tlingit First Nation
39 Te'Mexw Treaty Association
40 Teslin Tlingit Council
41 Tlatlasikwala First Nation
42 Ts'kw'aylaxw First Nation (Pavilion)
43 Tsawwassen First Nation
44 Tsay Keh Dene Band
45 Tsimshian Nation
46 Tsleil-Waututh Nation (Burrard)
47 Westbank First Nation
48 Wet'suwet'en Nation
49 Xaxli'p First Nation (Fountain)
50 Yale First Nation
51 Yekooche Nation
OTHER FIRST NATIONS INVOLVED IN TREATY NEGOTIATIONS
A Nisga'a Tribal Council
Approximate Boundaries of Traditional Territories
Produced under the Information Sharing Protocol by the Federal Treaty Negotiation Office, Indian and Northern Affairs Canada, and the Information Provision Branch, British Columbia Ministry of Aboriginal Affairs.
LOWER MAINLAND DETAIL
Scale 1:5 400 000
Scale 1:7 000 000
0 50 100 150 200 km
The lines on this map represent the approximate boundaries of traditional territories described in First Nation Statements of Intent to negotiate treaties which have been submitted to, and accepted by the B.C. Treaty Commission. They are illustrative only and may be updated in the future. Publication of this map does not imply that the First Nations, the Province of British Columbia, or the Government of Canada have agreed to the boundaries shown.
PACIFIC OCEAN
YUKON
N. W. T.
ALTA.
ALASKA
U. S. A.
Atlin
Lower Post
Good Hope Lake
Muncho Lake
Fort Nelson
Dease Lake
Ware
Fort St. John
Stewart
Hazelton
SMITHERS
TERRACE
PRINCE RUPERT
Houston
Burns Lake
Fort St. James
PRINCE GEORGE
KITIMAT
Kemano
Masset
Sandspit
QUESNEL
Bella Coola
Williams Lake
Clinton
KAMLOOPS
REVELSTOKE
SALMON ARM
VERNON
KELOWNA
MERRITT
PENTICTON
NELSON
KIMBERLEY
CRANBROOK
Port Hardy
NANAIMO
VANCOUVER
HOPE
VICTORIA

Acceptance of Claims for Negotiation

The criteria used by the federal government to determine if a claim will be accepted for negotiation were derived initially from the *1979 Baker Lake* decision. In this decision, Mr. Justice Mahoney elaborated on the *Calder* decision and established a common law test for determining whether there are continuing Aboriginal rights. In order for its comprehensive claims submission to be accepted, an Aboriginal group must demonstrate all of the following:

1. The Aboriginal group is, and was, an organized society.
2. The organized society has occupied the specific territory over which it asserts Aboriginal title since time immemorial. The traditional use and occupancy of the territory must have been sufficient to be an established fact at the time of assertion of sovereignty by European nations.
3. The occupation of the territory by the Aboriginal group was largely to the exclusion of other organized societies.
4. The Aboriginal group can demonstrate some continuing current use and occupancy of the land for traditional purposes.
5. The group's Aboriginal title and rights to resource use have not been dealt with by treaty.
6. Aboriginal title has not been eliminated by other lawful means.

The application of the claims acceptance criteria derived from *Baker Lake* has been amended in response to the 1990 Supreme Court judgement in the *Sparrow* case. This decision established a test for the unilateral ending of Aboriginal rights by lawful means. In order to establish that such lawful elimination has occurred, it must be demonstrated that the Crown exercised a clear and plain intention to do so. In response to the court's guidance, the federal government has undertaken a review of claims which have been rejected on the basis of supersession by law to determine if the *Sparrow* test leads to different conclusions concerning acceptability. New claims submissions are being reviewed in accordance with the *Sparrow* decision.

It is generally recognized that government funding is necessary for the research and preparation of claims submissions. The amounts of money required to assemble the documentation needed to substantiate a comprehensive claim are beyond the resources available to most Aboriginal groups.

Research funding is managed by the Research Funding Division of the Policy and Consultation Sector of the Department of Indian Affairs and Northern Development. This Research Funding Division is separate from the Comprehensive Claims Branch, thereby preserving a significant degree of autonomy between the claims preparation process and the federal government's claims negotiation program. Aboriginal groups that wish to prepare a comprehensive claims submission can apply to the Research Funding Division for a research grant. Such requests are evaluated and a decision is made on the merits of each individual case. Once a comprehensive claim is accepted and active negotiations begin, the Aboriginal party is provided with loan funding to support the negotiation process. The loans are repaid after settlement through deductions from the Aboriginal party's financial compensation payments.

Provincial and Territorial Involvement

Federal, provincial and territorial governments and Aboriginal groups are under no legal obligation to negotiate comprehensive claims settlements. As a matter of policy, however, the federal government is committed to resolving the claims of Aboriginal peoples through co-operation and negotiation. Negotiation is the best way to resolve conflicts between Native people and other Canadians, when Aboriginal peoples are claiming rights to lands and resources which are also utilized by others.

In the provinces, most of the lands and resources that are the subject of negotiations and that are required for the settlement of comprehensive claims are owned by the province and are under provincial jurisdiction. Moreover, by establishing certainty of title to lands and resources, claims settlements benefit the provinces. It is the position of the federal government that provincial governments must participate in comprehensive claims negotiations and must contribute to the provision of claims benefits to Aboriginal groups. The federal government is currently negotiating cost-sharing agreements with the governments of British Columbia, Newfoundland and Labrador, and Quebec.

Negotiations with provinces are often complex, reflecting the difficulty of fairly recognizing contributions of land and other non-cash benefits, the lack of clear legal obligations for governments to contribute, and the difficulty of predicting costs before an agreement has actually been negotiated with Aboriginal parties. Canada's goal in negotiating cost-sharing agreements is to provide a solid foundation for claims negotiations so that they can be effective, concluded in a reasonable amount of time, and properly implemented. Federal and provincial governments need to know where their respective responsibilities lie so that their negotiators can be provided with clear mandates.

In the Yukon and Northwest Territories, most lands and resources fall under federal jurisdiction. Nevertheless, territorial governments participate fully in claims negotiations and have made commitments to Aboriginal groups through the claims settlements.

Scope of Negotiations

Comprehensive claims settlements are negotiated to clarify the rights of Aboriginal groups to lands and resources, in a manner that will facilitate their economic growth and contribute to the development of Aboriginal self-government. Settlements are intended to ensure that the interests of Aboriginal groups in resource management and environmental protection are recognized, and that claimants share in the benefits of development.

In order to achieve these objectives, settlement agreements define a wide range of rights and benefits to be exercised and enjoyed by claimant groups. These rights and benefits usually include full ownership of certain lands in the area covered by the settlement; guaranteed wildlife harvesting rights; guaranteed participation in land, water, wildlife and environmental management throughout the settlement area; financial compensation; resource revenue-sharing; specific measures to stimulate economic development; and a role in the management of heritage resources and parks in the settlement area. Settlement rights are constitutionally protected and cannot be altered without the concurrence of the claimant group.

Due to the comprehensive nature of the items negotiated in a comprehensive claims settlement, and the complexity of the issues to be resolved before such a permanent agreement can be signed, negotiations typically take many years. Aboriginal peoples and governments often come to the table with fundamentally different conceptions of the nature of Aboriginal rights and the form which the final settlement should take. These differences must be resolved before settlements can be finalized. Negotiated settlements involve the legitimate rights of both Aboriginal peoples and non-Native peoples; consequently, these agreements cannot be concluded in a hasty or arbitrary fashion.

Some issues, such as arrangements for specific federal programs for Indians, do not belong in comprehensive claims settlements because they call for solutions that can be adjusted rapidly to adapt to changing needs. Since comprehensive claims settlements are constitutionally protected, they cannot offer such flexibility. The resolution of such issues is sought through discussions outside the comprehensive claims negotiation process. Beneficiaries of claims settlements retain their eligibility for normal government programs in accordance with general program criteria established from time to time.

Policy Review

The federal government's Claims Policy Statement of 1973 was clarified and reaffirmed in a 1981 statement on comprehensive claims policy entitled "In All Fairness." During the early 1980s, however, there was growing dissatisfaction among Aboriginal groups with respect to certain aspects of the policy, including the requirement for blanket extinguishment of Aboriginal rights in exchange for defined rights and benefits. This discontent was reflected in the 1983 report of the all-party Special Committee of the House of Commons on Indian Self-Government. It made several recommendations concerning the resolution of land claims.

By 1985, it had become clear that dissatisfaction with the existing policy was interfering with progress at the negotiating table. In July 1985, the Minister of the Department of Indian Affairs and Northern Development appointed a Task Force to Review Comprehensive Claims Policy and asked it to undertake a fundamental review of the current federal policy.

Following extensive consultations with Aboriginal groups, including those with whom claims were being negotiated, and with provincial and territorial governments, non-Aboriginal organizations and individuals, the Task Force released its report in March 1986. Its major recommendations included the broadening of policy objectives and application, the development of alternatives to extinguishment, an increase in the number of items negotiable in a claims settlement, and improvements in the process for negotiating and implementing agreements.

Revised 1986 Comprehensive Land Claims Policy

In December 1986, the Minister of the Department of Indian Affairs and Northern Development announced significant amendments to the Comprehensive Claims Policy, in response to the Task Force's recommendations. Some key elements of the revised policy are as follows:

1. **Exchange of Rights**
It is often stated that the federal government is seeking to end, or extinguish, all Aboriginal rights through claims settlements. This is not the case. The government's objective is to negotiate agreements that will provide certainty of rights to lands and resources in areas where Aboriginal rights have not yet been dealt with by treaty or other legal means. In doing so, the special rights of Aboriginal groups that are agreed upon are set out in constitutionally protected agreements or treaties.

   In order to avoid ambiguity and uncertainty, the federal government seeks confirmation from Aboriginal groups that the rights written down in claims settlements are the full extent of their special rights related to the subjects of the agreements. To accomplish this, Aboriginal groups are asked to relinquish undefined Aboriginal rights which they may have with respect to lands or resources, in favour of the rights and other benefits which are written down in the settlement agreement.

   Under the 1986 Comprehensive Land Claims Policy a claimant group may retain any Aboriginal rights that it may have with respect to the lands it will hold following a settlement, so long as such rights are not inconsistent with the final agreement. The policy also ensures that those Aboriginal rights which are not related to land and resources or to other subjects under negotiation will not be affected by the exchange of rights in the negotiated settlement.

2. **Self-Government**
The policy permits negotiators to include in comprehensive claims agreements a constitutionally entrenched commitment to negotiate self-government agreements. Self-government negotiations may take place at the same time as comprehensive claims negotiations, and are carried out in accordance with federal policy on community self-government negotiations. Negotiated self-government agreements are enacted by separate legislation, but the policy states that they will not receive constitutional protection until there is a general constitutional amendment to that effect.

   In 1991 Canada made a commitment to reconsider its policy on the constitutional protection of self-government agreements negotiated with comprehensive claims should the constitutional process then underway not succeed. It was noted that the positions of provincial and territorial governments would form part of this reconsideration.

3. **Resource Revenue-Sharing**
The 1986 policy makes it clear that the federal government is prepared to negotiate resource revenue-sharing with claimant groups, so they may share in the benefits of non-renewable resource development. A claimant group may receive a share of federal royalties derived from resource extraction throughout the area covered by the group's settlement agreement.

   Resource revenue-sharing arrangements do not imply that claimant groups have resource ownership rights. The federal or provincial government will be responsible for resource revenue instruments and must maintain its ability to adjust the fiscal regime. Existing or potential resource revenue-sharing arrangements arising out of comprehensive claims negotiations will be taken into account in any federal-territorial negotiations on resource revenues.

4. **Environmental Management**
The 1981 policy provided for enhanced Aboriginal involvement in environmental management through membership on advisory committees, boards and other similar bodies. The 1986 policy states that Aboriginal interests in environmental matters, particularly as these relate to wildlife management and the use of land and water, may also be addressed through participation in government bodies that have decision-making powers. Such arrangements must recognize that government has an overriding obligation to ensure resource conservation, to protect the interests of all users, to respect international agreements, and to manage renewable resources within its jurisdiction.

5. **Offshore Areas**
The 1986 policy statement clarified federal policy by noting that, if an Aboriginal group's traditional activities have extended to offshore areas, their claim settlement may include offshore wildlife harvesting rights. To the extent possible, negotiations are to be conducted in accordance with the same principles which are applied to land areas. Participation in environmental management regimes and resource-revenue sharing arrangements may also be negotiated with respect to offshore areas.

6. **Interim Measures**
The 1986 policy provides that appropriate interim measures may be established to protect

the interests of a claimant group while its claim is being negotiated.

7. **Implementation Plans**
The 1986 policy states that, in order for final agreements with claimant groups to be ratified by the federal government, they must be accompanied by implementation plans outlining the obligations of all parties. This will ensure efficient and timely implementation of the various elements of a settlement agreement.

Expansion of the Comprehensive Claims Process as Part of the Native Agenda

The fair and timely resolution of comprehensive clams is a priority of the Government of Canada. On September 25, 1990, the Prime Minister announced that, as part of a federal Native Agenda to address issues of concern to Aboriginal peoples in Canada, the process for the negotiation of comprehensive claims would be expanded. The previous six-claim limit on the number of negotiations which could be undertaken at one time was eliminated.

. . . .

SPECIFIC CLAIMS

Objectives of the Specific Claims Policy

The government's primary objective with respect to specific claims is to discharge its lawful obligation to Indian bands.

The government recognizes claims by Indian bands that disclose an outstanding lawful obligation — an obligation on the part of the federal government derived from the law. A lawful obligation may arise in any of the following circumstances:

- the non-fulfilment of a treaty or other agreement between Indians and the Crown;
- a breach of an obligation under the *Indian Act* or other statutes pertaining to Indians and the regulations under them;
- a breach of obligation arising out of government administration of Indian funds or other assets; and
- an illegal disposition of Indian land.

The government also acknowledges claims arising from the following circumstances:

- failure to provide compensation for reserve lands taken or damaged by the federal government or any of its agencies under authority; and
- fraud in connection with the acquisition or disposition of Indian reserve land by employees or agents of the federal government where the fraud can be clearly demonstrated.

Examples of specific claims:

- The Big Cove Indian Band in New Brunswick asserted that the sale of 202 hectares from the reserve did not follow the conditions of the band's surrender of lands in 1879, and submitted its claim in 1973. The claim was settled, and cash compensation of $3.2 million was paid to the band in 1988.
- The Lower Kootenay Indian Band asserted that 972 hectares of land promised in 1908 by Canada were never set apart as a reserve. The claim was submitted in 1984, and settled in 1989 for $4.7 million.

Treaty Land Entitlement (TLE) claims represent a subset of specific claims. They relate to a group of treaties that were signed with Indian bands, mainly in the prairie provinces. Under these treaties the size of a reserve was based on a number of hectares (usually 51) per person in the band. The population of each band was to be determined and the reserve land fixed according to surveys. However, not all band populations and lands were measured promptly or accurately. As a result, some bands have claimed outstanding entitlement for those band members who were not originally counted. Such claims are categorized as TLE claims.

The 1981 Policy Review

In 1973 the Department of Indian Affairs and Northern Development created the Office of Claims Negotiation, subsequently the Office of Native Claims. One negotiator with limited support staff was assigned to resolve both comprehensive and specific claims.

By 1981, only 12 of over 70 specific claims accepted for negotiation had been settled. Another 80 claims submissions still awaited a decision on whether they would be accepted for negotiation at all. Frustrations grew. A review of the policy and process was undertaken and a number of changes were announced in 1981.

As a result of the review, the criteria for acceptance of specific claims were expanded and new criteria for compensation were developed. Of particular note was the government's decision *not* to apply statutes of limitation or the doctrine of laches. Limitation statutes are federal or provincial statutes which prohibit taking a claim before the courts after a certain prescribed length of time. The doctrine of laches is a common law rule whereby the courts will not hear a claim if the claimant has, in the opinion of the court, waited too long to bring forward the claim. These defences would disqualify many Indian specific claims.

A major objective of the 1981 review was to articulate more clearly the objectives and criteria of the Specific Claims Policy. These were published in "Outstanding Business," a DIAND publication.

As a result of the 1981 review a separate branch was set up to deal with specific claims only. Nonetheless, by the end of the decade only three or four negotiated settlements were being achieved each year — fewer than the number of claims being submitted, with the result that the backlog of unresolved specific claims kept growing. The total settlement budget of approximately $15 million a year did not seem to be a major constraint, since it was not fully utilized in some years. Rather, the complexity and labour intensiveness of the process were repeatedly under-estimated, so that the process within both DIAND and the Department of Justice tended to be understaffed.

Three Main Criticisms

While the 1981 review resulted in some improvements, it fell short of responding to all concerns. Indians continued to argue that the Specific Claims program was:

1. too slow, with the result that too few claims were settled;
2. inherently unfair because of the government's multiple role as trustee of the Indian people, defender of the Crown's interests and judge for each claim submitted; and
3. overly restrictive in its acceptance criteria, thus excluding legitimate claims.

Minister's Meetings with Chiefs' Committee on Specific Claims

On October 10 and 11, 1990, the Minister of the Department of Indian Affairs and Northern Development met with 20 Indian leaders to discuss how to improve the process for settlement of specific claims. The Indian participants proposed that a working group be established and that Indian leaders across Canada be canvassed for their views. Chief Clarence T. Jules of the Kamloops Indian Band and Mr. Harry LaForme, then Commissioner of the Indian Commission of Ontario, were chosen to co-chair this group, which came to be known as the Chiefs' Committee on Specific Claims. On December 14, 1990, the co-chairs presented the Minister with a report which had already been approved by a Special Assembly of the Assembly of First Nations, the Chiefs of Ontario and the Indian Association of Alberta. The Chiefs' Committee recommended that:

1. substantially more resources, both human and financial, be dedicated to the settlement of specific claims;
2. an independent authority be established so that specific claims could be dealt with more fairly;
3. a joint Indian/government task force be established to analyze and make recommendations on policy and process measures; and
4. the processing of claims in the existing system be accelerated and not delayed because of implementing new measures.

Government Response

In January 1991, the Minister of the Department of Indian Affairs and Northern Development met with First Nations representatives in Toronto to discuss the recommendations in their report. The Prime Minister had already announced in September 1990, that the resolution of claims would be one of the four pillars of Canada's Native Agenda, the government's plan of action "to preserve the special place of First citizens in this country."

On April 23, 1991, the Prime Minister announced the new $355 million federal government initiative on Specific Claims to resolve claims more quickly, efficiently and fairly. The initiative involved the following major components.

1. **Increased Resources**
   Funds for payment under settlements were quadrupled from $15 million to $60 million annually. Additional staff were provided to DIAND and the Department of Justice to speed up the processing of claims.

2. **Administrative Policy Adjustments**
   As an immediate measure, the following administrative policy adjustments were approved in order to speed up the process.
   - The amount that the Minister of the Department of Indian Affairs and Northern Development is authorized to approve for payments of settlements without Treasury Board authority was increased from $1 million to $7 million. This change has enabled

departmental officials to forego the preparation and processing of a Treasury Board submission for settlements under $7 million.

- A "fast track" process was set up to resolve smaller claims still more quickly and efficiently. About one third of the claims settled to date have involved $500,000 or less. These claims accounted for less than two percent of total settlement funds paid to date.
- There is no limit to the number of claims that can be negotiated at any one time.
- Legal costs of bands no longer require the review and approval of the Department of Justice. Instead, legal costs are to be treated in the same manner as other negotiating costs. The negotiator, with the participation of the Department of Justice, will determine with the band at the outset of negotiations the legal fees which the government will be prepared to support.

3. **Pre-Confederation Claims**

The 1982 guideline restricting acceptance for negotiation of pre-Confederation claims was revoked. The 1982 guidelines excluded consideration of any claim based on events before 1867, "unless the federal government specifically assumed responsibility therefor."

As with all other specific claims, pre-Confederation claims must still demonstrate a lawful obligation of the government.

4. **The Indian Specific Claims Commission**

It was agreed that an independent authority be established to review specific claims.

The purpose of the Commission is:

- to review disputes between claimant bands and the government to determine whether, under the terms of the policy, a lawful obligation has been established and whether the compensation criteria which are applicable are the most appropriate; and
- when both parties agree, to assist the government and claimant bands in arranging mediation on any aspect of the negotiations.

After consideration of an appeal, the Commission makes its recommendations to the parties involved, including reports from time to time to the Governor in Council. Settlement amounts are still negotiated between the band and the government, and not by the Commission.

It is important to note that the Commission is transitional in nature, a feature agreed to by both the Chiefs' Committee on Specific Claims and the federal government.

5. **The Joint First Nation/Government Working Group (JWG) on Specific Claims Policy and Process**

In addition to the Commission, the Joint First Nations/Government Working Group on Specific Claims was created to consider criticism that the existing Specific Claims Policy and process are overly restrictive. The first meeting of the JWG was held in February 1992. The JWG will be reviewing and making recommendations on all the existing acceptance and compensation criteria upon which the Specific Claims Policy is based. The JWG will also make recommendations on the design of a dispute resolution system or process for resolving such claims between the federal government and First Nations. The group's recommendations will encompass the future evolution of the Indian Specific Claims Commission.

An "Evaluation Study on Claims" is presently underway. Objectives of this study are to examine claims that have been settled and those where negotiations have broken off in order to determine:

- strengths and weaknesses of the negotiation process and possible ways to improve this process;
- any trends or patterns which may have caused delays and avoidable aggravations in the negotiation process;
- the extent to which settlements have been implemented as promised or expected (e.g., were trust accounts established on time, and were intentions to establish reserves followed up in a timely fashion?);
- the effects of settlements, including the extent to which the specific claims settlements ameliorated the felt grievances of the bands; and
- recommendations on how the Specific Claims Policy and process could be improved.

Other studies include reviews of federal and provincial legislation having a bearing on claims and of alternative dispute resolution mechanisms.

A protocol setting out the agreed objectives of the JWG and describing the nature of the working relationship between the two parties was signed by the Minister and the National Chief of the Assembly of First Nations. Under this protocol, the JWG is required to provide quarterly progress reports to the Minister and the National Chief. A final report is expected by June 1993.

6. **Funding for Bands to do Research on Specific Claims**
The Department of Indian Affairs and Northern Development administers a contribution and loan program to assist Native participants in the specific claims process. In the fiscal year 1992/93, $7.8 million in contributions was available for the research, development and presentation of claims. The largest proportion of this amount was allocated to provincial Indian associations working on behalf of their member bands. In addition, loan funds totalling $5.4 million per year are available to assist claimant bands in negotiating the settlement of their specific claims.
The Research Funding Division in the Policy and Consultation Sector of DIAND is responsible for specific claims funding, as it is for comprehensive claims. The issue of how specific claims research funding should be allocated and how the research organizations should be evaluated will be a subject for discussion by the JWG.

. . . .

OTHER CLAIMS

There are a number of legitimate Native grievances that fall within the spirit of the comprehensive and specific claims policies, but do not meet the strict acceptance criteria of these two programs. These claims have been referred to as claims of a third kind. A number of these claims have been accepted by DIAND as requiring resolution, and the resolution of many of these grievances is being sought through negotiated settlements.

There appear to be two basic types of claims not covered by the existing program. Claims relating to Aboriginal title are similar to comprehensive claims: generally these involve situations where Aboriginal title has been lawfully dealt with, but where the process was not consistent with the reasonable standards of the time. The other type are situations relating to the Crown's responsibility to Native peoples which do not meet the criteria of the Specific Claims program, but which government believes should be dealt with on some other basis.

Claims Relating to Aboriginal Title

The Comprehensive Claims program does not accept claims where Aboriginal title has been dealt with by treaty or other legal means. However, in certain circumstances, even though the Aboriginal title was dealt with legally, the circumstances of that process may give rise to legitimate concerns by the Aboriginal group and government. For example, in the Northwest Territories, the federal government has undertaken negotiations with First Nations in the Treaty 11 and Treaty 8 areas where some of the terms of the treaties had not been fulfilled and the provisions of the treaties did not seem well suited to the North. In Ontario, Canada has joined the negotiations between the Golden Lake Algonquins and the Government of Ontario. The Golden Lake Algonquins claim that they never signed any of the treaties that cover their traditional lands, did not receive any treaty benefits, and are linguistically and culturally distinct from those First Nations that did sign the treaties. Canada and Ontario have agreed to share equally the costs of settlement of this claim.

Claims Relating to Federal Government Responsibility

The Specific Claims program does not accept claims where actions have not been in breach of the federal government's lawful obligations. However, in such cases there may, nonetheless, be legitimate grievances that could be resolved in a negotiated settlement. An example is the situation at Kanesatake, where a religious order disposed of land it owned but which was used by the Mohawk. Even though the case went to the highest court in the land and the court found against the Indians, the situation was considered to be unfair by government and a negotiated resolution is being pursued.

Several other claims of this kind have been received by the department, and detailed research is underway on each to determine if a legitimate grievance exists that could be settled by negotiation.

(c) Land Provisions of Modern Treaties†

See **Chapter 11, Part 7.**

JAMES BAY AND NORTHERN QUEBEC AGREEMENT AND THE NORTHEASTERN QUEBEC AGREEMENT[1]

While the James Bay and Northern Quebec Agreement (JBNQA) and subsequent Northeastern Quebec Agreement (NEQA) were essentially out-of-court settlements designed to resolve conflicts over construction of the James Bay hydroelectric development project (announced in 1971), they are regarded as Canada's first modern treaties. Signed in 1975 and 1978 respectively, these agreements have also come to be viewed as the benchmark for subsequent comprehensive claims agreements. Signatories to JBNQA were the Grand Council of the Crees of Quebec (representing eight Cree communities), the Northern Quebec Inuit Association, the government of Canada, the government of Quebec, the Quebec Hydro-Electric Commission (Hydro Quebec), the James Bay Energy Corporation, and the James Bay Development Corporation. NEQA was entered into between the same non-Aboriginal parties and the Naskapi Band of Quebec (Kobac Naskapi-Aeyouch), amending JBNQA.

The territory covered by JBNQA and NEQA is a vast area of northern Quebec amounting to roughly 410,000 square miles (1,061,900 square kilometres). The James Bay Crees and Inuit of Nunavik (northern Quebec) are allocated an area of 'primary interest' (basically their traditional land use areas or traditional territories) and an area of 'common interest' (overlapping land use area). With respect to the James Bay Crees, their area of primary interest amounts to some 23,510 square miles (35,000 square kilometres) south of the 55th parallel. Land administration is the responsibility of two public institutions: the James Bay Regional Council (JBRC) and the James Bay Development Corporation (JBDC). JBRC, made up of equal representation from the Crees, Naskapi and province of Quebec, has a legislative mandate from the province for purposes of municipal administration on Category II lands. The development corporation was created by Quebec to promote, plan and co-ordinate development in the territory. The Cree regional authority, composed of all corporations with jurisdiction over Category I lands, was also established. The authority represents Cree interests, and co-ordinates and administers all programs and services on Category I lands, if the communities so delegate.

The portion north of the 55th parallel, known as the Inuit area of primary interest, amounts to approximately 21,616 square miles (56,000 square kilometres). Administration of this region is undertaken by a public body, the Kativik regional government, and is thus referred to as the Kativik region. The Kativik regional government is responsible for land use planning, the environmental assessment procedures pursuant to the agreement, and the provision of public services.

Under JBNQA and NEQA, each Aboriginal party received specific rights to and interests in lands and resources within their primary interest area, which was divided into Category I (divided into IA and IB lands in the Cree region), II and III lands. Category I lands are for the exclusive use and benefit of the Aboriginal signatories. Each James Bay Cree community received approximately 2,158 square miles (approximately 5,589 square kilometres) of lands surrounding or adjacent to the community. Each Inuit community received title to an area of 3,130 square miles (approximately 8,106 square kilometres) allocated in a similar fashion. Although Quebec retained mineral rights, the Aboriginal beneficiaries were granted exclusive use of forest resources and harvesting.

Within the Cree region, title to Category IA lands is held by the Crown for Quebec. But in all other respects such lands are subject to the jurisdiction of the federal government, which is constitutionally responsible for their administration. Category IA lands are subject to the regime established under the *Cree-Naskapi (of Quebec) Act*. Category IB lands are fully transferred to the Aboriginal community landholding corporation and are not subject to

† Royal Commission on Aboriginal Peoples, "Land and Resources: Background", *Report of Royal Commission on Aboriginal Peoples: Resturing the Relationship*, vol. 2, chap. 4, Appenidx 4A at 720–32. Reproduced with the permission of the Minister of Public Works and Government Services, 2004, and courtesy of the Privy Council Office.

federal authority. The *Cree Villages and the Naskapi Village Act* makes Category IB land into village municipalities and established the Aboriginal municipal corporations whose make-up is identical to the landholding community corporations referred to above. Within the Inuit or Kativik region, Category I lands are not subdivided into IA or IB. The *Act respecting Northern Villages and the Kativik Regional Government* provides for local and regional organizational structures. Northern municipalities are established in Category I lands. Each municipal council is also responsible for administration of Category II lands.

With respect to the James Bay Crees, Category II lands comprise 25,130 square miles (approximately 65,086 square kilometres) south of the 55th parallel of latitude. Of this amount, Inuit have rights to 231 square miles (some 598.29 square kilometres). Category II lands for Inuit communities amount to 35,000 square miles (approximately 90,650 square kilometres) north of the 55th parallel and include a small allocation for the Whapmagoostui Crees. Within the Inuit allocation, 1,600 square miles (approximately 4,144 square kilometres) was later provided for the Naskapi band pursuant to NEQA. The Aboriginal parties have exclusive hunting, fishing and trapping rights, but Category II lands are also accessible by others for development purposes. In the event that development takes precedence over Aboriginal harvesting, the lands are to be replaced. Quebec retained title to and jurisdiction over these lands, although the Aboriginal communities share in land and resource management for hunting, fishing and trapping; tourism development; and forestry.

Category III lands, which make up the balance of land within the territory, are a unique type of provincial public lands. Both Aboriginal and non-Aboriginal people may hunt and fish on these lands, although the Aboriginal beneficiaries have exclusive rights to certain species (except migratory birds and marine animals). The Aboriginal parties also participate in land administration and development. The province, the James Bay Energy Corporation, Hydro Quebec, and the James Bay Development Corporation have specific rights to develop resources on Category III lands. However, depending on the jurisdictional nature of the project, either the federal or the provincial government must undertake an environmental impact assessment. (The exact meaning of this last provision has been, and continues to be, extremely contentious given Quebec's hydro development plans).

With respect to Category I lands, title is owned collectively by the appropriate Aboriginal government authority. The Cree and Naskapi governments exercise full authority with respect to local government, and the administration and management of lands, pursuant to the *James Bay and Northern Quebec Native Claims Settlement Act* and the *Cree-Naskapi (of Quebec) Act*. Local and regional administrative structures governing James Bay are parallel to municipalities in southern Quebec in terms of powers and authority. The powers of local government with respect to Category I lands include land and resource use and zoning; preparing land use plans; setting rules governing the use of lands and resources; regulating the construction and use of buildings; environmental protection; and hunting, fishing and trapping. However, with respect to the latter, wildlife harvesting by-laws must be submitted to the co-ordinating committee established pursuant to JBNQA, and the responsible minister can disallow them. (See the JBNQA wildlife regime, set out in Appendix 4B, for details.) No Category I lands can be sold or otherwise ceded except to the province.

The Aboriginal parties to the agreements also obtained the right of first refusal for outfitting within Category III lands for a period of 30 years from the execution of the agreements. However, the Aboriginal parties were not able to exercise this right in at least three non-Aboriginal applications out of every 10. The hunting, fishing and trapping co-ordinating committee established following the agreement is charged with overseeing this provision. (For details of the committee, see Appendix 4B.) In addition to compensation paid by Canada and Quebec, the beneficiaries were also entitled to a 25 per cent royalty share in provincial duties flowing from other forms of development, for example, mining and forestry, although this was later converted to a cash payment.

In addition to the types of access noted above, access is granted to Aboriginal lands and waters for public purposes. Government agents are authorized to enter Category I lands for the purpose of delivering public programs or services, and constructing or operating a public work or utility.

INUVIALUIT FINAL AGREEMENT

The 1984 comprehensive claims agreement between the Committee for Original Peoples' Entitlement (representing Inuvialuit of the western Arctic) and Canada transferred title to about 91,000 square kilometres to Inuvialuit. Of that amount, referred to as the Inuvialuit settlement region (ISR), Inuvialuit hold full surface and subsurface rights to approximately 12,800 square kilometres (Category A) and the surface rights to sand and gravel over another

78,200 square kilometres (Category B). Category A lands were distributed in blocks of approximately 1,700 square kilometres more or less near each of the six communities within the ISR. Fee simple absolute title includes the beds of all lakes, rivers and other water bodies found in Inuvialuit lands, although the Crown retains ownership of all waters in the ISR. Finally, a single block of approximately 2,000 square kilometres of fee simple absolute title in Cape Bathurst was conveyed. Title is collectively owned and managed through the Inuvialuit Land Corporation, a division of the Inuvialuit Regional Corporation.

The agreement also creates a special conservation regime governing the area between Alaska, the Yukon, and the Northwest Territories (known as the "Yukon North Slope"), including a new national park covering the western portion, as well as the creation of a territorial park (Herschel Island Park). Inuvialuit enjoy harvesting rights within both areas and participate in management activities. The balance of Inuvialuit harvesting and management rights with respect to lands and resources throughout ISR are set out in Appendix 4B.

Public right of access is subject to conditions that protect the area from damage, mischief and interference. The public has access to Inuvialuit lands without prior notice in case of emergency or to reach adjacent lands. The public may also enter Inuvialuit lands for recreation purposes if they receive the consent of Inuvialuit. Specifically, Inuvialuit agreed to allow the public to fish commercially or for sport on lands that do not surround the six communities, provided that individuals are registered with the appropriate authority (hunters and trappers committee or government agency). Government agents can enter Inuvialuit lands and use natural resources incidental to such access when delivering and managing programs and projects. Similarly, the government retained the right to manage fisheries on Category B lands. Further, the department of national defence has access for military exercises but must first negotiate an arrangement, including compensation.

Private access to Inuvialuit lands was granted so that non-Inuvialuit lands could be reached. As well, those holding resource rights on Inuvialuit lands are entitled to exercise such rights without alteration or interruption until such licences or permits terminate. In return, Canada remits to Inuvialuit any rents, fees or other payments from such third-party resource rights. With respect to future development, if such access requires a permanent right of way, developers are required to deal directly with the Inuvialuit administration commission and negotiate participation agreements, including rents for surface use, compensation and other benefits. With respect to sand and gravel on Inuvialuit lands, Inuvialuit agreed to reserve supplies to meet public community needs, direct private needs and, as a third priority, government projects. Removal of such materials requires a licence from or concessions to the Inuvialuit land administration.

Inuvialuit lands can be expropriated only by a federal cabinet order, subject to their receiving suitable alternative lands and cash compensation for loss of use and actual harvesting loss. Any disagreement concerning expropriated lands can be referred to arbitration (set out in the agreement). Similarly, Inuvialuit agreed to enter into negotiations in the event that any level of government requires Inuvialuit lands to meet public needs.

NUNAVUT FINAL AGREEMENT

The 1993 comprehensive claims agreement between Inuit of the Nunavut settlement area (as represented by the Tungavik Federation of Nunavut) and Canada is the first to create a new territory within Canada (Nunavut), which will be publicly governed with its own legislative assembly separate from the remainder of the Northwest Territories. Article 3 of the agreement sets out the boundaries of the new territory. Area A is a portion of the Arctic islands and the mainland of the eastern Arctic (including adjacent marine areas). Area B includes the Belcher Islands and associated islands, and adjacent marine areas in Hudson Bay. In addition, the area includes separate zones of waters and land-fast ice. Zone I comprises the waters north of the 61st parallel, subject to Canadian jurisdiction, seaward of the territorial sea boundary, and Zone II refers to those waters of James Bay, Hudson Bay and Hudson Strait that are not part of another land claim settlement or government jurisdiction. The outer land-fast ice zone is also defined in the agreement.

Article 19 of the agreement lays out Inuit rights to land within the new public territory (which is also divided into regional land use areas). 'Inuit-owned lands' are intended to provide Inuit with rights that promote economic self-sufficiency consistent with Inuit social and cultural needs and aspirations. Lands will therefore be selected near communities, include significant sites, and incorporate land use activities and patterns. Inuit-owned lands will take one of two forms: fee simple including surface and subsurface rights, and fee simple excluding surface and subsurface rights. Generally, Inuit title includes water except where water forms a boundary or is transboundary. There will be no Inuit lands in marine areas. Title will be owned collectively and vested in a designated Inuit organization (DIO), which is either Tungavik or a designated regional Inuit organization. Inuit title can be transferred only to another DIO, or in the case of land within a municipality, to Canada, the territorial government or a municipal corporation. The agreement also makes provisions for the future granting of certain Inuit lands to government for the purposes of public easements and the north warning system.

Quantum is as follows:

- North Baffin land use region: 86,060 square kilometres, consisting of at least 6,010 square kilometres in fee simple including surface and subsurface rights (first form), and approximately 80,050 square kilometres in fee simple excluding rights to surface and subsurface resources (second form);
- South Baffin Island land use region: 64,745 square kilometres, consisting of at least 4,480 square kilometres in the first form, and approximately 60,265 square kilometres in the second form of title;
- Keewatin Island land use region: 95,540 square kilometres, consisting of at least 12,845 square kilometres in the first form, and approximately 82,695 square kilometres in the second form;
- Kitikmeot East land use region: 36,970 square kilometres, consisting of at least 1,500 square kilometres in the first form, and approximately 35,470 square kilometres in the second form;
- Kitikmeot West land use region: at least 66,390 square kilometres, consisting of at least 9,645 square kilometres in the first form, and approximately 56,745 square kilometres in the second form;
- Sanikiluaq land use region: at least 2,486 square kilometres in the second form.

The agreement also establishes the following parks: Auyuittuq National Park (from a park reserve), Ellesmere Island National Park, a national park on north Baffin, and a national park on Wager Bay (the last is subject to the exchange of Inuit-owned lands). Establishment of territorial parks also will be considered. Inuit will be involved in the planning and management of parks through the negotiation of Inuit impact and benefits agreement (HBA). (See discussion of Auyuittuq National Park Reserve, Baffin Island, in Appendix 4B, for discussion of HBA.)

Inuit will have free and unrestricted access to harvest within the entire settlement area, including Category I and II lands, Crown lands, parks and conservation areas. As well, subject to Canada's rights and jurisdiction, Inuit will have the right to continue to use and harvest for domestic consumption in open waters in the outer land-fast ice zone. (See Appendix 4B for details of harvesting rights and management processes.) This right is subject to safety, conservation principles, bilateral agreements and land use activity. The last two conditions are rather expansive, as they refer to lands that are dedicated to military activity, owned in fee simple, granted in fee simple following ratification (if less than one square mile or 2.6 square kilometres) subject to an agreement for sale, or subject to a surface lease. However, renewal of surface leases is subject to Inuit rights. Pre-existing commercial rights to minerals on Inuit-owned lands continue following ratification of the agreement.

Designated Inuit organizations will have the right of first refusal throughout Nunavut to the following ventures: new lodges (sports or naturalist); wildlife propagation, cultivation or husbandry enterprises; and marketing wildlife (including parts and products). However, in all cases, if a DIO exercises this right and fails to establish an enterprise without just cause, the right may be declared by government as having lapsed.

Article 21 of the agreement outlines access rights to Inuit-owned lands within the Nunavut settlement area. Generally, non-Inuit may enter, cross or remain on Inuit-owned lands only with the consent of the appropriate DIO. All entry and access is subject to conditions to protect against damage, mischief and significant interference. The public may enter lands for emergency purposes, travel and recreation (including harvesting subject to the laws of general application). Public harvesting rights, however, can be removed where the DIO requires exclusive possession. Government agents can enter Inuit-owned lands to carry out public services, wildlife management and research (subject to the appropriate management board's approval), and the department of national defence can enter Inuit lands only after conclusion of an agreement with the DIO. In addition to the conditions stated earlier, third parties can enter Inuit lands for mineral exploration and/or development only with the consent of the DIO. Such consent may involve compensation.

Authorized agencies can expropriate Inuit-owned lands. However, there must first be an attempt to negotiate an agreement for the use or transfer of the land, and, failing that, public hearings must be held. Approval must be obtained from either the federal cabinet or territorial government, and compensation must be paid (as determined by the surface rights board created pursuant to the agreement).

UMBRELLA FINAL AGREEMENT BETWEEN COUNCIL FOR YUKON INDIANS, THE GOVERNMENT OF CANADA AND THE GOVERNMENT OF THE YUKON

The 1993 umbrella agreement between the Council for Yukon Indians (now the Council for Yukon First Nations) and the federal and territorial governments sets out the substantive benefits and processes that are to form the basis for individually negotiated First Nation claims agreements.[2] Four individual First Nation agreements were signed in 1994 with the Vuntut Gwich'in First Nation; the First Nation of Na-cho Ny'a'k Dun; the Teslin Tlingit Council; and the Champagne and Aishihik First Nations. Chapters 4, 5, 6 and 9 of the umbrella agreement contain the settlement lands provisions entailing quantum, how lands will be owned and managed by the communities, and the conditions for access to settlement lands.

Three different categories of lands are detailed — Category A, Category B and fee simple. Waters and water beds within the boundaries of a parcel form part of the settlement land. For Category A lands, Yukon First Nations will have rights equivalent to fee simple title to the surface of the land and full fee simple title to the subsurface. For Category B lands, First Nations will have rights equivalent to fee simple surface title only. Fee simple settlement lands will be the same as fee simple title as it is held by individuals. Note that the wording "equivalent to fee simple" for Category A and B lands was used intentionally in an attempt to avoid extinguishing any Aboriginal rights the First Nations may have. (In the preamble to the agreement, the parties acknowledge explicitly that First Nations wish to retain Aboriginal rights and titles with respect to settlement lands.) However, title to Category A and B lands is subject to pre-existing rights (less than fee simple); interests for the use of land or resources, and any renewals or replacements; and any right of way or easement contained in individual First Nation agreements. In return, any rents received by government are payable to the First Nation. Further, the First Nations are free to divest, reacquire, or deregister Category A and B lands. In doing so, the ceding, release and surrender of any Aboriginal claims or title or interest in the land is not affected.

The total amount of land for the requirements of all Yukon First Nations shall not exceed 16,000 square miles (41,439.81 square kilometres). That amount shall not contain more than 10,000 square miles (25,899.88 square kilometres) of Category A settlement land. Each First Nation agreement will set out whether existing reserves are to retain that status or to be selected as settlement land, thereby ceasing to be a reserve. As well, Yukon First Nations can convert land previously set aside into settlement land.[3] If the total amount of reserves and land set aside retained as settlement land by all the Yukon First Nations is less than 60 square miles (approximately 163 square kilometres), they will be able to select an additional amount of settlement land up to 60 square miles in total (see Table 1).

Chapter 10 of the agreement provides for the establishment of an additional category of lands[,] 'special management areas', which are for conservation purposes. Agreements outlining the rights and benefits of affected First Nations within such areas (that is, harvesting, participation in economic opportunities) are to be established.

First Nations will have the power to enact bylaws for use and occupancy, including setting rents or fees for third-party land use, land management, and establishing and keeping land records. Similarly, Yukon First Nations will have the authority to manage, administer, allocate and regulate the harvesting rights of Yukon Indians on settlement lands. (Refer to Yukon Umbrella Final Agreement, Appendix 4B, for details.)

In selecting lands, several restrictions apply. Privately owned land, or land that is subject to an agreement for sale or a lease, is not available, unless the owner consents. Likewise, leased land, land occupied or transferred to a federal, territorial or municipal government, is not available. Finally, land with public highways or rights of way or that forms a jurisdictional border is not available for selection.

Public right of access is subject to conditions to prevent damage, mischief and interference. Anyone has the right to enter settlement land in case of emergency. Anyone has the right to enter settlement land without the consent of the First Nation to reach adjacent non-settlement land for commercial or recreational purposes. Those holding licences can enter settlement land to exercise rights granted by such permits. Government agents can enter settlement land and use natural resources incidental to such access in order to deliver and manage programs and projects. Government will also retain fisheries management on Category B lands. Further, the department of national defence has the right of access to

TABLE 1: ALLOCATION OF SETTLEMENT LAND AMOUNT

	Category A		Fee Simple and Category B		Total		Allocation under 4.3.4	
	1	2	1	2	1	2	1	2
Carcross/Tagish First Nation	400	1,036	200	518	600	1,554	2.90	8
Champagne and Aishihik First Nations	475	1,230	450	1,165	925	2,396	12.17	32
Dawson First Nation	600	1,554	400	1,036	1,000	2,590	3.29	9
Kluane First Nation	250	648	100	259	350	907	2.63	7
Kwalin Dun First Nation	250	648	150	389	400	1,036	2.62	7
Liard First Nation	930	2,409	900	2,331	1,830	4,740	2.63	7
Little Salmon/Carmacks First Nation	600	1,555	400	1,036	1,000	2,590	3.27	8
First Nation of Nacho Nyak Dun	930	2,409	900	2,331	1,830	4,740	3.58	9
Ross River Dena Council	920	2,383	900	2,331	1,830	4,714	2.75	7
Selkirk First Nation	930	2,409	900	2,331	1,830	4,740	2.62	7
Ta'an Kwach'an Council	150	389	150	389	300	777	3.21	8
Teslin Tlingit Council	475	1,230	450	1,165	925	2,396	12.88	33
Vuntut Gwich'in First Nation	2,990	7,744	—	—	2,990	7,744	2.74	7
White River First Nation	100	259	100	259	200	518	2.72	7
TOTAL	10,000	25,900	6,000	15,540	16,000	41,440	60.00	155

Notes:
1 = Square miles.
2 = Approximate square kilometres (converted from square miles and rounded).

Source: Department of Indian Affairs and Northern Development, Umbrella Final Agreement Between the Government of Canada, the Council for Yukon Indians and the Government of the Yukon (1993), Chapter 9, Schedule A, p. 85.

undeveloped settlement land for military manoeuvres with the consent of the First Nation or, failing that, an order from the surface rights board established pursuant to the agreement.

On Category A lands, the public will need permission to hunt, except on defined waterfront rights of way. Similarly, those seeking to conduct mineral exploration will need the permission of the First Nation to look for minerals and will be required to negotiate in order to develop any mines. On category B lands, public access for non-commercial hunting will be permitted. Access to the subsurface for mining exploration and development will generally require the developer to negotiate an agreement outlining terms and conditions (with the First Nation or the surface rights board).

Although the parties recognize that settlement land is fundamental to the Yukon First Nations and therefore agree that expropriation should be avoided, authorized agencies can in fact expropriate settlement land. However, first there must be an attempt to negotiate an agreement for the use or transfer of the land, and failing that, public hearings must be held. Approval must be obtained from either the federal cabinet or territorial government, and compensation must be paid (as determined by the surface rights board).

THE SAHTU DENE AND METIS COMPREHENSIVE LAND CLAIM AGREEMENT AND THE GWICH'IN COMPREHENSIVE LAND CLAIM AGREEMENT

In August 1993 Canada signed a comprehensive claims agreement with the Sahtu (Slavey, Hare and Mountain Dene) and the Métis of the Sahtu region of the Northwest Territories. A separate comprehensive claims agreement was signed with the Gwich'in Tribal Council on behalf of the Gwich'in (also known as the Loucheaux) of the Northwest Territories and the Yukon in April 1992. Although the

Sahtu Dene and the Gwich'in are signatories of Treaty 11, and Metis people of the region received cash grants in return for surrendering their claims, the federal government agreed to enter into comprehensive claims negotiations with these nations because of unresolved differences with respect to the interpretation of their Aboriginal and treaty rights. The land provisions (Chapter 19 of the Sahtu Dene and Métis agreement and Chapter 18 of the Gwich'in agreement) are presented together here, as they are essentially identical.

The Gwich'in are to receive 16,264 square kilometres of lands in fee simple, except for subsurface and surface mines and mineral deposits and the right to develop those deposits. The Gwich'in are to obtain fee simple title, including subsurface and surface rights, to an additional 4,299 square kilometres; another 1,755 square kilometres of lands in fee simple, including mines and minerals; and a final 93 square kilometre block with title only to the subsurface mines and minerals, subject to existing rights and interests (the last parcel is known as "the Aklavik Lands"). The Sahtu Dene and Metis people are to receive title collectively to 39,624 square kilometres of lands in fee simple, without subsurface and surface rights to mines and mineral deposits. An additional 1,813 square kilometres in fee simple land, including subsurface and surface rights to minerals and mines, is to be transferred.

Both Gwich'in and Sahtu title will include ownership of those portions of the beds of inland waters contained within land boundaries, but will exclude boundary waters. The total quantum includes a category referred to as 'municipal lands', which are to provide the communities with local government boundaries for residential, commercial, industrial and traditional purposes. These lands may be conveyed to any person and if done, cease to be settlement lands. Such lands may also be made available for public purposes, such as road corridors, in return for compensation. With the exception of municipal lands, which are subject to real property taxation, no other settlement lands are subject to federal, territorial or municipal taxation.

The selection processes contained in the agreements outline the various criteria guiding the actual selection of lands. Noteworthy among them are the following: unless otherwise agreed, land subject to a fee simple interest, an agreement for sale, or a lease may not be selected; land that is administered or reserved by government (federal, territorial or municipal) may not be selected; and a sufficient amount of reasonably accessible Crown land is to be left for public purposes, including recreation and wildlife harvesting. As well, settlement lands may be expropriated by government for compensation (that is, sufficient alternative lands to restore total quantum).

Lands are to be owned collectively, and title cannot be conveyed to anyone except the Crown or a designated Aboriginal organization. In turn, the designated organization(s) will manage and control land use, and may charge rents or fees for use and occupancy. However, the Aboriginal organizations are expected to provide (and be compensated for) supplies of construction materials (sand, gravel, clay and others) and permit access to them if no alternative source is available.

The harvesting rights of the claims beneficiaries are similar to those outlined in other comprehensive claims agreements in which the Aboriginal parties possess exclusive and preferential harvesting rights on settlement lands as well as in protected areas and parks. Various bodies are established to oversee the management and regulation of wildlife, fisheries, land use and environmental screening of proposed development projects. Each body includes representation from the Aboriginal party, but the relevant minister retains ultimate decision-making authority.

Generally, only beneficiaries of the agreements are allowed access to settlement land. There are numerous exceptions. Access by any non-Aboriginal person is subject to conditions to prevent damage, mischief, alteration and interference. Further, permanent or seasonal camps are not allowed. Any person may enter land, and waters lying over such lands, in case of emergency. Members of the public have the right to use inland waters for travel or for recreation, but may harvest wildlife only for recreation (fish and migratory birds) in certain waters specified in schedules to the agreements. Government agencies or departments have the right to enter, cross and stay on settlement land to deliver programs and services or establish navigational aids. Further, if government, including the department of national defence, requires continuous use or occupancy of settlement land, it must negotiate an agreement with the Aboriginal parties.

As alluded to in the land provisions, parties with existing rights to use or operate on settlement land for commercial purposes shall continue to enjoy such rights, including associated benefits. Further, such rights are eligible for renewal, replacement and/or transfer. Commercial travel on waters and waterfront lands is allowed in the course of conduction commercial activity, although the most direct route must be taken with minimal use, and the Aboriginal party must be given prior notification. As well, access across lands and waters is allowed in order to reach adjacent lands for commercial purposes. Commercial fishing operations have the right of access to waterfront lands and waters.

Individuals and governments possessing mineral rights on settlement land are granted access for exploring, developing, producing or transporting minerals, provided that they have the agreement of the appropriate Aboriginal party or the surface rights boards created after each agreement. Further, those with mineral prospecting rights do not require a land use permit to exercise such rights, and are granted access to settlement land provided that notice is given to the appropriate Aboriginal party. Any party wishing to undertake oil and gas or mineral exploration on settlement land must first consult with the relevant Aboriginal party via the appropriate government agency. Consultations are to include such matters as the impact on the environment and wildlife, Aboriginal employment, and business opportunities and training. In turn, proposed developments may be subject to review by claims-based bodies that make recommendations, including conditions for mitigation, to the appropriate minister.

The Gwich'in agreement also contains the Yukon Transboundary Agreement between the Crown and the Gwich'in Tribal Council (Appendix C to the agreement). This agreement has to do with the rights of the Tetlit Gwich'in in the Fort McPherson group trapping area as well as in an adjacent area, which both fall under the auspices of the Yukon Umbrella Final Agreement. Specifically, the Tetlit Gwich'in and the Vuntut Gwich'in First Nation, the Dawson First Nation and the First Nation of Na-cho Ny'a'k Dun entered into an agreement in 1990 dealing with the interests of the Tetlit Gwich'in in an area included in the umbrella agreement. Essentially, the companion agreement sets out the provisions relating to those lands in the Yukon to which the Tetlit Gwich'in will receive title. It deals with the representation of both Aboriginal parties on the relevant interjurisdictional land and resource management bodies, and Tetlit Gwich'in harvesting rights in areas of overlapping traditional use. The rights and benefits set out in the companion agreement are the same as those outlined earlier.

Notes

1. This summary is based on the terms of the two agreements and on Rene Dussault and Louis Borgeat, *Administrative Law: A Treatise*, 2nd Ed., Volume 1, trans. Murray Rankin (Toronto: Carswell, 1985).
2. The communities that are party to the agreement are Carcross/Tagish First Nation, Champagne and Aishihik First Nations, Dawson First Nation, Kluane First Nation, Kwanlin Dunn First Nation, Liard First Nation, Little Salmon/Carmacks First Nation, First Nation of Na-cho Ny'a'k Dun, Ross River Dene Council, Selkirk First Nation, Ta'an Kwach'an Council, Teslin Tlingit Council, Vuntut Gwich'in First Nation, and White River First Nation.
3. In addition to existing reserves, other land had been set aside over the years throughout the Yukon for Indian use for housing, buildings and other purposes.

(d) *Nisga'a Final Agreement in Brief*[†]

See **Chapter 11, Part 7(h)**.

Preamble

The Final Agreement is intended to be the just and equitable settlement of the Nisga'a land question.

The Canadian courts have stated that reconciliation between Aboriginal and non-Aboriginal people is best achieved through negotiation and agreement, rather than through litigation and conflict. As such,

---

[†] *Nisga'a Final Agreement in Brief* (Ottawa: D.I.A.N.D., August 4, 1998) at 1–11. Ottawa: Indian and Northern Affairs Canada, 1998. Reproduced with the permission of the Minister of Public Works and Government Services, 2004. This material was produced solely by DIAND and not as a co-production between INAC and the government of British Columbia.

The document contains the following note:

> Please consult the *Nisga'a Final Agreement* for details concerning specific provisions. Find more information on the *Nisga'a Final Agreement* at www.aaf.gov.bc.ca/aaf/, www.inac.gc.ca or contact:
>
> Federal Treaty Negotiation Office, 2700-650 West Georgia Street, Vancouver, BC V6B 4N8.
> Telephone: (604) 775-7114 or toll free at 1-800-665-9320.
>
> B.C. Ministry of Aboriginal Affairs, 908 Pandora Avenue, Victoria, BC V8V 1X4.
> Telephone: (250) 356-8281 or toll free at 1-800-880-1022 PO Box 11576.

the Parties intend the Final Agreement to establish a new relationship based on mutual sharing and recognition.

The Parties intend that the Final Agreement will provide certainty with respect to ownership and use of lands and resources, and the relationship of laws within the Nass area.

General Provisions

The Nisga'a will continue to be an Aboriginal people under the *Constitution Act, 1982*.

The Nisga'a will continue to enjoy the same rights and benefits as other Canadian citizens.

Lands owned by the Nisga'a will no longer be reserve lands under the *Indian Act*.

The *Canadian Charter of Rights and Freedoms* will apply to the Nisga'a Government and its institutions.

Federal and provincial laws (such as the *Criminal Code of Canada*) will continue to apply to Nisga'a citizens and others on Nisga'a Lands.

The Treaty addresses the issue of certainty through a number of provisions. Key among these is a clause which provides that the Treaty is a full and final settlement of Nisga'a Aboriginal rights. Another provision clearly states that the Treaty exhaustively sets out the Nisga'a section 35 rights. There is also an agreement that the Nisga'a Aboriginal rights and title are modified and continue as set out in the Treaty. Finally, the Nisga'a agree to release any Aboriginal rights, including Aboriginal title, that are not set out in the Treaty or which are different in attributes or geographical extent from the Nisga'a section 35 rights set out in the Treaty.

The Final Agreement can only be amended with the consent of all three Parties. Canada would give consent to any proposed amendments by order of the Governor in Council, and British Columbia would do so by resolution of the Legislature.

Lands

The Nisga'a will own approximately 1,992 square kilometres of land in the lower Nass Valley. The land will be held in fee simple by the Nisga'a — the same kind of land ownership enjoyed by other landowners.

Nisga'a Lands will include approximately 1,930 square kilometres of transferred Crown land and 62 square kilometres of Indian reserves that will cease to be reserves on the effective date of the Treaty.

Nisga'a Lands will not include existing fee simple lands, or lands subject to agricultural leases and wood lot licenses.

Mineral Resources

The Nisga'a will own all subsurface resources on the Nisga'a Lands.

Interests within Nisga'a Lands

Existing legal interests on Nisga'a Lands will continue or be re-issued on their current terms. The Nisga'a, as the owners of the Nisga'a Lands, will be able to set conditions on any new interests it grants in the future.

Fee Simple Lands Outside Nisga'a Lands

Land contained within 18 Indian reserves outside of the Nisga'a Lands, and a small amount of adjacent land, will become fee simple lands owned by the Nisga'a and subject to provincial laws. The Nisga'a will own the subsurface resources of these lands.

The Nisga'a will also own an additional 15 parcels of fee simple land, totaling approximately 2.5 square kilometres. Subsurface resources on these lands will continue to be owned by the province and will be under provincial jurisdiction.

Commercial Recreation Tenure

The Nisga'a will receive a commercial recreation tenure for guiding which will operate under provincial laws.

Heritage Sites and Key Geographic Features

Important cultural sites will be protected through heritage site designation.

Some key geographic features will be renamed with Nisga'a names.

Parks and Ecological Reserve

British Columbia's authority and responsibilities over the Nisga'a Memorial Lava Bed Park and Gingietl Creek Ecological Reserve will continue.

Nisga'a history and culture are, and will be promoted as, the primary cultural features of the Park.

Nisga'a citizens have the right to use the lands and resources within the Park and Ecological Reserve for traditional purposes.

Water Volumes

Existing water licences will remain in place.

British Columbia will establish a Nisga'a water reservation of 300,000 cubic decametres of water per year to meet domestic, industrial and agricultural purposes.

Land Title

Nisga'a Lands will be owned by the Nisga'a. Any fee simple parcels within Nisga'a Lands that exist on the effective date will continue to be subject to the *Land Title Act* and the provincial land title system generally.

Individual parcels within Nisga'a Lands will initially be registered under a Nisga'a land title system and, following a transition period, may be registered under the provincial land title system.

Forest Resources

The Nisga'a will own all forest resources on Nisga'a Lands.

Existing licences will be in effect for a five year transition period to allow licensees to adjust their operations and will then be replaced by new licences. The licensees are required to meet certain obligations under the licences through the transition period and beyond, including silviculture obligations.

Following the transition period, the Nisga'a will manage forestry on Nisga'a Lands.

The Nisga'a Government will be able to implement forest management standards, provided that these meet or exceed provincial standards such as the *Forest Practices Code*.

Timber Processing

Provincial laws pertaining to the manufacture of timber products harvested on Crown lands will apply equally to timber harvested on Nisga'a Lands.

The Nisga'a will not establish a primary timber processing facility for 10 years after the effective date of the Treaty.

Forest Resources Outside Nisga'a Lands

The province agrees in principle to the Nisga'a purchase of forest tenure(s) with an aggregate allowable annual cut of up to 150,000 cubic metres. Any such acquisition would be subject to the *Forest Act*.

Access

There will be reasonable public access to Nisga'a Public Lands for non-commercial purposes such as hunting, fishing and recreation.

Residents of Nisga'a Lands who are not Nisga'a will have access to their private land.

The Nisga'a Government may make laws regulating public access for the purposes of public safety, protection of environmental, cultural or historic features, and protection of habitat.

The federal and provincial governments will have access to Nisga'a Lands for purposes such as the delivery or management of government services and emergency response. Likewise, representatives of the Nisga'a Government may, in accordance with the laws of general application, have temporary access to lands other than Nisga'a Lands for similar purposes.

Roads and Rights of Way

The province will continue to own the Nisga'a Highway (which is the main road through Nisga'a Lands) and will maintain the secondary provincial roads. The province may also acquire portions of Nisga'a Lands to create additional rights of way for road or public utility purposes.

The Nisga'a Government will regulate and maintain all Nisga'a roads.

Fisheries

Nisga'a citizens will have the right to harvest fish and aquatic plants subject to conservation requirements and legislation enacted to protect public health and safety.

Salmon

The Nisga'a will receive an annual allocation of salmon under the Treaty and harvest agreement, which will, on average, comprise approximately 26 percent of the Canadian Nass River total allowable catch. In addition, the Nisga'a will be able to sell their salmon, subject to monitoring, enforcement and laws of general application. A Harvest Agreement, separate from the Final Agreement, allows for the harvesting of sockeye and pink salmon.

If, in any year, there are no directed Canadian commercial or recreational fisheries for a species of Nass salmon, a Nisga'a commercial fishery will not be permitted for that species.

Steelhead

The Nisga'a have the right to harvest steelhead for domestic purposes.

Enhancement

The Nisga'a Government may conduct enhancement activities for Nass salmon with the approval of the Minister of Fisheries and Oceans.

Non-Salmon Species and Aquatic Plants

The Nisga'a may harvest non-salmon species. The allocation will be for domestic purposes, meaning that the harvest cannot be sold. The Final Agreement provides for a shellfish allocation and the Nisga'a may negotiate an allocation for other species, such as halibut and crab.

Fisheries Management

The Minister of Fisheries and Oceans and the province will retain responsibility for conservation and management of the fisheries and fish habitat, according to their respective jurisdictions. In addition, the Nisga'a Government may make laws to manage the Nisga'a harvest, if those laws are consistent with the Nisga'a Annual Fishing Plan approved by the Minister.

The Parties will establish and be represented on a Joint Fisheries Management Committee (JFMC) to facilitate the cooperative planning and conduct of Nisga'a fisheries and enhancement activities. The committee will make recommendations to the federal and provincial governments on these matters.

The Nisga'a will prepare a Nisga'a Annual Fishing Plan for all species of salmon and other fish. The Nisga'a Annual Fishing Plan will be reviewed by the JFMC and, if satisfactory, approved by the Minister of Fisheries and Oceans.

The agreement also provides for Nisga'a participation in any future regional or watershed-based fisheries management, should the need arise.

Lisims Fisheries Conservation Trust

The Trust will be established to promote conservation and protection of Nass area fish species, facilitate sustainable management of the fisheries for the benefit of all Canadians, and promote and support Nisga'a participation in the stewardship of the Nass fisheries.

Canada will contribute $10 million to this initiative and the Nisga'a will contribute $3 million.

Nisga'a Participation in the General Commercial Fishery

The Nisga'a will receive $11.5 million from Canada and B.C. to participate in the general commercial fishing industry.

The Nisga'a will not establish large-scale fish-processing facilities within eight years of the effective date of the Treaty.

Wildlife and Migratory Birds

The Nisga'a will receive a wildlife hunting allocation for domestic purposes in the Nass Wildlife Area. There are specific allocations for moose, grizzly bear and mountain goat. In the future, mammals other than these may be designated and an allocation established.

Hunting will be subject to conservation requirements and legislation enacted for the purposes of public health and safety. The Nisga'a right to hunt cannot interfere with other authorized uses of Crown land and does not preclude the Crown from authorizing uses of or disposing of Crown land, subject to certain considerations.

The Nisga'a may also harvest migratory birds, subject to laws of general application and appropriate international conventions.

Wildlife Management

The Minister of Environment, Lands and Parks is responsible for all wildlife. A wildlife committee will be established to promote cooperative management of the resource in the Nass area and advise the Minister on management and Nisga'a hunting matters. The committee will have equal representation from the Nisga'a and the province, with one representative from Canada.

The Nisga'a will develop an annual management plan for their hunt which will require provincial approval. The management plan will be reviewed by the wildlife committee and approved by the provincial Minister.

Nisga'a citizens who hunt outside the management area will be subject to provincial laws

Trade, Barter and Sale

The Nisga'a will be able to trade or barter wildlife, wildlife parts and migratory birds among themselves, or with other Aboriginal people. The Nisga'a harvest of wildlife is for domestic purposes.

Trapping

Trapping will be regulated in accordance with provincial laws.

Guiding

Guiding activities will continue to be subject to laws of general application.

The Nisga'a may receive a guide outfitter's certificate in the Nisga'a Lands, if a current certificate ceases to apply.

The Nisga'a will receive an angling licence for certain watercourses outside of the Nisga'a Lands.

Environmental Assessment and Protection

The Nisga'a Government will have the power to make laws relating to environmental assessment and protection. The environmental standards defined in these laws must meet or exceed federal and provincial standards.

The Nisga'a may undertake environmental assessments of proposed projects on their lands. Assessments will include public participation; and the results will be available to the public, except where information must remain confidential by law. Federal and provincial environmental assessment processes continue to apply on Nisga'a Lands.

Canada and British Columbia will participate in environmental assessments in cases where a project will have effects outside the Nisga'a Lands. To avoid duplication, the agreement provides for the harmonization of Nisga'a environmental assessments processes with those of Canada and British Columbia.

Nisga'a Government

The Nisga'a will be governed by the Nisga'a Lisims Government (central government) and four Nisga'a Village Governments.

Nisga'a Constitution

The Nisga'a will adopt a Constitution which will set out the terms of governance and recognize the rights and freedoms of Nisga'a citizens. The Constitution must be passed by at least 70 percent of the voters who participate in the vote to ratify the Final Agreement.

Relations with Individuals Who Are Not Nisga'a Citizens

The Nisga'a Government will be required to consult with other residents of Nisga'a Lands about decisions that significantly and directly affect them. Likewise, residents who are not Nisga'a will be able to participate in elected bodies that directly and significantly affect them. The means of participation can include opportunities to make representations, to vote for or seek election on Nisga'a Public Institutions, and to have the same means of appeal as Nisga'a citizens. Some local laws, such as traffic and transportation, will apply to other residents of Nisga'a Lands, but in the majority of cases Nisga'a laws will only pertain to Nisga'a citizens.

Transitional Provisions

The first elections for Nisga'a Government will be held no later than six months after the effective date of the Treaty. Prior to the elections, the Nisga'a Tribal Council will continue to manage Nisga'a affairs, in accordance with the transition provisions.

Legislative Jurisdiction and Authority

The Nisga'a Government will have the power to make laws required to carry out its responsibilities and exercise its authority under this agreement. In addition, the Nisga'a Government may make laws governing such things as Nisga'a citizenship; Nisga'a language and culture; Nisga'a property in Nisga'a Lands; public order, peace and safety; employment; traffic and transportation; the solemnization of marriages; child and family, social and health services; child custody, adoption, and education.

Federal and provincial laws continue to apply to Nisga'a citizens and Nisga'a Lands, and the relationship between these laws and Nisga'a laws has been clearly set out in the Final Agreement.

Administration of Justice

The Nisga'a Government may provide policing, correctional, and court services on Nisga'a Lands in accordance with the terms of the Treaty.

Police Services

If the Nisga'a Government decides to provide its own policing within Nisga'a Lands, it may do so with the approval of the Lieutenant Governor in Council. The Nisga'a Police Service will have the full range of police responsibilities and the authority to enforce Nisga'a, provincial and federal laws, including the *Criminal Code of Canada*, within the Nisga'a Lands. The police force will be required to meet provincial qualification, training and professional standards. It will also be independent and accountable.

Community Corrections Services

The Nisga'a may enter into agreements with Canada or British Columbia to provide community correctional services in accordance with generally accepted standards, and consistent with the needs and priorities of the Nisga'a Government.

Nisga'a Court

The Nisga'a may establish a Nisga'a Court for approval by the Lieutenant Governor in Council. The Nisga'a Court will adjudicate prosecutions and civil disputes arising under Nisga'a laws and review the administrative decisions of Nisga'a public institutions.

The judges will be appointed by the Nisga'a Government, according to a method of selection approved by the Lieutenant Governor in Council, and will comply with generally recognized principles of judicial fairness, independence and impartiality.

In proceedings where the accused could face imprisonment under Nisga'a law, he or she may elect to be tried in the Provincial Court of British Columbia.

Final decisions by the Nisga'a Court may be appealed to the Supreme Court of British Columbia on the same basis as decisions made at the Provincial Court of British Columbia.

Indian Act Transition

Provisions will be made to facilitate the transition from jurisdiction under the *Indian Act* to provincial or Nisga'a jurisdiction for such things as wills, administration of estates, and governance arrangements.

Capital Transfer and Loan Repayment

The cash settlement benefit of $190 million will be paid through capital transfers over a period of 15 years according to a schedule agreed to by the Parties.

The loans made by the Nisga'a to support their participation in Treaty negotiations over the years will be fully repaid over 15 years according to a schedule agreed to by the Parties.

Fiscal Relations

The Nisga'a Government will be responsible for ensuring the provision of programs and services at levels reasonably comparable to those generally available in northwest British Columbia.

Every five years, the Treaty requires the Parties to negotiate a fiscal financing agreement through which funding will be provided to the Nisga'a Government to enable the delivery of programs and services including health, education, social services, local services, capital asset maintenance and replacement, housing, and resource management.

The Fiscal Financing Agreement will take into account the Nisga'a Government's ability to raise its own revenues consistent with an own source revenue agreement. The first Own Source Revenue Agreement will provide for a phased-in contribution of Nisga'a revenues over a period of twelve years. After the initial agreement, the Own Source Revenue Agreement will be renegotiable every two years, if requested by any of the Parties.

The Treaty confirms that the funding of Nisga'a Government is a shared responsibility of the Parties and that it is the Parties' objective that, where feasible, the reliance of the Nisga'a Government and the Nisga'a Villages on transfers will be reduced over time.

Taxation

The Nisga'a Government will have the power to tax Nisga'a citizens on Nisga'a Lands.

The Nisga'a Government, Canada and British Columbia may negotiate tax delegation agreements for other taxes and the Parties may make agreements to coordinate their respective tax systems on Nisga'a Lands.

The *Indian Act* tax exemption for Nisga'a citizens will be eliminated after a transitional period of eight years for transaction (e.g. sales) taxes and 12 years for other (e.g. income) taxes.

Pursuant to a taxation agreement, the Nisga'a Government and Nisga'a Village Governments will be treated in the same way as municipalities for tax purposes.

Cultural Artifacts and Heritage

The Royal British Columbia Museum and the Canadian Museum of Civilization will return a portion of their collections of Nisga'a artifacts to the Nisga'a. The museums will also retain some collections of Nisga'a artifacts for public exhibitions.

The Nisga'a Government and the province will coordinate their activities to manage heritage sites within Nisga'a Lands to preserve their heritage value from activities which may otherwise adversely affect them.

Local and Regional Government Relations

Nisga'a Lands will continue to be part of the Electoral Area "A" in the Regional District of Kitimat-Stikine.

The Nisga'a and the Regional District may enter into servicing agreements or otherwise coordinate their activities with respect to common areas of responsibility.

Dispute Resolution

If disputes arise regarding the interpretation, application or implementation of the Treaty, the Parties will try to resolve them through cooperation and consultation. If the Parties are unable to resolve the dispute in this manner, they may resort to mediation or another form of dispute resolution that would facilitate the Parties' efforts to agree. If these efforts fail, the Parties will have recourse to arbitration, if they agree, or the British Columbia Supreme Court.

Eligibility and Enrolment

To be eligible to receive benefits from the Nisga'a Treaty, a person must meet enrolment criteria that are largely based on Nisga'a ancestry.

The task of determining eligibility will be carried out by an eight-member Enrolment Committee, which will create a register of names during an initial enrolment period. Thereafter, the Nisga'a Government will maintain the register. The decisions of the Enrolment Committee and the Nisga'a Government with respect to eligibility and enrolment are final and binding, within the bounds of an appeals process.

Ratification

The Final Agreement has no force or effect unless ratified by the Nisga'a, British Columbia, and Canada.

Those Nisga'a who are enrolled by the Enrolment Committee will vote on the agreement by secret ballot. A Ratification Committee, with Nisga'a, federal and provincial representatives, will oversee the conduct of the vote. To be approved, the agreement must be ratified by a majority (i.e., 50 percent plus one vote) of all eligible voters.

British Columbia and Canada will ratify the agreement in the British Columbia Legislature and Parliament, respectively, by the enactment of legislation giving effect to the Treaty.

Implementation

The Treaty will be implemented according to an Implementation Plan that is separate from the Final Agreement. The Implementation Plan sets out the steps to be taken to properly make the Treaty work on the ground. The plan will be for a term of ten years starting from the effective date of the Treaty.

(e) *Sechelt Agreement-in-Principle*†

See **Chapter 11, Part 7(k).**

[Editor's note: In late May 2000, the Sechelt announced that they would be withdrawing from the claims negotiations and taking their land claims to the courts instead. If final, this decision would deal a severe blow to the B.C. land claims process. The Sechelt negotiations had been the most advanced in the British Columbia Treaty Commission Process, which is dealing with claims from 51 B.C. bands.]

† "The Sechelt AIP Summary and Negotiations" from http://www.aaf.gov.bc.ca/aaf/nations/nations.htm. Last Update: April 1999 by Webmaster. Reproduced with permission of British Columbia Ministry of Aboriginal Affairs.

SUMMARY

General Provisions

The Sechelt Agreement-in-Principle (AIP) states that the Final Agreement will provide for the continued application of the *Canadian Charter of Rights and Freedoms* to the Sechelt government. It also provides that the Final Agreement will not alter the *Constitution of Canada*.

The Final Agreement will constitute the full and final settlement of all Sechelt claims to Aboriginal rights and Aboriginal title in Canada.

Sechelt Treaty Land

The Sechelt Indian Band currently owns its land in fee simple as a result of a self-government agreement implemented nearly 13 years ago. The Sechelt have self-government authority over their current lands.

The AIP provides that current Sechelt lands, about 1,031 hectares, will become Sechelt Treaty Land.

The Sechelt Indian Band will receive about 933 hectares of new lands. This will include about 288 hectares of rural land, and 645 hectares of urban land.

On one of the urban parcels, District Lot 7613, B.C. and the Sechelt Indian Band will share gravel and timber revenues. Each will receive 50 per cent of the forestry and gravel revenues from the effective date of the Final Agreement, until extraction levels of 52,222,810 metric tonnes of aggregate material and 143,342 cubic metres of merchantable timber are reached. The Sechelt will then receive 100% of the forest and gravel revenues.

The Sechelt Indian Band also owns another 25 hectares which will become Sechelt Treaty Land after the Final Agreement.

On the effective date, Sechelt Treaty Land will amount to approximately 1,988 hectares.

Fiscal Arrangements

The Sechelt Indian Band will receive $42 million in cash. This amount consists of $40 million to the Sechelt Prosperity Fund and $2 million to a Sechelt Transition Fund. During Final Agreement negotiations, the Parties will agree to a schedule of payments that will be paid out over a number of years.

Interests on Sechelt Land

Existing interests on Sechelt Treaty Land, such as road and cutting permits, guide outfitter licences and trap lines, rights of way and licences of occupation, will continue under their current terms.

The gravel lease with Construction Aggregates will also continue under its current terms.

Ownership of Resources on Sechelt Treaty Land

The Sechelt will own surface and subsurface resources on Sechelt Treaty Land.

Future Additions to Sechelt Treaty Land

For 24 years following the effective date, Sechelt may submit proposals to Canada and B.C. to have land that the Sechelt Indian Band has acquired or optioned become Sechelt Treaty Land.

The total area of the Sechelt Treaty Land shall not exceed a maximum of 3,055 hectares. The Sechelt Indian Band will not own subsurface resources on lands acquired after the effective date unless agreed by B.C.

Any lands to be added must meet certain defined criteria and be approved by Canada and B.C. For example, any lands the Sechelt may wish to add must be within an area defined as the Sechelt Area and must not result in any cost to Canada or B.C.

To ensure that municipal interests are considered, new Sechelt Treaty Land may not be created if it falls within the boundary of a municipality, unless the municipality agrees. Similarly, where Sechelt Land is acquired by Sechelt in an area of overlap with another First Nation, Sechelt Treaty Land may not be created without the consent of that First Nation.

Fisheries

The Sechelt have the right to harvest fish and marine plants, subject to conservation and public health and safety, for food, social and ceremonial purposes. The Sechelt will also receive 11 existing commercial fishing licences to assist the Sechelt Indian Band's participation in the general commercial fishery. The licences will operate on the same basis as all other commercial licences.

The Minister will retain overall responsibility for conservation and management of the fisheries and fish habitat.

Wildlife and Migratory Birds

Provincial and federal laws with respect to wildlife and wildlife management will apply on Sechelt Treaty Land.

The Sechelt will receive entitlements to hunt designated species of wildlife.

The Sechelt will develop an annual harvest plan for their harvest which will require provincial government approval.

They will also have the right to harvest migratory birds subject to applicable federal and provincial laws.

Forestry

The Sechelt will manage forest resources on Sechelt Treaty Land and will be responsible for conservation and protection. Management of the forest resources will meet or exceed established provincial forest practices, standards and laws.

Water

The Sechelt Indian Band may participate in any local government institution that may regulate water within the Sunshine Coast Regional District boundary.

The Sechelt will participate in any public water management process affecting the Sechelt Area.

Environmental Assessment and Protection

Federal and provincial environmental assessment processes and protection laws will apply to Sechelt Treaty Land.

Taxation

The existing *Indian Act* taxation exemptions will end. Sechelt members will begin paying transaction taxes 8 years following the effective date of the Final Treaty. Sechelt members will pay income tax 12 years following the effective date of the Final Treaty.

Governance

The parties agree that the existing Sechelt Indian Band governance arrangements, which have been in place for nearly 13 years, have been practical and successful. Under the *Sechelt Indian Band Self-Government Act*, the Sechelt Indian Band will continue to exercise a delegated model of law-making over Sechelt Treaty Land.

Culture and Heritage

The Sechelt Indian Band will have returned to them specified cultural artifacts currently held by British Columbia.

Federal and provincial laws relating to the establishment, management and protection of heritage resources will apply on Sechelt Treaty Land. The Sechelt Indian Band may participate in any public process respecting the planning or management of heritage resources affecting the Sechelt area.

Sechelt members will have the right to gather some items of a traditional nature on provincial Crown land. This gathering will be restricted to sustenance, medicinal or ceremonial purposes of a non-commercial nature. Sechelt may gather items such as: traditionally used plants, herbs, roots, berries, moss, ferns and bark. Before gathering of traditionally used trees can take place, arrangements must be reached with the appropriate Crown authority.

This gathering right will apply on lands within the Sechelt Area until those lands are sold or leased to a third party or required for federal or provincial authorized uses which are incompatible with gathering.

Implementation

A Sechelt Treaty implementation plan will be developed by a tripartite working group and concluded prior to ratifying the Final Agreement.

OTHER ARRANGEMENTS

The following initiatives fall outside the terms of the Sechelt AIP and will remain outside of the Final Treaty.

Economic Development

In order to assist the Sechelt Indian Band prepare for and assume new responsibilities it will acquire under a Final Agreement, Canada has provided a one-time payment of $1.5 million for economic development initiatives and planning.

Loan

The Province of British Columbia will provide the Sechelt Indian Band with a loan guarantee in the amount of $4 million on the effective date of the treaty. Repayment of this loan will be secured by the Sechelt's share of forestry and gravel revenues from Lot 7613.

Consultation

The Sechelt Indian Band, Canada and British Columbia are committed to continued open treaty negotiations.

Canada and British Columbia have already conducted extensive in-depth consultations during the Sechelt treaty negotiations. The Sechelt AIP was developed with the active involvement of, and input from, the Sunshine Coast Local Advisory Committee (LAC) and the Sechelt Treaty Advisory Committee (TAC).

The LAC represents third-party community-based and sectoral interests on the Sunshine Coast including representatives from forestry, aquaculture, business, commercial and sport fisheries, environmental, conservation, wildlife and labour groups. The TAC represents local government interests and includes representatives from the District of Sechelt, the Sunshine Coast Regional District, the Town of Gibsons, the District of Powell River and the Powell River Regional District. Both groups have committed extensive time and resources to the Sechelt treaty negotiations, providing invaluable advice to the provincial and federal negotiators. Bruce Milne, Mayor of the District of Sechelt, participates as a full member of the provincial negotiating team.

In all, more than 100 consultation meetings have been held with the LAC and TAC.

Next Steps

The Sechelt negotiations are the most advanced under the British Columbia Treaty Commission process. The Sechelt AIP will form the basis for Final Agreement negotiations. During this stage, public information sessions and consultations with the LAC and TAC will continue.

NEGOTIATIONS

October 1986 The *Sechelt Indian Band Self-Government Act* and *Sechelt Constitution* are declared in force. The Act provides for the delegation of specified federal governance powers to Sechelt. It also transfers to the Sechelt Indian Band, in fee simple title, control and ownership of its 33 reserves. B.C. subsequently enacts the *Sechelt Indian Government District Enabling Act*, which provides Sechelt with municipal-style governance over Sechelt lands.

July 1994 The Sechelt Indian Band files a statement of intent with the British Columbia Treaty Commission, declaring its desire to negotiate.

October 1994 Canada and B.C. establish the Sunshine Coast Local Advisory Committee (LAC) to provide advice on third party interests during treaty negotiations with Sechelt.

October 1994 B.C. establishes the Sechelt Treaty Advisory Committee (TAC) to provide advice to the provincial negotiating team on municipal issues.

December 1994 Sechelt, Canada and B.C. reach substantive agreement on a framework agreement.

February 1995 Sechelt tables its "Sechelt Land Claim Position Paper." This paper reflects the elements sought by Sechelt in a treaty.

August 1995 Sechelt, Canada and B.C. sign the Framework Agreement at a ceremony in Sechelt. Agreement-in-Principle negotiations begin.

June 1996 Canada and B.C. respond to Sechelt's position paper. Canada tables "Canada's Response to the Sechelt Land Claim Position Paper" and B.C. tables "Sechelt Treaty Negotiations Provincial Response."

November 1996 In response to Sechelt's request for information on the land and cash components of a treaty, Canada and B.C. table "Canada and British Columbia's Presentation of Land and Cash Scenarios for the Sechelt Treaty Negotiations." This paper sets out some scenarios that Canada and B.C. feel could be incorporated in a Final Agreement.

Aug. '95–July '97 The Parties hold open side table and main table meetings to discuss interests and negotiate the issues are reached by the Chief Negotiators on: amendment, dispute resolution, ratification of the Agreement-in-Principle (AIP) and the Final Agreement, eligibility, forestry management, subsurface resources, environmental management, culture and heritage, implementation, land use planning and general provisions.

August 1997 Canada and B.C. table a land and cash offer: "Canada's and British Columbia's Land and Cash Offer for the Sechelt Treaty Negotiations."

October 1997 Sechelt advises Canada and British Columbia that changes are required to the governments' preliminary offer.

Nov. '97–Aug. '98 Informal discussions concerning the offer. No formal negotiations.

September 1998 Formal negotiations begin, concurrent with consultations with Sunshine Coast LAC, the Sechelt TAC and other interested parties.

November 1998 Open side table meetings begin and consultations continue.

December 1998 British Columbia and Canada present a new land and cash offer to Sechelt Indian Band.

January 1999 Chief Negotiators release the Sechelt draft AIP for further consultation and internal reviews.

February 1999 Consultations on Sechelt Draft AIP continue and public information sessions are held. Chief Negotiators initial Sechelt draft AIP and recommend it for approval and signature by all Parties.

April 16, 1999 Canada, British Columbia and Sechelt Indian Band sign the Sechelt Agreement-in-Principle. Final Agreement negotiations begin.

(f) Land Claims Agreement Dispute Resolution†

See **Chaper 11, Part 7**.

NOTE

Although modern land claims agreements tend to follow a general framework, there are often significant differences in the way these complex documents approach such issues as finality, eligibility, the status of land, resource revenue sharing, self-government, third-party and public governmental interests, and dispute resolution. Dispute resolution is significant because it can play a key role in shaping of an agreement over time.

Nigel Bankes has analysed the dispute resolution provisions in three settlement documents — the 1984 *Inuvialuit Final Agreement*; the 1993 *Sahtu Dene and Metis Comprehensive Land Claim Agreement* (SA); and the *Agreement Between the Inuit of the Nunavut Settlement Area and Her Majesty the Queen in Right of Canada*. The analysis compares the way these agreements use four different kinds of dispute resolution forum: the ordinary courts (including judicial review of decisions of authorities established by the agreements); the quasi-judicial tribunals established under the agreements (e.g., land-use planning and wildlife management boards); arbitration (by settlement arbitration boards or panels and — in the case of the NFA — *ad hoc* arbitrators); and reference to third parties such as ministers or settlement implementation panels. The work also looks at the appointment of members of the settlement arbitration bodies; the kinds of matters that can be referred to arbitration; the legal effect of arbitration decisions; the rules regarding parties and procedures; and the dispute resolution experience to date. Bankes finds (at 303) that the three agreements contain "a bewildering potpourri of dispute settlement provisions, and [that] there is surprisingly little consistency either internally or between the agreements." He draws some general conclusions below.

EXTRACT

. . . .

What lessons can we learn from the above?

First, there is a dramatic difference between the dispute settlement model offered by the Inuvialuit Agreement and that offered by the SA and the NFA. In the case of the Inuvialuit Agreement, arbitration attains preeminent status as the means for resolving disputes between the parties. While the IFA does not preclude the parties to the agreement from electing to go to court rather than to arbitration (except of course where the same dispute has already been submitted to arbitration), it does allow either party to send a dispute to arbitration without the consent of the other party. This is not the case under the NFA and SA, where only a relatively narrow range of matters may be submitted to arbitration by the unilateral act of one party. It is per-

† Reproduced with permission of the Publisher from Nigel Bankes, "The Dispute Resolution Provisions of Three Northern Land Claims Agreements" in *Intercultural Dispute Resolution in Aboriginal Contexts* edited by Catherine Bell and David Kahane (Vancouver: UBC Press, 2004) at 319–20. Notes omitted.

haps not coincidental that the beneficiaries under both the SA and NFA have initiated important litigation in the courts concerning the interpretation of their agreement and have not undertaken arbitration, whereas the Inuvialuit have not resorted to the courts but have invoked the arbitration provisions of the IFA.[85] The IFA also stands out for the role it accords to industry with respect to certain categories of dispute and for the manner in which the agreement's arbitration panel is systematically accorded jurisdiction over particular categories of dispute rather than other bodies established by the agreement.

Second, it is clear that the parties have certainly not lavished on the subject of dispute settlement the sort of attention accorded to the subject by some more recent agreements, such as the Nisga'a Agreement. That agreement establishes a three-stage sequential procedure for resolving disagreements: (1) collaborative negotiations, (2) facilitated procedures using a neutral, and (3) formal adjudication using arbitral or judicial proceedings. Similarly, none of the three agreements explicitly contemplates using dispute settlement models based upon traditional laws and practices. While a particular panel might adopt procedures that are sensitive to traditional practices and languages, none of the agreements offers any guidance as to the adoption of such practices. So, in large part, we shall have to wait and see. The single experience to date with the Inuvialuit Agreement suggests that we should be slow to conclude that the parties have adopted dispute resolution mechanisms that are more culturally sensitive than those available from the courts.

Third, the overall impression of the entire basket of dispute resolution proceedings under all three agreements, but especially under the SA and NFA, is one of complexity, especially if one considers not just the arbitration provisions but also the various quasi-judicial boards created by other provisions of the agreements. This complexity seems unnecessary and may itself thwart rather than facilitate the resolution of disputes. There may be lessons here for the design of dispute resolution provisions in future land claims agreements.

This chapter has served as a preliminary inquiry only into the dispute settlement provisions of northern claims agreements. Other questions need to be asked in order to determine more precisely the effectiveness of the dispute resolution procedures that have been adopted for each of these agreements. Relevant questions would include the extent to which there are differences between the parties to the agreements that remain unresolved and the reasons why parties select particular dispute resolution techniques. In addition, we would benefit from a clearer understanding of the role of the implementation committees established under post-IFA land claims agreements, as well as the functional relationship between these committees and arbitration procedures.

12 Aboriginal Self-Government

(a) *Kaianerakowa*†

See **Chapter 12, Part 3(a).**

The Kaianerakowa, or Great Law of Peace, is the traditional centuries-old constitution of the Iroquois Confederacy. Kaianerakowa is impressive for its emphasis on discussion, checks and balances, and consensus. The following discussion of Kaianerakowa is from a published work that focuses on the Nation Office / traditionalist program for a separate Aboriginal justice system at Kahnawake, Quebec. As the work notes, although Kaianerakowa was originally in oral form, there are now several different written versions. See further, W.N. Fenton, *Parker on the Iroquois* (Syracuse, N.Y.: Syracuse University Press, 1968); and M.S. Baxendale and C. MacLaine, *This Land is Our Land: The Mohawk Revolt at Oka* (Montreal: Optimum, 1991), 91 *et seq.*

The traditionalists of the Nation Office Longhouse at Kahnawake view their right to a separate system of traditional justice as residing in many things, but most notably in treaty promises of separate institutions made to the Five Iroquois Nations by the Dutch in the 1664 Albany Treaty, and later ratified by the British. Within this treaty was enshrined the principle of the "Two Row Wampum," which established that

> ...if any English, Dutch or Indian (under the protection of the English) do any wrong, injury or violence to any of ye said [Iroquois] Princes, or their subjects, in any way whatsoever, if they complain to the Governor at New York or to the Officer in Chief at Albany, if the person so offending can be discovered, then that person shall suffer punishment and all due satisfaction shall be given, and the like shall be done for all other English Plantations.
>
> That if any Indians belonging to any of the [Iroquois] Sachims aforesaid, do any wrong, injury or damage to the English, Dutch or Indians under the protection of the English, if complaint be made to ye Sachims, and the person be discovered who did the injury, then the person so offending shall be punished and all just satisfaction shall be given to any of his Majesty's subjects in any Colony or other English Plantation in America.[1]

The Iroquois analogy for the institutional arrangement created by the Albany Treaty places each nation in a separate canoe or ship and envisions them moving side-by-side down the river of life, together, but independent of each other. Each nation keeps distinct in its boat all its laws, traditions and cultures, and anyone preferring the institutions and way of life offered by the other boat is free to leap to it, but not to return to their original craft. A choice must be made and adhered to, as a person straddling the water with a foot in each craft can never truly belong in either canoe or their cultures.[2] In the realm of the legal system, the Two Row Wampum means that an Iroquois offending against a non-Iroquois or fellow Iroquois must be tried by the laws of his own culture by which he was raised, and which bear relevance and importance to him, with a

---

† From E.J. Dickson-Gilmore, "Resurrecting the Peace: Traditionalist Approaches to Separate Justice in the Kahnawake Mohawk Nation" in R.A. Silverman and M.O. Nielsen, eds., *Aboriginal peoples and Canadian Criminal Justice* (1992) at 263–66 and 274–75. c1992. Reproduced with permission of Nelson, a division of Thomson Learning: www.thomsonrights.com. Fax (800) 730-2215. This is from an edited version of a paper by Dr. Dickson-Gilmore in Proceedings of the VI International Symposium, *Commission on Folk Law and Legal Pluralism*, Ottawa, Canada, August 14–18, 1990. Published by Butterworths Canada Ltd.

similar right accruing to non-Iroquois in similar circumstances.[3]

The essential cultural cargo carried by the Iroquois canoe is the Kaianerakowa, or Great Law of Peace. Since its inception sometime in the period "slightly before A.D. 1400 to A.D. 1600 or slightly before" (Tooker, 1978), the Great Law has been translated from its original form to a written text, of which three versions currently exist. The accounts are the Newhouse Version[4], the Chief's Version (1900)[5], and the Gibson Version (1899)[6], all of which are the result of nineteenth century efforts by Iroquois residing on the Six Nations reservation in Canada not only to preserve their political traditions (Fenton, 1975; Jennings, 1984), but to preserve them in a way which justified these as the foundation for governance of the reserve population. As a result, what emerged was a clearly defined system of traditional government and codified laws. How much of the result is of true antiquity and how much a function of the immediate needs of a nineteenth century community for a systemic, representative government will probably never be determined absolutely (Fenton, 1975); however, these three versions are the best *transcribed* traditional authorities available to modern researchers concerning the formation of the Iroquois Confederacy.[7]

In consulting these traditions, it is important to bear in mind a few important qualifications upon the use of traditions as historical documents. First, it must be acknowledged that there exist differences across the various versions of the traditions, most of which occur on the margins surrounding a core of common elements. As a result, there may not be any single version of the traditions of the formation of the League of the Five Nations which can be credited as in some way more authoritative than any other.[8] In the absence of such security, maximum accuracy may be achieved through presenting an amalgam of the various traditions which emphasises salient themes while acknowledging significant differences. This merely recognizes the reality that "a myth consists of all of its versions, and that inasmuch as all versions may be thought of as belonging together, they create a single identity for that myth" (Fenton, 1975).

In a similar vein, it is important to qualify all impressions of the Confederacy with the knowledge that these are based upon nineteenth and twentieth century reconstructions of original traditions which no longer exist in the nascent form, and that most modern transcriptions are removed from the "original" tradition by history, selective recall, and modern amendments.... While they might have origins in antiquity, oral traditions are by their very nature constantly adapting to changing social and historical circumstances; before they are committed to a literate record, such traditions cannot be wrong or dated, because there is no present version against which they can be measured. Therefore the Iroquois traditions currently extant, the Newhouse, Gibson and Chief's versions, must always be read in the context of their transcription, as this is what will explain much of their form and content.

The traditions describing the formation of the Confederacy are all agreed on one aspect, namely, that a period of protracted and debilitating warfare among the Five Nations constituted the principle motivation behind their unification.[9] When the fighting reached a dangerous fever pitch, two Mohawk peacemongers went among the Five Nations to cool the warriors with a message of "Peace and Power" (Scott, 1912) and unite them under the terms of an internal law of amity. This message, the Kaianerakowa, or Great Law of Peace, is a complex entity, and in its present form may be understood as consisting of two essential components or "layers". The first is a substratum which holds the defining principles — the spirit of the Iroquois Great Law — upon which the confederated Iroquois nations base their government and international relations. From this philosophical base springs the second layer of the Peace, which details in roughly 176 articles or "wampums", constitutional matters ranging from the mechanics of the process of confederation through to the appointment, tenure, and jurisdiction of government officials, and includes specific instructions relating to inter-and intra-Confederacy relations (Wallace, 1946).

For the present discussion, one of the most significant elements of the Kaianerakowa is its articulation of the decision-making process enlisted by traditional councils when meeting to determine matters of Confederacy or Nation business. Originally, these councils existed at three levels, from the highest Confederacy council through to the Nation and community councils, with process at the latter, lowest level appearing to be least formalized. The Confederacy council convened at Onondaga and was designed at the original confederation of the Five Nations to consist of fifty male "life chiefs" who were appointed — and could also be deposed — by the senior matrons of their clans. At the intermediate level of the individual Nation councils, these same Confederate sachems governed their respective national populations through processes similar to those characterising Confederacy government.

When in council the fifty Confederate sachems, their advisors and assistants, convened at the central Longhouse at Onondaga and effected a physical arrangement and political process which was apparently designed by Dekanawideh at the time of the formation of the Confederacy, and which was based upon traditional clan and moiety configurations. At this highest level, the Mohawk and Seneca sachems comprised one moiety, acting as the "older" or "elder" brothers to their opposing moiety of "younger brothers" composed of the representatives of the Cayugas and Oneidas (Tooker, 1978). These metaphorical siblings positioned themselves along either wall of the council Longhouse, facing each other over a fire which burned brightly whenever a congress was held. The fire was tended by the Onondaga Firekeepers, who were also members of the elder brother moiety, but whose roles as mediators of the council process placed them at one end of the Longhouse. From this position the Onondagas called the other nations to council, raised the matters to be deliberated and generally oversaw the process of deliberations "over the fire" (Barnes, 1984).

The council process was initiated when the Firekeepers passed an item of business to the elder brothers for their consideration; the Mohawks would discuss it among themselves and then refer the matter and their conclusions to the Senecas, who would debate them, possibly revising and returning their suggestions back to the Mohawks. This exchange would continue until the elder brothers reached a consensus, at which time the Mohawks passed their moiety's opinion over the fire to the younger brothers. The Cayuga and Oneida were then given an opportunity to ponder their opposite's opinion, and initiate an exchange like that previously occurring among their elder brothers. If the younger brothers agreed with Mohawk and Seneca positions, the Mohawks passed the concerted decision to the Onondagas, who could accept the outcome or, upon demonstrating its flaws, refer it back to the house for consideration (Barnes, 1984). If after extensive negotiations it became apparent that consonance was impossible, the Onondagas could suggest a possible resolution or, this and all efforts at conciliation being fruitless, the council fire would be covered with ashes, leaving the issue undetermined (Parker, 1916; Morgan, 1851).

The process of government at the level of the Nation councils did not differ greatly from that at the Confederacy council. Within the Mohawk Nation the nine representatives of the Turtle, Bear, and Wolf clans met in a council longhouse which is like that at Onondaga and adopted a similar seating plan and deliberation process. On one side of the house sat the Wolf clan, who called the Turtles their siblings and with them comprise one moiety; opposite to them was the Bear clan, which constituted the other moiety and referred to the Turtle and Wolf people as cousins. The Bear and Wolf leaders faced each other over a council fire tended by the Turtle clan leaders, who sat at one end and acted as Firekeepers and mediators.

The procedure of deliberations over this fire was structured along the same lines as that characterising the Confederate councils (Parker, 1916). Those wishing to bring an issue before the council would normally seek out a speaker or inferior war chief to communicate their business to the Turtle clan leaders, who as Firekeepers were responsible for adding it to the agenda and initiating it into the council session (Parker, 1916). Not all subjects raised were brought before the council; one of the most important tasks of the Firekeepers was to sift the matters brought by the speakers to determine which were of sufficient import to be included in a council session (Parker, 1916). When an important issue arose, it would be brought into deliberations first among the Turtle clan, who would discuss it among themselves and pass their opinions to the Wolf clan for their consideration. The Wolves would in turn consider the Turtle clan's recommendations and, if they found fault with them or wished them to alter them in anyway, they would return their suggestions for change to the Turtles. The Firekeepers would discuss the proposals of the Wolf leaders until they agreed among themselves either to accept the Wolves' changes or to return the issue back across the fire to them for further deliberation. This exchange would persist until the Turtle and Wolf clans agreed upon the best possible outcome, which the Turtles would then pass across the fire to the Bear clan, thereby initiating a further set of negotiations. When all clans finally reached an accord, the Turtle clan, having ensured that the outcome was consistent with the laws and principles of the Kaianerakowa, would return the council's decision to the people (Barnes, 1984). The remaining members of the Five Nations manifested variations on the Mohawk theme, as the number and arrangement of their clans and moieties dictated.

Although the Peace provided in great detail for the conduct of government among the Iroquois Nations, it is not nearly so clear regarding the practice of criminal justice.[10] Beyond the creation of specific prohibitions in regard to the behaviour of sachems, including murder (article 20) and gossip and involvement in "trivial affairs" (article 27), the

Peace as it currently exists does not appear to provide for the creation of mechanisms to respond to disputes and delicts among the people. In the absence of specific direction from the traditional law, the Nation Office/traditionalists of Kahnawake have looked to the spirit of traditional dispute resolution and the processes of the Mohawk Nation council for guidance, and have combined these in a "neo-tradition" of Mohawk criminal justice. Before elaboration of this proposed system can commence, however, the discussion must be diverted back into time, to inform the original traditions of dispute resolution among the Iroquois people.

Notes

1. New York Colonial Documents, London Documents II, p. 68.
2. Christine Deom, "Traditional Justice and the Conflict with the s. 107 Indian Act Court System at Kahnawake", (McGill Faculty of Law term essay, December 1988), 5–6.
3. *Two Row Wampum*, Mohawk Nation Office, n.d. (paper in author's possession).
4. This version was originally gathered and recorded in 1885 by a Canadian Mohawk named Seth Newhouse, who was also known as Dayodekane. It was later to be rejected by a Committee of the Chiefs at the Six Nations reservation in Ontario, who published their own account in 1912 (see note 5, below). Newhouse's account is that found in probably the best-known transcription, namely Arthur C. Parker, "The Constitutions of the Five Nations, or the Iroquois Great Book of Law", *The New York State Museum Bulletin*, (1916), p. 184; subsequently reprinted in William N. Fenton, *Parker on the Iroquois*, (Syracuse, N.Y.: Syracuse University Press, 1968). See also William N. Fenton, "Seth Newhouse's Traditional History and Constitution of the Iroquois Confederacy", *Proceedings of the American Philosophical Society*, (1949), no. 2, 93.
5. Compiled in large measure in reaction to the Newhouse Version by a Committee of the Chiefs of the Six Nations reservation in Brantford, Ontario. The involved chiefs were Peter Powless (Mohawk), Nicodemus Porter (Oneida), William Wage and Abram Charles (Cayuga), John A. Gibson (Seneca), Thomas Wm. Echo (Onondaga), Josiah Hill (Tuscarora; the Tuscaroras were accepted into the Confederacy around 1722, and although they have never received full equality within the Confederate Council, their addition led the Five Nations to become popularly known as the "Six Nations"), with the assistance of Chiefs Josiah Hill and J.W.M. Elliot as secretaries. Their account, signed and delivered in Oshwegan in 1900, was subsequently edited by Duncan C. Scott and published as "Traditional History of the Confederacy of the Six Nations", *Proceedings and Transactions of the Royal Society of Canada* 3rd ser., No. 5 (1912). See Paul A. Wallace, *The White Roots of Peace*, (Philadelphia: University of Philadelphia Press, 1946), p. vii.
6. This rendition was dictated by Chief John A. Gibson (also involved in the Chief's Version of 1900) to J.N.B. Hewitt in 1899 was revised by Chiefs Abram Charles, John Buck, Sr., and Joshua Buck from 1900–1914. The final product was translated from Mohawk into English by William N. Fenton and Simeon Gibson in 1943 and currently resides in the archives of the Bureau of American Ethnology. See Fenton, (1949), 158; Wallace (1946), vii.
7. Fenton, 1949, 158. Fenton refers here to two manuscripts, one recited in Onondaga by Chief John A. Gibson to J.N.B. Hewitt, apparently because Gibson was dissatisfied with both the Newhouse and Chiefs' Committee renditions. After Gibson died, his manuscript was revised by Hewitt and a number of learned men from the Six Nations reserve, including Gibson's two sons. Fenton translated it with help from Simeon Gibson in 1941. This version is accompanied by a version recited by John Gibson to A.A. Goldenweiser, which expanded on the version Gibson had given to Hewitt. Both manuscripts are held in the archives of the Bureau of American Ethnology, and Fenton believes together they offer the most satisfactory single account of the Confederacy. Paul A. W. Wallace included both these versions in his *White Roots of Peace* (1946).
8. See Fenton, 1975. 131–47; Englebrecht, 1985, 176–77.
9. See notes 5, 6, 7, above.
10. Although it does contain sections concerning laws of adoption (articles 66–70), emigration (articles 71–72), war (see "rights and powers of war", articles 79–91), treason or secession (article 92), and "protection of the house" (article 107).

(b) *Sechelt Indian Band Self-Government Act*†

See **Chapter 12, Part 3(c)(iii)(B)**.

BILL C–93

An Act relating to self-government for the Sechelt Indian Band

WHEREAS Parliament and the government of Canada are committed to enabling Indian bands that wish to exercise self-government on lands set apart for those bands to do so;

AND WHEREAS the members of the *Indian Act* Sechelt band, in a referendum held on March 15, 1986, approved of

† S.C. 1986, c. 27.

(a) the enactment of legislation substantially as set out in this Act for the purpose of enabling the Sechelt Band to exercise self-government over its lands, and
(b) the transfer by Her Majesty in right of Canada to the Sechelt Indian Band of fee simple title in all Sechelt reserve lands, recognizing that the Sechelt Indian Band would assume complete responsibility, in accordance with this Act, for the management, administration and control of all Sechelt lands;

NOW, THEREFORE, Her Majesty, by and with the advice and consent of the Senate and House of Commons of Canada, enacts as follows:

Short Title

1. This Act may be cited as the *Sechelt Indian Band Self-Government Act.*

Interpretation

2.(1) In this Act,

"Band" means the Sechelt Indian Band established by subsection 5(1);

"Council" means the Sechelt Indian Band Council referred to in section 8;

"District" means the Sechelt Indian Government District recognized by section 17;

"District Council" means the Sechelt Indian Government District Council established by subsection 19(1);

"Minister" means the Minister of Indian Affairs and Northern Development;

"Sechelt lands" means

(a) lands transferred to the Band under section 23, and
(b) lands that are declared by the Governor-in-Council and the Lieutenant-Governor-in-Council of British Columbia to be Sechelt lands for the purposes of this Act.

(2) For greater certainty, Sechelt lands do not include lands described in the definition "Sechelt lands" in subsection (1) where the lands have been sold or the title to the lands has been otherwise transferred.

3. For greater certainty, nothing in this Act shall be construed so as to abrogate or derogate from any existing aboriginal or treaty rights of the members of the Sechelt Indian Band, or any other aboriginal peoples of Canada, under section 35 of the *Constitution Act, 1982.*

Purposes of Act

4. The purposes of this Act are to enable the Sechelt Indian Band to exercise and maintain self-government on Sechelt lands and to obtain control over and the administration of the resources and services available to its members.

Sechelt Indian Band

5.(1) The Sechelt Indian Band is hereby established to replace the *Indian Act* Sechelt band.

(2) The *Indian Act* Sechelt band ceases to exist, and all its rights, titles, interests, assets, obligations and liabilities, including those of its band council, vest in the Sechelt Indian Band established under subsection (1).

Capacity and Powers of Band

6. The Band is a legal entity and has, subject to this Act, the capacity, rights, powers and privileges of a natural person and, without restricting the generality of the foregoing, may

(a) enter into contracts or agreements;
(b) acquire and hold property or any interest therein, and sell or otherwise dispose of that property or interest;
(c) expend or invest moneys;
(d) borrow money;
(e) sue or be sued; and
(f) do such other things as are conducive to the exercise of its rights, powers and privileges.

7. The powers and duties of the Band shall be carried out in accordance with its constitution.

Sechelt Indian Band Council

8. The Sechelt Indian Band Council shall be the governing body of the Band, and its members shall be elected in accordance with the constitution of the Band.

9. The Band shall act through the Council in exercising its powers and carrying out its duties and functions.

Band Constitution

10.(1) The constitution of the Band shall be in writing and may

(a) establish the composition of the Council, the terms of office and tenure of its members and procedures relating to the election of Council members;
(b) establish the procedures or processes to be followed by the Council in exercising the Band's powers and carrying out its duties;
(c) provide for a system of financial accountability of the Council to the members of the Band, including audit arrangements and the publication of financial reports;
(d) include a membership code for the Band;
(e) establish rules and procedures relating to the holding of referenda referred to in section 12 or subsection 21(3) or provided for in the constitution of the Band;
(f) establish rules and procedures to be followed in respect of the disposition of rights and interests in Sechelt lands;
(g) set out specific legislative powers of the Council selected from among the general classes of matters set out in section 14; and
(h) provide for any other matters relating to the government of the Band, its members or Sechelt lands.

(2) A membership code established in the constitution of the Band shall respect rights to membership in the *Indian Act* Sechelt band acquired under the *Indian Act* immediately prior to the establishment of that code.

11.(1) The Governor-in-Council may, on the advice of the Minister, by order, declare that the constitution of the Band is in force, if

(a) the constitution includes or provides for the matters set out in paragraphs 10(1)(a) to (f);
(b) the constitution has the support of a majority of the electors of the *Indian Act* Sechelt band or of the Sechelt Indian Band; and
(c) the Governor-in-Council approves the constitution.

(2) The support of a majority of the electors of the *Indian Act* Sechelt band or of the Sechelt Indian Band shall, for the purposes of this section, be established by a referendum held in accordance with the *Indian Referendum Regulations*.

Amendment to Band Constitution

12. The Governor-in-Council may, on the advice of the Minister, by order, declare in force an amendment to the constitution of the Band, if the amendment has been approved in a referendum held in accordance with the constitution of the Band and the Governor-in-Council approves the amendment.

Publication of Constitution and Amendments

13. The Minister shall cause to be published in the *Canada Gazette* the constitution or any amendment thereto forthwith on issuing an order declaring the constitution or amendment in force under this Act.

Legislative Powers of Council

14.(1) The Council has, to the extent that it is authorized by the constitution of the Band to do so, the power to make laws in relation to matters coming within any of the following classes of matters:

(a) access to and residence on Sechelt lands;
(b) zoning and land use planning in respect of Sechelt lands;
(c) expropriation, for community purposes, of interests in Sechelt lands by the Band;
(d) the use, construction, maintenance, repair and demolition of buildings and structures on Sechelt lands;
(e) taxation, for local purposes, of interests in Sechelt lands, and of occupants and tenants of Sechelt lands in respect of their interests in those lands, including assessment, collection and enforcement procedures and appeals relating thereto;
(f) the administration and management of property belonging to the Band;
(g) education of Band members on Sechelt lands;
(h) social and welfare services with respect to Band members, including, without restricting the generality of the foregoing, the custody and placement of children of Band members;
(i) health services on Sechelt lands;
(j) the preservation and management of natural resources on Sechelt lands;
(k) the preservation, protection and management of fur-bearing animals, fish and game on Sechelt lands;
(l) public order and safety on Sechelt lands;
(m) the construction, maintenance and management of roads and the regulation of traffic on Sechelt lands;
(n) the operation of businesses, professions and trades on Sechelt lands;
(o) the prohibition of the sale, barter, supply, manufacture or possession of intoxicants on

Sechelt lands and any exceptions to a prohibition of possession;

(p) subject to subsection (2), the imposition on summary conviction of fines or imprisonment for the contravention of any law made by the Band government;

(q) the devolution, by testate or intestate succession, of real property of Band members on Sechelt lands and personal property of Band members ordinarily resident on Sechelt lands;

(r) financial administration of the Band;

(s) the conduct of Band elections and referenda;

(t) the creation of administrative bodies and agencies to assist in the administration of the affairs of the Band; and

(u) matters related to the good government of the Band, its members or Sechelt lands.

(2) A law made in respect of the class of matters set out in paragraph (1)(p) may specify a maximum fine or a maximum term of imprisonment or both, but the maximum fine may not exceed two thousand dollars and the maximum term of imprisonment may not exceed six months.

(3) For greater certainty, the Council has the power to adopt any laws of British Columbia as its own law if it is authorized by the constitution to make laws in relation to the subject-matter of those laws.

(4) A law made by the Council may require the holding of a licence or permit and may provide for the issuance thereof and fees therefor.

15. The Council may exercise any legislative power granted to it by or pursuant to an Act of the legislature of British Columbia.

16. The *Statutory Instruments Act* does not apply to a law enacted by the Council.

Sechelt Indian Government District

17. There is hereby recognized the Sechelt Indian Government District, which shall have jurisdiction over all Sechelt lands.

18. The District is a legal entity and has the capacity, rights, powers and privileges of a natural person and, without restricting the generality of the foregoing, may

(a) enter into contracts or agreements;

(b) acquire and hold property or any interest therein, and sell or otherwise dispose of that property or interest;

(c) expend or invest moneys;

(d) borrow money;

(e) sue or be sued; and

(f) do such other things as are conducive to the exercise of its rights, powers and privileges.

19.(1) There is hereby established the Sechelt Indian Government District Council, which shall be the governing body of the District.

(2) The District Council shall consist of the members of the Council.

20. The District shall act through the District Council in exercising its powers and carrying out its duties and functions.

21.(1) Sections 17 to 20 shall come into force in accordance with this section.

(2) The Governor-in-Council may, subject to subsection (3), on the advice of the Minister, by order, declare that sections 17 to 20 are in force and transfer any of the powers, duties or functions of the Band or the Council under this Act or the constitution of the Band to the District, except those relating to membership in the Band and the disposition of rights or interests in Sechelt lands.

(3) The Governor-in-Council shall not make an order under subsection (2) unless he is satisfied that

(a) the legislature of British Columbia has passed legislation respecting the District and the legislation is in force in British Columbia; and

(b) the transfer of the powers specified in the order has been approved in a referendum held in accordance with the constitution of the Band.

(4) The Governor-in-Council may, on the advice of the Minister, by order, transfer any of the powers, duties and functions that were transferred to the District under subsection (2) back to the Band or the Council, as the case may be, if the legislation referred to in paragraph (3)(a) is amended.

(5) The Governor-in-Council shall not make an order under subsection (4) unless he is satisfied that the transfer of powers specified in the order has been approved in a referendum held in accordance with the constitution of the Band.

(6) The Governor-in-Council may, on the advice of the Minister, by order, declare that sections 17 to 20 are no longer in force and transfer the powers, duties and functions that were transferred to the District under subsection (2) back to the Band if the legislation referred to in paragraph (3)(a) is no longer in force.

22. The District may exercise any legislative power granted to it by or pursuant to an Act of the legislature of British Columbia.

Transfer of Lands

23.(1) The title to all lands, that were, immediately prior to the coming into force of this section, reserves, within the meaning of the *Indian Act*, of the *Indian Act* Sechelt band is hereby transferred in fee simple to the Band, subject to the rights, interests and conditions referred to in section 24.

(2) In subsection (1), "reserves" includes surrendered lands, within the meaning of the *Indian Act*, that have not been sold or the title to which has not been otherwise transferred.

(3) All rights and interests of the *Indian Act* Sechelt band in respect of the lands referred to in subsection (1) cease to exist on the coming into force of this section.

(4) Forthwith on the coming into force of this section the Governor-in-Council shall cause to be issued under the Great Seal of Canada letters patent confirming the transfer of, and describing, the lands referred to in subsection (1).

24. The fee simple title of the Band in the lands transferred to it under section 23 is subject to...[various exceptions regarding Crown mineral rights, existing third party interests, etc.]....

. . . .

25. The Band holds the lands transferred to it under section 23 for the use and benefit of the Band and its members.

Disposition of Sechelt Lands

26. The Band has full power to dispose of any Sechelt lands and any rights or interests therein but shall not do so except in accordance with the procedure established in the constitution of the Band.

Registration of Sechelt Lands

27.(1) Subject to subsection (2), particulars relating to all transactions respecting Sechelt lands shall be entered in the Reserve Land Register kept under section 21 of the *Indian Act*.

(2) This section does not apply with respect to any Sechelt lands that are registered pursuant to section 28.

28. The Council may make laws authorizing the registration, in accordance with the laws of British Columbia, of estates or interests in any Sechelt lands specified in the laws of the Council, and for that purpose may make laws making any laws of British Columbia applicable to those Sechelt lands.

. . . .

[Sections 29 and 30 make further provision for registration of lands.]

Sechelt Lands

31. For greater certainty, Sechelt lands are lands reserved for the Indians within the meaning of Class 24 of section 91 of the *Constitution Act, 1867*.

Moneys

32.(1) Moneys held by Her Majesty in right of Canada for the use and benefit of the *Indian Act* Sechelt band shall be transferred to the Band.

(2) Moneys transferred under this section shall be administered in accordance with the constitution and laws of the Band.

Funding

33. The Minister may, with the approval of the Governor-in-Council, enter into an agreement with the Band under which funding would be provided by the government of Canada to the Band in the form of grants over such period of time, and subject to such terms and conditions, as are specified in the agreement.

34. Any amounts required for the purposes of section 33 shall be paid out of such moneys as may be appropriated by Parliament for those purposes.

Application of Indian Act

35.(1) Subject to section 36, the *Indian Act* applies, with such modifications as the circumstances require, in respect of the Band, its members, the Council and Sechelt lands except to the extent that the *Indian Act* is inconsistent with this Act, the constitution of the Band or a law of the Band.

(2) For greater certainty, the *Indian Act* applies for the purpose of determining which members of the Band are "Indians" within the meaning of that Act.

(3) For greater certainty, section 87 of the *Indian Act* applies, with such modifications as the circumstances require, in respect of the Band and its members, who are Indians within the meaning of that Act, subject to any laws made by the Council in relation to the class of matters set out in paragraph 14(1)(e).

36. The Governor-in-Council may, on the advice of the Minister, by order declare that the *Indian Act* or any provision thereof does not apply to

(a) the Band or its members, or
(b) any portion of Sechelt lands, and may, on the advice of the Minister, by order revoke any such order.

Application of Laws of Canada

37. All federal laws of general application in force in Canada are applicable to and in respect of the Band, its members and Sechelt lands, except to the extent that those laws are inconsistent with this Act.

Application of Laws of British Columbia

38. Laws of general application of British Columbia apply to or in respect of the members of the Band except to the extent that those laws are inconsistent with the terms of any treaty, this or any other Act of Parliament, the constitution of the Band or a law of the Band.

. . . .

[Sections 39 to 41 relate to the application of natural resources laws.]

Application of By-laws

42. The by-laws of the *Indian Act* Sechelt band that are in force immediately before this Act comes into force remain in force on Sechelt lands that were, at that time, reserves, within the meaning of the *Indian Act*, of the *Indian Act* Sechelt band and in respect of the members of the Band to the extent that the by-laws are consistent with this Act, the constitution of the Band or a law of the Band.

Governor-in-Council and Ministers

43. The Governor-in-Council or any Minister of the Crown may exercise any powers and carry out any functions or duties that the Governor-in-Council or Minister, as the case may be, is authorized under the constitution of the Band to exercise or *carry out.*

Transitional Provisions

44.(1) The council of the *Indian Act* Sechelt band that is in office pursuant to the *Indian Act* immediately before the coming into force of section 5 shall be deemed to be the Council and to have been elected in accordance with the constitution of the Band.

(2) The council of the *Indian Act* Sechelt band referred to in subsection (1) shall continue in office as the Council until a new Council has been elected in accordance with the constitution of the Band.

(3) Any provisions of the *Indian Act* relating to elections of band councils and the qualification of persons to hold office as chief or councillor apply to the council of the *Indian Act* Sechelt band until a new Council has been elected in accordance with the constitution of the Band.

45.(1) The members of the *Indian Act* Sechelt band, immediately before the coming into force of this Act, are the members of the Sechelt Indian band immediately after the coming into force of the Act.

(2) For greater certainty, during any period after this Act comes into force but before the Band constitution comes into force the provisions of the *Indian Act* relating to membership apply in respect of the Sechelt Indian Band.

46. For greater certainty, during any period after this Act comes into force but before the constitution of the Band comes into force, the provisions of the *Indian Act* relating to the disposition of rights or interests in reserves, within the meaning of that Act, apply in respect of Sechelt lands.

Consequential Amendments

. . . .

Commencement

61. This Act or any provision thereof shall come into force on a day or days to be fixed by proclamation.

(c) *Vuntut Gwitchin First Nation Self-Government Agreement*†

See **Chapter 11, Part 7(f)** and **Chapter 12, Part 3(c)(iv)(A)**.

This Agreement made this 29th day of May, 1993

AMONG:

The Vuntut Gwitchin First Nation as represented by the Chief and Council (hereinafter referred to as the "Vuntut Gwitchin First Nation");

AND:

The Government of the Yukon as represented by the Government Leader of the Yukon on behalf of the Yukon (hereinafter referred to as "the Yukon");

AND:

Her Majesty the Queen in Right of Canada as represented by the Minister of Indian Affairs and Northern Development (hereinafter referred to as "Canada");

being the Parties (collectively referred to as "the Parties") to this Vuntut Gwitchin First Nation Self-Government Agreement (hereinafter referred to as "this Agreement").

. . . .

GENERAL

Definitions

1.1. In this Agreement:

"Act" includes ordinance;

"Citizen" means a citizen of the Vuntut Gwitchin First Nation as determined by the Constitution;

"Constitution" means the constitution of the Vuntut Gwitchin First Nation, in effect on the Effective Date, as amended from time to time;

"Consult or Consultation" means to provide:

(a) to the party to be consulted, notice of a matter to be decided in sufficient form and detail to allow that party to prepare its view on the matter,

(b) a reasonable period of time in which the party to be consulted may prepare its view on the matter, and an opportunity to present such views to the party obliged to consult, and

(c) full and fair consideration by the party obliged to consult of any views presented.

"Council for Yukon Indians" includes any successor to the Council for Yukon Indians and, in the absence of a successor, the Yukon First Nations;

"Effective Date" means the date on which this Agreement is brought into effect by the Self-Government Legislation;

"Emergency" includes apprehended, imminent or actual danger to life, health, safety, or the environment;

"Final Agreement" means the Vuntut Gwitchin First Nation Final Agreement between Canada, the Vuntut Gwitchin First Nation and the Government of the Yukon, initialled by the negotiators for the Parties the 31st day of May, 1992;

"Government" means Government of Canada or the Government of the Yukon, or both, depending on which government or governments have responsibility, from time to time, for the matter in question;

"Law" includes common law;

"Laws of General Application" means laws of general application as defined by common law, but does not include laws enacted by the Vuntut Gwitchin First Nation;

"Legislative Assembly" means the Council of the Yukon Territory as defined in the *Yukon Act*, R.S.C. 1985, c. Y–2;

"Legislation" includes Acts, Regulations, orders-in-council and bylaws;

"Minister" means the Minister or Ministers of Government charged by Legislation with the responsibility, from time to time, for the exercise of powers in relation to the matter in question;

† (May 29, 1993). Source of Information: Indian and Northern Affairs Canada. Reproduced with the permission of the Minister of Public Works and Government Services Canada, 1999.

"Regulation" includes a regulation or any instrument made in the execution of a power or authority conferred by an Act, but does not include laws enacted by the Vuntut Gwitchin First Nation;

"Self-Government Legislation" means the Legislation which brings this Agreement into effect;

"Settlement Agreement" has the same meaning as in the Final Agreement;

"Settlement Corporation" means a corporation as described in 20.4.2 of the Final Agreement, created by the Vuntut Gwitchin First Nation alone or together with one or more other Yukon First Nations;

"Settlement Land" means those lands identified as Settlement Land for the Vuntut Gwitchin First Nation;

"Settlement Legislation" has the same meaning as in the Final Agreement;

"Umbrella Final Agreement" means the Comprehensive Land Claim Umbrella Final Agreement between Canada, the Council for Yukon Indians and the Government of the Yukon, initialled by the negotiators for the parties to that Agreement on the 30th day of May 1992;

"Yukon First Nation" means one of the following:

- Carcross/Tagish First Nation;
- Champagne and Aishihik First Nations;
- Dawson First Nation;
- Kluane First Nation;
- Kwanlin Dun First Nation;
- Liard First Nation;
- Little Salmon/Carmacks First Nation;
- First Nation of Na'cho N'y'ak Dun;
- Ross River Dena Council;
- Selkirk First Nation;
- Ta'an Kwach'an Council;
- Teslin Tlingit Council;
- Vuntut Gwitchin First Nation; or
- White River First Nation;

"Yukon First Nations" means all of the Yukon First Nations defined as a Yukon First Nation;

"Yukon Indian People" means people enrolled under one of the Yukon First Nation Agreements in Accordance with the criteria established in Chapter 3 of the Umbrella final Agreement; and

"Yukon Law of General Application" means a Law of General Application enacted pursuant to the *Yukon Act*, R.S.C. 1985, c. Y–2.

Principles

2.1. The Vuntut Gwitchin First Nation has traditional decision-making structures and desires to maintain these traditional structures integrated with contemporary forms of government.

2.2. The Parties are committed to promoting opportunities for the well-being of Citizens equal to those of other Canadians and to providing essential public services of reasonable quality to all Citizens.

General Provisions

3.1. This Agreement shall not affect any aboriginal claim, right, title or interest of the Vuntut Gwitchin First Nation or of its Citizens.

3.2. This Agreement shall not affect the identity of the Citizens of the Vuntut Gwitchin First Nation as aboriginal people of Canada.

3.3. This Agreement shall not affect the ability of the aboriginal people of the Vuntut Gwitchin First Nation to exercise, or benefit from, any existing or future constitutional rights for aboriginal people that may be applicable to them.

3.4. Unless otherwise provided pursuant to this Agreement or in a law of the Vuntut Gwitchin First Nation enacted hereunder, this Agreement shall not affect the ability of Citizens to participate in and benefit from government programs for status Indians, non-status Indians or native people, as the case may be. Benefits under such programs shall be determined by the general criteria for such programs established from time to time.

3.5. Except for the purpose of determining which Citizens are "Indians" within the meaning of the *Indian Act*, R.S.C. 1985, c. I–5, the *Indian Act*, R.S.C. 1985, c. I–5, does not apply to Citizens, the Vuntut Gwitchin First Nation or Settlement Land.

3.6. This Agreement shall not:

3.6.1. affect the rights of Citizens as Canadian citizens; and

3.6.2. unless otherwise provided pursuant to this agreement or in a law of the Vuntut Gwitchin First Nation enacted hereunder, affect the entitlement of Citizens to all of the benefits, services, and protections of other citizens applicable from time to time.

3.7. Government may determine, from time to time, how and by whom any power or authority of Government set out in this agreement shall be exercised, other than the power to consent to an amendment pursuant to 6.2.

Ratification

4.1. Ratification of this Agreement shall be sought by the Parties and shall be ratified by each of the Parties in the following manner:

4.1.1. by Canada, by the Governor in Council;

4.1.2. by the Yukon, by the Commissioner in Executive Council; and

4.1.3. by the Vuntut Gwitchin First Nation, by the process set out in Schedule A of this Agreement.

Self-government Legislation

5.1. Prior to ratification of this Agreement, Government shall negotiate, with the Council for Yukon Indians, guidelines for drafting Self-Government Legislation that shall, among other things, take into account the provisions of this Agreement.

5.2. Government shall Consult the Council for Yukon Indians during the drafting of Self-Government Legislation.

5.3. Government shall Consult the affected Yukon First Nations during the drafting of any subsequent amendments to the Self-Government Legislation.

Amendment and Review

6.1. This Agreement may only be amended with the consent of the Parties.

6.2. Consent to any amendment pursuant to 6.1 may only be given on the part of:

6.2.1. Canada, by the Governor in Council;

6.2.2. the Yukon, by the Commissioner in Executive Council; and

6.2.3. the Vuntut Gwitchin First Nation, by the Chief and Council.

6.3. Where Government has concluded a self-government agreement with another Yukon First Nation which includes provisions more favourable than those in this Agreement, and where it would be practical to include those provisions in this Agreement, Government, at the request of the Vuntut Gwitchin First Nation shall negotiate with the Vuntut Gwitchin First Nation with a view to amending this Agreement to incorporate provisions no less favourable than those in the other self-government agreement.

6.4. A dispute arising from negotiations described in 6.3 may be referred by any Party to dispute resolution pursuant to 26.3.0 of the final agreement.

6.4.1. In any dispute arising pursuant to 6.3 an arbitrator shall have the authority set out in 26.7.3 of the Final Agreement.

6.5. The Parties shall make amendments to this Agreement which are required to give effect to orders or decisions of an arbitrator pursuant to 6.4.

6.6. Unless the Parties otherwise agree, the Parties shall review this Agreement within five years of the Effective Date of this Agreement for the purpose of determining whether:

6.6.1. other self-government agreements in Canada have more effectively incorporated self-government provisions respecting any matters considered in this Agreement;

6.6.2. other self-government agreements in Canada have more effectively incorporated implementation or financial transfer agreements;

6.6.3. this Agreement has been implemented in accordance with the implementation plan;

6.6.4. the negotiated transfer of programs, responsibilities and resources pursuant to this Agreement have been successful; and

6.6.5. this Agreement should be amended in accordance with 6.1 and 6.2 to reflect the outcome of the review.

Remedies

[Section 7 on Remedies includes an agreement by the parties not to challenge the validity of this Agreement.]

. . . .

Interpretation and Application of Law

8.1. Subject to 8.1.1, where there is any inconsistency or conflict between the provisions of the federal Self-Government Legislation and any other federal Legislation, the federal Self-Government Legislation shall prevail to the extent of the inconsistency or conflict.

8.1.1. Where there is any inconsistency or conflict between the provisions of the federal Self-Government Legislation and the Final Agreement or the Settlement Legislation, the Final Agreement or the Settlement Legislation shall prevail to the extent of the inconsistency or conflict.

8.2. Subject to 8.2.1, where there is any inconsistency or conflict between the provisions of Yukon Self-Government Legislation and any other Yukon Legislation, the Yukon Self-Government Legislation shall prevail to the extent of the inconsistency or conflict.

8.2.1. Where there is any inconsistency or conflict between the provisions of the Yukon Self-Government Legislation and the Final Agreement or the Settlement Legislation, the Final Agreement or the Settlement Legislation shall prevail to the extent of the inconsistency or conflict.

8.3. This Agreement is subject to the Final Agreement, and in the event of any inconsistency or conflict, the final Agreement shall prevail to the extent of the inconsistency or conflict.

8.4. Common law conflict of laws principles shall apply where a conflict of laws issue arises unless:

8.4.1. in the case of a conflict of laws issue arising between a law of the Vuntut Gwitchin First Nation and a law of another Yukon First Nation, the Vuntut Gwitchin First Nation and the other Yukon First Nation have otherwise agreed; or

8.4.2. in the case of a conflict of laws issue arising between a law of the Vuntut Gwitchin First Nation and a Law of General Application, the First Nation and Government have otherwise agreed.

8.5. Unless otherwise provided in this Agreement, the exercise of powers by the Vuntut Gwitchin First Nation pursuant to this Agreement shall not confer any duties, obligations or responsibilities on Government.

8.6. This Agreement shall be interpreted according to the *Interpretation Act*, R.S.C. 1985, c. I–21, with such modifications as the circumstances require.

8.7. The preamble and the principles in this Agreement are statements of the intentions of the Parties and shall only be used to assist in the interpretation of doubtful or ambiguous expressions in this Agreement.

8.8. Capitalized words or phrases shall have the meaning as defined in this Agreement.

8.9. Any reference in this Agreement to Legislation, an Act or a provision of an Act includes:

8.9.1. that Legislation, Act or provision of an Act, and any Regulations made thereunder, as amended from time to time; and

8.9.2. any successor Legislation, Act or provision of an Act.

8.10. Successor Legislation includes Yukon Legislation which replaces federal Legislation as a consequence of devolution of authority or responsibility from Canada to the Yukon.

8.11. The Supreme Court of the Yukon shall have jurisdiction in respect of any action or proceeding arising out of this Agreement or Self-Government Legislation.

8.12. Nothing in this Agreement shall be construed to limit the jurisdiction of the Federal Court of Canada as set forth in the *Federal Court Act*, R.S.C. 1985, c. F–7.

THE VUNTUT GWITCHIN FIRST NATION

Legal Status of the First Nation

9.1. Upon the Effective Date, the *Indian Act*, R.S.C. 1985, c. I–5, Old Crow Tribal Band shall cease to exist and its rights, titles, interests, assets, obligations and liabilities, including those of its band council, shall vest in the Vuntut Gwitchin First Nation.

9.2. The Vuntut Gwitchin First Nation is a legal entity and has the capacity, rights, powers and privileges of a natural person and without restricting the generality of the foregoing may:

9.2.1. enter into contracts or agreements;

9.2.2. acquire and hold property or any interest therein, sell or otherwise dispose of property or any interest therein;

9.2.3. raise, invest, expend and borrow money;

9.2.4. sue or be sued;

9.2.5. form corporations or other legal entities; and

9.2.6. do such other things as may be conducive to the exercise of its rights, powers and privileges.

9.3. The act of acquiring or the holding of any rights, liabilities or obligations by any entity described in 9.2, shall not be construed to affect any aboriginal right, title or interest of the Vuntut Gwitchin First Nation, its Citizens or their heirs, descendants or successors.

First Nation Constitution

10.1. The Vuntut Gwitchin First Nation Constitution shall:

10.1.1. contain the Vuntut Gwitchin First Nation citizenship code;
10.1.2. establish governing bodies and provide for their powers, duties, composition, membership and procedures;
10.1.3. provide for a system of reporting which may include audits through which the Vuntut Gwitchin First Nation government shall be financially accountable to its Citizens;
10.1.4. recognize and protect the rights and freedoms of Citizens;
10.1.5. provide for the challenging of the validity of laws enacted by the Vuntut Gwitchin First Nation and for the quashing of invalid laws;
10.1.6. provide for amending the Constitution by the Citizens; and
10.1.7. be consistent with this Agreement.

10.2. The Constitution may provide for any other matters relating to the Vuntut Gwitchin First Nation government or to the governing of Settlement Land, or of persons on Settlement Land.

10.3. The citizenship code established in the Constitution shall enable all persons enrolled under the Final Agreement to be Citizens.

Transitional Provisions

11.1. The Band Council of the *Indian Act*, R.S.C. 1985, c. I–5, Old Crow Indian Band that is in office on the Effective Date shall be deemed to be the governing body of the Vuntut Gwitchin First Nation until replaced in accordance with the constitution.

11.2. Any money held by Her Majesty in right of Canada for the use and benefit of the *Indian Act*, R.S.C. 1985, c. I–5, Old Crow Indian Band shall be transferred to the Vuntut Gwitchin First Nation, as soon as practicable after the Effective Date.

Delegation

12.1. The Vuntut Gwitchin First Nation may delegate any of its powers, including legislative powers, to:

12.1.1. a public body or official established by a law of the Vuntut Gwitchin First Nation;
12.1.2. Government, including a department, agency or official of Government;
12.1.3. a public body performing a function of government in Canada, including another Yukon First Nation;
12.1.4. a municipality, school board, local body, or legal entity established by Yukon law;
12.1.5. a tribal council;
12.1.6. the Council for Yukon Indians; or
12.1.7. any legal entity in Canada.

12.2. Any delegation under paragraphs 12.1.2 to 12.1.7 shall be made by written agreement with the delegate.

12.3. The Vuntut Gwitchin First Nation has the capacity to enter into an agreement to receive powers, including legislative powers, by delegation.

VUNTUT GWITCHIN FIRST NATION LEGISLATION

Legislative Powers

13.1. The Vuntut Gwitchin First Nation shall have the exclusive power to enact laws in relation to the following matters:

13.1.1. administration of Vuntut Gwitchin First Nation affairs and operation and internal management of the Vuntut Gwitchin First Nation;
13.1.2. management and administration of rights or benefits which are realized pursuant to the Final Agreement by persons enrolled under the Final Agreement, and which are to be controlled by the Vuntut Gwitchin First Nation; and
13.1.3. matters ancillary to the foregoing.

13.2. The Vuntut Gwitchin First Nation shall have the power to enact laws in relation to the following matters in the Yukon:

13.2.1. provision of programs and services for Citizens in relation to their spiritual and cultural beliefs and practices;

13.2.2. provision of programs and services for Citizens in relation to their aboriginal languages;

13.2.3. provision of health care and services to Citizens, except licensing and regulation of facility-based services off Settlement Land;

13.2.4. provision of social and welfare services to Citizens, except licensing and regulation of facility-based services off Settlement Land;

13.2.5. provision of training programs for Citizens subject to Government certification requirements where applicable;

13.2.6. adoption by and of Citizens;

13.2.7. guardianship, custody, care and placement of Vuntut Gwitchin First Nation children, except licensing and regulation of facility-based services off Settlement Land;

13.2.8. provision of education programs and services for Citizens choosing to participate, except licensing and regulation of facility-based services off Settlement Land;

13.2.9. inheritance, wills, intestacy and administration of estates of Citizens including rights and interests in Settlement Land;

13.2.10. procedures consistent with the principles of natural justice for determining the mental competency or ability of Citizens including administration of rights and interests of those found incapable of responsibility for their own affairs;

13.2.11. provision of services to Citizens for resolution of disputes outside the courts;

13.2.12. solemnization of marriage of Citizens;

13.2.13. licences in respect of matters enumerated in 13.1. 13.2 and 13.3 in order to raise revenue for Vuntut Gwitchin First Nation purposes;

13.2.14. other matters necessary to enable the Vuntut Gwitchin First Nation to fulfil its responsibilities under the Final Agreement or this Agreement; and

13.2.15. other matters ancillary to the foregoing.

13.3. The Vuntut Gwitchin First Nation shall have the power to enact laws of a local or private nature on Settlement Land in relation to the following matters:

13.3.1. use, management, administration, control and protection of Settlement Land;

13.3.2. allocation or disposition of rights and interests in and to Settlement Land, including expropriation by the Vuntut Gwitchin First Nation for the Vuntut Gwitchin First Nations's purposes;

13.3.3. use, management, administration and protection of natural resources under the ownership, control or jurisdiction of the Vuntut Gwitchin First Nation;

13.3.4. gathering, hunting, trapping or fishing and the protection of fish, wildlife and habitat;

13.3.5. control or prohibition of the erection and placement of posters and advertising signs or billboards;

13.3.6. licensing and regulating any person carrying on any business, trade, profession, or other occupation;

13.3.7. control or prohibition of public games, sports, races, athletic contests and other amusements;

13.3.8. control of the construction, maintenance, repair and demolition of buildings or other structures;

13.3.9. prevention of overcrowding or residences or other buildings or structures;

13.3.10. control of the sanitary condition of buildings or property;

13.3.11. planning, zoning and land development;

13.3.12. curfews, prevention of disorderly conduct and control or prohibition of nuisances;

13.3.13. control or prohibition of the operation and use of vehicles;

13.3.14. control or prohibition of the transport, sale, exchange, manufacture, supply, possession or consumption of intoxicants;

13.3.15. establishment, maintenance, provision, operation or regulation of local services and facilities;

13.3.16. caring and keeping of livestock, poultry, pets and other birds and animals, and impoundment and disposal of any bird or animal maltreated or improperly at-large, but the caring and keeping of livestock does not include game farming or game ranching;

13.3.17. administration of justice;

13.3.18. control or prohibition of any actions, activities or undertakings that constitute, or may constitute, a threat to public order, peace or safety;

13.3.19. control or prohibition of any activities, conditions or undertakings that constitute, or may constitute a danger to public health;

13.3.20. control or prevention of pollution and protection of the environment;

13.3.21. control or prohibition of the possession or use of firearms, other weapons and explosives;

13.3.22. control or prohibition of the transport of dangerous substances; and

13.3.23. other matters coming within the good government of Citizens on Settlement Land.

13.4. Emergency Powers

13.4.1. Off Settlement Land, in relation to those matters in 13.2, in any situation that poses an Emergency to a Citizen, Government may exercise a power conferred by Laws of General Application to relieve the Emergency, notwithstanding that laws of the Vuntut Gwitchin First Nation may apply to the Emergency.

13.4.2. A person acting pursuant to 13.4.1 shall, as soon as practicable, after determining that a person in an Emergency is a Citizen, notify the Vuntut Gwitchin First Nation of the action taken and transfer the matter to the responsible Vuntut Gwitchin First Nation authority, at which time the authority of the Government to act pursuant to 13.4.1 shall cease.

13.4.3. A person acting pursuant to 13.4.1 is not liable for any act done in good faith in the reasonable belief that the act was necessary to relieve an Emergency.

13.4.4. On Settlement Land, in relation to those matters in 13.4, in any situation that poses an Emergency to a person who is not a Citizen, the Vuntut Gwitchin First Nation may exercise a power conferred by laws of the Vuntut Gwitchin First Nation to relieve the Emergency, notwithstanding that a Law of General Application may apply to the Emergency.

13.4.5. A person acting pursuant to 13.4.4 shall, as soon as practicable, after determining that a person in an Emergency is not a Citizen, notify Government or where the person in an Emergency is a citizen of another Yukon First Nation, that Yukon First Nation, of the action taken and transfer the matter to the responsible authority, at which time the authority of the Vuntut Gwitchin First Nation to act pursuant to 13.4.4 shall cease.

13.4.6. A person acting pursuant to 13.4.4 is not liable for any act done in good faith in the reasonable belief that the act was necessary to relieve an Emergency.

13.4.7. Notwithstanding 13.5.0, in relation to powers enumerated in 13.3, Laws of General Application shall apply with respect to an Emergency arising on Settlement Land which has or is likely to have an effect off Settlement Land.

13.5. Laws of General Application

13.5.1. Unless otherwise provided in this Agreement, all laws of General Application shall continue to apply to the Vuntut Gwitchin First Nation, its Citizens and Settlement Land.

13.5.2. Canada and the Vuntut Gwitchin First Nation shall enter into negotiations with a view to concluding, as soon as practicable, a separate agreement or an amendment of this Agreement which will identify the areas in which the laws of the Vuntut Gwitchin First Nation shall prevail over federal Laws of General Application to the extent of any inconsistency or conflict.

13.5.2.1. Canada shall Consult with the Yukon prior to concluding the negotiations described in 13.5.2.

13.5.2.2. Clause 13.5.2 shall not affect the status of the Yukon as a party to the negotiations or agreements referred to in 13.6.0 or 17.0.

13.5.3. Except as provided in 14.0, a Yukon Law of General Application shall be inoperative to the extent that it provides for any matter for which provision is made in a law enacted by the Vuntut Gwitchin First Nation.

13.5.4. Where the Yukon reasonably foresees that a Yukon Law of General Application which it intends to enact may have an impact on a law of the Vuntut Gwitchin First Nation, the Yukon shall Consult with the Vuntut Gwitchin First Nation before introducing the Legislation into the Legislative Assembly.

13.5.5. Where the Vuntut Gwitchin First Nation reasonably foresees that a law of the Vuntut Gwitchin First Nation which it intends to enact may have an impact on a Yukon Law of General Application, the Vuntut Gwitchin First Nation shall Consult with the Yukon before enacting the law.

13.5.6. Where the Commissioner in Executive Council is of the opinion that the enactment of a law of the Vuntut Gwitchin First Nation has rendered a Yukon Law of General Application partially inoperative and that it would unreasonably alter the character of a Yukon

Law of General Application or that it would make it unduly difficult to administer that Yukon Law of General Application in relation to the Vuntut Gwitchin First Nation, Citizens or Settlement Land, the Commissioner in Executive Council may declare that the Yukon Law of General Application ceases to apply in whole or in part to the Vuntut Gwitchin First Nation, Citizens or Settlement Land.

13.5.7. Prior to making a declaration pursuant to 13.5.6, the Yukon shall:

13.5.7.1. Consult with the Vuntut Gwitchin First Nation and identify solutions, including any amendments to Yukon Legislation, that the Yukon considers would meet the objectives of the Vuntut Gwitchin First Nation; and

13.5.7.2. After Consultation pursuant to 13.5.6, where the Yukon and the Vuntut Gwitchin First Nation agree that the Yukon Law of General Application should be amended, the Yukon shall propose such amendment to the Legislative Assembly within a reasonable period of time.

13.6. Administration of Justice

13.6.1. The Parties shall enter into negotiations with a view to concluding an agreement in respect of the administration of Vuntut Gwitchin First Nation justice provided for in 13.3.17.

13.6.2. Negotiations respecting the administration of justice shall deal with such matters as adjudication, civil remedies, punitive sanctions including fine, penalty and imprisonment for enforcing any law of the Vuntut Gwitchin First Nation, prosecution, corrections, law enforcement, the relation of any Vuntut Gwitchin First Nation courts to other courts and any other matter related to aboriginal justice to which the Parties agree.

13.6.3. Notwithstanding anything in this Agreement, the Vuntut Gwitchin First Nation shall not exercise its power pursuant to 13.3.17 until the expiry of the time described in 13.6.6, unless an agreement is reached by the Parties pursuant to 13.6.1 and 13.6.2.

13.6.4. Until the expiry of the time described in 13.6.6 or an agreement is entered into pursuant to 13.6.1 and 13.6.2:

13.6.4.1. the Vuntut Gwitchin First Nation shall have the power to establish penalties of fines up to $5,000 and imprisonment to a maximum of six months for the violation of a law enacted by the Vuntut Gwitchin First Nation;

13.6.4.2. the Supreme Court of the Yukon Territory, the Territorial Court of Yukon, and the Justice of the Peace Court shall have jurisdiction throughout the Yukon to adjudicate in respect of a law of the Vuntut Gwitchin First Nation in accordance with the jurisdiction designated to those courts by Yukon Law except that any offence created under a law of the Vuntut Gwitchin First Nation shall be within the exclusive original jurisdiction of the Territorial Court of the Yukon;

13.6.4.3. any offence created under a law of the Vuntut Gwitchin First Nation shall be prosecuted as an offence against an enactment pursuant to the *Summary Convictions Act*, R.S.Y. 1986, c. 164 by prosecutors appointed by the Yukon; and

13.6.4.4. any term of imprisonment ordered by the Territorial Court of the Yukon pursuant to 13.6.4.1 shall be served in a correctional facility pursuant to the *Corrections Act*, R.S.Y., 1986, c. 36.

13.6.5. Nothing in 13.6.4 is intended to preclude:

13.6.5.1. consensual or existing customary practices of the Vuntut Gwitchin First Nation with respect to the administration of justice; or

13.6.5.2. programs and practices in respect of the administration of justice, including alternate sentencing or other appropriate remedies, to which the Parties agree before an agreement is concluded pursuant to 13.6.1 and 13.6.2.

13.6.6. The provisions in 13.6.4 are interim provisions and shall expire five years from the Effective Date or on the effective date of the agreement concluded pursuant to 13.6.1 and 13.6.2, whichever is earlier. If the Parties fail to reach an agreement pursuant to 13.6.1 and 13.6.2 during the five year period then the interim provisions shall extend for a further term ending December 31, 1999.

13.6.7. All new and incremental costs of implementing the interim provisions in 13.6.4 incurred by the Yukon shall be paid by Canada in accordance with guidelines to be negotiated by the Yukon and Canada.

Taxation

14.1. The Vuntut Gwitchin First Nation shall have the power to make laws in relation to:

14.1.1. taxation, for local purposes, of interests in Settlement Land, of occupants and tenants of Settlement Land in respect of their interests in those lands, including assessment, collection and enforcement procedures and appeals relating thereto;

14.1.2. other modes of direct taxation of Citizens (and, if agreed under 14.5.2, other persons and entities) within Settlement Land to raise revenue for Vuntut Gwitchin First Nation purposes; and

14.1.3. the implementation of measures made pursuant to any taxation agreement entered into pursuant to 15.1.

14.2. The Vuntut Gwitchin First Nation's powers provided for in 14.1 shall not limit Government's powers to levy tax or make taxation laws.

14.3. The Vuntut Gwitchin First Nation shall not exercise its power to make laws pursuant to 14.1.1 until the expiration of three years following the Effective Date, or until such earlier time as may be agreed between the Vuntut Gwitchin First Nation and the Yukon.

14.4. The Vuntut Gwitchin First Nation shall not exercise its power to make laws pursuant to 14.1.2 until the expiration of three years following the Effective Date.

14.5. After expiration of one year following the effective date of the Self-Government Legislation, or at such earlier time as may be agreed by Canada and the Vuntut Gwitchin First Nation, Canada and the Vuntut Gwitchin First Nation shall make reasonable efforts to negotiate agreements on:

14.5.1. the manner in which the Vuntut Gwitchin First Nation's power to make taxation laws under 14.1.2 shall be coordinated with existing tax systems; and

14.5.2. the extent, if any, to which the power provided for in 14.1.2 should be extended to apply to other persons and entities within Settlement Land.

14.6. When the Vuntut Gwitchin First Nation exercises its jurisdiction for, or assumes responsibility for the management, administration and delivery of, local services and as a consequence exercises property taxation powers under 14.1.1, the Yukon shall undertake to ensure a sharing of tax room in respect of property taxes consistent with equitable and comparable taxation levels.

14.6.1. To the extent that the Vuntut Gwitchin first Nation imposes property taxation for local purposes, the Yukon shall ensure that Yukon municipalities do not incur any consequential net loss.

14.6.2. The Vuntut Gwitchin First Nation and the Yukon shall enter into negotiations as necessary to provide for the efficient delivery of local services and programs.

14.7. Where, following the ratification date of this Agreement, Parliament enacts Legislation providing:

14.7.1. taxation powers to an Indian government other than those provided for in this Agreement; or

14.7.2. tax exemptions for an Indian government, or an entity or entities owned by an Indian government, other than those provided for in this Agreement, Canada shall, upon the request in writing of the Vuntut Gwitchin First Nation, recommend Legislation to the appropriate legislative authority to provide the Vuntut Gwitchin First Nation with those other powers or exemptions on the same terms as are set out in the Legislation which provides the powers or exemptions to the other Indian government or entity.

14.8. The Yukon Minister of Finance may enter into taxation agreements with the Vuntut Gwitchin First Nation.

Taxation Status

[This section confers on the Vuntut Gwitchin First Nation and on a subsidiary meeting certain requirements, the status of a public body performing a function of government in Canada for the purposes of paragraph 149(1)(c) of the *Income Tax Act*, S.C. 1970–71–72, c. 63, and exemption from income tax.]

Self-government Financial Transfer Agreement

16.1. Canada and the Vuntut Gwitchin First Nation shall negotiate a self-government financial transfer agreement in accordance with 16.3, with the objective of providing the Vuntut Gwitchin First Nation with resources to enable the Vuntut Gwitchin First Nation to provide public services at levels reasonably comparable to those generally prevailing in Yukon, at reasonably comparable levels of taxation.

. . . .

[Sections 16.2 to 16.5 deal with the negotiation and structure of the financial transfer agreement.]

16.6. Payments pursuant to the self-government financial transfer agreement shall be provided on an unconditional basis except where criteria or conditions are attached to the provision of funding for similar programs or services in other jurisdictions in Canada.

. . . .

[Sections 16.7 to 16.16 address other aspects of the financial transfer agreement.]

16.17. Nothing in 16.0 shall affect the ability of the Vuntut Gwitchin First Nation to exercise, or benefit from any rights that it may become entitled to under future provisions of the constitution of Canada.

Programs and Services

17.1. During the term of a self-government financing agreement the Vuntut Gwitchin First Nation and Government shall negotiate the assumption of responsibility by the Vuntut Gwitchin First Nation for the management, administration and delivery of any program or service within the Vuntut Gwitchin First Nation's jurisdiction, whether or not the Vuntut Gwitchin First Nation has enacted a law respecting such matter.

. . . .

[Sections 17.2 to 17.6 deal with other aspects of agreements to transfer control of programs or services.]

17.3.1. to provide resources adequate to ensure that the program or service to be offered by the Vuntut Gwitchin First Nation is of a level or quality equivalent to the Government program or service and existing program or service quality is not diminished;

17.3.2. to provide for mechanisms of cooperation and co-ordination, as appropriate, between the Vuntut Gwitchin First Nation government and governments at a local, territorial and federal level to ensure the effective and efficient delivery of the program or service;

17.3.3. to consider financial and administrative limitations and to promote administrative efficiency ad economies of scale;

17.3.4. to provide for local management and delivery of the program or service;

17.3.5. to provide mechanisms for negotiating basic common standards between Government and Vuntut Gwitchin First Nation programs and services; and

17.3.6. to identify the scope of the Parties' authority.

17.4. An agreement concluded pursuant to 17.1 shall include a program and service implementation plan and identify the training requirements to be addressed in that plan.

17.5. Canada and the Vuntut Gwitchin First Nation may agree to consolidate the funding provided for in an agreement entered into pursuant to 17.1 with the funding provided pursuant to the self-government financial transfer agreement, which consolidation may take effect either at the commencement of the next fiscal year or at the commencement of the term of the next self-government financial transfer agreement.

17.6. Any responsibility assumed by the Vuntut Gwitchin First Nation in an agreement entered into pursuant to 17.1 shall be funded by interim financing arrangements which shall be in accordance with 16.1.

Government of the Yukon Financial Contributions

18.1. The contribution of the Yukon shall be subtracted from the expenditure base of any fiscal transfer arrangement in effect at the time, and shall be calculated by Government to be the sum of [a number of designated factors]...

. . . .

but in all cases, the Yukon shall continue to have the capacity to provide to Yukon residents the services for which it remains responsible, at a level or quality comparable to those prevailing prior to assumption of responsibility by the Vuntut Gwitchin First Nation for the programs and services.

18.2. Any one-time net savings to the Yukon resulting from the Vuntut Gwitchin First Nations's assumption of responsibilities shall be paid by the Yukon to

Canada in instalments of an amount and in accordance with a schedule to be agreed upon.

. . . .

[Sections 18.3 and 18.4 deal with other aspects of the Yukon contribution.]

18.4. Should there be no fiscal transfer arrangement as contemplated in section 18.1 that is in effect at the time, then the Yukon contribution shall be provided for under an agreement to be negotiated by Canada and the Yukon, and shall be based on the stipulations enumerated in section 18.1.

. . . .

[Section 19.1 stipulates how any First Nation revenue capacity from a tax base should be considered when assessing First Nation funding.]

Laws of Canada and Yukon

20.1. The Vuntut Gwitchin First Nation has the power to adopt any Law of the Yukon or Canada as its own law in respect of matters provided for in this Agreement.

20.2. The *Statutory Instruments Act*, R.S.C. 1985, c. S–22, does not apply to a law enacted by the Vuntut Gwitchin First Nation.

Public Register of Laws and Notification Provisions

[The first parts of this section require a public register of all laws enacted by the Vuntut Gwitchin First Nation, and provide for related matters.]

. . . .

21.5. The Vuntut Gwitchin First Nation shall forward to Government a list of Citizens and any alterations to that list forthwith after they occur.

Financial Accountability

22.1. The Vuntut Gwitchin First Nation shall prepare, maintain and publish its accounts in a manner consistent with the standards generally accepted for governments in Canada.

[Section 23.0 provides for the creation of an implementation plan and s. 24.0 provides for mediation or arbitration of specified matters.]

(d) Proposed Charlottetown Accord†

See **Chapter 12, Part 5(b)**.

1. The *Constitution Act, 1867* is amended by adding thereto, immediately after section 1 thereof, the following section:

Canada Clause

"**2.**(1) The Constitution of Canada, including the *Canadian Charter of Rights and Freedoms*, shall be interpreted in a manner consistent with the following fundamental characteristics:

. . . .

(b) the Aboriginal peoples of Canada, being the first peoples to govern this land, have the right to promote their language, cultures and traditions and to ensure the integrity of their societies, and their governments constitute one of the three orders of government in Canada;

. . . .

(3) Nothing in this section derogates from the powers, rights or privileges of the Parliament or the Government of Canada, or of the legislatures or gov-

† Charlottetown Accord: *Draft Legal Text*, October 9, 1992 at 1–3, 14, 36–43, 48.

ernments of the provinces, or of the legislative bodies or governments of the Aboriginal peoples of Canada, including any powers, rights or privileges relating to language.

Aboriginal and treaty rights

(4) For greater certainty, nothing in this section abrogates or derogates from the aboriginal and treaty rights of the Aboriginal peoples of Canada.

. . . .

4. Sections 24 to 36 of [the *Constitution Act, 1867*] are repealed and the following substituted therefor:

. . . .

Constitution of Senate

"**21.**(1) ...
(c) [aboriginal representation]"

[Footnote: The number sixty-two is subject to future decisions on the number of guaranteed aboriginal seats. The issue of aboriginal representation and voting powers of aboriginal senators is to be discussed in the autumn of 1992, according to the Consensus Report.]

. . . .

8. The [*Constitution Act, 1867*] is further amended by adding thereto, immediately after section 91 thereof, the following section:

Application of class 24 of section 91

"**91A.** For greater certainty, class 24 of section 91 applies, except as provided in section 95E [which would have empowered the Alberta legislature to make laws in relation to Alberta Métis and Alberta Métis settlement lands, subject to federal paramountcy], in relation to all Aboriginal peoples of Canada."

[Section 23 of the Draft Legal Text would have protected (a) Métis land in Alberta from compulsory seizure and sale; (b) the *Metis Settlements Land Protection Act* from amendment by provincial legislation; and the Metis Settlements General Council from dissolution by federal or provincial laws. The August 22, 1992 Charlottetown Accord contained a provision that would have committed the federal government, Ontario, and the four western provinces to enter into a legally enforceable accord on Métis Nation issues. The latter accord would have included provisions for Métis self-government agreements, lands and resources.]

. . . .

24. Section 3 of the *Constitution Act, 1982* is repealed and the following substituted therefor:

Democratic rights of citizens

"**3.** Every citizen of Canada has the right to vote in an election of members of the House of Commons or of a legislative assembly of a province and to be qualified for membership therein."

[Section 24 of the Draft Legal Text would have amended the *Charter* with the effect that the right to vote guaranteed in s. 3 would not extend to a legislative assembly pursuant to Aboriginal self-government.]

. . . .

26. Subsection 32(1) of the said Act is amended by striking out the word "and" at the end of paragraph (a) thereof, by adding the word "and" at the end of paragraph (b) thereof and by adding thereto the following paragraph:

"(c) to all legislative bodies and governments of the Aboriginal peoples of Canada in respect of all matters within the authority of their respective legislative bodies."

27. The said Act is further amended by adding thereto, immediately after section 33 thereof, the following section:

Application of section 33 to aboriginal legislative bodies

"**33.1.** Section 33 applies to legislative bodies of the Aboriginal peoples of Canada with such modification, consistent with the purposes of the requirements of that section, as are appropriate to the circumstances of the Aboriginal peoples concerned."

. . . .

29. Section 35.1 of the said Act is repealed and the following substituted therefor:

Inherent right of self-government

"**35.1.**(1) The Aboriginal peoples of Canada have the inherent right of self-government within Canada.

Three orders of government

(2) The right referred to in subsection (1) shall be interpreted in a manner consistent with the recognition of the governments of the Aboriginal peoples of Canada as constituting one of three orders of government in Canada.

Contextual statement

(3) The exercise of the right referred to in subsection (1) includes the authority of duly constituted legislative bodies of the Aboriginal peoples, each within its own jurisdiction,

(a) to safeguard and develop their languages, cultures, economies, identities, institutions and traditions, and
(b) to develop, maintain and strengthen their relationship with their lands, waters and environment,

so as to determine and control their development as peoples according to their own values and priorities and to ensure the integrity of their societies.

Issues before court or tribunal

(4) Where an issue arises in any proceedings in relation to the scope of the inherent right of self-government, or in relation to an assertion of that right, a court or tribunal

(a) before making any final determination of the issue, shall inquire into the efforts that have been made to resolve the issue through negotiations under section 35.2 and may order the parties to take such steps as may be appropriate in the circumstances to effect a negotiated resolution; and
(b) in making any final determination of the issue, shall take into account subsection (3).

Land

(5) Neither the right referred to in subsection (1) nor anything in subsection 35.2(1) creates new aboriginal rights to land or abrogates or derogates from existing aboriginal or treaty rights to land, except as otherwise provided in self-government agreements negotiated under section 35.2.

Commitment to negotiate

35.2.(1) The government of Canada, the provincial and territorial governments and the Aboriginal peoples of Canada, including the Indian, Inuit and Métis peoples of Canada, in the various regions and communities of Canada shall negotiate in good faith the implementation of the right of self-government, including issues of

(a) jurisdiction,
(b) lands and resources, and
(c) economic and fiscal arrangements, with the objective of concluding agreements elaborating relationships between governments of Aboriginal peoples and the government of Canada and provincial or territorial governments.

. . . .

Where rights are treaty rights

(6) Where an agreement negotiated under this section

(a) is set out in a treaty or land claims agreement, or in an amendment to a treaty including a land claims agreement, or
(b) contains a declaration that the rights of the Aboriginal peoples set out in the agreement are treaty rights,

the rights of the Aboriginal peoples set out in the agreement are treaty rights under subsection 35(1).

Non-derogation

(7) Nothing in this section abrogates or derogates from the rights referred to in section 35 or 35.1, or from the enforceability thereof, and nothing in subsection 35.1(3) or in this section makes those rights contingent on the commitment to negotiate under this section.

Delay of justiciability

35.3.(1) Except in relation to self-government agreements concluded after the coming into force of this section, section 35.1 shall not be made the subject of judicial notice, interpretation or enforcement for five years after that section comes into force.

. . . .

Application of laws

35.4.(1) Except as otherwise provided by the Constitution of Canada, the laws of Canada and the laws of the provinces and territories continue to apply to the Aboriginal peoples of Canada, subject nevertheless to being displaced by laws enacted by legislative bodies of the Aboriginal peoples according to their authority.

Peace, order and good government in Canada

(2) No aboriginal law or any other exercise of the inherent right of self-government under section 35.1 may be inconsistent with federal or provincial laws that are essential to the preservation of peace, order and good government in Canada.

. . . .

Interpretation of treaty rights

35.6.(1) The treaty rights referred to in subsection 35(1) shall be interpreted in a just, broad and liberal manner taking into account their spirit and the context of the specific treaty negotiations relating thereto.

Commitment to processes to clarify, implement or rectify treaties

35.6.(2) The government of Canada is committed to establishing treaty processes to clarify or implement treaty rights and, where the parties agree, to rectify terms of treaties, and is committed, where requested by the Aboriginal peoples of Canada concerned, to participating in good faith in the process that relates to them.

[Section 35.6(3) would have committed the provincial and territorial governments to participating in the treaty processes referred to in s. 35.6(2), where invited by the federal government and the Aboriginal peoples concerned, or required to do so by treaty.]

Rights of the Aboriginal peoples of Canada guaranteed equally to both sexes

35.7. Notwithstanding any other provision of this Act, the rights of the Aboriginal peoples of Canada referred to in this Part are guaranteed equally to male and female persons.

Commitment to participate in constitutional conference

[**35.8.** The government of Canada and the provincial governments are committed to the principle that, before any amendment *described in section 45.1* is made,

(a) a constitutional conference that includes in its agenda an item relating to the proposed amendment, composed of the Prime Minister of Canada and the first ministers of the provinces will be convened by the Prime Minister of Canada; and
(b) the Prime Minister of Canada will invite representatives of the Aboriginal peoples of Canada to participate in the discussions on that item.]

[Footnote: The final wording of this provision (based on existing section 35.1 added in 1984) is to be revisited when the consent mechanism is finalized for section 45.1, at which time concerns will be addressed in respect of amendments directly referring to Aboriginal peoples in some but not all regions of Canada.]

Constitutional conferences

35.9.(1) At least four constitutional conferences on aboriginal issues composed of the Prime Minister of Canada, the first ministers of the provinces, representatives of the Aboriginal peoples of Canada and elected representatives of the governments of the territories shall be convened by the Prime Minister of Canada, the first to be held no later than 1996 and the three subsequent conferences to be held one every two years thereafter.

Agenda

(2) Each conference convened under subsection (1) shall have included in its agenda such items as are proposed by the representatives of the Aboriginal peoples of Canada.

. . . .

41. An amendment to the Constitution of Canada in relation to the following matters may be made by proclamation issued by the Governor General under the Great Seal of Canada only where authorized by resolutions of the Senate and House of Commons and of the legislative assembly of each province:

. . . .

[(c. 1) the number of senators by which the Aboriginal peoples of Canada are entitled to be represented in the Senate and the qualifications of such senators;]

[Footnote to c. 1: The issue of aboriginal representation is to be discussed in the autumn of 1992, according to the Consensus Report.]

. . . .

[**33.** The said Act is further amended by adding thereto, immediately after section 45 thereof, the following section:

Amendments where Aboriginal peoples of Canada directly referred to

"**45.1.**(1) An amendment to the Constitution of Canada that directly refers to, or that amends a provision that directly refers to, one or more of the aboriginal peoples of Canada or their governments [Footnote: A mechanism for obtaining aboriginal consent would be worked out prior to the tabling of a Constitution resolution in Parliament], including

(a) section 2, as it relates to the Aboriginal peoples of Canada [Footnote: A reference to any provision relating to aboriginal representation in the Senate would be added here], class 24 of section 91, and sections 91A, 95E and 127 of the Constitution Act, 1867; and
(b) section 25 and Part II of this Act and this section, may be made by proclamation issued by the Governor General under the Great Seal of Canada only where the amendment has been authorized in accordance with this Part and has received the substantial consent of the Aboriginal peoples so referred to.

Initiation of amendment procedures

(2) Notwithstanding section 46, the procedures for amending the Constitution of Canada in relation to any matter referred to in subsection (1) may be initiated by any of the Aboriginal peoples of Canada directly referred to as provided in subsection (1)."]

(e) *Pamajewon*†

See **Chapter 9, Part 5.**

R. v. Pamajewon is reproduced in part in **Reading 9(d)** at p. 350, as it relates to Aboriginal rights as well as to Aboriginal self-government. As can be seen there, the Supreme Court's comments on Aboriginal self-government were tentative at most. For portions of *Pamajewon* that relate especially to Aboriginal self-government, see paragraphs 24, 27, 30 and 41–43 in the *Pamajewon* extract.

† [*R.* v. *Jones*; *R.* v. *Gardner*], [1996] 2 S.C.R. 821, February 26, 1996 (decision) and August 21, 1996 (S.C.C. reasons: Lamer C.J.C., La Forest, Sopinka, Gonthier, Cory, McLachlin, Iacobucci and Major JJ, with L'Heureux-Dubé concurring in separate reasons); aff'g (1994), 21 O.R. (3d) 385 (O.C.A.: Dubin C.J.O. and Osborne J.A. A third judge, Blair J.A., retired before the judgment was rendered and took no part in it); dismissing appeals from convictions by Carr Prov. Ct. J. and Flaherty Prov. Ct. J.

(f) Highlights of *Report of the Royal Commission on Aboriginal Peoples*†

See **Chapter 12, Part 7.**

- The Queen and Parliament should issue a royal proclamation acknowledging mistakes of the past and committing governments to a new relationship.
- An aboriginal parliament should be created, to be known as the House of First Peoples.
- A wide-ranging public inquiry should be held into the origins and effects of residential schools.
- The Canadian Human Rights Commission should be authorized to inquire into the relocation of aboriginal communities and to recommend remedies to address the negative effects of relocations.
- All governments should recognize the inherent right of aboriginal self-government is [an aboriginal right affirmed in section 35(1) of] the Constitution.
- Ottawa should create a process to identify groups entitled to self-determination, based on a collective sense of national identity through things like history, language, traditions, sufficient size and a defined territorial base.
- Natives should be recognized as enjoying a unique form of dual citizenship, as citizens both of an aboriginal nation and of Canada.
- Aboriginal people living on their territory should pay personal income tax; those living off their territory should pay federal and provincial taxes.
- Federal and provincial governments should set up a Canada-wide agreement to establish common principles and directions to negotiate treaties with aboriginal nations.
- Land negotiations should be guided by the territory the nation traditionally used; current and projected population; economic and cultural needs; amount of land now held; amount of Crown land available in the area, and the nature of third-party interests.
- Permanent, independent treaty commissions should be established to oversee negotiations among federal, provincial and aboriginal governments.
- An independent lands and treaties tribunal should be created to decide on land claims, and to ensure that treaty negotiations are conducted and financed fairly.
- Federal and provincial governments should enter into long-term development deals with native nations to provide funding for economic development.
- Aboriginal governments should establish economic institutions that reflect the nation's values, are accountable and are protected from political interference.
- A national aboriginal development bank should be created to provide support to large-scale projects and raise capital for economic development.
- Programs for aboriginal entrepreneurs should be continued for at least 10 years.
- Tax credits should be extended to investors in aboriginal venture-capital corporations.
- Ottawa and the provinces should fund a major, 10-year initiative for employment development and training.
- Aboriginal communities should be allowed to make innovative use of social-assistance funds for employment and social development.
- The Department of Indian and Northern Affairs should be replaced with an aboriginal relations department and an Indian and Inuit services department.
- Aboriginal leaders should take a firm public stand supporting the right to freedom from violence for all community members, particularly women, children, elders and the disabled, and a zero-tolerance policy for violence against natives.
- Women should be assured of full and equal participation in decision-making bodies responsible for physical and emotional security.
- Federal and provincial governments should amend their legislation to recognize customary family laws in areas such as divorce, child custody and adoption.

† "Highlights of Report" [summary of some key recommendations of the *Report of the Royal Commission on Aboriginal Peoples*], *The Globe and Mail*, 22 November 1966, A8.

- Governments and other organizations should work out an action plan on health and social conditions, including a system of healing centres and lodges under aboriginal control; full support by mainstream health-service and social-service providers, and a community infrastructure program to address the most immediate health threats.
- Federal, provincial and territorial governments should commit themselves to training 10,000 aboriginal professionals in health and social services and ensure that student support is adequate to achieve that goal.
- Federal resources should be made available over the next 10 years to ensure adequate housing to all who need it on reserves while the provinces do the same in rural, northern and urban communities.
- All governments should help develop an aboriginal-controlled education system.
- School boards should be required, among other things, to institute aboriginal-language programs and hire aboriginal teachers and administrators in schools serving native students.
- An aboriginal peoples' international university should be created to promote traditional knowledge.
- The federal government should provide an annual grant of $10-million for five years to support an aboriginal-languages foundation.
- An aboriginal arts council should be established to foster arts and literature.
- A Canada-wide aboriginal youth policy should be developed, covering education, justice, health, sports and recreation and urban support programs.
- Governments should be prepared to negotiate with Metis representatives on self-government and to provide the nations with adequate land bases.
- Aboriginal representatives should be involved in all planning for future constitutional conferences and in the process of amending the Constitution, with a veto over any changes to sections regarding aboriginal rights.

(g) *People to People, Nation to Nation*†

See **Chapter 12, Part 7**.

The starting point is recognition that Aboriginal people are not, as some Canadians seem to think, an inconsequential minority group with problems that need fixing and outmoded attitudes that need modernizing. They are unique political entities, whose place in Canada is unlike that of any other people.

Because of their original occupancy of the country, the treaties that recognized their rights, the constitution that affirms those rights, and their continued cohesion as peoples, they are nations within Canada — collectivities with their own character and traditions, a right to their own autonomous governments, and a special place in the flexible federalism that defines Canada.

Seeking a better balance of political and economic power between Aboriginal and other Canadian governments was the core and substance of our work. Progress on other fronts, unless accompanied by this transformation, will simply perpetuate a flawed status quo.

Throughout our report, we emphasize the importance of an understanding of history. We cannot expect to usher in a new beginning unless we reckon first with the past.

We do not propose dwelling on the past. Neither Aboriginal nor non-Aboriginal people want that. But there must be an acknowledgement that great wrongs have been done to Aboriginal people.

There is little evidence of such an acknowledgement today. Indeed, just as the restoration of Aboriginal nations and cultures appears to be offering real hope for renewed well-being, a backlash is

† Royal Commission on Aboriginal Peoples, *People to People, Nation to Nation: Highlights from the Report of the Royal Commission on Aboriginal Peoples* (Ottawa: Canada Communication Group, 1996), chap. 5 at 126–27, 129–30, 132, 135–36, 138, 140–43. Notes omitted. Reproduced with the permission of the Minister of Public Works and Government Services, 2004 and courtesy of Privy Council Office.

developing — a reaction characterized by slogans like 'all Canadians are equal' and 'no special status' — but its premises are very wrong.

It is wrong to suggest that all people should be treated the same, regardless of inequalities in their situation.

It is wrong to turn a blind eye to the dispossession and racism that distort the circumstances of Aboriginal people and limit their life chances.

It is wrong to ignore the historical rights that Aboriginal people still enjoy as self-governing political entities — rights that Canada undertook to safeguard as we were struggling toward nationhood.

Proponents of the so-called 'equality' approach claim that renewal and restoration in the ways we propose will bring 'apartheid' to Canada. In the name of equality, they would deny Aboriginal people the chance to protect their distinctive cultures and fashion their societies in ways that reflect their values.

This way of thinking is the modern equivalent of the mind-set that led to the *Indian Act*, the residential schools, the forced relocations — and the other nineteenth-century instruments of assimilation.

. . . .

When constitutional issues are again the subject of intergovernmental negotiation, the following Aboriginal issues must be included:

- explicit recognition that section 35 of the *Constitution Act, 1982* includes the inherent right of self-government as an Aboriginal right
- a process for honouring and implementing treaty obligations
- a veto for Aboriginal peoples on amendments to sections of the constitution that directly affect their rights — section 91 (24) of the *Constitution Act, 1867* and sections 25, 35 and 35.1 of the *Constitution Act, 1982*
- recognition that section 91 (24) includes Metis people along with First Nations and Inuit
- constitutional protection for the Alberta *Metis Settlements Act*
- changes to section 91 (24) to reflect the broad self-governing jurisdiction Aboriginal nations can exercise as an inherent right and to limit federal powers accordingly

The statement of Canada's nationhood made by the constitution will never be complete until the relationship of respect and equality between Aboriginal and non-Aboriginal people that we envisage is represented there.

. . . .

HOW

The first step is for the government of Canada to make a clear commitment to renewing the relationship between Aboriginal and non-Aboriginal people, guided by the principles of recognition, respect, sharing and responsibility.

Change of this magnitude cannot be achieved by piecemeal reform of existing programs and services — however helpful any one of these reforms might be. It will take an act of national intention — a major, symbolic statement of intent, accompanied by the laws necessary to turn intentions into action.

This can best be done by a new Royal Proclamation, issued by the Queen as Canada's head of state and the historical guardian of the rights of Aboriginal peoples, and presented to the people of Canada in a special assembly called for the purpose.

The proclamation would set out the principles of the new relationship and outline the laws and institutions necessary to turn those principles into reality. It would not supplant but support and modernize the *Royal Proclamation of 1763*, which has been called Aboriginal peoples' *Magna Carta*.

The new proclamation would commit the government of Canada to making good on its proclaimed intentions by introducing new laws and institutions to implement them. The laws and institutions would come into being through companion legislation passed by Parliament:

- An Aboriginal Nations Recognition and Government Act, to permit the government of Canada, following processes and criteria set out in the act, to recognize Aboriginal nations and make interim arrangements to finance their activities.
- An Aboriginal Treaties Implementation Act, to establish processes and principles for recognized nations to renew their existing treaties or create new ones. This act would also establish several regional treaty commissions to facilitate and support treaty negotiations, which would be conducted by representatives of the governments concerned.
- An Aboriginal Lands and Treaties Tribunal Act, which would establish an independent body to decide on specific claims, ensure that treaty negotiations are conducted and financed fairly; and protect the interests of affected parties while treaties are being negotiated.
- An Aboriginal Parliament Act, to establish a body to represent Aboriginal Peoples within federal

governing institutions and advise Parliament on matters affecting Aboriginal people. (A constitutional amendment, to come later, would create a House of First Peoples, to become part of Parliament along with the House of Commons and the Senate.)

- An Aboriginal Relations Department Act and an Indian and Inuit Services Department Act, to set up two departments to replace the Department of Indian Affairs and Northern Development — one to implement the new relationship with Aboriginal Nations, the second to administer continuing services for groups that have not yet opted for self-government.

. . . .

To equip Aboriginal people for the tasks of nation building that lie ahead, structural change — new laws, new bodies to implement them — must be accompanied by measures to give people hope, new capacities for self-management, and the confidence to take charge in their communities and nations.

This requires early action in four areas: healing, economic development, human resources development, and Aboriginal institution building.

- **Healing of individuals, families, communities and nations**: Healing aims to restore physical, mental, emotional and spiritual health. It implies recovery for individuals and communities from the wounds of culture loss, paternalistic and sometimes racist treatment, and official policies of domination and assimilation.

  Healing is already under way in many communities, but the momentum needs to grow. It needs to be supported by schools, hospitals, family services. It needs to reach the young, the old, and everyone in between.

  Healing must build on Aboriginal traditions of mutual aid and community responsibility. It should include community and national leaders, whose approaches to decision making are sometimes distorted by their experiences of government under the *Indian Act*. Restoring communities and nations to unity and harmony is an extension of healing at the personal level. Such healing must accompany self-government.

- **Economic development**: Aboriginal people must have the tools to escape from the poverty that cripples them as individuals and as nations. Redistributing lands and resources will greatly improve their chances for jobs and a reasonable income. After that, the tools most urgently needed are capital for investment in business and industry and enhanced technical, management and professional skills to realize new opportunities.

  Hand in hand with improved economic conditions must come improved living conditions. We propose a major initiative to bring housing, water supplies and sanitation facilities up to standards that will reduce threats to health and help restore self-respect and initiative.

- **Accelerating development of human resources**: Activities of self-government, healing, community infrastructure development, and commercial enterprise will need many more trained people than are now available. Changes in the education system can generate better high school completion rates among Aboriginal students.

  We also propose a 10-year initiative to overcome education and training deficits by involving private companies, training institutions and governments in programs to encourage Aboriginal people to develop skills in a full range of technical, commercial and professional fields.

- **Institution building**: Most of the institutions governing Aboriginal life today originate outside Aboriginal communities. For the most part, they operate according to rules that fail to reflect Aboriginal values and preferences. In every sector of public life, there is a need to make way for Aboriginal institutions. Development of many of these institutions should proceed before self-governing nations emerge, but they should be designed to complement, not compete with, nation structures.

THE HIGH COST OF THE STATUS QUO

The case for a new deal for Aboriginal peoples rests on strong arguments for restorative justice and recognition of historical Aboriginal rights. It also rests on solid economic ground: Canada can no longer afford the status quo.

Eliminating the excess cost to Canadians of the policies of the past is a powerful argument for implementing the Commission's agenda for change.

- The cost of Aboriginal peoples' inability to obtain good jobs and earn reasonable incomes is very high. It takes the form of earnings Aboriginal people never receive, goods and services they do not add to the economy, and taxes they cannot pay.

- A smaller but still significant financial burden on taxpayers arises from the cost of remedial services to help Aboriginal people cope with the negative effects of their history of domination: higher than average use of welfare programs, housing subsidies, health and justice services.

. . . .

Cost of Government Assistance

In 1992–93, the latest year for which information on all governments is available, the federal government spent $6 billion dollars for Aboriginal people, mostly on programs for registered Indians and Inuit. Other governments (mainly the provinces) spent $5.6 billion — for a total of $11.6 billion.

Governments spend money on all citizens, mostly on programs to provide health care and education, stimulate the economy, facilitate transportation and so on. But the amount spent per person for Aboriginal people is 57 per cent higher than for Canadians generally.

. . . .

The Commission's agenda for change can substantially reduce the costs of Aboriginal marginalization, ill health and social distress. But changes of such magnitude will not be easy. Profound problems require solutions that deal with the root causes. Solutions, once identified and implemented, take time to come to fruition.

Canada stands to gain by acting on our proposals. Aboriginal people will gain by achieving greater productivity and higher incomes. Other Canadians will gain through reduced government spending and increased government revenues. Political, economic and social renewal can help Canada balance its books.

Our proposals will cost money, but they will also save money. Eventually, savings and new tax revenues will equal and then exceed the cost of the strategy. We estimate that it will take between 15 and 20 years of investment to reach that point.

Accordingly, we recommend strongly that governments increase their annual spending, so that five years after the start of the strategy, spending is between $1.5 and $2 billion higher than it is today, and that this level be sustained for some 15 years.

In considering the increased outlay we recommend, Canadians should keep four things in mind:

- The agenda for change will cost Canada significantly less than a continuation of the status quo, amended piecemeal here and there. The price tag on lost productivity and remedial measures to make up for poverty and other forms of disadvantage is four to five times higher than the cost of the measures we propose.
- Our recommendations constitute an interactive strategy. To work, they must reinforce each other. Implementing self-government and acquiring an increased land base will generate a powerful momentum for economic self-reliance. Economic well-being tends to improve health status. At the same time, progress in healing and education will produce stronger, more confident individuals with the skills and abilities to manage businesses and run governments.
- Changes will have to be negotiated with and implemented by Aboriginal people — in the way the choose. This means that the pace of change will be determined by the capacity of Aboriginal nations and communities to implement their chosen priorities — a capacity that is still developing.
- Governments are reassessing their role in society and cutting back public spending. It would be a travesty of justice, however, if concerted and effective action to rectify the results of a history of dispossession were abandoned on grounds of fiscal restraint. A great debt is owing, and Canadians cannot, in good conscience, default on it.

We estimate that half the potential gain from better social and economic conditions could be realized within the 20-year investment period. Beyond that point, social and economic recovery will continue under their own momentum. Over the 20-year period, the flow of financing should evolve in three stages:

- In the first five years, an immediate and major infusion of resources will be needed for all aspects of healing, economic stimulation, upgrading community infrastructure, and developing new institutions and human resources. By contrast, although structural reform will begin in these early years — nation building, recognition of self-government, and land and treaty processes — these activities will need only limited funding.
- At the end of the first five years, as more Aboriginal nations complete land and self-government negotiations, large outlays will be needed to settle land claims and implement self-government. Although we expect to see most claims settled

within the next 20 years, the cost of land settlements will be spread out over a longer period.

- After about 10 years, Aboriginal people and nations will begin to close the gap in economic self-reliance and contribute more to the financing of governments. The need for remedial programs will fall. The point where fiscal gains from our strategy begin to outstrip its costs will be reached within 20 years of the start of the strategy.

. . . .

Federal, provincial, territorial and Aboriginal governments will need to assume a share of the additional cost of the agenda for change. But the costs we describe will be borne in part by Aboriginal governments and financed through their own taxation efforts.

Federal, provincial and territorial governments will benefit greatly in the long term from

- reduced expenditures once the agenda for change begins to alleviate debilitating and costly conditions of Aboriginal life
- increased tax revenues as more Aboriginal people living off Aboriginal nation territories have jobs and decent incomes and pay taxes

As Commissioners we urge our fellow Canadians to commit the required resources to the actions we describe, to close the economic gap between Aboriginal and non-Aboriginal people by 50 per cent and improve social conditions in the next 20 years.

Perhaps it will take longer. But within the 20-year timeframe, enormous momentum for change can be generated. By 2016, Aboriginal people can be very much better off than they are today and moving steadily forward.

The result will be a large gain in human and financial terms for Aboriginal people — and, in the long term, much greater savings for all Canadians.

General Index

These references take the following form: **2(1)** indicates **Chapter 2, Part 1** of the **Main Text** section of the book; **11(7)(a)** indicates **Chapter 11, Part 7, heading (a)** of the **Main Text**. The notes in the text contain additional references to the **Chapter Readings** section of the book. For the location of these references, see the **Table of Section References** that follows this index.

ABORIGINAL PEOPLES **2(1)**
- Indians **1(3); 2**
- Inuit **1(3); 2(1); 2(3); 2(5)(b); 4(3); 11(7)(a); 11(7)(b); 11(7)(c); 11(7)(e); 11(7)(i); 12(3)(c)(iii)(A)**
- Métis **1(3); 2(1); 2(5)(c); 6(5); 10(5); 11(7)(f); 11(7)(g); 12(3)(c)(iii)(B); 12(5)(b)**

ABORIGINAL RIGHTS, ABORIGINAL TITLE **1(3); 3; 4; 77; 9; 10**
- Aboriginal concepts **3(3)**
- characterization **10(4)(c)**
- compensation **4(1)(g); 10(3)(f); 10(4)**
- *Constitution Act, 1982*, s. 35(1) **5(15); 6(6); 6(9)); 7(1) to 7(3); 7(4)(d)**
- content **4(1)(d); 7(4)(d)(i); 9(2) to 9(5); 10(7)(c); 12(5)**
- consultation, accomodation **10(6)**
- Crown honour **5(1); 7(4)(d)(iv); 8(3); 8(5)(b); 8(7); 8(8)(c); 8(8)(f); 8(9)(b); 8(9)(c); 10(6); 11(3)(e)**
- distinctive practices test **9(3)(e)**
- enforcement **4(1)(f)**
- evidence **10(3)(d); 10(4)(d)**
- extinguishment **4(1)(e); 9(2); 10(3)(h); 10(7)(f); 11(4)(b)**
- fiduciary aspects **7(4)(d)(iii); 8**
- identification **9(3); 10(3)(e)(iv); 10(7)(b)**
- infringement **7(4)(d)(iv); 9(4); 10(3)**
- justification **7(4)(d)(vii); 9(4); 10(3)(f); 10(6); 10(7)(g)**
- proof **4(1)(b); 4(3); 9(3)(e)**
- relationship between Aboriginal rights, title **9(3)(h); 10(2); 10(3)(e)**
- source or basis **3(5) to 3(14); 4(1)(a); 4(4); 9(3)(b); 9(3)(c); 10(1); 10(2); 10(3)(e)**
- sovereign incompatibility **10(4)(e)**

CONSTITUTIONAL AND LEGISLATIVE ENACTMENTS **6**
- *Canadian Bill of Rights* **2(4)(d)**
- *Constitution Act, 1867* **1(3); 2(3); 3(10); 6(3); 6(7); 6(8); 6(9); 10(3); 10(3)(h)**
- *Constitution Act, 1982* **1(3); 2(2); 6(6); 77; 8; 9; 10; 12(5)**
- *Indian Act* **1(3); 2(4); 2(8); 5(11); 5(12); 6(4); 6(8); 6(9); 10(3); 12(3)(b)(i); 12(6)**
- *Natural Resources Transfer Agreements* **1(3); 2(5)(c); 5(15); 6(5); 6(7)**

EQUALITY **2(4)(d) to 2(4)(g); 2(9)**

FIDUCIARY DUTIES **4(4); 7(4)(d)(iii); 8**
- character, scope **8(3) to 8(9); 10(7)(h)**
- content **8(6)**
- Crown honour **5(1); 5(14); 5(16); 8(3); 10(6)(a)**

HISTORY, PRE-HISTORY **1(3)**

LAND CLAIMS **1(3); 11**
- alternative approaches **11(3)**
- beneficiaries **2(7)**
- claims process **11(4)**
- comprehensive claims **11(4) to 11(7)**
- duty to negotiate **11(3)(e)**
- land claims agreements **11(5) to 11(7)**
- “other” claims **11(9)**
- specific claims **11(8)**

LEGISLATIVE JURISDICTION **6**
- *Constitution Act, 1867* **1(3); 2(3); 3(10); 6(3); 6(7); 6(8); 6(9); 10(3)**
- *Constitution Act, 1982* **1(3); 2(2); 6(6); 7; 8; 9; 10; 12(5)**
- inapplicability **6(3)(c)**
- inoperativeness **6(3)(b)**
- invalidity **6(3)(d)**
- *Indian Act* **1(3); 2(4); 2(8); 5(11); 5(12); 6(4); 6(8); 6(9); 10(3); 12(3)(b)(i); 12(6)**
- *Natural Resources Transfer Agreements* **1(3); 2(5)(c); 5(15); 6(5); 6(7)**
- Parliamentary sovereignty **6(2)**
- validity **6(3)(a)**

ROYAL PROCLAMATION OF 1763 **1(3); 3(6); 3(8); 3(9); 3(10); 3(11); 4(3)**

SELF-GOVERNMENT **12**
- Aboriginal perspectives **12(1)**
- Charlottetown **1(3); 5(9); 12(5)**
- common law, judicial **9(5); 10(3)(g); 12(3)(d); 12(4)**
- coordinated ethnic **12(3)(c)**
- federal policy **12(6)**
- legislated, negotiated **12(3)(b)**
- Royal Commission on Aboriginal Peoples **12(7)**
- separate ethnic **12(3)(c)(iv)**
- traditional **12(3)(a)**

SOCIAL CONDITIONS **1(2); 12(7)**

STATUS **2**
- claims beneficiaries **2(7)**
- *Constitution Act, 1867*, s. 91(24) **2(3)**
- *Constitution Act, 1982*, s. 35(1) **2(2)**
- equality **2(9)**
- *Indian Act*, status provisions **2(4); 2(8)**
- Inuit **2(5)(b)**
- Métis **2(5)(c)**
- non-status **2(5)(a)**
- problems **2(4)**
- treaty Indians **2(6)**

TREATIES **1(3); 2(6); 5**
- categories **5(3)**
- content **5(5)**
- Crown honour **5(1); 5(16); 11(3)(e)**
- defined **5(2)**
- duty to negotiate **11(3)(e)**
- interpretation, enforcement **5(8); 5(10) to 5(17)**
- participants **5(6); 5(12) to 5(14)**
- "non-territorial" **5(13)**
- problems **5(10); 5(17)**
- significance **5(1)**
- size **5(4)**
- status **5(7); 5(11) to 5(17)**

TREATY RIGHTS under s. 35 OF *CONSTITUTION ACT, 1982* (see also ABORIGINAL RIGHTS, ABORIGINAL TITLE) **5(7); 5(8); 5(9); 5(15); 5(16); 6(6)**

Table of Section References

1 Introduction 3

1(1) Scope of the Book 4
1(2) The People, the Change, and the Law 4
1(3) Mileposts 5

2 Who Is an Aboriginal Person? 13

2(1) Anthropological and Legal Descriptions 14
2(2) Section 35 Aboriginal Peoples 14
2(3) Section 91(24) Indians 14
2(4) Categories of *Indian Act* Indians 15
2(4)(a) *Indian Act* 15
2(4)(b) Pre-April 17, 1982 Eligibility Procedures 15
2(4)(c) Problems with Old System 15
2(4)(d) Movement for Change 16
2(4)(e) 1985 Eligibility Reforms 17
2(4)(f) Challenges Ahead 18
2(4)(g) *Corbiere v. Canada (Minister of Indian and Northern Affairs)* 19
2(5) Non-*Indian Act* Aboriginal Peoples 20
2(5)(a) Non-Status Indians 20
2(5)(b) Inuit 20
2(5)(c) Métis 20
2(6) Treaty Indians 21
2(7) Claims Agreement Beneficiaries 21
2(8) Self-Definition Possibilities 22
2(9) Aboriginal Status and Equality 22

3 Aboriginal Rights before *Calder* 30

3(1) Context 31
3(2) Background 31
3(3) Aboriginal Concepts 31
3(4) Descriptions and Questions 32
3(5) Source of Aboriginal Rights 33
3(6) Alternative Approaches 33
3(7) Interrelationships 34
3(8) Evolution of Approaches 34
3(9) The Royal Proclamation of 1763 34
3(10) *St. Catherine's Milling and Lumber Co. v. The Queen* 35
3(11) *Johnson and Graham's Lessee v. M'Intosh* 36
3(12) *Worcester v. Georgia* 37
3(13) *Connolly* 38
3(14) Shadow of *St. Catherine's* 39

4 Aboriginal Rights from *Calder* to *Guerin* 43

- **4(1)** *Calder* 44
  - **4(1)(a)** Source of Aboriginal Title 44
  - **4(1)(b)** Proof 45
  - **4(1)(c)** Effect of European Sovereignty 45
  - **4(1)(d)** Content 45
  - **4(1)(e)** Extinguishment 46
  - **4(1)(f)** Enforcement 46
  - **4(1)(g)** Compensation 46
- **4(2)** Post-*Calder* Years 46
- **4(3)** *Baker Lake* 47
- **4(4)** *Guerin* 47
- **4(5)** Turning Point? 48

5 Indian Treaties 51

- **5(1)** Significance 52
- **5(2)** Definition 52
- **5(3)** Main Categories 52
- **5(4)** Size 52
- **5(5)** Content 52
- **5(6)** Participants 53
- **5(7)** Status 53
- **5(8)** Interpretation And Enforcement 53
- **5(9)** Charlottetown Accord 54
- **5(10)** Treaty Problems 54
- **5(11)** *Simon* 55
- **5(12)** *Sioui* 55
- **5(13)** *Bear Island* 56
- **5(14)** *Badger* 56
- **5(15)** *Marshall* 58
- **5(16)** *Haida Nation* 59
- **5(17)** Clarification or Reconstruction? 60

6 Legislative Jurisdiction 65

- **6(1)** Overview 66
- **6(2)** Level One: Statutes and Parliamentary Sovereignty 66
- **6(3)** Level Two: *Constitution Act, 1867* 66
  - **6(3)(a)** Validity 66
  - **6(3)(b)** Inoperativeness 66
  - **6(3)(c)** Inapplicability 66
  - **6(3)(d)** Invalidity 67
- **6(4)** Level Three: Section 88 of *Indian Act* 67
- **6(5)** Level Four: *Natural Resources Transfer Agreements* 68
- **6(6)** Level Five: Section 35(1) of *Constitution Act, 1982* 68
- **6(7)** *Cardinal* 69
- **6(8)** *Dick* 69
- **6(9)** *Delgamuukw* 70
- **6(10)** *Kitkatla* 70
- **6(11)** More Challenges 71

7 *Constitution Act, 1982* and *Sparrow* 75

7(1) Changes to *Constitution Act, 1982* 76
7(2) Background 76
7(3) Questions 77
7(4) *Sparrow* 77
7(4)(a) Legal Situation before *Sparrow* 77
7(4)(b) Facts and Context 78
7(4)(c) Supreme Court's Decision 78
7(4)(d) Elements of Decision 79
7(4)(d)(i) Proof and Content 79
7(4)(d)(ii) Extinguishment 80
7(4)(d)(iii) Fiduciary Duties and Crown Honour 80
7(4)(d)(iv) Legal Status 80
7(4)(d)(v) Entrenchment 81
7(4)(d)(vi) Infringement 81
7(4)(d)(vii) Justification 81

8 Fiduciary Duties 86

8(1) Introduction 88
8(2) "Ordinary" Fiduciary Relationships 88
8(2)(a) Character and Scope 88
8(2)(b) Content 88
8(3) Source of Obligation 88
8(4) *Guerin* 89
8(4)(a) Facts 89
8(4)(b) Judgments 89
8(4)(c) Features 89
8(4)(d) Relationship to Land 90
8(5) *Sparrow* 90
8(5)(a) Judgment 90
8(5)(b) Features of *Sparrow* Duty 91
8(6) Content of Fiduciary Duty 91
8(6)(a) (a) *Guerin* Duty 91
8(6)(b) (b) Comparison with *Sparrow* Duty 92
8(7) General Trends 92
8(8) Modern Cases 93
8(8)(a) *Grand Council of the Crees* 93
8(8)(b) *Blueberry River* 93
8(8)(c) *Badger*, *Gladstone*, and *Delgamuukw* 94
8(8)(d) *Osoyoos* 95
8(8)(e) *Wewaykum* 95
8(8)(f) *Haida Nation* 97
8(9) Tentative Summary 98
8(9)(a) Special Fiduciary Obligation 98
8(9)(b) Specific Protection 98
8(9)(c) Related But Distinct Forms 98
8(9)(d) Scope of *Guerin* Duty 98
8(9)(e) Scope of *Sparrow* Duty 98
8(9)(f) Content 98
8(9)(g) Reconciliation 98
8(9)(h) Liberal Canons of Construction 98

9 Aboriginal Rights: I. . . . 108

9(1) Introduction . . . 109
9(2) *Mabo* . . . 109
9(3) *Van Der Peet* . . . 110
9(3)(a) Background . . . 110
9(3)(b) Basis of Aboriginal Rights: Land . . . 111
9(3)(c) Basis of Aboriginal Rights: Distinctive Societies . . . 112
9(3)(d) Section 35(1) . . . 112
9(3)(e) "Distinctive Practices" Test . . . 112
9(3)(f) A Missing Link? . . . 113
9(3)(g) McLachlin J.'s Criticisms . . . 113
9(3)(h) A Return to Land? . . . 114
9(4) *Gladstone* . . . 116
9(5) *Pamajewon* . . . 117

10 Aboriginal Rights: II . . . 125

10(1) Introduction . . . 126
10(2) *Adams* . . . 126
10(3) *Delgamuukw* . . . 127
10(3)(a) The Challenge . . . 127
10(3)(b) The Litigation . . . 127
10(3)(c) Changing Claims . . . 128
10(3)(d) Aboriginal Evidence . . . 129
10(3)(d)(i) Collective Oral Histories . . . 129
10(3)(d)(ii) Personal and Family Histories . . . 129
10(3)(d)(iii) Chiefs' Territorial Affidavits . . . 129
10(3)(d)(iv) Beyond Hearsay Exceptions . . . 130
10(3)(e) Aboriginal Title . . . 131
10(3)(e)(i) General Features . . . 131
10(3)(e)(ii) Exclusivity . . . 131
10(3)(e)(iii) Land Attachment . . . 132
10(3)(e)(iv) Identification . . . 132
10(3)(e)(v) Constitutional Status . . . 133
10(3)(e)(vi) Aboriginal Title and Other Aboriginal Rights . . . 133
10(3)(f) Justification . . . 133
10(3)(f)(i) Justification Goals . . . 133
10(3)(f)(ii) Justification in *Delgamuukw* . . . 134
10(3)(g) Self-Government . . . 134
10(3)(h) Extinguishment . . . 135
10(3)(h)(i) Provincial Jurisdiction under *Constitution Act, 1867* . . . 135
10(3)(h)(ii) Provincial Jurisdiction under Section 88 of *Indian Act* . . . 136
10(3)(h)(iii) A Case for Deferral? . . . 136
10(4) *Mitchell* . . . 136
10(4)(a) Recurring Questions . . . 136
10(4)(b) Background . . . 136
10(4)(c) Characterization . . . 137
10(4)(d) Evidence . . . 138
10(4)(e) Aboriginal Rights, Section 35(1), and Sovereign Incompatibility . . . 139
10(5) *Powley* . . . 140

10(6) *Haida Nation* 143
10(6)(a) Underlying Source and General Nature of s. 35(1) Duty to Consult . . . 143
10(6)(b) Parties Subject to Duty 144
10(6)(c) Scope of Duty 144
10(6)(d) Content of Duty 144
10(6)(e) Relationship between Forms of Justification 145
10(7) Basic Features 146
10(7)(a) General Aspects 146
10(7)(b) Identification 147
10(7)(c) Content 147
10(7)(d) Relationship to Crown 148
10(7)(e) Possession and Use 148
10(7)(f) Extinguishment and Restriction 148
10(7)(g) Justification 148
10(7)(h) Fiduciary Duty 149

11 Aboriginal Claims **162**
11(1) General Questionss 163
11(2) What Are Aboriginal Claims? 163
11(3) Alternative Approaches 163
11(3)(a) Courts 163
11(3)(b) Quasi-Judicial Tribunal 163
11(3)(c) Arbitration 163
11(3)(d) Representations before a Legislative Body 164
11(3)(e) Negotiations 164
11(4) Claims Process 164
11(4)(a) Procedure 164
11(4)(b) Development 163
11(5) Major Comprehensive Claims Agreements and Negotiations 166
11(6) Factors Influencing Settlement of Comprehensive Claims 167
11(6)(a) Issues 167
11(6)(b) Parties 168
11(6)(c) Non-Beneficiaries 168
11(6)(d) Development 168
11(6)(e) Other Forums 169
11(6)(f) Scope 169
11(6)(g) Other Factors 170
11(7) Some Key Land Claims Agreements 170
11(7)(a) 1971 Alaska Native Claims Settlement 170
11(7)(b) 1975 James Bay and Northern Quebec Agreement and 1978 Northeastern Quebec Agreement 171
11(7)(c) 1984 Western Arctic (Inuvialuit) Agreement 171
11(7)(d) 1992 Gwich'in Agreement 172
11(7)(e) 1993 Nunavut Agreement 172
11(7)(f) 1993 and Later Yukon Agreements 172
11(7)(g) 1993 Sahtu Dene and Metis Agreement 173
11(7)(h) Nisga'a Agreement 173
11(7)(i) 2003 Tlicho Agreement 176
11(7)(j) 2005 Labrador Agreement 177
11(7)(k) Sechelt Agreement-in-Principle 177
11(8) Some Specific Claims 178

11(9) "Other Claims" 178
11(9)(a) Oka 178
11(9)(a)(i) People 178
11(9)(a)(ii) Crisis 178
11(9)(a)(iii) Background 179
11(9)(a)(iv) Aftermath 180
11(9)(b) Ipperwash 180
11(10) Future Directions 180

12 Aboriginal Self-Government 190
12(1) Aboriginal Perspectives 191
12(2) The Debate 191
12(3) Possible Alternatives 191
12(3)(a) Traditional Self-government 191
12(3)(b) Legislated Self-Government 192
12(3)(b)(i) *Indian Act* Self-Government 192
12(3)(c) Negotiated Self-Government 193
12(3)(c)(i) Guaranteed Participation 193
12(3)(c)(ii) Public Government. 193
12(3)(c)(iii) Coordinated Ethnic Government 193
12(3)(c)(iii)(A) James Bay and Northern Quebec Agreement 194
12(3)(c)(iii)(B) Sechelt Indian Band Self-Government Act 194
12(3)(c)(iii)(C) Alberta Metis Settlements Legislation 194
12(3)(c)(iii)(D) Métis Act of Saskatchewan. 194
12(3)(c)(iv) Separate Ethnic Government 194
12(3)(c)(iv)(A) Vuntut Gwitchin First Nation Self-Government Agreement 195
12(3)(c)(iv)(B) Westbank Indian Self-Government Agreement 196
12(3)(d) Judicial Self-Government 196
12(4) A Common Law Right of Aboriginal Self-Government? 197
12(5) Formal Constitutional Route 198
12(5)(a) Road to Charlottetown 198
12(5)(b) Charlottetown Aboriginal Provisions 199
12(5)(c) Rejection of Charlottetown. 200
12(6) Federal Policy Route. 200
12(7) Royal Commission on Aboriginal Peoples 201
12(8) Assessment of Self-Government Initiatives 203

13 Concluding Note 212